CW01310360

studies in jazz

Institute of Jazz Studies
Rutgers—The State University of New Jersey
General Editors: Dan Morgenstern and Edward Berger

1. BENNY CARTER: A Life in American Music, *by Morroe Berger, Edward Berger, and James Patrick, 2 vols., 1982*
2. ART TATUM: A Guide to His Recorded Music, *by Arnold Laubich and Ray Spencer, 1982*
3. ERROLL GARNER: The Most Happy Piano, *by James M. Doran, 1985*
4. JAMES P. JOHNSON: A Case of Mistaken Identity, *by Scott E. Brown;* Discography 1917–1950, *by Robert Hilbert, 1986*
5. PEE WEE ERWIN: This Horn for Hire, *as told to Warren W. Vaché Sr., 1987*
6. BENNY GOODMAN: Listen to His Legacy, *by D. Russell Connor, 1988*
7. ELLINGTONIA: The Recorded Music of Duke Ellington and His Sidemen, *by W. E. Timner, 1988; 4th ed., 1996*
8. THE GLENN MILLER ARMY AIR FORCE BAND: Sustineo Alas/I Sustain the Wings, *by Edward F. Polic;* Foreword *by George T. Simon, 1989*
9. SWING LEGACY, *by Chip Deffaa, 1989*
10. REMINISCING IN TEMPO: The Life and Times of a Jazz Hustler, *by Teddy Reig, with Edward Berger, 1990*
11. IN THE MAINSTREAM: 18 Portraits in Jazz, *by Chip Deffaa, 1992*
12. BUDDY DeFRANCO: A Biographical Portrait and Discography, *by John Kuehn and Arne Astrup, 1993*
13. PEE WEE SPEAKS: A Discography of Pee Wee Russell, *by Robert Hilbert, with David Niven, 1992*
14. SYLVESTER AHOLA: The Gloucester Gabriel, *by Dick Hill, 1993*
15. THE POLICE CARD DISCORD, *by Maxwell T. Cohen, 1993*
16. TRADITIONALISTS AND REVIVALISTS IN JAZZ, *by Chip Deffaa, 1993*
17. BASSICALLY SPEAKING: An Oral History of George Duvivier, *by Edward Berger;* Musical Analysis *by David Chevan, 1993*
18. TRAM: The Frank Trumbauer Story, *by Philip R. Evans and Larry F. Kiner, with William Trumbauer, 1994*
19. TOMMY DORSEY: On the Side, *by Robert L. Stockdale, 1995*
20. JOHN COLTRANE: A Discography and Musical Biography, *by Yasuhiro Fujioka, with Lewis Porter and Yoh-ichi Hamada, 1995*
21. RED HEAD: A Chronological Survey of "Red" Nichols and His Five Pennies, *by Stephen M. Stroff, 1996*
22. THE RED NICHOLS STORY: After Intermission 1942–1965, *by Philip R. Evans, Stanley Hester, Stephen Hester, and Linda Evans, 1997*
23. BENNY GOODMAN: Wrappin' It Up, *by D. Russell Connor, 1996*
24. CHARLIE PARKER AND THEMATIC IMPROVISATION, *by Henry Martin, 1996*
25. BACK BEATS AND RIM SHOTS: The Johnny Blowers Story, *by Warren W. Vaché Sr., 1997*
26. DUKE ELLINGTON: A Listener's Guide, *by Eddie Lambert, 1998*
27. SERGE CHALOFF: A Musical Biography and Discography, *by Vladimir Simosko, 1998*
28. HOT JAZZ: From Harlem to Storyville, *by David Griffiths, 1998*
29. ARTIE SHAW: A Musical Biography and Discography, *by Vladimir Simosko, 2000*
30. JIMMY DORSEY: A Study in Contrasts, *by Robert L. Stockdale, 1998*
31. STRIDE!: Fats, Jimmy, Lion, Lamb and All the Other Ticklers, *by John L. Fell and Terkild Vinding, 1999*
32. GIANT STRIDES: The Legacy of Dick Wellstood, *by Edward N. Meyer, 1999*
33. JAZZ GENTRY: Aristocrats of the Music World, *by Warren W. Vaché Sr., 1999*
34. THE UNSUNG SONGWRITERS: America's Masters of Melody, *by Warren W. Vaché Sr., 2000*
35. THE MUSICAL WORLD OF J. J. JOHNSON, *by Joshua Berrett and Louis G. Bourgois III, 1999*
36. THE LADIES WHO SING WITH THE BAND, *by Betty Bennett, 2000*
37. AN UNSUNG CAT: The Life and Music of Warne Marsh, *by Safford Chamberlain, 2000*
38. JAZZ IN NEW ORLEANS: The Postwar Years Through 1970, *by Charles Suhor, 2001*
39. THE YOUNG LOUIS ARMSTRONG ON RECORDS: A Critical Survey of the Early Recordings, 1923–1928, *by Edward Brooks, 2002*
40. BENNY CARTER: A Life in American Music, Second Edition, *by Morroe Berger, Edward Berger, and James Patrick, 2 vols., 2002*
41. CHORD CHANGES ON THE CHALKBOARD: How Public School Teachers Shaped Jazz and the Music of New Orleans, *by Al Kennedy,* Foreword *by Ellis Marsalis Jr., 2002*
42. CONTEMPORARY CAT: Terence Blanchard with Special Guests, *by Anthony Magro, 2002*
43. PAUL WHITEMAN: Pioneer in American Music, Volume 1: 1890–1930, *by Don Rayno, 2003*
44. GOOD VIBES: A Life in Jazz, *by Terry Gibbs with Cary Ginell, 2003*
45. TOM TALBERT: His Life and Times; Voices From a Vanished World, *by Bruce Talbot, 2004*
46. SITTIN' IN WITH CHRIS GRIFFIN: A Reminiscence of Radio and Recording's Golden Years, *by Warren W. Vaché, 2005*
47. FIFTIES JAZZ TALK: An Oral Retrospective, *by Gordon Jack, 2004*
48. FLORENCE MILLS: Harlem Jazz Queen, *by Bill Egan, 2004*
49. SWING ERA SCRAPBOOK: The Teenage Diaries and Radio Logs of Bob Inman, 1936–1938, *by Ken Vail, 2005*

Studies in Jazz, No. 49

SWING ERA SCRAPBOOK
THE TEENAGE DIARIES & RADIO LOGS OF BOB INMAN
1936–1938

COMPILED BY KEN VAIL

The Scarecrow Press, Inc.
Lanham, Maryland,
and Oxford
2005

SCARECROW PRESS, INC.

Published in the United States of America
by Scarecrow Press, Inc.
A member of the Rowman & Littlefield Publishing Group
4720 Boston Way, Lanham, Maryland 20706
www.scarecrowpress.com

12 Hid's Copse Road
Cumnor Hill, Oxford OX2 9JJ, England

Copyright © Ken Vail 2005

All rights reserved. No part of this publication may be reproduced, stored in a retrieval system, or transmitted in any form or by any means, electronic, mechanical, photocopying, recording or otherwise without the prior permission of the publisher.

Library of Congress Cataloging-in-Publication Data

Inman, Bob, 1920–
  Swing era scrapbook : the teenage diaries & radio logs of Bob Inman, 1936–1938 /
  compiled by Ken Vail.
    p. cm. — (Studies in jazz ; np. 49)
  Includes index.
  ISBN 0-8108-5416-3 (alk. paper)
  1. Swing (Music)—History and criticism. 2. Radio music—History and criticism. 3. Inman, Bob, 1920– I Vail, Ken. II. Title. III. Series.
ML3518.I56 2005
781.65'4—dc22   2005042646

While the publishers have made every reasonable effort to trace the copyright owners for any or all of the photographs in this book, there may be some omissions of credits for which we apologise.

∞™ The paper used in this publication meets the minimum requirements of American National Standard for Information Sciences—Permanence of Paperfor Printed Library Materials, ANSI/NISO Z39.48-1992.

Acknowledgements

My grateful thanks to:
Bob Inman for his monumental effort in creating these invaluable Scrapbooks; also to Bob & Margaret Inman for proof-reading, suggestions and wonderful hospitality;
Brian Peerless for his valuable advice and sterling proof-reading;
Randy Sandke for his advice and comments;
Bruce Phillips, of Scarecrow, for his faith in the project;
Franz Hoffmann for his amazing series of books, Jazz Advertised;
Grant Elliott, Bob Frost, Dave Green, Jim Greig, Marty Grosz, Scott Hamilton, Dan Morgenstern, Hank O'Neal, Ken Peplowski, Bruce Phillips, Norman Saks, Randy Sandke and David Smith for help and encouragement at crucial moments.

All photographs from the collection of Bob Inman and the author, unless otherwise stated.

EDITOR'S FOREWORD

About 25 years ago, Ed Berger and I first set eyes on Bob Inman's unique scrapbooks. We knew then and there that they should be published, but were not then in a position to bring that about.

Happily, as he tells us in his introduction, Ken Vail encountered Bob, they became friends, and now this marvelous time-capsule is in your hands and you are about to embark on a journey through more than two-and-a-half years of the Swing Era at its height, from the vantage point of a dedicated fan.

Fans have not been treated well in jazz histories (Artie Shaw has been especially harsh), and it is seldom noted that without them there would have been no swing era. Of course they could be a nuisance, but when you get into the scrapbook, you will note how nice the musicians, almost without exception, were to Bob and his friends, not much more than 15 years of age when this project got started.

You will also note, as Bob's annotations, and his attendances at live events, get fully under way, that he is no ordinary fan, just looking for autographs and free photos. His comments are those of an increasingly sophisticated listener, and he has good ears and good taste. In fact, as this inveterate and incurable reader of vintage periodicals can attest to, he is hipper than a lot of the folks then writing about the music.

It's worth noting that he and his friends also love to dance; that relationship to the music called jazz, alas almost totally lost today, was such an important factor, and led these youngsters directly to the Savoy Ballroom. And they also discovered Harlem's Apollo.

Lest you should think that these pages are pure entertainment, or a kind of social history, pay close attention to what is contained herein. Bob's radio logs, of great documentary importance in and of themselves, are further illuminated by his annotations, noting soloists and even arrangers, often with additional commentary. The same goes for his often detailed listings of what he saw and heard at live performances, which take in dances (in venues including fancy and plain), broadcasts, and the stage shows that then were part and parcel of first-run motion picture theater fare. So you will be there with Bob and his friends at the Paramount, taking in Benny Goodman, and find out much more than contemporary reportage had to offer. And the boys will take you to 52nd Street, for a jam session lasting into dawn at the Onyx Club (from which appetite-whetting broadcasts include vocals — and trombone solos — by the one and only Leo Watson). Or the legendary Savoy battle of bands between Count Basie and Chick Webb.

From radio and live annotations, you will learn about repertoire that ranged far beyond what was recorded — and wouldn't we like to hear some of that stuff never recorded by the Basie band, featuring Lester Young and Herschel Evans, and things that Billie sang with them and nobody else!

There is much to learn here, about bands (such as Frankie Ward's Boston outfit — Bob likes their broadcasts and finds out about them by writing them their first fan letter) or forgotten studio series (such as *Bughouse Rhythm*, emanating from San Francisco). And did you know that the ill-fated Margaret (Queenie) Johnson broadcast regularly from Kansas City?

We see a photo of her, and that brings up another element: views of bands and players and singers not seen elsewhere, some taken by Bob and his friends, others clipped from long-gone sources — including a shot of Mezz Mezzrow's Harlem Uproar House band.

And there are letters, in response to fan mail, from among others Bunny Berigan (a particular Inman favorite), and even Dick Voynow. In a lighter vein, we enjoyed Bob's comments about girl singers — here, too, he had excellent taste — such as his first reaction to encountering Ella Fitzgerald: "She has a colossal (a favorite encomium) voice! A little fat and very nice." And he also has good judgment of songs, by the way.

In sum, this is a veritable cornucopia of first-hand information that supplements discographies and histories and adds to our perception of a key period in American music. Ken Vail's addition of represent-ative record dates and New York events adds context, and he has done a fine job preparing the Scrapbook for publication. But this is Bob Inman's work and we thank him for his nuttsy and truly super-colossal contribution to jazz documentation and history.

Dan Morgenstern
Director, Institute of Jazz Studies,
Rutgers University

FOREWORD BY BOB INMAN

I was born August 2, 1920, in Leonia, New Jersey. My father, an assistant minister at the Disciples First Church, NYC, played a poor "Salvation Army" style cornet when he met my mother, the organist at the same church, and married her in 1904. My father later became a noted authority on Latin America and wrote many books, taught at many colleges, befriended Latin American presidents, and advised Franklin Roosevelt on starting the 1935 "Good Neighbor Policy" with Latin America.

After moving from Leonia to Bronxville, New York, when I was five years old, I attended Bronxville Schools until my 1939 graduation. My brother kept me up late to hear radio jazz shows. I can still remember in 1934 when I danced with my older sisters, Anita and Joyce, and thrilled to the music of Glen Gray and the Casa Loma Orchestra at the Glen Island Casino. From that time until the present, big band jazz music has been my hobby and listening joy. What a thrill it was to get a radio from my mother at Christmas of 1935!

Bob Inman 1937

It was a pity that I didn't pay much attention to my mother's piano lessons. Sports were much more important to me than piano lessons. I still regret not playing the piano, but have always enjoyed both listening and singing.

From 1935 to the time I enlisted as an Aviation Cadet in February, 1943, I witnessed hundreds of jazz shows. I amassed seven big band jazz scrapbooks containing hundred of pictures and autographs along with logs of the numbers played by bands on thousands of radio broadcasts from 1935 to 1938.

How lucky I was to be in my late teens during the great flowering of jazz music. As Bronxville was one of the wealthiest towns in the United States, many of my schoolmates had cars and big allowances, making it conducive to visiting jazz hotels, nightclubs and radio shows. Every night, dozens of radio stations carried live band broadcasts. I usually won our game of tuning in many bands and picking out the bands' name by the sound. I had a very small allowance and no car to keep up with my wealthier classmates. My advantage over them was that I had a famous, internationally known father. Practically every morning, at school, I would greet my swing or "alligator" buddies with "Did you hear Benny last night?"

We visited New York City all day on many Saturdays. If we couldn't get a ride from one of our parents, we would hitch-hike about five miles to the 241st Street Lexington Avenue subway for the nickel ride to Grand Central Station. Sometimes we paid about thirty-five cents to get in the Paramount, Loew's State, Radio City, or the Apollo Theater in Harlem. I remember getting in line up around 42nd Street in the early morning to pay 35 cents to see Benny Goodman at the Paramount. We would see the movie and stage show twice for about six hours, sometimes sitting in the first few rows and watching the full theater go wild as the stage would rise with Goodman's band. A few jazz nuts were so excited that they had to get up and dance in the aisles. The second show, we would sit in the magnificent balcony. The huge organ was played between shows while people left and new arrivals got seated. Other bands we saw at the Paramount were Glen Gray, Charlie Barnet, Jimmie Lunceford, Hal Kemp, Tommy and Jimmy Dorsey, Bob Crosby, Isham Jones, Clyde McCoy, Mal Hallett, George Hall, Louis Armstrong, Joe Haymes, Ray Noble… and many more.

FOREWORD BY BOB INMAN

A subway nickel ride to Harlem's 125th Street Apollo Theater gave us a chance to see Ellington, Basie, etc., matinees along with practically all-black audiences. The Apollo's 11pm Wednesday amateur audition shows were sometimes broadcast over radio WMCA. It was very funny to hear the loud gong telling poor performers to give up and leave. It was on one of these shows that young Ella Fitzgerald got her start.

Our New York City Saturday lunch of a hot dog and orange juice cost us 15 cents. Remember, we usually only had one dollar to spend the whole day, including theaters, lunch, and subway rides. To get pictures, we visited the offices of Music Corporation of America, Rockwell-O'Keefe, CBS Artists Bureau, Mills Artists, Metronome magazine, Variety magazine, etc. We also visited the hotel rooms of any musicians we were lucky enough to find.

Some Saturdays we witnessed the famous CBS Saturday Night Swing Club radio broadcasts. I logged the numbers played on 80 of these 1936–1939 broadcasts, of which I witnessed 40 shows. When we couldn't get tickets by mail we would stand outside CBS studios at 485 Madison Avenue at 51st Street and beg for free tickets. Producers Ed Cashman and Al Rinker, announcers Paul Douglas, Dan Seymour and Melvin Allen, or musicians Bunny Berigan, Raymond Scott, Mannie Klein and others were kind enough to see that we young kids got into the small CBS studio to see their jazz show. Conductors of various shows included Lud Gluskin, Leith Stevens, Mark Warnow, Freddy Rich and Johnny Augustine.

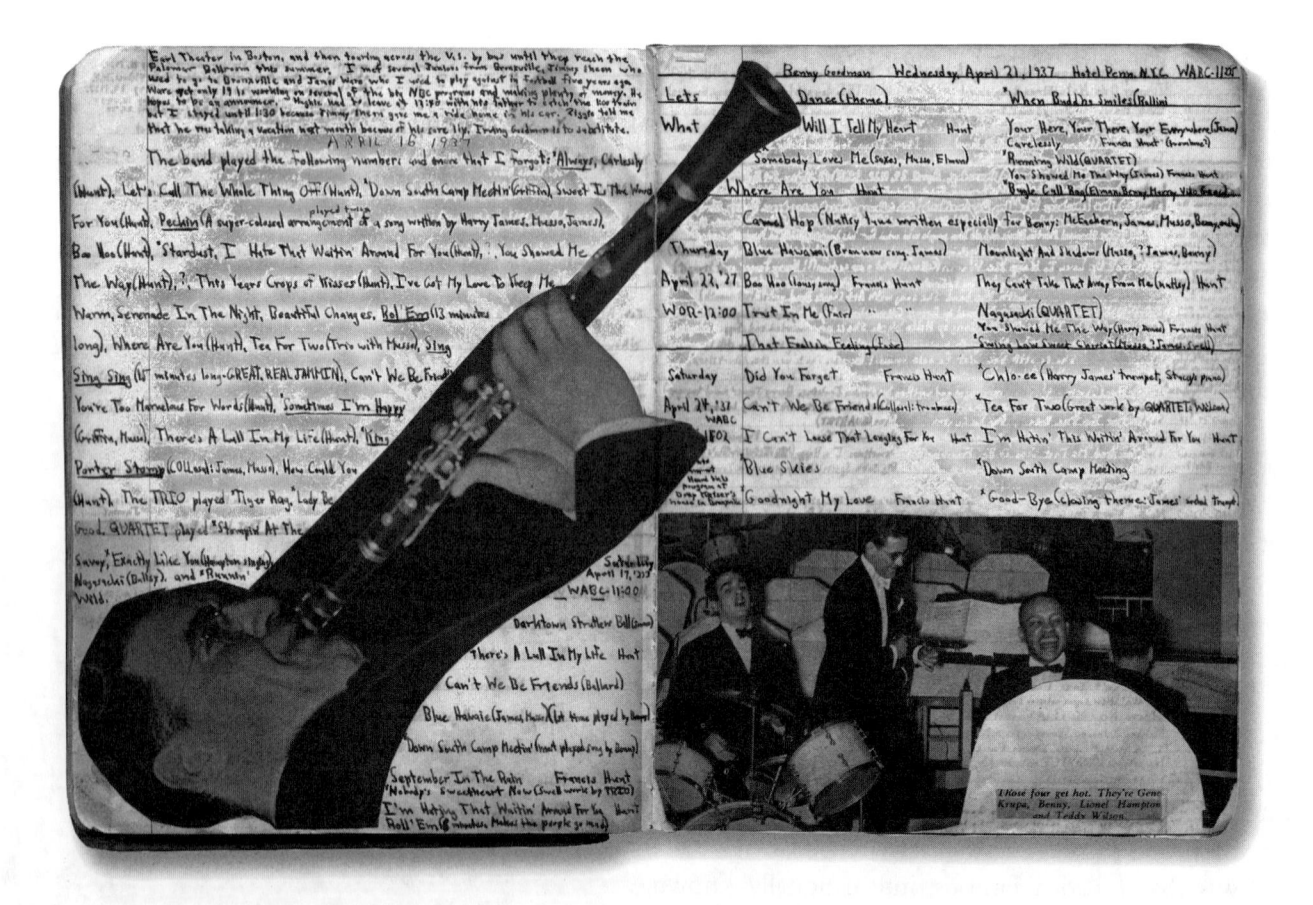

The first anniversary broadcast of the Saturday Night Swing Club was June 13, 1937, and was broadcast world-wide from midnight to 1:36AM. Paul Douglas and baseball announcer Mel Allen announced this swing session from the CBS Playhouse off Broadway at 48th Street. The 1500-plus audience heard music via remotes from the bands of Glen Gray (Palomar, Los Angeles), Bunny Berigan (Hotel Pennsylvania, NYC), Benny Goodman (Pittsburgh), and others. What a surprise to hear the voice of Edward R. Murrow from the Montmartre in Paris trying to correctly pronounce Stephane Grappelli and Django Reinhardt! A few years later Murrow startled the world with his vivid broadcasts from V-bombed London. The audience also saw and heard Duke Ellington with his small group, harpist Caspar Reardon, the Raymond Scott Quintet, the Adrian Rollini Trio, vocalist Kay Thompson, pianist Claude Thornhill, plus numbers from the regular CBS band under the direction of Leith Stevens. The final two jam session numbers included Carl Kress, Dick McDonough, Mannie Klein, Will Bradley (then known by his real name, Wilbur Schwictenberg), and Babe Russin. It was certainly an exciting and very late night for three 16-year-old kids, Jim Poe, Hugh Pastoriza, and myself. Jim Poe later became a movie script writer and won an Academy Award for "Around The World In Eighty Days".

I also enjoyed seeing the June 25, 1938, second anniversary CBS Swing Club show featuring Paul Douglas, Mel Allen, Duke Ellington, Slim and Slam, Connie Boswell, Bobby Hackett, the Modernaires, Jack and Charlie Teagarden, Raymond Scott, Mildred Bailey, Red Norvo, the Mills Brothers, Louis Armstrong, and others. I saw Bunny Berigan on dozens of CBS Swing Club shows. He left CBS to start his own band in February 1937. It never really got the top recognition it deserved. Maybe the easy-going Berigan didn't have enough discipline or business sense. Anyway, on the night of May 7, 1937, Poe, Pastoriza and myself watched the band from the entrance of the Hotel Pennsylvania's Madhattan Room because there was a cover charge and we didn't have enough money to pay it. Then we walked around looking for a way to get in at the back of the room and ended up in the Hotel Penn's dim cellar. We were lost until we found a door leading to the kitchen entrance to the Madhattan room. So we avoided the cover charge and had a ball talking with the Berigan band members.

All of our adventures were documented in my scrapbooks, a slice of history which my friend, Ken Vail, has now turned into this fascinating book. I hope it brings back golden memories for some of you, while giving a taste of "how it was" to younger readers.

Bob Inman 2002

INTRODUCTION BY KEN VAIL

In November 1991 I was enjoying my first jazz cruise in the Caribbean, aboard the SS Norway. One evening, my wife and I were invited to dine with Hank O'Neal and Shelley Shier, the producers of the Floating Jazz Festival. During the course of the meal, Hank said: "You know, you should meet Bob Inman!"

Bob and I met during that same cruise, became friends, and he told me about the seven scrapbooks he had kept as a teenager. Over the years he sent me xeroxes of various pages from the scrapbooks to help me with different projects. At the same time, without ever seeing the originals, I was trying to help Bob get the scrapbooks published. Eventually, in 2002, Bob persuaded me to buy the scrapbooks and I saw at last the remarkable social document that these teenage collections had become. I immediately set to work in an attempt to convert them into book form. *Swing Era Scrapbook* is the result of those efforts.

The early entries in the scrapbook are mainly radio logs, but after Bob's 16th birthday (August 1936) he begins to make forays into New York City to see his heroes in person, providing fascinating accounts of the treasure-house for jazz fans that was New York in the Swing Era. In writing these accounts Bob has used the colorful slang of the teenage swing fans of the Thirties and I have tried to retain the full flavour of these comments with a minimal amount of editing. I can only ask you to guess at the relative merits of *ballsy*; *nuttsy*; and *super-colossal*!

Another thing to remember when reading Bob's critical judgements is that, in many cases, he was hearing the musicians and the tunes for the very first time.

The layout of Radio Logs is always the same. First is the time of the broadcast, which is the time that Bob was listening, i.e. Eastern Standard Time. Next to the time is the station on which Bob was hearing the broadcast, e.g. WABC.

On the second line is the bandleader, headline singer, or program title, e.g. **FUN IN SWINGTIME**.

On the third line is the source of the program: either a commercial broadcasting studio or a theatre, hotel, ballroom or club with a live wire.

Next come the tune titles with vocalists where appropriate and, in brackets, Bob's teenage comments and observations.

On occasions, Bob has misheard the announced titles. In some instances, with the help of hindsight, I have been able to make corrections. On other occasions I have left Bob's phonetic interpretation or inserted *unknown title*.

The book begins with the New Year's Eve broadcasts from 31 December, 1935, and a map of the Manhattan midtown area which is the scene of much of the action related in these pages. I have added some monthly 'What's On in New York' boxes and recording sessions which I hope will give readers an overall perspective of the times but everything else is directly from the scrapbooks. All the photographs are from Bob Inman's collection.

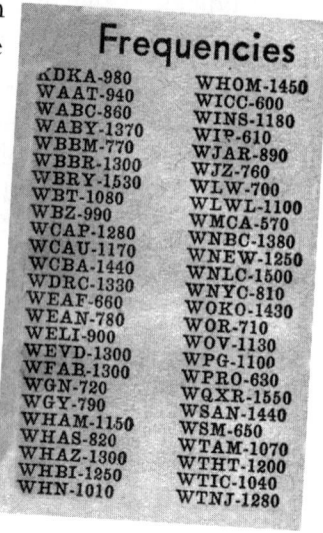

Frequencies

KDKA-980	WHOM-1450
WAAT-940	WICC-600
WABC-860	WINS-1180
WABY-1370	WIP-610
WBBM-770	WJAR-890
WBBR-1300	WJZ-760
WBRY-1530	WLW-700
WBT-1080	WLWL-1100
WBZ-990	WMCA-570
WCAP-1280	WNBC-1380
WCAU-1170	WNEW-1250
WCBA-1440	WNLC-1500
WDRC-1330	WNYC-810
WEAF-660	WOKO-1430
WEAN-780	WOR-710
WELI-900	WOV-1130
WEVD-1300	WPG-1100
WFAB-1300	WPRO-630
WGN-720	WQXR-1550
WGY-790	WSAN-1440
WHAM-1150	WSM-650
WHAS-820	WTAM-1070
WHAZ-1300	WTHT-1200
WHBI-1250	WTIC-1040
WHN-1010	WTNJ-1280

■ TUESDAY 31 DECEMBER 1935
NEW YEAR'S EVE BROADCASTS:

Time	Artist	Venue	Station
11:00	Abe Lyman	Hollywood Restaurant, NYC	?
11:15	Henry Halstead	Park Central Hotel, NYC	?
11:30	Louis Armstrong	Connie's Inn, NYC	WABC
11:45	Ray Noble	Rainbow Room, NYC	WJZ
11:45	Guy Lombardo	Hotel Roosevelt, NYC	WABC
12:00	Isham Jones	Hotel Lincoln, NYC	WABC
12:15	Ozzie Nelson	Hotel Lexington, NYC	WABC
12:30	Tommy Dorsey	Normandie Ballroom, Boston	WABC
12:30	Lucky Millinder	Baltimore, Maryland	WMCA
12:45	Vincent Lopez	Hotel Astor, NYC	WABC
01:00	George Olsen	College Inn, Chicago	WABC
01:00	Enric Madriguera	Morrison Hotel, Chicago	WJZ
01:10	Earl Hines	Grand Terrace, Chicago	NBC
01:15	Herbie Kay	Edgewater Beach Hotel, Chicago	WABC
01:15	Leon Belasco	Chez Paree, Chicago	NBC
01:30	Seymor Simons	Trianon Ballroom, Chicago	NBC
01:30	Jean Goldkette	?	WOR
01:30	Benny Goodman	Congress Hotel, Chicago	NBC
01:45	Frank Dailey	Meadowbrook, Cedar Grove, NJ	WABC
01:45	Ted Fio Rito	Netherlands-Plaza Hotel, Cincinnati	WOR
02:00	Freddy Martin	Waldorf-Astoria Hotel, NYC	NBC
02:15	Art Kassell	?	NBC
02:45	Paul Pendarvis	?	NBC
03:00	Al Kavelin	Blackstone Hotel, Chicago	WOR
03:15	Victor Young	?	WABC
03:15	Joe Sanders	Blackhawk Restaurant, Chicago	WOR
03:15	Joe Venuti	Palomar Ballroom, Los Angeles	WABC
03:30	Jack Hylton	Drake Hotel, Chicago	WBBA
04:45	Duke Ellington	Hotel Sherman, Chicago	WBBA

MIDTOWN NEW YORK CITY, New Year's Eve 1936 — *Swing Era Scrapbook* 1

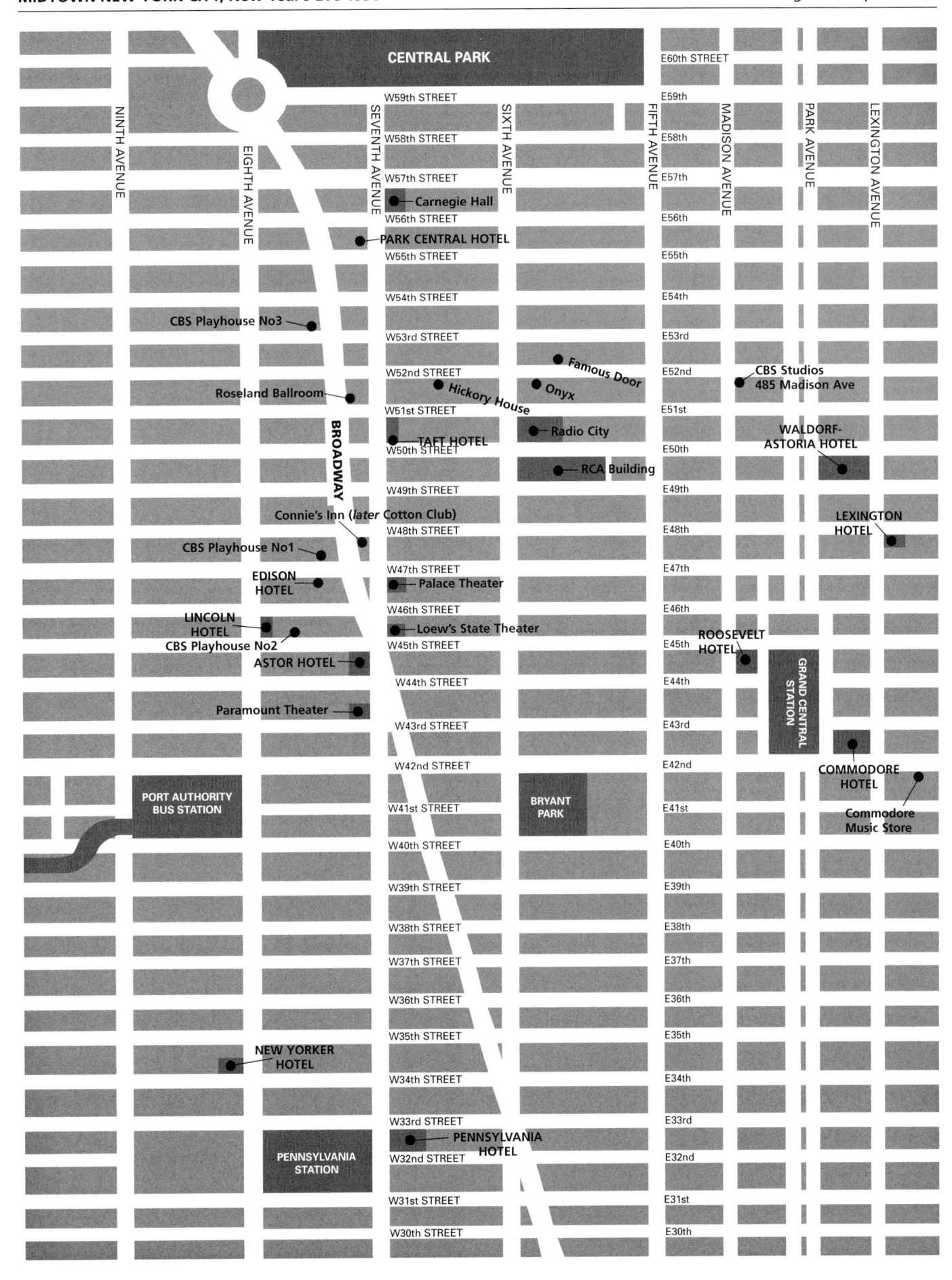

JANUARY 1936

Hotel Astor: **Vincent Lopez**
Hotel Lexington: **Ozzie Nelson**
Hotel Lincoln: **Isham Jones**
Rainbow Room: **Ray Noble**

Apollo Theater: **Fats Waller** (3–9); **Mills Brothers** (10–16); **Erskine Hawkins** (17–23); **Noble Sissle** (24–30)
Loew's State Theater: **Blanche Calloway Orchestra**
Paramount Theater: **Glen Gray Casa Loma Orchestra**

Connie's Inn: **Louis Armstrong**
Cotton Club: **Claude Hopkins Orchestra**
Hickory House: **Red Norvo Swing Sextet**
Onyx Club: **Riley & Farley**

■ SATURDAY 4 JANUARY 1936

RADIO LOGS

12:00 MIDNIGHT WMAQ
BENNY GOODMAN
Congress Hotel, Chicago
Blue Skies
With All My Heart (vocal: Helen Ward)
Eeny-Meeny-Miney-Mo (vocal: Helen Ward)
Star Dust
Dodging A Divorcee

■ SUNDAY 5 JANUARY 1936

RADIO LOGS

12:00 MIDNIGHT WMAQ
BENNY GOODMAN
Congress Hotel, Chicago
Unknown title
You Hit The Spot (vocal: Helen Ward)
Stompin' At The Savoy
Unknown title
King Porter Stomp
Sophisticated Lady
My Gal Sal

BENNY GOODMAN'S SENSATIONAL SWING BAND THE TALK OF THE MUSIC WORLD

JANUARY 1936

■ MONDAY 6 JANUARY 1936

RECORDING SESSION

RED NORVO AND HIS ORCHESTRA
Recording session for Decca in New York City.
Stew Pletcher (t); Eddie Sauter (mel); Donald McCook (cl); Herbie Haymer (ts); Dave Barbour (g); Pete Peterson (b); Bob White (d); Red Norvo (xyl); Trio (voc)
Gramercy Square / Polly Wolly Doodle (v3)

■ WEDNESDAY 8 JANUARY 1936

RECORDING SESSION

RED NORVO AND HIS ORCHESTRA
Recording session for Decca in New York City.
Stew Pletcher (t); Eddie Sauter (mel); Donald McCook (cl); Herbie Haymer (ts); Dave Barbour (g); Pete Peterson (b); Bob White (d); Red Norvo (xyl); Trio (voc)
Decca Stomp / The Wedding Of Jack And Jill (v3)

■ SUNDAY 12 JANUARY 1936

RADIO LOGS

12:00 MIDNIGHT WJZ
BENNY GOODMAN
Congress Hotel, Chicago
Farewell Blues
It's Been So Long (vocal: Helen Ward)
After You've Gone
No Other One (vocal: Helen Ward)
Star Dust
Dixieland Band (vocal: Helen Ward)
I'm Gonna Sit Right Down And Write Myself A Letter
That's You, Sweetheart (vocal: Helen Ward)
I Found A New Baby

■ TUESDAY 14 JANUARY 1936

RADIO LOGS

12:00 MIDNIGHT WMAQ
BENNY GOODMAN
Congress Hotel, Chicago
Yankee Doodle Never Went To Town (vocal: Helen Ward)
Cling To Me
Always
Alexander's Ragtime Band (vocal: Helen Ward)
Rosetta
I'm A Ding Dong Daddy (From Dumas)
Alone (vocal: Helen Ward)
Get Rhythm In Your Feet (vocal: Helen Ward)
Don't Blame Me
Goodbye

Opposite page: Benny Goodman's Band in Chicago (l to r): Jess Stacy (p), Harry Goodman (b), Allan Reuss (g), Helen Ward (voc), Gene Krupa (d), Benny, Dick Clark (ts), Harry Geller (t), Bill DePew (as), Ralph Muzzillo (t), Joe Harris (tb), Nate Kazebier (t), Hymie Shertzer (as), Red Ballard (tb), Art Rollini (ts)

■ FRIDAY 17 JANUARY 1936

RECORDING SESSION

MIKE RILEY, EDDIE FARLEY & THEIR ONYX CLUB BOYS
Recording session for Decca in New York City.
Eddie Farley (t/voc); Mike Riley (tb/voc); Frank Langone (cl); Conrad Lanoue (p); Arthur Ens (g); George Yorke (b); Vic Engle (d)
I'm Gonna Clap My Hands (vMR) / *I Wish I Were Aladdin* (vMR) / *Not Enough* (vMR) / *You're Wicky, You're Wacky, You're Wonderful* (vMR,EF)

■ MONDAY 20 JANUARY 1936

RECORDING SESSION

RED McKENZIE & HIS RHYTHM KINGS
Recording session for Decca in New York City.
Bunny Berigan (t); Forrest Crawford (cl); Babe Russin (ts); Frank Signorelli (p); Carmen Mastren (g); Sid Weiss (b); Stan King (d); Red McKenzie (comb/voc)
Sing An Old-Fashioned Song (vRM) / *I'm Building Up To An Awful Letdown* (vRM)

RADIO LOGS

12:00 MIDNIGHT WEAF
BENNY GOODMAN
Congress Hotel, Chicago
Farewell Blues
I'm Shooting High (vocal: Helen Ward)
Stompin' At The Savoy
Basin Street Blues (vocal: Joe Harris)
I'm Building Up To An Awful Letdown (vocal: Helen Ward)
Transcontinental
You Hit The Spot (vocal: Helen Ward)
I Surrender Dear
Yankee Doodle Never Went To Town (vocal: Helen Ward)

■ TUESDAY 21 JANUARY 1936

RADIO LOGS

12:00 MIDNIGHT WEAF
BENNY GOODMAN
Congress Hotel, Chicago
After You've Gone
Someday Sweetheart
It's Been So Long (vocal: Helen Ward)
You Forgot To Remember (vocal: Helen Ward)
Sandman

■ FRIDAY 24 JANUARY 1936

RECORDING SESSION

BENNY GOODMAN AND HIS ORCHESTRA
Recording session for Victor in Chicago.
Benny Goodman (cl); Harry Geller, Nate Kazebier, Ralph Muzillo (t); Red Ballard, Joe Harris (tb); Bill DePew, Hymie Shertzer (as); Art Rollini, Dick Clark (ts); Jess Stacy (p); Allan Reuss (g); Harry Goodman (b); Gene Krupa (d); Helen Ward (voc)
It's Been So Long (vHW) / *Stompin' At The Savoy* / *Goody-Goody* (vHW) / *Breakin' In A Pair Of Shoes*

RADIO LOGS

12:00 MIDNIGHT WMAQ
BENNY GOODMAN
Congress Hotel, Chicago
I Found A New Baby
It Must Have Been A Dream (vocal: Helen Ward)
Hooray For Love (vocal: Helen Ward)
Down South Camp Meetin'
I'm Shootin' High

■ SUNDAY 26 JANUARY 1936

RADIO LOGS

12:00 MIDNIGHT WJZ
BENNY GOODMAN
Congress Hotel, Chicago
Dear Old Southland
I'm Shootin' High (vocal: Helen Ward)
It Must Have Been A Dream (vocal: Helen Ward)
Big John Special
Lights Out (vocal: Helen Ward)
Someday Sweetheart
You're The Top (vocal: Helen Ward)
Stop, Look And Listen
The Broken Record (vocal: Helen Ward)
Alexander's Ragtime Band

■ MONDAY 27 JANUARY 1936

RECORDING SESSION

CAB CALLOWAY AND HIS ORCHESTRA
Recording session for Brunswick in Los Angeles.
Cab Calloway (voc); Lammar Wright, Doc Cheatham (t); DePriest Wheeler, Harry White, Claude Jones (tb); William Thornton Blue, Arville Harris (cl/as); Andrew Brown (bcl/as/bar); Walter Thomas (cl/ts/fl); Benny Payne (p); Morris White (g); Al Morgan (b); Leroy Maxey (d)
I Love To Sing-a (vCC) / *You're The Cure For What Ails Me* (vCC) / *Save Me, Sister* (vCC)

RADIO LOGS

12:00 MIDNIGHT WEAF
BENNY GOODMAN
Congress Hotel, Chicago
High Dive
You Hit The Spot (vocal: Helen Ward)
Mood Indigo/Sophisticated Lady (medley)
Goody Goody (vocal: Helen Ward)
Stompin' At The Savoy
Dixieland Band (vocal: Helen Ward)
That's You, Sweetheart
Breakin' In A Pair Of Shoes
Madhouse
You Forgot To Remember

■ TUESDAY 28 JANUARY 1936

RECORDING SESSION

WINGY MANONE AND HIS ORCHESTRA
Recording session for Vocalion in New York City.
Wingy Manone (t/voc); George Brunies (tb); Joe Marsala (cl); Gil Bowers (p); Carmen Mastren (g); Sid Weiss (b); Ray Bauduc (d)
Rhythm In My Nursery Rhymes (vWM) / *Old Man Mose* (vWM) / *The Broken Record* (vWM) / *Please Believe Me* (vWM)

RADIO LOGS

12:00 MIDNIGHT WMAQ
BENNY GOODMAN
Congress Hotel, Chicago
St. Louis Blues
Goody Goody (vocal: Helen Ward)
Thanks A Million
Walk, Jennie, Walk

■ WEDNESDAY 29 JANUARY 1936

RECORDING SESSION

FRANKIE TRUMBAUER AND HIS ORCHESTRA
Recording session for Brunswick in New York City.
Frankie Trumbauer (c-mel/as/ldr); Ed Wade, Charlie Teagarden (t); Jack Teagarden (tb); Johnny Mince (cl); Joe Cordaro (cl/as); Mutt Hayes (ts); Roy Bargy (p); George Van Eps (g); Art Miller (b); Stan King (d)
Flight Of A Haybag / *Breakin' In A Pair Of Shoes* / *Announcer's Blues*

RADIO LOGS

12:00 MIDNIGHT WMAQ
BENNY GOODMAN
Congress Hotel, Chicago
Always
Easy To Remember (vocal: Helen Ward)
I'm Building Up To An Awful Letdown (vocal: Helen Ward)
I Surrender Dear

■ FRIDAY 31 JANUARY 1936

RADIO LOGS

12:00 MIDNIGHT WMAQ
BENNY GOODMAN
Congress Hotel, Chicago
Big John Special
The Day I Let You Get Away (vocal: Helen Ward)
Someday, Sweetheart
It's Been So Long (vocal: Helen Ward)

FEBRUARY 1936

Hotel Astor: **Vincent Lopez**
Hotel Lexington: **Ozzie Nelson**
Rainbow Room: **Ray Noble**

Apollo Theater: **Teddy Hill** (7–13); **Duke Ellington** (14–20); **Earl Hines** (21–27); **Luis Russell** (28–)
Loew's State Theater: **Earl Hines** (14–20)
Paramount Theater: **Hal Kemp** (–4); **Isham Jones** (5–)

Connie's Inn: **Louis Armstrong** (–12); **Don Redman** (13–)
Cotton Club: **CLOSES 9th February**
Hickory House: **Wingy Manone**
Jack Dempsey's: **Red Norvo Swing Sextet**
Onyx Club: **Stuff Smith** (3–)
Famous Door: **Bunny Berigan** (10–)

■ SATURDAY 1 FEBRUARY 1936

RECORDING SESSION

GLEN GRAY AND THE CASA LOMA ORCHESTRA
Recording session for Decca in New York City.
Glen Gray (as/dir); Sonny Dunham, Grady Watts, Bobby Jones (t); Pee Wee Hunt (tb/voc); Billy Rauch, Fritz Hummel (tb); Clarence Hutchenrider (cl/as), Kenny Sargent (as/voc); Art Ralston (as/o/bsn); Pat Davis (ts); Mel Jenssen (vln); Joe Hall (p); Jack Blanchette (g); Stanley Dennis (b); Tony Briglia (d)
Moonburn (vPWH) / *My Heart And I* (vKS) / *Let Yourself Go* (vPWH) / *I'd Rather Lead A Band* (vPWH)

FATS WALLER & HIS RHYTHM
Recording session for Victor in New York City.
Herman Autrey (t); Gene Sedric (cl/ts); Fats Waller (p/voc); James Smith (g); Charles Turner (b); Yank Porter (d)
The Panic Is On (vFW) / *Sugar Rose* (vFW) / *Ooh! Look-a There, Ain't She Pretty?* (vFW) / *Moon Rose* (vFW) / *West Wind* (vFW) / *That Never-To-Be-Forgotten Night* (vFW) / *Sing An Old Fashioned Song* (vFW) / *Garbo Green* (vFW)

RADIO LOGS

12:00 MIDNIGHT WMAQ
BENNY GOODMAN
Congress Hotel, Chicago
You Hit The Spot (vocal: Helen Ward)
Yankee Doodle Never Went To Town (vocal: Helen Ward)
It Must Have Been A Dream
Down South Camp Meeting

■ SUNDAY 2 FEBRUARY 1936

RADIO LOGS

12:00 MIDNIGHT WJZ
BENNY GOODMAN
Congress Hotel, Chicago
Darktown Strutters' Ball
It's Been So Long (vocal: Helen Ward)
I Found A New Baby
I Feel Like A Feather In The Breeze (vocal: Helen Ward)
St. Louis Blues
West Wind (vocal: Helen Ward)
Roll Along, Prairie Moon
Goody Goody (vocal: Helen Ward)
Thanks A Million
After You've Gone

■ MONDAY 3 FEBRUARY 1936

RADIO LOGS

12:00 MIDNIGHT WEAF
BENNY GOODMAN
Congress Hotel, Chicago
Dodging A Divorcee
The Day I Let You Get Away (vocal: Helen Ward)
Sandman
Lights Out (vocal: Helen Ward)
My Honey's Lovin' Arms
Alone (vocal: Helen Ward)
Alexander's Ragtime Band
Star Dust
Eeny-Meeny-Miney-Mo (vocal: Helen Ward)
King Porter Stomp

■ TUESDAY 4 FEBRUARY 1936

RADIO LOGS

12:00 MIDNIGHT WMAQ
BENNY GOODMAN
Congress Hotel, Chicago
Truckin' (vocal: Helen Ward)
That's You, Sweetheart (vocal: Helen Ward)
What's The Name Of That Song? (vocal: Helen Ward)
Walk, Jennie, Walk

■ FRIDAY 5 FEBRUARY 1936

RECORDING SESSION

RED McKENZIE & HIS RHYTHM KINGS
Recording session for Decca in New York City.
Bunny Berigan (t); Al Philburn (tb); Forrest Crawford (cl); Babe Russin (ts); Frank Signorelli (p); Carmen Mastren (g); Sid Weiss (b); Stan King (d); Red McKenzie (comb/voc)
Don't Count Your Kisses (vRM) / *When Love Has Gone* (vRM) / *I Don't Know Your Name* (vRM) / *Moon Rose* (vRM)

FRANKIE TRUMBAUER AND HIS ORCHESTRA
Recording session for Brunswick in New York City.
Frankie Trumbauer (c-mel/as/voc/ldr); Ed Wade, Charlie Teagarden (t); Jack Teagarden (tb/voc); Johnny Mince (cl); Joe Cordaro (cl/as); Mutt Hayes (ts); Roy Bargy (p); George Van Eps (g); Art Miller (b); Stan King (d)
I Hope Gabriel Likes My Music (vJT,FT)

THURSDAY 6 FEBRUARY 1936

RADIO LOGS

12:00 MIDNIGHT WEAF
BENNY GOODMAN
Congress Hotel, Chicago
Farewell Blues
You Hit The Spot (vocal: Helen Ward)
On The Alamo
Honeysuckle Rose
What's The Name Of That Song? (vocal: Helen Ward)
Stompin' At The Savoy
Goody Goody (vocal: Helen Ward)
Rosetta
I'm Shooting High (vocal: Helen Ward)
Bugle Call Rag

SATURDAY 8 FEBRUARY 1936

RADIO LOGS

?? WMAQ
BENNY GOODMAN
Congress Hotel, Chicago
Remember
It's Great To Be In Love Again (vocal: Helen Ward)
Goody Goody (vocal: Helen Ward)
I Surrender, Dear

TUESDAY 11 FEBRUARY 1936

RECORDING SESSION

STUFF SMITH & HIS ONYX CLUB BOYS
Recording session for Vocalion in New York City.
Jonah Jones (t/voc); Stuff Smith (vln/voc); Raymond Smith (p); Bobby Bennett (g); Mack Walker (b); John Washington (d)
I'se A-Muggin'–Pt1 (vSS) / *I'se A-Muggin'–Pt2* (vSS) / *I Hope Gabriel Likes My Music* (vSS) / *I'm Putting All My Eggs In One Basket* (vSS)

MONDAY 24 FEBRUARY 1936

RECORDING SESSION

BUNNY BERIGAN AND HIS BOYS
Recording session for Vocalion in New York City.
Bunny Berigan (t); Joe Marsala (cl) and/or Bud Freeman (ts); Forrest Crawford (ts); Joe Bushkin (p); Dave Barbour (g); Mort Stuhlmaker (b); Dave Tough (d); Chick Bullock (voc)
It's Been So Long (vCB) / *I'd Rather Lead A Band* (vCB) / *Let Yourself Go* (vCB) / *Swing, Mister Charlie* (vCB)

RADIO LOGS

12:00 MIDNIGHT WEAF
BENNY GOODMAN
Congress Hotel, Chicago
Inka Dinka Doo
Lost (vocal: Helen Ward)
What Does It Matter?
Some of These Days
It's Been So Long (vocal: Helen Ward)
Blue Skies
It's Great To Be In Love Again (vocal: Helen Ward)
Honeysuckle Rose
Goody Goody (vocal: Helen Ward)

THURSDAY 27 FEBRUARY 1936

RECORDING SESSION

DUKE ELLINGTON AND HIS ORCHESTRA
Recording session for Brunswick in New York City.
Duke Ellington (p); Arthur Whetsel, Cootie Williams (t); Rex Stewart (c); Joe Nanton, Lawrence Brown (tb); Juan Tizol (v-tb); Barney Bigard (cl); Johnny Hodges (cl/ss/as); Otto Hardwick (as/bar); Harry Carney (cl/as/bar); Fred Guy (g); Hayes Alvis, Billy Taylor (b); Sonny Greer (d); Ivie Anderson (voc)
Isn't Love The Strangest Thing? (vIA) / *There Is No Greater Love* (vIA, BT out) / *Clarinet Lament (Barney's Concerto)* (BT, OH out) / *Echoes Of Harlem (Cootie's Concerto)* (BT, OH out)

FRIDAY 28 FEBRUARY 1936

RECORDING SESSION

DUKE ELLINGTON AND HIS ORCHESTRA
Recording session for Brunswick in New York City.
Duke Ellington (p); Arthur Whetsel, Cootie Williams (t); Rex Stewart (c); Joe Nanton, Lawrence Brown (tb); Juan Tizol (vtb); Barney Bigard (cl); Johnny Hodges (cl/ss/as); Pete Clark (as); Harry Carney (cl/as/bar); Fred Guy (g); Hayes Alvis, Billy Taylor (b); Sonny Greer (d); Ivie Anderson (voc)
Love Is Like A Cigarette (vIA, BT out) / *Kissin' My Baby Goodnight* (vIA, 2 takes) / *Oh Babe, Maybe Someday* (vIA, BT out)

SATURDAY 29 FEBRUARY 1936

RECORDING SESSION

GENE KRUPA'S SWING BAND
Recording session for Victor in Chicago.
Benny Goodman (cl); Roy Eldridge (t); Chu Berry (ts); Jess Stacy (p); Allan Reuss (g); Israel Crosby (b); Gene Krupa (d); Helen Ward (voc)
I Hope Gabriel Likes My Music / *Mutiny In The Parlor* (vHW) / *I'm Gonna Clap My Hands* (vHW) / *Swing Is Here*

MARCH 1936

Hotel Astor: **Vincent Lopez**
Hotel Lexington: **Ozzie Nelson**
Rainbow Room: **Ray Noble** (–10); **Glen Gray** (11–)

Apolio Theater: **Luis Russell** (–5); **Louis Armstrong** (6–12); **Leroy Smith** (13–19); **Claude Hopkins** (20–26); **Jimmie Lunceford** (27–)
Loew's State Theater: **Fats Waller** (20–26)

Connie's Inn: **Don Redman**
Hickory House: **Wingy Manone**
Jack Dempsey's: **Red Norvo Swing Sextet**
Onyx Club: **Stuff Smith**
Famous Door: **Bunny Berigan** (10–)

■ MONDAY 2 MARCH 1936

RECORDING SESSION

ANDY KIRK AND HIS TWELVE CLOUDS OF JOY
Recording session for Decca in New York City.
Andy Kirk (bsx/ldr); Harry Lawson, Paul King, Earl Thompson (t); Ted Donnelly, Henry Wells (tb); John Harrington (cl/as/bar); John Williams (as/bar); Dick Wilson (ts); Claude Williams (vln); Mary Lou Williams (p); Ted Brinson (g); Booker Collins (b); Ben Thigpen (d)
Walkin' And Swingin' / *Moten Swing* / *Lotta Sax Appeal*

■ TUESDAY 3 MARCH 1936

RECORDING SESSION

ANDY KIRK AND HIS TWELVE CLOUDS OF JOY
Recording session for Decca in New York City.
Andy Kirk (bsx/ldr); Harry Lawson, Paul King, Earl Thompson (t); Ted Donnelly, Henry Wells (tb); John Harrington (cl/as/bar); John Williams (as/bar); Dick Wilson (ts); Claude Williams (vln); Mary Lou Williams (p); Ted Brinson (g); Booker Collins (b); Ben Thigpen (d/voc); Pha Terrell (voc)
Git (vBT & band) / *All The Jive Is Gone* (vPT)

RADIO LOGS

?? WMAQ
BENNY GOODMAN
Congress Hotel, Chicago
It's Wonderful
You Hit The Spot (vocal: Helen Ward)
My Melancholy Baby
Transcontinental

Andy Kirk and his Twelve Clouds of Joy (below, l to r): Ted Brinson (g), Ted Donnelly (tb), Earl Thompson (t), Pha Terrell (voc), Paul King (t), Mary Lou Williams (p), Harry Lawson (t), Booker Collins (b), Dick Wilson (ts), John Williams (as), Ben Thigpen (d), John Harrington (as), Buddy Miller (bar), Andy Kirk.

■ WEDNESDAY 4 MARCH 1936

RECORDING SESSION

ANDY KIRK AND HIS TWELVE CLOUDS OF JOY
Recording session for Decca in New York City.
Andy Kirk (bsx/ldr); Harry Lawson, Paul King, Earl Thompson (t); Ted Donnelly, Henry Wells (tb); John Harrington (cl/as/bar); John Williams (as/bar); Dick Wilson (ts); Claude Williams (vln); Mary Lou Williams (p); Ted Brinson (g); Booker Collins (b); Ben Thigpen (d/voc)
Froggy Bottom (vBT) / *Bearcat Shuffle* / *Steppin' Pretty*

■ SATURDAY 7 MARCH 1936

RECORDING SESSION

ANDY KIRK AND HIS TWELVE CLOUDS OF JOY
Recording session for Decca in New York City.
Andy Kirk (bsx/ldr); Harry Lawson, Paul King, Earl Thompson (t); Ted Donnelly, Henry Wells (tb); John Harrington (cl/as/bar); John Williams (as/bar); Dick Wilson (ts); Claude Williams (vln); Mary Lou Williams (p); Ted Brinson (g); Booker Collins (b); Ben Thigpen (d)
Christopher Columbus / *Corky*

■ TUESDAY 10 MARCH 1936

RECORDING SESSION

WINGY MANONE AND HIS ORCHESTRA
Recording session for Vocalion in New York City.
Wingy Manone (t/voc); Ward Silloway (tb); Joe Marsala (cl); Eddie Miller (ts); Gil Bowers (p); Nappy Lamare (g/voc); Artie Shapiro (b); Ray Bauduc (d)
Shoe Shine Boy (vWM) / *West Wind* (vWM) / *Is It True What They Say About Dixie?* / *Goody Goody* (vWM)

■ WEDNESDAY 11 MARCH 1936

RECORDING SESSION

ANDY KIRK AND HIS TWELVE CLOUDS OF JOY
Recording session for Decca in New York City.
Andy Kirk (bsx/ldr); Harry Lawson, Paul King, Earl Thompson (t); Ted Donnelly, Henry Wells (tb); John Harrington (cl/as/bar); John Williams (as/bar); Dick Wilson (ts); Claude Williams (vln); Mary Lou Williams (p); Ted Brinson (g); Booker Collins (b); Ben Thigpen (d/voc)
I'se A-Muggin' (vBT) / *Until The Real Thing Comes Along* (vBT)

NOBLE SISSLE AND HIS ORCHESTRA
Recording session for Decca in New York City.
Noble Sissle (voc/ldr); Wendell Culley, Demas Dean, Clarence Brereton (t); Chester Burrill (tb); Sidney Bechet (cl/ss); Chauncey Haughton (cl/as); Gil White, Jerome Pasquall (ts); Oscar Madera (vln); Harry Brooks (p); Jimmy Miller (g); Jimmy Jones (b); Wilbert Kirk (d); Billy Banks, Lena Horne (voc)
That's What Love Did To Me (vLH) / *You Can't Live In Harlem* (vBB) / *I Wonder Who Made Rhythm* (vBB) / *'Tain't A Fit Night Out For Man Or Beast* (vNS) / *I Take To You* (vLH) / *Rhythm Of The Broadway Moon* (vNS)

Sidney Bechet

■ THURSDAY 12 MARCH 1936

RECORDING SESSION

MEZZ MEZZROW AND HIS SWING BAND
Recording session for Bluebird in New York City.
Frankie Newton (t); Mezz Mezzrow (cl); Bud Freeman (ts); Willie 'The Lion' Smith (p/voc); Albert Casey (g); Wellman Braud (b); George Stafford (d); Lucille Stewart (voc)
A Melody From The Sky (vLS) / *Lost* / *Mutiny In The Parlor* / *The Panic Is On* / *I'se A-Muggin'* (vWS & Band)

■ FRIDAY 13 MARCH 1936

RECORDING SESSION

STUFF SMITH & HIS ONYX CLUB BOYS
Recording session for Vocalion in New York City.
Jonah Jones (t/voc); Stuff Smith (vln/voc); James Sherman (p); Bobby Bennett (g); Mack Walker (b); Cozy Cole (d)
I Don't Want To Make History (vSS) / *'Tain't No Use* (vSS) / *After You've Gone* (vSS) / *You'se A Viper* (vJJ)

■ MONDAY 16 MARCH 1936

RADIO LOGS

11:00PM WMAQ
BENNY GOODMAN
Congress Hotel, Chicago
Madhouse
Mutiny In The Parlor (vocal: Helen Ward)
Yours Truly Is Truly Yours
Lost (vocal: Helen Ward)
Stompin' At The Savoy
Troublesome Trumpet (vocal: Helen Ward)

11:30PM WJZ
GLEN GRAY
Rainbow Room, NYC
Sweet Sue
Please Believe Me (vocal: Kenny Sargent)
Clap My Hands (vocal: Pee Wee Hunt)
So This Is Heaven (vocal: Kenny Sargent)
Wolverine Blues
With All My Heart (vocal: Kenny Sargent)
Mutiny On The Bandstand (vocal: Pee Wee Hunt)
Rose Room

12:00 MIDNIGHT WMAQ
FLETCHER HENDERSON
Grand Terrace, Chicago
Jim Town Blues
Rhythm In My Nursery Rhymes
Paradise
Trees
By Heck
Remember
Rug Cutters Swing

GALA OPENING
Wednesday, March 11th
in the
Rainbow Room

GLEN GRAY
and his famous
CASA LOMA
dance orchestra
Featuring songs by
PEE WEE HUNT and
KENNY SARGENT

SHEILA BARRETT
America's leading
satirist and mimic

JACK HOLLAND
and **JUNE HART**
Society's favorite dancers

NANO RODRIGO
and his tango rhumba orchestra

DINNER AND SUPPER DANCING
6:30 until 3 A.M. nightly except Sundays
FORMAL
Reservations Circle 6-1400
ROCKEFELLER CENTER ROOF

Glen Gray and the Casa Loma Orchestra opened at the Rainbow Room on Wednesday 11 March. Out front (above) are Billy Rauch, Art Ralston, Glen Gray, Clarence Hutchenrider and violinist Mel Jenssen conducting.
Right: The Casa Loma's 1935 brass section.

■ TUESDAY 17 MARCH 1936

RECORDING SESSION

TEDDY WILSON AND HIS ORCHESTRA
Recording session for Brunswick in New York City.
Ella Fitzgerald (voc); Frankie Newton (t); Jerry Blake (cl/as); Teddy Wilson (p); John Trueheart (g); Leemie Stanfield (b); Cozy Cole (d)
My Melancholy Baby (vEF) / *All My Life* (vEF) / *Christopher Columbus* / *I Know That You Know*

ADRIAN ROLLINI AND HIS ORCHESTRA
Recording session for Decca in New York City.
Irving Goodman (t); Art Drelinger (cl/ts); Adrian Rollini (bsx/vib); Jack Russin (p); Gwynn Nestor (g); George Hnida (b); Phil Sillman (d)
Tap Room Swing / *Swing Low* / *Stuff, Etc* / *Lessons In Love*

RADIO LOGS

10:00PM NBC
BENNY GOODMAN
"The Elgin Revue", Chicago
Alexander's Ragtime Band
From The Top Of Your Head (vocal: Helen Ward)
After You've Gone (BG Trio: Goodman, Krupa, Jess Stacy)
My Melancholy Baby
Bugle Call Rag

■ THURSDAY 19 MARCH 1936

RECORDING SESSION

BOB CROSBY AND HIS ORCHESTRA
Recording session for Decca in New York City.
Bob Crosby (voc/ldr); Phil Hart, Yank Lawson (t); Ward Silloway, Artie Foster (tb); Gil Rodin, Matty Matlock (cl/as); Noni Bernardi (as); Eddie Miller (cl/ts); Deane Kincaide (ts); Gil Bowers (piano); Nappy Lamare (g/voc); Bob Haggart (b); Ray Bauduc (d)
Christopher Columbus / *Ooh! Looka There! Ain't She Pretty?* (vBC) / *You're Toots To Me* (vBC) / *It's Great To Be In Love Again* (vBC)

■ FRIDAY 20 MARCH 1936

RECORDING SESSION

BENNY GOODMAN AND HIS ORCHESTRA
Recording session for Victor in Chicago.
Benny Goodman (cl); Harry Geller, Nate Kazebier, Pee Wee Erwin (t); Red Ballard, Joe Harris (tb); Bill DePew, Hymie Shertzer (as); Art Rollini, Dick Clark (ts); Jess Stacy (p); Allan Reuss (g); Harry Goodman (b); Gene Krupa (d); Helen Ward (voc)
Get Happy / Christopher Columbus / I Know That You Know

MUSIC CORPORATION OF AMERICA

745 FIFTH AVENUE, NEW YORK — 32 WEST RANDOLPH STREET, CHICAGO — OVIATT BUILDING, LOS ANGELES — UNION TRUST BUILDING, CLEVELAND — TOWER PETROLEUM, DALLAS

ADDRESS REPLY TO NEW YORK

March 20, 1936

Mr. Bob Inman
135 Pondfield Road
Bronxville, New York

Dear Mr. Inman:

I am sorry to say that BENNY GOODMAN will not be available for the time being, due to present contracts. However, there is a possibility that we could work out BERT BLOCK for you for approximately $450.00

I would appreciate hearing from you regarding this and assure you we will do everything possible to work out something satisfactory for you.

Awaiting your advice.

Sincerely,
MUSIC CORPORATION OF AMERICA

Willard Alexander
bc

With a typical teenager's nerve Bob, who could barely afford the $2 dinner at the Hotel Pennsylvania, had written to Willard Alexander of MCA asking how much it would cost to book the Benny Goodman Orchestra. Mr Alexander's polite response is shown above.

■ TUESDAY 24 MARCH 1936

RADIO LOGS

10:00PM NBC
BENNY GOODMAN
"The Elgin Revue", Chicago
Let Yourself Go
The Day I Let You Get Away (vocal: Helen Ward)
Unknown title
On The Alamo
Dixieland Band (vocal: Helen Ward)

■ WEDNESDAY 25 MARCH 1936

RECORDING SESSION

TOMMY DORSEY AND HIS ORCHESTRA
Recording session for Victor in New York City.
Tommy Dorsey (tb); Max Kaminsky, Sam Skolnick, Joe Bauer (t); Ben Pickering, Walter Mercurio (tb); Joe Dixon (cl/as/voc); Fred Stulce (as); Clyde Rounds (as/ts); Sid Block (ts); Dick Jones (p); William Schaffer (g); Gene Traxler (b); Dave Tough (d); Edythe Wright (voc)
You (vEW) / *Robins And Roses* (vEW) / *You Never Looked So Beautiful* / *You Started Me Dreaming* (vJD)

■ FRIDAY 27 MARCH 1936

RECORDING SESSION

TOMMY DORSEY AND HIS ORCHESTRA
Recording session for Victor in New York City.
Tommy Dorsey (tb); Max Kaminsky, Sam Skolnick, Joe Bauer (t); Ben Pickering, Walter Mercurio (tb); Joe Dixon (cl/as/voc); Fred Stulce (as); Clyde Rounds (as/ts); Sid Block (ts); Dick Jones (p); William Schaffer (g); Gene Traxler (b); Dave Tough (d); Edythe Wright (voc)
It's You I'm Talking About (vEW) / *Will I Ever Know It?* (vEW)

TOMMY DORSEY AND HIS CLAMBAKE SEVEN
Recording session for Victor in New York City.
Tommy Dorsey (tb); Max Kaminsky (t); Joe Dixon (cl); Sid Block (ts); Dick Jones (p); William Schaffer (g); Gene Traxler (b); Dave Tough (d); Edythe Wright (voc)
Rhythm Saved The World (vEW)

FLETCHER HENDERSON AND HIS ORCHESTRA
Recording session for Vocalion in Chicago.
Fletcher Henderson (p/ldr); Dick Vance, Joe Thomas, Roy Eldridge (t); Fernando Arbello, Ed Cuffee (tb); Buster Bailey (cl/as); Scoops Carry (as); Elmer Williams, Chu Berry (ts); Horace Henderson (p); Bob Lessey (g); John Kirby (b); Sid Catlett (d)
Christopher Columbus (pHH) / *Grand Terrace Swing [Big Chief De Sota]* (pFH) / *Blue Lou* (pHH) / *Stealin' Apples* (pFH)

■ SATURDAY 28 MARCH 1936

RECORDING SESSION

JIMMY DORSEY AND HIS ORCHESTRA
Recording session for Decca in Los Angeles.
Jimmy Dorsey (cl/as); George Thow (t); Toots Camarata (t/voc); Bobby Byrne, Don Mattison (tb/voc); Joe Yukl (tb); Jack Stacey (as); Fud Livingston (as/ts); Skeets Herfurt (ts); Bobby Van Eps (p); Roc Hillman (g/voc); Slim Taft (b); Ray McKinley (d/voc); Kay Weber, Bob Eberly (voc)
Tain't No Use (vTC,BB,RH) / *Welcome Stranger* (vKW) / *Serenade To Nobody In Particular* / *Robins And Roses* (vKW) / *Sing, Sing, Sing* (vTC,BB,RH)

MARCH 1936

Swing Era Scrapbook 11

■ SUNDAY 29 MARCH 1936

RECORDING SESSION

JIMMY DORSEY AND HIS ORCHESTRA
Recording session for Decca in Los Angeles.
Jimmy Dorsey (cl/as); George Thow (t); Toots Camarata (t/voc); Bobby Byrne, Don Mattison (tb/voc); Joe Yukl (tb); Jack Stacey (as); Fud Livingston (as/ts); Skeets Herfurt (ts); Bobby Van Eps (p); Roc Hillman (g/voc); Slim Taft (b); Ray McKinley (d/voc); Kay Weber, Bob Eberly (voc)
You Never Looked So Beautiful (vBE) / *Wah-Hoo!* (vTC,BB,RH) / *Is It True What They Say About Dixie?* (vBE) / *I'll Stand By* (vKW) / *What's The Reason (I'm Not Pleasin' You)?*

RADIO LOGS

8–9:00PM WJZ
SWING
BENNY GOODMAN Congress Hotel, Chicago
Stompin' At The Savoy
Dixieland Band (vocal: Helen Ward)
MEREDITH WILSON
Star Dust
ADRIAN ROLLINI'S TAP ROOM GANG
Tap Room Swing
FRANK FROEBA
After You've Gone
RED NORVO–MILDRED BAILEY
More Than You Know
The Day I Let You Get Away
STUFF SMITH
I'se A-Muggin'
KAY THOMPSON RHYTHM GIRLS
Goody Goody
You Hit The Spot
Honeysuckle Rose
Blue Moon
RAY NOBLE
The Very Thought Of You (vocal: Al Bowlly)
DICK McDONOUGH & CARL KRESS
Heatwave
RED NORVO
I Surrender Dear
RAY NOBLE
Truckin'
ADRIAN ROLLINI'S TAP ROOM GANG
Junk Man (harp: Casper Reardon)
BENNY GOODMAN
Dear Old Southland
RED NORVO
Deck Of Cards

■ MONDAY 30 MARCH 1936

RADIO LOGS

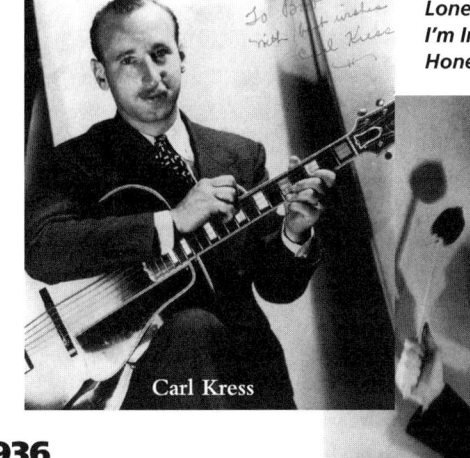

11:00PM WMAQ
BENNY GOODMAN
Congress Hotel, Chicago
Blue Skies
Everything's In Rhythm With My Heart (vocal: Helen Ward)
Minnie The Moocher's Wedding Day
Let's Face The Music And Dance (vocal: Helen Ward)
Walk, Jennie, Walk
Star Dust

It's Great To Be In Love Again (vocal: Helen Ward)
Breakin' In A Pair Of Shoes
On The Alamo
Goodbye (theme)

■ TUESDAY 31 MARCH 1936

RECORDING SESSION

ANDY KIRK AND HIS TWELVE CLOUDS OF JOY
Recording session for Columbia in New York City.
Andy Kirk (bsx/ldr); Harry Lawson, Paul King, Earl Thompson (t); Ted Donnelly, Henry Wells (tb); John Harrington (cl/as/bar); John Williams (as/bar); Dick Wilson (ts); Claude Williams (vln); Mary Lou Williams (p); Ted Brinson (g); Booker Collins (b); Ben Thigpen (d)
Puddin' Head Serenade

RADIO LOGS

10:00PM NBC
BENNY GOODMAN
"The Elgin Revue", Chicago
Back Home Again In Indiana
It's Been So Long (vocal: Helen Ward)
Blue Skies
Star Dust
You Hit The Spot (vocal: Helen Ward)

11:30PM WMCA
DON REDMAN
Connie's Inn, NYC
Chant Of The Weed (theme)
Truckin' (vocal: Don Redman)
Waitin' For Liza (vocal: Harlan Lattimore)
So This Is Heaven
Joe Louis Truck
Sugar Blues
Lonesome Cabin
I'm In The Mood For Love
Honeysuckle Rose

APRIL 1936

Hotel Astor: **Vincent Lopez**
Hotel Lexington: **Ozzie Nelson**
Rainbow Room: **Glen Gray**
Hotel Lincoln: **Tommy Dorsey** (1–)
Hotel New Yorker: **Bob Crosby**

Apollo Theater: **Jimmie Lunceford** (–2); **Willie Smith/Leadbelly** (3–9); **Cab Calloway** (10–16); **Willie Bryant** (17–23); **Buck & Bubbles / Bessie Smith / W.C.Handy** (24–30)
Loew's State Theater: **Cab Calloway** (24–30)
Roxy Theater: **Stuff Smith** (13–)

Connie's Inn: **Don Redman** (–27); **Leroy Smith** (29–)
Hickory House: **Wingy Manone**
Jack Dempsey's: **Red Norvo Swing Sextet**
Famous Door: **Bunny Berigan**
Onyx Club: **Stuff Smith**

Above: Bunny Berigan's Famous Door Band: Forrest Crawford, Red McKenzie, Mort Stuhlmaker, Eddie Condon & Bunny.

■ WEDNESDAY 1 APRIL 1936

RECORDING SESSION

HENRY 'RED' ALLEN
Recording session for Vocalion in New York City.
Henry 'Red' Allen (t/voc); J. C. Higginbotham (tb); Willie Humphrey (cl/as); Cecil Scott (ts); Norman Lester (p); Lawrence Lucie (g); Elmer James (b); Cozy Cole (d)
The Touch Of Your Lips (vHA) / *Lost* (vHA) / *I'll Bet You Tell That To All The Girls* (vHA) / *Every Minute Of The Hour* (vHA)

TEDDY HILL AND HIS ORCHESTRA
Recording session for Vocalion in New York City.
Teddy Hill (ts/ldr); Bill Dillard (t/voc); Frankie Newton, Shad Collins (t); Dicky Wells (tb); Russell Procope (cl/as); Howard Johnson (as); Cecil Scott (ts/bar); Sam Allen (p); John Smith (g); Richard Fulbright (b); Bill Beason (d)
Uptown Rhapsody

■ THURSDAY 2 APRIL 1936

RECORDING SESSION

ANDY KIRK AND HIS TWELVE CLOUDS OF JOY
Recording session for Decca in New York City.
Andy Kirk (bsx/ldr); Harry Lawson, Paul King, Earl Thompson (t); Ted Donnelly, Henry Wells (tb); John Harrington (cl/as/bar); John Williams (as/bar); Dick Wilson (ts); Claude Williams (vln); Mary Lou Williams (p); Ted Brinson (g); Booker Collins (b); Ben Thigpen (d); Pha Terrell (voc)
Until The Real Thing Comes Along (vPT)

■ FRIDAY 3 APRIL 1936

RECORDING SESSION

ANDY KIRK AND HIS TWELVE CLOUDS OF JOY
Recording session for Decca in New York City.
Andy Kirk (bsx/ldr); Harry Lawson, Paul King, Earl Thompson (t); Ted Donnelly, Henry Wells (tb); John Harrington (cl/as/bar); John Williams (as/bar); Dick Wilson (ts); Claude Williams (vln); Mary Lou Williams (p); Ted Brinson (g); Booker Collins (b); Ben Thigpen (d); Pha Terrell (voc)
Blue Illusion (vPT) / *Cloudy* (vPT)

RED McKENZIE & HIS RHYTHM KINGS
Recording session for Decca in New York City.
Bunny Berigan (t); Al Philburn (tb); Paul Ricci (cl); Babe Russin (ts); Frank Signorelli (p); Carmen Mastren (g); Sid Weiss (b); Stan King (d); Red McKenzie (comb/voc)
I Can't Get Started (vRM) / *I Can Pull A Rabbit Out Of My Hat* (vRM)

■ TUESDAY 7 APRIL 1936

RECORDING SESSION

CHICK WEBB ORCHESTRA
Recording session for Decca in New York City.
Ella Fitzgerald (voc); Mario Bauza, Taft Jordan, Bobby Stark (t); Sandy Williams, Claude Jones (tb); Edgar Sampson, Pete Clark (as); Elmer Williams (ts); Wayman Carver (ts/fl); Don Kirkpatrick (p); John Trueheart (g); Bill Thomas (b); Chick Webb (d)
Love, You're Just A Laugh (vEF) / *Crying My Heart Out For You* (vEF) / *Under The Spell Of The Blues* (vEF) / *When I Get Low I Get High* (vEF)

ANDY KIRK AND HIS TWELVE CLOUDS OF JOY
Recording session for Decca in New York City.
Andy Kirk (bsx/ldr); Harry Lawson, Paul King, Earl Thompson (t); Ted Donnelly, Henry Wells (tb); John Harrington (cl/as/bar); John Williams (as/bar); Dick Wilson (ts); Claude Williams (vln); Mary Lou Williams (p); Ted Brinson (g); Booker Collins (b); Ben Thigpen (d); Pha Terrell (voc)
Give Her A Pint (And She'll Tell It All) (vPT)

RADIO LOGS

10:00PM NBC
BENNY GOODMAN
"The Elgin Revue", Chicago
Christopher Columbus
Get Thee Behind Me Satan (vocal: Helen Ward)
Someday Sweetheart
I'm Gonna Sit Right Down And Write Myself A Letter (BG Trio: Stacy)
Goody Goody (vocal: Helen Ward)

■ WEDNESDAY 8 APRIL 1936

RECORDING SESSION

FATS WALLER & HIS RHYTHM
Recording session for Victor in New York City.
Herman Autrey (t); Gene Sedric (cl/ts); Fats Waller (p/voc); Albert Casey (g); Charles Turner (b); Arnold Boling (d); Elizabeth Handy (voc)
All My Life (vFW) / *Christopher Columbus* (vFW) / *Cross Patch* (vFW) / *It's No Fun* (vFW) / *Cabin In The Sky* (vFW) / *Us On A Bus* (vFW) / *Stay* (vFW,EH)

■ THURSDAY 9 APRIL 1936

RECORDING SESSION

FLETCHER HENDERSON AND HIS ORCHESTRA
Recording session for Victor in Chicago.
Fletcher Henderson (p/ldr); Dick Vance, Joe Thomas, Roy Eldridge (t); Fernando Arbello, Ed Cuffee (tb); Buster Bailey, Omer Simeon (cl/as); Elmer Williams, Chu Berry (ts); Horace Henderson (p); Bob Lessey (g); Israel Crosby (b); Sid Catlett (d)
I'm A Fool For Lovin' You (pHH) / *Moonrise On The Lowlands* (pHH) / *I'll Always Be In Love With You* (pFH) / *Jangled Nerves* (pHH)

WINGY MANONE AND HIS ORCHESTRA
Recording session for Bluebird in New York City.
Wingy Manone (t/voc); Joe Marsala (cl); Eddie Miller, Matty Matlock (cl/ts); Conrad Lanoue (p); Nappy Lamare (g/voc); Artie Shapiro (b); Ray Bauduc (d)
You Started Me Dreaming (vWM) / *Tormented* (vWM) / *Dallas Blues* (vWM) / *It's No Fun* (vWM) / *Rhythm Saved The World* (vWM) / *Swingin' At The Hickory House* (vWM,NL)

■ FRIDAY 10 APRIL 1936

RECORDING SESSION

ANDY KIRK AND HIS TWELVE CLOUDS OF JOY
Recording session for Decca in New York City.
Andy Kirk (bsx/ldr); Harry Lawson, Paul King, Earl Thompson (t); Ted Donnelly, Henry Wells (tb); John Harrington (cl/as/bar); John Williams (as/bar); Dick Wilson (ts); Claude Williams (vln); Mary Lou Williams (p); Ted Brinson (g); Booker Collins (b); Ben Thigpen (d)
Puddin' Head Serenade

■ MONDAY 13 APRIL 1936

RECORDING SESSION

BUNNY BERIGAN AND HIS BOYS
Recording session for Vocalion in New York City.
Bunny Berigan (t/voc); Art Shaw• or Paul Ricci* (cl); Forrest Crawford (ts); Joe Bushkin (p); Eddie Condon (g); Mort Stuhlmaker (b); Cozy Cole (d); Chick Bullock (voc)
A Melody From The Sky• (vCB) / *I Can't Get Started*• (vBB) / *A Little Bit Later On** (vCB) / *Rhythm Saved The World** (vCB)

BOB CROSBY AND HIS ORCHESTRA
Recording session for Decca in New York City.
Bob Crosby (voc/ldr); Phil Hart, Yank Lawson (t); Ward Silloway, Artie Foster (tb); Gil Rodin, Matty Matlock (cl/as); Noni Bernardi (as); Eddie Miller (cl/ts); Deane Kincaide (ts); Gil Bowers (piano); Nappy Lamare (g/voc); Bob Haggart (b); Ray Bauduc (d)
Muskrat Ramble / *Dixieland Shuffle*

■ TUESDAY 14 APRIL 1936

RADIO LOGS

10:00PM NBC
BENNY GOODMAN
"The Elgin Revue", Chicago
Inka Dinka Doo
I've Got The World On A String (vocal: Helen Ward)
Stompin' At The Savoy
Rosetta (BG Trio: BG, Krupa, **Teddy Wilson**)
King Porter Stomp

■ WEDNESDAY 15 APRIL 1936

RECORDING SESSION

TOMMY DORSEY AND HIS ORCHESTRA
Recording session for Victor in New York City.
Tommy Dorsey (tb); Max Kaminsky, Sam Skolnick, Joe Bauer (t); Ben Pickering, Walter Mercurio (tb); Joe Dixon (cl/as/voc); Fred Stulce (as); Bud Freeman, Bob Bunch (cl/ts); Dick Jones (p); William Schaffer (g); Gene Traxler (b); Dave Tough (d); Edythe Wright (voc)
You Never Looked So Beautiful (vEW) / *Stardust* (vEW) / *Ja-Da*

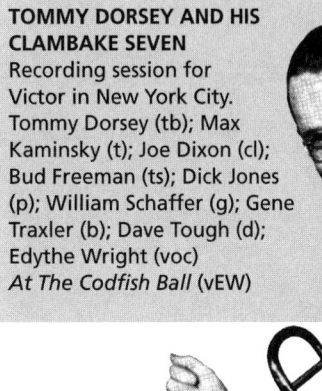

TOMMY DORSEY AND HIS CLAMBAKE SEVEN
Recording session for Victor in New York City.
Tommy Dorsey (tb); Max Kaminsky (t); Joe Dixon (cl); Bud Freeman (ts); Dick Jones (p); William Schaffer (g); Gene Traxler (b); Dave Tough (d); Edythe Wright (voc)
At The Codfish Ball (vEW)

> **Bob Crosby**
> AND HIS ORCHESTRA
> RKO BUILDING · ROCKEFELLER CENTER
> NEW YORK
>
> March 31, 1936
>
> Mr. Bob Inman
> 122 Pondfield Rd.
> Bronxville, N.Y.
>
> Dear Bob:
>
> I received your card and wish to take this opportunity to thank you for your interest in me and my orchestra.
>
> As you know, we are now located at the Hotel New Yorker, and may be heard from there over the Columbia network on Wednesday and Friday nights from eleven-thirty to twelve P.M., and on Saturday nights from twelve to twelve-thirty.
>
> The picture which you requested will be mailed to you within a very short time.
>
> Should you desire further information about the band, there is a good article on us in the April issue of Metronome.
>
> Trusting that our programs may continue to please you and hoping that I may receive your requests and comments, I remain
>
> Your friend,
> Bob Crosby
> Bob Crosby

■ TUESDAY 21 APRIL 1936

RECORDING SESSION

MIKE RILEY, EDDIE FARLEY & THEIR ONYX CLUB BOYS
Recording session for Champion in New York City.
Eddie Farley (t/voc); Mike Riley (tb/voc); Frank Langone (cl); Conrad Lanoue (p); Arthur Ens (g); George Yorke (b); Vic Engle (d)
There's Something In The Wind (vMR) / *The Old Oaken Bucket* (vMR)

RADIO LOGS

10:00PM NBC
BENNY GOODMAN
"The Elgin Revue", Chicago
I Found A New Baby
All My Life (vocal: Helen Ward)
Roll Along Prairie Moon
China Boy (BG Trio: BG, Krupa, Teddy Wilson)
You Can't Pull The Wool Over My Eyes (vocal: Helen Ward)

■ THURSDAY 23 APRIL 1936

RECORDING SESSION

BENNY GOODMAN AND HIS ORCHESTRA
Recording session for Victor in Chicago.
Benny Goodman (cl); Harry Geller, Nate Kazebier, Pee Wee Erwin (t); Red Ballard, Joe Harris (tb); Bill DePew, Hymie Shertzer (as); Art Rollini, Dick Clark (ts); Jess Stacy (p); Allan Reuss (g); Harry Goodman (b); Gene Krupa (d); Helen Ward (voc)
Stardust / *You Can't Pull The Wool Over My Eyes* (vHW) / *The Glory Of Love* (vHW) / *Remember* / *Walk, Jennie, Walk*

■ FRIDAY 24 APRIL 1936

RECORDING SESSION

BENNY GOODMAN TRIO
Recording session for Victor in Chicago.
Benny Goodman (cl); Teddy Wilson (p); Gene Krupa (d); Helen Ward (voc)
China Boy / *More Than You Know* / *All My Life* (vHW)

APRIL 1936   Swing Era Scrapbook   15

■ SATURDAY 25 APRIL 1936

RADIO LOGS

10:15PM WJZ
PAUL WHITEMAN Commercial

10:30PM WIP
WILLIE BRYANT Lincoln Theater, Philadelphia

11:00PM WHN
WINGY MANONE Hickory House, NYC

11:30PM WEAF
EARL HINES Grand Terrace, Chicago

12:00 MIDNIGHT WJZ
BENNY GOODMAN Congress Hotel, Chicago
Someday Sweetheart
Goody Goody (vocal: Helen Ward)
Christopher Columbus
All My Life (vocal: Helen Ward)
Blue Skies
I've Got A Heavy Date (vocal: Helen Ward)
Basin Street Blues (vocal: Joe Harris)
Dodging A Divorcee
Goodbye (theme)

12:30AM WHAS
MAL HALLETT Casa Madrid, Louisville, KY
Swing Fever (vocal: Buddy Welcome)
What's The Name Of That Song? (vocal: Clark Gillrum)
I'm Getting Sentimental Over You (Jimmy Styles' trombone)
I'se A-Muggin' (vocal: Buddy Welcome)
Solitude (vocal: Clark Gillrum)
Goody Goody (vocal: Lila Rose)
Honeysuckle Rose
Will Love Find A Way? (vocal: Clark Gillrum)

01:00AM WLW
EARL HINES Grand Terrace, Chicago

■ MONDAY 27 APRIL 1936

RECORDING SESSION

BENNY GOODMAN TRIO
Recording session for Victor in Chicago.
Benny Goodman (cl); Teddy Wilson (p); Gene Krupa (d); Helen Ward (voc)
Oh, Lady Be Good / Nobody's Sweetheart / Too Good To Be True (vHW)

FRANKIE TRUMBAUER AND HIS ORCHESTRA
Recording session for Brunswick in New York City.
Frankie Trumbauer (c-mel/as/ldr); Ed Wade, Charlie Teagarden (t); Jack Teagarden (tb/voc); Art Shaw (cl); Joe Cordaro (cl/as); Mutt Hayes (ts); Roy Bargy (p); Carl Kress (g); Art Miller (b); Stan King (d)
Somebody Loves Me (vJT) / *The Mayor Of Alabam'* (vJT&Band) / *Ain't Misbehavin'* (vJT) / *'S Wonderful*

■ TUESDAY 28 APRIL 1936

RADIO LOGS

10:00PM NBC
BENNY GOODMAN
"The Elgin Revue", Chicago
Darktown Strutters' Ball
Too Good To Be True (vocal: Helen Ward)
Unknown Title
Nobody's Sweetheart (BG Trio: BG, Krupa, Teddy Wilson)
Between The Devil And The Deep Blue Sea (vocal: Helen Ward)

■ WEDNESDAY 29 APRIL 1936

RADIO LOGS

12:00 MIDNIGHT WEAF
BENNY GOODMAN
Congress Hotel, Chicago
Farewell Blues
It's Been So Long
Stompin' At The Savoy
Lost (vocal: Helen Ward)
King Porter Stomp
I Never Knew
You (vocal: Helen Ward)
My Melancholy Baby
All My Life (vocal: Helen Ward)
Let Yourself Go

MAY 1936

Hotel Astor: **Vincent Lopez**
Hotel Lexington: **Bob Crosby** (13–)
Rainbow Room: **Glen Gray**
Hotel Lincoln: **Tommy Dorsey**
Hotel Pennsylvania: **Dick Stabile**

Apollo Theater: **Four Ink Spots/Hardy Bros band** (1–6); **Lucky Millinder** (7–14); **Willie Bryant** (15–21); **Noble Sissle** (22–28)
Loew's State Theater: **Lucky Millinder** (22–)
Paramount Theater: **Ray Noble** (13–19); **Louis Armstrong** (27–)

Connie's Inn: **Leroy Smith**
Hickory House: **Wingy Manone**
Famous Door: **Bunny Berigan** (Club CLOSES 9 May)
Onyx Club: **Stuff Smith**

■ SATURDAY 2 MAY 1936

RADIO LOGS

11:00PM WHN
WINGY MANONE Hickory House, NYC
11:30PM WJZ
GLEN GRAY
Rainbow Room, RKO Bldg, NYC
The Touch Of Your Hand (vocal: Kenny Sargent)
You Can Call It Swing (vocal: Pee Wee Hunt)
Can I Be Wrong? (vocal: Kenny Sargent)
Rose of The Rio Grande
Love Came Out of The Night (vocal: Kenny Sargent)
I'm Pictulated Over You (vocal: Pee Wee Hunt)
Avalon Town
Milenburg Joys

11:30PM WMCA
LEROY SMITH Connie's Inn, NYC

12:00 MIDNIGHT WABC
HENRY HALSTEAD St. Louis

12:30AM WIP
LUCKY MILLINDER
Lincoln Theater, Philadelphia
Red Rhythm (vocal: Edith Wilson)
Stompin' At The Savoy
Lost (vocal: Chuck Richards)
Keep The Rhythm Going (Edgar Hayes' piano)
Shoe Shine Boy
Tormented (vocal: Chuck Richards)
Stop, Look And Listen

■ SUNDAY 3 MAY 1936

RADIO LOGS

3:15PM WJZ
JOE VENUTI
In The Groove
Melody From The Sky (Tony Sacco's guitar)
Stompin' At The Savoy
Welcome Stranger (vocal: Mildred Fenton)
China Boy
Would You? (Tony Sacco's guitar)
Doin' Things
I Don't Want To Make History (vocal: Mildred Fenton)
There's Always A Happy Ending (Tony Sacco's guitar)

10:30PM WIP
LUCKY MILLINDER
Lincoln Theater, Philadelphia
Star Dust (theme)
Swingin' In E Flat
Rose Room
There Is No Greater Love (vocal: Chuck Richards)
Permit Me
Feelin' Gay
Same Old Way (written by J.C. Higginbotham, feat. pianist Edgar Hayes)
Ride, Red, Ride (feat. Red Allen)

11:35PM WEAF
EARL HINES
Grand Terrace, Chicago
Cavernism (theme)
Honeysuckle Rose
Stompin' At The Savoy
Rhythm Saved The World (vocal: Walter Fuller)
You Can't Pull The Wool Over My Eyes (vocal: Walter Fuller)
Rosetta
There's No Substitute For You (vocal: James Phillips)

■ MONDAY 4 MAY 1936

RECORDING SESSION

TEDDY HILL AND HIS ORCHESTRA
Recording session for Vocalion in New York City.
Teddy Hill (ts/ldr); Bill Dillard (t/voc); Frankie Newton, Shad Collins (t); Dicky Wells (tb); Russell Procope (cl/as); Howard Johnson (as); Cecil Scott (ts/bar); Sam Allen (p); John Smith (g); Richard Fulbright (b); Bill Beason (d)
At The Rugcutters' Ball / Blue Rhythm Fantasy / Passionette

■ TUESDAY 5 MAY 1936

RADIO LOGS

10:00PM NBC
BENNY GOODMAN
"The Elgin Revue", Chicago
Christopher Columbus
All My Life (vocal: Helen Ward)
After You've Gone (BG Trio: BG, Krupa, Teddy Wilson)
Remember
I Can't Give You Anything But Love (vocal: Helen Ward)

■ THURSDAY 7 MAY 1936

RECORDING SESSION

DON REDMAN AND HIS ORCHESTRA
Recording session for ARC in New York City.
Don Redman (cl/ss/as/voc/ldr); Reunald Jones, Shirley Clay, Sidney De Paris (t); Gene Simon, Benny Morton (tb); Edward Inge, Rupert Cole (cl/as); Harvey Boone (cl/as/bar); Robert Carroll (ts); Don Kirkpatrick (p); Talcott Reeves (g); Bob Ysaguirre (b); Manzie Johnson (d/vib); Harlan Lattimore (voc)
A Little Bit Later On (vDR) / *Lazy Weather* (vHL) / *Moonrise On The Lowlands* (vHL) / *I Gotcha* (vDR & Band)

■ FRIDAY 8 MAY 1936

RECORDING SESSION

WINGY MANONE AND HIS ORCHESTRA
Recording session for Bluebird in New York City.
Wingy Manone (t/voc); Joe Marsala (cl); Tommy Mace (as); Eddie Miller (ts); Conrad Lanoue (p); Carmen Mastren (g); Artie Shapiro (b); Sam Weiss (d)
Basin Street Blues (vWM) / *Hesitation Blues* (vWM) / *Sing Me A Swing Song* (vWM) / *Isn't Love The Strangest Thing?* (vWM) / *Every Once In A While* (vWM) / *Panama*

RADIO LOGS

11:30PM WJZ
Tribute To Duke Ellington
DUKE ELLINGTON Congress Hotel, Chicago (opening night)
Jumpy
GLEN GRAY Rainbow Room, NYC
Smoke Rings
We'll Rest At The End Of The Trail (vocal: Kenny Sargent)
Shades Of Hades
DUKE ELLINGTON Congress Hotel, Chicago (opening night)
Merry-Go-Round (Rex Stewart on cornet)
Echoes Of Harlem (Cootie Williams on trumpet)
CARL REVISO Hotel St. Francis, San Francisco
Peg O' My Heart
DUKE ELLINGTON Congress Hotel, Chicago (opening night)
Oh, Baby (vocal: Ivie Anderson)
Clarinet Lament

Below: Wingy Manone's little band at the Hickory House. Sid Weiss (b), Wingy Manone (t), Carmen Mastren (g), Joe Marsala (cl).

SUNDAY 10 MAY 1936

RADIO LOGS

3:15PM WJZ
JOE VENUTI
NYC
Lost (vocal: Mildred Fenton)
There Is No Greater Love (Tony Sacco's guitar)
It Happened (Tony Sacco's guitar)
Ain'tcha
You (Tony Sacco's guitar)
Sweet Sue
Rhythm Saved The World (vocal: Mildred Fenton)
What's The Name Of That Song? (Tony Sacco's guitar)
Swingerin'
Doing The Voom Voom

?? WIP
HARDY BROTHERS ORCHESTRA
Lincoln Theater, Philadelphia
Stomp It Off
I'll Follow You
Cavernism
Truckin'
Christopher Columbus
You Are My Lucky Star
Nitwit Serenade

11:00PM WHN
WINGY MANONE
Hickory House, NYC
Isle Of Capri (theme)
St. Louis Blues
Sweet Lorraine
Nickel In The Slot
Isn't Love The Strangest Thing

11:30PM WABC
TOMMY DORSEY
Lincoln Hotel, NYC
I'm Getting Sentimental Over You (theme)
Robins And Roses (vocal: Edythe Wright)
It Happened To End
Goody Goody (vocal: Three Esquires)
Don't Count Your Kisses (vocal: Edythe Wright, Jack Leonard)
Small Town Girl (vocal: Jack Leonard)
At The Codfish Ball (Clambake Seven, vocal: Edythe Wright)
In A Sentimental Mood
Four or Five Times

11:35PM WEAF
EARL HINES
Grand Terrace, Chicago
Goin' Home
At The Codfish Ball
It's You I'm Talking About
I'se A-Muggin' (vocal: Walter Fuller)
Sing Me A Swing Song
Rhythm Saved The World (vocal: Walter Fuller)
St. Louis Blues

12:00 MIDNIGHT WJZ
DUKE ELLINGTON
Congress Hotel, Chicago
Merry-Go-Round
Troubled Waters (vocal: Ivie Anderson)
In A Sentimental Mood
Stompy Jones
Echoes Of Harlem (Cootie Williams on trumpet)
I'm Satisfied (vocal: Ivie Anderson)
Sophisticated Lady (Lawrence Brown on trombone)
Jumpy

TUESDAY 12 MAY 1936

RECORDING SESSION

STUFF SMITH & HIS ONYX CLUB BOYS
Recording session for Vocalion in New York City.
Jonah Jones (t/voc); Stuff Smith (vln/voc); James Sherman (p); Bobby Bennett (g); Mack Walker (b); Cozy Cole (d)
Robins And Roses (vSS) / *I've Got A Heavy Date* (vSS& Band)

RADIO LOGS

10:00PM NBC
BENNY GOODMAN
"The Elgin Revue", Chicago
House Hop
Dixieland Band (vocal: Helen Ward)
Nobody's Sweetheart (BG Trio: BG, Krupa, Teddy Wilson)
More Than You Know
Farewell Blues

? WHN
WINGY MANONE
Hickory House, NYC
Jazz In Blue
Is It True What They Say About Dixie?
Dinah
Isn't Love The Strangest Thing?
Bugle Call Rag

12:00MIDNIGHT WMAQ
EARL HINES
Chicago
At The Codfish Ball
You Started Me Dreamin'
I'm A Fool For Loving You
Big John Special

WEDNESDAY 13 MAY 1936

RECORDING SESSION

CHARLIE BARNET AND HIS ORCHESTRA
Recording session for ARC in New York City.
Charlie Barnet (ss/as/ts/voc); Frank Amaral, Kermit Simmons (t); Joe Hostetter (t/voc); Buzz Smith, John Doyle (tb); George Vaughan, Don Morres (cl/as); Willard Brady (ts); Bob Parks (ts/voc); Horace Diaz (p); Frank Klinger (g); Sid Weiss (b); Julie Mendelson (d)
My First Thrill (vBP) / *The Swing Waltz* (vJH) / *Cross Patch* (vCB) / *Too Good To Be True* (vCB)

THURSDAY 14 MAY 1936

RECORDING SESSION

TEDDY WILSON AND HIS ORCHESTRA
Recording session for Brunswick in Chicago.
Roy Eldridge (t/voc); Buster Bailey (cl); Chu Berry (ts); Teddy Wilson (p); Bob Lessey (g); Israel Crosby (b); Sid Catlett (d)
Mary Had A Little Lamb (vRE) / *Too Good To Be True* / *Warmin' Up* / *Blues In C-Sharp Minor*

■ FRIDAY 15 MAY 1936

RADIO LOGS

12:15AM WEAF
DUKE ELLINGTON
Congress Hotel, Chicago
Every Minute Of The Hour
Jumpy
Troubled Waters
In A Sentimental Mood
Sumpin' 'Bout Rhythm
Love Is Like a Cigarette (vocal: Ivie Anderson)
Harlem Speaks

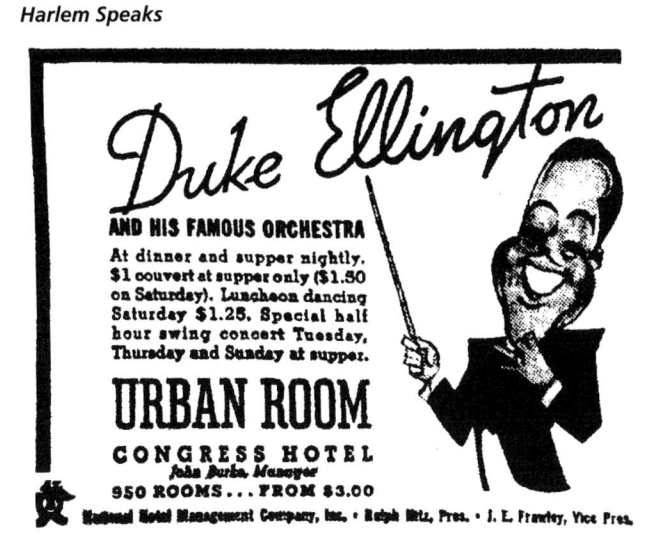

Duke Ellington AND HIS FAMOUS ORCHESTRA
At dinner and supper nightly. $1 couvert at supper only ($1.50 on Saturday). Luncheon dancing Saturday $1.25. Special half hour swing concert Tuesday, Thursday and Sunday at supper.
URBAN ROOM
CONGRESS HOTEL
John Burba, Manager
950 ROOMS...FROM $3.00
National Hotel Management Company, Inc. • Ralph Hitz, Pres. • J. E. Frawley, Vice Pres.

12:30AM WJZ
FLETCHER HENDERSON
Grand Terrace, Chicago (opening)
Christopher Columbus (theme)
Deep Sea Blues
Mutiny In The Parlor
I Got Plenty O' Nuttin'
Blue Skies
Sweet Sue
I'm A Fool For Loving You
Beautiful Lady In Blue
St. Louis Blues

■ SATURDAY 16 MAY 1936

RADIO LOGS

12:30AM WMCA
NOBLE SISSLE
Lincoln Theater, Philadelphia
Lady From Broadway
Robins And Roses
Melody From The Sky (vocal: Lena Horne)
White Heat
I'm Gonna Sit Right Down And Write Myself A Letter (vocal: Lena Horne)
All My Life (vocal: Billy Banks)
Ida, Sweet As Apple Cider
Goody Goody

■ SUNDAY 17 MAY 1936

RADIO LOGS

7:00PM WABC
TOMMY DORSEY
Lincoln Hotel, NYC
I'm Getting Sentimental Over You (theme)
You (vocal: Edythe Wright)
Small Town Girl (vocal: Jack Leonard)
Us On A Bus (vocal: Three Esquires)
Lost (vocal: Edythe Wright)
Darktown Strutters' Ball
It's You I'm Talking About (vocal: Edythe Wright)
What's The Name Of That Song? (vocal: Jack Leonard)
Mary Had A Little Lamb (vocal: Edythe Wright)
Love Is Like a Cigarette (vocal: Jack Leonard)
That's A-Plenty

12:00MIDNIGHT WJZ
DUKE ELLINGTON
Congress Hotel, Chicago
Clarinet Lament
Hyde Park
My Old Flame
Showboat Shuffle
Unknown Title
Oh Babe, Maybe Someday (vocal: Ivie Anderson)
Echoes Of Harlem
Rockin' In Rhythm

■ MONDAY 18 MAY 1936

RADIO LOGS

11:00PM WHN
WINGY MANONE
Hickory House, NYC
'Way Down Yonder In New Orleans
Sweet Sue
It's Been So Long

11:30PM WJZ
GLEN GRAY
Rainbow Room, NYC
China Girl
Tormented (vocal: Kenny Sargent)
I'm Gonna Sit Right Down And Write Myself A Letter (vocal: Pee Wee Hunt)
No Regrets (vocal: Kenny Sargent)
Christopher Columbus
Peg O' My Heart (vocal: Kenny Sargent)
I Can Pull A Rabbit Out Of The Hat (vocal: Pee Wee Hunt)
On The Alamo
Great Day

12:00MIDNIGHT WOR
DICK STABILE
Hotel Pennsylvania, NYC
You
Welcome Stranger (vocal: Bert Shaw)
Blue Skies
Melody From The Sky (vocal: Bert Shaw)
I Can't Get Started (vocal: Bert Shaw)
In A Sentimental Mood
I'll Bet You Tell That To All The Girls (vocal: Bert Shaw)
If You Love Me
Robins And Roses

■ TUESDAY 19 MAY 1936

RADIO LOGS

10:00PM NBC
BENNY GOODMAN
"The Elgin Revue", Chicago
Unknown Title
St. Louis Blues (vocal: Helen Ward)
'Way Down Yonder In New Orleans (BG Trio)
Star Dust
Honeysuckle Rose

■ WEDNESDAY 20 MAY 1936

RECORDING SESSION

LUCKY MILLINDER & MILLS BLUE RHYTHM BAND
Recording session for Columbia in New York City.
Lucky Millinder (voc/ldr); Wardell Jones, Shelton Hemphill (t); Henry 'Red' Allen (t/voc); George Washington (tb/voc); J.C.Higginbotham (tb); Willie Humphrey, Crawford Wethington (cl/as); Tab Smith (as); Joe Garland (cl/ts/bar); Edgar Hayes (p); Lawrence Lucie (g); Elmer James (b); O'Neil Spencer (d); Chuck Richards (voc)
Red Rhythm (vLM) / *Everything Is Still Okay* (vCR) / *Jes' Natch'ully Lazy* (vCR,GW) / *St. Louis Wiggle Rhythm*

■ THURSDAY 21 MAY 1936

RECORDING SESSION

HENRY 'RED' ALLEN
Recording session for Vocalion in New York City.
Henry 'Red' Allen (t/voc); J. C. Higginbotham (tb); Tab Smith (as); Cecil Scott (cl); Happy Cauldwell (ts); Jimmy Reynolds (p); Lawrence Lucie (g); Elmer James (b); Walter Johnson (d)
You (vHA) / *Tormented* (vHA) / *Nothing's Blue But The Sky* (vHA) / *Would You?* (vHA)

CAB CALLOWAY AND HIS ORCHESTRA
Recording session for Brunswick in New York City.
Cab Calloway (voc); Shad Collins, Irving Randolph, Lammar Wright (t); DePriest Wheeler, Keg Johnson, Claude Jones (tb); Garvin Bushell, Andrew Brown (cl/as); Ben Webster, Walter Thomas (ts); Benny Payne (p); Morris White (g); Milt Hinton (b); Leroy Maxey (d)
Love Is The Reason (vCC) / *When You're Smiling* (vCC) / *Jes' Natch'ully Lazy* (vCC) / *Are You In Love With Me Again?* (vCC)

■ FRIDAY 22 MAY 1936

RADIO LOGS

12:00MIDNIGHT WEAF
DUKE ELLINGTON
Congress Hotel, Chicago
Merry-Go-Round
Tormented (vocal: Ivie Anderson)
Showboat Shuffle
In A Sentimental Mood (Latest piece by Ellington)
Isn't Love The Strangest Thing? (vocal: Ivie Anderson)
Drifting Changes (vocal: Ivie Anderson)
Oh Babe, Maybe Someday (vocal: Ivie Anderson)
Echoes Of Harlem (Cootie Williams' trumpet)
Swing Low (Rex Stewart's cornet)

12:30AM WJZ
FLETCHER HENDERSON
Grand Terrace, Chicago
I Got Plenty O' Nuttin'
Do You Or Don't You Love Me? (vocal: Teddy Lewis)
My First Thrill (vocal: Teddy Lewis)
I Got Plenty O' Nuttin'
Honeysuckle Rose
Every Minute Of The Hour
Everybody's Swingin' It
The Moon Is Low

■ SATURDAY 23 MAY 1936

RECORDING SESSION

FLETCHER HENDERSON AND HIS ORCHESTRA
Recording session for Victor in Chicago.
Fletcher Henderson (p/ldr); Dick Vance, Joe Thomas, Roy Eldridge (t); Fernando Arbello, Ed Cuffee (tb); Buster Bailey, Jerome Pasquall (cl/as); Elmer Williams, Chu Berry (ts); Horace Henderson (p); Bob Lessey (g); Israel Crosby (b); Sid Catlett (d); Teddy Lewis (voc)
Where There's You, There's Me (vTL,pFH) / *Do You Or Don't You Love Me?* (vTL,pFH) / *Grand Terrace Rhythm* (pFH) / *Riffin'* (pHH) / *Mary Had A Little Lamb* (pHH)

MAY 1936   Swing Era Scrapbook   21

RADIO LOGS

12:30AM WIP
FATS WALLER
Lincoln Theater, Philadelphia
Ain't Misbehavin' (theme)
Christopher Columbus
Lovely Liza Lee
Cross Patch
Love Is Just Around The Corner
I Can't Give You Anything But Love
Tormented
Got A Feelin' You're Foolin'
Cavernism

■ SUNDAY 24 MAY 1936

This magnificent concert featured the bands of Joe Venuti, Wingy Manone, Art Shaw, Bob Crosby, Red Norvo, Stuff Smith, Bunny Berigan, Tommy Dorsey, Paul Whiteman, Adrian Rollini, Louis Armstrong, Frank Chase, Red Nichols, Memphis Five and Glen Gray as well as Caspar Reardon, Meade Lux Lewis, Carl Kress & Dick McDonough

RADIO LOGS

7:00PM WABC
TOMMY DORSEY
Lincoln Hotel, NYC
Mary Had A Little Lamb (vocal: Edythe Wright)
Love Came Out Of The Night (vocal: Jack Leonard)
Stop, Look And Listen
Me And The Moon
Goody Goody (vocal: Edythe Wright & Three Esquires)
You Started Me Dreaming (vocal: Jack Leonard)
Robins And Roses (vocal: Edythe Wright)
No Regrets (vocal: Jack Leonard)
Ja-Da
I'm Getting Sentimental Over You (theme)

10:30PM WIP
FATS WALLER
Lincoln Theater, Philadelphia
I've Got My Fingers Crossed
Sugar Rose
What's On Your Mind? (vocal: Three Palmer Brothers)
I'm Gonna Sit Right Down And Write Myself A Letter
Dinah
St. Louis Blues (Al Washington on clarinet)
Cross Patch
Honeysuckle Rose

11:00PM WHN
WINGY MANONE
Hickory House, NYC
Honeysuckle Rose
I'se A-Muggin'
'Way Down Yonder In New Orleans
Jazz Me Blues

■ MONDAY 25 MAY 1936

RADIO LOGS

11:00PM WHN
WINGY MANONE
Hickory House, NYC
Isle Of Capri (theme)
Is It True What They Say About Dixie?
Sweet Sue
That's A-Plenty

■ TUESDAY 26 MAY 1936

RADIO LOGS

10:00PM WEAF
BENNY GOODMAN
"The Elgin Revue", Chicago
Unknown Title
These Foolish Things (vocal: Helen Ward)
Nobody's Sweetheart (BG Trio)
Stompin' At The Savoy
Sing Me A Swing Song (vocal: Helen Ward)

11:00PM WHN
WINGY MANONE
Hickory House, NYC
Stompin' At The Savoy
Sweet Lorraine
Nickel In The Slot
Shine

11:00PM WEAF
FLETCHER HENDERSON
Grand Terrace, Chicago
How Do I Rate With You?
Swingin' Uptown
Jangled Nerves
Christopher Columbus (theme)

12:00 MIDNIGHT WABC
SLEEPY HALL
Meadowbrook, NJ
I'm Building Up To An Awful Letdown
Moonglow
Stompin' At The Savoy
Please Believe Me
Mama Don't Allow
Lost

Wingy Manone

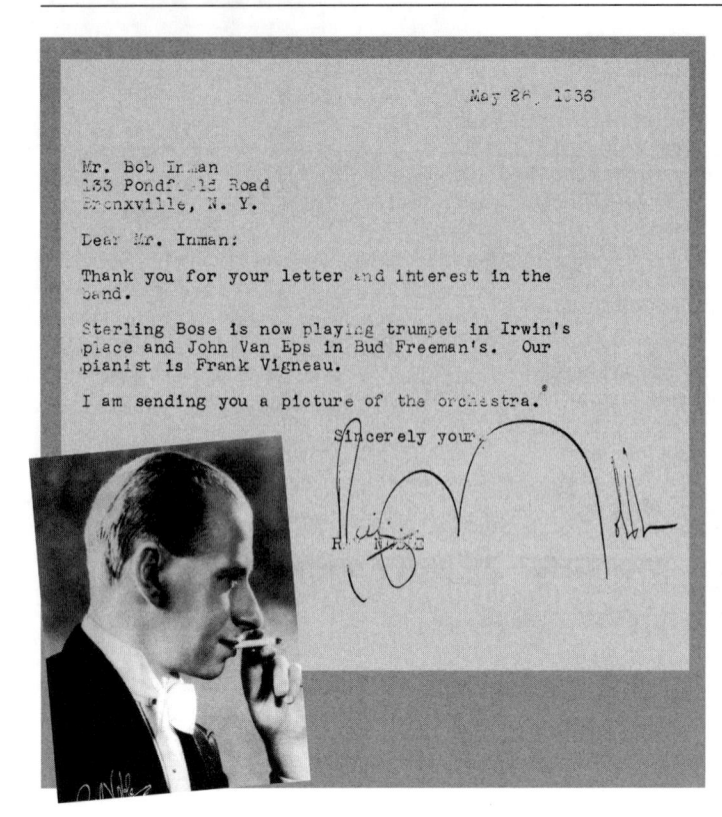

WEDNESDAY 27 MAY 1936

RECORDING SESSION

BENNY GOODMAN AND HIS ORCHESTRA
Recording session for Victor in New York City.
Benny Goodman (cl); Chris Griffin, Nate Kazebier, Pee Wee Erwin (t); Red Ballard, Murray McEachern (tb); Bill DePew, Hymie Shertzer (as); Art Rollini, Dick Clark (ts); Jess Stacy (p); Allan Reuss (g); Harry Goodman (b); Gene Krupa (d); Helen Ward (voc)
House Hop / *These Foolish Things* (vHW) / *Sing Me A Swing Song* (vHW) / *I Would Do Anything For You*

RADIO LOGS

10:45PM WEAF
CHARLIE BARNET
Glen Island Casino
When You're Low
Sunshine At Midnight (vocal: Joe Hope)
Spring In Vienna
Cross Patch (vocal: Charlie Barnet)
In A Little Wayside Inn
Dream Lullaby (theme)

THURSDAY 28 MAY 1936

RADIO LOGS

6:00PM WNEW
TOMMY DORSEY
Make-Believe Ballroom, NYC
I'm Getting Sentimental Over You (theme)
One Night In Monte Carlo (vocal: Edythe Wright)
Rhythm Saved The World (vocal: Edythe Wright)
Blue Moon
Rhythm In My Nursery Rhymes (vocal: Edythe Wright)
The Day I Let You Get Away (vocal: Edythe Wright & Three Esquires)
Honeysuckle Rose
At The Codfish Ball

11:00PM WHN
WINGY MANONE
Hickory House, NYC
Swingin' At The Hickory House
It's No Fun
Dallas Blues
Every Once In A While
I'll Be Glad When You're Dead, You Rascal, You

11:30PM WTIC
FLETCHER HENDERSON
Grand Terrace, Chicago
Riffin'
My First Thrill (vocal: Teddy Lewis)
Every Minute Of The Hour
Yeah, Man!

11:30PM WABC
TOMMY DORSEY
Lincoln Hotel, NYC
The Glory Of Love (vocal: Edythe Wright)
All My Life (vocal: Jack Leonard)
Sugar
There Is No Greater Love (vocal: Jack Leonard)
Christopher Columbus
I've Got A Heavy Date (vocal: Edythe Wright)
The Touch Of Your Lips (vocal: Jack Leonard)
Us On A Bus (vocal: Three Esquires)
Lost
Big John Special

FRIDAY 29 MAY 1936

RADIO LOGS

12:10AM WEAF
DUKE ELLINGTON
Congress Hotel, Chicago
Basin Street Blues
At A Fair With Rex (Exposition Swing?) (Rex Stewart on cornet)
Tormented (vocal: Ivie Anderson)
Ducky Wucky
Oh Babe, Maybe Someday (vocal: Ivie Anderson)
In A Sentimental Mood

12:30AM WJZ
FLETCHER HENDERSON
Grand Terrace, Chicago
Jangled Nerves
On The Beach At Bali-Bali
Mary Had A Little Lamb (vocal: Roy Eldridge)
Lost
St. Louis Blues

SUNDAY 31 MAY 1936

RADIO LOGS

7:15PM WABC
TOMMY DORSEY
Lincoln Hotel, NYC
Cross Patch (vocal: Edythe Wright)
Would You? (vocal: Jack Leonard)
Finger Buster
These Foolish Things (vocal: Edythe Wright)
Sugar Foot Stomp

JUNE 1936

Hotel Astor: **Vincent Lopez**
Hotel Lexington: **Bob Crosby** (13–)
Rainbow Room: **Glen Gray**
Hotel Lincoln: **Tommy Dorsey** (–9); **Dick Stabile** (10–)
Hotel Commodore: **Red Norvo**
Hotel Pennsylvania: **Joe Reichman**

Apollo Theater: **Fats Waller** (–4); **Earl Hines** (5–11); **Blanche Calloway** (12–18); **Chick Webb** (19–25); **Ethel Waters** (26–)
Paramount Theater: **Louis Armstrong** (–2);

Connie's Inn: **Valaida Snow** (3–)
Hickory House: **Wingy Manone**
Onyx Club: **Stuff Smith**

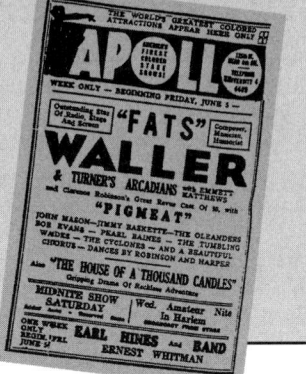

■ MONDAY 1 JUNE 1936

RECORDING SESSION

CHARLIE BARNET AND HIS ORCHESTRA
Recording session for Bluebird in New York City.
Charlie Barnet (ss/as/ts/voc); Frank Amaral, Kermit Simmons (t); Joe Hostetter (t/voc); Buzz Smith, John Doyle (tb); George Vaughan, Don Morres (cl/as); Willard Brady (ts); Bob Parks (ts/voc); Horace Diaz (p); Frank Klinger (g); Sid Weiss (b); Julie Mendelson (d); Laura Deane (v)
I'm An Old Cowhand (vJH) / *But Definitely* (vLD) / *Long Ago And Far Away* (vCB) / *When I'm With You* (vBP) / *Where Is My Heart?* (vJH) / *Empty Saddles* (vJH)

RADIO LOGS

11:00PM WHN
WINGY MANONE
Hickory House, NYC
Swingin' At The Hickory House
It's No Fun
Dallas Blues

■ TUESDAY 2 JUNE 1936

RECORDING SESSION

CHICK WEBB ORCHESTRA
Recording session for Decca in New York City.
Ella Fitzgerald (voc); Mario Bauza, Taft Jordan, Bobby Stark (t); Sandy Williams, Nat Story (tb); Edgar Sampson, Pete Clark (as); Ted McRae (ts); Wayman Carver (ts/fl); Don Kirkpatrick (p); John Trueheart (g); Bill Thomas (b); Chick Webb (d)
Sing Me A Swing Song (And Let Me Dance) (vEF) / *A Little Bit Later On* (vEF) / *Love, You're Just A Laugh* (vEF) / *Devoting My Time To You* (vEF) / *Go Harlem*

10:00PM WEAF
BENNY GOODMAN
"The Elgin Revue", NYC
Saw this program with Don Mortimer, Hugh Pastoriza, Nancy Long and Barbara Doyle. Left Bronxville at 9:10pm and got home at 12:00. Saw Benny Goodman walking from car into building. Asked for his signature but he said to wait until after the broadcast. Got signatures of Allan Reuss (guitar), Arthur Rollini (tenor sax), and Dick Clark (tenor sax) outside of building. Got trombonist Red Ballard's signature in studio before broadcast. After the broadcast got Pee Wee Erwin's, Nate Kazebier's, Gordon Griffin's, Helen Ward (vocalist), Bill Depew (sax), Teddy Wilson (piano), Murray McEachern (trombonist who replaced Joe Harris in May), Hymie Shertzer (alto sax), Gene Krupa (drums), Harry Goodman (bass) and Benny Goodman's signatures.
Ford Bond (announcer) talked before the program started and Eddie Dowling (comedian) warmed up the audience.

I Found A New Baby
I Can't Get Started (vocal: Helen Ward)
Someday Sweetheart (BG Trio)
Would You
Robins And Roses (vocal: Helen Ward)
I Would Do Anything For You (first trio; then orchestra)

■ WEDNESDAY 3 JUNE 1936

RADIO LOGS

10:30PM WHN
TOMMY 'RED' TOMPKINS
? Ballroom, NYC
Just You, Just Me
Welcome Stranger (vocal: Ted Napoleon)
Unknown Title
Mama Don't Allow (vocal: Silly Harris)
Moments Of Moments
Ride, Red, Ride (vocal: Sonny Genonson??)
Tormented
Zaz-Zuh-Zaz
Blue Skies

Red Norvo and his orchestra at the Commodore Hotel.

11:00PM WHN
CLYDEL MARSHALL
Connie's Inn, NYC
Keep The Rhythm Going
In A Sentimental Mood
Goody Goody (vocal: Bob McCrea)
Breakin' In A Pair Of Shoes
Lost (vocal: Ernie Powers)
Let Yourself Go

11:30PM WOR
MAL HALLETT
Trianon Ballroom, Chicago
The Glory Of Love (vocal: Buddy Welcome)
After Dark (vocal: Clark Yocum)
Gentleman Doesn't Believe (vocal: Clark Yocum)
Rhythm In My Nursery Rhymes (vocal: Nila Rose)
What's The Name Of That Song? / I'm Getting Sentimental Over You (vocal: Nila Rose)
I'se A-Muggin' (vocal: Buddy Welcome)
Thanks A Million (vocal: Clark Yocum)
Honeysuckle Rose

THURSDAY 4 JUNE 1936

RADIO LOGS

6:00PM WNEW
WINGY MANONE
Make-Believe Ballroom, NYC
Isle Of Capri (theme)
Swingin' At The Hickory House
Stompin' At The Savoy
Ol' Man Mose
Honeysuckle Rose
Dallas Blues
I'll Be Glad When You're Dead, You Rascal You
Isle Of Capri (theme)

7:15PM WOR
RED NORVO
Hotel Commodore, NYC
Stompin' At The Savoy
Lost
It Ain't Right
Someday, Sweetheart

FRIDAY 5 JUNE 1936

RECORDING SESSION

FATS WALLER & HIS RHYTHM
Recording session for Victor in New York City.
Herman Autrey (t); Gene Sedric (cl/ts); Fats Waller (p/voc); Albert Casey (g); Charles Turner (b); Arnold Boling (d)
It's A Sin To Tell A Lie (vFW) / *The More I Know You* (vFW) / *You're Not The Kind* (vFW) / *Why Do I Lie To Myself About You?* (vFW) / *Let's Sing Again* (vFW) / *Big Chief De Sota* (vFW)

SATURDAY 6 JUNE 1936

RADIO LOGS

11:00PM WABC
BOB CROSBY
Lexington Hotel, NYC
Summertime (theme)
Muskrat Ramble
Blazing The Trail (vocal: Frank Tennille)
Mary Had A Little Lamb (vocal: Bob Crosby)
Love Went Up In Smoke
Dixieland Band (vocal: Bob Crosby)
In A Sentimental Mood (vocal: Frank Tennille)
You Never Looked So Beautiful
Cryin' My Heart Out For You
Wolverine Blues

JUNE 1936

■ SUNDAY 7 JUNE 1936

RADIO LOGS

7:15PM WABC
TOMMY DORSEY
Lincoln Hotel, NYC
Goody Goody (vocal: Edythe Wright)
Would You? (vocal: Jack Leonard)
Robins And Roses (vocal: Edythe Wright)
Happy As The Day Is Long

■ MONDAY 8 JUNE 1936

RECORDING SESSION

FATS WALLER & HIS RHYTHM
Recording session for Victor in New York City.
Herman Autrey (t); Gene Sedric (cl/ts); Fats Waller (p); Albert Casey (g); Charles Turner (b); Yank Porter (d)
Black Raspberry Jam / Bach Up To Me / Fractious Fingering / Paswonky / Lounging At The Waldorf / Latch On

RADIO LOGS

11:00PM WHN
WINGY MANONE
Hickory House, 52nd Street, NYC
I Ain't Got Nobody
Whatcha Gonna Do When There Ain't No Swing?
It's No Fun
You Started Me Dreaming
Nickel In The Slot

11:30PM WJZ
GLEN GRAY
Rainbow Room, NYC
Say It With Music
There's Always A Happy Ending (vocal: Kenny Sargent)
Rhythm A La Carte (vocal: Pee Wee Hunt)
I'm Grateful To You
Eccentric
Sunshine At Midnight
Cross Patch (vocal: Pee Wee Hunt)
Blue Skies
I Found A New Baby

■ TUESDAY 9 JUNE 1936

RECORDING SESSION

BUNNY BERIGAN AND HIS BOYS
Recording session for Vocalion in New York City.
Chick Bullock (voc); Bunny Berigan (t); Jack Lacey (tb); Slats Long (cl); Joe Bushkin (p); Eddie Condon (g); Mort Stuhlmaker (b); Cozy Cole (d)
I Nearly Let Love Go Slipping Thru' My Fingers (vCB) / *But Definitely* (vCB) / *If I Had My Way* (vCB) / *When I'm With You* (vCB)

TOMMY DORSEY AND HIS ORCHESTRA
Recording session for Victor in New York City.
Tommy Dorsey (tb); Max Kaminsky, Sam Skolnick, Joe Bauer (t); Ben Pickering, Walter Mercurio (tb); Joe Dixon (cl/as/voc); Clyde Rounds (as); Bud Freeman, Bob Bunch (cl/ts); Dick Jones (p); Carmen Mastren (g); Gene Traxler (b); Dave Tough (d); Edythe Wright, Jack Leonard (voc)
Did I Remember? (vEW) / *You've Gotta Eat Your Spinach, Baby* (vEW) / *On The Beach At Bali-Bali* (vEW) / *No Regrets* (vJL) / *San Francisco* (vEW) / *That's A-Plenty*

■ WEDNESDAY 10 JUNE 1936

RECORDING SESSION

GLEN GRAY AND THE CASA LOMA ORCHESTRA
Recording session for Decca in New York City.
Glen Gray (as/dir); Sonny Dunham, Grady Watts, Bobby Jones (t); Pee Wee Hunt (tb/voc); Billy Rauch, Fritz Hummel (tb); Clarence Hutchenrider (cl/as), Kenny Sargent (as/voc); Art Ralston (as/o/bsn); Pat Davis (ts); Mel Jenssen (vln); Joe Hall (p); Jack Blanchette (g); Stanley Dennis (b); Tony Briglia (d)
Shades Of Hades / Copenhagen / Royal Garden Blues / Rose Of The Rio Grande / Jungle Jitters / Bugle Call Rag

RADIO LOGS

11:30PM WMCA
EARL HINES
Apollo Theater, NYC
Riffin'
Goin' Home
Christopher Columbus

■ THURSDAY 11 JUNE 1936

RECORDING SESSION

ART SHAW AND HIS ORCHESTRA
Recording session for Brunswick in New York City.
Art Shaw (cl/ldr); Willie Kelly (t); Mark Bennett (tb); Tony Zimmers (ts), Julie Schechter, Lou Klayman (vln); Sam Persoff (vla); Jimmy Oderich (cello); Fulton McGrath (p); Wes Vaughan (g/voc); Hank Wayland (b); Sammy Weiss (d); Peg La Centra (voc)
The Japanese Sandman / A Pretty Girl Is Like A Melody / I Used To Be Above Love (vWV) / *No Regrets* (vWV)

■ FRIDAY 12 JUNE 1936

RECORDING SESSION

BOB CROSBY AND HIS ORCHESTRA
Recording session for Decca in New York City.
Bob Crosby (voc/ldr); Zeke Zarchy, Yank Lawson (t); Ward Silloway, Warren Smith (tb); Gil Rodin, Matty Matlock (cl/as); Noni Bernardi (as); Eddie Miller (cl/ts); Deane Kincaide (ts); Joe Sullivan (piano); Nappy Lamare (g/voc); Bob Haggart (b); Ray Bauduc (d)
Pagan Love Song / Come Back, Sweet Papa (vNL) / *Sugar Foot Strut*

■ SATURDAY 13 JUNE 1936

RADIO LOGS

8:30PM WABC
SATURDAY NIGHT SWING SESSION No1
CBS Studios, NYC
The first program featured Bunny Berigan, Frank Trumbauer, Lee Wiley, Red Norvo and 'swing commentator', Paul Douglas.

■ MONDAY 15 JUNE 1936

RECORDING SESSION

BENNY GOODMAN AND HIS ORCHESTRA
Recording session for Victor in New York City.
Benny Goodman (cl); Chris Griffin, Nate Kazebier, Pee Wee Erwin (t); Red Ballard, Murray McEachern (tb); Bill DePew, Hymie Shertzer (as); Art Rollini, Dick Clark (ts); Jess Stacy (p); Allan Reuss (g); Harry Goodman (b); Gene Krupa (d); Helen Ward (voc)
In A Sentimental Mood / I Found A New Baby / My Melancholy Baby / Swingtime In The Rockies / These Foolish Things (vHW)

FRANKIE TRUMBAUER AND HIS ORCHESTRA
Recording session for Brunswick in New York City.
Frankie Trumbauer (c-mel/as/ldr); Russ Case, Charlie Teagarden (t); Jack Teagarden (tb/voc); Matty Matlock (cl); Joe Cordaro (cl/as); Eddie Miller (ts); Roy Bargy (p); Carl Kress (g); Art Miller (b); Ray Bauduc (d)
I'm An Old Cowhand (vJT) / *Diga Diga Doo*

■ TUESDAY 16 JUNE 1936

RECORDING SESSION

BENNY GOODMAN AND HIS ORCHESTRA
Recording session for Victor in New York City.
Benny Goodman (cl); Chris Griffin, Nate Kazebier, Pee Wee Erwin (t); Red Ballard, Murray McEachern (tb); Bill DePew, Hymie Shertzer (as); Art Rollini, Dick Clark (ts); Jess Stacy (p); Allan Reuss (g); Harry Goodman (b); Gene Krupa (d); Helen Ward (voc)
House Hop / There's A Small Hotel (vHW)

BOB CROSBY AND HIS ORCHESTRA
Recording session for Decca in New York City.
Bob Crosby (voc/ldr); Zeke Zarchy, Yank Lawson (t); Ward Silloway, Warren Smith (tb); Gil Rodin, Matty Matlock (cl/as); Noni Bernardi (as); Eddie Miller (cl/ts); Deane Kincaide (ts); Joe Sullivan (piano); Nappy Lamare (g/voc); Bob Haggart (b); Ray Bauduc (d)
Guess Who? (vBC) / *Cross Patch* (vBC) / *Big Chief De Sota* / *Mary Had A Little Lamb* (vBC) / *Savoy Blues*

■ FRIDAY 19 JUNE 1936

RECORDING SESSION

HENRY 'RED' ALLEN
Recording session for Vocalion in New York City.
Henry 'Red' Allen (t/voc); J. C. Higginbotham (tb); Tab Smith (as); Joe Garland (ts); Edgar Hayes (p); Lawrence Lucie (g); Elmer James (b); O'Neil Spencer (d)
Take My Heart (vHA) / *Chlo-e* (vHA) / *You're Not The Kind* (vHA) / *On The Beach At Bali-Bali* (vHA)

■ SATURDAY 20 JUNE 1936

RADIO LOGS

6:00PM WNEW
FATS WALLER
Make Believe Ballroom, NYC
Ain't Misbehavin'
Honeysuckle Rose (written by Fats Waller & Andy Razaf)
I'm Gonna Sit Right Down And Write Myself A Letter
A Handful Of Keys (written by Fats Waller)
Cross Patch
St. Louis Blues (Organ solo)
Sugar Rose (written by Fats Waller)
Christopher Columbus

8:00PM WABC
SATURDAY NIGHT SWING SESSION No2
CBS Studios, NYC
Program content unknown

■ SATURDAY 27 JUNE 1936

RADIO LOGS

8:00PM WABC
SATURDAY NIGHT SWING SESSION No3
CBS Studios, NYC
Program content unknown

■ SUNDAY 28 JUNE 1936

RADIO LOGS

12:00 MIDNIGHT WJZ
JIMMIE LUNCEFORD
Larchmont Casino, NY
Charmaine (vocal: Dan Grissom)
St. Louis Blues (Willie Smith)
Without A Shadow of A Doubt (vocal: Dan Grissom)
Moten Swing
Stompin' At The Savoy
Dream Boy (vocal: Sy Oliver)
Unsophisticated Lady
Harlem Shout

■ TUESDAY 30 JUNE 1936

RECORDING SESSION

BILLIE HOLIDAY & TEDDY WILSON ORCHESTRA
Recording session for Brunswick in NYC.
Jonah Jones (t); Harry Carney (cl/bar); Johnny Hodges (as); Teddy Wilson (p); Lawrence Lucie (g); John Kirby (b); Cozy Cole (d); Billie Holiday (v)
It's Like Reaching For The Moon / These Foolish Things / I Cried For You / Guess Who

RADIO LOGS

9:30PM WABC
BENNY GOODMAN
"Camel Caravan", Los Angeles
Always
There's A Small Hotel
I Found A New Baby

JULY 1936

Hotel Astor: **Hal Kemp**
Hotel Lexington: **Bob Crosby**
Rainbow Room: **Glen Gray**
Hotel Lincoln: **Dick Stabile**
Hotel Commodore: **Red Norvo**
Hotel Pennsylvania: **Joe Reichman**

Apollo Theater: **Teddy Hill** (3–9); **Valaida Snow** (10–16); **Hardy Brothers** (17–23); **Erskine Hawkins** (24–30)
Paramount Theater: **Bob Crosby** (15–21); **Red Nichols** (22–28)
Loew's State Theater: **Duke Ellington** (10–16); **Cab Calloway** (24–30)

Hickory House: **Joe Marsala/Eddie Condon**
Onyx Club: **Stuff Smith**

"In July 1936, after a long drive with my parents, brother John and sister Joyce, we visited friends in Los Angeles. Although I don't think my religious parents ever heard of Goodman they gave my brother permission to take us kids to see him at the Palomar Ballroom. I enjoyed the music so much that I kept dancing with my 17-yr-old sister away from the crowded dance floor. The Palomar manager called us into his office and threatened to arrest us if we continued to dance in the hallways of the Palomar. Boy, what a crime!"

■ WEDNESDAY 1 JULY 1936

RECORDING SESSION

WINGY MANONE AND HIS ORCHESTRA
Recording session for Bluebird in New York City.
Wingy Manone (t/voc); Mike Viggiano (cl); Tommy Mace (as); James Lamare (cl/ts); Conrad Lanoue (p); Jack LeMaire (g); Artie Shapiro (b); Abby Fisher (d)
River Man (vWM) / *Summer Holiday* (vWM) / *No Regrets* (vWM) / *Afterglow* (vWM) / *I Just Made Up With That Old Girl Of Mine* (vWM) / *You're Not The Kind* (vWM)

STUFF SMITH & HIS ONYX CLUB BOYS
Recording session for Vocalion in New York City.
Jonah Jones (t); Stuff Smith (vln/voc); James Sherman (p); Bobby Bennett (g); Mack Walker (b); Cozy Cole (d)
It Ain't Right (vSS) / *Old Joe's Hittin' The Jug* (vSS) / *Swing Time* / *Serenade For A Wealthy Widow*

■ TUESDAY 7 JULY 1936

RECORDING SESSION

JIMMY DORSEY AND HIS ORCHESTRA
Recording session for Decca in Los Angeles.
Jimmy Dorsey (cl/as); George Thow (t); Toots Camarata (t/voc); Bobby Byrne, Don Mattison (tb/voc); Joe Yukl (tb); Jack Stacey (as); Fud Livingston (as/ts); Skeets Herfurt (ts); Bobby Van Eps (p); Roc Hillman (g/voc); Slim Taft (b); Ray McKinley (d/voc)
Ah-Woo! Ah-Woo! To You (vTC,BB,RH) / *There's No Substitute For You* (vTC,BB,RH) / *Funiculi Funicula* / *Parade of The Milk Bottle Tops*

■ THURSDAY 9 JULY 1936

RADIO LOGS

12:00 MIDNIGHT WABC
BENNY GOODMAN
Palomar Ballroom, Los Angeles
Let's Dance (theme)
Christopher Columbus (Written by Chu Berry & Andy Razaf)
Star Dust (Written by Hoagy Carmichael)
Always (Written by Irving Berlin)
Too Good To Be True (vocal: Helen Ward)
Madhouse (Written by Jimmy Mundy)
More Than You Know (Written by Youmans-Rose-Eliscu)
Guess Who? (vocal: Helen Ward)
Minnie The Moocher's Wedding Day
Robins And Roses (vocal: Helen Ward)
Alexander's Ragtime Band

Benny Goodman and his orchestra spent July at Los Angeles' Palomar Ballroom (inset) and in the Hollywood studios making 'The Big Broadcast of 1937' (above).

■ FRIDAY 10 JULY 1936

RECORDING SESSION

BILLIE HOLIDAY & HER ORCHESTRA
Recording session for Vocalion in NYC.
Bunny Berigan (t); Artie Shaw (cl); Joe Bushkin (p); Dick McDonough (g); Pete Peterson (b); Cozy Cole (d); Billie Holiday (v)
Did I Remember? / No Regrets / Summertime / Billie's Blues

■ SATURDAY 11 JULY 1936

RADIO LOGS

8:00PM WABC
SATURDAY NIGHT SWING SESSION No4
CBS Studios, NYC
Program content unknown

12:00 MIDNIGHT WABC
BENNY GOODMAN
Palomar Ballroom, Los Angeles
Let's Dance (theme)
Blue Skies (Written by Irving Berlin)
When I'm With You (vocal: Helen Ward)
Remember (Written by Irving Berlin)
These Foolish Things (vocal: Helen Ward)
Back Home Again In Indiana
Goody Goody (vocal: Helen Ward) (Written by Matty Malneck-Johnny Mercer)
Someday, Sweetheart
Take My Heart (vocal: Helen Ward)
You Can't Pull The Wool Over My Eyes (vocal: Helen Ward)
Walk, Jennie, Walk (Written by Sam Wooding-Bob Schaffer)

■ THURSDAY 16 JULY 1936

RADIO LOGS

12.00 MIDNIGHT WABC
BENNY GOODMAN
Palomar Ballroom, Los Angeles
Let's Dance (theme)
House Hop (Written by Benny Goodman-Jimmy Mundy)
Mary Had A Little Lamb
St. Louis Blues (Written by W.C. Handy)
Robins And Roses (vocal: Helen Ward)
Big John Special
Truckin' (vocal: Helen Ward)
I Surrender Dear
Sing, Sing, Sing (vocal: Helen Ward)
I Can't Remember

■ FRIDAY 17 JULY 1936

RECORDING SESSION

DUKE ELLINGTON AND HIS ORCHESTRA
Recording session for Brunswick in New York City.
Duke Ellington (p), Arthur Whetsel, Cootie Williams (t), Rex Stewart (c), Joe Nanton, Lawrence Brown (tb), Juan Tizol (vtb), Barney Bigard (cl), Johnny Hodges (cl/ss/as), Otto Hardwick (as/bar), Harry Carney (cl/as/bar), Fred Guy (g), Hayes Alvis, Billy Taylor (b), Sonny Greer (d), Ivie Anderson (voc)
Shoe-Shine Boy (vIA, 2 takes) / *It Was a Sad Night in Harlem* (vIA) / *Trumpet in Spades (Rex's Concerto)* / *Yearning for Love (Lawrence's Concerto)* (2 takes)

RADIO LOGS

? WABC
CHARLIE BARNET
Glen Island Casino, New Rochelle, NY
Dear Old Southland
Stop, Look And Listen
You're Just The Kind
Christopher Columbus
Without A Shadow Of A Doubt (vocal: Joe Host)
Stompin' At The Savoy
These Foolish Things

■ SATURDAY 18 JULY 1936

RADIO LOGS

8:00PM WABC
SATURDAY NIGHT SWING SESSION No5
CBS Studios, NYC
Program content unknown

■ SUNDAY 19 JULY 1936

RADIO LOGS

? WEAF
JIMMIE LUNCEFORD
Larchmont Casino, Larchmont, NY
Jazznocracy (theme)
The Melody Man (vocal: Sy Oliver)
Vilia
Because You're You (vocal: Dan Grissom)
I'll Take The South (vocal: Trio)
Walkin' Through Heaven (vocal: Trio)
Rain (vocal: Trio)
On The Beach At Bali-Bali
Swing High
Rhythm Is Our Business

■ MONDAY 20 JULY 1936

RECORDING SESSION

ERSKINE HAWKINS AND HIS ORCHESTRA
Recording session for Vocalion in New York City.
Erskine Hawkins (t/ldr); Wilbur Bascomb, Marcellus Green, Sam Lowe (t); Edward Sims, Robert Range (tb); William Johnson (as); Jimmy Mitchelle (as/voc); Paul Bascomb (ts); Haywood Henry (cl/bar); Avery Parrish (p); William McLemore (g); Leemie Stanfield (b); James Morrison (d); Billy Daniels, Merle Turner (voc)
It Was A Sad Night In Harlem (vJM) / *Until The Real Thing Comes Along* (vBD) / *I Can't Escape From You* (vBD) / *Without A Shadow Of A Doubt* (vJM)

RADIO LOGS

? WEAF
JIMMIE LUNCEFORD
Larchmont Casino, NY
Honeysuckle Rose
Thunder (vocal: Dan Grissom)
Unsophisticated Sue (vocal: Trio)
Leaving Me (vocal: Dan Grissom)
?? Nana??
Sleepy Time Gal (vocal: Dan Grissom)
Rhythm Is Our Business

■ TUESDAY 21 JULY 1936

RADIO LOGS

8:45PM WOR
RED NORVO
Commodore Hotel, NYC
Queen Isabella (Decca Stomp)
If We Never Had Met (vocal: Lou Hurst)
Kick My Heart (vocal: Lou Hurst)
Take My Heart

9:30PM WABC
BENNY GOODMAN
"Camel Caravan", Los Angeles
Bugle Call Rag
These Foolish Things (vocal: Helen Ward)
Down South Camp Meeting
China Boy (BG Trio)
Farewell Blues

11:00PM WHN
LUCKY MILLINDER
Palisades Amusement Park, NJ
Star Dust
St. Louis Doodle
In A Sentimental Mood
Back Home Again In Indiana
Everything Is Still Okay (vocal: Chuck Richards)

11:30PM WPG
JAN SAVITT
Steel Pier, Atlantic City
Sleepy Time Gal
Take My Heart
Whispering
Stompin' At The Savoy
Serenade To A Wealthy Widow
She's Funny That Way (vocal: Dick Wharton)
Copenhagen
The Scene Changes
Sophisticated Lady
A Country Girl

■ WEDNESDAY 22 JULY 1936

RADIO LOGS

7:15PM WOR
RED NORVO
Commodore Hotel, NYC
Robins And Roses
These Foolish Things
I Never Knew
After You've Gone

■ THURSDAY 23 JULY 1936

RECORDING SESSION

JIMMY DORSEY AND HIS ORCHESTRA
Recording session for Decca in Los Angeles.
Jimmy Dorsey (cl/as); George Thow (t); Toots Camarata (t/voc); Bobby Byrne, Don Mattison (tb/voc); Joe Yukl (tb); Jack Stacey (as); Fud Livingston (as/ts); Skeets Herfurt (ts); Bobby Van Eps (p); Roc Hillman (g/voc); Slim Taft (b); Ray McKinley (d/voc)
Don't Look Now (vTC,BB,RH) / *It Ain't Right* (vDM) / *The Boston Tea Party* (vTC,BB,RH,DM) / *Mutiny In The Brass Section* / *Hollywood Pastime*

RADIO LOGS

7:35PM WHN
LUCKY MILLINDER
Palisades Amusement Park, NJ
Red Rhythm
Always (vocal: Allen Michels)
I Need You So (vocal: Chuck Richards)
Is It True What They Say About Dixie? (vocal: Red Allen)
Ride, Red, Ride
Merry-Go-Round

12.00 MIDNIGHT WABC
BENNY GOODMAN
Palomar Ballroom, Los Angeles
Sugar Foot Stomp
The Glory Of Love (vocal: Helen Ward)
You Forgot To Remember
Tain't No Use (vocal: Helen Ward & Benny Goodman)
I Would Do Anything For You
Afterglow (vocal: Helen Ward)
What Does It Matter?
I Found A New Baby
I Can't Get Started (vocal: Helen Ward)
Dear Old Southland

12.30AM WABC
CHARLIE BARNET
Glen Island Casino
Yeah, Man!
Robins And Roses (vocal: Barnet Rhythmairs)
My First Thrill
My Melancholy Baby
You're Not The Kind (vocal: Charlie Barnet)
I'm An Old Cowhand (vocal: Joe Host)
Sophisticated Lady
Stop, Look And Listen (vocal: Barnet Rhythmairs)
Dixieland Band (vocal: Charlie Barnet)
King Porter Stomp

■ FRIDAY 24 JULY 1936

RADIO LOGS

9.45PM WHN
STUFF SMITH
Onyx Club, 72 W52nd Street, NYC
I'se A-Muggin' (theme)
Mary Had A Little Lamb
It All Begins And Ends With You (by Frank Froeba)
Mendelssohn's Swing Song
Love Me Or Leave Me (Frank Froeba on piano)
You'se A Viper

10:00PM WHN
LUCKY MILLINDER
Palisades Amusement Park, NJ
There's Rhythm In Harlem
Everything Is Still Okay (vocal: Chuck Richards)
Swingin' In E-flat
Mood Indigo (vocal: Chuck Richards)
Some Of These Days (vocal: Lucky Millinder)
In A Sentimental Mood (vocal: Chuck Richards)
Star Dust (theme)

11:00PM WHN
JOE MARSALA-EDDIE CONDON
Hickory House, 52nd Street, NYC
Chicago (theme)
Basin Street Blues
Christopher Columbus
Stompin' At The Savoy
All My Life
Robins And Roses

■ SATURDAY 25 JULY 1936

RADIO LOGS

8:00PM WABC
SATURDAY NIGHT SWING SESSION No6
CBS Studios, NYC
Program content unknown

10.45PM WJZ
JIMMIE LUNCEFORD
Larchmont Casino, NY
Rhythm In My Nursery Rhymes (vocal: Willie Smith)
Black And Tan Fantasy
Yankee Doodle Never Went To Town
Jazznocracy (theme)

11:00PM WABC
BOB CROSBY
Lexington Hotel, NYC
Muskrat Ramble
I'm Just Beginning To Care
Oh, My Goodness (vocal: Bob Crosby)
The House Went Up In Smoke
I Take To You
Sunshine At Midnight (vocal: Bob Walker)
Here Comes Your Pappy (vocal: Nappy Lamare)
My First Thrill (vocal: Bob Crosby)
Wolverine Blues
Summertime (theme)

11:30PM WABC
HAL KEMP
Astor Hotel, NYC
But Definitely (vocal: Maxine Gray)
When The Bride Comes Home (vocal: Skinnay Ennis)
You're Not The Kind (vocal: Bob Allen)
Sing Me A Swing Song (vocal: Maxine Gray)
Tormented (vocal: Bob Allen)
Knock, Knock
The Scene Changes (vocal: Bob Allen)
Rigamarole
How I Miss You (theme)

12:00 MIDNIGHT WOR
ALEX BARTHA
Steel Pier, Atlantic City
Alexander's Ragtime Band (theme)
When The Bride Comes Home (vocal: Skinnay Ennis)
Don't Count Your Kisses
When I'm With You
Unknown Title
Robins And Roses (vocal: Bert Nickerson)
It's A Sin To Tell A Lie
Sittin' In The Sand
Tain't No Use
Let's Sing Again
Honeysuckle Rose
Riverboat Shuffle

12.30AM WABC
BENNY GOODMAN
Palomar Ballroom, Los Angeles
Alexander's Ragtime Band
Did I Remember?

Cross Patch
More Than You Know
Down South Camp Meeting
The Glory Of Love (vocal: Helen Ward)
Honeysuckle Rose
These Foolish Things (vocal: Helen Ward)
Minnie The Moocher's Wedding Day
Sing, Sing, Sing (vocal: Helen Ward)

■ WEDNESDAY 29 JULY 1936

RECORDING SESSION

DUKE ELLINGTON AND HIS ORCHESTRA
Recording session for Brunswick in New York City.
Duke Ellington (p); Arthur Whetsel, Cootie Williams (t); Rex Stewart (c); Joe Nanton, Lawrence Brown (tb); Juan Tizol (vtb); Barney Bigard (cl); Johnny Hodges (cl/ss/as); Otto Hardwick (as/bar); Ben Webster (ts); Harry Carney (cl/as/bar); Fred Guy (g); Hayes Alvis, Billy Taylor (b); Sonny Greer (d)
In a Jam (HA out) / *Exposition Swing* / *Uptown Downbeat (Blackout)* (BT out)

RADIO LOGS

9.30PM WHN
LUCKY MILLINDER
Palisades Amusement Park, NJ
Lucky Swings Out
Until The Real Thing Comes Along (vocal: Chuck Richards)
Ride, Red, Ride

■ THURSDAY 30 JULY 1936

RADIO LOGS

7.30PM WEAF
DICK McDONOUGH
Commercial, NYC
A Little Bit Later On
Knock Knock (vocal: Peg LaCentra)
St. Louis Blues
Did I Remember? (vocal: Peg LaCentra) (Adrian Rollini on vibraphone)
Christopher Columbus
Ain't Nobody's Business What I Do
You Hit The Spot

12.00 MIDNIGHT WABC
BENNY GOODMAN
Palomar Ballroom, Los Angeles
I Would Do Anything For You
Afterglow (vocal: Helen Ward)
Too Bad
In A Sentimental Mood
There's A Small Hotel (vocal: Helen Ward)
Walk, Jennie, Walk
Too Good To Be True (vocal: Helen Ward)
Someday, Sweetheart
Sing Me A Swing Song (vocal: Helen Ward)
Big John Special

12.30AM WEAF
FLETCHER HENDERSON
Grand Terrace, Chicago
I Wonder
Hidden Valley
Driftin' Along
Living From Day To Day

12.30AM WABC
CHARLIE BARNET
Glen Island Casino, New Rochelle, N.Y.
Tain't Good
My Blue Heaven
When I'm With You (vocal: Barnet Rhythmaires)
Down South Camp Meeting
These Foolish Things (vocal: Charlie Barnet)
Between The Devil And The Deep Blue Sea
Stompin' At The Savoy (vocal: Barnet Rhythmaires)
Living From Day To Day (vocal: Joe Host)

1.00AM WABC
DICK STABILE
Lincoln Hotel, NYC
I'm An Old Cowhand
Let Me Be The One In Your Heart
Organ Grinder Swing
Until Today
Blue Skies
It's A Sin To Tell A Lie (vocal: Bert Shaw)
You Can't Pull The Wool Over My Eyes

1.00AM WEAF
FLETCHER HENDERSON
Grand Terrace, Chicago
Blue Skies
Rug Cutter's Swing
River Man
Down South Camp Meeting
I'll Stand By
Jumpy Rhythm
Afterglow
Big John Special
Yeah, Man!

■ FRIDAY 31 JULY 1936

RADIO LOGS

? WHN
STUFF SMITH
Onyx Club, 72 W52nd Street, NYC
Until The Real Thing Comes Along
If We Never Meet Again
I Would Do Anything For You
(Frank Froeba piano solo)
Old Joe's Hittin' The Jug

8.15PM WJZ
JERRY SEARS
?
If We Never Meet Again
Organ Grinder's Swing
Until The Real Thing Comes Along (vocal: Irene Johnson)
Bugle Call Rag

9.30PM WHN
LUCKY MILLINDER
Palisades Amusement Park, NJ
Rhythm Of The Congo
Some Of These Days
When I Grow Too Old To Dream (vocal: Chuck Richards)
Shoe Shine Boy (vocal: Chuck Richards)
St. Louis Blues

W. C. Handy

AUGUST 1936

Hotel Astor: **Hal Kemp**
Hotel Lexington: **Bob Crosby** (–19); **Art Shaw** (21–)
Hotel Lincoln: **Dick Stabile**
Hotel Taft: **George Hall**
Hotel New Yorker: **Clyde Lucas**

Apollo Theater: **Luis Russell** (–6); **Willie Bryant** (7–13); **Cab Calloway** (14–20); **Mamie Smith / Sunset Royal Serenaders** (21–27); **Claude Hopkins** (28–)
Paramount Theater: **Phil Spitalny** (–4); **Lud Gluskin** (26–)

Hickory House: **Riley & Farley**
Onyx Club: **Stuff Smith**

■ SATURDAY 1 AUGUST 1936

RECORDING SESSION

FATS WALLER & HIS RHYTHM
Recording session for Victor in New York City.
Herman Autrey (t); Gene Sedric (cl/ts); Fats Waller (p/voc); Albert Casey (g); Charles Turner (b); Slick Jones (d)
I'm Crazy 'Bout My Baby (vFW) / *I Just Made Up With That Old Girl Of Mine* (vFW) / *Until The Real Thing Comes Along* (vFW) / *There Goes My Attraction* (vFW) / *The Curse Of An Aching Heart* (vFW) / *Bye Bye Baby* (vFW)

RADIO LOGS

8.00PM WABC
SATURDAY NIGHT SWING SESSION No7
CBS Studios, NYC
I Can't Get Started (Bunny Berigan & house band)
Shoe Shine Boy (Bunny Berigan & house band)
Arkansas Blues (Mound City Blue Blowers with Red McKenzie-Eddie Condon)
You Can't Pull The Wool Over My Eyes (Berigan, Joe Marsala, McKenzie, Condon)
Dardanella (Bunny Berigan & house band)
Riverboat Shuffle (Bunny Berigan & house band)
Takin' It On The Lam (Carl Kress & Dick McDonough)
Ain't Misbehavin' (Gogo DeLys singing with Bunny Berigan & house band)
Loveless Love (Bunny Berigan solo with house band)
Stompin' At The Savoy (Berigan, Joe Marsala, McKenzie, Condon, Kress, McDonough)

11.00PM WABC
BOB CROSBY
Lexington Hotel, NYC
The Glory Of Love
Sweet Mystery Of Love
Woman On My Weary Mind
I Take To You (vocal: Nappy Lamare)
If We Never Meet Again (vocal: Bob Walker)
Empty Saddles (vocal: Bob Crosby)
Big Chief De Sota
Summertime (theme)

11.15PM WHN
LUCKY MILLINDER
Palisades Amusement Park, NJ
A Solid Sender
Always
I Need You So (vocal: Chuck Richards)
Some Of These Days (vocal: ??)
Star Dust (theme)

Lots of luck "Lucky" Millinder

Dick McDonough (below left) and Carl Kress.

AUGUST 1936

12.30AM WABC
BENNY GOODMAN
Palomar Ballroom, Los Angeles
Let's Dance (theme)
Sing, Sing, Sing (vocal: Helen Ward)
Until The Real Thing Comes Along (vocal: Helen Ward)
Dream Awhile
Breakin' It Up
You Can't Pull The Wool Over My Eyes (vocal: Helen Ward)
Bugle Call Rag
These Foolish Things (vocal: Helen Ward)
You Forgot To Remember
On A Summer Holiday (vocal: Helen Ward)
I Found A New Baby
Goodbye (theme)

■ SUNDAY 2 AUGUST 1936

RADIO LOGS

8:30PM WOR
OZZIE NELSON
Palmer House, Chicago
I Nearly Let Love Go Slipping Through My Fingers
A Rendezvous With A Dream
Afterglow
Let's Sing Again
Cross Patch (vocal: Joy Hodges)
There's A Small Hotel
No Regrets (vocal: Ozzie Nelson)
Tain't No Use
Swamp Fire
You're Not The Kind

9.00PM WHN
LUCKY MILLINDER
Palisades Amusement Park, NJ
Lucky Swings Out
Stompin' At The Savoy
Merry-Go-Round
Everything Is Still Okay (vocal: Chuck Richards)
Red Rhythm
Until The Real Thing Comes Along (vocal: Chuck Richards)
Snaps And Go
Ride, Red, Ride

11.30PM WABC
BOB CROSBY
Lexington Hotel, NYC
Come Back, Sweet Papa
She Shall Have Music (vocal: Bob Walker)
Me And The Moon
Dixieland Shuffle
You Can't Pull The Wool Over My Eyes (vocal: Nappy Lamare)
Sweet Mystery Of Love
Muskrat Ramble
You're Not The Kind (vocal: Bob Crosby)
Pagan Love Song

12.00 MIDNIGHT WEAF
DUKE ELLINGTON
Cleveland, Ohio
Merry-Go-Round
Clarinet Lament (Barney Bigard on clarinet)
Isn't Love The Strangest Thing (vocal: Ivie Anderson)
At A Fair With Rex (Exposition Swing?) (Rex Stewart on cornet)
In A Sentimental Mood
Great Lake Stomp (vocal: Ivie Anderson)
Echoes of Harlem (Cootie Williams on trumpet)
Oh Babe, Maybe Someday (vocal: Ivie Anderson)

■ MONDAY 3 AUGUST 1936

RECORDING SESSION

CHARLIE BARNET AND HIS ORCHESTRA
Recording session for Bluebird in New York City.
Charlie Barnet (ss/as/ts/voc); George Kennedy, Irving Goodman, Kermit Simmons (t); Joe Hostetter (tb/voc); Buzz Smith, John Doyle (tb); George Vaughan, Don Morres (cl/as); Willard Brady, Bob Parks (ts); Horace Diaz (p); Buford Turner (g); Sid Weiss (b); Billy Flanagan (d); The Barnet Modernaires (v)
Until The Real Thing Comes Along (vCB) / *Make-Believe Ballroom* (vTBM) / *Bye Bye Baby* (vTBM) / *A Star Fell Out Of Heaven* (vJH) / *When Did You Leave Heaven?* (vCB) / *Always*

JIMMY DORSEY AND HIS ORCHESTRA
Recording session for Decca in Los Angeles.
Jimmy Dorsey (cl/as); George Thow (t); Toots Camarata (t/voc); Bobby Byrne, Don Mattison (tb/voc); Joe Yukl (tb); Jack Stacey (as); Fud Livingston (as/ts); Skeets Herfurt (ts); Bobby Van Eps (p); Roc Hillman (g/voc); Slim Taft (b); Ray McKinley (d/voc); Bob Eberly, Frances Langford (voc)
Easy To Love (vFL) / *Rap Tap On Wood* (vFL) / *So Do I* (vBE) / *One, Two, Button Your Shoe* (vBE)

RADIO LOGS

12:45PM WTIC
MERRY MADCAPS (Norman Cloutier)
Hartford, Conn
Sailing A Dreamboat (theme—vocal: Bob Ellis)
Farewell Blues
Until The Real Thing Comes Along (vocal: Bob Ellis)
Tain't No Use
Me And The Moon (vocal: Bob Ellis)
Shine

Norman Cloutier

■ TUESDAY 4 AUGUST 1936

RECORDING SESSION

JIMMY DORSEY AND HIS ORCHESTRA
Recording session for Decca in Los Angeles.
Jimmy Dorsey (cl/as); George Thow (t); Toots Camarata (t/voc); Bobby Byrne, Don Mattison (tb/voc); Joe Yukl (tb); Jack Stacey (as); Fud Livingston (as/ts); Skeets Herfurt (ts); Bobby Van Eps (p); Roc Hillman (g/voc); Slim Taft (b); Ray McKinley (d/voc); Bob Eberly (voc)
Chicken Reel / *Pennies From Heaven* (vBE) / *Dorsey Dervish (Waddlin' At The Waldorf)*

FLETCHER HENDERSON AND HIS ORCHESTRA
Recording session for Victor in Chicago.
Fletcher Henderson (p/ldr); Dick Vance, Joe Thomas, Roy Eldridge (t); Fernando Arbello, Ed Cuffee (tb); Buster Bailey, Jerome Pasquall (cl/as); Elmer Williams, Chu Berry (ts); Horace Henderson (p); Bob Lessey (g); Israel Crosby (b); Sid Catlett (d); Arthur 'Georgia Boy' Simpkins, Dick Vance, Roy Eldridge, Ed Cuffee (voc)
Shoe Shine Boy (vRE) / *Sing, Sing, Sing* (vGBS) / *Until Today* / *Knock, Knock, Who's There?* (vRE,EC) / *Jimtown Blues* / *You Can Depend On Me* (vDV)

Tommy Dorsey and his Orchestra with Dave Tough on drums and Bud Freeman on tenor sax.

RADIO LOGS

9:00PM WABC
TOMMY DORSEY
Texas Centennial, Dallas
I'm Getting Sentimental Over You (theme)
You've Gotta Eat Your Spinach, Baby (vocal: Edythe Wright)
The Scene Changes (vocal: Jack Leonard)
Sleep (swing style)
But Definitely (vocal: Three Esquires)
Four Or Five Times
Je Vous Adore
Maple Leaf Rag
Star Dust (vocal: Edythe Wright)
Happy As The Day Is Long

9:30PM WABC
BENNY GOODMAN
"Camel Caravan", Los Angeles
Big John Special
Nobody's Sweetheart (BG Trio)
When I'm With You
Darktown Strutters' Ball

11:15PM WTIC
MERRY MADCAPS (Norman Cloutier)
Tain't No Use
So Nice Of You (vocal: Eleanor Lane)
King Porter Stomp
A Pretty Girl Is Like A Melody (vocal: Eddie Halley)
My Melancholy Baby
Say Not
Jigglin' And Reelin'

1:00AM WABC
GEORGE HALL
Taft Hotel, NYC
These Foolish Things (vocal: Dolly Dawn)
Panama
But Definitely
Hidden Valley (vocal: Johnny McKeever)
Do You Or Don't You Love Me? (vocal: Dolly Dawn)
On Your Toes
Robins And Roses (vocal: Dolly Dawn's Patrol)
Just A-Wearyin' For You
Let's Sing Again (vocal: Johnny McKeever)

■ WEDNESDAY 5 AUGUST 1936

RECORDING SESSION

HENRY 'RED' ALLEN
Recording session for Vocalion in New York City.
Henry 'Red' Allen (t/voc); Rudy Powell (cl/as); Tab Smith (as); Cecil Scott (ts); Edgar Hayes (p); Lawrence Lucie (g); Elmer James (b); Cozy Cole (d)
When Did You Leave Heaven? (vHA) / *Am I Asking Too Much?* (vHA) / *Until Today* (vHA) / *Algiers Stomp*

JIMMY DORSEY AND HIS ORCHESTRA
Recording session for Decca in Los Angeles.
Jimmy Dorsey (cl/as); George Thow (t); Toots Camarata (t/voc); Bobby Byrne, Don Mattison (tb/voc); Joe Yukl (tb); Jack Stacey (as); Fud Livingston (as/ts); Skeets Herfurt (ts); Bobby Van Eps (p); Roc Hillman (g/voc); Slim Taft (b); Ray McKinley (d/voc); Bob Eberly, Frances Langford (voc)
I've Got You Under My Skin (vFL) / *Let's Call A Heart A Heart* (vBE)

■ THURSDAY 6 AUGUST 1936

RECORDING SESSION
ART SHAW AND HIS ORCHESTRA
Recording session for Brunswick in New York City.
Art Shaw (cl/ldr); Lee Castle, Dave Wade (t); Mike Michaels (tb); Tony Pastor (ts), Jerry Gray, Sam Rosenblum (vln); Sam Persoff (vla); Jimmy Oderich (cello); Joe Lippman (p); Gene Stultz (g); Ben Ginsberg (b); Sammy Weiss (d); Peg La Centra (voc)
South Sea Island Magic (vPLC) / *It Ain't Right* (vPLC) / *Sugar Foot Stomp* / *Thou Swell*

RADIO LOGS

7:30PM WTIC
MERRY MADCAPS (Norman Cloutier)
Hartford, Conn
Dinah
Why Shouldn't I?
Who's Sorry Now?
More Than You Know
Sweet Sue
Sailing A Dreamboat (theme)

8:30PM WHN
GLENA JANE THOMSON
Palisades Amusement Park, NJ
Star Dust (theme)
I'm Building Up To An Awful Letdown
It's Been So Long
Tormented
White Heat
All My Life
Rose Room
Every Now And Then
Afterglow
Nitwit Serenade
Star Dust (theme)

11:30PM WTIC
FLETCHER HENDERSON
Grand Terrace, Chicago
A Little Bit Later On
Sing Me A Swing Song
Remember
I Wonder
I Want To Be With You
Christopher Columbus (theme)

11:30PM WABC
DICK STABILE
Lincoln Hotel, NYC
Cross Patch
Did I Remember?
On The Beach At Bali-Bali
Me And The Moon
Shoe Shine Boy
When I'm With You (vocal: Bert Shaw)
Sweet Mystery Of Love
Ain't She Sweet (featuring 6 saxophones)
There's A Small Hotel
On The Air (theme)

12:00 MIDNIGHT WABC
BENNY GOODMAN
Palomar Ballroom, Los Angeles
Let's Dance (theme)
Three Little Words (One of Benny's best)
Sweet And Low (vocal: Helen Ward) (Benny swings out on a slow one)
It's A Sin To Tell A Lie (Lousy for Benny)
Sugar Foot Stomp (His best arrangement: swell muted trumpet; 5 clarinets)
You Turned The Tables On Me (vocal: Helen Ward) (Helen's best vocal)
If I Could Be With You One Hour Tonight
I Know That You Know
Sometimes I'm Happy (His best record)
The Glory Of Love (vocal: Helen Ward)
Hallelujah! (Fair)
Goodbye (theme)

12:30AM WABC
CHARLIE BARNET
Glen Island Casino, New Rochelle, N.Y.
Dream Lullaby (theme)
Always
Until The Real Thing Comes Along (vocal: Charlie Barnet)
Bye Bye Baby (vocal: Barnet Rhythmaires)
A Star Fell Out Of Heaven (vocal: Joe Host)
My Melancholy Baby (swell saxes; like Tommy Dorsey's)
You're Not The Kind (vocal: Charlie Barnet)
Make Believe Ballroom
These Foolish Things (vocal: Charlie Barnet)
My Blue Heaven (one of Barnet's best)
Toodle-oo (a swell hot piece)

■ FRIDAY 7 AUGUST 1936

RADIO LOGS

9.45PM WHN
STUFF SMITH
Onyx Club, 72 W52nd Street, NYC
I Got Rhythm
My Melancholy Baby
I Found A New Baby (Frank Froeba on piano)
Dinah

10.00PM WABC
ANDRÉ KOSTELANETZ-KAY THOMPSON'S RHYTHM SINGERS
(Commercial program sponsored by Chesterfield cigarettes), NYC
Let's Sing Again
Tormented (vocal: Ray Heatherton)
Cuban Swing
Swing (vocal: Kay Thompson)
Sunshine At Midnight (vocal: Kay Thompson)
Dance Of Inspiration
Take Me To The Opera
Stompin' At The Savoy

André Kostelanetz (below with his sax section) is the fiancé of Lily Pons the opera singer and conducts and arranges for his 45-piece orchestra on the Chesterfield Cigarette program over CBS.

■ SATURDAY 8 AUGUST 1936
RADIO LOGS

5:45PM WABC
CHARLIE BARNET
Glen Island Casino
I'm An Old Cowhand (vocal: Joe Host)
Robins And Roses (vocal: Barnet Rhythmaires)
When I'm With You (vocal: Barnet Rhythmaires)
Cross Patch (vocal: Charlie Barnet)
Rosetta
My First Thrill
King Porter Stomp
Night And Day
Anything Goes
Bye Bye Baby (vocal: Barnet Rhythmaires)
Down South Camp Meeting

8.00PM WABC
SATURDAY NIGHT SWING SESSION No8
CBS Studios, NYC
I Can't Get Started (theme–BUNNY BERIGAN & CBS band)
Between The Devil And The Deep Blue Sea (Bunny Berigan & CBS band)
Sweet Sue (DICK STABILE (cl/as) & CBS band)
Alexander's Ragtime Band (Bunny Berigan & CBS band)
Basin Street Blues (vocal by DOLLY DAWN with Bunny Berigan & band)
Cross Patch (Bunny Berigan & CBS band)
Let Yourself Go (J. GREEN on piano with CBS band)
I Got Rhythm (J. GREEN on piano with CBS band)

11.00PM WABC
BOB CROSBY
Lexington Hotel, NYC
Summertime (theme)
Sugar Foot Stomp
The Scene Changes (vocal: Bob Walker)
I Can't Escape From You (vocal: Bob Crosby)
Savoy Blues
I'll Never Let You Go (vocal: Nappy Lamare)
Until Today
Mary Had A Little Lamb (vocal: Bob Crosby)
Am I Asking Too Much? (vocal: Bob Walker)
Panama
Summertime (theme)

■ SUNDAY 9 AUGUST 1936
RADIO LOGS

2:05PM WJZ
FATS WALLER
Magic Key Program
It's A Sin To Tell A Lie
Until The Real Thing Comes Along
Crazy 'Bout My Baby

■ MONDAY 10 AUGUST 1936
RADIO LOGS

7:15PM WABC
GEORGE HALL
Taft Hotel, NYC
Make Believe
Ol' Man River
In A Sentimental Mood
Up On Your Toes
Christopher Columbus

■ TUESDAY 11 AUGUST 1936

RECORDING SESSION

LUCKY MILLINDER & MILLS BLUE RHYTHM BAND
Recording session for Columbia in New York City.
Lucky Millinder (voc/ldr); Wardell Jones, Shelton Hemphill, Henry 'Red' Allen (t); George Washington, J.C.Higginbotham (tb); Gene Mikell, Crawford Wethington (cl/as); Tab Smith (as); Joe Garland (cl/ts/bar); Edgar Hayes (p); Lawrence Lucie (g); Elmer James (b); O'Neil Spencer (d); Chuck Richards (voc)
Merry-Go-Round / Until The Real Thing Comes Along (vCR) / *In A Sentimental Mood* (vCR) / *Carry Me Back To Green Pastures* (vCR)

RADIO LOGS

2:15PM WABC
DICTATORS
CBS Studios, NYC
Mary Had A Little Lamb
Did I Remember?
The Way You Look Tonight
I Nearly Let Love Go Slipping Through My Fingers
Let's Sing Again
Take My Heart
I Can't Escape From You
The State Of My Heart
Sing Me A Swing Song
Doin' The Prom
But Definitely (theme)

9:00PM WABC
TOMMY DORSEY
Texas Centennial, Dallas
On The Beach At Bali-Bali (vocal: Edythe Wright)
Take My Heart (vocal: Jack Leonard)
Darktown Strutters' Ball
Guess Who? (vocal: Three Esquires)
I'm An Old Cowhand
Would You? (vocal: Edythe Wright, Jack Leonard, Three Esquires)
Royal Garden Blues
These Foolish Things (vocal: Edythe Wright)
That's A-Plenty
I'm Getting Sentimental Over You (theme)

9:30PM WABC
BENNY GOODMAN
"Camel Caravan", Los Angeles
I Know That You Know
Stompin' At The Savoy
Until The Real Thing Comes Along (vocal: Helen Ward)
Get Happy

■ WEDNESDAY 12 AUGUST 1936
RADIO LOGS

12:30PM WABC
MERRY MAKERS
CBS Studios, NYC
The Merry Makers are a CBS studio band with such well-known players as Bunny Berigan, Art Manners, Babe Russin, Bud Sheppard, Johnny Augustine, Dick Porter (piano), Lou Shoobe (bass), Vincent Maffay (guitar), and many others.
Stompin' At The Savoy
Without A Shadow Of A Doubt
Bye Bye Baby
I Want To Be With You
No Regrets

AUGUST 1936 *Swing Era Scrapbook* 37

Cross Patch
Afterglow
I'm Tootin' My Horn
Sunshine At Midnight
Oh! My Goodness

4:30PM WABC
INSTRUMENTALISTS
CBS Studios, NYC
Nagasaki (Art Manners playing hot clarinet)
If We Never Meet Again (Buddy Sheppard on violin)
Improvisation On A Piano (Marty Dale on piano; Johnny Williams, drums)
I'm Tootin' My Horn (Jerry Colonna playing trombone and singing)
Star Dust (Babe Russin swinging out on his tenor saxophone)

5:45PM WEAF
RED McKENZIE
NYC
In A Sentimental Mood (theme)
No Regrets
You're Not The Kind
Bye Bye Baby

6:00PM WABC
GEORGE HALL
Taft Hotel, NYC
These Foolish Things (vocal: Dolly Dawn)
Stompin' At The Savoy
It's Like Reaching For The Moon
Empty Saddles
Let's Sing Again
When A Lady Meets A Gentleman Down South

■ THURSDAY 13 AUGUST 1936

RECORDING SESSION

BENNY GOODMAN AND HIS ORCHESTRA
Recording session for Victor in Hollywood.
Benny Goodman (cl); Chris Griffin, Mannie Klein, Pee Wee Erwin (t); Red Ballard, Murray McEachern (tb); Bill DePew, Hymie Shertzer (as); Art Rollini, Dick Clark (ts); Jess Stacy (p); Allan Reuss (g); Harry Goodman (b); Gene Krupa (d); Helen Ward (voc)
You Turned The Tables On Me (vHW) / *Here's Love In Your Eyes* / *Pick Yourself Up* / *Down South Camp Meeting*

HUDSON-DeLANGE ORCHESTRA
Recording session for Brunswick in New York City.
Will Hudson (arr); Eddie DeLange (voc/ldr); James O'Connell, Harry Rausch, Ralph Hollenbeck (t); Edward Kolyer (tb); George Bohn, Hugh Hibbert (cl/as); Pete Brendel (as/bar); Ted Duane (cl/ts); Mark Hyams (p); Cliff Rausch (g); Doc Goldberg (b); Edward O'Hara (d); Ruth Gaylor (voc)
Grab Your Partner And Swing / *Cross Country Hop* / *Looking Down At The Stars* (vRG) / *What The Heart Believes* (vRG)

RADIO LOGS

7:00PM WABC
RED NICHOLS
"Atlantic Family Program"
Tain't No Use
Stay On The Right Side Of The Road
Then Came The Indians

9:00PM WABC
MARK WARNOW'S BLUE VELVET ORCHESTRA
CBS Studios, NYC
No Regrets
When I'm With You (vocal: Jerry Cooper)

Blues In G Minor
Summertime
Farewell Blues
Take My Heart (vocal: Jerry Cooper)
Runnin' Wild
They Didn't Remember

10:00PM WHN
STUFF SMITH
Onyx Club, 72 W52nd Street, NYC
Robins And Roses
There's A Small Hotel
Tea For Two (Frank Froeba on piano)
Old Joe's Hittin' The Jug
I'se A-Muggin' (theme)

10:30PM WOR
IRVING AARONSON
Ben Marden's Riviera, N.J.
Always
Dream Awhile (vocal: Skippy Carlstrom)
Until The Real Thing Comes Along
That's What Makes The World Go Round

11:00PM WABC
HAL KEMP
Astor Hotel, NYC
I Hate Your Face (vocal: Skinnay Ennis)
Tain't No Use
No Regrets (vocal: Bob Allen)
Knock Knock (vocal: Saxie Dowell)
Under A Texas Moon (vocal: Maxine Gray)
Rigamarole
A Rendezvous With You (vocal: Bob Allen)
I Get A Kick Out Of You (vocal: Maxine Gray)
When I'm With You (vocal: Skinnay Ennis)

11:30PM WABC
DICK STABILE
Lincoln Hotel, NYC
Is It True What They Say About Dixie?
Sweet Mystery of Love
Red Hot Penny
Without A Shadow of A Doubt
Ain't She Sweet
These Foolish Things (vocal: Bert Shaw)
Did I Remember?
Between The Devil And The Deep Blue Sea
But Definitely (vocal: Bert Shaw)
On The Air (theme)

11:30PM WTIC
FLETCHER HENDERSON
Grand Terrace, Chicago
Christopher Columbus (theme)
White Heat
Dancing Till Dawn
On Cocoanut Island
On The Beach At Bali-Bali
I Want To Be With You
Just Drifting Along

12:00 MIDNIGHT WABC
BENNY GOODMAN
Palomar Ballroom, Los Angeles
House Hop
You Turned The Tables On Me (vocal: Helen Ward)
St. Louis Blues (5 clarinets; 2 trombones; Benny's best clarinet)
There's A Small Hotel (vocal: Helen Ward) (swell bass)
Chinatown, My Chinatown (BG Trio) (poor piano)
Star Dust

Honeysuckle Rose (swell trombone & saxes; Goodman's clarinet)
The Glory Of Love (vocal: Helen Ward)
Remember

12:30AM WABC
CHARLIE BARNET
Glen Island Casino, New Rochelle, N.Y.
King Porter Stomp
When I'm With You (vocal: Modernaires)
Stompin' At The Savoy (vocal: Modernaires)
You're Not The Kind (vocal: Charlie Barnet)
Blue Skies
Me And The Moon (vocal: Modernaires)
Down South Camp Meeting

Charlie Barnet

1:00AM WENR
FLETCHER HENDERSON
Grand Terrace, Chicago
Sweet Sue
It All Depends On You
By Heck
Casa Loma Stomp
I Wonder
Down South Camp Meeting
Dixieland Band (vocal: Joe Thomas)
Christopher Columbus (theme)

■ FRIDAY 14 AUGUST 1936

RADIO LOGS

? WABC
JIMMY FERRALL/RHYTHMAIRES
CBS Studio, NYC
Sing Me A Swing Song
Take My Heart (vocal: Jimmy Ferrall)
I Got Rhythm
It's Got To Be Love
There's A Small Hotel
Mary Had A Little Lamb (Bud Sheppard on violin)

12:30PM WABC
CAPTIVATORS
CBS studio, NYC
The Captivators, Instrumentalists, Merry Makers, Rhythmaires, Dictators, etc. are all CBS bands. They all have about the same personnels.
Cross Patch
A Star Fell Out Of Heaven
On The Beach At Bali-Bali
You're Not The Kind

Robins And Roses
If We Never Meet Again
No Regrets
A Fine Romance
These Foolish Things
Where There's You There's Me

3.00PM WABC
SWEET AND HOT
CBS Studio, NYC
Honeysuckle Rose (theme)
Sing Me A Swing Song
Someday We'll Meet Again (Ruth Gerhart singing)
Lover
Spreadin' Rhythm Around (Dick Porter's piano)
Night And Day
Old Man Mose (Dick Porter, formerly of the Hickory House, playing piano)
Stars In My Eyes (Bud Sheppard playing a sweet violin)
Organ Grinder's Swing
Without A Shadow Of A Doubt (Ruth Gerhart singing)
Christopher Columbus
Tea For Two
Honeysuckle Rose (theme)

5:00PM WEAF
BUGHOUSE RHYTHM (DR JOHN MEAKEN)
San Francisco
Announced by G. Archibald Presby
Streamline Strut (written by Sidney Phillips: 4 E-flat clarinets; drums)
Farewell Blues (Arrangement to sound like Glen Gray)
Ain't Misbehavin' (written by Thomas 'Fats' Waller)
Man From Brandyville (written by Lawrence King-Lee Morton)

5.15PM WEAF
JAN SAVITT
Philadelphia
Alexander's Ragtime Band
These Foolish Things (vocal: Carlotta Dale)
Am I Asking Too Much?
Blue Room
Take My Heart (vocal: Dick Horten)

7:30PM WEAF
DICK McDONOUGH BAND
Commercial, NYC
You Hit The Spot
I Know That You Know
Tain't No Use (vocal: Peg LaCentra)
Japanese Sandman
Until The Real Thing Comes Along (vocal: Peg LaCentra)
Farewell Blues
You Hit The Spot

9.00PM WTIC
MERRY MADCAPS (Norman Cloutier)
Hartford, Conn
Sweet Sue
Take My Heart (vocal: Ed Holly)
Some Of These Days
Empty Saddles (vocal: Ed Holly)
Get Happy
You're Not The Kind
Tain't No Use
There's A Small Hotel (vocal: Ed Holly)
But Definitely
Sailing A Dreamboat (theme)

9:45PM WHN
STUFF SMITH
Onyx Club, 72 W52nd Street, NYC
I'se A-Muggin' (theme)

Pick Yourself Up
You're Not The Kind
Love Me Or Leave Me (Frank Froeba on piano)
Here Comes The Man With The Jive

10:00PM WABC
ANDRÉ KOSTELANETZ
Commercial sponsored by Chesterfield Cigarettes.
Too Good To Be True
There's A Small Hotel (vocal: Ray Heatherton)
Bamba
Bye Bye Baby (vocal: Kay Thompson & her 8 rhythm girls)
I Can't Remember (vocal: Ray Heatherton)
I'm Yours (vocal: Kay Thompson)
Take Me Out To The Ball Game

1:30AM WCAU
JAN SAVITT
CBS studio, Philadelphia
Another CBS studio band in Philadelphia.
Out Of Space (theme)
Not For All The Rice In China
Easter Parade
Heat Wave
Chansonette
I Get A Kick Out Of You
Stars In My Eyes
Harlemania

■ SATURDAY 15 AUGUST 1936

RADIO LOGS

5:30PM WABC
CHARLIE BARNET
Glen Island Casino, New Rochelle, N.Y.
I've Lost Another Sweetheart (theme)
Swingtime In the Rockies (same arrangement as Benny Goodman uses)
Me And The Moon (vocal: Modernaires)
My Melancholy Baby (A swell swing number)
I Can't Escape From You (vocal: Joe Host)
Until Today (vocal: Joe Host)
So Nice Of You (vocal: Joe Host)
Bye Bye Baby (vocal: Modernaires)
Dixieland Band (vocal: Charlie Barnet) (Poor vocal by Charlie)
Would You? (vocal: Joe Host) (Nice saxes)
Honeysuckle Rose (Best arrangement: swell clarinet; bass; saxes; trumpet; piano)
When Did You Leave Heaven? (vocal: Joe Host) (Swell new sweet number)

6:00pm WABC
DICTATORS (CBS BAND)
CBS Studio, NYC
Nothin's Blue But The Sky
Until Today
Hay Straw
There Isn't Any Limit To My Love
Let's Sing Again
Let Yourself Go

8.00PM WABC
SATURDAY NIGHT SWING SESSION No9
CBS Studios, NYC
This program started about a month ago and is on every Saturday. Guest stars appear with Bunny Berigan every week. George Hogan and Paul Douglas are the announcers. The show is produced by Phil Cohan and his assistant, Ed Cashman.
I Can't Get Started (theme—Bunny Berigan & house band conducted by Leith Stevens)
On Your Toes (Bunny Berigan & house band conducted by Leith Stevens)
Sensation (Bunny Berigan & house band cond. by Leith Stevens—written by Eddie Edwards of ODJB)
There's Religion In Rhythm (vocal by Willard Robison with house band)
Sophisticated Lady (Babe Russin on saxophone with house band)
Chinatown, My Chinatown (Babe Russin again, on tenor saxophone, with house band)
Limehouse Blues (Bunny Berigan & house band conducted by Leith Stevens)
Ochi Chornya (Bunny Berigan trumpet solo with house band)
Let's Go Barrelhouse (vocal by Willard Robison-Bunny Berigan. Written by Robison.)

10:00PM WHN
STUFF SMITH
Onyx Club, 72 W52nd Street, NYC
Swing Mister Charlie
A Fine Romance
Emaline (Frank Froeba on piano)
Organ Grinder's Swing
I'se A-Muggin' (theme)

11:00PM WJZ
RILEY & FARLEY
Hickory House, 52nd Street, NYC
Let's Sing Again
Bye Bye Baby
Song of The Islands
I'm A Lone Cowboy
You Took Advantage Of Me
I Never Knew I Could Love Anybody
Crazy Rhythm
Rip Van Winkle
If You Love Me
The Music Goes Round And Around (theme)

11:30PM WABC
HAL KEMP
Astor Hotel, NYC
I Can't Escape From You (vocal: Maxine Gray)
Will You Know Me When I'm Famous? (vocal: Skinnay Ennis)
Monopoly (vocal: Bob Allen)
Biwangi
You Don't Love Right (vocal: Skinnay Ennis)
I'll Never Let You Go (vocal: Maxine Gray)
Shoe Shine Boy
Hands Across The Table

■ SUNDAY 16 AUGUST 1936

RADIO LOGS

7:00PM WABC
CLYDE LUCAS
Hotel New Yorker, NYC
Too Good To Be True
These Foolish Things
Until Today
You Dropped Me Like A Red Hot Penny (vocal: Clyde Lucas)
A Lonely Gondolier (vocal: Lyn Lucas)
Organ Grinder's Swing (Swell vocal arrangement)
Parlez-Moi D'Amour (Terrible-7 violins)

7:30PM WOR
IRVING AARONSON
Ben Marden's Riviera, N.J.
Blue Skies (Best arrangement–nice sax, trumpets and piano)
When I'm With You (vocal: Skippy Carlstrom)
Too Good To Be True (vocal: Bobby Nicholson/Lola Bob)
Monopoly (vocal: Lola Bob)

8:00PM WABC
AMERICA DANCES
CBS Studios, NYC
Another CBS program, on once a week with guest stars.
On The Air (theme)
Take My Heart (Lud Gluskin Orchestra)
In A Sentimental Mood (Lud Gluskin Orchestra)
Tormented (Blue Flames vocal quartet)
Fascinating Rhythm / Crazy Rhythm / I Got Rhythm (medley)
When I'm With You (vocal by Gogo de Lys)
St. Louis Blues (Casper Reardon playing the harp)
Stars In My Eyes
It Ain't Right (Blue Flames vocal quartet)
Sophisticated Lady
'Way Down Yonder In New Orleans (Casper Reardon–Gogo De Lys)
Star Dust

10:45PM WICC
LUIS RUSSELL
Pleasure Beach BR, Bridgeport, Conn
Swing With Luis
Until The Real Thing Comes Along (vocal: Bobbie Caston)
Everybody Calls It Swing
Take My Heart (vocal: Sonny Woods)

11:30PM WABC
BOB CROSBY
Lexington Hotel, NYC
Summertime (theme)
Royal Garden Blues
Did I Remember? (vocal: Bob Walker)
But Definitely (vocal: Bob Crosby)
Star Dust
I Take To You (vocal: Nappy Lamare)
Tin Roof Blues (Ward Silloway's trombone)
I Can't Escape From You (vocal: Bob Crosby)
The Scene Changes (vocal: Bob Walker)
Wolverine Blues

■ MONDAY 17 AUGUST 1936
RADIO LOGS

12:30PM WABC
MERRY MAKERS
CBS Studios, NYC
The Merry Makers are a CBS studio band with such well-known players as Bunny Berigan, Art Manners, Babe Russin, Bud Sheppard, Johnny Augustine, Dick Porter (piano), Lou Shoobe (bass), Vincent Maffay (guitar), and many others.
52nd Street Fever
These Foolish Things
Nobody's Sweetheart
Sweet Mystery of Love
You Can't Pull The Wool Over My Eyes
The Scene Changes
Morocco
Stars In My Eyes
Dinah
But Definitely
Sing, Baby, Sing

1:30PM WABC
RHYTHMAIRES
CBS studios, NYC
Why Do I Lie To Myself About You?
First Rose of Spring
Sing, Baby, Sing
Until Today
Stompin' At The Savoy
Why Do I Lie To Myself About You?

2:30PM WABC
MANHATTAN MATINÉE
CBS studios, NYC
Swell. Another weekly CBS program with guest stars. Announcer: Bert Parks
Shine On Your Shoes (Mark Warnow's Orchestra)
Cross Patch (Mark Warnow's Orchestra)
Stars In My Eyes (Ruth Carheart singing)
Jazznocracy
Bye Bye Baby (4 Eaton Boys singing)
Swing Mister Charlie
Someday We'll Meet Again (Russell Door singing)
All Dressed Up Tonight And No Place To Go (Ruth Carheart singing)
Wild Party
You Can't Pull The Wool Over My Eyes (Doris Kerr & 4 Eaton Boys singing)
Monday In Manhattan (theme)

5:30PM WABC
VIRGINIA VERRILL
CBS studios, NYC
You're Not The Kind (vocal: Virginia Verrill)
I Never Knew (vocal: Virginia Verrill)
I Can't Pretend (vocal: Virginia Verrill)

7:00PM WABC
LORETTA LEE
CBS studios, NYC
Bye Bye Baby (vocal: Loretta Lee)
Did I Remember? (vocal: Loretta Lee)
I Can't Escape from You (orchestra)
The Scene Changes (vocal: Loretta Lee)
Lulu's Back In Town (vocal: Loretta Lee)
Deep South (theme)

7:15PM WOR
IRVING AARONSON
Ben Marden's Riviera, N.J.
Doin' The Riviera
Sunshine At Midnight
Sing Me A Swing Song
You're Not The Kind
Swingola

9:00PM WABC
JAN SAVITT
CBS studio, Philadelphia
Another CBS studio band in Philadelphia.
Music Makes Me
Why Do I Lie To Myself About You?
Shoe Shine Boy
I've Got A Note
The Way You Look Tonight
Organ Grinder's Swing
Are You My Love?
The Continental
Anything Goes
Good Green Acres At Home
Look In Love

12:00 MIDNIGHT WEAF
RILEY & FARLEY
Hickory House, 52nd Street, NYC
You Took Advantage Of Me
Just Driftin' Along (vocal: Ed Farley)
Wabash Blues
I'm Gonna Clap My Hands (vocal: Ed Farley)
Farewell Blues
Afterglow
Oh, Dear! What Can The Matter Be? (vocal: Ed Farley & Mike Riley)
When Buddha Smiles
Rip Van Winkle (vocal: Ed Farley)

When I'm With You (vocal: Mike Riley)
No Regrets (vocal: Ed Farley)

12:15AM WTIC
MERRY MADCAPS (Norman Cloutier)
Organ Grinder's Swing
The Stars Weep (vocal: Bob Ellis)
Did I Remember? (vocal: Bob Ellis)
Sweet Mystery of Love

12:30AM WABC
CHARLIE BARNET
Glen Island Casino, New Rochelle, N.Y.
Colossal. Charlie Barnet is my favourite band now besides Benny Goodman.
Swingtime In The Rockies (Charlie Barnet's sax playing is colossal)
Until The Real Thing Comes Along (vocal: Charlie Barnet) (swell song)
Me And The Moon (vocal: Modernaires) (Barnet's Modernaires were formerly with Fred Waring)
Darktown Strutters' Ball (swell sax accompaniment to trumpet solo)
Take My Heart
Stop, Look And Listen (vocal: Modernaires) (slide trombones; fine vocal by Modernaires)
'Way Down Yonder In New Orleans (ordinary arrangement except for sax solo)
Did I Remember To Tell You That I Love You?
Make Believe Ballroom (vocal: Modernaires) (Modernaires' best singing on swell new song)
Down South Camp Meeting (great arrangement by Fletcher Henderson)

1:00AM WENR
FLETCHER HENDERSON
Grand Terrace, Chicago
Henderson has fine orchestra and writes fine arrangements but the band plays too ragged. They can't play smoothly. Their solos are excellent.
Mary Had A Little Lamb (Good arrangement of a bad song: Buster Bailey on clarinet)
Dancing Till Dawn (Terrible song)
All My Life (Poor vocal: nice saxes swinging out on slow song)
Blue Lou (One of Henderson's best songs: swell trumpet by Roy Eldridge and sax by Chu Berry)
Tea For Two (Fair: nice piano by Henderson)
You Can't Pull The Wool Over My Eyes (Eldridge, Bailey do nice work)
Rose Room (Swell song: nice saxes, especially Chu Berry's tenor)
I Would Do Anything For You (Great arrangement, played too ragged)
The Moon Is Low (Eldridge, Berry, doing more fine work)
Christopher Columbus (theme)

■ TUESDAY 18 AUGUST 1936

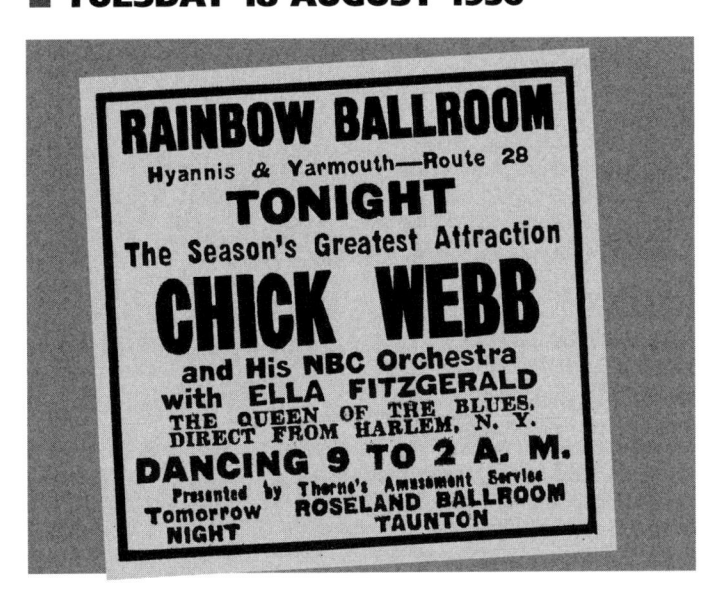

RAINBOW BALLROOM
Hyannis & Yarmouth—Route 28
TONIGHT
The Season's Greatest Attraction
CHICK WEBB
and His NBC Orchestra
with ELLA FITZGERALD
THE QUEEN OF THE BLUES
DIRECT FROM HARLEM, N. Y.
DANCING 9 TO 2 A. M.
Presented by Thorne's Amusement Service
Tomorrow ROSELAND BALLROOM
NIGHT   TAUNTON

RADIO LOGS

2:30PM WABC
DICTATORS
CBS studios, NYC
Knock Knock
These Foolish Things
It Ain't Right
So Nice Of You
The Way You Look Tonight

5:00PM WABC
JIMMY FERRALL
CBS studios, NYC
You're Not The Kind Of A Girl For A Boy Like Me
Empty Saddles
Everything I Have Is Yours
It's Love Again
It's Like Reaching For The Moon

9:00PM WABC
TOMMY DORSEY
Dallas, Texas
Swell. Tommy Dorsey is playing on the Ford Commercial program.
She Shall Have Music (good swing arrangement of a terrible song)
Mary Had A Little Lamb (vocal: Edythe Wright)
In A Sentimental Mood (Nice swinging with 2 slide trombones)
Riffin' (Bud Freeman does plenty of 'hot' work on tenor; Dave Tough on drums)
Long Ago And Far Away (vocal: Jack Leonard) (too sweet)
Ja-Da (great work by Tommy on trombone; fair solo by Max Kaminsky)
It's A Sin To Tell A Lie (vocal: Jack Leonard) (terrible song: nice trombone)
I'm Confessin' (one of TDs best arrangements: swell sax & trumpet teams; Freeman & Tough swell)
When I'm With You (vocal: Edythe Wright) (fair)
Weary Blues (EXCELLENT: unsurpassed work by Freeman, Dorsey, Kaminsky & Tough)

9:30PM WABC
BENNY GOODMAN
"Camel Caravan", Los Angeles
I Got Rhythm (Excellent, nuttsy, colossal: what ballsy slide trombones, sax, piano)
Between The Devil And The Deep Blue Sea (vocal: Helen Ward)
Sugar Foot Stomp (Ballsy, nuttsy: 5 clarinets; swell trumpet; trombone)

10:45PM WLW
JOE HAYMES
Moonlight Gardens, Coney Island, Cincinnati, Ohio
Colossal.
Swing Low (by Joe Haymes: nuttsy trumpet and saxes)
You Started Me Dreaming (vocal: Honey Burns)
Swingin' For The King (vocal: Cliff Weston) (by Joe Haymes)
Blue Illusion (Just like Red Nichols' 'Wailin' To The Four Winds': nuttsy trumpet)
My Melancholy Baby (vocal: Cliff Weston) (nuttsy saxes)

11:30PM WABC
DICK STABILE
Lincoln Hotel, NYC
Swell. Dick Stabile plays alto sax
On The Air (theme)
You Can't Pull The Wool Over My Eyes (vocal: Dick Stabile)
On A Cocoanut Island (vocal: Bert Shaw)
Top Hat (A year-old song played in nice swing style)
Did I Remember? (six saxophones)
Blue Skies (one of Dick's best arrangements: what a sax!)
I Can't Escape From You (vocal: Bert Shaw)
I Take To You (vocal: Bert Shaw) (six saxophones: nuttsy clarinet)
When I'm With You (vocal: Dick Stabile)
Honeysuckle Rose (six saxophones: nuttsy; nice string bass)

11:35PM WEAF
FLETCHER HENDERSON
Grand Terrace, Chicago
Bye Bye Baby
Sing, Baby, Sing
St. Louis Blues
But Definitely
Stompin' At The Savoy
Jangled Nerves
Christopher Columbus (theme)

11:45PM WABC
RHYTHMAIRES
CBS studios, NYC
It Ain't Right
Me And The Moon
Oh, My Goodness
Rendezvous With A Dream
Swamp Fire

12:00 MIDNIGHT WEAF
PAUL WHITEMAN
Casa Manana, Ft Worth, Texas
Fair. Too large an orchestra
Why? (Nice solo by Frankie Trumbauer)
Monopoly (vocal: Ramona)
You Took Advantage Of Me
Tormented (vocal: Jack Teagarden)
You Can't Pull The Wool Over My Eyes (vocal: Darelle Alexander)
Summer Breeze
Sunshine At Midnight
Nobody's Sweetheart (vocal: Jack Teagarden)
The Stars Weep (vocal: Ramona)
On The Alamo

12:30AM WEAF
JOE VENUTI
Casa Manana, Ft Worth, Texas
Joe Venuti plays a 'hot' violin. Swell on 'hot' numbers; sweet numbers are bad.
Bugle Call Rag (Swell drum licks; fine arrangement; great fiddling)
When I'm With You (vocal: Donald Dorsey) (Terrible)
Satan's Holiday (Not much orchestra but swell violin by Joe Venuti)
Too Good To Be True (vocal: Mildred Fenton) (Lousy)
Christopher Columbus (Nuttsy sax: fine arrangement but played too fast; fine bass with violin)
Lone Star (vocal: Donald Dorsey) (Terrible)
Nagasaki
Is It True What They Say About Dixie? (vocal: Mildred Fenton)
Fiddlesticks

1:00AM WABC
GEORGE HALL
Hotel Taft, NYC
Tain't No Use
When The Moon Hangs High (vocal: Johnny McKeever)
You Can't Pull The Wool Over My Eyes (vocal: Dolly Dawn & Dawn Patrol)
Cradle Song
Did I Remember? (vocal: Johnny McKeever)
Knock Knock
San Francisco
Bye Bye Baby (vocal: Dolly Dawn)
Soon

1:00AM WENR
FLETCHER HENDERSON
Grand Terrace, Chicago
Shanghai Shuffle
She Shall Have Music
Milenberg Joys
Did I Remember?

You Dropped Me Like A Red Hot Penny
Blue Lou
It's You I'm Talkin' About!
Hocus Pocus
Knock Knock

■ WEDNESDAY 19 AUGUST 1936

RECORDING SESSION

BOB CROSBY AND HIS ORCHESTRA
Recording session for Decca in New York City.
Bob Crosby (voc/ldr); Zeke Zarchy, Yank Lawson (t); Ward Silloway, Warren Smith (tb); Gil Rodin, Matty Matlock (cl/as); Noni Bernardi (as); Eddie Miller (cl/ts); Deane Kincaide (ts); Bob Zurke (piano); Nappy Lamare (g/voc); Bob Haggart (b); Ray Bauduc (d)
My Kingdom For A Kiss (vBC) / *Through The Courtesy of Love* (vBC) / *Peter Piper* (vBC) / *Woman On My Weary Mind* / *Royal Garden Blues*

RADIO LOGS

12:30PM WABC
MERRY MAKERS
CBS Studios, NYC
The Merry Makers are a CBS studio band with many well-known players including Bunny Berigan, Art Manners, Babe Russin, etc.
Christopher Columbus
Until Today
You've Gotta Eat Your Spinach Baby
Without A Shadow Of A Doubt
Knock Knock
A Fine Romance
I'll Never Let You Go
Sing, Sing, Sing
There's A Small Hotel
Doin' The Prom

3:45PM WABC
GOGO DE LYS
CBS studios, NYC
To Be Alone With You (theme)
Did I Remember? (vocal: Gogo De Lys)
I'll Never Let You Go (vocal: Gogo De Lys)
A Star Fell Out Of Heaven (vocal: Gogo De Lys)
Boston Tea Party (vocal: Gogo De Lys)
You're Not The Kind (vocal: Gogo De Lys)

4:30PM WABC
INSTRUMENTALISTS
CBS Studios, NYC
Another CBS studio band. Great
After You've Gone (Artie Manners going to town on the clarinet)
The Turkey is Going To Swing Tonight (Vincent Maffay playing sweet guitar)
Dizzy Drumming (Nuttsy. Johnny Williams playing the drums)
Take My Heart (Thelma Filla, guest, playing a sweet violin)
Strike Up The Band (Babe Russin playing the tenor saxophone)

5:30PM WABC
BUDDY CLARK
CBS Studios, NYC
Two In Love (theme)
No Regrets (vocal: Buddy Clark)
Oh, My Goodness! (vocal: Buddy Clark)
My Heart Stood Still (vocal: Buddy Clark)
I'm An Old Cowhand (vocal: Buddy Clark)
Christopher Columbus (Band)
Sweet Mystery of Love (vocal: Buddy Clark)

AUGUST 1936

7:00PM WABC
LEE WILEY
CBS Studios, NYC
I'm Coming, Virginia (theme)
I Can't Get Started (vocal: Lee Wiley)
Take My Heart (vocal: Lee Wiley)
Too Good To Be True (Band)
Glad To Be Unhappy (vocal: Lee Wiley)

To Bob Sincerely Lee Wiley

11:30PM WABC
BOB CROSBY
Lexington Hotel, NYC
This is Bob Crosby's last broadcast from the Lexington Hotel in NYC.
Summertime (theme)
South Rampart Street Parade (Written by drummer Ray Bauduc)
My Kingdom For A Kiss (vocal: Bob Crosby)
Here Comes Your Pappy (vocal: Nappy Lamare)
Sweet Misery Of Love (vocal: Bob Walker)
Bye Bye Baby (vocal: Bob Crosby)
Dixieland Shuffle (nice solos by Eddie Miller, Matty Matlock, Nappy Lamare)
Peter Piper (vocal: Bob Crosby)
Without A Shadow Of A Doubt (vocal: Bob Walker)
Pagan Love Song (best arrangement: Ray Bauduc; Bob Haggart; Yank Lawson)

12:15AM WTIC
MERRY MADCAPS (Norman Cloutier)
Hartford, Conn
Tain't No Use
On A Summer Holiday (vocal: Bob Ellis)
Let's Sing Again (vocal: Bob Ellis)
But Definitely

1:00AM WENR
FLETCHER HENDERSON
Grand Terrace, Chicago
Big John Special (One of Henderson's best pieces: swell trumpets; saxes)
Stompin' At The Savoy
These Foolish Things
Unknown Title
Dancing 'Til Dawn
Mary Had A Little Lamb
Shoe Shine Boy
Stop, Look, And Listen
Blue Minor
Christopher Columbus (theme)

■ THURSDAY 20 AUGUST 1936

RECORDING SESSION
WINGY MANONE AND HIS ORCHESTRA
Recording session for Bluebird in New York City.
Wingy Manone (t/voc); Al Mastren (tb); Mike Viggiano (cl); Joe Marsala (cl/as); James Lamare (cl/ts); Conrad Lanoue (p); Jack LeMaire (g); Artie Shapiro (b); Sam Weiss (d); Sally Sharon (voc)
It Can Happen To You (vWM) / *It's The Gypsy In Me* (vWM) / *Cottage By The Moon* (vWM) / *And They Said It Wouldn't Last* (vWM) / *Fancy Meeting You* (vWM) / *A Good Man Is Hard To Find* (vWM,SS)

RADIO LOGS

6:00PM WNEW
BARNET'S MODERNAIRES
Make Believe Ballroom
Blue Moon
Moonglow
Stompin' At The Savoy
Make Believe Ballroom

9:00PM WABC
MARK WARNOW'S BLUE VELVET ORCHESTRA
CBS Studios, NYC
Without A Shadow Of A Doubt
When I'm With You (Loretta Lee singing)
Swing Fugue In E Flat (Nuttsy, written by Mark Warnow: trumpet; clarinet)
Land Of Degradation (Clyde Barrie, Negro, singing a spiritual song)
Me And The Moon (Redheaded Loretta Lee vocalizing)
Whispering
By Heck
Soft Lights And Sweet Music

10:00PM WHN
STUFF SMITH
Onyx Club, 72 W52nd Street, NYC
I'se A-Muggin' (theme)
Unknown Title
Star Dust
Tea For Two
When I'm So Close To You
If We Never Meet Again (Joe Bushkin at piano)
You'se A Viper (by Stuff Smith)

11:30PM WABC
CHARLIE BARNET
Glen Island Casino, New Rochelle, N.Y.

Charlie Barnet

Bye Bye Baby (vocal: Charlie Barnet & Modernaires)
My Melancholy Baby
When I'm With You (vocal: Modernaires)
Darktown Strutters' Ball
Me And The Moon (vocal: Modernaires)
Blue Skies
Robins And Roses (vocal: Modernaires)
My First Thrill (vocal: Modernaires)
Dixieland Band (vocal: Charlie Barnet)
Yeah, Man!
Between The Devil And The Deep Blue Sea

12:00 MIDNIGHT WABC
BENNY GOODMAN
Palomar Ballroom, Los Angeles
I Know That You Know
These Foolish Things (vocal: Helen Ward)
Here's Love In Your Eyes
You Turned The Tables On Me (vocal: Helen Ward)
Swingtime In The Rockies
You're Not The Kind (vocal: Helen Ward)
Always
Without A Shadow Of A Doubt (vocal: Helen Ward)
When Did You Leave Heaven?
Sugar Foot Stomp
Goodbye (theme)

1:00AM WOR
JOE HAYMES
Coney Island, Cincinnati
Joe Haymes has another new band. He has one of the finest tenor sax men I have ever heard. Cliff Weston plays the trumpet.
You Can't Pull The Wool Over My Eyes (vocal: Cliff Weston)
A Pretty Girl Is Like A Melody (Neat arrangement: no solos)
Should I? (Nice clarinet, trombone, trumpet, piano and sax)
All My Life (vocal: Honey Burns)
All Right, All Right (vocal: Cliff Weston) (A take-off on Major Bowes)
Sophisticate (Swell swing arrangement of a slow song: nuttsy sax team)
Papa Tree-Top Tall (vocal: Cliff Weston) (Written by Hoagy Carmichael)
Tormented (vocal: Honey Burns)
Happy As The Day Is Long

■ FRIDAY 21 AUGUST 1936

RECORDING SESSION

BENNY GOODMAN AND HIS ORCHESTRA
Recording session for Victor in Hollywood.
Benny Goodman (cl); Chris Griffin, Sterling Bose, Pee Wee Erwin (t); Red Ballard, Murray McEachern (tb); Bill DePew, Hymie Shertzer (as); Art Rollini, Dick Clark, Vido Musso (ts); Jess Stacy (p); Allan Reuss (g); Harry Goodman (b); Gene Krupa (d)
St. Louis Blues / Love Me Or Leave Me / Bugle Call Rag

BENNY GOODMAN QUARTET
Lionel Hampton (vib); Teddy Wilson (p); Benny Goodman (cl); Gene Krupa (d)
Moonglow

STUFF SMITH & HIS ONYX CLUB BOYS
Recording session for Vocalion in New York City.
Jonah Jones (t); Stuff Smith (vln/voc); James Sherman (p); Bobby Bennett (g); Mack Walker (b); Cozy Cole (d)
Knock Knock, Who's There? (vSS) / *Bye Bye Baby* (vSS) / *Here Comes The Man With The Jive* (vSS & Band)

RADIO LOGS

12:30pm WABC
CAPTIVATORS
CBS studio, NYC
The Captivators, Instrumentalists, Merry Makers, Rhythmaires, Dictators, etc. are all CBS bands. They all have about the same personnels.
Oh, My Goodness
Me And The Moon
It Ain't Right
Rendezvous With A Dream
Sing, Baby, Sing
Did I Remember?
I'm An Old Cowhand
Swamp Fire
Sweet Sue

3:00pm WABC
SWEET AND HOT
CBS Studios, NYC
Cross Patch (Lud Gluskin & his orchestra)
Stars In My Eyes (Ruth Carheart singing)
Crazy Rhythm (Lud Gluskin & his orchestra)
Would You Have A Cup Of Jello With Me? (Eaton Boys singing)
Smoke Gets In Your Eyes
Bobbin' Up And Down (Raymond Scott playing piano)
Hidden Valley (Ruth Carheart singing)
When A Lady Meets A Gentleman Down South (Eaton Boys singing)
Swingin' For The King
Me And The Moon (Art Gentry singing)
Honeysuckle Rose (theme)

7:00pm WABC
VIRGINIA VERRILL
CBS Studios, NYC
Afterglow (vocal: Virginia Verrill)
You Dropped Me Like A Red Hot Penny (vocal: Virginia Verrill)
Take My Heart (vocal: Virginia Verrill)
You Can't Pull The Wool Over My Eyes (vocal: Virginia Verrill)
Afterglow (vocal: Virginia Verrill) (introduced by Virginia last month)

7:30pm WELI
CECIL DOWNES
Coconut Grove, Bridgeport, Conn
You're A Heavenly Thing
Goodbye (vocal: Vera Cruse)
I Found A New Baby
Singin' The Blues
I Surrender Dear
I'll Get By (vocal: Jerry Packard)
House Jack Built For Jill
Bye Bye Baby
A Star Fell Out Of Heaven (vocal: Vera Cruse)

9:00pm WTIC
MERRY MADCAPS (Norman Cloutier)
Hartford, Conn
Sailing A Dreamboat (theme)
Blue Skies
Sing Me A Swing Song
Bye Bye Baby
A Pretty Girl Is Like A Melody (vocal: Ed Holly)
It's Got To Be Love
Original Dixieland One-Step
Peanut Vendor
China Boy
Sailing A Dreamboat (theme)

9:45pm WHN
STUFF SMITH
Onyx Club, 72 W52nd Street, NYC
Here Comes The Man With The Jive
It All Begins And Ends With You
St. Louis Blues

10:15pm WLW
JOE HAYMES
Coney Island, Cincinnati
Organ Grinder's Swing
Lost In My Dreams (vocal: Ronnie Chase)
After You've Gone (vocal: Honey Burns)
If We Never Meet Again (vocal: Cliff Weston)

■ SATURDAY 22 AUGUST 1936

RADIO LOGS

5:30pm WABC
CHARLIE BARNET
Glen Island Casino, New Rochelle, N.Y.
I've Lost Another Sweetheart (theme)
Always
So Nice Of You (vocal: Charlie Barnet)
Make Believe Ballroom (vocal: Modernaires)
A Star Fell Out Of Heaven (vocal: Joe Host)

Rosetta
Charlie Barnet's History Of Jazz
Stop, Look And Listen (vocal: Modernaires)
My Melancholy Baby
'Way Down Yonder In New Orleans

7:30PM WELI
CECIL DOWNS
Cocoanut Grove, Bridgeport, Conn
'Tain't No Use
Am I Asking Too Much? (vocal: Vera Cruse)
St. Louis Blues
Until Today (vocal: Jerry Packard)
Basin Street Blues
Christopher Columbus
Whatcha Gonna Do When There Ain't No Swing
After You've Gone

8:00PM WABC
SATURDAY NIGHT SWING SESSION No10
CBS Studio, NYC
I Can't Get Started (theme) (Bunny Berigan & house band)
You Can't Pull The Wool Over My Eyes (Bunny Berigan & house band)
Slippin' Around (Miff Mole on trombone with house band)
Dardanella (Bunny Berigan playing trumpet with swell saxes of house band)
Stompin' At The Savoy (Fred Waring's Swing Octet)
Loveless Love (Bunny Berigan taking a swell trumpet solo with house band)
You're Not The Kind (Bunny Berigan & Leith Stevens' house band)
Mood Hollywood (Lennie Hayton playing piano with the house band)
Wang Wang Blues (Bunny Berigan with the house band)

9:30PM WHN
STUFF SMITH
Onyx Club, 72 W52nd Street, NYC
I Don't Want To Make History
Summertime
In A Sentimental Mood
Take My Heart
I'm A Ding Dong Daddy (From Dumas)
I'se A-Muggin' (theme)

9.45PM WHN
LUCKY MILLINDER
Palisades Amusement Park, NJ
Star Dust (theme)
Lucky Swings Out
Carry Me Back To Green Pastures
Red Rhythm

10.30PM WHN
LUCKY MILLINDER
Palisades Amusement Park, NJ
Merry-Go-Round
Until The Real Thing Comes Along
In The Shade Of The Old Apple Tree
St. Louis Wiggle (Written by Lucky Millinder)

11:00PM WABC
ART SHAW
Hotel Lexington, NYC
Art Shaw plays the clarinet with his 'sweet swing' orchestra. He opened at the Lexington yesterday, following Bob Crosby.

I URGE THOSE who enjoy being first to get in as soon as possible on the Artie Shaw music, now being Columbaired from the Bob Crosby-vacated Hotel Lexington. The former New Havener's clarinet comes very close to Benny Goodman's, which is as near perfect as any swing musician would care to come, and the orchestral ideas are something new in the much-affected modern manner. I give you Master Shaw as a certain best bet.

It Ain't Right (vocal: Peg LaCentra)
Out Of Nowhere
There's A Small Hotel (vocal: Peg LaCentra)
I'm One Step Ahead Of My Shadow (vocal: Tony Pastor)
St. Louis Blues
King Of Swing (vocal: Peg LaCentra)
In A Sentimental Mood
South Sea Island Magic (vocal: Peg LaCentra)

11.15PM WHN
LUCKY MILLINDER
Palisades Amusement Park, NJ
Back Home Again In Indiana
I Need You So (vocal: Chuck Richards)
Always
Ride, Red, Ride

11.30PM WABC
HAL KEMP
Hotel Astor, NYC
Until The Real Thing Comes Along
Rigamarole
Monopoly (vocal: Bob Allen)
Me And The Moon (vocal: Maxine Gray)
When Did You Leave Heaven? (vocal: Skinnay Ennis)
Mean To Me
You Turned The Tables On Me (vocal: Bob Allen)
You Don't Love Right (vocal: Skinnay Ennis)
Long Ago And Far Away

12:15AM WLW
JOE HAYMES
Coney Island, Cincinnati
Papa Tree-Top Tall (vocal: Cliff Weston) (Written by Hoagy Carmichael)
Take My Heart (vocal: Honey Burns)
You Can't Pull The Wool Over My Eyes (vocal: Cliff Weston)
On A Summer Holiday (vocal: Honey Burns)
Should I?

Joe Haymes

12:30AM WABC
BENNY GOODMAN
Palomar Ballroom, Los Angeles
Let's Dance (theme)
I Got Rhythm (Swell slide trombones: nice sax by Rollini)
When I'm With You (vocal: Helen Ward) (Fair sweet song with nice vocal)
Remember (Arthur Rollini takes a fine, swingy, sweet solo: nice sax team)
Knock, Knock (vocal: Helen Ward) (A terrible song of puns–some original)
Sometimes I'm Happy (One of Benny's smoothest and best songs)
Between The Devil And The Deep Blue Sea (vocal: Helen Ward)
Who? (BG Trio) (Lousy number)
If I Could Be With You One Hour Tonight (Reuss swell on guitar)
Sing, Sing, Sing (vocal: Helen Ward) (fine work by Krupa & Harry Goodman)
Goodbye (theme)

12:30AM WABC
GEORGE HALL
Taft Hotel, NYC
A Star Fell Out Of Heaven (vocal: Dolly Dawn)
Organ Grinder's Swing
One Rose (vocal: Johnny McKeever)
Is It True What They Say About Dixie?
You'll Have To Swing It
Pale Hands
I'm An Old Cowhand (vocal: Dolly Dawn)
The Way You Look Tonight (vocal: Johnny McKeever)
Swamp Fire
If You Ask me How Much I Love You (theme)

■ MONDAY 24 AUGUST 1936

RECORDING SESSION

TEDDY WILSON AND HIS ORCHESTRA
Recording session for Brunswick in Los Angeles.
Lionel Hampton (vib); Teddy Wilson (p); Gordon Griffin (t); Benny Goodman (cl); Vido Musso (ts); Allan Reuss (g); Harry Goodman (b); Gene Krupa (d); Helen Ward, Red Harper (voc)
You Came To My Rescue (vHW) / *Here's Love In Your Eyes* (vHW) / *You Turned The Tables On Me* (vRH, BG out) / *Sing, Baby, Sing* (vRH, BG out)

RADIO LOGS

12:30PM WABC
MERRY MAKERS
CBS Studios, NYC
The Merry Makers are a CBS studio band with such well-known players as Bunny Berigan, Art Manners, Babe Russin, Bud Sheppard, Johnny Augustine, Dick Porter (piano), Lou Shoobe (bass), Vincent Maffay (guitar), and many others.
Christmas Night In Harlem
Afterglow
Dinah
Until Today
I Can Pull A Rabbit Out Of My Hat
Sweet Mystery Of Love
Sweet Sue
Without A Shadow Of A Doubt
I'm An Old Cowhand

1:30PM WABC
RHYTHMAIRES
CBS studios, NYC
Boston Tea Party
When I'm With You
Tain't No Use
Old Louisiana
I'm Tootin' My Horn

2:30PM WABC
MANHATTAN MATINÉE
CBS studios, NYC
Another weekly CBS program with guest stars. Announcer: Bert Parks
San Francisco
Me And The Moon
The Scene Changes
Bojangles Of Harlem
Harlem Heat
Bye Bye Baby
Bill Bailey
Guess Who? (vocal: Bert Parks)
I Can't Get Started (vocal: Margaret McCrae)
Let's Sing Again
Doh, Ray, Me
Cross Patch

7:00PM WABC
LORETTA LEE
CBS Studios, NYC
Deep South (theme)
I'll Never Let You Go (vocal: Loretta Lee)
South Sea Island Magic (vocal: Loretta Lee)
Bye Bye Baby (vocal: Loretta Lee)
Shoe Shine Boy (vocal: Loretta Lee)
Eeny-Meeny-Miney-Mo (vocal: Loretta Lee)
Deep South (theme)

7:15PM WABC
GEORGE HALL
Tap Room, Hotel Taft, NYC
Indian Tom Toms
Indian Love Call
Rose Marie
Stars Weep
My Kingdom For A Kiss
Never Gonna Dance
Swamp Fire

9.00PM WHN
LUCKY MILLINDER
Palisades Amusement Park, NJ
Mood Indigo
Take My Heart
Merry-Go-Round
In The Shade Of The Old Apple Tree
Red Rhythm

1:45AM WOR
STUFF SMITH
Onyx Club, 72 W52nd Street, NYC
Stompin' At The Savoy
Pick Yourself Up
The Man With The Jive
Ride, Red, Ride

■ TUESDAY 25 AUGUST 1936

RADIO LOGS

2.30PM WABC
DICTATORS
CBS studio, NYC
Oh, My Goodness!
I Can't Escape From You (vocal: Mary Alcott)
Do You Or Don't You Love Me? (vocal: Mary Alcott)
Sweet Mystery Of Love
Did I Remember? (vocal: Mary Alcott)
These Foolish Things

5.00PM WABC
JIMMY FERRALL
CBS studio, NYC
I've Waited A Lifetime (theme)
I Can't Escape From You (vocal: Jimmy Ferrall)
I Need You Night And Day (vocal: Jimmy Ferrall)
Where There's You There's Me (Mark Warnow Orchestra)
I Can't Get Started (vocal: Jimmy Ferrall)
Love Will Tell (vocal: Jimmy Ferrall)
I've Waited A Lifetime (theme)

9:00PM WABC
TOMMY DORSEY
Dallas, Texas
Cross Patch (vocal: Edythe Wright)
Dream Awhile (vocal: Jack Leonard)
Big John Special (Written by Fletcher Henderson: better than Goodman)
When Did You Leave Heaven? (vocal: Edythe Wright) (Nice sweet tune)
I've Got A Note (vocal: Three Esquires) (Nuttsy trombone)
Until Today (vocal: Rosemary Lane)
Sugar Foot Stomp
Always With You (Written by Tommy Dorsey)
St. Louis Blues

9:30PM WABC
BENNY GOODMAN
"Camel Caravan", Los Angeles
Hallelujah
Here's Love In Your Eyes
You Came To My Rescue
Your Minstrel Man
Star Dust
Sing, Sing, Sing

10:45PM WLW
JOE HAYMES
Coney Island, Cincinnati
Papa Tree Top Tall (vocal: Cliff Weston)
You're Not The Kind (vocal: Honey Burns)
Swing Low (Written and arranged by Joe Haymes: nuttsy trumpet)
The Way You Look Tonight (vocal: Ronnie Chase)

11.30PM WICC
DICK STABILE
Hotel Lincoln, NYC
Cross Patch
Did I Remember?
Tain't No Use
Sweet Mystery Of Love
San Francisco
Until The Real Thing Comes Along
My Kingdom For A Kiss
Ain't She Sweet
Two Sides To Every Story (vocal: Bert Shaw)
I Got Rhythm

11.30PM ?
FLETCHER HENDERSON
Grand Terrace, Chicago
Limehouse Blues
Sad Night In Harlem
Down South Camp Meetin'
On The Beach At Bali-Bali
Until The Real Thing Comes Along
Yeah, Man!

12:30AM WABC
GEORGE HALL
Taft Hotel, NYC
There Goes My Attraction
When I'm With You (vocal: Dolly Dawn)
'Way Down Yonder In New Orleans
South Sea Island Magic (vocal: Johnny McKeever)
San Francisco (From movie of the same name)
Wake Up And Sing (vocal: Dolly Dawn & the Dawn Patrol)
Just A-Wearyin' For You
Two Sides To Every Story (vocal: Dolly Dawn)
Would You? (vocal: Johnny McKeever)
Stompin' At The Savoy
If You Ask Me How Much I Love You (theme)

12:45AM WTIC
MERRY MADCAPS (Norman Cloutier)
Hartford, Conn
Sailing A Dreamboat (theme)
Boston Tea Party
All Dressed Up And No Place To Go (vocal: Eleanor Lane)
More Than You Know (vocal: Ed Holly)
If We Never Meet Again (vocal: Ed Holly)
Sailing A Dreamboat (theme)

■ WEDNESDAY 26 AUGUST 1936

RECORDING SESSION

BENNY GOODMAN QUARTET
Recording session for Victor in Los Angeles.
Lionel Hampton (vib/voc); Teddy Wilson (p); Benny Goodman (cl); Gene Krupa (d)
Dinah / Vibraphone Blues (vLH)

BENNY GOODMAN TRIO
Teddy Wilson (p); Benny Goodman (cl); Gene Krupa (d); Lionel Hampton (voc)
Exactly Like You (vLH)

RED NORVO AND HIS ORCHESTRA
Recording session for Brunswick in New York City.
Red Norvo (xyl/ldr); Bill Hyland, Stew Pletcher, Eddie Meyers (t); Leo Moran (tb); Slats Long (cl/as); Frank Simeone (as); Herbie Haymer (ts); Joe Liss (p); Dave Barbour (g); Pete Peterson (b); Maurice Purtill (d); Mildred Bailey (voc)
It All Begins And Ends With You (vMB) / *A Porter's Love Song To A Chambermaid* (vMB) / *I Know That You Know* / *Picture Me Without You* (vMB)

RADIO LOGS

12:30PM WABC
MERRY MAKERS
CBS studios, NYC
Stompin' At The Savoy
Rendezvous With A Dream
Just Driftin' Along
Ad Lib
Dream Awhile
Sizzlin' Sam
Nothing's Blue But The Sky
So Nice Of You
Finale In E-flat

3.45PM WABC
DICTATORS
CBS Studios, NYC
Bye Bye Baby
Driftin' Along
I Can't Escape From You
Without A Shadow of A Doubt
I'll Take The South

4:30PM WABC
INSTRUMENTALISTS
CBS Studios, NYC
Inka Dinka Doo (Art Manners playing clarinet)
The Man I Love (Thelma Filla playing a nice sweet violin)
I'm Tootin' My Horn (Jerry Colonna playing trombone and singing)
Rose In The Dark (Written by Raymond Scott: Maffay on guitar; Scott on piano)
Crazy Rhythm (Babe Russin playing tenor sax)

7.00PM WABC
LEE WILEY
CBS Studios, NYC
I'm Coming, Virginia (theme)
Me And The Moon (vocal: Lee Wiley)
Make Believe (vocal: Lee Wiley)
The Glory Of Love (band)
Until The Real Thing Comes Along (vocal: Lee Wiley)

10:00PM WHN
STUFF SMITH
Onyx Club, 72 W52nd Street, NYC
Bye Bye Baby
You're Not The Kind
All My Life (Frank Froeba piano solo)
Goody Goody

11.15PM WHN
LUCKY MILLINDER
Palisades Amusement Park, NJ
Dallas Bender
Empty Saddles (vocal: Chuck Richards)
Swing Me Crazy (Written by Lucky Millinder)
Clarinet Marmalade
Star Dust (theme)

11.30PM WABC
JAY FREEMAN
Paradise Restaurant, NYC
San Francisco
Sweet Sue
Empty Saddles
Sweet Mystery Of Love
It's The Gypsy In Me
It's A Sin To Tell A Lie
I Can't Escape From You (vocal: Jimmy Richards)
You Dropped Me Like A Red Hot Penny
You're Not The Kind
Nobody's Sweetheart

■ THURSDAY 27 AUGUST 1936

RADIO LOGS

1:45PM WABC
DORIS KERR
CBS Studios, NYC
Swing It
Did I Remember?
If We Never Meet Again
Bye Bye Baby
The Very Thought Of You

6:00PM WABC
LORETTA LEE
CBS Studios, NYC
Deep South (theme: vocal by Loretta Lee)
Shine (vocal: Loretta Lee)
Rendezvous With A Dream (vocal: Loretta Lee)
It Ain't Right (Mark Warnow Orchestra)
There Is No Greater Love (vocal: Loretta Lee)
Me And The Moon (Mark Warnow Orchestra)
Deep South (theme)

11.30PM WTIC
FLETCHER HENDERSON
Grand Terrace, Chicago
Let's Get Together
Sing, Baby, Sing
Driftin' Along
Bye Bye Baby
You Can't Pull The Wool Over My Eyes

12:00 MIDNIGHT WABC
CHARLIE BARNET
Glen Island Casino, New Rochelle, N.Y.
I've Lost Another Sweetheart (theme)
Charlie Barnet's History Of Jazz (vocal: Charlie Barnet) (Great: 7 mins long)
So Nice Of You (vocal: Charlie Barnet) (Barnet has a swell, natural voice)
Three Little Words (Nuttsy sax team and great sax solo work by Barnet)
Make Believe Ballroom (vocal: Modernaires) (Written by Andy Razaf-Winiger)
Until The Real Thing Comes Along (vocal: Charlie Barnet) (This is my favourite song now)
Stompin' At The Savoy (vocal: Modernaires) (Stale tune, but great words)
These Foolish Things (vocal: Charlie Barnet) (Swell song with a swell vocal)
Yeah, Man! (Same as Fletcher Henderson's *Hotter Than 'Ell*: colossal tenor by Barnet)

■ FRIDAY 28 AUGUST 1936

RADIO LOGS

12:30PM WABC
CAPTIVATORS
CBS studio, NYC
The Captivators, Instrumentalists, Merry Makers, Rhythmaires, Dictators, etc. are all CBS bands. They all have about the same personnels.
Christopher Columbus (Bunny Berigan; Babe Russin)
Hidden Valley
I'm Tootin' My Horn (Babe Russin; Jerry Colonna's trombone)
Dixieland Shuffle
Even Though It's The Colour Of Your Eyes
A Fine Romance
You Dropped Me Like A Red Hot Penny
When I'm With You
I Can't Escape From You
Bye Bye Baby

1:30PM WABC
RHYTHMAIRES
CBS studio, NYC
I've Waited A Lifetime (theme: vocal by Jimmy Ferrall)
Boston Tea Party
Did I Remember? (vocal: Jimmy Ferrall)
Get Happy
If We Never Meet Again (vocal: Jimmy Ferrall)
Vampin' A Co-ed
Jangled Nerves
Love Is Like A Melody (vocal: Jimmy Ferrall)
Swingtime In The Rockies
I Take To You
I'm An Old Cowhand

5:00PM SFO
BUGHOUSE RHYTHM (Dr John Meaken)
San Francisco
Announced by G. Archibald Presby
Ride, Red, Ride (Paul Hare, trumpet)
Blues In E-Flat (vocal: Gladys Swartout) (Paul Hare, trumpet)
The Village Cut-up (Written by Dr Meaken, piano)
Madhouse

5:30PM WABC
BUDDY CLARK
CBS Studios, NYC
It's You In Love (theme)
Empty Saddles (vocal: Buddy Clark)
But Definitely (vocal: Buddy Clark)
Mean To Me (vocal: Buddy Clark)
Love, What Are You Doing To Me? (Mark Warnow Band)
It's You In Love (theme)

5:45PM SFO
HAZEL SCOTT
My Heart Is Under The Spell of The Blues (theme)
I Never Knew
If I Could Be With You One Hour Tonight
Body And Soul
Sugar
A Good Man Is Hard To Find

9.35PM WHN
LUCKY MILLINDER
Palisades Amusement Park, NJ
Some Of These Days
Red Rhythm
Star Dust (theme)

9:45PM WHN
STUFF SMITH
Onyx Club, 72 W52nd Street, NYC
I've Got A Heavy Date
There's A Small Hotel
It Ain't Right
I Found A New Baby (Frank Froeba piano solo)
I'se A-Muggin' (theme)

10:15PM WLW
JOE HAYMES
Moonlight Gardens, Cincinnati
Bye Bye Baby (vocal: Cliff Weston)
You're Not The Kind (vocal: Honey Burns)
Sitting On The Moon (vocal: Cliff Weston)
All My Life (vocal: Honey Burns)

11.15PM WHN
LUCKY MILLINDER
Palisades Amusement Park, NJ
Star Dust (theme)
Merry-Go-Round (Written by Duke Ellington: nice trumpets; nuttsy sax)
Swing Me Crazy (Fair)
Until The Real Thing Comes Along (vocal: Chuck Richards) (Nuttsy saxes: great vocal)
Ride, Red, Ride (Written by Lucky Millinder: nuttsy trombones; colossal trumpet by Red Allen)

11.30PM WABC
DICK STABILE
Hotel Lincoln, NYC
Me And The Moon (vocal: Bert Shaw)
No Regrets (vocal: Bert Shaw)
Organ Grinder's Swing
It's A Sin To Tell A Lie (vocal: Bert Shaw)
Knock, Knock
These Foolish Things
Without A Shadow Of A Doubt (vocal: Frank Fleming)
The Glory Of Love (vocal: Bert Shaw)
When I'm With You

The long-awaited Dick Stabile Orchestra is finally a reality. After a Boston engagement and a short road tour, Dick's band moved into the Hotel Lincoln, New York City. This spot has had a 50% business increase, and it looks like Dick and the boys will stay there quite a while.

The Stabile unit airs frequently on national networks and really plays a nifty broadcast. Much of the arranging is done by Dick himself and George Kaetz. Reed work is featured, and there are plenty of those fine Stabile sax and clarinet solos.

1:00AM WABC
GEORGE HALL
Taft Hotel, NYC
Christopher Columbus
I Can't Escape From You
My Kingdom For A Kiss (vocal: Johnny McKeever)
Too Good To Be True
You Can't Pull The Wool Over My Eyes (vocal: Dolly Dawn)
When A Lady Meets A Gentleman Down South
Afterglow
Back Home Again In Indiana
If You Ask Me How Much I Love You (theme)

■ SATURDAY 29 AUGUST 1936
RADIO LOGS

5:50PM WABC
CHARLIE BARNET
Glen Island Casino, New Rochelle, N.J.
Down South Camp Meetin' (Arranged by Fletcher Henderson: nuttsy; 5 clarinets)
Me And the Moon (vocal: Modernaires) (Swell vocal, song, saxes)
Three Little Words (Colossal! Superb saxes with marvelous trumpets)
Four Or Five Times (Easily best sax team I have ever heard)
Midnight And You / Sweet Mystery Of Love / I Can't Escape From You (Medley of sweet songs, pretty good: Charlie Barnet and Benny Goodman are my bands now)
Darktown Strutters' Ball (Great trumpet team and colossal sax by Barnet)
She Shall Have Music / Moonglow (vocal: Modernaires)
A Star Fell Out Of Heaven (vocal: Hal Dickinson) (Good sweet piece)
'Way Down Yonder In New Orleans (Barnet's tenor sax is superb)

8:00PM WABC
SATURDAY NIGHT SWING SESSION No11
CBS Studio, NYC
Cross Patch (Bunny Berigan playing nice trumpet with colossal saxes)
St. Louis Blues (Casper Reardon playing a great swing harp)
Oh, Lady Be Good (Written by George Gershwin: marvelous clarinet & bass)
Keep On The Right Side Of The Road (Lee Wiley singing)
Jazz Me Blues (Great clarinet, drums, bass and saxes)
I Can Pull A Rabbit Out of My Hat
I Can't Get Started (Bunny Berigan trumpet solo)
King Of Swing

9.15PM WHN
CAB CALLOWAY
Palisades Amusement Park, NJ
Minnie The Moocher (theme) (Written by Cab Calloway)
Oh, Lady Be Good (vocal: Cab Calloway)
Until The Real Thing Comes Along (vocal: Bennie Payne)
Hi-De-Ho (vocal: Cab Calloway)
Sweet Sue (guitar by Morris White)

9.45PM WHN
STUFF SMITH
Onyx Club, 72 W52nd Street, NYC
Christopher Columbus
If We Never Meet Again (vocal: Stuff Smith)
Three Little Words (Frankie Froeba's piano solo)
After You've Gone

10.45PM WHN
CAB CALLOWAY
Palisades Amusement Park, NJ
My Blue Heaven (vocal: Cab Calloway)
Love Is The Reason (vocal: Cab Calloway)
When You're Smiling (vocal: Cab Calloway)
Some Of These Days (vocal: Cab Calloway)

11.00PM WABC
ART SHAW
Hotel Lexington, NYC
Christopher Columbus
It Ain't Necessarily So (vocal: Peg LaCentra)
I Used To Be Above Love (vocal: Gene Stone)
Summer Holiday (vocal: Peg LaCentra)
Is It True What They Say About Dixie?
I Can't Escape From You (vocal: Peg LaCentra)
Star Dust (Written by Hoagy Carmichael: best arrangement)
Me And The Moon (vocal: Peg LaCentra)
Sugar Foot Stomp

An over-night success at the Lexington Hotel in New York was scored by Art Shaw, who plays an agile swing clarinet in front of a unique ork. Shaw's combination consists of three brass, one sax, two violins, viola, cello, guitar, piano, drums, and string-bass.

11:05PM WJZ
RILEY & FARLEY
Hickory House, 52nd Street, NYC
Afterglow
Oh, Dear! What Can The Matter Be? (vocal: Ed Farley & Mike Riley)
Cottage By the Moon
Jingle Bells (vocal: Mike Riley)
I'm An Old Cowhand
Wabash Blues
Rip Van Winkle
Rendezvous With A Dream
I'm Gonna Clap My Hands (vocal: Ed Farley)
Farewell Blues
Afterglow
I'm Gonna Clap My Hands (Written by Farley & Riley)
The Music Goes Round And Around (Written by Farley & Riley)

11.15PM WHN
CAB CALLOWAY
Palisades Amusement Park, NJ
Minnie The Moocher (theme) (Written by Cab Calloway)
The Beggar (vocal: Cab Calloway)
Sylvia (Pretty good arrangement of a terrible song)
Jes' Natch'ully Lazy (vocal: Cab Calloway) (Cab doing some of his cannibalistic singing)

11.30PM WABC
HAL KEMP
Astor Hotel, NYC
When Did You Leave Heaven? (vocal: Skinnay Ennis) (Ennis is the band's drummer)
Organ Grinder's Swing
You're Not The Kind (vocal: Bob Allen)
There's A Small Hotel (vocal: Maxine Gray)
Bye Bye Baby
Monopoly (vocal: Bob Allen)
You Don't Love Right (vocal: Skinnay Ennis)
A Fine Romance (vocal: Bob Allen & Maxine Gray)
Honey, Please Don't Turn Sour On Me
I'll Never Let You Go

12:00 MIDNIGHT WOR
BOB CROSBY
Steel Pier, Atlantic City, N.J.
Poppa, Come Back Home
The Scene Changes (vocal: Bob Walker)
I Can't Escape From You (vocal: Bob Crosby)
Dixieland Shuffle (Very Dixielandish piece recorded for Decca)
I'll Never Let You Go (vocal: Nappy Lamare)
Until Today (vocal: Kay Weber) (Both Crosby and Weber used to be with Dorsey Brothers)
Peter Piper (vocal: Bob Crosby)
Take My Heart (vocal: Bob Walker)
Muskrat Ramble

Right: Bob Crosby and his Orchestra in Atlantic City.

12:30AM WTIC
MERRY MADCAPS (Norman Cloutier)
Hartford, Conn
Sailing A Dreamboat (theme)
Let's Face The Music And Dance
Gotta Dance My Way To Heaven (vocal: Eleanor Lane)
Solitude
Nothing's Blue But The Sky (vocal: Ed Holly & Eleanor Lane)
Memories Of You
You've Gotta Eat Your Spinach, Baby
My Blue Heaven
Farewell Blues
Cross Patch
Sailing A Dreamboat (theme)

■ SUNDAY 30 AUGUST 1936

RADIO LOGS

6:45PM WABC
CLYDE LUCAS
Hotel New Yorker, NYC
You Can't Pull The Wool Over My Eyes
Shoe Shine Boy / You're Not The Kind / Sweet Mystery Of Love
Give Me That Old Fashioned Swing (Trio)
My Heart's At Thy Sweet Voice
Why Do I Lie To Myself About You?
Did I Remember? (vocal: Lyn Lucas)

8.00PM WABC
AMERICA DANCES
CBS Studios, NYC
On The Air (theme) (Nuttsy theme)
Great Day (vocal: Blue Flames)
I'm Grateful To You (vocal: Buddy Clark)
A Waltz Dream
Dodging A Divorcee (vocal: Gogo De Lys) (Special words)
A Star Fell Out Of Heaven
Robins And Roses (vocal: Blue Flames)
Threequanta???? (vocal: Chiquita)
I Can't Escape From You (vocal: Buddy Clark)
No Regrets
Until The Real Thing Comes Along (vocal: Gogo De Lys)
Limehouse Blues

9.00PM WHN
CAB CALLOWAY
Palisades Amusement Park, NJ
Minnie The Moocher (theme)
Honeysuckle Rose (vocal: Cab Calloway)
Zaz-Zuh-Zaz (vocal: Cab Calloway)
Ol' Man Mose (vocal: Cab Calloway)
The Big Roar
Minnie The Moocher (theme)

11.15PM WHN
CAB CALLOWAY
Palisades Amusement Park, NJ
Blue Skies (vocal: Cab Calloway)
Between The Devil And The Deep Blue Sea (vocal: Cab Calloway)
I've Got The World On A String (vocal: Cab Calloway)
I've Gotta Right To Sing The Blues
Rain

11.30PM WABC
ART SHAW
Hotel Lexington, NYC
Nightmare (theme) (Colossal clarinets)
Thou Swell
The Glory Of Love
I'm Just Beginning To Care (vocal: Peg LaCentra)
Take My Heart (vocal: Peg LaCentra)
One Step Ahead of My Shadow (vocal: Tony Pastor)
St. Louis Blues
It Ain't Right (vocal: Peg LaCentra)
South Sea Island Magic (vocal: Peg LaCentra)
The King Of Swing (vocal: Peg LaCentra)

11.35PM WEAF
FLETCHER HENDERSON
Grand Terrace, Chicago
Christopher Columbus (theme)
I Just Made Up With That Old Girl Of Mine
Did I Remember? (vocal: Arthur Lee 'Georgia Boy' Simpkins)
Sing Me A Swing Song (Written by Adams-Carmichael)
Bugle Blues (Colossal piece: nice trumpet team; Eldridge great)
Swingtime In The Rockies (Same arrangement as Goodman, Barnet)
Sing, Baby, Sing (Chu Berry great on tenor sax)
Just Driftin' Along (Terrible song)
Sing, Sing, Sing (vocal: 'Georgia Boy' Simpkins)
Christopher Columbus (theme) (Music by Chu Berry, words by Andy Razaf)

12.00 MIDNIGHT WABC
CHARLIE BARNET
Glen Island Casino, New Rochelle, N.Y.
I've Lost Another Sweetheart (theme)
Always (Charlie Barnet is one of the finest tenor sax men today!)
You're Not The Kind (vocal: Charlie Barnet) (Nuttsy sweet song)
Bye Bye Baby (vocal: Barnet Modernaires)
If We Never Meet Again (vocal: Hal Dickinson)
King Porter Stomp (Practically same arrangement as Goodman)
History Of Jazz (Several songs: Africa; Dixieland band; arrangements; no swing; swing; *Dear Old Southland*)
Stop, Look, And Listen (vocal: Barnet Modernaires) (Nuttsy)
I'm An Old Cowhand (vocal: Hal Dickinson)
Tain't Good! (Fair: Barnet's tenor sax stealing the show)

■ MONDAY 31 AUGUST 1936

RECORDING SESSION

HENRY 'RED' ALLEN
Recording session for Vocalion in New York City.
Henry 'Red' Allen (t/voc); Albert Nicholas (cl); Pete Clark (as); Ted McRae (ts); Clyde Hart (p); Lawrence Lucie (g); John Kirby (b); Cozy Cole (d)
Darling, Not Without You (vHA) / *I'll Sing You A Thousand Love Songs* (vHA) / *Picture Me Without You* (vHA) / *Out Where The Blues Begin* (vHA)

JIMMIE LUNCEFORD AND HIS ORCHESTRA
Recording session for Decca in New York City.
Jimmie Lunceford (ldr); Eddie Tompkins, Paul Webster, Sy Oliver (t); Elmer Crumbley, Russell Bowles, Eddie Durham (tb); Willie Smith, Earl Carruthers (cl/as/bar); Laforet Dent (as); Dan Grissom (cl/as); Joe Thomas (cl/ts); Edwin Wilcox (p); Al Norris (g); Moses Allen (b); Jimmy Crawford (d)
Organ Grinder's Swing

RADIO LOGS

12:30PM WABC
MERRY MAKERS
CBS Studios, NYC
The Merry Makers are a CBS studio band with such well-known players as Bunny Berigan, Art Manners, Babe Russin, Bud Sheppard, Johnny Augustine, Dick Porter (piano), Lou Shoobe (bass), Vincent Maffay (guitar), and many others.
Bye Bye Baby
Did I Remember?
Diga Diga Doo
Begin The Beguine
Big Chief De Sota
Until The Real Thing Comes Along
Is It True What They Say About Dixie?
When I'm With You
Bye Bye Blues
Tain't No Use

6:00PM WABC
DICTATORS (CBS Band)
CBS Studios, NYC
Without A Shadow Of A Doubt
When Did You Leave Heaven?
In A Little English Inn
Sing, Baby, Sing

7.00PM WABC
JIMMY FERRALL/RHYTHMAIRES
CBS studio, NYC
Take My Heart
Me And The Moon
Doin' The Prom
More Than You
I Can't Escape From You

7.15PM WOR
IRVING AARONSON
Ben Marden's Riviera, N.J.
San Francisco
I Can't Escape From You
Mary Had A Little Lamb
The Glory Of Love (WHAT A TERRIBLE BROADCAST!)

8.30PM WOR
OZZIE NELSON
Palmer House, Chicago
Without A Shadow Of A Doubt
Suppose I Had Never Met You
It's A Sin To Tell A Lie
Swamp Fire
There's A Small Hotel
The Glory Of Love
Is It True What They Say About Dixie?
She Shall Have Music
Doin' The Prom

SEPTEMBER 1936

Hotel Lexington: **Art Shaw**
Hotel Lincoln: **Dick Stabile**
Hotel Taft: **George Hall**
Hotel New Yorker: **Clyde Lucas**

Apollo Theater: **Claude Hopkins** (–3); **Louis Armstrong** (4–10); **Duke Ellington** (11–17); **Ethel Waters** (18–24); **Jimmie Lunceford** (25–)
Paramount Theater: **Shep Fields** (–8); **Vincent Lopez** (9–22); **Will Osborne** (23–)
Loew's State Theater: **Noble Sissle** (11–17)

Cotton Club Downtown: **Cab Calloway/Bill Robinson** (opens 24)
Hickory House: **Riley & Farley**
Onyx Club: **Stuff Smith; Billie Holiday** (added to bill on 2nd)

■ TUESDAY 1 SEPTEMBER 1936

RECORDING SESSION

JIMMIE LUNCEFORD AND HIS ORCHESTRA
Recording session for Decca in New York City.
Jimmie Lunceford (ldr); Eddie Tompkins, Paul Webster (t); Sy Oliver (t/voc); Elmer Crumbley, Russell Bowles, Eddie Durham (tb); Willie Smith (cl/as/bar/voc); Earl Carruthers (cl/as/bar); Laforet Dent (as); Dan Grissom (cl/as/voc); Joe Thomas (cl/ts); Edwin Wilcox (p); Al Norris (g); Moses Allen (b); Jimmy Crawford (d)
On The Beach At Bali-Bali (vSO) / *Me And The Moon* (vTrio) /
Living From Day To Day (vDG) / *'Tain't Good* (vTrio)

RADIO LOGS

11.45AM WABC
RHYTHMAIRES
CBS studio, NYC
Doin' The Prom
Out Where The Blues Begin
So Nice Of You
Until The Real Thing Comes Along
Knock, Knock

2.30PM WABC
DICTATORS
CBS studio, NYC
I'm Tootin' My Horn
If We Never Meet Again
Fancy Meeting You
My Cabin In The Ozarks
Bojangles Of Harlem

3.45PM WABC
GOGO DE LYS
CBS studio, NYC
To Be Alone With You (theme)
No Regrets (vocal: Gogo De Lys)
When A Lady Meets A Gentleman Down South (Mark Warnow Orchestra)
How Deep Is The Ocean? (vocal: Gogo De Lys)
Just Driftin' Along (Mark Warnow Orchestra)
Love Will Tell (vocal: Gogo De Lys)
To Be Alone With You (theme)

5.00PM WABC
JIMMY FERRALL
CBS studio, NYC
I've Waited A Lifetime (theme)
You're Not The Kind (vocal: Jimmy Ferrall)
Empty Saddles (vocal: Jimmy Ferrall)
Bye Bye Baby (Mark Warnow Orchestra)
Midnight Blue (vocal: Jimmy Ferrall)
I've Waited A Lifetime (theme)

6.00PM WABC
PATTI CHAPIN
CBS studio, NYC
Dream Awhile (vocal: Patti Chapin)
Roses Of Picardy (vocal: Patti Chapin)
When A Lady Meets A Gentleman Down South (Mark Warnow Orchestra)
Me And The Moon (vocal: Patti Chapin)

9:30PM WABC
BENNY GOODMAN
"Camel Caravan", NYC
Three Little Words

On The Alamo
Always

12:30AM WEAF
JOE VENUTI
Casa Manana, Ft Worth, Texas
Stars Weep / Sweet Mystery Of Love
Runnin' Ragged
These Foolish Things (vocal: Mildred Fenton)
Christopher Columbus
Harlem Heat
When I'm With You / Summer Breeze
Dinah (vocal: Mildred Fenton)
Parade Of The Milk Bottle Tops (Written by Joe McCarthy & Jimmy Dorsey)

Joe Venuti

1:00AM WABC
GEORGE HALL
Taft Hotel, NYC
I'm An Old Cowhand (vocal: Dolly Dawn & Johnny McKeever)
Speak To Me Of Love (vocal: Dolly Dawn)
Sing, Baby, Sing
Empty Saddles In The Old Corral (vocal: Johnny McKeever)
Twenty-Four Hours A Day (vocal: Dolly Dawn's Patrol)
Tea For Two
Knock, Knock
The Way You Look Tonight (vocal: Johnny McKeever)
Stompin' At The Savoy (Written by Benny Goodman, Chick Webb, Edgar Sampson)

1.00AM WENR
FLETCHER HENDERSON
Grand Terrace, Chicago
Christopher Columbus (theme)
Uptown Shuffle
It's You I'm Talking About
Riffin'
But Definitely
Down South Camp Meetin'
Where There's You, There's Me
I'll Stand By (vocal: 'Georgia Boy' Simpkins)
My Blue Heaven
Nobody's Sweetheart
Christopher Columbus (theme)

■ WEDNESDAY 2 SEPTEMBER 1936

RADIO LOGS

12:30PM WABC
MERRY MAKERS
CBS studio, NYC
Tain't No Use
Did I Remember? (Bunny Berigan's trumpet; Buddy Sheppard's violin)
Bye Bye Baby
Swing, Swing Mother-In-Law (Babe Russin's tenor sax; Johnny Williams' drums; Bunny Berigan's trumpet)
A Star Fell Out Of Heaven
Meet Me On The Down Beat
Close To Me
I Take To You

2:45PM WABC
DICTATORS
CBS studio, NYC
Pick Yourself Up

When Did You Leave Heaven (vocal: Virginia Verrell)
Bojangles Of Harlem

5:00PM WABC
MARK WARNOW-MARGARET McCRAE
CBS studio, NYC
Do You Or Don't You Love Me (vocal: Margaret McCrae)
Without A Shadow Of A Doubt (vocal: Margaret McCrae)
But Definitely (Mark Warnow Orchestra)
You're Not The Kind (vocal: Margaret McCrae)
Cross Patch (Mark Warnow Orchestra)
I'll Never Let You Go (vocal: Margaret McCrae)

5:30PM WABC
BUDDY CLARK
CBS studio, NYC
South Sea Island Magic
Between The Devil And The Deep Blue Sea
When Did You Leave Heaven
Tain't No Use
I Want The Whole World To Know I Love You
Doin' the Prom
Two In Love (theme)

11:00PM WABC
CLYDE LUCAS
Hotel New Yorker, NYC
You Dropped Me Like A Red Hot Penny
If We Never Meet Again (vocal: Lyn Lucas)
Would You?
It's A Sin To Tell A Lie
Give Me That Old Fashioned Swing (vocal: Trio)
Through The Courtesy Of Love
Organ Grinder's Swing (best arrangement)
Trees

11:00PM WMCA
CLAUDE HOPKINS
Apollo Theater, NYC
Ja-Da
Until The Real Thing Comes Along (vocal: Orlando Robeson)

Claude Hopkins

■ THURSDAY 3 SEPTEMBER 1936

RADIO LOGS

12.00 MIDNIGHT WABC
CHARLIE BARNET
Glen Island Casino
I've Lost Another Sweetheart (theme)
Three Little Words
Stop, Look, And Listen (vocal: Barnet Modernaires)
Jangled Nerves
It's The Talk Of The Town
Four Or Five Times
Stompin' At The Savoy
Yeah, Man! (This was an all-swing program)

■ FRIDAY 4 SEPTEMBER 1936

RADIO LOGS

12:30PM WABC
MERRY MAKERS
CBS Studios, NYC
The Merry Makers are a CBS studio band with such well-known players as Bunny Berigan, Art Manners, Babe Russin, Bud Sheppard, Johnny Augustine, Dick Porter (piano), Lou Shoobe (bass), Vincent Maffay (guitar), and many others.
Organ Grinder's Swing
When Did You Leave Heaven?
Tain't No Use
Until Today
Too Bad

12:45PM WABC
CAPTIVATORS
CBS Studios, NYC
Bye Bye Baby
Rendezvous With A Dream
When A Lady Meets A Gentleman Down South
Empty Saddles
There Goes The One I Love (Babe Russin on sax)

1:30PM WABC
RHYTHMAIRES
CBS Studios, NYC
I've Waited A Lifetime (theme)
Sing, Sing, Sing
Until Today (vocal: Jimmy Ferrall)
Knock, Knock
I'm An Old Cowhand (vocal: Jimmy Ferrall)
My Kingdom For A Kiss
I Can't Escape from You (vocal: Jimmy Ferrall)
When Did You Leave Heaven?
Until The Real Thing Comes Along (vocal: Jimmy Ferrall)
Swamp Fire
Sing, Baby, Sing

3:00PM WABC
SWEET AND HOT
CBS Studio, NYC
Honeysuckle Rose (theme)
Boston Tea Party (Lud Gluskin & his orchestra)
Out Of The World (Ruth Carheart singing)
Tain't No Use (Lud Gluskin & his orchestra)
Mad Dogs And Englishmen (Four Eaton Boys singing)
You're Not The Kind (Ruth Carheart singing)
Nagasaki (Four Eaton Boys singing)
My Romance
Bye Bye Baby (Art Gentry [one of the Eaton Boys] singing)
Big Chief De Sota
Honeysuckle Rose (theme)

5.00PM WEAF
BUGHOUSE RHYTHM
San Francisco
Big Chief De Sota (Written by Fernando Arbello & Andy Razaf)
Beebe (Written by Jimmy Dorsey: played by Dr. Meakin's Ork with J. Harrington on sax)
That's A-Plenty
DISCUSSION on 3 types of swing music: Dixieland Stomp; Gut Bucket Swing; Bounce Tempo
Rubber Heels (Written by pianist/leader Dr. John Meakin)

9:00PM WTIC
MERRY MADCAPS (Norman Cloutier)
Hartford, Conn
Sailing A Dreamboat (theme)
Let's Face The Music And Dance

A Rendezvous With A Dream (vocal: Ed Holly)
Solitude
Nothing's Blue But The Sky (vocal: Ed Holly)
Memories Of You
Sing Me A Swing Song (vocal: Ed Holly)
My Blue Heaven
It's Like Reaching For The Moon (vocal: Ed Holly)
Farewell Blues
Cross Patch

9.45PM WHN
STUFF SMITH
Onyx Club, 72 W52nd Street, NYC
You'se A Viper (vocal: Stuff Smith)
Please Leave Me Alone
Church Mouse On A Spree (Frankie Froeba's piano solo)
Knock, Knock (vocal: Stuff Smith with band)

■ SATURDAY 5 SEPTEMBER 1936

RADIO LOGS

5.30PM WABC
CHARLIE BARNET
Glen Island Casino, New Rochelle, N.Y.
I've Lost Another Sweetheart (theme)
Symphony In Riffs (Nuttsy)
Sad Night In Harlem (vocal: Barnet Modernaires) / *Without A Shadow of A Doubt* / *Through The Courtesy Of Love*
Riffin'
You're Not The Kind (vocal: Charlie Barnet)
It All Begins And Ends With You
Sing, Baby, Sing
Me And The Moon (vocal: Barnet Modernaires)
On A Cocoanut Island
Toodle-Oo (Written by Charlie Barnet)

8:00PM WABC
SATURDAY NIGHT SWING SESSION No12
CBS Studio, NYC
I Can't Get Started (theme) (Bunny Berigan with house band)
Shoe Shine Boy (Bunny Berigan with house band led by Mark Warnow)
Harmonica Ride (Cappy Berry and Harmonica Band)
You're Not The Kind (Bunny Berigan with house band)
Honeysuckle Rose (Frank Froeba playing a piano solo)
Church Mouse On A Spree (Frank Froeba playing a piano solo)
Swing, Swing Mother-In-Law (Bunny Berigan with house band)
Star Dust (Bunny Berigan trumpet solo)
Voodoo (Cappy Berry and Harmonica Band)
I Found A New Baby (Bunny Berigan with house band)

■ SUNDAY 6 SEPTEMBER 1936

RADIO LOGS

4:30PM WOR
MAL HALLETT
Steel Pier, Atlantic City, N.J.
Boston Tea Party (theme) (Written by trumpeter Frank Ryerson)
She Shall Have Music (vocal: Buddy Welcome)
Sweet Mystery Of Love (vocal: Clark Yocum)
I'm An Old Cowhand (vocal: Buddy Welcome)
In A Little Gypsy Tea Room (vocal: Jerry Perkins)
We're In The Money (vocal: Clark Yocum)
It's A Sin To Tell A Lie (vocal: Jerry Perkins)
Dixieland Band (vocal: Buddy Welcome)
Let's Sing Again (vocal: Clark Yocum)
Big John Special
Why Do I Lie To Myself About You? (vocal: Buddy Welcome)

MONDAY 7 SEPTEMBER 1936

RADIO LOGS

1.30PM WABC
RHYTHMAIRES
CBS studio, NYC
When A Lady Meets A Gentleman Down South
A Star Fell Out Of Heaven
Oh, You
A Fine Romance
Sweet Georgia Brown
Take My Heart

3:00PM WJZ
MANHATTERS
NBC Studio Band, NYC
Solitude (theme)
Swingtime In The Rockies
My Kingdom For A Kiss
52nd Street Fever (vocal: Louis Julian)
You're Not The Kind (vocal: Louis Julian)
Night In Manhattan
Me And The Moon (vocal: Louis Julian)
Stompin' At The Savoy
If We Never Meet Again (vocal: Louis Julian)
Would You Have A Cup Of Java With Me?
Solitude (theme)

5:30PM WABC
VIRGINIA VERRILL
CBS Studios, NYC
I Take To You (vocal: Virginia Verrill)
When Did You Leave Heaven? (vocal: Virginia Verrill)
My Baby Just Cares For Me (Mark Warnow Orchestra)
Tain't Good (vocal: Virginia Verrill)

10:45PM WHN
DUKE ELLINGTON
Palisades Park, NJ
Swing Low (A very fast number with trumpet like Eldridge)
Echoes Of Harlem (Written by Duke Ellington; superb cornet)
Oh Babe, Maybe Someday (vocal: Ivie Anderson)
In A Sentimental Mood (Written by Duke Ellington)

Duke Ellington

12:00 MIDNIGHT WPG
MAL HALLETT
Steel Pier, Atlantic City
Boston Tea Party (theme) (Written by trumpeter Frank Ryerson)
Is It True What They Say About Dixie? (vocal: Buddy Welcome)
Sunshine At Midnight (vocal: Clark Yocum)
Swing Fever (Swell new song with Buddy Welcome on sax)
When It's Twilight On The Trail (vocal: Clark Yocum)
Ol' Man River
The State Of My Heart (Clark Yocum on guitar)
The Glory Of Love (vocal: Buddy Welcome)
Big Chief De Sota

TUESDAY 8 SEPTEMBER 1936

RECORDING SESSION

ERSKINE HAWKINS AND HIS ORCHESTRA
Recording session for Vocalion in New York City.
Erskine Hawkins (t/ldr); Wilbur Bascomb, Marcellus Green, Sam Lowe (t); Edward Sims, Robert Range (tb); William Johnson (as); Jimmy Mitchelle (as/voc); Paul Bascomb (ts); Haywood Henry (cl/bar); Avery Parrish (p); William McLemore (g); Leemie Stanfield (b); James Morrison (d); Billy Daniels, Merle Turner (voc)
Swinging In Harlem / *Coquette* (vBD) / *Big John Special* / *A Swingy Little Rhythm*

RADIO LOGS

11.45AM WABC
RHYTHMAIRES
CBS studio, NYC
Doin' The Prom
Until Today
A Fine Romance
Did I Remember?
You Dropped Me Like A Red Hot Penny

2:30PM WABC
DICTATORS
CBS studio, NYC
Would You Have A Cup Of Java With Me?
Midnight Blue
Me And The Moon
My Kingdom For A Kiss
Boy Meets Girl

9:30PM WABC
BENNY GOODMAN
"Camel Caravan", Steel Pier, Atlantic City, N.J.
Inka Dinka Doo (Superb trumpets and clarinet by Goodman)
You Turned The Tables On Me (vocal: Helen Ward)
Jingle Bells (5 clarinets; nuttsy trumpet & sax solos)
If I Could Be With You One Hour Tonight (Reuss on guitar great; better than record)
Chinatown, My Chinatown (BG Trio)

WEDNESDAY 9 SEPTEMBER 1936

RECORDING SESSION

FATS WALLER & HIS RHYTHM
Recording session for Victor in New York City.
Herman Autrey (t); Gene Sedric (cl/ts); Fats Waller (p/voc); Albert Casey (g); Charles Turner (b); Slick Jones (d)
S'posin' (vFW) / *Copper Colored Gal* (vFW) / *I'm At The Mercy of Love* / *Floatin' Down To Cotton Town* (vFW) / *La-De-De, La-De-Da* (vFW)

SEPTEMBER 1936

RADIO LOGS

12:30PM WABC
MERRY MAKERS
CBS Studios, NYC
The Merry Makers are a CBS studio band with many well-known players.
Runnin' A Temperature
You Came To My Rescue
Swing, Swing Mother-In-Law
Tain't No Use
South Sea Island Magic
Swingtime In The Rockies
Just Driftin' Along
Boston Tea Party
Midnight Blue
Jangled Nerves

9:00PM WABC
CHESTERFIELD DANCE TIME
NYC
Sponsored by Chesterfield Cigarettes. The announcer is David Ross.
Did I Remember? (vocal: Ray Heatherton)
Carina Mucho (Rhumba played by André Kostelanetz Orchestra)
A New Sun In The Sky (vocal: Kay Thompson & her Rhythm Singers)
Stars In My Eyes (vocal: Ray Heatherton)
Alone Together (vocal: Kay Thompson)
Put On Your Old Grey Bonnet (vocal: Kay Thompson & her Singers)

10:30pm WHN
STUFF SMITH
Onyx Club, 72 W52nd Street, NYC
It All Begins And Ends With You (vocal: Jonah Jones)
I Surrender Dear (Frank Froeba piano solo)
Until The Real Thing Comes Along (vocal: Billie Holiday)
Underneath The Music Box

12:00 MIDNIGHT WPG
MAL HALLETT
Steel Pier, Atlantic City, N.J.
Let's Sing Again (vocal: Buddy Welcome & Clark Yocum)
The Glory Of Love (vocal: Buddy Welcome)
I Surrender, Dear / I'm Surprised
Big John Special (Practically same Henderson arrangement as Goodman uses)
Without A Shadow Of A Doubt (vocal: Clark Yocum)
Nitwit Serenade (Buddy Welcome's sax is great; great sax team)
All My Life (vocal: Billy??)
Wobbly Walk (vocal: Buddy Welcome & band) (Nuttsy sax, clarinet, vocal)

■ THURSDAY 10 SEPTEMBER 1936

RADIO LOGS

9:00PM WABC
MARK WARNOW
CBS Studios, NYC
A Star Fell Out Of Heaven
Close To Me (vocal: Morton Downey)
Swing Feud (Written by Mark Warnow)
Sing Me A Swing Song (vocal: Lee Wiley)
Tia Juana
Off To Philadelphia In The Morning (vocal: Morton Downey)
My Blue Heaven

11:35PM WEAF
FLETCHER HENDERSON
Grand Terrace, Chicago
Without A Shadow of A Doubt
If We Never Meet Again
Magnolias In The Moonlight
Riffin'

12:00 MIDNIGHT WABC
CHARLIE BARNET
Glen Island Casino
Make Believe Ballroom (vocal: Barnet Modernaires)
If We Never Meet Again
Charlie Barnet's History Of Jazz
These Foolish Things (vocal: Charlie Barnet)
Three Little Words
It's The Talk Of The Town

■ FRIDAY 11 SEPTEMBER 1936

RADIO LOGS

12:30PM WABC
CAPTIVATORS
CBS Studios, NYC
There Goes My Attraction
It Can Happen To You
I'm An Old Cowhand
I Give My Heart To You
You Turned The Tables On Me
Why Do I Lie To Myself About You?
Tain't No Use
Until Today
Color Of Your Eyes

5:45PM WOR
HAZEL SCOTT
Grand Central Palace
Three Little Words
The Man I Love
Nagasaki
Don't Cry When He Is Gone

Sincerely Hazel Scott

9:00PM WTIC
MERRY MADCAPS (Norman Cloutier)
Hartford, Conn
Sailing A Dreamboat (theme)
In A Sentimental Mood
Three Little Words (vocal: Ed Holly)
Would You?
You Can't Pull The Wool Over My Eyes (vocal: Ed Holly)
Boston Tea Party
When Did You Leave Heaven? (vocal: Ed Holly)
Hobo On Park Avenue
So Nice Of You (vocal: Ed Holly)
The Way You Look Tonight

10:00PM WABC
ANDRÉ KOSTELANETZ
CBS Studios, NYC
Fancy Meeting You
Take My Heart (vocal: Ray Heatherton)
Blow, Gabriel, Blow (vocal: Kay Thompson & Rhythm Singers)
For You (vocal: Ray Heatherton)
You're O.K.
Time On My Hands (vocal: Kay Thompson)
Sing, Sing, Sing (vocal: Rhythm Singers)
Everybody Knows My Baby

10:45PM WABC
VIRGINIA VERRILL
CBS Studios, NYC
Do You Or Don't You Love Me? (vocal: Virginia Verrill)
Did I Remember? (vocal: Virginia Verrill)
Afterglow (Mark Warnow Orchestra)
Not Without You (vocal: Virginia Verrill)

Virginia Verrill

11:15PM WEAF
FLETCHER HENDERSON
Grand Terrace, Chicago
Christopher Columbus (theme)
Sing, Baby, Sing
Jangled Nerves
Did I Remember? (vocal: 'Georgia Boy' Simpkins)
Sing Me A Swing Song
King Porter Stomp (New arrangement)
Christopher Columbus (theme)

11:30PM WABC
BENNY GOODMAN
Ritz-Carlton Hotel, Boston
Love Me Or Leave Me (Poor for Goodman's band)
Until The Real Thing Comes Along (vocal: Helen Ward)
Here's Love In Your Eyes
Honeysuckle Rose (Marvelous: one of Goodman's best)
Midnight Blue (vocal: Helen Ward)
I Found A New Baby (Another one of Goodman's best)
Remember (Tenor sax by Rollini; trombone by McEachern)
Star Dust (Best arrangement of a swell song in swing style)
Down South Camp Meeting (Nuttsy arrangement by Henderson)

12.00 MIDNIGHT WABC
ART SHAW
Hotel Lexington, NYC
Nightmare (Nuttsy opening and closing theme)
Take My Word
It Ain't Right (vocal: Peg LaCentra)
A Star Fell Out Of Heaven (vocal: Gene Stone)
Over A Bowl Of Sushi-aki (vocal: Peg LaCentra)
Until Today (vocal: Peg LaCentra)
Ain't Misbehavin'
These Foolish Things (vocal: Peg LaCentra)
After Sundown

SATURDAY 12 SEPTEMBER 1936
RADIO LOGS

8:00PM WABC
SATURDAY NIGHT SWING SESSION No13
CBS Studio, NYC
I Can't Get Started (theme) (Bunny Berigan with house band)
Stompin' At The Savoy (Bunny Berigan with house band)
Kiddin' On The Fiddle (Al Duffy, composer, on violin with house band)
Limehouse Blues (Johnny Williams going nuttsy on drums with house band)
Sugar Foot Stomp (Art Shaw on clarinet with String Quartet)
Sometimes I Feel Like A Motherless Child (Lee Wiley vocal with house band)
Serenade For A Wealthy Widow (Written by Reginald Foresythe)
Until Today (Bunny Berigan playing trumpet and singing with house band)
The Boston Tea Party (Bunny Berigan with house band)

11.00PM WABC
ART SHAW
Hotel Lexington, NYC
Sugar Foot Stomp
South Sea Island Magic (vocal: Peg LaCentra)
Fancy Meeting You (vocal: Peg LaCentra)
Star Dust
Pick Yourself Up (vocal: Tony Pastor)
I'm All Dressed Up (vocal: Peg LaCentra)
The King Of Swing (vocal: Peg LaCentra)

11:10PM WJZ
RILEY & FARLEY
Hickory House, 52nd Street, NYC
Honeysuckle Rose
I Wish You Were My Love Affair
I Never Knew

Rip Van Winkle (vocal: Ed Farley) (Written by Riley & Farley)
It's A Sin To Tell A Lie
The Man With The Jive
Until Today

12.00 MIDNIGHT WOR
MAL HALLETT
Marine Ballroom, NJ
Is It True What They Say About Dixie? (vocal: Buddy Welcome)
No Regrets (vocal: Clark Yocum)
I'm Getting Sentimental Over You (Jimmy Skyles on trombone)
The State Of My Heart (vocal: Clark Yocum)
On The Beach At Bali-Bali (vocal: Buddy Welcome)
In A Little Gypsy Tea Room (vocal: Clark Yocum)
I'm An Old Cowhand (vocal: Buddy Welcome)
I Give My Heart To You (vocal: Clark Yocum)
Big Chief De Sota (Written by Fernando Arbello & Andy Razaf)

12.30AM WABC
DICK STABILE
Hotel Lincoln, NYC
If We Never Meet Again (vocal: Bert Shaw)
A High Hat, A Piccolo, And A Cane (vocal: Bert Shaw)
Two Sides To Every Story
Sing Me A Swing Song
It Can Happen (vocal: Bert Shaw)

1.00AM WENR
FLETCHER HENDERSON
Grand Terrace, Chicago
Christopher Columbus (theme) (Written by Chu Berry)
Blue Lou
Did I Remember? (vocal: 'Georgia Boy' Simpkins)
Stompin' At The Savoy (Same arrangement as Goodman)
Remember (Same arrangement as Goodman)
Until The Real Thing Comes Along (vocal: 'Georgia Boy' Simpkins)
Madhouse
Lonesome Night
Swing Is The Thing
The Moon Is Low

SUNDAY 13 SEPTEMBER 1936
RADIO LOGS

7:15PM WNEW
HAROLD ARDEN
Rustic Cabin, Palisades, NJ
I Surrender Dear
Living From Day To Day
I Want The Whole World To Know I Love You
Tain't No Use

8:00PM WABC
AMERICA DANCES
CBS Studios, NYC
June Night / Sometimes I'm Happy / Linger Awhile
When Did You Leave Heaven? (vocal: Buddy Clark)
Doin' The Prom (Lud Gluskin's Orchestra)
Never More
South American Joe (vocal: Buddy Clark)
Tain't Good (vocal: Blue Flames)
No Regrets (vocal: Gogo De Lys)
Chinatown, My Chinatown

11:35PM WEAF
FLETCHER HENDERSON
Grand Terrace, Chicago
Mary Had A Little Lamb
Bye Bye Baby
Fancy Meeting You

St. Louis Blues
If We Never Meet Again (vocal: 'Georgia Boy' Simpkins)
Livin' From Day To Day
I'll Never Let You Go (vocal: Dick Vance)
Some Of These Days

12.00 MIDNIGHT WPG
MAL HALLETT
Steel Pier, Atlantic City, NJ
Boston Tea Party (theme)
She Shall Have Music (vocal: Buddy Welcome)
A Star Fell Out Of Heaven (vocal: Clark Yocum)
China Boy
Sweet Mystery Of Love (vocal: Clark Yocum)
I'm Shooting High (vocal: Buddy Welcome)
I Surrender Dear
I'll Get By
Ask Me (Colossal swing song: nuttsy rhythm section)
Afterglow (vocal: Clark Yocum)
Honeysuckle Rose (Unsurpassable brass, reed sections)
Boston Tea Party (theme)

12.00 MIDNIGHT WABC
ART SHAW
Hotel Lexington, NYC
Nightmare (theme) (Nuttsy theme: too short to record)
Without A Shadow Of A Doubt (vocal: Peg LaCentra)
The Glory Of Love (vocal: Peg LaCentra)
Out Of Nowhere
You're Not The Kind (vocal: Peg LaCentra)
I Can't Escape From You
You Can't Pull The Wool Over My Eyes (vocal: Tony Pastor)
Until The Real Thing Comes Along

12.30AM WABC
FRANK DAILEY
Meadowbrook Ballroom, NJ
Gypsy Violins (theme)
Bojangles Of Harlem
These Foolish Things (vocal: Ann Lee Davies)
Organ Grinder's Swing
There's A Small Hotel
I Got Rhythm (vocal: Ann Lee Davies)
Night And Day
The Make Believe Ballroom (vocal: Ann Lee Davies)
Two Sides To Every Story
Did I Remember? (vocal: Bill Lang)
Gypsy Violins (theme)

Frank Dailey's Meadowbrook Ballroom

1.00AM WENR
FLETCHER HENDERSON
Grand Terrace, Chicago
Christopher Columbus (theme) (Written by Chu Berry)
Symphony In Riffin'
All My Life (Exceptionally smooth saxes with nice swing)
Big Chief De Sota (Written by Fernando Arbello & Andy Razaf)
Nana
We're In The Money
Far In The Night
By Heck!
Star Dust

■ MONDAY 14 SEPTEMBER 1936

RADIO LOGS

11:15PM WEAF
FLETCHER HENDERSON
Grand Terrace, Chicago
Too Bad
Sing, Sing, Sing
Fancy Meeting You
If We Never Meet Again (vocal: 'Georgia Boy' Simpkins)
I Got Rhythm

■ TUESDAY 15 SEPTEMBER 1936

RECORDING SESSION

CAB CALLOWAY AND HIS ORCHESTRA
Recording session for Brunswick in New York City.
Cab Calloway (voc); Shad Collins, Irving Randolph, Lammar Wright (t); DePriest Wheeler, Keg Johnson, Claude Jones (tb); Garvin Bushell, Andrew Brown (cl/as); Ben Webster, Walter Thomas (ts); Benny Payne (p); Morris White (g); Milt Hinton (b); Leroy Maxey (d)
Copper Colored Gal (vCC) / *Frisco Flo* (vCC) / *The Wedding Of Mr & Mrs Swing* (vCC) / *The Hi-De-Ho Miracle Man* (vCC)

BEN POLLACK AND HIS ORCHESTRA
Recording session for Brunswick in New York City.
Ben Pollack (d*/voc/ldr); Harry James, Shorty Sherock, Charlie Spivak (t); Bruce Squires, Glenn Miller (tb); Irving Fazola (cl); Opie Cates (as); Dave Matthews (ts); Ray Cohen (vln); Freddy Slack (p); Frank Frederico (g); Thurman Teague (b); Sammy Taylor (d); Carol Mackay, Lois Still (voc)
*I'm One Step Ahead Of My Shadow** (vLS) / *Thru' The Courtesy Of Love** (vBP) / *I Couldn't Be Mad At You* (vCM)
Joe Price (steel guitar) added:
Song Of The Islands

RADIO LOGS

9:30PM WABC
BENNY GOODMAN
"Camel Caravan", Boston
I Found A New Baby
Pick Yourself Up (Nuttsy trombone, trumpet team and clarinet)
Swingtime In The Rockies (Nuttsy sax and trumpet)
These Foolish Things (vocal: Helen Ward)
Minnie The Moocher's Wedding Day (One of Goodman's best arrangements)

10:30PM WJZ
VINCENT LOPEZ
CBS Studio, NYC
Organ Grinder's Swing
It's A Sin To Tell A Lie (vocal: Fred Lowery)
Pick Yourself Up (From new movie "Swing Time" with Rogers-Astaire)

Bye Bye Baby (vocal: Edith Dick)
Until The Real Thing Comes Along (Stanley Woods on sax)
When A Lady Meets A Gentleman Down South (vocal: Edith Dick)
I'm Getting Sentimental Over You (trombone)
Knock, Knock (Written by Vincent Lopez)

11:30PM WJZ
RILEY & FARLEY
Hickory House, 52nd Street, NYC
The Music Goes Round And Around (theme)
I Wish You Were My Love Affair
Did I Remember? (vocal: Ed Farley)
Get Happy
Me And The Moon
Just Drifting Along (vocal: Ed Farley)
Let's Sing Again (vocal: Mike Riley)
Rip Van Winkle (vocal: Ed Farley) (Written by Riley & Farley)
Robins And Roses
Solitude (vocal: Ed Farley)
San Francisco

12:30AM WJZ
JIMMY DORSEY
Cotton Club, Culver City, Calif
Sandman (theme)
Boston Tea Party (vocal: Dorsey Trio) (Colossal)
No Regrets (vocal: Bob Eberly)
Stompin' At The Savoy (Best arrangement of this song: nuttsy)
A Star Fell Out Of Heaven (vocal: Martha Tilton)
Funiculi, Funicula
You (vocal: Bob Eberly)
I'm An Old Cowhand (vocal: Dorsey Trio)
When I'm With You (vocal: Bob Eberly)
St. Louis Blues
Sandman (theme)

1.00AM WENR
FLETCHER HENDERSON
Grand Terrace, Chicago
Christopher Columbus (theme) (Written by Chu Berry)
I Got Plenty O' Nuttin'
Shoe Shine Boy (vocal: 'Georgia Boy' Simpkins)
Going Home
Without A Shadow Of A Doubt
Down South Camp Meeting
No Regrets (vocal: 'Georgia Boy' Simpkins)
Stompin' At The Savoy
If I Could Be With You One Hour Tonight (vocal: 'Georgia Boy' Simpkins)
Madhouse (Roy Eldridge's trumpet is wonderful)

■ WEDNESDAY 16 SEPTEMBER 1936

RECORDING SESSION

BEN POLLACK AND HIS ORCHESTRA
Recording session for Brunswick in New York City.
Ben Pollack (d/voc/ldr); Harry James, Shorty Sherock, Charlie Spivak (t); Bruce Squires, Glenn Miller (tb); Irving Fazola (cl); Opie Cates (as); Dave Matthews (ts); Ray Cohen (vln); Freddy Slack (p); Frank Frederico (g); Thurman Teague (b); Sammy Taylor (d); Jim Hardy (voc)
Jimtown Blues / Now Or Never (vJH)

BEN POLLACK / THE DEAN AND HIS KIDS
Recording session for Vocalion in New York City.
Ben Pollack (d/ldr); Harry James (t/voc); Bruce Squires (tb); Irving Fazola (cl); Dave Matthews (ts); Freddy Slack (p); Frank Frederico (g); Thurman Teague (b)
Spreadin' Knowledge Around / Zoom Zoom Zoom (vHJ)

RADIO LOGS

12:30PM WABC
MERRY MAKERS
CBS Studios, NYC
Sing, Sing, Sing
I Can't Pretend
Rhe Ta Ta Da Te De Tee De Dee De Da La
If We Never Meet Again
Swing, Swing Mother-In-Law
A Fine Romance
Twiddlin' My Thumbs
Two Sides To Every Story
Bye Bye Baby

10:30PM WHN
STUFF SMITH
Onyx Club, 72 W52nd Street, NYC
Pick Yourself Up
Please Leave Me Alone (Written by Riley & Farley)
Church Mouse On A Spree (Frank Froeba piano solo on own song)
Bugle Blues

11:15PM ?
FOUR INK SPOTS
Studio, NYC
Swing Mister Charlie
Midnight Blue
A High Hat, A Piccolo, And A Cane
The Old Spinning Wheel
Sing, Sing, Sing

11:30PM WABC
BENNY GOODMAN
Ritz-Carlton Hotel, Boston
King Porter Stomp (New arrangement, better: nice sax; trumpet)
You Turned The Tables On Me (vocal: Helen Ward)
Stompin' At The Savoy
Body And Soul (BG Trio) (Swell slow piece)
Sing, Baby, Sing (vocal: Helen Ward) (Not good for Goodman)
Three Little Words (Colossal: clarinet; trombone; trumpets; drums)
Here's Love In Your Eyes
Midnight Blue (vocal: Helen Ward) (Poor song but nice trumpet)
Pick Yourself Up (Nuttsy trumpets, trombones)
Swingtime In The Rockies (A new swing tune)

12:00 MIDNIGHT WPG
ALEX BARTHA
Steel Pier, Atlantic City
Alexander's Ragtime Band
Why Do I Lie To Myself About You?
South Sea Island Magic
Swamp Fire
When Did You Leave Heaven?
Rigamarole
You're Not The Kind (sung by 'Miss California' Johnson)
Sophisticated Swing
Stompin' At The Savoy
Shoe Shine Boy

12:30AM WOR
JOE SANDERS
Blackhawk Restaurant, Chicago
Until The Real Thing Comes Along (vocal: Joe Sanders)
I've Got Trouble With My Shadow (vocal: Joe Sanders)
I Can't Escape From You
Let's Face The Music And Dance (vocal: Jack Swift)
Slew Foot (vocal: Joe Sanders)
I Could Be In Heaven (vocal: Jack Swift)
Shoe Shine Boy
Sing, Sing, Sing
When Did You Leave Heaven?

12.30AM WABC
DICK STABILE
Hotel Lincoln, NYC
Me And The Moon
Long Ago And Far Away (vocal: Bert Shaw)
I'm An Old Cowhand (vocal: Dick Stabile)
You Came To My Rescue (vocal: Frank Fleming)
When I'm With You
I Take To You
A Star Fell Out Of Heaven
Honeysuckle Rose
Empty Saddles

■ THURSDAY 17 SEPTEMBER 1936

RECORDING SESSION

ART SHAW AND HIS ORCHESTRA
Recording session for Brunswick in New York City.
Art Shaw (cl/ldr); Lee Castle, Zeke Zarchy (t); Mike Michaels (tb); Tony Pastor (ts/voc), Jerry Gray, Ben Plotkin (vln); Sam Persoff (vla); Jimmy Oderich (cello); Joe Lippman (p); Gene Stultz (g); Ben Ginsberg (b); Sammy Weiss (d); Peg La Centra (voc)
You're Giving Me A Song And A Dance (vPLC) / *Darling, Not Without You* (vPLC) / *One, Two, Button Your Shoe* (vTP) / *Let's Call A Heart A Heart* (vPLC)

RADIO LOGS

6:00PM WNEW
ORIGINAL DIXIELAND JAZZ BAND
'Make Believe Ballroom', NYC
Original Dixieland One-Step
Sensation
Bluin' The Blues

7:15PM WABC
MARK WARNOW
CBS Studios, NYC
Doin' The Prom
You Turned The Tables On Me (vocal: Lee Wiley)
Swing Fugue In E-Flat
(Tune teasers)
When Did You Leave Heaven? (vocal: Jimmy Brierley)
Here Comes The King
Until The Real Thing Comes Along (vocal: Lee Wiley)
Darktown Strutters' Ball

■ FRIDAY 18 SEPTEMBER 1936

RADIO LOGS

5.00PM WEAF
BUGHOUSE RHYTHM
San Francisco
Boston Tea Party (Written by Frank Ryerson, trumpet with Hallett)
Delirium (Written by Arthur Schutt: played by Dr. Meakin (p), g, cl, tpt, dms, sax)
Tain't No Use (Written by Burton Lane: introduced by Jimmy Dorsey)
Hobo On Park Avenue (written by Will Hudson: Hudson wrote 'Moonglow', 'Tormented', 'White Heat', 'Jazznocracy' etc.)

11:15PM WEAF
FLETCHER HENDERSON
Grand Terrace, Chicago
When I'm With You
I Wonder
If We Never Meet Again

12.30AM WABC
DICK STABILE
Hotel Lincoln, NYC
San Francisco
Two Sides To Every Story (vocal: Bert Shaw)
The Stars Weep (vocal: Bert Shaw)
Between The Devil And The Deep Blue Sea
Through The Courtesy Of Love
Until Today (vocal: Bert Shaw)
You Dropped Me Like A Red Hot Penny
Sweet Mystery of Love
I Got Rhythm
Did I Remember?

■ SATURDAY 19 SEPTEMBER 1936

RADIO LOGS

11:15PM WABC
ART SHAW
Lexington Hotel, NYC
Pick Yourself Up (vocal: Tony Pastor)
When Your Lover Has Gone (vocal: Peg LaCentra)
You're Giving Me A Song And A Dance
Nightmare (theme) (Nuttsy opening and closing theme: clarinets)

11:30PM WABC
BENNY GOODMAN
Ritz-Carlton Hotel, Boston
Let's Dance (theme)
Alexander's Ragtime Band
You're Not The Kind (vocal: Helen Ward)
When Did You Leave Heaven?
When Buddha Smiles
In A Sentimental Mood (Superb trombone by McEachern)
Riffin' At The Ritz (New song, just introduced)
Sometimes I'm Happy
Sing, Sing, Sing (vocal: Helen Ward)
Goodbye (theme)

11:30PM WABC
TED LEWIS
Mayfair Casino, Chicago
Copenhagen
Mexicali Rose
Sing, Sing, Sing
Close Your Pretty Eyes (vocal: Ted Lewis)
Polka Dot Stomp
Did I Remember?

■ SUNDAY 20 SEPTEMBER 1936

RADIO LOGS

11:00 WABC
JIMMIE LUNCEFORD
Nixon Grand Th, Philadelphia
Black And Tan Fantasy
Rhythm Is Our Business
Star Dust
Sophisticated Lady
My Blue Heaven
All My Life

■ MONDAY 21 SEPTEMBER 1936

RADIO LOGS

2:30PM WABC
MANHATTAN MATINÉE
CBS studios, NYC
When Did You Leave Heaven?
Doin' The Prom
Swing, Swing Mother-In-Law
Where Green Grass Grows Around
When I'm With You (vocal: Jimmy Brierley)
Bye Bye Baby
Love Will Tell
Mary Had A Little Lamb
It Ain't Right
Monday In Manhattan (theme)

■ TUESDAY 22 SEPTEMBER 1936

RADIO LOGS

9:30PM WABC
BENNY GOODMAN
"Camel Caravan", Boston
Walk, Jennie, Walk
Tain't No Use (vocal: Helen Ward) (Colossal, marvelous saxes)
Sometimes I'm Happy
Tiger Rag (BG Trio)

12:00 MIDNIGHT WEAF
PAUL WHITEMAN
Casa Manana, Texas
Rose Of The Rio Grande (Colossal)
Two Sides To Every Story (vocal: Trio) (Colossal: marvelous saxes)
Why Do I Lie To Myself About You? (vocal: Darelle Alexander)
In A Sentimental Mood
Tain't No Use (vocal: Jack Teagarden)
I Can't Escape From You (vocal: Ramona Davis)
Bojangles Of Harlem (Written by Jerome Kern, from "Swing Time")
Bye Bye Baby (vocal: Ramona Davis)
Until Today
Rhapsody In Blue (opening and closing theme)

12:30AM WEAF
JOE VENUTI
Casa Manana, Texas
On The Alamo
Until The Real Thing Comes Along (vocal: Mildred Fenton)
Hocus Pocus
Dream Awhile (vocal: Mildred Fenton)
Introduction To A G String (Written by Joe Venuti)
Ol' Man River
Cream Puff
Nagasaki

Joe Venuti and Paul Whiteman have been playing at Billy Rose's Casa Manana all summer at the Fort Worth Fair.

1:00AM WENR
FLETCHER HENDERSON
Grand Terrace, Chicago
Christopher Columbus (theme)
It Happened In Chicago
Please Don't Turn Your Back On Me
Remember (Same arrangement as Goodman's: played too fast)
Lonesome Night
Swing Low
When I'm With You
Jamaica Shout
I Would Do Anything For You (Written by Claude Hopkins)
Jim Town Blues
Christopher Columbus (theme)

■ WEDNESDAY 23 SEPTEMBER 1936

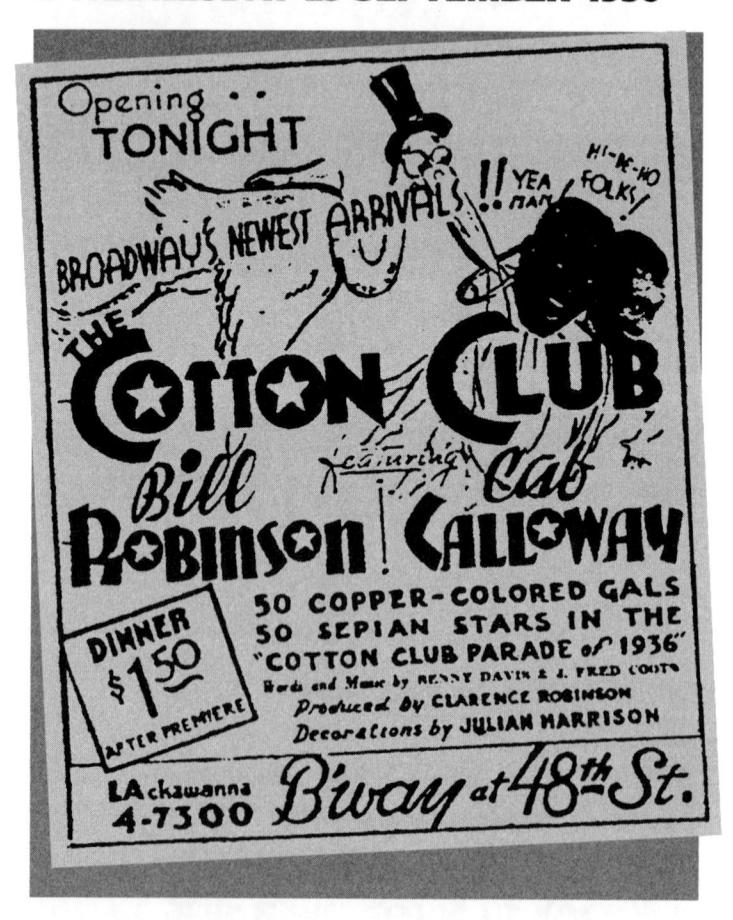

RADIO LOGS

8:00PM WOR
CAB CALLOWAY
Cotton Club, NYC
This is the first night that Calloway has played at the "new" Cotton Club. The "new" Cotton Club is the "old" Connie's Inn on Broadway and 48th Street.
I'm At The Mercy Of Love (vocal: Cab Calloway)
Alabama Barbecue (vocal: Cab Calloway)
That's What You Mean To Me (vocal: Cab Calloway)
Suzy Q (vocal: Cab Calloway) (From 'The Cotton Club of 1936')
Frisco Flo (vocal: Cab Calloway) (From 'The Cotton Club of 1936')
Jingle Of The Jungle (vocal: Cab Calloway) (From 'The Cotton Club of 1936')
The Hi-De-Ho Miracle Man (vocal: Cab Calloway) (From 'The Cotton Club of 1936')
Minnie The Moocher (theme)

SEPTEMBER 1936 — Swing Era Scrapbook 63

9:00PM WABC
ANDRÉ KOSTELANETZ
Chesterfield program, NYC
I'm An Old Cowhand (André Kostelanetz 45-piece band)
The Way You Look Tonight (vocal: Ray Heatherton)
Rhumba??
Hallelujah (vocal: Kay Thompson & Rhythm Singers)
Say Not (vocal: Ray Heatherton)
I'm Getting Sentimental Over You (vocal: Kay Thompson)
Dance For Me My Darling (Tango by André Kostelanetz 45-piece band)
Louisiana Hayride (vocal: Kay Thompson & Rhythm Singers)
Shine (André Kostelanetz 45-piece band: 17 violins)

The New Cotton Club Opens

With Bill Robinson and Cab Calloway heading its elaborate revue, there could be little doubt that the "new" Cotton Club, which found itself opening at Broadway and Forty-eighth Street on Thursday evening, would turn out an Entertainment. Two more pulse-quickening darktown strutters have never come hi-de-hoing and yeah-maning down from Harlem than the stars selected for this show. And to abet them the management collected as nifty a cast of sepia entertainers as ever flashed a toothy smile.

Of course, it is easy to say that there will never be another colored show like some of those they used to do up at the—not the "old" but the old, OLD Cotton Club. And it is true that, in spots, this downtown incarnation grows a bit tedious and dull, which is something a colored show is just not supposed to do. But this department testifies that you'll go a long way to see better numbers than Calloway singing "Frisco Flo," the amazing Kaloah doing her "ripple" dance, the hoofing Berry Brothers, the "tramp' band or Robinson, Calloway and the girls taking away "That Copper-Colored Gal o' Mine." For the better part of the revue (which was a bit too long on opening night, anyhow), it is first-class Negro entertainment—and there isn't much entertainment that can beat it.

Top: Cab Calloway and his Orchestra, stars of the new Cotton Club revue downtown at Broadway and Forty-eighth Street.

10:30PM WHN
STUFF SMITH
Onyx Club, 72 W52nd Street, NYC
Stuff Smith plays a hot violin and Jonah Jones plays a hot trumpet. Counting himself, Stuff has 6 men in his "jam" band.
Old Joe's Hittin' The Jug (vocal: Stuff Smith)
A Fine Romance (vocal: Stuff Smith) (From 'Swing Time')
Sophisticated Lady (Solo on piano by Frank Froeba)
I Got Rhythm

11:00PM ?
WILL HUDSON-ED DeLANGE
Raymor Ballroom, Boston
Hobo On Park Avenue (theme)
Organ Grinder's Swing
The First Thing I Knew Was You (vocal: Ruth Gaylor)
Honeysuckle Rose
Monopoly Swing

11:30PM WABC
BENNY GOODMAN
Ritz-Carlton Hotel, Boston
Let's Dance (theme)
Sugar Foot Stomp
You Turned The Tables On Me (vocal: Helen Ward)
You Forgot To Remember (Baritone sax instead of tenor on record)
Peter Piper (vocal: Helen Ward) (A clever tongue-twister)
How Am I To Know (BG Trio)
Riffin' At The Ritz (Written by Benny: swell saxes; trumpets include Sterling Bose)
Until The Real Thing Comes Along (vocal: Helen Ward)
I Would Do Anything For You
Here's Love In Your Eyes (From 'Big Broadcast of 1937')

12:00 MIDNIGHT WPG
ALEX BARTHA
Steel Pier, Atlantic City, NJ
Alexander's Ragtime Band (theme)

The House Jack Built For Jill
Here's Love In Your Eyes
South Sea Island Magic
Papa Tree Top Tall
Dream Awhile
When Did You Leave Heaven?
I Never Knew
You're Not The Kind (vocal: Carl White)
It's The Gypsy In Me
If We Never Meet Again
Jangled Nerves

■ THURSDAY 24 SEPTEMBER 1936

RECORDING SESSION

CHARLIE BARNET AND HIS ORCHESTRA
Recording session for Bluebird in New York City.
Charlie Barnet (ss/as/ts/voc); George Kennedy, Irving Goodman, Kermit Simmons (t); Sonny Lee, John Doyle (tb); George Vaughan, Don Morres (cl/as); Willard Brady, Murray Williams (ts); Horace Diaz (p); Scoop Thomson (g); Sid Weiss (b); Billy Flanagan (d); The Barnet Modernaires (v)
The Milkman's Matinee (vTBM) / *Rainbow On The River* (vCB) / *Did You Mean It?* (vCB) / *You Do The Darndest Things, Baby* (vCB) / *It's Love I'm After* (vCB) / *Sing, Baby, Sing* (vCB)

RADIO LOGS

7:15PM WABC
MARK WARNOW
CBS Studios, NYC
The Way You Look Tonight
Alkenza (vocal: Tito Gizar)
Summertime
You're Not The Kind (vocal: Margaret McCrae)
Begin The Beguine
If We Never Meet Again (vocal: Tito Gizar)
Honeysuckle Rose
A Star Fell Out Of Heaven

11:05PM WJZ
RILEY & FARLEY
Hickory House, 52nd Street, NYC
I'm Gonna Sit Right Down And Write Myself A Letter
The Land Of Jazz
I Never Knew
Harmonica Ride
Rip Van Winkle
When I'm With You
Basin Street Blues
Oh Dear, What Can The Matter Be? (vocal: Ed Farley)
The Music Goes Round And Around (theme)

11:30PM WOR
CAB CALLOWAY
Cotton Club, NYC
Minnie The Moocher (theme)
Sweet Sue (vocal: Cab Calloway)
You're Not The Kind (vocal: Cab Calloway)
Belles Of Harlem
Blue Skies
Until The Real Thing Comes Along (vocal: Bennie Payne)
Copper Colored Gal Of Mine (vocal: Cab Calloway)
The Hi-De-Ho Miracle Man (vocal: Cab Calloway) (From 'The Cotton Club of 1936')
Oh, Lady Be Good
Minnie The Moocher (theme)

11:30PM WMCA
TEDDY HILL
Savoy Ballroom, NYC
Uptown Rhapsody (theme)
Big Chief De Sota
Did I Remember?
My Blue Heaven (vocal: Bill Dillard)
King Porter Stomp
Lonesome Night
Honeysuckle Rose
Until The Real Thing Comes Along (vocal: Bill Dillard)
Sensation
Uptown Rhapsody (theme)

FRIDAY 25 SEPTEMBER 1936

RADIO LOGS

11:30PM WMCA
TEDDY HILL
Savoy Ballroom, NYC
Stompin' At The Savoy (theme)
'Way Down Yonder In New Orleans
These Foolish Things
Down Home Rag
Paradise (vocal: Bill Dillard)
Blue Rhythm Fantasy
Vagabond Song
I Can't Escape From You
Happy As The Day Is Long

12:00 MIDNIGHT WOR
CAB CALLOWAY
Cotton Club, NYC
Everybody Swing (vocal: Cab Calloway)
That's What You Mean To Me (vocal: Cab Calloway)
Organ Grinder's Swing (vocal: Cab Calloway)
Rain (vocal: Cab Calloway)
Sylvia (vocal: Bennie Payne)
The Hi-De-Ho Miracle Man (vocal: Cab Calloway)
Copper Colored Gal Of Mine (vocal: Cab Calloway)
White Heat

SATURDAY 26 SEPTEMBER 1936

RADIO LOGS

10:00PM WIXBS
BLANCHE CALLOWAY
Baltimore, Maryland
Until The Real Thing Comes Along
Sing, Sing, Sing (vocal: Blanche Calloway)
When Did You Leave Heaven?
You Stepped Out Of A Dream
Just Met Up With That Gal Of Mine
Sad Night In Harlem (vocal: Blanche Calloway)
Organ Grinder's Swing
Roll Them Bones (theme)

11:00PM WABC
ART SHAW
Lexington Hotel, NYC
Nightmare (theme)
Tain't No Use
Pick Yourself Up (vocal: Tony Pastor)
Darling, Not Without You (vocal: Peg LaCentra)
Japanese Sandman
If We Never Meet Again (vocal: Peg LaCentra)
Ain't Misbehavin' (vocal: Tony Pastor)

You're Giving me A Song And A Dance
It Ain't Right
Nightmare (Nuttsy opening and closing theme: clarinets)

12:30AM WMCA
NOBLE SISSLE
Nixon-Grand Theater, Philadelphia
Truckin'
Organ Grinder's Swing
No Regrets (vocal: Lena Horne)
Afterglow
Polka-Dot Stomp
Black And Tan Fantasy
Lost (vocal: Lena Horne)
You
White Heat

SUNDAY 27 SEPTEMBER 1936

RADIO LOGS

11:00PM WABC
ART SHAW
Lexington Hotel, NYC
Did I Remember? (vocal: Peg LaCentra)
When Did You Leave Heaven? (vocal: Tony Pastor)
Until Today (vocal: Peg LaCentra)
A Star Fell Out Of Heaven (vocal: Gene Stone)

TUESDAY 29 SEPTEMBER 1936

RECORDING SESSION

BILLIE HOLIDAY & HER ORCHESTRA
Recording session for Vocalion in NYC.
Bunny Berigan (t); Irving Fazola (cl); Clyde Hart (p); Dick McDonough (g); Artie Bernstein (b); Cozy Cole (d); Billie Holiday (v)
A Fine Romance / I Can't Pretend / One, Two, Button Your Shoe / Let's Call A Heart A Heart

RADIO LOGS

9:30PM WABC
BENNY GOODMAN
"Camel Caravan", NYC
Star Dust
Riffin' At The Ritz (New swing song by Bill Miller, titled by Helen Ward)
Body And Soul (BG Trio)
Sing, Sing, Sing (vocal: Helen Ward) (Special 5-mins arrangement: colossal)

WEDNESDAY 30 SEPTEMBER 1936

RECORDING SESSION

DON REDMAN AND HIS ORCHESTRA
Recording session for ARC in New York City.
Don Redman (cl/ss/as/voc/ldr); Reunald Jones, Otis Johnson, Harold Baker (t); Gene Simon, Benny Morton, Quentin Jackson (tb); Edward Inge, Rupert Cole (cl/as); Harvey Boone (cl/as/bar); Robert Carroll (ts); Don Kirkpatrick (p); Clarence Holiday (g); Bob Ysaguirre (b); Sid Catlett (d); Harlan Lattimore (voc)
Who Wants To Sing My Love Song? (vHL) / *Too Bad* (vDR) / *We Don't Know From Nothin'* (vDR) / *Bugle Call Rag*

OCTOBER 1936

Hotel Pennsylvania: **Benny Goodman** (1–)
Hotel Commodore: **Mal Hallett** (2–)
Hotel Lincoln: **Dick Stabile**
Hotel Taft: **George Hall**
Hotel New Yorker: **Will Osborne** (8–)
Rainbow Room: **Ray Noble**

Apollo Theater: **Fats Waller** (2–8); **Noble Sissle** (9–15); **Chick Webb** (16–22); **Sunset Royal Serenaders** (23–29); **Lucky Millinder** (30–)
Paramount Theater: **Clyde Lucas** (21–)
Loew's State Theater: **Don Redman** (9–15); **Lucky Millinder** (16–22); **Tommy Dorsey/Lee Wiley** (23–29);

Cotton Club Downtown: **Cab Calloway/Bill Robinson**
Hickory House: **Riley & Farley**
Onyx Club: **Stuff Smith**

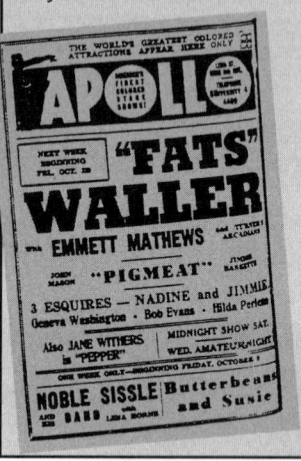

■ THURSDAY 1 OCTOBER 1936

RECORDING SESSION

WINGY MANONE AND HIS ORCHESTRA
Recording session for Bluebird in New York City.
Wingy Manone (t/voc); Mike Viggiano (cl); Joe Marsala (cl/as); James Lamare (cl/ts); Conrad Lanoue (p); Jack LeMaire (g); Artie Shapiro (b); George Wettling (d)
In The Groove (vWM) / *Let Me Call You Sweetheart* (vWM) / *Easy Like* (vWM) / *I Can't Pretend* (vWM) / *Floatin' Down To Cotton Town* (vWM) / *A Fine Romance* (vWM)

■ FRIDAY 2 OCTOBER 1936

RADIO LOGS

11:30PM WABC
BENNY GOODMAN
Hotel Pennsylvania, NYC
Let's Dance (theme)
Down South Camp Meetin'
When Did You Leave Heaven? (vocal: Helen Ward)
After You've Gone (BG Trio)
Peter Piper (vocal: Helen Ward) (A clever tongue-twister)
Swingtime In The Rockies
More Than You Know
Sing, Baby, Sing (vocal: Helen Ward)
I Can't Escape From You
Riffin' At The Ritz

■ SATURDAY 3 OCTOBER 1936

Went in on train at 5.15 with Hugh Pastoriza, Mr Pastoriza and Cynthia Doyle. Went to 485 Madison Avenue where we saw the Saturday Night Swing Session broadcast (6:45 to 7:15). Got the autographs of Bunny Berigan (trumpet); Dave Wade (trumpet); Nat Natoli (trumpet); Johnny Williams (drums); Babe Rusin (sax); Elliot 'Jonah' Jones (trumpet w Stuff Smith); Cozy Cole (drums w Stuff Smith); Bobby Bennett (guitar w Stuff Smith); Stuff Smith (violin); Caspar Reardon (harp); Lee Wiley (vocalist); Hank Ross (sax w Freddy Rich); and Joe Vargas (trombone w Rich). Freddy Rich conducted the regular band. Stuff Smith had his 6-piece jam band there as a guest from the Onyx Club and Caspar Reardon was guest harpist and Lee Wiley was guest vocalist. I didn't get the autographs of Freddy Rich (director), Art Manners (clarinet), Lou Shoobe (bass), Vincent Maffay (guitar) and a few others.

6.45PM WABC
SATURDAY NIGHT SWING SESSION No14
Studio 1, CBS Studios, NYC
I Can't Get Started (Bunny Berigan & house band)
Washington & Lee Swing
Organ Grinder's Swing (Colossal: best number played; written by Will Hudson)
Man With The Jive (Stuff Smith and his 6-piece Onyx Club band)
Tain't Good (Caspar Reardon playing on the harp: swell)
Georgia On My Mind (Lee Wiley singing with Williams and Berigan)
Oh, Lady Be Good (Stuff Smith & Band: Jonah Jones on trumpet)
I Can't Get Started (Bunny Berigan trumpet solo)
Wang Wang Blues

Mr Pastoriza took us to Schrafft's restaurant to eat afterwards. We then went to the Hotel Pennsylvania where Benny Goodman opened 2 days ago for a 6-month's engagement. We talked to him for 5 minutes. Cynthia Doyle had dinner with him the night before. Vido Musso has taken Dick Clark's place on the sax; Sterling Bose has taken Nate Kazebier's place on trumpet; and Pee Wee Erwin has stayed in California.

■ MONDAY 5 OCTOBER 1936

RADIO LOGS

7:15PM WOR
MAL HALLETT
Hotel Commodore, NYC
Mal Hallett just opened up at the Palm Room, Hotel Commodore, on October 2 for a month or so's engagement.
Boston Tea Party (theme by Frank Ryerson, trumpeter in band)
No Regrets (vocal: Clark Yocum)
I'm Getting Sentimental Over You (Jimmy Skyles on trombone)
I'm An Old Cowhand (vocal: Buddy Welcome) (whole band singing with Buddy)
State Of My Heart (vocal: Clark Yocum)
When Did You Leave Heaven? (vocal: Clark Yocum)
Stars Weep
Big Chief De Sota

■ TUESDAY 6 OCTOBER 1936

RADIO LOGS

9:30PM WABC
BENNY GOODMAN
"Camel Caravan", NYC
I Know That You Know
When Buddha Smiles
Peter Piper (vocal: Helen Ward) (new tongue twister)
China Boy (BG Trio)

■ WEDNESDAY 7 OCTOBER 1936

RECORDING SESSION

BENNY GOODMAN AND HIS ORCHESTRA
Recording session for Victor in New York City.
Benny Goodman (cl); Chris Griffin, Zeke Zarchy, Ziggy Elman (t); Red Ballard, Murray McEachern (tb); Bill DePew, Hymie Shertzer (as); Art Rollini, Vido Musso (ts); Jess Stacy (p); Allan Reuss (g); Harry Goodman (b); Gene Krupa (d); Helen Ward (voc)
When A Lady Meets A Gentleman Down South (vHW) / *You're Giving Me A Song And Dance* (vHW) / *Organ Grinder's Swing* / *Peter Piper* (vHW) / *Riffin' At The Ritz* / *Alexander's Ragtime Band*

■ THURSDAY 8 OCTOBER 1936

RADIO LOGS

8:45PM WICC
FRANKIE WARD
Normandie Ballroom, Boston
Fair
China Boy
You're Not The Kind
When I'm With You
Thou Swell
The Moon Is Grinning At Me
Jangled Nerves

■ FRIDAY 9 OCTOBER 1936

RADIO LOGS

11:15PM WOR
MAL HALLETT
Hotel Commodore, NYC
Good. Buddy Welcome, who sings, plays sax & clarinet, is one of my favourite vocalists and a fine tenor sax player.
The Gentleman Obviously Doesn't Believe (vocal: Buddy Welcome)
Humoresque (Frankie Carle on piano)
It Can Happen To You / *Night And Day* / *A Star Fell Out Of Heaven*
On The Beach At Bali-Bali (vocal: Buddy Welcome) (whole band singing with Buddy)
Christopher Columbus
Boston Tea Party (theme)

11:30PM WABC
BENNY GOODMAN
Hotel Pennsylvania, NYC
Let's Dance (theme)
Alexander's Ragtime Band
You Turned The Tables On Me (vocal: Helen Ward)
If I Could Be With You One Hour Tonight
Me Without You (vocal: Helen Ward)
Blue Skies

Tiger Rag (BG Trio)
You're Giving Me A Song And A Dance (vocal: Helen Ward)
Love Me Or Leave Me
Sometimes I'm Happy

12:00 MIDNIGHT WEAF
FLETCHER HENDERSON
Grand Terrace, Chicago
Not a very good program. Terrible!
Christopher Columbus (theme) (recorded for Melotone)
King Porter Stomp
The Melody Plane
Stompin' Serenade
If We Never Meet Again (vocal: 'Georgia Boy' Simpkins)
Sing, Baby, Sing
Who Loves You? (vocal: 'Georgia Boy' Simpkins)
Until Today
When Did You Leave Heaven? (vocal: 'Georgia Boy' Simpkins)
After You've Gone

12:30AM WJZ
BOB CROSBY
Hotel St. Nicholas, St.Paul-Minneapolis
Crosby just opened up yesterday at St.Paul-Minneapolis. Kay Weber, who used to be with Bob Crosby in the Dorsey Brothers Band (1934–35) just joined the band three weeks ago. Joe Sullivan, pianist, joined about six weeks ago.
Sugar Foot Strut
Until Today (vocal: Kay Weber)
What Is This Thing Called Love? (vocal: Eddie Miller)
My Kingdom For A Kiss (vocal: Bob Crosby)
I Take To You (vocal: Nappy Lamare)
Dixieland Shuffle (written by bass player in band; 21-yr-old Bob Haggart)
Peter Piper (vocal: Bob Crosby)
When Did You Leave Heaven? (vocal: Kay Weber)
Panama (colossal work by Bauduc on drums, Haggart and Miller)

Below: The Bob Crosby Orchestra with Kay Weber and Joe Sullivan (third from left, back row).

■ SATURDAY 10 OCTOBER 1936

Hugh Pastoriza got 2 passes in the mail to see this week's Swing Session so he and I went in by the Subway at 5:00 and went to the Columbia Broadcasting System, 485 Madison Avenue, where the broadcast originated in Studio 1. The guest stars on this broadcast were Teddy Wilson, famed hot 22yr-old colored pianist and Adrian Rollini, bass sax and vibraphone player. Got the autographs of Teddy Wilson, Frank Worrell (guitar in CBS band), Adrian Rollini, Paul Douglas (announcer for program), Ernie White (clarinet in CBS band), Johnny Williams (drummer in CBS band who used to play with the Original Memphis Five and is one of Ray Bauduc's best friends), and Bunny Berigan (one of the greatest trumpeters that ever lived). I saw this same broadcast last week and have now gotten the autographs of everybody except the bass, piano, trumpet and sax player and director Freddy Rich.

Adrian Rollini on bass sax for *Tap Room Swing*.

6.45PM WABC
SATURDAY NIGHT SWING SESSION No15
Studio 1, CBS Studios, NYC
Colossal. Better than last week.
I Can't Get Started (opening theme: Bunny Berigan with Freddie Rich's CBS house band)
Fight On Pennsylvania (Colossal saxes and 4 trumpets in band)
Stop, Look And Listen (Band, featuring 2 trombones; Berigan; trumpet and Frank Worrell, guitar)
Honeysuckle Rose (Adrian Rollini playing vibraphone)
I'm An Old Cowhand (Blue Flames; quartet of 3 women, 1 man singing the nuts! Hank Ross swell)
You Turned The Tables On Me (Babe Russin colossal on tenor sax)
Tea For Two (Teddy Wilson on piano with Johnny Williams on drums)
Ida, Sweet As Apple Cider (Teddy Wilson on piano, Johnny Williams on drums)
Tap Room Swing (written by Adrian Rollini; played by Babe Russin, Ward Lay (saxes); Adrian Rollini (bass sax); Bunny Berigan (trumpet); Teddy Wilson (piano); Frankie Worrell (guitar); Johnny Williams (drums))
I Know That You Know (Teddy Wilson on piano)
St. Louis Blues (Jerry Colonna trombone solo)

■ SUNDAY 11 OCTOBER 1936

RADIO LOGS

11:30PM WJZ
GLEN GRAY
Congress Casino, Chicago
This is the first night that Glen Gray has played at the Congress Hotel. Goodman and Ellington played here last spring and now Glen Gray has opened up for the winter.
I'm An Old Cowhand
Until The Real Thing Comes Along (vocal: Kenny Sargent)
Stompin' Around (Johnny Davis nuttsy on tenor sax)
Between The Devil And The Deep Blue Sea (vocal: Pee Wee Hunt)
Bugle Call Rag (3 trombones: Hutchenrider on clarinet)
Smoke Rings (opening and closing theme written by Hutchenrider)

12:00 MIDNIGHT WMCA
STUFF SMITH
Onyx Club, 72 W52nd Street, NYC
Stuff Smith and his 6-piece "jam" band have been playing at the Onyx Club, 72 W52nd Street, for about 5 months and are leaving for California in February. Cozy Cole, drummer, and Jonah Jones, trumpeter, are featured with Stuff Smith who plays the violin.
I'se A-Muggin' (theme)
Oh, Lady Be Good
Gypsy Fiddles Were Playing (vocal: 3 Spirits Of Rhythm)
I've Got A Heavy Date
Cocktails For Two (Teddy Bunn featured on guitar)
There's A Small Hotel
Swing At The Onyx Club (whole Band vocalizing)

12:00 MIDNIGHT WOR
LOUIS PRIMA
Blackhawk Restaurant, Chicago
Not very good. Louis Prima plays hot trumpet and features Pee Wee Russell on clarinet. Just opened at the Blackhawk weeks ago.
Sing, Sing, Sing (theme)
You Can't Pull The Wool Over My Eyes (vocal: Louis Prima)
Out Where The Blues Begin (vocal: Velma Raye)
Unknown title
Tin Roof Blues
My Heart Wants To Dance (vocal: Velma Raye)
You're Still In My Dreams (vocal: Velma Raye)
Chapel In The Moonlight (vocal: Velma Raye)
Star Dust (vocal: Louis Prima)
I Still Want You (written by Louis Prima)

12:00 MIDNIGHT WJZ
FLETCHER HENDERSON
Grand Terrace, Chicago
Christopher Columbus (theme)
Jangled Nerves (colossal trombone; tenor sax by Chu Berry)
Fancy Meeting You
Close To Me
Happy As The Day Is Long
If We Never Meet Again (vocal: 'Georgia Boy' Simpkins)
The Stampede (an old swing song written by Fletcher Henderson)
Magnolias In The Moonlight
Madhouse (same arrangement as Goodman uses)
Everybody Calls It Swing
Sing, Sing, Sing (nuttsy brass section)
Christopher Columbus (theme)

■ MONDAY 12 OCTOBER 1936

RECORDING SESSION

HENRY 'RED' ALLEN
Recording session for Vocalion in New York City.
Henry 'Red' Allen (t/voc); Gene Mikell (cl); Tab Smith (as); Ted McRae (ts); Clyde Hart (p); Danny Barker (g); John Kirby (b); Cozy Cole (d)
Midnight Blue (vHA) / *Lost In My Dreams* (vHA) / *Sitting On The Moon* (vHA) / *Whatcha Gonna Do When There Ain't No Swing?* (vHA)

■ TUESDAY 13 OCTOBER 1936

RADIO LOGS

5:30PM WABC
INSTRUMENTALISTS
CBS Studios, NYC
I'm An Old Cowhand
Blues
Meet Me On The Downbeat
Stompin' Around
Runnin' Wild
Blend Of All Instrumentalists (theme)

9:30PM WABC
BENNY GOODMAN
"Camel Caravan", NYC
Blue Skies (better than recording for Victor: nuttsy trumpet and sax by Rollini)
Organ Grinder Swing (Colossal: nuttsy saxes; swell trumpets; nuttsy trumpet; swell sax by Vido Musso)
When A Lady Meets A Gentleman Down South (vocal: Helen Ward)
Jam Session (new one written and arranged by James Mundy)

■ WEDNESDAY 14 OCTOBER 1936

RECORDING SESSION

JIMMIE LUNCEFORD AND HIS ORCHESTRA
Recording session for Decca in New York City.
Jimmie Lunceford (ldr); Eddie Tompkins, Paul Webster (t); Sy Oliver (t/voc); Elmer Crumbley, Russell Bowles, Eddie Durham (tb); Willie Smith (cl/as/bar/voc); Earl Carruthers (cl/as/bar); Laforet Dent (as); Dan Grissom (cl/as/voc); Joe Thomas (cl/ts); Edwin Wilcox (p); Al Norris (g); Moses Allen (b); Jimmy Crawford (d)
Muddy Water (vTrio) / *I Can't Escape From You* (vDG) / *Harlem Shout*

RADIO LOGS

11:00PM WEAF
GLEN GRAY
Congress Casino, Chicago
Cross Patch (vocal: Pee Wee Hunt)
There's A Small Hotel (vocal: Kenny Sargent)
Dardanella
I Can't Give You Anything But Love (vocal: Connie Boswell)
Boston Tea Party (vocal: Pee Wee Hunt)
Rose Room (great tenor sax by Pat Davis)
Maniac's Ball

11:00PM WABC
BENNY GOODMAN
Hotel Pennsylvania, NYC
Let's Dance (theme)
For Sentimental Reasons (vocal: Helen Ward) (swell new arrangement)
Here's Love In Your Eyes
Did You Mean It? (vocal: Helen Ward) (fair new song)
To Mary With Love
When Buddha Smiles
When Did You Leave Heaven? (vocal: Helen Ward)
Jam Session (Vido Musso's colossal tenor sax; GREAT trumpet solo)
You Turned The Tables On Me (vocal: Helen Ward) (nuttsy)
House Hop

An unusual picture of Benny Goodman, without spectacles, taken at the Hotel Pennsylvania by Hugh Pastoriza.

■ THURSDAY 15 OCTOBER 1936

RECORDING SESSION

LUCKY MILLINDER & MILLS BLUE RHYTHM BAND
Recording session for Columbia in New York City.
Lucky Millinder (voc/ldr); Wardell Jones, Shelton Hemphill, Henry 'Red' Allen (t); George Washington, J.C.Higginbotham (tb); Gene Mikell, Crawford Wethington (cl/as); Tab Smith (as); Joe Garland (cl/ts/bar); Billy Kyle (p); Lawrence Lucie (g); John Kirby (b); O'Neil Spencer (d); Chuck Richards (voc)
Balloonacy / Barrelhouse / The Moon Is Grinning At Me (vCR) */ Showboat Shuffle*

■ FRIDAY 16 OCTOBER 1936

RADIO LOGS

11:45PM WABC
BENNY GOODMAN
Hotel Pennsylvania, NYC
You're Giving Me A Song And A Dance (vocal: Helen Ward)
Love Me Or Leave Me (colossal)
Some Of These Days (BG Trio) (swell)
Picture Me Without You (vocal: Helen Ward) (fair)
Swingtime In The Rockies

12:00 MIDNIGHT WEAF
FLETCHER HENDERSON
Grand Terrace, Chicago
Christopher Columbus (theme)
Swingtime In The Rockies
I Can't Pretend
Milenberg Joys (nice sax team: Chu Berry swell on tenor)
No Regrets (vocal: 'Georgia Boy' Simpkins)
The Stampede (written by Fletcher Henderson)
If We Never Meet Again (vocal: 'Georgia Boy' Simpkins)
When Did You Leave Heaven? (terrible)
Until Today (stinky)
After You've Gone (swell: Buster Bailey on clarinet)
Christopher Columbus (theme)

12:15AM WMCA
STUFF SMITH
Onyx Club, 72 W52nd Street, NYC
Stuff Smith plays a hot violin and Jonah Jones plays a hot trumpet. Counting himself, Stuff has 6 men in his "jam" band.
Christopher Columbus
Star Dust / Love Is The Sweetest Thing / Until The Real Thing Comes Along
Aristocrat Of Harlem
Stuff Stomp

12:30AM WABC
DICK STABILE
Hotel Lincoln, NYC
Unknown title (nuttsy alto sax by Dick Stabile)
Swingtime In The Rockies
A Star Fell Out Of Heaven (vocal: Bert Shaw)
Swamp Fire (Dick Stabile is the nuttsiest soprano sax player)
Two Sides To Every Story (vocal: Bert Shaw)
A Woman Can Change Her Mind
I'm An Old Cowhand (vocal: Dick Stabile)
The Stars Weep (vocal: Bert Shaw)
Midnight Blue
A High Hat, A Piccolo And A Cane (vocal: Dick Stabile & Bert Shaw)
Tea On The Terrace (vocal: Bert Shaw)

SATURDAY 17 OCTOBER 1936

RADIO LOGS

6.45PM WABC
SATURDAY NIGHT SWING SESSION No16
Studio 1, CBS Studios, NYC
I Can't Get Started (theme) (Bunny Berigan on trumpet)
On Wisconsin (Bunny Berigan's alma mater)
Stompin' At The Savoy (Frank Worrell, guitar; colossal saxes; Berigan nuttsy)
Jamboree Jones (vocal: Modernaires) (written by Johnny Mercer)
I'm Tootin' My Horn (marvelous trumpets with Berigan, nice saxes)
I Got Rhythm (Duet: Buddy Sheppard, violin; Frank Worrell, guitar)
In A Little Spanish Town (Berigan on trumpet; nice rhythm section)
Limehouse Blues (colossal sax team: Berigan MARVELOUS on trumpet)
Bye Bye Baby (vocal: Modernaires) (swell)
Three Little Words (Berigan's trumpet; Babe Russin's sax; White's clarinet)
Boston Tea Party (swell)

11:15PM WIXBI
HENRY HALSTEAD
Raymor Ballroom, Boston
Until The Real Thing Comes Along
You'll Have To Swing It
That's A-Plenty
There'll Be Some Changes Made
Tain't No Use

Lucky Millinder Orchestra (below) play Loew's State (16–22nd).

12:30AM WMCA
TOMMY DORSEY
Nixon-Grand Theater, Philadelphia
Peter Piper (vocal: Edythe Wright)
A Star Fell Out Of Heaven (vocal: Jack Leonard)
A High Hat, A Piccolo And A Cane (vocal: Three Esquires)
You Turned The Tables On Me
Trombone Man (specially written for Tommy Dorsey)
Dancing With You (vocal: Three Esquires)
My Blue Heaven
I'll Always Be In Love With You
I Can't Escape From You (vocal: Jack Leonard)

12:35AM WOR
BENNY GOODMAN
Hotel Pennsylvania, NYC
Blue Skies
You Turned The Tables On Me (vocal: Helen Ward)
Jam Session
How Am I To Know? (BG Trio)
Did You Mean It? (vocal: Helen Ward)
Star Dust

■ SUNDAY 18 OCTOBER 1936

RECORDING SESSION

TOMMY DORSEY AND HIS ORCHESTRA
Recording session for Victor in New York City.
Tommy Dorsey (tb); Max Kaminsky, Steve Lipkins, Joe Bauer (t); Ben Pickering, Walter Mercurio (tb); Joe Dixon (cl/as/voc); Clyde Rounds (as); Bud Freeman, Bob Bunch (cl/ts); Dick Jones (p); Carmen Mastren (g); Gene Traxler (b); Dave Tough (d); Edythe Wright, Jack Leonard (voc)
After You've Gone / For Sentimental Reasons (vJL) / *A High Hat, A Piccolo And A Cane* (vTrio) / *Close To Me* (vJL) / *Sleep* / *Another Perfect Night Is Ending* (vJL) / *Maple Leaf Rag*

■ MONDAY 19 OCTOBER 1936

RECORDING SESSION

RED NORVO AND HIS ORCHESTRA
Recording session for Brunswick in New York City.
Red Norvo (xyl/ldr); Bill Hyland, Stew Pletcher, Eddie Meyers (t); Al Mastren (tb); Hank D'Amico (cl/as); Frank Simeone (as); Herbie Haymer (ts); Joe Liss (p); Dave Barbour (g); Pete Peterson (b); Maurice Purtill (d); Mildred Bailey, Lou Hirst (voc)
It Can Happen To You (vMB) / *Now That Summer Is Gone* (vMB) / *Peter Piper* (vMB) / *When Is A Kiss Not A Kiss?* (vLH)

Red Norvo

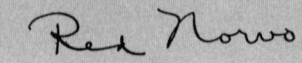

■ TUESDAY 20 OCTOBER 1936

RADIO LOGS

9:30PM WABC
BENNY GOODMAN
"Camel Caravan", NYC
Love Me Or Leave Me (nuttsy: just recorded last month; Musso on sax)
Some Of These Days (BG Trio) (very good: especially Krupa)
Did You Mean It? (vocal: Helen Ward) (swell new song)
Honeysuckle Rose (nice trombone by McEachern; sax by Musso was colossal; great trumpet)

■ WEDNESDAY 21 OCTOBER 1936

RADIO LOGS

11:05PM WABC
BENNY GOODMAN
Hotel Pennsylvania, NYC
Let's Dance (theme)
Down South Camp Meetin' (nuttsy: clarinets, etc)
Midnight Blue (vocal: Helen Ward) (swell new song: Chris Griffin's swell trumpet)
A Fine Romance (COLOSSAL swinging: Krupa's drums; swell trumpet)
I Can't Escape From You (vocal: Helen Ward) (McEachern's trombone)
Here's Love In Your Eyes
Who? (BG Trio)
To Mary With Love
My Gal Sal (one of Goodman's best arrangements: Musso's baritone sax)
You're Giving Me A Song And A Dance (vocal: Helen Ward)

RECORDING SESSION

BILLIE HOLIDAY & TEDDY WILSON ORCHESTRA
Recording session for Brunswick in NYC.
Irving Randolph (t); Vido Musso (cl); Ben Webster (ts); Teddy Wilson (p); Allan Reuss (g); Milt Hinton (b); Gene Krupa (d); Billie Holiday (v)
Easy To Love / With Thee I Swing / The Way You Look Tonight

■ FRIDAY 23 OCTOBER 1936

RADIO LOGS

6:10PM WNEW
TOMMY DORSEY
'Make Believe Ballroom', NYC
When Did You Leave Heaven? (vocal: Edythe Wright)
Maple Leaf Rag (colossal trumpet; clarinet; sax by Bud Freeman)
Midnight Blue (vocal: Jack Leonard)
Sleep (swing tempo: nuttsy bass; nice clarinet)
You're Not The Kind (vocal: Edythe Wright)
In The Groove (original swing song: nuttsy)
I'm Getting Sentimental Over You (theme)

Tommy Dorsey and his orchestra opened at Loew's State today for a one-week run at the Times Square theater.

11:30PM WABC
BENNY GOODMAN
Hotel Pennsylvania, NYC
Let's Dance (theme)
Three Little Words
For Sentimental Reasons (vocal: Helen Ward)
Minnie The Moocher's Wedding Day (colossal: saxes; sax; clarinet)
Picture Me Without You (vocal: Helen Ward)
Tiger Rag (BG Trio) (excellent work by all three, especially Wilson)
Peter Piper (vocal: Helen Ward)
Stompin' At The Savoy (written by Edgar Sampson, introduced by Goodman)
Goody Goody (vocal: Helen Ward) (introduced by Goodman last May)
Sing, Sing, Sing (vocal: Helen Ward) (colossal original arrangement: Krupa's drums)

SATURDAY 24 OCTOBER 1936

I got 3 passes to this week's Swing Session at the CBS Studios, 485 Madison Avenue, so I took Hugh Pastoriza and Harold Johnson in to see it. We went in by train. The guest stars of this broadcast were Claude Thornhill, famous pianist, formerly with Ray Noble and Russ Morgan who is now playing with commercial studio bands such as André Kostelanetz' Chesterfield Band; Tommy Dorsey, greatest trombonist who is now playing a week's engagement at Loew's State Theater, NYC, with his band; Gogo DeLys, CBS woman vocalist. I got the autographs of Raymond Scott (pianist with CBS band), Gogo DeLys, Ward Lay (bassist with CBS Band), Claude Thornhill (guest pianist) and Russ Genner (trombone). I couldn't get Tommy Dorsey's autograph because he left too soon. I didn't get the autographs of Johnny Augustine (director of band), one sax player, and one trumpet player.

Gogo DeLys

6.45PM WABC
SATURDAY NIGHT SWING SESSION No17
Studio 1, CBS Studios, NYC
I Can't Get Started (theme) (Bunny Berigan's trumpet; directed by Johnny Augustine)
Roar, Lion, Roar (nuttsy swing arrangement of Columbia's song: nuttsy bass)
Organ Grinders' Swing (best arrangement I ever heard of this favorite song by Will Hudson: Johnny Williams on drums; 3 clarinets; 4 muted trumpets; Hank Ross on tenor and Bunny Berigan on trumpet were colossal.)
I'm Getting Sentimental Over You (Tommy Dorsey on trombone)
That's A-Plenty (Williams, drums; Dorsey, trombone; Berigan, trumpet & sax team were marvelous)
We've Got The Same Kind Of Rhythm (Gogo DeLys singing a new rhythm number)
Bach Invention (as original) (Claude Thornhill on piano)
Bach Invention (with swing) (Claude Thornhill on piano: nuttsy)
Chopin's Waltz in B Minor (as original) (Claude Thornhill on piano)
Chopin's Waltz in B Minor (with swing) (Claude Thornhill on piano: colossal)
Mendelssohn's Caprice (with and without swing) (Claude Thornhill on piano)
Flight Of The Bumble Bee (Claude Thornhill on piano; 4 trumpets; saxes; drums)
Can't We Be Friends (Claude Thornhill on vibraphone with band)
Loveless Love (Bunny Berigan trumpet solo: super-colossal)
After You've Gone (Berigan's trumpet; Dorsey's trombone; Thornhill's piano; Lay's bass; Worrell's guitar; Williams' drums)
By Heck (nice arrangement of swell old tune: nice clarinet, bass)

11:30PM WJZ
RAY NOBLE
Rainbow Room, NYC
Band includes Charlie Spivak (t); Will Bradley (tb); Glenn Miller (tb); Johnny Mince
By The Fireside (theme)
When I'm With You (vocal: Al Bowlly)
'Way Down Yonder In New Orleans
There's Something In The Air
Did You Mean It?
Talking To My Heart (vocal: Al Bowlly)
Chinatown, My Chinatown
Goodnight Sweetheart (closing theme)

12:30AM WMCA
LUCKY MILLINDER
Nixon-Grand Theater, Philadelphia
Swell. Saw them last month. Band includes Red Allen (t); George Washington (tb); J. C. Higginbotham (tb); Tab Smith (as); Billy Kyle (p); Lawrence Lucie (g); John Kirby (b); O'Neil Spencer (d)
Star Dust (theme) (whole band singing)
Lucky Swings Out (written by Lucky Millinder: nuttsy)
The Moon Is Grinning At Me (vocal: Chuck Richards)
I'll Be Loving You Always (vocal: Talmadge 'Tab' Smith)
Until The Real Thing Comes Along (vocal: Chuck Richards)
St. Louis Wiggle Rhythm (great sax; piano by Billy Kyle)
Mood Indigo (marvelous slow-swing tenor sax)
Red Rhythm (original number written for Henry 'Red' Allen)

12:30AM WOR
BENNY GOODMAN
Hotel Pennsylvania, NYC
Helen Ward's last night with the band for a couple of weeks as she heads off to Reno for a divorce.
Let's Dance (theme)
I Know That You Know
Midnight Blue (vocal: Helen Ward)
Star Dust
Sing, Baby, Sing (vocal: Helen Ward)
Sometimes I'm Happy (smoothest and yet hottest arrangement)
Walk, Jennie, Walk
It's Been So Long (vocal: Helen Ward)
King Porter Stomp
You're Not The Kind (vocal: Helen Ward)

1:00AM WOR
LEON BELASCO
Hotel Netherland-Plaza, Cincinnati
Here's Love In Your Eyes
If We Never Meet Again (vocal: Lavern Andrews)
Speakeasy
Papa Tree Top Tall (vocal: Lavern Andrews)

■ MONDAY 26 OCTOBER 1936

RECORDING SESSION

JIMMIE LUNCEFORD AND HIS ORCHESTRA
Recording session for Decca in New York City.
Jimmie Lunceford (ldr); Eddie Tompkins, Paul Webster (t); Sy Oliver (t/voc); Elmer Crumbley, Russell Bowles, Eddie Durham (tb); Willie Smith (cl/as/bar/voc); Earl Carruthers (cl/as/bar); Laforet Dent (as); Dan Grissom (cl/as/voc); Joe Thomas (cl/ts); Edwin Wilcox (p); Al Norris (g); Moses Allen (b); Jimmy Crawford (d)
This Is My Last Affair (vDG) / *Running A Temperature* (vSO)

■ TUESDAY 27 OCTOBER 1936

RECORDING SESSION

MIKE RILEY, EDDIE FARLEY & THEIR ONYX CLUB BOYS
Recording session for Decca in New York City.
Eddie Farley (t); Mike Riley (tb/voc); unknown cl, p, g, b, d
Trouble Don't Like Music (vMR) / *A High Hat, A Piccolo And A Cane* (vMR) / *Hey, Hey* (vMR) / *With Thee I Swing* (vMR)

RADIO LOGS

9:30PM WABC
BENNY GOODMAN
Camel Caravan program, NYC
'Camel Caravan' is a one-hour program broadcast every Tuesday night and sponsored by Camel cigarettes. Benny Goodman and Georgie Stoll furnish the music and guest stars appear each week. Rupert Hughes is the master of ceremonies. This series started last June.
I Got Rhythm (colossal: Krupa's drums; Musso's sax; Stacy's piano; 2 trombones)
Jam Session (written by Jimmy Mundy: Musso's sax; trumpet)
Tiger Rag (BG Trio)
Alexander's Ragtime Band

■ THURSDAY 29 OCTOBER 1936

RECORDING SESSION

CHICK WEBB ORCHESTRA
Recording session for Decca in New York City.
Ella Fitzgerald (voc); Mario Bauza, Taft Jordan, Bobby Stark (t); Sandy Williams, Nat Story (tb); Louis Jordan, Pete Clark (as); Ted McRae (ts), Wayman Carver (ts/fl); Tommy Fulford (p); John Trueheart (g); Beverly Peer (b); Chick Webb (d)
(If You Can't Sing It) You'll Have To Swing It (vEF) / *Swinging On The Reservation* (vEF) / *I've Got The Spring Fever Blues* (vEF) / *Vote For Mr. Rhythm* (vEF)

RADIO LOGS

6.00PM WNEW
CAB CALLOWAY
Make Believe Ballroom, NYC
Make Believe Ballroom is a program broadcast daily from 5 to 7pm. Every night, Martin Block plays records and has an orchestra or individual as a guest once a week. Cab Calloway and his band are now playing at the New Cotton Club which just opened up last month. Cab and his band seem to be making a great comeback with such guys as Keg Johnson on trombone, etc.
Make Believe Ballroom (vocal: Cab Calloway) (nice clarinets; guitar; sax)
Copper Colored Gal (vocal: Cab Calloway) (from *Cotton Club Parade of 1936*)
Until The Real Thing Comes Along (vocal: Bennie Payne)
Sweet Sue (vocal: Cab Calloway) (smooth brass with clarinets; swell bass)
I Ain't Got Nobody (vocal: Cab Calloway) (nuttsy: guitar; saxes; etc)
The Hi-De-Ho Miracle Man (vocal: Cab Calloway) (from *Cotton Club Parade of 1936*)
Sylvia (vocal: Bennie Payne) (nice trumpet and saxes)
Some Of These Days (vocal: Cab Calloway) (Johnson's trombone; guitar; clarinet)
Minnie The Moocher (vocal: Cab Calloway) (opening & closing theme written by Cab Calloway)

■ FRIDAY 30 OCTOBER 1936

RECORDING SESSION

ART SHAW AND HIS ORCHESTRA
Recording session for Brunswick in New York City.
Art Shaw (cl/ldr); Lee Castle, Zeke Zarchy (t); Mike Michaels (tb); Tony Pastor (ts/voc), Jerry Gray, Frank Siegfield (vln); Sam Persoff (vla); Bill Schumann (cello); Joe Lippman (p); Tony Gattuso (g); Ben Ginsberg (b); George Wettling (d); Peg La Centra (voc)
The Skeleton In The Closet / *There's Something In The Air* (vPLC) / *Take Another Guess* (vPLC) / *There's Frost On The Moon* (vPLC)

RADIO LOGS

11:30PM WABC
BENNY GOODMAN
Hotel Pennsylvania, NYC
Let's Dance (theme)
I Would Do Anything For You
When Did You Leave Heaven? (vocal: Margaret McCrae)
Minnie The Moocher's Wedding Day (nice saxes with trumpets)
For Sentimental Reasons (vocal: Margaret McCrae)
When Buddha Smiles (colossal saxes: nice tenor solo by Arthur Rollini)
China Boy (BG Trio)
When A Lady Meets A Gentleman Down South (vocal: Margaret McCrae)
I Can't Escape From You (vocal: Margaret McCrae)
Down South Camp Meetin'

Margaret McCrae (above) sings with the Benny Goodman Band at the Pennsylvania while Helen Ward (left) obtains a divorce in Reno.

■ SATURDAY 31 OCTOBER 1936

RADIO LOGS

12.00 NOON WABC
THE CAPTIVATORS
CBS Studios, NYC
I'm Talking To My Heart
Swing, Swing Mother-in-Law
The Stars Weep
I'm In A Dancing Mood

4.45PM WABC
MERRY MAKERS
CBS Studios, NYC
When Did You Leave Heaven?
Let's Take A Trip To Jamaica
Who?
I'm Tootin' My Horn
I Would Sing To The Moon

6.45PM WABC
SATURDAY NIGHT SWING SESSION No18
Studio 1, CBS Studios, NYC
Johnny Augustine conducted the CBS Band. Announcer: Dan Seymour. Produced by Phil Cohan and Ed Cashman.
I Can't Get Started (theme) (Bunny Berigan on trumpet)
March, March On Down The Field (Yale's song in nuttsy swing style; colossal saxes; Berigan great)
Stop, Look, And Listen (COLOSSAL: Frank Worrell's guitar; trombones)
Did You Mean It? (Blue Flames [3 girls, 1 man] singing: good)
Livery Stable Blues (Original Dixieland Jazz Band: Nick LaRocca (t); Russel Robinson (p); Larry Shields (cl); Eddie Edwards (tb); Tony Sbarbaro (d). 5-piece band started in 1908; couldn't read music then; disbanded in 1924 but are now back together with a 14-piece band recording for Victor.)
Tiger Rag (14-piece Dixieland band)
There Goes My Attraction (Blue Flames singing)
Dardanella (Berigan's muted trumpet; great saxes; drums by Johnny Williams)
Down By The Old Mill Stream (Bunny Berigan trumpet solo: swing style)
Runnin' Wild (swell brass: Russ Genner on trombone; Berigan colossal)

12.00 MIDNIGHT WABC
TOMMY DORSEY
Levaggi's, Boston
Colossal.
That's A-Plenty
Stop, Look, And Listen
Dancing With You (vocal: Jack Leonard)
In The Groove

■ TUESDAY 3 NOVEMBER 1936 (ELECTION DAY)

RADIO LOGS

9:30PM WABC
BENNY GOODMAN
Camel Caravan program, NYC
Bugle Call Rag (COLOSSAL: new arrangement with Benny's clarinet; Krupa's drums; McEachern's trombone; Musso's sax; Bose's trumpet)
Swingtime In The Rockies (better than the recording, especially Benny; Krupa; Bose)

■ WEDNESDAY 4 NOVEMBER 1936

RADIO LOGS

11:00PM WABC
BENNY GOODMAN
Hotel Pennsylvania, NYC
I Found A New Baby
I Would Do Anything For You
Here's Love In Your Eyes
There's Something In The Air (vocal: Margaret McCrae)
Sometimes I'm Happy (colossal: great trumpet, sax, and clarinet)
Body And Soul (BG Trio) (Teddy Wilson does the best work on this piece)
It's De-Lovely (vocal: Margaret McCrae)
In A Sentimental Mood (nice trumpet and trombone)
Did You Mean It? (vocal: Margaret McCrae)
Jam Session

■ THURSDAY 5 NOVEMBER 1936

RECORDING SESSION

BENNY GOODMAN AND HIS ORCHESTRA
Recording session for Victor in New York City.
Benny Goodman (cl); Chris Griffin, Zeke Zarchy, Ziggy Elman (t); Red Ballard, Murray McEachern (tb); Bill DePew, Hymie Shertzer (as); Art Rollini, Vido Musso (ts); Jess Stacy (p); Allan Reuss (g); Harry Goodman (b); Gene Krupa (d); Ella Fitzgerald (voc)
Somebody Loves Me / *'Tain't No Use* (vBG) / *Bugle Call Rag* / *Jam Session* / *Goodnight, My Love* (vEF) / *Take Another Guess* (vEF) / *Did You Mean It?* (vEF)

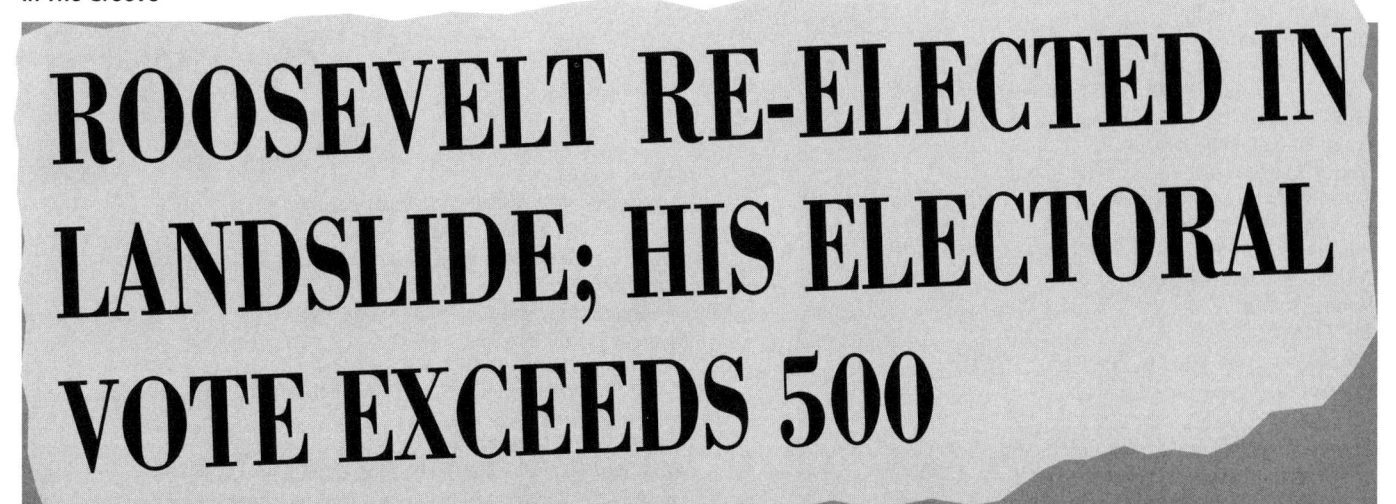

ROOSEVELT RE-ELECTED IN LANDSLIDE; HIS ELECTORAL VOTE EXCEEDS 500

■ FRIDAY 6 NOVEMBER 1936

RECORDING SESSION

WOODY HERMAN AND HIS ORCHESTRA
Recording session for Decca in New York City.
Woody Herman (cl/as/voc/ldr); Clarence Willard, Kermit Simmons (t); Joe Bishop (fh); Neal Reid (tb); Murray Williams, Don Watt (as); Saxie Mansfield, Bruce Wilkins (ts); Nick Hupfer (vln); Horace Diaz (p); Chick Reeves (g); Walter Yoder (b); Frank Carlson (d)
Wintertime Dreams (vWH) / *Someone To Care For Me* (vWH)

RADIO LOGS

11.00PM WJZ
COUNT BASIE
Grand Terrace, Chicago
This is the first broadcast by Count Basie. He has a comparatively new band. It is very good but a little ragged.
Streamline Strut (swell piano; clarinet; Basie plays the piano)
I'll Always Be In Love With You (nice trombone; clarinet)
I Surrender Dear (vocal: Jimmy Rushing)

11.15PM WABC
MAL HALLETT
Hotel Commodore, NYC
Copper Colored Gal
Chapel In The Moonlight (vocal: Jerry Perkins w Glee Club)
There's Something In The Air (vocal: Buddy Welcome)
I Want The Whole World To Know I Love You (vocal: Jerry Perkins)
Moonlight On The Chesapeake (vocal: Jerry Perkins)
We're In The Money (vocal: Jerry Perkins) (swell)
Boston Tea Party (original theme)

11.30PM WABC
BENNY GOODMAN
Hotel Pennsylvania, NYC
Let's Dance (theme)
Alexander's Ragtime Band (just recorded for Victor last week)
If We Never Meet Again (nice sax and trumpet)
Oh, Lady Be Good (too slow: nice tenor by Musso and drums by Krupa)
You Turned The Tables On Me (vocal: Margaret McCrae)
I Got Rhythm (colossal: Stacy's piano; Krupa's drums; Musso's swell tenor)
Until The Real Thing Comes Along (vocal: Margaret McCrae)
Star Dust
Who? (BG Trio)
Picture Me Without You (vocal: Margaret McCrae)
Walk, Jennie, Walk

12.00 MIDNIGHT WOR
CLAUDE HOPKINS
Roseland Ballroom, NYC
I Would Do Anything For You (opening & closing theme)
Mr Ghost Goes To Town (written by Will Hudson)
Make Believe Ballroom
Singin' In The Rain
When Did You Leave Heaven? (vocal: Marjorie Rank)
Somebody Loves Me (vocal: Fred Norman) (swell trumpet; bass)
King Porter Stomp (nice sax team; trumpet)
Too Much Imagination (vocal: Marjorie Rank)
Hodge-Podge
Aw, Shucks!
I Would Do Anything For You (closing theme)

12.20AM WMCA
STUFF SMITH
Onyx Club, 72 W52nd Street, NYC
Swell. WHAT JAMMING!
If We Never Meet Again
Organ Grinder's Swing
I'se A-Muggin' (theme)

1.45AM WMCA
TEDDY HILL
Savoy Ballroom, NYC
Stompin' At The Savoy
I Never Knew
When Did You Leave Heaven?
Symphony In Riffs
Three Little Words (Sam Allen at the piano)
Down Home Rag
I Can't Escape From You
Paradise (nuttsy sax team)
Deep Forest

■ SATURDAY 7 NOVEMBER 1936

I got 2 old tickets to see this week's broadcast but Hughie and I couldn't get to see it because we got there 5 minutes late. We listened to it in a taxicab outside the studios. Afterwards we got the autographs of Loretta Lee and Earl Hines, famed colored pianist, who were guests on the program. Earl Hines and his Orchestra are now playing a week's engagement at the Apollo Theater, 125th St, NYC, and are next going to Troy, NY and then to the Grand Terrace in Chicago. He is one swell guy. We also talked to Hank Ross, tenor sax in CBS band. He said that he used to play with Rubinoff, Roger Wolfe Kahn and Benny Goodman. He recorded 'Moonglow' with Goodman, on Columbia. Babe Russin has left the CBS band. His place was taken by George Van Eps, present sax with Ray Noble.

6.45PM WABC
SATURDAY NIGHT SWING SESSION No19
Studio 1, CBS Studios, NYC
I Can't Get Started (opening theme) (Bunny Berigan on trumpet)
Across The Field
My Melancholy Baby
Rosetta (EARL HINES)
Dodging A Divorcee (Dave Wade, trumpet)
Half Of Me (Truckin' On Sunday Night) (LORETTA LEE singing)
Wolverine Blues (The Breakdown Eight)
There's A Small Hotel
After You've Gone (EARL HINES on piano: colossal)
Three Little Words (The Breakdown Eight, featuring Babe Russin)
Swing, Swing Mother-in-Law (LORETTA LEE singing: Dave Wade on trumpet; Lou Shoobe on bass)

MONDAY 9 NOVEMBER 1936

RECORDING SESSION

JONES-SMITH INCORPORATED
Recording session for Vocalion in Chicago.
Carl 'Tatti' Smith (t); Lester Young (ts); Count Basie (p); Walter Page (b); Jo Jones (d); Jimmy Rushing (voc)
Shoe Shine Boy (2 takes) / *Evenin'* (vJR) / *Boogie Woogie* (vJR) / *Oh, Lady Be Good*

MILDRED BAILEY & HER ORCHESTRA
Recording session for Vocalion in NYC.
Ziggy Elman (t); Art Shaw° (cl); Johnny Hodges* (as); Francis Lowe (ts); Teddy Wilson (p); Dave Barbour (g); John Kirby (b); Cozy Cole (d); Mildred Bailey (v)
°*For Sentimental Reasons* (vMB) / °**It's Love I'm After* (vMB) / °*'Long About Midnight* (vMB) / *More Than You Know* (vMB)

TUESDAY 10 NOVEMBER 1936

RECORDING SESSION

WOODY HERMAN AND HIS ORCHESTRA
Recording session for Decca in New York City.
Woody Herman (cl/as/voc/ldr); Clarence Willard, Kermit Simmons (t); Joe Bishop (fh); Neal Reid (tb); Murray Williams, Don Watt (as); Saxie Mansfield, Bruce Wilkins (ts); Nick Hupfer (vln); Horace Diaz (p); Chick Reeves (g); Walter Yoder (b); Frank Carlson (d)
The Goose Hangs High (vWH) / *Now That Summer is Gone* (vWH) / *I Can't Pretend* (vWH) / *Old-Fashioned Swing* (vWH)

Cynthia Doyle, Barbara Stuart, Cynthia Lake, Nancy Long, Harvey Pinger, Dick Morningstar, Hugh Pastoriza and I went into NYC on the 6:14pm train to see Benny Goodman in the Madhattan Room at the Hotel Pennsylvania. We each paid $2 for a dinner. Mr. Pastoriza was chaperon. We stayed there from 6:45 until 11:20. Teddy Wilson played during intermissions.

The Trio (Goodman, Wilson & Krupa) played: *Nobody's Sweetheart; Someday Sweetheart;* and *Who?* Goodman and the band had to broadcast over the Camel Caravan at 9:30 so they were absent for about an hour. Bert Block and his Band substituted and were pretty good. I got autographs of most of Goodman's Band.

RADIO LOGS

9:30PM WABC
BENNY GOODMAN
Camel Caravan program, NYC
You Turned The Tables On Me (vocal: Ella Fitzgerald)
House Hop
Who? (BG Trio)

12.30AM WMCA
CHICK WEBB
Savoy Ballroom, NYC
Chick Webb, Negro drummer, has one of the finest swing bands in the country today. Ella Fitzgerald is an unsurpassable vocalist. Webb is going to play opposite Lucky Millinder at the Savoy next week.
Memphis Blues
Spring Fever Blues (vocal: Ella Fitzgerald)
Go Harlem (great sax & trombone: nice drumming by Chick Webb)
Down Home Rag
Vote For Mr Rhythm (vocal: Ella Fitzgerald)
I May Be Wrong (vocal: Taft Jordan) (nice trumpet; sax)
Stop, Look, And Listen
Royal Garden Blues
Stompin' At The Savoy (closing theme played in its entirety)

WEDNESDAY 11 NOVEMBER 1936

RADIO LOGS

11:00PM WABC
BENNY GOODMAN
Hotel Pennsylvania, NYC
Three Little Words (McEachern's trombone; Musso's tenor sax)
To Mary With Love (nice trombone and trumpet)
You Can Tell She Comes From Dixie (vocal: Margaret McCrae) (lousy)
Sing, Baby, Sing (lousy)
If We Never Meet Again (nice trumpet; saxes, etc)
There's Something In The Air (vocal: Margaret McCrae)
Some Of These Days (BG Trio) (they use the same introduction on all songs)
Darktown Strutters' Ball (swell: 5 clarinets)
Midnight Blue (vocal: Margaret McCrae)
Love Me Or Leave Me (nuttsy: Musso; Stacy; Reuss, etc)

11.30PM WMCA
EARL HINES
Apollo Theater, NYC
Swell.
Cavernism (theme)
I Know That You Know (nuttsy trumpets; great piano)
When Did You Leave Heaven?

11.30PM WEAF
GLEN GRAY
Congress Hotel, Chicago
Good.
Smoke Rings (theme) (written by Clarence Hutchenrider, clarinetist)
Through The Courtesy Of Love (vocal: Kenny Sargent)
Skeleton In The Closet (vocal: Pee Wee Hunt)
So Do I (vocal: Kenny Sargent)
Swing Low, Sweet Chariot
Tain't Good, Like A Nickel Made Of Wood (vocal: Pee Wee Hunt)
Rhythm Of The River (written by Clarence Hutchenrider, clarinetist)
Chant Of The Jungle

12.00 MIDNIGHT WJZ
COUNT BASIE
Grand Terrace, Chicago
Marvelous piano playing by Count Basie.
Moten Swing (opening theme)
The South Side Stomp
Tea For Two
The Glory Of Love (vocal: Jimmy Rushing)
Shout And Do It
But Definitely
Hot Coffee
Yeah, Man!

12.00 MIDNIGHT WOR
CAB CALLOWAY
Cotton Club, NYC
Good.
The Wedding Of Mr And Mrs Swing (vocal: Cab Calloway)
Did I Remember? (vocal: Bennie Payne)
Make Believe Ballroom (vocal: Cab Calloway)
When You're Smiling (vocal: Cab Calloway)
The Beggar (vocal: Bennie Payne)
Save Me Sister
I've Got You Under My Skin (vocal: Cab Calloway)
Get A Little Closer, Babe

THURSDAY 12 NOVEMBER 1936

RADIO LOGS

6.35PM WNEW
CHARLIE BARNET
Make Believe Ballroom, NYC
Nuttsy.
Milk Man's Matinee (vocal: Modernaires)
Dixieland Band (vocal: Charlie Barnet)
Until The Real Thing Comes Along (vocal: Charlie Barnet)
King Porter Stomp (colossal tenor sax by Barnet; trumpet by Irving Goodman)
Make Believe Ballroom (vocal: Modernaires) (program theme)

11.00PM WABC
ART SHAW
French Casino, NYC
Nightmare (opening & closing theme)
The Way You Look Tonight
Summertime (vocal: Peg LaCentra)
Take Another Guess (vocal: Tony Pastor)
You're Giving Me A Song And A Dance (vocal: Peg LaCentra)
In A Sentimental Mood
There's Something In The Air (vocal: Peg LaCentra)
Skeleton In The Closet (nuttsy drums; trumpet; sax by Pastor)
Darling, Not Without You (vocal: Peg LaCentra)
At Sundown (great: drums; trumpet; sax and clarinet by Art Shaw)

11.15PM WOR
MAL HALLETT
Hotel Commodore, NYC
Terrible on sweet numbers. Good on swing tunes. Stuart Anderson (sax), Buddy Welcome (sax), Joe Carbonaro (bass), Charlie Blake (drums), and Frank Ryerson (tpt) are the good guys in the band.
Make Believe Ballroom
Swing Fever (vocal: Buddy Welcome)
Darling, Not Without You / Lonesome Guitar / I Would Sing To The Moon
There's Something In The Air (vocal: Buddy Welcome)
Did I Remember? (vocal: Jerry Perkins)

Frank Ryerson

Stuart Anderson

11.15PM WAAB
RED NICHOLS
Raymor Ballroom, Boston
Wail Of The Winds (original opening and closing theme)
South Sea Island Magic
Midnight Blue
Sing Me A Swing Song (vocal: The Songcopators)
Darling, Not Without You
There's Music In The Air
Jamboree Jones

12:00 MIDNIGHT WOR
BENNY GOODMAN
Hotel Pennsylvania, NYC
Swingtime In The Rockies (great drumming; Musso's tenor sax; Elman's trumpet)
Goodnight My Love (vocal: Margaret McCrae)
St. Louis Blues (nuttsy: Benny's best clarinet work; Krupa; Zarchy's trumpet)
Tain't No Use (vocal: Benny Goodman) (marvelous trumpet; Benny's funny singing)
When Did You Leave Heaven? (vocal: Margaret McCrae)
After You've Gone (BG Trio) (great work by all 3, especially Benny)
On The Alamo (smooth saxes with piano: slow clarinet)
It's De-Lovely (vocal: Margaret McCrae) (swell new song)
If We Never Meet Again (trumpet; Musso's tenor)

■ FRIDAY 13 NOVEMBER 1936
RADIO LOGS
11.15PM WOR
MAL HALLETT
Hotel Commodore, NYC
Honeysuckle Rose (colossal, nuttsy)
Easy To Love (vocal: Jerry Perkins)
Where The Lazy River Goes By (vocal: Buddy Welcome)
I've Got Something In My Eye
Talking To My Heart (vocal: Jerry Perkins)
It's Love I'm After
South Sea Island Magic (vocal: Clark Yocum & Glee Club)
Boston Tea Party (theme) (written by trumpeter Frank Ryerson)

11.30PM WMCA
CHICK WEBB
Savoy Ballroom, NYC
Great.
'Way Down Yonder In New Orleans (colossal: tenor; trumpet & drums)
You've Got To Swing It (vocal: Ella Fitzgerald)
Boston Tea Party (nice tenor)
Don't Be That Way
When Did You Leave Heaven?
Honeysuckle Rose (vocal: Ella Fitzgerald) (marvelous)
Organ Grinder's Swing
Confessin' (vocal: Taft Jordan)
Stompin' At The Savoy (closing theme) (written by Edgar Sampson)

11.35PM WJZ
GLEN GRAY
Congress Hotel, Chicago
Swell.
Pennies From Heaven (vocal: Kenny Sargent)
Papa Tree Top Tall (vocal: Pee Wee Hunt)
For Sentimental Reasons (vocal: Kenny Sargent)
Jazz Me Blues
Out Of Space
Beale Street Blues (vocal: Pee Wee Hunt)
Casa Loma Stomp (marvelous trombone; sax by Pat Davis)
Smoke Rings (theme) (written by clarinetist Clarence Hutchenrider)

■ SATURDAY 14 NOVEMBER 1936
RADIO LOGS
11:00PM WABC
BENNY GOODMAN
Hotel Pennsylvania, NYC
Helen Ward returned to the band tonight.
Let's Dance (theme)
I Know That You Know
You're Giving Me A Song And A Dance (vocal: Helen Ward)
There's Something In The Air
In A Sentimental Mood (Chris Griffin's trumpet)
Peter Piper (vocal: Helen Ward)
Tiger Rag (BG Trio) (excellent: Benny playing in lower register; Krupa)
For Sentimental Reasons (vocal: Helen Ward)
When Buddha Smiles
More Than You Know (BG Trio) (excellent work by Teddy Wilson)

12.00 MIDNIGHT WJZ
GLEN GRAY
Congress Hotel, Chicago
Smoke Rings (theme) (recorded for Brunswick)
Casino Capers (lousy)
The Night We Met (vocal: Kenny Sargent) (fair)
Between The Devil And The Deep Blue Sea (vocal: Pee Wee Hunt)
Love Is A Powerful Thing (vocal: Kenny Sargent)
Shades Of Hades (nuttsy)

Star Dust
Bye Bye Baby (vocal: Pee Wee Hunt)
Bugle Call Rag (marvelous, colossal: best arrangement)

12.10AM WEAF
COUNT BASIE
Grand Terrace, Chicago
Yeah, Man! (marvelous: trumpet; drums; piano by Count Basie, etc)
Christopher Columbus
Confessin' (vocal: Jimmy Rushing)
Dear Old Southland
Rhythm In My Nursery Rhymes (vocal: Jimmy Rushing)

12.45AM WOR
CLAUDE HOPKINS
Roseland Ballroom, NYC
I Would Do Anything For You (theme)
Soft Horn
When I'm With You

1.30AM WBBM
ROY ELDRIDGE
Three Deuces, Chicago
King Porter Stomp (trumpet by Eldridge; alto by Scoops Carry)
That Thing (nice bass by Charles 'Truck' Parham)
China Boy (Zutty Singleton's drums; David Young on tenor sax)
Heckler's Hop (marvelous trumpet by Roy Eldridge; Singleton's drums)

■ MONDAY 16 NOVEMBER 1936

RADIO LOGS

9.15PM WAAB
BERT BLOCK
Raymor Ballroom, Boston
Moonglow (theme) (written by Will Hudson: swell)
I'll Sing You A Thousand Love Songs
Did I Remember? (vocal: Bill Johnson)
You Turned The Tables On Me (vocal: Bill Hitchcock)
Dream Awhile

9.30PM WJZ
TOMMY DORSEY
KOOL Program, NYC
Bye Bye Baby
Star Dust
Happy As The Day Is Long

11.30PM WJZ
COUNT BASIE
Grand Terrace, Chicago
Moten Swing (theme)
Jangled Nerves
Ebony Rhapsody
Boogie Woogie
Shout And Scream
House Hop
The Glory Of Love (vocal: Jimmy Rushing)
Harlem Shout
Moten Swing (theme)

■ TUESDAY 17 NOVEMBER 1936

RECORDING SESSION

HENRY 'RED' ALLEN
Recording session for Vocalion in New York City.
Henry 'Red' Allen (t/voc); Gene Mikell (cl); Tab Smith (as); Cecil Scott (ts); Clyde Hart (p); Danny Barker (g); John Kirby (b); Cozy Cole (d)
Did You Mean It? (vHA) / *In The Chapel In The Moonlight* (vHA) / *Here's Love In Your Eye* (vHA) / *When My Dreamboat Comes Home* (vHA)

RADIO LOGS

9.00PM ?
DICK STABILE SEXTET
Ben Bernie Program, NYC
Star Dust

9.30PM WABC
BENNY GOODMAN
Camel Caravan program, NYC
Dinah (BG Quartet) (excellent)
Sugar Foot Stomp (COLOSSAL: great trumpet; saxes; Krupa)
You're Giving Me A Song And A Dance (vocal: Helen Ward) (nuttsy new song recorded 3 weeks ago: nice trumpet)
Down South Camp Meetin' (swell trumpet; saxes; 5 clarinets)

■ WEDNESDAY 18 NOVEMBER 1936

RECORDING SESSION

BENNY GOODMAN QUARTET
Recording session for Victor in New York City.
Lionel Hampton (vib); Teddy Wilson (p); Benny Goodman (cl); Gene Krupa (d)
Sweet Sue, Just You / *My Melancholy Baby* / *Tiger Rag*

ELLA FITZGERALD AND HER SAVOY EIGHT
Recording session for Decca in New York City.
Ella Fitzgerald (voc); Taft Jordan (t); Sandy Williams (tb); Pete Clark (cl); Teddy McRae (ts/bar); Tommy Fulford (p); John Trueheart (g); Beverly Peer (b); Chick Webb (d)
My Last Affair / *Organ Grinder's Swing*

TOMMY DORSEY AND HIS ORCHESTRA
Recording session for Victor in New York City.
Tommy Dorsey (tb); Max Kaminsky, Steve Lipkins, Joe Bauer (t); Ben Pickering, Walter Mercurio (tb); Joe Dixon (cl/as/voc); Clyde Rounds (as); Bud Freeman, Bob Bunch (cl/ts); Dick Jones (p); Carmen Mastren (g); Gene Traxler (b); Dave Tough (d); Edythe Wright, Jack Leonard (voc)
Head Over Heels In Love (vEW) / *May I Have The Next Romance With You?* (vJL) / *Where Are You?* (vJL) / *That Foolish Feeling* (vEW) / *There's Frost On The Moon* (vEW)

RADIO LOGS

11:00PM WABC
BENNY GOODMAN
Hotel Pennsylvania, NYC
This is possibly Lionel Hampton's first broadcast with the band.
Jingle Bells (fair: trumpet; Musso's sax)
Goodnight My Love (vocal: Helen Ward) (just recorded this month)
Oh, Lady Be Good (swell: trombone team; Musso's sax)
Take Another Guess (vocal: Helen Ward)
My Melancholy Baby (swell: saxes; trumpets; Musso's sax)
I Got Rhythm (nuttsy: trumpets; Musso's sax; Elman's trumpet)

NOVEMBER 1936

Easy To Love (Jess Stacy's piano, etc)
Between The Devil And The Deep Blue Sea (vocal: Helen Ward)
Exactly Like You (BG Quartet) (Lionel Hampton singing and playing vibes)
Riffin' At The Ritz (nuttsy: saxes)

11.30PM WHN
WOODY HERMAN
Brooklyn Roseland
Royal Garden Blues (clarinet)
Rose Room (sax by Saxie Mansfield)
Old Fashioned Swing (trombone)
I've Got You Under My Skin
Basin Street Blues (vocal: Woody Herman)

■ THURSDAY 19 NOVEMBER 1936

RECORDING SESSION

BILLIE HOLIDAY & TEDDY WILSON ORCHESTRA
Recording session for Brunswick in NYC.
Jonah Jones (t); Benny Goodman (cl); Ben Webster (ts); Teddy Wilson (p); Allan Reuss (g); John Kirby (b); Cozy Cole (d); Billie Holiday (v)
Pennies From Heaven / That's Life I Guess / I Can't Give You Anything But Love

ELLA FITZGERALD AND HER SAVOY EIGHT
Recording session for Decca in New York City.
Ella Fitzgerald (voc); Taft Jordan (t); Sandy Williams (tb); Pete Clark (cl); Teddy McRae (ts/bar); Tommy Fulford (p); John Trueheart (g); Beverly Peer (b); Chick Webb (d)
Shine / Darktown Strutters' Ball

■ FRIDAY 20 NOVEMBER 1936

RECORDING SESSION

LUCKY MILLINDER & MILLS BLUE RHYTHM BAND
Recording session for Columbia in New York City.
Lucky Millinder (voc/ldr); Wardell Jones, Shelton Hemphill, Henry 'Red' Allen (t); George Washington, J.C.Higginbotham (tb); Gene Mikell, Crawford Wethington (cl/as); Tab Smith (as); Joe Garland (cl/ts/bar); Billy Kyle (p); Lawrence Lucie (g); John Kirby (b); O'Neil Spencer (d); Chuck Richards (voc)
Big John Special / Mr. Ghost Goes To Town / Callin' Your Bluff / Algiers Stomp

RADIO LOGS

1.50AM WBBM
ROY ELDRIDGE
Three Deuces, Chicago
Shoe Shine Boy
Basin Street Blues
Nagasaki
You Can Depend On Me (vocal: Gladys Palmer)
Bugle Blues (marvelous trumpet by Roy)
A High Hat, A Piccolo, And A Cane
I Got Rhythm

■ SATURDAY 21 NOVEMBER 1936

Dick Morningstar and I went to New York City by Subway to see this week's Swing Session. We just got there in time. Will Hudson (composer, arranger, and orchestra leader), Margaret McCrae (vocalist), and part of Lucky Millinder's Band (Henry 'Red' Allen: trumpet, Tab Smith: alto sax, sax, piano) were the guests. Got the autographs of Mark Warnow (director of CBS band), Lou Shoobe (bass in CBS band), Pete Pumiglio (sax in CBS band), Dave Hamilton (sax in CBS band), Will Hudson, Henry 'Red' Allen, and Lucky Millinder.

6.45PM WABC
SATURDAY NIGHT SWING SESSION No20
Studio 1, CBS Studios, NYC
I Can't Get Started (opening theme) (Bunny Berigan on trumpet)
Notre Dame Victory March
Jazzeroo (drums by Johnny Williams; Berigan; Shoobe on bass, etc)
Body And Soul (HENRY 'RED' ALLEN singing and playing trumpet)
Ride, Red, Ride (Lucky Millinder singing; Red Allen on trumpet)
Mr Ghost Goes To Town (Will Hudson, composer, conducting; Berigan on trumpet)
It's De-Lovely (MARGARET McCRAE singing)
I Can't Get Started (Bunny Berigan trumpet solo)
Organ Grinder's Swing (Will Hudson, composer, conducting)

The Lucky Millinder brass section (left, l to r): George Washington, J. C. Higginbotham, Henry "Red" Allen, Wardell Jones, Shelton "Scad" Hemphill.

After the broadcast we decided to go and see Benny Goodman for a few minutes without paying. We got to the Madhattan Room just as the Quartet were finishing. I got Lionel Hampton's autograph and he told me to take his cigarette as he left me by the bandstand to play with the Quartet. We heard the whole band play: *You're Not The Kind* (vocal by Helen Ward); *Always*; *Where The Lazy River Goes By* (vocal by Helen Ward); and *You Can Tell She Comes From Dixie* (vocal by Helen Ward).

11:00PM WABC
BENNY GOODMAN
Hotel Pennsylvania, NYC
Let's Dance (theme)
King Porter Stomp (great, but not as good as the Victor recording)
Where The Lazy River Goes By (vocal: Helen Ward) (swell)
Somebody Loves Me (good arrangement of nuttsy old swing tune)
An Apple A Day (vocal: Helen Ward)
Dinah (BG Quartet) (great work by Hampton)
You Turned The Tables On Me (vocal: Helen Ward) (great)
When Buddha Smiles (marvelous sax section)
Easy To Love (Jess Stacy's piano)
I Found A New Baby (Krupa's drums)
Goodbye (closing theme)

■ SUNDAY 22 NOVEMBER 1936

RADIO LOGS

2.30PM WJZ
TOMMY DORSEY
Magic Key Program, NYC
I'm Getting Sentimental Over You
There's Frost On The Moon (vocal: Edythe Wright)
For Sentimental Reasons (vocal: Jack Leonard)
That's A-Plenty

■ MONDAY 23 NOVEMBER 1936

RECORDING SESSION

BUNNY BERIGAN AND HIS ORCHESTRA
Recording session for Brunswick in New York City.
Bunny Berigan (t); Red Jessup (tb); Toots Mondello (as); Babe Russin (ts); Joe Bushkin (p); Eddie Condon (g); Mort Stuhlmaker (b); George Wettling (d); Art Gentry (voc)
That Foolish Feeling (vAG) / *Where Are You?* (vAG) / *In A Little Spanish Town*

HUDSON-DeLANGE ORCHESTRA
Recording session for Brunswick in New York City.
Will Hudson (arr); Eddie DeLange (voc/ldr); James O'Connell, Harry Rausch, Jimmy Blake (t); Edward Kolyer (tb); George Bohn, Hugh Hibbert (cl/as); Pete Brendel (as/bar); Ted Duane (cl/ts); Mark Hyams (p); Cliff Rausch (g); Doc Goldberg (b); Edward O'Hara (d); Fredda Gibson (voc)
Remember When (vEDL) / *I'll Never Tell You I Love You Again* (vFG) / *If We Never Meet Again* (vFG) / *Midnight At The Onyx*

■ TUESDAY 24 NOVEMBER 1936

RECORDING SESSION

TOMMY DORSEY AND HIS ORCHESTRA
Recording session for Victor in New York City.
Tommy Dorsey (tb); Max Kaminsky, Ray McKinney, Joe Bauer (t); Ben Pickering, Walter Mercurio (tb); Joe Dixon (cl/as/voc); Clyde Rounds (as); Bud Freeman, Bob Bunch (cl/ts); Dick Jones (p); Carmen Mastren (g); Gene Traxler (b); Dave Tough (d); Edythe Wright, Jack Leonard, Three Esquires (voc)
Tea On The Terrace (vEW) / *I'm In A Dancing Mood* (vJL) / *Keeping Out of Mischief Now* / *Jamboree* (vEW,3E)

RADIO LOGS

9:30PM WABC
BENNY GOODMAN
Camel Caravan program, NYC
Stompin' At The Savoy (BG Quartet) (super-colossal work by Hampton)
St. Louis Blues (colossal: clarinet; Elman's trumpet; 5 clarinets; saxes)
Take Another Guess (vocal: Helen Ward) (swell new song)
When You And I Were Young, Maggie (ballsy: saxes; Elman's trumpet; Krupa)

■ WEDNESDAY 25 NOVEMBER 1936

RADIO LOGS

11:00PM WABC
BENNY GOODMAN
Hotel Pennsylvania, NYC
Let's Dance (theme)
Jam Session (colossal trumpet; swell Musso tenor)
Tain't Good (vocal: Helen Ward)

Mean To Me (Krupa's drumming; Musso's swell tenor)
Goodnight My Love (vocal: Helen Ward) (fair: Musso's tenor)
Here's Love In Your Eyes (not so good)
Pick Yourself Up (not as good as the record: Benny's clarinet below standard)
Until The Real Thing Comes Along (vocal: Helen Ward) (nuttsy)
Sweet Sue (BG Quartet) (great work by Wilson & Hampton)
It's De-Lovely (vocal: Helen Ward)
Honeysuckle Rose (marvelous jamming)

11.30PM WMCA
BLANCHE CALLOWAY
Apollo Theater, NYC
If We Never Meet Again (Tommy Stevenson singing and playing trumpet)

12.30AM WJZ
COUNT BASIE
Grand Terrace, Chicago
Jangled Nerves
I'll Always Be In Love With You
Tea On The Terrace (vocal: Jimmy Rushing)
Drop Me Off At Harlem
Rhythm In My Nursery Rhymes (vocal: Jimmy Rushing)
Limehouse Blues

■ THURSDAY 26 NOVEMBER 1936

RADIO LOGS

11.30PM WJZ
COUNT BASIE
Grand Terrace, Chicago
Streamline Strut
Drop Me Off At Harlem
Tea On The Terrace (vocal: Jimmy Rushing)
Happy Feet
Shoe Shine Boy
But Definitely (vocal: Jimmy Rushing)
Easy To Love (lousy)
Ebony Rhapsody (clarinet; Basie on piano; sax)

12:00 MIDNIGHT WOR
BENNY GOODMAN
Hotel Pennsylvania, NYC
Roger Lyons announced.
I Would Do Anything For You (fair trumpet; swell solid bassing by Harry Goodman)
You're Giving Me A Song And A Dance (vocal: Helen Ward) (trumpet; sax)
You Can Depend On Me (not very good)
If We Never Meet Again (trumpet)
Stompin' At The Savoy (BG Quartet) (Wilson & Hampton were great)
Three Little Words (ballsy: Stacy's piano; Krupa's drums; Goodman; McEachern; Musso)
Tain't Good (vocal: Helen Ward) (Swell introduction: trumpet; Stacy; Krupa)
When You And I Were Young, Maggie (Krupa; Elman; Goodman)
Did You Mean It? (vocal: Helen Ward) (Musso's tenor sax; Krupa)
Organ Grinder's Swing (swell but not as good as recording: trumpet; Musso's sax)

12.30AM WOR
WOODY HERMAN
Roseland Ballroom, NYC
Swell.
Blue Prelude (theme) (nuttsy: featuring trombone by Neil Reid)
Limehouse Blues (colossal: featuring Frank Carlson on drums)
Darling, Not Without You (vocal: Woody Herman)
Blue Skies (Clarence Willard on cornet; Saxie Mansfield's tenor)
Basin Street Blues (vocal: Woody Herman) (Woody's clarinet)
Sing, Baby, Sing (lousy)
Without The Shadow Of A Doubt (vocal: Woody Herman)
Old Fashioned Swing (vocal: Woody Herman) (Mansfield's tenor)

I Can't Pretend (vocal: Woody Herman) (nuttsy sweet song)
The Goose Hangs High (vocal: Woody Herman)
Weary Blues (Joe Bishop; Carlson's drums)
Blue Prelude (theme) (written by Isham Jones)

■ FRIDAY 27 NOVEMBER 1936

RADIO LOGS

11.30PM WNEW
WILLIE BRYANT
Ubangi Club, NYC
This is Willie Bryant's first broadcast over WNEW.
It's Over Because We're Through (theme)
King Porter Stomp (nice trumpet; tenor; trombone)
When Did You Leave Heaven? (Johnny Russell's tenor; Charlie Frazier's flute)
A Star Fell Out Of Heaven? (Johnny Russell's tenor; Charlie Frazier's flute)
Chimes At The Meeting
Swingtime In The Rockies (too weak; ragged)
If We Never Meet Again (trumpet)
Symphony In Riffs
It's Over Because We're Through (theme)

11.35PM WJZ
COUNT BASIE
Grand Terrace, Chicago
Count Basie has a swell new swing band which originated in Kansas City. Jimmy Rushing is a lousy vocalist but Basie is a nuttsy piano player. He used to play piano in Bennie Moten's Kansas City Band.
You're Too Good To Be True
Rose Room
It's De-Lovely
Tea On The Terrace (vocal: Jimmy Rushing)
Thanksgiving
Jangled Nerves (nuttsy song: trumpet; trombone; tenor sax)

12.00 MIDNIGHT WJZ
GLEN GRAY
Congress Hotel, Chicago
Smoke Rings (theme)
Pennies From Heaven (vocal: Kenny Sargent)
Papa Tree Top Tall (vocal: Pee Wee Hunt) (Sonny Dunham's trumpet)
For Sentimental Reasons (vocal: Kenny Sargent) (3 trombones; Hutchenrider)
Jazz Me Blues (ballsy: Pat Davis on tenor; Hunt's trombone, etc)
Out Of Space (Clarence Hutchenrider on clarinet)
Beale Street Blues (vocal: Pee Wee Hunt) (ballsy: Sonny Dunham's trumpet)
Weary Blues (colossal: Hunt's trombone; Hutchenrider; Dunham; Davis)
Smoke Rings (theme)

12.30AM WNEW
MAL HALLETT
Hotel Commodore, NYC
Boston Tea Party (theme)
Sweetheart, Let's Grow Old Together (vocal: Jerry Perkins)
La Golondrina (tango: lousy)
My Melancholy Baby (slow foxtrot: lousy)
Boston Tea Party (vocal: Buddy Welcome) (theme in its entirety: ballsy)
Did I Remember? (vocal: Jerry Perkins)
Make Believe Ballroom (vocal: Buddy Welcome) (colossal tenor)
Love Marches On
Boston Tea Party (theme)

12.30AM WABC
DICK STABILE
Hotel Lincoln, NYC
Of Thee I Swing, Baby (vocal: Bert Shaw)
Midnight Blue (vocal: Bert Shaw)
All's Fair In Love And War
The Night is Young (vocal: Frank Fleming)
You Turned The Tables On Me

Love Me Or Leave Me
I'm Talking To My Heart (vocal: Frank Fleming)
Bye Bye Baby (vocal: Bert Shaw)
A Perfect Lover (vocal: Bert Shaw)
Tain't Good, Like A Nickel Made Of Wood

■ SATURDAY 28 NOVEMBER 1936

Mortimer, Jones, Johnson, Pinger, Pastoriza, Morningstar and myself saw this week's Saturday Swing Session. Morningstar and I saw the Stanford-Columbia football game at the Polo Grounds in the afternoon. Got the autographs of Mary Lou Williams (guest pianist who plays and arranges with Andy Kirk's band), Andy Kirk, John Williams (1st sax in Kirk band), Johnny Augustine (conductor of CBS band), Adrian Rollini (guest who played bass sax, vibraphone and fountain pen), Mike Miolla (trumpet), Pete Pumiglio (sax), George Hogan (announcer), Shirley Howard (guest vocalist), Nat Natoli (trumpet), Bernie Ladd (sax), Frank Victor (guest guitar player), and Vincent Maffay (guitar).

Andy Kirk

Mary Lou Williams

6.45PM WABC
SATURDAY NIGHT SWING SESSION No21
Studio 1, CBS Studios, NYC
I Can't Get Started (opening theme) (Bunny Berigan on trumpet)
By Heck (colossal arrangement of ballsy old song: bass; trumpet)
I Never Slept A Wink Last Night (MARY LOU WILLIAMS' nuttsy piano solo)
Tea For Two (MARY LOU WILLIAMS piano solo: marvelous)
I Found A New Baby (CBS Band really going to town: Berigan's trumpet; 4 saxes; 2 trombones)
Solitude (SHIRLEY HOWARD singing with accompaniment by Bunny Berigan)
Unnamed Original (Adrian ROLLINI on vibes; Frank Victor on guitar; Lou Shoobe on bass)
Swing Low (Adrian ROLLINI on bass sax with Berigan, Victor & Johnny Williams)
Down By The Old Mill Stream (Bunny Berigan trumpet solo)
Swing, Swing Mother-in-Law (Berigan's trumpet; 3 clarinets; 2 trombones; drums)

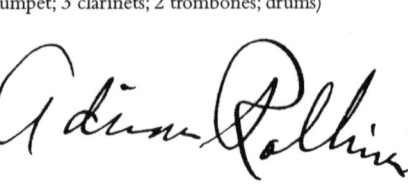

11.30PM WMCA
CHICK WEBB
Savoy Ballroom, NYC
Big John Special (Taft Jordan on trumpet)
Crying My Heart Out (vocal: Ella Fitzgerald)
Big Chief De Sota
I'll Sing You A Thousand Love Songs (vocal: Charles Linton)
Don't Be That Way
Cream Puff
This Is My Last Affair (vocal: Ella Fitzgerald)
Stompin' At The Savoy (closing theme) (written by Edgar Sampson)

12.15AM WJZ
GLEN GRAY
Congress Hotel, Chicago
Hold Me Tight (vocal: Kenny Sargent)
Diane
I'm Getting Sentimental Over You (3 trombones)
Me And The Moon (vocal: Pee Wee Hunt)
Solitude
Pagan Love Song
Goblin Band
Smoke Rings (theme)

12.30AM WOR
JOE HAYMES
Lake Wood, N.J.
Midnight
Rosetta
To Mary With Love
The Wedding Of Mr And Mrs Swing (vocal: Cliff Weston)
Chapel In The Moonlight (vocal: Don McKinley)
St. Louis Blues
Lost In My Dreams (vocal: Cliff Weston)
Should I?
Lost In Your Arms (vocal: Honey Burns)
Sitting On The Moon (vocal: Cliff Weston)
Did You Mean It?
If We Never Meet Again (vocal: Cliff Weston)
Organ Grinder's Swing
For Sentimental Reasons (vocal: Honey Burns)
A Chapel In The Moonlight

NOVEMBER 1936

■ SUNDAY 29 NOVEMBER 1936

RECORDING SESSION

FATS WALLER & HIS RHYTHM
Recording session for Victor in Chicago.
Herman Autrey (t); Gene Sedric (cl/ts); Fats Waller (p/voc); Albert Casey (g); Charles Turner (b); Slick Jones (d)
Hallelujah! Things Look Rosy Now (vFW) / *Hallelujah! Things Look Rosy Now* / *'Tain't Good* (vFW) / *'Tain't Good* / *Swingin' Them Jingle Bells* (vFW) / *Swingin' Them Jingle Bells* / *A Thousand Dreams Of You* (vFW) / *A Thousand Dreams Of You* / *A Rhyme For Love* (vFW) / *I Adore You* (vFW)

■ MONDAY 30 NOVEMBER 1936

RECORDING SESSION

ART SHAW AND HIS ORCHESTRA
Recording session for Brunswick in New York City.
Art Shaw (cl/ldr); Lee Castle, Zeke Zarchy (t); Buddy Morrow (tb); Tony Pastor (ts/voc), Jerry Gray, Frank Siegfield (vln); Sam Persoff (vla); Bill Schumann (cello); Joe Lippman (p); Tony Gattuso (g); Ben Ginsberg (b); George Wettling (d); Peg La Centra (voc)
Love And Learn (vPLC) / *Moon Face* (vPLC) / *The Same Old Line* / *You Can Tell She Comes From Dixie* (vPLC)

Left: Art Shaw and his vocalist, Peg La Centra.

DECEMBER 1936

Hotel Pennsylvania: **Benny Goodman**
Hotel Commodore: **Mal Hallett**
Hotel Lincoln: **Dick Stabile**
Hotel Taft: **George Hall**
Hotel New Yorker: **Abe Lyman**
Rainbow Room: **Ray Noble**

Apollo Theater: **Mills Brothers/Ovie Alston** (4–10); **Bessie Smith/Erskine Hawkins** (11–17); **Luis Russell** (18–24); **Claude Hopkins** (25–31)
Paramount Theater: **Art Shaw** (9–); **Glen Gray** (23–)

Cotton Club Downtown: **Cab Calloway/Bill Robinson**
Hickory House: **3T's: Frank Trumbauer, Jack & Charlie Teagarden**
Onyx Club: **Stuff Smith**

■ TUESDAY 1 DECEMBER 1936

RADIO LOGS

9:30pm WABC
BENNY GOODMAN
Camel Caravan program, NYC
I Would Do Anything For You (Elman's trumpet; Krupa)
Tain't Good (vocal: Helen Ward) (swell new song)
There's Something In The Air (vocal: Helen Ward) (swell)
Swing Low, Sweet Chariot (Musso's sax; Elman's great trumpet)

10.30pm WOR
MAL HALLETT
Hotel Commodore, NYC
Boston Tea Party (theme)
Oh Say, Can You Swing? (vocal: Buddy Welcome) (Charlie Blake's drums)
One Never Knows, Does One?
Estelle (written and played on the piano by Frankie Carle)
Why Do I Lie To Myself? (vocal: Buddy Welcome)
And So Do I (vocal: Jerry Perkins)
Ol' Man River
Make Believe Ballroom (vocal: Buddy Welcome)
You've Got Something
Never Should Have Told You So

■ WEDNESDAY 2 DECEMBER 1936

RECORDING SESSION

BENNY GOODMAN TRIO/QUARTET
Recording session for Victor in New York City.
Lionel Hampton (vib); Teddy Wilson (p); Benny Goodman (cl); Gene Krupa (d)
Tiger Rag (trio, LH out) / *Stompin' At The Savoy* / *Whispering*

RADIO LOGS

11:00pm WABC
BENNY GOODMAN
Hotel Pennsylvania, NYC
Dan Seymour announced.
Sunny Disposish (good: trumpet; trombone)
Star Dust (nuttsy arrangement of Hoagy Carmichael's great song)
When A Lady Meets A Gentleman Down South (vocal: Helen Ward)
You Can Depend On Me (not very good)

Down South Camp Meetin' (Benny's clarinet exceptionally good; saxes; clarinets)
Midnight Blue (vocal: Helen Ward) (Elman's hot trumpet)
Sugar Foot Stomp (marvelous: saxes; clarinets; trumpet; Krupa)
Sometimes I'm Happy (colossal: saxes; Musso's tenor; trumpet)
Remember (swell: McEachern's trombone; Musso's solo not as good as Rollini's)
Where The Lazy River Goes By (vocal: Helen Ward) (swell new song)
House Hop (swell: written and arranged by Jimmy Mundy)

11.30pm WMCA
DON REDMAN
Apollo Theater, NYC
I've Got You Under My Skin (vocal: Louise Carroll & Band)
'Long About Midnight

■ THURSDAY 3 DECEMBER 1936

RECORDING SESSION

WOODY HERMAN AND HIS ORCHESTRA
Recording session for Decca in New York City.
Woody Herman (cl/as/voc/ldr); Clarence Willard, Kermit Simmons (t); Joe Bishop (fh); Neal Reid (tb); Murray Williams, Don Watt (as); Saxie Mansfield, Bruce Wilkins (ts); Nick Hupfer (vln); Horace Diaz (p); Chick Reeves (g); Walter Yoder (b); Frank Carlson (d)
Mr. Ghost Goes To Town / *Better Get Off Your High Horse* (vWH)

RADIO LOGS

6.30pm WNEW
CHICK WEBB
Make Believe Ballroom, NYC
Let's Get Together (theme)
Clap Hands, Here Comes Charlie (good: Taft Jordan, trumpet; Chick Webb, drums)
That Man Is Here Again (vocal: Ella Fitzgerald) (written by Edgar Sampson)
Don't Be That Way (featuring Chick Webb on drums)
Spring Fever Blues (vocal: Ella Fitzgerald) (nuttsy, colossal)
Honeysuckle Rose (vocal: Ella Fitzgerald) (swell, ballsy)
You'll Have To Swing It (vocal: Ella Fitzgerald) (swell)
House Hop
Organ Grinder's Swing (vocal: Ella Fitzgerald)

■ FRIDAY 4 DECEMBER 1936

RECORDING SESSION

ADRIAN ROLLINI TRIO
Recording session for Decca in New York City.
Adrian Rollini (vib); Frank Victor (g); Haig Stephens (b)
Vibrollini / *Driftin'*

RADIO LOGS

7.15PM WOR
JULIE WINTZ
New Jersey
When My Dreamboat Comes Home
Tain't No Use
The Night Is So Young
Doin' The Suzy-Q

11.30PM WMCA
CHICK WEBB
Savoy Ballroom, NYC
Jamaica Shout (tenor, etc)
There's Something In The Air (vocal: Ella Fitzgerald)
Riffin' At The Ritz
Love, What Are You Doing To My Heart? (vocal: Charles Linton)
The Duke Swings Low
I'm An Old Cowhand
Bye Bye Baby
A Little Bit Later On (vocal: Ella Fitzgerald)
Harlem Heat (saxes: tenor; clarinet; ballsy drums)

11.30PM WNEW
WILLIE BRYANT
Ubangi Club, NYC
You Can't Pull The Wool Over My Eyes (vocal: Willie Bryant)
Blue Interlude (Johnny Russell featured on tenor sax)
Naughty Waltz
Star Dust
Cavernism
Dear Old Southland

12.00 MIDNIGHT WJZ
GLEN GRAY
Congress Hotel, Chicago
Smoke Rings (theme)
Diane (pretty good: Pat Davis' sweet tenor; trumpet)
Pennies From Heaven (vocal: Kenny Sargent)
The Moon Is Grinning At Me (vocal: Pee Wee Hunt)
I've Got You Under My Skin (vocal: Kenny Sargent)
Swing Low, Sweet Chariot (sax; clarinet by Hutchenrider)
Paramour (written by Clarence Hutchenrider, clarinettist)
Lazy Bones (vocal: Pee Wee Hunt)
Bugle Call Rag (ballsy: trombones; drums; saxes)

12.30AM WEAF
JACK TEAGARDEN (3T's)
Hickory House, 52nd Street, NYC
Teagarden/Trumbauer Band's first broadcast. Just opened 2 days ago at the Hickory House. Poor arrangements but good vocals and fine solos.
Basin Street Blues (vocal: Jack Teagarden) (opening theme)
You Turned The Tables On Me (vocal: Jack Teagarden)
The Mayor Of Alabam' (Frankie Trumbauer; Jack Teagarden)
Honeysuckle Rose (Caspar Reardon playing harp with the band)
When Did You Leave Heaven? (Frank Carter singing and playing piano)
Wild Cat (Charlie Teagarden's trumpet; Frankie Trumbauer's alto)
Ode To A Chimney Sweep (written and arranged by Russ Case)
Christmas Night In Harlem (Jack Teagarden singing, playing muted trombone)
Junk Man (Caspar Reardon playing harp)
You Took Advantage Of Me
Tea For Two
Oh, Lady Be Good

12.45AM WJZ
EARL HINES
Grand Terrace, Chicago
Swell. First night at Grand Terrace after long tour.
Deep Forest (theme)
Liza
Easy To Love (vocal: Ida James)
Inspiration

■ SATURDAY 5 DECEMBER 1936

Pastoriza, Morningstar and myself went into NYC by subway to see broadcast. Red McKenzie and his 3-piece band who are now playing at McKenzie's Restaurant and Fred Waring's Octet were guests. Got the autographs of McKenzie, Eddie Condon (guitar in McKenzie's Band), Joe Bushkin (piano in McKenzie's Band), Joe Marsala (clarinet in McKenzie's Band), on a picture of McKenzie and of Abe Cholden (new sax player with CBS band).

6.45PM WABC
SATURDAY NIGHT SWING SESSION No22
Studio 1, CBS Studios, NYC
I Can't Get Started (theme) (Bunny Berigan on trumpet)
One, Two, Button Your Shoe
Clarinet Marmalade (Berigan, Condon, Marsala, Bushkin, McKenzie)
Formal Night In Harlem (Johnny Williams on chimes, drums; Berigan; Maffay)
Jamboree Jones (Fred Waring Octet: 1 female, 7 males singing the nuts)
Tain't Good (Fred Waring Octet: 1 female, 7 males singing the nuts)
I've Got The World On A String (Red McKenzie singing)
Star Dust (Bunny Berigan trumpet solo)
'Way Down Yonder In New Orleans (McKenzie singing; Berigan; Condon)
Crazy Rhythm (ballsy: saxes; Berigan; Williams' drumming)

11:07PM WABC
BENNY GOODMAN
Hotel Pennsylvania, NYC
Let's Dance (theme)
Mean To Me (good: Musso's tenor)
You're My Best Bet (vocal: Helen Ward) (fair)
If I Could Be With You One Hour Tonight
An Apple A Day (vocal: Helen Ward)
Organ Grinder's Swing (new introduction: Musso's swell tenor)
Dinah (BG Trio)
Take Another Guess (vocal: Helen Ward)
Goodbye (closing theme)

11.30PM WMCA
CHICK WEBB
Savoy Ballroom, NYC
Henderson Stomp (clarinets: nuttsy)
You're The Only One To Blame (vocal: Ella Fitzgerald)
Back Home Again In Indiana (Sandy Williams' trombone; Taft Jordan's trumpet)
Milenberg Joys (vocal: Ella Fitzgerald)
Organ Grinder's Swing (vocal: Ella Fitzgerald) (ballsy vocal)

■ MONDAY 7 DECEMBER 1936

RADIO LOGS

7.15PM WOR
HAL KEMP
Arcadia Ballroom, Philadelphia
Something Has Happened To Me (vocal: Skinnay Ennis)
You've Got Something (vocal: Bob Allen)
A Fine Romance (vocal: Maxine Gray)
Serenade For A Wealthy Widow

7.20PM WJZ
BUGHOUSE RHYTHM
San Francisco
Jitters (Walter Kellsy playing hot violin with Dr Meakin's Band)
Papa Tree Top Tall (written by Hoagy Carmichael: startling key changes)

■ TUESDAY 8 DECEMBER 1936

RADIO LOGS

4.15PM WEAF
CHICK WEBB
NYC
Let's Get Together (theme) (swell theme with nuttsy drum intro by Chick Webb)
After You've Gone (saxes; Taft Jordan's trumpet; trombone)
Blue Lou (nuttsy: rhythm section; sax; muted trumpet)
Rhythm In My Soul
Someday, Sweetheart (vocal: Charles Linton) (what saxes!)
Big John Special (Taft Jordan playing great trumpet)
Facts And Figures (nuttsy drumming by Chick Webb)
Springtime In The Rockies
When Did You Leave Heaven? (vocal: Charles Linton)
Stompin' At The Savoy (closing theme)
Ella Fitzgerald was absent from the band for the week 7–11 December; possibly to have an abortion.

9.00PM WNEW
MAL HALLETT
Hotel Commodore, NYC
Boston Tea Party (opening and closing theme)
Make Believe Ballroom (vocal: Buddy Welcome)
In The Chapel In The Moonlight (vocal: Jerry Perkins)
Spring Fever (piano solo by Frankie Carle, with drummer Charlie Blake)
The Night Is Young And You're So Beautiful
It's De-Lovely
It Was In A Little Gypsy Tea Room (vocal: Jerry Perkins & Band)
I'm An Old Cowhand (vocal: Buddy Welcome & Band)
For Sentimental Reasons
I'll Cling To The Moon
Another Perfect Night Is Ending
Copper Colored Gal (lousy)

9:30PM WABC
BENNY GOODMAN
Camel Caravan program, NYC
Mean To Me (saxes; Musso's tenor; Krupa)
The World Is Waiting For The Sunrise (BG Trio) (swell work by all three)
Darling, Not Without You (vocal: Helen Ward) (nuttsy new song)
Shine (Elman's trumpet; Krupa)

10.30PM WOR
MAL HALLETT
Hotel Commodore, NYC
It's Love I'm After (vocal: Buddy Welcome)
You've Got Something (from *Red, Hot and Blue*)
Big Chief De Sota
Ridin' High (Frankie Carle on piano)
The Dixieland Band (vocal: Buddy Welcome)
The Lonesome Road (vocal: Glee Club)
That's Life, I Guess (vocal: Buddy Welcome) (swell: saxes)
Sweetheart, Let's Grow Old Together (vocal: Jerry Perkins) (stinks)
On The Beach At Bali-Bali (vocal: Buddy Welcome & Band) (swell)

■ WEDNESDAY 9 DECEMBER 1936

RECORDING SESSION

BENNY GOODMAN AND HIS ORCHESTRA
Recording session for Victor in New York City.
Benny Goodman (cl); Chris Griffin, Irving Goodman, Ziggy Elman (t); Red Ballard, Murray McEachern (tb); Bill DePew, Hymie Shertzer (as); Art Rollini, Vido Musso (ts); Jess Stacy (p); Allan Reuss (g); Harry Goodman (b); Gene Krupa (d); Helen Ward (voc)
When You And I Were Young, Maggie / *Gee! But You're Swell* (vHW) / *Smoke Dreams* (vHW) / *Swing Low, Sweet Chariot*

ANDY KIRK AND HIS TWELVE CLOUDS OF JOY
Recording session for Decca in New York City.
Andy Kirk (bsx/ldr); Harry Lawson, Paul King, Earl Thompson (t); Ted Donnelly, Henry Wells (tb); John Harrington (cl/as/bar); John Williams (as/bar); Dick Wilson (ts); Claude Williams (vln); Mary Lou Williams (p); Ted Brinson (g); Booker Collins (b); Ben Thigpen (d); Pha Terrell, Harry Mills (voc)
Fifty Second Street (vHM & Band) / *The Lady Who Swings The Band* (vHM) / *What Will I Tell My Heart?* (vPT) / *Dedicated To You* (vPT)

RADIO LOGS

11:00PM WABC
BENNY GOODMAN
Hotel Pennsylvania, NYC
John-Allen Wolf announced.
Swing Low, Sweet Chariot (swell: Stacy's piano; Krupa's drumming; trumpet)
Pennies From Heaven (vocal: Helen Ward) (good)
Always (colossal: Musso's tenor; Krupa; McEachern's trombone)
For Sentimental Reasons (vocal: Helen Ward)
When You And I Were Young, Maggie (nuttsy: piano; Elman's trumpet)
Blues In E-Flat (BG Quartet) (just improvising, slow tempo blues: Wilson)
Did You Mean It? (vocal: Helen Ward)
Somebody Loves Me (O.K.: Musso's tenor sax)
Jam Session (swell: Ziggy Elman's trumpet)

■ FRIDAY 11 DECEMBER 1936

Edward VIII abdicates; Duke of York succeeds him as George VI

RADIO LOGS

11.30PM WMCA
CHICK WEBB
Savoy Ballroom, NYC
Clarinet Marmalade
Riffin' At The Ritz
Pennies From Heaven (vocal: Charles Linton)
Boston Tea Party
Someday, Sweetheart (vocal: Charles Linton)
Stop, Look, And Listen
After You've Gone
Melody Man

12.00 MIDNIGHT WJZ
GLEN GRAY
Congress Hotel, Chicago
Dardanella
So Do I (vocal: Kenny Sargent)
You're Too Good To Be True (vocal: Pee Wee Hunt)
I Can't Pretend (vocal: Kenny Sargent)
California, Here I Come
Tain't Good, Like A Nickel Made Of Wood (vocal: Pee Wee Hunt)
Rhythm Of The River
Pagan Love Song
Smoke Rings (theme)

12.00 MIDNIGHT WOR
CAB CALLOWAY
Cotton Club, NYC
I Love To Sing-a (vocal: Cab Calloway)
It's De-Lovely (vocal: Cab Calloway)
Keep That Hi-De-Ho In Your Soul (vocal: Cab Calloway)
Poinciana
Poor Little Butterfly
Monopoly Swing
I'm At The Mercy Of Love
Hot Stuff

12.30AM WEAF
JACK TEAGARDEN (3T's)
Hickory House, 52nd Street, NYC
Basin Street Blues (vocal: Jack Teagarden) (opening theme)
Tain't Good (vocal: Jack Teagarden) (Charlie Teagarden trumpet solo)
'S Wonderful (2 Teagardens & Frankie Trumbauer "going to town")
Did You Mean It? (vocal: Jack Teagarden)
I'm An Old Cowhand (vocal: Jack Teagarden)
Liza (Adele Girard playing harp with the band)
Fare Thee Well To Harlem (vocal: Jack Teagarden)
Eclipse (Frankie Trumbauer's alto sax)
Mr T From Tennessee (vocal: Jack Teagarden) (swell words)
Little Old Lady
Between The Devil And The Deep Blue Sea
I Got Rhythm

■ SATURDAY 12 DECEMBER 1936

Mr Morningstar drove Dick Morningstar, Pinger, Pastoriza and myself into NYC in the morning. We went to MCA and got pictures of Norvo and Basie. We then went (11:00am) to the Paramount Theater where we saw the movie 'Pennies From Heaven' with Bing Crosby and Louis Armstrong. This picture was lousy but Armstrong was great. Art Shaw and his band were on the stage with Peg LaCentra (vocalist), Jane Cooper (tap dancer), Al Bernie (comedian), and The Modernaires (4 men singers). *Nightmare* (Shaw's theme), *Organ Grinder's Swing, Ding Dong Daddy* (featuring Tony Pastor singing and playing tenor sax), *Let's Dance* (The Modernaires), *Milkman's Matinée* (The Modernaires), *Jamboree Jones, Sometimes I'm Happy* (The Modernaires), *Streamline* (Shaw's Band), *It Ain't Necessarily So* (Peg LaCentra), *You Turned The Tables On Me* (Peg LaCentra), *King Of Swing* (Peg LaCentra and The Modernaires). Hughie had to go home. We went to the Swing broadcast over WABC at 6:45. This show was broadcast to South America. Jack Teagarden, Charlie Teagarden, Frank Trumbauer, Caspar Reardon, Teddy Wilson, The Blue Flames (quartet) and Frank Ayalla (Spaniard who conducted band with Freddie Rich) were the guests. A Spaniard announced all the songs in Spanish along with Paul Douglas.

This picture of Frankie Trumbauer playing C-melody sax and Vincent Maffay playing the guitar was taken at the Saturday Night Swing Session on Saturday December 12, 1936 at about 6:55pm when, along with Jack Teagarden, Charlie Teagarden, Lou Shoobe (bass), Johnny Williams (drums), they were playing *Basin Street Blues*. The 3T's, who are with Paul Whiteman's band are now playing a month's engagement at the Hickory House on 52nd Street. Vincent Maffay is employed by CBS and plays regularly with the CBS Band.

6.45PM WABC
SATURDAY NIGHT SWING SESSION No23
Studio 1, CBS Studios, NYC
I Can't Get Started (opening theme) (Bunny Berigan on trumpet)
Pick Yourself Up (colossal: WHAT A MARVELOUS SAX TEAM!!!)
Basin Street Blues (Jack & Charlie Teagarden, Frank Trumbauer with Vincent Maffay, Lou Shoobe & Johnny Williams)
I Got Rhythm (Teagardens, Trumbauer with Vincent Maffay, Lou Shoobe & Johnny Williams)
Handful Of Keys (TEDDY WILSON doing a swell piano solo)
St. Louis Blues (Frank Ayalla conducting CBS Band: SAXES; Berigan's muted trumpet)
Junk Man (Caspar Reardon on harp; 2 Teagardens; Trumbauer: nuttsy)
Singin' The Blues (Blue Flames: 1 male, 3 females singing)
La Cumparsita (tango featuring Bunny Berigan on trumpet)
My Melancholy Baby (NUTTSY: trombone team; Pete Pumiglio's clarinet; Hamilton's tenor)

RADIO LOGS

11:30PM WABC
BENNY GOODMAN
Hotel Pennsylvania, NYC
Let's Dance (theme)
Get Happy (Swell: fast tempo)
Smoke Dreams (vocal: Helen Ward) (played for first time over the radio)
Copper Colored Gal
Easy To Love
Minnie The Moocher's Wedding Day
Goodnight My Love (vocal: Helen Ward)
Whispering (BG Quartet)
You Can Tell She Comes From Dixie (vocal: Helen Ward)
I Found A New Baby
Goodbye (closing theme)

12.00 MIDNIGHT WJZ
GLEN GRAY
Congress Hotel, Chicago
A Study In Brown
Love, What Are You Doing To My Heart? (vocal: Kenny Sargent)
Four Score And Seven Years Ago (vocal: Pee Wee Hunt)
Midnight Blue (vocal: Kenny Sargent)
Shades Of Hades
The Moon Is Grinning At Me (vocal: Pee Wee Hunt)
Jelly Roll Blues
I Got Rhythm

■ SUNDAY 13 DECEMBER 1936

RADIO LOGS

5.30PM WOR
FRANK DAILEY
Meadowbrook, N.J.
Here's Love In Your Eyes
Star Dust
I'm In A Dancing Mood
Basin Street Blues
A Woman's Got A Right To Change Her Mind (vocal: Ann Lee Davis)
He's A Humdinger
I Got Rhythm
What You Mean To Me
By Heck
Gypsy Violins (theme)

■ TUESDAY 15 DECEMBER 1936

RADIO LOGS

4.15PM WTIC
CHICK WEBB
NBC Studios, NYC
Mr Ghost Goes To Town (Taft Jordan playing great trumpet)
In My Seclusion (vocal: Charles Linton) (ballsy saxes; piano)
Harlem Heat (nuttsy: trumpet; tenor sax)
I've Got You Under My Skin (Louis Jordan on sax)
Honeysuckle Rose (vocal: Ella Fitzgerald)
Royal Garden Blues (ballsy, best on program: Taft Jordan's trumpet; Sandy Williams' trombone)

9.00PM WNEW
MAL HALLETT
Hotel Commodore, NYC
That's Life I Guess (vocal: Buddy Welcome)
Mickey Mouse's Birthday Party
You've Got Everything (vocal: Jerry Perkins)
On The Beach At Bali-Bali (vocal: Buddy Welcome & Band)
Estelle (Frankie Carle on piano)
It's Love I'm After
The Night Is Young And You're So Beautiful
For Sentimental Reasons
Angry

9:30PM WABC
BENNY GOODMAN
Camel Caravan program, NYC
Get Happy (COLOSSAL: Benny playing low register clarinet; Stacy; McEachern)
Smoke Dreams (vocal: Helen Ward) (swell new song: Stacy's piano)
An Apple A Day (Ziggy Elman's trumpet; Musso's tenor)
Walk, Jennie, Walk (Krupa's drumming; McEachern's trombone)

■ WEDNESDAY 16 DECEMBER 1936

RECORDING SESSION

REX STEWART & HIS 52ND STREET STOMPERS
Recording session for Master Records in Hollywood.
Rex Stewart (c); Lawrence Brown (tb); Johnny Hodges (ss/as); Harry Carney (cl/bar); Duke Ellington (p); Brick Fleagle (g); Billy Taylor (b); Jack Maisel (d)
Rexatious / Lazy Man's Shuffle

DECEMBER 1936

RADIO LOGS

11:00PM WABC
BENNY GOODMAN
Hotel Pennsylvania, NYC
Bert Parks announced.
When Buddha Smiles (nuttsy slow tempo: Rollini's tenor; colossal saxes)
You Turned The Tables On Me (vocal: Helen Ward) (swell)
The Skeleton In The Closet (good: Musso's tenor; Krupa's drumming)
St. Louis Blues (BALLSY-COLOSSAL: saxes; Benny's clarinet; 5 clarinets; Elman's trumpet)
There's Frost On The Moon (vocal: Helen Ward) (nuttsy new song)
After You've Gone (BG Trio) (Teddy Wilson's piano)
Darling, Not Without You (vocal: Helen Ward) (another swell sweet song)
Love Me Or Leave Me (SWELL: Musso's tenor; Stacy's piano; Reuss' guitar)
Jingle Bells (nuttsy arrangement of lousy song: trumpet; Musso; clarinets)

11.30PM WMCA
ERSKINE HAWKINS
Apollo Theater, NYC
Willie Bryant announces this Amateur Hour from the Apollo Theater.
Organ Grinder's Swing (swell slow tempo: trumpet; clarinet)
In The Chapel In The Moonlight (vocal: Billy Daniels)

Below: The Hudson-DeLange Orchestra.

■ THURSDAY 17 DECEMBER 1936

RADIO LOGS

6.00PM WNEW
HUDSON-DeLANGE
Make Believe Ballroom, NYC
Will Hudson writes and arranges for the band while Eddie DeLange directs and sings. Band is a year-and-a-half old, personnel is same except for 1 man. Hudson wrote *Organ Grinder's Swing*, *You're Not The Kind* and *Tormented*.
Hobo On Park Avenue (opening theme) (written by Will Hudson)
Midnight At The Onyx (new song by Will Hudson, swell: clarinets; tenor; trumpet)
Mr Ghost Goes To Town (written by Will Hudson, swell: saxes; brass; tenor)
How Was I To Know (vocal: Eddie DeLange) (words by DeLange, music by Will Hudson)
I'll Never Say I Love You (vocal: Fredda Gibson) (written by Will Hudson: slow)
Organ Grinder's Swing (vocal: Eddie DeLange) (nuttsy trumpet)
Remember When (vocal: Eddie DeLange) (written by Will Hudson)
The Moon Is Grinning At Me (vocal: Fredda Gibson) (written by Hudson, ballsy: tenor)
Monopoly Swing (NUTTSY)

9.30PM WNEW
TOMMY DORSEY
Roseland Ballroom, NYC
I'm Getting Sentimental Over You (theme)
Head Over Heels In Love (vocal: Edythe Wright)
For Sentimental Reasons (vocal: Jack Leonard)
Bugle Call Rag

Pennies From Heaven
A High Hat, A Piccolo, And A Cane (vocal: Three Esquires)
I'm In A Dancing Mood (vocal: Jack Leonard)
Tea On The Terrace (vocal: Edythe Wright)
Organ Grinder's Swing
That's A-Plenty

11.30PM WJZ
EARL HINES
Grand Terrace, Chicago
Cream Of The Crop (vocal: Walter Fuller) (written by Earl Hines)
Talking To My Heart
Liza
When Did You Leave Heaven? (vocal: Ida James)
Inspiration (written by Earl Hines)
It's De-Lovely
Here's Love In Your Eye
When I Grow Too Old To Dream

12:00 MIDNIGHT WOR
BENNY GOODMAN
Hotel Pennsylvania, NYC
Jerry Lawrence announced.
Let's Dance (theme)
Three Little Words (COLOSSAL: trumpet)
Smoke Dreams (vocal: Helen Ward)
Blue Skies
For Sentimental Reasons (vocal: Helen Ward)
It's De-Lovely (vocal: Helen Ward) (Elman's trumpet)
I Can't Give You Anything But Love (BG Quartet) (great work by Hampton & Wilson)
Down South Camp Meetin'
You're My Best Bet (vocal: Helen Ward) (good new song)
Swing Low, Sweet Chariot (lousy intro: Musso's tenor; trumpet)
Goodbye (closing theme)

■ FRIDAY 18 DECEMBER 1936

RECORDING SESSION

HUDSON-DeLANGE ORCHESTRA
Recording session for Brunswick in New York City.
Will Hudson (arr); Eddie DeLange (voc/ldr); James O'Connell, Harry Rausch, Jimmy Blake (t); Edward Kolyer (tb); George Bohn, Hugh Hibbert (cl/as); Pete Brendel (as/bar); Ted Duane (cl/ts); Mark Hyams (p); Cliff Rausch (g); Doc Goldberg (b); Edward O'Hara (d)
Love Song Of A Half-Wit, Pt1 / Love Song Of A Half-Wit, Pt2 / How Was I To Know? (vEDL) / *Am I Intruding?*

BEN POLLACK AND HIS ORCHESTRA
Recording session for Variety in Hollywood.
Ben Pollack (voc/ldr); Harry James, Shorty Sherock, Charlie Spivak (t); Bruce Squires, Glenn Miller (tb); Irving Fazola (cl); Opie Cates (as); Dave Matthews (ts); Ray Cohen (vln); Freddy Slack (p); Frank Frederico (g); Thurman Teague (b); Sammy Taylor (d)
In A Sentimental Mood / Deep Elm / Peckin' (vBP & Band) / *The Moon Is Grinning At Me* (vBP)

Helen Ward left Benny Goodman today to marry Albert Marx. It's too bad that she left for she sure did have one swell voice. She was one of my favorite vocalists. She had just gotten a divorce in October.

RADIO LOGS

11.30PM WMCA
CHICK WEBB
Savoy Ballroom, NYC
Facts And Figures
Make Believe Ballroom (vocal: Ella Fitzgerald)
It Happens To The Best Of Friends
There's Heaven In My Heart (vocal: Charles Linton)
Riffin'
Limehouse Blues
My Heart On Fire (vocal: Ella Fitzgerald)
Down Home Rag
Stompin' At The Savoy
Let's Get Together (theme)

12.00 MIDNIGHT WJZ
GUS ARNHEIM
Congress Hotel, Chicago
St. Louis Blues
Take Another Guess (vocal: June Robbins)
For Sentimental Reasons
Mr Ghost Goes To Town

12.10AM WABC
DICK STABILE
Hotel Lincoln, NYC
Vibraphonia (Adrian Rollini playing vibes with Frank Victor on guitar)
Gee, But You're Swell (vocal: Bert Shaw)
Dear Diary
If My Heart Could Only Talk
I'm The Cuban Cary
Is She Really The One For Me?

■ SATURDAY 19 DECEMBER 1936

RECORDING SESSION

BARNEY BIGARD & HIS JAZZOPATORS
Recording session for Master Records in Hollywood.
Cootie Williams (t); Juan Tizol (vtb); Barney Bigard (cl); Harry Carney (bar); Duke Ellington (p); Billy Taylor (b); Sonny Greer (d)
Clouds In My Heart / Frolic Sam / Caravan / Stompy Jones

I took Mortimer down to see this week's Saturday Swing Session. Got the autographs of Abe Cholden (sax), Ernie White (sax/clarinet), Harry Preble (trumpet, formerly with CBS band), Billy Gussak (drummer who took the place of Johnny Williams), Frank Victor (guest guitarist), Harry Volpa (guest guitarist), Doris Kerr (guest vocalist), and Lud Gluskin (musical director of CBS).

6.45PM WABC
SATURDAY NIGHT SWING SESSION No24
Studio 1, CBS Studios, NYC
Christmas Night In Harlem
Sensation (8-piece CBS Swing Band)
Swingin' The Scales (Harry Volpa, Frank Victor, Lou Shoobe)
An Apple A Day
Between The Devil And The Deep Blue Sea
In A Little Spanish Town (Bunny Berigan trumpet solo)
Pagan Fantasy
I Found A New Baby
Until Today (Bunny Berigan singing)
Raggin' The Scale

RADIO LOGS

12.00 MIDNIGHT WNEW
MIKE RILEY
Club Caliente, 66 W52nd Street, NYC
Hey, Hey
I Never Knew
'Way Down Yonder In New Orleans
I'll Sing You A Thousand Love Songs
Honeysuckle Rose
I'm Getting Sentimental Over You
Jazz Me Blues
The Music Goes Round And Around (theme)

12.35AM WOR
WOODY HERMAN
Roseland Ballroom, NYC
Blue Prelude (theme)
Oh, Say, Can You Swing It?
So Do I (vocal: Woody Herman)
Mr Ghost Goes To Town
Tea On The Terrace
Rose Room
Wait
Weary Blues

■ MONDAY 21 DECEMBER 1936

RECORDING SESSION

DUKE ELLINGTON AND HIS ORCHESTRA
Recording session for Master Records in Hollywood.
Duke Ellington (p); Wallace Jones or Arthur Whetsel, Cootie Williams (t); Rex Stewart (c); Joe Nanton, Lawrence Brown (tb); Juan Tizol (vtb); Barney Bigard (cl); Johnny Hodges (cl/ss/as); Otto Hardwick (as/bar); Ben Webster (ts); Harry Carney (cl/as/bar); Fred Guy (g); Hayes Alvis, Billy Taylor (b); Sonny Greer (d)
Scattin' At The Cotton Club / Black Butterfly (BT out)

■ TUESDAY 22 DECEMBER 1936

RADIO LOGS

4.15PM WEAF
CHICK WEBB
Savoy Ballroom, NYC
Jangled Nerves
There's Something In The Air (vocal: Ella Fitzgerald)
Bugle Call Rag
Charmaine (vocal: Charles Linton)
Memphis Blues
The Duke Swings Out
Copenhagen Swing
Let's Get Together (theme)

9:30PM WABC
BENNY GOODMAN
Camel Caravan program, NYC
Copper Colored Gal
King Porter Stomp
Oh, Lady Be Good (BG Trio)
Troublesome Trumpet (vocal: Benny Goodman) (Ziggy Elman's trumpet)

■ WEDNESDAY 23 DECEMBER 1936

RECORDING SESSION

ART SHAW AND HIS ORCHESTRA
Recording session for Brunswick in New York City.
Art Shaw (cl/ldr); Lee Castle, Zeke Zarchy (t); Buddy Morrow (tb); Tony Pastor (ts/voc), Jerry Gray, Frank Siegfield (vln); Sam Persoff (vla); Bill Schumann (cello); Joe Lippman (p); Tony Gattuso (g); Ben Ginsberg (b); George Wettling (d)
Sobbin' Blues / Copenhagen / Cream Puff / My Blue Heaven

ART SHAW AND HIS STRINGS
Recording session for Brunswick in New York City.
Art Shaw (cl/ldr); Jerry Gray, Frank Siegfield (vln); Sam Persoff (vla); Bill Schumann (cello); Joe Lippman (p); Tony Gattuso (g); Ben Ginsberg (b); George Wettling (d)
Streamline / Sweet Lorraine

RADIO LOGS

12.45AM WABC
DUKE ELLINGTON
Sebastian's Cotton Club, LA
Yearning For Love (Lawrence Brown's trombone)
Oh, Babe, Maybe Someday (vocal: Ivie Anderson)
In A Sentimental Mood

12.55AM WWL
BOB CROSBY
Roosevelt Hotel, New Orleans
Jim Town Blues (colossal)
Summertime (theme) (played in full: swell)

Christmas greetings from Mr & Mrs Teddy Wilson

1.15AM WMAQ
EARL HINES
Grand Terrace, Chicago
Live And Learn (vocal: Walter Fuller)
Trust In Me
Nobody's Sweetheart
Please Keep Me In Your Dreams (vocal: Ida James)

THURSDAY 24 DECEMBER 1936

RECORDING SESSION

FATS WALLER & HIS RHYTHM
Recording session for Victor in New York City.
Herman Autrey (t); Gene Sedric (cl/ts); Fats Waller (p/voc); Albert Casey (g); Charles Turner (b); Slick Jones (d/vib)
Havin' A Ball (vFW) / *I'm Sorry I Made You Cry* (vFW) / *Who's Afraid Of Love?* (vFW) / *Please Keep Me In Your Dreams* (vFW) / *One In A Million* (vFW) / *Nero* (vFW)

FRIDAY 25 DECEMBER 1936

RADIO LOGS

6.35PM WABC
THE DICTATORS
CBS Studios, NYC
Love Marches On
Fooled
Sweet For The Eyes
Swingin' On The Swanee Shore

10.30PM WOR
CAB CALLOWAY
Cotton Club, NYC
Hot Stuff
Half Of Me (vocal: Cab Calloway)
My Melancholy Baby (vocal: Cab Calloway)
You're Giving Me A Song And A Dance (vocal: Cab Calloway)
Midnight Lullaby (vocal: Cab Calloway)
Frisco Flo (vocal: Cab Calloway)
Dixie, Where Jazz Was Born

11.00PM WNEW
STUFF SMITH
Onyx Club, 72 W52nd Street, NYC
Chopsticks (colossal jamming by Smith on violin; Jonah Jones on trumpet; Cozy Cole on drums)
Old Fashioned Swing
Swing, Mr Charlie
Old Joe Is Hittin' The Jug
Pick Yourself Up

11.30PM WNEW
OVIE ALSTON
Ubangi Club, NYC
Royal Garden Blues (theme)
Rigamarole
Did I Remember? (vocal: Clarence Lee)
Someday Sweetheart
Exactly Like You (vocal: Ovie Alston)
Black And Blue (vocal: Clarence Lee)
Organ Grinder's Swing

DECEMBER 1936

12.15AM WJZ
GUS ARNHEIM
Congress Hotel, Chicago
Rosetta
That's What You Mean To Me (vocal: June Robbins)
Anything But Love (vocal: Harry He??)

12.30AM WOR
WOODY HERMAN
Roseland Ballroom, NYC
Blue Prelude (theme) (written by trumpeter Joe Bishop)
Boston Tea Party
Basin Street Blues (vocal: Woody Herman)
Sing, Baby, Sing
I've Got You Under My Skin
Old Fashioned Swing (vocal: Woody Herman) (swell)
Pennies From Heaven
Blue, Turning Grey, Over You
I'll Forsake All Others
Weary Blues
Blue Prelude (theme)

12.30AM WABC
DICK STABILE
Hotel Lincoln, NYC
Love Marches On (vocal: Bert Shaw)
Tea On The Terrace
Talking To My Heart
Chapel In The Moonlight (vocal: Bert Shaw)
Easy To Love
Dust On The Moon
Rainbow On The River
Between The Devil And The Deep Blue Sea

12.30AM WWL
BOB CROSBY
Roosevelt Hotel, New Orleans
St. Louis Blues
I Can't Believe You Really Love Me (vocal: Kay Weber)
The Way You Look Tonight (vocal: Kay Weber)
Summertime (theme)

12.30AM WEAF
JACK TEAGARDEN (3T's)
Hickory House, 52nd Street, NYC
'S Wonderful
Christmas Night In Harlem
Old Christmas Tree
I've Got You Under My Skin
I'm An Old Cowhand (vocal: Jack Teagarden)
I Got Rhythm
With Plenty Of Money And You
There's Frost On The Moon
'Way Down Yonder In New Orleans
Chapel In The Moonlight
Diane
Lazy River
Tea For Two

1.15AM WNEW
STUFF SMITH
Onyx Club, 72 W52nd Street, NYC
Oh, Lady Be Good
12th Street Rag
Jingle Bells
I'se A-Muggin' (theme)

■ SATURDAY 26 DECEMBER 1936

Went into NYC by train where I took my brother, Slim, to see this week's broadcast. Paul Douglas announced and Leith Stevens conducted the CBS Band. Bunny Berigan, featured trumpet, missed this broadcast for the first time since the first Swing session on June 13 because of illness. Tommy Dorsey, greatest living trombonist, and Fats Waller, great Negro swing pianist/vocalist/showman, who both record for Victor with their orchestras were guest stars. I got their autographs on their pictures. Also got the autographs of Dave Wade (trumpet) and Lloyd Williams (trumpet).

6.45PM WABC
SATURDAY NIGHT SWING SESSION No25
Studio 1, CBS Studios, NYC
I Can't Get Started (theme featuring Dave Wade on trumpet)
Jazzeroo (CBS Band "going to town": marvelous sax section; rhythm section)
The Toy Trumpet (written by Raymond Scott: Dave Hamilton, sax; Pete Pumiglio, cl; Lou Shoobe; Billy Gussak)
One, Two, Button Your Shoe (Babe Russin, sax)
I'm Crazy 'Bout My Baby (FATS WALLER singing and playing piano)
Hallelujah (Thomas 'Fats' Waller, radio's harmful little armful, doing a piano solo)
Cornfed
I'm Getting Sentimental Over You (TOMMY DORSEY trombone solo with CBS Band)
Ain't Misbehavin' (Tommy Dorsey on trombone: swell)
Mr Ghost Goes To Town
Honeysuckle Rose (We sat within 5 feet of Waller and Dorsey as they jammed out on 5 choruses of Waller's own composition)

RADIO LOGS

11:00PM WABC
BENNY GOODMAN
Hotel Pennsylvania, NYC
Dear Old Southland
Easy To Love
Smoke Dreams
Troublesome Trumpet
Sometimes I'm Happy
Skeleton In The Closet
I'm Coming, Virginia
In A Sentimental Mood
Always
Goodbye (theme)

12.20AM WOR
MAL HALLETT
Hotel Commodore, NYC
Organ Grinder's Swing
Basin Street Blues (vocal: Buddy Welcome)
Oh, Say, Can You Swing It?

12.30AM WMCA
BLANCHE CALLOWAY
Nixon Grand Theater, Philadelphia
Lady's Bagatelle
Organ Grinder's Swing
Tain't No Use
House Hop

12.50AM WOR
WOODY HERMAN
Roseland Ballroom, NYC
Wonderful Wintertime Dreams
It Happened Down In Dixieland (vocal: Woody Herman) (COLOSSAL)

■ SUNDAY 27 DECEMBER 1936

RADIO LOGS

12.45AM WEAF
BOB CROSBY
Roosevelt Hotel, New Orleans
Darktown Blues
The Day I Let You Get Away (vocal: Nappy Lamare)
Pennies From Heaven (vocal: Bob Crosby)
Sweet Lorraine

■ TUESDAY 29 DECEMBER 1936

RECORDING SESSION

HENRY 'RED' ALLEN
Recording session for Vocalion in New York City.
Henry 'Red' Allen (t/voc); ? (cl); Tab Smith (as); ? (ts/bar); Billy Kyle (p); Danny Barker (g); Johnny Williams (b); Alphonse Steele (d)
I Adore You (vHA) / *He Ain't Got Rhythm* (vHA) / *This Year's Kisses* (vHA) / *Let's Put Our Heads Together* (vHA)

RADIO LOGS

9.15PM WNEW
MAL HALLETT
Hotel Commodore, NYC
That's Life, I Guess (vocal: Buddy Welcome) (ballsy)
Copper Colored Gal
One Never Knows, Does One? (vocal: Jerry Perkins)
Angry
Boston Tea Party (theme)

09:30PM WABC
BENNY GOODMAN
Camel Caravan program, NYC
Bugle Call Rag
I Can't Give You Anything But Love (BG Sextet) (nuttsy: Musso & Elman with the Quartet)
Exactly Like You

12.00 MIDNIGHT WNEW
WOODY HERMAN
Roseland Ballroom, NYC
Blue Prelude (theme) (written by trumpeter Joe Bishop)
Blue Lou
Please Care For Me (vocal: Woody Herman)
Royal Garden Blues
Tea On The Terrace (vocal: Woody Herman)
Blue Skies
I've Had The Blues So Long
Liza
Blue Prelude (theme) (nuttsy)

12.40AM WWL
BOB CROSBY
Hotel Roosevelt, New Orleans
Nuttsy.
If I Could Have You (vocal: Bob Crosby)
Easy To Love (vocal: Kay Weber)
Basin Street Blues (vocal: Bob Crosby)
So Do I (vocal: Bob Crosby)
Pagan Love Song (COLOSSAL)
Summertime (theme) (swell)

■ WEDNESDAY 30 DECEMBER 1936

RECORDING SESSION

BENNY GOODMAN AND HIS ORCHESTRA
Recording session for Victor in New York City.
Benny Goodman (cl); Chris Griffin, Irving Goodman, Ziggy Elman (t); Red Ballard, Murray McEachern (tb); Bill DePew, Hymie Shertzer (as); Art Rollini, Vido Musso (ts); Jess Stacy (p); Allan Reuss (g); Harry Goodman (b); Gene Krupa (d); Jimmy Rushing, Margaret McCrae (voc)
He Ain't Got Rhythm (vJR) / *Never Should Have Told You* (vMMC) / *This Year's Kisses* (vMMC) / *You Can Tell She Comes From Dixie* (vMMC)

RADIO LOGS

11:00PM WABC
BENNY GOODMAN
Hotel Pennsylvania, NYC
An Apple A Day (vocal: Margaret McCrae)
Aunt Hagar's Blues
I'm Betting On You (vocal: Margaret McCrae)
Sugar Foot Stomp
Dinah (BG Quartet)
Goodbye (closing theme)

12.40AM WWL
BOB CROSBY
Hotel Roosevelt, New Orleans
That's What You Mean To Me (vocal: Bob Crosby)
She's Funny That Way (vocal: Bob Crosby)
Savoy Blues
My Kingdom For A Kiss (vocal: Bob Crosby)
Sweet Lorraine (Eddie Miller, tenor; Joe Sullivan, piano)
Summertime (theme)

DECEMBER 1936

■ THURSDAY 31 DECEMBER 1936

NEW YEAR'S EVE BROADCASTS:

Time	Artist	Venue	Station
11:15	Les Brown	Trianon Ballroom, Cleveland	WEAF
11:15	Eddie Duchin	Hotel Plaza, NYC	WOR
11:15	Ozzie Nelson	Hotel Lexington, NYC	WABC
11:15	Harold Stern	Fulton Royal, Brooklyn	WJZ
11:30	Dick Stabile	Hotel Lincoln, NYC	WABC
11:30	Cab Calloway	Cotton Club, NYC	WOR
11:30	Johnny Burkhart	Kentucky Hotel, Louisville, Ky	WHAS
11:30	Rita Rio	Hotel Governor Clinton, NYC	WJZ
11:45	Guy Lombardo	Roosevelt Hotel, NYC	WABC
11:45	Leo Reisman	Waldorf-Astoria Hotel, NYC	WOR
11:45	Ray Noble	Rainbow Room, NYC	WEAF
12:00	Benny Goodman	Hotel Pennsylvania, NYC	WABC
12:00	Guy Lombardo	Roosevelt Hotel, NYC	WOR
12:00	Russ Morgan	French Casino, NYC	WEAF
12:00	Woody Herman	Roseland Ballroom, NYC	WNEW
12:10	Count Basie	Roseland Ballroom, NYC	WNEW
12:15	Vincent Lopez	Hotel Astor, NYC	WABC
12:15	Mal Hallett	Hotel Commodore, NYC	WOR
12:15	3 T's	Hickory House, NYC	WJZ
12:30	Abe Lyman	Hotel New Yorker, NYC	WABC
12:30	Horace Heidt	Biltmore Hotel, NYC	WOR
12:30	Emil Coleman	Iridium Room, NYC	WJZ
12:45	Jerry Freeman	Paradise Restaurant, NYC	WABC
12:45	Benny Goodman	Hotel Pennsylvania, NYC	WOR
01:00	Henry Busse	Chez Paree, Chicago	WJZ
01:00	Gus Arnheim	Congress Hotel, Chicago	WOR
01:00	George Olsen	Edgewater Beach Hotel, Chicago	WABC
01:15	Roger Pryor	Hotel Sherman, Chicago	WOR
01:15	Kings Jesters	Bismarck Hotel, Chicago	WJZ
01:15	Frankie Masters	Stevens Hotel, Chicago	WABC
01:30	Carl Ravazza	Hotel Book-Cadillac, Detroit	WABC
01:30	Earl Hines	Grand Terrace, Chicago	WJZ
01:30	Shep Fields	Arcadia Restaurant, Philadelphia	WOR
01:45	Red Norvo	Blackhawk Restaurant, Chicago	WOR
01:45	Bobby Meeker	Hotel Jefferson, St. Louis	WABC
01:45	Bob LaRue	Hotel LaSalle, Detroit	WJZ
02:00	Larry Funk	Brown Palace Hotel, Denver	WABC
02:00	Al Kavelin	Blackstone Hotel, Chicago	WOR
02:00	Art Kassel	?	WJZ
02:00	Stuff Smith	Onyx Club, NYC	WMCA
02:15	Emerson Gill	William Penn Hotel, Pittsburgh	WJZ
02:15	Bob Young	Salt Lake City	WABC
02:15	Chick Webb	Savoy Ballroom, NYC	WMCA
02:15	Kay Kyser	Trianon Ballroom, Chicago	WOR
02:30	Nick Stuart	Reno, Nevada	WABC
02:30	Benny Meroff	Hotel Netherland-Plaza, Cincinnati	WOR
02:45	George Hall	Hotel Taft, NYC	WABC
02:45	Duke Ellington	Sebastian's Cotton Club, LA	WOR
03:00	Phil Harris	Palomar Ballroom, LA	WABC
03:00	Sterling Young	Wilshire Bowl, LA	WOR
03:00	Griff Williams	Mark Hopkins Hotel, SF	WJZ
03:15	Larry Lee	Beverly Wilshire Hotel, LA	WABC
03:15	George Breeze	Hotel Senator, Sacramento	WJZ
03:15	Phil Harris	Palomar Ballroom, LA	WOR
03:20	Earl Simmon	San Francisco	WJZ
03:30	Harry Owens	Royal Hawaiian Hotel, Hawaii	WABC
03:30	Francis Lyons	Hotel Francis Drake, SF	WOR
03:30	Jan Garber	Cocoanut Grove, Ambassador Hotel, LA	WJZ

RADIO LOGS

11.15PM WEAF
LES BROWN
Trianon Ballroom, Cleveland
Organ Grinder's Swing
Ain't Misbehavin'
Riffin' At The Ritz

11.30PM WABC
DICK STABILE
Blue Room, Hotel Lincoln, NYC
I'm The Cuban Cary
Will I Discover? (vocal: Bert Shaw)
Twinkle, Twinkle, Little Star (vocal: Billie Trask)
Easy To Love (vocal: Bert Shaw)
On The Air (theme)

11.30PM WOR
CAB CALLOWAY
Cotton Club, NYC
Nagasaki
Keep That Hi-De-Ho In Your Soul (vocal: Cab Calloway)
The Hi-De-Ho Miracle Man (vocal: Cab Calloway)
Chinese Rhythm
The Roar

12.00 MIDNIGHT WABC
BENNY GOODMAN
Hotel Pennsylvania, NYC
Let's Dance (opening theme)
Swingtime In The Rockies
Star Dust
Take Another Guess (vocal: Margaret McCrae)
Goodbye (closing theme)

12.10AM WNEW
COUNT BASIE
Roseland Ballroom, NYC
Huff Puff
Organ Grinder's Swing
The Glory Of Love (vocal: Jimmy Rushing)
Limehouse Blues
Jangled Nerves
Thanksgiving
Moten Swing (theme)

12.15AM WJZ
JACK TEAGARDEN (3T's)
Hickory House, 52nd Street, NYC
Honeysuckle Rose
Swingin' On The Swanee Shore
Goose Hangs High
Liza (harp: Caspar Reardon)
Nagasaki
The Peanut Vendor

12.45AM WOR
BENNY GOODMAN
Hotel Pennsylvania, NYC
Let's Dance (opening theme)
When You And I Were Young, Maggie
There's Something In The Air (vocal: Margaret McCrae)
I Got Rhythm (BGQuartet)
St. Louis Blues
Remember

1.30AM WJZ
EARL HINES
Grand Terrace, Chicago
Avalon
Marjorie
Rock And Ride
Cavernism (theme)

1.45AM WOR
RED NORVO
Blackhawk Restaurant, Chicago
You're My Best Bet (vocal: Stew Pletcher)
Did You Mean It? (vocal: Mildred Bailey)
Rosetta
Dear Old Southland
More Than You Know (vocal: Mildred Bailey)

2.00AM WMCA
STUFF SMITH
Onyx Club, 72 W52nd Street, NYC
I'se A-Muggin' (theme)
Heaven
Swing, Swing Mother-in-Law
I'm An Old Cowhand (vocal: 6 Spirits Of Rhythm)
If We Never Meet Again
Stuff Stomp

2.15AM WMCA
CHICK WEBB
Savoy Ballroom, NYC
Let's Get Together (theme)
House Hop
Until The Real Thing Comes Along (vocal: Ella Fitzgerald & Charles Linton)
Jam Session
Love, What Are You Doing To My Heart? (vocal: Charles Linton)
Mr Ghost Goes To Town
Copenhagen
This Is My Last Affair (vocal: Ella Fitzgerald)
Bugle Call Rag

2.30AM WABC
NICK STUART
Reno, Nevada
Tea On The Terrace
Organ Grinder's Swing
The Night Is Young
It Ain't Right
Bugle Call Rag

2.30AM WOR
BENNY MEROFF
Hotel Netherland-Plaza, Cincinnati
Get Happy
Basin Street Blues
Tiger Rag
It Ain't Right

2.45AM WOR
DUKE ELLINGTON
Sebastian's Cotton Club, LA
East St. Louis Toodle-Oo (theme)
Big Chief De Sota
I'm Satisfied (vocal: Ivie Anderson)
Oh, Babe, Maybe Someday (vocal: Ivie Anderson)
Organ Grinder's Swing
Ring Dem Bells

3.00AM WABC
PHIL HARRIS
Palomar Ballroom, LA
It's De-Lovely
Goose Hangs High
Rhyme For Love
Goodnight My Love (vocal: Judy Janas)

3.15AM WOR
PHIL HARRIS
Palomar Ballroom, LA
Under The Spell Of The Voodoo Drums
There's Frost On The Moon (vocal: Judy Janas)
You Can Tell She Comes From Dixie (vocal: Phil Harris)
Chapel In The Moonlight

Chick Webb

JANUARY 1937

Hotel Pennsylvania: **Benny Goodman**
Hotel Commodore: **Mal Hallett**
Hotel Lincoln: **Dick Stabile** (–?); **Isham Jones** (?–)
Hotel Taft: **George Hall**
Hotel New Yorker: **Abe Lyman**
Hotel Lexington: **Ozzie Nelson**
Hotel Astor: **Vincent Lopez**
Rainbow Room: **Ray Noble**

Apollo Theater: **Teddy Hill** (1–7); **Willie Bryant** (8–14); **Fats Waller** (15–21); **Chick Webb** (22–28); **Willie Bryant** (29–)
Paramount Theater: **Glen Gray** (–5); **Ray Noble** (13–)
Loew's State Theater: **Fats Waller** (8–14); **Jimmie Lunceford** (29–)

Cotton Club Downtown: **Cab Calloway/Bill Robinson**
Hickory House: **3T's: Frank Trumbauer, Jack & Charlie Teagarden**
Onyx Club: **Stuff Smith**

■ SATURDAY 2 JANUARY 1937

Hughie and I went in by subway to see this week's broadcast. We met Roddy Snow, H. Pinger, Morningstar and Mortimer there. The guests were Claude Hopkins, famous Negro pianist who leads his own band, and Joe Sodja, a swell, young, new guitar player, and his accompanist, pianist Nat Jaffe. Got their autographs and Cliff Natalie (trumpet), Ben Chorney (?) (bass), Glenn Miller (trombone) and Jules Jacob (sax).

6.45PM WABC
SATURDAY NIGHT SWING SESSION No26
Studio 1, CBS Studios, NYC
I Can't Get Started (theme) (Bunny Berigan on trumpet)
Pick Yourself Up (CBS Band playing swell: brass; saxes; Maffay's guitar)
I Never Knew
Three Little Words (CLAUDE HOPKINS on piano)
Vampin' A Co-ed (CLAUDE HOPKINS on piano)
Organ Grinder's Swing (one of their best arrangements: BALLSY)
Love Me Or Leave Me (DORIS KERR singing: great)
Down By The Old Mill Stream (Bunny Berigan trumpet solo)
China Boy (JOE SODJA on guitar with Nat Jaffe on piano)
Sheik Of Araby (JOE SODJA on guitar with Nat Jaffe on piano)
Who's Sorry Now (JOE SODJA on guitar with Nat Jaffe on piano)
Hand In Glove (CBS Band)

RADIO LOGS

2.10AM WGN
RED NORVO
Blackhawk Restaurant, Chicago
In The Middle Of A Kiss
Dream Awhile (vocal: Mildred Bailey)
Star Dust
Bye Bye Baby (vocal: Stew Pletcher)
St. Louis Blues (vocal: Mildred Bailey)
Love Me Or Leave Me

■ MONDAY 4 JANUARY 1937

RADIO LOGS

7.15PM WJZ
BUGHOUSE RHYTHM
San Francisco
Nobody Lied (gut-bucket style: written & arranged by Wilbert Baranco)
Glockenspiel (classical piece showing swing chimes)
Stompin' At The Savoy (EDSON GILSON playing swing chimes)
Love Song Of A Half-Wit (written by Will Hudson: his latest)

11.30PM WEAF
RAY NOBLE
Rainbow Room, NYC
One, Two, Button Your Shoe
Under Your Spell (vocal: Howard Berry)
The Way You Look Tonight
Easy To Love
Now
There's Something In The Air
You're Everything Faithful
The Touch Of Your Lips

11.30PM WABC
RED NICHOLS
Mayfair Casino, Cleveland, Ohio
Wailing Of The Winds
You're My Best Bet (vocal: Songcopators)
Ida
Swinging On The Swanee (vocal: Songcopators)
Three Little Words (vocal: Songcopators)
Christopher Columbus
Midnight Blue
Silver Threads Among The Gold
You've Got That Certain Something
Stop, Look, And Listen (vocal: Songcopators)
Troublesome Trumpet
Goodnight My Love (vocal: Jack Wilshire)

11.45PM WJZ
EARL HINES
Grand Terrace, Chicago
Nobody's Sweetheart
Love And Learn (vocal: Walter Fuller)
I Never Should Have Told You So (vocal: Ida James)
Here's Love In Your Eye (vocal: Walter Fuller)
Keep Me In Your Dreams (vocal: Ida James)
Cavernism (theme)

12.00 MIDNIGHT WJZ
GUS ARNHEIM
Congress Hotel, Chicago
Take Another Guess (vocal: June Robbins)
May I Have The Next Romance With You? (vocal: Ray Foster)
Nagasaki
I Can't Give You Anything But Love
There's Frost On The Moon (vocal: June Robbins)

You've Got Something (vocal: Ray Foster)
Smoke Dreams (vocal: June Robbins)
St. Louis Blues
Ain't Misbehavin'
Easy To Love

12.00 MIDNIGHT WOR
MAL HALLETT
Hotel Commodore, NYC
Lousy.
I Love You From Coast To Coast
If My Heart Could Only Talk (vocal: Jerry Perkins)
I'm In A Dancing Mood
Easy To Love (vocal: Jerry Perkins)
Ink Spots (FRANKIE CARLE on piano)
Big Chief De Sota
Summer Nights
I Was Saying To The Moon
I'm An Old Cowhand
Japanese Sandman
It's Love I'm After (vocal: Buddy Welcome)

■ TUESDAY 5 JANUARY 1937

RADIO LOGS

4.00PM WEAF
CHICK WEBB
Savoy Ballroom, NYC
Nuttsy.
Vote For Mr Rhythm (vocal: Ella Fitzgerald)
Jamboree
Darling, Not Without You (vocal: Charles Linton)
Swing Your Feet
Blue Lou
You Turned The Tables On Me (vocal: Ella Fitzgerald)
'Way Down Yonder In New Orleans
House Hop
There's Something In The Air
Let's Get Together (theme)

7.15PM WOR
JOE HAYMES
Lakewood, N.J.
Darn Good.
Jingle Bells (Benny Goodman's arrangement)
A Call To Arms (vocal: Barry McKinley)
Blue Lou
Tain't No Use (vocal: Barbara Burns)
White Star Of Sigma Nu

7.15PM WOR
SKEETER PALMER
Murray's, Tuckahoe, N.Y.
Fair.
Nothing Till Now (theme)
Me And The Moon
Midnight Blue
Make Believe Ballroom

9.00PM WNEW
MAL HALLETT
Hotel Commodore, NYC
On The Beach At Bali-Bali (vocal: Buddy Welcome)
Honeysuckle Rose
Serenade In The Night
She Shall Have Music
Hallelujah (vocal: Buddy Welcome)
Angry
Boston Tea Party (theme)

9.30PM WABC
BENNY GOODMAN
Camel Caravan program, NYC
He Ain't Got Rhythm (vocal: Frances Hunt) (latest song by Irving Berlin: swell singing by new vocalist)
Limehouse Blues (BG Trio) (Gene Krupa sick with 'flu, so Hampton plays drums)
Goodtime Charlie (Elman's trumpet, etc)

11.00PM WMCA
FRANKIE WARD
Hotel Bradford, Boston
Fair.
I'm In A Dancing Mood
Back Home Again In Indiana
Three Little Words
Mr Ghost Goes To Town
Thou Swell

12.00 MIDNIGHT WNEW
WOODY HERMAN
Roseland Ballroom, NYC
Colossal.
Blue Skies
I'll Forsake All Others
Weary Blues
Basin Street Blues (vocal: Woody Herman)
Ol' Man Mose (vocal: Woody Herman)
I Can't Give You Anything But Love (arranged by Gordon Jenkins)
Tea On The Terrace (vocal: Woody Herman)
Diga Diga Doo

12.30AM WMCA
CHICK WEBB
Savoy Ballroom, NYC
That's Life, I Guess (vocal: Ella Fitzgerald)
Big Chief De Sota
Together We Live (vocal: Louis Jordan)
Cream Puff
Sing Me A Swing Song (vocal: Ella Fitzgerald)
Limehouse Blues
Swinging On The Reservation (vocal: Ella Fitzgerald)

12.40AM WWL
BOB CROSBY
Hotel Roosevelt, New Orleans
I've Got You Under My Skin (vocal: Kay Weber)
Did You Mean It? (vocal: Bob Crosby)

■ WEDNESDAY 6 JANUARY 1937

RADIO LOGS

3.15AM WABC
BENNY GOODMAN
NYC
Special broadcast to England. Vocalist Frances Hunt joined the band two days ago.
Goodnight My Love (vocal: Frances Hunt)
Stompin' At The Savoy (Murray McEachern's trombone)
Swing Low Sweet Chariot (Elman; Musso)
Always
Bugle Call Rag
Dinah (BG Quartet)
Body And Soul (BG Trio)

JANUARY 1937

Isham Jones

11.00PM WABC
ISHAM JONES
Hotel Lincoln, NYC
Opening night at the Lincoln Hotel. This is a NEW Isham Jones Band.
There's Something In The Air
Skeleton In The Closet (vocal: Eddie Stone)
I Can't Get Started (vocal: Joe Martin)
One, Two, Button Your Shoe (vocal: Eddie Stone)
So Do I (vocal: Joe Martin)
Devil's Holiday
Pennies From Heaven
California, Here I Come
Liza
Easy To Love (vocal: Joe Martin)
I'll See You In My Dreams (theme)

11.00PM WNEW
SIX SPIRITS OF RHYTHM
Onyx Club, 72 W52nd Street, NYC
Stuff Smith is on a week's vacation. Wellman Braud is on bass with Teddy Bunn (guitar).
Some Of These Days
I Surrender Dear
Papa Tree Top Tall
Gypsy Fiddler
One, Two, Button Your Shoe
Fooled Again
That's Why I'm Blue (written by Teddy Bunn, guitar player)

11.30PM WEAF
GLEN GRAY
Rainbow Room, NYC
For Sentimental Reasons (vocal: Kenny Sargent)
I Love You From Coast To Coast (vocal: Pee Wee Hunt)
The Way You Look Tonight (vocal: Kenny Sargent)
Back Home Again In Indiana (Sonny Dunham's trumpet)
I Cried For You (vocal: Kenny Sargent)
The Moon Is Grinning At Me (vocal: Pee Wee Hunt)
So Do I
Pagan Love Song

■ THURSDAY 7 JANUARY 1937

RECORDING SESSION
TOMMY DORSEY AND HIS ORCHESTRA
Recording session for Victor in New York City.
Tommy Dorsey (tb); Bunny Berigan, Steve Lipkins, Joe Bauer, Bob Cusumano (t); Les Jenkins, Artie Foster (tb); Joe Dixon (cl/as); Fred Stulce, Clyde Rounds (as); Bud Freeman (ts); Dick Jones (p); Carmen Mastren (g); Gene Traxler (b); Dave Tough (d); Edythe Wright, Jack Leonard, Three Esquires (voc)
The Goona Goo (vEW) / *If My Heart Could Only Talk* (vJL) / *Mr. Ghost Goes To Town* / *Lookin' Around Corners For You* (v3E)

RADIO LOGS
9.15PM WOR
RED NORVO
Blackhawk Restaurant, Chicago
With Plenty Of Money And You (vocal: Stew Pletcher)
Clap Hands, Here Comes Charlie
Georgia On My Mind (vocal: Mildred Bailey)
That's A-Plenty
Now That Summer Is Gone

10.00PM WOR
CAB CALLOWAY
Cotton Club, NYC
Sweet Sue (vocal: Cab Calloway)
My Melancholy Baby (vocal: Cab Calloway)
Belles Of Harlem
Zaz-Zuh-Zaz (vocal: Cab Calloway)
The Beggar (vocal: Bennie Payne)
I Learned About Love From Her (vocal: Cab Calloway)
The Night is Young (vocal: Cab Calloway)
Some Of These Days (vocal: Cab Calloway)

■ FRIDAY 8 JANUARY 1937

RECORDING SESSION
RED NORVO AND HIS ORCHESTRA
Recording session for Brunswick in Chicago.
Red Norvo (xyl/ldr); Bill Hyland, Stew Pletcher, Eddie Sauter (t); Al Mastren (tb); Hank D'Amico (cl/as); Frank Simeone (as); Herbie Haymer (ts); Joe Liss (p); Dave Barbour (g); Pete Peterson (b); Maurice Purtill (d); Mildred Bailey (voc)
A Thousand Dreams Of You (vMB) / *Smoke Dreams* (vMB) / *Slummin' On Park Avenue* (vMB) / *I've Got My Love To Keep Me Warm* (vMB)

RADIO LOGS
5.30PM WABC
DORIS KERR
CBS Studios, NYC
Maybe Someday (vocal: Doris Kerr)
May I Have The Next Romance With You? (vocal: Doris Kerr)
You Swing (vocal: Doris Kerr)

9.30PM WOR
RED NORVO
Blackhawk Restaurant, Chicago
That's Love (vocal: Mildred Bailey)
I'm An Old Cowhand (vocal: Maurice Purtill)
Dream Awhile (vocal: Mildred Bailey)
I Never Knew
Gone (vocal: Mildred Bailey)
Chapel In The Moonlight
Is That Religion? (vocal: Mildred Bailey)
I Got Rhythm

■ SATURDAY 9 JANUARY 1937

Went to New York City with Hugh Pastoriza, Saturday January 9. We left Bronxville at 9:15 am and took the subway to Mt. Vernon. We went to the Music Corp. of America (MCA) where we got pictures of Tommy Dorsey and Count Basie for nothing and to the Columbia Broadcasting System where we ordered pictures of Vincent Maffay (guitar), Frank Trumbauer and Adrian Rollini. We then went to Loew's State Theater where we saw Thomas 'Fats' Waller and his Band on the stage. He was the nuts. He had 5 saxes, 5 rhythm and 6 brass players. He played *Marie* (Fats singing and playing piano), *Until The Real Thing Comes Along* (Fats singing-piano), *Darktown Lullaby* (swell Negress singing), *You Turned The Tables On Me* (Negress singing), *When Did You Leave Heaven?*, *Tea For Two* (colossal piano solo by Fats), *I Would Do Anything For You* (featuring Slick Jones on drums), *St. Louis Blues* (Al Washington holding a clarinet note for 2 minutes), *Keep On Smiling* (Emmett Matthews singing and playing tenor sax). We went around to the stage door and got Fats Waller to autograph his picture and the autographs of George James (alto sax), Slick Jones (drums), Edward 'Andy' Anderson (trumpet), C.E. Smith (trumpet), Al Casey (guitar), George Wilson (trombone). We then went over to Rockwell-O'Keefe to see if we could get some pictures. They didn't have any but we met Mr. O'Keefe.

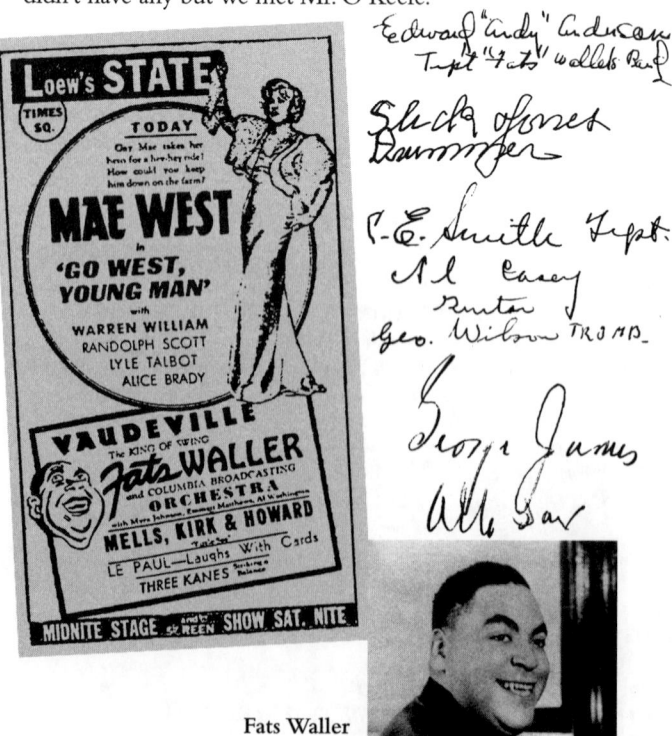

Fats Waller

At 2:00pm we paid 55 cents and went in the Roseland Ballroom, Broadway at 51st Street. Woody Herman's Band and Count Basie's Band played alternately for one hour each from 2 to 6 o'clock. Both bands are the nuts. Herman's is only about 3 months old and is composed of a lot of men from Isham Jones' old band. Woody Herman sings and plays a swell clarinet. Count Bill Basie used to play piano in Bennie Moten's Kansas City Band and just started his present band 7 months ago. He has played in Kansas City, Grand Terrace Café, Chicago, and now at Roseland in NYC. Both bands have 4 rhythm, Herman's band has 4 brass, 5 reeds while Basie has 4 reeds and 5 brass. James Rushing sings for Basie. We got the autographs of all the musicians in Count Basie's Band on a picture of Basie and ten of Woody Herman's Band on a small picture of Herman which he gave to us.

Basie's Band played: *Unknown title* / *Too Bad* (Rushing) / *Unknown title* / *Blue Lou* / *If We Never Meet Again* (Rushing) / *Unknown title* / *Wild Party* / *My First Thrill* / *My Blue Heaven* (Rushing) / *Tea For Two* / *Riffin' At The Ritz* (same arrangement as Benny Goodman uses) / *I Surrender Dear* / *Unknown title* / *Big Chief De Sota* / *Skeleton In The Closet* / *Unknown title* / *Unknown title* / *Pennies From Heaven* (Rushing) / *Unknown title* / *But Definitely* / *I Ain't Got Nobody* (Rushing) / *Dinah* (Rushing) / *Unknown title* / *Nagasaki* (Rushing with Band) / *Moten Swing* (theme).

Woody Herman played *Blue Prelude* (theme featuring Neil Reid on trombone and Nick Hupfer on violin) / *On The Alamo* / *Blue Lou* / *Trust In Me* (Herman vocal) / *Liza* / *Unknown title* / *Tain't Good* / *Unknown title* / *Weary Blues*. Broadcast over WOR at 5:00pm: *Blue Prelude* (theme) / *Blue Lou* / *I Can't Give You Anything But Love* / *I'll Forsake All Others* (Herman vocal) / *Mr. Ghost Goes To Town* / *Tea On The Terrace* / *Old Fashioned Swing* (Herman & Band vocal) / *For Sentimental Reasons* / *Inka Dinka Doo*.

Woody Herman

Count Basie

We then went over to 485 Madison Avenue where we saw the Saturday Night Swing Broadcast at 6:45. Numbers played were *I Can't Get Started* (theme featuring Bunny Berigan on trumpet) / *An Apple A Day* (CBS Band) / *Honeysuckle Rose* (Al Rinker's vocal Swing Octet with 7 males and 1 female, partly made of the 4 Modernaires) / *Stop, Look, And Listen* (colossal arrangement by CBS Band — Manners' clarinet) / *Sing, Sing, Sing* (Hazel Scott playing piano) / *Unknown title* (Hazel Scott) / *Loveless Love* (Bunny Berigan trumpet solo) / *A Call To Arms* (muted trumpets, saxes) / *Twilight In Turkey* (written by Raymond Scott and played by Johnny Williams-drums; Dave Harris-sax; Dave Wade-trumpet; Pete Pumiglio-clarinet; Lou Shoobe-bass; Raymond Scott-piano with the lights turned out in the studio) / *Stompin' At The Savoy* (Rinker's octet) / *Wang Wang Blues*.

Got the autographs of Al Rinker, Hazel Scott, Art Manners (clarinet) and Leith Stevens (director).

RADIO LOGS

9.30PM WOR
RED NORVO
Blackhawk Restaurant, Chicago
A Porter's Love Song (vocal: Mildred Bailey)
Basin Street Blues (vocal: Stew Pletcher)
Midnight Blue (vocal: Mildred Bailey)
Rosetta
Smoke Dreams (vocal: Mildred Bailey)
Bye Bye Baby (vocal: Stew Pletcher)
Body And Soul
Shoutin' In That Amen Corner (vocal: Mildred Bailey)

9.50PM WJZ
FATS WALLER
I'm Crazy 'Bout My Baby (vocal: Fats Waller)
Ooh, Looka There, Ain't She Pretty? (vocal: Fats Waller)

10.30PM WEAF
GLEN GRAY
Rainbow Room, NYC
Remember
I'll Sing You A Thousand Love Songs (vocal: Kenny Sargent)
Tain't Good (vocal: Pee Wee Hunt)
Darling, Not Without You (vocal: Kenny Sargent)
Zig Zag
I've Got You Under My Skin (vocal: Kenny Sargent)
Lazy Bones (vocal: Pee Wee Hunt)
I'm Getting Sentimental Over You (5 trombones)
Should I?
Smoke Rings (theme)

12.30AM WMCA
TEDDY HILL
Nixon-Grand Theater, Philadelphia
Swingtime In The Rockies
Organ Grinder's Swing
Honeysuckle Rose
Make Believe Ballroom
Sensation
Deep Forest

■ SUNDAY 10 JANUARY 1937

RADIO LOGS

2.00PM WJZ
CARL KRESS-DICK McDONOUGH
Magic Key program, NYC
Stage Fright (original composition)
Heat Wave

10.30PM WOR
CAB CALLOWAY
Hotel Roosevelt, New Orleans
Nobody's Sweetheart
So Do I
Bugle Call Rag
The Hi-De-Ho Miracle Man (vocal: Cab Calloway)
Sylvia
Keep That Hi-De-Ho In Your Soul (vocal: Cab Calloway)
St. Louis Blues

■ MONDAY 11 JANUARY 1937

RECORDING SESSION

ADRIAN ROLLINI TRIO
Recording session for Decca in New York City.
Adrian Rollini (vib); Frank Victor (g); Haig Stephens (b)
Rebound / Jitters

■ TUESDAY 12 JANUARY 1937

RECORDING SESSION

BILLIE HOLIDAY & HER ORCHESTRA
Recording session for Vocalion in NYC.
Jonah Jones (t); Edgar Sampson (cl/as); Ben Webster (ts); Teddy Wilson (p); Allan Reuss (g); John Kirby (b); Cozy Cole (d); Billie Holiday (v)
One Never Knows, Does One? / I've Got My Love To Keep Me Warm / If My Heart Could Only Talk / Please Keep Me In Your Dreams

RADIO LOGS

4.05PM WEAF
CHICK WEBB
Savoy Ballroom, NYC
Swell. Exceptionally smooth for a Negro band.
Honeysuckle Rose
Swinging For The King (Taft Jordan's trumpet; Chick Webb's drumming)
Living In Seclusion (vocal: Louis Jordan) (swell vocal; saxes)
Stompin' At The Savoy (fast tempo: trombone; tenor sax; Taft's high trumpet)
There's Frost On The Moon (vocal: Ella Fitzgerald & Charles Linton)
Tain't Good (vocal: Ella Fitzgerald) (nice swing clarinet; Chick Webb's drums)
Harlem Heat (Taft Jordan's trumpet; tenor; clarinet; clarinets with brass; Chick Webb's drumming)
Swinging On The Reservation (vocal: Ella Fitzgerald) (ballsy drumming)
Let's Get Together (theme) (foxtrot: very good)

7.15PM WOR
FRANK DAILEY
Meadowbrook, N.J.
Good.
Until The Real Thing Comes Along
Hand In Glove (vocal: Frankie Hope)
Pennies From Heaven
Hallelujah!
May I Have The Next Dance?
Gypsy Violins (theme)

9.00PM WNEW
MAL HALLETT
Hotel Commodore, NYC
Boston Tea Party (theme) (written by 1st trumpeter, Frank Ryerson)
It's De-Lovely (vocal: Barbara Jason) (to be married next month)
Night (vocal: Jerry Perkins) (17-yr-old vocalist from Chicago)
Love Marches On
The Lonesome Road (vocal: Mal Hallett's Glee Club)
Sittin' On The Moon (vocal: Buddy Welcome) (sax/clarinet player)
Ah, But Is It Love?
You're Everything Sweet (vocal: Buddy Welcome)
So Do I (vocal: Jerry Perkins)

9:30PM WABC
BENNY GOODMAN
Camel Caravan program, NYC
It's De-Lovely (vocal: Frances Hunt)
Ridin' High
With Plenty Of Money And You (vocal: Frances Hunt)

10.30PM WOR
CAB CALLOWAY
Cotton Club, NYC
Plenty good.
Swing, Swing, Swing (vocal: Cab Calloway)
Emaline (vocal: Cab Calloway)
Mr Ghost Goes To Town
Minnie The Moocher's Wedding Day (vocal: Cab Calloway)
I Ain't Got Nobody (vocal: Cab Calloway)

10.30PM WAAB
HUDSON-DeLANGE
Raymor Ballroom, Boston
Hobo On Park Avenue (theme)
The Moon Is Grinning At Me (vocal: Fredda Gibson)
Swing, Swing Mother-in-Law
Ain't-cha Glad (vocal: Eddie DeLange)
Monopoly Swing
Hobo On Park Avenue (theme)

■ WEDNESDAY 13 JANUARY 1937

RADIO LOGS

6.45PM WMCA
STUFF SMITH
Commercial program, NYC
Alexander's Ragtime Band (COLOSSAL: Stuff Smith's violin; Jonah Jones' trumpet; tenor)
Pennies From Heaven (vocal: Ella Fitzgerald) (Sandy Williams' trombone)
Ol' Man River (featuring Jonah Jones on trumpet: NUTTSY; tenor)
When A Lady Meets A Gentleman Down South (vocal: Ella Fitzgerald)
12th Street Rag (Smith's hot violin was colossal)
It's De-Lovely (vocal: Ella Fitzgerald) (short Ella vocal with whole band singing)

7.30PM WEAF
CHARLIE BARNET
Motor Boat Show, Grand Central Palace
Fair. Barnet plays a swell tenor.
Christopher Columbus
Stop, Look And Listen (vocal: Modernaires)
Oh, Say, Can You Swing?
Did You Mean It? (vocal: Modernaires)
Sailin' (theme)

8.00PM WAAB
HUDSON-DeLANGE
Raymor Ballroom, Boston
Pennies From Heaven (vocal: Eddie DeLange)
You Turned The Table On Me (vocal: Fredda Gibson)
Mr Ghost Goes To Town
Hobo On Park Avenue (theme)

8.15PM WOR
COUNT BASIE
Roseland Ballroom, NYC
Nuttsy.
Yeah, Man!
Walking Through The Park (written by Basie, nuttsy: Lester Young's tenor; trumpet)
Evenin' (vocal: Jimmy Rushing)
Streamline Strut (Lester Young's tenor; Basie's piano)
Moten Swing (theme) (nuttsy)

9.30PM WGN
RED NORVO
Blackhawk Restaurant, Chicago
Gone (vocal: Mildred Bailey)
Decca Stomp
Goodnight My Love (vocal: Mildred Bailey)
Bye Bye Baby (vocal: Stew Pletcher)

10.10PM WMCA
FRANKIE WARD
Hotel Bradford, Boston
Good.
Mr Ghost Goes To Town
Please Keep Me In Your Dreams
Easy To Love

I'll Always Be In Love With You
Rainbow On The River (vocal: Ethel ?)
Thou Swell

11.00PM WABC
BENNY GOODMAN
Hotel Pennsylvania, NYC
Bert Parks announced.
I Want To Be Happy (Musso's tenor; Elman's trumpet; very smooth brass)
There's Frost On The Moon (vocal: Frances Hunt)
Alexander's Ragtime Band (marvelous clarinet)
Goodnight My Love (vocal: Frances Hunt)
Riffin' At The Ritz (ballsy: Musso's tenor; Elman's trumpet)
It's De-Lovely (vocal: Frances Hunt)
Three Little Words
One Never Knows Does One? (vocal: Frances Hunt)
Tain't Good (vocal: Frances Hunt)
Jam Session (swell: just recorded)
Goodbye (closing theme)

■ THURSDAY 14 JANUARY 1937

RECORDING SESSION

BENNY GOODMAN AND HIS ORCHESTRA
Recording session for Victor in New York City.
Benny Goodman (cl); Chris Griffin, Harry James, Ziggy Elman (t); Red Ballard, Murray McEachern (tb); Bill DePew, Hymie Shertzer (as); Art Rollini, Vido Musso (ts); Jess Stacy (p); Allan Reuss (g); Harry Goodman (b); Gene Krupa (d); Frances Hunt (voc)
Goodnight My Love (vFH) / *I Want To Be Happy* / *Chlo-e (Song Of The Swamp)* / *Rosetta*

CHICK WEBB ORCHESTRA
Recording session for Decca in New York City.
Ella Fitzgerald (voc); Mario Bauza, Taft Jordan, Bobby Stark (t); Sandy Williams, Nat Story (tb); Louis Jordan, Pete Clark (as); Ted McRae (ts); Wayman Carver (ts/fl); Tommy Fulford (p); John Trueheart (g); Beverly Peer (b); Chick Webb (d)
Take Another Guess (vEF) / *Love Marches On* (vTrio)

ELLA FITZGERALD WITH THE MILLS BROTHERS
Ella Fitzgerald, The Mills Brothers (voc), Bernard Addison (g)
Big Boy Blue

RADIO LOGS

9.15PM WOR
RED NORVO
Blackhawk Restaurant, Chicago
Swell.
You're My Best Bet (vocal: Stew Pletcher) (trumpeter)
Goodnight My Love (vocal: Mildred Bailey)
Smoke Dreams (vocal: Mildred Bailey)
Dear Old Southland

10.00PM WOR
CAB CALLOWAY
Cotton Club, NYC
Good.
Hot Stuff (vocal: Cab Calloway)
Smoke Dreams (vocal: Bennie Payne)
Rosetta (vocal: Cab Calloway)
It Ain't Necessarily So (vocal: Cab Calloway)
It Happened Down In Dixieland (vocal: Cab Calloway)
My Melancholy Baby (vocal: Cab Calloway)
Copper Colored Gal (vocal: Cab Calloway)
Nagasaki (vocal: Cab Calloway)

11.30PM WABC
RED NICHOLS
New Mayfair Casino, Cleveland, Ohio
Fair.
Wail Of The Winds (theme)
Gee, But You're Swell (vocal: Songcopators)
I've Got You Under My Skin (vocal: Songcopators)
There's Something In The Air
There'll Be Some Changes Made
Alexander's Ragtime Band
Coast To Coast (vocal: Jack Wilshire)
Old Black Joe
I Can Pull A Rabbit Out Of My Hat
Dese Dem Dose
South Sea Island Magic (vocal: Songcopators)
Dodging A Divorcee
Tain't Good (vocal: Arline Owens)

11.45PM WJZ
EARL HINES
Grand Terrace, Chicago
Deep Forest (theme)
Love And Learn (vocal: Walter Fuller)
I Never Should Have Told You (vocal: Ida James)
Talkin' To My Heart
Keep Swingin'
Keep Me In Your Dreams (vocal: Ida James)

12.00 MIDNIGHT WOR
BENNY GOODMAN
Hotel Pennsylvania, NYC
Bert Parks announced.
I Want To Be Happy (solid drums by Krupa; Musso's swell tenor; Stacy's piano; Elman's trumpet)
This Year's Crop Of Kisses (vocal: Frances Hunt) (nuttsy new song: clarinet with Stacy's piano; Krupa)
Somebody Loves Me (just recorded: Musso's tenor; trumpet)
If We Never Meet Again (good: Elman's trumpet; Musso's tenor)
Sugar Foot Stomp (COLOSSAL)
Easy To Love (Stacy's intro; Elman's trumpet)
He Ain't Got Rhythm (vocal: Frances Hunt)
Limehouse Blues (BG Quartet)
There's Something In The Air (vocal: Frances Hunt)
House Hop

■ FRIDAY 15 JANUARY 1937

RADIO LOGS

9.30PM **WOR**
RED NORVO
Blackhawk Reataurant, Chicago
Pennies From Heaven
With Plenty of Money And You (vocal: Stew Pletcher) (trumpeter)
I've Got You Under My Skin (vocal: Mildred Bailey)
Sing, Baby, Sing

12.30AM **WEAF**
LES BROWN
Trianon Ballroom, Cleveland, Ohio
Les Brown and his Duke Blue Devil Band is only a half year old. All its members went to Duke University, N. Carolina last year. Fair.
Yesterdays (theme)
Tea On The Terrace
Goodnight My Love
Copper Colored Gal
Easy To Love
Someone To Care For Me
Everybody Swing
So Do I
Jingle Bells

■ SATURDAY 16 JANUARY 1937

Hugh Pastoriza, his cousin from England, and I went down by train to see this week's Swing Broadcast held at 485 Madison Avenue, NYC at 6:45. Fats Waller (comical Negro pianist), The Symphonettes (girl vocal trio), and Glenn Miller (trombone player formerly with Ray Noble) were guests. I got the autograph of Glenn Miller in the book 'Rhythm On Record' on a picture of Ray Noble's 1936 band. Also got Jerry Colonna's autograph who was in the small audience at the broadcast. He is employed by CBS and plays trombone. Paul Douglas and George Hogan announced this program. This program was dedicated to the welcoming of radio station WPRO, Providence, R.I. to the chain of Columbia stations.

Jerry Colonna

6.45PM **WABC**
SATURDAY NIGHT SWING SESSION No28
Studio 1, CBS Studios, NYC
I Can't Get Started (theme) (featuring Bunny Berigan on trumpet)
Papa Tree Top Tall (colossal: saxes, brass, bass, Johnny Williams' drums)
Raggin' The Scale (Russ Genner's trombone; Lou Shoobe's bass; Art Manners' clarinet)
Hallelujah (Thomas 'Fats' Waller singing in his comical way and 'beating out' on the piano)
St. Louis Blues (Waller playing a COLOSSAL piano: aided by Berigan. Waller then left for the Apollo Theater where he is playing this week)
Somebody Loves Me (NUTTSY: Berigan; Wade; Natoli; Miolla; Genner; Vargas in muted brass section)
I'm Doin' That Thing (swell vocal by girl trio, Symphonettes, with their arranger Hugh Martin on piano)
Old Fashioned Love (Berigan trumpet solo marvelous: Leith Stevens directed band)
Community Swing (Glenn Miller directing his own composition: BALLSY; Pumiglio's clarinet)

HOTEL PENNSYLVANIA

After the broadcast we took a taxi over to the Hotel Pennsylvania, 7th Avenue & 33rd Street, where we met Nancy Long, a girl friend from Scarsdale, and Mr. Pastoriza and went to see Benny Goodman's Band from 7.30 to 11.30. We sat at a table next to the band and had a $2 dinner (the cheapest). Besides dancing with Nancy (too crowded to dance much) Hughie and I got the autographs of all the band in the book Rhythm On Record. This book was written by Hilton R. Schleman, published in England, costs $2.50 in the U.S. and has an introduction by Johnny Hammond. It lists all the recordings, with their personnels, from 1906 to 1936. Every time I had one of the guys autograph it they would ask where I got the book and spend a long time looking through it. In this way I got acquainted with many members of the band. This Benny Goodman Band sure is the best going. Gene Krupa, best swing drummer to ever live, is a showman when he drums. He chews gum and moves his whole body, especially his hands, arms, legs and head. Teddy Wilson (colored), although only 23 years-old, is the greatest pianist that ever lived. We talked with him about some of the recordings he has made. He said that he would send us each a picture of himself. Since he is a negro he is not allowed to play with Goodman's white band, but he plays with the Trio and Quartet nightly at the Hotel Pennsylvania. He also plays solo piano during intermissions. Lionel Hampton, who used to play in Les Hite's Band and in Paul Howard's Quality Serenaders in Los Angeles, played drums and vibraphone in his own band at LA's Paradise Club until he got the call from Benny last summer. When Benny Goodman's Band played at the Palomar Ballroom in LA during July and August, they used to go over to the Paradise and listen to Hampton. Goodman was so impressed that he had Hampton come to the Hotel Pennsylvania last November. He has been playing, and singing, with the Quartet ever since. Since he is a Negro he isn't usually allowed to play with the band but last week, when Gene Krupa got the influenza, Lionel played drums with the whole band. He sure can play them swell. He is supposed to be the greatest vibraphone player to ever live. Of course, everybody knows that Benny Goodman is the greatest clarinet player to ever live. So you see you have a Trio and a Quartet which consists of the greatest musicians and exponents on their respective instruments that has ever been known. We got the autographs of : Jess Stacy (one of the greatest white piano players), Gene Krupa, Gordon Griffin, Harry James (new trumpeter from Ben Pollack's band who replaced Irving Goodman last week), Allen Reuss, Harry Goodman, Arthur Rollini, Vido Musso (Rollini and Musso seemed to be the greatest of friends. – they played checkers during intermissions), Ziggy Elman, Herman Shertzer, Bill DePew, Frances Hunt (new vocalist who has a swell voice but I still don't like her personality much — what a flirt!), Murray McEachern (Canadian trombonist who is only 23 and can play almost every instrument, had a baby son last month), and Red Ballard who has been trombonist with the band ever since it started.

We met Benny's secretary, Mr. Chapin, who seemed to be about 18-yrs-old. He took us upstairs to the 7th floor, to the room where he and Benny sleep. he showed us fan mail which he answers and many pictures of Benny and a few of the band that we had never seen. He gave us one picture, the only one for which he had duplicates, of Benny playing the clarinet. I got Benny to autograph this picture to me. After talking with Chapin in his room for about 15 minutes we went downstairs. Chapin said that Benny and his band were planning to leave the Hotel Penn this May, go on a tour of the South, and end up on the west coast in July. There is a possibility of Benny going to Europe in 1939.

The numbers played while we were there were: *There's Frost On The Moon* (vocal by Frances Hunt); *Here's Love In Your Eye*; *I Can't Escape From You* (vocal by Frances Hunt); *Remember*; *After You've Gone* (Trio); *Stompin' At The Savoy* (Quartet); *I'm Coming Virginia* (Quartet); *I Got Rhythm* (Quartet); *This Year's Kisses* (vocal by Frances Hunt); *Easy To Love*; *Chlo-e*; *Honeysuckle Rose* (Griffin's trumpet; McEachern's trombone); *An Apple A Day* (Elman's muted trumpet); *Darling, Not Without You* (vocal by Frances Hunt; Elman's trumpet); *It's De-Lovely* (vocal by Frances Hunt); *Love Marches On* (vocal by Frances Hunt); *One Never Knows, Does One?* (vocal by Frances Hunt); *Oh, Lady Be Good*; *There's Frost On The Moon* (vocal by Frances Hunt); *Goodnight My Love* (vocal by Frances Hunt); *Easy To Love* (Harry James' trumpet); *Stardust*; and *A Fine Romance*.

Teddy Wilson piano solos during intermissions included: *My Old Flame*; *Stardust*; *Honeysuckle Rose*; *Sweet Lorraine*; *I Can't Give You Anything But Love*, etc.

At 11:00pm the band broadcast over CBS (WABC). Bert Parks announced.

Let's Dance (theme) (opening theme with muted trumpets, etc)
Down South Camp Meetin' (Griffin's trumpet; 4 clarinets; sax section)
Love Marches On (Vocal: Frances Hunt) (swell new song)
Rosetta (smooth arrangement featuring Red Ballard on trombone; Musso)
When You And I Were Young Maggie (what saxes!! Ziggy Elman's trumpet)
One Never Knows, Does One? (Vocal: Frances Hunt) (we stood almost next to her)
Chlo-e (Harry James' trumpet, etc)
I Know That You Know
Who? (BG Trio) (Krupa stole the show, he was marvelous: what a drummer!!!)
Where The Lazy River Goes By (Vocal: Frances Hunt) (Ziggy Elman's trumpet)
King Porter Stomp (MARVELOUS arrangement: Griffin's trumpet)
Goodbye (closing theme) (featuring Harry James' trumpet)

At 11:30, right after the broadcast, we left and got the 11:40 train.

RADIO LOGS

5.00PM WOR
WOODY HERMAN
?
Head Over Heels In Love (vocal: Woody Herman)
Trust In Me (vocal: Woody Herman)
How Ya Gonna Keep 'em Down On The Farm
So Do I
The Goose Hangs High

9.00PM WAAB
HUDSON-DeLANGE
Raymor Ballroom, Boston
You Turned The Tables On Me (vocal: Fredda Gibson)
Monopoly Swing
It Seems I've Done Something Wrong Again (vocal: Eddie DeLange)
Alexander's Ragtime Band
Hobo On Park Avenue (theme)

12.45AM WMCA
LUIS RUSSELL
Nixon-Grand Theater, Philadelphia
Everybody Calls It Swing
So Do I (vocal: Sonny Woods)
I Got Rhythm

■ MONDAY 18 JANUARY 1937

RADIO LOGS

6.45PM WMCA
STUFF SMITH
Commercial program, NYC
This program is a commercial sponsored by Lucidin. It is on every Monday, Wednesday and Friday at 6:45. It is a swell jam program.
Basin Street Blues (trumpet solo by Jonah Jones: swell, a la Armstrong)
That Man Is Here Again (vocal: Ella Fitzgerald) (written by Edgar Sampson)
Clouds (Stuff Smith's COLOSSAL violin)
A Chapel In The Moonlight (vocal: Ella Fitzgerald) (lousy song)
Honeysuckle Rose (Edgar Sampson's tenor; Sandy Williams' trombone)

8.00PM WAAB
HUDSON-DeLANGE
Raymor Ballroom, Boston
I've Got You Under My Skin (vocal: Eddie DeLange)
Basin Street Blues (vocal: Fredda Gibson)
Through The Courtesy Of Love (vocal: Fredda Gibson)
Love Song Of The Catskills

10.50PM WAAB
HUDSON-DeLANGE
Raymor Ballroom, Boston
Somebody Loves Me (vocal: Fredda Gibson)
Organ Grinder's Swing (vocal: Eddie DeLange)
Hobo On Park Avenue (theme)

11.30PM WNEW
STUFF SMITH
Onyx Club, 72 W52nd Street, NYC
Old Fashioned Love
If We Never Meet Again
Louisiana
Old Joe's Hittin' The Jug
Organ Grinder's Swing
I'se A-Muggin' (theme)

Stuff Smith

■ TUESDAY 19 JANUARY 1937

RECORDING SESSION

MILDRED BAILEY & HER ORCHESTRA
Recording session for Vocalion in Chicago.
Roy Eldridge (t); Scoops Carry (as); Herbie Haymer (ts); Teddy Cole (p); Johnny Collins (g); Truck Parham (b); Zutty Singleton (d); Mildred Bailey (v)
My Last Affair (vMB) / *Trust In Me* (vMB) / *Where Are You?* (vMB) / *You're Laughing At Me* (vMB)

TOMMY DORSEY AND HIS ORCHESTRA
Recording session for Victor in New York City.
Tommy Dorsey (tb); Bunny Berigan, Steve Lipkins, Joe Bauer, Bob Cusumano (t); Les Jenkins, Artie Foster (tb); Joe Dixon (cl/as); Fred Stulce, Clyde Rounds (as); Bud Freeman (ts); Dick Jones (p); Carmen Mastren (g); Gene Traxler (b); Dave Tough (d); Edythe Wright
Who'll Buy My Violets? / *On A Little Bamboo Bridge* (vEW) / *How Could You?* (vEW) / *Melody In F*

RADIO LOGS

9.00PM WNEW
MAL HALLETT
Hotel Commodore, NYC
50 Million Sweethearts Can't Be Wrong (vocal: Buddy Welcome)
Tea On The Terrace (vocal: Jerry Perkins)
The Girl Of My Dreams (vocal: Buddy Welcome)
Night (vocal: Jerry Perkins)
Inkspots (Pianist FRANKIE CARLE who can play 2500 notes in a minute)
Big Boy Blue (vocal: Buddy Welcome)
Japanese Sandman
Goodnight My Love (vocal: Jerry Perkins)
Swing Fevers (vocal: Buddy Welcome)

9:30PM WABC
BENNY GOODMAN
Camel Caravan program, NYC
I Want To Be Happy
Tiger Rag (BG Trio)
Swing Low, Sweet Chariot (Musso; Elman)

■ WEDNESDAY 20 JANUARY 1937

RADIO LOGS

6.45PM WMCA
STUFF SMITH
Commercial program, NYC
This program is a commercial sponsored by Lucidin. It is on every Monday, Wednesday and Friday at 6:45. It is a swell jam program.
Nagasaki
Rhythm Jamboree (vocal: Ella Fitzgerald)
Sweet Sue (Jonah Jones' trumpet; Sandy Williams' trombone)
There's Frost On The Moon (vocal: Ella Fitzgerald)

8.00PM WAAB
HUDSON-DeLANGE
Raymor Ballroom, Boston
Pennies From Heaven
Alexander's Ragtime Band
Where Am I? (vocal: Fredda Gibson)

9.30PM WHN
WOODY HERMAN
Brooklyn Roseland
Blue Prelude (theme) (colossal slow theme)
I Can't Give You Anything But Love, Baby (waltz–foxtrot)
Tea On The Terrace (vocal: Woody Herman) (new song by Vee Lawnhurst)

JANUARY 1937

Old Fashioned Swing (vocal: Woody Herman) (Saxie Mansfield's tenor; nuttsy piano; Neil Reid's trombone)
Blue Prelude (theme) (Neil Reid's trombone; Nick Hupfer's violin)

11.00PM WABC
BENNY GOODMAN
Hotel Pennsylvania, NYC
Ol' Man River (short, only fair)
Smoke Dreams (vocal: Frances Hunt) (swell new song from movie 'After The Thin Man')
Mr. Ghost Goes To Town (colossal trumpet!!)
Gone (swell song from movie 'Love On The Run': McEachern's trombone)
Swingtime In The Rockies (Musso's tenor; Krupa's drumming; trumpet)
Tea For Two (BG Quartet)
There's Frost On The Moon (vocal: Frances Hunt)
Ridin' High (swell: trumpet)
You Can Tell She Comes From Dixie (vocal: Frances Hunt)
Jam Session (Musso's tenor; Elman's trumpet; Krupa)

■ THURSDAY 21 JANUARY 1937

RECORDING SESSION

COUNT BASIE AND HIS ORCHESTRA
Recording session for Decca in New York City.
Buck Clayton, Joe Keyes, Carl Smith (t); Dan Minor, George Hunt (tb); Caughey Roberts (as); Lester Young, Herschel Evans (ts); Jack Washington (bar); Count Basie (p); Claude Williams (g); Walter Page (b); Jo Jones (d); Jimmy Rushing (voc)
Honeysuckle Rose / *Pennies From Heaven* (vJR) / *Swinging At The Daisy Chain* / *Roseland Shuffle*

RADIO LOGS

9.15PM WOR
RED NORVO
Blackhawk Restaurant, Chicago
Bughouse (nuttsy: tenor; piano)
I've Got My Love To Keep Me Warm (vocal: Mildred Bailey)
It Had To Be You (smooth brass; trombone)
Snowball (vocal: Mildred Bailey)
I Know That You Know

10.00PM WOR
CAB CALLOWAY
Cotton Club, NYC
Howard G. Burns announced.
Mr Ghost Goes To Town (tenor; drums; trumpet)
Pennies From Heaven (vocal: Bennie Payne)
Formal Night In Harlem (vocal: Cab Calloway)
Under The Spell Of The Voodoo Drum (vocal: Cab Calloway)
The Bug Walk (trombone, etc.)
I Learned About Love From Her (vocal: Cab Calloway)
Jitterbug Shuffle (Jones' trombone)
White Heat (colossal: trumpet; tenor)

10.30PM WEAF
JIMMY DORSEY
Kraft Music Hall, Hollywood
I'll Sing You A Thousand Love Songs (vocal: Bing Crosby)
Cowboy Reel (JIMMY DORSEY's Band swinging out in gutbucket style: JD's alto; trumpet; saxes)
So Do I (vocal: Bing Crosby)
I'm In A Dancing Mood

11.30PM WABC
ISHAM JONES
Hotel Lincoln, NYC
Jones' new band just opened 2 weeks ago at the Lincoln, replacing Dick Stabile. Eddie Stone, violin player and swell vocalist, has been with Jones for almost 8 years.
I'll See You In My Dreams (theme) (written by Isham Jones)
Big Boy Blue (vocal: Eddie Stone) (tenor)
I'll Forsake All Others (vocal: Joe Martin)
Papa Tree Top Tall (tenor, trumpet)
Easy To Love (vocal: Joe Martin)
Mix Up (Nuttsy tenor, trumpet)
Summer Nights
Mama Don't Allow (vocal: Eddie Stone)
I Never Knew
You'll Simply Have To Swing It (vocal: Eddie Stone)
The Night Is Young

11.45PM WJZ
EARL HINES
Grand Terrace, Chicago
Deep Forest (theme)
Skeleton In The Closet (vocal: Walter Fuller)
Tea On The Terrace (vocal: Ida James)
One In A Million
It's De-Lovely

12.00 MIDNIGHT WOR
BENNY GOODMAN
Hotel Pennsylvania, NYC
Let's Dance (theme)
Three Little Words (McEachern's trombone; Musso's tenor; swell ending)
With Plenty Of Money And You (vocal: Frances Hunt) (swell sax team)
Chlo-e (old, old song: Krupa's steady drumming; Harry James' trumpet)
Ol' Man River (short, fair: no solos)
Star Dust (COLOSSAL: just like Victor recording; Benny's clarinet)
Stompin' At The Savoy (BG Quartet) (Hampton's vibes are colossal)
It's De-Lovely (vocal: Frances Hunt) (from the movie 'Red Hot And Blue')
Never Should Have Told You (vocal: Frances Hunt) (swell)
Oh, Lady Be Good (McEachern's trombone)
Bugle Call Rag (COLOSSAL: McEachern; Rollini; Elman)

■ FRIDAY 22 JANUARY 1937

RECORDING SESSION

BUNNY BERIGAN AND HIS ORCHESTRA
Recording session for Brunswick in New York City.
Bunny Berigan, Harry Greenwald, L. Brown (t); Ford Leary (tb); Matty Matlock (cl); Hymie Shertzer (as); Art Drelinger (ts); Les Burness (p); Tom Morgan (g); Arnold Fishkind (b); Manny Berger (d); Art Gentry (voc)
The Goona Goo (vAG) / *Who's Afraid Of Love?* (vAG) / *One In A Million* (vAG) / *Blue Lou*

RADIO LOGS

6.45PM WMCA
STUFF SMITH
Commercial program, NYC
This program is a commercial sponsored by Lucidin. It is on every Monday, Wednesday and Friday at 6:45. It is a swell jam program.
This Is My Last Affair (vocal: Ella Fitzgerald)
Shine

10.30PM WOR
TOMMY DORSEY
Meadowbrook, N.J.
Nuttsy. Heard this program at Vi Barnard's house.
Head Over Heels In Love (vocal: Edythe Wright)
If My Heart Could Only Talk (vocal: Jack Leonard)
Fool By My Side
Dancing With You (vocal: Jack Leonard & Three Esquires)
Marie (vocal: Jack Leonard) (COLOSSAL: lousy vocal by Leonard but whole band sang the nuts)

The Goona Goo (vocal: Edythe Wright) (swell, just recorded: Max Kaminsky's trumpet)
Mr Ghost Goes To Town (NUTTSY: Bud Freeman's tenor; Kaminsky's trumpet)
Music Hall Rag (swell: Bud Freeman; Kaminsky; Dave Tough's drums)

11.15PM WNAC
HUDSON-DeLANGE
Raymor Ballroom, Boston
Am I Intruding? (vocal: Eddie DeLange)
Mr Ghost Goes To Town
Tea On The Terrace (vocal: Fredda Gibson)
Hobo On Park Avenue (theme) (played in full)

1.45AM WOR
RED NORVO
Blackhawk Restaurant, Chicago
COLOSSAL.
Mr Ghost Goes To Town (BALLSY: tenor; drums)
Who's That Knocking At My Heart? (vocal: Stew Pletcher)
Nagasaki (stupendous)

■ SATURDAY 23 JANUARY 1937

Hughie couldn't go to this week's broadcast so I took David Low (his first). Mr. Pastoriza drove us over to the subway. When in the city we walked around trying to get pictures, but without success. We went to the broadcast at 6:30. Caspar Reardon (swing harpist), Doris Kerr (vocalist), and Chick Lindsey (20-yr-old Negro guitarist and vocalist from Norfolk, Virginia) were guests. Since I had all their autographs except Lindsey's, I only got his. I got Vince Maffay, guitar player, to autograph his picture. Leith Stevens conducted.

Chick Lindsey

6.45PM WABC
SATURDAY NIGHT SWING SESSION No29
Studio 1, CBS Studios, NYC
I Can't Get Started (theme featuring Bunny Berigan on trumpet hitting some high ones)
Panamania (Russ Genner's trombone; Raymond Scott's piano; Lou Shoobe's bass; Berigan's trumpet)
You Turned The Tables On Me (smooth saxes; Dave Harris' nuttsy tenor)
Washboard Blues (CASPAR REARDON playing harp with aid of Johnny Augustine's violin)
Washington & Lee Swing (brass section of Mike Miolla, Dave Wade, Nat Natoli)
He Ain't Got Rhythm (nuttsy looking DORIS KERR singing; Miolla, Wade, Natoli, Berigan)
Powerhouse (Monkey Wrench Song) (written by Raymond Scott: Billy Gussak, drums; Dave Wade, trumpet & xylophone; Shoobe; Pumiglio and Dave Harris' nuttsy tenor)
Pick Yourself Up (Berigan trumpet solo; Billy Gussak's drumming)
I Would Do Anything For You / China Boy (CHICK LINDSEY playing guitar and doing tricky vocals)
Runnin' Wild (swell: Genner & Joe Haymes on trombones; Pumiglio, Manners, Harris, White on saxes)

RADIO LOGS

5.00PM WOR
COUNT BASIE
Roseland Ballroom, NYC
Heard this program at David Low's apartment in NYC.
Yeah, Man!
Shoe Shine Boy
Mary Had A Little Lamb

Margie (vocal: Jimmy Rushing)
Swinging At The Daisy Chain (original)
The Glory of Love (vocal: Jimmy Rushing)
Limehouse Blues
Unknown Title (swell)

9.00PM WAAB
HUDSON-DeLANGE
Raymor Ballroom, Boston
Peter Piper
I've Got You Under My Skin (vocal: Eddie DeLange)
Knock Knock
Through The Courtesy Of Love (vocal: Fredda Gibson)

10.45PM WABC
BENNY GOODMAN
Hotel Pennsylvania, NYC
Let's Dance (theme)
Darktown Strutters' Ball (COLOSSAL: McEachern's great lowdown trombone)
Easy To Love (from the movie 'Red Hot And Blue': Harry James' trumpet; saxes)
Ballad In Blue (marvelous sax section: Arthur Rollini's tenor solo)
Love Marches On (vocal: Frances Hunt)
Madhouse (stupendous trumpet by Ziggy Elman; Stacy's ballsy piano; Rollini)

11.15PM WOR
TOMMY DORSEY
Meadowbrook, N.J.
Nuttsy. Heard this program at Nancy Long's house in Scarsdale.
I'm Getting Sentimental Over You (theme) (Tommy Dorsey's great trombone)
Tea On The Terrace (vocal: Edythe Wright) (nice muted trumpet)
The Night Will Never End (vocal: Jack Leonard)
Organ Grinder's Swing (vocal: Three Esquires) (Bud Freeman's tenor)
Swing That Music (swell: Bud Freeman's tenor; Dave Tough's drums, etc.)

12.30AM WEAF
ANDY KIRK
Trianon Ballroom, Cleveland
Although I have heard many Andy Kirk recordings for Decca, this is the first time I have heard him broadcast. Pha Terrell leads the band, Andy Kirk plays the sax. The band features Mary Lou Williams on the piano. She is the wife of Johnny Williams, the sax player.
Walkin' And Swingin' (written and arranged by Mary Lou Williams [26])
Mary Had A Little Lamb
Until The Real Thing Comes Along (vocal: Pha Terrell)
Honeysuckle Rose (nuttsy: trombone; Dick Wilson's swell tenor)
Froggy Bottom (vocal: Ben Thigpen) (written and arranged by Mary Lou Williams)
Make Believe Ballroom (lousy)
Will I Remember? (vocal: Pha Terrell)
Avalon (nuttsy clarinet; trombone team; Williams' piano; Wilson's tenor)
Clouds (theme)

Pha Terrell

■ MONDAY 25 JANUARY 1937

RECORDING SESSION

BILLIE HOLIDAY & TEDDY WILSON ORCHESTRA
Recording session for Brunswick in NYC.
Buck Clayton (t); Benny Goodman (cl); Lester Young (ts); Teddy Wilson (p); Freddie Green (g); Walter Page (b); Jo Jones (d); Billie Holiday (v)
He Ain't Got Rhythm / This Year's Kisses / Why Was I Born? / I Must Have That Man

JANUARY 1937

RADIO LOGS

6.45PM WMCA
STUFF SMITH
Commercial program, NYC
This program is a commercial sponsored by Lucidin. It is on every Monday, Wednesday and Friday at 6:45. It is a swell jam program.
Darktown Strutters' Ball
Tain't Good, Like A Nickel Made Of Wood (vocal: Ella Fitzgerald)
Star Dust (swell: Jonah Jones' muted trumpet; baritone sax by Edgar Sampson)
You Dropped Me Like A Red Hot Penny (vocal: Ella Fitzgerald)
Bugle Call Rag (Stuff's violin; Cozy Cole's drums; Sandy Williams' trombone)
Love Marches On (vocal: Ella Fitzgerald)
Dinah (theme)

■ TUESDAY 26 JANUARY 1937

RECORDING SESSION

JIMMIE LUNCEFORD AND HIS ORCHESTRA
Recording session for Decca in New York City.
Jimmie Lunceford (ldr); Eddie Tompkins, Paul Webster (t); Sy Oliver (t/voc); Elmer Crumbley, Russell Bowles, Eddie Durham (tb); Willie Smith (cl/as/bar/voc); Earl Carruthers (cl/as/bar); Laforet Dent (as); Dan Grissom (cl/as/voc); Joe Thomas (cl/ts/voc); Edwin Wilcox (p); Al Norris (g); Moses Allen (b); Jimmy Crawford (d)
He Ain't Got Rhythm (vJT) / *Linger Awhile* (vDG) / *Honest And Truly* (vDG) / *Slumming On Park Avenue* (vTrio)

RADIO LOGS

9.00PM WHN
ERSKINE HAWKINS
Harlem Uproar Club, NYC
The Harlem Uproar Club is on Broadway at 51st Street.
When Did You Leave Heaven? (vocal: ?) (tenor)
That's Life I Guess (trumpet)
When I Grow Too Old To Dream (vocal: ?)

9.15PM WNEW
MAL HALLETT
Hotel Commodore, NYC
You're Everything Sweet (vocal: Buddy Welcome)
Ridin' High (FRANKIE CARLE on piano)
Get Happy

9:30PM WABC
BENNY GOODMAN
Camel Caravan program, NYC
I Want To Be Happy (record released today)
Runnin' Wild (BG Quartet)
This Year's Crop Of Kisses (vocal: Frances Hunt) (Musso's tenor)
Alexander's Ragtime Band

10.30PM WOR
CAB CALLOWAY
Cotton Club, NYC
Goodnight, My Love (vocal: Cab Calloway)
I Love To Sing-a (vocal: Cab Calloway)
The Goona Goo (Doc Cheatham's trumpet; Eddie Barefield's alto; Bennie Payne's piano)
It Ain't Necessarily So (vocal: Cab Calloway)
Hot Stuff (Ben Webster's swell tenor)
Summer Nights (vocal: Bennie Payne)
Copper Colored Gal (vocal: Cab Calloway)

11.15PM WEAF
JAN SAVITT
KYW Studios, Philadelphia
Swell.
I Can't Lose That Longing For You
Mr Ghost Goes To Town
Rainbow On The River
Quaker City Jazz

■ WEDNESDAY 27 JANUARY 1937

RADIO LOGS

8.30PM WHN
CLAUDE HOPKINS
Brooklyn Roseland
I Would Do Anything For You (theme/vocal: Beverly White)
Bye Bye Baby
Goodnight, My Love (vocal: Beverly White)
Sunday (vocal: Beverly White)
Somebody Loves Me (vocal: Fred Norman)
Swingin' Down The Lane (vocal: Beverly White)
I Love You Truly
King Porter Stomp (trumpet; clarinet)
There's Something In The Air (vocal: Beverly White)

10.30PM WOR
CAB CALLOWAY
Cotton Club, NYC
Sweet Sue (vocal: Cab Calloway)
Sweet Lorraine (vocal: Cab Calloway)
Mr Ghost Goes To Town
Devil's Kitchen (vocal: Cab Calloway)

11.00PM WABC
BENNY GOODMAN
Hotel Pennsylvania, NYC
Let's Dance (theme)
Clap Hands! Here Comes Charlie (Ziggy Elman's trumpet; Musso's tenor; saxes)
One Never Knows, Does One? (vocal: Frances Hunt) (Vido Musso's tenor)
He Ain't Got Rhythm (vocal: Frances Hunt) (by Irving Berlin, from 'On The Avenue')
An Apple A Day (trumpet)
Runnin' Wild (BG Quartet) (good, but not up to standard)
Sometimes I'm Happy (NUTTSY, very slow: trumpet; Musso's tenor)
Walk, Jennie, Walk (McEachern's trombone; Krupa's drums)
Goodbye (closing theme) (played in its entirety)

11.30PM WMCA
CHICK WEBB
Apollo Theater, NYC
Spring Fever Blues (vocal: Ella Fitzgerald)
There's Frost On The Moon (vocal: Ella Fitzgerald/Charles Linton/Louis Jordan)

■ THURSDAY 28 JANUARY 1937

RECORDING SESSION
GLEN GRAY AND THE CASA LOMA ORCHESTRA
Recording session for Decca in New York City.
Glen Gray (as/dir); Sonny Dunham, Grady Watts, Frank Zullo (t); Pee Wee Hunt (tb/voc); Billy Rauch, Fritz Hummel (tb); Clarence Hutchenrider (cl/as), Kenny Sargent (as/voc); Art Ralston (as/o/bsn); Pat Davis (ts); Mel Jenssen (vln); Joe Hall (p); Jack Blanchette (g); Stanley Dennis (b); Tony Briglia (d)
You're Laughing At Me (vKS) / *I've Got My Love To Keep Me Warm* (vKS) / *Swing High, Swing Low* (vPWH) / *Please Keep Me In Your Dreams* (vKS)

RADIO LOGS

10.30PM WHN
TEMPO KING
Hollywood Restaurant, NYC
Swell jamming by Joe Marsala, Marty Marsala, Joe Bushkin and probably George Wettling on drums. The Hollywood Restaurant is on Broadway at 48th Street.
Basin Street Blues (theme/vocal: Tempo King) (Marty Marsala's trumpet)
Clarinet Marmalade (featuring Joe Marsala on clarinet)
Let's Call A Heart A Heart (vocal: Tempo King)
I Cried For You (featuring Joe Marsala on clarinet; Joe Bushkin on piano)
This Is My Last Affair (vocal: Tempo King)
I Would Do Anything For You (vocal: Tempo King)
Rosetta (Bushkin; 2 Marsala's)

12.00 MIDNIGHT WOR
BENNY GOODMAN
Hotel Pennsylvania, NYC
Ridin' High (trumpet)
You're Laughing At Me (vocal: Frances Hunt)
Easy To Love (Stacy's piano; James' trumpet)
There's Frost On The Moon (vocal: Frances Hunt)
Dinah (BG Quartet) (great work by Hampton)
Goodnight, My Love (vocal: Frances Hunt)
Madhouse (Elman; Stacy)
Smoke Dreams (vocal: Frances Hunt)
Remember (Musso's tenor)
House Hop

■ FRIDAY 29 JANUARY 1937

RECORDING SESSION
TOMMY DORSEY AND HIS ORCHESTRA
Recording session for Victor in New York City.
Tommy Dorsey (tb); Bunny Berigan, Jimmy Welch, Joe Bauer, Bob Cusumano (t); Les Jenkins, Red Bone (tb); Joe Dixon (cl/as); Fred Stulce, Clyde Rounds (as); Bud Freeman (ts); Dick Jones (p); Carmen Mastren (g); Gene Traxler (b); Dave Tough (d); Jack Leonard (voc)
You're Here, You're There, You're Everywhere (vJL) / *Song Of India* / *Marie* (vJL & Band) / *Dedicated To You* (vJL)

RADIO LOGS

6.45PM WMCA
STUFF SMITH
Commercial program, NYC
This program is a commercial sponsored by Lucidin. It is on every Monday, Wednesday and Friday at 6:45. It is a swell jam program.
Sing, Baby, Sing
Pennies From Heaven (vocal: Ella Fitzgerald)
Nobody's Sweetheart (Smith's violin; sax)
Spring Fever Blues (vocal: Ella Fitzgerald) (nuttsy song)

10.30PM WOR
TOMMY DORSEY
Meadowbrook, N.J.
COLOSSAL. Heard this program at Carolyn Bade's house in Hartsdale.
How Could You? (vocal: Edythe Wright)
May I Have The Next Romance? (vocal: Jack Leonard)
Song Of India (Dave Tough's drums; Bud Freeman)
It's De-Lovely (vocal: Edythe Wright & Three Esquires)
Maple Leaf Rag (Freeman's tenor; Kaminsky)
Troubles Don't Like Music (vocal: Edythe Wright & Three Esquires)
If I Should (vocal: Edythe Wright & Three Esquires)
Memphis Blues (super-nuttsy)
For You (vocal: Jack Leonard & Three Esquires)
Nagasaki

11.15PM WOR
WOODY HERMAN
Roseland Ballroom, NYC
Blue Lou (nuttsy: Saxie Mansfield's tenor)
Trust In Me (vocal: Woody Herman) (swell sweet song)

12.15AM WOR
MAL HALLETT
Hotel Commodore, NYC
Night (vocal: Jerry Perkins)
My Love Dreams Never Come True (vocal: Buddy Welcome)
Ridin' High (FRANKIE CARLE on piano)
The Goona Goo (vocal: Buddy Welcome)

12.30AM WEAF
ANDY KIRK
Trianon Ballroom, Cleveland
Kirk's band is playing at the Trianon Ballroom, Cleveland and features Mary Lou Williams on the piano, Pha Terrell's vocals, and Dick Wilson's tenor sax.
You Turned The Tables On Me (tenor)
I Never Slept A Wink Last Night
Goodnight, My Love (vocal: Pha Terrell)
You Do The Darnedest Things, Baby
Spring Holiday (MARY LOU WILLIAMS on piano)
When I'm With You (vocal: Pha Terrell)
Make Believe Ballroom
Sepian Jazz

■ SATURDAY 30 JANUARY 1937

Hughie Pastoriza and I were driven over to the subway at 9:30am. We got into NYC at 10:45. I went over to have some pictures taken of myself (4 for a dime). We then went to 1587 Broadway where W. C. Handy's Music Publishing Inc. is. We had him autograph the book 'Rhythm On Record'. I then went over to 17 E 49th St where I got a picture of Jimmie Lunceford and a picture of his band from Lunceford's manager, Harold Oxley. I also got two pictures of Thomas 'Fats' Waller in the same building from Philip Ponce, Waller's manager. We then went to see Jimmie Lunceford and his band at Loew's State Theater, 46th & Broadway. We got in at 11:45am for a quarter. I'm afraid that Jimmie and his band aren't nearly as good as they used to be. Their arrangements are too spectacular, but it is still a good band.
Jazznocracy (theme)
Rhythm Is Our Business (Vocal: Willie Smith) (Paul Webster's trumpet)
Organ Grinder's Swing (lousy trumpet; Al Norris' guitar; clarinet)
For Dancers Only (Lunceford's interpretation of swing; Smith's alto)
Yankee Doodle Never Went To Town (Vocal: Mabel Scott)
Swing It, Gate (Vocal: Mabel Scott)
My Blue Heaven (Vocal: Trio–Sy Oliver, Eddie Tompkins, Willie Smith)
Nobody (played in the style of Ellington, Lombardo, Louis, and Whiteman)
Nagasaki (Eddie Tompkins; Paul Webster; Joe Thomas' tenor)

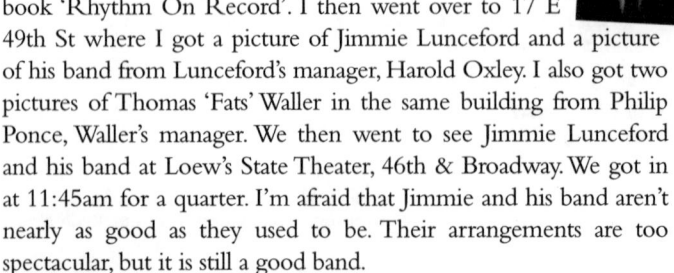

After seeing Lunceford, we didn't stay to see the movie. We went around to the stage door on 46th Street and got the autographs of James Crawford (drums), Elmer Crumbley (trombone), Joe Thomas (sax), Al Norris (guitar), Edwin Wilcox (piano) and Eddie Tompkins (trumpet, vocals), on a picture of Lunceford's band. After that, at 2:30, we went down to the Hotel Penn, 33rd at 7th Ave, where we went to Mr Chapin's room on the 7th floor (769). He wasn't there. We then went to Macy's where we looked at radios and records. At 4:00pm we went to Rockwell-O'Keefe, Rockefeller Center, where we met Vincent Prior who let us look through his files of pictures. He gave us each 15. We got to the Columbia Studios, where the Swing Session is held, early. We got Tommy Dorsey to autograph 'Rhythm On Record.'

6.45PM WABC
SATURDAY NIGHT SWING SESSION No30
Studio 1, CBS Studios, NYC
Chicken And Waffles (introductory theme)
I Can't Get Started (theme featuring Bunny Berigan on trumpet)
Happy Birthday (Dave Harris' tenor; Pumiglio's clarinet; Genner's trombone; Williams; Berigan)
Stompin' At The Savoy (COLOSSAL: Art Manners' clarinet; Harris; Berigan)
I'm Getting Sentimental Over You (Tommy Dorsey & trombone introduced by David Ross)
Trombone Man (NUTTSY: Edythe Wright; 3 Esquires; Blue Flames; Dorsey & CBS band)
Star Dust (STUPENDOUS singing by the Blue Flames: 1 man; 3 girls)
Love And Learn (Ernie White's clarinet; Dave Harris' tenor; Maffay's guitar)
Melody In F (Bunny Berigan trumpet solo: never heard Berigan better)
Big John Special (NUTTSY-COLOSSAL: Art Manners' sax; Dorsey; Berigan)
Panamania (swell new song: Lou Shoobe's bass; Genner; Raymond Scott's piano)
Happy Birthday (played for President F. D. Roosevelt for 2nd time)

Tommy Dorsey and band are leaving the Meadowbrook, N. J. this Wednesday (Feb 3). Bunny Berigan, who is starting his own band is going to replace Dorsey there.

RADIO LOGS

09.00PM WNEW
MAL HALLETT
Hotel Commodore, NYC
You've Got Something
Who's Afraid Of Love (vocal: Buddy Welcome)
Inkspots (FRANKIE CARLE on piano)
Bouncy Rhythm (vocal: Buddy Welcome) (written by trumpeter Frank Ryerson)
Rockin' Chair (vocal: Teddy Grace)
I Can't Lose That Longing For You (vocal: Jerry Perkins)
Boston Tea Party (theme)

12.30AM WMCA
CHICK WEBB
Savoy Ballroom, NYC
Stompin' At The Savoy (theme) (played in full)
Goodnight, My Love (vocal: Ella Fitzgerald) (arranged by Al Feldman for Goodman & Webb)
Blue Lou
One Never Knows, Does One? (vocal: Charles Linton)
Swinging For The King
Swinging On The Reservation (vocal: Ella Fitzgerald) (written by Wayman Carver)

2.00AM WGN
RED NORVO
Blackhawk Restaurant, Chicago
Whatcha Gonna Do When There Ain't No Swing? (vocal: Mildred Bailey)
I'm An Old Cowhand (vocal: Stew Pletcher)
Mr Ghost Goes To Town
Take Another Guess (vocal: Mildred Bailey)
You're My Best Bet (vocal: Stew Pletcher)
It's Love I'm After
Nagasaki

FEBRUARY 1937

Hotel Pennsylvania: **Benny Goodman**
Hotel Commodore: **Mal Hallett** (–18); **Tommy Dorsey** (19–)
Hotel Lincoln: **Isham Jones**
Hotel Taft: **George Hall**
Hotel Lexington: **Ozzie Nelson**
Rainbow Room: **Glen Gray**

Apollo Theater: **Willie Bryant** (–4); **Jimmie Lunceford** (5–11); **Louise Beavers** (12–18); **Lucky Millinder** (19–25); **Fletcher Henderson** (26–)
Loew's State Theater: **Buck & Bubbles** (19–25)

Cotton Club Downtown: **Cab Calloway/Bill Robinson**
Hickory House: **3T's: Frank Trumbauer, Jack & Charlie Teagarden** (–16); **Mike Riley** (17–)
Onyx Club: **Stuff Smith**

■ TUESDAY 2 FEBRUARY 1937

RECORDING SESSION

CLAUDE HOPKINS AND HIS ORCHESTRA
Recording session for Decca in New York City.
Claude Hopkins (p/ldr); Shirley Clay, Jabbo Smith, Lincoln Mills (t); Floyd Brady, Fred Norman, Vic Dickenson (tb); Gene Johnson, Chauncey Haughton, Ben Smith (as); Bobby Sands (ts); Walter Jones (g); Abe Bolar (b); Pete Jacobs (d); Beverley White (voc)
Sunday (vBW) / *No No Nora* (vBW) / *Swingin' Down The Lane* (vBW)

RADIO LOGS

8.00PM WNEW
MAL HALLETT
Hotel Commodore, NYC
Who's Afraid Of Love (vocal: Buddy Welcome)
Stormy Weather (vocal: Teddy Grace) (swell vocalist)
Bouncy Rhythm (vocal: Buddy Welcome) (written by trumpeter Frank Ryerson)
I Can't Lose That Longing For You (vocal: Jerry Perkins)
Inkspots (FRANKIE CARLE on piano)
I'm The Lady Who Swings The Band (vocal: Teddy Grace)
Organ Grinder's Swing (Anderson's tenor)
Sometimes I'm Happy

9.00PM WHN
ERSKINE HAWKINS
Harlem Uproar Club, NYC
Campus Serenade (theme) (featuring trumpet of Erskine Hawkins)
I Found A New Baby (Hawkins' trumpet; tenor; trombone)
If You Should Ever Leave (vocal: Jimmy Mitchelle)
Darktown Strutters' Ball (trumpet; saxes; drums; tenor)
Body And Soul
Flying Off The Handle
Painting The Town Red
This Is My Last Affair
Uproar Shout

9:30PM WABC
BENNY GOODMAN
Camel Caravan program, NYC
Goodnight, My Love (vocal: Frances Hunt)
Ida, Sweet As Apple Cider (BG Quartet)
Sing, Sing, Sing (COLOSSAL: Krupa's drumming)

Gene Krupa

■ WEDNESDAY 3 FEBRUARY 1937

RECORDING SESSION

BENNY GOODMAN QUARTET
Recording session for Victor in New York City.
Lionel Hampton (vib); Teddy Wilson (p); Benny Goodman (cl); Gene Krupa (d)
Ida, Sweet As Apple Cider / *Tea For Two* / *Runnin' Wild*

9.00PM WEAF
TOWN HALL TONIGHT
RCA Building, NYC

Cynthia Doyle took me in to see the Ipana Toothpaste broadcast over WEAF at 9:00pm. Her brother, Henry, drove Mrs Doyle, Barbara Lynebury, Cynthia and myself into NYC by car. The broadcast is called 'Town Hall Tonight' and features comedian Fred Allen; his wife, Portland Hoffa; the announcer, Harry Von Zell; Peter Van Steeden's Orchestra; the Mighty Allen Art Players; and several guest vocalists, etc. I recognized Mannie Klein on trumpet and Carl Kress on guitar in Van Steeden's Band. After the broadcast we went into one of the drug stores in the RCA Building where, to our surprise, we found about ten of the guys in Glen Gray's Band having something to eat. Of course, Glen Gray & his Band were appearing in the Rainbow Room of Rockefeller Center. We then drove home. Heard Goodman broadcast in the car. Just got home as Goodman concluded at 11:30.

RADIO LOGS

11.00PM WABC
BENNY GOODMAN
Hotel Pennsylvania, NYC
This Is My Last Affair (vocal: Frances Hunt)
Japanese Sandman
Nobody's Sweetheart (BG Trio)
Goodbye (intermission theme)
This Year's Crop Of Kisses (vocal: Frances Hunt)
Love Me Or Leave Me
Tea For Two (BG Quartet) (colossal work by whole quartet)
Anything Goes (vocal: Frances Hunt) (nuttsy introduction)

11.30PM WEAF
GLEN GRAY
Rainbow Room, NYC
Always (Stan Dennis' bass; Pat Davis' tenor)
Please Keep Me In Your Dreams (vocal: Kenny Sargent)
I Love You From Coast To Coast (vocal: Pee Wee Hunt)
You're Laughing At Me (vocal: Kenny Sargent)
Study In Brown
The Moon Is Grinning At Me (vocal: Pee Wee Hunt)
Moonlight And Cotton (latest tune by arranger Gene Gifford)
Should I (Davis; Dunham; Hall)
Smoke Rings (theme)

12.00 MIDNIGHT WNEW
WOODY HERMAN
Roseland Ballroom, NYC
Mr Ghost Goes To Town (very original arrangement: Frank Carlson's drums)
I Can't Give You Anything But Love (arranged by Gordon Jenkins)
I'll Forsake All Others (vocal: Woody Herman) (nuttsy song)
Liza
Davenport Blues (written by Bix: Herman's clarinet; Saxie Mansfield's tenor)
Weary Blues (BALLSY: clarinets; Neil Reid's trombone; Woody's clarinet; drums)
Wintertime Dreams (vocal: Woody Herman) (Hupfer's violin)
Blue Prelude (theme)

FEBRUARY 1937 Swing Era Scrapbook 115

■ THURSDAY 4 FEBRUARY 1937

RECORDING SESSION

GLEN GRAY AND THE CASA LOMA ORCHESTRA
Recording session for Decca in New York City.
Glen Gray (as/dir); Sonny Dunham, Grady Watts, Frank Zullo (t); Pee Wee Hunt (tb/voc); Billy Rauch, Fritz Hummel (tb); Clarence Hutchenrider (cl/as), Kenny Sargent (as/voc); Art Ralston (as/o/bsn); Pat Davis (ts); Mel Jenssen (vln); Joe Hall (p); Jack Blanchette (g); Stanley Dennis (b); Tony Briglia (d)
A Study In Brown / Whoa, Babe! (vPWH) / *The Goblin Band / Paramour*

WINGY MANONE AND HIS ORCHESTRA
Recording session for Bluebird in New York City.
Wingy Manone (t/voc); George Brunies (tb); Matty Matlock (cl); Joe Marsala (ts); Conrad Lanoue (p); Jack LeMaire (g); Artie Shapiro (b); Danny Alvin (d)
Formal Night In Harlem (vWM) / *Sweet Lorraine* (vWM) / *Boo Hoo* (vWM) / *You Showed Me The Way* (vWM) / *I Can't Lose That Longing For You* (vWM) / *Oh, Say! Can You Swing?* (vWM)

RADIO LOGS

5.30PM WNEW
MAKE BELIEVE BALLROOM
NYC
The Make Believe Ballroom is a program that is on several hours a day with many sponsors. Martin Block, who originated the program, is master of ceremonies. On tonight's 2nd Anniversary Program (5.30–7.00pm), instead of playing recordings, he is having many guest stars
Let's Dance At Make Believe Ballroom (vocal: Andy Razaf)
(Lyricist Andy Razaf sings, accompanied by the composer Paul Denniker on piano)
12th Street Rag (STUFF SMITH, his violin, and 5-piece jam band from the Onyx Club)
Dinah (vocal: Dolly Dawn) (Dolly, from the Hotel Taft, singing with Stuff Smith's Band)
I've Got You Under My Skin (Stuff Smith's violin; Jonah Jones' trumpet, etc)
Love Will Tell (vocal: Johnny McKeever) (with George Hall's Band from the Hotel Taft)
Nola (VINCENT LOPEZ from Hotel Astor on piano)
Trust In Me (vocal: Billy Muir) (with Billy Hayes' Band from the Hotel Edison)
A Little Bit Later On (vocal: Chick Bullock) (with Bunny Berigan's new Band)
TED HUSING, CBS announcer, kidding around with Martin Block
(Record of 'Drifting Tide')
Tiger Rag (vocal: Four Eaton Boys) (with Art Gentry and Ray Block, arranger, at piano)
BENNY GOODMAN wishing Martin Block good luck
(Record of 'Sandman')
Burning Down The House I Was Brought Up In (Landt Trio & White)
GLEN GRAY giving his regards to Martin Block
(Record of 'Royal Garden Blues')
The Hi-De-Ho Miracle Man (vocal: Cab Calloway) (Cab with his own Band)
WOODY HERMAN giving congratulations
(Record of Woody's 'Better Get Off Your High Horse')
GUY LOMBARDO, from Hotel Roosevelt, giving his congratulations to Martin Block
BOB CROSBY, who is now on tour, giving regards
(Record of 'Pagan Love Song')
BILL SIMPSON, WNEW engineer, and bandleader ABE LYMAN congratulating Martin
Organ Grinder's Swing (vocal: Ella Fitzgerald) (with CHICK WEBB Band: nuttsy)

REGINALD FORSYTHE, English composer, giving congratulations
(Record of 'Dodging A Divorcee')
FRANK LAMARE from Arcadia Ballroom;
SHEP FIELDS, who is now at Georgia Tech, Georgia
Gee, But You're Swell (vocal: Louis Jordan) (with CHICK WEBB Band)
TOMMY DORSEY, from Hopewell, Va, giving congratulations
(Record of 'Getting Sentimental Over You')
Happy Days Are Here Again (DICK ROBERTSON and his Band)
JIMMY LUNCEFORD, sailing for Europe, giving congratulations
(Record of 'This Is My Last Affair')
With Plenty Of Money And You (vocal: Chick Bullock) (with piano accompaniment)
CHARLIE BARNET & 4 MODERNAIRES giving best wishes
(Records of 'Milk Man's Matinee' & "Way Down Yonder In New Orleans')

10.40PM WHN
TEMPO KING
Hollywood Restaurant, NYC
I've Got You Under My Skin (vocal: Tempo King)
There's A Small Hotel (vocal: Tempo King)
When Did You Leave Heaven? (vocal: Tempo King)
I Can't Escape From You (vocal: Tempo King)
Honeysuckle Rose
Basin Street Blues (theme)

11.30PM WABC
ISHAM JONES
Hotel Lincoln, NYC
Liza
I Can't Lose That Longing For You (vocal: Joe Martin)
The Skeleton In The Closet (vocal: Eddie Stone)
Thanks For Everything (Jones' latest song)
Oh, Say, Can You Swing? (vocal: Eddie Stone)
If My Heart Could Only Talk
Floating On A Bubble
Was It Rain? (vocal: Joe Martin)
Old Fashioned Swing (vocal: Eddie Stone)
May I Have The Next Romance?
I'll See You In My Dreams (theme) (written by Isham Jones)

12.00 MIDNIGHT WOR
BENNY GOODMAN
Hotel Pennsylvania, NYC
Announced by Roger Lyon.
When You And I Were Young, Maggie (Elman's trumpet with Krupa's drums)
Gee, But You're Swell (vocal: Frances Hunt) (Hunt sings this about half as well as Helen Ward)
Mean To Me (nuttsy arrangement of swell song: Musso's great tenor; saxes)
Ida, Sweet As Apple Cider (BG Quartet) (introduced by Benny: great work by Benny and Lionel)
Summer Nights (vocal: Frances Hunt) (trombone)
My Melancholy Baby (McEachern's trombone; Stacy's piano backing; saxes; brass)
I Found A New Baby (colossal: intro; Krupa; brass; Benny; James; Rollini)
There's Something In The Air (vocal: Frances Hunt)
More Than You Know (nuttsy: slow, concise swing; saxes; tenor; trumpet)
Changes (colossal saxes: trumpet; Musso's tenor; Stacy's piano)

12.30AM WJZ
FRANK TRUMBAUER
Hickory House, NYC
'S Wonderful (Trumbauer's alto sax; trumpet)
Basin Street Blues (vocal: Ford Leary) (trombone)
Hand In Glove (vocal: Frances Lane) (lousy)
I'm An Old Cowhand (vocal: Ford Leary) (swell)
Rosetta (vocal: Al Stuart) (great trumpet)
William Tell (trumpet; drums; alto sax)
Three Little Words (vocal: Frances Lane) (trombone)
I Got Rhythm (FRANK CARTER piano solo)
I Know That You Know (vocal: Four Modernaires)
Pagan Love Song (alto sax; trumpet; trombone)

■ FRIDAY 5 FEBRUARY 1937

RADIO LOGS

6.45PM WMCA
STUFF SMITH
Commercial program, NYC
This program is a commercial sponsored by Lucidin. It is on every Monday, Wednesday and Friday at 6:45. It is a swell jam program.
Alexander's Ragtime Band
An Apple A Day (vocal: Ella Fitzgerald)
I'll Chase The Blues Away (vocal: Ella Fitzgerald)
Marie (COLOSSAL: tenor; Jonah Jones' trumpet; vocals)

10.00PM WOR
BUNNY BERIGAN
Meadowbrook, N.J.
Heard this program at Nancy Long's house in Scarsdale.
I Can't Get Started (theme) (featuring Bunny Berigan's trumpet)
Slummin' On Park Avenue
There's Something In The Air (vocal: Caesar Cole?)
The Goona Goo (vocal: Bunny Berigan)
May I Have The Next Romance With You?
'Way Down Yonder In New Orleans
Now
Oh Baby, What I Wouldn't Do
Chinatown, My Chinatown

1.40AM WOR
RED NORVO
Blackhawk Restaurant, Chicago
Slummin' On Park Avenue
Smoke Dreams (vocal: Mildred Bailey)
St. Louis Blues (vocal: Mildred Bailey)
Who's That Knockin' At My Door (vocal: Stew Pletcher)
I'll Chase The Blues Away
Trust In Me (vocal: Mildred Bailey)
Nagasaki

■ SATURDAY 6 FEBRUARY 1937

Hughie and I went in by subway to see this week's Swing broadcast. Since we got to Grand Central at 6:00pm we went over to the Commodore Music Shop, 144 E 42nd Street. We each bought a picture of two jam bands. One had Eddie Condon (guitar), Henry Red Allen (trumpet), Joe Marsala (clarinet), Joe Bushkin (piano) and Morty Stuhlmaker (bass). The other had Bunny Berigan (trumpet), Eddie Condon (guitar), Red McKenzie (vocalist), Morty Stuhlmaker (bass), Joe Bushkin (piano), and Forrest Crawford (tenor). We also bought three Victor records for two dollars: Benny Goodman's *Never Should Have Told You* and *You Can Tell She Comes From Dixie* (25560); *Rosetta* and *I Want To Be Happy* (25510); and Tommy Dorsey's *Mr. Ghost Goes To Town* (with Berigan, Freeman, Tough, etc) and *Lookin' Around Corners For You* (25509). Milton Gabler, who owns Commodore shop, said that Benny Goodman had been buying Ella Fitzgerald records before we came in.

6.45PM WABC
SATURDAY NIGHT SWING SESSION No31
Studio 1, CBS Studios, NYC
Chicken And Waffles (Introductory theme)
I Can't Get Started (theme) (featuring Bunny Berigan on trumpet)
Hallelujah (Berigan's colossal trumpet; Dave Harris' tenor; Johnny Williams' drums, etc)
Organ Grinder's Swing (COLOSSAL: Berigan; clarinets; brass section of Natoli, Miolla, Roselli, Vargas, Genner)
Ain't Misbehavin' (Gogo De Lys singing the nuts: she has everything; Berigan)
There's A Small Hotel (colossal slow, sweet-swing arrangement: clarinet team of White, Harris, Manners, Pumiglio)
White Star Of Sigma Nu (Joe Haymes directing CBS Band with Pumiglio's swell clarinet, Charlie Bush's drums and Mike Michaels' trombone)
St. Louis Blues (STUPENDOUS: Haymes directing his own arrangement with Art Manners' alto sax, Mike Michaels' trombone, Ernie White's clarinet)
The Goona Goo (3 Wallace Sisters with Frank Marx, arranger, on the piano: good)
Now (Bunny Berigan trumpet solo: without doubt, Berigan and Beiderbecke are greatest trumpeters)
Swing, Swing Mother-in-Law (Raymond Scott at piano with CBS Band, playing his own composition)

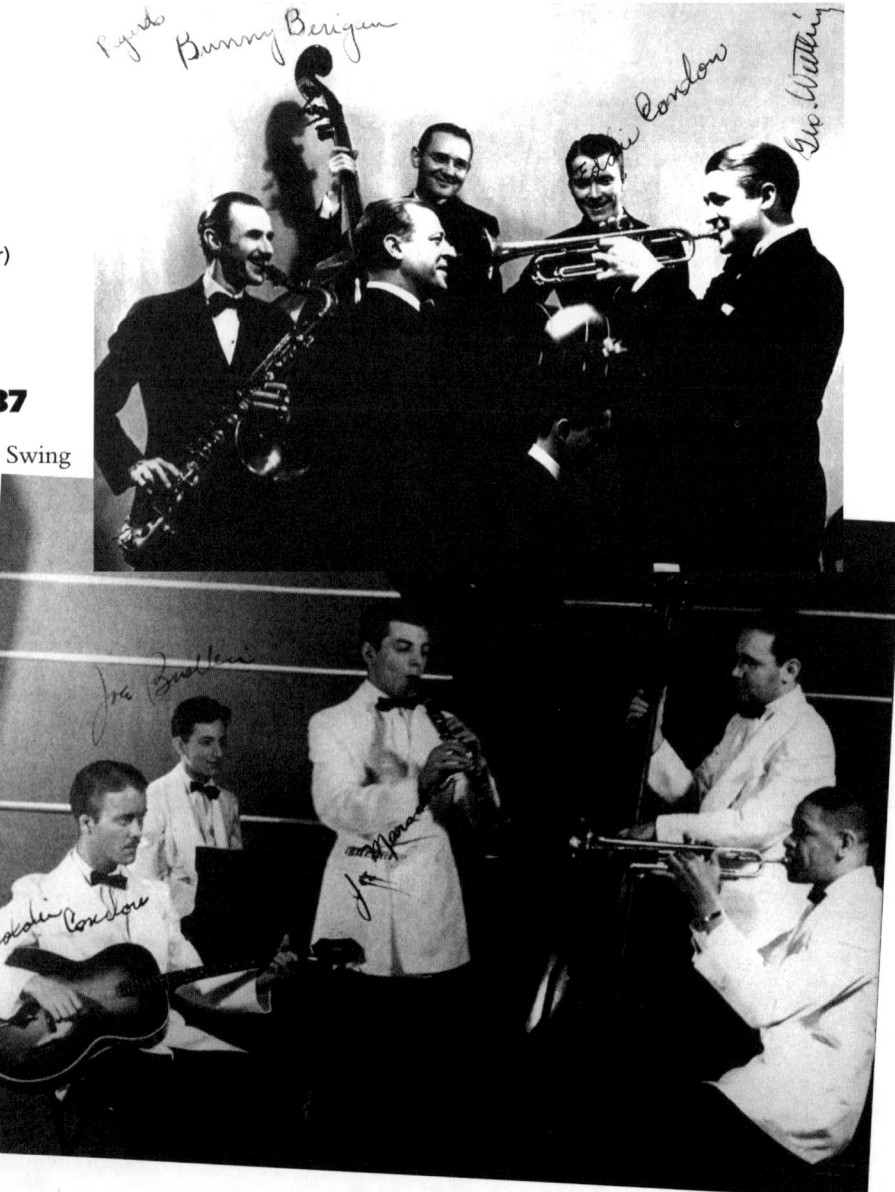

After the broadcast I got the autographs of Joe Haymes, Charlie Bush and Mike Michaels in 'Rhythm On Record'. Got autograph of Bunny Berigan on picture. Went to David Low's house for the night.

■ SUNDAY 7 FEBRUARY 1937

RADIO LOGS

9.15PM WAAB
RED NORVO
Blackhawk Restaurant, Chicago
I've Got My Love To Keep Me Warm
Gee, But You're Swell (vocal: Stew Pletcher)
Body And Soul
There's Frost On The Moon (vocal: Mildred Bailey)
Oh, Lady Be Good
I Got Rhythm

■ MONDAY 8 FEBRUARY 1937

RECORDING SESSION

BOB CROSBY AND HIS ORCHESTRA
Recording session for Decca in New York City.
Bob Crosby (voc/ldr); Andy Ferretti, Yank Lawson (t); Ward Silloway, Mark Bennett (tb); Gil Rodin, Matty Matlock (cl/as); Noni Bernardi (as); Eddie Miller (cl/ts); Deane Kincaide (ts); Bob Zurke (piano); Nappy Lamare (g/voc); Bob Haggart (b); Ray Bauduc (d)
Old Spinning Wheel / Gin Mill Blues / If I Had You (vBC) / *Between The Devil And The Deep Blue Sea*

LIONEL HAMPTON AND HIS ORCHESTRA
Recording session for Victor in New York City.
Lionel Hampton (vib/voc/d); Ziggy Elman (t); Hymie Shertzer, George Koenig (as); Vido Musso, Art Rollini (ts); Jess Stacy (p); Allan Reuss (g); Harry Goodman (b); Gene Krupa (d)
This Is My Last Affair (vLH) / *Jivin' The Vibes / The Mood That I'm In* (vLH) / *Stomp* (dLH)

■ TUESDAY 9 FEBRUARY 1937

RADIO LOGS

9:30PM WABC
BENNY GOODMAN
Camel Caravan program, NYC
He Ain't Got Rhythm (vocal: Frances Hunt) (swell tune)
I Got Rhythm (BG Quartet) (colossal work by Quartet)
Ridin' High (trumpet; Benny)

10.30pm WOR
CAB CALLOWAY
Cotton Club, NYC
Rosetta (swell: Ben Webster's tenor; Payne's piano; Doc Cheatham's trumpet; clarinets)
Serenade In The Night (vocal: Cab Calloway)
Swing, Swing, Swing (vocal: Cab Calloway) (written by Calloway)
Summer Nights (vocal: Cab Calloway) (lousy song)
The Hi-De-Ho Miracle Man (vocal: Cab Calloway)
Tea On The Terrace (vocal: Cab Calloway)
The Goona Goo (vocal: Cab Calloway)
Some Of These Days (vocal: Cab Calloway) (flute; great vocal by Cab)
Minnie The Moocher (theme)

■ WEDNESDAY 10 FEBRUARY 1937

RECORDING SESSION

EARL HINES AND HIS ORCHESTRA
Recording session for Vocalion in Chicago.
Earl Hines (p/ldr); Charlie Allen, Milton Fletcher (t); Walter Fuller (t/voc); Louis Taylor, William Franklin, Trummy Young (tb); Darnell Howard (cl/as/vln); Omer Simeon (cl/as/bar); Budd Johnson (ts); Lawrence Dixon (g); Quinn Wilson (b); Wallace Bishop (d); Ida Mae James (voc)
Flany Doodle Swing / Pianology / Rhythm Sundae / Inspiration / I Can't Believe That You're In Love With Me (vIMJ) / *Honeysuckle Rose* (Quartet–OS,BJ,EH,WB)

RADIO LOGS

9.15PM WOR
BUNNY BERIGAN
Meadowbrook, N.J.
I Can't Get Started (theme) (featuring Bunny Berigan's trumpet)
Serenade In The Night (lousy song well played)
Blue Lou (Bunny's colossal trumpet; drums; saxes)
You're Laughing At Me (vocal: Louise Wallace) (swell song; Bunny's trumpet)
June Night (Art Drelinger's tenor; Bunny's muted trumpet; piano)

9.30PM WHN
JOE HAYMES
Brooklyn Roseland
St. Louis Blues (colossal: same arrangement as record on Vocalion, piano; drums; tenor; clarinet; trumpet)
It's Love I'm After (vocal: Cliff Weston)
Big Boy Blue (SWELL: fair trumpet; great tenor; clarinet)
Midnight (theme) (ballsy theme)

10.30PM WOR
CAB CALLOWAY
Cotton Club, NYC
Damn good.
Mr Ghost Goes To Town (written by Will Hudson: great tenor; trumpet)
When My Dreamboat Comes Home (vocal: Cab Calloway)
Big Boy Blue (vocal: Cab Calloway) (Ben Webster's swell tenor; Claude Jones' trombone; clarinet)
Save Me Sister (vocal: Cab Calloway)
Hot Stuff
Unknown Title (swell arrangement; trombones; saxes; piano; Barefield's alto)
What Will I Tell My Heart? (vocal: Bennie Payne)
Nagasaki (vocal: Cab Calloway) (Webster; Jones; Cheatham)

11.00PM WABC
BENNY GOODMAN
Hotel Pennsylvania, NYC
This Is My Last Affair (vocal: Frances Hunt)
I've Got My Love To Keep Me Warm (trumpet; Stacy; Krupa; Benny)
St. Louis Blues (NUTTSY, very slow tempo, slower than the record: Benny; clarinets; James)
This Year's Kisses (vocal: Frances Hunt) (Musso's tenor)
Minnie The Moocher's Wedding Day (ballsy saxes & brass: colossal Harry James trumpet; what an arrangement!!)
After You've Gone (BG Trio) (great work by all three)
You're Laughing At Me (vocal: Frances Hunt)
Boo Hoo (vocal: Frances Hunt) (just written by Carmen Lombardo)

11.30PM WMCA
JIMMIE LUNCEFORD
Apollo Theater, NYC
Pretty good. Sailing for Europe next week.
Organ Grinder's Swing (over arranged: Al Norris' guitar; clarinet; trumpet)
Dear Old Southland (2 trumpet solos; Willie Smith's tenor)

11.30PM WEAF
GLEN GRAY
Rainbow Room, NYC
Smoke Rings (theme)
May I Have The Next Romance? (vocal: Kenny Sargent)
Oh, Babe! What Can The Matter Be (vocal: Pee Wee Hunt)
Too Marvelous For Words (vocal: Kenny Sargent)
Sugar Foot Stomp (Hutchenrider's clarinet; Hunt's trombone)
Paramour (Pat Davis' swell, sweet tenor; Tony Briglia's drums; brass – Watts, Zullo, Dunham)
The Goona Goo (vocal: Pee Wee Hunt) (Pat Davis' tenor; Dunham's trumpet; Dennis' bass)
I Cried For You (vocal: Kenny Sargent) (trombones: Hunt, Rauch, Hummel)
When Will I Know? (Hutchenrider, recorded on Decca)

12.00 MIDNIGHT WNEW
WOODY HERMAN
Roseland Ballroom, NYC
Blue Prelude (theme) (nuttsy theme featuring Reid's trombone; Hupfer's violin)
Mr Ghost Goes To Town (Frank Carlson's drums; Saxie Mansfield's tenor; Herman's clarinet)
I Can't Pretend (vocal: Woody Herman) (ballsy new song recorded on Decca)
Jazz Me Blues (nuttsy: Reid's trombone; Herman's clarinet; Carlson's drums)
This Year's Crop Of Kisses (vocal: Woody Herman)
My Blue Heaven (swell: clarinets; Woody's clarinet; saxes; Joe Bishop's flugelhorn)
Wait (vocal: Woody Herman) (nuttsy new song: Woody is one nuttsy vocalist and a swell guy)
I Can't Give You Anything But Love (special arrangement by Gordon Jenkins)

12.35AM WOR
COUNT BASIE
Chatterbox, Hotel William Penn, Pittsburgh
Great! Basie's piano is colossal. Lester Young, Jo Jones' drums and Buck Clayton's trumpet are the high points of the band.
You Do The Darndest Things, Baby (vocal: Jimmy Rushing) (Basie's piano)
Swinging At The Daisy Chain (Lester Young's tenor)
Riffin'
I Cried For You (vocal: Jimmy Rushing)
Oh, Lady Be Good (Count Basie's nuttsy piano; trumpet; Herschel Evans' tenor)
Yeah, Man!
Moten Swing (theme)

■ THURSDAY 11 FEBRUARY 1937

RECORDING SESSION

LUCKY MILLINDER & MILLS BLUE RHYTHM BAND
Recording session for Variety in New York City.
Lucky Millinder (voc/ldr); Charlie Shavers, Carl Warwick, Harry Edison (t); Sandy Watson, Wilbur De Paris (tb); Tab Smith (as); Eddie Williams, Ronald Haynes, Harold Arnold (ts); Billy Kyle (p); Danny Barker (g); John Williams (b); Lester Nichols (d/vib)
Blue Rhythm Fantasy / Prelude To A Stomp / Rhythm Jam / Jungle Madness

RADIO LOGS

12.00 MIDNIGHT WOR
BENNY GOODMAN
Hotel Pennsylvania, NYC
Heard this program at Cynthia Doyle's house.
Chlo-e (Harry James' trumpet)
With Plenty Of Money And You (vocal: Frances Hunt)
Mean To Me
Who? (BG Trio) (Lionel Hampton playing drums)
Summer Nights (vocal: Frances Hunt)
Sometimes I'm Happy (colossal: Harry James' trumpet)
Goodtime Charlie
Goodbye (closing theme)

■ FRIDAY 12 FEBRUARY 1937

RADIO LOGS

12.10AM WOR
MAL HALLETT
Hotel Commodore, NYC
You're Not The Kind (vocal: Teddy Grace)
Copper Colored Gal
Sometimes I'm Happy (trombones)
I'm The Lady Who Swings The Band (vocal: Teddy Grace)
Estelle (original piece by FRANKIE CARLE at the piano)
Mary Lou (Anderson's swell tenor; trumpet)
Angry (Anderson's swell tenor; trumpet)

12.30AM WEAF
FRANK TRUMBAUER
Hickory House, 52nd Street, NYC
Fair. Last broadcast of Trumbauer from Hickory House. Mike Riley & band are replacing him this coming Wednesday when Trumbauer leaves for Florida. He is going to rejoin Paul Whiteman next month.
Pickin' The Blues (theme)
I'd Climb The Highest Mountain
Slummin' On Park Avenue (vocal: 4 Modernaires)
Blue Room / My Blue Heaven
I'm An Old Cowhand (vocal: Ford Leary)
52nd Street (latest song by Kahn-Chaplin)
Oh, Yazoo (vocal: Frances Lane) (harpist)
I'm Getting Sentimental Over You (vocal: Ford Leary)
I Know That You Know (vocal: 4 Modernaires)
Singin' The Blues (theme)

1.00AM WOR
COUNT BASIE
Chatterbox, Hotel William Penn, Pittsburgh
Ballsy! Count Basie used to play piano in Bennie Moten's Band in Kansas City until Moten died in 1935. Played in Kansas, Grand Terrace Chicago, and Roseland Ballroom in NYC before going to Hotel William Penn.
Marjorie (Lester Young's swell tenor; Count Basie's piano; Walter Page's bass)
Swing, Brother, Swing (Clayton's trumpet; Lester Young's tenor; Jo Jones' drums)
You Do The Darndest Things, Baby (vocal: Jimmy Rushing) (nice sax section; Evans' tenor)
Streamline Strut (Lester Young's tenor; Dan Minor's trombone; Buck Clayton's trumpet)
Magnolias In The Moonlight (clarinet; Clayton's trumpet; tenor)
My Blue Heaven (vocal: Jimmy Rushing)
Organ Grinder's Swing (Lester Young's great tenor; Jo Jones' drums; Page's bass)
I Got Rhythm
Moten Swing (theme)

1.30AM WOR
RED NORVO
Blackhawk Restaurant, Chicago
Nuttsy!
Slummin' On Park Avenue (vocal: Stew Pletcher) (swell new song: Bill Hyland's trumpet, etc)
Goodnight, My Love (vocal: Mildred Bailey) (Herb Haymer's tenor)
Decca Stomp (COLOSSAL! Saxes with Red Norvo's soft, subtle xylophone; Haymer's clarinet)
An Apple A Day (vocal: Stew Pletcher) (nuttsy: saxes & clarinet; Purtill's drums with Red)
What Will I Tell My Heart? (vocal: Mildred Bailey) (Herb Haymer's tenor)
A Thousand Dreams Of You (vocal: Mildred Bailey) (lousy song but nice vocal)
Exactly Like You (Bill Hyland's trumpet; Purtill's drums; supported by Pete Peterson's bass; Red McGarvey's guitar)
Take Another Guess (vocal: Mildred Bailey) (Bill Miller's swell piano; brass section)
Nagasaki (Red Norvo's ballsy xylophone; trumpet; Haymer; Purtill; clarinet)

FEBRUARY 1937

■ SATURDAY 13 FEBRUARY 1937

Since Hughie couldn't go to see this week's broadcast I took Cynthia Doyle and Nancy Long in to see this week's broadcast. We had a nuttsy time. Before going to the broadcast at 485 Madison Ave, we went over to the Commodore Music Shop and bought some magazines. We then walked up to 51st Street at Madison where the broadcast takes place. Caspar Reardon (swing harpist who appears as guest on many programs), Chick Webb (4ft 6ins tall Negro drummer who leads his own band at the Savoy Ballroom) and Ella Fitzgerald (Negro vocalist with Webb's band, she has a colossal voice, is a little fat, and is very nice) were guests. After the broadcast I got the autographs of Chick Webb, Theodore McRae (tenor with Webb's band), Thomas Fulford (piano in Webb's band), and Taft Jordan (trumpet in Webb's band) all on a picture of Chick Webb. I also got Ella Fitzgerald's autograph on a picture of her. Sat in front row. This was one of the best swing broadcasts yet held.

6.45PM WABC
SATURDAY NIGHT SWING SESSION No32
Studio 1, CBS Studios, NYC
Chicken And Waffles (Introductory theme)
I Can't Get Started (theme) (featuring Bunny Berigan on trumpet)
Hail West Virginia (swell arrangement: Lou Shoobe's bass; Johnny Williams' drums)
Bugle Call Rag (COLOSSAL: Art Manners' clarinet; brass section of Berigan, Williams, Miolla, Roselli)
Spring Fever Blues (Ella Fitzgerald singing the nuts with aid of CBS Band, Webb, McRae)
Love And Learn (Berigan; Shoobe; Maffay; Russ Genner and Joe Vargas' trombones, etc)
Melody In F (Bunny Berigan's trumpet solo was marvelous: how he sends me!!)
Formal Night In Harlem (Berigan's muted trumpet; Webb's drums; McRae's tenor; Shoobe's bass)
St. Louis Blues (Caspar Reardon harp feature: CBS Band's backing was better than Reardon; Joe Vargas' nuttsy muted trombone)
Clap Hands, Here Comes Charlie (ballsy: clarinet section of Pumiglio, Manners, Harris)
This Is My Last Affair (Ella Fitzgerald singing 4 feet from us: she is the nuts)
By Heck (repeated by request: rhythm section of Shoobe, Maffay, Williams, Raymond Scott)

RADIO LOGS

12:30AM WIR
FLETCHER HENDERSON
Nixon-Grand Theater, Philadelphia
Good. Lousy vocalists.
Christopher Columbus (theme) (nuttsy trumpet)
Jim Town Blues (swell muted trumpet; Chu Berry's tenor)
Alexander's Ragtime Band (Chu Berry's tenor)
Back In Your Own Backyard (violin; Henderson's piano; Chu Berry's tenor)
When Dreams Come True (Henderson's piano)
It's Wearing Me Down (vocal: Dorothy Derrick) (a torch song written by Henderson)
You Turned The Tables On Me (vocal: Dick Vance) (sung by trumpeter Vance)
Happy As The Day Is Long

■ SUNDAY 14 FEBRUARY 1937

RADIO LOGS

10:15PM WIR
FLETCHER HENDERSON
Nixon-Grand Theater, Philadelphia
Lousy except for swell solos by Chu Berry on tenor; Buster Bailey on clarinet, and the trumpet (Emmett Berry?).
Love And Learn (trumpet; clarinet; tenor)
This Is My Last Affair (vocal: Dorothy Derrick)
St. Louis Blues (vocal: Jerry Baker)
Down South Camp Meeting
Honeysuckle Rose (Chu Berry's colossal tenor; clarinets; Henderson's piano; swell)
'Way Down Yonder In New Orleans (vocal: Emmett Berry)
King Porter Stomp (ballsy arrangement: trumpet; Chu Berry's great tenor; trombone)
Christopher Columbus (theme) (nuttsy trumpet)

11:15PM WOR
JIMMY DORSEY
Sebastian's Cotton Club, LA
Skeleton In The Closet (vocal: Ray McKinley) (trombone)
I'm In A Dancing Mood (vocal: Bob Eberly)
Swing High, Swing Low (vocal: Vicki Joyce) (Jimmy's clarinet; nuttsy tenor; trumpet)
Sandman (theme) (swell, slow theme)

■ MONDAY 15 FEBRUARY 1937

RECORDING SESSION

ANDY KIRK AND HIS TWELVE CLOUDS OF JOY
Recording session for Decca in New York City.
Andy Kirk (bsx/ldr); Harry Lawson, Paul King, Earl Thompson (t); Ted Donnelly, Henry Wells (tb); John Harrington (cl/as/bar); John Williams (as/bar); Earl Miller (as); Dick Wilson (ts); Claude Williams (vln); Mary Lou Williams (p); Ted Brinson (g); Booker Collins (b); Ben Thigpen (d); Pha Terrell (voc)
Wednesday Night Hop / Skies Are Blue (vPT) / ***Downstream*** (vPT) / ***In The Groove***

ART SHAW AND HIS ORCHESTRA
Recording session for Brunswick in New York City.
Art Shaw (cl/ldr); Lee Castle, Zeke Zarchy (t); Buddy Morrow (tb); Tony Pastor (ts/voc), Jerry Gray, Frank Siegfield (vln); Sam Persoff (vla); Bill Schumann (cello); Joe Lippman (p); Tony Gattuso (g); Ben Ginsberg (b); George Wettling (d); Peg La Centra (voc)
Love Is Good For Anything That Ails You (vPLC) / ***No More Tears*** (vPLC) / ***Moonlight And Shadows*** (vPLC) / ***Was It Rain?*** (vPLC)

Letter (Yankee Network, Station WEAN, Crown Hotel, Providence, R.I.)

February 15, 1937

Dear Mr. Inman:

I regret exceedingly the delay in answering your letter but I have been out of town and have just returned. With reference to your request I will be very glad to outline to you the personell of the orchestra through its several metamorphosis. The Band started out with the following personell.

Bob Conzelman - drums; Jimmy Hartwell - clarinet; Bix Beiderbecke - cornet; Abe Cholden - tenor sax; Bob Gillette - banjo; Ole Vangsness - bass; Al Gandi - Trombone; and Dick Voynow - piano.

The band then changed as a result of the following. The Bass player was a dental school graduate and wanted to practice dentistry. He was surplanted by Min Leibrook. Bob Conzelman had to return to Chicago. He was surplanted by Vic Moore and Abe Cholden also had to return to Chicago. He was surplanted by George Johnson.

It was this band that made all the recordings and it remained as outlined until Bix Beiderbecke left to go with Gene Goldkett. He was surplanted by Jimmy Mc Partland.

With reference to Benny Goodman, Dave Tough, Bud Freeman, Teschmacher and several others, these boys all played with me at some time or another during the time prior to the organization of the Wolverines, at which time I was booking only as a jobbing orchestra and we were all very young, being around 19 or 20.

At that time also Don Murray, Chuck Cheney and Glen Scoville jobbed with us occasionally. However, during this entire jobbing period, Bix and I always were in the band.

(2)

I get to New York occasionally and if you like I should be very glad to meet you and give you any further information you desire.

May I be so bold as to ask just what you do?

Yours very truly,

Richard F. Voynow
~~Sales Manager~~
~~WEAN~~

RFV:jk

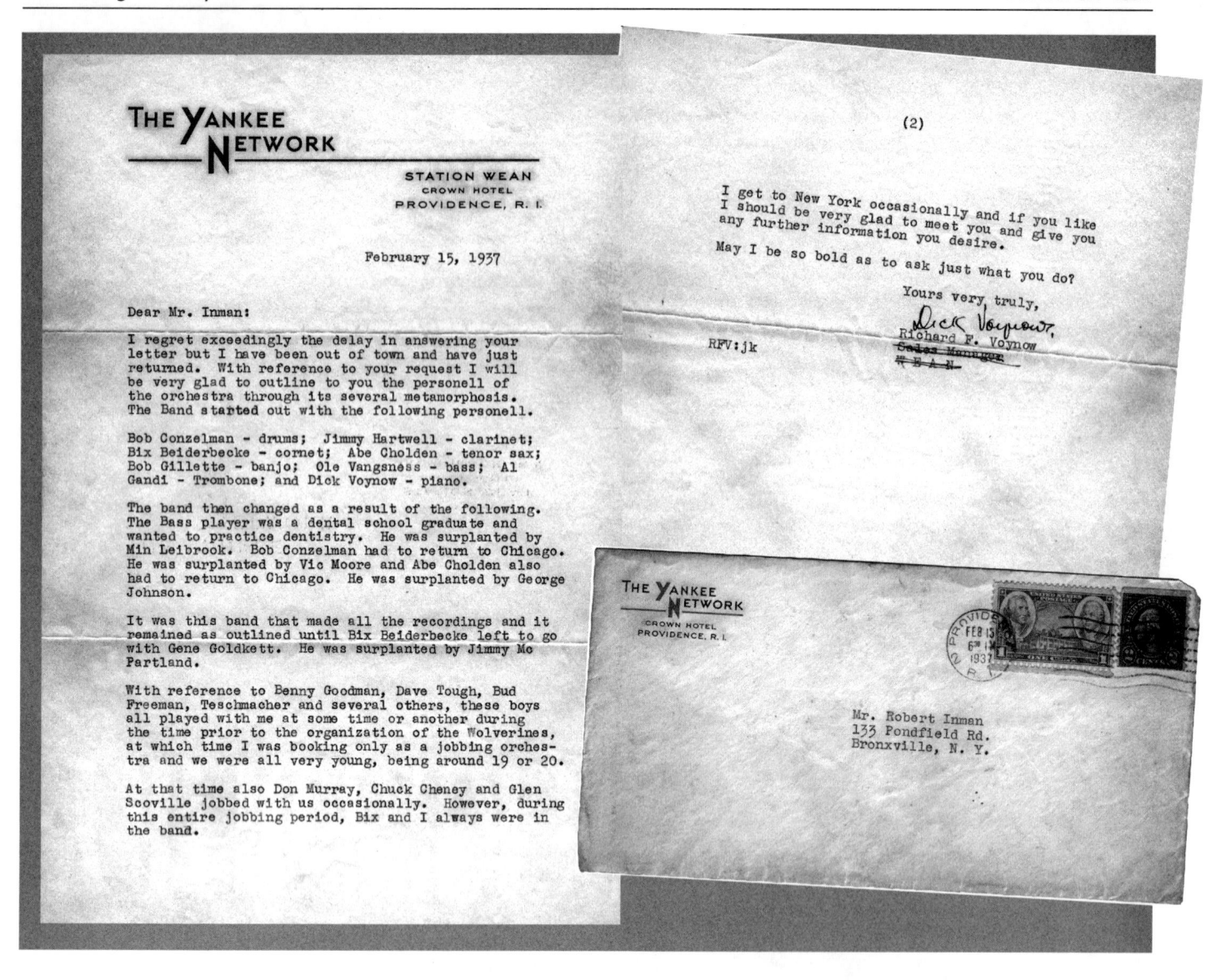

Envelope addressed to:
Mr. Robert Inman
133 Pondfield Rd.
Bronxville, N. Y.

RADIO LOGS

7:15PM WJZ
BUGHOUSE RHYTHM
San Francisco
Announced by G. Archibald Presby. Nuttsy swing program with swing comments.
'Way Down Yonder In New Orleans (published in 1922 by Creamer-Layton: Dr Meakin's Band: tenor; piano)
Skeleton In The Closet (introduced by Louis Armstrong, written by Arthur Johnson: trumpet)
Rose Room (Wallace Harlow Burgess, cornet; John Harrington's clarinet)
Keepin' Out Of Mischief Now (written by Fats Waller and Andy Razaf: tenor)

9.00PM WHN
ERSKINE HAWKINS
Harlem Uproar Club, NYC
Swell. Erskine Hawkins is a nuttsy trumpet player. Whoever the tenor sax or alto sax player is, he sure is the nuts. Hawkins also plays the sax… maybe it's him!
Campus Serenade (theme) (nuttsy slow swing theme)
After You've Gone (vocal: Jimmy Mitchelle) (trumpet; tenor)
House Hop (Jimmy Mundy arrangement; a little ragged)
What Will I Tell My Heart? (ballsy tenor)
Someday, Sweetheart (colossal: tenor; trumpet)
I Can't Escape From You (great: piano)
I'm Painting The Town Red (vocal: Jimmy Mitchelle)
When I Grow Too Old To Dream (vocal: Jimmy Mitchelle)

■ TUESDAY 16 FEBRUARY 1937

RECORDING SESSION

GLEN GRAY AND THE CASA LOMA ORCHESTRA
Recording session for Decca in New York City.
Glen Gray (as/dir); Sonny Dunham, Grady Watts, Frank Zullo (t); Pee Wee Hunt (tb/voc); Billy Rauch, Fritz Hummel (tb); Clarence Hutchenrider (cl/as), Kenny Sargent (as/voc); Art Ralston (as/o/bsn); Pat Davis (ts); Mel Jenssen (vln); Joe Hall (p); Jack Blanchette (g); Stanley Dennis (b); Tony Briglia (d)
Too Marvelous For Words (vKS) / *Zig-Zag* / *Sentimental And Melancholy* (vKS) / *Drifting Apart*

RADIO LOGS

09:30PM WABC
BENNY GOODMAN
Camel Caravan program, NYC
I'll Keep Warm All Winter
Trust In Me (vocal: Frances Hunt)
Nobody's Sweetheart (BG Trio)
Darktown Strutters' Ball (Elman's trumpet)

WEDNESDAY 17 FEBRUARY 1937

RECORDING SESSION

BUNNY BERIGAN AND HIS ORCHESTRA
Recording session for Brunswick in New York City.
Bunny Berigan, Harry Greenwald, L. Brown (t); Ford Leary (tb); Matty Matlock (cl); Hymie Shertzer (as); Art Drelinger (ts); Les Burness (p); Tom Morgan (g); Arnold Fishkind (b); Manny Berger (d); Johnny Hauser (voc)
I'm Gonna Kiss Myself Goodbye (vJH) / *Big Boy Blue* (vJH) / *Dixieland Shuffle* / *Let's Do It*

TOMMY DORSEY AND HIS ORCHESTRA
Recording session for Victor in New York City.
Tommy Dorsey (tb); Bunny Berigan, Jimmy Welch, Joe Bauer, Andy Ferretti (t); Les Jenkins, Red Bone (tb); Slats Long (cl/as); Fred Stulce, Clyde Rounds (as); Bud Freeman (ts); Dick Jones (p); Carmen Mastren (g); Gene Traxler (b); Dave Tough (d); Edythe Wright, Jack Leonard, Three Esquires (voc)
Sweet Is The Word For You (vJL) / *In A Little Hula Heaven* (vEW) / *I'll Dream My Way To Heaven* (v3E)

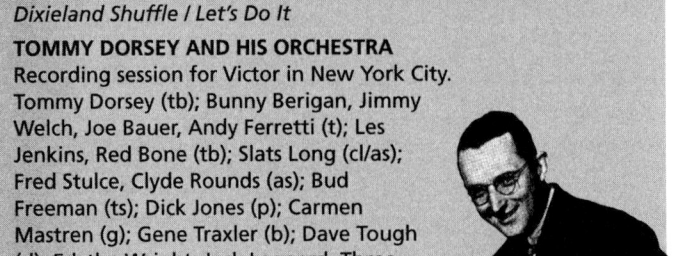

RADIO LOGS

11.00PM WABC
BENNY GOODMAN
Hotel Pennsylvania, NYC
Heard two numbers from this program in Sis Doyle's car.
Roll 'Em (colossal)
The Goona Goo (vocal: Frances Hunt)

11.40PM WEAF
GLEN GRAY
Rainbow Room, NYC
Smoke Dreams (theme)
Honeysuckle Rose (vocal: Pee Wee Hunt) (Hutchenrider's clarinet)
I'll Keep You In My Dreams (vocal: Kenny Sargent)
So Do I (vocal: Kenny Sargent)
Always (Hutchenrider; Pat Davis' tenor; Sonny Dunham's trumpet)
I Can't Lose That Longing For You (vocal: Kenny Sargent)
Rhythm On The River (Clarence Hutchenrider's clarinet; Pat Davis' tenor; very slow)
Put On Your Old Grey Bonnet (vocal: Pee Wee Hunt) (Davis; Joe Hall's piano; Rauch's trombone)

12.00 MIDNIGHT WNEW
WOODY HERMAN
Roseland Ballroom, NYC
Ballsy.
It Happened Down In Dixieland (vocal: Woody Herman) (BALLSY: Reid's trombone; Saxie Mansfield's tenor)
I'll Forsake All Others (vocal: Woody Herman)
Fan It (vocal: Woody Herman) (Reid; Mansfield; Carlson's drums; Bishop's flugel horn)
D-Minor Blues (written by Joe Bishop; Mansfield; Herman's clarinet)
Royal Garden Blues (Reid; Mansfield)
Trust In Me
Blue Prelude (theme)

THURSDAY 18 FEBRUARY 1937

RECORDING SESSION

BILLIE HOLIDAY & TEDDY WILSON ORCHESTRA
Recording session for Brunswick in NYC.
Red Allen (t); Cecil Scott (cl); Prince Robinson (ts); Teddy Wilson (p); Jimmy McLin (g); John Kirby (b); Cozy Cole (d); Billie Holiday (v)
The Mood That I'm In / *You Showed Me The Way* / *Sentimental And Melancholy* / *This Is My Last Affair*

TOMMY DORSEY AND HIS ORCHESTRA
Recording session for Victor in New York City.
Tommy Dorsey (tb); Bunny Berigan, Jimmy Welch, Joe Bauer, Andy Ferretti (t); Les Jenkins, Red Bone (tb); Slats Long (cl/as); Fred Stulce, Clyde Rounds (as); Bud Freeman (ts); Dick Jones (p); Carmen Mastren (g); Gene Traxler (b); Dave Tough (d); Jack Leonard (voc)
Thanks For Everything (vJL) / *Liebestraum* / *Mendelssohn's Spring Song*

RADIO LOGS

6.00PM WNEW
GLEN GRAY
Make Believe Ballroom, NYC
Heard this program at Sis Doyle's house. NUTTSY.
Smoke Dreams (theme) (Billy Rauch's trombone; clarinets of Gray and Hutchenrider)
The Goblin Band (rhythm section of Stan Dennis, bass; Hall, piano; Tony Briglia, drums; Blanchette)
May I Have The Next Romance (vocal: Kenny Sargent)
Whoa, Babe (vocal: Pee Wee Hunt)
Sentimental And Melancholy (vocal: Kenny Sargent) (to be recorded on Decca)
Study In Brown (nuttsy slow piece: brass section of Sonny Dunham, Grady Watts & Frank Zullo)
Between The Devil And The Deep Blue Sea (vocal: Pee Wee Hunt)
For You (vocal: Kenny Sargent) (Jack Blanchette's guitar: very sweet old song, swell)
Casa Loma Stomp (written for band several years ago by Gene Gifford who now arranges for band)

10.15PM WHN
TEMPO KING
Hollywood Restaurant, NYC
Joe Marsala (clarinet), Marty Marsala (trumpet), Joe Bushkin (piano), Eddie Condon (guitar), Artie Shapiro (bass), Al Seidel (drums).
This Is My Last Affair (vocal: Tempo King) (2 Marsala's; Bushkin; Condon)
I Would Do Anything For You (vocal: Tempo King)

Tempo King

■ FRIDAY 19 FEBRUARY 1937

RADIO LOGS

12.15AM WOR
TOMMY DORSEY
Hotel Commodore, NYC
Dorsey features his own trombone, Bud Freeman's tenor, Dave Tough's drums, Pee Wee Erwin's trumpet, and has a rhythm section composed of Dick Jones (piano/arranger), Gene Traxler (bass), Carmen Mastren (guitar). Joe Dixon plays clarinet. The band opened tonight at the Commodore Hotel.
Marie (vocal: Jack Leonard & Band) (Tommy's trombone; trumpet; Freeman's tenor)
Song Of India (Joe Dixon's clarinet; trumpet. Just recorded last month!)
Dancing With You (vocal: Jack Leonard & Three Esquires) (written by Tommy Dorsey)
Swing That Music (vocal: Three Esquires) (written & titled after Louis Armstrong's new book—Bud Freeman's great tenor; Dave Tough's drums)
I'm Getting Sentimental Over You (theme) (nuttsy theme written by Ned Washington & George Bassman)

■ SATURDAY 20 FEBRUARY 1937

RECORDING SESSION

RAYMOND SCOTT QUINTETTE
Recording session for Master in NYC.
Raymond Scott (p/ldr); Dave Wade (t); Pete Pumiglio (cl); Dave Harris (ts); Lou Shoobe (b); Johnny Williams (d)
Minuet In Jazz / Twilight In Turkey / The Toy Trumpet / Powerhouse

RADIO LOGS

4.30PM WABC
ART SHAW
Meadowbrook, N.J.
Heard this program at Sis Doyle's house. Shaw started his own band last August at the Lexington Hotel, NYC. He is a noted swing clarinet player and features "sweet-swing" with 2 violins, 1 viola, 1 cello, 2 reed, 3 brass and 4 rhythm.
Nightmare (theme) (nuttsy theme with stringed instruments and clarinets: too short to record)
At Sundown (Tony Pastor's tenor; Zeke Zarchy's trumpet; Art Shaw's clarinet)
Goodnight, My Love (vocal: Peg LaCentra) (Joe Lippman's piano; George Wettling's drums)
Skeleton In The Closet (Zeke Zarchy's trumpet; clarinets; Shaw; Pastor; Wettling)
Pennies From Heaven (vocal: Peg LaCentra)
The Girl Friend (George Wettling's drums)

Half Of Me (vocal: Peg LaCentra)
The Night Is Young (Jerry Gray, violin; Ben Plotkin, violin; Sam Persoff, viola; Jimmy Oderich, cello)
Love And Learn
Coming Through the Rye
Nightmare (theme)

6.45PM WABC
SATURDAY NIGHT SWING SESSION No33
Studio 1, CBS Studios, NYC
First Swing session broadcast this year that I have not seen. Heard at my house with Hughie.
Chicken And Waffles (Introductory theme)
Nero (trumpet not by Berigan, probably Dave Wade: nice brass section, etc)
Powerhouse (Dave Harris, Pete Pumiglio, Dave Wade, Raymond Scott, Lou Shoobe, Johnny Williams)
Star Dust (Leith Stevens directing band: Johnny Williams' bells; Vincent Maffay's guitar; saxes)
Just Naturally Swinging (Guitar duet: Tony Colucci and Johnny Cali)
That's Life, I Guess (sung by BLUE FLAMES: 1 male, 3 females. Swell)
Twilight In Turkey (Scott Quintet: Williams; Wade; Dave Harris, tenor; Scott, piano)
Dardanella (What saxes!!! trumpet by Wade?; bass clarinet)
Unknown title (CHAUNCEY MOREHOUSE, drummer, playing vibraphone: swell)
Swing High, Swing Low

11.00PM WABC
BENNY GOODMAN
Hotel Pennsylvania, NYC
Heard this program at Robcliff Jones' house in Bronxville.
Chlo-e (nuttsy: Harry James' trumpet)
You Showed Me The Way (vocal: Frances Hunt)
Roll 'Em (COLOSSAL, STUPENDOUS: Mary Lou Williams' arrangement; Benny's great clarinet; Musso's tenor; Krupa; Stacy's nuttsy piano)
Smoke Dreams (vocal: Frances Hunt)
I'll Keep Warm All Winter (nuttsy: Harry James' trumpet)
This Is My Last Affair (vocal: Frances Hunt) (swell trumpet)
I Got Rhythm (BG Quartet) (introduced by Benny: Hampton's great vibes)
Star Dust
Goodbye (closing theme)

11.30PM WMCA
CHICK WEBB
Savoy Ballroom, NYC
Heard this program at Robcliff Jones's house. NUTTSY!
Stompin' At The Savoy (theme) (written by Chick Webb, Benny Goodman and Edgar Sampson)
Sugar Foot Stomp
You'll Have To Swing It (vocal: Ella Fitzgerald)
Stop, Look And Listen
You're Laughing At Me (vocal: Louis Jordan)
Jangled Nerves
Feelin' Low (vocal: Ella Fitzgerald)
Swinging On The Reservation (vocal: Ella Fitzgerald) (Wayman Carver's flute)

12.00 MIDNIGHT WJZ
GUS ARNHEIM
Congress Hotel, Chicago
Heard this program at Robcliff Jones's house.
Say It With Music (theme) (swell swing theme)
Love Is Good For Anything That Ails You (vocal: June Robbins)
I've Got My Love To Keep Me Warm
Slummin' On Park Avenue
Dedicated To You (vocal: Ray Foster)
Oh Say, Can You Swing? (vocal: Don Hamilton)
This Is My Last Affair (vocal: June Robbins)
Too Bad
You're Laughing At Me

■ SUNDAY 21 FEBRUARY 1937

RADIO LOGS

12.00 MIDNIGHT WEAF
GUS ARNHEIM
Congress Hotel, Chicago
Who's That Knocking At My Heart? (vocal: Don Hamilton)
This Year's Crop Of Kisses (vocal: June Robbins)
Blue Skies (nice tenor; brass; saxes)
You're Here, You're There, You're Everywhere (vocal: Ray Foster)
I Can't Break The Habit Of You (vocal: Don Hamilton)
This Is My Last Affair (vocal: June Robbins)
Jungle Drums
Swing High, Swing Low (vocal: Don Hamilton)
Dedicated To You (vocal: Ray Foster)
I've Got My Love To Keep Me Warm (vocal: June Robbins)

■ MONDAY 22 FEBRUARY 1937

RECORDING SESSION

FATS WALLER & HIS RHYTHM
Recording session for Victor in New York City.
Herman Autrey (t); Gene Sedric (cl/ts); Fats Waller (p/voc); Albert Casey (g); Charles Turner (b); Slick Jones (d/vib)
You're Laughing At Me (vFW) / *I Can't Break The Habit Of You* (vFW) / *Did Anyone Ever Tell You?* (vFW) / *When Love Is Young* (vFW) / *The Meanest Thing You Ever Did Was Kiss Me* (vFW)

RADIO LOGS

9.00AM WABC
CBS STUDIO BAND
CBS Studios, NYC
Twinkle Twinkle Little Star
This Year's Crop Of Kisses (vocal: Ruth Gaylor) (formerly with Hudson-DeLange Ork)
Oh, Susanna, Dust Off That Old Pianna (vocal: 4 Eaton Boys)
Now
There's Something In The Air

09.15PM WHN
ERSKINE HAWKINS
Harlem Uproar House, NYC
Nuttsy.
Big Boy Blue (vocal: Jimmy Mitchelle) (ballsy: saxes; trumpet)
Whoa, Babe (swell: tenor; trumpet)
Viper's Swing (written by one of the guys in the band: trumpet; tenor)
Campus Serenade (theme) (what a theme!! ballsy!)

■ TUESDAY 23 FEBRUARY 1937

RADIO LOGS

4.15PM WJZ
CHICK WEBB
Savoy Ballroom, NYC
Facts And Figures
You Showed Me The Way (vocal: Ella Fitzgerald)
Easy To Love
Swingin' Along
The Mayor Of Alabam' (vocal: Louis Jordan)
Rusty Hinge
Goodnight, My Love (vocal: Ella Fitzgerald)
That's A-Plenty

9.00PM WHN
ERSKINE HAWKINS
Harlem Uproar House, NYC
Organ Grinder's Swing
Cocktail Rhythm
Jam Session

9:30PM WABC
BENNY GOODMAN
Camel Caravan program, NYC
Always (Rollini; McEachern)
Roll 'Em (super-colossal: brass; saxes; Stacy; trombone team; tenor; Benny)
Boo Hoo (vocal: Frances Hunt)
Liza (BG Quartet) (ballsy introduction)

■ WEDNESDAY 24 FEBRUARY 1937

RADIO LOGS

6.50PM WMCA
STUFF SMITH
Commercial program, NYC
Blue Prelude (Sandy Williams' trombone; Jonah Jones' trumpet)
You Came To My Rescue (vocal: Ella Fitzgerald)
'Way Down Yonder In New Orleans
An Apple A Day (vocal: Ella Fitzgerald)

10.20PM WMCA
FRANKIE WARD
Hotel Bradford Roof, Boston
St. Louis Blues (nuttsy: drums, clarinet, etc)
Someone To Care For Me
Big John Special

10.30PM WOR
CAB CALLOWAY
Cotton Club, NYC
Honeysuckle Rose (vocal: Cab Calloway)
Was It Rain?
Big Boy Blue (vocal: Cab Calloway)
Whispering (vocal: Cab Calloway)
My Melancholy Baby
The Lady From Mayfair (vocal: Cab Calloway) (first time on radio: lousy)
Peckin' (vocal: Cab Calloway) (nuttsy: clarinet; trombone; great tenor)
Some Of These Days (vocal: Cab Calloway) (great vocal by Cab)

11.00PM WABC
BENNY GOODMAN
Hotel Pennsylvania, NYC
You Showed Me The Way (vocal: Frances Hunt)
Stompin' At The Savoy (Rollini; McEachern)
I Can't Lose That Longing For You (vocal: Frances Hunt)
I Want To Be Happy (Musso; Elman)
There's Something In The Air (vocal: Frances Hunt) (swell trumpet)
Ida, Sweet As Apple Cider (BG Quartet) (introduced by Benny)
It's The Mood That I'm In (vocal: Frances Hunt)
I Wish I Knew (McEachern; James; Musso)
Goodbye (closing theme)

11.30PM WJZ
GLEN GRAY
Rainbow Room, NYC
Zig Zag (Stan Dennis' bass)
Too Marvelous For Words (vocal: Kenny Sargent)
The Moon Is Grinning At Me (vocal: Pee Wee Hunt)
May I Have The Next Romance? (vocal: Kenny Sargent)
Between The Devil And The Deep Blue Sea (vocal: Pee Wee Hunt)
Beale Street Blues (vocal: Pee Wee Hunt)
I've Got My Love To Keep Me Warm (vocal: Kenny Sargent)
Should I? (Davis; Hall; Hutchenrider)
Smoke Rings (theme)

11.40PM WMCA
LUCKY MILLINDER
Apollo Theater, NYC
Sundays Are The Best For Somebody Else But Me (pianist/composer singing—Billy Kyle?)
Rhythm Jam (featuring Cousin Charlie, new young 3rd trumpeter with band—Charlie Shavers?)

12.00 MIDNIGHT WABC
TOMMY DORSEY
Hotel Commodore, NYC
I'm Getting Sentimental Over You You (theme) (slow, sweet opening & closing theme)
Head Over Heels In Love (vocal: Edythe Wright) (Dorsey's muted trombone; Bud Freeman)
Dedicated To You (vocal: Jack Leonard)
Liebestraum (classical piece in swing style: Tommy's trombone; Freeman's tenor; Joe Dixon's clarinet; Dave Tough's drums)
Lookin' Around Corners For You (vocal: Three Esquires) (trumpet; Tommy)
Passionette (lousy)
On A Little Bamboo Bridge (vocal: Edythe Wright)
Marie (vocal: Jack Leonard & Band) (written by Irving Berlin)
Memphis Blues (Tommy's trombone; trumpet; Joe Dixon's clarinet; Dave Tough's drums)
Smoke Dreams (vocal: Edythe Wright & Three Esquires)
That's A-Plenty (Dixon's swell clarinet; Tommy; Freeman's tenor sax)

12.30AM WOR
COUNT BASIE
Chatterbox, Hotel William Penn, Pittsburgh
Rhythm In My Soul
Dear Old Southland
For Sentimental Reasons (vocal: Jimmy Rushing)
Oh, Lady Be Good
Somebody Loves Me (vocal: Jimmy Rushing)
You Do The Darndest Things, Baby (vocal: Jimmy Rushing)
Dancing Derby
Yeah, Man!

■ THURSDAY 25 FEBRUARY 1937

RADIO LOGS

6.00PM WNEW
JERRY HOLDEN
Make Believe Ballroom, NYC
Fair. This is the first time that this orchestra has broadcast over the radio.
Swingin' At The Make Believe Ballroom (theme)
All's Fair In Love And War
I Can't Give You Anything But Love, Baby
Big Boy Blue
I Cried For You
All Of Me (trombone; tenor)

11.00PM WABC
TOMMY DORSEY
Hotel Commodore, NYC
This Year's Crop Of Kisses (vocal: Edythe Wright)
You're Here, You're There, You're Everywhere (vocal: Jack Leonard)
Who'll Buy My Violets?s (Dixon; Tommy; trumpet; Freeman's tenor)
Organ Grinder's Swing (great work by trumpeter and Freeman; Tommy)
Twinkle, Twinkle, Little Star (vocal: Edythe Wright)
May I Have The Next Romance With You? (vocal: Jack Leonard)
Blue Lou (nuttsy tune; saxes)
Swing That Music (vocal: Three Esquires) (Freeman's tenor sax; Tommy's trombone)

FEBRUARY 1937

12.00 MIDNIGHT WOR
BENNY GOODMAN
Hotel Pennsylvania, NYC
I've Got My Love To Keep Me Warm
Goodnight, My Love (vocal: Frances Hunt)
Swingtime In The Rockies (Musso; Benny; Griffin)
You're Laughing At Me (vocal: Frances Hunt)
Somebody Loves Me (saxes; Elman; Musso)
How Could You? (vocal: Frances Hunt)
Serenade In The Night
Liza (BG Quartet)
You Showed Me The Way (vocal: Frances Hunt) (James' trumpet)
Jam Session (Musso; Elman)
Goodbye (closing theme)

■ FRIDAY 26 FEBRUARY 1937

RECORDING SESSION

RED McKENZIE & HIS RHYTHM KINGS
Recording session for Variety in New York City.
Dave Wade (t); Pete Pumiglio (cl); Dave Harris (ts); Raymond Scott (p); ? (g); Lou Shoobe (b); Johnny Williams (d); Red McKenzie (voc)
Sweet Lorraine (vRM) / *Wanted* (vRM)

RADIO LOGS

6.45PM WMCA
STUFF SMITH
Commercial program, NYC
This program is a commercial sponsored by Lucidin. It is on every Monday, Wednesday and Friday at 6:45. It is a swell jam program.
He Ain't Got Rhythm
An Apple A Day (vocal: Ella Fitzgerald)
Serenade In The Night
That Man is Here Again (vocal: Ella Fitzgerald) (ballsy)
Ol' Man River (Jonah Jones; Stuff Smith's violin; trombone)

12.00 MIDNIGHT WJZ
BOB CROSBY
Congress Hotel, Chicago
Colossal! Bob Crosby's first night at the Congress Hotel. Heard this program in Eddie Fisher's car driving home from Scarsdale.
Wolverine Blues (Matlock's or Mince's clarinet)
Stormy Weather (vocal: Kay Weber)
One, Two, Button Your Shoe (vocal: Bob Crosby)
Dogtown Blues (Yank Lawson's trumpet; Eddie Miller's tenor)
If I Had You (Yank Lawson's great trumpet)
Easy To Love (vocal: Kay Weber)
Pagan Love Song (Lawson; Miller; Bob Haggart; Ray Bauduc)
Summertime (theme) (nuttsy theme)

■ SATURDAY 27 FEBRUARY 1937

Hughie and I went in to see this week's Swing Session. I went by subway and he went by train. Since I had plenty of time I went over to 42nd Street and got some pictures, 4 for a dime, of myself. Are they ever rare!?! I met Hughie at the broadcasting place (485 Madison Ave) at 6:20. Ramona Davis (girl pianist and vocalist with Paul Whiteman since 1932), Al Duffy (violinist who has played with the Arkansas Travelers, California Ramblers, and Roger Wolfe Kahn's band), and Red McKenzie (white American vocalist born in 1903 who organised famous Mound City Blue Blowers and formerly sang with Whiteman) were this week's guest stars. I got the autographs of McKenzie, Duffy, and Ramona in the book 'Rhythm On Record'. Also got Ramona's autograph on her picture, and Dave Harris's autograph (he plays tenor sax with CBS Band) on a piece of paper. Harris used to be named Hamilton. I've got his autograph using both names.

Sincerely Dave Harris

Ramona Davis

6.45PM WABC
SATURDAY NIGHT SWING SESSION No34
Studio 1, CBS Studios, NYC
Chicken And Waffles (Introductory theme)
I Can't Get Started (theme) (featuring Bunny Berigan on trumpet)
How Could You? (Dave Harris' tenor; Pete Pumiglio's clarinet; Raymond Scott)
Let's Go Barrelhouse (RAMONA singing and playing piano with the aid of Berigan, Art Manners, Lou Shoobe, Frank Worrell, Williams)
Kiddin' On The Fiddle (AL DUFFY playing his own song on his violin)
Bunny Berigan's start as a trumpet player, playing with a carnival band.
Somebody Loves Me (brass section of Berigan, Williams, Wade, Miolla, Vargas, Genner)
I Can't Get Started (RED McKENZIE singing a nuttsy vocal with aid of Berigan)
Melody In G (Raymond Scott Quintet: Dave Harris, ts; Pete Pumiglio, cl; ?t; Lou Shoobe, b; Johnny Williams, d. They played this directly in front of us. Harris stepped on my toe while playing)
Ozarks Are Calling Me Home (RAMONA singing and playing piano)
Stop, Look, And Listen (STUPENDOUS: clarinets, brass, Frank Worrell's guitar)

RADIO LOGS

??PM ?
ART SHAW
Meadowbrook, N.J.
Tea On The Terrace
Easy To Love
When A Lady Meets A Gentleman Down South
Trust In Me
Cream Puff
Can't You Tell?
Ain't Misbehavin'
Was It Rain? (vocal: Peg LaCentra)

11.00PM WABC
BENNY GOODMAN
Hotel Pennsylvania, NYC
I heard this program at Nancy Long's house.
I Wish I Knew (McEachern; Musso)
Too Marvelous For Words (vocal: Frances Hunt)
Mean To Me (Musso's tenor sax with trumpets)
You Showed Me The Way (vocal: Frances Hunt) (James' trumpet; McEachern's trombone)
Anything Goes (solid rhythm section)
Swing Low, Sweet Chariot (Musso; Elman; saxes)
Remember (Rollini's tenor; McEachern)
Limehouse Blues (BG Quartet) (nuttsy)
This Is My Last Affair (vocal: Frances Hunt) (James' trumpet)
Changes (nuttsy saxes; James' trumpet)
Goodbye (closing theme)

11.30PM WMCA
CHICK WEBB
Savoy Ballroom, NYC
Copenhagen
Unknown Title
I Want To Be Happy

12.07AM WJZ
BOB CROSBY
Congress Hotel, Chicago
The Night Is Young
With Plenty of Money And You (vocal: Bob Crosby) (Eddie Miller's swell tenor sax)
Gin Mill Blues (written by Joe Sullivan, formerly with band: featuring Bob Zurke's piano)
Come Back, Sweet Papa (vocal: Nappy Lamare) (Eddie Miller's tenor; Yank Lawson's trumpet)
Did You Mean It? (vocal: Bob Crosby) (Lawson; clarinet)
Bugle Call Rag (Lawson; Bob Haggart's bass; Ray Bauduc's drums; Miller)

■ SUNDAY 28 FEBRUARY 1937

RADIO LOGS

9.15PM WGN
RED NORVO
Blackhawk Restaurant, Chicago
Smoke Dreams (vocal: Mildred Bailey) (ballsy)
It Had To Be You
With Plenty Of Money And You (vocal: Stew Pletcher)
What Will I Tell My Heart? (vocal: Mildred Bailey)
Honeysuckle Rose

MARCH 1937

Hotel Pennsylvania: **Benny Goodman**
Hotel Commodore: **Tommy Dorsey**
Hotel New Yorker: **Bob Crosby**
Hotel Lincoln: **Isham Jones**
Hotel Taft: **George Hall**
Hotel Lexington: **Ozzie Nelson**
Rainbow Room: **Glen Gray**

Apollo Theater: **Fletcher Henderson** (–4); **Earl Hines** (5–11); **Jesse Stone/Buck & Bubbles** (12–18); **Count Basie** (19–25); **Cab Calloway** (26–)
Paramount Theater: **Benny Goodman** (3–23); **Eddie Duchin** (24–)
Loew's State Theater: **Fats Waller** (20–26)

Cotton Club Downtown: **Cab Calloway** (–16); **Duke Ellington** (17–)
Hickory House: **Mike Riley / Joe Marsala**
Onyx Club: **Stuff Smith**

■ MONDAY 1 MARCH 1937

RADIO LOGS

7.15PM WJZ
BUGHOUSE RHYTHM
San Francisco
Rigamarole (written by Harold Mooney)
The Goona Goo (piano: arrangement by Dr Meakin)
Hector, The Garbage Collector (written by Earl C. Showers; sung by Saunders King)

9.00PM WHN
ERSKINE HAWKINS
Harlem Uproar House, NYC
Nuttsy.
Campus Serenade (theme)
My Buddy (vocal: Jimmy Mitchelle)
Goodnight, My Love (vocal: Jimmy Mitchelle)
Star Dust (vocal: Jimmy Mitchelle) (Hawkins' trumpet)
Roses Of Picardy (vocal: Jimmy Mitchelle)
Formal Night In Harlem (vocal: Jimmy Mitchelle)
Coquette (bass sax; Hawkins' trumpet)
St. Louis Blues (vocal: Jimmy Mitchelle) (trumpet; piano)
Big John Special (a little ragged; trumpet)

9.30PM WJZ
TOMMY DORSEY
Kool-Raleigh Commercial, NYC
Jamboree (vocal: Edythe Wright & Three Esquires)
Dedicated To You (vocal: Jack Leonard)
'Way Down Yonder In New Orleans
Two Cigarettes In The Dark (theme)

10.00PM WJZ
CHICK WEBB
Studio program, NYC
Ella Fitzgerald COLOSSAL.
I Found A New Baby (NUTTSY: Wayman Carver's flute; McRae's tenor; Fulford's piano; Williams' trombone; Taft Jordan's trumpet)
Swing, Mr Charlie (vocal: Four Inkspots)
What Will I Tell My Heart? (vocal: Ella Fitzgerald) (swell song)
Oh Dear, What Can The Matter Be? (Jordan's trumpet; Webb's drums; tenor)
You Showed Me The Way (vocal: Ella Fitzgerald) (great vocal on swell song; Jordan; Webb's drums)
Cross Patch (vocal: Four Inkspots) (Charles Fuqua-guitar; Jerry Daniels; Ivory Watson; Orville Jones)
Stompin' At The Savoy (written by Edgar Sampson: Jordan; saxes; brass)

MARCH 1937

■ TUESDAY 2 MARCH 1937

RECORDING SESSION

FLETCHER HENDERSON AND HIS ORCHESTRA
Recording session for Vocalion in New York City.
Fletcher Henderson (p/ldr); Dick Vance, Russell Smith, Emmett Berry (t); George Washington, Ed Cuffee, J. C. Higginbotham (tb); Jerry Blake (cl/as/voc); Hilton Jefferson (as); Elmer Williams, Chu Berry (ts); Lawrence Lucie (g); Israel Crosby (b); Walter Johnson (d); Dorothy Derrick (voc)
What Will I Tell My Heart? (vDD) / *It's Wearing Me Down* (vDD) / *Slumming On Park Avenue* (vJB) / *Rhythm Of The Tambourine*

Betty Grahl got some tickets to see this week's Camel Caravan from the CBS 53rd Street Playhouse from 9:30 to 10:30pm. Her parents drove Hughie, Mary Elma Riddel and myself in. The regular Camel Caravan originated in Hollywood but since Goodman is in NYC he broadcasts there. Frances Hunt wasn't present tonight and Bill DePew was replaced by George Koenig last week. Bert Parks announced. I got the autographs of arranger Jimmy Mundy, Vido Musso, Lionel Hampton and George Koenig.

9:30PM WABC
BENNY GOODMAN
Camel Caravan program, NYC
Stompin' At The Savoy (program theme played at 9:25)
Alexander's Ragtime Band
Star Dust (muted brass section)
Ridin' High (James' trumpet; Krupa)
Somebody Loves Me (Musso; James)
Bugle Call Rag (McEachern; Rollini; Elman)
Sometimes I'm Happy (Harry James' trumpet; Musso)
WILLIAMS' COLLEGE GLEE CLUB singing 3 numbers (9:55)
Makin' Whoopee (Harry James' trumpet)
Dinah (BG Quartet) (Hampton and Benny really sending each other)
Goodbye (closing theme) (James' trumpet: 10:25)
Got home at 12:15am.

RADIO LOGS

12.15AM WNEW
WOODY HERMAN
Roseland Ballroom, NYC
Smoke Dreams (vocal: Woody Herman)
I Can't Give You Anything But Love, Baby
I'm Face To Face With Love (vocal: Woody Herman)
Blue Prelude (theme)

12.35AM WOR
RED NORVO
Blackhawk Restaurant, Chicago
Riffin' At The Ritz
Easy To Love (vocal: Mildred Bailey) (in honor of Cole Porter)
Night And Day (in honor of Cole Porter)
I've Got You Under My Skin (vocal: Mildred Bailey) (in honor of Cole Porter)
I'll Chase The Blues Away (vocal: Mildred Bailey)
It Had To Be You
Rockin' Chair (vocal: Mildred Bailey)
I Know That You Know

■ WEDNESDAY 3 MARCH 1937

RECORDING SESSION

CAB CALLOWAY AND HIS ORCHESTRA
Recording session for Variety in New York City.
Cab Calloway (voc); Shad Collins, Irving Randolph, Lammar Wright (t); DePriest Wheeler, Keg Johnson, Claude Jones (tb); Garvin Bushell, Andrew Brown (cl/as); Ben Webster, Walter Thomas (ts); Bennie Payne (p); Morris White (g); Milt Hinton (b); Leroy Maxey (d)
I Don't Know If I'm Comin' Or Goin' (vCC) / *My Gal Mezzanine* (vCC) / *That Man Is Here Again* (vCC) / *Peckin'* (vCC) / *Congo* (vCC) / *Swing, Swing, Swing* (vCC)

RADIO LOGS

5.45PM WABC
BLUE FLAMES
CBS Studios, NYC
Swing, Swing Mother-In-Law (written by Raymond Scott)
Singin' The Blues (written by Frank Trumbauer)
You're Just A Little Different
He Ain't Got Rhythm (written by Irving Berlin)
This Year's Kisses (written by Irving Berlin)

10.30PM WOR
CAB CALLOWAY
Cotton Club, NYC
I Don't Know If I'm Coming Or Going (vocal: Cab Calloway) (from *Cotton Club Parade*)
I've Got My Love To Keep Me Warm (vocal: Cab Calloway) (swell song)
Little White Lies (Jones' trombone; Cheatham's trumpet; Webster's tenor)
The Lady From Mayfair (vocal: Cab Calloway)
Twinkle, Twinkle, Little Star (Webster's tenor)
Peckin' (swell tune: clarinet; Webster's tenor)
St. James Infirmary (vocal: Cab Calloway)
Some Of These Days (vocal: Cab Calloway) (great vocal by Cab; flute)

11.00PM WABC
BENNY GOODMAN
Hotel Pennsylvania, NYC
The Benny Goodman band opened today at the Paramount Theater, Times Square, doubling up with the Hotel Pennsylvania engagement.
Goodnight, My Love (vocal: Frances Hunt)
What Can I Say After I Say I'm Sorry?
You Showed Me The Way (vocal: Frances Hunt) (nuttsy song, introduced by Benny: James' trumpet; McEachern's trombone)
I Know That You Know (colossal work by Benny; Krupa)
Sugar Foot Stomp
Slummin' On Park Avenue (vocal: Frances Hunt)
Liza (BG Quartet) (they are playing this at the Paramount Theater)
Sometimes I'm Happy (Harry James; Musso)
How Could You? (vocal: Frances Hunt)
Goodbye (closing theme)

11.30PM WMCA
FLETCHER HENDERSON
Apollo Theater, NYC
Down South Camp Meeting
Rhythm Of The Tambourine (trumpet; Chu Berry's tenor; Buster Bailey's clarinet; J.C. Higginbotham's trombone)
Christopher Columbus (theme)

■ THURSDAY 4 MARCH 1937

RECORDING SESSION

HENRY 'RED' ALLEN
Recording session for Vocalion in New York City.
Henry 'Red' Allen (t/voc); Buster Bailey (cl); Tab Smith (as); Sonny Fredericks (ts); Billy Kyle (p); Danny Barker (g); Johnny Williams (b); Alphonse Steele (d)
After Last Night With You (vHA) / *Goodnight, My Lucky Day* (vHA) / *There's A Kitchen Up In Heaven* (vHA) / *I Was Born To Swing* (vHA)

■ FRIDAY 5 MARCH 1937

RECORDING SESSION

DUKE ELLINGTON AND HIS ORCHESTRA
Recording session for Master Records in New York City.
Duke Ellington (p); Wallace Jones or Arthur Whetsel, Cootie Williams (t); Rex Stewart (c); Joe Nanton, Lawrence Brown (tb); Juan Tizol (vtb); Barney Bigard (cl); Johnny Hodges (cl/ss/as); Otto Hardwick (as/bsx); Harry Carney (cl/as/bar); Fred Guy (g); Hayes Alvis, Billy Taylor (b); Sonny Greer (d); Ivie Anderson (voc)
The New Birmingham Breakdown (HA out) / *Scattin' At The Kit Kat* (BT out) / *I've Got To Be A Rug Cutter* (vIA plus HC,RS,HA) / *The New East St. Louis Toodle-O* (BT out)

GLEN GRAY AND THE CASA LOMA ORCHESTRA
Recording session for Decca in New York City.
Sonny Dunham, Grady Watts, Frank Zullo (t); Pee Wee Hunt (tb/voc); Billy Rauch, Fritz Hummel (tb); Clarence Hutchenrider (cl/as); Kenny Sargent (as/voc); Danny d'Andrea (as); Art Ralston (as/o/bsn); Pat Davis (ts); Joe Hall (p); Jack Blanchette (g); Stanley Dennis (b); Tony Briglia (d)
I'd Be A Fool Again (vKS) / *You're Here, You're There, You're Everywhere* (vKS) / *Was It Rain?* (vKS) / *Love Is Good For Anything That Ails You* (vPWH) / *One, Two, Three Little Hours* (vKS)

RADIO LOGS

11.45PM WMCA
CHICK WEBB
Savoy Ballroom, NYC
Great.
The Goona Goo (vocal: Ella Fitzgerald) (Chick Webb's drums; Taft Jordan's trumpet)
So They Say (vocal: Ella Fitzgerald) (new song: good)
House Hop

12.00 MIDNIGHT WJZ
BOB CROSBY
Congress Hotel, Chicago
Nuttsy. They sure do dish out that Dixieland stuff!!
Summertime (theme)
Wolverine Blues
I've Got My Love To Keep Me Warm (vocal: Kay Weber)
Here Comes Your Pappy (vocal: Nappy Lamare)
One, Two, Button Your Shoe (vocal: Bob Crosby)
Muskrat Ramble (Yank Lawson's trumpet; Eddie Miller's tenor; Haggart's bass)
Black And Blue (vocal: Eddie Miller) (Miller's tenor; Bob Zurke's piano)
Jamboree

■ SATURDAY 6 MARCH 1937

Mrs Pinger drove Harvey Pinger, Dick Morningstar, Hughie and myself to the Woodlawn subway at 8:00 in the morning. We all paid 40 cents to go see Benny Goodman and his Band at the Paramount Theater, Broadway at 43rd Street, where he started last Wednesday and is to be there several weeks. Since Goodman has come in they have raised the price to 40 cents and opened the doors at 8:30 instead of 10:30. It was almost a riot. It was so overcrowded, with people in the aisles, and everybody got so excited over Benny's music and made so much noise. We got in the theater at 9:15, saw the movie 'Maid of Salem' twice, and Benny Goodman's stage show twice, and got out of the theater at 3:00pm. Goodman and Band sure were great. In the last show a fellow in the audience got up and trucked. Benny Goodman wore a tuxedo while the band wore light blue coats and black pants.
PERSONNEL: Benny Goodman (clarinet); Arthur Rollini, Herman Shertzer, George Koenig, Vido Musso (saxes); Harry James, Gordon Griffin, Ziggy Elman (trumpets); Murray McEachern, Red Ballard (trombones); Jess Stacy (piano); Allan Reuss (guitar); Harry Goodman (bass); Gene Krupa (drums); Frances Hunt (vocals)

Let's Dance (theme)
Bugle Call Rag (Benny; Rollini; Elman; McEachern)
Star Dust (James' trumpet; Benny; brass section)
Alexander's Ragtime Band (Benny; brass; saxes)
I've Got My Love To Keep Me Warm (vocal: Frances Hunt)
He Ain't Got Rhythm (vocal: Frances Hunt)
Goodnight, My Love (vocal: Frances Hunt)
Between The Devil And The Deep Blue Sea (vocal: Frances Hunt) (encore)
Tiger Rag (BG Trio) (COLOSSAL work by the Trio)
Body And Soul (BG Trio) (good work by the Trio)
Dinah (BG Quartet) (Lionel Hampton was great)
I Got Rhythm (BG Quartet) (Hampton on vibes, also aiding Wilson on piano)
Stompin' At The Savoy (BG Quartet) (nuttsy)
Sing, Sing, Sing (super-colossal: Krupa; Musso; Benny)

At 3:00 we went around to the stage door where Pinger wanted to get some autographs. He got a few and I got Herman Shertzer's.

Herman Shertzer

> Doubling from his Hotel Pennsylvania engagement, Benny Goodman brought his band to the stage of the Paramount Theatre in New York recently and shattered all records, with 21,000 paid admissions during the opening day.
>
> Crowds began to assemble at 6:30 in the morning on Goodman's opening day, and at 7:30 the police reserves were called out. At 12:30 over 9,000 tickets had been sold, and the police were called again.
>
> At the 1:30 stage appearance of the band their rhythm proved so irresistible that people danced in the aisles! About this time the crowd in front of the Paramount was so terrific that passers-by were forced to walk in the street.
>
> Paramount grossed $58,000 during Goodman's first week, with a rather weak motion picture the only other attraction offered.

Hughie had to go home at about 12:00 so he missed the Saturday Swing broadcast. We just messed around, going into hotel lobbies, etc., until six o'clock. I then left Dickie and Pinger and went to Schrafft's Restaurant on Fifth Avenue at 45th Street where I met Cynthia Doyle and Nancy Long. I took them to this week's Saturday Swing broadcast. We met Dickie and Pinger again there. Paul Starrett (ukulele player and arranger for CBS Band), Earl 'Fatha' Hines (great Negro piano player who is spending this week at the Apollo Theater in Harlem and is to be at the Nixon-Grand Theater in Philadelphia next week with his band) and the Carroll Sisters (3 girl singers–fair) were this week's guests along with Tommy Dorsey's whole band, which was picked up from the Palm Room of the Hotel Commodore. Besides announcer Paul Douglas there was a new announcer. I got Earl Hines' autograph in 'Rhythm On Record' and the autographs of the following new guys in the CBS Band: Bob Michels (bass), Larry Heggins (sax), and Mickey Bloom (trumpeter with Hal Kemp who took Bunny Berigan's place on this broadcast). As Bunny Berigan was absent they left out the old theme.

PERSONNEL: Leith Stevens, Raymond Scott, Bob Michels, Johnny Williams, Frankie Worrell, Mickey Bloom, Nat Natoli, Dave Wade, Jimmy Rosselli, Russ Genner, Joe Vargas, Pete Pumiglio, Art Manners, Dave Harris, Larry Heggins.

Time changed from 6:45—7:15 to 7:00—7:30. Not as good because it makes it difficult to catch the 7:40 train for Bronxville.

7.00PM WABC
SATURDAY NIGHT SWING SESSION No35
Studio 1, CBS Studios, NYC
Nero (new theme) (nuttsy)
Pick Yourself Up (swell)
Georgia Jubilee (good: written by pianist Arthur Schutt)
Japanese Sandman (EARL HINES at piano with aid of Williams' drums and Michels' bass)
Twelfth Street Rag (EARL HINES: a little disappointed in Hines tonight, his piano playing a little too intricate)
Reckless Night On Board An Ocean Liner (Raymond Scott's own number played by his Quintet: Dave Harris, Pete Pumiglio, Dave Wade, Johnny Williams, Bob Michels & Scott)
Honeysuckle Rose (THREE CARROLL SISTERS, pretty good: marvelous song written by Fats Waller)
Swing That Music (TOMMY DORSEY'S whole band with the Three Esquires from the Hotel Commodore: Bud Freeman's tenor; Tommy's trombone)
Liebestraum (TOMMY DORSEY'S whole band from the Hotel Commodore, nuttsy: Bud Freeman's tenor; Dave Tough's drums; Johnny Mince's clarinet; Pee Wee Erwin's trumpet. Mince & Erwin just joined Dorsey.)
After You've Gone (PAUL STARRETT, arranger, playing the nuts on a ukulele)

After the broadcast Cynthia, Nancy and I went down to the Hotel Commodore just to look in on Tommy Dorsey's band: *Marie* (Marvelous, sung by Jack Leonard with aid of band's voices), *Stardust, Trombone Man* (history of Tommy's trombone with Edythe Wright & Three Esquires), *Song Of India* and *You Took Advantage Of Me*. We then got the 8:35 train for Bronxville and went to an Open House at the High School until 12:15.

RADIO LOGS

12.40AM WIP
MAL HALLETT
Nixon-Grand Theater, Philadelphia
Great. A big improvement over their recent stay at the Hotel Commodore in New York City. Teddy Grace is one of the finest hot woman vocalists there is.
The Goona Goo (vocal: Buddy Welcome & Teddy Grace) (colossal arrangement of swell song: tenor)
St. Louis Blues (vocal: Teddy Grace) (swell trumpet by Ryerson?; Anderson's tenor)
Whoa, Babe (vocal: Buddy Welcome)
Alligator Crawl (FRANKIE CARLE piano solo: fair)
Basin Street Blues (vocal: Buddy Welcome) (Carle's swell piano; sax section)
Boston Tea Party (theme) (swell theme written by trumpeter/arranger Ryerson)

■ SUNDAY 7 MARCH 1937

RADIO LOGS

9.15PM WGN
RED NORVO
Blackhawk Restaurant, Chicago
You Showed Me The Way (vocal: Mildred Bailey)
Swing High, Swing Low
Night And Day (six minutes long)
Is That Religion? (vocal: Mildred Bailey)

■ MONDAY 8 MARCH 1937

RECORDING SESSION

COOTIE WILLIAMS & HIS RUGCUTTERS
Recording session for Variety in New York City.
Cootie Williams (t); Joe Nanton (tb); Johnny Hodges (ss/as); Harry Carney (bar); Duke Ellington (p); Hayes Alvis (b); Sonny Greer (d)
I Can't Believe That You're In Love With Me / Downtown Uproar / Diga Diga Doo / Blue Reverie / Tiger Rag

RADIO LOGS

7.15PM WJZ
BUGHOUSE RHYTHM
San Francisco
Farewell Blues
Sweet Sue (Edson Gilson on vibraphone)
I Wish I Could Shimmy Like My Sister Kate (written by A.J.Piron)

9.30PM WJZ
TOMMY DORSEY
Kool-Raleigh Commercial, NYC
Two Cigarettes In The Dark (theme)
Swing That Music (vocal: Three Esquires)
In A Little Hula Heaven (vocal: Edythe Wright)
Ja-Da

■ TUESDAY 9 MARCH 1937

RADIO LOGS

9:30PM WABC
BENNY GOODMAN
Camel Caravan program, NYC
Camel Hop
You Showed Me The Way (vocal: Frances Hunt)
Ol' Man River
Shine (BG Quartet)

9.50PM WHN
ERSKINE HAWKINS
Harlem Uproar House, NYC
Nuttsy.
I Found A New Baby
I've Been A Fool Again (vocal: D. Lloyd)
I'm Painting The Town Red (vocal: Jimmy Mitchelle)
Goodnight, My Love (vocal: 4 Palmer Brothers)
My Blue Heaven (vocal: Jimmy Mitchelle) (ballsy: saxes; drums)
Swingin' In Harlem (NUTTSY: saxes; trumpet; tenor)
Campus Serenade (theme)

■ WEDNESDAY 10 MARCH 1937

RECORDING SESSION

TOMMY DORSEY AND HIS ORCHESTRA
Recording session for Victor in New York City.
Tommy Dorsey (tb); Pee Wee Erwin, Joe Bauer, Andy Ferretti (t); Les Jenkins, Red Bone (tb); Johnny Mince (cl/as); Fred Stulce, Mike Doty (as); Bud Freeman (ts); Dick Jones (p); Carmen Mastren (g); Gene Traxler (b); Dave Tough (d); Edythe Wright, Jack Leonard (voc)
They All Laughed (vEW) / *I've Got Beginner's Luck* (vEW) / *Wanted* (vJL) / *Blue Danube / Dark Eyes*

HUDSON-DeLANGE ORCHESTRA
Recording session for Master in New York City.
Will Hudson (arr); Eddie DeLange (voc/ldr); Charles Mitchell, Howard Schaumberger, Jimmy Blake (t); Edward Kolyer (tb); George Bohn, Gus Bivona (cl/as); Pete Brendel (as/bar); Ted Duane (cl/ts); Mark Hyams (p); Bus Etri (g); Doc Goldberg (b); Nat Pollard (d); Ruth Gaylor (voc)
Stardust / College Widow / You're My Desire (vRG) / *Bugle Call Rag / The Maid's Night Off*

RADIO LOGS

11.00PM WABC
BENNY GOODMAN
Hotel Pennsylvania, NYC
You Showed Me The Way (vocal: Frances Hunt)
I've Got My Love To Keep Me Warm (James' trumpet)
With Plenty Of Money And You (vocal: Frances Hunt)
Bugle Call Rag (recorded for Victor, played in *Big Broadcast Of 1937*)
Stompin' At The Savoy (BG Quartet) (ballsy: screwy introduction)
Sweet Is The Word For You (vocal: Frances Hunt)
The Goona Goo (vocal: Frances Hunt)
Roll 'Em (arranged by Mary Lou Williams: Stacy; Musso; Benny; brass)
Goodbye (closing theme)

11.33PM WMCA
EARL HINES
Apollo Theater, NYC
Swell.
I Can't Believe That You're In Love With Me (vocal: Ida James) (nuttsy song, swell vocal)
After You've Gone (Hines' piano; trumpet; drums; clarinet, etc)

12.00 MIDNIGHT WABC
TOMMY DORSEY
Hotel Commodore, NYC
Pee Wee Erwin, formerly with Benny Goodman and Ray Noble, isn't any Berigan or Kaminsky, but he is darn good. Program announcer: André Baruch.
How Could You? (vocal: Edythe Wright) (Dorsey's trombone; Erwin's trumpet; Freeman)
Goodnight, My Love (vocal: Jack Leonard) (lousy)
Melody In F (Dorsey's muted trombone; saxes; Erwin's trumpet; Freeman; Joe Dixon)
Lookin' Around Corners For You (vocal: Three Esquires) (Jack Leonard; Joe Bauer; Allen Starr)
Jamboree (vocal: Edythe Wright & Three Esquires) (only fair)
Twinkle, Twinkle, Little Star (vocal: Edythe Wright) (Dave Tough's drums)
Carelessly (vocal: Jack Leonard) (lousy)
Spring Song In Swing (by Mendelssohn: Johnny Mince's clarinet; Erwin)
Thanks For Everything (vocal: Jack Leonard) (swell song with nice vocal; saxes; Freeman; Erwin)
Down South Camp Meeting (Fletcher Henderson arrangement, BALLSY: Erwin's trumpet)
I'm Getting Sentimental Over You (theme)

■ THURSDAY 11 MARCH 1937

RECORDING SESSION

HUDSON-DeLANGE ORCHESTRA
Recording session for Master in New York City.
Will Hudson (arr); Eddie DeLange (voc/ldr); Charles Mitchell, Howard Schaumberger, Jimmy Blake (t); Edward Kolyer (tb); George Bohn, Gus Bivona (cl/as); Pete Brendel (as/bar); Ted Duane (cl/ts); Mark Hyams (p); Bus Etri (g); Doc Goldberg (b); Nat Pollard (d); Ruth Gaylor (voc)
Sophisticated Swing / Wake Up And Live (vRG) / *Back In Your Arms* (vEDL) / *Never In A Million Years* (vRG)

RADIO LOGS

11.00PM WABC
TOMMY DORSEY
Hotel Commodore, NYC
This Year's Kisses (vocal: Edythe Wright)
Carelessly (vocal: Jack Leonard) (very new song: foxtrot)
Liebestraum (Dorsey's trombone; Mince's clarinet; Freeman's tenor; Erwin's trumpet)
When The Poppies Bloom Again (vocal: Three Esquires) (Freeman; Tough)
Who'll Buy My Violets? (saxes; Erwin's trumpet; Freeman; Tommy)
I Can't Break The Habit Of You (vocal: Edythe Wright)
May I Have The Next Romance With You? (vocal: Jack Leonard)
Blue Danube Waltz (Swing! Freeman; Tough; Mince; Erwin and Tommy together)
Where Are You? (vocal: Jack Leonard)
Bugle Call Rag (Freeman; Erwin; Tommy; Mince; Tough's drums)

11.30PM WABC
ISHAM JONES
Hotel Lincoln, NYC
Good. Kenneth Roberts announced from the Blue Room of the Hotel Lincoln.
One In A Million (piano; tenor, etc)
I Can't Lose That Longing For You (vocal: Joe Martin)
Swing High, Swing Low (vocal: Eddie Stone)
Thanks For Everything (vocal: Joe Martin)
Slummin' On Park Avenue (vocal: Eddie Stone)
Too Marvelous For Words (vocal: Joe Martin)
Now You're Talking My Language (vocal: Eddie Stone)
Just To Remind You (vocal: Joe Martin) (latest song by Isham Jones)
The Trouble With Me Is You (tenor: nuttsy)
I've Been A Fool Again (vocal: Eddie Stone)
Goodbye Forever (closing theme)

12.00 MIDNIGHT WOR
BENNY GOODMAN
Hotel Pennsylvania, NYC
Howard Barnes announced.
Clap Hands! Here Comes Charlie (nuttsy: Benny; saxes; brass; Krupa; tenor; trumpet)
This Is My Last Affair (vocal: Frances Hunt) (nuttsy song, great vocal: James' trumpet)
You Forgot To Remember (McEachern; Benny; Arthur Rollini's swell tenor with Krupa)
You're Laughing At Me (vocal: Frances Hunt) (swell song, nice vocal: James' trumpet; Musso's tenor)
He Ain't Got Rhythm (vocal: Frances Hunt) (introduction by Krupa)
Oh, Lady Be Good (brass & sax sections swingin' out)
You Showed Me The Way (vocal: Frances Hunt) (what a nuttsy sweet song: James' trumpet)
Limehouse Blues (BG Quartet) (Benny always announces what the Quartet is going to play: Lionel Hampton is colossal but I have heard better Quartet numbers)
I Can't Lose That Longing For You (vocal: Frances Hunt) (Musso's tenor)
Honeysuckle Rose (saxes; brass; Krupa; McEachern; Musso with colossal brass backing; James)

■ FRIDAY 12 MARCH 1937

RADIO LOGS

12.00 MIDNIGHT WJZ
BOB CROSBY
Congress Hotel, Chicago
Super-Colossal at times; other times great. Wonderful trombone work; Miller's great tenor, Bauduc's drums, etc.
Summertime (theme)
Between The Devil And The Deep Blue Sea
Summer Nights (vocal: Kay Weber)
With Plenty Of Money And You (vocal: Bob Crosby)
Gin Mill Blues (COLOSSAL: Miller; Zurke's piano; Bauduc)
You Showed Me The Way (Miller; trombone)
Was It Rain?
Pagan Love Song (Miller; Haggart; Lawson)

Below: Autographs of the Bob Crosby Band on a postcard received from Chicago.

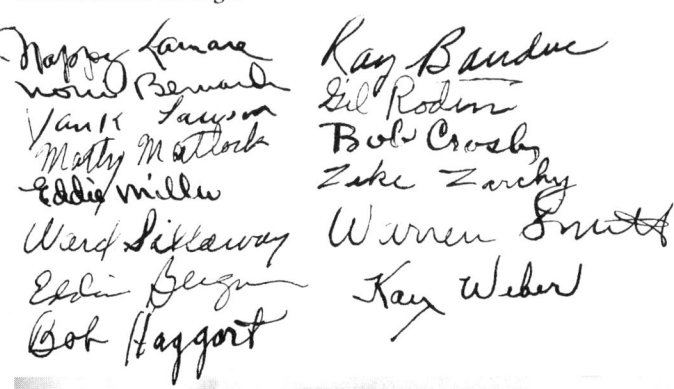

SATURDAY 13 MARCH 1937

Morningstar, Pinger and I went down with the Reserve Basketball team on the bus to Horace Mann High School at 2:00pm. We beat them 24–18, and had a swim in their pool. Pinger, Morningstar and I then took the subway down to see the broadcast at 485 Madison Avenue. We got there at 6:30 and got in on old passes. Duke Ellington and his whole band and Caspar Reardon (swing harpist) were the guests on this week's broadcast. Ellington (famed Negro leader, composer, arranger, piano player) and his band just arrived in NYC two weeks ago from a long road trip. They played at Sebastian's Cotton Club in Culver City, California, for quite some time. This is the first time they have been in NYC for almost a year. They were at the Savoy Ballroom with Chick Webb last Sunday night and are opening at the Cotton Club this coming Wednesday, replacing Cab Calloway. We (Hughie and I) never saw such a super-colossal broadcast. Many pressmen were there and more people witnessed this broadcast than any previous ones. Many pictures were taken. Paul Douglas and Melvin Allen announced the show and the full personnels were:

CBS Band: Leith Stevens (leader); Pete Pumiglio, Art Manners (clarinets); Dave Harris, Hank Ross (saxes); Raymond Scott (piano); Lou Shoobe (bass); Frank Worrell (guitar); Johnny Williams (drums); Joe Vargas, Russ Genner (trombones); Nat Natoli, Lloyd Williams, Dave Wade, Mickey Bloom (trumpets).

DUKE ELLINGTON ORCHESTRA: Duke Ellington (piano); Fred Guy (guitar); Billy Taylor, Hayes Alvis (bass); Sonny Greer (drums); Barney Bigard, Johnny Hodges, Otto Hardwick, Harry Carney (saxes); Joe Nanton, Juan Tizol, Lawrence Brown (trombones); Rex Stewart, Cootie Williams, Arthur Whetsel (trumpets); Ivie Anderson (vocals).

7.00PM WABC
SATURDAY NIGHT SWING SESSION No36
Studio 1, CBS Studios, NYC
Showboat Shuffle (CBS Band under direction of Leith Stevens: Dave Harris' tenor; Johnny Williams' drums)
Caravan (Hodges' alto; Cootie Williams' trumpet; Ellington; Bigard. Played in the dark)
Oh, Babe, Maybe Someday (IVIE ANDERSON singing the nuts with Ellington Band: Hodges; Bigard; 3 trombones; 2 basses, etc. She sure can sing and she dances around plenty while doing so.)
Trumpet In Spades (featuring Rex Stewart on the cornet. No high notes but very tricky)
In A Sentimental Mood (CASPAR REARDON, intoduced by Ellington & Paul Douglas, going the nuts on his harp with the aid of the CBS Band: Art Manners' very soft clarinet; Mickey Bloom's trumpet; Shoobe's bass, etc.)
Harlem Uproar (Played with the lights out by Cootie Williams group. Ellington's piano; Hodges; Hardwick's bass sax; Greer's drums)
East St. Louis Toodle-Oo (Ellington's theme since 1927. Chimes and drums by Greer; Cootie Williams' trumpet; Joe Nanton's trombone; Ellington's piano; Bigard's clarinet, etc.)
Sophisticated Lady; Black Beauty; Solitude (Medley of Ellington piano solos played with the lights out)
It Don't Mean A Thing If It Ain't Got That Swing (CBS Band)
This concluded the broadcast but Raymond Scott's Quintet played another number because everybody was "in the groove" after the wonderful show that Ellington had put on.
Twilight In Turkey (Harris' tenor; Wade; Shoobe; Williams)

After the broadcast we had a short talk with trumpeter Mickey Bloom who really can swing out, but doesn't get much of a chance in the Hal Kemp Band. Since we didn't have time to catch the 7:40 train we went to see Tommy Dorsey's Band at the Palm Room of the Hotel Commodore. We got the autographs of Andy Ferretti (trumpet), Bud Freeman (tenor), Mike Doty (sax), Johnny Mince (clarinet) and Pee Wee Erwin (trumpet formerly with Ray Noble and Benny Goodman). Ferretti and Mince just came from Bob Crosby's Band two weeks ago. We talked to all of them about who they used to play with and how Erwin left Goodman last summer to stay in Los Angeles, but how he couldn't get a job because of the unions. We had to take the 8:35 train home.

Members of the CBS Band (left): Nat Natoli, unknown, Mickey Bloom (trumpets); Russ Genner, Joe Vargas (trombones) and Johnny Williams (drums). Inset: Duke Ellington

MARCH 1937

RADIO LOGS

12.00 MIDNIGHT WJZ
BOB CROSBY
Congress Hotel, Chicago
Jamboree (Matlock's clarinet; Silloway's trombone)
You're Laughing At Me (vocal: Kay Weber)
I Can't Lose That Longing For You (vocal: Bob Crosby)
Dixieland Shuffle (Silloway; Miller; Zurke's piano)
Boo Hoo (vocal: Nappy Lamare)
Goodnight My Love (Matlock's clarinet, etc)
South Rampart Street Parade (written by Ray Bauduc)
Summertime (theme)

12.30AM WABC
BENNY GOODMAN
Hotel Pennsylvania, NYC
House Hop (Krupa; Benny; saxes)
Gee, But You're Swell (vocal: Frances Hunt)
When You And I Were Young, Maggie
More Than You Know (BG Trio)
The Camel Hop (McEachern; trumpet; Musso)
Slummin' On Park Avenue (vocal: Frances Hunt)
Trust In Me (vocal: Frances Hunt)
Liza (BG Quartet)
Smoke Dreams (vocal: Frances Hunt)
Goodbye (closing theme)

■ SUNDAY 14 MARCH 1937

There was a Sunday afternoon jam session at Masters Recording Studio which I only found out about later. The session was produced by Helen Oakley for Irving Mills to launch the Master and Variety record labels. Duke Ellington, Artie Shaw, Ella Fitzgerald, Chick Webb, Frankie Newton, Mezz Mezzrow, George Wettling and Eddie Condon and many others took part.

Jam Session at Masters: Ella Fitzgerald (right) accompanied by Billy Kyle; Benny Goodman (below) accompanied by Chick Webb and Joe Bushkin.

■ TUESDAY 16 MARCH 1937

RADIO LOGS

9:30PM WABC
BENNY GOODMAN
Camel Caravan program, NYC
I Know That You Know
Body And Soul (BGTrio)
When Buddha Smiles (Rollini's tenor sax)
Limehouse Blues (BG Quartet)

■ WEDNESDAY 17 MARCH 1937

RECORDING SESSION

CAB CALLOWAY AND HIS ORCHESTRA
Recording session for Variety in New York City.
Cab Calloway (voc); Shad Collins, Irving Randolph, Lammar Wright (t); DePriest Wheeler, Keg Johnson, Claude Jones (tb); Garvin Bushell, Andrew Brown (cl/as); Ben Webster, Walter Thomas (ts); Bennie Payne (p); Morris White (g); Milt Hinton (b); Leroy Maxey (d)
Wake Up And Live (vCC) / *Goodnight, Baby* (vCC) / *Manhattan Jam*

JIMMY DORSEY AND HIS ORCHESTRA
Recording session for Decca in Los Angeles.
Jimmy Dorsey (cl/as); Joe Meyer (t); Toots Camarata (t/voc); Bobby Byrne, Don Mattison (tb/voc); Bruce Squires (tb); Len Whitney (as); Fud Livingston (as/ts); Charles Frazier (ts); Freddie Slack (p); Roc Hillman (g/voc); Jack Ryan (b); Ray McKinley (d/voc); Bob Eberly, Josephine Tumminia (voc)
The Blue Danube Waltz (vJT) / *Slap That Bass* (vBE) / *They All Laughed* (vDM) / *They Can't Take That Away From Me* (vBE) / *Let's Call The Whole Thing Off* (vDM)

TOMMY DORSEY AND HIS ORCHESTRA
Recording session for Victor in New York City.
Tommy Dorsey (tb); Pee Wee Erwin, Joe Bauer, Andy Ferretti (t); Les Jenkins, Red Bone (tb); Johnny Mince (cl/as); Fred Stulce, Mike Doty (as); Bud Freeman (ts); Dick Jones (p); Carmen Mastren (g); Gene Traxler (b); Dave Tough (d); Edythe Wright, Jack Leonard (voc)
Turn Off The Moon (vJL) / *Jammin'* (vEW) / *I've Got Rain In My Eyes* (vEW)

Duke Ellington and Orchestra open at the Cotton Club in New York tonight, replacing Cab Calloway.

RADIO LOGS

11.15PM WABC
BENNY GOODMAN
Hotel Pennsylvania, NYC
Makin' Whoopee (James' trumpet; brass; Benny)
This Is My Last Affair (vocal: Frances Hunt) (James' trumpet)
Chinatown, My Chinatown (BG Trio)
You Showed Me The Way (vocal: Frances Hunt) (James' trumpet)

■ THURSDAY 18 MARCH 1937

RECORDING SESSION

FATS WALLER & HIS RHYTHM
Recording session for Victor in New York City.
Herman Autrey (t); Gene Sedric (cl/ts); Fats Waller (p/voc); Albert Casey (g); Charles Turner (b); Slick Jones (d/vib)
Cryin' Mood (vFW) / *Where Is The Sun?* (vFW) / *You've Been Reading My Mail* (vFW) / *To A Sweet Pretty Thing* (vFW) / *Old Plantation* (vFW) / *Spring Cleaning* (vFW)

RADIO LOGS

11.30PM WOR
DUKE ELLINGTON
Cotton Club, NYC
East St. Louis Toodle-Oo (theme)
Harlem Speaks (Rex Stewart's cornet; Hodges; Hardwick etc)
Caravan (trombone; Bigard; Cootie Williams; Hodges)
One, Two, Button Your Shoe (vocal: Ivie Anderson) (swell arrangement by Duke)
Pennies From Heaven (vocal: Ivie Anderson) (Cootie Williams; Hodges; Greer)
Mexicali Rose (vocal: Ivie Anderson)
Sophisticated Lady (one of the greatest songs ever written: Hodges; what a sax section!! Nanton)
Rockin' In Rhythm (Ellington's piano; 2 basses; Bigard; muted trumpet; saxes)

12.00 MIDNIGHT WOR
BENNY GOODMAN
Hotel Pennsylvania, NYC
This Year's Crop Of Kisses (vocal: Frances Hunt)
Camel Hop (ballsy: McEachern; nuttsy trumpet; Musso)
I've Got My Love To Keep Me Warm (Krupa; trumpet)
Shine (BG Quartet) (super-ballsy: one of their best numbers)
Chlo-e (introduction by Stacy: Harry James' trumpet)
You Showed Me The Way (vocal: Frances Hunt) (nuttsy: Harry James' trumpet)
Then my radio tube burnt out!

■ FRIDAY 19 MARCH 1937

Bob's friend, Don Mortimer goes to the Madhattan Room of the Pennsylvania Hotel in New York City with Adrian Hasse, Len Poor and Ralph Bean:
"When we got there Happy Felton and his Band were playing while Benny Goodman's Band were fulfilling a wonderful engagement at the Paramount Theater in Times Square. Since I had been out of town for ten weeks I asked a waiter how Benny Goodman and the band were coming along. He told me they were just as good as ever. He also said that Benny had been offered an additional six weeks at the Paramount but turned it down because the men in his band didn't want to stay there any longer. Benny's band finally arrived at about 11:00pm. I think

the band is as fine as it ever was with the exception of the saxes which cannot seem to get adjusted. George Koenig, the new sax with the band, is O.K. I think he fits into the groove very well. The brass section is the best ever to have been with Benny. Both trombones are stupendous. The three trumpets of Griffin, Elman and James are swell with the possible exception of Griffin who doesn't take as many solos as he used to. Harry James, the new third trumpet, who has recently been added to the band, is wonderful. He really sends me. The rhythm section is still tops with Stacy and Krupa outstanding. The band's playing of Mary Lou Williams' *Roll 'Em* is something to get excited about. I think this piece is as good as the playing of *Sing, Sing, Sing* which was Benny's outstanding piece of 1936. I had talks with most of the men in Benny's band. I had a swell one with Murray McEachern who told me of the pictures he would give me on our next meeting at the Penn. He also gave me a balling-out for misinterpreting him for having said that he preferred sweet music to swing. He exclaimed that I had stated this wrongly but he does greatly enjoy the type of music which is played by Tommy Dorsey. He says this is his idea of good sweet music—not like that of Guy Lombardo. I thoroughly agree with him on this point."

The personnel of the band was: Rollini; Shertzer; Koenig; Musso; McEachern; Ballard; Elman; Griffin; James; Krupa; Stacy; Reuss and Harry Goodman (Wilson & Hampton in Quartet).

The tunes played while I was there were: *Minnie The Moocher's Wedding Day, Swing Is The Word For It* (Vocal: Frances Hunt), *Changes, This Year's Kisses* (vocal: Frances Hunt), *You Showed Me The Way* (vocal: Frances Hunt), *I've Got My Love To Keep Me Warm, Alexander's Ragtime Band, He Ain't Got Rhythm* (vocal: Frances Hunt), *Sometimes I'm Happy, I Wish I Knew, Smoke Dreams* (vocal: Frances Hunt), *Swing Low Sweet Chariot, Chinatown* (TRIO), *Oh! Lady Be Good* (TRIO), *Dinah* (QUARTET), *Stompin' At The Savoy* (QUARTET), *I Got Rhythm* (QUARTET), *Goodnight My Love* (vocal: Frances Hunt), *How Could You?* (vocal: Frances Hunt), *This Is My Last Affair, Roll 'Em*.

RADIO LOGS

11.45PM WMCA
CHICK WEBB
Savoy Ballroom, NYC
Heard in Kilborn Gordon's car coming home from Scarsdale.
You Showed Me The Way (vocal: Ella Fitzgerald)
Down Home Rag
Stompin' At The Savoy (theme)

■ SATURDAY 20 MARCH 1937

7.00PM WABC
SATURDAY NIGHT SWING SESSION No37
CBS Playhouse, 251 W45th Street, NYC

I went into NYC by myself on the subway at 11:45am. I went to Macy's and bought a radio tube for my radio and Benny Goodman's recording of *When You And I Were Young, Maggie* and *Swing Low, Sweet Chariot* (Victor 25492). I then went up to Roseland at 51st Street where I was supposed to meet Don Mortimer at 2:00pm. Since he wasn't there and I had seen Woody Herman and thought Henry Biagini was lousy, I didn't go in. However, Mortimer went in and got the autographs of both bands and said that Biagini was good. I went over to Rockwell-O'Keefe on the 23rd Floor at Rockefeller Centre where I met Vincent Prior, publicity director, who handles all the pictures for Rockwell-O'Keefe. I was there about an hour talking to Prior about bands and pictures. I met Glen Gray there. I went looking through their files with Prior and I got pictures of Bunny Berigan, Glenn Miller, Bob Crosby's vocal trio (Eddie Miller, Nappy Lamare & Frank Tennille), Kay Weber, The old Dorsey Brothers Band, Tommy and Jimmy Dorsey together, Glen Gray's Band, and an old one of Louis Armstrong. I then went down Broadway, going in all the music stores looking for pictures and old records. In Vims Music Store I met a fellow who has a lot of old records and who proof-read 'Rhythm On Record' and used to work for Columbia Record Company. I then went over to the Commodore Music Shop where the head, Milton Gabler, showed me pictures of the Swing Session held last Sunday at the Savoy Ballroom with the bands of Benny Goodman, Count Basie, Chick Webb etc. He said I could have gone if I had known about it. I bought three records: Bob Crosby's *If I Had You* and *Gin Mill Blues* (Decca 1170); Jimmy Dorsey's *Parade Of The Milk Bottle Tops* and *Don't Look Now* (Decca 941); Mildred Bailey's Swing Band playing *When Day Is Done* and *Someday, Sweetheart* (Vocalion 3057). I then went over and up to the CBS Playhouse, 251 W45th Street, where this week's Saturday Night Swing session was taking place. This theater holds many more people than the studio did. Before the broadcast we noticed Ina Ray Hutton (girl orchestra leader) and all of Les Brown's Duke University Blue Devils Band sitting right in front of us. I got Ina's autograph in 'Rhythm On Record' and seven members of Les Brown's band.

After the broadcast I got the autographs of announcer Melvin Allen and Bud Hulick (a comedian whose partner is Stoopnagle), Art Shaw in 'Rhythm On Record' and Eddie Condon (guitarist who watched the broadcast) and George Wettling (drummer in Shaw's Band) on a picture. It was raining out and there were so many autograph hunters, they were hard to get.

Above: The Tommy Dorsey Band at the Hotel Commodore. Dorsey is at far left; trumpets are Joe Bauer, Andy Ferretti and Pee Wee Erwin; Dave Tough on drums and Gene Traxler on bass. In the front row are Carmen Mastren on guitar and Johnny Mince, Mike Doty, Bud Freeman and Fred Stulce on saxes.
Inset: Tough, Traxler and pianist Dick Jones. Photographs by Bob's friend, Hugh Pastoriza.
Bottom right: Edythe Wright.

We then took the subway over to the Palm Room of the Hotel Commodore where we stayed outside from 8 until 10 just listening to the band and getting their autographs in 'Rhythm On Record'. We had a nuttsy time talking to all the guys. Edythe Wright is the nuts. I made friends with pianist and arranger Dick Jones. He told me all about the band's history, etc. We also met the secretary to Dorsey's Band, Tommy Linehan and manager Bob Burns. Linehan is a swell guy. He got us pictures of Wright and Dorsey and got Dorsey to autograph one of them. The band played:
Song Of India
How Could You? (vocal: Edythe Wright)
This Year's Kisses (vocal: Edythe Wright)
Slummin' On Park Avenue
Down South Camp Meeting (Pee Wee Erwin; Mince)
May I Have The Next Romance With You? (vocal: Jack Leonard)
Liebestraum
Star Dust
Dark Eyes (COLOSSAL: Mince; Freeman; Tough)
Thanks For Everything (vocal: Jack Leonard) (Freeman; Erwin)
Sugarfoot Stomp (Erwin)
I'm Getting Sentimental Over You (theme)

MARCH 1937

RADIO LOGS

12.00 MIDNIGHT WABC
BENNY GOODMAN
Hotel Pennsylvania, NYC
Jam Session (Musso; Elman; Krupa)
You Showed Me The Way (vocal: Frances Hunt)
Star Dust (Harry James' trumpet)
I Got Rhythm (BG Quartet)
Too Marvelous For Words (vocal: Frances Hunt)
Minnie The Moocher's Wedding Day (nuttsy: saxes; brass)
I Can't Lose That Longing For You (vocal: Frances Hunt) (Musso's tenor)
Roll 'Em (colossal arrangement by Mary Lou Williams)
Swingtime In The Rockies
Goodbye (closing theme)

■ MONDAY 22 MARCH 1937

RECORDING SESSION

FLETCHER HENDERSON AND HIS ORCHESTRA
Recording session for Vocalion in New York City.
Fletcher Henderson (p/ldr); Dick Vance, Russell Smith, Emmett Berry (t); George Washington, Ed Cuffee, J. C. Higginbotham (tb); Jerry Blake (cl/as/voc); Hilton Jefferson (as); Elmer Williams, Chu Berry (ts); Lawrence Lucie (g); Israel Crosby (b); Walter Johnson (d)
Stampede / Back In Your Own Backyard / Rose Room / Great Caesar's Ghost

RED NORVO AND HIS ORCHESTRA
Recording session for Brunswick in Chicago.
Red Norvo (xyl/ldr); Bill Hyland, Stew Pletcher, Eddie Sauter (t); Al Mastren (tb); Hank D'Amico (cl/as); Frank Simeone, Charles Lamphere (as); Herbie Haymer (ts); Joe Liss (p); Dave Barbour (g); Pete Peterson (b); Maurice Purtill (d)
Remember / Liza / I Would Do Anything For You / Jiving The Jeep

GLENN MILLER AND HIS ORCHESTRA
Recording session for Decca in New York City.
Glenn Miller (tb/ldr); Charlie Spivak, Manny Klein (t); Sterling Bose (t/voc); Jesse Ralph, Harry Rodgers (tb); Hal McIntyre (cl/as); George Siravo (as); Jerry Jerome, Carl Biesecker (ts); Howard Smith (p); Dick McDonough (g); Ted Kotsoftis (b); George Simon (d); Doris Kerr, The Tune Twisters (voc)
Peg O' My Heart / Wistful And Blue (vDK) / *How Am I To Know?* (vDK) / *Anytime, Anyday, Anywhere* (vSB,TTT) / *Moonlight Bay / I'm Sitting On Top Of The World*

■ TUESDAY 23 MARCH 1937

RECORDING SESSION

MILDRED BAILEY & HER ORCHESTRA
Recording session for Vocalion in Chicago.
Bill Hyland, Stew Pletcher, Eddie Sauter (t); Alex Mastren (tb); Hank D'Amico (cl/as); Frank Simeone (as); Herbie Haymer (ts); Joe Liss (p); Dave Barbour (g); Pete Peterson (b); Maurice Purtill (d); Red Norvo (xyl); Mildred Bailey (v)
Never In A Million Years (vMB) / *There's A Lull In My Life* (vMB) / *Rockin' Chair* (vMB) / *Little Joe* (vMB)

CHU BERRY & HIS STOMPY STEVEDORES
Recording session for Variety in New York City.
Hot Lips Page (t/voc); George Matthews (tb); Buster Bailey (cl); Chu Berry (ts); Horace Henderson (p); Lawrence Lucie (g); Israel Crosby (b); Cozy Cole (d)
Now You're Talking My Language (vHLP) / *Back Home Again In Indiana / Too Marvelous For Words* (vHLP) / *Limehouse Blues*

Mrs. Pinger drove Harvey Pinger and myself to the subway. We met Mortimer, Morningstar, and Johnson at the CBS Playhouse on Broadway where Benny Goodman broadcasts on 'Camel Caravan'. Since Hymie Shertzer was sick Milt Yaner, formerly with Ray Noble, took his place.

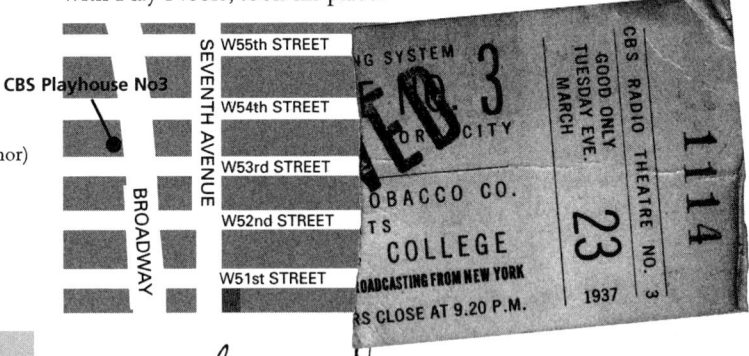

9:30PM WABC
BENNY GOODMAN
Camel Caravan program, NYC
Let's Dance (theme)
Roll 'Em
I've Got My Love To Keep Me Warm
This is My Last Affair (vocal: Frances Hunt)
Camel Hop
You Showed Me The Way (vocal: Frances Hunt)
I Found A New Baby
Stompin' At The Savoy (BGQuartet)
Sugar Foot Stomp (Harry James' trumpet)
Goodbye (theme)

RADIO LOGS

11:45pm WMCA
Chick Webb
Savoy Ballroom, NYC
I Got A Guy (vocal: Ella Fitzgerald)
Memphis Blues
Someday, Sweetheart (vocal: Charles Linton)
Honeysuckle Rose
House Hop
Let's Get Together (theme)

12.00 MIDNIGHT WNEW
WOODY HERMAN
Roseland Ballroom, NYC
Where Are You? (vocal: Woody Herman)
Memphis Blues
I'm Face To Face With Love
You Showed Me The Way (vocal: Woody Herman)

■ WEDNESDAY 24 MARCH 1937

RECORDING SESSION

CHICK WEBB ORCHESTRA
Recording session for Decca in New York City.
Ella Fitzgerald (voc); Mario Bauza, Taft Jordan, Bobby Stark (t); Sandy Williams, Nat Story (tb); Louis Jordan, Pete Clark (as); Ted McRae (ts), Wayman Carver (ts/fl); Tommy Fulford (p); John Trueheart (g); Beverly Peer (b); Chick Webb (d)
You Showed Me The Way (vEF) / *Cryin' Mood* (vEF) / *Love Is The Thing, So They Say* (vEF) / *Wake Up And Live* (vEF & trio)
The band also record tracks without Ella: *Rusty Hinge* (vLJ) / *It's Swell Of You* (vLJ) / *Clap Hands, Here Comes Charley* / *That Naughty Waltz*

David Low invited Cynthia Doyle, Barbara Doyle, Cynthia Lake, Ed Morley and myself to dinner at his house at 53 E66th Street in N.Y.C. After eating dinner we all took taxis down to the Madhattan Room of the Hotel Pennsylvania, arriving at 8:15. Since we didn't get any dinner we only had to pay the cover charge. I didn't get any autographs and didn't talk to anybody except Chapin (Benny's secretary) and Teddy Wilson. We talked about different articles written on Benny (Cue, Sun, Down Beat, etc), how hard the engagement was at the Paramount, pictures of the band, etc. While were were there, from 8:15 to 11:15, the band played: *Rosetta* (Ballard; Musso); *Chlo-e*; *Alexander's Ragtime Band*: then the band rested while Teddy Wilson 'jammed out' on *I Cried For You; Slummin' On Park Avenue; He Ain't Got Rhythm*. Then the band played *Slummin' On Park Avenue* (vocal by Frances Hunt); *?; You Showed Me The Way* (vocal by Frances Hunt: James' trumpet); *Oh, Lady Be Good; This Is My Last Affair* (vocal by Frances Hunt); *He Ain't Got Rhythm* (vocal by Frances Hunt); *Makin' Whoopee; When Buddha Smiles; One Never Knows, Does One?* (vocal by Frances Hunt); *Sweet Is The Word For You* (vocal by Frances Hunt); *Down South Camp Meeting* (Griffin; 5 clarinets); *Gee, But You're Swell* (vocal by Frances Hunt: Krupa's drums); *The Goona Goo* (vocal by Frances Hunt); *Sometimes I'm Happy* (Colossal: James; Musso); *Three Little Words*, and others. We missed the Trio and Quartet tonight. We got the 11:35 train home. David slept at my house.

■ THURSDAY 25 MARCH 1937

Mr. Pastoriza drove Hughie, Roddy Snow, Harvey Pinger and me to the Palm Room of the Hotel Commodore in New York to see the Tommy Dorsey Orchestra. They played:

Song Of India (Pee Wee Erwin's trumpet)
You're Laughing At Me (vocal: Jack Leonard)
Stop, Look And Listen
Dark Eyes
Blue Danube
Sweet is The Word For It (vocal: Jack Leonard)
Beale Street Blues (Les Jenkins' trombone)
Slummin' On Park Avenue

You're Here, You're There, You're Everywhere (vocal: Three Esquires)
Sugarfoot Stomp
Dedicated To You (vocal: Jack Leonard)
Swing That Music (vocal: Three Esquires)
There's Something In The Air (vocal: Jack Leonard)

RADIO LOGS

12.00 MIDNIGHT WOR
BENNY GOODMAN
Hotel Pennsylvania, NYC
Alexander's Ragtime Band
You're Laughing At Me (vocal: Frances Hunt)
Down South Camp Meeting
You Showed Me The Way (vocal: Frances Hunt)
Roll 'Em (colossal arrangement by Mary Lou Williams)
I Can't Lose That Longing For You (vocal: Frances Hunt) (Musso's tenor)
Runnin' Wild (BG Quartet)
Somebody Loves Me (superb sax section)
Sweet Is The Word For You (vocal: Frances Hunt)
Darktown Strutters' Ball

■ FRIDAY 26 MARCH 1937

RECORDING SESSION

COUNT BASIE AND HIS ORCHESTRA
Recording session for Decca in New York City.
Buck Clayton, Ed Lewis, Bobby Moore (t); Dan Minor, George Hunt (tb); Caughey Roberts (as); Lester Young, Herschel Evans (ts); Jack Washington (bar); Count Basie (p); Freddie Green (g); Walter Page (b); Jo Jones (d); Jimmy Rushing (voc)
Exactly Like You (vJR) / *Boo-Hoo* (vJR) / *The Glory Of Love* / *Boogie-Woogie* (vJR)

TEDDY HILL AND HIS ORCHESTRA
Recording session for Bluebird in New York City.
Teddy Hill (ts/ldr/voc); Bill Dillard (t/voc); Frankie Newton, Shad Collins (t); Dicky Wells (tb); Russell Procope (cl/as); Howard Johnson (as); Cecil Scott (ts/bar); Sam Allen (p); John Smith (g); Richard Fulbright (b); Bill Beason (d); Beatrice Douglas (voc)
The Love Bug Will Bite You (vBand) / *Would You Like To Buy A Dream?* (vBD) / *Big Boy Blue* (vBD,TH) / *Where Is The Sun?* (vBD) / *The Harlem Twister* / *My Marie*

Roddy Snow, who lives in Washington but is spending his Easter vacation in Bronxville, and myself went down to Grand Central Station on the 6:39pm train and took the subway from there over to Times Square and down to the Pennsylvania Hotel at 7th Avenue and 33rd Street. We recognized Joe Marsala in the lobby. He has his band now playing at the Hickory House on 52nd Street. We got his autograph, he is a swell guy.

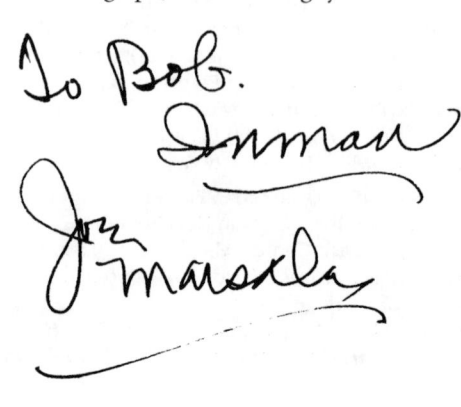

Three photographs of the 1927 Ben Pollack Orchestra. The angled photograph is the one that Bob had Benny and Harry Goodman autograph. Right: Layout of the Madhattan Room. The solid dots represent the tables at which Bob and his friends sat.

We had a hell of a time getting in because the head-waiter said that one of us would have to buy dinner. Not that we couldn't eat the dinner, but we aren't the richest people in the world. Since most of the tables were reserved we had to go over in the corner. After more arguments with the waiters about getting better tables, and not eating, we finally got a good table near the band. We sure were lucky that we didn't have to spend two dollars for dinner, because you are supposed to if you come before 9:30. At 8:30 Harold Johnson, Hugh Pastoriza and Robcliff Jones came in and joined us. Hal and Robcliff had to buy something to eat (red wine). At about 8:00 Roddy and I talked with Lionel Hampton about how he used to play with Louis Armstrong and how he liked it better now. He offered us cigarettes. His breath indicated that he had been drinking. At about 8:45 another party from Bronxville came in (Cynthia Doyle, Edith Russell, Emmy Neiley, Ed Pennell, Henry Pennell, etc) and at about 9:00 still another party from Bronxville came in (Barbara Doyle, Nancy Long and Tommy Doyle). We all danced with them off and on. Jones brought down a camera and took 16 action photos of the band. I got Benny and Harry Goodman to autograph a ten-year-old picture of the Ben Pollack Band at Atlantic City that included the Goodman brothers, Jack Teagarden, Gil Rodin, Dick Morgan, Al Harris, Larry Binyon and Vic Breidis.

Benny and Harry were very much interested in this picture, calling several members of the band over and asking where I got the picture. Then they began recalling old times, where they used to play and how Benny was only 17 when the picture was taken and how he had changed but how Harry still looked the same. Since Johnny Hammond was sitting at the same table I got his autograph. He is secretary to UHCA and is a noted authority on jazz. I got Gene Krupa and Red Ballard to autograph a picture with them, Benny, Bill DePew, Nate Kazebier and Martha Raye in it. Gene remarked how sunburnt he was in the picture. Since I took this book down I got Vido Musso, Gene Krupa, Hymie Shertzer, Art Rollini,

Gordon Griffin, Ziggy Elman (Harry Finkelman) and Teddy Wilson to autograph it. All of them were greatly interested in this book. I sure did have a nuttsy time. The numbers played, as far as I can remember, were:

SET 1: *Remember; What Will I Tell My Heart?; Riffin' At The Ritz; He Ain't Got Rhythm* (vocal by Frances Hunt); *House Hop*. SET 2: *Nobody's Sweetheart* (BG Trio); *Body And Soul* (BG Trio); *Dinah* (BG Quartet); *Stompin' At The Savoy* (BG Quartet); *I Got Rhythm* (BG Quartet). SET 3: *They Can't Take That Away From Me* (vocal by Frances Hunt); *Let's Call The Whole Thing Off* (vocal by Frances Hunt); *Goodnight My Love* (vocal by Frances Hunt); *Slummin' On Park Avenue* (vocal by Frances Hunt; Musso's tenor); *Down South Camp Meetin'* (5 clarinets; Griffin's trumpet). SET 4: *I Can't Lose That Longing For You* (vocal by Frances Hunt); *Always; You Showed Me The Way* (vocal by Frances Hunt); *Sing, Sing, Sing* (Super-colossal: 12 minutes long with solos by Krupa; Benny; Musso; James; Stacy). SET 5: *I've Got My Love To Keep Me Warm; Too Marvelous For Words* (vocal by Frances Hunt); *Makin' Whoopee; This Year's Kisses* (vocal by Frances Hunt); *Can't We Be Friends?* (great: brass section with Krupa); *I Found A New Baby* (Elman; Rollini). SET 6: *Somebody Loves Me; You're Laughing At Me* (vocal by Frances Hunt; Elman's trumpet); *Roll 'Em* (super-colossal: about 15 minutes; Krupa; Benny; Musso; Stacy); *There's Something In The Air* (vocal by Frances Hunt; Griffin's trumpet; Musso); *Three Little Words*. SET 7: *This Is My Last Affair* (vocal by Frances Hunt); *When Buddha Smiles* (Rollini).
BROADCAST over WABC at 11:30 with Bert Parks announcing: *Camel Hop; You Showed Me The Way* (vocal by Frances Hunt); *Down South Camp Meetin'; Trust In Me* (vocal by Frances Hunt); *Changes; Oh, Lady Be Good; Sweet Sue* (BG Quartet); *He Ain't Got Rhythm* (vocal by Frances Hunt); *I Want To Be Happy* (Musso; James); *Goodbye* (closing theme).
At 12:15: *Oh, Lady Be Good* (BG Trio); *Runnin' Wild* (BG Trio); *Dinah* (BG Quartet); *Stompin' At The Savoy* (BG Quartet); and *I Got Rhythm* (BG Quartet).
We had to leave at 12:45 to catch the last train (1:00am) to Bronxville. Got home at 2:00am.

RADIO LOGS

10:30PM WHN
JOE MARSALA
Hickory House, 144 W52nd Street, NYC
Keep Smilin' At Trouble
May I Have The Next Romance With You? (featuring Adele Girard, harp)
Oh, Sister! Ain't That Hot (featuring Joe Bushkin)
This Is My Last Affair
Swing High, Swing Low
I Want A Little Girl

12:00 MIDNIGHT WJZ
BOB CROSBY
Congress Hotel, Chicago
I've Got Beginner's Luck (vocal: Bob Crosby)
Picture Me Without You (vocal: Kay Weber)
She's Funny That Way (Eddie Bergman's violin)
Smoke Dreams (vocal: Bob Crosby) (Eddie Miller's tenor)
Dixieland Shuffle (ballsy)
The Night Is Young
Now
Summertime (theme) (played in full)

12:00 MIDNIGHT WNEW
WOODY HERMAN
Roseland Ballroom, NYC
Blue Prelude (theme)
The Lady From Mayfair

12.30AM WABC
MAL HALLETT
Meadowbrook, N.J.
Swell vocalist/clarinet player Buddy Welcome; nuttsy vocalist Teddy Grace, but a lousy vocalist in 17-yr-old Jerry Perkins.
Boston Tea Party (theme) (swell foxtrot theme written by Frank Ryerson)
Oh, Say, Can You Swing? (vocal: Buddy Welcome)
Was It Rain? (vocal: Jerry Perkins) (lousy)
She Lived Down In Our Alley (vocal: Buddy Welcome) (first time on radio)
Choir Boy (vocal: Jerry Perkins)
Tea For Two (FRANKIE CARLE piano feature)
Between The Devil And The Deep Blue Sea (vocal: Teddy Grace)
I Adore You (vocal: Jerry Perkins)
Big Boy Blue

■ SATURDAY 27 MARCH 1937

RECORDING SESSION

ADRIAN ROLLINI AND HIS ORCHESTRA
Recording session for Master in New York City.
Jonah Jones (t); Sid Stoneburn (cl); Fulton McGrath (p); Dick McDonough (g); George Hnida (b); Al Sidell (d); Adrian Rollini (vib)
Slap That Bass / Let's Call The Whole Thing Off

RADIO LOGS

7.00PM WABC
SATURDAY NIGHT SWING SESSION No38
CBS Playhouse No2, NYC
I didn't see this broadcast, but Mortimer, Morningstar, Snow, and Johnson did. Annette Hanshaw, vocalist, was in the audience.
Swing High, Swing Low (swell: great trumpet; rhythm; Russ Genner & Joe Vargas on trombones)
Star Dust (Raymond Scott on harpsichord; clarinet team of Pumiglio, Manners, Harris, Ross; muted brass)
Rebound (ADRIAN ROLLINI on vibes; Haig Stephens, bass; Frank Victor, guitar: swell)
Liza (swell old song by Irving Berlin: Dave Harris' tenor; Russ Genner's trombone)
Twilight In Turkey (Raymond Scott Quintet: Scott, Harris, Wade, Shoobe, Williams, Pumiglio)
Powerhouse (Raymond Scott Quintet: Scott, Harris, Wade, Shoobe, Williams, Pumiglio)
Organ Grinder's Swing (Leith Stevens conducting CBS Band: colossal clarinets, saxes, bass)
The Jitters (ADRIAN ROLLINI Trio; just recorded for Decca; good)
That's A-Plenty

MARCH 1937

11.30PM WABC
BENNY GOODMAN
Hotel Pennsylvania, NYC
Roll 'Em
You Showed Me The Way (vocal: Frances Hunt)
Love Me Or Leave Me
Ridin' High

Harvey Pinger and I went up to the Bronxville Field Club about a mile from my house at 9:30pm where the Easter College Prom was held. It cost $2.50 per person to get in so we climbed in the window. I was the only guy without formal dress. Lucky Millinder had a band here last fall but now he has a completely new band with the exception of saxman Tab Smith, drummer O'Neil Spencer and vocalist Chuck Richards. I don't think this new band is quite as good as the old band (had Henry Red Allen, J.C. Higginbotham, George Washington, Elmer James, Edgar Hayes, Lawrence Lucie, George Mikell, Crawford Wethington, Joe Garland and Scad Hemphill) although it is the nuts. Some great work is done by saxmen Tab Smith and Eddie Williams, trumpeters Charlie Shavers, Harry Edison and Carl Warwick, pianist Billy Kyle who comes from Philadelphia, is only 19 years-old and is supposed to be a second Teddy Wilson. Others in the band are Sandy Watson (trombone), Specs Arnold (tenor sax), John Williams (bass) and Danny Barker (guitar) with, of course, good old Lucky Millinder leading and singing in his original way. I got the autographs of the whole band on a picture of Lucky Millinder. The band played most of the time from 9.30pm to 2.45am having very little intermissions. Some of their numbers were: *Nagasaki, Lucky Swings Out, East St. Louis Toodle-Oo, Organ Grinder's Swing, Bugle Call Rag, Ride Red Ride* (with 3 trumpets instead of 1, as Red Allen used to do it), *Blue Rhythm Fantasy* (just recorded for Variety), *Jungle Madness*, etc.

■ SUNDAY 28 MARCH 1937
RADIO LOGS

10.50PM WHN
JOE MARSALA
Hickory House, 144 W52nd Street, NYC
Oh, Sister! Ain't That Hot (featuring Joe Bushkin)
Clarinet Marmalade (muted trumpet by Marty Marsala)

11.00PM WABC
RED NICHOLS
College Inn, Chicago
Wail Of The Winds (theme) (colossal theme)
I'm Talking Through My Heart
My Little Buckaroo
Star Dust
Wake Up And Live
Pagan Love Song
Wail Of The Winds (theme)

11.30PM WOR
DUKE ELLINGTON
Cotton Club, NYC
Scattin' At The Kit Kat
Where is The Sun?
I've Got My Love To Keep Me Warm
Slummin' On Park Avenue
This Year's Crop Of Kisses
I've Got To Be A Rugcutter (vocal: Ivie Anderson & Trio)
Echoes Of Harlem
Rockin' In Rhythm
April In Paris
Truckin' (vocal: Ivie Anderson)

■ MONDAY 29 MARCH 1937
RADIO LOGS

7:15PM WJZ
BUGHOUSE RHYTHM
San Francisco
Night Ride (Edson Gilson playing kettle drums in Vic Berton style)
When You And I Were Young, Maggie (arranged by Jimmy Mundy)
Stumblin' (featuring Dr. John Meakin on piano)
52nd Street (written by Sammy Cahn & Saul Chaplin)

11:00PM WMCA
FRANKIE WARD
Penthouse, Hotel Bradford, Boston
Moonlight And Shadows (vocal: Carmen Trudeau)
I Surrender, Dear (Ward's bassoon)
This Year's Crop Of Kisses (Ward on vibraphone)
Trust In Me
St. Louis Blues

11:30PM WABC
JAY FREEMAN
Paradise Restaurant, NYC
It's Swell Of You
Just A Quiet Evening
One In A Million
Theme (colossal trumpet)

11.40PM WEAF
GLEN GRAY
Rainbow Room, RCA Building, NYC

Last broadcast of Glen Gray from the Rainbow Room. Below they can be seen lined up on the roof at Rockefeller Center.

This Is My Last Affair (vocal: Pee Wee Hunt)
May I Have The Next Romance? (vocal: Kenny Sargent)
The Sheik of Araby (5 clarinets: swell)
When Love Is Young (vocal: Kenny Sargent)
Whoa, Babe! (vocal: Pee Wee Hunt)
You're Here, You're There, You're Everywhere (vocal: Kenny Sargent)
I Got Rhythm (nuttsy: Brass; Hutchenrider)
Smoke Rings (theme)

12.00 MIDNIGHT WOR
TOMMY DORSEY
Hotel Commodore, NYC
How Could You? (vocal: Edythe Wright)
Too Marvelous For Words (vocal: Jack Leonard)
Beale Street Blues
Rain In My Eyes (vocal: Edythe Wright)
Marie (vocal: Jack Leonard & Band) (Tommy; Erwin; Freeman; Tough)
On A Little Bamboo Bridge (vocal: Edythe Wright)
You Showed Me The Way (vocal: Jack Leonard)
Organ Grinder's Swing (vocal: Three Esquires)

Tommy Dorsey's Three Esquires: Jack Leonard, Axel Stordahl, and Joe Bauer

12.00 midnight WJZ
BOB CROSBY
Congress Hotel, Chicago
Jamboree
I've Got My Love To Keep Me Warm (vocal: Kay Weber)
Struttin' With Some Barbecue (Matty Matlock's clarinet)
How Could You? (vocal: Bob Crosby)
You're Driving Me Crazy (The BobCats)
Here Comes Your Pappy (vocal: Nappy Lamare)
This is My Last Affair (vocal: Kay Weber)
Steppin' Pretty (Warren Smith's trombone; Bob Zurke's piano)

■ **TUESDAY 30 MARCH 1937**

RECORDING SESSION

GLEN GRAY AND THE CASA LOMA ORCHESTRA
Recording session for Decca in New York City.
Walter Smith, Grady Watts, Frank Zullo (t); Pee Wee Hunt (tb/voc); Billy Rauch, Fritz Hummel (tb); Clarence Hutchenrider (cl/as), Kenny Sargent (as/voc); Danny d'Andrea (as); Art Ralston (as/o/bsn); Pat Davis (ts); Joe Hall (p); Jack Blanchette (g); Stanley Dennis (b); Tony Briglia (d)
There's A Lull In My Life (vKS) / *Would You Like To Buy A Dream?* (vKS) / *Never In A Million Years* (vKS) / *I Remember* (vKS)

RADIO LOGS

9:30PM WABC
BENNY GOODMAN
Camel Caravan program, NYC

Down South Camp Meetin'
How Could You? (vocal: Frances Hunt)
Can't We Be Friends? (Ballard's trombone; Musso; Benny)
Chinatown, My Chinatown (BGQuartet)

11:00PM WMCA
FRANKIE WARD
Penthouse, Hotel Bradford, Boston
I've Got My Love To Keep Me Warm
When Love is Young
Swing High, Swing Low
Little Old Lady (Ward on vibraphone)

11.20PM WABC
TOMMY DORSEY
Hotel Commodore, NYC
You Showed Me The Way (vocal: Jack Leonard)
Down South Camp Meetin' (Freeman; clarinets)

11.30PM WNEW
ED FARLEY
Club Evergreen, N.J.
Farley used to have a band with Mike Riley, but Farley left a few months ago to form his own band. I like Farley's band better.
The Trouble With Me Is You
Night And Day (Farley's trumpet)
By Heck (arranged by Paul Williams)

12.00 MIDNIGHT WNEW
WOODY HERMAN
Roseland Ballroom, NYC
If I Could Be With You One Hour Tonight
September In May (vocal: Woody Herman)
My Home Town Band (vocal: Woody Herman)
I Can't Give You Anything But Love, Baby (arrangement by Gordon Jenkins)
Sweet Is The Word For You (vocal: Woody Herman)
I'm Sitting On Top of The World
Face To Face (vocal: Woody Herman)
Ostrich Walk

12.30AM WMCA
TEDDY HILL
Savoy Ballroom, NYC
Stompin' At The Savoy (opening theme)
Honeysuckle Rose
Where Is The Sun? (vocal: Beatrice Douglas)
Back Home Again In Indiana
Springtime In The Rockies
Would You Like To Buy A Dream? (vocal: Beatrice Douglas)
Big John Special
The Love Bug
Uptown Rhapsody (closing theme)

■ **WEDNESDAY 31 MARCH 1937**

RECORDING SESSION

BILLIE HOLIDAY & TEDDY WILSON ORCHESTRA
Recording session for Brunswick in NYC.
Cootie Williams (t); Harry Carney (cl/bar); Johnny Hodges (as); Teddy Wilson (p); Allan Reuss (g); John Kirby (b); Cozy Cole (d); Billie Holiday (v)
Carelessly / *How Could You?* / *Moanin' Low*

JAM SESSION AT VICTOR
Recording session for Victor in NYC.
Bunny Berigan (t); Tommy Dorsey (tb); Fats Waller (p); Dick McDonough (g); George Wettling (d)
Honeysuckle Rose / *Blues*

RADIO LOGS

10:15PM WMCA
FRANKIE WARD
Penthouse, Hotel Bradford, Boston
This Year's Crop Of Kisses
Was It Rain? (vocal: Carmen Trudeau)
The Goona Goo (trumpet; saxes; Ward's bassoon; tenor)
You Showed Me The Way (vocal: Carmen Trudeau)
Honeysuckle Rose

10:30PM WHN
JOE MARSALA
Hickory House, 144 W52nd Street, NYC
Wolverine Blues
Sweet Mama (Joe Marsala's clarinet; drums)
Head Over Heels In Love (vocal: Adele Girard)
Wanted (Marty Marsala's trumpet, etc)
Basin Street Blues (trumpet; piano; Joe's clarinet: nuttsy)
Honeysuckle Rose (ADELE GIRARD on harp: good)
Jazz Me Blues (BALLSY: Both Marsala's; swell violin; piano; harp)

11.05PM WABC
BENNY GOODMAN
Hotel Pennsylvania, NYC
You Showed Me The Way (vocal: Frances Hunt)
Blue Skies
St. Louis Blues
Mean To Me (nuttsy: Musso's tenor)
Trust In Me (vocal: Frances Hunt)
Runnin' Wild (BG Quartet)
It's The Mood That I'm In (vocal: Frances Hunt)

11:30PM WOR
DUKE ELLINGTON
Cotton Club, NYC
Colossal.
In A Jam (Ellington; Bigard; Williams; Stewart; Hodges' great sax)
Black Butterfly (sax; trombone)
Scattin' At The Kit Kat (ballsy: brass, sax)
Let's Go Ballyhoo (vocal: Ivie Anderson) (swell)
Lost Ecstasy (vocal: Ivie Anderson)
Downtown Uproar (Cootie Williams' Rugcutters: Cootie; Johnny Hodges)
Never In A Million Years (vocal: Ivie Anderson)
Trumpet In Spades (Stewart's cornet)
East St. Louis Toodle-Oo (theme)

12:00 MIDNIGHT WJZ
BOB CROSBY
Congress Hotel, Chicago
Can't Help Lovin' Dat Man (Miller; Matlock; Zurke; Smith)
Carelessly (vocal: Kay Weber)
It's The Mood That I'm In (vocal: Bob Crosby)
When My Dreamboat Comes Home
On A Little Bamboo Bridge (Lawson; Miller; Smith)
Love Is Good For Anything That Ails You (vocal: Bob Crosby)
Sweet Lorraine (vocal: Nappy Lamare)
Farewell Blues (vocal: Nappy Lamare)
Summertime (theme)

12:30AM WOR
TOMMY DORSEY
Commodore Hotel, NYC
How Could You?
Where Are You? (vocal: Jack Leonard)
Beale Street Blues (Tommy; Erwin; Freeman)
They Can't Take That Away From Me (vocal: Jack Leonard)
They All Laughed (vocal: Edythe Wright)
Easy To Remember (swing style)
Too Marvelous For Words (vocal: Jack Leonard)
That's A-Plenty

APRIL 1937

Hotel Pennsylvania: **Benny Goodman** (–29); **Bunny Berigan** (30–)
Hotel Commodore: **Tommy Dorsey**
Hotel New Yorker: **Lennie Hayton** (8–)
Hotel Lincoln: **Isham Jones**
Hotel Taft: **George Hall**
Hotel Lexington: **Ozzie Nelson**

Apollo Theater: **Teddy Hill** (2–8); **Chick Webb** (9–15); **Don Redman** (16–22); **Claude Hopkins** (23–29); **Tiny Bradshaw** (30–)
Paramount Theater: **Louis Armstrong** (3–23); **Eddie Duchin** (24–)
Loew's State Theater: **Ted Lewis** (1–14); **Horace Heidt** (15–21); **Cab Calloway** (22–28)

Cotton Club Downtown: **Duke Ellington**
Hickory House: **Joe Marsala**
Onyx Club (re-opens at 62 W52nd Street): **Stuff Smith**

THURSDAY 1 APRIL 1937

RECORDING SESSION

BILLIE HOLIDAY & HER ORCHESTRA
Recording session for Vocalion in NYC.
Eddie Tompkins (t); Buster Bailey (cl); Joe Thomas (ts); Teddy Wilson (p); Carmen Mastren (g); John Kirby (b); Alphonse Steele (d); Billie Holiday (v)
Where Is The Sun? / Let's Call The Whole Thing Off / They Can't Take That Away From Me / I Don't Know If I'm Comin' Or Goin'

BUNNY BERIGAN AND HIS ORCHESTRA
Recording session for Victor in New York City.
Bunny Berigan (t/voc); Cliff Natalie, Steve Lipkins (t); Ford Leary (tb/voc); Frank d'Annolfo (tb); Slats Long, Henry Freeman (cl/as); Clyde Rounds, George Auld (ts); Joe Lippman (p); Tom Morgan (g); Arnold Fishkind (b); George Wettling (d); Carol McKay (voc)
You Can't Run Away From Love Tonight (vCM) / *'Cause My Baby Says It's So* (vBB) / *Carelessly* (vCM) / *All Dark People Are Light On Their Feet* (vFL)

APRIL 1937

RADIO LOGS

6:00PM WNEW
DUKE ELLINGTON
Make Believe Ballroom, NYC
Colossal.
Merry-Go-Round (colossal)
On The Sunny Side of The Street (vocal: Ivie Anderson)
It Don't Mean A Thing If It Ain't Got That Swing (vocal: Ivie Anderson)
Creole Love Call (SUPER-COLOSSAL: Joe Nanton's muted trombone; trumpet; Bigard)
Never In A Million Years (vocal: Ivie Anderson)
Trumpet In Spades (Stewart's cornet)
East St. Louis Toodle-Oo (theme)

11:30PM WABC
ISHAM JONES
Hotel Lincoln, NYC
Good.
I Told The Birds (vocal: Eddie Stone)
You're Part Of Me
I've Got My Love To Keep Me Warm (vocal: Joe Martin)
It's The Mood That I'm In (vocal: Eddie Stone)
Twilight In Turkey (ballsy)
Just To Remind You (written by Isham Jones)
Boo Hoo (vocal: Eddie Stone)
Where Are You? (vocal: Joe Martin)
Rosetta (vocal: Eddie Stone) (Bobby Jones' trumpet)

12.00 MIDNIGHT WOR
BENNY GOODMAN
Hotel Pennsylvania, NYC
Swingtime In The Rockies (Musso; James)
Sentimental And Melancholy (Benny)
Can't We Be Friends? (Musso; Benny)
This Year's Crop Of Kisses (Benny playing solo instead of vocal)
Ol' Man River (SWELL)
Always (Benny's clarinet; swell trumpets)
Let's Call The Whole Thing Off
Ida (BG Quartet) (same as record)
Chlo-e (saxes; James; Stacy)
Somebody Loves Me (saxes; Benny)

■ FRIDAY 2 APRIL 1937

RADIO LOGS

10:15PM WMCA
FRANKIE WARD
Penthouse, Hotel Bradford, Boston
Too Marvelous For Words (vocal: Carmen Trudeau)
Swing High, Swing Low
Black Bottom Stomp (Ward on vibraphone; trumpet; saxes)
You Showed Me The Way (vocal: Carmen Trudeau)
Big John Special

12:00 MIDNIGHT WJZ
BOB CROSBY
Congress Hotel, Chicago
Heard this program at Nancy Long's house.
Between The Devil And The Deep, Blue Sea
Was It Rain? (vocal: Kay Weber)
Slummin' On Park Avenue (Smith; Miller's tenor)
Boo Hoo (vocal: Nappy Lamare)
Gin Mill Blues (super-colossal: Zurke; Miller; Matlock)
You Showed Me The Way (vocal: Bob Crosby)
South Rampart Street Parade
Summertime (theme)

1:30AM WOR
JOE SANDERS
Blackhawk Restaurant, Chicago
Rusty Hinge
This Year's Crop Of Kisses
King Porter Stomp
Found

2:00AM WBBH
ROY ELDRIDGE
Three Deuces, Chicago
The Buzzard (written by Roy Eldridge)
You Showed Me The Way
I'll Sing You A Thousand Love Songs (CLEO BROWN on piano)
Smoke Dreams (colossal trumpet by Roy)
Honeysuckle Rose
I Surrender Dear (vocal: Cleo Brown)
The Lady In Red
Jamboree

■ SATURDAY 3 APRIL 1937

RADIO LOGS

This broadcast was held at Studio No1, 485 Madison Avenue. Melvin Allen and Paul Douglas announced. Now, Stuff Smith is even better than Joe Venuti, making him the best hot violinist there is.

7.00PM WABC
SATURDAY NIGHT SWING SESSION No39
CBS Studio No1, 485 Madison Ave, NYC
Chicken And Waffles (Introductory theme)
How Could You? (CBS Band directed by Leith Stevens: saxes; Harris' tenor)
Georgia Jubilee (trumpet)
Limehouse Blues (STUFF SMITH and Onyx Club Band: Smith's violin; Jonah Jones' trumpet; Cozy Cole's drums)
Here Comes The Man With The Jive (STUFF SMITH and Onyx Club Band: Smith's colossal violin & vocals)
Somebody Loves Me (colossal arrangement: brass; clarinets; trumpet; saxes; Williams' drums)
Sweet Sue (CBS Band arranger playing ukulele)
Love And Learn (swell: saxes; clarinet)
Stompin' At The Onyx Club (STUFF SMITH and Onyx Club Band: piano; Jones' trumpet; Cole's drums)
Swing, Swing Mother-In-Law (written by Raymond Scott: saxes; trumpet)

11.00PM WABC
BENNY GOODMAN
Hotel Pennsylvania, NYC
Heard this program at Barbara Doyle's house.
Mr. Ghost Goes To Town (Harry James' trumpet)
There's A Lull In My Life (vocal: Frances Hunt)
Camel Hop
You Showed Me The Way (vocal: Frances Hunt)
Slummin' On Park Avenue

They Can't Take That Away From Me (vocal: Frances Hunt)
Tiger Rag (BG Trio) (marvelous work)
Sometimes I'm Happy (Griffin; Musso)
Sing, Sing, Sing (super-colossal arrangement: Krupa; Musso; James; Stacy)

12:00 MIDNIGHT WJZ
BOB CROSBY
Congress Hotel, Chicago
Heard first half of this program at Barbara Doyle's house, then ran home to hear the rest. Colossal!
Hallelujah (Zurke; Miller; Smith; Lawson)
Moonlight And Shadows (vocal: Kay Weber)
Jazz Lips
They All Laughed (vocal: Bob Crosby)
Sugar Foot Strut
'Way Down Yonder In New Orleans (vocal: Nappy Lamare)
Sentimental And Melancholy (vocal: Kay Weber) (Miller's tenor)
Honeysuckle Rose (Matlock; Smith; Bauduc, etc)

12:30AM WIP
CHICK WEBB
Nixon-Grand Theater, Philadelphia
Ballsy. Just left the Savoy ballroom a few weeks ago. Is now on tour, playing this week at the Nixon-Grand Theater and then on to the Howard Theater in Washington, D.C.
Sugar Foot Stomp (trombone; trumpet; piano; tenor)
I Can't Break The Habit Of You (vocal: Ella Fitzgerald)
Thou Swell (Taft Jordans trumpet, etc)
Charmaine (vocal: Charles Linton)
Swing Low, Sweet Chariot (arranged by Jimmy Mundy: tenor; trumpet)
The Mayor Of Alabam' (vocal: Louis Jordan) (tenor; trumpet)
Clap Hands, Here Comes Charlie (Webb's drums; tenor)
Let's Get Together (theme)

2:00AM WBBH
ROY ELDRIDGE
Three Deuces, Chicago
Guess Who?
I May Be Wrong
Swing, Brother, Swing
Body And Soul
With Plenty Of Money And You
Happy As The Day Is Long
Shine

■ SUNDAY 4 APRIL 1937

RADIO LOGS

10:39PM WHN
JOE MARSALA
Hickory House, 144 W52nd Street, NYC
Joe Marsala lives at the Hotel Plymouth, 49th Street off Broadway.
Just A Little Girl
Swing High, Swing Low (Adele Girard on harp)
I Never Knew
Sweet Is The Word For You
Clarinet Marmalade

11:10PM WABC
RED NICHOLS
College Inn, Chicago
By Heck
Old Fashioned Love (vocal: Arline Owens)
I've Got My Love To Keep Me Warm
Boo Hoo (vocal: Jack & Arline Owens)
Miss Annabelle Lee (Zimmers' tenor)
When My Dreamboat Comes Home
Summer Nightss
O Sole Mio

What Will I Tell My Heart?
Wail Of The Winds (theme)

11:30PM WOR
DUKE ELLINGTON
Cotton Club, NYC
Nuttsy. Announced by J. Howard Doyle.
The Jive Stomp (Hardwick's bass sax; Bigard's clarinet; brass section; Williams' trumpet)
Mood Indigo (colossal trio of Tricky Sam Nanton-trombone; Arthur Whetsel-trumpet; Bigard-clarinet)
Never In A Million Years (vocal: Ivie Anderson) (trombone)
Christopher Columbus (trumpet; Hodges' sax; Bigard's clarinet)
Uptown Downbeat (Bigard; Stewart; clarinets)
Trust In Me (vocal: Ivie Anderson) (Bigard; trumpet)
Tiger Rag (5 minutes of jamming: Bigard; Hardwick?; Tizol; Hodges; Bigard)

12:30AM WABC
ISHAM JONES
Hotel Lincoln, NYC
This is My Last Affair
They Can't Take That Away From Me (vocal: Joe Martin)
Slummin' On Park Avenue (vocal: Eddie Stone)
Just To Remind You (written by Isham Jones)
A Session Of Jam
You're Laughin' At Me
Now You're Talkin' My Language (vocal: Joe Martin)
It's Swell Of You (vocal: Eddie Stone)
Now The Whole World Knows (vocal: Joe Martin)
Was It Rain?

■ MONDAY 5 APRIL 1937

RADIO LOGS

07.15PM WJZ
BUGHOUSE RHYTHM
San Francisco
Very descriptive announcing by G. Archibald Presby. GREAT.
Swinging On The Reservation (written by Chick Webb: played by Dr John Meakins' Band)
Exactly Like You (muted brass; clarinets; trombone; saxes: nuttsy)
Dr Heckle & Mr Jive (written by Dick McDonough)
Mr Ghost Goes To Town (written by Will Hudson last year, very popular, relaxed swing tune: saxes answering brass; nuttsy drums and guitar solos; trumpet)

12:00 MIDNIGHT WJZ
BOB CROSBY
Congress Hotel, Chicago
Can't Help Lovin' Dat Man
May I Have The Next Romance? (vocal: Kay Weber)
South Rampart Street Parade
Wild Irish Rose (BobCats jamming)
They All Laughed (vocal: Bob Crosby) (arranged by Bob Haggart)
Tin Roof Blues (Smith's trombone; Matlock's clarinet)
Pagan Love Song (Lawson; Miller's tenor; Ray Bauduc's drums; Bob Haggart's bass)

12:00 MIDNIGHT WOR
TOMMY DORSEY
Hotel Commodore, NYC
I'm Getting Sentimental Over You (theme) (Dorsey's trombone)
I've Got Beginner's Luck (vocal: Edythe Wright)
When Love Is Young
Liebestraum (Tough; Freeman; Erwin)
I'll Dream My Way To Heaven (vocal: Three Esquires)
It's The Mood That I'm In (vocal: Edythe Wright)
Mr Ghost Goes To Town (Tough's drums)
You're Here, You're There, You're Everywhere (vocal: Jack Leonard)
Swing That Music (Bud Freeman's tenor)

■ TUESDAY 6 APRIL 1937

Went down on the 7:31 train with Don Mortimer who saw Benny last night at the Penn. We walked over 52nd Street and looked at all the restaurants (Onyx Club, Hickory House, etc). Went over to the CBS Playhouse No3 on Broadway where we waited at the stage door. The Hammerstein Music Hall just got out so I got a couple of autographs. We met Harry James who gave Mortimer a ticket to get into the Benny Goodman Camel Caravan broadcast. After waiting about another half-hour Ziggy Elman finally got me a ticket. After the broadcast at 10:25 we went over and tried, without success, to see Stuff Smith and Joe Marsala on 52nd Street. We got the 10:45 train home.

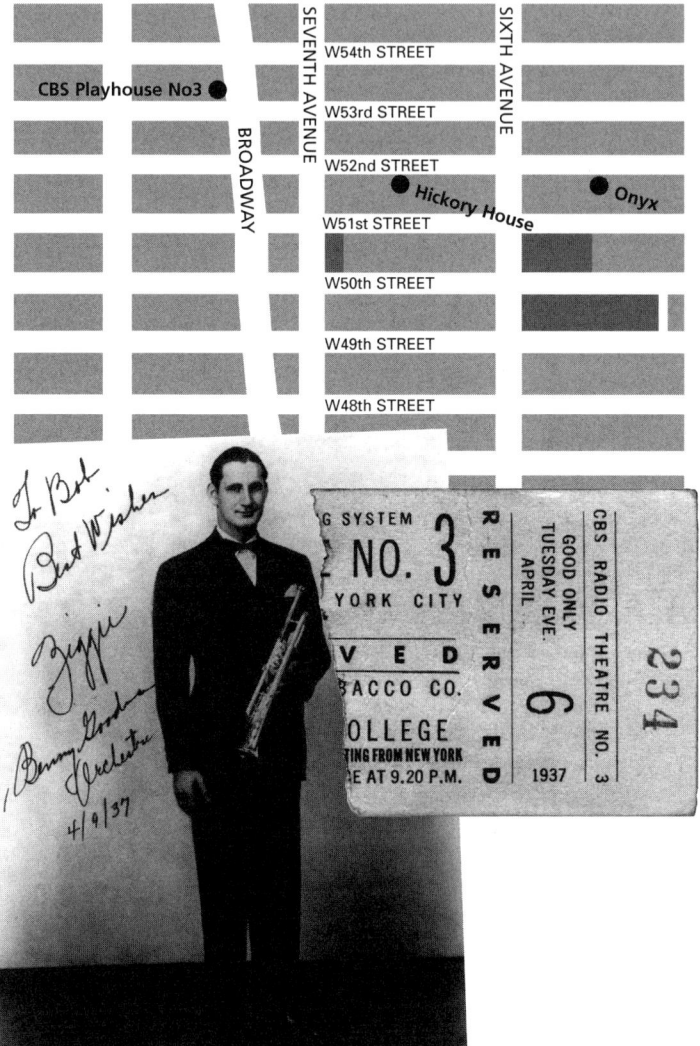

9:30PM WABC
BENNY GOODMAN
Camel Caravan program, NYC
Let's Dance (theme)
I've Got My Love To Keep Me Warm (Harry James' trumpet)
Where Are You? (vocal: Frances Hunt) (very new song)
Oh, Lady Be Good (McEachern; Musso)
Mr. Ghost Goes To Town (ballsy: Harry James' trumpet)
There's A Lull In My Life (vocal: Frances Hunt)
Swingtime In The Rockies (Benny; Elman)
Tea For Two (BG Quartet)
Swing Low Sweet Chariot

RADIO LOGS

11:00PM WABC
TOMMY DORSEY
Hotel Commodore, NYC
Beale Street Blues (Pee Wee Erwin's trumpet; Bud Freeman's tenor; Dave Tough's solid drums)
Jamboree (vocal: Edythe Wright & Three Esquires)
I Can't Lose That Longing For You (vocal: Edythe Wright)
Dark Eyes (Johnny Mince's clarinet; Tough; Freeman)
You Showed Me The Way (vocal: Jack Leonard)
I Never Knew (Mince; Freeman; Tough)

12:00 MIDNIGHT WNEW
WOODY HERMAN
Roseland Ballroom, NYC
You Showed Me The Way (vocal: Woody Herman)
Just To Remind You (vocal: Woody Herman)
Can't We Be Friends?
If My Heart Could Only Talk (vocal: Woody Herman)
Spring Fever Blues (vocal: Woody Herman)
You Look Lovely Tonight (vocal: Woody Herman)
Blue Skies

12:30AM WMCA
WILLIE BRYANT
Savoy Ballroom, NYC
It's Over Because We're Through (theme)
King Porter Stomp
Prelude To A Stomp
Star Dust (vocal: Arnold Adams)
Calling Your Bluff
Viper's Moan (Joe Thomas' trumpet)
More Than You Know
There Is No Greater Love
Jam Session (Jimmy Mundy arrangement)

■ WEDNESDAY 7 APRIL 1937

RADIO LOGS

10:35PM WHN
JOE MARSALA
Hickory House, 144 W52nd Street, NYC
Wolverine Blues (9 minutes long: Joe Marsala's clarinet; Marty's trumpet; Joe Bushkin)
No More Tears (Adele Girard on harp)
I've Got My Love To Keep Me Warm
Several songs by **The Three Peppers** (piano; guitar; bass)
Keep Smilin' At Trouble

11.05PM WABC
BENNY GOODMAN
Hotel Pennsylvania, NYC
Where Are You? (vocal: Frances Hunt) (swell)
Moonlight And Shadows (Harry James' trumpet)
You Showed Me The Way (vocal: Frances Hunt) (swell)
Roll 'Em
I've Got My Love To Keep Me Warm
Dinah (BG Quartet)
Can't We Be Friends? (Red Ballard's trombone)
How Could You? (vocal: Frances Hunt)

11:30PM WOR
DUKE ELLINGTON
Cotton Club, NYC
East St. Louis Toodle-Oo (theme) (nuttsy theme)
Jumpy
Sophisticated Lady
I Take Your Hand

Raymond Scott

Daybreak Express (introduced and written by Ellington: imitates train)
Where Is The Sun?
I've Got To Be A Rug-Cutter (vocal: Ivie Anderson & Trio) (new piece)
I'm Satisfied (vocal: Ivie Anderson)
The Land Of Jam
The New East St. Louis Toodle-Oo (theme) (recorded but not yet released by Master Records)

12:00 MIDNIGHT WJZ
BOB CROSBY
Congress Hotel, Chicago
Wabash Blues
What Will I Tell My Heart?
Slummin' On Park Avenue
Dixieland Shuffle
'Way Down Yonder In New Orleans (vocal: Nappy Lamare)
The Mood That I'm In
This Is My Last Affair (vocal: Bob Crosby)
Wolverine Blues

12:00 MIDNIGHT WABC
TOMMY DORSEY
Hotel Commodore, NYC
I've Got Beginner's Luck (vocal: Edythe Wright)
Dedicated To You (vocal: Jack Leonard)
Blue Danube Waltz
Wanted (vocal: Jack Leonard)
Ja-Da
On A Little Bamboo Bridge (vocal: Edythe Wright)
Mr Ghost Goes To Town (Tough's drums)
Where Are You? (vocal: Jack Leonard)
Bugle Call Rag

■ THURSDAY 8 APRIL 1937

RADIO LOGS

6:00PM WNEW
RAYMOND SCOTT
Make Believe Ballroom, NYC
Minuet In Jazz
A Reckless Night On Board An Ocean Liner (Pumiglio; Harris; Wade)
The Toy Trumpet (Dave Wade's rasping muted trumpet; Johnny Williams' drums; Pumiglio)
Dead End Blues (Wade's trumpet; Harris' tenor; Pumiglio's clarinet; solid rhythm section)
Power House (Wade; Harris; Williams)
Twilight In Turkey (great theme composed by pianist Raymond Scott)

9:30PM WAAB
FRANKIE WARD
Penthouse, Hotel Bradford, Boston
Gee, But You're Swell
Sometimes I'm Happy
Was It Rain? (vocal: Carmen Trudeau)
Swinging On The Reservation

10:45PM WHN
JOE MARSALA
Hickory House, 144 W52nd Street, NYC
I Cried For You
When Did You Leave Heaven

■ FRIDAY 9 APRIL 1937

RECORDING SESSION

DUKE ELLINGTON AND HIS ORCHESTRA
Recording session for Master Records in New York City.
Duke Ellington (p); Arthur Whetsel, Cootie Williams (t); Rex Stewart (c); Joe Nanton, Lawrence Brown (tb); Juan Tizol (vtb); Barney Bigard (cl); Johnny Hodges (cl/ss/as); Otto Hardwick (as/bsx); Harry Carney (cl/as/bar); Fred Guy (g); Hayes Alvis, Billy Taylor (b); Sonny Greer (d); Ivie Anderson (voc)
There's A Lull In My Life (vIA) / *It's Swell Of You* (vIA) / *You Can't Run Away From Love Tonight* (vIA)

FATS WALLER & HIS RHYTHM
Recording session for Victor in New York City.
Herman Autrey (t); Gene Sedric (cl/ts); Fats Waller (p/voc); Albert Casey (g); Charles Turner (b); Slick Jones (d/vib)
You Showed Me The Way (vFW) / *You Showed Me The Way* / *Boo Hoo* / *The Love Bug Will Bite You* / *San Anton'* (vFW) / *San Anton'* / *I've Got A New Lease On Love* (vFW) / *I've Got A New Lease On Love* / *Sweet Heartache* (vFW) / *Sweet Heartache* / *Honeysuckle Rose* (vibSJ)

RADIO LOGS

12:10AM WJZ
BOB CROSBY
Congress Hotel, Chicago
The Old Spinning Wheel (just released on Decca: Matlock; Lawson; Zurke)
I Can't Lose That Longing For You (vocal: Bob Crosby) (Matlock; Miller; Lawson)
In A Minor Mood (Zurke; Miller with Bauduc; Matlock; Smith; Lawson)
Woman On My Weary Mind (Matlock; clarinets; Miller; Smith)
You Showed Me The Way (vocal: Bob Crosby) (Lawson; Matlock)
What Is This Thing Called Love? (Miller; not enough time to play)

SATURDAY 10 APRIL 1937

RADIO LOGS

7.00PM WABC
SATURDAY NIGHT SWING SESSION No40
CBS Studios, NYC
Conducted by Leith Stevens; announced by Mel Allen and Paul Douglas.
Nero (Swell)
They All Laughed (Latest song by George Gershwin: sax solos by Harris & Pumiglio)
I Found A New Baby (JOE MARSALA'S swell clarinet; played in honor of pianist Joe Sullivan who made the record with the Chicago Rhythm Kings)
Improvisation (Just jammin' the blues in B-flat: Williams' drums)
Study In Brown (Exactly like Glen Gray's Decca recording: Dave Harris's tenor)
Big Boy Blue (Sung by the FOUR STARS Quartet)
Reckless Night On Board An Ocean Liner (Raymond Scott's Quintet: good)
Darktown Strutters' Ball (LOU 'RED' EVANS playing an ocarina/sweet potato: very short but swell)
Oh, Lady Be Good (LOU 'RED' EVANS doing an encore on his 'hot potato')
Heat Wave (Colossal: brass; saxes; Harris' saxs)

11.00PM WABC
BENNY GOODMAN
Hotel Pennsylvania, NYC
Heard this program at Betty Landon's house.
I Found A New Baby (wonderful)
September In The Rain (vocal: Frances Hunt)
Makin' Whoopee (nuttsy)
Sentimental And Melancholy
Slummin' On Park Avenue (vocal: Frances Hunt)
Camel Hop
You Showed Me The Way (vocal: Frances Hunt)
Shine (BG Quartet)
Wake Up And Sing
Sugar Foot Stomp (James' trumpet)

11:15PM WAAB
HUDSON-DeLANGE
Raymor Ballroom, Boston
Hobo On Park Avenue (theme)
Never In A Million Years
Midnight At The Onyx
Night And Day (vocal: Eddie DeLange)
Star Dust

Two clarinettists currently appearing in New York City: Joe Marsala (above), resident at the Hickory House and guest on the 40th Saturday Night Swing Session; and Benny Goodman (right), resident at the Hotel Pennsylvania with his Orchestra.

12:00 MIDNIGHT WJZ
BOB CROSBY
Congress Hotel, Chicago
Heard this program at Betty Landon's house.
Carelessly
Fidgety Feet
Smoke Dreams (vocal: Bob Crosby)
Here Comes Your Pappy (vocal: Nappy Lamare)
It's The Mood That I'm In
They All Laughed (vocal: Bob Crosby)
Bugle Call Rag (Matlock; Lawson, etc)

12:30AM WIP
LUCKY MILLINDER
Nixon-Grand Theater, Philadelphia
Heard at Betty Landon's house. Lucky Millinder sure has got a great new band.
Balloonacy
The Moon Is Grinning At Me (vocal: Chuck Richards)
Whispering (featuring Billy Kyle, new young pianist)
Having A Ball
Blue Rhythm Fantasy
What Will I Tell My Heart? (vocal: Chuck Richards)
Jump Steady (Tab Smith's great alto sax, etc)
Luckyology

■ SUNDAY 11 APRIL 1937

RADIO LOGS

10:30PM WHN
JOE MARSALA
Hickory House, 144 W52nd Street, NYC
Wolverine Blues (Joe Marsala's clarinet; Marty Marsala's trumpet; violin; Joe Bushkin's piano; drums)
Alexander's Ragtime Band (vocal: Three Peppers) (Marty; Joe; Bushkin)
I Found A New Baby (Marty; Bushkin; ballsy, soft-swing violin; Adele Girard's harp; Ray Biondi's violin; Danny Alvin's drums)
Singin' The Blues (Joe's clarinet; Marty's trumpet)
Keep Smilin' At Trouble (Marty; Ray's violin; Alvin's drums; Artie Shapiro's bass)
Nothin' But The Blues (nuttsy theme)

11:05PM WABC
LENNIE HAYTON
Terrace Room, Hotel New Yorker, NYC
Flying Fingers (written by Lennie Hayton)
I'll Never Tell You I Love You (vocal: Paul Barry)
Spring Cleaning (trumpet; piano; clarinet)
Little Old Lady (vocal: Paul Barry)
Sweet is The Word For You (vocal: Paul Barry)
Mr Ghost Goes To Town

■ MONDAY 12 APRIL 1937

RADIO LOGS

7:15PM WJZ
BUGHOUSE RHYTHM
San Francisco
Nuttsy. Great descriptive announcing by G. Archibald Presby.
Spring Fever Blues (nuttsy fairly new song by David Bauer & Sam Warner: trumpet; tenor; saxes)
Dinah (THE VILLAGE CUT-UPS: Williams Sisters vocalizing; clarinet; vibraharp; guitar; bass; piano & choir: swell vocal and vibes)
Boston Tea Party (tenor sax; trumpet; drums; clarinets)

7:30PM WEAF
MIDGE WILLIAMS
Rockefeller Centre, NYC
Jerry Sears directed the orchestra. Williams has made several records with jam bands and sings with Jesse Owens' colored Band.
It's High Time (vocal: Midge Williams)
What Harlem Is To Me (vocal: Midge Williams)
Study In Brown (vocal: Midge Williams)
When Love Is Young (vocal: Midge Williams)
Moonlight And Shadows (vocal: Midge Williams)
It Don't Mean A Thing (vocal: Midge Williams)

8:00PM WAAB
HUDSON-DeLANGE
Raymor Ballroom, Boston
Sweet Lorraine
Wake Up And Live
Number 2A
Sophisticated Swing
I've Got My Love To Keep Me Warm (vocal: Eddie DeLange)

09:00PM WJZ
GOOD TIME SOCIETY
Rockefeller Centre, NYC
Jam Session (Teddy Hill Band)
An Apple A Day (vocal: Four Inkspots)
The Love Bug Will Bite You (vocal: Anda Randolph)
Nobody's Sweetheart (ballsy: Sam Allen's piano; bass; Newton's trumpet)
There's A Lull In My Life (vocal: Eddie Matthews)
With Plenty Of Money And You (vocal: Four Inkspots)
My Blue Heaven (Teddy Hill Band) (swell)

11:00PM WMCA
FRANKIE WARD
Penthouse, Hotel Bradford, Boston
September In The Rain (vocal: Carmen Trudeau)
This Year's Crop Of Kisses
Too Marvelous For Words (vocal: Carmen Trudeau)
At The Jazz Band Ball (swell: bass; tenor; vibes; trumpet)
I Surrender Dear (colossal arrangement: what a marvelous sax section; trumpet)
You Showed Me The Way (vocal: Carmen Trudeau)
Honeysuckle Rose (trumpet; saxes; clarinet; vibes)
This Is My Last Affair (vocal: Carmen Trudeau)
After You've Gone (tenor; trombone, etc)

12:00 MIDNIGHT WJZ
BOB CROSBY
Congress Hotel, Chicago
Every Monday night the band has a jam session. This is the fourth.
Between The Devil And The Deep Blue Sea (arranged by Bob Haggart: Matlock; Lawson; Miller; Smith)
Trust In Me (vocal: Kay Weber) (arranged by Bob Zurke: Eddie Miller's great tenor)
Coquette (Bauduc's drums; Lawson's trumpet; Miller's tenor; Matlock's clarinet)
I Can't Lose That Longing For You (vocal: Bob Crosby) (Yank Lawson)
Gin Mill Blues (written by Joe Sullivan: featuring Zurke's piano; Miller's tenor)
'Way Down Yonder In New Orleans (vocal: Nappy Lamare) (Lawson; Matlock; Zurke; Miller; Smith)
Jamboree (great arrangement by Bob Haggart: Matlock; Miller's swell tenor)

12:00 MIDNIGHT WOR
TOMMY DORSEY
Hotel Commodore, NYC
I Can't Break The Habit Of You (vocal: Edythe Wright)
September In The Rain (vocal: Jack Leonard)
Dancing With Mince (colossal: Mince; Erwin)
To A Sweet, Pretty Thing (vocal: Three Esquires) (Freeman; Mince)
My Blue Heaven (colossal clarinet by Johnny Mince; Erwin; Dorsey; Freeman)
It's The Mood That I'm In (vocal: Edythe Wright)
Dark Eyes (This guy Mince is simply super-colossal on clarinet: Erwin; Freeman; Tough)
Too Marvelous For Words (great sax section)
Memphis Blues (Erwin; Dorsey; Freeman)
I'm Getting Sentimental Over You (theme)

■ TUESDAY 13 APRIL 1937

RECORDING SESSION

WILLIE 'THE LION' SMITH AND HIS CUBS
Recording session for Decca in New York City.
Dave Nelson (t); Buster Bailey (cl); Robert Carroll (ts); Willie 'The Lion' Smith (p); Jimmy McLin (g); Ellsworth Reynolds (b); Eric Henry (d)
The Swampland Is Calling Me / More Than That / I'm All Out Of Breath / I Can See You All Over The Place

RADIO LOGS

8:45PM WHN
ERSKINE HAWKINS
Harlem Uproar House, NYC
Swell. Announced by Charles F. McCarthy.
Limehouse Blues
What Will I Tell My Heart? (vocal: Jimmy Mitchelle) (Paul Bascomb's great tenor sax)
Does Your Heart Beat For Me? (vocal: Trio)
When My Dreamboat Comes Home (vocal: Jimmy Mitchelle) (bass sax; piano; saxes; trumpet)
I've Been A Fool Again (Hawkins' trumpet)

Marie (vocal: Jimmy Mitchelle) (real swingin' out: tenor)
Rosetta (vocal: Jimmy Mitchelle)
The Viper's Swing (trombone; trumpet; sax)

9:30PM WABC
BENNY GOODMAN
Camel Caravan program, NYC
Oh, Lady Be Good (Benny; McEachern; Musso)
September In The Rain (vocal: Frances Hunt)
Nagasaki (BG Quartet) (great all round work)
Minnie The Moocher's Wedding Day (ballsy: Harry James' trumpet; saxes)

11:00PM WAAB
HUDSON-DeLANGE
Raymor Ballroom, Boston
Pennies From Heaven
Mr Ghost Goes To Town (vocal: Eddie DeLange)
Through The Courtesy of Love
Night And Day (vocal: Eddie DeLange)
Sophisticated Lady

■ WEDNESDAY 14 APRIL 1937

RECORDING SESSION

LIONEL HAMPTON AND HIS ORCHESTRA
Recording session for Victor in New York City.
Lionel Hampton (vib/voc); Cootie Williams (t); Lawrence Brown (tb); Mezz Mezzrow (cl); Johnny Hodges (as); Jess Stacy (piano); Allan Reuss (g); John Kirby (b); Cozy Cole (d)
Buzzin' 'Round With The Bee (vLH) / *Whoa, Babe!* (vLH) / *Stompology*

NOBLE SISSLE AND HIS ORCHESTRA
Recording session for Variety in New York City.
Noble Sissle (voc/ldr); Wendell Culley, Demas Dean, Clarence Brereton (t); Chester Burrill (tb); Sidney Bechet (cl/ss); Chauncey Haughton (cl/as); Gil White, Jerome Pasquall (ts); Oscar Madera (vln); Erskine Butterfield (p); Jimmy Miller (g); Jimmy Jones (b); Wilbert Kirk (d)
Bandana Days / *I'm Just Wild About Harry* / *Dear Old Southland* (vNS)

RADIO LOGS

11.05PM WABC
BENNY GOODMAN
Hotel Pennsylvania, NYC
Sweet is The Word For You (vocal: Frances Hunt)
Moonlight And Shadows (Musso; James)
Alexander's Ragtime Band
Star Dust (colossal: brass; saxes; Harry James' trumpet)
Roll 'Em (super-colossal arrangement: Stacy; Krupa; Musso; Benny)
Boo Hoo (vocal: Frances Hunt)
Exactly Like You (BG Quartet) (Lionel Hampton singing)
I Can't Lose That Longing For You (vocal: Frances Hunt)
Jammin' (Musso)

11:30PM WJZ
WILL OSBORN
Hotel Netherland-Plaza, Cincinnati
Fair.
'Way Down Yonder In New Orleans
The Goona Goo (vocal: Dorothy Rogers)
What Will I Tell My Heart? (vocal: Will Osborn)
That Foolish Feeling
Where Are You?
Mr Ghost Goes To Town
This is My Last Affair
It's The Mood That I'm In
Too Marvelous For Words (vocal: Will Osborn)
Tea On The Terrace (theme)

12:00 MIDNIGHT WJZ
BOB CROSBY
Congress Hotel, Chicago
Muskrat Ramble
May I Have The Next Romance? (vocal: Kay Weber)
Boo Hoo (vocal: Nappy Lamare) (Miller)
Dogtown Blues (Zurke; clarinets; Lawson)
To A Sweet, Pretty Thing (vocal: Bob Crosby)
Hallelujah (Matlock; Zurke; Smith; Bauduc; Miller)
September In The Rain (vocal: Kay Weber)
Panama (Miller; Lawson; Matlock; Smith)

12:00 MIDNIGHT WABC
TOMMY DORSEY
Hotel Commodore, NYC
Kenneth Roberts announced.
How Could You? (vocal: Edythe Wright)
September In The Rain (vocal: Jack Leonard)
Song Of India (Tough; Dorsey; Erwin; Freeman)
To A Sweet, Pretty Thing (vocal: Three Esquires)
Dippermouth Blues (Mince; Tough; Freeman)
Marie (vocal: Jack Leonard & Band) (Dorsey; Freeman; Erwin)
Unknown Title (Freeman; clarinets; Tough)
Rain In My Eyes (vocal: Edythe Wright) (swell new song)
That's A-Plenty (colossal: Erwin; Mince; Freeman; Tough)
I'm Getting Sentimental Over You (theme)

■ THURSDAY 15 APRIL 1937

RECORDING SESSION

TOMMY DORSEY AND HIS ORCHESTRA
Recording session for Victor in New York City.
Tommy Dorsey (tb); Pee Wee Erwin, Joe Bauer, Andy Ferretti (t); Les Jenkins, Red Bone (tb); Johnny Mince, Fred Stulce, Mike Doty (cl/as); Bud Freeman (ts); Howard Smith (p); Carmen Mastren (g); Gene Traxler (b); Dave Tough (d); Edythe Wright (voc)
Wake Up And Live (vEW) / *Nola* / *Satan Takes A Holiday* / *Stop, Look And Listen*

TOMMY DORSEY AND HIS CLAMBAKE SEVEN
Recording session for Victor in New York City.
Tommy Dorsey (tb); Pee Wee Erwin (t); Johnny Mince (cl); Bud Freeman (ts); Howard Smith (p); Carmen Mastren (g); Gene Traxler (b); Dave Tough (d); Edythe Wright (voc)
The Milkman's Matinee (vEW) / *Twilight In Turkey* / *He's A Gypsy From Poughkeepsie* (vEW) / *Alibi Baby* (vEW)

RADIO LOGS

10:30PM WHN
JOE MARSALA
Hickory House, 144 W52nd Street, NYC
Great. Real jammin'.
Let's Call The Whole Thing Off
Slummin' On Park Avenue (vocal: Three Peppers)
If I Had My Way (vocal: Three Peppers)
I Want A Little Girl (vocal: Joe Marsala) (Bushkin)
I Cried For You (played twice: in sweet and swing)
When A Lady Meets A Gentleman Down South (vocal: Joe Bushkin) (swell hot vocal)
The Blues (theme played in full: colossal clarinet by Joe)

■ FRIDAY 16 APRIL 1937

RECORDING SESSION

NOBLE SISSLE'S SWINGSTERS
Recording session for Variety in New York City.
Noble Sissle (ldr); Sidney Bechet (cl/ss); Jimmy Miller (g); Jimmy Jones (b); Wilbert Kirk (d); Billy Banks (voc)
Okey-Doke / *Characteristic Blues* (vBB)

Mr Pastoriza, Hughie and myself went down to see Benny Goodman's band at the Hotel Pennsylvania by subway. Since we spent some time hunting for film for the camera that Hughie brought along to take pictures of the band, we didn't get there until 9:40pm. Since we got a table far away from the band we left the table and stood around where the band was all night. I only had to pay 85 cents the whole evening. We didn't do any dancing. Hughie took about 16 pictures. We got Lionel Hampton and Teddy Wilson to pose for us. We talked to Ziggy Elman, Arthur Rollini, Gene Krupa, Lionel Hampton and Teddy Wilson but I only got one autograph (McEachern's on a picture in this book). Mr Chapin, secretary, told us that he didn't have any pictures and that the band was leaving the Penn the 28th of April, going to the Savoy Ballroom, Roseland Ballroom, Metropolitan Theater in Boston, and then touring across the US by bus until they reach the Palomar Ballroom this summer. I met several Juniors from Bronxville, Jimmy Sheen who used to go to Bronxville, and James Ware who I used to play against in football five years ago. Ware, yet only 19, is working on several of the big NBC programs and making plenty of money. He hopes to be an announcer. Hughie had to leave at 12:40 with his father to catch the 1:00 train but I stayed until 1:30 because Jimmy Sheen gave me a ride home in his car. Ziggy told me that he was taking a vacation next month because of his sore lip. Irving Goodman is to substitute.

The band played the following numbers and more that I forgot: *Always, Carelessly* (Frances Hunt), *Let's Call The Whole Thing Off* (Frances Hunt), *Down South Camp Meetin'* (Griffin), *Sweet Is The Word For You* (Frances Hunt), *Peckin'* (A super-colossal arrangement, played twice, of a song written by Harry James: James, Musso), *Boo Hoo* (Frances Hunt), *Stardust, I'm Hatin' This Waiting Around For You* (Frances Hunt), *Unknown Title, You Showed Me The Way* (Frances Hunt), *Unknown Title, This Year's Crop Of Kisses* (Frances Hunt), *I've Got My Love To Keep Me Warm, Serenade In The Night, Changes, Roll 'Em* (13 minutes long), *Where Are You?* (Frances Hunt), *Tea For Two* (TRIO plus Musso), *Sing, Sing, Sing* (15 minutes long – GREAT. REAL JAMMIN'), *Can't We Be Friends?, Too Marvelous For Words* (Frances Hunt), *Sometimes I'm Happy* (Griffin, Musso), *There's A Lull In My Life* (Frances Hunt), *King Porter Stomp* (COLOSSAL, James, Musso), *How Could You?* (Frances Hunt), *Tiger Rag* (TRIO), *Oh, Lady Be Good* (TRIO), *Stompin' At The Savoy* (QUARTET), *Exactly Like You* (QUARTET, Hampton singing), *Nagasaki* (QUARTET, Ballsy), *Runnin' Wild* (QUARTET).

RADIO LOGS

2:15AM WGN
ROY ELDRIDGE
Three Deuces, Chicago
Sing, Sing, Sing (Roy Eldridge's great trumpet; tenor; piano; Zutty's drums)
There's A Lull In My Life
Christopher Columbus (Roy's trumpet; Zutty's drums; tenor)

APRIL 1937

■ SATURDAY 17 APRIL 1937

Hughie Pastoriza and I were driven by his mother to the subway at 241st Street at 8.45am. Upon arriving in New York City we went to the Music Corporation of America (MCA) in the Squibb Building on Fifth Avenue. We each got pictures of Benny Goodman (4), Mildred Bailey, Gene Krupa, Tommy Dorsey, Count Basie (2) all for nothing. We then went down to the Paramount Theater at 43rd Street & Broadway where we paid 25 cents to get in to see the movie *Swing High, Swing Low* (fair) and, in person, Louis Armstrong and his Band. We were in the theater from 10:15 to 2:15, seeing the stage show twice. On the whole I thought Louis' band was very good but there were too many tap dancers mixed in with the show. Louis is still one of the great trumpeters and has a wonderful personality. Louis and the band played:

When It's Sleepy Time Down South (swell theme)
Swing That Music (Louis' trumpet; Madison's tenor)
Copper Colored Gal (accompaniment to dancers)
Boo Hoo (vocal: Bobbie Caston) (Louis' regular vocalist)
Tiger Rag (accompaniment to more tap dancers)
Black And Tan Fantasy (accompaniment to dancers)
When My Dreamboat Comes Home (vocal: Sonny Woods)
What Will I Tell My Heart? (vocal: Sonny Woods)
Ol' Man River (vocal: Sonny Woods) (Woods' best vocal)
My Blue Heaven (vocal: Sonny Woods)
Skeleton In The Closet (vocal: Louis Armstrong) (Louis singing and playing the song he introduced: swell)
St. Louis Blues (Red Allen's trumpet; Leo Mosley's trombone; Pops Foster's bass)
I Hope Gabriel Likes My Music (Louis; Red Allen; Higginbotham's trombone; Luis Russell's piano; Bingie Madison's tenor; Paul Barbarin's drums)

Afterwards we went around to the stage door where we got the autographs of the guys in the band that we didn't get in the theater. I got the autograph of Luis Russell on a picture of himself, the autograph of Louis Armstrong on an old picture of himself, and the autographs of the whole band except the guitar on a picture of the band. The following were in the band: Henry 'Red' Allen, Shelton Hemphill, Louis Bacon (trumpets); J.C. Higginbotham, Leo Mosley, James Archey (trombones); Bingie Madison, Al Nicholas, Pete Clark, Charlie Holmes (saxes); Luis Russell (piano); George 'Pops' Foster (bass); Paul Barbarin (drums) and the guitar player Lee Blair. Since Hughie took his expensive camera down we took pictures of the stage show and also got Henry 'Red' Allen, Higginbotham and Paul Barbarin to pose for us outside the theater (*below*).

Louis Armstrong's brass section (l to r): J. C. Higginbotham, Henry 'Red' Allen, James Archey, Louis Bacon, Leo Mosley, Shelton Hemphill

At 3:30 we went up to Rockwell-O'Keefe at the RKO Building to see Vincent Prior and get some pictures. Prior was out of town but we got some pictures of Bob Crosby and Louis Armstrong. As we were leaving we happened to meet Ed Cashman, director of the Saturday Night Swing session held at 7:00pm over WABC, in the elevator. He recognized us since we have been to see so many broadcasts, and asked us if we were going to the broadcast tonight. We told him that we didn't get any passes this week. He said that if we went there at six o'clock and mentioned his name we could get in to see the broadcast. Before doing that, however, we went up to the Hotel Plymouth, 143 W49th Street, where we looked up Ziggy Elman (trumpeter with Benny Goodman's Band) and Vido Musso (sax with Goodman's Band). Since they were both out we wrote a note to Ziggy saying that we had been there and asking for a picture of himself. After leaving the hotel we dropped in at the Harlem Uproar House (Broadway at 51st Street) but Erskine Hawkins wasn't there. We ran into Vido Musso in the street. He remembered me and shook hands with me and told us that we could get a picture of him at the Conn Musical Instrument Store, 117 West 48th Street. We went there and met William H. Shine who gave us pictures of Vido Musso, Bunny Berigan (2), and Sonny Dunham. he said to come around next week when he would have some more pictures of musicians to give us since there are three made of each person and he only uses one. We also went to the Selmer Music Store, 113 W48th, but pictures cost one dollar there. We then went over to the Capital Hotel at 8th Avenue and 51st Street where Harry James (trumpeter with Goodman's band) lives. Since he wasn't in we wrote him a note asking for pictures of himself. We then went over to the Saturday Night Swing session an hour early at 485 Madison Avenue so we could get in without any trouble. Billy Kyle, young new pianist with Lucky Millinder's Band was to be the featured guest. It also marked the return of Bunny Berigan after an absence of a month traveling in the New England States with his own new band. We had a short talk with Bunny about his trip. He autographed 2 of his pictures. I also had a long talk with pianist Billy Kyle. He sure is one swell guy. He said that his favorite piano player was Art Tatum, the blind colored pianist. He was telling me how he met Teddy Wilson, seeing Duke Ellington's band at the Cotton Club and of the jam session he was in several Sundays ago with Goodman, Shaw, Ellington, Marsala, Webb, Wettling, Basie, Condon, Mezzrow, etc [at Master Records Studio, 14th March]. Since Lucky Millinder and his drummer O'Neil Spencer were there with Kyle I got their autographs. Kyle is going to be at the Savoy with Millinder's Band for a week starting tomorrow, playing opposite Teddy Hill's Band.

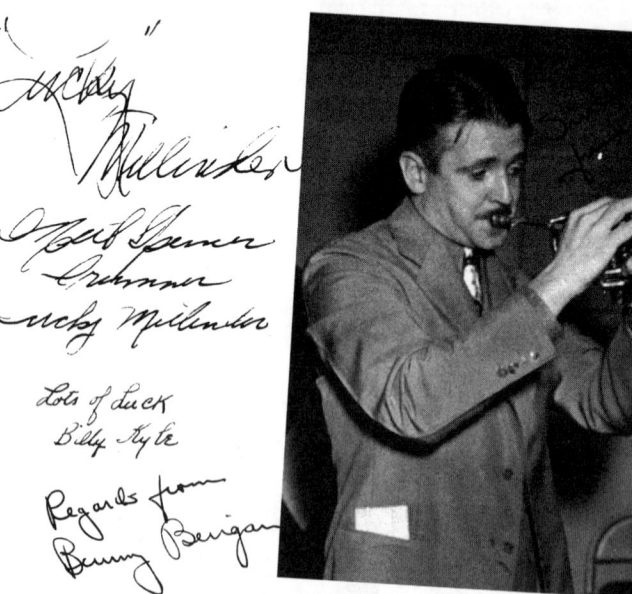

7.00PM WABC
SATURDAY NIGHT SWING SESSION No41
CBS Studio No1, 485 Madison Ave, NYC
Leith Stevens: Raymond Scott; Dave Harris; Pete Pumiglio; Art Manners; Hank Ross; Russ Genner; Joe Vargas; Dave Wade; Nat Natoli; Lloyd Williams; Bunny Berigan; Lou Shoobe; Frankie Worrell; Johnny Williams; Billy Kyle; O'Neil Spencer
Waddlin' At The Waldorf (written by Jimmy Dorsey: Art Manners' alto sax; saxes; Shoobe's bass)
This is My Last Affair (swell ballad: CBS Band directed by Leith Stevens: Berigan's trumpet)
I Can't Get Started (Dave Wade playing muted trumpet welcoming Bunny Berigan back)
Careless Love (one of those GREAT trumpet solos by Bunny Berigan)
Minuet In Jazz (Raymond Scott Quintet: Harris; Pumiglio; Wade; Shoobe; Williams; Scott)
Blue Room (marvelous arrangement: brass section and saxes; Berigan's trumpet)
Whispering (BILLY KYLE playing WONDERFUL piano with CBS Band with O'Neil Spencer on drums)
I Got Rhythm (BILLY KYLE again with O'Neil Spencer & CBS Band. Colossal)
Dinner Music For A Pack Of Hungry Cannibals (Raymond Scott Quintet)
Swanee River (Berigan directing CBS Band: Harris' tenor)

RECORDING SESSION
ANDY KIRK AND HIS TWELVE CLOUDS OF JOY
Recording session for Decca in New York City.
Andy Kirk (bsx/ldr); Harry Lawson, Paul King, Earl Thompson (t); Ted Donnelly, Henry Wells (tb); John Harrington (cl/as/bar); John Williams (as/bar); Earl Miller (as); Dick Wilson (ts); Mary Lou Williams (p); Ted Brinson (g); Booker Collins (b); Ben Thigpen (d); Pha Terrell (voc)
Worried Over You (vPT) / *Foolin' Myself* (vPT) / *I'm Glad For Your Sake* (vPT) / *I'll Get Along Somehow* (vPT)

RADIO LOGS

2:30PM WJZ
BOB CROSBY
Congress Hotel, Chicago
Slummin' On Park Avenue (Miller; Lawson; Smith)
Sentimental And Melancholy (vocal: Kay Weber)
To A Sweet, Pretty Thing (vocal: Bob Crosby) (Lawson)
Tin Roof Blues (Smith; Matlock)
Trust In Me (vocal: Kay Weber)
I Love You Just Enough (vocal: Kay Weber) (Miller; Matlock; Bauduc)
Smoke Dreams (vocal: Bob Crosby)
Steppin' Pretty (arranged by Mary Lou Williams)

8:00PM WAAB
ART SHAW
Raymor Ballroom, Boston
Shaw's new band—no violins.
Nightmare (theme)
Slummin' On Park Avenue
How Could You?
Someday, Sweetheart
I've Got My Love To Keep Me Warm
Cream Puff

11.00PM WABC
BENNY GOODMAN
Hotel Pennsylvania, NYC
Darktown Strutters' Ball
There's A Lull In My Life (vocal: Frances Hunt)
Can' t We Be Friends? (Red Ballard's trombone)
Blue Hawaii (first time played by Benny: James; Musso)
Down South Camp Meetin' (most-played tune by Benny)
September In The Rain (vocal: Frances Hunt)
Nobody's Sweetheart (BG Trio) (swell)
I'm Hatin' This Waitin' Around For You (vocal: Frances Hunt)
Roll 'Em (8-minute version– makes the audience go mad)

11:30PM WMCA
TEDDY HILL
Savoy Ballroom, NYC
Stompin' At The Savoy (theme)
Symphony In Riffs
Big Boy Blue (vocal: Teddy Hill & Bill Dillard)
Blue Rhythm Fantasy
Twilight In Turkey
I Got Rhythm
Paradise (vocal: Bill Dillard)
Study In Brown
Ja-Da

12:00 MIDNIGHT WJZ
BOB CROSBY
Congress Hotel, Chicago
Sugarfoot Stomp
What Will I Tell My Heart? (vocal: Kay Weber)
There'll Be Some Changes Made (vocal: Bob Crosby)
Half Of Me
When My Dreamboat Comes Home
It's The Mood That I'm In
Woman On My Weary Mind (vocal: Nappy Lamare)
I've Got My Love To Keep Me Warm (vocal: Kay Weber)
Pagan Love Song

12:30AM WMCA
COUNT BASIE
Nixon-Grand Theater, Philadelphia
Moten Swing (theme)
Shout And Feel It
Old Fashioned Love
Mary Had A Little Lamb (vocal: Jimmy Rushing)
King Porter Stomp
This Year's Kisses (vocal: Billie Holiday)
Dear Old Southland
Somebody Loves Me (vocal: Jimmy Rushing)
Swinging At The Daisy Chain
Yeah, Man!

■ SUNDAY 18 APRIL 1937

RADIO LOGS

3:00PM WEAF
BOB CROSBY
Congress Hotel, Chicago
An afternoon jam session sponsored by *Down Beat* to raise money for recovering pianist Joe Sullivan. Johnny Dodds (clarinet) and Baby Dodds (drums) guest with the band.
Rachmaninov's Prelude (combined with Fats Waller's ZONKY)
Dogtown Blues (written by Bob Haggart)
Between The Devil And The Deep Blue Sea
Just Strolling (written by Joe Sullivan, played by Bob Zurke)
South Rampart Street Parade (written by Ray Bauduc)
Gin Mill Blues (written by Joe Sullivan: featuring Bob Zurke's wonderful piano)

6:30PM WOR
FUN IN SWINGTIME
WOR Studios, NYC
Del Schubert announces. Tim & Irene are the lousy comedians on the program. The band sounds like the CBS Saturday Night Swing band. [It is the Bunny Berigan Orchestra]
Chicken And Waffles (very short introductory theme, very fast: nuttsy)
I Can't Get Started (regular theme featuring Bunny Berigan's muted trumpet)
The Goona Goo (Bunny Berigan's trumpet; ballsy tenor; drums; brass, etc)
Trees (sweet song played in swing style: saxes; clarinets; brass; Bunny's trumpet)
Sweet Sue (LENNIE HAYTON, guest, playing a fair piano)
Am I Blue? (ballsy arrangement: Bunny's trumpet?; Art Drelinger's tenor)

■ MONDAY 19 APRIL 1937

RECORDING SESSION

ERSKINE HAWKINS AND HIS ORCHESTRA
Recording session for Vocalion in New York City.
Erskine Hawkins (t/ldr); Wilbur Bascomb, Marcellus Green, Sam Lowe (t); Edward Sims, Robert Range (tb); William Johnson (as); Jimmy Mitchelle (as/voc); Paul Bascomb (ts); Haywood Henry (cl/bar); Avery Parrish (p); William McLemore (g); Leemie Stanfield (b); James Morrison (d); Billy Daniels, Merle Turner (voc)
'Way Down Upon The Swanee River / Dear Old Southland / Uproar Shout / If You Leave Me (vJM)

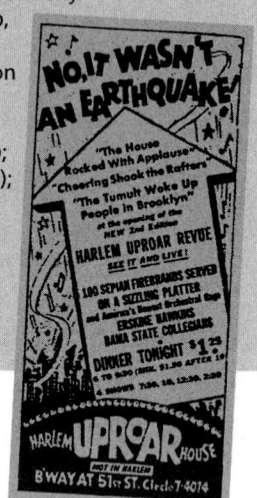

RADIO LOGS

7:15PM WJZ
BUGHOUSE RHYTHM
San Francisco
Announced by G. Archibald Presby. This is the last broadcast in this series. GREAT.
Christmas Night In Harlem (written 3 years ago by Raymond Scott: tenor)
Big John Special (written & arranged by Fletcher Henderson, medium swing: tenor; trumpet; Meakins' piano)
Listen To The Mocking Bird (written by Alice Hawthorne, swell swing arrangement: flute; trumpet; tenor; clarinet)
Copenhagen (written by Charles Davis in 1924 depicting capital city of Denmark. Davis also wrote 'The Jim Town Blues' in 1925: trombones; piano)

7:30PM WEAF
MIDGE WILLIAMS
Rockefeller Centre, NYC
As Long As You've Got Your Health (vocal: Midge Williams)
Solitude (vocal: Midge Williams)
How Could You? (Jerry Sears' Band)
The Moon is In The Sky (vocal: Midge Williams)
In The Shade Of The Old Apple Tree (vocal: Midge Williams) (Miff Mole's trombone)

8:00PM WAAB
ART SHAW
Raymor Ballroom, Boston
Night And Day
Whoa, Babe (vocal: Tony Pastor)
There's A Lull In My Life (Shaw's clarinet)
Big John Special
Nightmare (theme)

9:00PM WJZ
GOODTIME SOCIETY
Studio, NYC
Unknown Title (nuttsy piece by Teddy Hill Band)
Let's Call The Whole Thing Off (vocal: Four Inkspots)
Spring Fever Blues
Ja-Da

11:15PM WNAC
ART SHAW
Raymor Ballroom, Boston
Down South Camp Meeting
Smoke Dreams (vocal: Dorothy Howe)
Someday, Sweetheart
Swing High, Swing Low

■ TUESDAY 20 APRIL 1937

RADIO LOGS

9:30PM WABC
BENNY GOODMAN
Camel Caravan program, NYC
Swingtime In The Rockies (Musso; saxes; Benny; Krupa; Elman)
They Can't Take That Away From Me (vocal: Frances Hunt) (colossal: saxes; Benny)
More Than You Know (BG Trio)
Changes (saxes; James; Musso)

10:45PM WMEA
FRANKIE WARD
Penthouse, Hotel Bradford, Boston
How Could You? (vocal: Carmen Trudeau)
Sweet is The Word For You
Blue Skies
This Is My Last Affair (vocal: Carmen Trudeau)

11:05PM WABC
TOMMY DORSEY
Hotel Commodore, NYC
Melody In F (Bud Freeman)
I'll Dream My Way To Heaven (vocal: Three Esquires)
Mendelssohn's Spring Song (Mince; Erwin; Freeman; Tommy)
In A Little Hula Heaven (vocal: Edythe Wright)
Where Are You? (vocal: Jack Leonard)
Satan Takes A Holiday (COLOSSAL: clarinets; Tough; Freeman)
There's A Lull In My Life (vocal: Edythe Wright) (saxes; Freeman)
Beale Street Blues (Tommy; Freeman; Pee Wee Erwin)

■ WEDNESDAY 21 APRIL 1937

RECORDING SESSION

CLAUDE HOPKINS AND HIS ORCHESTRA
Recording session for Decca in New York City.
Claude Hopkins (p/ldr); Shirley Clay, Jabbo Smith, Lincoln Mills (t); Floyd Brady, Fred Norman, Vic Dickenson (tb); Arville Harris (cl/as/ts); Gene Johnson, Ben Smith (as); Bobby Sands (ts); Walter Jones (g); Abe Bolar (b); George Foster (d); Beverley White (voc)
Honey (vBW) / *June Night* (vBW) / *Church Street Sobbin' Blues* / *My Kinda Love* (vBW)

JOE MARSALA'S CHICAGOANS
Recording session for Variety in New York City.
Marty Marsala (t); Joe Marsala (cl); Ray Biondi (vln); Joe Bushkin (p); Adele Girard (harp); Eddie Condon (g); Artie Shapiro (b); Danny Alvin (d)
Wolverine Blues / Chimes Blues / Jazz Me Blues

RADIO LOGS

11.05PM WABC
BENNY GOODMAN
Hotel Pennsylvania, NYC
Let's Dance (theme)
What Will I Tell My Heart? (vocal: Frances Hunt)
Somebody Loves Me (saxes; Musso; Elman)
Where Are You? (vocal: Frances Hunt)
When Buddha Smiles (Rollini)
You're Here, You're There, You're Everywhere (James' trumpet)
Carelessly (vocal: Frances Hunt)
Runnin' Wild (BG Quartet)
You Showed Me The Way (vocal: Frances Hunt) (James' trumpet)
Bugle Call Rag (Elman; Benny; McEachern; Musso; Krupa)

APRIL 1937

8:00PM WAAB
ART SHAW
Raymor Ballroom, Boston
Because I Love You
Too Marvelous For Words (vocal: Dorothy Howe)
My Blue Heaven
Panamania
Nightmare (theme)

11:30PM WMCA
DON REDMAN
Apollo Theater, NYC
Good.
This Is My Last Affair (vocal: Louis McCall)
(Don Redman's clarinet)
I'm An Old Cowhand (trumpet; trombone)

11:30PM WOR
DUKE ELLINGTON
Cotton Club, NYC
Colossal. J. Howard Doyle announced.
Birmingham Breakdown
There's A Lull In My Life (vocal: Ivie Anderson)
I've Got To Be A Rugcutter (vocal: Ivie Anderson & Trio) (Hodges; trombones)
Ebony Rhapsody (vocal: Ivie Anderson) (Nanton' trombone; Bigard's clarinet; Greer's chimes; saxes; piano)
Black Butterfly (bass sax; Lawrence Brown's trombone: very slow tempo)
Slippery Horn (Bigard's clarinet; Hodges with Williams; Tizol's trombone; basses)
Alabama Home (Rex Stewart's muted trumpet; Hodges)
East St. Louis Toodle-Oo (theme) (played in full: Rex Stewart; Barney Bigard)

12:00 MIDNIGHT WABC
TOMMY DORSEY
Hotel Commodore, NYC
Wake Up And Live (vocal: Edythe Wright)
Sweet is The Word For You (vocal: Jack Leonard)
Who'll Buy My Violets? (Mince; Freeman)
Star Dust (vocal: Edythe Wright) (Tommy's great trombone)
Dark Eyes (Mince; Erwin; Freeman; Dorsey; Tough)
Dedicated To You (vocal: Jack Leonard) (Tommy's muted trombone)
Jammin' (vocal: Edythe Wright) (REAL jammin')
Never In A Million Years (vocal: Jack Leonard)
Swing That Music (vocal: Three Esquires)

12:00 MIDNIGHT WJZ
BOB CROSBY
Congress Hotel, Chicago
Summertime (theme)
Jamboree (Matty Matlock's clarinet; Eddie Miller's tenor; Warren Smith's trombone: nuttsy)
Summer Nights (vocal: Kay Weber) (Miller's great, slow tenor; Matlock's clarinet)
Struttin' With Some Barbecue (Yank Lawson's trumpet; Miller; Matlock; Bauduc)
They All Laughed (vocal: Bob Crosby) (Matlock; Lawson: swell song, colossal swing ending)
Little Rock Getaway (Bob Zurke's piano; Bauduc's drums; Miller's tenor: super-colossal)
Hula Heaven (Miller's tenor, Bob Zurke's piano; Ray Bauduc's drums; Matlock's clarinet, etc)
Moonlight And Shadows (vocal: Kay Weber) (Warren Smith's nuttsy trombone; Matlock; Miller)
Sweet Lorraine (Matlock; Miller with Haggart & Bauduc; Lawson's trumpet; Zurke; Lamare's guitar)

■ THURSDAY 22 APRIL 1937

RADIO LOGS

8:00PM WAAB
ART SHAW
Raymor Ballroom, Boston
Night And Day
Someday, Sweetheart
Smoke Dreams (vocal: Dorothy Howe)
Blue Skies
How Could You? (vocal: Tony Pastor)

12.00 MIDNIGHT WOR
BENNY GOODMAN
Hotel Pennsylvania, NYC
Camel Hop (nuttsy tune written especially for Benny: McEachern; James; Musso; Benny)
Blue Hawaii (brand new song: James' trumpet)
Boo Hoo (vocal: Frances Hunt) (lousy song)
Trust In Me (vocal: Frances Hunt)
That Foolish Feeling (fair)
Moonlight And Shadows (Musso; James; Benny)
They Can't Take That Away From Me (vocal: Frances Hunt) (nuttsy)
Nagasaki (BG Quartet)
You Showed Me The Way (vocal: Frances Hunt) (James' trumpet)
Swing Low, Sweet Chariot (swell: Musso; James)

■ FRIDAY 23 APRIL 1937

RECORDING SESSION

TEDDY HILL AND HIS ORCHESTRA
Recording session for Bluebird in New York City.
Teddy Hill (ts/ldr); Bill Dillard (t/voc); Frankie Newton, Shad Collins (t); Dicky Wells (tb); Russell Procope (cl/as); Howard Johnson (as); Cecil Scott (ts/bar); Sam Allen (p); John Smith (g); Richard Fulbright (b); Bill Beason (d); Beatrice Douglas (voc)
I Know Now (vBD) / *The Lady Who Couldn't Be Kissed* (vBD) / *The You And Me That Used To Be* (vBD) / *A Study In Brown* / *Twilight In Turkey* / *China Boy*

TEDDY WILSON AND HIS ORCHESTRA
Recording session for Bluebird in New York City.
Teddy Wilson (p/ldr); Harry James (t); Buster Bailey (cl); Johnny Hodges (as); Allen Reuss (g); John Kirby (b); Cozy Cole (d); Helen Ward (voc)
There's A Lull In My Life (vHW) / *It's Swell Of You* (vHW) / *How Am I To Know?* (vHW) / *I'm Coming, Virginia*

RADIO LOGS

11:30PM WMCA
LUCKY MILLINDER
Savoy Ballroom, NYC
Heard this program at Babs Underhill's house at Scarsdale.
You Took My Heart
Let's Get Together
I've Got You Under My Skin
Hallelujah
There's Somebody Else But Me
Having A Ball

■ SATURDAY 24 APRIL 1937

Hughie Pastoriza, Dick Morningstar and myself took the 7:19 train up to White Plains where we went to The Westchester County Center where Joe Haymes and Richard Himber were playing. We didn't have enough money to get in (costs $1.10), so we waited outside for the guys in Haymes' band to come in. I got the autographs of Joe and 9 of the guys on a picture of Joe Haymes. Since there weren't any trains for an hour, we hitch-hiked home. Got home at 10:00pm. We didn't get to hear any tunes by the band.

RADIO LOGS

2:30PM WJZ
BOB CROSBY
Congress Hotel, Chicago
I've Got Beginner's Luck (Miller; Matlock)
Too Marvelous For Words (vocal: Kay Weber) (Matlock; Miller)
That Foolish Feeling (vocal: Bob Crosby) (Lawson; Zurke; Smith)
Dixieland Shuffle (Smith; Miller; Matlock; Lawson)
Struttin' With Some Barbecue (Miller's tenor, etc)
I've Got My Love To Keep Me Warm (vocal: Kay Weber)
You Showed Me The Way (vocal: Bob Crosby)
Between The Devil And The Deep Blue Sea

7.00PM WABC
SATURDAY NIGHT SWING SESSION No42
CBS Studio No1, 485 Madison Ave, NYC
I Found A New Baby
Someday, Sweetheart (Eddie Condon, guitar and Ray Biondi, violin – from the Hickory House: swell)
Too Marvelous For Words (CBS Band under the direction of Leith Stevens)
Honeysuckle Rose (LES LIEBER, only about 20 yrs-old, playing that 4-inch hot fife)
Nobody's Sweetheart (LES LIEBER doing an encore: he sure can swing on that thing!)
Okey-Doke (NOBLE SISSLE with SIDNEY BECHET playing the soprano sax as only he can)
Characteristic Blues (NOBLE SISSLE with SIDNEY BECHET)
How Could You?
Keep Smilin' At Trouble (Eddie Condon, guitar, and Ray Biondi, violin, really jamming)
It Don't Mean A Thing

11.00PM WABC
BENNY GOODMAN
Hotel Pennsylvania, NYC
Heard this program at Dottie Kaiser's house in Bronxville.
Did You Forget? (vocal: Frances Hunt)
Can't We Be Friends? (colossal: Ballard's trombone)
I Can't Lose That Longing For You (vocal: Frances Hunt)
Blue Skies
Goodnight, My Love (vocal: Frances Hunt)
Chlo-e (Harry James' trumpet; Stacy's piano)
Tea For Two (BG Quartet) (great work by Wilson)
I'm Hatin' This Waitin' Around For You (vocal: Frances Hunt)
Down South Camp Meetin'
Goodbye (closing theme) (James' muted trumpet)

11:45PM WMCA
TEDDY HILL
Savoy Ballroom, NYC
Nuttsy.
The You And Me That Used To Be (vocal: Bill Dillard)
Always
Swingtime In The Rockies
I Know That You Know (featuring Shad Collins' trumpet)

12:00 MIDNIGHT WJZ
BOB CROSBY
Congress Hotel, Chicago
South Rampart Street Parade (colossal: Matty Matlock's clarinet; brass section)
September In The Rain (vocal: Kay Weber) (Eddie Bergman's violin; Miller's slow tenor; Matlock)
Boo Hoo (vocal: Nappy Lamare)
Just Strolling (colossal piece written by Joe Sullivan: Bob Zurke's super-great piano; Lamare's guitar)
I Can't Lose That Longing For You (vocal: Bob Crosby) (Miller's ballsy tenor; Lawson)
On A Little Bamboo Bridge (Lawson; Miller w Bauduc; Smith; Matlock)
Sentimental And Melancholy (vocal: Kay Weber)
Honeysuckle Rose (Smith; Bauduc, etc)

APRIL 1937

12:30AM WMCA
JIMMIE LUNCEFORD
Nixon-Grand Theater, Philadelphia
Jazznocracy (theme) (swell theme: trumpet)
Running A Temperature (vocal: Sy Oliver)
Honest And Truly (vocal: Dan Grissom) (trumpet)
Margie (trombones; tenor; trumpet)
Organ Grinder's Swing (overdone: some parts OK)
I'm Nuts About Screwy Music (vocal: Willie Smith)
Tain't Good (vocal: Trio) (vocal trio: Willie Smith; Eddie Tompkins; Sy Oliver)
Bugle Call Rag (guitar; tenor; trumpet: great ending)

3:00AM WBZ
TEDDY HILL
Savoy Ballroom, NYC
Uptown Rhapsody (theme)
Swing In The Spring (Frankie Newton's trumpet)
Big Boy Blue (vocal: Bill Dillard)
Twilight In Turkey (WONDERFUL)
Sensation (clarinets; trombone, etc)
My Blue Heaven (vocal: Bill Dillard)
China Boy (Sam Allen's piano)
The You And Me That Used To Be (vocal: Bill Dillard)
Study In Brown
Marie
The Love Bug Will Bite You (3 trumpets)
Uptown Rhapsody (theme) (Newton's trumpet)

■ SUNDAY 25 APRIL 1937

RADIO LOGS

6:30PM WOR
FUN IN SWINGTIME
WOR Studios, NYC
Del Schubert announces. The Bunny Berigan Orchestra.
Swanee River (Berigan's trumpet; Art Drelinger's tenor)
Never In A Million Years (great sax section, etc)
Ah, Sweet Mystery Of Life (Bunny Berigan's trumpet; saxes)
Star Dust (featuring Bunny Berigan's trumpet; solid rhythm section; saxes)
What Will I Tell My Heart?

■ MONDAY 26 APRIL 1937

RECORDING SESSION

LIONEL HAMPTON AND HIS ORCHESTRA
Recording session for Victor in New York City.
Lionel Hampton (vib/voc/p/d); Buster Bailey (cl); Johnny Hodges (as); Jess Stacy (piano); Allan Reuss (g); John Kirby (b); Cozy Cole (d)
On The Sunny Side Of The Street (vLH) / *Rhythm, Rhythm [I Got Rhythm]* / *China Stomp [Chinatown]* (pLH-JS) / *I Know That You Know* (dLH)

WOODY HERMAN AND HIS ORCHESTRA
Recording session for Decca in New York City.
Woody Herman (cl/as/voc/ldr); Clarence Willard, Kermit Simmons (t); Joe Bishop (fh); Neal Reid (tb); Murray Williams, Don Watt (as); Saxie Mansfield, Bruce Wilkins (ts); Nick Hupfer (vln); Horace Diaz (p); Chick Reeves (g); Walter Yoder (b); Frank Carlson (d)
Dupree Blues (vWH) / *Doctor Jazz* (vWH) / *Trouble In Mind* (vWH) / *It Happened Down In Dixieland* (vWH)

RADIO LOGS

9:00pm WJZ
GOOD TIME SOCIETY
CBS Studios, NYC
Twilight In Turkey (TEDDY HILL'S Band: trumpet; drums)

You Showed Me The Way (vocal: Four Inkspots)
A Study In Brown (TEDDY HILL'S Band: sax; trombone)
Whoa, Babe (vocal: Four Inkspots)
I Know That You Know (sax; piano; trumpet)
(theme)

Teddy Hill and his Band

11:00PM WMCA
FRANKIE WARD
Penthouse, Hotel Bradford, Boston
This Year's Crop of Kisses (sax; Frankie Ward's vibraphone)
Was It Rain? (vocal: Carmen Trudeau)
History Of Jazz Band—At The Jazz Band Ball (sax; vibes; trumpet; oboe; clarinets; drums)
Where Is The Sun? (vocal: Carmen Trudeau) (swell song)
Beginner's Luck

11:30PM ??
PAUL WHITEMAN
Drake Hotel, Chicago
Night And Day (written by Cole Porter)
Sonny Boy (vocal: Jack Teagarden)
New Love (vocal: Jimmy Brierley) (played for first time: written by band's violinist, Matt Malneck)
Heat Wave
What Will I Tell My Heart?
Was It Rain? (vocal: Jimmy Brierley)
Love Me Or Leave Me (vocal: Jack Teagarden) (Charlie Teagarden's trumpet)
Little Girl Blue
Bugle Call Rag

12:00 MIDNIGHT WJZ
BOB CROSBY
Congress Hotel, Chicago
The Old Spinning Wheel (colossal: intro; Bauduc; Lawson; Matlock; Zurke's piano)
What Will I Tell My Heart? (vocal: Kay Weber) (Warren Smith's trombone; Zurke; Lawson)
Slummin' On Park Avenue (arranged by Matty Matlock: Miller's great tenor; Lawson's trumpet)
There'll Be Some Changes Made (vocal: Bob Crosby) (colossal vocal; Miller; Matlock's clarinet)
Tin Roof Blues (BOBCATS: Smith's slow, moaning, swinging, super-colossal trombone; Matlock)
Here Comes Your Pappy (vocal: Nappy Lamare) (Eddie Miller; Haggart's solid bass; Matlock's clarinet)
Just Strolling (written by Joe Sullivan: colossal piano by Bob Zurke; Lamare's guitar; slow clarinets)
Royal Garden Blues (Matlock's swell clarinet; Smith's trombone; Lawson; Miller's tenor)

12:00 MIDNIGHT WOR
TOMMY DORSEY
Hotel Commodore, NYC
This Year's Kisses (vocal: Edythe Wright)
Never In A Million Years (vocal: Jack Leonard)
Easy To Remember (swing arrangement)
There's A Lull In My Life (vocal: Edythe Wright)
52nd Street (vocal: Edythe Wright & Three Esquires)
Song Of India (Tough's drums; Dorsey; Erwin; Freeman)
The Milk Man's Matinee (vocal: Edythe Wright)
Marie (vocal: Jack Leonard & band) (GREAT: Tommy Dorsey and Bud Freeman especially)
Down South Camp Meetin' (wonderful: saxes; brass)
I'm Getting Sentimental Over You (theme)

■ TUESDAY 27 APRIL 1937

RECORDING SESSION
DUKE ELLINGTON AND HIS ORCHESTRA
Recording session for Master Records in New York City.
Duke Ellington (p); Wallace Jones, Cootie Williams (t); Rex Stewart (c); Joe Nanton, Lawrence Brown (tb); Juan Tizol (vtb); Barney Bigard (cl); Johnny Hodges (cl/ss/as); Otto Hardwick (as/bsx); Harry Carney (cl/as/bar); Fred Guy (g); Hayes Alvis, Billy Taylor (b); Sonny Greer (d); Ivie Anderson (voc)
Azure / The Lady Who Couldn't Be Kissed

RADIO LOGS

8:45PM WHN
ERSKINE HAWKINS
Harlem Uproar House, NYC
Nuttsy. Brothers Paul Bascomb (tenor sax) and Wilbur Bascomb (trumpet) are in the band. Ray Sanders announced.
I Found A New Baby (wonderful: Paul Bascomb's tenor; Hawkins' trumpet; brass; rhythm)
Big Boy Blue (vocal: Jimmy Mitchelle) (super-colossal saxes with trumpet; nice long clarinet solo)
Trust In Me
That's Life I Guess (vocal: Wilbur Bascomb) (nuttsy song: just how I feel now)
I've Got My Love To Keep Me Warm (vocal: Jimmy Mitchelle) (Avery Parrish's swell piano solo)
If You Leave Me (vocal: Jimmy Mitchelle) (ballsy song: Paul Bascomb's tenor; trumpet)
Swingin' In Harlem (great: saxes and brass; drums; marvelous tenor; trumpet; bass sax)
Campus Serenade (theme)

9:30PM WABC
BENNY GOODMAN
Camel Caravan program, NYC
Remember (colossal, better than record: McEachern's smooth trombone; Musso's great tenor)
Nagasaki (BG Quartet)
All The World Is Oaksie-Doaksie (vocal: Frances Hunt & Benny Goodman) (written especially for Jack Oakie and Camel Caravan)
Roll 'Em (super-wonderful: Stacy; Benny; muted wa-wa brass; Krupa)

10:30PM WOR
DUKE ELLINGTON
Cotton Club, NYC
Marvelous. Nobody can touch the Duke and his particular swing style!! Nothing can be said to give Duke and his band as much credit as they deserve. They are one of the oldest, swinginest, and best bands in the history of jazz. Roger Lyons announced.
The Duke Steps Out (trumpet; trombone; tenor; Tizol; Hardwick; bass)
Yearning For Love (a trombone concerto by Lawrence Brown: rather slow, wonderful trombone)
I Kiss Your Hand, Madame (Barney Bigard's clarinet; Johnny Hodges' alto; trombones; Williams)
Big Chief De Sota (written by Fernando Arbello: Hodges; Williams; biting brass)
There's A Lull In My Life (vocal: Ivie Anderson) (Hardwick; saxes; Stewart's trumpet)
China Boy (featuring Johnny Hodges on soprano sax: marvelous)
Azure (Bigard's wonderful slow clarinet; great baritone sax; very slow tempo: swell)
Showboat Shuffle (written and arranged by Ellington: Stewart; saxes)

11:00PM WABC
TOMMY DORSEY
Hotel Commodore, NYC
Song Of India (Tough's drum intro; Dorsey's muted high trombone; Erwin's swell trumpet; reeds)
It's The Mood That I'm In (vocal: Edythe Wright) (swell song; fair arrangement)
'Way Down Yonder In New Orleans (Pee Wee Erwin's trumpet; rest cut out for station ident)
Twilight In Turkey (Dick Jones' piano; Tough's drums; Erwin; Bud Freeman's wonderful tenor; Mince)
Nola (Mince; Freeman; Dorsey's muted trombone; Jones; saxes: good)
Marie (vocal: Jack Leonard & band) (Tommy Dorsey; Erwin; Bud Freeman)
Jamboree (vocal: Edythe Wright, Jack Leonard & Three Esquires)

■ WEDNESDAY 28 APRIL 1937

RECORDING SESSION
LUCKY MILLINDER & MILLS BLUE RHYTHM BAND
Recording session for Variety in New York City.
Lucky Millinder (voc/ldr); Charlie Shavers, Carl Warwick, Harry Edison (t); Alfred Cobbs, Wilbur De Paris (tb); Tab Smith (as); Eddie Williams, Ben Williams, Harold Arnold (ts); Billy Kyle (p); Danny Barker (g); John Williams (b); Lester Nichols (d/vib); Chuck Richards
The Lucky Swing / Let's Get Together

RADIO LOGS

9:00PM WHN
WOODY HERMAN
Roseland Ballroom, NYC
GREAT. This band has gone places the past few months. It is marvelous, colossal. 45-minute program announced by John Lang.
There's A Lull In My Life (vocal: Woody Herman) (sounds just like Isham Jones who Woody used to be with)
Royal Garden Blues (colossal: Neil Reid's trombone; Saxie Mansfield's tenor; Herman's clarinet; Joe Bishop)
I Can't Give You Anything But Love (special arrangement by Gordon Jenkins: Nick Hupfer's violin; clarinets)
Turn Off The Moon (vocal: Woody Herman)
Diga Diga Doo (wonderful swing arrangement: Frank Carlson's swell drums; Joe Bishop's flugelhorn; Woody's clarinet)
Memphis Blues (vocal: Woody Herman) (marvelous swing arrangement of W.C.Handy's old tune: piano; Carlson's drums; super-colossal vocal and clarinet by Woody; trombones)
Hometown Band (just written by the bass player with the band, Walter E. Yoder: Frank Carlson's drums; Joe Bishop's flugelhorn)
Sweet is The Word For You (vocal: Woody Herman) (Hupfer's violin)
Squeeze Me (nuttsy song by Fats Waller: Mansfield's great tenor; Bishop; Kermit Simmons' trumpet)
Ol' Man Mose (vocal: Woody Herman & band) (written by Louis Armstrong: stupendous vocal by Woody with whole band)
Was It Rain?
Blue Prelude (theme) (nuttsy slow theme)

10:00PM WMCA
FRANKIE WARD
Penthouse, Hotel Bradford, Boston
Announced by John Riley. Personnel: Frankie Ward; Eddie Brown, Sill Scafati, Charles Whitmore (trumpets); Bob Hohler, Frank Taylor (trombones); Jim Brunton, Gene Rosati (saxes); Frank Bellizia (piano); Fred Whiting (bass); Fred

Moynahan (drums); Carmen Trudeau (vocal).
The You And Me That Used To Be (vocal: Carmen Trudeau) (swell song: saxes)
At The Jazz Band Ball (arranged by Brad Fallon: Gene Rosati's tenor; Ward's vibes; Brown's trumpet)
Too Marvelous For Words (vocal: Carmen Trudeau) (featuring bassoon by Ward; tenor)
Swing High, Swing Low
Ja-Da (nuttsy: tenor; trumpet; clarinet)

10:15PM WOR
JOE SANDERS
Blackhawk Restaurant, Chicago
You're Here, You're There, You're Everywhere
I Wish I Were In Love Again (vocal: Joe Sanders)
Jammin' (vocal: Joe Sanders) (trombone; clarinet; trumpet by Jack Gillespie)
Time Out For Love (vocal: Joe Sanders)
I'll Never Forget That I Love You (theme)

11.00PM WABC
BENNY GOODMAN
Hotel Pennsylvania, NYC
Bert Parks announced.
Johnny One Note (Elman; Benny; Stacy)
Blue Hawaii (Harry James' trumpet)
That Foolish Feeling (vocal: Frances Hunt)
Goodbye (closing theme played in full: James' trumpet)
Trust In Me (vocal: Frances Hunt)
Ida, Sweet As Apple Cider (BG Quartet) (slow & fast tempo)
Carelessly (vocal: Frances Hunt) (McEachern's trombone)
I Want To Be Happy (Musso's tenor; Elman's trumpet)
More Than You Know (ballsy medium tempo: James; Musso; brass; saxes)

■ THURSDAY 29 APRIL 1937

RECORDING SESSION

BARNEY BIGARD & HIS JAZZOPATORS
Recording session for Variety in New York City.
Rex Stewart (c); Juan Tizol (vtb); Barney Bigard (cl); Harry Carney (bar); Duke Ellington (p); Billy Taylor (b); Sonny Greer (d)
Lament For A Lost Love / Four And One-Half Street / Demi-Tasse / Jazz A La Carte

HENRY 'RED' ALLEN
Recording session for Vocalion in New York City.
Henry 'Red' Allen (t/voc); Glyn Paque (cl); Tab Smith (as); Harold Arnold (ts); Luis Russell (p); Danny Barker (g); Johnny Williams (b); Paul Barbarin (d)
Sticks And Stones (vHA) / **Meet Me In The Moonlight** (vHA) / **Don't You Care What Anyone Says?** (vHA) / **A Love Song Of Long Ago** (vHA)

RADIO LOGS

6.00PM WNEW
MAKE BELIEVE BALLROOM
WNEW Studios, NYC
Martin Block runs the 'Make Believe Ballroom' every night from 5:30 to 7:00. He usually plays records but since the Benny Goodman Band got 20,000 of the 40,000 votes cast for bands, they were there in person tonight.
Let's Dance (theme) (Benny's good old theme)
Minnie The Moocher's Wedding Day (great saxes; brass; Benny; Krupa)
You Showed Me The Way (vocal: Frances Hunt) (what a song and what a band!!! Harry James; McEachern)
Benny thanked Martin Block and all the people who voted for his band in the Band Popularity Contest.
Oh, Lady Be Good (BG Trio) (Benny, as usual, introduced each member)
I've Got My Love To Keep Me Warm (colossal, what a sax section!!! Harry James' great trumpet)

September In The Rain (vocal: Peg LaCentra) (Peg LaCentra is replacing Frances Hunt as singer in the band. She worked with Art Shaw's Band until last month)
I Got Rhythm (BG Quartet) (introduced by Benny: colossal clarinet; great vibes)
You Turned The Tables On Me (vocal: Helen Ward) (she is now married, and stopped singing several months ago but appears as a special guest. She is still wonderful – still the best female vocalist there is)
I Found A New Baby (wonderful, colossal: Ziggy Elman's trumpet; Rollini's tenor; Benny)
Goodbye (closing theme) (Harry James' muted trumpet)

12.00 MIDNIGHT WOR
BENNY GOODMAN
Hotel Pennsylvania, NYC
This is the Benny Goodman Band's final broadcast from the Pennsylvania. They will be replaced tomorrow night by Bunny Berigan (former Goodman trumpeter) and his band.
Alexander's Ragtime Band (Benny's clarinet)
September In The Rain (vocal: Peg LaCentra)
'Cause My Baby Says It's So (Harry James' trumpet; Benny)
The You And Me That Used To Be (vocal: Frances Hunt)
Mr. Ghost Goes To Town (NUTTSY: James' trumpet)
There's A Lull In My Life (vocal: Peg LaCentra)
Liza (BG Quartet)
How Could You? (vocal: Frances Hunt)
Sometimes I'm Happy (MARVELOUS: Griffin's trumpet; Musso's tenor)
Big John Special (nuttsy piece: saxes; James; brass)

■ FRIDAY 30 APRIL 1937

RADIO LOGS

12:15AM WJZ
BOB CROSBY
Congress Hotel, Chicago
Between The Devil And The Deep Blue Sea (GREAT: Lawson; Matlock; Smith; Miller)
Carelessly (vocal: Kay Weber) (swell sweet ballad: Eddie Miller's swell tenor with Bauduc's drums)
They All Laughed (vocal: Bob Crosby) (Yank Lawson's trumpet; Matlock's clarinet; solid bass by Bob Haggart)
Honeysuckle Rose (trumpet section; Lawson; Miller; swell clarinet by Matlock; Smith's great trombone; Bauduc)

12.30AM WABC
BENNY GOODMAN
Hotel Statler, Boston
From Station WEEI.
Let's Dance (theme)
Love Me Or Leave Me (great: Benny's clarinet; Musso's tenor; Stacy's piano; Reuss's guitar; James' trumpet)
Never In A Million Years (vocal: Peg LaCentra) (Benny; saxes; Harry James' trumpet)
Moonlight And Shadows (lousy song: Benny; fair tenor by Musso; sax section; great trumpet by Harry James)
There's A Lull In My Life (vocal: Peg LaCentra) (swell song: Ziggy Elman's muted sweet trumpet; saxes; brass)
Camel Hop (trumpet intro; saxes-brass; McEachern's ballsy trombone; super-colossal trumpet by Harry James; Musso; Benny)
They Can't Take That Away From Me (vocal: Peg LaCentra) (wonderful: saxes; Benny's great clarinet)
Limehouse Blues (BG Quartet) (outstanding work by all four, especially Benny & Teddy)
Between The Devil And The Deep Blue Sea (vocal: Peg LaCentra) (COLOSSAL: wonderful arrangement; good vocal; James; Benny)
I Found A New Baby (wonderful: intro; Krupa; saxes-brass; Benny; James; Rollini's tenor sax)
You Showed Me The Way (vocal: Peg LaCentra) (Sis Doyle did it a few months ago–but no more: James; McEachern; Benny)

X Marks The Spot—

by Bob Inman

From BRONXVILLE HIGH SCHOOL MIRROR:

With school gradually coming to a close, we seem to have regents marking more spots than any x's will. Regardless of regents, however, we must have our night life. With Benny Goodman and Red Norvo out of town, the heart of dance music has gone. Duke Ellington and Jimmy Dorsey plus the numerous jam bands around town are the only things left for those who like their swing. If you like a lot of sepian floor show, plenty of the Duke's music, and have a dollar and a half, the Cotton Club is the place. For a quiet evening for just dancing, the very modern Terrace Room of the Hotel New Yorker is the place. Jimmy Dorsey's music has a distinctive style with dusky June Richmond and drummer man, Ray McKinley, furnishing plenty of comedy.

For anyone who hasn't been to the Savoy Ballroom in Harlem, life just isn't complete. Not only do they have continuous dancing to two of the leading colored bands, but the dancing on the floor is terrific. I know of no place in the world where both white and black people get together and let themselves relax as they dance to the real "in the groove" music. The "Lindy Hop" is the usual dance, with enough rhythm to keep the floor actually going up and down. If you happen to be there Saturday night around 12:30 (it's open till 4:00) the "Lindy Hop" contest will give you a certain feeling and sensation for rhythm that you've never realized before. Some people like to dance. Others like to watch the orchestras and dancers, while still others like to study the psychology of the negroes, their humor and nonchalance. Don't let anybody tell you that the Savoy is a dirty place, either. It's one of our most modern ballrooms. Don't miss a show like the Savoy.

The smaller spots along 52nd Street and in Greenwich Village are where the jam bands play to be watched rather than danced to. Although Nick's Tavern in Greenwich Village has continuous entertainment featuring Bobby Hackett's subdued swing combination, it also has dancing. The most moderate prices prevail here and the atmosphere is excellent. Hackett's technique on the trumpet makes him one of the greatest. Three members of his band used to play along with Benny Goodman "way back when" in Chicago.

Of course you all know of the Hickory House and Onyx Club on 52nd Street. Joe Marsala, of the Hickory House, not only swings it but gives you a grand time with his smile and cordiality. Then there's "Stuff" Smith with his hot violin and band at the Onyx. This swing tends toward jungle rhythm.

If you visit all these places, you'll know the greatest swing circuit in the world.

■ SATURDAY 1 MAY 1937

RADIO LOGS

7.00pm WABC
SATURDAY NIGHT SWING SESSION No43
CBS Studio No1, 485 Madison Ave, NYC
Announced by Paul Douglas and Mel Allen. Leith Stevens conducted CBS Band.
Scattin' At The Kit-Kat (great song by Duke Ellington: Manners' alto; saxes; brass; Williams' drums)
You're Not The Kind (SUPER-COLOSSAL: What a song!!! What a band!!! clarinet; saxes; trumpet; brass)
Star Dust (ADELE GIRARD, girl swing harpist, from the Hickory House playing great harp; Williams' drums)
Dark Eyes (Russian classic in swing style, played by TOMMY DORSEY's Band from the Hotel Commodore: stupendous clarinet by Johnny Mince; GREAT trumpet by Pee Wee Erwin; wonderful tenor by Bud Freeman; Dave Tough's colossal drums; Dorsey)
Jammin' (GREAT! REAL jammin' by whole DORSEY Band, especially Mince; Erwin: vocal by EDYTHE WRIGHT)
Adam's Apple (LOU RED EVANS playing a swell swing song, first time on air)
Sweet Sue (Encore by LOU RED EVANS; solid rhythm section)
The Girl With The Light Blue Hair (Raymond Scott Quintet playing his latest composition: medium tempo; Pumiglio; Wade; Harris)
Powerhouse (Encore by Scott's Quintet: Wade's trumpet; Dave Harris' tenor; Johnny Williams' drums; Lou Shoobe's bass; Pumiglio)
By Heck! (WONDERFUL: Bunny Berigan?; Shoobe; saxes)

12:00 MIDNIGHT WJZ
BOB CROSBY
Congress Hotel, Chicago
Warren Smith, the hot trombonist who replaced Mark Bennett several months ago, was rumored as joining up with Benny Goodman last June. He joined Abe Lyman's band instead and then to Crosby's Band. Mark Bennett is now with Ruby Newman.
The Old Spinning Wheel (wonderful: Matlock; Lawson; Miller; Bob Zurke's great piano)
You Showed Me The Way (vocal: Bob Crosby) (Warren Smith's trombone; Lawson; Matlock; marvelous vocal)
Slummin' On Park Avenue (Miller's tenor; Smith's swell trombone; Lawson)
When Love Is Young (vocal: Kay Weber) (lousy song-fair arrangement-good vocal: Miller)
At The Jazz Band Ball (ballsy old piece: Matty Matlock; Miller's great tenor; Bauduc; Smith's trombone)
To A Sweet And Pretty Thing (vocal: Bob Crosby) (lousy song, but another great relaxed vocal)
Jamboree (colossal: intro by brass; Smith's trombone with clarinets; Matlock's dirty clarinet in Pee Wee style; Miller's relaxed tenor; Smith again really taking off)
Summertime (theme) (Zeke Zarchy's trumpet?; Miller's tenor)

■ SUNDAY 2 MAY 1937

RADIO LOGS

6:30pm WOR
FUN IN SWINGTIME
WOR Studios, NYC
Bunny Berigan and his Band opened last Friday at the Madhattan Room of the Hotel Pennsylvania, replacing Benny Goodman's Band.
Boo Hoo (Berigan's trumpet; Leary's trombone; Drelinger)
You Showed Me The Way
Carelessly (Bunny Berigan's trumpet solo)
Kiss Me Again

THE EVENT OF THE YEAR
NUTTINGS ON THE CHARLES WALTHAM TONIGHT
The Greatest Swing Band in America
The Swingmaster in person
BENNY GOODMAN
and the Goodman Quartet, With Teddy Wilson, Gene Kruppa & Lionel Hampton
Dancing 8 to 1 A.M. Admission $1 plus tax
TOMORROW NIGHT—Directly After Coast to Coast Broadcast—NORTH SHORE GARDENS, Salem
Only Other Mass. Appearance, Thursday, Cook's Butterfly Ballroom, Springfield

■ MONDAY 3 MAY 1937

RADIO LOGS

9:00PM WHN
ERSKINE HAWKINS
Harlem Uproar House, NYC
Announced by Ray Sanders.
Campus Serenade (theme) (ballsy theme: Hawkins' high trumpet; sax section)
When I Grow Too Old To Dream (vocal: Jimmy Mitchelle) (swing style: Paul Bascomb's tenor; trumpet)
I Can't Lose That Longing For You (vocal: Jimmy Mitchelle)
When My Dreamboat Comes Home (great bass sax, super-colossal arrangement: trumpet)
Any Time, Any Day, Any Where (trombone; nuttsy tenor in Don Redman style; Avery Parrish's piano)
Dear Old Southland (GREAT: brass; saxes; drums; muted trumpet; tenor sax; trumpet; bass sax)
The Uproar Shout (COLOSSAL: bass sax in Otto Hardwick style; swell trumpet; piano; tenor like Chu Berry)
Big John Special (swell tune: ragged saxes and trumpets. What a tenor sax!!! trumpet; piano)

■ TUESDAY 4 MAY 1937

RECORDING SESSION

STUFF SMITH & HIS ONYX CLUB BOYS
Recording session for Decca in New York City.
Jonah Jones (t); Buster Bailey (cl); Stuff Smith (vln/voc); Clyde Hart (p); Bobby Bennett (g); Mack Walker (b); Cozy Cole (d)
Twilight In Turkey / Where Is The Sun? (vSS) / Upstairs / Onyx Club Spree (vSS) / Onyx Club Stomp (vSS)

RADIO LOGS

8:45PM WHN
ERSKINE HAWKINS
Harlem Uproar House, NYC
This fellow Paul Bascomb is a great tenor sax player. There is also a swell bass sax player. Poor drummer and trombonist.
Whoa, Babe! (Bascomb's tenor)
Moonlight And Shadows (lousy)
When The Poppies Bloom Again
Old Folks At Home (swell: Bascomb's tenor; Hawkins' trumpet; Parrish's piano)
Does Your Heart Beat For Me? (vocal: Jimmy Mitchelle) (Bascomb's tenor)
What Will I Tell My Heart? (vocal: Trio [Mitchelle/Edward Sims/Robert Range]) (nuttsy tenor)
Swingtime In The Rockies (tenor; Hawkins' trumpet; Parrish's piano)
St. Louis Blues (weak trombone; great tenor; piano; muted trumpet)

9:30PM WABC
BENNY GOODMAN
Camel Caravan program, NYC
I Want To Be Happy (Musso; James; Benny)
Never In A Million Years (vocal: Peg LaCentra) (Harry James' trumpet)
'Cause My Baby Says It's So (fair song from new film *The Singing Marine*: Benny; James)
Runnin' Wild (BG Quartet) (wonderful)

10:30PM WOR
DUKE ELLINGTON
Cotton Club, 48th Street, NYC
The Cotton Club is open every night for dinner and after supper.
The Jig Waltz (Bigard's fast clarinet; Cootie Williams' great trumpet; Sonny Greer's drums; saxes)
Old Plantation (vocal: Ivie Anderson) (intro by Williams' trumpet; Joe Nanton's wa-wa trombone; typical Barney Bigard clarinet–slow, long high notes; great sax run; wa-wa brass)
Caravan (8 members of band led by Barney Bigard: Tizol; Williams; Harry Carney's ballsy baritone sax; Bigard; Nanton)
I've Got To Be A Rugcutter (vocal: Ivie Anderson & Trio) (Ellington's piano intro; trumpet; Greer's drums; Bigard's clarinet; great baritone & tenor sax)
Azure (Ellington's latest piece, somewhat in the same style as 'Mood Indigo': trio of Bigard's clarinet, Nanton's trombone and Whetsel's trumpet playing slow and soft)
Christopher Columbus (swing tune written by Fletcher Henderson but arranged by Ellington: Hodges; Whetsel's muted trumpet)
Clarinet Lament (written by Ellington and Bigard: Bigard's great slow–not intricate–clarinet. I have never heard a style like Bigard's—he is wonderful)
Jive Stomp (Ellington's piano; Harry Carney's baritone sax; saxes; Stewart's trumpet; Bigard; brass)
East St. Louis Toodle-Oo (theme) (written by Ellington in 1926)

11:05PM WABC
FRANK DAILEY
Meadowbrook, N.J.
Swell. Great tenor sax player with band. Announced by Bert Parks.
Oh, Lady Be Good (clarinet; brass; tenor)
That Foolish Feeling (vocal: Louise Wallace)
My Melancholy Baby (swell tenor sax; clarinet)
Turn off The Moon (vocal: Louise Wallace)
Dinah (slow: saxes; trombone; stinky accordion)
Without Your Love (vocal: Louise Wallace)
Honeysuckle Rose (trumpet; tenor; clarinet)
Gypsy Violins (theme) (slow)

11:30PM WABC
GUS ARNHEIM
Hotel New Yorker, NYC
The Love Bug Will Bite You (Joe Dixon's swell clarinet; trombone; piano)
Blue Hawaii (vocal: Ray Foster) (typical sweet Dixon clarinet solo)
Crazy Rhythm (great trombone; saxes vibes; Dixon; trumpet)
Swing, Swing Mother-In-Law (vocal: John Hamilton) (Joe Dixon; trumpet)
Sentimental And Melancholy (vocal: June Robbins) (trombone)
Exactly Like You (Joe Dixon's clarinet; trumpet; drums; tenor)
Alone With You (vocal: Ray Foster) (Joe Dixon's clarinet)
You're Driving Me Crazy (Joe Dixon's swell clarinet)
You Showed Me The Way (vocal: June Robbins)
Say It With Music (theme)

■ WEDNESDAY 5 MAY 1937

RADIO LOGS

9:00PM WABC
ANDRÉ KOSTELANETZ
Chesterfield Cigarette program, NYC
Announced by David Ross. André Kostelanetz' 45-piece band can really swing out when given the chance. Since Kostelanetz was sick, Harry Hoffman conducted.
May I Have The Next Romance?
Group Of English Folk Songs (vocal: Chorus)
March Á La Swing (Toots Mondello's clarinet?)
The Last Rose Of Summer (vocal: Lily Pons)
Slap That Bass (vocal: Chorus) (GREAT: basses; saxes; chorus)
Vilia (vocal: Lily Pons) (classical piece)

9:45PM WHN
HENRY BIAGINI
Roseland Ballroom, NYC
Good.
Big Boy Blue (tenor; clarinet)
September In The Rain (vocal: Selva Castle)
Exactly Like You (tenor; clarinet; piano; bass)
There's A Lull In My Life (vocal: Bill Schiller)
Clarinet Marmalade (tenor; clarinet; trumpet)
Shall We Dance? (vocal: Bill Schiller)
When I Take My Sugar To Tea
Love, What Are You Doing To My Heart? (vocal: Selva Castle)
Limehouse Blues (great: tenor; trumpet)

The Skeleton In The Closet (vocal: Selva Castle) (tenor)
When Love Is Young (vocal: Bill Schiller)
Darktown Strutters' Ball (vocal: ?) (clarinet)
One, Two, Three Little Hours (vocal: Bill Schiller)
I Can't Break The Habit Of You (trumpet)

10:30PM WOR
DUKE ELLINGTON
Cotton Club, NYC
MARVELOUS.
The Haywood Breakdown (COLOSSAL: Cootie Williams' trumpet; Hardwick's bass sax; Bigard; clarinets)
Azure (destined to become one of the biggest hits of 1937: wonderful—so soft and slow)
Drop Me Off At Harlem (vocal: Ivie Anderson) (piano intro; trombone; bass saxes with muted trumpet)
Sumpin' 'Bout Rhythm (vocal: Ivie Anderson) (trumpet intro; Hodges; bass sax; sax section with Greer's drums)
You Can't Run Away From Love (very slow foxtrot: Harry Carney's nuttsy baritone sax; Hodges' swell alto; trombone. Swell)
The Lady Who Couldn't Be Kissed (very new: Carney's baritone sax; Rex Stewart's trumpet; trombone)
In A Sentimental Mood (written by Ellington last year, what a super-colossal sweet piece: saxes; trombone)
Land Of Jam (Hardwick's bass sax; Williams' & Whetsel's trumpets; Hodges; Bigard)
Scattin' At The Kit-Kat (GREAT: trumpet intro; saxes with wa-wa brass; Williams' trumpet)

11:05PM WABC
BUNNY BERIGAN
Hotel Pennsylvania, NYC
Bunny Berigan, greatest living trumpetist, started his own band about 3 months ago under the management of Rockwell-O'Keefe. He opened last Friday at the Madhattan Room of the Hotel Pennsylvania, replacing Benny Goodman's Band. Announced by Bert Parks.
The You And Me That Used To Be
Swanee River (Art Drelinger's swell tenor; Berigan's great trumpet; Leary's trombone)
Wake Up And Live (vocal: Carol McKay) (good: Drelinger's slow tenor)
Big John Special (wonderful piece, arranged by Fletcher Henderson: saxes; trombone; Bunny)
September In The Rain (vocal: Ford Leary)
Trees (swell: Bunny's trumpet; saxes)
I'm Gonna Kiss Myself Goodbye (vocal: Ford Leary)
It's Swell Of You (vocal: Carol McKay)
Kiss Me Again

11:30PM WMCA
TINY BRADSHAW-EDGAR HAYES
Apollo Theater, NYC
Star Dust (Edgar Hayes piano solo with band: swell)
Goin' Places (Tiny Bradshaw directing band, swell: sax; clarinet)

11:30PM WABC
GUS ARNHEIM
Hotel New Yorker, NYC
John Allen Wolf announced.
Little Old Lady
Am I Wasting My Time? (vocal: Ray Foster)
What Will I Tell My Heart? (vocal: June Robbins)
Angry (Joe Dixon's ballsy clarinet; drums; trombone)
Star Dust (nuttsy: sax section; tenor sax)
Oh, Say, Can You Swing? (vocal: John Hamilton)
You're My Everything
Stars Fell On Alabama
Silent Love
The Goona Goo

12:00 MIDNIGHT WJZ
BOB CROSBY
Congress Hotel, Chicago
Between The Devil And The Deep Blue Sea (Lawson's trumpet; Miller's tenor; Matlock)
Trust In Me (vocal: Kay Weber) (Miller)
In A Little Hula Heaven (Miller; Matlock; Lawson; Zurke; Bauduc; Haggart's solid bassing)
You Showed Me The Way (vocal: Bob Crosby) (Yank Lawson's trumpet; Matlock; Smith)
Gin Mill Blues (colossal: Miller's long tenor; Zurke's long piano; Matlock; clarinets; Bauduc)
To A Sweet And Pretty Thing (vocal: Bob Crosby) (Lawson)
Summer Nights (vocal: Kay Weber)
Honeysuckle Rose (Lamare; Lawson; Matlock, etc)

■ THURSDAY 6 MAY 1937

HINDENBURG CRASHES IN FLAMES IN LAKEHURST

RECORDING SESSION

TOMMY DORSEY AND HIS ORCHESTRA
Recording session for Victor in New York City.
Tommy Dorsey (tb); Pee Wee Erwin, Joe Bauer, Andy Ferretti (t); Les Jenkins, Red Bone (tb); Johnny Mince, Fred Stulce, Mike Doty (cl/as); Bud Freeman (ts); Howard Smith (p); Carmen Mastren (g); Gene Traxler (b); Dave Tough (d); Edythe Wright, Jack Leonard (voc)
Love Is Never Out Of Season (vJL) / *Our Penthouse On Third Avenue* (vJL) / *Mountain Music* (vEW) / *Good Mornin'* (vEW)

RADIO LOGS

8:32PM WOR
CHARLES DORNBERGER
Hotel Roosevelt, NYC
Announced by Roger Lyon. Fair.
They Can't Take That Away From Me
Moonglow
Boo Hoo
A Sailboat In The Moonlight
Wake Up And Live
Where Is The Sun?
Rusty Hinge
The Moon Is In The Sky (vocal: Bill Wendell)
Answer
Where Are You?

10:30PM WMCA
FRANKIE WARD
Penthouse, Hotel Bradford, Boston
When Love Is Young (Ward's bassoon; saxes)

This Year's Crop Of Kisses (Ward's vibraharp; trumpet)
At The Jazz Band Ball (tenor; Ward's vibes; trumpet; strong rhythm section; clarinets; Ward's bassoon)
Where Is The Sun? (vocal: Carmen Trudeau)
Swing High, Swing Low
Swamp Fire (swell: brass; drums; rhythm)

Autographs of the Frankie Ward Band sent on a postcard from the Hotel Bradford in Boston

FRIDAY 7 MAY 1937

RECORDING SESSION

CHARLIE BARNET AND HIS ORCHESTRA
Recording session for Bluebird in New York City.
Charlie Barnet (ss/as/ts/voc); Irving Goodman, Frank Amaral, Al Stuart (t); Bob Fishel, James Curry (tb); Henry Galtman (cl/as); Joe Estren, Dave Gotwalls (as); Kurt Bloom (ts/voc); John Nicolini (p); Tom Morgan (g); Bob Elden (b); Buddy Schutz (d); Kathleen Long (v)
The First Time I Saw You (vCB) / *In Your Own Little Way* (vKL) / *You're Looking For Romance* (vKB) / *Love Is A Merry-go-round* (vKL) / *A Sailboat In The Moonlight* (vKB) / *He Walked Right In* (vKB,KL)

BUNNY BERIGAN
Madhattan Room, Hotel Pennsylvania, NYC

Hugh Pastoriza, Jim Poe and myself took the 9:04pm train into 138th Street from where we walked over to 140th Street and Lenox Avenue where the Savoy Ballroom is located. We tried to get in, but since it was formal night we had to go elsewhere (Teddy Hill's Band and Billy Hicks' Sizzlin' Six were playing there, and Willie Bryant is at the Apollo Theater for the week). We talked for a while to a guy who works at the Savoy. Benny Goodman and Chick Webb are going to play opposite each other this coming Tuesday. We then took the subway down to the Pennsylvania Hotel. After watching Bunny Berigan's Band from the hallway next to the Madhattan Room for a while, we saw Ed Gage, Wayman and two girls from Bronxville. We then happened to find a door leading to the kitchen, walked a long way round until finally coming to the kitchen entrance into the Madhattan Room. In this way we got in for nothing!

Bunny Berigan, considered by me and many others as the greatest living trumpeter, used to play with Benny Goodman's band; he then had his own small band at the 800 Club on 52nd Street and played on CBS' 'Saturday Night Swing Session' every Saturday night from June 1936 to February 1937; then under the management of Rockwell-O'Keefe he started his own Big Band. Berigan recognized us from seeing us at the Saturday Night Swing Sessions, and spoke to us. We made great friends with George Wettling, the drummer in the band. He really is about the best drummer there is besides Krupa. He is quite a drinker. He told us how he, Bunny Berigan, Tommy Dorsey, Fats Waller, and Dick McDonough made the Victor record of *Honeysuckle Rose* and *Blues*. They had all had plenty to drink and were feeling good except for Dorsey. Because of that, and because they didn't have any music to read, it really was a 'jam session at Victor.' He told us that we could get some swell pictures of himself and some other guys out of the next issue of Look magazine. Wettling sure is a swell guy. He was with us the whole night except when playing or drinking cocktails in the kitchen. We got his autograph on a piece of paper and in the book 'Rhythm On Record' under Paul Mares' Friars Society Orchestra. Wettling formerly played with Jack Hylton's American band and with Art Shaw's Band from December 1936 to March 1937.

We also talked with bassist Fishkind, trombonist Frankie D'Annolfo and pianist/arranger Joe Lippman. Trumpeter Cliff Natalie is the brother of Nat Natoli and they have both played on the Saturday Night Swing Sessions. Tenor saxist Clyde Rounds used to be with Tommy Dorsey and trumpeter Steve Lipkins was with Joe Venuti and Tommy Dorsey. The band played: *Stardust* / *Swanee River* / *There's A Lull In My Life* / *They Can't Take That Away From Me* / *Organ Grinder's Swing* / *Never In A Million Years* / *Boo Hoo* (vocal: Ford Leary) / *Carelessly* / *They All Laughed* / *Too Marvelous For Words* (vocal: Carol McKay) / *Wake Up And Live* (vocal: Carol McKay) / *It's Swell of You* (vocal: Carol McKay) / *Peckin'* / *Black Bottom* etc.

SATURDAY 8 MAY 1937

Trip to New York City

Hughie Pastoriza, Jim Poe and myself took the 12:40 train into NYC. We got off at Grand Central and went up to see the members of the Original Dixieland Jazz band at 30 West 58th Street, where they live, but since they are appearing with Xavier Cugat at the Paramount Theater this week they weren't there. We then went over to 799 Seventh Avenue where Mills Artists are located. We went into a private office where we met some guy who manages the new Variety and Master Records put out by Irving Mills. He gave us an issue of Jazz World (a magazine printed in Holland which we lost later in the day). His secretary gave us pictures of Duke Ellington (2 of band, 1 of him), Cab Calloway's Band, Hudson-DeLange (3 of band, 1 of DeLange). We then went to Bach Instruments at 128 West 48th Street but weren't able to get any pictures. Poe bought some drumsticks. We then went over to Rockwell-O'Keefe, on the 23rd Floor of the Rockefeller Center, where we met Vincent Prior. He told us he was leaving the offices to go out to Columbus, Ohio, with Glen Gray's Casa Loma orchestra, acting as an understudy to Gray's road manager who is supposed to be the best road manager there is. At Columbus he was leaving Gray's Band to go and meet Bob Crosby's Band in Illinois where he is going to travel around with the band. He will probably manage a band himself some day. He told us that Woody Herman left Roseland Ballroom last week and is at the Normandie Ballroom in Boston for 10 days. Before saying goodbye he gave us pictures of Pee Wee Hunt, Glen Gray's band, Louis Armstrong (1 of band, 4 of Louis), Bob Crosby's Band, 3 of Andy Kirk's Band, Peg LaCentra, Claude Hopkins' Band, and Woody Herman. We then went over to Conn where we asked W. H. Shine if they had any new pictures to give us. Since they had just moved he told us to come back for them in a few weeks. There we met Russell G. Mason who represents Conn in Westchester County and who lives in Mount Vernon. He offered us a ride home but we declined since we were staying in to see the Swing Session. We then went over to a magazine store to ask if we could sell any issues of Life, but they are only worth 35 cents apiece now. We then went over to the Public Library and looked up old articles on jazz. After that we went to the Hot Club, 144 E42nd Street, where we met Milt Gabler who owns the store. Hughie bought Tommy Dorsey's Victor record of *Twilight In Turkey / Milkman's Matinee* and Duke Ellington's *East St. Louis Toodle-Oo / I've Got To Be A Rugcutter* (first record released by Master).

Went up to the CBS Studios at 485 Madison Avenue where we tried to get in on an old ticket, without success. After asking people, however, we finally succeeded in getting three tickets. We only got the autographs of Leslie Lieber and new trombonist J. D. Smith who replaced Joe Vargas.

7.00PM WABC
SATURDAY NIGHT SWING SESSION No44
CBS Studio No1, 485 Madison Ave, NYC
Announced by Paul Douglas and Mel Allen. Leith Stevens conducted the CBS Band: Dave Wade, Jimmy Rosselli, Lloyd Williams, Nat Natoli (trumpets); Russ Genner, J. D. Smith (trombones); Hank Ross, Dave Harris, Art Manners, Pete Pumiglio (saxes); Raymond Scott (piano); Frankie Worrell (guitar); Lou Shoobe (bass); Johnny Williams (drums). Guests: Duke Ellington (piano); Les Lieber (penny whistle); Chauncey Morehouse (vibes); Joan Edwards (vocals).
Chicken And Waffles (theme)
Satan Takes A Holiday (S. Clayton's new song: Harris' tenor; Williams' drums; saxes; clarinets)
Opus No1 (CHAUNCEY MOREHOUSE, guest, playing vibraharp)
Royal Garden Blues (colossal: brass; saxes; Harris' tenor; Pumiglio's clarinet; Wade's trumpet)
Swing Session (DUKE ELLINGTON, guest, playing his new composition dedicated to the Saturday Night show)
Solitude / In A Sentimental Mood (DUKE ELLINGTON piano solos of his own compositions)
They All Laughed (Leith Stevens directing CBS Band. Nuttsy piece: brass; saxes, etc)
This Is My Last Affair (JOAN EDWARDS, guest, singing and playing piano)
Copper Colored Gal (JOAN EDWARDS, guest, singing and playing piano)
Who's Sorry Now (LES LIEBER, guest, playing penny whistle)
Some Of These Days (LES LIEBER, guest, playing penny whistle)
Scattin' At The Kit-Kat (written by Duke Ellington: Dave Harris' tenor; Williams' great drumming)

Duke Ellington and Chauncey Moorhouse left in the middle of the broadcast. After the show we went over to the Hot Club again and played records and took a picture of Milt Gabler. We would have gone to the Hotel Commodore but nobody was there. Got the 9:05 train home from Grand Central.

RADIO LOGS

11:00PM WABC
BUNNY BERIGAN
Hotel Pennsylvania, NYC
Announced by Bert Parks.
Was That The Human Thing To Do?
It's Swell Of You (vocal: Carol McKay)
All Dark People Are Light On Their Feet
You Can't Run Away from Love
Am I Blue?
Trees
You Showed Me The Way (vocal: Carol McKay)
'Cause My Baby Says It's So (vocal: Bunny Berigan)
Summer Nights
King Porter Stomp

11:30PM WMCA
TEDDY HILL
Savoy Ballroom, NYC
Announced by Joe Tobin.
Stompin' At The Savoy (theme)
I Never Knew
When Two Love Each Other (vocal: Bill Dillard)
Stop, Look, And Listen (trumpet; trombone)
Honeysuckle Rose (trombone)
Rhythm Fantasy (trombone; clarinet)
Charmaine (Sam Allen's piano; trumpet)
Sugar Blues
Sensation
Deep Forest (Sam Allen's piano)

■ SUNDAY 9 MAY 1937

RADIO LOGS

06:30PM WOR
FUN IN SWINGTIME
WOR Studios, NYC
Bunny Berigan and his Band.
Black Bottom
It's Swell Of You (vocal: Carol McKay)
'Cause My Baby Says It's So (vocal: Bunny Berigan)
Melody In F

10:30PM WAAB
WOODY HERMAN
Normandie Ballroom, Boston
Too Marvelous For Words (vocal: Woody Herman)
Weary Blues
Squeeze Me
You Showed Me The Way (vocal: Woody Herman)
In The Middle Of A Kiss
Doctor Jazz (vocal: Woody Herman)
Tin Roof Blues

■ MONDAY 10 MAY 1937

RADIO LOGS

9:00PM WHN
RED NORVO
Hotel Gibson, Cincinnati, Ohio
Appearing at the Florentine Room of the Hotel Gibson.
Theme (colossal: One of the best themes ever written)
Mean To Me (wonderful: trumpet; Herb Haymer's tenor; Hank D'Amico's clarinet; Bill Miller's piano; Norvo's xylophone)
This Is My Last Affair (vocal: Mildred Bailey) (great sax section)
Too Marvelous For Words (vocal: Stew Pletcher) (trumpet; Red; saxes)
Liza (trumpet; Norvo's xylophone; Haymer's nuttsy, solid tenor)
Dedicated To You (vocal: Mildred Bailey) (wonderful vocal)
Carelessly (Eddie Sauter arrangement of nuttsy song)
Little Joe (vocal: Mildred Bailey)
I Know That You Know (super-Colossal: Red's xylophone; Herb Haymer's tenor; Hank D'Amico's clarinet; Mastren's trumpet)

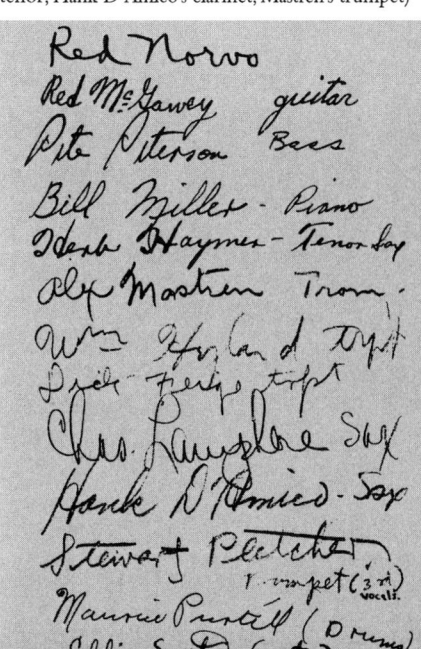

The autographs of the Red Norvo band were signed at the Blackhawk in Chicago and sent to Bob on a postcard.

12:00 MIDNIGHT WJZ
BOB CROSBY
Congress Hotel, Chicago
This is the last swing concert broadcast of Bob Crosby, but not the last broadcast. He leaves the Congress Hotel this coming Thursday (13th) night.
Jamboree (NUTTSY: Smith's trombone; Matlock's clarinet; Miller's tenor)
Wake Up And Live (vocal: Bob Crosby) (Miller's typical tenor; Matlock; Zurke's piano)
Unknown Title (7 BobCats jamming: Miller with Bauduc; Zurke; Lawson; Smith)
Trust In Me (vocal: Kay Weber) (Miller's swell tenor sax)
At The Jazz Band Ball (arranged by Bob Haggart: Matlock; Miller; Warren Smith's original hot trombone; continued jamming of whole rhythm section on background; Bauduc's great)
Just Strolling (written by Joe Sullivan depicting a boy just walking nowhere: Zurke's wonderful piano; Lamare)
They All Laughed (vocal: Bob Crosby) (real swingin' out by whole band on a popular ballad)
Steppin' Pretty (GREAT: Miller's marvelous tenor with Bauduc; wa-wa brass with saxes; Matlock)
Summertime (theme) (written by George Gershwin)

There was an incredible sight on Lenox Avenue and 140th Street Tuesday, May 11. Mounted police, the fire department, deputy inspectors, and a score of ordinary cops were required to keep in check a mob of ten thousand souls who were fighting to get into the Savoy Ballroom to hear the battle of the century between Benny Goodman and Chick Webb's orchestras. About four thousand people actually managed to jam their way into the Savoy, where four or five cops were stationed on the Goodman bandstand to maintain law and order.

■ TUESDAY 11 MAY 1937

RECORDING SESSION

BILLIE HOLIDAY & TEDDY WILSON ORCHESTRA
Recording session for Columbia in NYC.
Buck Clayton (t); Buster Bailey (cl); Johnny Hodges (as); Lester Young (ts); Teddy Wilson (p); Allan Reuss (g); Artie Bernstein (b); Cozy Cole (d); Billie Holiday (v)
Sun Showers / Yours And Mine / I'll Get By / Mean To Me

RADIO LOGS

9:30PM WABC
BENNY GOODMAN
Camel Caravan program, NYC
Alexander's Ragtime Band (swell: Benny)
Blue Hawaii (swing arrangement of lousy piece from film *Waikiki Wedding*: James)
Sweet Sue (BG Quartet) (not as good as record)
Peckin' (Harry James' great tune played for first time on air: Benny; Musso; James)

Below: A monumental meeting of two great swing bands at the Savoy Ballroom. By general consent (and Benny Goodman and Gene Krupa agreed) the clear winner was the amazing Chick Webb and his Orchestra, aided by Ella Fitzgerald.

MAY 1937

9:45PM WAAB
WOODY HERMAN
Normandie Ballroom, Boston
Maple Leaf Rag
Sweet Is The Word (vocal: Woody Herman)
Blue Skies
Dupree Blues

10:35PM WOR
DUKE ELLINGTON
Cotton Club, NYC
Roger Lyons announced.
All God's Chillun Got Rhythm (vocal: Ivie Anderson) (half of band singing: little instrumentation)
Swing Low (Rex Stewart's great long intricate trumpet passage; saxes; Harry Carney's nuttsy baritone; Cootie Williams' high screeching trumpet; Hodges)
Clarinet Lament (magnificent clarinet by Barney Bigard: soft, muffled–not sharp–but broad tone)
Every Day (Bigard's clarinet; trumpet; real swingin' out by 6 brass)
There's A Lull In My Life (vocal: Ivie Anderson) (Harry Carney's baritone; saxes with brass; trombones)
I've Got To Be A Rugcutter (vocal: Ivie Anderson & Trio) (on Master Records)
Azure (destined to become one of the biggest hits of 1937: wonderful—so soft and slow)

11:05PM WABC
GUS ARNHEIM
Hotel New Yorker, NYC
Great. Ralph Edwards announced.

Sincerely, Gus Arnheim

Serenade In The Night
April In Paris
I Surrender, Dear
Just One More Chance
Carelessly (vocal: Ray Foster)
Chinatown, My Chinatown (nuttsy: Joe Dixon's clarinet; saxes; trumpet; tenor sax; xylophone)
This Year's Crop Of Kisses (vocal: June Robbins) (tenor sax)
Sweet Lorraine (Joe Dixon's straight clarinet; brass)
Too Bad (vocal: John Hamilton) (piano; saxes; swell vocal)
You're My Everything
The Goona Goo (Arnheim's piano; trumpet, etc)
I Got Rhythm (trumpet; tenor sax)

12:00 MIDNIGHT WABC
FRANK DAILEY
Meadowbrook, N.J.
My Melancholy Baby
Good-Bye To Love
Scattin' At The Kit-Kat
Let's Kiss And Make Up
When Two Love Each Other
That Foolish Feeling (vocal: Louise Wallace)
The Rockin' Chair Swing (too much accordion, but good)
September In The Rain

■ WEDNESDAY 12 MAY 1937

RECORDING SESSION

TOMMY DORSEY AND HIS ORCHESTRA
Recording session for Victor in New York City.
Tommy Dorsey (tb); Pee Wee Erwin, Joe Bauer, Andy Ferretti (t); Les Jenkins, Red Bone (tb); Johnny Mince, Fred Stulce, Mike Doty (cl/as); Tony Antonelli (ts); Howard Smith (p); Carmen Mastren (g); Gene Traxler (b); Dave Tough (d)
Humoresque / Goin' Home

RADIO LOGS

9:00PM WHN
HENRY BIAGINI
Roseland Ballroom, NYC
William Tell (tenor)
They Can't Take That Away From Me
Spring Fever Blues
Trust In Me (vocal: Bill Schiller)
As Long As You've Got Your Health
Turn Off The Moon (vocal: Bill Schiller)
'Way Down Yonder In New Orleans (trumpet)
You Showed Me The Way (vocal: Bill Schiller)
Memphis Blues (trombone; clarinet; tenor)

11:00PM WABC
BUNNY BERIGAN
Hotel Pennsylvania, NYC
September In The Rain
Kiss Me Again (Bunny Berigan's trumpet; Gene Kinsey's clarinet; Georgie Auld's tenor; Leary's trombone)
Carelessly (vocal: Carol McKay)
Boo Hoo (vocal: Ford Leary) (trombone and vocal)
Too Marvelous For Words (vocal: Carol McKay) (clarinet)
The Goona Goo (vocal: Bunny Berigan) (Auld's tenor)
They All Laughed (vocal: Carol McKay)
You Can't Run Away From Love
Mahogany Hall Stomp

■ THURSDAY 13 MAY 1937

RECORDING SESSION

BUNNY BERIGAN AND HIS ORCHESTRA
Recording session for Victor in New York City.
Bunny Berigan, Cliff Natalie, Steve Lipkins (t); Ford Leary (tb/voc); Frank d'Annolfo (tb); Sid Perlmutter, Joe Dixon (cl/as); Clyde Rounds, George Auld (ts); Joe Lippman (p); Tom Morgan (g); Arnold Fishkind (b); George Wettling (d); Sue Mitchell (voc)
The First Time I Saw You (vFL) / *Love Is A Merry-go-round* (vSM) / *The Image Of You* (vSM) / *I'm Happy, Darling, Dancing With You* (vSM) / *Swanee River*

ART SHAW AND HIS NEW MUSIC
Recording session for Brunswick in New York City.
Art Shaw (cl/ldr); John Best, Malcolm Crain, Tom di Carlo (t); Harry Rogers, George Arus (tb); Les Robinson, Art Masters (as); Tony Pastor (ts/voc); Fred Petry (ts); Les Burness (p); Al Avola (g); Ben Ginsberg (b); Cliff Leeman (d)
All Alone / All God's Chillun Got Rhythm (vTP) / *It Goes To Your Feet* (vTP) / *Because I Love You*

RADIO LOGS

11:15PM WNAC
WOODY HERMAN
Normandie Ballroom, Boston
Carelessly (vocal: Woody Herman)
Too Marvelous For Words (vocal: Woody Herman)

11:45PM WABC
MERRY MAKERS
CBS Studio, NYC
Maybe
There's A Lull In My Life
The Moon Is In The Sky
Carelessly
How Could You?

12:00 MIDNIGHT WNEW
JOE MARSALA
Hickory House, 144 W52nd Street, NYC
Farewell Blues
Basin Street Blues
Let's Call The Whole Thing Off
Rosetta
This Is My Last Affair
I Want A Little Girl
When A Lady Meets A Gentleman Down South

12:15AM WOR
BUNNY BERIGAN
Hotel Pennsylvania, NYC
It Looks Like Rain In Cherry Blossom Lane (vocal: Carol McKay)
Star Dust (vocal: Carol McKay) (COLOSSAL: Berigan; Lippman's piano; saxes; great blues vocal)
Mr Ghost Goes To Town (NUTTSY: Georgie Auld's great tenor; Berigan; Wettling's drums)
They All Laughed (vocal: Carol McKay) (swell introduction; smooth saxes; Berigan)
Royal Garden Blues (tenor)

■ FRIDAY 14 MAY 1937

RECORDING SESSION

DUKE ELLINGTON AND HIS ORCHESTRA
Recording session for Master Records in New York City.
Duke Ellington (p); Wallace Jones, Cootie Williams (t); Rex Stewart (c); Joe Nanton, Lawrence Brown (tb); Juan Tizol (vtb); Barney Bigard (cl); Johnny Hodges (cl/ss/as); Otto Hardwick (as/bsx); Harry Carney (cl/as/bar); Fred Guy (g); Hayes Alvis, Billy Taylor (b); Sonny Greer (d); Ivie Anderson (voc)
Caravan / *Azure*

■ SATURDAY 15 MAY 1937

RADIO LOGS

2:30PM WJZ
CHICK WEBB
Savoy Ballroom, NYC
What A Shuffle! (written by Chick Webb)
I Can't Break The Habit Of You (vocal: Ella Fitzgerald)
Take It From The Top (latest Webb composition: first time on the air)
Where Are You? (vocal: Charles Linton)
I Found A New Baby
Rusty Hinge
There's A Lull In My Life (vocal: Ella Fitzgerald)
That's A-Plenty
Caravan
Let's Get Together (theme)

7.00PM WABC
SATURDAY NIGHT SWING SESSION No45
CBS Studio No1, 485 Madison Ave, NYC
Jazzeroo (Leith Stevens directing the CBS Band)
Tiger Fantasy (MANNIE KLEIN, formerly with Benny Goodman, now with NBC, playing good trumpet)
Too Marvelous For Words (CBS Band: Genner's trombone; tenor; saxes; muted trumpet)
Honey, Won't You Please Come Home (TRIO from Onyx Club (piano, guitar & drums: Don Frye–p; Teddy Bunn–g; Leo Watson–d)
Handful Of Keys (ONYX TRIO: Bunn's guitar)
Satan Takes A Holiday (COLOSSAL: clarinets; Williams' drums; Harris' tenor; brass section)
They All Laughed (Guest SUE MITCHELL, girl singing the nuts for first time on radio: she has a low voice and is to join Bunny Berigan's Band soon)
Twilight In Turkey (Raymond Scott Quintet: Dave Harris' great send-out tenor; Wade, etc)
Waddlin' At The Waldorf (swell song written by Jimmy Dorsey: Manners' alto sax; saxes)
Chicken And Waffles (theme)

11:00PM WOR
DUKE ELLINGTON
Cotton Club, NYC
Caravan
Frolic Sam
Solace (first time over air, written by Duke & Bigard: very slow–similar to *Azure*)

11:15PM WAAB
GLENN MILLER
Raymor Ballroom, Boston
Moonlight Serenade (theme)
On Moonlight Bay (whole band singing; Carney's drums; Boses trumpet)
Where Are You?
How Am I To Know? (vocal: Vi Mele)
Honeysuckle Rose
Moonlight Serenade (theme)

11:18PM WABC
BUNNY BERIGAN
Hotel Pennsylvania, NYC
Love Is A Merry-Go-Round
'Cause My Baby Says It's So (vocal: Bunny Berigan)
Big John Special

11:30PM WMCA
CHICK WEBB
Savoy Ballroom, NYC
Jam Session (McRae's tenor)
Holiday In Harlem (vocal: Ella Fitzgerald) (clarinet)
The Naughty Waltz
Charmaine
Take It From The Top (latest Webb composition: tenor; trumpet)
Clap Hands, Here Comes Charlie (Webb's swell drums)
So They Say (vocal: Ella Fitzgerald) (nuttsy song; great vocal)
Copenhagen (trombone; clarinets; wa-wa brass; clarinet)

1:30AM WOR
DICK STABILE
William Penn Hotel, Pittsburgh
Wake Up And Live (vocal: Paula Kelly)
Turn Off The Moon (vocal: Bert Shaw)
Maybe (vocal: Paula Kelly)
Sweet is The Word For You
Where Is The Sun?
Honeysuckle Rose
You Showed Me The Way (vocal: Bert Shaw)
Was It Rain? (vocal: Bert Shaw)
He Ain't Got Rhythm

■ SUNDAY 16 MAY 1937

RADIO LOGS

6:30PM WOR
BUNNY BERIGAN
WOR Studios, NYC
Toodle-Oo
They All Laughed (intro; saxes; Bunny; Leary)
You Can't Run Away From Love
Nobody's Sweetheart

MAY 1937

The Woody Herman Orchestra (l to r): Woody, Tommy Linehan, unidentified, unidentified, Saxie Mansfield, unidentified, unidentified, Clarence Willard, unidentified, Frank Carlson, Walt Yoder, Joe Bishop, Bruce Wilkins, Neal Reid.

9:30PM WAAB
WOODY HERMAN
Normandie Ballroom, Boston
Easy To Remember
Turn Off The Moon (vocal: Woody Herman)
Liza
They Can't Take That Away From Me
I Can't Give You Anything But Love
Carelessly (vocal: Woody Herman)
Doctor Jazz (vocal: Woody Herman)
My Blue Heaven
Coquette
How Am I To Know?
Blue Prelude (theme)

10:30PM WOR
DUKE ELLINGTON
Cotton Club, 48th Street, NYC
The Sheik Of Araby (trombone; Rex Stewart's trumpet; Hardwick's bass sax; Greer's drums)
Rose Room (marvelous old song: Bigard's magnificent intricate clarinet with wa-wa brass; Ellington's swell piano; Hodges)
It's Swell Of You (vocal: Ivie Anderson) (Bigard; swell trombone; trumpet)
Downtown Uproar (Cootie Williams Group: Williams' clear-toned trumpet; Hodges' great soprano sax with Hardwick's bass sax; Carney's baritone; Greer's swell drum breaks; Ellington's ballsy tinkling piano; trombone)
All God's Chillun Got Rhythm (vocal: Ivie Anderson) (Bigard; marvelous vocal)
Sad Night In Harlem (vocal: Ivie Anderson) (nuttsy Hodges; 2 basses; Bigard's clarinet behind Ivie's great vocal)
The Land Of Jam (Carney's colossal baritone; Stewart, Hodges; Williams' trumpet; Bigard)
Azure (ballsy: this will be a hit tune by September)
Scattin' At The Kit-Kat (one of Ellington's greatest pieces)

■ MONDAY 17 MAY 1937

RECORDING SESSION

TEDDY HILL AND HIS ORCHESTRA
Recording session for Bluebird in New York City.
Teddy Hill (ts/ldr); Bill Dillard (t/voc); Shad Collins, Dizzy Gillespie (t); Dicky Wells (tb); Russell Procope (cl/as); Howard Johnson (as); Robert Carroll (ts); Sam Allen (p); John Smith (g); Richard Fulbright (b); Bill Beason (d)
San Anton' (vBD) / *I'm Happy, Darling, Dancing With You* / *Yours And Mine* (vBD) / *I'm Feelin' Like A Million* (vBD) / *King Porter Stomp* / *Blue Rhythm Fantasy*

RADIO LOGS

10:30PM WOR
DUKE ELLINGTON
Cotton Club, 48th Street, NYC
Hyde Park (colossal: trumpet; Carney's baritone; Bigard's clarinet; Hodges; Whetsel's trumpet)
Old Plantation (vocal: Ivie Anderson) (from the *Cotton Club Parade*: trombone; Bigard's clarinet; Greer's solid drumming; saxes)
Trust In Me (vocal: Ivie Anderson) (nuttsy: Cootie Williams' real swing trumpet; Bigard)
Big Chief De Sota (written by Fernando Arbello: swell Hodges; Cootie hitting some real high notes. What jammin'!!! Bigard's clarinet; very solid 5-man rhythm section)
Azure (in response to many requests! Bigard's soft, muted clarinet; Carney's baritone sax)
Merry-Go-Round (written by Ellington—one of his best: Hodges; marvelous high screeching trumpet; trombone team; Bigard's marvelous clarinet; Hardwick's bass sax; super-colossal ending with whole band jamming)

Tiger Rag (Bigard's clarinet after introduction by Ellington's piano; Otto Hardwick's long bass sax solo with rhythm section; great original long trombone solo by either Nanton or Tizol; Bigard's low-high, high-low long clarinet solo—what a style!!! Rex Stewart's low trumpet; very long bass solo with Ellington's little piano inputs. 10 minutes long!)

11:15PM WNAC
GLENN MILLER
Raymor Ballroom, Boston
Moonlight Serenade (theme)
Smoke Dreams (Sterling Bose's trumpet)
Wistful And Blue (vocal: Vi Mele)
Night Over Shanghai
I Got Rhythm (Sterling Bose's trumpet)
Swinging On The Reservation
Moonlight Serenade (theme)

May 17, 1937

Mr. Bob Inman
133 Pondfield Rd.
Bronxville, N.Y.

Dear Mr. Inman:

I have your very nice letter, and certainly found a lot in it that was of considerable interest. Under separate cover, I have sent you autographs of the boys as you requested.

I do hope you could come into the Hickory some night and watch us work and possibly have a little chat.

Cordially,

Joe Marsala

9:30PM WABC
BENNY GOODMAN
Camel Caravan program, NYC
Jam Session (Musso's tenor; James' trumpet; Benny)
Big John Special (super-colossal: James' trumpet)
There's A Lull In My Life (vocal: Peg LaCentra) (nuttsy)
Diga Diga Doo (BG Quartet)

11:00PM WABC
GUS ARNHEIM
Hotel New Yorker, NYC
Blue Hawaii (vocal: Ray Foster)
Mary Lou (nuttsy: trumpet; drums)
Man In The Moon (vocal: June Robbins)
Alibi Baby (vocal: John Hamilton)
Where Or When (vocal: Ray Foster)
You're Driving Me Crazy (great: solid drums; neat trumpet; swinging brass section; Arnheim's piano; Joe Dixon's magnificent clarinet with drums)
Just A Quiet Evening
Carelessly (vocal: Ray Foster)
Sweet Is The Word For You

■ TUESDAY 18 MAY 1937

RECORDING SESSION

BENNY GOODMAN QUARTET
Recording session for Columbia in New York City.
Lionel Hampton (vib); Teddy Wilson (p); Benny Goodman (cl); Gene Krupa (d)
Diga Diga Doo

ART SHAW AND HIS NEW MUSIC
Recording session for Brunswick in New York City.
Art Shaw (cl/ldr); John Best, Malcolm Crain, Tom di Carlo (t); Harry Rogers, George Arus (tb); Les Robinson, Henry Freeman (as); Tony Pastor (ts/voc); Fred Petry (ts); Les Burness (p); Al Avola (g); Ben Ginsberg (b); Cliff Leeman (d)
Night And Day / I Surrender, Dear / Blue Skies / Someday, Sweetheart

RADIO LOGS

8:00PM WAAB
GLENN MILLER
Raymor Ballroom, Boston
Moonlight Serenade (theme)
On Moonlight Bay
Turn Off The Moon
Was It My Heart?
How Could You? (vocal: Vi Mele)
You Can't Run Away From Love (Jesse Ralph's trombone)
Moonlight Serenade (theme)

■ WEDNESDAY 19 MAY 1937

Went down to visit model houses on bus with school history class. Hugh Pastoriza, Jim Poe and myself stayed in New York after the class came home. We went to see Vincent Prior at Rockwell-O'Keefe. He gave us a great big picture of Peg LaCentra. Went to Gale, Metronome and Decca records. Got some postcards of Teddy Hill, Four Inkspots at Gale; nothing at Metronome; picture of Chick Webb band at Decca. Went to the Commodore Music Store where I bought Bob Crosby's *Between The Devil And The Deep Blue Sea / The Old Spinning Wheel* (Decca 1196); Cootie Williams' *Diga Diga Doo / I Can't Believe That You're In Love With Me* (Variety 555) and, for Maurine Van Meter, Jimmy Dorsey's *Mutiny In The Brass Section / All God's Chillun Got Rhythm* (Decca 1256).

RADIO LOGS

8:45PM WAAB
GLENN MILLER
Raymor Ballroom, Boston
Moonlight Serenade (theme)
I've Got My Love To Keep Me Warm
Let's Call The Whole Thing Off
I Never Knew (vocal: Vi Mele)
Star Dust
On Moonlight Bay
Lady Who Couldn't Be Good
Moonlight Serenade (theme)

9:00PM WHN
HENRY BIAGINI
Roseland Ballroom, NYC
September In The Rain (vocal: Selva Castle)
They All Laughed (vocal: Bill Schiller)
Big Boy Blue (trumpet)
Where Are You? (vocal: Bill Schiller)
Ja-Da (clarinet; piano; tenor)
For You (vocal: Bill Schiller)
I'm Hatin' This Waitin' Around (vocal: Selva Castle)
The Moon Is In The Sky / In Your Own Little Way
My Blue Heaven
What Will I Tell My Heart? (vocal: Bill Schiller)
When Two Love Each Other (vocal: Selva Castle)
Runnin' Wild
Carelessly

11:00PM WABC
BUNNY BERIGAN
Hotel Pennsylvania, NYC
It Looks Like Rain In Cherry Blossom Lane
Black Bottom
Too Marvelous For Words

11:15PM WNAC
GLENN MILLER
Raymor Ballroom, Boston
Moonlight Serenade (theme)
Humoresque
How Am I To Know? (vocal: Vi Mele)
It's Swell Of You
Down South Camp Meeting
You're Here, You're There, You're Everywhere (vocal: Vi Mele)

■ THURSDAY 20 MAY 1937

RECORDING SESSION

JOHNNY HODGES AND HIS ORCHESTRA
Recording session for Variety in New York City.
Cootie Williams (t); Barney Bigard (cl); Johnny Hodges (ss/as); Otto Hardwick (as); Harry Carney (bar); Duke Ellington (p); Fred Guy (g); Hayes Alvis (b); Sonny Greer (d); Buddy Clark (voc)
Foolin' Myself (v BC) / *A Sailboat In The Moonlight* (vBC) / *You'll Never Go To Heaven* (vBC) / *Peckin'* (vBC)

RADIO LOGS

9:45PM WAAB
GLENN MILLER
Raymor Ballroom, Boston
Down South Camp Meeting
How Am I To Know? (vocal: Vi Mele)
It's Swell Of You
Three Little Words (Sterling Bose's trumpet)

10.00PM WEAF
JIMMY DORSEY
Kraft Music Hall, Hollywood
In A Little Hula Heaven (vocal: Bing Crosby) (Bing's singing and whistling the nuts with Jimmy Dorsey's band; Jack Ryan's bass)
Never In A Million Years (vocal: Bing Crosby) (Jimmy Dorsey's nuttsy alto sax)
Limehouse Blues (vocal: Bing Crosby) (great vocal by Bing with fine backing by Jimmy Dorsey's band)
Carelessly (vocal: Bing Crosby) (good vocal of fairly good song with Dorsey Band)
September In The Rain (vocal: Connee Boswell) (guest star Boswell's singing the nuts)
Basin Street Blues (vocal: Connee Boswell) (same arrangement as Decca recording; Crosby aiding)
Parade Of The Milk Bottle Tops (JIMMY DORSEY's Band: written by Pat McCarthy: trombone; Ray McKinley's drums; ballsy tenor; Joe Meyer's trumpet; Dorsey's wonderful alto sax; clarinets; rhythm section)

11:30PM WOR
DUKE ELLINGTON
Cotton Club, 48th Street, NYC
Harlem Speaks (nuttsy piece: Stewart's trumpet; Hodges; Williams' great trumpet; Alvis' bass; Harry Carney's colossal baritone sax; Joe Nanton's magnificent muted wa-wa trombone)
Solace (one of Ellington's latest numbers featuring Barney Bigard's slow, soft clarinet)
Caravan (super-colossal: Tizol's trombone; Bigard's clarinet; Williams' trumpet; Carney's baritone)
Ebony Rhapsody (vocal: Ivie Anderson) (nuttsy song a few years old: Greer's bells; saxes; moaning brass; piano; Cootie)
Tomorrow Is Another Day (typical Ellington saxes with strong rhythm section)
Echoes Of The Jungle (Stewart's wonderful, tricky, muted trumpet; Bigard's very soft, good clarinet; Hodges with wa-wa brass; Nanton's wa-wa trombone; nice tom-tom drumming by Greer throughout)
Poor Little Rich Girl (fast foxtrot: Carneys wonderful baritone; Williams' straight trumpet; Barney Bigard's clarinet; Greer's tricky but steady drumming; trumpet; trombone)
Kissin' My Baby Goodnight (vocal: Ivie Anderson) (Hodges' nuttsy soprano sax; Williams' trumpet)

11:45PM WNAC
GLENN MILLER
Raymor Ballroom, Boston
Moonlight Serenade (theme)
Honeysuckle Rose (Hal McIntyre's clarinet)
How Could You? (vocal: Vi Mele)
Night And Day (waltz: fair)
Trust In Me (vocal: Vi Mele)
Night Over Shanghai
Moonlight Serenade (theme)

12:00 MIDNIGHT WOR
BUNNY BERIGAN
Hotel Pennsylvania, NYC
Swell. Announced by Howard Doyle.
Boo Hoo (vocal: Ford Leary)
You Showed Me The Way (vocal: Carol McKay) (nuttsy)
Was That The Human Thing To Do?
They All Laughed (vocal: Carol McKay) (ballsy)
Am I Blue? (Bunny's colossal trumpet; Auld's tenor)
The You And Me That Used To Be (vocal: Ford Leary)
Royal Garden Blues (Bunny and whole band really swingin' out!)
September In The Rain (vocal: Ford Leary) (saxes)
Star Dust (vocal: Carol McKay) (colossal: Bunny's trumpet; what a slow arrangement!)
The Goona Goo (vocal: Bunny Berigan) (Recorded on Brunswick)

12:30AM WEAF
CHARLIE BARNET
Kinmore Hotel, Albany, N.Y.
Swing Low, Sweet Chariot (Jimmy Mundy arrangement)
This Is My Last Affair (vocal: Kathleen Lane)
Night And Day (trumpet; Barnet's tenor: great)

Rockin' Chair Swing (swell saxes; trumpet; clarinet; drums; Barnet's tenor)
Clarinet Lament (colossal: clarinet; trombone; wonderful saxes and brass; clarinet swell but not as good as Bigard)
In Your Own Little Way (vocal: Kathleen Lane) (trombone)
Trees (saxes; trumpet; Barnet's swell tenor sax–like Musso)
You're Precious To Me (lousy arrangement of a stinky piece)
September In The Rain (swell song: fair)
The You And Me That Used To Be (vocal: Kathleen Lane) (nuttsy tenor)
Dear Old Southland (wonderful old piece, marvelous arrangement: muted trumpet; saxes; Barnet's typical tenor sax; piano beating it out with drums; high trumpet; solid bassing)

■ FRIDAY 21 MAY 1937

RADIO LOGS

11:40PM WMCA
CHICK WEBB
Savoy Ballroom, NYC
You Showed Me The Way (vocal: Ella Fitzgerald)
Blue Lou (Jordan; Williams, etc)
Thou Swell (Taft Jordan's swell swing trumpet; nice up and down clarinet)
Dedicated To You (vocal: Ella Fitzgerald) (Ella's usual very fine vocalizing; Ted McRae's tenor sax)
When You And I Were Young, Maggie (somewhat like Goodman's arrangement)
Let's Get Together (theme)

■ SATURDAY 22 MAY 1937

Bob's friend, Don Mortimer, saw Benny Goodman at the Metropolitan Theater in Boston before going on to the Raymor Ballroom to see the new Glenn Miller Band. Here he describes the visit to see Glenn Miller's Band:

"Len Poor, Phil Lees, Park Collins, Bob Will and myself went down to the Raymor Ballroom and saw Glenn Miller and his very new band. I talked to Glenn, Jerry Jerome, and Glenn's manager, who are swell fellows. Through the three of them I found out that Miller's band is to stay at the Raymor for another week and then will be followed by Charlie Barnet. Glenn and band are then going on the road and will land up in New York in June (probably at the New Yorker Hotel). The manager told me that the letter I wrote them a few weeks ago was the first fan letter that the band had received. He told me he would get Glenn to autograph a picture for me and send it. The band was colossal for a new band. I have never seen a brass section with such a surprising sense of rhythm. Sterling Bose and Tweet Peterson were wonderful on trumpets, while Jesse Ralph played some colossal trombone. Bud Smith, another trombonist, took no solos but, in my opinion, was really in the groove. Eak Kenyon, the drummer, is popular as hell with the Boston cats and really is fine with the sticks. He was with Nye Mayhew recently in Boston. Chummy McGregor was swell on piano, Jerry Jerome was swell on tenor and Hal McIntyre was colossal on clarinet. He plays it much like Johnny Mince. Glenn does not play the trombone except on one number, *Jammin'*, by his Clambake Seven. Vi Mele is a wonderful vocalist and I expect she will go places. Benny Goodman came in late in the evening and stood and talked to me about the band. The best songs played were *I Got Rhythm* (Miller's own arrangement), *Honeysuckle Rose, On Moonlight Bay* and his theme song [*Moonlight Serenade*] which he wrote and arranged but which has no name."

Below: The Benny Goodman Band on stage at the Metropolitan Theater in Boston. Benny is out front and Don Mortimer's photograph also shows Jess Stacy, Gene Krupa, Gordon Griffin, Ziggy Elman, Murray McEachern, Allen Reuss, Vido Musso, Hymie Shertzer, Art Rollini and George Koenig. Harry Goodman and Harry James were missing and Red Ballard hidden at the time the photograph was taken.

RADIO LOGS

1:45PM WOR
DICK STABILE
William Penn Hotel, Pittsburgh
The Image Of You (vocal: Bert Shaw)
To A Sweet, Pretty Thing (vocal: Bert Shaw) (clarinet; trumpet)
Mountain Music (vocal: Paula Kelly) (Stabile's clarinet)
Where Or When (vocal: Bert Shaw) (Stabile's tenor sax)
Wake Up And Live (vocal: Paula Kelly)

3:00PM WJZ
CHICK WEBB
Savoy Ballroom, NYC
Memphis Blues (Taft Jordan's nuttsy trumpet; wonderful baritone sax; Pete Clark's clarinet)
I've Got Rain In My Eyes (vocal: Ella Fitzgerald) (swell arrangement of swell piece; ballsy alto sax)
Jamaica Shout (Webb's drums; baritone sax; Jordan's trumpet; Fulford's piano; Ted McRae's nuttsy, jerky tenor sax)
Holiday In Harlem (vocal: Ella Fitzgerald) (thin clarinet)
Copenhagen (Fulford's piano super-colossal; 4 clarinets with wa-wa brass; clarinet; Sandy Williams' trombone; bass sax; McRae; Webb)
Stompin' At The Savoy (arranged by Edgar Sampson: clarinet; tenor)
Harlem Congo (Webb's drums; clarinet; trumpet; trombone: marvelous)
I'm In A Crying Mood (vocal: Ella Fitzgerald) (written by Webb, arranged by Al Feldman)
Jam Session (Webb; McRae's tenor; Jordan's trumpet)
Let's Get Together (theme)

7.00PM WABC
SATURDAY NIGHT SWING SESSION No46
CBS Studio No1, 485 Madison Ave, NYC
Hallelujah (Leith Stevens directing CBS Band: swell muted trumpet; Harris' tenor)
Nagasaki (Guest guitarist JOE SODJA playing magnificent original swing guitar)
I Never Knew (JOE SODJA doing a guitar encore: never heard such an original guitar)
Caravan (Williams' tom-toms: super-colossal arrangement with whole band swingin')
The Girl With The Light Blue Hair (Raymond Scott Quintet: Pumiglio; Wade; Harris)
The Toothache (Raymond Scott Quintet playing his latest piece)
Isle Of Capri (vocal and trumpet by that grand character, WINGY MANONE)
The You And Me That Used To Be (colossal song: Dave Harris' tenor; saxes; brass section)
Swingin' At The Hickory House (ballsy swingin' with WINGY MANONE'S trumpet; Pumiglio; Harris)
Crazy Rhythm (CBS Band going the balls: nuttsy)

11:30PM WMCA
CHICK WEBB
Savoy Ballroom, NYC
Go Harlem (Chick Webb's drums)
There's A Lull In My Life (vocal: Ella Fitzgerald)
September In The Rain (vocal: Charles Linton)
I Found A New Baby (Wayman Carver's flute; trumpet; tenor)
Mayor Of Alabam' (vocal: Louis Jordan) (Jordan's alto sax; Fulford's piano)
Big John Special (NUTTSY: piano; trumpet; Webb)
You Showed Me The Way (vocal: Ella Fitzgerald)
Chick Webb Stomp (written by Webb; trumpet; Carver's flute)
Let's Get Together (theme)

12:00 MIDNIGHT WNEW
JOE MARSALA
Hickory House, 144 W52nd Street, NYC
Someday, Sweetheart (nuttsy: Joe Bushkin's piano; Joe Marsala's clarinet; Ray Biondi's violin; Adele Girard's swell harp)
They Can't Take That Away From Me (vocal: Adele Girard) (swell song but busy vocal)
Christopher Columbus (Marty Marsala's trumpet; Ray Biondi's swell swing violin; Girard's fair harp; Bushkin's nuttsy piano; Marsala's typical clarinet; Danny Alvin's drums; Shapiro's bass)

Where Is The Sun? (vocal: unk male) (Marty's trumpet; Girard's harp; Joe Bushkin's piano; Joe's clarinet)
Jazz Me Blues (Marty Marsala's straight jam trumpet; Girard's harp; Joe Marsala's clarinet; Danny Alvin's drums)
Carelessly (Marty Marsala's trumpet; Girard's harp; Ray Biondi's non-swing violin; Joe's clarinet)
Honeybun (vocal: unk male) (fast tempo: Marty & Joe Marsala jammin' together; Eddie Condon's guitar)

■ SUNDAY 23 MAY 1937
RADIO LOGS

6:30PM WOR
FUN IN SWINGTIME
WOR Studios, NYC
Del Schubert announces. Tim & Irene are the lousy comedians on the program. The Bunny Berigan Orchestra are the stars.
September In The Rain
Frankie & Johnny

10:45PM WOR
DUKE ELLINGTON
Cotton Club, 48th Street, NYC
Caravan
Scattin' At The Kit-Kat (released last week on Master: saxes; Cootie Williams)
I've Got To Be A Rugcutter (vocal: Ivie Anderson & Trio)
Time On My Hands / Without A Song / Tea For Two (Vincent Youman medley: all 3 are nuttsy pieces & Ellington's arrangements are superb; what saxes!!!)
Jive Stomp (hot trombone; Ellington's simple, swing piano; Harry Carney's ballsy baritone sax; colossal sax run with trumpet; Bigard)

RAYMOR 253 HUNTINGTON AVE.
DANCING EVERY EVENING
THE SPONSORS OF CASA LOMA, RAY NOBLE, BOB CROSBY, NOW PRESENT
the new swing sensation
GLENN MILLER
AND HIS 15 PIECE BAND
DON'T MISS THEM — NO ADVANCE IN PRICES
A limited number of Glenn Miller Recordings to early patrons

■ MONDAY 24 MAY 1937

RECORDING SESSION

ELLA FITZGERALD AND HER SAVOY EIGHT
Recording session for Decca in New York City.
Ella Fitzgerald (voc); Taft Jordan (t); Sandy Williams (tb); Louis Jordan (as); Teddy McRae (ts/bar); Tommy Fulford (p); Bobby Johnson (g); Beverly Peer (b); Chick Webb (d)
All Over Nothing At All / If You Ever Should Leave / Everyone's Wrong But Me / Deep In The Heart Of The South

RADIO LOGS

8:00PM WAAB
GLENN MILLER
Raymor Ballroom, Boston
Let's Call The Whole Thing Off
You Can't Run Away From Love
How Could You? (vocal: Vi Mele)
Lady Who Couldn't Be Kissed
I Never Knew (vocal: Vi Mele)
There's A Lull In My Life
St. Louis Blues

11:05PM WJZ
CHICK WEBB
Goodtime Society, NYC
I've Got a Dime (vocal: Ella Fitzgerald)
Caravan (muted trumpet; Webb's drums)
Whoa Babe (vocal: Ella Fitzgerald) (very original vocal)
Unknown Title (Sandy Williams' trombone; Taft Jordan's trumpet; clarinet)

12:00 MIDNIGHT WNEW
JOE MARSALA
Hickory House, 144 W52nd Street, NYC
Keep Smilin' At Trouble
They Can't Take That Away From Me (vocal: Adele Girard)
Royal Garden Blues
Where Is The Sun?
Honeysuckle Rose
Singin' The Blues
Rosetta

■ TUESDAY 25 MAY 1937

RECORDING SESSION

WINGY MANONE AND HIS ORCHESTRA
Recording session for Bluebird in New York City.
Wingy Manone (t/voc); Al Mastren (tb); Joe Marsala (cl/as); Babe Russin (ts); Conrad Lanoue (p); Jack LeMaire (g/voc); Artie Shapiro (b); Danny Alvin (d)
The Image Of You (vWM) / *Don't Ever Change* (vWM) / *Life Without You* (vWM) / *You're Precious To Me* (vWM) / *It Must Be Religion* (vWM,JLM) / *The Prisoner's Song* (vWM)

RADIO LOGS

9:30PM WABC
BENNY GOODMAN
Camel Caravan program, NYC
Love Me Or Leave Me (super-colossal: Musso; James; Benny; Krupa)
Chlo-e (Stacy's intro; Krupa; saxes; brass; Benny; James; Stacy)
I'm Hatin' This Waitin' Around (vocal: Peg LaCentra)
Avalon (BG Quartet) (really swingin' out)

11:30PM WAAB
GLENN MILLER
Raymor Ballroom, Boston
Let's Call The Whole Thing Off
Humoresque
September In The Rain (vocal: Vi Mele)
Night And Day
Wistful And Blue (vocal: Vi Mele)
St. Louis Blues

■ WEDNESDAY 26 MAY 1937

RECORDING SESSION

TOMMY DORSEY AND HIS ORCHESTRA
Recording session for Victor in New York City.
Tommy Dorsey (tb); Pee Wee Erwin, Joe Bauer, Andy Ferretti (t); Les Jenkins, Red Bone (tb); Johnny Mince, Fred Stulce, Mike Doty (cl/as); Bud Freeman (ts); Howard Smith (p); Carmen Mastren (g); Gene Traxler (b); Dave Tough (d); Jack Leonard (voc)
You're Precious To Me (vJL) / *Happy Birthday To Love* (vJL) / *Strangers In The Dark* (vJL) / *Beale Street Blues*

RADIO LOGS

9:30PM WHN
HENRY BIAGINI
Roseland Ballroom, NYC
Swell. There are some swell swing guys in this band, especially the pianist and tenor sax player.
Me, Myself And I (vocal: Bill Schiller)
I Can't Break The Habit Of You (vocal: Selva Castle)
You'll Never Go To Heaven (vocal: Bill Schiller)
Satan Takes A Holiday (vocal: Al Fatso) (colossal)
That's A-Plenty (drums; trumpet; clarinet; sax)
I'll Always Be In Love With You (nuttsy old piece)

11:05PM WABC
BUNNY BERIGAN
Hotel Pennsylvania, NYC
All Dark People Are Light On Their Feet (vocal: Ford Leary) (George Auld's tenor sax)
The Image Of You (vocal: Sue Mitchell) (new vocalist: swell high trumpet with smooth saxes)
Mahogany Hall Stomp (Bunny's fair trumpet; Auld's swell tenor sax; Bunny)
I Can't Get Started (colossal)
Peckin' (super-colossal swing hit song by trumpeter Harry James; Bunny up high)
Wake Up And Live (vocal: Sue Mitchell)
Mr Ghost Goes To Town (marvelous: real jammin' featuring George Wettling's great drumming; Auld's long, ballsy tenor solo; Ford Leary's trombone in Miff Mole style; Bunny)
Toodle-Oo (vocal: Bunny Berigan) (tenor; trombone; Wettling; clarinet)

11:15PM WNAC
GLENN MILLER
Raymor Ballroom, Boston
I'm Sitting On Top Of The World
Where Are You? (vocal: Vi Mele)
I'm Bubbling Over With Love

Wistful And Blue (vocal: Vi Mele)
On Moonlight Bay

■ THURSDAY 27 MAY 1937

RECORDING SESSION

HUDSON-DeLANGE ORCHESTRA
Recording session for Brunswick in New York City.
Will Hudson (arr); Eddie DeLange (voc/ldr); Charles Mitchell, Howard Schaumberger, Jimmy Blake (t); Edward Kolyer, Jack Andrews (tb); George Bohn, Gus Bivona (cl/as); Pete Brendel (as/bar); Ted Duane (cl/ts); Mark Hyams (p); Bus Etri (g); Doc Goldberg (b); Nat Pollard (d)
Magnolia / I Know That You Know / If I Could Be With You One Hour Tonight / I Never Knew

RADIO LOGS

9:45PM WAAB
GLENN MILLER
Raymor Ballroom, Boston
Night Over Shanghai
Turn Off The Moon
Jammin' (vocal: Vi Mele)
Star Dust
I Got Rhythm (colossal)

10.00PM WEAF
JIMMY DORSEY
Kraft Music Hall, Hollywood
How Could You? (vocal: Bing Crosby) (nuttsy vocal with great backing by Jimmy Dorsey's Swingsters)
You're Here, You're There, You're Everywhere (vocal: Bing Crosby)
Time On My Hands (vocal: Bing Crosby) (with Jimmy Dorsey's band & Paul Taylor Chorus)
Flight Of The Bumble Bee (swung by JIMMY DORSEY's Band: Dorsey's E-flat tenor; trombone; piano)
Where Are You? (vocal: Bing Crosby) (colossal sweet song, with Paul Taylor Chorus)

11:15PM WNAC
GLENN MILLER
Raymor Ballroom, Boston
Humoresque
Time On My Hands
It's Swell Of You
Down South Camp Meetin'

Glenn Miller

■ FRIDAY 28 MAY 1937

RECORDING SESSION

DON REDMAN AND HIS ORCHESTRA
Recording session for Variety in New York City.
Don Redman (cl/ss/as/voc/ldr); Reunald Jones, Otis Johnson, Harold Baker (t); Gene Simon, Benny Morton, Quentin Jackson (tb); Edward Inge, Rupert Cole (cl/as); Harvey Boone (cl/as/bar); Robert Carroll (ts); Don Kirkpatrick (p); Bob Lessey (g); Bob Ysaguirre (b); Sid Catlett (d); The Swing Choir (voc)
Stormy Weather (vTSC) / *Exactly Like You* (vTSC) / *The Man On The Flying Trapeze* (vDR) / *On The Sunny Side Of The Street* (vTSC) / *Swingin' With The Fat Man* / *Sweet Sue* / *That Naughty Waltz*

RADIO LOGS

11.30PM WMCA
JESSE OWENS
Savoy Ballroom, NYC
Owens started his own band about 3 months ago. He's no musician but has a fine personality. He was the champion of the 1936 Olympic Games held in Germany. He plays the sax.
My Gal Sal (Cedric Wallace on bass)
Where Are You? (vocal: Danny Logan)
Basin Street Blues
Song Of India (ragged: same arrangement as Dorsey)
Scattin' At The Kit Kat (trumpet; trombone)
On The Sunny Side Of The Street (vocal: Band)
The Indian Jubilee (written by Nicholas Rodriguez, pianist with band)

12.00 MIDNIGHT WABC
BENNY GOODMAN
Cornell University, Ithaca, N.Y.
The Navy Bill Prom Dance opposite Bob Crosby Band. Last year Goodman played at Ohio State University, this year it's Red Norvo and Noble Sissle.
Let's Dance (theme)
Sugar Foot Stomp (marvelous arrangement: Benny's clarinet; Harry James' colossal trumpet; Krupa)
They Can't Take That Away From Me (vocal: Peg LaCentra) (nuttsy song, swell vocal: Benny; saxes)
Peckin' (new super-colossal swing tune by Harry James: Benny's great clarinet; James' magnificent trumpet; Musso; Krupa)
Where Are You? (vocal: Peg LaCentra) (swell present day hit: I wish I knew where she was)
Makin' Whoopee (Benny's clarinet; marvelous trumpet solo by Harry James)
I'm Hatin' This Waitin' For You (vocal: Peg LaCentra) (fair song, regular arrangement)
Nagasaki (BG Quartet) (introduced by Benny: marvelous work by all, especially Hampton)
The You And Me That Used To Be (vocal: Peg LaCentra) (ballsy ballad)
Roll 'Em (magnificent swing piece written and arranged for Benny by Mary Lou Williams)

12.30AM WABC
RED NORVO/NOBLE SISSLE
Senior prom, Ohio State University
Norvo and Sissle are playing opposite each other tonight in Ohio. Norvo has it all over Sissle. Benny Goodman and Bob Crosby are playing at the Cornell Navy Bill Dance.
Far Above Cayuga's Waters (RED NORVO played this in honor of Cornell where Benny Goodman and Bob Cosby are playing tonight. Goodman, on his broadcast 5 minutes ago, saluted O.S.U. with *Roll'Em*)
Moonlight And Shadows (fair song but swell arrangement: saxes; RED NORVO's xylophone)
Never In A Million Years (vocal: Mildred Bailey)
Gee, But You're Swell (NOBLE SISSLE Band play while Norvo Band rests. Fair)
Swamp Fire (NOBLE SISSLE Band again: lousy arrangement of a fair swing piece)
The Love Bug Will Bite You (vocal: Mildred Bailey & Band) (Maurice Purtill's solid drums with RED NORVO's band)
Hallelujah (RED NORVO: brass section; fast sax section; Red's xylophone; Haymer's great tenor)
You're Precious To Me / Carelessly / Tropical Moonlight (NOBLE SISSLE Band playing a medley: Sidney Bechet's clarinet)
Night Ride (NOBLE SISSLE Band. Nuttsy, fairly new, swing piece: drums; brass; clarinets; saxes; trombones; trumpet; Bechet's clarinet)

Noble Sissle

■ SATURDAY 29 MAY 1937

Hugh Pastoriza and myself took the 7:19 train from Bronxville up to County Center, White Plains. It cost me 15 cents up by train and 70 cents to get in. Hughie brought his father's $100 Kodak along and we both brought several pictures to get autographed. We waited outside for an hour. We first met Ziggy Elman and Murray McEachern. Like the rest of the band they were wearing plain brown suits, white shoes, white shirts, and yellow ties. We shook hands with them and got them to autograph a picture taken by Hughie at the Hotel Penn. Hughie took a picture of me standing with them. We then went across the street where we met George Koenig and Harry James walking around. I got James' autograph on the same picture taken by Hughie, who then took a picture of them with me. Harry told us that the band was going to be at the Steel Pier in Atlantic City the next night. Koenig spent quite some time fixing my tie. We then met Vido Musso and Harry Goodman walking around together. Vido was glad at seeing us and shook hands with me while Hughie took a picture of us. We then got Allan Reuss to pose for a picture. At about 8:30, when it began to get dark, we went in. It certainly is a big place. I soon got hot as hell although the temperature outside must have been about 75°. There must have been 10,000 (capacity) people there. There were balcony seats which cost $1.75. The only thing they served was beer which I don't like.

Below: Bob Inman with Ziggy Elman & Murray McEachern.
Opposite page: Bob with Harry James & George Koenig.
Inset: Bob with Allen Reuss.
Bottom: Benny Goodman and the band on stage.
All photographs by Hugh Pastoriza

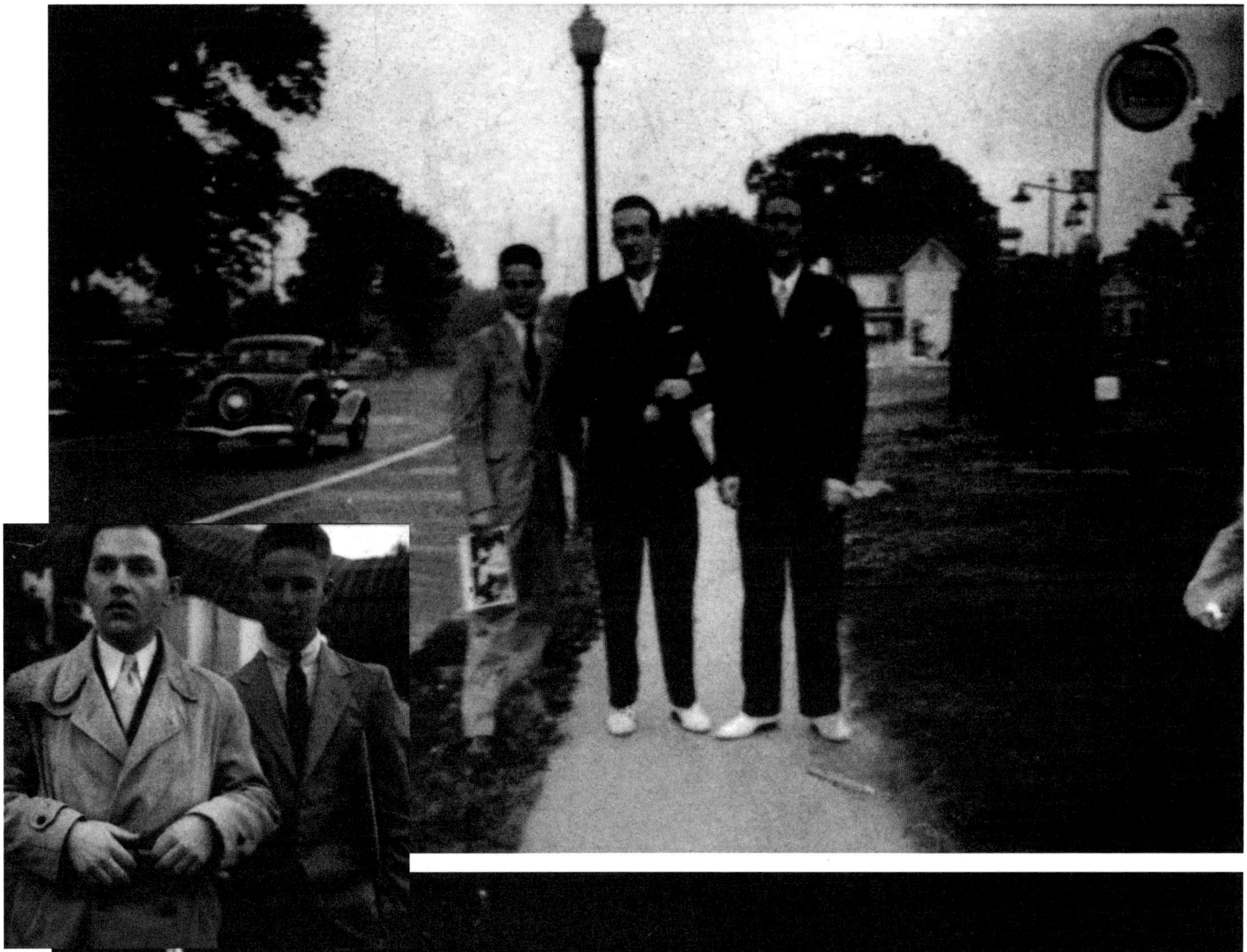

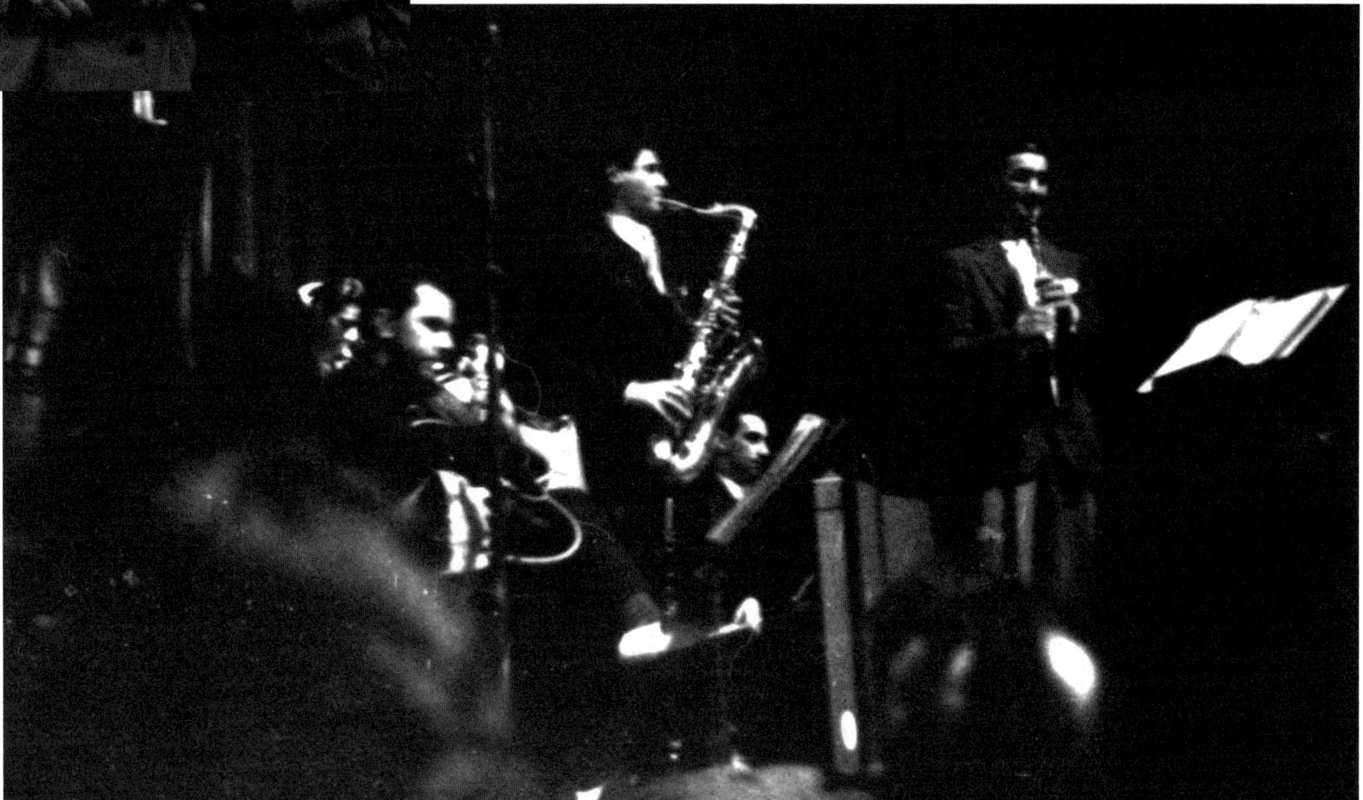

Most of my friends from Bronxville were there: Morningstar, Johnson, Pinger, Von Shilgan, Poe, Robcliff Jones, Burpee, Ferrall, Branum, Bevelaque, etc. Several older girls that I knew were there but Nancy Long was the only one that I knew real well. I didn't do any dancing but just stood around the band. They played on a high platform. The intermissions were very short and the following are the numbers played:

When You And I Were Young, Maggie; September In The Rain (vocal by Peg LaCentra); *Sandman* (Harry James' trumpet); *Unknown title* (long trumpet solo by Chris Griffin); *Peckin'* (James' trumpet); *Chlo-e; Carelessly* (vocal by Peg LaCentra, McEachern's trombone); *Unknown title* (Elman, Musso); *Unknown title; Camel Hop; I've Got My Love To Keep Me Warm* (I'll never forget this song and who used to like it so much); *Never In A Million Years* (vocal by Peg LaCentra, Griffin's trumpet); *Between The Devil And*

Action pictures by Hugh Pastoriza of the Benny Goodman Band in action on the stage of Westchester County Center.
Below: A publicity shot of vocalist Peg LaCentra.

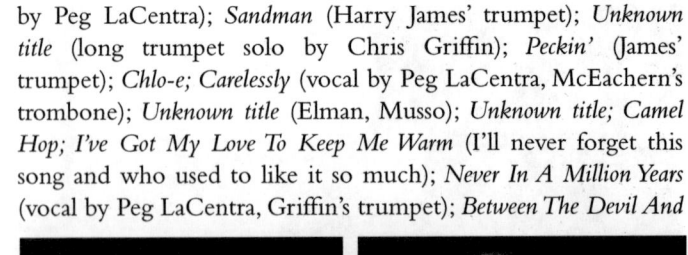

The Deep Blue Sea (vocal by Peg LaCentra, James' trumpet); *Sometimes I'm Happy* (Griffin's trumpet, saxes); *Roll 'Em; Stardust* (James' trumpet); *Oh, Lady Be Good* (Musso, James); *Blue Hawaii* (James' trumpet); *I'm Hatin' This Waitin' Around* (vocal by Peg LaCentra); *This Is My Last Affair* (vocal by Peg LaCentra, James' trumpet); *Swingtime In The Rockies* (Ziggy Elman's trumpet); *Can't We Be Friends?* (Ballard's trombone); *Where Are You?* (vocal by Peg LaCentra); *Blue Skies* (Rollini, Elman); *St. Louis Blues* (10-minutes long: first 3-minutes played exactly as recording but then what jamming by the whole band! Solos by Stacy, Krupa, Musso, James, Benny); *You Showed Me The Way* (vocal by Peg LaCentra); *Down South Camp Meetin'* (Griffin's trumpet); *Somebody Loves Me* (Musso, James); *They Can't Take That Away From Me* (vocal by Peg LaCentra); *King Porter Stomp* (10-minutes long: James, Musso, Benny, McEachern); *When Buddha Smiles* (Rollini); *Goodnight, My Love* (vocal by Peg LaCentra); *Big John Special* (James); *Always* (Rollini, McEachern); *There's A Lull In My Life* (vocal by Peg LaCentra); *Sing, Sing, Sing* (8-minutes long); *Alexander's Ragtime Band; Let's Call The Whole Thing Off* (vocal by Peg LaCentra); *Jam Session* (Musso, Elman); *Unknown title* (James' trumpet); *Too Marvelous For Words* (vocal by Peg LaCentra); *Minnie The Moocher's Wedding Day* (James, saxes); *September In The Rain* (vocal by Peg LaCentra); *Bugle Call Rag* (Rollini, James); *Remember* (Rollini); *The You And Me That Used To Be* (vocal by Peg LaCentra); *Peckin'; Sugar Foot Stomp* (James); *Goodbye* (closing theme). The Quartet played 5 numbers at about 12:15: *Nagasaki; Avalon; Stompin' At The Savoy; There's A Lull In My Life; I Got Rhythm*.

It ended at 1:35am. Robcliff Jones' chauffeur drove Hughie, Pinger, Robcliff, Nancy and myself to Nancy Long's house in Scarsdale where we got something to eat. We then drove home, getting to bed at 3:00am.

RADIO LOGS

7.00PM WABC
SATURDAY NIGHT SWING SESSION No47
CBS Studio No1, 485 Madison Ave, NYC
Mel Allen and Paul Douglas announced. Guests are Joe Bushkin, Art Gentry, Bunny Berigan and Tommy Dorsey.
How Could You?
Blues (Guest soloist TOMMY DORSEY)
Pagan Love Song (TOMMY DORSEY on trombone; Mickey Bloom on trumpet; Joe Bushkin's piano)
Slap That Bass (ART GENTRY singing; Lou Shoobe's bass)
Ostrich Walk (Williams' drums; tenor sax; clarinet; trumpet)
Singin' The Blues (JOE BUSHKIN on piano)
They All Laughed (JOE BUSHKIN on piano)
You Can't Run Away From Love Tonight (BUNNY BERIGAN Band from the Pennsylvania Hotel)
Frankie And Johnny (BUNNY BERIGAN Band from the Pennsylvania Hotel)
Wang Wang Blues (CBS Band)

11:00PM WABC
BUNNY BERIGAN
Hotel Pennsylvania, NYC
When I Think Of You (vocal: Carol McKay)
The Goona Goo (vocal: Bunny Berigan)
The You And Me That Used To Be (vocal: Ford Leary)
Trees
Frankie And Johnny (GREAT)

11:30PM WJZ
BOB CROSBY
Aragon Ballroom, Chicago
The Old Spinning Wheel
There's A Lull In My Life (vocal: Kay Weber)
They All Laughed (vocal: Bob Crosby)
Sweet Leilani
'Way Down Yonder In New Orleans (vocal: Nappy Lamare)
Never In A Million Years (vocal: Kay Weber)
At The Jazz Band Ball
There'll Be Some Changes Made (vocal: Bob Crosby)

12:00 MIDNIGHT WABC
GLEN GRAY
Palomar Ballroom, LA
Swing Low, Sweet Chariot
There's A Lull In My Life (vocal: Kenny Sargent)
Swing High, Swing Low (vocal: Pee Wee Hunt)
I Know Now (vocal: Kenny Sargent)
Sugar Foot Stomp
Whoa, Babe (vocal: Pee Wee Hunt)
I Cried For You
I Got Rhythm

12:30AM WEAF
HUDSON-DeLANGE
Playland Casino, Rye, N.Y.
Star Dust (guitar; trumpet; clarinet: SWELL)
The Little Things (vocal: Eddie DeLange) (recent tune written by Will Hudson & Eddie DeLange)
Mr Ghost Goes To Town (written and arranged by Will Hudson)
This Year's Crop Of Kisses (vocal: Band) (drums)
You're My Desire (vocal: Nan Wynn) (great)
Maid's Night Off (written and arranged by Will Hudson)
Magnolia (Duane's tenor; piano)
Unnamed tune (written by Will Hudson)

■ SUNDAY 30 MAY 1937
RADIO LOGS

2.25PM WJZ
TOMMY DORSEY
Magic Key program, NYC
I'm Getting Sentimental Over You (theme) (Tommy Dorsey's trombone)
Good Morning (vocal: Edythe Wright) (just released on Victor last week: Dorsey; Bud Freeman's tenor)
Marie (vocal: Jack Leonard & Band) (one of the most popular records ever made!!! Dorsey's trombone; Pee Wee Erwin's trumpet; Bud Freeman's tenor)

7:15PM WAAB
BOB CROSBY
Aragon Ballroom, Chicago
Gin Mill Blues
If I Had You (vocal: Bob Crosby)
Panamania (Miller; Lawson; Smith; Matlock)
Summertime (theme)

■ MONDAY 31 MAY 1937
RADIO LOGS

9:45PM WAAB
GLENN MILLER
Raymor Ballroom, Boston
White Star Of Sigma Nu
Night And Day (lousy)
You're Here, You're There, You're Everywhere (vocal: Vi Mele)
Shoe Shine Boy (Sterling Bose's trumpet)
Caravan

JUNE 1937

Hotel Pennsylvania: **Bunny Berigan** (on the roof)
Hotel New Yorker: **Gus Arnheim**
Hotel Lexington: **Andy Iona** (23–)

Apollo Theater **Louis Armstrong** (–3); **Count Basie** (4–10); **Lucky Millinder** (11–18); **Duke Ellington** (19–24); **Erskine Hawkins** (25–)
Paramount Theater: **Ozzie Nelson** (2–15); **Clyde Lucas** (27–)
Loew's State Theater: **Erskine Hawkins** (3–9); **Wingy Manone** (24–30)

Cotton Club Downtown: **Duke Ellington** (–13th when club closes for summer)
Hickory House: **Joe Marsala**
Onyx Club: **John Kirby/Spirits of Rhythm**

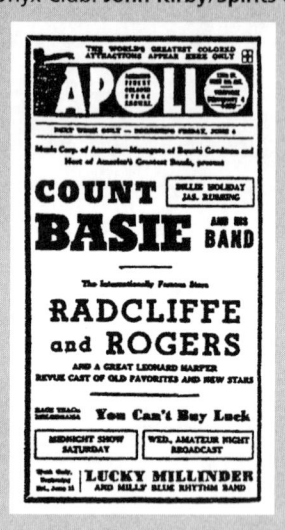

■ TUESDAY 1 JUNE 1937

RECORDING SESSION

BILLIE HOLIDAY & TEDDY WILSON ORCHESTRA
Recording session for Columbia in NYC.
Buck Clayton (t); Buster Bailey (cl); Lester Young (ts); Teddy Wilson (p); Freddie Green (g); Walter Page (b); Jo Jones (d); Billie Holiday (v)
Foolin' Myself (vBH) / *Easy Living* (vBH) / *I'll Never Be The Same* (vBH) / *I've Found A New Baby*

RADIO LOGS

9:30PM WABC
BENNY GOODMAN
Camel Caravan program, NYC
Madhouse (colossal: James; Stacy; Krupa)
They All Laughed (vocal: Peg LaCentra)
Limehouse Blues (BG Quartet)

11:00PM WAAB
GLENN MILLER
Raymor Ballroom, Boston
How Could You? (vocal: Vi Mele)
Sweet Leilani
I'm Bubbling Over With Love
Wistful And Blue (vocal: Vi Mele)
Anytime, Anyplace, Anywhere (Sterling Bose's trumpet)

11:05PM WEAF
HUDSON-DeLANGE
Playland Casino, Rye, N.Y.
Never In A Million Years (vocal: Nan Wynn)
Unknown Title (trumpet; saxes; drums)
Don't Kiss Me Again (vocal: Eddie DeLange) (recent tune written by Will Hudson & Eddie DeLange)
Hobo On Park Avenue (written by Will Hudson)
I Never Knew
There's A Lull In My Life (vocal: Nan Wynn)
Midnight At The Onyx (written by Will Hudson)
I Know That You Know

11:30PM WABC
FRANK DAILEY
Meadowbrook, N.J.
Oh, Lady Be Good
Never In A Million Years (vocal: Louise Wallace)
Swing High, Swing Low (vocal: Louise Wallace)
Purple Shade
How Could You? (vocal: Louise Wallace)
St. Louis Blues
Without Your Love (vocal: Louise Wallace)
Mountain Music (drums; tenor; trumpet)
It Looks Like Rain In Cherry Blossom Lane (vocal: Louise Wallace)

■ WEDNESDAY 2 JUNE 1937

RADIO LOGS

11:05PM WABC
BUNNY BERIGAN
Hotel Pennsylvania Roof, NYC
Last night, Tuesday 1 June, Bunny and the Band moved from the Madhattan Room to the Roof of the Hotel Pennsylvania for the rest of the summer. Announced by Mel Allen.
September In The Rain
Toodle-Oo (vocal: Bunny Berigan)
Wake Up And Live (vocal: Ruth Bradley)
The First Time I Saw You
Was That The Human Thing To Do?
Too Marvelous For Words
Am I Blue?
Love Is A Merry-Go-Round (vocal: Ruth Bradley)
Swanee River

■ FRIDAY 4 JUNE 1937

BRONXVILLE HIGH
The traditional Junior-Senior Banquet was held Friday night, June fourth, amid a festivity of color... and service by the competent sophomore waiters.
Beneath green and yellow streamers, swinging Japanese lanterns, and a blue moon, everyone was soon dancing to the rhythmic swing of Jack Montgomery's Orchestra. It is the general opinion that this is the best orchestra Bronxville has had this year.

I attended this swell dance because I waited on the tables. Jack Montgomery played with very little intermission from 9:30 to 1:15. He certainly has got a great up-and-coming band: 10 pieces. Great tenor sax player named Jack Peck, guitarist and vocalist Harry Massey. Have nuttsy swing Quartet. Leader Montgomery also sings and plays vibraphone. The band is playing steady in Mount Kisco on route 117. I met Montgomery and the manager. Said they would send me their picture. Trumpeter used to play with Gordon Griffin in White Plains. Band played: *White Heat, Riffin' At The Ritz, Marie, Honeysuckle Rose*, etc.

SATURDAY 5 JUNE 1937

RADIO LOGS

7.00PM WABC
SATURDAY NIGHT SWING SESSION No48
CBS Studio No1, 485 Madison Ave, NYC
Mel Allen and Paul Douglas announced. Guests are Willie 'The Lion' Smith, Sharkey Bonano, and Joe Sodja.
Pick Yourself Up (Leith Stevens directing CBS Band: swell)
Passionette (WILLIE 'THE LION' SMITH playing piano as only he can: swell)
I'm All Out Of Breath (WILLIE 'THE LION' SMITH on piano again)
Satan Takes A Holiday (SUPER-Colossal arrangement: Williams' drums; clarinets; Harris' tenor)
Jazz Me Blues (SHARKEY BONANO, trumpet, and 6-piece Dixieland jam band from Greenwich Village going the balls: trombone; bass; piano; clarinet, etc)
Livery Stable Blues (SHARKEY BONANO's gang doing an encore: real New Orleans swing)
The You And Me That Used To Be (great arrangement, great piece: brass; saxes)
Sheik Of Araby / Who's Sorry Now? (JOE SODJA playing marvelous guitar: colossal)
Tiger Rag (JOE SODJA again, even more marvelous guitar. How he swings!!)
Scattin' At The Kit-Kat

10:30PM ?
ART SHAW
The Willows, Pittsburgh
Super-Colossal, marvelous. Heard this program at Carolyn Bade's house in Hartsdale.
Night And Day
There's A Lull In My Life
Blue Hawaii
Message To The Moon
Was It Rain?
Let's Call The Whole Thing Off

11:00PM WAAB
GLENN MILLER
Raymor Ballroom, Boston
On Moonlight Bay
How Am I To Know? (vocal: Vi Mele)
Gone With The Wind
Twilight In Turkey

12:30AM WEAF
HUDSON-DeLANGE
Playland Casino, Rye, N.Y.
If I Could Be With You (nuttsy piece: good trumpet; tenor; clarinet)
Carelessly (vocal: Nan Wynn)
Dallas Blues (vocal: Eddie DeLange) (trumpet just like Harry James)
The Maid's Night Off (written by Will Hudson: trumpet; clarinet)
You're My Desire (vocal: Nan Wynn)
No. 15 (latest by Will Hudson, to get a regular title soon: drums; clarinets)
Where Are You? (vocal: Eddie DeLange)
Bugle Call Rag (swell Hudson arrangement: trumpet; guitar; clarinet; drums)
I Never Knew

SUNDAY 6 JUNE 1937

RADIO LOGS

10:30PM WOR
NYE MAYHEW
Glen Island Casino, New Rochelle, N.Y.
Swell.
I Can't Lose That Longing For You
This Is My Last Affair (vocal: Helen Reynolds)
Stop, Look, And Listen (nuttsy: trumpet; piano)
Carelessly
Meet Me In The Moonlight
Honeysuckle Rose (nuttsy trombone; trumpet; tenor)
I've Got You Under My Skin
Lassus Trombone (tenor; trumpet; 3 trombones; piano)
It's Love I'm After (vocal: Helen Reynolds)

11:05PM WABC
GUS ARNHEIM
Hotel New Yorker, NYC
Budd Johnson and Skippy Martin are chief arrangers. Clarinetist Joe Dixon left the band several weeks ago to join Bunny Berigan's Band at the Penn. Irving Fazola replaced Dixon.
I'm Happy, Darling, Dancing With You (vocal: Ray Foster) (very new song: clarinet; drums)
How Could You? (vocal: June Robbins) (Beigel's or Carlson's trumpet; Bill Covey's tenor)
In A Little Roadside Rendezvous (vocal: John Hamilton) (very slow: played for first time over radio)
Christopher Columbus (Beigel's trumpet; Bill Covey's tenor; Ralph Copsey's trombone; Stan Kenton's piano)
Turn Off The Moon (vocal: Ray Foster) (saxes: Covey; Shoop; John Hamilton)
Is This Gonna Be My Lucky Summer? (vocal: June Robbins) (another new song: fair)
Where Or When
Love Is A Merry-Go-Round (vocal: June Robbins) (swell song: fair)

MONDAY 7 JUNE 1937

RADIO LOGS

9:00PM WJZ
EDGAR HAYES
Goodtime Society, NBC Studios, NYC
Great. This is Edgar Hayes' month-old band now playing at the Savoy Ballroom. He used to play piano and arrange for Lucky Millinder's Blue Rhythm band. He plays a nuttsy swing piano.

Edgar Steps Out (colossal swing tune: great muted trumpet; Hayes' piano; drums; brass)
Caravan (Ellington's composition played somewhat in style of Lucky Millinder's old band: nuttsy)
Alabama Bound / One In A Million (vocal: Four Inkspots)
Peckin' (great swing stuff: trumpet; dirty clarinet; tenor; biting brass)

11:05PM WABC
GUS ARNHEIM
Hotel New Yorker, NYC
Looking For Love
Mean To Me (trumpet; clarinet)
Night Over Shanghai (vocal: June Robbins)
You're Driving Me Crazy (nuttsy: trumpet; clarinet)
You Can't Run Away From Love Tonight (vocal: Ray Foster) (great: tenor)
They All Laughed (vocal: John Hamilton) (nuttsy song written by George Gershwin: clarinet)
Sweet And Lovely
It Must Be True
My Silent Love

12:00 MIDNIGHT WOR
NYE MAYHEW
Glen Island Casino, New Rochelle, N.Y.
Fair.
You Showed Me The Way
Little Old Lady
I've Got My Love To Keep Me Warm
Swing High, Swing Low
Night And Day
Hors D'Oeuvres (tenor; clarinet; drums)
Love Locked Out / Love Is The Sweetest Thing
The Goona Goo

TUESDAY 8 JUNE 1937

RECORDING SESSION
DUKE ELLINGTON AND HIS ORCHESTRA
Recording session for Master Records in New York City.
Duke Ellington (p); Wallace Jones, Cootie Williams (t); Rex Stewart (c); Joe Nanton, Lawrence Brown (tb); Juan Tizol (vtb); Barney Bigard (cl); Johnny Hodges (cl/ss/as); Otto Hardwick (as/bsx); Harry Carney (cl/as/bar); Fred Guy (g); Hayes Alvis, Billy Taylor (b); Sonny Greer (d); Ivie Anderson (voc)
All God's Chillun Got Rhythm (HA out) / *All God's Chillun Got Rhythm* (vIA and HC,RS,HA) / *Alabamy Home* (vIA)

RADIO LOGS
9:30PM WABC
BENNY GOODMAN
Camel Caravan program, NYC
Walk, Jennie, Walk (James' trumpet; Krupa; Benny)
When It's Sleepy Time Down South (new arrangement: James' trumpet)
Star Dust
Marie (BG Quartet)

WEDNESDAY 9 JUNE 1937

RECORDING SESSION
FATS WALLER & HIS RHYTHM
Recording session for Victor in New York City.
Herman Autrey (t); Gene Sedric (cl/ts); Fats Waller (p/voc); Albert Casey (g); Charles Turner (b); Slick Jones (d)
Smarty (vFW) / *Don't You Know Or Don't You Care?* (vFW) / *Lost Love* (vFW) / *I'm Gonna Put You In Your Place* (vFW) / *Blue, Turning Grey Over You* (vFW)

GLENN MILLER AND HIS ORCHESTRA
Recording session for Brunswick in New York City.
Glenn Miller (tb/ldr); Charlie Spivak, Manny Klein, Sterling Bose (t); Jesse Ralph, Harry Rodgers (tb); Hal McIntyre (cl/as); George Siravo (as); Jerry Jerome, Carl Biesecker (ts); Howard Smith (p); Dick McDonough (g); Ted Kotsoftis (b); George Simon (d)
I Got Rhythm / *Sleepy Time Gal* / *Community Swing* / *Time On My Hands*

RADIO LOGS
9:30PM WHN
ANTHONY TRINI
Roseland Ballroom, NYC
Plenty O.K. This band sure plays some swell numbers but is ragged in spots. Swell tenor sax.
After You've Gone
This Is My Last Affair
I Surrender Dear
Night And Day
Old Fashioned Swing (tenor: nuttsy)
Dedicated To You (vocal: Anthony Trini) (Trini also played violin)
As Long As I Live
September In The Rain (vocal: Sonny Sontag)
Swing Low, Sweet Chariot
I Would Do Anything For You (vocal: June Bennett)
Song Of India
Riffin' At The Ritz
Big John Special (nuttsy)

11:05PM WABC
BUNNY BERIGAN
Hotel Pennsylvania Roof, NYC
Announced by Jerry Lawrence.
Never In A Million Years
Poor Robinson Crusoe
The Image Of You (vocal: Ruth Bradley)
Louis (swell swing solos: Bunny; Auld's tenor; clarinet)
You're Gonna Wake Up And Think You're Dreaming (vocal: Ruth Bradley)
Mr. Ghost Goes To Town (clarinet; Wettling's drums; trombone; sax)
'Cause My Baby Says It's So (vocal: Bunny Berigan)
Mahogany Hall Stomp

THURSDAY 10 JUNE 1937

RADIO LOGS
10.00PM WEAF
JIMMY DORSEY
Kraft Music Hall, Hollywood
It Looks Like Rain In Cherry Blossom Lane (vocal: Bing Crosby) (Jimmy Dorsey's band)
They Can't Take That Away From Me (vocal: Bing Crosby) (Jimmy Dorsey's band)
Casey Jones (vocal: Bing Crosby) (Jimmy Dorsey's band)
There's A Lull In My Life (vocal: Bing Crosby) (with Jimmy Dorsey's band)
Too Marvelous for Words (vocal: Harriet Hilliard)
Our Penthouse On Third Avenue (vocal: Harriet Hilliard)
Hollywood Pastimes (JIMMY DORSEY's Band: great)
Waddlin' At The Waldorf (JIMMY DORSEY's Band: Jimmy's alto sax)

FRIDAY 11 JUNE 1937

RECORDING SESSION
FATS WALLER
Recording session for Victor in New York City.
Fats Waller (p)
Keepin' Out Of Mischief Now / *Star Dust* / *Basin Street Blues* / *Tea For Two* / *I Ain't Got Nobody*

RADIO LOGS
12.30AM WEAF
FLETCHER HENDERSON
Grand Terrace Café, Chicago
It's Wearing Me Down (vocal: Chuck Richards)
House Hop
Moonlight And Shadows (vocal: Chuck Richards)
Back Home Again In Indiana
If You Should Ever Leave (vocal: Chuck Richards)
S'posin'

SATURDAY 12 JUNE 1937

RECORDING SESSION
TOMMY DORSEY AND HIS ORCHESTRA
Recording session for Victor in New York City.
Tommy Dorsey (tb); Pee Wee Erwin, Joe Bauer, Andy Ferretti (t); Les Jenkins, Red Bone (tb); Johnny Mince, Fred Stulce, Mike Doty (cl/as); Bud Freeman (ts); Howard Smith (p); Carmen Mastren (g); Gene Traxler (b); Dave Tough (d); Edythe Wright, Jack Leonard (voc)
That Stolen Melody / *Barcarolle* / *Hymn To The Sun*

TOMMY DORSEY AND HIS CLAMBAKE SEVEN
Recording session for Victor in New York City.
Tommy Dorsey (tb); Pee Wee Erwin (t); Johnny Mince (cl); Bud Freeman (ts); Howard Smith (p); Carmen Mastren (g); Gene Traxler (b); Dave Tough (d); Edythe Wright (voc)
Is This Gonna Be My Lucky Summer? (vEW) / *If You Ever Should Leave* (vEW) / *Who'll Be The One This Summer?* (vEW) / *Don't Ever Change* (vEW) / *Our Love Was Meant To Be* (vEW) / *Posin'* (vEW)

I got two tickets mailed to me for this Swing Session. This is a special hour and a half program celebrating one year of Swing Sessions sponsored by the Columbia Broadcasting System. It starts at midnight. Mrs Pastoriza drove Hughie, Jim Poe, and myself at 10:45pm. We got there at 11:50 and all the seats were taken except the box seats. So we entered them, which were the best seats. Don Mortimer, who just got home from school, gave me his camera to take pictures. I took 16 pictures but only a few came out. Duke Ellington's Jam Ensemble kept rehearsing *Frolic Sam* before the broadcast. It sure was great. It was just recorded on Variety. Announcer Melvin Allen came out before the broadcast and introduced Paul Douglas. The regular CBS Band, under the direction of Leith Stevens, was larger: 5 trumpeters—Mannie Klein, Jimmy Rosselli, Dave Wade, Lloyd Williams, Nat Natoli; 3 trombones—Wilbur Schwichtenburg; Russ Genner, Joe Vargas; pianist Raymond Scott; drummer Johnny Williams; bassist Lou Shoobe; guitarist Frankie Worrell; and 4 saxes—Pete Pumiglio, Art Manners, Dave Harris and Hank Ross (played in Benny Goodman's Columbia recording of *Moonglow*). There must have been at least 1500 people at this broadcast in CBS Playhouse No1, just off Broadway at 48th Street. Although it was an hour and a half long it was marvelous and the whole audience was kept very well entertained. The broadcast of the Quintette from Paris, France, didn't come over very well. It was 6 o'clock in the morning there. Of course, the parts of the broadcast that we could see were the best. Therefore, Duke Ellington's Ensemble, Thompson Rhythm Singers (which included Al Rinker who used to be one of the Whiteman Rhythm Boys), Kress & McDonough, and the two last jam session numbers really 'sent me' the most. We must have looked quite important, taking notes and pictures up in a box, because the CBS cameraman on the stage below took a picture of us. There were many photographers in the front row, probably from swing magazines. After the broadcast we got the autographs of trombonist Wilbur Schwichtenberg, guest guitarist Dick McDonough, guest pianist Claude Thornhill, and guest vocalist Kay Thompson. Mrs Pastoriza then drove us home, arriving at 3:00am.

12.00 MIDNIGHT WABC
SATURDAY NIGHT SWING SESSION No49
CBS Playhouse No1, 48th Street, NYC
Mel Allen and Paul Douglas announced.
Panamania (Mannie Klein's trumpet; Schwichtenberg's trombone; Leith Stevens directing)
Frolic Sam (DUKE ELLINGTON; Harry Carney; Cootie Williams; Juan Tizol; Barney Bigard; Hayes Alvis)
Ain't Misbehavin' (CASPER REARDON on harp)
Swing, Swing Mother-In-Law (CBS Band: Klein; Genner)
Rebound (ADRIAN ROLLINI Trio: Rollini's vibes; Frank Victor's guitar; Haig Stephens' bass)
It Had To Be You (KAY THOMPSON, guest vocalist)
Am I Blue? (BUNNY BERIGAN Orchestra from the Hotel Pennsylvania)
Powerhouse (Raymond Scott Quintet: Harris' tenor; Williams' drums, etc)
I Got Rhythm (GLEN GRAY Band from the Palomar Ballroom in Los Angeles)
The Devil is Afraid Of Music (GLEN GRAY Band from the Palomar Ballroom in Los Angeles with vocal by Pee Wee Hunt)
Crazy Rhythm (LES LIEBER, guest, on hot fife)
Nobody's Sweetheart (LES LIEBER, guest, on hot fife)
Djangology (QUINTET OF THE HOT CLUB OF FRANCE from Paris)
Limehouse Blues (QUINTET OF THE HOT CLUB OF FRANCE from Paris)
Breakup (QUINTET OF THE HOT CLUB OF FRANCE from Paris)

Left: The scene in the studio as the augmented CBS Band swing out.
Above: Bob Inman's autographed programme.

The Swing Session's Called To Order (CBS Band)
Classics In Jazz (CLAUDE THORNHILL on piano)
Flight Of The Bumble Bee (CLAUDE THORNHILL on piano)
There's A Lull In My Life (BENNY GOODMAN TRIO from Pittsburgh, Pa)
Nagasaki (BENNY GOODMAN Quartet from Pittsburgh, Pa)
Whoa, Babe! (KAY THOMPSON Rhythm Singers: 8 girls, 2 boys and Al Rinker)
Caravan (CBS Band: Wade; Klein – arranged by Paul Starrett)
Chicken A La Swing (Dick McDonough & Carl Kress doing a swell guitar duet with CBS band)
I Know That You Know (Dick McDonough & Carl Kress encore)
Twilight In Turkey (Raymond Scott Quintet)
Three Little Words (impromptu jam session – one of the best things I ever heard with Johnny Williams; Hank Ross; Dave Wade; Lou Shoobe; Pete Pumiglio; Carl Kress and Claude Thornhill)
Blues In E-Flat (a second jam session and last number: Johnny Williams' drums; Lou Shoobe's bass; Art Manners' clarinet; Mannie Klein directing and playing magnificent trumpet; Dick McDonough's guitar and Claude Thornhill on piano)
Chicken And Waffles (closing theme)

RADIO LOGS

11.30PM WJZ
JIMMIE LUNCEFORD
Lido Casino, Larchmont, N.Y.
Melody Man
Rockin' Chair Swing
Tain't No Good
Rain In My Heart
So Rare (vocal: Dan Grissom & Sy Oliver)
Organ Grinder's Swing
Rhythm is Our Business

■ SUNDAY 13 JUNE 1937

RADIO LOGS

11.30PM WJZ
JIMMIE LUNCEFORD
Lido Casino, Larchmont, N.Y.
Tidal Wave
Me, Myself And I
Oh, Boy! (vocal: Sy Oliver)
So Rare (vocal: Dan Grissom & Sy Oliver) (nuttsy)
Yankee Doodle Never Went To Town (vocal: Willie Smith)
Dear Old Southland

■ MONDAY 14 JUNE 1937

RECORDING SESSION

MEZZ MEZZROW AND HIS ORCHESTRA
Recording session for Victor in New York City.
Sy Oliver (t); J. C. Higginbotham (tb); Mezz Mezzrow (cl); Happy Cauldwell (ts); Sonny White (p); Bernard Addison (g); Pops Foster (b); Jimmy Crawford (d)
Blues In Disguise / *That's How I Feel Today* / *Hot Club Stomp* / *The Swing Session's Called To Order*

CLAUDE THORNHILL AND HIS ORCHESTRA
Recording session for Vocalion in New York City.
Claude Thornhill (p/vib/ldr); Manny Klein, Charlie Spivak (t); Jack Lacey (tb); Toots Mondello, Jess Carneol (as); Babe Russin (ts); Eddie Powell (bar/fl); Artie Bernstein (b); Chauncey Morehouse (d); Maxine Sullivan, Jimmy Farrell (voc)
Whispers In The Dark (vJF) / *Harbor Lights* (vJF) / *Stop! You're Breaking My Heart* (vMS) / *Gone With The Wind* (vMS)

■ TUESDAY 15 JUNE 1937

RECORDING SESSION

BILLIE HOLIDAY & HER ORCHESTRA
Recording session for Vocalion in NYC.
Buck Clayton (t); Edmond Hall (cl); Lester Young (ts); Teddy Wilson (p); Freddie Green (g); Walter Page (b); Jo Jones (d); Billie Holiday (v)
Me, Myself And I / *A Sailboat In The Moonlight* / *Born To Love* / *Without Your Love*

JIMMIE LUNCEFORD AND HIS ORCHESTRA
Recording session for Decca in New York City.
Jimmie Lunceford (ldr); Paul Webster (t); Eddie Tompkins, Sy Oliver (t/voc); Elmer Crumbley, Russell Bowles, Eddie Durham (tb); Willie Smith (cl/as/bar/voc); Earl Carruthers (cl/as/bar); Ed Brown (as); Dan Grissom (cl/as/voc); Joe Thomas (cl/ts/voc); Edwin Wilcox (p); Al Norris (g); Moses Allen (b); Jimmy Crawford (d)
Coquette (vDG) / *The Merry-Go-Round Broke Down* (vSO & Band) / *Ragging The Scale* / *Hell's Bells* / *For Dancers Only*

Jimmie Lunceford

RADIO LOGS

9:30PM WABC
BENNY GOODMAN
Camel Caravan program, NYC
Dear Old Southland
House Hop
September In The Rain (vocal: Peg LaCentra)
The Sheik Of Araby (BG Quartet)

■ WEDNESDAY 16 JUNE 1937

RECORDING SESSION

BARNEY BIGARD & HIS JAZZOPATORS
Recording session for Variety in New York City.
Rex Stewart (c); Juan Tizol (vtb); Barney Bigard (cl); Harry Carney (bar); Duke Ellington (p); Fred Guy (g); Billy Taylor (b); Sonny Greer (d); Sue Mitchell (voc)
Get It Southern Style (vSM) / *Moonlight Fiesta* / *Sponge Cake And Spinach* / *If You're Ever In My Arms Again* (vSM)
Bandleader Charlie Barnet plays maraccas on *Moonlight Fiesta*.

■ THURSDAY 17 JUNE 1937

RADIO LOGS

12.00 MIDNIGHT WEAF
FLETCHER HENDERSON
Grand Terrace Café, Chicago
King Porter Stomp
Good Morning (vocal: Chuck Richards)
Chris And His Gang (written by Fletcher Henderson)
If You Should Ever Leave (vocal: Chuck Richards)
Jangled Nerves (Chu Berry's great tenor)
Star Dust (vocal: Chuck Richards) (vibraphone)
S'posin' (vocal: Chuck Richards)
Tiger Rag (great)

12.00 MIDNIGHT WEAF
CHARLIE BARNET
Hickory Lodge, Larchmont, N.Y.
Opening night for Barnet at the Hickory Lodge (formerly the Post Lodge).
I've Lost Another Sweetheart (theme)
Caravan
Echoes Of Harlem
Love Is a Merry-Go-Round (vocal: Al Stewart)
Carelessly
They Can't Take That Away From Me
Clarinet Lament
Dear Old Southland
Puerto Rican Dreams
Oh, Babe, Maybe Someday (vocal: Al Stewart)
Admiration (ran out of time)

■ FRIDAY 18 JUNE 1937

RECORDING SESSION

BUNNY BERIGAN AND HIS ORCHESTRA
Recording session for Victor in New York City.
Bunny Berigan, Irving Goodman, Steve Lipkins (t); Morey Samuel, Sonny Lee (tb); Sid Perlmutter, Joe Dixon (cl/as); Clyde Rounds, George Auld (ts); Joe Lippman (p); Tom Morgan (g); Arnold Fishkind (b); George Wettling (d); Ruth Gaylor (voc)
All God's Chillun Got Rhythm (vRG) / *The Lady From Fifth Avenue* (vRG) / *Let's Have Another Cigarette* (vRG)

■ SATURDAY 19 JUNE 1937

RECORDING SESSION

HENRY 'RED' ALLEN
Recording session for Vocalion in New York City.
Henry 'Red' Allen (t/voc); Bingie Madison (cl); Tab Smith, Charlie Holmes (as); Harold Arnold (ts); Luis Russell (p); Danny Barker (g); Pops Foster (b); Paul Barbarin (d)
Till The Clock Strikes Three (vHA) / *The Merry-go-round Broke Down* (vHA) / *You'll Never Go To Heaven* (vHA) / *The Miller's Daughter, Marianne* (vHA)

RADIO LOGS

7.30PM WABC
SATURDAY NIGHT SWING SESSION No50
CBS Studio No1, 485 Madison Ave, NYC
Trumpeter Frankie Newton and pianist Nat Jaffe are the guests.
Swing Session Called To Order
I Found A New Baby
'Cause My Baby Says Its So
Lullaby To A Lamp Post
There's No Two Ways About It
Waddlin' At The Waldorf

12:00 MIDNIGHT WABC
BENNY GOODMAN
Sunhurry Road, Columbus, Ohio
Heard this program at Babs Underhill's house in Scarsdale.
Swingtime In The Rockies
There's A Lull In My Life (vocal: Peg LaCentra)
St. Louis Blues
I'm Hatin' This Waitin' Around (vocal: Peg LaCentra)
Body And Soul (BG Trio)
Peckin'
They Can't Take That Away From Me (vocal: Peg LaCentra)
Shine (BG Quartet)
Can't We Be Friends? (Ballard's trombone)

■ MONDAY 21 JUNE 1937

My brother John and myself drove down in our Chevrolet car to see Duke Ellington and his Orchestra which started a week's engagement at the Apollo Theater last Friday. Each week the Apollo gets some well-known colored band. Erskine Hawkins is coming next week; then Jimmie Lunceford, and later, Chick Webb. There was only one movie which we only saw a little of, but the stage show was very long with Ellington's band, the dancers and comedians. We paid 30 cents for orchestra seats. The Duke & his Band and Ivie Anderson were simply super-colossal. What a marvelous band!! Outstanding were: Rex Stewart, Cootie Williams, Juan Tizol, Harry Carney, Barney Bigard, Duke Ellington's rippling piano, and the solid rhythm section featuring two basses together and counter rhythm. Unusual was the fact that there was a 7-man brass section instead of the usual 6. Freddy Jenkins, whom Rex Stewart succeeded in early 1935 made the 4th trumpet (left to right: Stewart, Jenkins, Williams, Whetsel). Bassist Billy Taylor was added to the band in early 1935 at the same time that handsome Hayes Alvis succeeded Wellman Braud. The following numbers were played strictly by the band alone (the band also accompanied dancers, etc beforehand): *East St. Louis Toodle-Oo* (theme written by Ellington in 1924 and recorded at least three different times—recently on Master 101, features Cootie Williams' rubber-muted trumpet); *Trumpet In Spades* (featuring Rex Stewart's marvelous rubber wa-wa muted trumpet); *Caravan* (recent composition with great solos by Juan Tizol and his smooth valve-trombone, Bigard's colossal clarinet, Cootie Williams' steel muted trumpet, Harry Carney's baritone sax); *There's A Lull In My Life* (just released this month on Master; Ivie Anderson doing marvelous vocal; Harry Carney's soft baritone; Cootie Williams' trumpet); *All God's Chillun Got Rhythm* (Ivie Anderson singing with a chorus of the whole band, just as she sang it in the very recent picture 'A Day At The Races.' Nuttsy); *Get What You Can While You Can* (Ivie Anderson singing a long vocal with little musical aid by the band but with comic sayings from the mouths of Sonny Greer, Otto Hardwick, etc.); *I've Got To Be A Rugcutter* (Recorded on Master 101). Funny clowning and dancing by Freddy Jenkins, Ivie Anderson truckin' and singing with trio of Hayes Alvis, Harry Carney and Rex Stewart, Bigard's clarinet, Carney's baritone, Hodges' alto, Williams' and Stewart's trumpets); and finally the closing number with some great jamming by Freddy Jenkins, Williams and Carney. Got home at 4:45pm.

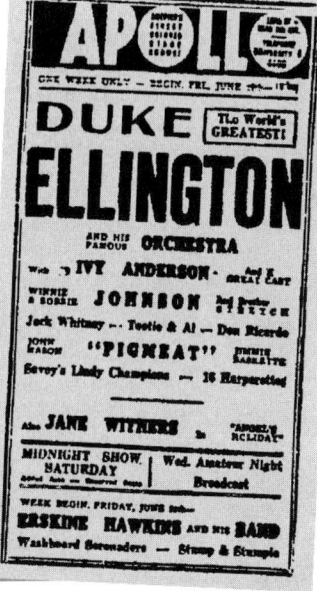

Don Mortimer and myself borrowed bicycles and left Bronxville at 7:45pm in a terrible rain storm which, except for about 30 minutes, continued all night. We got thoroughly wet through to the skin but it was fun just the same. We got to the Lido Casino on the Boston Post Road in Larchmont at about 8:35 where we waited outside for Lunceford and his boys to arrive in cars. We got their autographs (except 4: Willie Smith, Moses Allen, Paul Webster and Earl Carruthers) on a picture of the band, and Lunceford's autograph on a picture of himself. Don Mortimer took about 5 pictures of different guys, some standing with me, all posed.

We didn't have quite enough money so we watched from outside from 9:30 to 10:15. An awning kept us from getting any wetter than we were. We got the autographs of Lunceford, Joe Thomas (ballsy guy and a great tenor sax player), Dan Grissom (sax & vocalist), Eddie Tompkins (trumpet, vocal), Sy Oliver (trombone, vocal), Elmer Crumbley (trombone), Ed Durham (trombone), Russell Bowles (trombone), Edwin Wilcox (piano), James Crawford (drums) and Al Norris (guitar). Some of the numbers that the band played were: *I'm Nuts About Screwy Music* (vocal by Willie Smith), *Dream Boy* (vocal by Dan Grissom), *Remember When* (vocal by Dan Grissom), *So Rare* (ballsy new song with vocal by Grissom & Oliver), *Because You're You* (vocal by Dan Grissom) etc.

Jimmie Lunceford's rhythm section (l to r, above): pianist Edwin Wilcox, drummer James Crawford, bassist Moses Allen and guitarist Al Norris.

We then cycled over to the Hickory Lodge in Larchmont and stood at the doorway and heard Charlie Barnet and his nuttsy band playing in the Hickory Club which just opened for the first time last week. Barnet and his Band have a 6-week contract there and are thinking of going to the French Casino in August. Last summer Barnet had one of the best bands in the country at Glen Island Casino, New Rochelle, N.Y. This winter he got a new band, having a small piece combination playing at the Motor Boat Show and last month having his present band playing at the Kinmare Hotel in Albany, a weekend at the Raymor Ballroom in Boston, and now at the Hickory Lodge for at least six weeks. We didn't get to see but a few of the guys:

pianist John Nicolini, trombonist John Sarnelli, vocalist/trombonist Bob Fishel who said he sang with Red Norvo last summer at the Commodore Hotel, drummer Buddy Schutz, etc. I think saxist Joe Estren got the autographs of the rest of the band for us. Mortimer got some of the guys to pose for pictures and also got special permission to go in and take several pictures while the band broadcasted at 11:30. Barnet sure has got a swell band, especially smooth, although it isn't as good as last summer. For some reason he doesn't seem to sing any more, but his great tenor sax playing and clarineting is still the feature of the band. After the broadcast we left at about 12:20. It was still raining and we were stopped by a policeman who wanted to know why we were riding around so late. He let us go and we arrived home at 1:10am

This was also the night when 23-year-old Joe Louis became World Heavyweight Boxing Champion by stopping James J. Braddock in the 8th round at Comiskey Park in Chicago.

■ TUESDAY 22 JUNE 1937

RADIO LOGS

9:30PM WABC
BENNY GOODMAN
Camel Caravan program, NYC
I Got Rhythm (James; Musso)
A Handful Of Keys (BG Quartet)
The You And Me That Used To Be (vocal: Peg LaCentra)
Mean To Me

12.30AM WMCA
COUNT BASIE
Savoy Ballroom, NYC
Moten Swing (theme)
King Porter Stomp
Where Are You? (vocal: Billie Holiday)
Blue Ball

WEDNESDAY 23 JUNE 1937

RECORDING SESSION

JIMMY DORSEY AND HIS ORCHESTRA
Recording session for Decca in Los Angeles.
Jimmy Dorsey (cl/as); Joe Meyer (t); Toots Camarata (t/voc); Bobby Byrne, Don Mattison (tb/voc); Bruce Squires (tb); Len Whitney (as); Fud Livingston (as/ts); Charles Frazier (ts); Freddie Slack (p); Roc Hillman (g/voc); Jack Ryan (b); Ray McKinley (d/voc); Bob Eberly (voc)
Flight Of The Bumble Bee / The Moon Got In My Eyes (vBE) / *After You* (vDM) / *All You Want To Do Is Dance* (vBE) / *It's The Natural Thing To Do* (vDM)

RAYMOND SCOTT QUINTETTE
Recording session for Master in NYC.
Raymond Scott (p/ldr); Dave Wade (t); Pete Pumiglio (cl); Dave Harris (ts); Lou Shoobe (b); Johnny Williams (d)
Reckless Night On Board An Ocean Liner / Dinner Music For A Pack Of Hungry Cannibals

At 2:15pm Mrs Pastoriza drove Hughie, Jim Poe and myself to the subway at 241st Street in Mount Vernon from where we went to the city. We sure did have a lot of fun on the subway with some girl. After getting off, Poe went to some pool to swim while we went to see William Shine at the Conn Instrument Store. He told us that he didn't have any pictures as yet, but to come around next week. We then walked up to the Squibb Building on Fifth Avenue, to the Music Corporation of America, where we got 2 pictures of Edythe Wright and Peg LaCentra. We then walked down to Rockefeller Center where we met Vincent Prior at Rockwell-O'Keefe. He certainly is a swell guy. We had about 15 minutes with him. He warned me about the hold-ups at the Savoy when I told him that I was going there. When I asked why Rockwell-O'Keefe had dropped mananging Bunny Berigan's new band, he told us that the band was always 'getting drunk' so they let MCA take over the band. With such fine new men as clarinetist Joe Dixon, trombonist Sonny Lee, and trumpeter Irving Goodman, the band is steadily improving and should go places. Prior gave us pictures of: Woody Herman's Band, Sonny Dunham (2), Glenn Miller, and 5 of Glen Gray's Band. After that, at about 5:30, we went over to 799 7th Avenue, to Mills Artists, where we met Poe. Hughie left us at this point to keep a dinner engagement. We first went in and met one of the secretaries who gave me two foreign swing magazines: Hot Jazz (French) and De Jazz Wereld (Dutch). She left at 6:00 but we stayed and waited for Al Brackman (the man directly under Irving Mills) to come back and give us some pictures of the Raymond Scott Quintet. During that time we got ahold of many of the Master and Variety steel pressed recordings yet to be released. We played many of them. Some of them were Johnny Williams' (Scott Quintet) Band playing *Little Old Lady* and *52nd Street Stomp*; Barney Bigard's Jazzopators playing *Get It Southern Style* and *If You're Ever In My Arms Again*; and Ellington's records of *All God's Chillun Got Rhythm*, one with Ivie Anderson – the other a jam combination. I then went into another room and, from a special file, took out pictures of: Frankie Newton (trumpet), Earl Hines (piano), Caspar Reardon (harp), Raymond Scott (piano), Dolly Dawn (vocals), Lucky Millinder's band, Cab Calloway, part of Calloway's Band, Duke Ellington (6), and 5 of Ellington's Band. At about 6:30 some guy came in for an audition. He, 2 other guys, Poe and myself were in this little room. He was a copy of Fats Waller except that he can't play the piano well. Poe had his drumsticks along and accompanied him. The guy said that they would put him on the Saturday Night Swing Session this coming Saturday. Finally, at about 7:30, Al Brackman came but he didn't give us any pictures so we left. We took the subway up to the Savoy Ballroom, 140th Street at Lenox Avenue, where we paid 50 cents to go in at 9:30. Billy Hicks' Sizzlin' Six and Count Basie were

Caspar Reardon

Sonny Dunham

Raymond Scott

the two bands there tonight. Basie has been there for about two weeks and plans to stay 3 more — then going up to the Ritz-Carlton Hotel in Boston. Hicks always plays off and on at the Savoy. We got the autographs of all the guys in his band which included trombonist Fernando Arbello (formerly with Fletcher Henderson, Claude Hopkins and Chick Webb), Edmond Hall (formerly with Claude Hopkins in 1935), etc. They were pretty good.

We got all the autographs of the guys in Count Basie's Band. He has one of the best bands in the country – it's so relaxed. John Hammond says it's the best. Outstanding are tenor saxmen Lester Young & Herschel Evans; trumpeters Buck Clayton & Bobby Moore; pianist Count Basie; bassist Walter Page; drummer Jo Jones; and vocalist Billie Holiday, sensational blues singer, the greatest since Bessie Smith.

Fernando Arbelo – trombone
Edmond Hall
Scippy – Drums
Billy Hicks
Al Hall – Bass
Leroy Jones – Guitar
Cyril Haynes (Pianist)

Billy Hicks and his Sizzlin' Six

George Wettling and the brass section

Mortimer, who had joined us at the Savoy, and I had to leave at 12:20. We didn't do any dancing but were fascinated by watching the dancers do the Lindy hop, truckin', peckin', shag, etc. Basie's Band played the following numbers, and more: *Sometimes I'm Happy* (Evans' tenor), *I Surrender Dear* (Jimmy Rushing vocal), *House Hop, Boo Hoo, My First Thrill, Riffin' At The Ritz, I've Got My Eye On You* (Lester Young, Evans), *Pennies From Heaven* (Rushing vocal), *Jam Session, Always, Louise* (Evans), *Me, Myself And I* (Billie Holiday vocal), *Blue Ball* (Colossal: Evans' tenor, Lester's tenor), *Dreamboat, Mayflower* (Bobby Moore's trumpet, Young's tenor) etc. Too bad Billie Holiday didn't sing more numbers. After having a very enjoyable evening at the Savoy, we had to catch the 1:15 train from 138th Street to our homes in Bronxville.

Earlier in the evening Mortimer had gone to see Bunny Berigan and his Band at the Hotel Pennsylvania Roof where he took the photographs shown on this page. The personnel was: Bunny Berigan, Irving Goodman, Steve Lipkins (trumpets); Sonny Lee, Morey Samuel (trombones); Sid Perlmutter, Joe Dixon, Clyde Rounds, George Auld (saxes); Joe Lippman (piano); Tom Morgan (guitar); Arnold Fishkind (bass); George Wettling (drums); Ruth Bradley (vocals). They played: *It Looks Like Rain In Cherry Blossom Lane; There's A Lull In My Life; Trees; You Can't Run Away From Love; Was It Rain?; They All Laughed; All God's Chillun Got Rhythm; Mr Ghost Goes To Town; Someday Sweetheart; Ubangi Man; Black Bottom; Star Dust.*

Bunny Berigan at the Hotel Pennsylvania Roof

George Wettling

■ THURSDAY 24 JUNE 1937

RADIO LOGS

10.00PM WEAF
JIMMY DORSEY
Kraft Music Hall, Hollywood
They All Laughed (vocal: Bing Crosby) (Jimmy Dorsey's band)
Let's Call The Whole Thing Off (vocal: Bing Crosby & Constance Bennett)
Was It Rain? (vocal: Bing Crosby) (Jimmy Dorsey's clarinet)
Then I'll Be Happy (vocal: Bing Crosby) (Ray McKinley's drums)
There's A Lull In My Life (vocal: Bing Crosby) (tenor sax; saxes)
Put On Your Old Grey Bonnet (JIMMY DORSEY's Band: Joe Meyer's trumpet; piano; drums; Hillman's guitar)

■ FRIDAY 25 JUNE 1937

RECORDING SESSION

BUNNY BERIGAN AND HIS ORCHESTRA
Recording session for Victor in New York City.
Bunny Berigan, Irving Goodman, Steve Lipkins (t); Morey Samuel, Sonny Lee (tb); Sid Perlmutter, Joe Dixon (cl/as); Clyde Rounds, George Auld (ts); Joe Lippman (p); Tom Morgan (g); Arnold Fishkind (b); George Wettling (d); Ruth Gaylor (voc)
Roses In December (vRG) / *Mother Goose* (vRG) / *Frankie And Johnny* / *Mahogany Hall Stomp*

RADIO LOGS

9.00PM WJZ
LOUIS ARMSTRONG
Fleischmann Yeast program
When It's Sleepy Time Down South (theme) (nuttsy)
They All Laughed (Madison's tenor; Luis Russell's piano; Louis' trumpet)
Cuban Pete (Barbarin's drums)
Honeymoonin' In Manhattan (written by Louis Armstrong & Horace Gerlach)
Dinah

10.00PM WABC
TOMMY DORSEY
Kool Cigarette program
Wake Up And Live (vocal: Edythe Wright)
Strangers In The Dark (vocal: Jack Leonard)
Three Little Words (Johnny Mince; Tommy Dorsey)

■ SATURDAY 26 JUNE 1937

RADIO LOGS

5:00PM WABC
FRANK DAILEY
Meadowbrook, N.J.
A swell band except for a lousy accordion that ruins many fine arrangements.
Scattin' At The Kit-Kat
Having A Wonderful Time (vocal: Louise Wallace)
Carelessly
How Could You? (vocal: Louise Wallace)
Star Dust
On The Isle Of Kitchy-mi-boko
My Melancholy Baby
September In The Rain
Stumblin'
After You've Gone
Speakin' Of Dreams
Gypsy Violins (theme)

7.30PM WABC
SATURDAY NIGHT SWING SESSION No51
CBS Studio No1, 485 Madison Ave, NYC
Count Basie and Kay Thompson are the guests.
Hallelujah
Dinner Music For A Pack Of Hungry Cannibals (Raymond Scott Quintet)
Ain't Misbehavin'
Prince Of Wails (COUNT BASIE's marvelous, simple, original piano with CBS Band)
Boogie Woogie (COUNT BASIE playing marvelous swing piano and great vocal by JIMMY RUSHING)
The You And Me That Used To Be (great arrangement: Leith Stevens directing the CBS Band)
How Could You? (KAY THOMPSON, foremost gal rhythm singer, doing a marvelous vocal)
Reckless Night On Board An Ocean Liner (Raymond Scott Quintet going the nuts)
Crazy Rhythm (great arrangement for CBS Band: Harris' tenor; brass section)

David Low and I went up to see Lucky Millinder and Band at the Bronxville Field Club. We met Pastoriza, Johnson, Morningstar, O'Brien, Ryan, Revill, etc., up there. Because it was so expensive we didn't go in, but watched from a window directly next to the band. The band was plenty good. This is the third time I have seen Millinder at the Field Club with his second band. The only change from the band that we heard last time was that a girl vocalist has taken Chuck Richards' place. Chuck is now vocalizing for Fletcher Henderson. I don't know the girl's name but she sounded pretty good. Drummer O'Neil Spencer took several sweet vocals also. Outstanding in the band are pianist Billy Kyle, alto saxist Tab Smith, tenor saxist 'Specs' Arnold, and nice trumpet solos by all three trumpeters: Charlie Shavers, Carl Warwick and Harry Edison. I didn't get any autographs because I already have them all. Right now, I would say that Billy Kyle and Tab Smith are the only ones that are very, very fine. As I remember, here are a few numbers that the band played: *Marie; Dedicated To You; Organ Grinder's Swing; Showboat Shuffle; September In The Rain; Trust In Me; Merry-Go-Round; Star Dust* (Warwick's trumpet); *Big John Special; The You And Me That Used To Be; Ride, Red, Ride* (Great: their specialty); *You Showed Me The Way* (girl vocalist); and many others.

Bronxville Field Club
COLLEGE PROM
Saturday, June 26, 1937

Lucky Millinder
WITH MILLS BLUE RHYTHM BAND
9:30 until 2:30

AGE LIMIT BOYS
17 years and over

$3.50 per couple — Members
$4.00 per couple — Non-Members
STAGS — $3.00

RADIO LOGS

11:00PM WABC
BUNNY BERIGAN
Hotel Pennsylvania Roof, NYC
Was That The Human Thing To Do? (Joe Dixon)
Peckin' (Berigan)
It's Swell Of You (vocal: Ruth Bradley)
The Goona Goo (recorded on Brunswick)
If You Love Each Other (vocal: Ruth Bradley)
Black Bottom (Sonny Lee's swell trombone)
Wake Up And Live (vocal: Ruth Bradley) (Berigan; Auld)
Royal Garden Blues (Berigan; Auld; Dixon; Lee)
I Can't Get Started (theme)

11:05PM WJZ
WOODY HERMAN
Willows, nr Pittsburgh
There's A Lull In My Life (vocal: Woody Herman)
Weary Blues (Reid's trombone)
Where Is The Sun?
Doctor Jazz (vocal: Woody Herman) (another nuttsy vocal from Woody)
Gone With The Wind (vocal: Jenny Kaye)
It Happened Down In Dixieland (vocal: Woody Herman & Band)

11:30PM WOR
RED NORVO
Maurice Casino, Asbury Park, N.J.
I Know That You Know
Never In A Million Years (vocal: Mildred Bailey)
Slap That Bass
It Looks Like Love
The Love Bug Will Bite You (vocal: Mildred Bailey)
Turn Off The Moon
They Can't Take That Away From Me
Hallelujah

11.45PM WJZ
HUDSON-DeLANGE
Playland Casino, Rye, N.Y.
Hobo On Park Avenue (theme)
If I Could Be With You (trumpet; clarinet)
You're My Desire (vocal: Nan Wynn & Band) (SWELL)
Popcorn Man (vocal: Nan Wynn & Band)
Don't Kiss Me Again (vocal: Eddie DeLange)
Midnight At The Onyx (written by Will Hudson: great)

12.00 MIDNIGHT WNEW
JOE MARSALA
Hickory House, 144 W52nd Street, NYC
Wolverine Blues
Basin Street Blues
Jazz Me Blues
Singin' The Blues
St. Louis Blues
Farewell Blues
Bugle Blues

12.30AM WEAF
CHARLIE BARNET
Hickory Lodge, Larchmont, N.Y.
Somebody Loves Me
The You And Me That Used To Be (vocal: Gail Reese)
Lullaby To A Lamp Post
When Love Is Young
A Sailboat In The Moonlight (vocal: Kurt Bloom)
Rockin' Chair Swing
Caravan
Carelessly (vocal: Gail Reese)
Admiration
I've Lost Another Sweetheart (theme)

1:40AM WOR
EARL HINES
Trans-Atlantic Auditorium, L.A.
Fair.
Margie
Song Of India
Jammin' (vocal: Trummy Young)
I'll Never Tell You I Love You (vocal: Ida James)
Clarry (?) Doodle

■ SUNDAY 27 JUNE 1937

RADIO LOGS

11.00PM WABC
GUS ARNHEIM
Hotel New Yorker, NYC
Scattin' At The Kit-Kat
A Sailboat In The Moonlight (vocal: Ray Foster)
They Can't Take That Away From Me (vocal: June Robbins)
The Merry-Go-Round Broke Down (lousy song but good swing arrangement)
So Rare (vocal: Ray Foster)
Marquetta (clarinet; swell tenor; vibraphone; swell trumpet)
Love Is A Merry-Go-Round (vocal: June Robbins)
They All Laughed (vocal: John Hamilton)

11.30PM WICC
MIKE RILEY
Pleasure Beach Ballroom, Bridgeport, Conn
Study In Brown (trumpet; loud drums)
Sweet Leilani (lousy)
Ja-Da (good)
How Could You? (vocal: Lila Rose) (sang with Mal Hallett's Band a few months ago)
I'm Hatin' This Waitin' Around (vocal: Mike Riley)
Good Morning (vocal: Lila Rose) (trombone; tenor sax)
I Never Knew (Riley's trombone; loud drums; tenor sax on swell solo)
Mountain Music (vocal: Mike Riley) (trombone)
You Showed Me The Way (vocal: Mike Riley)

■ MONDAY 28 JUNE 1937

RADIO LOGS

11.05PM WABC
GUS ARNHEIM
Hotel New Yorker, NYC
Strangers In The Dark (vocal: June Robbins)
Honeysuckle Rose
Cuban Pete
Easy Living (vocal: June Robbins)
After Sundown
I'm Happy, Darling, Dancing With You

11.30PM WEAF
CHARLIE BARNET
Hickory Lodge, Larchmont, N.Y.
I've Lost Another Sweetheart (theme)
Marie (Barnett's great tenor; trombone; trumpet)
Echoes Of Harlem (COLOSSAL: Barnett's tenor)
Love Is A Merry-Go-Round (vocal: Gail Reese)
The Image of You
Tomorrow Is Another Day
You're My Desire
The Way You Look Tonight (vocal: Gail Reese)
Dusk In A Chinese Cemetery
You're Looking For Romance
Song Of India (the Dorsey arrangement)
Honeysuckle Rose

12.00 MIDNIGHT WNEW
JOE MARSALA
Hickory House, 144 W52nd Street, NYC
Marie (Joe Marsala's clarinet; Marty Marsala's trumpet)
They Can't Take That Away From Me (vocal: Adele Girard)
Blue Skies (2 Marsala brothers; Girard's harp; Ray Biondi's violin)
Body And Soul (Joe Bushkin's piano; Girard; Marsalas, etc)
Singin' The Blues (colossal clarinet by Joe)
Star Dust (Girard's harp; Bushkin's piano, etc)
Bugle Call Rag (Art Shapiro's bass; Danny Alvin's drums)

1.00AM WOR
COUNT BASIE
Savoy Ballroom, NYC
Yeah, Man! (tenor; Clayton's trumpet)
You Do The Darnedest Things, Baby (vocal: Jimmy Rushing)
Dear Old Southland (Basie's piano, etc)
I Can't Get Started (vocal: Billie Holiday)
St. Louis Blues (vocal: Jimmy Rushing) (long intro; 2 tenors; Walter Page's bass solo; Basie's piano; Jones' drums; trumpet; trombone)
Roseland Shuffle (Evans' tenor; Basie's piano; Jones' drums; very solid rhythm section)
Me, Myself And I (vocal: Billie Holiday) (marvelous vocal)
Baby Girl (Moore's trumpet; Minor's trombone; tenor; Basie's piano)
Thanksgiving (Lester Young's tenor; trumpet; Evans' tenor)

■ TUESDAY 29 JUNE 1937

Roddy Snow just came up from Washington, D.C. to visit for two days and then go to New England. We were driven to the subway by my brother at 2:00pm. That afternoon we went around getting pictures. Roddy got a lot more than I did because I already had most of them. I got a picture of Kay Weber from Rockwell-O'Keefe, where I saw Prior. Got 3 pictures of Edythe Wright, 2 pictures of Bunny Berigan, a picture of Ruth Bradley, 3 of Red Norvo, one of the Tommy Dorsey Trio, one of vocalist Billie Holiday, and from Mills Artists: one of Ina Ray Hutton, Rex Stewart, Duke Ellington, and from Consolidated: a picture of Earl Hines. After that we walked up and down Broadway noticing that Wingy Manone and his New Orleans Band was playing at Loew's State Theater and that Duke Ellington and Band were going to play there next week. We then took the subway up to 125th Street in Harlem where we paid 25 cents each to go in the Apollo Theater and see the stage show featuring Erskine Hawkins and his band along with 'Charlie Chan at the Olympics'. I was disappointed in Hawkins' screeching show-off trumpet but the band was pretty good, having good arrangements and a definite style of its own, somewhat like Jimmie Lunceford's band. The band played: *Campus Serenade* (theme); *There's A Lull In My Life* (Muriel Togue–new vocalist); *I've Got My Love To Keep Me Warm; Nagasaki; Dear Old Southland; Where Are You?* (Muriel Togue); *Too Marvelous For Words* (Togue); *They Can't Take That Away From Me* (Togue); *Three Little Words* (featuring the piano of Avery Parrish); *Trust In Me; Swingin' In Harlem; When My Dreamboat Comes Home* (vocalist Jimmy Mitchelle).

Erskine Hawkins and his Harlem Uproar Band

Peg LaCentra

Ina Ray Hutton

We then took the subway down to the Hotel Pennsylvania at 33rd Street and Seventh Avenue where we took the elevator up to the roof, arriving there at 9:20; the cover charge of 75 cents going on at 9:30, which we paid. Berigan's band is great. It has improved a great deal since I saw it in May. We had long talks with most of the guys. They were interested in us because we had so many pictures. Bunny autographed 2 pictures of himself for me; one of which he hadn't seen yet. Also got the whole band to autograph a picture of Berigan. No pictures of the band have been taken as yet. Also got the autograph of the songwriter who wrote *Gee, But You're Swell; June Night*, etc. who has just written some new pieces for Berigan to play. The personnel of the band is: Georgie Auld (tenor sax), Sid Perlmutter (lead alto sax), Joe Dixon (clarinet), Clyde Rounds (sax); Irving Goodman, Steve Lipkins (trumpets); Sonny Lee, Morey Samuels (trombones); Joe Lippman (piano, arranger); Tom Morgan (guitar); Arnold Fishkind (bass); George Wettling (drums). Was with Irving Goodman for quite a while. He says Ellington has one of the best bands; his brother Freddy is playing trumpet in Long Island; Peg LaCentra just left his brother's band, but he didn't know the new vocalist. Asked me if I was the guy who had a picture of him and Ziggy. I told him I was and he asked me if I could get him one. Wettling remembered me and asked for the picture that we took of him in May but I haven't got one as yet. He still drinks plenty. Talked to Sonny Lee about picture I had of him with Benny Goodman's recording band taken in '34 at the Columbia Studios in NYC when they made 8 records including *Emaline*. Joe Dixon and Clyde Rounds, both of whom used to be with Tommy Dorsey, said that Dorsey was a swell guy but hard to work for so they quit the band. Vocalist Ruth Bradley, who succeeded Sue Mitchell told us that she used to sing with Ruby Newman at the Rainbow Room and before that she played sax and clarinet with Ina Ray Hutton's All-Girl Orchestra. Trombonist Les Jenkins, who plays with Tommy Dorsey, came in at about 11:35 and talked with all the boys. He is very popular and a great trombone player. We were with Joe Dixon's brother from Boston who is about our age and plays trombone. We left at 12:45. A few numbers played were: *Where Or When* (Ruth Bradley); *The You And I That Used To Be* (Ruth Bradley); *Peckin'; Swanee River; A Sailboat In The Moonlight; So Rare* (Ruth Bradley); *I Can't Get Started* (Bunny Berigan); *Rockin' Chair Swing; Lady From Fifth Avenue* (Ruth Bradley); *Mr. Ghost Goes To Town; Stardust; Love Is A Merry-Go-Round* (Ruth Bradley); *Frankie And Johnny* (best number played by Berigan); *Last Night*.

SWING HIGH!
ON THE SKY-COOLED
PENNSYLVANIA ROOF
BUNNY BERIGAN
and his orchestra
Dinner and supper dancing every evening except Sunday
Open for luncheon, too
HOTEL
PENNSYLVANIA
33RD STREET AND 7TH AVENUE

On their broadcast over WABC at 11:00, announced by Bert Parks, they played: *You're Gonna Wake Up Some Day* (Ruth Bradley); *A Message From The Man In The Moon* (Ruth Bradley); *Kiss Me Again; Poor Robinson Crusoe* (Sonny Lee's trombone, George Auld's tenor); *They All Laughed* (Ruth Bradley); *Louise* (Auld's tenor, Dixon's clarinet, Lee's trombone, Berigan's trumpet); *You Can't Run Away From Love* (Ruth Bradley); *Swanee River* (Berigan's trumpet, Auld's tenor).

In the next two weeks, Bunny and the Band are going to be replaced by Tommy Dorsey's Band when Berigan's Band goes to play at the Pavillion Royale in Long Island for the summer.

RECORDING SESSION

MILDRED BAILEY & HER ORCHESTRA
Recording session for Vocalion in New York.
Buck Clayton (t); Edmond Hall (cl); Herschel Evans (ts); James Sherman (p); Freddie Green (g); Walter Page (b); Jo Jones (d); Mildred Bailey (v)
If You Should Ever Leave (vMB) / *The Moon Got In My Eyes* (vMB) / *Heaven Help This Heart Of Mine* (vMB) / *It's The Natural Thing To Do* (vMB)

RADIO LOGS

6:00pm WAAT
BUNNY BERIGAN
WAAT Studios, Jersey City, N.J.
SWELL.
I Can't Get Started (theme)
Dark Eyes (part of band jamming; Bunny; Sonny Lee's trombone; Wettling; Dixon)
Wang Wang Blues (very old piece; Joe Lippman's very solid piano sender)
BUNNY BERIGAN interviewed by announcer: Born in Wisconsin, November 2, 1907; First name is Bernard; First played violin; Married for 6 years; Has 2 children.

9:30pm WABC
BENNY GOODMAN
Camel Caravan program, Los Angeles
This is the first of a new series, a half-hour program now called Benny Goodman's Swing School, which features Benny exclusively without Jack Oakie and guests.
Alexander's Ragtime Band
Peckin'
Sweet Leilani (BG Trio)
Avalon (BG Quartet)
When It's Sleepy Time Down South (trumpet)
Sing, Sing, Sing (Krupa; brass, etc)

LISTEN TONIGHT! Benny Goodman EMPEROR OF SWING
BENNY GOODMAN'S "SWING SCHOOL"
Every Tuesday night at 8:30 pm E.S.T. (9.30 pm E.D.S.T.), 7:30 pm C.S.T., 6:30 pm M.S.T., 5:30 pm P.S.T., over WABC-Columbia Network.
COLUMBIA COAST-TO-COAST
GET A LIFT WITH A CAMEL

11.30pm WNEW
CONNIE McLEAN
Kit Kat Club, NYC
Mr Ghost Goes To Town
Summer Nights
Slap That Bass
Rockin' Chair
Christopher Columbus
Happy Birthday To Love
Siboney

■ WEDNESDAY 30 JUNE 1937

RECORDING SESSION

FLETCHER HENDERSON AND HIS ORCHESTRA
Recording session for Vocalion in Chicago.
Fletcher Henderson (p/ldr); Dick Vance, Russell Smith, Emmett Berry (t); John McConnell, Albert Wynn, Ed Cuffee (tb); Jerry Blake (cl/as/voc); Hilton Jefferson (cl/as); Elmer Williams, Chu Berry (ts); Lawrence Lucie (g); Israel Crosby (b); Pete Suggs (d); Chuck Richards (voc)
If You Ever Should Leave (vCR) / *Posin'* (vCR) / *All God's Chillun Got Rhythm* (vJB) / *Chris And His Gang*

RADIO LOGS

08:10pm WOR
WINGY MANONE
Jay C. Flippen's program
Isle Of Capri (vocal: Wingy Manone) (Wingy singing and playing trumpet)

12:00 midnight WJZ
WOODY HERMAN
Willows, nr Pittsburgh
Colossal.
Blue Prelude (theme) (nuttsy)
Blue Skies
There's A Lull In My Life (vocal: Woody Herman)
Blue Lou
Basin Street Blues (vocal: Woody Herman)
Ain't Misbehavin' (vocal: Jenny Kaye)
You Showed Me The Way (vocal: Woody Herman)
Davenport Blues
That's A-Plenty
Can't We Be Friends?

Bob had written to Dave Tough's **Hide-Hitter's Hangout** column in *Metronome*. This is Dave's published reply:

Mr. R. I. of Bronxville, New York, pondering over the futility of it all, wonders perplexedly if he should practice on a drum or on a pad; split good cymbals to make them sizzle; how to tell a good cymbal from a bad one; who is good and who is bad, and how good is who if he is good and when and where and why, and who do you think you are and why don't you go back where you came from.

Mr. R. I. has me right alongside of him in that private fog of his, but although it's with considerable trepidation I'll try to answer anything once.

He can make more noise, have more fun, and very probably get better results by practicing on a complete set. It's so often the things you hit and when that are more important than the beats themselves.

In answer to the second question I should recommend a Chinese sizzle cymbal in preference to splitting up a good Turkish cymbal. That sort of thing rarely works out with any success.

The third question, however, stops me in my tracks. Tentatively I should say that a good cymbal for him is one that sounds good to him. Or isn't it? That's the only way to judge a cymbal. Maybe R. I. means that he doesn't know what he likes. Does he? Is he trying to get whimsical on us? Mr. R. I., are you really pulling that left leg of mine—the nice leg that pounces on my high-hat? Don't you like cymbals at all?

But I can say this, sir, that Chick Webb is much better than whom and who and he's good and he's very good and he does everything there is to be done to a drum and he does it beautifully and sometimes he plays with such stupefying technique that he leaves you in a punch drunk stupor and ecstatically bewildered as this sentence has wound up to be.

P. S.: Mr. R. I. thinks *he's* confused.

JULY 1937

Hotel Pennsylvania: **Bunny Berigan** (–6); **Tommy Dorsey** (7–)
Hotel New Yorker: **Gus Arnheim** (–28); **Phil Napoleon** (29–)
Hotel Astor: **Ted Lewis** (5–)

Apollo Theater: **Ethel Waters/Eddie Mallory** (2–8); **Jimmie Lunceford** (9–15); **Edgar Hayes** (16–22); **Major Bowes** (23–29); **Cab Calloway** (30–)
Paramount Theater: **Mal Hallett** (21–)
Loew's State Theater: **Duke Ellington** (1–7); **Lucky Millinder** (22–28); **Gus Arnheim** (29–)

Hickory House: **Joe Marsala**
Onyx Club: **John Kirby/Spirits of Rhythm**

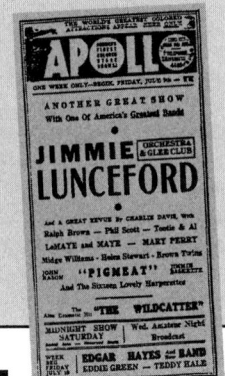

■ THURSDAY 1 JULY 1937

RECORDING SESSION

HUDSON-DeLANGE ORCHESTRA
Recording session for Brunswick in New York City.
Will Hudson (arr); Eddie DeLange (voc/ldr); Charles Mitchell, Howard Schaumberger, Jimmy Blake (t); Edward Kolyer, Jack Andrews (tb); George Bohn, Gus Bivona (cl/as); Pete Brendel (as/bar); Ted Duane (cl/ts); Mark Hyams (p); Bus Etri (g); Doc Goldberg (b); Nat Pollard (d); Nan Wynn (voc)
Popcorn Man (vNW) / *Yours And Mine* (vNW) / *I'm Feelin' Like A Million* (vNW)

RADIO LOGS

3.30PM WABC
ALEX BARTHA
Steel Pier, Atlantic City, N.J.
Heard this program at Nancy Long's house in Scarsdale.
This Is My Last Affair
It Looks Like Rain In Cherry Blossom Lane (vocal: Bert Nickerson)
Boo Hoo
Where Or When
Gee, But You're Swell

10.00pm WEAF
JIMMY DORSEY
Kraft Music Hall, Hollywood
Smarty (vocal: Bing Crosby) (Jimmy Dorsey's band)
It's The Natural Thing To Do (vocal: Bing Crosby)
All You Want To Do Is Dance (vocal: Bing Crosby) (written by Johnny Burke & Arthur Johnson)
Flight Of The Bumble Bee (JIMMY DORSEY's Band: Dorsey's alto sax; Byrne's trombone; Slack's piano)
The Moon Got In My Eyes (vocal: Bing Crosby)

11.45PM WABC
MERRY MAKERS
CBS Studios, NYC
Rusty Hinge (tenor)
Good Morning
The Lady From Fifth Avenue
You Can't Run Away From Love
We Can't Go On This Way

■ FRIDAY 2 JULY 1937

RECORDING SESSION

GLEN GRAY AND THE CASA LOMA ORCHESTRA
Recording session for Decca in Los Angeles.
Glen Gray (as/dir); Walter Smith, Grady Watts, Frank Zullo (t); Pee Wee Hunt (tb/voc); Billy Rauch, Fritz Hummel (tb); Clarence Hutchenrider (cl/as); Kenny Sargent (as/voc); Art Ralston (as/o/bsn); Danny d'Andrea (as); Pat Davis (cl/ts/fl); Joe Hall (p); Jack Blanchette (g); Stanley Dennis (b); Tony Briglia (d)
Yours And Mine (vKS) / *Let 'Er Go* / *I'm Feeling Like A Million* (vPWH) / *I May Be Wrong* (vPWH)

RADIO LOGS

5:00PM WJZ
MANHATTERS
NBC Studio Band, NYC
Satan Takes A Holiday (Cappy Reed on drums)
All God's Chillun Got Rhythm (vocal: Mildred Fenton)
The Lady Who Couldn't Be Kissed
Never In A Million Years (vocal: Mildred Fenton)

10.00PM WJZ
TOMMY DORSEY
Kool Cigarette program
Comedian Jack Pearl left the program last week. Now Tommy Dorsey & Band have whole program with some lousy tenor singer.
Song Of India
There's A Lull In My Life (vocal: Edythe Wright)
Marie (vocal: Jack Leonard & Band) (shorter than record: Pee Wee Erwin)
52nd Street (vocal: Edythe Wright & Three Esquires) (Novelty, mostly vocal)
My Melancholy Baby / Time On My Hands (vocal: Jack Leonard) (medley featuring Tommy Dorsey's trombone)
I Can't Give You Anything But Love, Baby (vocal: Edythe Wright)
Swing That Music (nuttsy: Bud Freeman's fast tenor; Dorsey's great trombone)
I'm Getting Sentimental Over You (theme)

"Posin": Edythe Wright indulges in some banter with Johnny Mince and Bud Freeman. Also visible are Tommy Dorsey and trumpeter Andy Ferretti.

11.05PM WABC
GUS ARNHEIM
Hotel New Yorker, NYC
The Old Spinning Wheel (trumpet; tenor sax; clarinet)
Gone With The Wind (vocal: Ray Foster)
The Lady Who Couldn't Be Kissed (vocal: John Hamilton)
When Buddha Smiles (trumpet; drums; piano; clarinet)
So Rare (vocal: Ray Foster)
The You And Me That Used To Be (vocal: June Robbins)
You're Looking For Romance
Sweet Leilani
Love Is A Merry-Go-Round (vocal: June Robbins)
Say It With Music (theme)

11:30PM WOR
RED NORVO
Steel Pier, Atlantic City, N.J.
Marvelous, Colossal!! Saxist Herbie Haymer is great. He is so relaxed, like the whole band. Great trumpeter, good clarinetist in Hank D'Amico. Mildred Bailey can't be beat as a vocalist. What a broadcast!!! Playing opposite Jan Savitt at Steel Pier.
Slap That Bass (Peterson's bass; tenor, etc)
The You And Me That Used To Be (vocal: Mildred Bailey)
I Surrender, Dear (magnificent: trombone; clarinet; tenor; Red; trumpet)
Clap Hands! Here Come Charlie
This Is My Last Affair (vocal: Mildred Bailey)
It Had To Be You (Red's xylophone; tenor, etc)
They All Laughed (vocal: Mildred Bailey)
Nagasaki (Red; Haymer's tenor; trumpet; brass section; clarinet: super-marvelous)

12:00 MIDNIGHT WEAF
JAN SAVITT
Million Dollar Pier, Atlantic City, N.J.
O.K.
You Were Born To Love (vocal: Carlotta Dale)
The Miller's Daughter Marianne (vocal: Bon-Bon Tunnell)
Sensation (swell Dixieland style: trumpet; trombone)
You Can't Run Away From Love (vocal: Dick Wharton)
Our Penthouse On Third Avenue (vocal: Carlotta Dale)
Davenport Blues (great: trumpet; clarinet)
You'll Never Go To Heaven (vocal: Bon-Bon Tunnell)
Yankee Doodle (swell: trombone; saxes)
I Know Now (vocal: Dick Wharton)

12:30AM WEAF
OZZIE NELSON
Million Dollar Pier, Atlantic City, N.J.
Fair.
Peckin' (swell arrangement: no vocal)
Hallelujah (vocal: Shirley Lloyd)
Never In A Million Years (vocal: Ozzie Nelson)
A Study In Brown (swell: baritone sax)
A Message From The Man In The Moon (vocal: Ozzie Nelson)
I'm Bubbling Over (vocal: Shirley Lloyd)
'Cause My Baby Says It's So
Where Or When
Exactly Like You (baritone sax; trumpet; brass)

1:00AM WOR
COUNT BASIE
Savoy Ballroom, NYC
Moten Swing (theme) (nuttsy theme: tenor sax)
Southside Stomp (Herschel Evans' tenor sax; Buck Clayton's muted trumpet; Jo Jones' drums)
Where Are You? (vocal: Jimmy Rushing) (commercial tune swung out: swell tenor sax)
Happy Feet (colossal: Basie's piano; Jones' solid drums; great trumpet; tenor sax)
Too Marvelous For Words (vocal: Billie Holiday) (swell: soft muted trumpet by Clayton)
One O'Clock Jump (Lester Young's colossal tenor sax; Dan Minor's good trombone; Buck Clayton's real jam muted trumpet; Walter Page's great bass)

Boo Hoo (vocal: Jimmy Rushing) (Basie's ballsy piano; Evans' tenor; trumpet)
Whatcha Gonna Do When There Ain't No Swing (vocal: Billie Holiday) (colossal piece: great vocal)
Moten Swing (Young's ballsy tenor sax; sax section; trumpet: great swing tune)

■ SATURDAY 3 JULY 1937

RADIO LOGS

8.00PM WABC
SATURDAY NIGHT SWING SESSION No52
CBS Studio No1, 485 Madison Ave, NYC
EXCELLENT. Announced by Mel Allen and Paul Douglas.
Nagasaki (great standard played by CBS Band: Harris' tenor; Williams' drums)
I've Got To Be A Rugcutter (IVIE ANDERSON & TRIO with Ellington Sextet)
Back Room Romp (DUKE ELLINGTON Sextet: Carney's great baritone sax)
Too Marvelous For Words (Leith Stevens directing CBS Band: swell brass section)
Swing, Brother, Swing (BILLIE HOLIDAY with a sensational vocal: piano)
Scattin' At The Kit-Kat (colossal: CBS Band with Dave Harris' tenor)
After You've Gone (Paul Starrett, CBS arranger, playing a colossal ukulele)
Dinah (really nuttsy jammin' by DUKE ELLINGTON on piano; Sonny Greer on drums; Hayes Alvis on bass; Harry Carney on baritone; Tricky Sam Nanton on trombone; and Rex Stewart and Cootie Williams on trumpets)

11:00PM WABC
BUNNY BERIGAN
Hotel Pennsylvania Roof, NYC
Great. Much improvement over two months ago.
Black Bottom (Wettling's solid drums; Bunny, etc)
So Rare (vocal: Ruth Bradley)
If I Had You (Sonny Lee's trombone; Auld's tenor sax)
The Lady From Fifth Avenue (vocal: Ruth Bradley)
All God's Chillun Got Rhythm (vocal: Ruth Bradley)
I'm Happy, Darling, Dancing With You (vocal: Ruth Bradley)
'Cause My Baby Says It's So (vocal: Bunny Berigan)
Mahogany Hall Stomp (Berigan; Auld; Lee; Dixon)
I Can't Get Started (theme)

11:30PM WABC
FRANK DAILEY
Meadowbrook, N.J.
Swell spots but terrible accordion. Louise Wallace is a swell vocalist.
Scattin' At The Kit-Kat
You're My Desire (vocal: Louise Wallace)
Mountain Music
Southland Serenade (vocal: Louise Wallace)
Oh, Lady Be Good
Star Dust
Image Of You
Having A Wonderful Time (vocal: Louise Wallace)
My Melancholy Baby
On The Trail Of The Lonesome Pine
Stompin' At The Savoy
Gypsy Violins (theme)

12:00 MIDNIGHT WPG
RED NORVO
Steel Pier, Atlantic City, N.J.
Marvelous.
Slap That Bass (Norvo's xylophone; long relaxed trumpet solo; Bill Miller's piano; Haymer's tenor)
This Is My Last Affair (vocal: Mildred Bailey) (super-colossal vocal)
Heaven Help This Heart Of Mine (trumpet; Norvo's xylophone; Haymer's tenor; trombone)
A Porter's Love Song (trumpet; Norvo; Hank D'Amico's swell long clarinet; drums)
'Long About Midnight (vocal: Mildred Bailey) (great song; trombones;

saxes; drums)
Turn Off The Moon (D'Amico's clarinet; Norvo; Haymer's swell relaxed tenor; trumpet)
The You And Me That Used To Be (vocal: Mildred Bailey) (trumpet; D'Amico's clarinet)
Do You Ever Think Of Me? (NUTTSY: Norvo's xylophone; saxes; brass; D'Amico's clarinet; trumpet)

12:30AM WEAF
FLETCHER HENDERSON
Grand Terrace, Chicago
Good.
Christopher Columbus (theme) (composed by Henderson last year)
Liza (swell, recorded on Decca)
If You Should Ever Leave
Old King Cole
Stealin' Apples (Fletcher Henderson's piano; Chu Berry's marvelous tenor)
Mountain Music
Posin' (trumpet; clarinet)
Jangled Nerves (wonderful tenor sax; trumpet)
Don't You Care What Anyone Says? (vocal: male vocalist) (tenor sax)
Tiger Rag

12:30AM WABC
GLEN GRAY
Palomar Ballroom, LA
Smoke Rings (theme)
A Study In Brown (recorded on Decca: Walter Smith's trumpet)
Strangers In The Dark (vocal: Kenny Sargent)
Jammin' (vocal: Pee Wee Hunt)
Where Or When (vocal: Kenny Sargent)
Goblin Market
I May Be Wrong (vocal: Pee Wee Hunt)
How Am I To Know (6 saxes; nuttsy clarinet)
Casa Loma Stomp (written by arranger Gene Gifford)

■ SUNDAY 4 JULY 1937

RADIO LOGS

5:00PM WOR
RED NORVO
Steel Pier, Atlantic City, N.J.
Jammin' (trumpet; Norvo's xylophone; brass, etc)
More Than You Know (vocal: Mildred Bailey)
Carelessly (Herbie Haymer's nuttsy tenor sax)
All God's Chillun Got Rhythm (Purtill's drums)
The Love Bug Will Bite You (vocal: Mildred Bailey)
Mean To Me (Haymer's tenor; Norvo's xylophone; D'Amico's clarinet)
Never In A Million Years (vocal: Mildred Bailey)
Rhythm Roundup (swell: trombone; Haymer's tenor sax)

9:30PM WPG
OZZIE NELSON
Million Dollar Pier, Atlantic City, N.J.
There's A Lull In My Life (vocal: Shirley Lloyd)
Peckin'
'Cause My Baby Says It's So
Basin Street Blues
Never In A Million Years (vocal: Ozzie Nelson)

11.05PM WABC
GUS ARNHEIM
Hotel New Yorker, NYC
Alibi Baby (vocal: John Hamilton)
Message From The Moon (vocal: June Robbins)
The Image Of You (vocal: Ray Foster)
Mean To Me (swell trumpet)
The Moon Got In My Eyes (vocal: Ray Foster)
The Love Bug Will Bite You
Let's Call The Whole Thing Off (vocal: June Robbins)
Dancing Under The Stars (vocal: Ray Foster)

11:30PM WOR
LOUIS ARMSTRONG
Maurice Casino, Asbury Park, N.J.
Great.
Alexander's Ragtime Band
September In The Rain (vocal: Bobbie Caston)
All God's Chillun Got Rhythm (Henry Allen's trumpet)
Cuban Pete (vocal: Louis Armstrong)
Ida, Sweet As Apple Cider (Bingie Madison's tenor sax, etc)
What Will I Tell My Heart? (vocal: Sonny Woods) (tenor sax)
Swing That Music (vocal: Louis Armstrong) (written by Armstrong)
When It's Sleepy Time Down South (vocal: Louis Armstrong)

12:00 MIDNIGHT WOR
NYE MAYHEW
Glen Island Casino, New Rochelle, N.Y.
Lousy.
I'm Happy, Darling, Dancing With You
Speak Easy (trumpet; tom-toms; tenor sax)
I'm Hatin' This Waitin' Around (vocal: Douglas Newman)
When
I've Got My Love To Keep Me Warm
Tain't No Use
I Get A Kick Out Of You
Cheek To Cheek
The Goona Goo
Japanese Sandman

12:30AM WPG
RED NORVO
Steel Pier, Atlantic City, N.J.
Announced by Ray Morgan.
Clap Hands, Here Comes Charlie
There's A Lull In My Life (vocal: Mildred Bailey)
Turn Off The Moon
Without Your Love (nuttsy piece; trumpet)
St. Louis Blues (vocal: Mildred Bailey)
Jammin' (Haymer's tenor; trumpet)
The You And Me That Used To Be (vocal: Mildred Bailey)
Do You Ever Think Of Me? (theme) (ballsy: Norvo; D'Amico's clarinet)

12:30AM WEAF
FLETCHER HENDERSON
Grand Terrace, Chicago
Posin' (vocal: Chuck Richards) (trumpet)
All God's Chillun Got Rhythm
Unknown Title (written by Fletcher Henderson)
Where Or When (vocal: Chuck Richards)
Honeysuckle Rose (Chu Berry's tenor sax; Blake's clarinet)

■ MONDAY 5 JULY 1937

RADIO LOGS

12:00 NOON WABC
SWINGIN' THE BLUES
CBS Studios, NYC
Announced by Jerry Lawrence.
Jazz Me Blues (Dixieland-style, nuttsy jammin': trumpet; great tenor sax solo; Pumiglio's clarinet; Williams' ballsy drums)
Basin Street Blues (marvelous slow, blue trumpet in the style of Marty Marsala; short clarinet solo; ending)
Royal Garden Blues (drum intro with cow-bells, etc; tenor sax by Harris or Ross; Williams drum break; slow breakaway ending with solid rhythm section)
Mood Indigo (one of Duke Ellington's greatest pieces: soft, muffled clarinet; muted trumpet)

12:45AM WABC
GLEN GRAY
Palomar Ballroom, Los Angeles
Blue Room
It's Swell Of You (vocal: Kenny Sargent)
On The Isle Of Kitchy-mi-boko (vocal: Pee Wee Hunt)
Chinatown, My Chinatown

1:00AM WOR
COUNT BASIE
Savoy Ballroom, NYC
I Found A New Baby
Never In A Million Years (vocal: Billie Holiday)
There's A Lull In My Life

■ TUESDAY 6 JULY 1937

RECORDING SESSION

BENNY GOODMAN AND HIS ORCHESTRA
Recording session for Victor in Hollywood.
Benny Goodman (cl); Chris Griffin, Harry James, Ziggy Elman (t); Red Ballard, Murray McEachern (tb); George Koenig, Hymie Shertzer (as); Art Rollini, Vido Musso (ts); Jess Stacy (p); Allan Reuss (g); Harry Goodman (b); Gene Krupa (d)
Peckin' / Can't We Be Friends? / Sing, Sing, Sing Part 1 / Sing, Sing, Sing Part 2

RADIO LOGS

9:30PM WABC
BENNY GOODMAN
Camel Caravan program, Los Angeles
The second half-hour program now called Benny Goodman's Swing School.
Blue Skies (Harry James' trumpet)
Swingtime In The Rockies (Musso; Elman)
Body And Soul (BG Trio)
A Handful Of Keys (BG Quartet)
Can't We Be Friends?
Bugle Call Rag (Harry James' trumpet)

11.00PM WEAF
HUDSON-DeLANGE
Playland Casino, Rye, N.Y.
Dallas Blues (vocal: Eddie DeLange)
You're My Desire (vocal: Nan Wynn & Band)
Lost Again (vocal: Eddie DeLange)
Caravan (clarinets; Duane's tenor)
Sophisticated Swing
Let's Call The Whole Thing Off
If I Could Be With You
Hobo On Park Avenue (theme) (played in full)

11:05PM WABC
BUNNY BERIGAN
Hotel Pennsylvania Roof, NYC
Mel Allen announced.
The You And Me That Used To Be (vocal: Ruth Bradley)
Who'll Be My Romance This Summer? (vocal: Ruth Bradley)
You Can't Run Away From Love Tonight (vocal: Ruth Bradley)
The Prisoner's Song
Poor Robinson Crusoe (Dixon; Auld)
Love Is A Merry-Go-Round (vocal: Ruth Bradley)
Swanee River
The Image Of You (vocal: Ruth Bradley) (Berigan's trumpet)
Louise (Georgie Auld's tenor sax; Sonny Lee's trombone; Bunny)

11:30PM WABC
RED NORVO
Steel Pier, Atlantic City, N.J.
Announced by George Foster.
I Know That You Know (colossal arrangement: Haymer's tenor; trombone; Norvo; great ending)
Never In A Million Years (vocal: Mildred Bailey) (Bailey singing as only she can: she's colossal!!!)
Without Your Love (swell slow foxtrot: Haymer's tenor; Hyland's trumpet; trombone)
Carelessly (Haymer's short tenor solo; trumpet; trombone; Norvo's low-down xylophone)
Honeysuckle Rose (vocal: Mildred Bailey) (stupendous song sung by The Queen of Swing)
Drop Me Off At Harlem (Ellington piece with typical Ellington saxes; Norvo; D'Amico)
They Can't Take That Away From Me (vocal: Mildred Bailey) (swell)
Do You Ever Think Of Me? (theme)

12.30AM WABC
TOMMY DORSEY
Pavillon Royale, Long Island, N.Y.
Wake Up And Live (vocal: Edythe Wright)
The Morning After (vocal: Jack Leonard)
Barcarolle (another old classic in swing style)
There's A Lull In My Life (vocal: Edythe Wright)
Canadian Capers (TD's dirty trombone; Freeman's tenor; Mince; Tough's drums)
Our Penthouse On Third Avenue (vocal: Jack Leonard) (lousy song)
Humoresque (arranged by TD and Paul Wetstein: recorded on Victor 25600)
Once In A While (vocal: Edythe Wright & Three Esquires)
Liza (great: Bud Freeman really sending me with his tenor sax solo, and Johnny Mince doing his bit on clarinet)

Tommy Dorsey

■ WEDNESDAY 7 JULY 1937

RECORDING SESSION

BENNY GOODMAN AND HIS ORCHESTRA
Recording session for Victor in Hollywood.
Benny Goodman (cl); Chris Griffin, Harry James, Ziggy Elman (t); Red Ballard, Murray McEachern (tb); George Koenig, Hymie Shertzer (as); Art Rollini, Vido Musso (ts); Jess Stacy (p); Allan Reuss (g); Harry Goodman (b); Gene Krupa (d); Betty Van (voc)
Roll 'Em / When It's Sleepy Time Down South / Afraid To Dream (vBV) / Changes

REX STEWART & HIS 52ND STREET STOMPERS
Recording session for Master Records in New York City.
Rex Stewart (c); Freddy Jenkins (t); Johnny Hodges (ss/as); Harry Carney (cl/bar); Duke Ellington (p); Brick Fleagle (g); Hayes Alvis (b); Jack Maisel (d)
Back Room Romp (A Contrapuntal Stomp) / Love In My Heart (Swing, Baby, Swing) / Sugar Hill Shim-Sham / Tea And Trumpets

COUNT BASIE AND HIS ORCHESTRA
Recording session for Decca in New York City.
Buck Clayton, Ed Lewis, Bobby Moore (t); Dan Minor, George Hunt (tb); Earle Warren (as); Lester Young, Herschel Evans (ts); Jack Washington (bar); Count Basie (p); Freddie Green (g); Walter Page (b); Jo Jones (d); Jimmy Rushing (voc)
Smarty / One O'Clock Jump / Listen My Children, And You Shall Hear (vJR) / John's Idea

BOB CROSBY AND HIS ORCHESTRA
Recording session for Decca in New York City.
Bob Crosby (voc/ldr); Zeke Zarchy, Yank Lawson (t); Ward Silloway, Warren Smith (tb); Matty Matlock (cl/as); Bill DePew (as); Eddie Miller (cl/ts); Gil Rodin (ts); Bob Zurke (piano); Nappy Lamare (g/voc); Bob Haggart (b); Ray Bauduc (d); Kay Weber (voc)
Whispers In The Dark (vKW) / Stop, You're Breaking My Heart (vBC) / The Loveliness Of You (vBC) / You Can't Have Everything (vKW)

Dick Morningstar and Bob drive up to spend 10 days with Hughie Pastoriza at his place near Wolfeboro on Lake Winnipesaukee in New Hampshire.

RADIO LOGS

10.45PM WEAF
JOHNNY O'BRYAN
San Francisco, Cal
The You And Me That Used To Be (all tunes feature O'Bryan's swell harmonica)
Blue Prelude
Runnin' Wild

11.05PM WABC
TOMMY DORSEY
Pavillon Royale, Long Island, N.Y.
Never In A Million Years (vocal: Jack Leonard)
Hymn To The Sun (lousy: Dorsey's trombone)
Star Dust (vocal: Edythe Wright) (nuttsy: Dorsey's trombone)
Satan Takes A Holiday (swell, written by Larry Clinton: Dave Tough's drums)
The Morning After (vocal: Jack Leonard)
The Stolen Melody (Pee Wee Erwin's trumpet; Freeman's nuttsy tenor; Mince)
Once In A While (vocal: Edythe Wright & Three Esquires)
I've Got To Swing (swell: Mince; Tough; Howard Smith's piano; Freeman; Tommy)

12.00 MIDNIGHT WNEW
JOE MARSALA
Hickory House, 144 W52nd Street, NYC
SWELL: REAL swing.
Wolverine Blues (Marty Marsala's trumpet; Girard's harp)
Gone With The Wind (vocal: Adele Girard)
Blue Skies (Marty Marsala's trumpet; Joe's clarinet)
Body And Soul (featuring Adele Girard's swell harp)
All Of Me (Joe Bushkin's piano; 2 Marsalas; guitar)
Farewell Blues (same as Delta Four's Decca record: nuttsy)

12.30AM WJZ
WOODY HERMAN
Willows, nr Pittsburgh, Pa
WONDERFUL. Great Dixieland stuff. Real swing artists. Herman has a grand swing voice and a sentimental one.
Alexander's Ragtime Band (great: Herman's clarinet; Carlson's drums; Yoder's bass)
September In The Rain (vocal: Woody Herman) (Saxie Mansfield's swell tenor sax)
My Blue Heaven (Herman's swell clarinet; saxes; Joe Bishop's flugel horn)
How Am I To Know? (featuring Saxie Mansfield)
Was It Rain?
Doctor Jazz (vocal: Woody Herman) (Reid's trombone; Yoder's bass)
Can't We Be Friends (Reid; Yoder; clarinet)
I'm Confessin' (Mansfield; Reid)
Blue Lou (Herman's clarinet; Mansfield)

1.30AM WOR
COUNT BASIE
Savoy Ballroom, NYC
GREAT. So relaxed.
Yeah, Man! (Clayton's trumpet; Herschel Evans' tenor: used to be called *Hotter Than Hell*)
Me, Myself And I (vocal: Billie Holiday) (nuttsy piece: Billie singing as only she can!)
Rhythm In My Nursery Rhymes (vocal: Jimmy Rushing)
Roseland Shuffle (recorded on Decca 1141: Basie's swell boogie-woogie piano)
Swinging At The Daisy Chain (Basie's piano; Page's solid bassing; Jo Jones' drums; trumpet)
I Must Have That Man (vocal: Billie Holiday) (grand old piece: great vocal by red-headed Billie)
Dinah (vocal: Jimmy Rushing) (Count Basie's typical piano)
Thanksgiving (Evans' tenor; Basie; trumpet)

■ THURSDAY 8 JULY 1937

RECORDING SESSION

JIMMIE LUNCEFORD AND HIS ORCHESTRA
Recording session for Decca in New York City.
Jimmie Lunceford (ldr); Paul Webster (t); Eddie Tompkins, Sy Oliver (t/voc); Elmer Crumbley, Russell Bowles, Eddie Durham (tb); Willie Smith (cl/as/bar/voc); Earl Carruthers (cl/as/bar); Ed Brown (as); Dan Grissom (cl/as/voc); Joe Thomas (cl/ts/voc); Edwin Wilcox (p); Al Norris (g); Moses Allen (b); Jimmy Crawford (d)
Posin' (vWS & Band) / The First Time I Saw You (vDG) / Honey, Keep Your Mind On Me (vDG) / Put On Your Old Grey Bonnet (vET)

RADIO LOGS

11.30PM WABC
RED NORVO
Steel Pier, Atlantic City, N.J.
GREAT!
All God's Chillun Got Rhythm
There's A Lull In My Life (vocal: Mildred Bailey)
Sweet Is The Word For You
Slap That Bass (trumpet; Haymer's tenor sax)
Rockin' Chair (vocal: Mildred Bailey) (GREAT)
Decca Stomp [Queen Isabella] (NUTTSY: Norvo; Haymer)
The Love Bug Will Bite You (vocal: Mildred Bailey) (swell)
Hallelujah (Haymer's nuttsy tenor sax; Norvo's xylophone)

■ FRIDAY 9 JULY 1937

RECORDING SESSION

RED NORVO AND HIS ORCHESTRA
Recording session for Brunswick in New York City.
Red Norvo (xyl/ldr); Louis Mucci, George Wendt, Stew Pletcher (t); Al Mastren (tb); Charles Lamphere, Hank D'Amico (cl/as); Len Goldstein (as); Herbie Haymer (ts); Bill Miller (p); Red McGarvey (g); Pete Peterson (b); Maurice Purtill (d); Mildred Bailey (voc)
Everyone's Wrong But Me (vMB) / *Posin'* / *The Morning After* (vMB) / *Do You Ever Think Of Me?*

RADIO LOGS

8:30PM WHDH
CLAUDE HOPKINS
Canobie Lake Park, Salem, N.H.
Good.
I Would Do Anything For You (theme)
Swingtime In The Rockies
Never In A Million Years (vocal: Beverly 'Baby' White)
Just You (Hopkins soloing on piano)
My Dear (Hopkins' piano; Pete Jacobs' drums)
Margie (vocal: Beverly 'Baby' White) (swell old piece)
Plantation Swing
Marie (vocal: Beverly 'Baby' White) (great vocal)
Sometimes I'm Happy (NUTTSY: tenor sax)

9:00PM WAAB
FRANKIE WARD
Nautical Plaza, Revere Beach, Mass
Darn good.
I Surrender Dear (great, one of Ward's best arrangements: nuttsy saxes; Ward's xylophone)
They Can't Take That Away From Me (swell tune but way over-played: tenor sax)
Where Are You? (vocal: Carmen Trudeau)
Copenhagen (swell: Ward's vibes; Gene Rosati's tenor sax)
Never In A Million Years
What Will I Tell My Heart? (vocal: Carmen Trudeau)
Satan Takes A Holiday
Love Is Good (vocal: Carmen Trudeau)

CANOBIE LAKE PARK
Beautiful New Ballroom—SALEM, N.H.
TONIGHT
America's Greatest Colored Pianist
CLAUDE HOPKINS
and his famous colored orchestra
Admission 65c tax incl.
Check Dancing every Wed., Thurs., Sat.
Tune in WHDH 8:30 to 9 P.M. Every Wed., Thurs., Fri., Sat.

Front row: Claude Hopkins, piano; Jabbo Smith, trumpet; Vic Dickenson, trombone; Beverly White, vocalist; Ben Smith, sax; Joe Jones, guitar. Standing: Abe Baker, bass; Gene Johnson, sax; Shirley Clay, trumpet; Bobby Sands, sax; Chauncey Haughton, sax; Fred Norman, trombone; Lincoln Mills, trumpet; Pete Jacobs, drums.

10.00PM WJZ
TOMMY DORSEY
Kool Cigarette Program, NYC
Swell.
Dark Eyes (Dorsey's muted trombone; Mince; Erwin)
Our Penthouse On Third Avenue (vocal: Jack Leonard)
Beale Street Blues (COLOSSAL: Erwin; Freeman; 4 clarinets; Mince)
The First Time I Saw You (vocal: Morton Bowe) (guest)
Posin' (vocal: Edythe Wright) (solos by Dave Tough; Bud Freeman; Pee Wee Erwin; Mince; Dorsey)
Whispering (vocal: Jack Leonard)
Avalon (very short, featuring Dorsey's trombone)
Japanese Sandman (short, featuring Johnny Mince's clarinet)
That's A-Plenty (GREAT: Mince; Erwin; Freeman)
I'm Getting Sentimental Over You (theme)

11:30PM WABC
BOB CROSBY
Ritz-Carlton Hotel, Boston
Summertime (theme)
At The Jazz Band Ball (Miller; Bauduc; Smith; Matlock)
Carelessly (vocal: Kay Weber)
Stop, You're Breaking My Heart (vocal: Bob Crosby)
Gin Mill Blues (COLOSSAL: Zurke's piano; Miller)
To A Sweet And Pretty Thing (vocal: Bob Crosby)
Stumblin' (8 BOBCATS)
Never In A Million Years (vocal: Kay Weber)
South Rampart Street Parade

12.00 MIDNIGHT WEAF
JAN SAVITT
Million Dollar Pier, Atlantic City, N.J.
O.K. Nuttsy on some numbers but terrible on others.
Quaker City Jazz (theme) (trombone)
Riverboat Shuffle (great: trombone; trumpet)
You Were Born To Love (vocal: Carlotta Dale)
I Know Now (vocal: Dick Wharton)
Copenhagen (SWELL: clarinet; trombone; trumpet)
Love Is A Merry-Go-Round (vocal: Bon Bon Tunnell)
The Image Of You (vocal: Carlotta Dale)
Turkey In The Straw (trumpet; clarinet)
A Message From The Man In The Moon (vocal: Dick Wharton)
Where Or When (vocal: Carlotta Dale)
The Ghost Of Casey Jones (vocal: Bon Bon Tunnell)

12.30AM WJZ
FLETCHER HENDERSON
Grand Terrace Café, Chicago
GOOD.
Blue Lou (trumpet; Israel Crosby's bass; tenor)
Love Is Never Out Of Season (vocal: Chuck Richards)
Old King Cole (Chu Berry's tenor)
If You Should Ever Leave (vocal: Chuck Richards)

Caesar's Ghost (clarinet; Berry's tenor; trumpet)
Posin' (vocal: Chuck Richards) (from the *New Grand Terrace Revue* written by Sammy Cahn & Saul Chaplin)
Jangled Nerves (excellent: Chu Berry's tenor)
They Can't Take That Away From Me (vocal: Chuck Richards)
Tiger Rag (great: Chu Berry's tenor; trombones)
Christopher Columbus (theme)

■ SATURDAY 10 JULY 1937

RECORDING SESSION

TOMMY DORSEY AND HIS ORCHESTRA
Recording session for Victor in New York City.
Tommy Dorsey (tb); Pee Wee Erwin, Joe Bauer, Andy Ferretti (t); Les Jenkins, Red Bone (tb); Johnny Mince, Fred Stulce, Mike Doty (cl/as); Bud Freeman (ts); Howard Smith (p); Carmen Mastren (g); Gene Traxler (b); Russ Isaacs (d); Edythe Wright (voc)
The Things I Want / *Allegheny Al* (vEW)

TOMMY DORSEY AND HIS CLAMBAKE SEVEN
Recording session for Victor in New York City.
Tommy Dorsey (tb); Pee Wee Erwin (t); Johnny Mince (cl); Bud Freeman (ts); Howard Smith (p); Carmen Mastren (g); Gene Traxler (b); Russ Isaacs (d); Edythe Wright (voc)
My Cabin Of Dreams (vEW) / *You're My Desire* (vEW) / *Am I Dreaming?* (vEW) / *In My Meditations* (vEW)

RADIO LOGS

6.00PM WEAF
WILLIE BRYANT
NBC Studios, NYC
Plenty O.K.
It's Over Because We're Through (theme)
This And That (George Matthews' nuttsy trombone)
Steak And Potatoes (vocal: Willie Bryant)
Liza (Otis Johnson's trumpet; saxes; trombone)
Never In A Million Years (vocal: Arnold Adams) (Adams is guitarist with the band)
Where Are You?
'Way Down Yonder In New Orleans
St. Louis Blues (vocal: Willie Bryant) (swell piano)
Riffin' At The Ritz
It's Over Because We're Through (theme)

8.00PM WABC
SATURDAY NIGHT SWING SESSION No53
CBS Studio No1, 485 Madison Ave, NYC
Heard this program in a store in Wolfeboro, N.H.
Unknown Title
I Got Rhythm (JOHNNY CALI & TONY GATTUSO good guitar duet)
Swing Guitars (JOHNNY CALI & TONY GATTUSO good guitar duet)
Caravan (Ellington's great piece: saxes)
Beale Street Blues (TOMMY DORSEY'S CLAMBAKE 7)
Alibi Baby (EDYTH WRIGHT & TOMMY DORSEY'S CLAMBAKE 7)
My Little Friend (GOGO DE LYS singing an unusual vocal)
Down South Camp Meetin' (CBS Band)
The Toothache (Raymond Scott Quintet playing its latest piece. They are leaving soon to make a movie in Hollywood)

11.30PM WABC
GUS ARNHEIM
Hotel New Yorker, NYC
The Moon Got In My Eyes (vocal: Ray Foster)
Peckin'
Easy Living (vocal: June Robbins)
It's The Natural Thing To Do
Say It With Music (theme)

12.00 MIDNIGHT WNEW
JOE MARSALA
Hickory House, 144 W52nd Street, NYC
Night Over Shanghai (vocal: Adele Girard)
Oh, Sister, Ain't That Hot!
Night And Day (vocal: Adele Girard)
Royal Garden Blues
Singin' The Blues (written by Frankie Trumbauer: Joe Marsala's clarinet)
Copenhagen (Joe Bushkin's piano)

■ SUNDAY 11 JULY 1937

George Gershwin Dies Of Brain Tumour In Hollywood

RADIO LOGS

6:30PM WOR
FUN IN SWINGTIME
WOR Studios, NYC
Bunny Berigan Orchestra.
Was It Rain? (Georgie Auld; Sonny Lee; Joe Lippman)
Peckin' (saxes; Bunny)
The Prisoner's Song (Bunny; Georgie Auld; Joe Dixon)
I Can't Get Started (theme)

■ MONDAY 12 JULY 1937

RADIO LOGS

8.00PM WEAF
CHICK WEBB
'Goodtime Society', NYC
NUTTSY. Fitzgerald is tops.
What A Shuffle!
If You Should Ever Leave (vocal: Ella Fitzgerald)
I Never Knew (Ted McRae's sharp tenor sax: swell)
Stop! You're Breaking My Heart (vocal: Ella Fitzgerald)
Clap Hands! Here Comes Charlie

8.30PM WJZ
PAUL WHITEMAN
Fort Worth, Texas
Played in honor of George Gershwin who died yesterday.
Rhapsody In Blue (one of George Gershwin's greatest pieces)
Summertime (Jack Teagarden's wonderful trombone)

12.00 MIDNIGHT WOR
TOMMY DORSEY
Hotel Pennsylvania Roof, NYC
Good Morning (vocal: Edythe Wright)
Love Is Never Out Of Season (vocal: Jack Leonard) (Freeman's tenor; Mince's clarinet)
Who'll Buy My Violets? (wonderful: Dorsey's trombone; Tough's drums; Freeman; Erwin)
So Rare (vocal: Edythe Wright)
Liza (Dorsey's trombone; Mince's marvelous clarinet; Bud Freeman's tenor sax)
Once In A While (vocal: Jack Leonard & Three Esquires) (written by Tommy Dorsey)
My Blue Heaven
The Morning After (vocal: Jack Leonard) (written by Tommy Dorsey)
Jammin' (vocal: Edythe Wright)

12:00 MIDNIGHT WABC
BOB CROSBY
Ritz-Carlton Hotel, Boston
The Old Spinning Wheel (Bauduc's drums; Lawson's trumpet; Zurke)
The Loveliness Of You (vocal: Bob Crosby)
Lovin' Sam (Warren Smith's great trombone; Miller's tenor)
September In The Rain (vocal: Kay Weber)
Stop, You're Breaking My Heart (vocal: Bob Crosby)
They All Laughed (vocal: Bob Crosby) (nuttsy piece: swell vocal)
Just Strolling (written by Joe Sullivan, featuring Bob Zurke)
There's A Lull In My Life (vocal: Kay Weber) (Miller's tenor)
Wolverine Blues (Bauduc's drums; clarinet, etc)

12.30AM WABC
GLEN GRAY
Palomar Ballroom, Los Angeles
Sweet Lorraine
Where Or When (vocal: Kenny Sargent)
Without Your Love (vocal: Kenny Sargent)
Narcissus (written by Gene Gifford-Bishop)
I Remember (vocal: Kenny Sargent) (written by cornetist Grady Watts)
Chinatown, My Chinatown
Old King Cole (vocal: Pee Wee Hunt)
When You're Smiling
Stompin' At The Savoy

■ TUESDAY 13 JULY 1937

Dick Morningstar and myself are spending 10 days with Hughie Pastoriza at his place near Wolfeboro on Lake Winnipesaukee in New Hampshire. We came up by car last Wednesday and are leaving this Friday by train. Since the Pavilion at Alton Bay was going to have Mal Hallett's Band play there for one day we decided to take the canoe trip of 15 miles down there. We left at 10:30 that morning: the three of us and our blankets, food, suits, etc. The water was exceptionally rough, making travel slow. We stopped off for lunch at uninhabited Rattlesnake Island. We then continued down to Alton Bay where we ate and made our beds, moving all our materials and the canoe around to the backyard

Lake Winnipesaukee, New Hampshire

of some house about 60 yards off the water. Dickie and Hughie went for a motor boat ride at 7:00 for 50 cents. We met Nancy Long driving to Camp Kehouha, about 5 miles from here. She had to drive on to camp so she couldn't come and see Mal Hallett, as much as she wanted to. We went into the Pavilion at 8:05, paying the price of 99 cents. Hallett's Band started playing at 8:35 and it got very crowded after a while. Hallett is very tall, about 6ft 6ins. When his band really swings out it is wonderful but he has to spoil it with waltzes and poorly arranged sweet commercial tunes. The band is very versatile having 5 vocalists; drummer Charlie Blake, guitarist Clark Yocum, saxist/clarinetist Buddy Welcome who weighs about 250 pounds, 17-yr-old Jerry Perkins who was discovered by Hallett last year working at the Trianon Ballroom in Chicago, and Teddy Grace. To me, Teddy Grace and Buddy Welcome are easily the best. Perkins has a good voice but it's too sweet for me. Yocum is fair on commercial tunes and Blake is pretty weak on 2 or 3 of his own special numbers. Welcome and Teddy Grace take most of the vocals, just about all of the 'hot' ones. Teddy Grace is almost tops as far as feminine vocalists go. She has red hair, seems rather old and is only fair looking, but what a nuttsy, low, hot voice. Welcome is a great big man with a swell, original voice who also plays plenty of clarinet. Trumpeter/arranger Frank Ryerson, who composed Hallett's theme *Boston Tea Party*, was absent, being home with a cold, and one of the saxists was missing making the band minus 2 men. Outstanding musicians were tenor saxist Stuart Anderson and bassist Joe Carbonara who weighs 320 pounds. Anderson is simply marvelous on that sax of his, giving it plenty of gut-bucket kick. Showman Carbonara really slaps that bass like nobody's business. Drummer Charlie Blake, trumpeter Mike McMickle and clarinetist Buddy Welcome were also very good. Pianist Frankie Carle is way too 'corny'.

Some of the tunes the band played were: *Dixieland Band* (Buddy Welcome vocal); *Always; Dear Old Southland; Basin Street Blues; Between The Devil And The Deep Blue Sea* (Teddy Grace vocal); *Honeysuckle Rose; The Goona Goo; Slap That Bass; Stardust; Swingtime In The Rockies; St. Louis Blues* (Teddy Grace vocal and Stuart Anderson); *There's A Lull In My Life* (Clark Yocum vocal); *Where Are You?* (Clark Yocum vocal); *Rockin' Chair Swing* (Teddy Grace doing a longer vocal than she did on the Decca recording); *Twilight In Turkey; In A Little Gypsy Tea Room* (Jerry Perkins vocal); *I Got Rhythm; Little Old Lady* (Jerry Perkins vocal); *Wake Up And Live; The Lady Who Swings The Band* (Teddy Grace vocal); *I Can't Lose That Longing For You* (Jerry Perkins vocal); *I Can't Give You Anything But Love* (Teddy Grace vocal); *Sometimes I'm Happy; Whoa Babe; I Know Now* (Jerry Perkins vocal); *You're Looking For Romance* (Clark Yocum vocal).

Mal Hallett (left) and his Band (below)

RADIO LOGS

9:30 PM WABC
BENNY GOODMAN
Camel Caravan program, Los Angeles
The third half-hour program now called Benny Goodman's Swing School.
Star Dust
Sugar Foot Stomp
More Than You Know (BG Trio)
St. Louis Blues (MEYER ALEXANDER's CHORUS)
Nagasaki (BG Quartet)
Truckin'
King Porter Stomp

11:05 PM WABC
BUNNY BERIGAN
Pavillon Royale, Long Island, N.Y.
Trees (swing-style: featuring Bunny)
It Looks Like Rain In Cherry Blossom Lane (vocal: Ruth Bradley)
If I Had You (Bunny's low-down trumpet; Dixon; Auld)
Rockin' Chair Swing (nuttsy piece: Joe Dixon's clarinet; Georgie Auld's tenor)
The Prisoner's Song (Bunny's muted trumpet; Morgan's guitar; Lippman; Auld; Dixon)
The Lady From Fifth Avenue (vocal: Ruth Bradley) (Georgie Auld's bouncy tenor)
Rose Room (Bunny; saxes; Lee's trombone)
I'm Happy, Darling, Dancing With You (Bunny; Joe Lippman's piano)

12.30 AM WABC
TOMMY DORSEY
Hotel Pennsylvania Roof, NYC
Mountain Music (Tough's drums; Dorsey's trombone; Erwin; Johnny Mince's clarinet)
The Morning After (vocal: Jack Leonard)
Satan Takes A Holiday
Once In A While (vocal: Three Esquires)
Posin' (vocal: Edythe Wright)
Night Over Shanghai (vocal: Jack Leonard)
Goin' Home (arranged by Tommy Dorsey & Carmen Mastren: Smith's piano; Mince)
There's A Lull In My Life (vocal: Edythe Wright)
Bugle Call Rag (Bud Freeman's GREAT tenor sax)

■ WEDNESDAY 14 JULY 1937

RECORDING SESSION

WILLIE 'THE LION' SMITH AND HIS CUBS
Recording session for Decca in New York City.
Frankie Newton (t); Buster Bailey (cl); Pete Brown (as); Willie 'The Lion' Smith (p); Jimmy McLin (g); John Kirby (b); O'Neil Spencer (d/voc)
Get Acquainted With Yourself (vO'NS) / *Knock Wood* (vO'NS) / *Peace, Brother, Peace* (vO'NS) / *The Old Stamping Ground* (vO'NS)

RADIO LOGS

11.05 PM WABC
TOMMY DORSEY
Hotel Pennsylvania Roof, NYC
Love Is Never Out Of Season (vocal: Jack Leonard)
Liebestraum (one of Dorsey's swing arrangements of a classic: Tommy; Freeman; Mince)
The Morning After (vocal: Jack Leonard)
Song Of India (Tommy's trombone; Erwin; Freeman)
Once In A While (vocal: Three Esquires) (Jack Leonard, Joe Bauer, Odd Stordahl)
Marie (Tommy etc)
I'm Getting Sentimental Over You (theme)

12.00 MIDNIGHT WEAF
PAUL WHITEMAN
Fort Worth, Texas
Liebestraum (lousy arrangement by drummer Larry Gomar)
Gone With The Wind (vocal: Jimmy Brierley)
Oriental Yoga (vocal: Jack Teagarden)
Tango Of Roses
St. Louis Blues (vocal: Jack Teagarden) (trombone & vocal by the one and only Jack Teagarden)
In A Sentimental Mood (Al Gallodoro's great alto sax)
Siboney (rhumba)
Rhapsody In Blue (tribute to George Gershwin)

12.00 MIDNIGHT WNEW
JOE MARSALA
Hickory House, 144 W52nd Street, NYC
Gone With The Wind (vocal: Adele Girard)
Marie (Joe Bushkin's swell piano)
Basin Street Blues (vocal: Joe Marsala)
Oh, Sister, Ain't That Hot!
I Cried For You (Marty Marsala's trumpet; Girard's harp; Alvin's drums; Shapiro's bass)
Christopher Columbus (Marty; Girard, etc.)

12.30 AM WJZ
FLETCHER HENDERSON
Grand Terrace Café, Chicago
Back Home Again In Indiana (tenor sax; trumpet)
After All
Heaven Help This Heart of Mine (vocal: Chuck Richards)
Love Is Never Out Of Season (vocal: Chuck Richards)
If You Should Ever Leave (vocal: Chuck Richards) (alto sax)
My Gal Sal (vibraphone; Chu Berry's tenor)
Star Dust
Posin' (vocal: Chuck Richards)
Rhythm Of The Tambourine

1.30 AM WWL
GLENN MILLER
Hotel Roosevelt, New Orleans
Moonlight Serenade (theme)
Down South Camp Meetin'
If I Put My Heart In My Song (vocal: Kathleen Lane)
Shine
When I Look Into Your Eyes
How Could You? (vocal: Kathleen Lane)
Turn Off The Moon
Anytime, Anyday, Anywhere (vocal: Sterling Bose)
You're Here, You're There, You're Everywhere (vocal: Kathleen Lane)
Three Little Words (Jerry Jerome's tenor sax)
Moonlight Serenade (theme)

■ FRIDAY 16 JULY 1937

RADIO LOGS

11:30 PM WABC
BOB CROSBY
Ritz-Carlton Hotel, Boston
Between The Devil And The Deep Blue Sea (Lawson's trumpet; Miller's great tenor sax; Smith's trombone)
There's A Lull In My Life (vocal: Kay Weber)
Little Rock Getaway (written by Joe Sullivan, featuring Bob Zurke; Miller)
Wake Up And Live (vocal: Bob Crosby)
Tin Roof Blues (8 BOBCATS: Zurke; Smith, etc)
Stop, You're Breaking My Heart (vocal: Bob Crosby) (clarinet; Miller; Lawson)
Too Marvelous For Words (vocal: Kay Weber) (clarinet; Miller; Lawson)
Pagan Love Song (Lawson; Miller; Haggart's bass; Bauduc)
Summertime (theme)

12.15AM WMCA
ART SHAW
Wildwood, N.J.
Swell. Peg LaCentra is back with the band after being absent with Benny Goodman's Band.
I've Got You Under My Skin (vocal: Tony Pastor) (tenor saxist singing hot with whole band chorusing)
Where Or When (vocal: Peg LaCentra) (Tom DiCarlo's trumpet; Art Shaw's swell clarinet)
My Blue Heaven (fast tempo: Shaw's clarinet)
Hold Your Hat (Les Burness' piano; Arus' trombone; Pastor's tenor)

12.30AM WJZ
FLETCHER HENDERSON
Grand Terrace Café, Chicago
If You Should Ever Leave (vocal: Chuck Richards)
St. Louis Blues
Rockin' Chair Swing (tenor sax)
Jim Town Blues (trumpet; tenor)
Our Penthouse On Third Avenue (vocal: Chuck Richards)
Posin' (vocal: Chuck Richards)
They Can't Take That Away From Me (vocal: Chuck Richards)
Clarinet Marmalade (4 clarinets: swell)

1.30AM WWL
GLENN MILLER
Hotel Roosevelt, New Orleans
Shine
Simply Grand (vocal: Kathleen Lane)
Community Swing
The Merry-Go-Round Broke Down (vocal: Kathleen Lane & Band)
My Gal Sal
You Can't Run Away From Love Tonight (Carl Biesecker's sax)
Humoresque
Stop! You're Breaking My Heart (vocal: Kathleen Lane)
Caravan (Jerry Jerome's tenor sax; Hal McIntyre's clarinet)
Too Marvelous For Words (vocal: Kathleen Lane)

■ SATURDAY 17 JULY 1937

RADIO LOGS

8.00PM WABC
SATURDAY NIGHT SWING SESSION No54
CBS Studio No1, 485 Madison Ave, NYC
Heard this program in a store in Wolfeboro, N.H.
Heat Wave (CBS Band: great sax section!! 4 clarinets; tenor sax)
Blues (ART SHAW playing COLOSSAL clarinet: he is one of THE greatest)
So Rare (swell commercial piece, Leith Stevens directing CBS Band: trumpet; Ross' tenor sax)
Body And Soul (NAT JAFFE, pianist and arranger, playing nice piano with bassist Art Shapiro)
Oh, Lady Be Good (NAT JAFFE, pianist and arranger, playing nice piano with bassist Art Shapiro)
Annie Laurie (MAXINE SULLIVAN doing NUTTSY vocal with CBS Band)
Peckin' (Harry James wrote the music, Ben Pollack the words: Hank Ross' tenor)
Sweet Sue (LES LIEBER playing the nuts on that hot fife of his: swell)
I Found A New Baby (LES LIEBER playing an encore)
Swing Session Called To Order (written by Larry Clinton: Billy Gussak's drums; clarinet)

11:00PM WABC
BUNNY BERIGAN
Pavillon Royale, Long Island, N.Y.
I Can't Get Started (theme) (nuttsy theme featuring Berigan on muted trumpet)
Am I Blue? (super-colossal: Georgie Auld's tenor sax; Berigan; Sonny Lee; Wettling)
A Message From The Man In The Moon (vocal: Ruth Bradley) (Joe Dixon's clarinet)
Ubangi Man (recent composition by Bunny Berigan: Auld's tenor; Wettling; Lee's trombone)
How Carelessly
Louise (swell arrangement of very old piece: Auld; Dixon's clarinet; Lee; Bunny, etc)
You Can't Run Away From Love Tonight (vocal: Ruth Bradley)
Love Is A Merry-Go-Round (vocal: Ruth Bradley) (swell, recorded last month)
Wang Wang Blues (jam outfit of the band: Berigan's trumpet; Joe Dixon's clarinet; Sonny Lee's trombone; Joe Lippman's piano; Wettling's nuttsy drumming)
How Deep Is The Ocean? (colossal: saxes; Bunny; Sonny Lee's swell trombone; Georgie Auld's tenor; Joe Lippman's piano; brass, etc)
The Goona Goo (vocal: Bunny Berigan) (recorded on Brunswick: Wettling & Lippman ballsy)

11.30PM WABC
GUS ARNHEIM
Hotel New Yorker, NYC
The Image Of You (vocal: Ray Foster)
Tomorrow's Another Day (vocal: June Robbins)
Nagasaki (trumpet; Fazola's clarinet)
First Time I Saw You
The Loveliness Of You (vocal: Ray Foster)
It's The Natural Thing To Do (vocal: John Hamilton)
Whispers In The Dark (vocal: Ray Foster)
Between The Devil And The Deep Blue Sea
The Moon Got In My Eyes (vocal: Ray Foster)
Cuban Pete

12.00 MIDNIGHT WJZ
PAUL WHITEMAN
Texas Exposition of 37
Dodging A Divorcee
It Looks Like Rain In Cherry Blossom Lane (vocal: Jimmy Brierley)
Oriental Yoga (vocal: Jack Teagarden)
The Merry-Go-Round Broke Down
Garden Of Weeds (Jack Teagarden, Charlie Teagarden & Frankie Trumbauer doing swell)
The Mother-In-Law's Necktie Party (vocal: Jack Teagarden)
Gone With The Wind (vocal: Jimmy Brierley)
Rhapsody In Blue (theme)

12.00 MIDNIGHT WNEW
JOE MARSALA
Hickory House, 144 W52nd Street, NYC
Royal Garden Blues
Night And Day (Adele Girard's harp)
Night Over Shanghai (vocal: Adele Girard)
I Found A New Baby

1:30AM WWL
GLENN MILLER
Hotel Roosevelt, New Orleans
Honeysuckle Rose (arranged by Glenn Miller)
Turn Off The Moon (Sterling Bose's trumpet)
How Could You? (vocal: Kathleen Lane)
Time On My Hands
Stompin' At The Savoy (Jesse Ralph's trombone)
Whispers In The Dark (vocal: Kathleen Lane)
White Star Of Sigma Nu (Miller's arrangement)
You're Here, You're There, You're Everywhere (vocal: Kathleen Lane)
Moonlight Serenade (theme)

■ SUNDAY 18 JULY 1937

RADIO LOGS

6:30PM WOR
FUN IN SWINGTIME
WOR Studios, NYC
Swell: Bunny Berigan Orchestra
Toodle-Oo (Bunny; Auld; Sonny Lee)
The Goona Goo (no vocal)
Rose Room (Lee; Berigan; Dixon; BALLSY)
All God's Chillun Got Rhythm (swell)

■ MONDAY 19 JULY 1937

Bob goes to spend ten days with Don Mortimer at his summer cottage in Madison, Connecticut.

This picture was taken by Elmer Hollingshead from the hotel at Madison, Connecticut. It shows the Yacht Club where Bob swam during his stay at Don Mortimer's summer cottage.

Tonight is the last broadcast of the Casa Loma Band from the Palomar Ballroom where they have been playing for the past month. Benny Goodman's Band is replacing them the 21st of July. The Casa Loma Band still isn't as good as it was four years ago. Bobby Jones was succeeded by Frankie Zullo; Sonny Dunham by Walter Smith; and Dan D'Andrea was added on sax and violin when Glen Gray replaced Mel Jensen as leader.

RADIO LOGS

8.00pm WJZ
WILLIE BRYANT
'Goodtime Society', NYC
This And That (short trombone solo by George Matthews; screwy tenor; rasping trumpet; bass sax)
Slap That Bass (vocal: Four Inkspots) (only fair arrangement: Orville Jones on bass)
Hallelujah (ragged, but good arrangement: drums; nice piano; weak clarinet)
Cross Patch (vocal: Four Inkspots) (2 guitars and bass doing fair vocal)
It's Over Because We're Through (theme) (Sidney DeParis on trumpet)

11:30pm WICC
ZINN ARTHUR
Nichol's Pinebrook Country Club
Good.
Peckin' (tenor sax; trumpet)
Turn Off The Moon (vocal: Zinn Arthur)
Satan Takes A Holiday
Where Are You? (vocal: Zinn Arthur)
What'll I Do? (clarinet; trombone; tenor)
Star Dust (vocal: Zinn Arthur)
Marie (clarinet; trombone; trumpet; piano)
Basin Street Blues (vocal: Zinn Arthur)

12:00 MIDNIGHT WABC
BOB CROSBY
Ritz-Carlton Hotel, Boston
In A Minor Mood (Eddie Miller's tenor sax; clarinet; Smith's trombone; Bob Zurke's great piano; Yank Lawson's great jam trumpet)
Tomorrow Is Another Day (vocal: Kay Weber) (Eddie Miller's tenor sax)
They All Laughed (vocal: Bob Crosby) (tenor sax; Lawson's trumpet)
Dogtown Blues (written by 21-yr-old bassist Bob Haggart: Yank Lawson's trumpet; swell clarinet; Bob Zurke's colossal piano)
There'll Be Some Changes Made (vocal: Bob Crosby) (nuttsy old piece: Miller; Matlock)
You Can't Have Everything (vocal: Kay Weber) (swell vocal; Eddie Miller's tenor)
Love Is Just Around The Corner (vocal: Nappy Lamare) (marvelous sax by Miller following vocal; Matlock's clarinet)
Summertime (theme) (second chorus by Eddie Miller on tenor sax)

The Ritz Roof
BOB CROSBY
And HIS ORCHESTRA

ANOTHER CROSBY FOR THE MOVIES

When the carefully laid plans of Major Pictures, producers of Mae West and Bing Crosby productions, materialize, Bob Crosby, fifth and youngest of the Crosby brothers, Bing, Everett, Ted and George, will blossom forth as the screen competitor of his celebrated big brother, the famous Bing.

Bob Crosby, popular radio band leader and singing star, has a famous name and a famous brother but he has realized a lifelong ambition within the past fortnight by making good on his own merits. The versatile young baritone is now the proud possessor of a screen contract which definitely places him among the leading personalities of the Major Pictures studio.

12.30am WABC
GLEN GRAY
Palomar Ballroom, Los Angeles
Smoke Rings (theme)
Sheik Of Araby
Where Or When (vocal: Kenny Sargent)
Gotta Go (vocal: Pee Wee Hunt)
Night Over Shanghai (vocal: Kenny Sargent)
Shades Of Haiti
The Love Bug Will Bite You (vocal: Pee Wee Hunt)
Rhythm Of The River (slow tempo: clarinet)
Twilight In Turkey (Tony Briglia's drums; clarinet; Davis' tenor)

1:00am WNEW
LEO MOSLEY
Barnes Tavern, Nr Pelham, N.Y.
Harry Kramer announced.
Ol' Man River (Mosley's trombone; trumpet; piano; solid bass; tenor sax)
Blue Memories (vocal: Skeets Tolbert)
Twilight In Turkey (trombone; clarinet; piano; Mosley's strange horn–half sax, half trombone)
The Man With The Funny Horn (vocal: Leo Mosley & Skeets Tolbert) (nuttsy: trombone; drums)
There's A Lull In My Life
Melody In F (nuttsy swingin' clarinet by Skeets; Fred Jefferson on piano; John Drummond's bass; Mosley on his horn)
I Got Rhythm (vocal: Leo Mosley) (swell clarinet; trumpet)

1:30am WWL
GLENN MILLER
Hotel Roosevelt, New Orleans
Jimmy Wilson announced.
Moonlight Serenade (theme) (written by Miller but unnamed)
Satan Takes A Holiday (Peterson's trumpet)

St. Louis Blues (marvelous arrangement: Jerry Jerome's tenor; Sterling Bose's trumpet; Hal McIntyre's clarinet; wa-wa brass section; Jesse Ralph's trombone)
Star Dust (another colossal arrangement, Miller certainly can arrange wonderfully: Hal McIntyre's clarinet; Sterling Bose)
Wake Up And Live (Tweet Peterson's trumpet; Jerry Jerome's tenor sax; Eak Kenyon on drums)
Basin Street Blues (vocal: Kathleen Lane) (pretty good vocal: Hal McIntyre's clarinet)
Little Old Lady (stinky song–very short)
Night And Day (great song: Carl Biesecker's tenor; brass)
Moonlight Serenade (theme)

■ TUESDAY 20 JULY 1937

RECORDING SESSION

TOMMY DORSEY AND HIS ORCHESTRA
Recording session for Victor in New York City.
Tommy Dorsey (tb); Pee Wee Erwin, Joe Bauer, Andy Ferretti (t); Les Jenkins, Walter Mercurio (tb); Johnny Mince, Fred Stulce, Skeets Herfurt (cl/as); Bud Freeman (ts); Howard Smith (p); Carmen Mastren (g); Gene Traxler (b); Dave Tough (d); Edythe Wright, Jack Leonard (voc)
Have You Got Any Castles, Baby? (vJL) / *You've Got Something There* (vEW) / *Night And Day* / *Smoke Gets In Your Eyes*

TOMMY DORSEY AND HIS CLAMBAKE SEVEN
Recording session for Victor in New York City.
Tommy Dorsey (tb); Pee Wee Erwin (t); Johnny Mince (cl); Bud Freeman (ts); Howard Smith (p); Carmen Mastren (g); Gene Traxler (b); Dave Tough (d); Edythe Wright (voc)
All You Want To Do Is Dance (vEW) / *Having A Wonderful Time* (vEW) / *After You* (vEW) / *Stardust On The Moon* (vEW)

RADIO LOGS

9:30PM WABC
BENNY GOODMAN
Camel Caravan program, Los Angeles
The fourth half-hour program now called Benny Goodman's Swing School.
Smiles (marvelous: trumpet)
Caravan (super-magnificent: Krupa's tom-toms; Benny's GREAT clarinet; Harry James' marvelous trumpet; nuttsy ending)
Tea For Two (BG Quartet)
Swing Low Sweet Chariot (Musso; James)
Camel Hop (M ALEXANDER's SWING CHORUS singing the nuts with aid of Goodman)
Tiger Rag (BG Trio)
After The Ball Is Over
They Can't Take That Away From Me (vocal: Betty Van) (Benny's new vocalist)

11:05PM WABC
BUNNY BERIGAN
Pavillon Royale, Long Island, N.Y.
How Deep Is The Ocean (BALLSY: Auld; Dixon)
Frankie And Johnny (BALLSY: Lippman on piano; Auld; Bunny; Wettling)
I Can't Get Started (swell saxes; Berigan's trumpet: BALLSY)
Never In A Million Years (vocal: Ruth Bradley)
'Cause My Baby Says It's So (vocal: Bunny Berigan)
Swanee River
The Morning After (vocal: Ruth Bradley) (swell drums by George Wettling)
The Prisoner's Song

11:15PM WOR
JOE HAYMES
Lido Club, Larchmont, N.Y.
Great. Sure is good to hear Joe Haymes again. He's a swell guy and some arranger!
Scattin' At The Kit-Kat (Mike Michaels' trombone)
The Image Of You (vocal: Barbara 'Honey' Burns)
Dark Eyes (vocal: Barbara 'Honey' Burns) (trombone; Charlie Bush's drums: great)
Me, Myself And I (vocal: Clyde Rogers) (Dave Frankel's great trumpet; tenor sax; clarinet)

11:17PM WMCA
FRANKIE WARD
Nautical Plaza, Revere Beach, Mass
Nuttsy. Very smooth, but the whole band swings.
I Surrender Dear (one of Ward's best arrangements: what saxes!)
They Can't Take That Away From Me (swell commercial tune: Ward's alto)
Carelessly (vocal: Carmen Trudeau)
Honeysuckle Rose (Brad Gowans' cornet; Bob Hohler's trombone; Ward's xylophone; sax)
Never In A Million Years (Frankie Ward's swell xylophone; Gowans' cornet: very smooth)
Oh, Lady Be Good (good alto sax; Ward's subtle xylophone; Hohler's ride trombone; sax)
What Will I Tell My Heart? (vocal: Carmen Trudeau) (fair vocal; trombone; saxes)
St. Louis Blues (saxes & brass; Hohler's real swingin' trombone with Fred Moynahan's drums)
Where Are You? (vocal: Carmen Trudeau) (another current commercial pop: good vocal)
The Goona Goo (Ward's fair bassoon playing: pretty weak backing by band)

12.30AM WABC
TOMMY DORSEY
Hotel Pennsylvania Roof, NYC
Ralph Edwards announced.
Stolen Melody (Johnny Mince's clarinet)
Where Or When (vocal: Jack Leonard)
Hymn To The Sun (Bud Freeman's tenor; clarinet)
Once In A While (vocal: Three Esquires)
I May Be Wrong (swell: Bud Freeman's tenor; Gene Traxler's solid bass; Dave Tough; trombone)
The Things I Want (vocal: Edythe Wright) (nuttsy: Dorsey; Freeman; saxes)
Marie (vocal: Jack Leonard & band) (one of the biggest record sellers on Victor: Erwin's trumpet; Bud Freeman's GREAT tenor)
Happy Birthday To Love (vocal: Jack Leonard) (commercial tune: tricky saxes)
Royal Garden Blues (Dorsey's trombone; Mince's clarinet; ballsy arrangement; Bud Freeman's MARVELOUS tenor; Dave Tough's cymbals; brass, etc)
I'm Getting Sentimental Over You (theme) (so smooth and nuttsy)

1:30AM WWL
GLENN MILLER
Hotel Roosevelt, New Orleans
Moonlight Serenade (theme)
Moonlight Bay (short chorus sung by whole band; Eak Kenyon's drums; McIntyre; Bose's trumpet)

Simply Grand (vocal: Kathleen Lane) (written/arranged by Chummy McGregor: nuttsy)
Down South Camp Meetin' (F Henderson's arrangement: Bose's trumpet; clarinets; saxes: nuttsy)
Star Dust (similar to Goodman arrangement: brass in intro but no clarinet; later Hal McIntyre's clarinet)
I'm Bubbling Over (Tweet Peterson's trumpet; Hal McIntyre's clarinet)
Where Is The Sun? (vocal: Kathleen Lane) (swell vocal on swell song; Carl Biesecker's short tenor sax solo)
Humoresque (Sterling Bose's typical straight swinging trumpet; McIntyre's clarinet; Jerome's tenor)
Honeysuckle Rose (saxes on first chorus; Kenyon's short drum breaks; Jerome's tenor; McIntyre)
Moonlight Serenade (theme)

■ WEDNESDAY 21 JULY 1937
RADIO LOGS

11.30PM WMCA
EDGAR HAYES
Apollo Theater, NYC
St. Louis Blues (Hayes' typical piano)

12.00 MIDNIGHT WNEW
JOE MARSALA
Hickory House, 144 W52nd Street, NYC
Clarinet Marmalade
Bugle Call Rag

12.30AM WJZ
WOODY HERMAN
Willows, nr Pittsburgh, Pa
Stupendous.
Blue Hawaii (vocal: Sharri Kaye) (Frank Carlson's drums)
Patch Up Your Heart (vocal: Woody Herman)
That's A-Plenty (Herman's colossal clarinet)
Doctor Jazz (vocal: Woody Herman)
East Of The Sun (featuring Saxie Mansfield's tenor sax)
Love Me (vocal: Sharri Kaye)
Can't We Be Friends? (Saxie Mansfield; Reid's trombone)
Blue Prelude (theme)

1:30AM WWL
GLENN MILLER
Hotel Roosevelt, New Orleans
Moonlight Serenade (theme)
Community Swing (written by Miller: recorded on Brunswick)
If I Put My Heart In My Song (vocal: Kathleen Lane)
The Lady Who Couldn't Be Kissed (Sterling Bose's trumpet)
Whispers In The Dark (vocal: Kathleen Lane)
Anytime, Anyday, Anywhere (vocal: Sterling Bose) (recorded on Decca featuring Bose's singing & trumpet)
You Can't Run Away From Love Tonight (Hal McIntyre; Biesecker's sax)
Loveless Love (very short: McIntyre's clarinet)
Gone With The Wind (vocal: Kathleen Lane) (nice vocal)
I'm Sitting On Top Of The World (saxes; Jerome's tenor; McIntyre's clarinet)
Isle Of Capri (small jam band playing the nuts: McIntyre; Kenyon)
Moonlight Serenade (theme)

■ THURSDAY 22 JULY 1937
RECORDING SESSION

ART SHAW AND HIS NEW MUSIC
Recording session for Brunswick in New York City.
Art Shaw (cl/ldr); John Best, Malcolm Crain, Tom di Carlo (t); Harry Rogers, George Arus (tb); Les Robinson, Harry Freeman (as); Tony Pastor (ts/voc); Fred Petry (ts); Les Burness (p); Al Avola (g); Ben Ginsberg (b); Cliff Leeman (d); Peg La Centra (voc)
Afraid To Dream (vPLC) / *If You Should Ever Leave* (vPLC) / *Sweet Adeline* (vTP) / *How Dry I Am*

RADIO LOGS

6:45PM WOR
JOE HAYMES
Lido Club, Larchmont, N.Y.
The Love Bug Will Bite You (vocal: Clyde Rogers)
Caravan (nuttsy: great tenor sax)
September In The Rain (vocal: Barbara 'Honey' Burns)
I'll Never Tell You I Love You (vocal: Barbara 'Honey' Burns)
White Star Of Sigma Nu (written by Haymes)

1:30AM WWL
GLENN MILLER
Hotel Roosevelt, New Orleans
Moonlight Serenade (theme)
White Star Of Sigma Nu (written by Joe Haymes, Miller's arrangement: Jerome's tenor; Bose's trumpet)
Simply Grand (vocal: Kathleen Lane)
Humoresque (Trombone team; saxes; Sterling Bose's swell trumpet; McIntyre's clarinet; Jerome's tenor)
Peg O' My Heart (Biesecker's tenor; McIntyre's clarinet; rather short)
Stop! You're Breaking My Heart (Swell new song: Jerome's tenor; clarinets; trombones)
Where Are You? (vocal: Kathleen Lane) (Much requested piece: saxes; brass; clarinet; small fill-in solos)
You're Here, You're There, You're Everywhere (vocal: Kathleen Lane)
When Day Is Done (Peterson's trumpet; Biesecker's tenor; McIntyre's clarinet)
I Got Rhythm (Recorded on Brunswick: McIntyre; Jesse Ralph's ballsy trombone; Jerome; muted trumpet; piano; Kenyon's drums)
Moonlight Serenade (theme)

■ FRIDAY 23 JULY 1937
RECORDING SESSION

GLEN GRAY AND THE CASA LOMA ORCHESTRA
Recording session for Decca in Los Angeles.
Glen Gray (as/dir); Walter Smith, Grady Watts, Frank Zullo (t); Pee Wee Hunt (tb/voc); Billy Rauch, Fritz Hummel (tb); Clarence Hutchenrider (cl/as), Kenny Sargent (as/voc); Art Ralston (as/o/bsn); Danny d'Andrea (as); Pat Davis (cl/ts/fl); Joe Hall (p); Jack Blanchette (g); Stanley Dennis (b); Tony Briglia (d)
Swing Low, Sweet Chariot / *Smoke Rings* / *Casa Loma Stomp* / *For You* (vKS) / *Always*

RADIO LOGS

7:45PM WEAF
BUGHOUSE RHYTHM
San Francisco
Dr John Meakin directs the band and plays piano. This is National Bughouse Rhythm Week — as Benny Goodman remarked last week: 'What's that?'
Formal Night In Harlem (trumpet)
Liebestraum (George Druck's smooth trombone; clarinet; baritone sax; swell trombone; nuttsy trumpet; long drum solos; nuttsy ending)

The Maid's Night Off (written by Will Hudson, fast becoming a hit: nuttsy saxes at beginning; nuttsy trumpet breaks probably by Harlow Burgess; J Harrington's great tenor sax solo, followed by short drum break by Edson Gilson)

9:00PM WHDH
LARRY GADSBY
Riverview Beach, Neponset Bridge, Mass
LOUSY.
Sophisticated Swing (theme)
Rosetta
'Cause My Baby Says It's So
A Sailboat In The Moonlight (vocal: Larry Gadsby)
Star Dust
Our Penthouse On Third Avenue

10.00PM WJZ
TOMMY DORSEY
Kool Cigarette Program, NYC
Wake Up And Live (vocal: Edythe Wright) (Pee Wee Erwin's trumpet)
Night Over Shanghai (vocal: Jack Leonard) (Pee Wee Erwin's trumpet)
Satan Takes A Holiday (NUTTSY: Dave Tough's drums; Freeman's GREAT tenor in place of Dorsey's trombone; swell sax chorus; clarinets. Dorsey hasn't taken a solo yet—he must be sick!)
Trouble Don't Like Music (vocal: Edythe Wright & Three Esquires) (Dave Tough's drums; saxes; trumpets; Pee Wee Erwin)
Dancing In The Dark
Dancing On The Ceiling (vocal: Jack Leonard)
I Kiss Your Hand, Madame
Down South Camp Meetin' (arranged by Henderson: saxes; clarinets; brass; Erwin's trumpet; Freeman)

10:25PM WMCA
FRANKIE WARD
Nautical Plaza, Revere Beach, Mass
There's A Lull In My Life
They Can't Take That Away From Me (vocal: Carmen Trudeau)
Peckin'
Where Is The Sun? (vocal: Carmen Trudeau)
Satan Takes A Holiday (Frankie Ward's bassoon; drums; tenor sax)
Honeysuckle Rose (trumpet; saxes; trombone)
Strollin' Through The Park (vocal: Carmen Trudeau & band) (trombone; xylophone)

11:30PM WABC
BOB CROSBY
Ritz-Carlton Hotel, Boston
Can't Help Lovin' Dat Man (Lawson; Matlock; Bob Zurke; Smith)
Whispers In The Dark (vocal: Kay Weber) (Miller's tenor sax)
The Lady From Fifth Avenue (vocal: Bob Crosby) (Matlock)
Muskrat Ramble (GREAT: Smith's trombone; Miller's nuttsy tenor; Lamare's guitar; Matlock; Lawson)
The Loveliness Of You (vocal: Bob Crosby) (saxes; Matlock's clarinet; swell trumpet by Lawson; Zurke; Bauduc)
When My Dreamboat Comes Home (vocal: Nappy Lamare) (Miller; Smith's trombone; Bauduc)
I Know Now (vocal: Kay Weber) (swell)
Twilight In Turkey (simply stupendous: Matlock; Miller; Smith; Lawson)

11:30PM WEAF
HUDSON-DeLANGE
Playland Casino, Rye, N.Y.
Hobo On Park Avenue (theme) (swell theme written by Will Hudson)
Jealous Blues (vocal: George 'GiGi' Bohn) (Bohn plays sax in the band)
Caravan (Ted Duane's tenor; clarinet; trumpet)
Lost Again (vocal: Eddie DeLange) (nuttsy song written by Will Hudson: saxes; brass)
The Maid's Night Off (becoming a big hit: Jimmy Blake's trumpet; clarinet)
The You And Me That Used To Be (vocal: Nan Wynn & Band)
The Fireman's Ball (written by Will Hudson–very new, ballsy: Jimmy Blake)
You're My Desire (vocal: Nan Wynn) (WONDERFUL, great vocal: Ed Kolyer's trombone)

Unnamed (swell hot piece: trumpet)
Bugle Call Rag (Skeets Dolan's drums; Bus Etri's swell guitar; Mark Hyams' piano)

11:30PM WOR
DICK STABILE
Steel Pier, Atlantic City, N.J.
Fair. Stabile features himself on the alto sax. He is darn good but corny at times.
Good Morning
So Rare (vocal: Bert Shaw)
A Study In Brown
The Lady Who Couldn't Be Kissed
Our Penthouse On Third Avenue (vocal: Bert Shaw)
Gone With The Wind (vocal: Bert Shaw)

12:30AM WEAF
JOE VENUTI
Castle Farms, Cincinnati, Ohio
Plenty good.
Between The Devil And The Deep Blue Sea (swell: Venuti's violin; spotty trumpet; clarinet)
Where Or When (vocal: Dan Darcy) (Darcy plays drums in the band)
Someday Sweetheart (Venuti's violin; swell tenor sax; muted trumpet; nice jamming)
Trust In Me (vocal: Trudi Mack) (nuttsy arrangement: wa-wa muted brass)
I Got Rhythm (vocal: Bob McCracken) (Venuti's violin; swell clarinet; nice piano; drums)
Yours And Mine (vocal: Dan Darcy)
Star Dust (vocal: Trudi Mack) (swell trombone; trumpet; Joe's nuttsy violin)
I Know Now (vocal: Dan Darcy)
Exactly Like You (damn good arrangement: muted unforced trumpet; Venuti's violin; tenor sax)

12.30AM WJZ
MIKE RILEY
New Penn Club, Pittsburgh, Pa
The Music Goes Round And Around (theme) (written by Riley & Ed Farley last year)
The Things I Want
My Blue Heaven (vocal: Mike Riley & Band)
Ja-Da (Riley's swell trombone)
I Can't Give You Anything But Love, Baby (vocal: Marion Miller)
Whispering (Riley's muted trombone; saxes)
Stay On The Right Side (vocal: Marion Miller)
On The Isle Of Kitchy-Mi-Boko (tenor sax)
You Showed Me The Way (vocal: Mike Riley) (great trumpet)
Where Or When (vocal: Marion Miller)

1:00AM WNEW
LEO MOSLEY
Barnes Tavern, Nr Pelham, N.Y.
Nuttsy. Mel Wright announced. The Barnes Tavern is open from 8:30 to 4:00am.
The Subway To Barnes (great, real swing: piano; trumpet; clarinet; Mosley's horn; bass)
September In The Rain
The Man With The Funny Little Horn (vocal: Leo Mosley, Band & Trio)
No, No, Brother, I Ain't The Man (vocal: Leo Mosley & Skeets Tolbert) (written by Mosley)
Ring Dem Bells (piano in place of bells; really fine, fast tenor; Mosley's trombone)
Caravan (Leo Mosley's swell trombone; muted trumpet; keen clarinet: fast tempo)
Blue Fantasy (only fair: no solos except for Mosley)

1:30AM WWL
GLENN MILLER
Hotel Roosevelt, New Orleans
Moonlight Serenade (theme)
Honeysuckle Rose (brass & sax intro; trumpet; Jerome's tenor; Ralph's trombone)
When I Look Into Your Eyes (Jesse Ralph's sweet trombone; trumpet)
The Merry-Go-Round Broke Down (vocal: Kathleen Lane & Band) (stinking-lousy song)
Time On My Hands (recorded on Brunswick, swell: saxes; muted brass; Peterson's trumpet)

Three Little Words (fast tempo: brass v. saxes; McIntyre's swell, long clarinet solo; Jerome's tenor)
Whispers In The Dark (vocal: Kathleen Lane) (Tweet Peterson's muted trumpet; Ralph's sweet trombone)
Shine (McIntyre's colossal clarinet; whole band really swinging out)
Gone With The Wind (vocal: Kathleen Lane)
St. Louis Blues (saxes v. brass; Bose's trumpet; Jerome's tenor; McIntyre; Ralph)
Moonlight Serenade (theme)

■ SATURDAY 24 JULY 1937
RADIO LOGS

6:45PM WABC
BOB CROSBY
Ritz-Carlton Hotel, Boston
South Rampart Street Parade
Gone With The Wind (vocal: Kay Weber)
Gin Mill Blues (GREAT: Zurke; Matlock)
If I Had You (vocal: Bob Crosby)
High Society (8 BOBCATS: MARVELOUS)
Tomorrow Is Another Day (vocal: Kay Weber)

8.00PM WABC
SATURDAY NIGHT SWING SESSION No55
CBS Studio No1, 485 Madison Ave, NYC
Announced by Mel Allen and Paul Douglas.
Panamania (nuttsy swing tune: great dirty trombone; fair piano; Stevens directing CBS Band)
Nola (HOWARD SMITH, pianist with Tommy Dorsey Orch from Hotel Penn playing nuttsy piano)
Crazy Rhythm (HOWARD SMITH playing swell piano with Billy Gussak, drums, and Charlie Barber on bass)
Shame On You (Leith Stevens directing CBS Band: fair song)
Slap That Bass (THREE SYMPHONETTES, girls, singing with Hugh Martin's piano and Barber's bass)
Dippermouth Blues (SHARKEY BONANO & His Sharks Of Rhythm, 6-piece jam band from Nick's Tavern: Bonano's swell trumpet; George Brunies' great muted trombone; nuttsy piano. What an ending!! Everybody jammin')
Panama (GREAT!! SHARKEY BONANO's Band again sending me: clarinet; trombone; piano)
Tea For Two (SWELL: CBS Band, vibraphone; stupendous saxes; trombones; piano)
Darktown Strutters' Ball (GREAT: Charlie Barber, formerly with Fred Waring & Russ Morgan, on bass)
Nagasaki (Leith Stevens directing CBS Band: saxes intro; tenor sax; clarinet)

9:55PM WMCA
FRANKIE WARD
Nautical Plaza, Revere Beach, Mass
Love Is A Merry-Go-Round (vocal: Carmen Trudeau)
Wolverine Blues
Where Are You? (vocal: Carmen Trudeau)
My Blue Heaven (trombone; trumpet; drums; bassoon; clarinet)
Carelessly (vocal: Carmen Trudeau) (trombone; tenor)
Where Or When

11:00PM WABC
BUNNY BERIGAN
Pavillon Royale, Long Island, N.Y.
I Can't Get Started (theme) (recorded by Berigan last year on Vocalion)
Black Bottom (very old jazz piece: Berigan's muted trumpet; Wettling)
Easy Living (vocal: Ruth Bradley) (nuttsy: fairly new ballad that is a great hit)
Ubangi Man (written by Berigan: Georgie Auld's tenor; Berigan's nuttsy trumpet with Wettling's cymbals; Lee's trombone; Dixon; Lippman's piano)
The Lady From Fifth Avenue (vocal: Ruth Bradley) (Bunny; Auld's SWELL tenor; Wettling)
Russian Lullaby (COLOSSAL: Wettling's tom-toms; Fishkind's solid bassing; Auld's marvelous tenor sax; Joe Dixon's clarinet backed by Wettling; Berigan's high note trumpet)
Strangers In The Dark (vocal: Ruth Bradley) (swell commercial tune)

Satan Takes A Holiday (NUTTSY: peachy slow intro; Wettling's great drumming; Berigan's great high screeching trumpet; marvelous rhythm section)
Rockin' Chair Swing (a swell piece but played a little too fast: Joe Dixon's marvelous clarinet; Lee's great trombone; Auld's nuttsy tenor; Wettling)
Poor Robinson Crusoe (DAMN good: trombone team; Berigan's trumpet; Auld playing marvelous, long, tenor solo; great Joe Dixon clarinet; whole band swinging out at the end)
I Can't Get Started (theme)

12:00 MIDNIGHT WEAF
JOE VENUTI
Castle Farms, Cincinnati, Ohio
SWELL.
Unknown Title
It Looks Like Rain In Cherry Blossom Lane (vocal: Dan Darcy)
Parade To A G-string
Wake Up And Live (vocal: Trudi Mack) (nuttsy: wa-wa brass; drums; trumpet; clarinet)
I Got Rhythm (vocal: Bob McCracken & Band) (GREAT: Venuti's violin; clarinet)
Bugle Call Rag (colossal: Venuti's violin; tenor sax; drum breaks)
How Could You? (vocal: Trudi Mack) (swell: drum break after vocal; brass)
Louise (Venuti's violin; swell tenor sax; trombones; brass; drums)
September In The Rain (vocal: Dan Darcy)

12:00 MIDNIGHT WPG
DICK STABILE
Steel Pier, Atlantic City, N.J.
GOOD.
Gone With The Wind (vocal: Bert Shaw)
Honeysuckle Rose (Stabile's clarinet and sax)
The Image Of You (vocal: Bert Shaw)
They All Laughed (vocal: Paula Kelly)
'Cause My Baby Says It's So (vocal: Paula Kelly)
Satan Takes A Holiday
Rosetta (vocal: Dick Stabile) (Castello's trumpet)

12:30AM WABC
BENNY GOODMAN
Palomar Ballroom, Los Angeles
EXCELLENT, MARVELOUS! This is Goodman's first broadcast from the Palomar Ballroom in Los Angeles. He opened there last Wednesday. He left the Hotel Penn at the end of April, went on an extensive road tour by bus up in New England and across the US to Los Angeles where he is making a movie while doing at least a 6-week engagement at the Palomar. I heard this program at Don Mortimer's summer home in Madison, Connecticut.
Let's Dance (opening theme) (features the brass section)
Caravan (magnificent arrangement of Ellington's tune: Benny's clarinet with brass and Krupa's tom-toms; Harry James' super-colossal high trumpet followed by short chorus by the Trio; Krupa's solo tom-toms)
Yours And Mine (vocal: Betty Van) (Betty Van replaced Peg LaCentra in the last week of June: she's pretty good)
The Sheik Of Araby (brass intro; saxes; James' great trumpet; trombone)
Afraid To Dream (vocal: Betty Van) (very new song: nuttsy saxes with brass & Benny's clarinet; Stacy's piano behind swell vocal; Benny; Krupa)
Peckin' (sensational tune written by Ben Pollack and Harry James about 6-months ago– now a national hit: it was released on Victor 25621 yesterday; MARVELOUS; sensational brasses; Benny's magnificent clarinet; Harry James' stupendous trumpet; Musso's tenor; Krupa's solid drumming)
A Handful Of Keys (BG Quartet) (good piano; nuttsy vibes)
I Can't Give You Anything But Love (vocal: Betty Van) (brass intro: saxes with Stacy's piano; James' swingin' trumpet; stupendous arrangement; nuttsy vocal)
Smiles (very old piece: Benny's clarinet; Harry James' trumpet is again a standout; saxes; trombones-brass; Krupa's great drumming)
Remember (grand old Irving Berlin tune recorded on Victor 25329: McEachern's short, nuttsy, smooth trombone; Benny's long clarinet solo with saxes backing; Rollini's nuttsy tenor sax; McEachern)
Big John Special (great swing tune written & arranged by Fletcher Henderson: Harry James' 2 trumpet solos; Benny's short clarinet solo; Jess Stacy's wonderful piano solo followed by a magnificent built-up trumpet solo by Harry James)

1:30AM WWL
GLENN MILLER
Hotel Roosevelt, New Orleans
Moonlight Serenade (theme)
MEDLEY: **Let's Call The Whole Thing Off / They All Laughed** (medley from *Shall We Dance* movie starring Fred Astaire & Ginger Rogers)
The Moon Got In My Eyes (vocal: Kathleen Lane)
Loveless Love (McIntyre's clarinet)
Sweet Leilani (vocal: Kathleen Lane)
Isle Of Capri
Star Dust
Night And Day
Where Is The Sun? (vocal: Kathleen Lane)
Doin' The Jive (vocal: Kathleen Lane & Band) (written by Chummy McGregor)
Moonlight Serenade (theme)

While up at Don Mortimer's cottage in Madison, Connecticut, I got the following records from the store in Madison: Benny Goodman Quartet's *Tea For Two / Runnin' Wild* (Victor 25529); Benny Goodman Quartet's *Sweet Sue / My Melancholy Baby* (Victor 25473); Lionel Hampton's *Stompology* / Hot Club of France's *Swing Guitars* (Victor 25601); Lionel Hampton's *Rhythm, Rhythm / China Stomp* (Victor 25586); Lionel Hampton's *Sunny Side Of The Street / I Know That You Know* (Victor 25592); Bunny Berigan's *Swanee River / Love Is A Merry-Go-Round* (Victor 25588); Bunny Berigan's *Mahogany Hall Stomp* / Shafter Octet's *Chopin's Ghost* (Victor 25622); Tommy Dorsey's *Twilight In Turkey / The Milkman's Matinee* (Victor 25568); and Duke Ellington's *The Mooche / Mood Indigo* (Victor 24486).

The Benny Goodman Band at the Palomar Ballroom in Los Angeles: Harry Goodman (bass); Gene Krupa (drums); Harry James, Ziggy Elman, Chris Griffin (trumpets); Vido Musso, Hymie Shertzer, Art Rollini, George Koenig (saxes)

■ SUNDAY 25 JULY 1937

RADIO LOGS

2:30PM WOR
JOHNNY HAUSER
Grossinger Country Club, Ferndale, N.Y.
Johnny Hauser started his band about 4 months ago. He was formerly a star vocalist with Paul Whiteman's Band. He has a swell voice and his band is darn good.
I Can't Give You Anything But Love, Baby
Born To Love (vocal: Patricia Carroll)
What Will I Tell My Heart?
I've Got You Under My Skin / Easy To Love / May I Have The Next Romance With You?
The Mayor Of Alabam' (vocal: Johnny Hauser & Band) (nuttsy: trumpet)
My Cabin Of Dreams (vocal: Johnny Hauser) (written by Nick Kenny and introduced last week by Hauser's Band)
Rosetta (vocal: Johnny Hauser) (trumpet)

5:00PM WOR
DICK STABILE
Steel Pier, Atlantic City, N.J.
Ray Morgan announced.
All God's Chillun Got Rhythm (vocal: Paula Kelly)
Gone With The Wind (vocal: Bert Shaw) (Stabile's alto sax)
Posin' (vocal: Dick Stabile) (swell rhythm intro; Stabile's clarinet; drums)
The Image Of You (vocal: Bert Shaw)

The First Time I Saw You (vocal: Paula Kelly)
The Clock Strikes Three
Where Or When (vocal: Bert Shaw)
Rosetta (vocal: Dick Stabile) (swell hot vocal)
On The Air (theme)

11.05PM WABC
GUS ARNHEIM
Hotel New Yorker, NYC
GOOD.
Marcheta (swell: Irving Fazola's clarinet; tenor sax; trumpet)
Night Over Shanghai (vocal: June Robbins)
It Looks Like Rain In Cherry Blossom Lane (vocal: Ray Foster) (nuttsy tenor sax; trumpet; piano)
The Loveliness Of You (vocal: Ray Foster)
You'll Never Go To Heaven (vocal: John Hamilton & Band)
Easy Living (vocal: June Robbins) (grand piece: swell saxes; brass)
Peckin' (Harry James' piece: trumpet; swell tenor sax; fair vibes; trumpet)

11.30PM WICC
RAY BELAIRE
Pleasure Beach BR, Bridgeport, Conn
Fair. Good arrangements but rather poor musicians.
A Study In Brown (tenor sax; trumpet)
Heaven Help This Heart of Mine (vocal: Sylvia King)
Satan Takes A Holiday (trumpet; lousy clarinet; too loud drums; tenor)
The Image Of You (vocal: Sylvia King)
Mean To Me (lousy drums; tenor sax; trombone)
When It's Sleepy Time Down South (vocal: Sylvia King)
If You Should Ever Leave
After You've Gone

12:00 MIDNIGHT WPG
ALEX BARTHA
Steel Pier, Atlantic City, N.J.
Alexander's Ragtime Band (tenor; drums)
Where or When
Satan Takes A Holiday (lousy)
I Know Now (vocal: Bert Nickerson)
They All Laughed (vocal: Carl White)
It Looks Like Rain In Cherry Blossom Lane (vocal: Carl White)
Honeysuckle Rose
You Were Born To Love (vocal: Bert Nickerson)
I Can't Give You Anything But Love, Baby (clarinet)

1:30AM WWL
GLENN MILLER
Hotel Roosevelt, New Orleans
Simply Grand (vocal: Kathleen Lane) (written & arranged by Chummy McGregor)
Anytime, Anyday, Anywhere (vocal: Sterling Bose) (featuring Bose's singing & trumpet)
Gone With The Wind (vocal: Kathleen Lane) (swell vocal by beautiful Lane)
Honeysuckle Rose (Bose's swell trumpet; Jerry Jerome's long, nuttsy tenor sax; Jesse Ralph's great trombone; Hal McIntyre's swell clarinet)

■ MONDAY 26 JULY 1937

RECORDING SESSION

ANDY KIRK AND HIS TWELVE CLOUDS OF JOY
Recording session for Decca in New York City.
Andy Kirk (bsx/ldr); Harry Lawson, Paul King, Earl Thompson (t); Ted Donnelly, Henry Wells (tb); John Harrington (cl/as/bar); John Williams (as/bar); Earl Miller (as); Dick Wilson (ts); Mary Lou Williams (p); Ted Brinson (g); Booker Collins (b); Ben Thigpen (d); Pha Terrell (voc)
A Mellow Bit Of Rhythm / In My Wildest Dreams (vPT) / *Better Luck Next Time* (vPT) / *With Love In My Heart* (vPT)

RADIO LOGS

8.00PM WJZ
WILLIE BRYANT
'Goodtime Society', NYC
St. Louis Blues (vocal: Willie Bryant) (swell long piano solo in style of Teddy Wilson)
Mary Had A Little Lamb (vocal: Four Inkspots) (lousy song)
Honeysuckle Rose (clarinet; swell tenor in style of Lester Young; trumpet; swell piano)
It's Over Because We're Through (theme)

11:15PM WOR
NYE MAYHEW
Glen Island Casino, New Rochelle, N.Y.
Charles Kibling announced. Lousy. Bob Mayhew plays trumpet and Jack and Nye Mayhew play saxes. All three used to play for Paul Whiteman.
A Sailboat In The Moonlight
Strangers In The Dark
Big Boy Blue
Night Over Shanghai
Estalie (Spanish tune)

A CHANGE IN POLICY IS NOW IN EFFECT AT
GLEN ISLAND CASINO
Shore Road, New Rochelle, N. Y.
HEREAFTER THERE WILL BE NO COVER OR MUSIC CHARGE TO DINNER GUESTS
Our usual moderate prices will prevail.
Featuring Nightly,
NYE MAYHEW
and his Orchestra, with Carolyn Hughes, vocalist.

11:30PM WMCA
FRANKIE WARD
Nautical Plaza, Revere Beach, Mass
Too Marvelous For Words (vocal: Carmen Trudeau) (tenor sax)
Remember (Irving Berlin's old piece—good: Frankie Ward's vibes; tenor sax)
Strollin' In The Park (vocal: Carmen Trudeau & band)
They Can't Take That Away From Me (swell, fast tempo: tenor sax)
Eccentric (old piece swung out on: Fred Moynahan's drum breaks; trombones)

12:00 MIDNIGHT WABC
BOB CROSBY
Ritz-Carlton Hotel, Boston
The Girl Friend (Eddie Miller's tenor sax; Lawson's trumpet; Miller again; Bob Zurke; Smith)
I Know Now (vocal: Kay Weber) (Miller's tenor sax on first chorus; Yank Lawson's trumpet on chorus following vocal; clarinet)
Stop, You're Breaking My Heart (vocal: Bob Crosby) (real Dixieland-style: Bauduc's drums; clarinet; Miller; Lawson)
Woman On My Weary Mind (good: Miller; Smith)
Here Comes Your Pappy (vocal: Nappy Lamare) (Miller's tenor behind vocal; clarinet; Lawson)
Little Rock Getaway (featuring Bob Zurke's piano; Miller)
There's A Lull In My Life (vocal: Kay Weber) (singing the nuts; Miller's standout tenor again)
Sweet Lorraine (clarinet; Miller; Lawson; Zurke; Haggart's nuttsy bass solo; Bauduc)

1:30AM WWL
GLENN MILLER
Hotel Roosevelt, New Orleans
Every Monday night is request night at the Roosevelt. People are interviewed over the radio and request their favorite song.
How Could You? (vocal: Kathleen Lane) (Hal McIntyre's swell clarinet)
Where Are You? (fair, swell song but drawn out: McIntyre's typical clarinet)
Stompin' At The Savoy (Jesse Ralph's trombone; Bose's trumpet; Jerome's tenor)
Night And Day (McIntyre's clarinet; muted trumpet)
It Looks Like Rain In Cherry Blossom Lane (lousy: muted wa-wa trumpet)
Star Dust (similar to Goodman's: nice trumpet; nuttsy clarinet by Hal McIntyre)

■ TUESDAY 27 JULY 1937

RECORDING SESSION

ANDY KIRK AND HIS TWELVE CLOUDS OF JOY
Recording session for Decca in New York City.
Andy Kirk (bsx/ldr); Harry Lawson, Paul King, Earl Thompson (t); Ted Donnelly (tb); Henry Wells (tb/voc); John Harrington (cl/as/bar); John Williams (as/bar); Earl Miller (as); Dick Wilson (ts); Mary Lou Williams (p); Ted Brinson (g); Booker Collins (b); Ben Thigpen (d); Pha Terrell (voc)
What's Mine Is Yours (vPT) / **Why Can't We Do It Again?** (vHW) / **The Key To My Heart** (vPT) / **I Want To Be A Gypsy** (vPT)

RADIO LOGS

9:30PM WABC
BENNY GOODMAN
Camel Caravan program, Los Angeles
The fifth half-hour program now called Benny Goodman's Swing School.
The Sheik Of Araby (James' swell trumpet; Benny)
I Can't Give You Anything But Love (STUPENDOUS: James; Stacy)
Marie (BG Trio) (swell)
They All Laughed (M ALEXANDER's SWING CHORUS singing the nuts)
I Got Rhythm (BG Trio) (marvelous)
Afraid To Dream (vocal: Betty Van) (nuttsy: swell Benny)
Jam Session (Musso; James' trumpet)

11:08PM WABC
BUNNY BERIGAN
Pavillon Royale, Long Island, N.Y.
When Two Love Each Other (vocal: Ruth Bradley)
Swanee River (arranged by Berigan & Larry Clinton: Berigan; Georgie Auld's tenor)
You Can't Run Away From Love Tonight (vocal: Ruth Bradley)
I'm Happy, Darling, Dancing With You (vocal: Ruth Bradley) (swell: Auld's tenor)
Mahogany Hall Stomp (Berigan's muted trumpet; Lee's trombone; Auld's tenor; brass)
The You And Me That Used To Be (vocal: Ruth Bradley)
Royal Garden Blues (Auld's short tenor intro; Wettling's solid drums; Berigan's swell trumpet; Auld's COLOSSAL tenor; Lee's real swing trombone; Bunny again)

11:30PM WEAF
HUDSON-DeLANGE
Playland Casino, Rye, N.Y.
Darktown Strutters' Ball (Duane's tenor; Etri's guitar solo; Blake's trumpet; Gus Bivona's clarinet)
Star Dust (little too fast: brass intro; saxes; guitar; trumpet; clarinet)
It's Swell Of You (vocal: Nan Wynn) (great vocal: Ed Kolyer's trombone)
If I Could Be With You (long brass intro: saxes; trumpet; trombone; clarinet)
Back In Your Arms (vocal: Eddie DeLange) (Ted Duane's sweet, nuttsy tenor; clarinet)
I'd Do Anything Because I Love You (vocal: George Bohn) (trumpet; clarinet)

When You Gotta Swing, You Gotta Swing It (Hudson's latest: tenor; Dolan's drums; trumpet; guitar)
You're My Desire (vocal: Nan Wynn) (how I love this song, great vocal: GREAT trombone)
Magnolia (short guitar solo; Gus Bivona's long, swell clarinet solo; guitar; nuttsy trumpet; swell drums)
Hobo On Park Avenue (theme)

12.30AM WABC
TOMMY DORSEY
Hotel Pennsylvania Roof, NYC
Allegheny Al (vocal: Edythe Wright)
Love Is A Merry-Go-Round (vocal: Jack Leonard)
Barcarolle (Dorsey's muted trombone; Freeman; solid bass; Freeman)
Once In A While (vocal: Edythe Wright & Three Esquires)
I've Got The Blues (swell: clarinets; Dorsey)
Posin' (vocal: Edythe Wright) (Erwin; Freeman; Mince; Tough; Dorsey)
Humoresque (Dorsey's trombone; Smith's piano; Erwin)
The Morning After (vocal: Jack Leonard) (written by Tommy Dorsey)
I May Be Wrong (nuttsy: Dorsey; Freeman)
Jammin' (Fast as hell! Mince; Erwin)

1:30AM WWL
GLENN MILLER
Hotel Roosevelt, New Orleans
Community Swing (recorded on Brunswick)
If I Put My Heart In My Song (vocal: Kathleen Lane) (nuttsy vocal)
They Can't Take That Away From Me / Let's Call The Whole Thing Off / They All Laughed (medley from *Shall We Dance* movie starring Fred Astaire & Ginger Rogers)
Shoe Shine Boy (vocal: Sterling Bose) (New Orleansian Sterling Bose's singing & trumpet)
White Star Of Sigma Nu (Jerome's tenor; Kenyon's drums)
The Moon Got In My Eyes (vocal: Kathleen Lane) (good vocal on fair song, getting popular)
Humoresque (McIntyre's good clarinet; Jerry Jerome's fine, full-toned tenor sax)
Stop! You're Breaking My Heart (vocal: Kathleen Lane) (good tune)
St. Louis Blues (Bose's trumpet; Jerome's tenor; McIntyre; Ralph; swell brass)

■ WEDNESDAY 28 JULY 1937

Bob returns home to Bronxville.

RADIO LOGS

11.00PM WABC
TOMMY DORSEY
Hotel Pennsylvania Roof, NYC
Me, Myself, And I (vocal: Edythe Wright) (swell: Mince's clarinet; Freeman; Dorsey)
Strangers In The Dark (vocal: Jack Leonard)
Who'll Buy My Violets? (nuttsy: Mince; Erwin; Freeman with Tough; Dorsey)
The Things I Want (vocal: Edythe Wright) (swell song: Dorsey's trombone on first chorus)
Night And Day (swell: Dorsey's muted trombone; Howard Smith's piano)
I Know Now (vocal: Jack Leonard) (Tommy Dorsey's muted trombone)
Melody In F (one of Dorsey's BEST classics: Mince; Freeman; Dorsey)
So Rare (vocal: Edythe Wright) (nuttsy piece: Dorsey's trombone)
Mendelssohn's Spring Song (great: Mince; Tough; Erwin; Freeman; Dorsey)

■ THURSDAY 29 JULY 1937

RADIO LOGS

11:30PM WICC
ZINN ARTHUR
Nichol's Pinebrook Country Club, Conn
Hodge-Podge
Sweet Leilani (vocal: Zinn Arthur)
Satan Takes A Holiday

Lament O Gitano (vocal: Zinn Arthur)
Cross Country Hop (written by Will Hudson)
Goodbye (vocal: Zinn Arthur)
Rose Room
There's A Small Hotel (vocal: Zinn Arthur)
Bongo (written by Zinn Arthur: trombone; clarinet)

12:30AM WABC
BENNY GOODMAN
Palomar Ballroom, Los Angeles
When You And I Were Young, Maggie (Musso's gut-bucket tenor; Harry James; Krupa)
Afraid To Dream (vocal: Betty Van) (just released today on Victor, will be a big hit)
The Lady Who Couldn't Be Kissed (McEachern's trombone; Musso's tenor)
Someday Sweetheart (BG Trio) (recorded on Victor 25181: unsurpassable work by all three)
Darktown Strutters' Ball
Love Is A Merry-Go-Round (vocal: Betty Van)
Avalon (BG Quartet) (marvelous: fast tempo)
How Could You? (vocal: Betty Van)
I Found A New Baby (GREAT, recorded on Victor 25355: James; Musso; Benny)

■ FRIDAY 30 JULY 1937

RECORDING SESSION

BENNY GOODMAN QUARTET
Recording session for Victor in Hollywood.
Lionel Hampton (vib); Teddy Wilson (p); Benny Goodman (cl); Gene Krupa (d)
Avalon / Handful Of Keys / The Man I Love

TEDDY WILSON AND HIS ORCHESTRA
Recording session for Brunswick in Los Angeles.
Benny Goodman (cl); Harry James (t); Vido Musso (ts); Teddy Wilson (p); Allan Reuss (g); Harry Goodman (b); Gene Krupa (d); Boots Castle (voc)
You're My Desire (vBC) /*Remember Me* (vBC) / *The Hour Of Parting* (vBC) / *Coquette*

RADIO LOGS

10.00PM WJZ
TOMMY DORSEY
Kool Cigarette Program, NYC
I heard this program at Helen Devlin's house in Bronxville.
Humoresque (Erwin; Tommy; Smith's piano)
So Rare (vocal: Edythe Wright)
East Of The Sun (vocal: Jack Leonard)
In My Solitude
Ain't Misbehavin' (vocal: Edythe Wright)
Liza (good, but too short!)

11:05PM WABC
PHIL NAPOLEON
Hotel New Yorker, NYC
This is the first time I ever heard Phil Napoleon's Band, formed this month, which replaced Gus Arnheim at the Hotel New Yorker yesterday. He used to play trumpet with the Memphis Five. His band doesn't sound very good to me. He features 'Whispering swing.' Kenneth Roberts announced.
Tomorrow Is Another Day (vocal: Dorothy Howe) (she formerly sang with Art Shaw's band)
Darktown Strutters' Ball (fair: Napoleon's fair trumpet)
It Looks Like Rain In Cherry Blossom Lane (vocal: Billy Pritchard) (tenor sax)
That's A-Plenty (Napoleon's good trumpet; nice clarinet; very weak sax section; trombones)
The First Time I Saw You (vocal: Dorothy Howe)
Rusty Hinge (vocal: Ford Leary) (Leary, trombonist, was formerly with Bunny Berigan's band)
Harbor Lights (vocal: Billy Pritchard)
Sugar Foot Stomp
Washboard Blues (vocal: Ford Leary) (lousy, too much violins: Napoleon; Leary's trombone)

11:30PM WABC
BOB CROSBY
Ritz-Carlton Hotel, Boston
Between The Devil And The Deep Blue Sea (Lawson; Miller)
Where Or When (vocal: Kay Weber) (Zurke; Miller)
The Lady From Fifth Avenue (vocal: Bob Crosby) (Miller)
Unknown Title (featuring Bob Zurke's piano: marvelous)
There'll Be Some Changes Made (vocal: Bob Crosby) (arranged by Matlock)
Coquette (nuttsy)
I Know Now (vocal: Kay Weber)
Twilight In Turkey (great: Miller; Zurke; Lawson)

11:30PM WEAF
HUDSON-DeLANGE
Playland Casino, Rye, N.Y.
Sweet Lorraine
Darktown Strutters' Ball
Carelessly (vocal: Nan Wynn)
Caravan
Have You Got Any Castles? (vocal: George Bohn)
No. 32
I'm Feeling Like A Million (vocal: Nan Wynn)
Where Are You?
Fireman's Ball

12:15AM WABC
RED NORVO
Coney Island, Cincinnati, Ohio
WONDERFUL!
The You And Me That Used To Be (vocal: Mildred Bailey)
Posin' (swell arrangement: no vocal)
Honeysuckle Rose (vocal: Mildred Bailey)
Love Me Or Leave Me (great)

12.30AM WEAF
MIKE RILEY
Castle Farms, Cincinnati, Ohio
Fair: Mike Riley has laryngitis so he can't sing tonight.
Blue Skies
Am I Dreaming?
How Could You?
Blue Hawaii
They All Laughed
I'm Hatin' This Waitin' Around
Where Or When (vocal: Marion Miller)

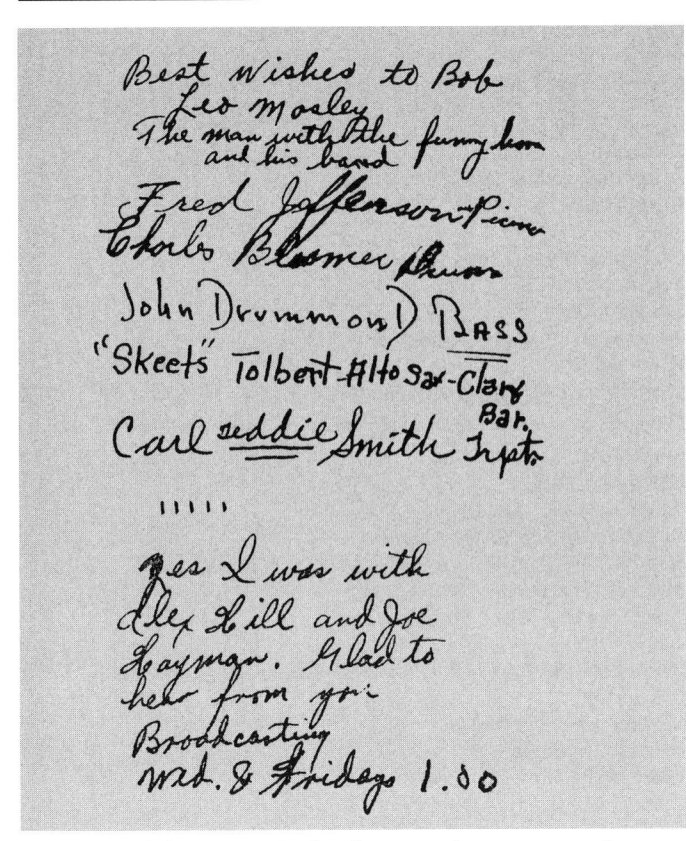

Bob received the Leo Mosley band autographs on a postcard on July 30th. It is interesting to note the signature of trumpeter Carl "Teddie" Smith. Carl was formerly with Count Basie and was nominally co-leader with Jo Jones of the famous Smith-Jones Incorporated sessions. Over the years he has been known to us as Carl "Tatti" Smith, presumably as a result of mis-hearing. I wonder if his double underlining of "Teddie" signified his frustration with the mistaken nomenclature.

■ SATURDAY 31 JULY 1937

I bought three records today at Ferris' Music Store in Bronxville. They were: Count Basie's *Boogie Woogie / Exactly Like You* (Decca); Count Basie's *One O'Clock Jump / John's Idea* (Decca 1363); and Andy Kirk's *Cloudy / Puddin' Head Serenade* (Decca 1208).

RADIO LOGS

4.30PM WEAF
WILLIE BRYANT
NYC
Swell.
South Side Stomp
Caravan
Afraid To Dream
Oh, Lady Be Good
Tea On The Terrace
Congo

9:15PM WHN
ANTHONY TRINI
Roseland Ballroom, NYC
Twelfth Street Rag
When You And I Were Young, Maggie
When Two Love Each Other
China Boy

Satan Takes A Holiday
Basin Street Blues (vocal: June Bennett)
You're My Desire
Jam Session
Confessin' (vocal: June Bennett)

9:45PM WMCA
DICK McGINLEY
Nautical Plaza, Revere Beach, Mass
Blue Skies
Satan Takes A Holiday
White Heat

11:04PM WABC
BUNNY BERIGAN
Pavillon Royale, Long Island, N.Y.
Born To Love (vocal: Ruth Bradley)
All God's Chillun Got Rhythm (vocal: Ruth Bradley)
The Morning After
Frankie And Johnny
The Image Of You (vocal: Ruth Bradley)
Russian Lullaby
A Message From The Man In The Moon (vocal: Ruth Bradley)
The Prisoner's Song
I Can't Get Started (theme)

12.00 MIDNIGHT WEAF
MIKE RILEY
Castle Farms, Cincinnati, Ohio
A Study In Brown
Good Morning (vocal: Marion Miller)
I Never Knew
Mountain Music
Today I'm A Man
My Blue Heaven (vocal: Mike Riley)
Sweet Leilani
Posin'
The Music Goes Round And Around (theme)

12:30AM WHN
RED NORVO
Coney Island, Cincinnati, Ohio
Turn Off The Moon
There's A Lull In My Life (vocal: Mildred Bailey)
Clap Hands! Here Comes Charlie
Heaven Help This Heart Of Mine (vocal: Mildred Bailey)
Jammin'
Hallelujah!

12:30AM WABC
BENNY GOODMAN
Palomar Ballroom, Los Angeles
Mean To Me (grand arrangement of old standard tune)
Afraid To Dream (vocal: Betty Van)
Caravan (super-marvelous: Benny; Stacy; James; Krupa)
Chlo-e (recorded on Victor 25531: Harry James' trumpet; Jess Stacy's piano solo)
Dinah (BG Quartet) (nuttsy, fast: much different from recording on Victor 25398)
There's A Lull In My Life (vocal: Betty Van) (wonderful arrangement of swell hit tune)
Spain (old tune played by Goodman for first time over radio: Benny; James' trumpet; SWELL)
When Buddha Smiles (GREAT – recorded on Victor 25258: Art Rollini's tenor)
Walk, Jennie, Walk (swell – recorded on Victor 25329: James' short trumpet; Krupa)

1:30AM WWL
GLENN MILLER
Hotel Roosevelt, New Orleans
Community Swing
Simply Grand (vocal: Kathleen Lane)
You're Here, You're There, You're Everywhere (vocal: Kathleen Lane)

AUGUST 1937

Hotel Pennsylvania: **Tommy Dorsey**; Frank Dailey subs for one week (21–28) while Dorsey plays the Steel Pier in Atlantic City
Hotel New Yorker: **Phil Napoleon**
Hotel Astor: **Ozzie Nelson** (2–)

Apollo Theater: **Cab Calloway** (–5); 'Skating Along' (6–12); **Claude Hopkins** (13–19); 'All-Girl Revue' (20–26); **Blanche Calloway** (27–)
Paramount Theater: **Mal Hallett** (–3); **Phil Spitalny** (4–10);
Loew's State Theater: **Gus Arnheim** (–4); **Will Osborne** (12–18); **Chick Webb** (19–25)

Hickory House: **Joe Marsala**
Onyx Club: **John Kirby/Spirits of Rhythm**

Young America's Favorite
OPENING MONDAY NIGHT
the One and Only
Ozzie Nelson
and his orchestra featuring
LOVELY SHIRLEY LLOYD
and Bob DuPont, the Lathrops and the Olympic Trio.
Dinners from $2. Cover charge (after 10 p.m.) 75c weekdays, $1 Saturdays and holiday eves.
ASTOR ROOF
HOTEL ASTOR – TIMES SQUARE

■ SUNDAY 1 AUGUST 1937

RADIO LOGS

5.00PM WOR
TOMMY DORSEY
Steel Pier, Atlantic City, N.J.
Allegheny Al (vocal: Edythe Wright) (Dorsey's muted trombone; Mince's clarinet)
The Morning After (vocal: Jack Leonard) (Tommy Dorsey's swell smooth trombone)
Barcarolle (swell: Erwin; Freeman; Erwin again)
Once In A While (vocal: Edythe Wright & Three Esquires)
I've Got The Blues (great: Freeman; clarinets; Dorsey's long, muted solo)
Posin' (vocal: Edythe Wright) (swell: lousy piece but nuttsy solos by Erwin; Freeman; Mince; Tough; Dorsey)
Humoresque (Dorsey's trombone; Erwin; Mince's long solo; Smith's piano; Dorsey)

Happy Birthday To Love (vocal: Jack Leonard)
I May Be Wrong (ballsy: Freeman, etc)
Jammin' (vocal: Edythe Wright)

12:30AM WHN
RED NORVO
Coney Island, Cincinnati, Ohio
MARVELOUS!
Blue Skies
If You Should Ever Leave (vocal: Mildred Bailey)
Body And Soul
Slap That Bass
More Than You Know (vocal: Mildred Bailey) (GREAT)
Where Or When
'Long About Midnight (vocal: Mildred Bailey) (COLOSSAL)
Nagasaki

1:30AM WWL
GLENN MILLER
Hotel Roosevelt, New Orleans
I'm Sitting On Top Of The World
If I Put My Heart In My Song (vocal: Kathleen Lane)
The Lady Who Couldn't Be Kissed
Shoe Shine Boy (vocal: Sterling Bose)
Shine
Whispers In The Dark (vocal: Kathleen Lane)
Whispering
Do You Ever Think Of Me?
Japanese Sandman
Where Is The Sun? (vocal: Kathleen Lane)
St. Louis Blues

■ MONDAY 2 AUGUST 1937

Today is my birthday. I am now 17-years-old. My brother gave me the Benny Goodman record of *Roll 'Em / Afraid To Dream* (Victor 25627).

RECORDING SESSION

BENNY GOODMAN QUARTET
Recording session for Victor in Hollywood.
Lionel Hampton (vib); Teddy Wilson (p); Benny Goodman (cl); Gene Krupa (d)
Smiles / Liza

RADIO LOGS

12:00 MIDNIGHT WABC
BOB CROSBY
Ritz-Carlton Hotel, Boston
The Old Spinning Wheel (wonderful)
Never In A Million Years (vocal: Kay Weber)
They All Laughed (vocal: Bob Crosby)
Tin Roof Blues
You Can't Have Everything (vocal: Kay Weber)
If I Had You (vocal: Bob Crosby)
Bugle Call Rag

■ TUESDAY 3 AUGUST 1937

RADIO LOGS

9:30PM WABC
BENNY GOODMAN
Camel Caravan program, Los Angeles
The sixth half-hour program now called Benny Goodman's Swing School.
Always
The Merry-Go-Round Broke Down

Where Or When (BG Trio)
Three Little Words (MEYER ALEXANDER's SWING CHORUS)
Twilight In Turkey (BG Quintet) (Harry James plus Quartet)
Changing Of The Guard (vocal: Pat O'Malley) (Harry James' trumpet)
It Looks Like Rain In Cherry Blossom Lane
I Found A New Baby

11:15PM WEAF
FLETCHER HENDERSON
Grand Terrace, Chicago
O.K.
Posin'
Rhythm Of The Tambourine
Having A Wonderful Time (vocal: Chuck Richards)
Honeysuckle Rose

11:30PM WEAF
HUDSON-DeLANGE
Playland Casino, Rye, N.Y.
SWELL.
Stop! You're Breaking My Heart (vocal: Nan Wynn)
Magnolia
You've Got Something There (vocal: Eddie DeLange)
Dallas Blues (vocal: GiGi Bohn)
Popcorn Man (vocal: Nan Wynn & Band)
Number 32 (written by Hudson)
Fireman's Ball
You're My Desire (vocal: Nan Wynn)
The Image Of You (vocal: GiGi Bohn)
Hobo On Park Avenue (theme)

12.00 MIDNIGHT WNEW
WILLIE BRYANT
Savoy Ballroom, NYC
GOOD.
Blue Rhythm Fantasy (theme) (nuttsy new theme played in its entirety)
Harlem Special
A Study In Brown
A Sailboat In The Moonlight
So Rare
Where Or When
Cavernism (Sonny White's nice piano solo)
Honeysuckle Rose
King Porter Stomp

12:30AM WHN
RED NORVO
Coney Island, Cincinnati, Ohio
SIMPLY GRAND!
Turn Off The Moon
Never In A Million Years (vocal: Mildred Bailey)
Jammin'
Everyone's Wrong But Me (vocal: Mildred Bailey)
If You Should Ever Leave (vocal: Mildred Bailey)
Without Your Love
Shoutin' In That Amen Corner (vocal: Mildred Bailey)
I Know That You Know

12.30AM WABC
TOMMY DORSEY
Hotel Pennsylvania Roof, NYC
All God's Chillun Got Rhythm
Night Over Shanghai (vocal: Jack Leonard)
Satan Takes A Holiday
You've Got Something There (vocal: Edythe Wright)
Our Penthouse On Third Avenue (vocal: Jack Leonard)
Dark Eyes
The Morning After (vocal: Jack Leonard) (Tommy Dorsey's muted trombone)
Beale Street Blues

■ WEDNESDAY 4 AUGUST 1937

RECORDING SESSION

ART SHAW AND HIS NEW MUSIC
Recording session for Brunswick in New York City.
Art Shaw (cl/ldr); John Best, Malcolm Crain, Tom di Carlo (t); Harry Rogers, George Arus (tb); Les Robinson, Harry Freeman (as); Tony Pastor (ts/voc); Jules Rubin (ts); Les Burness (p); Al Avola (g); Ben Ginsberg (b); Cliff Leeman (d); Peg La Centra, Leo Watson (voc)
Am I In Love? (vPLC) / *Fee Fi Fo Fum* (vLW) / *Please Pardon Us, We're In Love* (vPLC) / *The Chant* / *The Blues–Part 1* / *The Blues–Part 2*

RADIO LOGS

12.00 MIDNIGHT WNEW
JOE MARSALA
Hickory House, 144 W52nd Street, NYC
Jazz Me Blues
Marie
Gone With The Wind
Blue Skies
Embraceable You
Farewell Blues
Dallas Blues

12.00 MIDNIGHT WEAF
PAUL WHITEMAN
Fort Worth, Texas
Is It True Somebody Loves Me (vocal: Jack Teagarden)
The Night Is Young (vocal: Jimmy Brierley)
Gone With The Wind (vocal: Jimmy Brierley)
Me, Myself And I
Love's Old Sweet Song
Mendelssohn's Spring Song

■ THURSDAY 5 AUGUST 1937

RECORDING SESSION

CHARLIE BARNET AND HIS ORCHESTRA
Recording session for Variety in New York City.
Charlie Barnet (ss/as/ts/voc); Frankie Newton, Jack Koven, Jimmy Milazzo (t); Bob Fishel, John d'Agostino (tb); Harry Carrel, Ernie Diven (as); Kurt Bloom (ts); Ludwig Flato (p); George Cuomo (g); John Kirby or Harry Sulkin (b); Joe Dale (d); The Four Stars (v)
Shame On You (vCB) / *Emperor Jones* / *If You're Ever In My Arms Again* (vTFS)

RADIO LOGS

12:30AM WABC
BENNY GOODMAN
Palomar Ballroom, Los Angeles
I heard this program at Betty Nicholson's house in Scarsdale with Carolyn Bade. I'll never forget this night! If only I could remember more of it!
Let's Dance (theme)
Peckin'
Stardust On The Moon (vocal: Betty Van)
I've Got My Love To Keep Me Warm (Right In The Groove!)
Swingtime In The Rockies (beautiful trombones and saxes therein)
All Over Nothing At All (vocal: Betty Van) (simply super-colossal: Stacy's piano)
Who? (BG Trio) (eloquence tripled: an easy, fastish tempo, complete relaxation)
It Looks Like Rain In Cherry Blossom Lane (James' trumpet with piano backing)
Limehouse Blues (BG Quartet) (more marvelous work, by Hamp especially)
Stompin' At The Savoy (Arthur Rollini's real swell tenor; McEachern, etc)

1:30AM WWL
GLENN MILLER
Hotel Roosevelt, New Orleans
Satan Takes A Holiday
If I Put My Heart In My Song (vocal: Kathleen Lane)
The Lady Who Couldn't Be Kissed
Star Dust
Loveless Love
Honeysuckle Rose
The Moon Got In My Eyes (vocal: Kathleen Lane)
Whispering
Do You Ever Think Of Me?
Japanese Sandman
You're Here, You're There, You're Everywhere (vocal: Kathleen Lane)

■ FRIDAY 6 AUGUST 1937

RECORDING SESSION

MAXINE SULLIVAN
Recording session for Vocalion in New York City.
Maxine Sullivan (voc); Frankie Newton (t); Buster Bailey (cl); Pete Brown (as); Babe Russin (ts); Claude Thornhill (p); John Kirby (b); O'Neil Spencer (d)
Loch Lomond (vMS) / *I'm Coming, Virginia* (vMS) / *Annie Laurie* (vMS) / *Blue Skies* (vMS)

Maxine Sullivan

RADIO LOGS

10.00PM WJZ
TOMMY DORSEY
Kool Cigarette Program, NYC
I Know Now (vocal: Jack Leonard)
Night And Day
Sleepy Time Gal (vocal: Jack Leonard)
Star Dust (vocal: Edythe Wright)
All God's Chillun Got Rhythm

11:30PM WABC
BOB CROSBY
Ritz-Carlton Hotel, Boston
Ain't Misbehavin'
Whispers In The Dark (vocal: Kay Weber)
Gone With The Wind (vocal: Kay Weber)
Jamboree (Bauduc; Matlock)
Summertime (theme)

■ SATURDAY 7 AUGUST 1937

RECORDING SESSION

BUNNY BERIGAN AND HIS ORCHESTRA
Recording session for Victor in New York City.
Bunny Berigan (t/voc); Irving Goodman, Steve Lipkins (t); Al George, Sonny Lee (tb); Mike Doty, Joe Dixon (cl/as); Clyde Rounds, George Auld (ts); Joe Lippman (p); Tom Morgan (g); Hank Wayland (b); George Wettling (d); Gail Reese (voc)
Let 'Er Go (vGR) / *Turn On That Red-Hot Seat* (vGR) / *I Can't Get Started* (vBB) / *The Prisoner's Song*

Hugh Pastoriza, Roddy Snow, Howard Shepard and myself left Bronxville at 8pm in Howard's car. We arrived at Playland, Rye (11 miles from Bronxville) at 8.30 and went on the big roller coaster twice as well as another exciting ride. Both gave us a great thrill. At 9.00 we went into the Playland Casino where we got a table near the band. Because it was Saturday we had to pay $1.65 apiece: $1.25 for dinner and 0.40 cover charge. I wasn't hungry so I got a glass of champagne which was very good, but cheap stuff. We got the autographs of the whole band on a picture of the band. Leaders Will Hudson and Eddie DeLange also autographed a picture of themselves that I had. Will Hudson is only with the band half of the time; spending two weeks with it and then two weeks away from it. He happened to be there tonight. All he did was sit around, talk, and read a newspaper. He is one of the finest musical composers that the world has known, and also a great arranger. He writes and arranges most of the tunes the band plays. Irving Mills, who manages the band, and Eddie DeLange usually supply the words to Hudson's tunes. Eddie DeLange is quite a showman. He never wears a tie, always having a scarf instead. He leads the band at all times, except when doing one of his swell, sentimental vocals. Nan Wynn and saxist GiGi Bohn are the other two vocalists. Nan Wynn replaced Ruth Gaylor several months ago. Wynn is very pretty, kind of Spanish looking. Her personality is fair, very nice but a little dumb. Her vocals are splendid. Saxist GiGi Bohn takes very few vocals. He has a fair hot voice. Outstanding musicians in the band were cornetist Jimmy Blake, trombonist Ed Kolyer, tenor saxist Ted Duane, saxist Gi Gi Bohn, guitarist Bus Etri, clarinetist Gus Bivona, and bassist Ed Goldberg. Blake tops them all with

Composer/arranger Will Hudson (left) with his co-leader, singer Eddie DeLange.

his real swing cornet. He joined the band several months ago, coming from Boston. He is always very sure of his notes and doesn't ruin his playing by hitting high notes as so many trumpeters do. Ed Kolyer takes hardly any hot trombone licks but he has a marvelous sweet tone and is very smooth on sweet songs. Ted Duane is definitely a hot tenor sax soloist and is above average. GiGi Bohn never takes any solos, but he leads one of the finest sax sections today. Guitarist Bus Etri plays plenty screwy hot licks on his guitar, a very good soloist and a pretty fair rhythm man. Big, husky clarinetist Gus Bivona is another new member of the band (the other three saxists have been with the band since it started) and plays swell clarinet. Although I believe the rhythm section is the poorest part of the band, I would say that bassist Ed Goldberg is always there with a nice tone. Although Skeets Dolan's drumming is a great improvement on Ed O'Hara, Dolan is still a little too loud. This is the last night of the band's 6-week engagement at the Playland Casino. On Sunday they go down to Baltimore and then have a rest, making records all week. They are to be at Atlantic City starting the 21st of August. We had to leave at 11.30 even though the place was open until 2.00am.

RADIO LOGS

7:00PM WABC
BOB CROSBY
Ritz-Carlton Hotel, Boston
In A Minor Mood
Where Or When (vocal: Kay Weber)
Have You Got Any Castles, Baby? (vocal: Bob Crosby)
Twilight In Turkey (Miller; Lamare; Matlock)

8.00PM WABC
SATURDAY NIGHT SWING SESSION No56
CBS Studio No1, 485 Madison Ave, NYC
Waddlin' At The Waldorf (nuttsy: Hank Ross's nuttsy sax; Gussak's drums)
Darktown Strutters' Ball (LOU 'RED' EVANS going the balls)
Satan Takes A Holiday (LOU 'RED' EVANS)
By Heck (Artie Shapiro's nuttsy bass)
On The Sunny Side Of The Street (CAB CALLOWAY singing the balls with part of his band: Chu Berry, tenor sax; Chauncey Haughton, clarinet; Doc Cheatham, trumpet; Bennie Payne, piano. I still think Chu Berry is the greatest living sax player. SUPER-COLOSSAL)
So Rare (Leith Stevens directing the CBS Band)
Ain't Misbehavin' (CASPAR REARDON on harp)
Oh, Lady Be Good (CAB CALLOWAY singing : Doc Cheatham on trumpet)
Farewell Blues (Hank Ross' tenor)

11:00PM WABC
BUNNY BERIGAN
Pavillon Royale, Long Island, N.Y.
Am I Blue?
The Image of You (vocal: Gail Reese)
Ubangi Man (Lee; Auld; Berigan; Wettling)
My Cabin Of Dreams (vocal: Gail Reese)
Swanee River
A Message From The Man In The Moon (vocal: Gail Reese)
Louise (Auld; Dixon)
Born To Love (vocal: Gail Reese)
The Prisoner's Song

11.30PM WMCA
WILLIE BRYANT
Savoy Ballroom, NYC
This 'n' That
Basin Street Blues
We Can't Go On This Way
Liza (Charles Frazier's tenor sax)
St. Louis Blues (vocal: Willie Bryant)
Dark Eyes

12.00 MIDNIGHT WNEW
JOE MARSALA
Hickory House, 144 W52nd Street, NYC
Harlem Joys (Marty Marsala's trumpet; Girard's harp; Bushkin's piano)
Night Over Shanghai (Adele Girard's harp)
I Know That You Know (vocal: Adele Girard)
Singin' The Blues
Muskrat Ramble
I'll See You Again

12:30AM WABC
BENNY GOODMAN
Palomar Ballroom, Los Angeles
Changes
Afraid To Dream (vocal: Betty Van)
It Looks Like Rain In Cherry Blossom Lane
Me, Myself And I (vocal: Betty Van)
When It's Sleepy Time Down South
The Merry-Go-Round Broke Down
The You And Me That Used To Be (vocal: Betty Van)
Shine (BG Quartet) (Hampton's vibes outstanding)
Cherry
Bugle Call Rag

■ SUNDAY 8 AUGUST 1937

Harvey Pinger, Roddy Snow and myself left Bronxville at 2.00 this afternoon and went down to 52nd Street by subway. We wanted to go to the Onyx Club but we found that it is closed on Sundays. So we went over to the Hickory House on 52nd Street between Sixth and Seventh Avenues. We entered the Hickory House at 3.30 and sat down at a table where we had a round of drinks. This is the first time that I have been down to the Hickory House. It is one of the most famous jam places in New York City. To get in you have to buy a drink and you can sit at a table or around the large oval bar in the middle of which Marsala's Band plays. We were there from 3.30 to 6.00. Every Sunday afternoon they have a jam session from 3 to 6 and then they don't play until 10.30 when, with short intermissions, they continue until 3.30 in the morning. Because I had met Joe Marsala before, at the Hotel Pennsylvania when Benny Goodman was there, he recognized me. During the first intermission Marsala was at the far end of the room when he happened to notice me. He smiled, waved, and came over and shook hands with me and sat at our table for about ten minutes. He sure is a swell fellow. I asked him several questions concerning the band, etc. He told me that Hugues Panassie, the French authority on jazz who wrote the book 'Hot Jazz', wanted Marsala to bring his band over to Paris where the Fair is now going on. As yet, however, union trouble has prevented this. I told him that I saw drummer George Wettling playing with Bunny Berigan's Band. At this, he replied that he was trying to get Wettling back because the present drummer, Danny Alvin, was only fair and Wettling was great. He also said that Wettling and Condon both came from Chicago and have been the best of friends for a long time and that they both drink way too much. In fact, Eddie Condon drank so much that he had to retire from the band in June to take a rest and stop drinking. When Condon left the band temporarily, violinist Ray Biondi changed over to guitar, giving the present personnel: Joe Marsala (clarinet); Marty Marsala (trumpet); Ray Biondi (guitar); Joe Bushkin (piano); Artie Shapiro (bass); Danny Alvin (drums), and Adele Girard (female harpist who does some pitiful vocalizing). She's good looking and a good harp player, but that's about all. The 2 Marsala Brothers, Bushkin, and Shapiro are very fine swing musicians and really swell fellows. They are all so friendly. After the next set, Joe Marsala and Bushkin autographed a picture containing Marsala, Bushkin, Condon, Morty Stuhlmaker and Henry 'Red' Allen. Joe said that he wished he could get this picture saying that it was a 'kick.' I also got Joe Marsala and bassist Sid Weiss to autograph my book 'Rhythm On Record'.

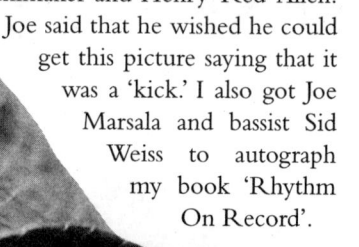

Adele Girard

AUGUST 1937

Left: On the stand at the Hickory House are Danny Alvin, Ray Biondi, Adele Girard, Art Shapiro, Joe Marsala, Joe Bushkin

Sid Weiss, who used to play at the Hickory House with Wingy Manone's Band (included Manone, Weiss, Carmen Mastren and Joe Marsala) is now living in Washington, D.C., where his wife is president of the Hot Club which Roddy Snow attends. Weiss has a nuttsy brother, Sam, who plays plenty of drums. Sid, who also played with Charlie Barnet's Band at the Glen Island Casino last summer, sat in with Marsala's Band in place of Shapiro. He sure did some swell bassing. During the next set, while the band was playing, Joe Marsala motioned for me to come up to the bar. Naturally I was quite embarrassed with everybody looking at me. He told me that Eddie Condon had just come in and was sitting on the other side of the bar. He said that I should go around and show him the picture. I did this with great pride. Condon autographed it for me and I had a little chat with him, Sid Weiss, and some other fellow who was sitting with them. He looked something like John Hammond, but wasn't. I then went back to our table and got the autographs of Biondi and Shapiro. Some of the numbers the band played were: *Marie* / *I Found A New Baby* (featuring three trumpets of Marty Marsala, Joe Bushkin, and Ray Biondi) / *Gone With The Wind* (sung by Adele Girard) / *Blue Skies* / *Farewell Blues*. We left for home at 6.15, taking the subway.

RADIO LOGS

6:00PM WABC
PHIL HARRIS
Texas Exposition
Blue Bonnet (vocal: Phil Harris)
I Know Now (vocal: Ruth Robins)
Heaven Help This Heart Of Mine (vocal: Art Jarrett)
Dardanella
There's A Lull In My Life (vocal: Leah Raye)
Stormy Weather (vocal: Art Jarrett)
Stop! You're Breaking My Heart (vocal: Phil Harris)
Whispers In The Dark (vocal: Ruth Robins)
Rose Room (theme)

6:30PM WOR
FUN IN SWINGTIME
WOR Studios, NYC
Bunny Berigan Orchestra.
Tain't So
Remember
'Cause My Baby Says It's So (Georgie Auld; Joe Dixon)
I Can't Get Started (theme)

■ MONDAY 9 AUGUST 1937

Roddy Snow, Hugh Pastoriza, Robcliff Jones and myself took the 11:50 train from Bronxville on Monday night. I had been swimming all day at Jones' Beach on Long Island, saw 'Artists And Models,' a movie with Jack Benny, Louis Armstrong etc., and Phil Spitalny's All-Girl Orchestra (terrible) at the Paramount Theater on Times Square, and arrived home in Bronxville at 10pm. At 10.30 Roddy Snow came over to my house and reminded me that I was to go to New York City to stay out all night as we had planned. So, at 11:30 we all sneaked out of our houses, I sneaked down the stairs in my stockinged feet unlocking the door so I could get in the next morning. Robcliff climbed down a rope out of his window, Hughie almost woke his strict parents by practically falling out of his second storey window to the ground. Roddy didn't have anything to worry about because he lives in Washington, D.C. and is visiting his sister in Fleetwood, and she doesn't care. I didn't want to make this trip because I didn't have a cent to my name and I was out all night the previous Thursday. But Roddy said he would treat me and my parents were in Long Island for the night (Hilda was here), so I went.

We were all excited at going into the city at such a late time. We were all very jovial and must have looked very funny among the other passengers on the train who were all tired, most of them sleeping. After arriving at Grand Central, we took the shuttle subway over to Times Square and from there the subway down to 33rd Street and Seventh Avenue, where the Hotel Pennsylvania is located. We arrived at the Roof where Tommy Dorsey's Band was playing at 12:40. We immediately got a table across from the band. Of course, we each had to pay the cover charge of 0.75 apiece for 50 minutes of music and fun, but we didn't mind because we were out to have a good time. Much to our surprise we found that Donald Budge and Gene Mako were among the very few people there. You know that Budge is the world's greatest amateur tennis player, and both he and Mako were on the Davis Cup team that defeated England three weeks ago. Budge danced a little so it was possible for me to get his autograph on the back of Dorsey's picture that I had brought along. Many pictures were taken of Mako, Budge and Dorsey together. Budge pretended to play the guitar while Dorsey played trombone, and Mako really did play the drums. In fact, Mako replaced the regular drummer, Dave Tough, for 20 minutes playing with the band. Although a pretty lousy drummer, Mako was funny. The whole band got to fooling around and none of them did particularly good work; they were even sloppy.

Dorsey's Band started something comparatively new several months ago when they began to play several swing arrangements of old classics (*Marie, Song Of India, Mendelssohn's Spring Song,*

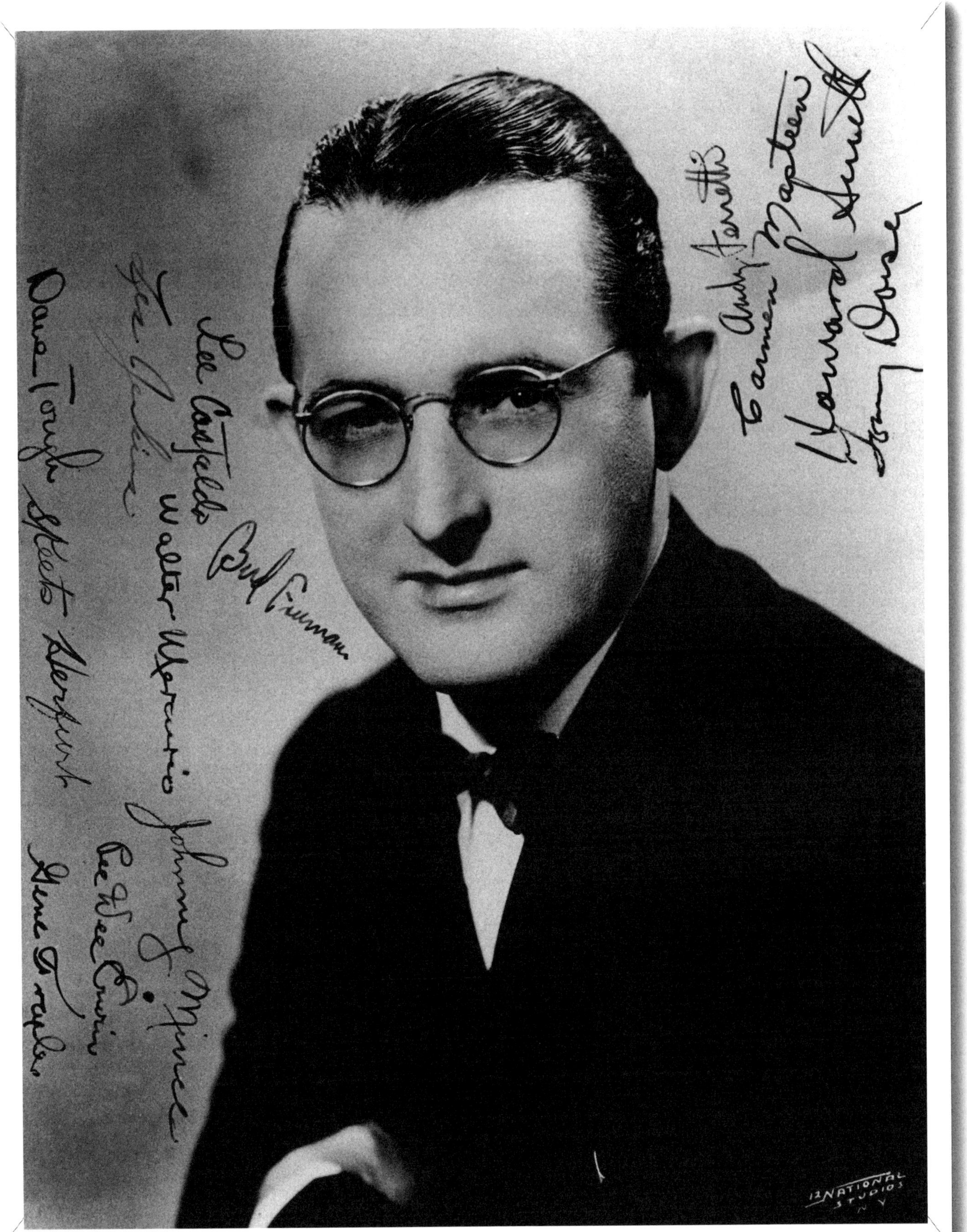
NATIONAL STUDIOS N Y

Melody In F, Who'll Buy My Violets, Humoresque, Barcarolle, etc). They made a tremendous hit and the Victor recordings sold like fire. They were very good, but now they are being over-played by Dorsey. I think it would do him good to stop making records for a while and go on tour and get in the groove by playing more of the old standard hot tunes. He is still the nuts when he plays such tunes as *Honeysuckle Rose, Beale Street Blues* (to be released on a 12" Victor record), *That's A-Plenty, Ja-Da, Royal Garden Blues, Down South Camp Meetin'*, etc. Another thing is the trouble that Dorsey has with the men in his band. Dorsey always did want his own way and seemed to like himself a little bit more than the other fellow, but just the same he was always very nice and smiling. Several months ago saxmen Joe Dixon and Clyde Rounds left the band because they couldn't get along with Tommy. Then trumpeter Max Kaminsky left, then trumpeter Steve Lipkins went, pianist Dick Jones was fired and, just a few weeks ago, saxist Mike Doty had an argument with Tommy and he left. Skeets Herfurt, who used to play with the old Dorsey Brothers' band and then Jimmy' band, replaced Doty. Herfurt is a fine alto sax soloist, a swell guy, and a good vocalist. Because of that Dorsey is getting rid of trumpeter Joe Bauer who sang with the Three Esquires. Also, a few weeks ago trombonist Red Bone left the band for an unknown reason. Walter Mercurio, who played with Dorsey's Band in 1936, is back replacing Bone on first trombone. Lee Castaldo, formerly trumpeter with Art Shaw and Red Norvo, is to replace Bauer next week. The only thing that Dorsey played that sent me was a 12-minute version of *Honeysuckle Rose* with Bud Freeman and Dorsey taking long, swell solos. I got the autographs of the whole band (except for Stulce, Bauer, Stordahl, Leonard and Wright) on a picture of Tommy Dorsey.

During the second intermission I went over and had a ten-minute talk with Dave Tough. I told him that I was the one that wrote a letter to his column in Metronome. In this letter I asked many questions about drumming and kidded around very much. He published my letter in the July issue and it was one of the funniest things I have ever read. He said that he thought Gene Krupa was the best white drummer but that Chick Webb was the greatest drummer that ever lived. Tough thinks that Bauduc is a good drummer, but Webb thinks that Bauduc is the greatest. Who the hell IS the greatest drummer? Tough told me how he, Krupa and Wettling all used to play together in Chicago and how he used to play with Bix Beiderbecke and Benny Goodman. He says that Beiderbecke was the greatest cornetist that ever lived. He also mentioned Zutty Singleton and Roy Eldridge as very fine musicians. After the band had stopped playing we talked to Andy Ferretti about how late the Hickory House and Onyx Club stayed open. He told us that they both stayed open until 4:00 and that the Savoy Ballroom in Harlem closed earlier on Monday night, so we took the subway up to 52nd Street. We decided to go and spend the rest of the night at the Onyx Club. On the way past the Hickory House, however, we met Joe Marsala. He came up and shook hands with me again and we talked with him on the street for about ten minutes. He told us that he started to play the clarinet when he was 9-years-old and that he was now 31. He then guessed all our ages. We didn't go in the Hickory House because I had been there the day before. We went over to the Onyx Club and went in at about 2:15. It was the first time that any of us had been there. It is very small, but modern and air-conditioned. We went in and sat at a table but soon left it when we found that we had to pay $1.50 apiece at all tables. We stood at the bar. To our surprise I recognized bassist Ed Goldberg and drummer Skeets Dolan from the Hudson-DeLange Band that we saw on Saturday night. We stood with them until they left about a half hour later. Goldberg treated me to a drink. The band was led by John Kirby and we spent a long time admiring the real relaxed swing that these Negroes played. It's marvelous. Everybody in the band is a very fine swing artist, except I wasn't impressed by the drumming of O'Neil Spencer. He was too loud and showed-off a bit, but he did a swell vocal on *The Old Stamping-Ground* (recently recorded on Decca with Willie 'The Lion' Smith). Each tune the band played lasted anywhere from 5-minutes to 15. The personnel of the band was: John Kirby (bassist formerly with Fletcher Henderson); Buster Bailey (clarinetist formerly with Millinder, Sissle, Henderson); Leo Watson (trombone and hot vocalist who played drums on 2 numbers); Frankie Newton (trumpeter formerly with Teddy Hill's Band); Don Frye (pianist); and Pete Brown (saxist). Looking around I noticed that Charlie Barnet was eating at a table and Claude Thornhill (pianist) was at another table. Finally, at about 3:00am, Barnet took out his tenor sax and Sal Franzella (a boy from New Orleans who just left Ted Lewis' band) took his clarinet and they sat in with the band. What a GREAT jam session it was!! It lasted for 45 minutes. During the next intermission, in which Maxine Williams [Sullivan] sang, Roddy and I went back to get autographs. We had a swell talk with Frankie Newton who took us out in the back of the Onyx where John Kirby and Leo Watson were sitting talking. Newton introduced all of us and we all chatted for the next ten minutes about the bygone days of Fletcher Henderson, Cab Calloway, Chu Berry, automobiles, etc. We left at 4:00am when the Onyx closed and took the subway home. We got home at 7:00am.

Frank Newton
O'Neil Spencer (drums)
John Kirby
Leo Watson
Pete Brown (Alto)

THE ONYX

"THE CRADLE OF SWING"

JOHN KIRBY

WITH

LEO AND HIS SPIRITS OF RHYTHM

FEATURING

BUSTER BAILEY AND FRANK NEWTON

62 WEST 52ND, NEW YORK

RECORDING SESSION

COUNT BASIE AND HIS ORCHESTRA
Recording session for Decca in New York City.
Buck Clayton, Ed Lewis, Bobby Moore (t); Dan Minor, Benny Morton, Eddie Durham (tb); Earle Warren (as/voc); Lester Young, Herschel Evans (ts); Jack Washington (bar); Count Basie (p); Freddie Green (g); Walter Page (b); Jo Jones (d); Jimmy Rushing (voc)
Good Morning Blues (vJR) / *Our Love Was Meant To Be* (vEW) / *Time Out* / *Topsy*

RADIO LOGS

8.00PM WJZ
WILLIE BRYANT
'Goodtime Society', NYC
Twelfth Street Rag
For Dancers Only
Dear Old Southland
Blue Rhythm Fantasy (theme)

11:30PM WICC
ZINN ARTHUR
Nichol's Pinebrook Country Club, Conn
Old King Cole
A Message From The Man In The Moon (vocal: Zinn Arthur)
Rose Room
I've Got My Love To Keep Me Warm (vocal: Zinn Arthur)
Twilight In Turkey
Hands Across The Table
For You (vocal: Zinn Arthur)
Organ Grinder's Swing
Carelessly
Marie

12:00 MIDNIGHT WABC
BOB CROSBY
Ritz-Carlton Hotel, Boston
Sugar Foot Strut
That Old Feeling (vocal: Kay Weber)
My Cabin Of Dreams (vocal: Bob Crosby)
Gin Mill Blues
All God's Chillun Got Rhythm (vocal: Nappy Lamare)
Have You Got Any Castles, Baby? (vocal: Bob Crosby)
Tomorrow Is Another Day (vocal: Kay Weber)
Pagan Love Song (Miller; Lawson)

12.00 MIDNIGHT WNEW
JOE MARSALA
Hickory House, 144 W52nd Street, NYC
Clarinet Marmalade
Where Or When (vocal: Adele Girard)
Harlem Joys
It Looks Like Rain In Cherry Blossom Lane

12.30AM WABC
TOMMY DORSEY
Hotel Pennsylvania Roof, NYC
I'm Getting Sentimental Over You (theme)
Allegheny Al (vocal: Edythe Wright) (Bud Freeman; Howard Smith)
Love Is Never Out Of Season (vocal: Jack Leonard)
Liebestraum
The Things I Want (vocal: Edythe Wright)
Canadian Capers (Johnny Mince's clarinet)
The Morning After (vocal: Jack Leonard)
Goin' Home
So Rare (vocal: Edythe Wright)
That's-A-Plenty (Mince; Freeman; Tough)

1:30AM WWL
GLENN MILLER
Hotel Roosevelt, New Orleans
Humoresque (Bose's trumpet; Jerry Jerome's tenor)
If I Put My Heart In My Song (vocal: Kathleen Lane)
Shine (McIntyre's clarinet)
Where Are You? (vocal: Kathleen Lane)
Anytime, Anyday, Anywhere (vocal: Sterling Bose) (Sterling Bose's trumpet)
Where Is The Sun? (vocal: Kathleen Lane)
Caravan
You're Here, You're There, You're Everywhere (vocal: Kathleen Lane)
St. Louis Blues (Jerry Jerome's tenor; Bose's trumpet; Jesse Ralph's trombone)

TUESDAY 10 AUGUST 1937

RECORDING SESSION

WOODY HERMAN AND HIS ORCHESTRA
Recording session for Decca in New York City.
Woody Herman (cl/as/voc/ldr); Clarence Willard, Kermit Simmons (t); Joe Bishop (fh); Neal Reid (tb); Jack Ferrier, Deane Kincaide (as); Saxie Mansfield, Bruce Wilkins (ts); Nick Hupfer (vln); Tommy Linehan (p); Oliver Mathewson (g); Walter Yoder (b); Frank Carlson (d)
Stardust On The Moon (vWH) / *The Lady From Fifth Avenue* (vWH) / *Don't You Know Or Don't You Care?* (vWH) / *Double Or Nothing* (vWH)

EARL HINES AND HIS ORCHESTRA
Recording session in Chicago.
Earl Hines (p/ldr); Charlie Allen, Milton Fletcher (t); Walter Fuller (t/voc); Louis Taylor, William Franklin, Trummy Young (tb); Darnell Howard (cl/as/vln); Omer Simeon (cl/as/bar); Budd Johnson (ts); Lawrence Dixon (g); Quinn Wilson (b); Wallace Bishop (d); Madeline Green (voc)
Blue Skies (vMG) / *Hines Rhythm* / *A Mellow Bit Of Rhythm* / *Ridin' A Riff*

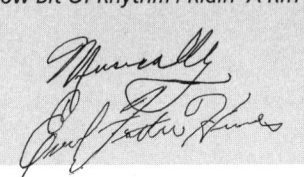

RADIO LOGS

9:30PM WABC
BENNY GOODMAN
Camel Caravan program, Los Angeles
The seventh half-hour program now called Benny Goodman's Swing School.
Let's Dance (theme)
Remember (Rollini; McEachern)
Me, Myself, And I (vocal: Benny Goodman)
A Sailboat In The Moonlight (BG Trio)
Mother Goose Marches On (MEYER ALEXANDER's SWING CHORUS)
Shine (BG Quartet)
Swing, Benny, Swing (Bloch & Sully with MEYER ALEXANDER's SWING CHORUS)
Sing, Sing, Sing (Krupa; Musso; James)
Goodbye (closing theme)

11:05PM WABC
BUNNY BERIGAN
Pavillon Royale, Long Island, N.Y.
GREAT, MARVELOUS! Saxist Mike Doty replaced Sid Perlmutter with the Band a few weeks ago. Kenneth Roberts announced.
Wake Up And Live
Rose Room (MARVELOUS: nuttsy saxes; Joe Lippman's great piano; Georgie Auld's short, but nuttsy tenor sax; ditto for Joe Dixon's clarinet; Berigan's trumpet)

Roses In December (vocal: Gail Reese) (swell arrangement: Berigan's muted trumpet; Lee)
Russian Lullaby (COLOSSAL: Berigan; Wettling; Auld; Dixon; brass section; ending)
I'm Feeling Like A Million (vocal: Gail Reese) (Lippman & Wettling behind vocal; Berigan)
Poor Robinson Crusoe (simply MAGNIFICENT: Berigan; Auld; Dixon; Lee; drums)
You Can't Run Away From Love (vocal: Gail Reese) (commercial but great)
Frankie And Johnny (super-colossal, better than the record: Berigan; Wettling; Auld; Dixon)

11:30PM WEAF
LES BROWN
Playland Casino, Rye, N.Y.
I'm Coming Virginia
Strangers In The Dark
The Image Of You
Heart Of Stone (vocal: Jack Wilmot)
Sleepy Time Gal
Gone With The Wind (vocal: Jack Wilmot)
When You Wore A Tulip (swell: trumpet; tenor sax; clarinet; trombones)
Whispers In The Dark
Bugle Call Rag
Yesterdays (theme) (nuttsy slow theme)

12:00 MIDNIGHT WNEW
WILLIE BRYANT
Savoy Ballroom, NYC
Announced by Martin Block.
Wednesday Night Hop
Lindy Hop (GREAT: nuttsy piano; tenor sax)
South Side Stomp (NUTTSY: tenor sax; piano)
You're My Desire
If I Could Only Count On You
For Dancers Only
Between The Devil And The Deep Blue Sea
Coquette
Blue Rhythm Fantasy (theme)

12.30AM WABC
TOMMY DORSEY
Hotel Pennsylvania Roof, NYC
How Could You? (vocal: Edythe Wright)
Love Is A Merry-Go-Round (vocal: Jack Leonard)
Blue Danube Waltz
Once In A While (vocal: Edythe Wright)
Sugarfoot Stomp
I Know Now (vocal: Jack Leonard)
Hymn To The Sun
The Things I Want (vocal: Edythe Wright)
Weary Blues

■ WEDNESDAY 11 AUGUST 1937

RADIO LOGS

12.30AM WABC
TOMMY DORSEY
Hotel Pennsylvania Roof, NYC
You've Got Something There (vocal: Edythe Wright)
Our Penthouse On Third Avenue (vocal: Jack Leonard)
Barcarolle (Erwin; Freeman; Mince)
The Morning After (vocal: Jack Leonard)
Royal Garden Blues
The Things I Want (vocal: Edythe Wright)
Humoresque
Have You Got Any Castles, Baby? (vocal: Jack Leonard)
Bugle Call Rag

■ THURSDAY 12 AUGUST 1937

RECORDING SESSION

ERSKINE HAWKINS AND HIS ORCHESTRA
Recording session for Vocalion in New York City.
Erskine Hawkins (t/ldr); Wilbur Bascomb, Marcellus Green, Sam Lowe (t); Edward Sims, Robert Range (tb); William Johnson (as); Jimmy Mitchelle (as/voc); Paul Bascomb (ts); Haywood Henry (cl/bar); Avery Parrish (p); William McLemore (g); Leemie Stanfield (b); James Morrison (d); Billy Daniels, Merle Turner (voc)
I'll See You In My Dreams / *Red Cap* (vJM) / *I'll Get Along Somehow* (vJM) / *I Found A New Baby*

RADIO LOGS

11:30PM WICC
ZINN ARTHUR
Nichol's Pinebrook Country Club, Conn
Linger Awhile
You're My Desire (vocal: Zinn Arthur)
Stop! You're Breaking My Heart (vocal: Zinn Arthur)
Oh, Lady Be Good
A Message From The Man In The Moon (vocal: Zinn Arthur)
Rose Room
Goodbye (vocal: Zinn Arthur)
Bongo

12:00 MIDNIGHT WNEW
WILLIE BRYANT
Savoy Ballroom, NYC
Blue Rhythm Fantasy (theme) (played in full)
Hallelujah
The Goona Goo
Stardust On The Moon
Congo
Satan Takes A Holiday
Call Your Bluff

12:30AM WABC
BENNY GOODMAN
Palomar Ballroom, Los Angeles
Makin' Whoopee (NUTTSY: saxes & brass; Harry James' trumpet; Benny)
You Turned The Tables On Me (vocal: Betty Van) (sounds great after a long time)
Cherry
Caravan (MAGNIFICENT – best arrangement I ever heard: Krupa; James)
I'm Getting Sentimental Over You (first time Goodman has played this great piece: Musso; James)
Runnin' Wild (BG Quartet) (their usual fine work)
Alexander's Ragtime Band (SWELL: no solos except Benny's; whole band jivin')
More Than You Know (BG Trio) (simply grand playing in fairly slow tempo)
All Over Nothing At All (vocal: Betty Van)

■ FRIDAY 13 AUGUST 1937

RECORDING SESSION

CHARLIE BARNET AND HIS ORCHESTRA
Recording session for Variety in New York City.
Charlie Barnet (ss/as/ts); Frankie Newton, Jack Koven, Jimmy Milazzo (t); Bob Fishel, John d'Agostino (tb); Harry Carrel, Ernie Diven (as); Kurt Bloom (ts); Ludwig Flato, Joe Myrow (p); George Cuomo (g); John Kirby or Harry Sulkin (b); Joe Dale (d)
Surrealism / *Lullaby To A Lamp Post* / *Overheard In A Cocktail Lounge* / *Merry Widow On A Spree*

AUGUST 1937

RADIO LOGS

7:45PM WEAF
BUGHOUSE RHYTHM
San Francisco
Announced by G. Archibold Presby. Excellent.
Midnight At The Onyx
Big Boy Blue (extra nuttsy arrangement)
Big John Special (written by Horace Henderson: nuttsy trumpet; tenor sax)

8.30PM WHDH
CAB CALLOWAY
Canobie Lake Park, N.H.
Nobody's Sweetheart (Chu Berry; Claude Jones)
There's A Lull In My Life (vocal: Cab Calloway) (Chu Berry)
Knick-Knacks
My Melancholy Baby (vocal: Cab Calloway)
Honeysuckle Rose (vocal: Cab Calloway)
Sylvia (vocal: Bennie Payne)
Jitterbug Special

10.00PM WJZ
TOMMY DORSEY
Kool Cigarette Program, NYC
Liebestraum
You've Got Something There (vocal: Jack Leonard)
When We're In Love (vocal: Jack Leonard)
Louise
Can't We Be Friends? (vocal: Edythe Wright)
Swing That Music

KIMBALL'S STARLIGHT
On Route 128, at South Lynnfield
TONIGHT—CHECK DANCING
ALLEN CURTIS
TOMORROW NIGHT
The Swing Sensation
ART SHAW
AND HIS FAMOUS ORCHESTRA
with PEG LA CENTRA
Direct from the French Casino, New York City

11:00PM WABC
PHIL NAPOLEON
Hotel New Yorker, NYC
The Miller's Daughter, Marianne
Washboard Blues (vocal: Ford Leary)
My Little Fraternity Pin (vocal: Billy Pritchard)
Satan Takes A Holiday
You're My Desire (vocal: Dorothy Howe)
Milenburg Joys
It Looks Like Rain In Cherry Blossom Lane (vocal: Billy Pritchard)
Where Or When (vocal: Dorothy Howe)
Alexander's Ragtime Band (vocal: Ford Leary)
Original Dixieland One-Step

11:30PM WEAF
COUNT BASIE
Hotel Ritz-Carlton, Boston
Moten Swing (theme)
Yeah, Man! (Lester Young; Buck Clayton; Herschel Evans)
Louise (Herschel Evans)
I Must Have That Man (vocal: Billie Holiday)
When My Dreamboat Comes Home (vocal: Jimmy Rushing)
Swinging At The Daisy Chain (Lester Young; Count Basie)
Me, Myself And I (vocal: Billie Holiday)
Smarty (vocal: Jimmy Rushing)
Perfidia
After You've Gone (Jo Jones; Buck Clayton; Walter Page; Herschel Evans)

11:30PM WEAF
LES BROWN
Playland Casino, Rye, N.Y.
Turn Off The Moon (Jack Atkins' trumpet)
You're My Desire (vocal: Jack Wilmot)
A Little Bit Later On
Where Or When (vocal: Jack Wilmot)
St. Louis Blues
More Than You Know

Count Basie

■ SATURDAY 14 AUGUST 1937

RADIO LOGS

6:00PM WJZ
JAN SAVITT
Pittsburgh, Pa
Remember Me (vocal: Bon Bon Tunnell)
Our Penthouse On Third Avenue (vocal: Carlotta Dale)
Love Is On The Air Tonight
I Know That You Know (vocal: Dick Wharton)
Strangers In The Dark
Cross Country
Yours And Mine (vocal: Carlotta Dale)
Smarty (vocal: Carlotta Dale)
In Little Town (vocal: Dick Wharton)
Posin' (vocal: Bon Bon Tunnell)

8.00PM WABC
SATURDAY NIGHT SWING SESSION No57
CBS Studio No1, 485 Madison Ave, NYC
Frolic Sam
Who's Sorry Now? (BUSTER BAILEY on clarinet)
Limehouse Blues (BUSTER BAILEY on clarinet)
Dardanella
Dark Eyes (BUNNY BERIGAN ORCHESTRA from the Pavillon Royale in Long Island)
The Prisoner's Song (BUNNY BERIGAN ORCHESTRA from the Pavillon Royale in Long Island)
Thief In The Night (NAT JAFFE on piano)
Someday, Sweetheart (NAT JAFFE on piano)
I Know That You Know (BUSTER BAILEY on clarinet)
Nagasaki
Chicken And Waffles (theme)

9:30PM WEAF
JACK MEAKIN
San Francisco
Same orchestra as on 'Bughouse Rhythm'.
Riverboat Shuffle
Ain't Misbehavin'
Norwegian Dance No.7
Midnight At The Onyx (Hall's clarinet)
Canadian Capers (Meakin's piano)

11:00PM WABC
BUNNY BERIGAN
Pavillon Royale, Long Island, N.Y.
You're Gonna Wake Up Some Morning
I Can't Believe That You're In Love With Me (wonderful: Berigan's real blue, muted trumpet; Dixon; Auld)
All God's Chillun Got Rhythm (vocal: Gail Reese) (Wettling; Dixon)
Trees (swell swing arrangement: brass; Auld)
Remember (colossal: Bunny; saxes; Auld)
The Lady From Fifth Avenue (vocal: Gail Reese) (Auld; Berigan)
Let's Have Another Cigarette (vocal: Gail Reese)
Rockin' Chair Swing (Dixon; Auld; Lee)
The Image Of You (vocal: Gail Reese)
Kiss Me Again (GREAT: Berigan; Auld; Dixon; Lee)

11:30PM WEAF
LES BROWN
Playland Casino, Rye, N.Y.
The You And Me That Used To Be
Exactly Like You
Gone With The Wind (vocal: Jack Wilmot)
They Can't Take That Away From Me
Rocking Chair
There's A Lull In My Life (vocal: Jack Wilmot)
Feather Your Nest
My Blue Heaven

11.30PM WOR
CAB CALLOWAY
Reid Beach Casino, Asbury Park, N.J.
Caravan (ballsy: Chu Berry's tenor)
They Can't Take That Away From Me (vocal: Cab Calloway)
The Love Bug Will Bite You (vocal: Cab Calloway)
Twilight In Turkey
Where Or When (vocal: Bennie Payne)
Three Swings And Out
Ride, Red, Ride
Minnie The Moocher (theme)

11:30PM WNEW
WILLIE BRYANT
Savoy Ballroom, NYC
Blue Rhythm Fantasy (theme) (played in full)
The Love Bug Will Bite You
Midnight At The Onyx (what a tenor sax!! clarinet; trumpet)
It Looks Like Rain In Cherry Blossom Lane (vocal: Willie Bryant)
Twelfth Street Rag (arranged by Fred Norman featuring Sonny White's swell piano)
Sophisticated Swing (SWELL: trombone)
When Irish Eyes Are Smiling

12:00 MIDNIGHT WABC
COUNT BASIE
Hotel Ritz-Carlton, Boston
Announced by Art King.
Moten Swing (theme)
I Found A New Baby
Too Marvelous For Words (vocal: Billie Holiday)
He Ain't Got Rhythm (vocal: Jimmy Rushing)
Oh, Lady Be Good (Lester Young's great tenor; drums; piano)

12.00 MIDNIGHT WNEW
Joe Marsala
Hickory House, 144 W52nd Street, NYC
Harlem Joys
Where Or When (vocal: Adele Girard)
Marie (WONDERFUL: 2 Marsala's; Adele Girard's harp, etc)
My Cabin Of Dreams (Marty Marsala's trumpet)
Rosetta (what jammin'!!! Marty Marsala's muted trumpet; Joe Bushkin's piano)
Honeysuckle Rose (Girard's swell harp; Shapiro's bassing; Bushkin's great piano)
I Found A New Baby

12.00 MIDNIGHT WEAF
GUS ARNHEIM
Castle Farms, Cincinnati, Ohio
It's The Natural Thing To Do (vocal: Ray Foster)
Solitude
The Loveliness of You (vocal: Ray Foster)
Coquette (Irving Fazola's clarinet; piano; trumpet)
Night Over Shanghai (vocal: June Robbins)
Peckin' (screwy intro: tenor sax; Fazola; trumpet)
A Sailboat In The Moonlight (vocal: Ray Foster)
High, Wide And Handsome (clarinet; bass; drums)
It Looks Like Rain In Cherry Blossom Lane (vocal: Ray Foster)
Say it With Music (theme)

12:30AM WABC
BENNY GOODMAN
Palomar Ballroom, Los Angeles
Chlo-e (SWELL: Stacy's introduction; Benny; Harry James' trumpet)
Me, Myself And I (vocal: Betty Van) (James; Musso)
A Sailboat In The Moonlight (BG Trio) (good)
I Found A New Baby (GREAT: Benny; James; Rollini)
It Looks Like Rain In Cherry Blossom Lane (James' trumpet; trombone)
Avalon (BG Quartet)
Sometimes I'm Happy (STUPENDOUS: Griffin's trumpet; Musso)
I'm Feeling Like A Million (vocal: Betty Van) (lousy song, swell arrangement)
Roll 'Em (MAGNIFICENT: brass section; Stacy's long piano solo; Goodman's clarinet; Harry James)

1:30AM WWL
GLENN MILLER
Hotel Roosevelt, New Orleans
On Moonlight Bay (swell–whole band singing: Kenyon's drums; Bose's trumpet)
Gone With The Dawn (vocal: Kathleen Lane) (swell sentimental piece)
They Can't Take That Away From Me / Let's Call The Whole Thing Off / They All Laughed (medley from *Shall We Dance* movie starring Fred Astaire & Ginger Rogers)
Peg O' My Heart (recorded on Decca–good: McIntyre's clarinet)
Shine (McIntyre's clarinet)
The Moon Got In My Eyes (vocal: Kathleen Lane) (clarinet)
Caravan (Jerome's tenor; McIntyre; Kenyon)
Where Is The Sun? (vocal: Kathleen Lane)
Pagan Love Song (trombone; clarinet)

2:00AM KXBY
COUNTESS JOHNSON
Antler's Club, Kansas City, Mo
Living From Day To Day
Moten Swing (10-minutes long: piano; tenor)
If I Put My Heart In My Song
Posin' (vocal: Earl Jackson) (Earl Jackson also plays sax)
I Know Now (vocal: ?)
Boogie Woogie (piano intro: great tenor sax in Chu Berry-style; trumpet)
Nitwit Serenade (time only permitted 2 choruses of this Will Hudson piece: tenor; trumpet; piano)

2:40AM WBBM
HORACE HENDERSON
Swingland Café, Chicago
Chris And His Gang (theme) (colossal theme, written & arranged by Horace Henderson)
Jangled Nerves (Alvin Burroughs featured on drums: nuttsy, real fast tenor; cornet; trombone)
King Porter Stomp (Eddie Sims' nice trumpet; trombone; tenor sax; typical ending)
Unnamed tune (nuttsy piano work; trumpet; that same ballsy tenor sax; bass solo)
Twilight In Turkey (great swing arrangement: tricky trombone; tenor sax)
Hoppin' Off (trumpet; fair trombone; wonderful tenor sax; good trumpet; piano; clarinet)
Blue Lou (written by Edgar Sampson: wa-wa trumpet; nice trombone; long tenor sax solo; trumpet)

3:00AM WJZ
WILLIE BRYANT
Savoy Ballroom, NYC
'Way Down Yonder In New Orleans
Big Boy Blue
Stardust On The Moon (vocal: Arnold Adams)
When Irish Eyes Are Smiling
The You And Me That Used To Be
Eli's Stomp
That Naughty Waltz
Blue Rhythm Fantasy (theme)

SUNDAY 15 AUGUST 1937

RADIO LOGS

6:30PM WOR
FUN IN SWINGTIME
WOR Studios, NYC
Bunny Berigan Orchestra.
Feelin' Like A Million
Satan Takes A Holiday
Tomorrow Is Another Day

MONDAY 16 AUGUST 1937

RECORDING SESSION

LIONEL HAMPTON AND HIS ORCHESTRA
Recording session for Victor in Hollywood.
Lionel Hampton (vib/voc/p/d); Jonah Jones (t); Eddie Barefield (cl); Clyde Hart (piano); Bobby Bennett (g); Mack Walker (b); Cozy Cole (d)
Confessin' (vLH) / *Drum Stomp [Crazy Rhythm]* (dLH) / *Piano Stomp [Shine]* (pLH-CH) / *I Surrender Dear*

RADIO LOGS

8.00PM WJZ
WILLIE BRYANT
'Goodtime Society', NYC
Sugarfoot Stomp
Peace, Brother, Peace (first time played on air)
Oh, Lady Be Good
Blue Rhythm Fantasy (theme)

12:00 MIDNIGHT WABC
COUNT BASIE
Hotel Ritz-Carlton, Boston
Old Fashioned Love
I'll Always Be In Love With You
Swing, Brother, Swing (vocal: Billie Holiday)
With Plenty of Money And You (Herschel Evans)
Our Love Was Never Meant To Be (vocal: Earl Warren)
Energetic Stomp (written by Count Basie)
There's A Lull In My Life (vocal: Billie Holiday)
Roseland Shuffle (Herschel Evans; Jo Jones)

12.30AM WABC
TOMMY DORSEY
Hotel Pennsylvania Roof, NYC
Me, Myself And I (vocal: Edythe Wright)
Have You Got Any Castles, Baby? (vocal: Jack Leonard)
Melody In F
Once In A While (vocal: Jack Leonard)
Marie (vocal: Jack Leonard & Band) (Pee Wee Erwin's trumpet)
Song Of India
A Message From The Man In The Moon (vocal: Edythe Wright)
Beale Street Blues

TUESDAY 17 AUGUST 1937

RADIO LOGS

9:30PM WABC
BENNY GOODMAN
Camel Caravan program, Los Angeles
The eighth half-hour program now called Benny Goodman's Swing School.
Let's Dance (theme)
That Naughty Waltz (Musso; McEachern)
Satan Takes A Holiday (Krupa; Stacy; Musso)
So Rare (BG Trio)
Let's Have Another Cigarette (MEYER ALEXANDER's Swing Chorus)
Liza (BG Quartet)
Chlo-e (Stacy)
Caravan
Goodbye (closing theme)

Two scenes from 'Hollywood Hotel' which Benny Goodman and his band are making in Hollywood.

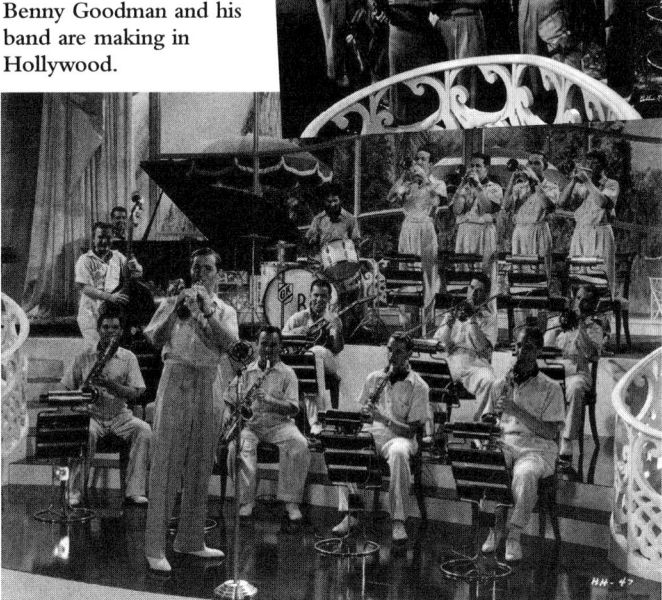

11:05PM WABC
BUNNY BERIGAN
Pavillon Royale, Long Island, N.Y.
A Sailboat In The Moonlight
You Can't Have Everything (vocal: Gail Reese) (Wettling; Dixon)
Roses In December (vocal: Gail Reese)
Swanee River (Georgie Auld)
Let Her Go (vocal: Gail Reese)
Tain't So (Dixon; Auld)
Stop! You're Breaking My Heart
I Can't Get Started (theme)

11:30PM WEAF
LES BROWN
Playland Casino, Rye, N.Y.
The Image Of You
A Sailboat In The Moonlight
Feather Your Nest
Am I In Love? (vocal: Jack Wilmot)
Swamp Fire
Whispers In The Dark
Robins And Roses
That Old Feeling (vocal: Jack Wilmot)
Bugle Call Rag
Sleepy Time Gal

11.30PM WOR
MIKE RILEY
Manhattan Beach Casino, Brooklyn
Marie
Song Of The Islands
My Blue Heaven (vocal: Mike Riley)
Whispering (Mike Riley's trombone)
Do You Ever Think Of Me?
Star Dust (vocal: Mike Riley)
When You And I Were Young, Maggie
Am I Dreaming?
I May Be Wrong

12:00 MIDNIGHT WNEW
WILLIE BRYANT
Savoy Ballroom, NYC
Hallelujah
The Goona Goo (Claude Green's baritone sax)
Stardust On The Moon
Congo (vocal: Charles Frazier)
Satan Takes A Holiday
Calling Your Bluff (Sonny White's piano)

12.30AM WABC
TOMMY DORSEY
Hotel Pennsylvania Roof, NYC
The Lady From Fifth Avenue (vocal: Edythe Wright)
The Morning After (vocal: Jack Leonard)
Dark Eyes (Privin; Mince)
Where Or When (vocal: Jack Leonard)
Ja-Da (Freeman; Erwin)
Christopher Columbus (Henderson theme)
You've Got Something There (vocal: Edythe Wright)
Who'll Buy My Violets?
Happy Birthday To Love (vocal: Jack Leonard)
I'm Getting Sentimental Over You (theme)

■ WEDNESDAY 18 AUGUST 1937

RECORDING SESSION

BUNNY BERIGAN AND HIS ORCHESTRA
Recording session for Victor in New York City.
Bunny Berigan, Irving Goodman, Steve Lipkins (t); Al George, Sonny Lee (tb); Mike Doty, Joe Dixon (cl/as); Clyde Rounds, George Auld (ts); Joe Lippman (p); Tom Morgan (g); Hank Wayland (b); George Wettling (d); Gail Reese (voc)
Why Talk About Love? (vGR) / *Caravan* / *A Study In Brown*

RADIO LOGS

11.00PM WABC
TOMMY DORSEY
Hotel Pennsylvania Roof, NYC
The Things I Want (vocal: Edythe Wright)
Love Is A Merry-Go-Round (vocal: Jack Leonard)
A Stolen Melody (Bud Freeman's sax)
The Lady Who Couldn't Be Kissed (vocal: Edythe Wright)
Mendelssohn's Spring Song (Erwin; Mince)
Night Over Shanghai (vocal: Jack Leonard)
Methuselah Goes A-Riding (vocal: Edythe Wright)
Tomorrow Is Another Day (vocal: Edythe Wright)
That's A-Plenty (Mince; Erwin)

11.30PM WMCA
CLAUDE HOPKINS
Apollo Theater, NYC
I May Be Wrong
Sunday (vocal: Beverly White) (Joe Smith's trumpet)

12.00 MIDNIGHT WNEW
JOE MARSALA
Hickory House, 144 W52nd Street, NYC
Wolverine Blues (Joe Bushkin's piano)
Where Or When (vocal: Adele Girard)
My Cabin Of Dreams
Clarinet Marmalade
Basin Street Blues
Marie
Posin'

12.00 MIDNIGHT WEAF
PAUL WHITEMAN
Texas Exposition, Dallas, Texas
In A Sentimental Mood (Al Gallodoro's alto sax)
Me, Myself And I (vocal: Jack Teagarden)
Dinah (vocal: Jack Teagarden)
The You And Me That Used To Be (Harry Goldfield's trumpet)
Satan Takes A Holiday (arranged by Roy Bargy)
After You've Gone (vocal: Jack Teagarden)

12.30AM WEAF
FLETCHER HENDERSON
New Grand Terrace, Chicago
Avalon
If You Should Ever Leave (vocal: Chuck Richards)
Clarinet Marmalade
I Won't Take No For An Answer
Posin' (vocal: Chuck Richards)
Honeysuckle Rose (Emmett Berry's trumpet)
It Looks Like Rain In Cherry Blossom Lane (vocal: Chuck Richards)
Yeah, Man! (Dick Vance's trumpet; Hilton Jefferson's alto sax; Elmer Williams' clarinet)
They Can't Take That Away From Me (vocal: Chuck Richards)
Tiger Rag (Dick Vance's trumpet)
Christopher Columbus (theme)

2.00PM KXBY
COUNTESS JOHNSON
Antlers Club, Kansas City, Mo
I Never Knew
Star Dust (vocal: Bill Noland)
Froggy Bottom
Walkin' Through Heaven (vocal: Bill Noland)
Posin'
What Will I Tell My Heart? (vocal: Connie Dean)
Boogie Woogie

■ THURSDAY 19 AUGUST 1937

RADIO LOGS

11.30PM WOR
MIKE RILEY
Manhattan Beach Casino, Brooklyn
I Never Knew
Swing Low, Sweet Chariot
Memories Of You (vocal: Mike Riley)
The Merry-Go-Round Broke Down (vocal: Art Dano)
On The Isle Of Kitchy-mi-boko
Today I'm A Man (vocal: Mike Riley)
The First Time I Saw You
The Music Goes Round And Around (theme)

12:30AM WNEW
WILLIE BRYANT
Savoy Ballroom, NYC
Marie (vocal: Arnold Adams) (Arnold Adams plays guitar in the band)
Blue Room (Claude 'Fats' Green's clarinet)
If I Can Count On You (vocal: Arnold Adams)

Sweet And Swingy (first time played: written by Harry White)
Honeysuckle Rose (Sonny White's piano)
Twelfth Street Rag (arranged by Fred Norman)
Eli's Stomp (written by trombonist Eli Robinson)

12:30AM WABC
BENNY GOODMAN
Palomar Ballroom, Los Angeles
The Merry-Go-Round Broke Down
The Lady Who Couldn't Be Kissed
Where Or When (BG Trio)
Minnie The Moocher's Wedding Day
It Looks Like Rain In Cherry Blossom Lane
Let's Have Another Cigarette (vocal: Betty Van)
Sweet Sue (BG Quartet)
Spain
Peckin'
Goodbye (closing theme)

■ FRIDAY 20 AUGUST 1937

RECORDING SESSION

HUDSON-DeLANGE ORCHESTRA
Recording session for Brunswick in New York City.
Will Hudson (arr); Eddie DeLange (voc/ldr); Charles Mitchell, Howard Schaumberger, Jimmy Blake (t); Edward Kolyer, Jack Andrews (tb); George Bohn, Gus Bivona (cl/as); Pete Brendel (as/bar); Ted Duane (cl/ts); Mark Hyams (p); Bus Etri (g); Doc Goldberg (b); Nat Pollard (d)
Mr. Sweeney's Learned To Swing / Travelin' Down The Trail / Goin' Haywire

All today's programs were heard at my brother-in-law Al Winter's (he married my sister Winona) house in Bayside, Long Island.

RADIO LOGS

5:30PM WOR
BOB CROSBY
Great Lakes Expo, Cleveland, Ohio
In A Minor Mood (Bob Zurke's piano)
Where Or When (vocal: Kay Weber) (nuttsy muted trumpet by Zeke Zarchy; Eddie Miller's short, wholesome tenor)
If I Had You (vocal: Bob Crosby) (Bob Zurke's piano much different from solo on record; Miller's ballsy tenor; Yank Lawson's real swing Dixieland trumpet; Matlock's nuttsy clarinet; Smith's great dirty trombone)
Dixieland Shuffle

7:45PM WEAF
BUGHOUSE RHYTHM
San Francisco
Announced by G. Archibold Presby as only he can. A special program for the 'kiddies' educating them on swing.
Jingle Bells (Lawrence Coler's bass sax; Harlow Burgess' trumpet: arranged by Spud Murphy)
Old King Cole (Very similar to *Christopher Columbus*)
Three Blind Mice (colossal, written by Frank Trumbauer: Raymond Harrington's wonderful tenor sax; John Meakin's piano; Burgess' trumpet simply magnificent)

10.00PM WJZ
TOMMY DORSEY
Kool Cigarette Program, NYC
Hymn To The Sun (another classic: Dorsey's trombone; Mince's good clarinet; Erwin's swell trumpet; Freeman's wonderful tenor)
Have You Got Any Castles, Baby? (vocal: Jack Leonard)
The Big Apple (vocal: Edythe Wright & Band) (played for first time on the air, the Big Apple is a new dance that started in the south a few months ago and is now becoming very popular: poor vocal)
For You (vocal: Jack Leonard)

Sophisticated Lady (Dorsey's trombone)
Under A Blanket Of Blue (vocal: Edythe Wright)
I've Got To Swing (Mince's clarinet; Smith's swell piano; Dorsey; Freeman)

11:05PM WABC
PHIL NAPOLEON
Hotel New Yorker, NYC
The First Time I Saw You (vocal: Dorothy Howe)
My Blue Heaven (Ford Leary's trombone)
Medley
Love Me (vocal: Dorothy Howe)
That's A-Plenty
Sweet Like You (vocal: Ford Leary)
Sweet Night (vocal: Dorothy Howe)
Beale Street Blues (Milt Yaner's clarinet)

11:30PM WNEW
WILLIE BRYANT
Savoy Ballroom, NYC
Honeysuckle Rose (arranged by Edgar Sampson: Arnold Adams' solid guitar; clarinet; real gut-bucket tenor sax; trumpet; Sonny White's piano)
Steak And Potatoes (vocal: Willie Bryant) (trumpet; great tenor; trombone)
MEDLEY: *If You Should Ever Leave / My Cabin Of Dreams / How Can You Forget?* (vocal: Arnold Adams)
Marie (vocal: Arnold Adams) (trumpet)
Star Dust (vocal: Arnold Adams) (Claude Green's sax; Gene Prince's trumpet; Eli Robinson's trombone)
The Love Bug Will Bite You (vocal: Willie Bryant) (trumpet; sax; piano)
A Study In Brown (Prince Robinson's sax)
Blue Rhythm Fantasy (theme) (Harry Fredericks' trumpet)

12:00 MIDNIGHT WABC
COUNT BASIE
Hotel Ritz-Carlton, Boston
Shoot The Likker (Eddie Durham's trombone; Buck Clayton's trumpet; Herschel Evans' tenor)
Easy Living (vocal: Billie Holiday)
The You And Me That Used To Be (vocal: Jimmy Rushing)
Baby Girl
I Cried For You (vocal: Billie Holiday)
Boogie Woogie (vocal: Jimmy Rushing)
Honeysuckle Rose
Swinging At The Daisy Chain

12:30AM WEAF
LES BROWN
Playland Casino, Rye, N.Y.
More Than You Know
Gone With the Wind (vocal: Jack Wilmot)
I'm Coming, Virginia
You're My Desire (vocal: Jack Wilmot)
Turn Off The Moon
Heart Of Stone
Exactly Like You
That Old Feeling (vocal: Jack Wilmot)
Rigamarole
Me, Myself And I

1:30AM WWL
GLENN MILLER
Hotel Roosevelt, New Orleans
Stompin' At The Savoy (Jesse Ralph's trombone; Jerry Jerome's tenor; Hal McIntyre's clarinet)
Where Is The Sun? (vocal: Kathleen Lane)
They Can't Take That Away From Me / Let's Call The Whole Thing Off / They All Laughed (medley from *Shall We Dance* movie starring Fred Astaire & Ginger Rogers)
Sweet Leilani
White Star Of Sigma Nu
Simply Grand (vocal: Kathleen Lane) (written by pianist Chummy MacGregor)
Satan Takes A Holiday (Eak Kenyon's drums)

■ SATURDAY 21 AUGUST 1937

I spent this past week at my married sister's house in Bayside, Long Island. On the way home to Bronxville I decided to stay in New York City for several hours. I arrived there at 3:30 and first went up to the RKO Building to see Vincent Prior at Rockwell-O'Keefe. To my disgust it was closed, so I walked along 52nd Street for a while and then I decided to go to the Center Music Store at Rockefeller Center just to see what the store was like. It is the nuts: modern in every respect. I bought Art Shaw's record of *I Surrender Dear / Blue Skies* (Brunswick 7907) released last month. I then went over to Broadway at 46th Street where Chick Webb's Band is playing a week at Loew's State Theater. I paid 55 cents and went in at 4:15. The whole show was very good. Webb has a great band and is considered by many (Tough, etc) to be the greatest drummer that ever lived. I still like Krupa better. Webb is a hunchback and stands about 5 feet. There is none faster than he but his taste isn't always what it should be. Outstanding musicians in the band are: trumpeters Taft Jordan and Bobby Stark, trombonist Sandy Williams, and tenor saxist Ted McRae. Wayman Carver is probably the best swing flute player in the world. The following were numbers played: *Let's Get Together* (theme); *Harlem Congo* (Taft Jordan's trumpet, Williams' trombone, Louis Jordan's clarinet); *I Ought To Have My Head Examined* (Louis Jordan's vocal); *September In The Rain* (Charles Linton vocal); *King Porter Stomp* (Bobby Stark's trumpet, McRae's tenor sax, Williams' trombone); *Sweet Sue* (played by a Quartet: Webb on drums, Beverly Peer on bass, Thomas Fulford on piano, Wayman Carver on flute & clarinet); *There's A Lull In My Life* (Ella Fitzgerald vocal); *Whoa, Babe* (Ella Fitzgerald vocal); *This Is My Last Affair* (Ella Fitzgerald singing as only she can); *Royal Garden Blues* (marvelous; Fitzgerald leading the band and Webb beating the drums something terrific).

After leaving the theater at 7:00 I went over to 485 Madison Avenue where the Saturday Night Swing Sessions are held every Saturday. I certainly have missed seeing this broadcast. Last winter I saw 25 of them. The last one I saw was the anniversary on June 12th. I didn't have tickets to this broadcast but a girl happened to have some extra tickets and gave me one, so I got in without any trouble. I went up to the 22nd Floor, where they broadcast, at 7:20, a half-hour early. The guests on this program were Charlie Barnet (tenor saxist who is a millionaire and has his own band), Les Lieber (hot fife player who works in the CBS Publishing Department), Roland Dupont (a trombonist who arranges many pieces for the CBS band), and the Swingtet (2 girls and 2 boys who just came back from Jack Hylton's Band in England). The CBS Band's personnel has several new members while the Raymond Scott Quintet is in Hollywood. This band sure does sound marvelous! Without a doubt, it is one of the best bands in existence. The only real outstanding soloists, however, are Hank Ross on tenor sax and Art Manners on clarinet. The directors Ed Cashman and Phil Cohan (2 swell guys) were both there and Paul Douglas and Melvin Allen announced.

I got a few autographs after the broadcast, then left the building and walked in the rain down to the Commodore Music Store on E42nd Street where they were just closing up. Since they knew me, they stayed open 10 minutes longer. I bought the following records: Barney Bigard's Jazzopators' *Frolic Sam / Clouds In My Heart* (Variety 525); Gotham Stompers' *My Honey's Lovin' Arms / Alabamy Home* (Variety 629); Billie Holiday's *Me, Myself And I /*

Charles Linton, vocalist with Chick Webb's Band.

Without Your Love (Vocalion 3593); Mildred Bailey's *Rockin' Chair / Little Joe* (Vocalion 3553); Bix Beiderbecke's *Jazz Me Blues / At The Jazz Band Ball* (Vocalion 3042); and Teddy Wilson's *There's A Lull In My Life / It's Swell Of You* (Brunswick 7884). I then took the 9:05 train home.

AUGUST 1937

RADIO LOGS

4:45PM WEAF
WILLIE BRYANT
Savoy Ballroom, NYC
Sugar Foot Stomp
Blue Room
Love Is The Thing (vocal: Willie Bryant) (nuttsy vocal)
South Side Stomp (Andy Gibson's trumpet)

5:30PM WOR
BOB CROSBY
Great Lakes Expo, Cleveland, Ohio
Top Street Blues (written by Bob Zurke)
Whispers In The Dark (vocal: Kay Weber)
Stop! You're Breaking My Heart (vocal: Bob Crosby)
All God's Chillun Got Rhythm (vocal: Nappy Lamare)
The Loveliness Of You (vocal: Bob Crosby)
Muskrat Ramble
Gone With The Wind (vocal: Kay Weber)
Bugle Call Rag
Summertime (theme)

7:00PM WABC
COUNT BASIE
Hotel Ritz-Carlton, Boston
Bugle Call Rag (Herschel Evans' tenor; Lester Young; Eddie Durham's trombone)
I Can't Get Started (vocal: Billie Holiday)
Rhythm In My Nursery Rhymes (vocal: Jimmy Rushing)
Thanksgiving (Lester Young; Ed Lewis)

8.00PM WABC
SATURDAY NIGHT SWING SESSION No58
CBS Studio No1, 485 Madison Ave, NYC
Farewell Blues (arranged by Will Biettel: Willie Kelly's good muted trumpet)
Oh, Lady Be Good (WILL BIETTEL playing a special instrument: colossal)
Three Little Words (WILL BIETTEL again, really sendin' 'em; drums)
Swing Session Called To Order (marvelous: CBS Band)
It's The Talk Of The Town (CHARLIE BARNET playing great sax)
Rosetta (CHARLIE BARNET playing marvelous tenor sax as only he can)
Stop, Look And Listen (SWINGTET vocalizing: 2 boys and 2 girls)
'Cause My Baby Says It's So (Hank Ross' ballsy tenor; Kelly's trumpet)
Crazy Rhythm (LES LIEBER's wonderful fife playing)
Sweet Sue (LES LIEBER again, really swinging on double fifes)
I Found A New Baby (wonderful, CBS Band: Ross; Kelly)

11:00PM WABC
BUNNY BERIGAN
Pavillon Royale, Long Island, N.Y.
You Can't Have Everything (vocal: Gail Reese)
Yours And Mine (vocal: Gail Reese)
A Study In Brown (wonderful, by far the best arrangement of this song: Bunny; Lee's trombone)
A Message From The Man In The Moon (vocal: Gail Reese)
Russian Lullaby (simply marvelous: strong rhythm section, especially Wettling's drums and Fishkind's bass; Berigan's unusual muted trumpet solo at beginning; Auld's typical swell tenor sax; Dixon's typical clarinet; Bunny again in different style)
That Foolish Feeling (vocal: Gail Reese)
'Cause My Baby Says It's So (vocal: Bunny Berigan)
Feelin' Like A Million
Yes! We Have No Bananas (wonderful! Bunny; Auld; Dixon; strong, nuttsy rhythm section; Wettling's drums; Lee)

11:30PM WMCA
WILLIE BRYANT
Savoy Ballroom, NYC
Yours And Mine
When I Grow Too Old To Dream
You Showed Me The Way (Jimmy Archey's trombone)
Prelude To A Stomp
Lindy Hop (nuttsy: Jimmie Lunceford and Billy Hicks just said hello and greeted Willie)
St. Louis Blues (vocal: Willie Bryant) (nuttsy vocal)

12.00 MIDNIGHT WNEW
JOE MARSALA
Hickory House, NYC
Harlem Joys (Marty Marsala's trumpet; Bushkin's piano)
They Can't Take That Away From Me (vocal: Adele Girard)
Marie
Rosetta (Danny Alvin's drums; Bushkin's piano)
Mandy (Marty Marsala's trumpet)
Star Dust
Caravan

12:30AM WABC
BENNY GOODMAN
Palomar Ballroom, Los Angeles
This is Betty Van's last night with the band.
Down South Camp Meetin' (wonderful: exactly like the Victor recording)
Me, Myself And I (vocal: Betty Van) (wonderful: James' great trumpet; Musso; Krupa)
Can't We Be Friends? (Red Ballard's swell sweet trombone; James; Musso; brass)
Nagasaki (BG Quartet) (another excellent swing masterpiece by all four)
Let's Have Another Cigarette (vocal: Betty Van) (Musso's swell tenor on 1st chorus)
Smiles (nuttsy: Benny; James' long, great straight solo)
A Sailboat In The Moonlight (BG Trio) (not nearly as good as the Quartet)
I Can't Give You Anything But Love (MARVELOUS: James; Stacy; great sax section; colossal biting brass; ballsy ending)
That Naughty Waltz (great: Benny; McEachern; James; Musso; James again)

1:30AM WWL
GLENN MILLER
Hotel Roosevelt, New Orleans
I'm Sitting On Top Of The World (swell–recently released on Decca)
Gone With The Wind (vocal: Kathleen Lane)
Peckin' (marvelous clarinet by Hal McIntyre; Bose's nuttsy trumpet)
Star Dust (nuttsy swing arrangement: Peterson's trumpet; McIntyre's clarinet)
If I Put My Heart In My Song (vocal: Kathleen Lane) (nuttsy ballad)
Whispering / Do You Ever Think Of Me? / Japanese Sandman (medley)
Stop! You're Breaking My Heart (vocal: Kathleen Lane)
Honeysuckle Rose (great: McIntyre's clarinet)

■ SUNDAY 22 AUGUST 1937

RADIO LOGS

5:00PM WOR
TOMMY DORSEY
Steel Pier, Atlantic City, N.J.
Allegheny Al (vocal: Edythe Wright) (fine, solid bassing by Gene Traxler; Mince's clarinet)
I Know Now (vocal: Jack Leonard) (swell new commercial piece: Tommy's trombone)
Blue Danube (Strauss classic: Tommy; Mince; Tough; Erwin)
Once In A While (vocal: Edythe Wright & Three Esquires) (very sweet but good)
The Big Apple (vocal: Edythe Wright & Band) (Dave Tough's nuttsy, steady drumming; Traxler)
Yours And Mine (vocal: Jack Leonard) (another sweet commercial piece but swell)
Humoresque (swell: Tommy; Smith's piano; Mince's clarinet; Tough; Erwin)
Tomorrow Is Another Day (vocal: Edythe Wright) (Dorsey's trombone)
Weary Blues (wonderful: Tough's real grooving; Mince's great clarinet; Erwin's marvelous trumpet; Freeman doing magnificently, one of the best tenor solos I ever heard)

5:30PM WOR
BOB CROSBY
Great Lakes Expo, Cleveland, Ohio
Between The Devil And The Deep Blue Sea (Yank Lawson; Warren Smith)
I Know That You Know (vocal: Kay Weber)
Stop! You're Breaking My Heart (vocal: Bob Crosby)
Twilight In Turkey (arranged by Dean Kincaide)

10:00PM WPG
HUDSON-DeLANGE
Million Dollar Pier, Atlantic City, N.J.
If I Had You
No Name (written by Will Hudson)
Darktown Strutters' Ball (Jimmy Blake's trumpet)
Where Are You? (vocal: Ed DeLange)
The Maid's Night Off (Ed Kolyer's trombone)
Whispers In The Dark (vocal: Nan Wynn)
I'm Feelin' Like A Million (vocal: Nan Wynn)
The Loveliness Of You (vocal: Gigi Bohn)

11:35PM WABC
PHIL NAPOLEON
Hotel New Yorker, NYC
Darktown Strutters' Ball
Heavenly (vocal: Dorothy Howe)
Alexander's Ragtime Band (vocal: Ford Leary)
Let Her Go
Blue Bayou (arranged by Napoleon, played for first time over air)
Clarinet Marmalade (clarinet; Napoleon's good wa-wa trumpet; tenor sax)
Can I Forget You? (vocal: Dorothy Howe)
Harbor Lights

12:00 MIDNIGHT WPG
ALEX BARTHA
Steel Pier, Atlantic City, N.J.
They All Laughed (vocal: Carl White)
I Know Now (vocal: Bert Nickerson)
Posin' (vocal: Carl White)
I Love You (vocal: Bert Nickerson)
Me, Myself And I
Bugle Call Rag
How Could You? (vocal: Betty Phillips) (Betty Phillips is 14-yrs-old)
I'm Hatin' This Waitin' Around (vocal: Betty Phillips)
You're My Desire (vocal: Carl White)
Have You Got Any Castles, Baby? (vocal: D. Hammond)
You Were Born To Love (vocal: Bert Nickerson)

12:30AM WEAF
ANDY KIRK
Grand Terrace Café, Chicago
Until The Real Thing Comes Along (theme)
A Mellow Bit Of Rhythm (WONDERFUL: Dick Wilson's nuttsy tenor sax; swell trumpet)
I Never Slept A Wink Last Night (Mary Lou Williams' great piano solo: she's tops!)
If You Should Ever Leave (vocal: Pha Terrell) (trumpet; Dick Wilson's tenor sax)
Walkin' And Swingin' (marvelous, smooth relaxed swing: Ted Donnelly's ballsy trombone; Mary Lou Williams' piano; Dick Wilson's tenor sax)
Posin' (very relaxed, no vocal: very original arrangement)
I Love You From Coast To Coast (Mary Lou Williams' peachy piano)
Where Or When (vocal: Henry Wells) (fair)

1:30AM WWL
GLENN MILLER
Hotel Roosevelt, New Orleans
Night And Day
The Moon Got In My Eyes (vocal: Kathleen Lane)
Humoresque (Bose's trumpet; Jerry Jerome's tenor)
Time On My Hands (Jesse Ralph's trombone)
Loveless Love (McIntyre's clarinet)

Whoa, Babe (Jerry Jerome's tenor)
Whispers In The Dark (vocal: Kathleen Lane) (trumpet)
Stompin' At The Savoy
How Am I To Know? (vocal: Kathleen Lane)

■ MONDAY 23 AUGUST 1937

RADIO LOGS

8.00PM WJZ
WILLIE BRYANT
'Goodtime Society', NYC
Eli's Stomp (written by Eli Robinson: sax; Fats Green's clarinet; trumpet)
When Irish Eyes Are Smiling (arranged by Al Gibson: Sonny White's piano)
The Love Bug Will Bite You (vocal: Willie Bryant)
Congo (written by Harry White: Prince Robinson's tenor sax)

10:00PM WPG
HUDSON-DeLANGE
Million Dollar Pier, Atlantic City, N.J.
Stop! You're Breaking My Heart (vocal: Nan Wynn)
Sophisticated Swing (Ed Kolyer's trombone)
Dallas Blues (vocal: Gigi Bohn)
You've Got Something There (vocal: Ed DeLange)
Fireman's Ball (written by Will Hudson)
Darktown Strutters' Ball
Sweet Lorraine
Lost Again (vocal: Ed DeLange)
Grab Your Partner (vocal: Ed DeLange)
It Looks Like Rain In Cherry Blossom Lane (vocal: Nan Wynn)

11:30AM WABC
TOMMY DORSEY
Steel Pier, Atlantic City, N.J.
How Could You? (vocal: Edythe Wright)
Have You Got Any Castles, Baby? (vocal: Jack Leonard)
Goin' Home (Mince; Erwin)
Once In A While (vocal: Edythe Wright & Three Esquires)
Liza (Freeman; Mince; Tough)
The Big Apple (vocal: Edythe Wright & Band)
Yours And Mine (vocal: Jack Leonard)
Liebestraum (Dave Tough's drums)
Tomorrow Is Another Day (vocal: Edythe Wright)

12.00 MIDNIGHT WNEW
JOE MARSALA
Hickory House, 144 W52nd Street, NYC
Nuttsy.
China Boy
Whispers In The Dark (vocal: Adele Girard) (pretty lousy: Girard's harp)
Muskrat Ramble (marvelous: 2 Marsala brothers playing some GREAT stuff; Bushkin's piano)
Basin Street Blues (more colossal relaxed jam swing: Joe's outstanding clarinet; Marty etc)
My Cabin Of Dreams (good: Girard's harp; Bushkin's solid sender piano; Joe)

12:00 MIDNIGHT WABC
COUNT BASIE
Hotel Ritz-Carlton, Boston
MARVELOUS. COLOSSAL. GREAT.
Energetic Stomp (GREAT, written by Basie: Lester Young's tenor; Clayton's trumpet; trombone; Basie's piano)
They Can't Take That Away From Me (vocal: Billie Holiday) (good vocal: trumpet)
Good Morning Blues (vocal: Jimmy Rushing) (written by Basie and recorded 2 weeks ago)
Moten Twist (written by trombonist Eddie Durham: nuttsy tenor sax; trumpet; Jones' solid drums)
Tea For Two (marvelous: Clayton's muted trumpet; tenor; Basie's colossal piano; Page's bass)

Whatcha Gonna Do When There Ain't No Swing? (vocal: Billie Holiday) (colossal, great)
The Glory Of Love (vocal: Jimmy Rushing) (Clayton's nuttsy, soft muted trumpet; Jones' drums; Young's GREAT tenor)
Oh, Lady Be Good (Basie sending me something terrific; trumpet; trombone; tenor sax)
One O'Clock Jump (magnificent, what a rhythm section!!! Basie's marvelous piano; tenor sax)

1:30AM WWL
GLENN MILLER
Hotel Roosevelt, New Orleans
NUTTSY: reception on the radio is very clear tonight.
Moonlight Serenade (theme)
On Moonlight Bay (rather weak brass, otherwise swell: McIntyre's clarinet)
If I Put My Heart In My Song (vocal: Kathleen Lane) (swell vocal: how I love this song!!)
Anytime, Anyday, Anywhere (vocal: Sterling Bose) (Bose's good trumpet)
Star Dust (nuttsy arrangement: Bose's neat trumpet; McIntyre's clarinet)
Peckin' (more-or-less regular arrangement, like Ben Pollack's, but good)
Gone With The Wind (vocal: Kathleen Lane)
The Lady Who Couldn't Be Kissed (lousy song but fair arrangement: no solos)
Where Is The Sun? (vocal: Kathleen Lane)
Community Swing (great, written by Miller: Bose's trumpet; McIntyre's clarinet)
Moonlight Serenade (theme)

■ TUESDAY 24 AUGUST 1937

RECORDING SESSION

CAB CALLOWAY AND HIS ORCHESTRA
Recording session for Variety in New York City.
Cab Calloway (voc); Doc Cheatham, Irving Randolph, Lammar Wright (t); DePriest Wheeler, Keg Johnson, Claude Jones (tb); Garvin Bushell, Andrew Brown (cl/as); Chu Berry, Walter Thomas (ts); Benny Payne (p); Morris White (g); Milt Hinton (b); Leroy Maxey (d)
Moon At Sea (vCC) / ***I'm Always In The Mood For You*** (vCC) / ***She's Tall, She's Tan, She's Terrific*** (vCC)

RADIO LOGS

9:30PM WABC
BENNY GOODMAN
Camel Caravan program, Los Angeles
Let's Dance (theme)
Sometimes I'm Happy (marvelous example of sweet swing: trumpet; Musso)
Minnie The Moocher's Wedding Day (COLOSSAL example of fast swing: magnificent brass chorus; James' grand trumpet; Benny)
My Cabin Of Dreams (BG Trio) (very new: good, but too commercial)
Bye Bye Pretty Baby (MEYER ALEXANDER's Swing Chorus singing the nuts with Goodman band)
Stompin' At The Savoy (BG Quartet) (nuttsy, especially Hampton: much different from record)
A Sailboat In The Moonlight (vocal: Martha Tilton) (swell arrangement of a lousy piece)
Roll 'Em (magnificent: Stacy's great piano solo much different from record; James' long nuttsy solo)
Goodbye (closing theme)

11:30PM WEAF
LES BROWN
Playland Casino, Rye, N.Y.
SWELL.
Yesterdays (theme) (colossal slow theme written by Jerome Kern several years ago)
Dancing Blue Devils (nuttsy: swell tenor sax; nice clarinet; great trumpet; saxes; piano)
Strangers In The Dark (vocal: Jack Wilmot) (swell arrangement: tenor; beautiful trumpet)
Feather Your Nest (great, recorded on Decca: good trumpet; swell tenor; clarinet; trombone)
Am I In Love? (very smooth saxes; good arrangement)
Caravan (played unusually fast: nice smooth trombone; trumpet à la Eldridge; clarinet)
You're My Desire (vocal: Jack Wilmot) (nuttsy trumpet à la James; swell clarinet; tenor sax; trumpet)
Me, Myself And I (wonderful tenor sax; colossal trumpet à la Beiderbecke)
There's A Lull In My Life (vocal: Jack Wilmot) (fair vocal; muted trombone; clarinet)
Big John Special (swell trumpet except a little screechy; clarinet; saxes; trombone)

12:00 MIDNIGHT WNEW
WILLIE BRYANT
Savoy Ballroom, NYC
Blue Rhythm Fantasy (theme) (great theme: clarinet etc)
Darktown Strutters' Ball (vocal: Willie Bryant) (arranged by Fred Norman: sax; trumpet)
Coquette (Sonny White's swell piano; soft muted trumpet; good clarinet; sax)
Love Is The Thing, So They Say (vocal: Willie Bryant) (arranged by Eli Robinson)
Honeysuckle Rose (ballsy: Charlie Frazier's colossal tenor sax; trumpet; White's nuttsy piano)
The Goona Goo (Arnold Adams' solid guitar; Fats Green's great baritone sax: swell)
Twelfth Street Rag (featuring Sonny White's peachy piano tickling)

■ WEDNESDAY 25 AUGUST 1937

RADIO LOGS

8:00PM WICC
ZINN ARTHUR
Nichol's Pinebrook Country Club, Conn
Goodbye (vocal: Zinn Arthur)
Bongo (written by Zinn Arthur)
Yours And Mine (vocal: Zinn Arthur)

10:00PM WPG
HUDSON-DeLANGE
Million Dollar Pier, Atlantic City, N.J.
Lazy
Wake Up And Live (vocal: Nan Wynn)
Midnight At The Onyx (written by Will Hudson)
The Maid's Night Off (written by Will Hudson)
You've Got Something There (vocal: Ed DeLange)
No.321 (written by Will Hudson)
It Looks Like Rain In Cherry Blossom Lane (vocal: Nan Wynn)
Have You Got Any Castles, Baby? (vocal: Gigi Bohn)
If I Had You (Jimmy Blake's trumpet; Bus Etri's guitar)
Back In Your Arms (Gus Bivona's clarinet)

11:05PM WABC
FRANK DAILEY
Hotel Pennsylvania Roof, NYC
Good. While Tommy Dorsey is playing a week at the Steel Pier in Atlantic City, Dailey is filling in for him.
Oh, Lady Be Good
Afraid To Dream (vocal: Louise Wallace)
'Way Down Yonder In New Orleans (vocal: Joe Mooney) (Mooney is the blind accordion player in the band)
Don't You Know Or Don't You Care?
You Are The Reason For My Love (vocal: Louise Wallace) (nice tenor sax)
The Loveliness Of You (fair muted trumpet)
Stumbling (swell: trombones; clarinet; sax)
Strangers In The Dark (vocal: Louise Wallace)
Stompin' At The Savoy

11:30PM WABC
TOMMY DORSEY
Steel Pier, Atlantic City, N.J.
Good. Ralph Schumacher announced.
Me, Myself And I (vocal: Edythe Wright)
I Know Now (vocal: Jack Leonard)
Barcarolle (good: Freeman; Mince, etc)
Once In A While (vocal: Edythe Wright & Three Esquires)
The Big Apple (vocal: Edythe Wright & Band)
Whispers In The Dark (vocal: Jack Leonard)
Melody In F (great: Freeman; Mince)
Feelin' Like A Million (vocal: Edythe Wright)
I May Be Wrong (colossal: saxes)
Swing That Music (vocal: Three Esquires) (Mince; Dorsey)
I'm Getting Sentimental Over You (theme)

12.00 MIDNIGHT WNEW
JOE MARSALA
Hickory House, 144 W52nd Street, NYC
Harlem Joys (swell: Marty Marsala's trumpet; Girard's short harp solo; Joe Bushkin's colossal piano with swell bassing of Artie Shapiro; Joe's clarinet)
Afraid To Dream (slow commercial foxtrot swung by Marsala's men: Girard's fair, long harp solo followed by Bushkin's swell piano solo; Ray Biondi's swell guitar solo; Joe)
Rosetta (nuttsy old standard tune: Marty & Joe taking the first chorus together, sounding great; Girard's good harp; Bushkin's marvelous piano; Joe's simply grand blues clarinet; Marty's nuttsy trumpet at end)
I Know Now (vocal: Adele Girard) (lousy vocal)
Caravan (great: Alvin's fair tom-toms; Girard; Joe Marsala's colossal long clarinet solo; whole band really jammin'!!)
Singin' The Blues (nuttsy slow piece: Girard's good harp; Bushkin; Marty, etc)
I Found A New Baby (Joe's clarinet; Bushkin's marvelous piano; Alvin's drum solo; 3 trumpets; Shapiro's bass)

12.00 MIDNIGHT WEAF
PAUL WHITEMAN
Billy Rose Aquacade, Dallas, Texas
Satan Takes A Holiday (arranged by Roy Bargy)
All God's Chillun Got Rhythm (vocal: Jack Teagarden)
Old Fashioned Love (vocal: Jack Teagarden)
Nagasaki (Roy Bargy's piano)

12:30AM WEAF
ANDY KIRK
Grand Terrace Café, Chicago
GREAT!
Riffs (colossal: nice trumpet; Ben Thigpen's cymbals; Dick Wilson's grand tenor sax)
Posin' (Mary Lou Williams' swell long, introductory piano solo; Dick Wilson's nice tenor)
Foolin' Myself (vocal: Pha Terrell) (Mary Lou Williams; Dick Wilson's tenor)
Caravan (pretty fast but plenty OK: trumpet; Dick Wilson's colossal tenor sax, really great and original; Thigpen's nice solid drums)
If You Should Ever Leave (vocal: Pha Terrell) (so smooth: Wilson's tenor sax)
Froggy Bottom (vocal: Ben Thigpen) (wonderful, written by Williams: nice piano intro followed by Wilson, then a swell trumpet; grand guitar solo)
Can I Forget You? (vocal: Henry Wells) (trombone team: only fair)
Bugle Call Rag (wonderful original arrangement: nuttsy trumpet; nice clarinet with wa-wa brass section; swell short trombone solo; trumpet again; Wilson)
Unknown title (great long solo by Wilson; good trombone; Williams' GRAND piano; clarinet)
Clouds (closing theme) (trumpet)

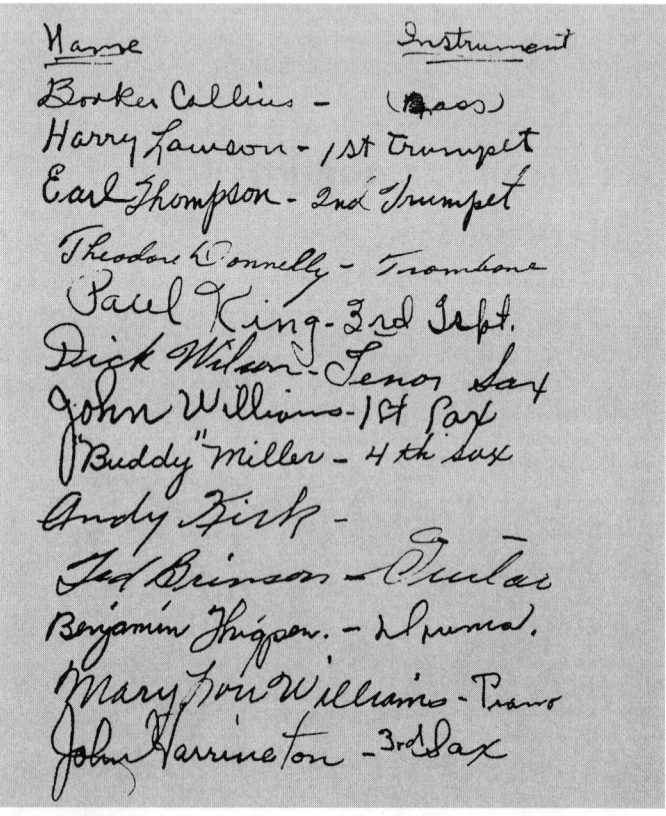

Autographed postcard from the Andy Kirk Band.

1:30AM WWL
GLENN MILLER
Hotel Roosevelt, New Orleans
This is the band's last night (after almost 3 months) at the Roosevelt Hotel in New Orleans. Tomorrow they open at the Hotel Adolphus in Dallas.
On Moonlight Bay (vocal: Band)
Gone With The Wind (vocal: Kathleen Lane) (swell vocal: how I love this song!!)
They Can't Take That Away From Me / Let's Call The Whole Thing Off / They All Laughed (medley from *Shall We Dance* movie starring Fred Astaire & Ginger Rogers)
Sweet Leilani
Jazz Me Blues (Miller's small band: McIntyre; Bose; Miller; Kenyon)
The Moon Got In My Eyes (vocal: Kathleen Lane)
The Lady Who Couldn't Be Kissed (Peterson's trumpet)
How Am I To Know? (vocal: Kathleen Lane)

■ THURSDAY 26 AUGUST 1937

RECORDING SESSION

BEN POLLACK AND HIS ORCHESTRA
Recording session for Decca in Los Angeles.
Ben Pollack (ldr); Ray Woods, Joe Meyer, Muggsy Spanier (t); Joe Yukl (tb); Ben Kanter, Bud Carlton (cl/as); Artie Quenzer, Mort Friedman (ts); Al Beller (vln); Bob Laine (p); Garry McAdams (g); Francis Palmer (b); Graham Stevenson (d); Frances Hunt (voc)
Song Of The Islands (vFH) / *Song Of The Islands* / *I'm Yours For The Asking* (vBP)

CLAUDE THORNHILL AND HIS ORCHESTRA
Recording session for Brunswick in New York City.
Claude Thornhill (p/vib/ldr); Manny Klein, Charlie Spivak (t); Jack Lacey (tb); Toots Mondello, Jess Carneol (as); Babe Russin (ts); Eddie Powell (bar/fl); Artie Bernstein (b); Chauncey Morehouse (d); Maxine Sullivan, Barry McKinley (voc); string section
You And I Know (vBMK) / *An Old Flame Never Dies* (vBMK) / *Ebb Tide* (vBMK) / *Don't Save Your Love* (vMS)

RADIO LOGS

5.30PM WOR
FREDDIE CARLON
Pioneer Palace, Cleveland, Ohio
Blue Skies (nuttsy original arrangement: drums; trombone)
The First Time I Saw You
Big Boy Blue (good: fair trumpet; very good tenor sax; nice clarinet; that sax again)
Meet Me In The Moonlight (lousy)
Ja-Da (kind of slow, but good: too soft piano; very good tenor sax; swell trumpet)

12:00 MIDNIGHT WNEW
WILLIE BRYANT
Savoy Ballroom, NYC
This And That (some swell, relaxed swing by whole band; trumpet)
House Hop (weak intro, otherwise very good: Sonny White's colossal, simple piano; trumpet)
Stardust On The Moon (pretty lousy)
Steak And Potatoes (vocal: Willie Bryant) (recorded a few years ago on Victor: nuttsy sax; trombone)
Honeysuckle Rose (played two ways: waltz style, then colossal swingin'; sax)
Scattin' At The Kit-Kat (swell: trumpet; nuttsy trombone; weak saxes)

12:30AM WEAF
ANDY KIRK
Grand Terrace Café, Chicago
Until The Real Thing Comes Along (theme)
Stop! You're Breaking My Heart
The Folks Who Live On The Hill (vocal: Henry Wells)
I Know Now (vocal: Henry Wells) (Wilson's ballsy tenor; Williams)
Yeah, Man!
If You Should Ever Leave (vocal: Pha Terrell)
Posin'
Worried Over You (vocal: Pha Terrell)
Unknown title (marvelous clarinet; Wilson; trombone)

12:30AM WABC
BENNY GOODMAN
Palomar Ballroom, Los Angeles
Benny's band now has a new vocalist. It's Martha Tilton who formerly sang with Jimmy Dorsey's Band. She is very good but she doesn't have any distinct style and doesn't swing very well.
Remember (wonderful: McEachern's very smooth trombone; Musso's swell tenor)
Stardust On The Moon (vocal: Martha Tilton) (good: Musso's nice slow tenor sax)
Sunny Disposish (colossal: marvelous solos by Benny; James; McEachern)
Let's Have Another Cigarette (vocal: Martha Tilton) (swell vocal; Musso's slow tenor sax)
Who? (BG Trio) (great: long solos by all three — Wilson outstanding)
Me, Myself And I (vocal: Martha Tilton) (grand arrangement: Benny; Musso; Krupa)
Smiles (BG Quartet) (Wilson's great piano solo; Hampton's colossal work)
When It's Sleepy Time Down South (MARVELOUS: Benny; James; Musso)
Swing Low, Sweet Chariot (swell, very fast: Musso's long sax solo; trumpet)
This Is My Last Affair (vocal: Martha Tilton) (MARVELOUS: Harry James)

?? ??
CHARLIE JOHNSON
Paradise Club, Atlantic City, N.J.
White Heat (George Stafford's drums)
King Porter Stomp
Whoa, Babe (Charlie Johnson's piano)

2.00AM KXBY
COUNTESS JOHNSON
Antlers Club, Kansas City, Mo
Big Chief De Sota
A Sailboat In The Moonlight (vocal: Bill Noland)
Froggy Bottom
What Will I Tell My Heart? (vocal: Connie Dean)
I Never Knew
Moonglow
St. Louis Blues (vocal: Bill Noland)
Dinah

■ FRIDAY 27 AUGUST 1937

RADIO LOGS

8:30PM WHDH
CHICK WEBB
Canobie Lake Park, Salem, N.H.
Let's Get Together (theme)
Clap Hands, Here Comes Charlie
You Showed Me The Way (vocal: Ella Fitzgerald)
When You And I Were Young, Maggie (Jimmy Mundy arrangement)
September In The Rain (vocal: Charles Linton)
Big John Special
Chick Webb Stomp
Sugar Foot Stomp

10.00PM WJZ
TOMMY DORSEY
Kool Cigarette Program, NYC
Goin' Home (Howard Smith's piano)
Yours And Mine (vocal: Jack Leonard)
Me, Myself And I (vocal: Edythe Wright)
My Silent Love
After You've Gone (vocal: Edythe Wright)
Marie (vocal: Jack Leonard & Band)
I'm Getting Sentimental Over You (theme)

11:30PM WNEW
WILLIE BRYANT
Savoy Ballroom, NYC
Harlem Special
The Goona Goo (Claude Green's baritone sax)
Talk With Sax (vocal: Charlie Frazier)
Medley (incl If You Should Ever Leave) (vocal: Arnold Adams)
Calling Your Bluff (Sonny White's piano)
King Porter Stomp
Blue Rhythm Fantasy (theme)

12:00 MIDNIGHT WABC
COUNT BASIE
Hotel Ritz-Carlton, Boston
Abadias
Have You Got Any Castles, Baby?

Jivin' The Keys
I Don't Know If I'm Comin' Or Goin' (vocal: Billie Holiday)
If You Should Ever Leave (vocal: Jimmy Rushing)
I Ain't Got Nobody (vocal: Jimmy Rushing)
A Sailboat In The Moonlight (vocal: Billie Holiday)
Doggin' Around (colossal: written by Herschel Evans)

SATURDAY 28 AUGUST 1937

RADIO LOGS

4:30PM WEAF
WILLIE BRYANT
Savoy Ballroom, NYC
When Irish Eyes Are Smiling (arranged by 2nd trumpeter, Andy Gibson)
Peace, Brother, Peace (vocal: Willie Bryant)
Medley
For Dancers Only
Paradise (arranged by Edgar Robinson, clarinetist)
Prelude To A Stomp (Claude 'Fats' Green's clarinet)
Dark Eyes (arranged by Charles Dixon; Sonny White's piano)

11:30PM WNEW
WILLIE BRYANT
Savoy Ballroom, NYC
Today is bassist Norman Frank's birthday.
Naughty Waltz (Gene Prince's trombone; Charlie Frazier's sax)
Basin Street Blues
It Looks Like Rain In Cherry Blossom Lane (whole audience sang)
Eli's Stomp (written by trombonist Eli Robinson)
You Showed Me The Way (Sonny White's piano)
Marie (vocal: Arnold Adams)

11:30PM WJZ
ANDY KIRK
Grand Terrace Café, Chicago
Keep It In The Groove
Stop! You're Breaking My Heart
Where Or When (vocal: Henry Wells)
If You Should Ever Leave (vocal: Pha Terrell)
Smarty
Posin'
Worried Over You (vocal: Pha Terrell)
All The Jive Is Gone
Avalon

12.05AM WNEW
JOE MARSALA
Hickory House, 144 W52nd Street, NYC
Clarinet Marmalade
Whispers In The Dark (Girard's harp)
Night Over Shanghai (vocal: Adele Girard)
Marie (Joe Bushkin's piano; Marty Marsala's trumpet)
My Cabin Of Dreams
Muskrat Ramble (Danny Alvin's drums)
So Rare (Bushkin; Marty Marsala)
Posin' (Girard's harp)

12:30AM WABC
BENNY GOODMAN
Palomar Ballroom, Los Angeles
The Lady Who Couldn't Be Kissed (Rollini; McEachern)
A Sailboat In The Moonlight (vocal: Martha Tilton) (trumpet)
Jam Session (Musso; Elman's trumpet; Krupa)
So Rare (BG Trio) (Much too commercial)
Peckin' (GREAT: Benny; James; Musso)
All Over Nothing At All (vocal: Martha Tilton) (Stacy; McEachern)
Limehouse Blues (BG Quartet) (colossal)
I'd Like To See Some More Of Samoa (vocal: Martha Tilton) (Stacy)
Caravan (wonderful: Krupa; Benny; brass; Harry James)

1.15AM WHAS
HORACE HENDERSON
Skoller's Swingland Café, Chicago
Song of India
Wearing Me Down (vocal: Walter Fuller)
Everybody Loves My Baby
I Know That You Know
Chris And His Gang (theme)

2.00AM KXBY
COUNTESS JOHNSON
Antlers Club, Kansas City, Mo
Marie
When I'm With You (vocal: Bill Noland)
Posin'
Gone With The Wind (vocal: Bill Noland)
Baby, Keep From My Heart (vocal: Bill Noland)

2.40AM WBBH
HORACE HENDERSON
Skoller's Swingland Café, Chicago
I Never Knew
Noah's Ark
The Sheik Of Araby
Back Home Again In Indiana
Jangled Nerves

Margaret 'Countess' Johnson

SUNDAY 29 AUGUST 1937

RADIO LOGS

2.40PM WJZ
TOMMY DORSEY
Mackey Program, NBC Studios, NYC
Song Of India (Pee Wee Erwin's trumpet)
The Big Apple (vocal: Edythe Wright & Band) (Carmen Mastren's guitar)
I'm Getting Sentimental Over You (theme)

6:30PM WOR
FUN IN SWINGTIME
WOR Studios, NYC
Bunny Berigan Orchestra.
A Study In Brown (Georgie Auld; Sonny Lee)
Ubangi Man (written by Berigan)

8:30PM WABC
KAY THOMPSON / ADELE GIRARD
Good Gulf Program, NYC
So Rare (vocal: Kay Thompson & Three Rhythm Boys) (including Al Rinker)
Marie (Adele Girard's harp)
Big Boy Blue (vocal: Kay Thompson & Three Rhythm Boys)

11:30PM WICC
BILLY BROOKS
Pleasure Beach Park, Bridgport, Conn
Rose Room
Heaven Help This Heart of Mine (vocal: Elyse Cooper)
Song Of India
Having A Wonderful Time (vocal: Frances Garrett)
Yours And Mine
Afraid To Dream
Sweet Georgia Brown
Copenhagen
The Folks Who Live On The Hill
Alibi Baby (vocal: Frances Garrett & Billy Brooks)
If You Should Ever Leave (vocal: Elyse Cooper)
Jazz Me Blues

12:30AM WEAF
ANDY KIRK
Grand Terrace Café, Chicago
Too Marvelous For Words (vocal: Henry Wells)
You're My Desire (vocal: Pha Terrell)
Yours And Mine
Posin' (Mary Lou Williams' marvelous piano introduction)
The Moon Got In My Eyes
Roll 'Em (magnificent: Mary Lou Williams; clarinet)
The Folks Who Live On The Hill (vocal: Henry Wells)
Wednesday Night Hop (GREAT: clarinet)

■ MONDAY 30 AUGUST 1937

I played golf today with Pop, Slim, and Al Winters. The N.Y. Giants baseball team replaced the Chicago Cubs in first place in the National League today for the first time since July 15th. Let's hope the Giants take the National League Pennant again!

Joe Louis just retained his heavyweight boxing championship by beating Welshman Tommy Farr.

RADIO LOGS

8.00PM WJZ
WILLIE BRYANT
'Goodtime Society', NYC
Today is Willie Bryant's birthday.
Darktown Strutters' Ball
Rose Room (Prince Robinson's sax)
South Side Stomp (Charlie Frazier's sax)
Blue Rhythm Fantasy (theme)

10:45PM WMCA
FRANKIE WARD
Nautical Plaza, Revere Beach, Mass
Whispers In The Dark (vocal: Carmen Trudeau) (Ward's bassoon)
Love Is A Merry-Go-Round (vocal: Carmen Trudeau) (Brad Gowans' trumpet)
Wolverine Blues (Ward's tenor sax; Ed Brown's clarinet; Frank Taylor's trombone; Fred Moynahan's drums)

11:15PM WJZ
ANDY KIRK
Grand Terrace Café, Chicago
Keep It In The Groove
The Folks Who Live On The Hill
Where or When (vocal: Henry Wells)
A Study In Brown (trumpet; sax)

11:30PM WIP
MAL HALLETT
Wildwood, N.J.
Satan Takes A Holiday
The You And Me That Used To Be (vocal: Teddy Grace)
Where Are You? (vocal: Jerry Perkins)
Red Hot Heat (vocal: Teddy Grace) (swell tune: Anderson's tenor sax)
Moonlight On The Highway (vocal: Jerry Perkins) (Anderson's nuttsy tenor sax)
Alexander's Ragtime Band (swell trumpet; Anderson's grooving tenor sax)
I Know Now (vocal: Jerry Perkins) (lousy)
That's A-Plenty (swell: Blake's solid drumming; Bob Alexy's trumpet; sax)
Let's Have Another Cigarette (vocal: Jerry Perkins) (good tune)
Boston Tea Party (theme)

11:35PM WICC
ZINN ARTHUR
Nichol's Pinebrook Country Club, Conn
Posin'
So Rare
Stop! You're Breaking My Heart (vocal: Zinn Arthur)
Yours And Mine (vocal: Zinn Arthur)
Oh, Lady Be Good
The Moon Got In My Eyes
Rose Room
Whispers In The Dark
My Blue Heaven

12.00 MIDNIGHT WOR
TOMMY DORSEY
Hotel Pennsylvania Roof, NYC
Satan Takes A Holiday
Have You Got Any Castles, Baby? (vocal: Jack Leonard)
Barcarolle
Love Is A Merry-Go-Round (vocal: Jack Leonard)
Christopher Columbus (super-colossal swing tune: Erwin's trumpet)
The Morning After (vocal: Jack Leonard)
Sleep
Yours And Mine (vocal: Jack Leonard)
Bugle Call Rag (super-colossal: magnificent solos by Freeman; Erwin; Dorsey)

12:00 MIDNIGHT WABC
COUNT BASIE
Hotel Ritz-Carlton, Boston
Marvelous.
Moten Swing (theme) (colossal theme written by Bennie Moten)
Milenburg Joys (marvelous: Clayton's nice trumpet; Page's bass solo; colossal tenor sax)
Let's Call The Whole Thing Off (vocal: Billie Holiday) (magnificent work by Basie & Page together)
Smarty (vocal: Jimmy Rushing) (more magnificent work by rhythm section; Basie's solo)
September In The Rain (vocal: Earle Warren) (some swell relaxed swing!)
You're Precious To Me (swinging a commercial tune: Jo Jones' solid drumming; trumpet)
Them There Eyes (vocal: Billie Holiday) (ballsy arrangement of swell piece: great vocal)
Boogie Woogie (vocal: Jimmy Rushing & Band) (marvelous: Basie's piano; Page's bass; colossal vocal)
Bugle Call Rag (trumpet; Basie's ballsy piano; nuttsy guitar solo; trombone; Young's magnificent, long tenor sax solo. This version is simply tops—what a trumpet!!!)

12:30AM WENR
ANDY KIRK
Grand Terrace Café, Chicago
Why Can't We Dream Again? (vocal: Henry Wells)
Mr. Ghost Goes To Town (Dick Wilson's tenor sax)
With Love In My Heart (vocal: Pha Terrell)
Big John Special (Mary Lou Williams' piano)

The You And Me That Used To Be
A Lot Of Stuff
You're My Desire (vocal: Pha Terrell)
King Porter Stomp
Twilight In Turkey (Ben Thigpen's drums)
Clouds (closing theme)

1.15AM WBBH
HORACE HENDERSON
Skoller's Swingland Café, Chicago
Avalon
Dancing Under The Stars (vocal: 'Georgia Boy' Simpkins)
I Wish I Were Twins
China Boy
Sugar Foot Stomp
Sweet Georgia Brown (Burke's trombone)
Star Dust (vocal: Walter Fuller)
How Could You?
Sultan Serenade

2.00AM KXBY
COUNTESS JOHNSON
Antlers Club, Kansas City, Mo
Christopher Columbus
It Looks Like Rain In Cherry Blossom Lane
Until The Real Thing Comes Along (vocal: Bill Noland)
If You Were Mine (vocal: Bill Noland)
After You've Gone

■ TUESDAY 31 AUGUST 1937

RECORDING SESSION

CAB CALLOWAY AND HIS ORCHESTRA
Recording session for Variety in New York City.
Cab Calloway (voc); Doc Cheatham, Irving Randolph, Lammar Wright (t); DePriest Wheeler, Keg Johnson, Claude Jones (tb); Garvin Bushell, Andrew Brown (cl/as); Chu Berry, Walter Thomas (ts); Bennie Payne (p); Morris White (g); Milt Hinton (b); Leroy Maxey (d)
Go South, Young Man (vCC) / *Mama, I Wanna Make Rhythm* (vCC) / *Hi-De-Ho Romeo* (vCC) / *Queen Isabella* / *Savage Rhythm*

BEN POLLACK AND HIS ORCHESTRA
Recording session for Decca in Los Angeles.
Ben Pollack (ldr); Ray Woods, Joe Meyer, Muggsy Spanier (t); Joe Yukl (tb); Ben Kanter, Bud Carlton (cl/as); Artie Quenzer, Mort Friedman (ts); Al Beller (vln); Bob Laine (p); Garry McAdams (g); Francis Palmer (b); Graham Stevenson (d); Frances Hunt (voc)
Have You Ever Been In Heaven? (vFH) / *If You Should Ever Leave* (vFH) / *Mama, I Wanna Make Rhythm* (vFH) / *I'm Dependable* (vBP)

RADIO LOGS

9:30PM WABC
BENNY GOODMAN
Camel Caravan program, Los Angeles
Heard this program at Nancy Long's house in Scarsdale.
Let's Dance (theme)
Camel Hop (colossal: James; Musso)
La Cucaracha (lousy piece: nuttsy tenor sax)
Whispers In The Dark (BG Trio) (fair)
The Blue Danube (MEYER ALEXANDER's Swing Chorus)
Vibraphone Blues (BG Quartet) (MARVELOUS)
Swing Song (MEYER ALEXANDER's Swing Chorus)
The Dixieland Band (vocal: Martha Tilton) (NUTTSY)
House Hop (swell)
Goodbye (closing theme)

?? ??
CHARLIE JOHNSON
Paradise Club, Atlantic City, N.J.
Casa Loma Stomp
Marie (vocal: Amos Bond)
Four In A Bar
For Dancers Only
Jam Session

11:15PM WJZ
ANDY KIRK
Grand Terrace Café, Chicago
Heard this program at Nancy Long's house.
I Know Now
Posin'
Cloudy
The Big Apple (Donnelly's trombone; Kirk's alto sax)
Clouds (closing theme)

11:30PM WJZ
LES BROWN
Playland Casino, Rye, N.Y.
Keepin' Out Of Mischief
The One Rose Left In My Heart (vocal: Jack Wilmot)
Exactly Like You
That Old Feeling (vocal: Jack Wilmot)
King Porter Stomp (Jack Atkins' trumpet)
Gone With The Wind (vocal: Jack Wilmot)
My Blue Heaven
We'll Ride The Tide Together (vocal: Jack Wilmot)
Bugle Call Rag (Les Brown's clarinet)
Ramona

12:00 MIDNIGHT WNEW
WILLIE BRYANT
Savoy Ballroom, NYC
My Wild Irish Rose
For Dancers Only
Medley of Popular Songs
Caravan (Charlie Frazier's sax)
Oh, Lady Be Good (arranged by Edgar Sampson; Green's trombone; White's piano)
Twelfth Street Rag (arranged by Fred Norman: Sonny White's piano)
Sweet And Swingy (new song by trumpeter Andy Gibson)

12.30AM WABC
TOMMY DORSEY
Hotel Pennsylvania Roof, NYC
Twelfth Street Rag (Smith's piano)
Where Or When? (vocal: Jack Leonard)
Night And Day (nice corny saxes; Bud Freeman)
Strangers In The Dark (vocal: Jack Leonard)
Mendelssohn's Spring Song (Tommy Dorsey; Freeman; Mince, etc)
An Old Flame Never Dies (vocal: Jack Leonard)
Smoke Gets In Your Eyes
Happy Birthday To Love (vocal: Jack Leonard)
So Rare
Happy As The Day Is Long (good: nice saxes; Erwin's swell trumpet; Freeman)
I'm Getting Sentimental Over You (theme)

12:30AM WENR
ANDY KIRK
Grand Terrace Café, Chicago
Caravan
Froggy Bottom (vocal: Ben Thigpen)
Worried Over You (vocal: Pha Terrell)
We're In The Money (vocal: Pha Terrell)
The Folks Who Live On The Hill
What Will I Tell My Heart?
Just Foolin' Myself (vocal: Pha Terrell)
Jam Session
Clouds (closing theme)

SEPTEMBER 1937

Hotel Pennsylvania: **Tommy Dorsey**
Hotel Commodore: **Tommy Dorsey** (30–)
Hotel New Yorker: **Benny Meroff**

Apollo Theater: **Blanche Calloway** (–2); **Chick Webb** (3–9); **Don Redman** (10–16); **Willie Bryant** (17–23); **Duke Ellington** (24–30)
Paramount Theater: **Shep Fields** (1–7); **Hudson-DeLange** (22–28)
Loew's State Theater: **Jimmy Dorsey** (10–16); **Chick Webb** (17–23); **Enric Madriguera** (24–30)

Cotton Club: **Cab Calloway** (reopens 21st)
Hickory House: **Joe Marsala**
Onyx Club: **John Kirby/Spirits of Rhythm**

■ WEDNESDAY 1 SEPTEMBER 1937

The All-Stars just beat the Green Bay Packers at Chicago, 6–0.

RADIO LOGS

12:30AM WEAF
ANDY KIRK
Grand Terrace Café, Chicago
A Study In Brown (good: trumpet)
If You Should Ever Leave (vocal: Pha Terrell)
Yours And Mine (fair)
Walkin' And Swingin' (colossal: trombone team; Mary Lou Williams' GREAT piano; Dick Wilson)
Down Stream (vocal: Pha Terrell) (nuttsy sweet tune: swell vocal from sweet-voiced Terrell)
Posin' (Mary Lou Williams' super-colossal piano; Dick Wilson's typical nuttsy sax solo)
Harbor Lights (vocal: Henry Wells) (lousy)
Yeah, Man! (marvelous: clarinet; Dick Wilson's two solos)
I Got Rhythm (great: trombone; clarinet)

■ THURSDAY 2 SEPTEMBER 1937

Went to radio station WINS (1800 kilocycles, 118 E58th Street, NYC) with my brother today to get the Hudson-DeLange record of *You're My Desire* and *Back In Your Arms* (Master 132). I won it two weeks ago on Jack Bennett's 'Noon Day Frolic' program on which he plays records and has people guess the orchestras playing, and also has contests between bands on recordings. I met him personally and he is a swell fellow.

I heard the Dick Stabile broadcast this evening on short wave (49 meter band) over my brother's nuttsy All-Wave Grunow Radio which he bought two years ago. He goes back to Ohio to teach school tomorrow but he is leaving his radio!

I received this picture of Will Hudson and Eddie DeLange from Jack Bennett today, Thursday, September 2, 1937. Bennett is the WINS announcer that runs the Noon Day Frolics every day over WINS at 12:45 to 1:30pm. He plays records over these programs and has two different kinds of contests: one where you guess the orchestras and another where he has a contest betweeen two bands— all recorded of course. Two weeks ago I won the contest in guessing 12 bands without a mistake. So today I went to WINS (118 E58th Street) and saw Jack Bennett who gave me this picture and the autographed record of Hudson-DeLange playing *You're My Desire* and *Back In Your Arms* (Master 132).

RADIO LOGS

11:35PM W8XAL
DICK STABILE
Moonlight Gardens, Coney Island, Ohio
Fair.
The Image Of You (vocal: Bert Shaw)
Caravan
Harbor Lights (vocal: Bert Shaw)
'Cause My Baby Says It's So (vocal: Paula Kelly)
Star Dust (Stabile's fair alto sax)
Wake Up And Live (vocal: Paula Kelly)
So Rare (vocal: Bert Shaw)
I Never Knew (nuttsy trumpet)
Lost My Rhythm, Lost My Man

?? ??
CHARLIE JOHNSON
Paradise Club, Atlantic City, N.J.
Everybody Shuffle
St. Louis Blues (vocal: Amos Bond)
Clarinet Marmalade
Carelessly (vocal: Nan Snow)
Song Of India

12:10AM WNEW
WILLIE BRYANT
Savoy Ballroom, NYC
WONDERFUL.
Sugar Foot Stomp (GREAT: colossal trumpet solo; clarinet; whole band really goin')
Tea On The Terrace (swell arrangement by Al Gibson of swell tune: Sonny White's piano)
When I Grow Too Old To Dream (good arrangement of lousy piece: saxes; trumpet)
When Irish Eyes Are Smiling (colossal arrangement: Eli Robinson's trombone; Prince Robinson's good tenor sax)
Peace, Brother, Peace (written by Clarence Williams last month: trumpet; great tenor)
Eli's Stomp (written & arranged by Eli Robinson: swell clarinet; piano)

12:30AM WEAF
ANDY KIRK
Grand Terrace Café, Chicago
The Loveliness Of You (vocal: Henry Wells)
The Lady From Fifth Avenue
Whispers In The Dark (vocal: Henry Wells)
Posin'

12:30AM WABC
BENNY GOODMAN
Palomar Ballroom, Los Angeles
Blue Skies (wonderful, slower tempo than record: McEachern; trumpet; Benny)
Let's Have Another Cigarette (vocal: Martha Tilton) (nuttsy piece: Musso's sweet sax)
It Looks Like Rain In Cherry Blossom Lane (good: James' 2 solos; trombone team; Benny)
Body And Soul (BG Trio) (swell, especially Wilson's piano)
The Dixieland Band (vocal: Martha Tilton) (colossal: swell vocal; McEachern's sweet trombone; Benny)
On The Alamo (wonderful medium smooth swing: solid saxes; Stacy; Benny)
Me, Myself And I (vocal: Martha Tilton) (swell arrangement of good piece: James; Musso; Benny)
A Handful Of Keys (BG Quartet) (wonderful)
Truckin' (vocal: Martha Tilton) (nuttsy piece: James' colossal solo; Benny)
Goodbye (closing theme) (written and arranged by Gordon Jenkins)

2.05AM WBBH
HORACE HENDERSON
Skoller's Swingland Café, Chicago
'Way Down Yonder In New Orleans

Mountain Music (vocal: 'Georgia Boy' Simpkins)
Blue Skies (Burke's trombone)
Yeah, Man!
Posin' (vocal: Walter Fuller)
King Porter Stomp
Go For Yourself

FRIDAY 3 SEPTEMBER 1937

RECORDING SESSION

BUNNY BERIGAN AND HIS ORCHESTRA
Recording session for Victor in New York City.
Bunny Berigan (t/voc); Irving Goodman, Steve Lipkins (t); Al George, Sonny Lee (tb); Mike Doty, Joe Dixon (cl/as); Clyde Rounds, George Auld (ts); Joe Lippman (p); Tom Morgan (g); Hank Wayland (b); George Wettling (d); Gail Reese (voc)
Sweet Varsity Sue (vGR) / *Gee, But It's Great To Meet A Friend* (vGR & band) / *Ebb Tide* (vGR) / *Have You Ever Been In Heaven?* (vGR) / *Mama, I Wanna Make Rhythm* (vBB)

RADIO LOGS

10:30PM WMCA
FRANKIE WARD
Nautical Plaza, Revere Beach, Mass
Where Or When
'Way Down Yonder In New Orleans (vocal: Carmen Trudeau)
Peckin'
Feelin' Like A Million (Brad Gowans' trumpet)
The You And Me That Used To Be (Frank Taylor's trombone)

11:30PM WABC
COUNT BASIE
Hotel Ritz-Carlton, Boston
Oh, Lady Be Good (Lester Young's tenor)
Love Is In The Air Tonight (vocal: Earle Warren)
Heaven Help This Heart Of Mine (vocal: Billie Holiday)
Good Morning Blues (vocal: Jimmy Rushing)
A Study In Brown (vocal: Jimmy Rushing)
My Cabin Of Dreams (vocal: Jimmy Rushing)
I Got Rhythm (Earle Warren's clarinet; Buck Clayton's trumpet; Herschel Evans' sax)
Moten Swing (theme) (theme played in full)

11:30PM WMCA
WILLIE BRYANT
Savoy Ballroom, NYC
WONDERFUL.
King Porter Stomp
Sophisticated Swing
You're My Desire (dedicated to clarinetist/baritone saxist Claude 'Fats' Green who married Clarissa Cumberback today)
A Study In Brown
Willie Bryant talks with ERSKINE HAWKINS
The Big Apple
Willie Bryant talks with track star JESSE OWENS
Big John Special

12:15AM WMCA
SONNY DUNHAM
Wildwood, N.J.
Margie (Sonny Dunham on trumpet and trombone; Stewie McKay's sax; Tommy Reo's trombone)
My Future Just Passed
Casa Loma Stomp
Song Of India
Saratoga

12:45AM WEAF
ANDY KIRK
Grand Terrace Café, Chicago
Deep In The Heart Of The South (vocal: Pha Terrell)
Honeysuckle Rose (Andy Kirk's clarinet; Dick Wilson's tenor)
I Know Now (vocal: Henry Wells)
Avalon (Dick Wilson's tenor; Ted Donnelly's trombone)
The Big Apple

■ SATURDAY 4 SEPTEMBER 1937

Going back to the night before (Friday) when Freddy Patrick drove Hughie, Roddy Snow, Jim Poe, Carolyn Bade, Nancy Long and myself up to Playland at Rye where we had a wonderful time on the amusements; we didn't have enough money to go in the Casino and see Les Brown's Band. Anyway, that night we decided to go into NYC the next day. However, it ended up that Hughie went in early to see an eye doctor and I left Bronxville, alone, at 11:00am, hitch-hiked to the subway and arrived at radio station WINS (1180 kilocycles— owned by N.Y. American Journal) at 118 E58th Street where I met Hughie. We witnessed the Noon Day Frolic Show from 12:45 to 1:30 in a tiny little room. This program is a daily feature managed and announced by Jack Bennett who plays records and has contests as to who the bands are. Several weeks ago I won one of these contests and received a record by Hudson-DeLange. After talking with Bennett (he likes Tommy Dorsey's Band best and dislikes Negro music) we left WINS and went to see Prior at Rockwell-O'Keefe, only to find it closed. We then went to the Conn Musical Instrument Store to find that closed as well; then to Mills Artists which was also closed; then to the Music Corporation of America where a fellow told us that the picture department had moved from the 29th Floor to the 16th Floor. So he took us down to the 16th Floor where he gave us pictures of Mildred Bailey, Red Norvo, Tommy Dorsey, Bunny Berigan, Gail Reese, Louise Wallace, Count Basie, Jimmy Rushing, etc.

We walked down to Times Square and as we passed Loew's State Theater we noticed that Jimmy Dorsey's Band is going to play a week's engagement there from this coming Thursday.

We then went down to 42nd Street where we stopped at Vims Radio Store where we met this fellow who runs the record department and who proof-read 'Rhythm On Record.' He told us that this book was out of print and was worth more than it's original price. He told us how he knew Milt Gabler and how he was going to England next year to get several thousand English HMV Records from a closed house that belongs to his friend. He is going to start an extensive collection of records with these. He autographed Hugh's 'Rhythm On Record' but I didn't have mine along. After leaving him we went over to the Commodore Music Shop, our good old stand-by music store which Milt Gabler owns. We spent an hour there playing records and talking to the two boy clerks and Milt. We listened to the new Victor album consisting of four 12-inch records by Benny Goodman, Fats Waller, Bunny Berigan and Tommy Dorsey. It's wonderful,

Bunny Berigan (left) and his vocalist, Gail Reese (above).

but costs $5.00. I finally bought the Mills Blue Rhythm Band's record of *African Lullaby* and *Swingin' In E-Flat* (Columbia 3038-D) and, together, Hughie and I got Red Norvo's *Bughouse* and *Blues In E-Flat* (Columbia 3079-D). So far today we've tried five music stores to get Goodman's Columbia record of *Junk Man* and *Ol' Pappy* without success. Finally, at 7 o'clock, we went up to 485 Madison Avenue to try and get into the Saturday Night Swing Session without passes. We were very lucky in meeting Al Brown, a guy our age who knows some people in the Swing Session. So he got us in without any trouble. We were very much delighted in noting that Mannie Klein (one of the best trumpet players) and Toots Mondello had joined the regular CBS Band. Mondello is considered by many as the leading sax player in the world. He used to play with Benny Goodman's Band and has since been working in various radio studio orchestras such as André Kostelanetz'. Mannie Klein has the same background as Mondello: he too played with Goodman, only earlier than Mondello, and then went into radio. Mondello is little and fat but is a very nice fellow and Klein is rather short, very popular, and a great guy. We got their autographs and Hughie took several pictures of them; one of Mannie with his arm around me. Also had a talk with Art Manners and took his picture.

Bob Inman with Mannie Klein   Toots Mondello

Joe Vargas and Art Manners   Ella Fitzgerald

The personnel of the CBS Band this week, under the direction of Leith Stevens, is: Toots Mondello, Art Manners, Hank Ross, Andy Young, saxes; Nat Natoli, Jimmy Rosselli, Mannie Klein, Willie Kelly, trumpets; Joe Vargas, Earle Ison, trombones; Lou Shoobe, bass; Frankie Worrell, guitar; Sam Weiss, drums and pianist ??? Guests on this week's broadcast are Walter Gross (nuttsy swing pianist), Chick Webb and part of his band including Ella Fitzgerald (direct from the Apollo Theater where Webb's band is doing a week's engagement). Paul Douglas and Mel Allen were again the announcers, and Phil Cohan and Ed Cashman were on hand to direct the whole program. Cashman remembered us and spoke to us. After the broadcast we got the autographs of Sam Weiss (colossal drummer who is brother to Sid Weiss), Chick Webb, Joe Saunders (manager of the Webb Band), and Beverly Peer (bassist with Webb's Band). Hughie took many pictures of the broadcast and got Ella Fitzgerald to pose for a picture after the broadcast. I never hope to see such a super-colossal broadcast again. It was absolutely tops. We got the 9:05 train home, even though it was raining.

8.00PM WABC
SATURDAY NIGHT SWING SESSION No60
CBS Studio No1, 485 Madison Ave, NYC
Opening theme (Hank Ross' tenor sax; Weiss' drums)
Stompin' At The Savoy (NUTTSY: Manners; Klein; Ross; Klein again)
The You And Me That Used To Be (what saxes!! Ross; Klein)
Honeysuckle Rose (WALTER GROSS' nuttsy piano solo with Weiss drumming)
Royal Garden Blues (WONDERFUL: Klein; Ross; swell clarinet)
Sweet Sue (CHICK WEBB QUINTET: Thomas Fulford, piano; Beverly Peer, bass; Wayman Carver, flute; clarinet; Chick Webb, drums)
In A Little Spanish Town (CHICK WEBB QUINTET: colossal; Webb's GREAT drumming)
Swing, Brother, Swing (ELLA FITZGERALD and CBS Band: GREAT)
Japanese Sandman (WALTER GROSS piano solo)
Get Happy (CBS Band, colossal: Klein; brass; saxes)
Chicken And Waffles (short closing theme: Sam Weiss' swell drumming; saxes; brass)

RADIO LOGS

4:45PM WEAF
WILLIE BRYANT
Savoy Ballroom, NYC
St. Louis Blues (vocal: Willie Bryant)
Between The Devil And The Deep Blue Sea (vocal: Willie Bryant)
Lindy Hoppers (Sonny White's piano)

9:45PM WMCA
FRANKIE WARD
Nautical Plaza, Revere Beach, Mass
So Rare (vocal: Carmen Trudeau) (Brad Gowans' trumpet)
My Blue Heaven (Ward's tenor sax)
Whispers In The Dark (Fred Moynahan's drums)
Posin' (vocal: Carmen Trudeau)

11:00PM WABC
BENNY MEROFF
Hotel New Yorker, NYC
Terrible! Bert Parks announced.
They All Laughed
Tomorrow Is Another Day
Oh, Lady Be Good
Sweet Leilani
The Peanut Vendor
The Miller's Daughter, Marianne / Moonlight On The Highway / Make A Wish (MEDLEY)
A Study In Brown / Sophisticated Lady / I'm Getting Sentimental Over You / Smoke Gets In Your Eyes (MEDLEY)
He Ain't Got Rhythm

11:30PM WMCA
WILLIE BRYANT
Savoy Ballroom, NYC
Fair. Announcer: Sam Brown. This is the last broadcast of Bryant from the Savoy. Eddie Mallory's Band takes Bryant's place tomorrow.
Darktown Strutters' Ball (vocal: Willie Bryant) (great. Prince Robinson's nice relaxed tenor sax; Sonny White's piano)
Somebody Loves Me (swell old piece arranged by Edgar Sampson: Sonny White's piano; weak sax section)
I Know Now (Wallace Jones' trumpet)
So Rare
Stardust On The Moon
Satan Takes A Holiday (Prince Robinson's tenor sax)
Love Is The Thing So They Say (vocal: Willie Bryant)
Limehouse Blues (clarinet; sax)

12.00 MIDNIGHT WNEW
JOE MARSALA
Hickory House, 144 W52nd Street, NYC
Wolverine Blues
Whispers In The Dark (vocal: Adele Girard)
I Want A Little Girl
Oh, Sister! Ain't That Hot?
Tin Roof Blues
Afraid To Dream
St. Louis Blues

12.00 MIDNIGHT WJZ
PAUL WHITEMAN
Fort Worth, Texas
The Darktown Strutters' Ball
I Know Now (vocal: Jimmy Brierley)
Until The Real Thing Comes Along (vocal: Jack Teagarden)
The Shag
The Wheel Of The Wagon (terrible)
St. Louis Blues (vocal: Jack Teagarden)
Star Dust (featuring 2 Teagardens; Al Gallodoro)
Raisin' The Rent (vocal: Jack Teagarden)
Farewell Blues (colossal)

12:30AM WABC
BENNY GOODMAN
Palomar Ballroom, Los Angeles
This is Benny Goodman's last night at the Palomar in Los Angeles. On 9th September they open a 10-day engagement at the Dallas Exposition in Texas.
Dear Old Southland (great: James' short solo; McEachern; sax; Stacy)
So Rare (vocal: Martha Tilton) (good, but too commercial; James; Benny)
St. Louis Blues (wonderful: great solos by Benny and James; nice ending)
They Can't Take That Away From Me (vocal: Martha Tilton) (swell: nice & sweet)
Big John Special (colossal: James; Stacy's great solo)
Where Or When (BG Trio) (fair: trio play too many commercial pieces)
So You Won't Sing (vocal: Martha Tilton) (swell: very new piece; Benny)
Smiles (BG Quartet) (swell: very old piece)
Sugar Foot Stomp (colossal: James' great muted trumpet)

1.00AM WHAS
HORACE HENDERSON
Skoller's Swingland Café, Chicago
I Never Knew
Body And Soul (vocal: Walter Fuller)
Swing Low, Sweet Chariot
Was It Rain? (vocal: 'Georgia Boy' Simpkins)
Financial Love
Big Boy Blue (vocal: Walter Fuller)
Never In A Million Years (vocal: 'Georgia Boy' Simpkins)
Between The Devil And The Deep Blue Sea
Whoa, Babe!

2.00AM KXBY
COUNTESS JOHNSON
Antlers Club, Kansas City, Mo
Blue Skies
I Know Now (vocal: Bill Noland)
Dedicated To You (vocal: Leonard Brown)
Hanging Around My Home (vocal: Bill Noland)
Organ Grinder's Swing

2.40AM WBBH
HORACE HENDERSON
Skoller's Swingland Café, Chicago
China Boy
Big John Special
Honeysuckle Rose
Blue Lou
Chris And His Gang (theme)

SUNDAY 5 SEPTEMBER 1937

RECORDING SESSION

LIONEL HAMPTON AND HIS ORCHESTRA
Recording session for Victor in Hollywood.
Lionel Hampton (vib/voc/d); Ziggy Elman (t); Vido Musso (cl/ts); Art Rollini (ts); Jess Stacy (p); Allan Reuss (g); Johnny Miller (b); Cozy Cole (d)
The Object Of My Affection (vLH) / *Judy* (vLH) / *Baby, Won't You Please Come Home?* (vLH) / *Everybody Loves My Baby* (vLH) / *After You've Gone* (v,dLH) / *I Just Couldn't Take It Baby* (vLH)

RADIO LOGS

5:00PM WOR
MAL HALLETT
Steel Pier, Atlantic City, N.J.
Moonlight On The Highway (vocal: Jerry Perkins) (good arrangement)
This Is My Last Affair (vocal: Teddy Grace) (great: Stuart Anderson's tenor)
Milenburg Joys (swell arrangement: nice trombone; Bob Alexy's swell trumpet)
Let's Have Another Cigarette (vocal: Jerry Perkins) (swell commercial hit)
I Got Rhythm (Frankie Carle's fair piano solo with band)
Spring Fever Blues (vocal: Teddy Grace) (wonderful: trumpet)
Swing High, Swing Low (vocal: Buddy Welcome) (good: nice, corny piano by Carle; Blake's drums; Anderson)
That's A-Plenty (wonderful: Bob Alexy's swell trumpet; Anderson's GREAT tenor sax)
The Dixieland Band (vocal: Buddy Welcome) (clarinet by Welcome also)
Boston Tea Party (theme)

ROSELAND BALLROOM – Taunton
SUNDAY MIDNITE
Only Appearance of
CAB CALLOWAY
IN PERSON and His World Famous ORCHESTRA
Concert 11 to 12
Dancing 12 to 4 a.m.

KIMBALL'S STARLIGHT
On Route 128, at South Lynnfield
TONIGHT—CHECK DANCING
FRAN RITCHIE
SAT.—JACK DELMAR and his famous band from Phila.
SUNDAY MIDNITE
LOUIS ARMSTRONG

6:00PM WABC
PHIL HARRIS
Pan-American Casino, Dallas, Texas
This is Phil Harris' last broadcast from Texas. Benny Goodman's Band is to replace him at the end of this week.
Rose Room (theme) (swell theme)
Dardanella (nice trumpet)
Whispers In The Dark (written by brother of Ruth Robbins who sings with Harris' Band)
Posin' (vocal: Phil Harris) (one of Harris' typical 'lazy' vocals)
Coquette
Afraid To Dream (vocal: Art Jarrett) (Jarrett is not a regular in the Band but appears in the floor show)
So Rare (vocal: Art Jarrett)
You Can't Run Away From Love Tonight (vocal: Phil Harris)
When I Dream About Hawaii (vocal: Ruth Robbins)

6:30PM WOR
FUN IN SWINGTIME
WOR Studios, NYC
Del Schubert announces. The Bunny Berigan Orchestra.
Me, Myself And I
Can't Help Lovin' Dat Man O' Mine (Auld; Dixon)

11.00PM WBBH
HORACE HENDERSON
Skoller's Swingland Café, Chicago
Song of India
Imagination (vocal: Walter Fuller)
Rug Cutter's Swing
Rhythm In My Nursery Rhymes

11:15PM WMAQ
ANDY KIRK
Grand Terrace Café, Chicago
Blue Skies
Posin' (Dick Wilson's tenor; Ted Donnelly's trombone)
A Study In Brown
Foolin' Myself (vocal: Pha Terrell)

11:30PM WICC
VAL JEAN
Pleasure Beach Park, Bridgport, Conn
A Study In Brown
Where Is The Sun?
Harbor Lights
Tea On The Terrace
Where Or When
Wabash Blues
Trust In Me (9-yr-old Sammy Kataldall??)
On The Isle Of Kitchy-mi-boko
Afraid To Dream
In The Shadow Of Love (theme)

12:30AM WEAF
ANDY KIRK
Grand Terrace Café, Chicago
The Big Apple (Ted Donnelly's trombone)
Yours And Mine (vocal: Henry Wells)
The Folks Who Live On The Hill
Zonky (written by Claude Hopkins: Mary Lou Williams' piano)
Can I Forget You? (vocal: Henry Wells)
Down Stream (vocal: Pha Terrell)
Jim Jam (Paul King's swell trumpet; Dick Wilson's tenor)
Posin' (Mary Lou Williams' great piano)
Clouds (closing theme, vocal: Henry Wells)

1.30am WHAS
HORACE HENDERSON
Skoller's Swingland Café, Chicago
Back Home Again In Indiana
Our Penthouse On Third Avenue
Alexander's Ragtime Band
Marie
A Study In Brown
How Could You? (vocal: Walter Fuller)
Away From Me
All By Myself
Jam Session

■ MONDAY 6 SEPTEMBER 1937 (LABOR DAY)

RECORDING SESSION

BENNY GOODMAN AND HIS ORCHESTRA
Recording session for Victor in Hollywood.
Benny Goodman (cl); Chris Griffin, Harry James, Ziggy Elman (t); Red Ballard, Murray McEachern (tb); George Koenig, Hymie Shertzer (as); Art Rollini, Vido Musso (ts); Jess Stacy (p); Allan Reuss (g); Harry Goodman (b); Gene Krupa (d); Martha Tilton (voc)
Bob White (vMT) / *Sugar Foot Stomp* / *I Can't Give You Anything But Love, Baby* (vMT) / *Minnie The Moocher's Wedding Day*

RADIO LOGS

12:00 NOON WABC
SWINGIN' THE BLUES
CBS Studios, NYC
Charles Starr announced.
Dallas Blues (nuttsy piece and arrangement: swell dirty trombone; Ross' tenor?)
I Ain't Got Nobody (wonderful tenor sax; colossal trumpet & trombone)
I'm Coming Virginia (super-colossal tenor sax solo; nuttsy clarinet; great old-style trombone in style of Bill Rank)
Am I Blue? (that great tenor sax again; nice clarinet; a Warren Smith-type trombone solo; swell short vibraphone solo; some nuttsy solid bassing)

8.00PM WJZ
WILLIE BRYANT
'Goodtime Society', NYC
Willie Bryant's last night at the Savoy Ballroom was Saturday 4th. He played last night (5th) at Bridgeport, Connecticut.
Limehouse Blues (Green's clarinet)
Paradise (Andy Gibson's trumpet)
Blue Rhythm Fantasy (theme)

12:00 MIDNIGHT WABC
COUNT BASIE
Hotel Ritz-Carlton, Boston
Heard part of this program in Fred Patrick's house, coming home from Carolyn Bade's house in Hartsdale. Hugh Sargent announced.
Prince Of Wails (Buck Clayton's trumpet)
How Could You? (vocal: Billie Holiday)
Have You Got Any Castles, Baby?
Evenin' (vocal: Jimmy Rushing) (colossal tune, such a swinging tempo: marvelous slow tenor sax with Jo Jones' ballsy drumming; wonderful vocal)
Abadias (Buck Clayton's muted trumpet at start; another of those flowing tenor sax solos)
Swing, Brother, Swing (vocal: Billie Holiday) (NUTTSY piece: Billie at her best)
I Ain't Got Nobody (vocal: Jimmy Rushing) (Basie's super-colossal piano tickling & Page's bass)
Doggin' Around (written by Herschel Evans with his ballsy tenor sax; Basie's simply marvelous piano; real jammin' at end–clarinet)
Moten Swing (theme)

12:30AM WEAF
ANDY KIRK
Grand Terrace Café, Chicago
Until The Real Thing Comes Along (theme)
The Top Of The World (written by Mary Lou Williams; trombone; Wilson's tenor; clarinet)
Dedicated To You (vocal: Pha Terrell) (sweet commercial tune, but good; no solos)
Yeah, Man! (SWELL: high clarinet; Paul King's nice trumpet; Dick Wilson's ballsy tenor)
The Loveliness Of You (vocal: Henry Wells) (Mary Lou Williams' piano intro; nice vocal)
If I Could Count On You (vocal: Henry Wells) (swell piece: another good vocal)
Dear Old Southland (Mary Lou Williams' colossal piano intro; Dick Wilson's typical oozing tenor; another long-noted clarinet that really sends me!)
I'll Get Along Somehow (vocal: Pha Terrell) (nuttsy sweet piece–especially words: swell vocal)
Jam Session (Goodman's arrangement: Dick Wilson's good tenor; Paul King's swell trumpet)
The Lady From Fifth Avenue (lousy song: swell intro, Wilson's tenor and drums)

■ TUESDAY 7 SEPTEMBER 1937

RECORDING SESSION

HENRY 'RED' ALLEN
Recording session for Vocalion in New York City.
Henry 'Red' Allen (t/voc); Ed Hall (cl); Tab Smith (as); Sammy Davis (ts); Billy Kyle (p); Danny Barker (g); Johnny Williams (b); Alphonse Steele (d)
I Owe You (vHA) / *Have You Ever Been In Love?* (vHA) / *Is It Love Or Infatuation?* (vHA) / *Can I Forget You?* (vHA)

FATS WALLER & HIS RHYTHM
Recording session for Victor in New York City.
Herman Autrey (t); Gene Sedric (cl/ts); Fats Waller (p/voc); Albert Casey (g); Charles Turner (b); Slick Jones (d)
You've Got Me Under Your Thumb (vFW) / *Beat It Out* (vFW) / *Our Love Was Meant To Be* (vFW) / *I'd Rather Call You Baby* (vFW) / *I'm Always In The Mood For You* (vFW) / *She's Tall, She's Tan, She's Terrific* (vFW) / *You're My Dish* (vFW) / *More Power To You* (vFW)

RADIO LOGS

9:30PM WABC
BENNY GOODMAN
Camel Caravan program, Los Angeles
Heard this program at Hugh Pastoriza's house in Bronxville.
Let's Dance (theme)
Oh, Lady Be Good (swell arrangement: McEachern's trombone; Musso)
So Rare (vocal: Martha Tilton) (James' trumpet)
I Surrender Dear (RED NORVO playing some colossal, soft, subtle swing on his xylophone with Goodman's band. Norvo's Band replaces Goodman at the Palomar tonight)
Down South Camp Meetin' (nuttsy)
Rockin' Chair (short theme by MEYER ALEXANDER's Swing Chorus to introduce Mildred Bailey)
The Moon Got In My Eyes (vocal: Mildred Bailey) (poor song but Mildred singing as only she can)
Smiles (BG Quartet) (wonderful swinging by all, especially Hampton)
Stompin' At The Savoy
Sugar Foot Stomp (colossal arrangement: clarinets; Harry James' long muted trumpet solo)
Goodbye (closing theme)

12:00 MIDNIGHT WNEW
EDDIE MALLORY
Savoy Ballroom, NYC
Peckin' (Don Byas's sax)
I've Got To Have You
Sweet Georgia Brown
Without Your Love
Honeysuckle Rose (Mallory's trumpet)
Happy As The Day Is Long (Don Byas's sax)
King Porter Stomp (Mallory's trumpet)

12.30AM WABC
TOMMY DORSEY
Hotel Pennsylvania Roof, NYC
You've Got Something There (vocal: Edythe Wright)
An Old Flame Never Dies (vocal: Jack Leonard)

Night And Day
Once In A While (vocal: Jack Leonard)
Who'll Buy My Violets?
If You Were Someone Else (vocal: Edythe Wright)
Smoke Gets In Your Eyes
Yours And Mine (vocal: Jack Leonard)
I May Be Wrong
Goodbye Jonah (vocal: Edythe Wright)

1.00AM KRLD
GLENN MILLER
Hotel Adolphus, Dallas
On Moonlight Bay (whole band singing: Irving Fazola on clarinet; Sterling Bose's trumpet)
Sweet Leilani (vocal: Kathleen Lane) (Fazola on clarinet)
Stop, You're Breaking My Heart (vocal: Kathleen Lane) (Jerry Jerome's swell sax)
Peckin' (nuttsy: Fazola's clarinet; Bob Price's trumpet; Jesse Ralph's ballsy trombone)
Gone With The Wind (vocal: Kathleen Lane)
Humoresque (Chummy McGregor's piano; swell solos by Sterling Bose, clarinetist, Jerry Jerome)
Wistful And Blue (BALLSY smooth piece)

WEDNESDAY 8 SEPTEMBER 1937

RECORDING SESSION

TOMMY DORSEY AND HIS ORCHESTRA
Recording session for Victor in New York City.
Tommy Dorsey (tb); Pee Wee Erwin, Lee Castle, Andy Ferretti (t); Les Jenkins, Walter Mercurio (tb); Johnny Mince, Fred Stulce, Skeets Herfurt (cl/as); Bud Freeman (ts); Howard Smith (p); Carmen Mastren (g); Gene Traxler (b); Dave Tough (d); Jack Leonard (voc)
In The Still Of The Night (vJL) / *Who Knows?* (vJL) / *If It's The Last Thing I Do* (vJL) / *I May Be Wrong*

RADIO LOGS

11:30PM WMCA
CHICK WEBB
Apollo Theater, NYC
Strictly Jive (written by Chick Webb, featuring Bobby Stark's trumpet)
Shine (vocal: Ella Fitzgerald)
I May Be Wrong (program theme)

12.00 MIDNIGHT WNEW
JOE MARSALA
Hickory House, 144 W52nd Street, NYC
Keep Smilin' At Trouble
Whispers In The Dark (Girard's harp)
Marie (Joe Bushkin's piano)
I'm Afraid To Dream (vocal: Adele Girard)
The Big Apple
It Looks Like Rain In Cherry Blossom Lane

12.00 MIDNIGHT WEAF
PAUL WHITEMAN
Fort Worth, Texas
Honeysuckle Rose
After You've Gone (vocal: Jack Teagarden) (Roy Bargy's piano; Charlie Teagarden's trumpet)
The Wheel Of The Wagon (terrible)
It's The Natural Thing To Do
Goodbye Jonah
Church Mouse On A Spree (arranged by Roy Bargy)
Rhapsody In Blue (theme)

12:30AM WEAF
ANDY KIRK
Grand Terrace Café, Chicago
The Big Apple (nuttsy swing arrangement: nice clarinet & trombone; swell sax solo)
Can I Forget You? (vocal: Henry Wells) (lousy, way too commercial: no solos)
Stop! You're Breaking My Heart (nuttsy arrangement: clarinet; Williams; Wilson)
Wednesday Night Hop (colossal, written by Kirk: Dick Wilson; Paul King; wa-wa brass; trombone)
Then You Kissed Me (vocal: Pha Terrell) (good: first time on radio)
Posin' (swell arrangement, but over-played: honors to Mary Lou Williams and Dick Wilson)
Worried Over You (vocal: Pha Terrell) (wonderful sweet piece: Wilson's tenor sax)
Walkin' And Swingin' (written by Mary Lou Williams: Ted Donnelly's ballsy trombone; Williams; Dick Wilson)
Caravan (written by Duke Ellington who was at the Grand Terrace last night)

THURSDAY 9 SEPTEMBER 1937

RADIO LOGS

6:00PM WNEW
FATS WALLER
Martin Block's Make Believe Ballroom
Ain't Misbehavin' (theme)
Christopher Columbus (Al Casey's guitar)
Don't You Know Or Don't You Care (vocal: Fats Waller) (dedicated to his wife)
Basin Street Blues
Marie (vocal: Fats Waller) (Al Casey's guitar)
Tea For Two (piano solo)
I'm Gonna Sit Right Down And Write Myself A Letter (vocal: Fats Waller)
A Handful Of Keys (piano solo)
Honeysuckle Rose (vocal: Fats Waller) (Al Casey's guitar)

11:30PM WNEW
EDDIE MALLORY
Savoy Ballroom, NYC
Bugle Call Blues
Desperately In Love
After You've Gone
I Love You Truly (Don Byas's sax)
Baby, Won't You Marry Me? (vocal: Eddie Mallory)
Sweet And Lovely
Caravan (Tyree Glenn's trombone)

12:00 MIDNIGHT WPG
ALEX BARTHA
Steel Pier, Atlantic City, N.J.
Alexander's Ragtime Band
Remember Me (vocal: Bert Nickerson)
That Old Feeling (vocal: D. Hammond)
Where Or When (vocal: Carl White)
Out Of The Blue (Bartha's theme played in full)
Between The Devil And The Deep Blue Sea
Don't You Know Or Don't You Care (vocal: Bert Nickerson)
They All Laughed (vocal: Carl White)
Turn Off The Moon (vocal: D. Hammond)

12:30AM WABC
RED NORVO
Palomar Ballroom, Los Angeles
This is the first coast-to-coast broadcast of Norvo's Band from the Palomar where it opened two days ago, replacing Benny Goodman's great band.
Posin' (vocal: Mildred Bailey) (recently recorded on Brunswick: swell arrangement)
Heaven Help This Heart Of Mine (vocal: Mildred Bailey) (nuttsy piece: grand vocal)

SEPTEMBER 1937

The Loveliness Of You (another commercial tune, swung out on: Herbie Haymer's sax)
A Porter's Love Song (nuttsy: Hank D'Amico's nice clarinet; Haymer's tenor sax)
Gone With The Wind (vocal: Mildred Bailey) (Haymer's ballsy tenor sax; Norvo's xylophone)
Clap Hands, Here Comes Charlie (swell: Haymer's sax; trumpet)
It's The Natural Thing To Do (vocal: Mildred Bailey)
Bugle Call Rag (WONDERFUL: Haymer's colossal tenor sax; D'Amico's grand clarinet with Purtill's cymbals; Red's GREAT xylophone playing; Purtill's nice drum break; ending)

12:30AM WABC
ANDY KIRK
Grand Terrace Café, Chicago
Posin' (Mary Lou Williams' piano)
So Rare (vocal: Henry Wells)
A Lot Of Stuff (Mary Lou Williams' piano)
King Porter Stomp
My Cabin Of Dreams (vocal: Henry Wells)
The Folks Who Live On The Hill (vocal: Pha Terrell)
Stardust On The Moon (vocal: Henry Wells)
Bugle Call Rag
A Study In Brown (Dick Wilson's tenor sax)
Clouds (closing theme)

1:00AM KRLD
GLENN MILLER
Hotel Adolphus, Dallas
Shine (Irving Fazola; Jerry Jerome's tenor sax)
Time On My Hands
How Could You? (vocal: Kathleen Lane)
Whispers In The Dark (vocal: Kathleen Lane)
The Lady Who Couldn't Be Kissed (Sterling Bose's trumpet; Jerry Jerome's tenor sax)
Gone With The Wind (vocal: Kathleen Lane)
St. Louis Blues (COLOSSAL: Fazola great on clarinet)

2:00AM KXBY
COUNTESS JOHNSON
Antler's Club, Kansas City, Mo
Moten Swing
One Rose
Organ Grinder's Swing
Honeysuckle Rose (colossal, very similar to Basie's arrangement: tenor sax)
When Did You Leave Heaven? (vocal: Leonard Brown)
The Glory Of Love
Caravan (nuttsy piano; trumpet)

2.00AM WBBM
HORACE HENDERSON
Skoller's Swingland Café, Chicago
Chris And His Gang (theme)
Sweet Georgia Brown
Where Are You? (vocal: 'Georgia Boy' Simpkins) (swell sweet arrangement: trumpet; tenor sax)
Liza
Posin' (vocal: 'Georgia Boy' Simpkins) (clarinet)
China Boy
Good Morning (vocal: 'Georgia Boy' Simpkins)
Farewell Blues (wonderful: tenor sax)

2:45AM KSL
RED NORVO
Palomar Ballroom, Los Angeles
EXCELLENT. If only there wasn't so much static.
Smoke Dreams (vocal: Mildred Bailey) (nuttsy sweet piece: usual great vocal)
Remember (Norvo's band cartainly has a wonderful, distinctive style. The whole band sends me! MARVELOUS)
They Can't Take That Away From Me (vocal: Mildred Bailey) (D'Amico's clarinet; Haymer's tenor)

Swing Era Scrapbook 255

■ FRIDAY 10 SEPTEMBER 1937

RECORDING SESSION

CHU BERRY & HIS STOMPY STEVEDORES
Recording session for Variety in New York City.
Irving Randolph (t); Keg Johnson (tb); Chu Berry (ts); Bennie Payne (p/voc); Danny Barker (g); Milt Hinton (b); Leroy Maxey (d)
Chuberry Jam / Maelstrom / My Secret Love Affair (vBP) */ Ebb Tide*

■ SATURDAY 11 SEPTEMBER 1937

RECORDING SESSION

TOMMY DORSEY AND HIS CLAMBAKE SEVEN
Recording session for Victor in New York City.
Tommy Dorsey (tb); Pee Wee Erwin (t); Johnny Mince (cl); Bud Freeman (ts); Howard Smith (p); Carmen Mastren (g); Gene Traxler (b); Dave Tough (d); Edythe Wright, Jack Leonard (voc)
The Lady Is A Tramp (vEW) */ Tears In My Heart* (vEW) */ Josephine* (vJL) */ If The Man In The Moon* (vJL)

BEN POLLACK AND HIS PICK-A-RIB BOYS
Recording session for Decca in Los Angeles.
Ben Pollack (d/ldr); Muggsy Spanier (t); Ted Vesely (tb); Ben Kanter (cl); King Guion (ts); Bob Laine (p); Garry McAdams (g); Francis Palmer (b); Peggy Mann (voc)
Boogie Woogie / California, Here I Come / My Wild Irish Rose / Alice Blue Gown / Cuddle Up A Little Closer (vPM) */ Can't You Hear Me Calling, Caroline?* (vPM)

RADIO LOGS

5:45PM WOR
DICK STABILE
Billy Rose's Aquacade, Cleveland, Ohio
All God's Chillun Got Rhythm (vocal: Paula Kelly)
Have You Got Any Castles, Baby? (vocal: Dick Stabile)
They All Laughed (vocal: Paula Kelly)
The Skipper (written by Dick Stabile: swell clarinet by Stabile; drums)

8.00PM WABC
SATURDAY NIGHT SWING SESSION No61
CBS Studio No1, 485 Madison Ave, NYC
Waddling At The Waldorf (CBS Band under the direction of Leith Stevens)
China Boy (guest JIMMY DORSEY playing swell clarinet with his drummer, Ray McKinley, going to town!)
It's The Natural Thing To Do (commercial tune by CBS band: Ross' nice tenor sax; fair piano; Ross again; super sax section!!)
Body And Soul (blind pianist ALEC TEMPLETON playing first a straight melody; then as the Americans would like it; and then as the Europeans would like it. He is a classical pianist but can really swing out!)
Bach Goes To Town (written by ALEC TEMPLETON and played by him on piano: very swingy but a little too intricate. Templeton says that if Bach lived now he would be a jazz player)
Caravan (SUPER-COLOSSAL! Manny Klein's nuttsy muted trumpet)
Shoe Shine Boy (JUNE RICHMOND, Dorsey's Negro vocalist, singing the nuts)
Blues In B-Flat (slow number really jammed out on: Jimmy Dorsey; Klein; Ross; Mondello; McKinley; Templeton; Shoobe. GRAND!!)

11:00PM WABC
JIMMIE LUNCEFORD
Valley Dale, nr Columbus, Ohio
Avalon (Joe Thomas' sax; Eddie Tompkins' trumpet)
Posin' (vocal: Willie Smith & Trio)
Count Me Out (vocal: Dan Grissom)
Annie Laurie (Joe Thomas' sax)
Honest And Truly (vocal: Dan Grissom)

Teasing Tessie Brown (vocal: Eddie Tompkins)
Would You Like To Buy A Dream?
For Dancers Only

11:30PM WMCA
EDDIE MALLORY
Savoy Ballroom, NYC
Bugle Call Blues
Desperately In Love
I Love You Truly (Don Byas's sax)
Baby, Won't You Marry Me? (vocal: Eddie Mallory)
Caravan (Mallory's trumpet)
Blue Brass

12:00 MIDNIGHT WABC
RED NORVO
Palomar Ballroom, Los Angeles
SUPER-GRAND. I heard this program at Nancy Long's house in Scarsdale.
Russian Lullaby (colossal: Herbie Haymer; Hank D'Amico)
If You Should Ever Leave (vocal: Mildred Bailey)
All God's Chillun Got Rhythm
Everyone's Wrong But Me (vocal: Mildred Bailey)
Me, Myself, And I (vocal: Mildred Bailey)
Paradise (written by Irving Berlin, nuttsy: Red's great xylophone playing!)
'Long About Midnight (vocal: Mildred Bailey) (wonderful: colossal vocal)
Nagasaki (5-minutes long: Super! Wonderful! Magnificent!)

1.00AM WBBM
HORACE HENDERSON
Skoller's Swingland Café, Chicago
Chris And His Gang (theme)
Rosetta (vocal: Walter Fuller)
All By Myself (vocal: 'Georgia Boy' Simpkins)
'Way Down Yonder In New Orleans
Blue Lou
I Got Rhythm

■ SUNDAY 12 SEPTEMBER 1937
RADIO LOGS

6:00PM WABC
BENNY GOODMAN
Pan American Casino, Dallas, Texas
I heard this program at Nancy Long's house in Scarsdale with Don Mortimer. Goodman is doing a 10-day engagement at the Dallas Exposition.
Satan Takes A Holiday (a different arrangement: Rollini; James; Stacy)
Yours And Mine (vocal: Martha Tilton) (swell: nuttsy saxes)
La Cucaracha (lousy piece but very good arrangement: Musso)
Stardust On The Moon (vocal: Martha Tilton) (great saxes: Musso's tenor)
Ida, Sweet As Apple Cider (BG Quartet) (longer and much better than record)
Bob White (vocal: Martha Tilton) (very new song – nuttsy: Harry James)
When It's Sleepy Time Down South (colossal: Musso's sax; James)
Walk, Jennie, Walk (better than record: James' nuttsy solo; Krupa; Rollini)
Me, Myself And I (vocal: Martha Tilton) (Musso's good tenor sax; James)
Where Or When (BG Trio) (not very good)

1:00AM KRLD
GLENN MILLER
Hotel Adolphus, Dallas
Night And Day (Jesse Ralph's trombone)
You're Here, You're There, You're Everywhere (vocal: Kathleen Lane)
Shine (Hal McIntyre's clarinet)
Sleepytime Gal
Peckin' (Sterling Bose's trumpet; Hal McIntyre's clarinet)
If I Put My Heart In My Song (vocal: Kathleen Lane)
I'm Bubbling Over (Jerry Jerome's tenor sax; Hal McIntyre's clarinet)
How Am I To Know? (vocal: Kathleen Lane)
Honeysuckle Rose
Unnamed Theme [Moonlight Serenade] (written by Miller)

1.30AM WBBM
HORACE HENDERSON
Skoller's Swingland Café, Chicago
Between The Devil And The Deep Blue Sea
Blue Skies
It's Wearing Me Down (vocal: 'Georgia Boy' Simpkins)
Remember
Yeah, Man!
Big John Special
Never In A Million Years
Sultan Serenade

■ MONDAY 13 SEPTEMBER 1937

School started today. How I wish summer was just beginning. I had a swell summer but football looks hopeful.

RECORDING SESSION

BILLIE HOLIDAY & HER ORCHESTRA
Recording session for Vocalion in NYC.
Buck Clayton (t); Buster Bailey (cl); Lester Young (ts); Claude Thornhill (p); Freddie Green (g); Walter Page (b); Jo Jones (d); Billie Holiday (v)
Getting Some Fun Out of Life / Who Wants Love? / Trav'lin' All Alone / He's Funny That Way

RADIO LOGS

7:45PM WNAC
JAN SAVITT
KYW Studios, Philadelphia
Swell.
If You Should Ever Leave (vocal: Carlotta Dale) (swell sweet trombone, smooth)
Sensation (nuttsy: swell trumpet; nice clarinet; corny trombone, but good)
My Cabin Of Dreams (vocal: Dick Wharton) (3 trombones; swell clarinet)
Swamp Fire (colossal: swell trumpet; dirty trombones and brass; weak saxes)
Quaker City Jazz (theme) (swell fast theme; wa-wa brass etc)

8:00PM WBRY
DICK STABILE
Billy Rose's Aquacade, Cleveland, Ohio
Good.
'Cause My Baby Says It's So (vocal: Paula Kelly)
The Loveliness Of You (vocal: Bert Shaw)
Satan Takes A Holiday (swell: Dick Stabile's alto sax)
Let's Call The Whole Thing Off (vocal: Dick Stabile & Paula Kelly)
Am I In Love? (vocal: Bert Shaw)
Posin' (vocal: Dick Stabile) (swell)
The First Time I Saw You (vocal: Paula Kelly)
That Old Feeling (vocal: Paula Kelly)
Caravan (alto sax)

8.30PM WJZ
WILLIE BRYANT
'Goodtime Society', NYC
High Jive
Twelfth Street Rag
Blue Rhythm Fantasy (theme)

12:00 MIDNIGHT WOR
TOMMY DORSEY
Hotel Pennsylvania, NYC
You And I Know (vocal: Edythe Wright)
If It's The Last Thing I Do (vocal: Jack Leonard)
Who'll Buy My Violets?
Once In A While (vocal: Jack Leonard)
You've Got Something There (vocal: Edythe Wright)

SEPTEMBER 1937

Just A Simple Melody (vocal: Jack Leonard)
So Many Memories
Beale Street Blues

12:30AM WABC
ANDY KIRK
Grand Terrace Café, Chicago
The You And Me That Used To Be (vocal: Pha Terrell)
The Folks Who Live On The Hill (vocal: Pha Terrell)
Stop! You're Breaking My Heart
Roll 'Em
The Moon Got In My Eyes (vocal: Henry Wells)
Posin'
So Rare (vocal: Henry Wells)
I Never Slept A Wink Last Night (Mary Lou Williams' piano)

1:00AM KRLD
GLENN MILLER
Hotel Adolphus, Dallas
Satan Takes A Holiday (Kenyon's drums; Fazola's clarinet)
Stop, You're Breaking My Heart (vocal: Kathleen Lane)

■ TUESDAY 14 SEPTEMBER 1937

RADIO LOGS

9:30PM WABC
BENNY GOODMAN
Camel Caravan program, Dallas, Texas
Let's Dance (theme)
Makin' Whoopee (great: Benny; James; brass & saxes)
Loch Lomond (vocal: Martha Tilton & Benny Goodman) (swell solos by James & Musso)
Don't You Know Or Don't You Care (BG Quartet) (colossal: very new piece)
Peckin' (played by request: solos by Benny; James; Musso)
Powerhouse (colossal arrangement à la Scott: band change instruments; Benny on sax; Rollini on clarinet; Harry James on drums; Ziggy Elman on piano; McEachern on trumpet and bells; swell solo by Benny on tenor sax)
Bob White (vocal: Martha Tilton) (nuttsy: latest tune by Johnny Mercer)
Basin Street Blues (JACK TEAGARDEN, now with Paul Whiteman, singing and playing trombone: Benny; Krupa)
Bugle Call Rag (super-colossal: Benny; McEachern & Teagarden; Rollini; Elman)
Goodbye (closing theme)

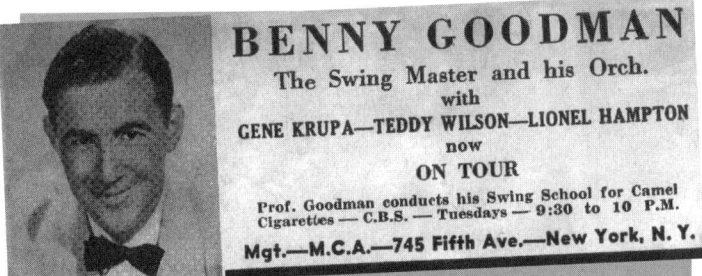

■ WEDNESDAY 15 SEPTEMBER 1937

RECORDING SESSION

WILLIE 'THE LION' SMITH AND HIS CUBS
Recording session for Decca in New York City.
Frankie Newton (t); Buster Bailey (cl); Pete Brown (as); Willie 'The Lion' Smith (p); Jimmy McLin (g); John Kirby (b); O'Neil Spencer (d/voc)
Blues, Why Don't You Let Me Alone? / I've Got To Think It Over (vO'NS) / *Achin' Hearted Blues* (vO'NS) / *Honeymoonin' On A Dime* (vO'NS)

■ THURSDAY 16 SEPTEMBER 1937

Nancy Long, Robcliff Jones and myself went to see Jimmy Dorsey and his band at Loew's State Theater in New York City. This was my second time seeing this band in one week. We got in in time to hear the second show and we decided to stay on and see another stage show. The shows were almost the same as when I saw them last Saturday except that there were a few changes in the songs played. *Old Man Harlem* was played featuring Ray McKinley's drumming, and June Richmond sang *Shoe Shine Boy*. The final change was that they played *Caravan* featuring the colossal trombone work of Bobby Byrne. After the last show we went out and talked to some of the fellows in the band and I took pictures of some of them standing with Jones and Nancy, but none of them were any good because it was night when I took them. I had lengthy talks with all of the band and Roc Hillman gave me his address for the following week when the band would play a date in Ohio. I had one colossal time!

Below: Jimmy Dorsey and the band on the stage of Loew's State Theater.
Bottom: A Jimmy Dorsey poster outside the theater.

Jimmy Dorsey and his Orchestra.
Back row: Freddie Slack, Don Mattison, Bruce Squires, Jimmy, Ray McKinley, Jack Ryan, Leonard Whitney
Middle row: Toots Camarata, Shorty Sherock, Dave Matthews, Roc Hillman
Front row: Bobby Byrne, Bob Eberly, Charlie Frazier

RADIO LOGS

? WSAN
JAN SAVITT
KYW Studios, Philadelphia, Pa
Alexander's Ragtime Band
Turkey In The Straw
I Know Now
A Study In Brown

■ FRIDAY 17 SEPTEMBER 1937

RECORDING SESSION

BUSTER BAILEY & HIS RHYTHM BUSTERS
Recording session for Vocalion in NYC.
Frankie Newton (t); Buster Bailey (cl); Pete Brown (as); Don Frye (p); James McLin (g); John Kirby (b); O'Neil Spencer (d)
Afternoon In Africa / Dizzy Debutante

ART SHAW AND HIS NEW MUSIC
Recording session for Brunswick in New York City.
Art Shaw (cl/ldr); John Best, Malcolm Crain, Tom di Carlo (t); Harry Rogers, George Arus (tb); Les Robinson, Harry Freeman (as); Tony Pastor (ts/voc); Fred Petry (ts); Les Burness (p); Al Avola (g); Ben Ginsberg (b); Cliff Leeman (d); Bea Wain, Leo Watson (voc)
It's A Long, Long Way To Tipperary / I've A Strange New Rhythm In My Heart (vLW) / *If It's The Last Thing I Do* (vBW) / *Nightmare / Shoot The Likker To Me, John Boy* (vLW) / *Free Wheeling* (vLW)

Bob's friend, Don Mortimer, goes to New York by himself and visits Loew's State Theater:

"I saw Chick Webb and his colossal band. The outstanding members were Chick himself who can really pound those drums, Taft Jordan and Bobby Stark on trumpets, Sandy Williams on trombone, Tommy Fulford on piano and Teddy McRae on the tenor. Ella Fitzgerald was the greatest thing on the program in my opinion. I have never heard any woman sing real relaxed swing the way she did. It was simply STUPENDOUS. After seeing two shows I went out to the stage entrance where I stood in the rain and talked to all of the guys in the band, as well as taking pictures of them and Ella Fitzgerald, Helen Oakley(swing critic) and Al Feldman, Webb's arranger."

Above: Chick Webb (2) and Helen Oakley at the stage entrance of Loew's State.

Charles Linton, Ella Fitzgerald and Chick Webb on the stage of Loew's State

RADIO LOGS

11:30PM WMCA
EDDIE MALLORY
Savoy Ballroom, NYC
SWELL. I heard this program at Sis Doyle's house in Bronxville.
Peckin' (Mallory's nice trumpet)
I May Be Wrong
Baby, I Want You (swell chorus singing)
Star Dust (wonderful tenor sax and piano)
Sweethearts On Parade (Tyree Glenn's trombone)
Blue Grass (colossal piece written by Eddie Mallory featuring his trumpet)

■ SATURDAY 18 SEPTEMBER 1937

Don Mortimer, Hugh Pastoriza and myself took the 2:38 train into 125th Street where we got off and walked over to Seventh Avenue where the Apollo Theater is located. We paid 30 cents each and went in and saw the 80-minute stage show featuring Willie Bryant and his swell band. Besides Bryant's band there were many dancers and singers, and a lousy movie. We were inside the theater from 3:30 to 6:30. It was a pretty good floor show with that rare personality, Willie Bryant, stealing the show. He looks as though he is white, seldom smiles, but has a great sense of humor. Numbers by the band included: *Blue Rhythm Fantasy* (super-colossal theme written by Billy Kyle); *Coquette* (featuring Fats Green's baritone sax, Prince Robinson's clarinet, Wallace Jones' trumpet); *You're My Desire; I'm Counting On You* (vocal by guitarist Arnold Adams); *It's Over Because We're Through* (Willie Bryant singing his old theme song); *My Cabin Of Dreams* (Ivy Johnson singing); *So Rare* (Ivy Johnson singing again); *For Dancers Only* (wonderful — a recent smash hit swing tune). Bryant started this band 9 weeks ago. It includes Prince Robinson (tenor saxist in his forties); Charles Frazier (sax); Claude Green (sax); Wallace Jones (trumpet); Harry Fredericks (trumpet); Andy Gibson (trumpet); Eli Robinson (trombone, formerly with Lucky Millinder); Arnold Adams (guitar); Sonny White (piano, swell); Norman Frank (bass), and a few others. After taking a few pictures of the band which never came out, we took the 6th Avenue EL down to Grand Central.

After buying some Super-X film for Hughie's camera we walked up to 485 Madison Avenue where the Swing Session was to go on the air in 35 minutes. Mortimer had a special pass from Milt Gabler but Hughie and I had to ask people if they had extra tickets until we finally got in. The guests on this week's program were Thomas 'Fats' Waller (Negro showman and pianist), Les Lieber (young fife player who works in the CBS Publicity Department), Joseph Miro (pianist & composer), and Larry Wynn's Winners (4 Negroes and white Larry Wynn making up a swell vocal group). Paul Douglas and Mel Allen were, as usual, the announcers. Ed Cashman was also there but Cohan wasn't.

The personnel of the CBS under the direction of Leith Stevens was: Billy Gussak (drums); Frankie Worrell (guitar); Lou Shoobe (bass); Jimmy Dale (piano); Joe Vargas (trombone); Roland Dupont (trombone); Toots Mondello (sax); Art Manners (sax); Hank Ross (sax); George Tudor (sax); Willie Kelly (trumpet); Nat Natoli (trumpet); Jimmy Rosselli (trumpet); Lloyd Williams (trumpet). We got good seats together and enjoyed this excellent broadcast immensely. Hughie and Don took several pictures but only a few came out. After the broadcast I got the autographs of Les Lieber and Sonny Salad.

Left: Les Lieber

Willie Bryant

To Bob from Leslie Lieber

With love Sonny Salad

SEPTEMBER 1937

8.00PM WABC
SATURDAY NIGHT SWING SESSION No62
CBS Studio No1, 485 Madison Ave, NYC
Swing Session Called To Order (CBS Band going the nuts: Toots Mondello's clarinet)
Alligator Crawl (genial FATS WALLER playing a super-colossal piano: Gussak's drums)
Don't You Know Or Don't You Care (FATS WALLER playing and singing: Mondello; bass; drums)
Always (11-yr-old SONNY SALAD from Schenectady playing a fair clarinet with band)
Surrealism (composer JOSEPH MIRO playing piano: Mondello on flute; Gussak's drums)
Big Boy Blue (LARRY WYNN'S WINNERS singing swell: piano)
My Cabin Of Dreams (LARRY WYNN'S WINNERS singing)
Frolic Sam (super-colossal arrangement: Hank Ross' great tenor sax solo)
Dinah (A jam session!!! With Fats Waller, Toots Mondello on clarinet, Roland Dupont on trombone, Willie Kelly on trumpet, Hank Ross, guitar and bass)

Ad Lib on *Dinah*
The boys at CBS are still whispering about Fats Waller's ad lib line on a recent Saturday night swing show, when Paul Douglas, in calling out *Dinah* for a jam session, asked in what key it ought to be played. Manny Klein suggested E-flat and Babe Russin, A-flat, but Fats shouted coast-to-coast, "Dinah's okay in any flat!"

After the broadcast we went to the Hot Club (Commodore Music Shop). Hughie and I bought *Blues* by Art Shaw on Brunswick. We also bought the Victor Album consisting of 4 12-inch records by Goodman, Berigan, Tommy Dorsey and Fats Waller. I bought Edgar Hayes' *Stompin' At The Renny* and *Laughin' At Life* (Decca 1416).

Don and Hughie took the 9:05 train home but I took the subway up to 140th Street and Lenox Avenue where I arrived at the Savoy Ballroom at 9:30. Before going in I noticed in a store next to the Savoy a big picture of Bennie Moten's Band of 1934 when Count Basie and Jimmy Rushing were with the band. The guy wouldn't sell this rare picture. I finally went into the Savoy where it was already very crowded. Eventually I met Fred Patrick from Hartsdale, and Paul Mallory, Ed Johnson and Elmer Hollingshead from Scarsdale. We stayed together the whole evening and had a wonderful time watching the two swell bands really go to town, and the marvelous dancers on the floor. There is continuous dancing until 4:00am to the music of the Sultan Serenaders and Eddie Mallory's Band. Both Negroes and white people mix, even when dancing. And what dancers they are! They Truck, Lindy-hop, Big Apple, Suzy-Q, and Shag. Much to our regret we didn't have any girls along to dance with. How we did want to dance! We finally left at 12:50 to catch the 1:10 train home.

As for the bands they were all you wanted. The Sultan Serenaders from the South had 3 saxes, 4 rhythm and a few brass. Outstanding were one of their saxists, a clarinetist, and the bassist. Eddie Mallory's Band is composed of 5 saxes, 4 trombones, 4 trumpets (counting Eddie Mallory who plays a swell trumpet) and 4 rhythm. His band can play exceptionally smooth and hot and has its own particular style, having all its arrangers within the band including Mallory who also composes and sings besides directing. The band isn't very well known yet but should go to the top soon. It has been going for almost 2 years although it has been on tour for practically all that time. Tonight closes a three-week engagement at the Savoy. Tomorrow they go on another extended road trip. Most of the men are

Eddie Mallory

from the middle west. Eddie Mallory told me how he used to direct the Mills Blue Rhythm Band in 1933 when Edgar Hayes was a member. He said that he quit that job because there were too many leaders. Back in 1931 he had a band in Chicago including trombonist Keg Johnson and pianist Teddy Wilson among others. I don't know the full personnel of the band except for the autographs shown here. Outstanding musicians in the band are the drummer, tenor saxist Don Byas, and trombonist-xylophonist-arranger Tyree Glenn. The band does a lot of chorus singing, differing from Don Redman's style in that they stay on the melody.

[autographs: Eddie Mallory; Ted Sturgis – bass; Joe Keyes – trumpet; Don Byas – tenor sax; Pascal McRae; Tyree Glenn – trombone; Leslie Corley – guitar; Wilbourn ? – bar. sax; John Skates – piano]

■ SUNDAY 19 SEPTEMBER 1937

RADIO LOGS

12:45AM WABC
BOB CROSBY
Valley Dale, Columbus, Ohio
Squeeze Me (Bob Zurke; Eddie Miller)
When My Dreamboat Comes Home
Pagan Love Song
Whispers In The Dark (vocal: Kay Weber)
My Cabin Of Dreams (vocal: Bob Crosby)

■ MONDAY 20 SEPTEMBER 1937

RECORDING SESSION

DUKE ELLINGTON AND HIS ORCHESTRA
Recording session for Master Records in New York City.
Duke Ellington (p); Arthur Whetsel, Cootie Williams, Freddie Jenkins (t); Rex Stewart (c); Joe Nanton, Lawrence Brown (tb); Barney Bigard (cl); Johnny Hodges (cl/ss/as); Otto Hardwick (as/bsx); Harry Carney (cl/as/bar); Fred Guy (g); Billy Taylor (b); Sonny Greer (d)
Chatterbox / Jubilesta / Diminuendo In Blue / Crescendo In Blue / Harmony In Harlem / Dusk In The Desert

RADIO LOGS

12:00 NOON WABC
CBS HOUSE BAND
'Swingin' The Blues', NYC
Nothing But The Blues (Willie Kelly's trumpet; Art Manners' clarinet)
Beale Street Blues (Billy Gussak's drums; Toots Mondello's clarinet)
Blue Turning Grey Over You (vocal: Willis Kelly) (Marty Dale's piano; Roland Dupont's trombone)
Singin' The Blues (Roland Dupont's trombone; Sammy Weiss' drums)

11:30PM WABC
CAB CALLOWAY
Cotton Club, NYC
Preview broadcast from the Cotton Club where Cab Calloway opens tomorrow night.
Go South Young Man (vocal: Cab Calloway) (Chu Berry's tenor)
I'm Always In The Mood For You (vocal: Cab Calloway)
I'm A Hi-De-Ho Romeo (vocal: Cab Calloway)
She's Tall, She's Tan, She's Terrific (vocal: Cab Calloway)
The Harlem Bolero (vocal: Cab Calloway)
Nightfall In Louisiana (vocal: Cab Calloway)
The Bill Robinson (vocal: Cab Calloway)
Minnie The Moocher (vocal: Cab Calloway) (played in full)

12:30AM WEAF
ANDY KIRK
Grand Terrace Café, Chicago
Big John Special
Can I Forget You? (vocal: Henry Wells)
We're In The Money (vocal: Pha Terrell)
I Know Now (vocal: Henry Wells)
My Cabin Of Dreams (vocal: Henry Wells)
Stop! You're Breaking My Heart
Posin'
King Porter Stomp

■ TUESDAY 21 SEPTEMBER 1937

RECORDING SESSION

BEN POLLACK AND HIS PICK-A-RIB BOYS
Recording session for Decca in Los Angeles.
Ben Pollack (d/ldr); Muggsy Spanier (t); Ted Vesely (tb); Ben Kanter (cl); Happy Lawson (ts); Bob Laine (p); Garry McAdams (g); Francis Palmer (b); Peggy Mann (voc)
If It's The Last Thing I Do (vPM) / *I'm In My Glory* (vPM) / *You Made Me Love You* (vPM) / *The Snake Charmer*

RADIO LOGS

9:30PM WABC
BENNY GOODMAN
Camel Caravan program, Kansas City, Mo
Let's Dance (theme)
My Honey's Lovin' Arms (wonderful piece: Musso)
Yours And Mine (vocal: Martha Tilton) (nuttsy)
The Man I Love (BG Quartet) (nuttsy: slow and swinging)
One O'Clock Jump (written by Count Basie and played in his honor: Stacy's nuttsy piano intro; Musso's tenor; McEachern's colossal trombone; Benny; James' wonderful trumpet with saxes; marvelous ending with whole band. SUPER-GRAND)
Am I Blue? (vocal: Martha Tilton) (ballsy: Benny; Stacy)
Avalon (BG Quartet) (wonderful)
Marie (colossal: very new Fletcher Henderson arrangement; great solos by Elman, Rollini, McEachern)
Madhouse (magnificent: Stacy; James)
Goodbye (closing theme)

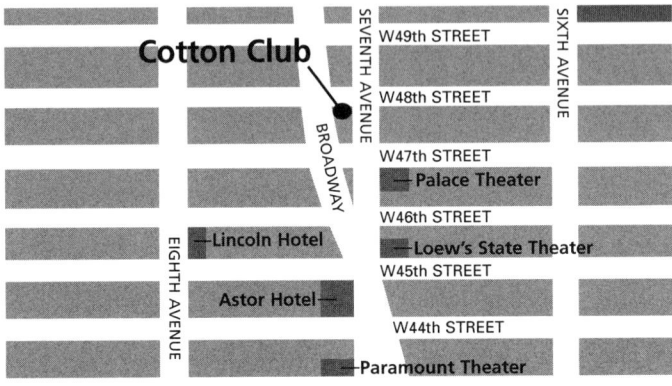

WEDNESDAY 22 SEPTEMBER 1937

RECORDING SESSION

FLETCHER HENDERSON AND HIS ORCHESTRA
Recording session for Vocalion in New York City.
Fletcher Henderson (p/ldr); Dick Vance, Russell Smith, Emmett Berry (t); John McConnell, Albert Wynn, Ed Cuffee (tb); Jerry Blake (cl/as/voc); Hilton Jefferson (cl/as); Elmer Williams, Ben Webster (ts); Lawrence Lucie (g); Israel Crosby (b); Pete Suggs (d/vib); Chuck Richards (voc)
Let 'Er Go (vJB) / *Worried Over You* (vCR) / *What's Your Story, What's Your Jive?* (vJB) / *Trees* (vCR)

RED NORVO AND HIS ORCHESTRA
Recording session for Brunswick in Los Angeles.
Red Norvo (xyl/ldr); Louis Mucci, George Wendt, Stew Pletcher (t); Al Mastren (tb); Charles Lamphere, Hank D'Amico (cl/as); Len Goldstein (as); Herbie Haymer (ts); Bill Miller (p); Red McGarvey (g); Pete Peterson (b); Maurice Purtill (d); Mildred Bailey (voc)
Tears In My Heart (vMB) / *Worried Over You* / *Clap Hands, Here Comes Charlie* / *Russian Lullaby*

THURSDAY 23 SEPTEMBER 1937

RADIO LOGS

10:00PM WAAB
BLANCHE CALLOWAY
Southland, Boston
All I Want (theme)
Caravan
You Showed Me The Way
St. Louis Blues

11:00PM WABC
CAB CALLOWAY
Cotton Club, NYC
Queen Isabella (nuttsy: clarinet; tenor; trombone)
On The Sunny Side Of The Street (vocal: Cab Calloway) (swell, slow tempo: Chu Berry's tenor; trumpet)
The Big Apple (vocal: Cab Calloway) (good: trumpet; sax)
All God's Chillun Got Rhythm (vocal: Cab Calloway)
They Can't Take That Away From Me (vocal: Cab Calloway)
I'm A Hi-De-Ho Romeo (vocal: Cab Calloway)
Just A-Wearyin' For You (vocal: Bennie Payne)

FRIDAY 24 SEPTEMBER 1937

RADIO LOGS

9:00PM WAAB
WOODY HERMAN
Normandie Ballroom, Boston
Where Or When (vocal: Woody Herman)
Strangers In The Dark (vocal: Woody Herman)
St. Louis Blues (Saxie Mansfield's tenor)
Dupree Blues (vocal: Woody Herman)
Where Or When (vocal: Woody Herman)
Tin Roof Blues (super-colossal)

10.00PM WJZ
TOMMY DORSEY
Kool Cigarette Program, NYC
Song Of The Volga Boatman
Unknown Title
Goodbye, Jonah (vocal: Edythe Wright)
Unknown Title (vocal: Jack Leonard)

11:30PM WABC
CAB CALLOWAY
Cotton Club, NYC
Mama, I Want To Swing (vocal: Cab Calloway)
Satan Takes A Holiday (fair: lousy drums)
Way Down Upon The Swanee River
Moon At Sea (vocal: Cab Calloway)
Caravan (fair: drums; trumpet)
I Surrender Dear (vocal: Cab Calloway)
Down South Camp Meetin'

12:00 MIDNIGHT WNEW
JOE MARSALA
Hickory House, 144 W52nd Street, NYC
Caravan (swell swinging: Joe's clarinet)
Whispers In The Dark (vocal: Adele Girard)
Oh, Sister, Ain't That Hot
Star Dust
Harlem Joys
Mandy

12:30AM WMCA
LUCKY MILLINDER
Savoy Ballroom, NYC
Star Dust (theme) (nuttsy theme featuring Billy Kyle's swell piano)
Clementine
Balloonacy (written by alto saxist Tab Smith)
I've Got You Under My Skin (only fair)
Big John Special (colossal: Smith's alto sax; Charlie Shavers' trumpet)
A Study In Brown
Marie (featuring 3 choruses of Billy Kyle's piano)
Swanee River (vocal: Billy Kyle & band) (swell: rather long)

■ SATURDAY 25 SEPTEMBER 1937

After a strenuous football scrimmage in the morning I decided to go into the city. I left, alone, at 2:00 and hitch-hiked to the subway. At 3:30 I arrived at the Apollo Theater where I paid 30 cents for orchestra seats even though it was very crowded. As usual, the stage show lasted for an hour. It was very good, but a bit cheap. Of course, Ellington's band was wonderful. Most of the show was based around tunes written by Duke Ellington: *Solitude, Sophisticated Lady, In a Sentimental Mood, It Don't Mean A Thing*, etc.

The following numbers were played by Ellington's Band:
Crescendo In Blue (a nuttsy piece written by Ellington last week: Bigard's clarinet)
In the Shade of the Old Apple Tree (Jenkins' nuttsy muted trumpet, Hodges' alto sax, Nanton's ballsy wa-wa plunger trombone)
Lady Who Couldn't Be Kissed (played to the accompaniment of the Four Step Brothers; Carney's baritone)
Trumpet In Spades (Rex Stewart trumpet solo; marvelous)
All God's Chillun Got Rhythm (Ivie Anderson singing the nuts)
He Does Me So Much Good (a comic number with Ivie Anderson; Otto Hardwick and Sonny Greer doing the talking)
A conversation between Ivie Anderson and Rex Stewart's miraculous talking trumpet.
Troubled Waters (Ivie Anderson again singing marvelously)
I've Got To Be A Rug Cutter (Ivie Anderson with vocal trio consisting of bassist Hayes Alvis, Harry Carney and Rex Stewart)

After leaving the Apollo, I took the subway to 485 Madison Avenue where I met Peter Macey with his sister and cousin from Ossining, N.Y. Macey's father sells time on the radio so he gets tickets to programs. He took me in to the Saturday Night Swing Session on one of his tickets. The program was as follows:
SATURDAY NIGHT SWING SESSION No63
Panamania (Dupont's trombone)
Unknown Title
There's A Small Hotel (Rosselli's trumpet)
Unknown Title (Karawanis Brothers)
Casa Loma Stomp (Karawanis Brothers again)
Organ Grinder's Swing (short introduction to Hudson-DeLange)
Popcorn Man (Hudson-DeLange)
I'll Never Be The Same (Hazel Scott singing)
Shindig (Nuttsy: Lloyd Williams' trumpet)

RADIO LOGS

8:30PM WAAB
WOODY HERMAN
Normandie Ballroom, Boston
Remember Me (vocal: Woody Herman)
Am I In Love? (vocal: Woody Herman)
Twilight In Turkey (arranged by Deane Kincaide)
Strangers In The Dark (vocal: Woody Herman)
It Happened Down In Dixieland (vocal: Woody Herman & Band)
Old Man Moon (Kermit Simmons' trumpet)
The Dream In My Heart (vocal: Woody Herman)
Weary Blues (super-colossal: Neil Reid's trombone; Woody's clarinet)
Rose Room (ballsy song: Nick Hupfer's violin)
Blue Prelude (theme)

11:00PM WNEW
BOBBIE TROTTER
La Casino, Jamaica, Long Island, N.Y.
Fair. Bobbie Trotter, 22-yr-old Negro girl, started her band last month.
The Loveliness Of You
Sister Kate
Ol' Man Mose
You Took Advantage Of Me
Marie
Nobody's Sweetheart
Original Dixieland One-Step

11:30PM WMCA
LUCKY MILLINDER
Savoy Ballroom, NYC
Star Dust (theme) (nuttsy theme featuring Billy Kyle's swell piano)
Double Breasted Lips (written by alto saxist Tab Smith: good Smith alto)
When Irish Eyes Are Smiling (Billy Kyle's ballsy piano; Smith's alto sax)
Star Dust (vocal: Trevor Bacon) (regular theme played in full)
Honeysuckle Rose
Come! Come!
Blue Rhythm Fantasy

■ MONDAY 27 SEPTEMBER 1937

RECORDING SESSION

MILDRED BAILEY & HER ORCHESTRA
Recording session for Vocalion in Los Angeles.
Louis Mucci, George Wendt, Stew Pletcher (t); Alex Mastren (tb); Hank D'Amico (cl/as); Len Goldstein, Charles Lamphere (as); Herbie Haymer (ts); Bill Miller (p); Red McGarvie (g); Pete Peterson (b); Maurice Purtill (d); Red Norvo (xyl); Mildred Bailey (v)
Bob White (vMB) / *Just A Stone's Throw From Heaven* (vMB) / *Loving You* (vMB) / *Right Or Wrong* (vMB)

RADIO LOGS

12:00 NOON WABC
CBS HOUSE BAND
'Swingin' The Blues', NYC
Royal Garden Blues (Art Manners' clarinet; Willie Kelly's trumpet; Hank Ross' great tenor sax)
Basin Street Blues (vocal: Willie Kelly) (clarinet)
Farewell Blues (colossal: Ross' dirty tenor sax)
Livery Stable Blues (nuttsy)
Junk Man Blues (swell: comical vocal; clarinet)

8.00PM WJZ
WILLIE BRYANT
'Goodtime Society', NYC
When I Grow Too Old To Dream (Bryant's band swingin' out swell)
St. Louis Blues (vocal: Willie Bryant) (nuttsy: saxes; Sonny White's piano)
Blue Rhythm Fantasy (theme)

■ TUESDAY 28 SEPTEMBER 1937

RECORDING SESSION

WINGY MANONE AND HIS ORCHESTRA
Recording session for Bluebird in New York City.
Wingy Manone (t/voc); Joe Marsala (cl/as); Babe Russin (ts); Conrad Lanoue (p); Jack LeMaire (g); Artie Shapiro (b); Danny Alvin (d)
I Ain't Got Nobody (vWM) / *I've Got My Heart Set On You* (vWM) / *Everything You Said Came True* (vWM) / *Getting Some Fun Out Of Life* (vWM) / *Jazz Me Blues* (vWM) / *Laugh Your Way Through Life* (vWM)

RADIO LOGS

10:00PM WABC
BENNY GOODMAN
Camel Caravan program, Cleveland, Ohio
Let's Dance (theme)
St. Louis Blues (nuttsy: Harry James' swell trumpet; great work by Benny; saxes)
Me, Myself And I (vocal: Martha Tilton) (grand arrangement: James; Musso's gut-bucket tenor sax)
I'm Getting Sentimental Over You (BG Trio) (swell: 2 tempos)
Wrappin' It Up (wonderful arrangement of Henderson piece: James)
I'm A Ding Dong Daddy (From Dumas) (BG Quartet) (grand)
That Old Feeling (vocal: Martha Tilton) (swell ballad: smooth saxes; Martha singing the nuts)
Caravan (super-marvelous: Harry James; Krupa; Benny)
Goodbye (closing theme)

■ WEDNESDAY 29 SEPTEMBER 1937

RADIO LOGS

9:30PM CKLW
JOE SANDERS
Blackhawk Restaurant, Chicago
The Moon Got In My Eyes
They Can't Take That Away From Me
Loving You (vocal: Vic Scherzinger)

10:00PM WEAF
JOHNNY HAUSER
New Mayfair Casino, Cleveland
The Mayor Of Alabam'
Everything You Said Came True
If I Could Be With You
A Gold Mine In The Sky (vocal: Johnny Hauser)

10:30PM WABC
FRANK DAILEY
Meadowbrook, N.J.
I Saw A Kiss A-Sailing (vocal: Louise Wallace) (tenor sax; clarinet; Joe Mooney's accordion)
Something To Sing About (tenor sax, etc)
That Old Feeling (vocal: Louise Wallace)
St. Louis Blues (swell: nuttsy trumpet; tenor sax; clarinet; accordion)
Once In A While (vocal: Louise Wallace)
My Melancholy Baby (very good: swell tenor sax; nice clarinet; lousy accordion)
Yours And Mine (vocal: Louise Wallace)
Stumbling (good: Mooney's accordion; nice clarinet again)
You're My Desire (vocal: Louise Wallace)
Scattin' At The Kit Kat (accordion; high clarinet; jerky tenor sax)
Gypsy Violins (theme) (swell opening & closing theme, rather slow)

11:30PM WMCA
DUKE ELLINGTON
Apollo Theater, NYC
Passion (a recent tune by Ellington: Hodges' colossal alto sax; Cootie Williams' trumpet)
Azure (written by Ellington several months ago – very slow: Carney's baritone sax)

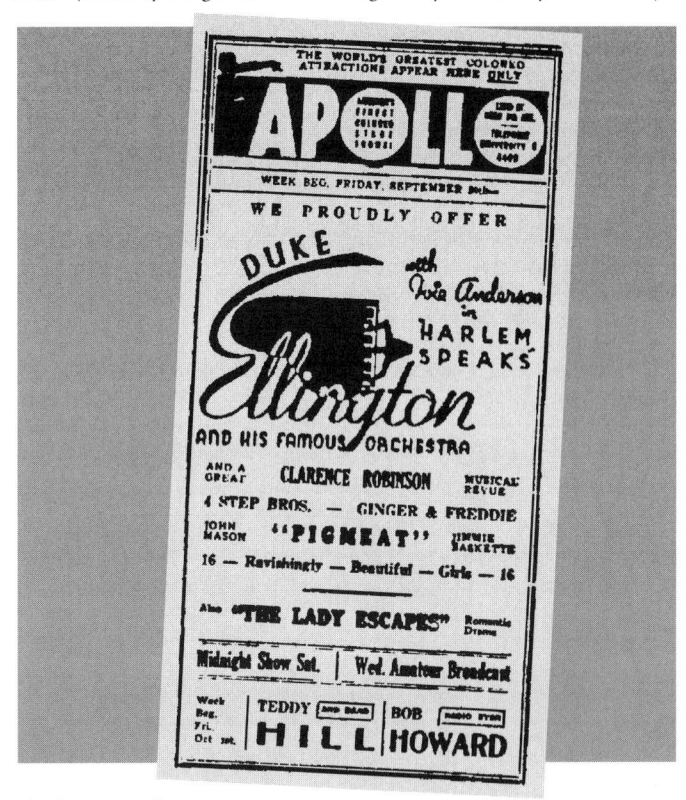

12:30AM WABC
RED NORVO
Palomar Ballroom, Los Angeles
So Rare (vocal: Stew Pletcher) (swell: Herbie Haymer's wonderful tenor sax)
Loving You (vocal: Mildred Bailey) (swell new piece: Mastren's smooth trombone)
Tears In My Heart (vocal: Mildred Bailey) (colossal new tune: Haymer's nuttsy, dirty, oozing tenor sax; Stew Pletcher's short trumpet solo)
Roses In December (muted trumpet on first chorus; Miller's piano; Haymer's tenor sax)
Shoutin' In That Amen Corner (vocal: Mildred Bailey) (nuttsy vocal)
A Porter's Love Song (nuttsy: Red; D'Amico's clarinet; Haymer's tenor)
Round The Old Deserted Farm (vocal: Mildred Bailey) (recently written by Willard Robison)
Bugle Call Rag (wonderful original arrangement: Haymer's grand tenor solo; Purtill's cymbals; Hank D'Amico's swell clarinet; Norvo's nuttsy xylophone playing; Purtill's drum break)

■ THURSDAY 30 SEPTEMBER 1937

Tommy Dorsey and his Orchestra open at the Palm Room of the Hotel Commodore in New York City.

RADIO LOGS

9.30PM WHN
CLAUDE HOPKINS
Roseland Ballroom, NYC
Baptist Moan (nuttsy swinging: swell tenor sax)
My Cabin Of Dreams (vocal: Beverly White) (too long: nice trumpet)
I Know That You Know (featuring Hopkins' typical, swell piano; drums)
Swingin' Down The Lane (vocal: Beverly White) (Hopkins' ballsy piano; bass)
June Night (vocal: Beverly White & Band) (fair tenor sax & clarinet)
All God's Chillun Got Rhythm (vocal: Beverly White) (grand: trumpet)
The Maid's Night Off (nuttsy: swell trumpet and trombone solos; tenor sax)
Sunday (vocal: Beverly White) (Hopkins' colossal piano on first chorus; trombone; tenor sax)
I Would Do Anything For You (theme / vocal: Beverly White)

11:30PM WABC
CAB CALLOWAY
Cotton Club, NYC
The Big Apple (vocal: Cab Calloway & Band) (good in parts: clarinet; tenor)
Rhapsody Melody (swell new sweet piece: nice saxes & brass; Chu Berry's sax)
Way Down Upon The Swanee River (good: Chu Berry's colossal tenor sax; trombones)
Just A-Wearyin' For You (OK: Berry's short tenor sax solo)
Little White Lies (swell: grand trumpet; Keg Johnson's trombone; Chu Berry again)
Marie (vocal: Cab Calloway) (smooth trombone; swell trumpet; clarinet; sax)
Zaz-Zuh-Zaz (vocal: Cab Calloway & Band)
I Got Rhythm (vocal: Cab Calloway) (Chu Berry's marvelous tenor sax; clarinet; trumpet)

OCTOBER 1937

Hotel Pennsylvania: **Benny Goodman** (11–)
Hotel Commodore: **Tommy Dorsey**
Hotel New Yorker: **Glen Gray** (8–)
Hotel Lincoln: **Isham Jones** (6–)

Apollo Theater: **Lucky Millinder** (1–7); **Tiny Bradshaw** (8–14); **Luis Russell** (15–21); **Ethel Waters/Eddie Mallory** (22–28); **Fletcher Henderson** (29–)
Paramount Theater: **Benny Meroff** (6–26)
Loew's State Theater: **Fletcher Henderson** (–6); **Horace Heidt** (7–13)

Cotton Club: **Cab Calloway**
Hickory House: **Joe Marsala**
Onyx Club: **John Kirby / Spirits of Rhythm**

■ SATURDAY 2 OCTOBER 1937

Today I bought 4 records at Ferris' Music Store: Benny Goodman's *Sugar Foot Stomp* and *I Can't Give You Anything But Love* (Victor 25678); Count Basie's *Good Morning Blues* and *Our Love Was Meant To Be* (Decca 1446); Glen Gray's *For You* and *Casa Loma Stomp* (Decca 1412); and Teddy Wilson's *Big Apple* and *You Can't Stop Me From Dreaming* (Brunswick 7954).

RADIO LOGS

7.30PM WABC
SATURDAY NIGHT SWING SESSION No64
CBS Studio No1, 485 Madison Ave, NYC
A new time: 7:30. Mel Allen & Paul Douglas again announcing. However, this swing session wasn't up to standard.
Sugar (CBS Band directed by Leith Stevens: Hank Ross' tenor sax)
Canadian Capers (TOMMY DORSEY playing fast, swell trombone; piano; saxes)
A Porter's Love Song (VI MELE singing and playing piano)
Mr. Ghost Goes To Town (lousy: VI MELE playing fair piano)
A Study In Brown (written & arranged by Larry Clinton who was in the control room: very short, showing how tunes are arranged)
The Big Dipper (latest composition of Larry Clinton's: nuttsy; clarinet)
Chinatown, My Chinatown (JOE SODJA playing marvelous, intricate guitar)
Get It Southern Style (ALICE KING singing good with Joe Sodja's guitar)
Marie (A jam session!!! With Joe Sodja's colossal guitar; Dorsey's nuttsy dirty trombone solo; Mondello's swell clarinet; Ross' tenor; Alice King)

11:30PM WABC
BOB CROSBY
Book-Cadillac Hotel, Detroit
SWELL. I heard this program at Maurine Van Meter's house in Bronxville.
Between The Devil And The Deep Blue Sea
I Know Now (vocal: Kay Weber)
Stop! You're Breaking My Heart (vocal: Bob Crosby)
Squeeze Me
Strangers In The Dark (vocal: Kay Weber)
Here Comes Your Pappy (vocal: Nappy Lamare)
Remember Me
The Old Spinning Wheel
Summertime (theme)

12:15AM WMCA
JOE MARSALA
Hickory House, 144 W52nd Street, NYC
Rosetta
Singin' The Blues

12:30AM WABC
RED NORVO
Palomar Ballroom, Los Angeles
Clap Hands! Here Comes Charlie (swell, rather slow: Norvo's xylophone; Herbie Haymer)
Worried Over You (vocal: Mildred Bailey) (colossal: how I feel this song)
Roses In December (trumpet on first chorus; Bill Miller's ballsy piano; Haymer)
Remember (super-colossal: marvelous saxes at beginning; trumpet; Red; Haymer)
Me, Myself And I (vocal: Mildred Bailey) (reassuring that Bailey is still tops: Haymer)
Where Or When (tricky arrangement: Norvo's sweet xylophone; swell cymbal playing)
A Stone's Throw From Heaven (vocal: Mildred Bailey) (first time on radio)
I Got Rhythm (wonderful, fast tempo: Norvo; Haymer's nuttsy sax; trumpet)

■ MONDAY 4 OCTOBER 1937

RADIO LOGS

10:30PM WNEW
JACK MONTGOMERY
NY
Everything You Said Came True (vocal: Jack Peck)
That Old Feeling
Yours To Command (a little ragged; trumpet)
Jangled Nerves (Peck's swell sax; trumpet; trombone)

11:05PM WEAF
JOHNNY HAUSER
New Mayfair Casino, Cleveland, Ohio
So Rare (vocal: Johnny Hauser)
A Gold Mine In The Sky (vocal: Johnny Hauser)
After You (vocal: Johnny Hauser)
Body And Soul
Dinah (vocal: Johnny Hauser)
If I Could Count On You
Big John Special
Sailing Home
Me, Myself And I

11:30PM WEAF
WOODY HERMAN
Normandie Ballroom, Boston
Royal Garden Blues (Neil Reid's trombone; Saxie Mansfield's nuttsy tenor; clarinet)
In The Still Of The Night (vocal: Woody Herman)
My Cabin Of Dreams (swell: Mansfield's tenor sax; Herman's clarinet)
Am I In Love? (vocal: Woody Herman) (snazzy sweet vocal)
It Happened Down In Dixieland (vocal: Woody Herman) (wonderful: Mansfield; Reid)
Flugelhorn Blues (vocal: Woody Herman) (colossal slow blues: marvelous solos by Bishop; Mansfield; Reid)
Davenport Blues (super-colossal, slow blues relaxed swing: Mansfield; Bishop; Herman's dirty Dixieland clarinet; swell saxes; Reid's marvelous blues trombone)
The Image Of You (rather short: Woody Herman's typical swell clarinet; drums)
Blue Prelude (theme) (marvelous slow, smooth theme written by Isham Jones: Reid's trombone)

12:00 MIDNIGHT WOR
TOMMY DORSEY
Hotel Commodore, NYC
You And I Know (vocal: Edythe Wright)
Whispers In The Dark (vocal: Jack Leonard)
The Barcarolle
Once In A While (vocal: Edythe Wright & Three Esquires) (swell, very smooth)
Night And Day (good: nice sax run; Howard Smith's short piano solo; Dorsey)
The Big Apple (vocal: Edythe Wright)
If It's The Last Thing I Do (vocal: Jack Leonard) (swell new sweet piece)
Hymn To The Sun
Have You Got Any Castles, Baby? (vocal: Jack Leonard)
Happy As The Day Is Long

■ TUESDAY 5 OCTOBER 1937

RADIO LOGS

WABC-CBS: Jack Oakie College (Camel Cigarettes); Benny Goodman's Swing Band; Wm. Austin, impersonator; Stuart Erwin: WHAS WDRC WBT WPRO WBBM WPG WOKO WCAU (sw-6.06-11.83)
With the beginning of the fall season, collegians once more matriculate at Jack Oakie's College, under the watchful eye of Oakie, his football coach, Raymond Hatton, Professor William Austin, of the English Department, Georgie Stoll of the Department of Music, and Benny Goodman and his Swing School. President Oakie and his professors take up the first half-hour in musical and comic lessons from Hollywood, and Professor Goodman teaches swing from Baltimore on the second half-hour. Professor Hatton is a well-known stage and screen comedian; Austin of the English Department is an English character actor, known for his highbrow English impersonations. After the first week of the College, the swing lessons of Benny Goodman will be continued from the Hotel Pennsylvania in New York City.

10:00PM WABC
BENNY GOODMAN
Camel Caravan program, Baltimore
Let's Dance (theme)
Love Me Or Leave Me (nuttsy: excellent solos by Vido Musso; Jess Stacy; Allan Reuss; wonderful trumpet, probably by Harry James)
The Moon Got In My Eyes (vocal: Martha Tilton) (Musso's short passages; Benny)

In The Shade Of The Old Apple Tree (wonderful: saxes carrying 1st chorus; James' short solo; Benny's marvelous clarinet; trombone team; James' 2nd hot solo)
Whispers In The Dark (BG Trio) (good, but commercial: Wilson's piano outstanding)
Honeysuckle Rose (great, fairly fast: solid saxes and biting brass with Benny's nuttsy clarinet; James' super-marvelous, rasping trumpet; 'die-off' ending)
Limehouse Blues (BG Quartet) (grand: excellent work especially on last chorus)
Loch Lomond (vocal: Martha Tilton) (lousy piece but swell swinging)
One O'Clock Jump (GREAT!! Benny's latest gigantic killer: Stacy; Musso's swell sax; good trombone; Harry James)
Goodbye (closing theme)

Martha Tilton

WEDNESDAY 6 OCTOBER 1937

RADIO LOGS

11:30PM WMCA
LUCKY MILLINDER
Apollo Theater, NYC
When Irish Eyes Are Smiling (swell: Tab Smith's nuttsy alto; Charlie Shavers' trumpet)
Blue Rhythm Fantasy (Smith's colossal alto; nuttsy trumpet; nice clarinet; Billy Kyle's piano)

12:00 MIDNIGHT WABC
TOMMY DORSEY
Hotel Commodore, NYC
I'm Feeling Like A Million (vocal: Edythe Wright)
The Morning After (vocal: Jack Leonard)
Humoresque
If It's The Last Thing I Do (vocal: Jack Leonard)
The Dipsy-Doodle (vocal: Edythe Wright) (introduced yesterday)
Remember Me (vocal: Jack Leonard)
Who'll Buy My Violets?
So Many Memories
Swing That Music

12:08AM WEAF
WOODY HERMAN
Normandie Ballroom, Boston
Exactly Like You
Don't You Know Or Don't You Care (vocal: Woody Herman) (Mansfield's tenor sax)
My Blue Heaven (ballsy arrangement: Mansfield's nice sax; Herman's clarinet)
You're My Desire (vocal: Woody Herman) (too commercial but swell ballad)
Easy To Remember (nuttsy swing arrangement: Bishop's horn; clarinet; sax)
Dancing Under The Stars (vocal: Woody Herman) (very new song: OK)

THURSDAY 7 OCTOBER 1937

RECORDING SESSION

BUNNY BERIGAN AND HIS ORCHESTRA
Recording session for Victor in New York City.
Bunny Berigan, Irving Goodman, Steve Lipkins (t); Al George, Sonny Lee (tb); Mike Doty, Joe Dixon (cl/as); Clyde Rounds, George Auld (ts); Joe Lippman (p); Tom Morgan (g); Hank Wayland (b); George Wettling (d); Gail Reese (voc)
I'd Love To Play A Love Scene (vGR) / *I Want A New Romance* (vGR) / *Miles Apart* (vGR) / *A Strange Loneliness* (vGR)

FATS WALLER & HIS RHYTHM
Recording session for Victor in New York City.
Herman Autrey (t); Gene Sedric (cl/ts); Fats Waller (p/voc); Albert Casey (g); Charles Turner (b); Slick Jones (d)
How Can I? (vFW) / *The Joint Is Jumpin'* (vFW) / *A Hopeless Love Affair* (vFW) / *What Will I Do In The Morning?* (vFW) / *How Ya, Baby?* (vFW) / *Jealous Of Me* (vFW)

RADIO LOGS

8:00PM WHN
JIMMY DORSEY
Hotel Netherland-Plaza, Cincinnati, Ohio
Tain't No Use (vocal: Trio) (swell: Freddy Slack's ballsy piano after vocal)
Yours And Mine (vocal: Bob Eberly)
Whispers In The Dark (vocal: Bob Eberly)
Flight Of The Bumble Bee (featuring Jimmy Dorsey's fast alto sax; trombone)
Sweet Leilani (vocal: Bob Eberly)

9:30PM WHN
FLETCHER HENDERSON
Roseland Ballroom, NYC
Christopher Columbus (theme) (arranged and popularized by Henderson)
Clarinet Marmalade (Jerry Blake's clarinet)
All God's Chillun Got Rhythm (vocal: Jerry Blake)
Worried Over You (vocal: Chuck Richards)
Chris And His Gang (colossal tune: clarinet)
Whispers In The Dark (vocal: Chuck Richards)
St. Louis Blues (nuttsy tenor sax solo; nice trumpet; Jerry Blake's swell clarinet)
Let 'Er Go (vocal: Jerry Blake) (18-yr-old Israel Crosby's swell bass solo; fair clarinet; tenor sax)
It's Wearing Me Down (vocal: Chuck Richards) (colossal sweet piece and swell vocal)
Avalon (nuttsy: trumpet; tenor sax; clarinet; trombone)

10:00PM WABC
CAB CALLOWAY
Cotton Club, NYC
Mama, I Wanna Make Rhythm (vocal: Cab Calloway) (Chu Berry's nuttsy tenor sax)
Nightfall In Louisiana (vocal: Cab Calloway) (very slow new piece: Chu Berry)
Caravan (pretty good: Keg Johnson's sweet trombone; Berry's wonderful sax again)
If It's The Last Thing I Do
Have You Met Miss Jones? (vocal: Cab Calloway) (first time on the radio)
She's Tall, She's Tan, She's Terrific (vocal: Cab Calloway) (swell: Doc Cheatham's trumpet; Chu Berry)
The Shag (lousy)
Sweet Sue (vocal: Cab Calloway) (good: Johnson's trombone; Cheatham's trumpet; Berry)

11:00PM WJZ
JIMMY DORSEY
Hotel Netherland-Plaza, Cincinnati, Ohio
Sandman (theme) (swell theme recorded for Decca)
Arkansas Traveler (colossal: Jimmy Dorsey's fair clarinet; nuttsy tenor sax; Jack Ryan's bass)
Star Dust (Bobby Byrne's sell trombone followed by a nice sweet muted trumpet)
I'm Getting Sentimental Over You (featuring Bobby Byrne's good high trombone)
After You (vocal: Don Mattison) (ballsy arrangement: Slack's colossal piano; tenor sax)
Once In A While (vocal: Bob Eberly)
Parade Of The Milk Bottle Tops (wonderful: Camarata's trumpet; Ray McKinley; Dorsey)
An Old Flame Never Dies (vocal: Bob Eberly) (fair: way too commercial)
I Cried For You (nuttsy: Dorsey's nice clarinet with wa-wa brass; Slack's piano)
They Can't Take That Away From Me (vocal: Bob Eberly) (swell tune)
Dusk In Upper Sandusky (didn't have time to play it all)
Sandman (theme)

12:00 MIDNIGHT WABC
BOB CROSBY
Book-Cadillac Hotel, Detroit
Summertime (theme) (swell theme written by the late George Gershwin)
Panama (good: outstanding solos by Eddie Miller on tenor; Yank Lawson; Matlock; Warren Smith)
Roses In December (vocal: Kay Weber) (Miller's tenor; Lawson's short trumpet solo)
Have You Got Any Castles, Baby? (vocal: Bob Crosby) (too commercial: Miller; Matlock)
Tin Roof Blues (The 8 Bobcats producing some wonderful, slow, inspired Dixieland: Warren Smith's ballsy blues trombone; Matlock's great clarinet solo)
Love Is Just Around The Corner (vocal: Nappy Lamare) (Matlock's clarinet)
The First Time I Saw You (vocal: Bob Crosby) (nuttsy: Lawson; Matlock; Miller; Bauduc)
That Old Feeling (vocal: Kay Weber) (swell tune: Miller's tenor; Warren Smith)
At The Jazz Band Ball (marvelous: Matlock; Smith; Miller; Bauduc's drum solo)

FRIDAY 8 OCTOBER 1937

On Friday night Carolyn Bade, Anne Wilson, Babs Underhill, Maurine Van Meter, George Fick, Jim Poe and Jim Branham came to my house. Wonderful time with Carolyn Bade.

RADIO LOGS

10:00PM WBZ
TOMMY DORSEY
Kool Cigarette program, NYC
Humoresque
Yours And Mine (vocal: Jack Leonard)
Who's Sorry Now?
Farewell To Arms (vocal: Jack Leonard)
Jammin' (vocal: Edythe Wright)

11:30PM WHN
SAVOY SULTANS
Savoy Ballroom, NYC
Jealous
Among My Souvenirs (nuttsy: real solid drums; tenor sax)
You're My Desire
I Can't Give You Anything But Love
Sophisticated Swing (good: nice high, muted trumpet)
Just Because You're You (grand piece but a weak arrangement)
Linger Awhile

12:00 MIDNIGHT WJZ
EARL HINES
New Grand Terrace, Chicago
Deep Forest (theme) (nuttsy: Hines' piano; tenor sax)
You're Driving Me Crazy (nice trumpet; Hines' piano)
The Loveliness Of You
I Know That You Know
I Can't Believe That You're In Love With Me (vocal: Ida James)
Rose Room
Inspiration
A Mellow Bit Of Rhythm (colossal: tenor sax)
Ridin' A Riff
I Never Knew

■ SATURDAY 9 OCTOBER 1937

Spent the morning at Jim Mumma's house. Played football against Gorton there losing 6–0. Saturday night I went to Nancy Long's house. Swell time with Carolyn.

RADIO LOGS

7:00PM WEAF
JAN SAVITT
Philadelphia
Smarty (vocal: Carlotta Dale)
The Lady Is A Tramp (vocal: Carlotta Dale)
Peckin' (Joe Wood's trumpet)
Strange New Rhythm In My Heart (Cole Porter tune: Joe Kearns' clarinet)
Gone With The Wind (vocal: Bon Bon Tunnell)
I'm Just A Country Boy (vocal: Bon Bon Tunnell)
That Old Feeling (vocal: Carlotta Dale)

7.00PM WABC
SATURDAY NIGHT SWING SESSION No65
CBS Studio No1, 485 Madison Ave, NYC
Riverboat Shuffle (Colossal; nice clarinet; swell trumpet; bully saxes)
Star Dust (SAL FRANZELLA playing a wonderful clarinet)
Who? (SAL FRANZELLA again going the nuts with rhythm section)
I'm Coming, Virginia (CBS Band going the nuts in slow tempo)
Bob White (NAN WYNN, girl vocalist formerly with Hudson-DeLange, going the nuts)
St. Louis Blues (W. C. HANDY playing a muted trumpet)
East St. Louis (W. C. HANDY's latest composition played marvelously by the CBS Band under Leith Stevens trumpet; saxes; clarinets)
Honeysuckle Rose (FLETCHER HENDERSON playing swell piano)
It's Wearing Me Down (CHUCK RICHARDS singing swell: very good song)
Scattin' At The Kit Kat (CBS Band: ballsy; drums; saxes; brass)

■ SUNDAY 10 OCTOBER 1937

Played touch football in afternoon with Fred Patrick, Hollingshead, Paul Hallsey, and Fick. Had dinner at Jim Poe's house with Carolyn Bade, Nancy Long, Bobby Van Schilgan and Jim. Excellent time with Carolyn.

RADIO LOGS

11:30AM WNEW
SUNDAY MORNING SWING CONCERT
Criterion Theater, NYC
Inaugural program, with MARTIN BLOCK as Master of Ceremonies
After You (WNEW Studio Band: This band has got something; nice tenor sax)
Firecrackers (WNEW Studio Band doing an encore: nice drum break)
Black Bottom (Guest BUNNY BERIGAN playing wonderfully inspired trumpet; drums; trombone)
Caravan (MICKY MOZART, 16-yr-old boy, playing a swing harp: only fair)
If You Should Ever Leave (HELEN WARD, now a housewife, singing the nuts)
St. Louis Blues (SAMMY SPERGEL swingin' it on electric guitar: lousy)
A Study In Brown (WNEW Studio Band: lousy clarinet; fair wa-wa trombone; trumpet)
Ubangi Man (written & played by BUNNY BERIGAN: swell tenor sax; trombone; fair drums)
MEDLEY: *Organ Grinder Swing / The Merry-Go-Round Broke Down / Mr Ghost Goes To Town* (MICKY MOZART's harp)
You Can't Stop Me From Dreaming (WNEW Studio Band: tenor sax; trombone)
Honeysuckle Rose (Zippy's good violin on first chorus; BUNNY BERIGAN's marvelous low-down, dirty, swinging trumpet; fair clarinet; good trombone)
Between The Devil And The Deep Blue Sea (HELEN WARD singing good)
Russian Lullaby (WNEW Studio Band with BUNNY BERIGAN's wonderful trumpet: nuttsy)
La Cumparsita
Have You Got Any Castles, Baby?
Whoa, Babe (WNEW Studio Band: crappy drummer)

10:00PM WAAB
WOODY HERMAN
Normandie Ballroom, Boston
Muskrat Ramble (stupendous: Neil Reid; Saxie Mansfield's tenor; Woody; Frankie Carlson's drums)
Love Me Or Leave Me (Clarence Willard's trumpet)
In The Still Of The Night (vocal: Woody Herman)
That Old Feeling (vocal: Woody Herman)
Doctor Jazz (vocal: Woody Herman) (colossal)

■ MONDAY 11 OCTOBER 1937

I had dinner at Carolyn Bade's house in Hartsdale with Anne Wilson, Maurine Van Meter, Jim Poe and Hugh Pastoriza. Excellent time with Carolyn. She had 32 people at her house so we went out driving.

Swing Music Status Assured

Reception of Benny Goodman's Band at the Pennsylvania Settles All Argument.

By ALTON COOK,
World-Telegram Radio Editor.

There should be no misgivings about the status of swing music this season. The last couple of days have brought emphatic straws simply swirling around in the votes. Here's the evidence:—

Benny Goodman took his loud swing band into the Pennsylvania Hotel for the season Monday night, and the place was crowded. That, of course, is true of almost any big band's opening. Outside the ball room door stood a crowd of people, no notion of going in to brave the cover charge but standing with determination and tapping feet to Goodman's music. The hotel tried to disperse them occasionally. They melted each time and came back to tap toes contentedly. I never saw that before.

For his WABC broadcast last night, Benny Goodman moved into one of the New York theater studios. The announcer moved out to lead the usual studio applause after each swing tune and got not mere applause but cheers.

* * *

■ TUESDAY 12 OCTOBER 1937

RADIO LOGS

12:00 NOON WABC
CBS HOUSE BAND
'Swingin' The Blues', NYC
Columbus Day. I heard this program in Jim Branham's car with Hugh Pastoriza, Anne Wilson, Maurine Van Meter, and Carolyn Bade. Since we have no school today we went to Mt. Kisco to have a super-colossal time on a picnic. These past 4 days I've had a marvelous time with Carolyn!!
Aunt Hagar's Blues
Memphis Blues
Nothin' But The Blues
Crazy Blues

10:00PM WABC
BENNY GOODMAN
Camel Caravan, CBS Playhouse, NYC
Let's Dance (theme)
Satan Takes A Holiday (nuttsy: very original arrangement; Krupa; James; Stacy)
Let's Have Another Cigarette (vocal: Martha Tilton) (nice tenor sax)
Ciribiribin (featuring Harry James' excellent trumpet solo)
Roses In December (BG Trio) (very sweet but Wilson's marvelous piano work)
Somebody Loves Me (one of Benny's smoothest arrangements: Musso; James)
I Got Rhythm (BG Quartet) (COLOSSAL: all 4 great, especially Wilson)
You're Out Of This World (vocal: Martha Tilton) (very new song: trombone; Stacy)
Smiles (magnificent: Harry James' great solo; Benny)
Goodbye (closing theme)

11:00PM WABC
TOMMY DORSEY
Hotel Commodore, NYC
In The Mission By The Sea (vocal: Jack Leonard) (lousy song, recorded today)
A Simple Melody (swell new piece: Howard Smith's nuttsy piano)
My Secret Love Affair (vocal: Edythe Wright) (good: another new piece)
Mendelssohn's Spring Song (swell: Mince's clarinet; Erwin; Freeman)
If You Were Someone Else (vocal: Edythe Wright)
Once In A While (vocal: Edythe Wright & 3 Esquires) (swell sweet piece: Dorsey)
The Dipsy-Doodle (vocal: Edythe Wright)
Farewell My Love (vocal: Jack Leonard) (lousy: another stinking sweet song)
Symphony In Riffs (swell: Freeman; tricky sax runs; Dorsey; Tough)

■ WEDNESDAY 13 OCTOBER 1937

RECORDING SESSION

COUNT BASIE AND HIS ORCHESTRA
Recording session for Decca in New York City.
Buck Clayton, Ed Lewis, Bobby Hicks (t); Dan Minor, Benny Morton, Eddie Durham (tb); Earle Warren (as/voc); Lester Young, Herschel Evans (ts); Jack Washington (bar); Count Basie (p); Freddie Green (g); Walter Page (b); Jo Jones (d); Jimmy Rushing (voc)
I Keep Remembering (vJR) / *Out The Window* / *Don't You Miss Your Baby?* (vJR) / *Let Me Dream* (vEW)

RADIO LOGS

6:45PM WABC
FRANK DAILEY
Meadowbrook, N.J.
Swell: a real solid smooth band. Jerry Lawrence announced.
Miles Apart (vocal: Louise Wallace)
Messin' At The Meadowbrook (recently written by Frank Dailey: swell)
Once In A While (vocal: Louise Wallace) (swell: going to be a tremendous hit)
Someday Sweetheart (great: clarinet; sax)
On The Trail Of The Lonesome Pine
That Old Feeling

11:00PM WABC
BENNY GOODMAN
Hotel Pennsylvania, NYC
In The Shade Of The Old Apple Tree
That Old Feeling (vocal: Martha Tilton) (swell piece: no solos)
Moonlight On The Highway (good: James' short, fair solo; Stacy's nice solo)
Whispers In The Dark (BG Trio) (introduced as usual by Benny)
The Moon Got In My Eyes (vocal: Martha Tilton) (good, but lousy words: Musso)
Chlo-e (swell: Stacy's piano intro & solo; James' trumpet)
Avalon (BG Quartet) (introduced by Benny: nuttsy, especially Benny & Hampton)
I'd Like To See Some More Of Samoa (vocal: Martha Tilton) (fair)
Caravan (excellent: James' nuttsy solo; Krupa's drums; Benny)
Satan Takes A Holiday (very original arrangement: James; Benny)

■ THURSDAY 14 OCTOBER 1937

RECORDING SESSION

TOMMY DORSEY AND HIS ORCHESTRA
Recording session for Victor in New York City.
Tommy Dorsey (tb); Pee Wee Erwin, Lee Castle, Andy Ferretti (t); Les Jenkins, Earle Hagen (tb); Johnny Mince, Fred Stulce, Skeets Herfurt (cl/as); Bud Freeman (ts); Howard Smith (p); Carmen Mastren (g); Gene Traxler (b); Dave Tough (d); Edythe Wright, Jack Leonard (voc)
Getting Some Fun Out of Life (vEW) / *In The Mission By The Sea* (vJL) / *Moanin' In The Mornin'* (vEW) / *Down With Love* (vEW) / *Who?* (vJL & Band) / *The Dipsy Doodle* (vEW)

TOMMY DORSEY AND HIS CLAMBAKE SEVEN
Recording session for Victor in New York City.
Tommy Dorsey (tb); Pee Wee Erwin (t); Johnny Mince (cl); Bud Freeman (ts); Howard Smith (p); Carmen Mastren (g); Gene Traxler (b); Dave Tough (d); Edythe Wright (voc)
Nice Work If You Can Get It (vEW) / *You're A Sweetheart* (vEW)

RADIO LOGS

6.00PM WNEW
MAKE BELIEVE BALLROOM
CBS Studio, NYC
The Make Believe Ballroom is a program that is on several hours a day with many sponsors. Martin Block, who originated the program, is master of

ceremonies. On tonight's program, instead of playing recordings, he is having BUNNY BERIGAN and his band.
WONDERFUL! Bunny Berigan's Band is almost tops in every department; especially its original arrangements and unsurpassed and original solos.
A Study In Brown (nuttsy, very original arrangement: Bunny's trumpet; Auld; Dixon; Lee)
Why Talk About Love? (vocal: Gail Reese) (nice new song with that certain swing)
Let 'Er Go (vocal: Gale Reese) (swell, recently released on Victor: Sonny Lee's ballsy muted trombone)
That Old Feeling (vocal: Gail Reese) (Carolyn's favorite song now: Wettling's drums)
Frankie And Johnny (colossal: first chorus taken by sax section; Bunny's marvelous plunger trumpet backed by Wettling's nuttsy, solid drums; Auld's short tenor sax solo; Bunny again on a great unmuted solo; Auld again on a long marvelous solo with Wettling; Joe Dixon's wonderful, typical clarinet; Sonny Lee's swell trombone; Hank Wayland's colossal bass solo; George Wettling's ballsy drum solo; wonderful ending with whole band swinging)
I Want A New Romance (vocal: Gale Reese) (very new, and a swell tune, slow & swinging: Bunny)
Caravan (a 'different' arrangement of Ellington's great hit: Berigan's plunger trumpet; Lee's smooth trombone; nuttsy clarinets with Wettling's cymbals)
The Prisoner's Song (wonderful, fast, swingin': Berigan; Auld; Lee; Dixon)

7:00PM WHN
JIMMY DORSEY
Hotel Netherland-Plaza, Cincinnati, Ohio
Dorsey Dervish
Star Dust
I'm Getting Sentimental Over You
An Old Flame Never Dies (vocal: Bob Eberly)

■ FRIDAY 15 OCTOBER 1937

I met Carolyn at the train and Hughie met Nancy Long. We all went up to Maurine Van Meter's house. Carolyn and I went out walking alone. What a beautiful night, and what a girl!!!

RADIO LOGS

9:30PM WJZ
TOMMY DORSEY
Hotel Commodore, NYC
The Dipsy-Doodle (vocal: Edythe Wright)
If It's The Last Thing I Do (vocal: Jack Leonard)
Who? (vocal: Jack Leonard) (another 'Marie')
Soon
Love, You Funny Thing
I'll String Along With You (vocal: Edythe Wright)
My Blue Heaven

Jack Leonard

Tommy Dorsey

■ SATURDAY 16 OCTOBER 1937

RADIO LOGS

7.30PM WABC
SATURDAY NIGHT SWING SESSION No66
CBS Studio No1, 485 Madison Ave, NYC
Excellent. Paul Douglas announced. This broadcast featured stars from the Onyx Club which is managed by Joe Helbock, who's birthday is today.
After You (swell: CBS Band directed by Leith Stevens)
Darling Nellie Gray (MAXINE SULLIVAN, from the Onyx Club, singing swell with the Onyx Club Band led by bassist John Kirby with clarinetist Buster Bailey, trumpeter Frankie Newton, saxist Pete Brown, drummer O'Neil Spencer, trombonist Leo Watson and pianist Don Frye)
It Don't Mean A Thing (CBS Band going the nuts on Duke Ellington's old piece: swell tenor; trumpet)
Liza (LES LIEBER playing his usual excellent hot fife)
Honeysuckle Rose (LES LIEBER again, playing double-fife)
Oh, Lady Be Good (super-ballsy jam session with Onyx Club Band plus STUFF SMITH who just came to New York: Bailey's wonderful clarinet backed by John Kirby's solid bass; great trumpet chorus by Frankie Newton; Stuff Smith's real low-down, swingin' violin; Pete Brown's colossal alto sax; Leo Watson's marvelous hot vocal without words)
Loch Lomond (MAXINE SULLIVAN again singing slowly and nuttsy; Newton's trumpet)
Farewell Blues (colossal! CBS Band: excellent brass and sax sections; dirty trombone; Shoobe's wonderful solid bass solo; Hank Ross' marvelous tenor sax)

9:30PM WAAB
BLANCHE CALLOWAY
Southland, Boston
Gone With The Wind
Bugle Blues (featuring Harmonica Willie)
Rollin' Sam (vocal: Blanche Calloway)
Blue Lou

11:00PM WABC
BENNY GOODMAN
Hotel Pennsylvania, NYC
House Hop
So Many Memories (vocal: Martha Tilton)
My Honey's Lovin' Arms
Bob White (vocal: Martha Tilton)
Roses In December (BG Trio)
Marie
I'm A Ding Dong Daddy (From Dumas) (BG Quartet)
Loch Lomond (vocal: Martha Tilton)
Roll 'Em

11:30PM WMCA
TEDDY HILL
Savoy Ballroom, NYC
Always (nuttsy: Irving Berlin's grand old piece)
Prelude To A Stomp
Honeysuckle Rose
My Blue Heaven (vocal: Bill Dillard)

■ SUNDAY 17 OCTOBER 1937

RADIO LOGS

11:30AM WNEW
SUNDAY MORNING SWING CONCERT
International Casino, NYC
Unknown title (WNEW Studio Band directed by Merle Pitt)
The Dipsy Doodle (EDYTHE WRIGHT singing with Tommy Dorsey Band)
My Blue Heaven (SUE MITCHELL singing the nuts)
Beale Street Blues (MILT HERTH playing a nice organ)
Church Street Sobbin' Blues (swell: Merle Pitt's WMEW Studio Band)
Rosetta (featuring ZIPPO and his violin: lousy)

Canadian Capers (TOMMY DORSEY's Band: lousy piece but swell trombone by Dorsey)
Black And Tan Fantasy (MILT HERTH at organ again)
Trees (JACK LEONARD singing very sweetly with TOMMY DORSEY Band)
Sophisticated Swing (WNEW Studio Band: good)
They All Laughed (SUE MITCHELL singing colossally: she's plenty O.K.)
Sweet Sue (SAMMY SPERGEL going lousy on his electric guitar)
Swing That Music (TOMMY DORSEY Band: Tommy's superb trombone!)
The Old Grey Bonnet (MILT HERTH at organ again)
Rigamarole (WNEW Studio Band: good drumming)
Song Of India (TOMMY DORSEY Band: Tommy's nice trombone!)
Midnight In A Madhouse (WNEW Studio Band concluding program)

■ MONDAY 18 OCTOBER 1937

RECORDING SESSION

ART SHAW AND HIS NEW MUSIC
Recording session for Brunswick in New York City.
Art Shaw (cl/ldr); John Best, Malcolm Crain, Tom di Carlo (t); Harry Rogers, George Arus (tb); Les Robinson, Harry Freeman (as); Tony Pastor (ts/voc); Jules Rubin (ts); Les Burness (p); Al Avola (g); Ben Ginsberg (b); Cliff Leeman (d); Dolores O'Neil (voc)
Let 'Er Go / A Strange Loneliness (vDO'N) / Monsoon / I'm Yours / Just You, Just Me / Free For All

RADIO LOGS

7:00PM WHN
JIMMY DORSEY
Hotel Netherland-Plaza, Cincinnati, Ohio
They All Laughed
Let's Call A Heart A Heart
You And I Know

■ TUESDAY 19 OCTOBER 1937

I bought 12 old records today at Ferris' Music Store in Bronxville. I got all 12 for 3 dollars or 25 cents apiece. There were 2 Brunswicks and 10 Victors: Frankie Trumbauer's *Break It Down* and *Juba Dance* (Brunswick 6763); Duke Ellington's *Bundle Of Blues* and *Get Yourself A New Broom* (Brunswick 6607); Fletcher Henderson's Connie's Inn Orchestra *Sugar Foot Stomp* and *Singin' The Blues* (Victor 22721); Duke Ellington's *Bugle Call Rag* and *Dinah* (Victor 22938); Duke Ellington's *Mississippi* and *Flaming Youth* (Victor 24057); Duke Ellington's *Doin' The Voom Voom* and *Swanee Shuffle* (Victor 24121); Louis Armstrong's *That's My Home* and *Hobo, You Can't Ride This Train* (Victor 24200); Louis Armstrong's *You'll Wish You'd Never Been Born* and *I Hate To Leave You Now* (Victor 24204); Bennie Moten's *New Orleans* and *Lafayette* (Victor 24216); Louis Armstrong's *Hustlin' And Bustlin' For Baby* and *I Gotta Right To Sing The Blues* (Victor 24233); Duke Ellington's *Cocktails For Two* and *Live And Love Tonight* (Victor 24617); and Duke Ellington's *I Met My Waterloo* (Victor 24719-B) backed by Jerry Johnson's *Missouri Misery* (Victor 24719-A).

RADIO LOGS

12:00 NOON WABC
CBS HOUSE BAND
'Swingin' The Blues', NYC
Jazz Me Blues (colossal: magnificent solos by tenor sax; trumpet; trombone; solid drums)

Deep Forest (written by Earl Hines—wonderful: rubber wa-wa dirty muted trumpet; slow blue ending)
Beale Street Blues (trumpeter Willis Kelly singing swell; swell solid drumming; clarinets)
A Good Man Is Hard To Find

10:00PM WABC
BENNY GOODMAN
Camel Caravan, CBS Playhouse, NYC
Let's Dance (theme)
Sunny Disposish (swell: Benny; Harry James)
So Many Memories (vocal: Martha Tilton) (Vernon Brown's trombone)
Remember Me (BG Trio) (fair)
Roll 'Em (colossal: Stacy; Krupa; Benny; James)
Rose Room (a new, diferent, arrangement: Musso with trombone; Stacy)
Everybody Loves My Baby (BG Quartet) (wonderful)
Popcorn Man (vocal: Martha Tilton) (new piece written by Will Hudson: James)
Darktown Strutters' Ball (magnificent: Benny; Harry James' great solo; Musso; clarinets; Krupa)
Goodbye (closing theme)

■ WEDNESDAY 20 OCTOBER 1937

RADIO LOGS

11:00PM WABC
BENNY GOODMAN
Hotel Pennsylvania, NYC
Stardust On The Moon (vocal: Martha Tilton) (fair commercial tune: Musso)
Dear Old Southland (nuttsy: James' high trumpet intro; tenor; Stacy)
So Many Memories (vocal: Martha Tilton) (swell sweet piece in typical Goodman style)
One O'Clock Jump (WONDERFUL: Stacy; Musso; Vernon Brown, etc)
Body And Soul (BG Trio) (one of the grandest pieces ever written!!)
Me, Myself And I (vocal: Martha Tilton) (swell arrangement: James' short solo; Benny)
Sweet Sue (BG Quartet) (pure nuttsy unsurpassable improvisation)
When It's Sleepy Time Down South (slower tempo than record: Benny; James; Musso)
Camel Hop (Vernon Brown's fair trombone)

12:00 MIDNIGHT WEAF
WOODY HERMAN
Normandie Ballroom, Boston
SWELL.
Weary Blues (colossal: Neil Reid's wonderful blues trombone; Yoder's solid bass; Herman)
You're My Desire (vocal: Woody Herman)
It Happened Down In Dixieland (vocal: Woody Herman) (WONDERFUL: Herman's great vocal & chorus; Saxie Mansfield)
I Can't Give You Anything But Love (Gordon Jenkins' special arrangement)
Can I Forget You? (vocal: Woody Herman)
MEDLEY: **You And I Know / If You Were Someone Else**
In The Still Of The Night (vocal: Woody Herman)
Twilight In Turkey (swell original arrangement: Frank Carlson's solid drumming)

12:00 MIDNIGHT WABC
TOMMY DORSEY
Hotel Commodore, NYC
Fair.
Getting Some Fun Out Of Life (vocal: Edythe Wright)
Everything You Said Came True (vocal: Jack Leonard)
It's My Turn Now (vocal: Edythe Wright)
Marie (vocal: Jack Leonard & Band) (too fast)
The Dipsy-Doodle (vocal: Edythe Wright)
In A Mist (written by Bix Beiderbecke: Smith's piano; clarinet)
Who? (vocal: Jack Leonard) (another 'Marie')
Goodbye Jonah (vocal: Edythe Wright)

12:30AM WABC
BOB CROSBY
Palomar Ballroom, Los Angeles
Colossal.
Summertime (theme) (grand slow theme written by the late George Gershwin)
Bob White (great relaxed swing: Yank Lawson's trumpet; Miller's tenor; clarinet)
Roses In December (vocal: Kay Weber) (swell: Miller's grand tenor; clarinet)
The First Time I Saw You (vocal: Bob Crosby) (Lawson's sending solo; Matlock; Miller; Bauduc)
Gin Mill Blues (super-grand: Bob Zurke's magnificent piano throughout; Eddie Miller's colossal, relaxed tenor sax, Matty Matlock's clarinet; Ray Bauduc's marvelous drum breaks)
Remember Me (vocal: Bob Crosby) (rather silly words but a big hit: nice swingy ending)
She's Tall, She's Tan, She's Terrific (vocal: Nappy Lamare) (Matlock's clarinet; Smith's trombone; Lawson's trumpet)
That Old Feeling (vocal: Kay Weber) (again, Miller's tenor sax steals the show; clarinet)
South Rampart Street Parade (written by Ray Bauduc and arranged by Bob Haggart: rhythm section; Matlock's fast, low-registered clarinet with Bauduc's great backing; whole band jamming; what a marvelous SWING band, so relaxed!)

■ THURSDAY 21 OCTOBER 1937

My favorite bands right now are (not in order): Benny Goodman, Red Norvo, Bob Crosby, Duke Ellington, Bunny Berigan, Count Basie, Woody Herman.

Count Basie and Billie Holiday open tonight at the Meadowbrook in New Jersey for two weeks.

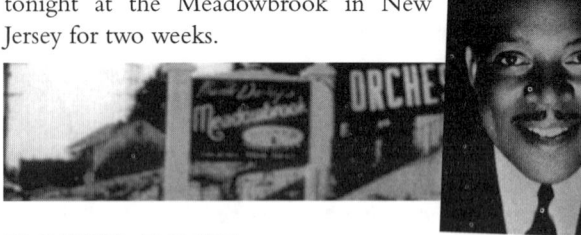

RADIO LOGS

11:00PM WABC
CAB CALLOWAY
Cotton Club, NYC
Swell. Chu Berry's tenor sax solos are still great and outstanding and make every number worthwhile.
Have You Met Miss Jones? (vocal: Cab Calloway)
Rustle Of Swing
I Love To Sing-a (vocal: Cab Calloway)
You Do Me Good (vocal: Cab Calloway)
Save Me, Sister (vocal: Cab Calloway)
Chinese Rhythm (vocal: Cab Calloway)
'Way Down Yonder In New Orleans (vocal: Cab Calloway)
Minnie The Moocher (theme, vocal: Cab Calloway) (theme played in full with vocal)

11:30PM WJZ
JIMMY DORSEY
Congress Hotel, Chicago
This is Dorsey's opening night at the Congress Casino of the Congress Hotel in Chicago.
Sandman (theme) (nuttsy slow theme recorded 2 years ago on Decca)
Just Lately (vocal: Bob Eberly) (swell new sweet piece: Camarata's trumpet; clarinet)
Have You Got Any Castles, Baby? (vocal: Bob Eberly) (lousy piece: Dorsey's clarinet)
Flight Of The Bumble Bee (good: sweet trombone; Slack's nice piano; drums; Dorsey)
You And I Know (vocal: Bob Eberly) (another nice commercial: sweet trumpet)

I Cried For You (nuttsy arrangement: Dorsey's clarinet and wa-wa brass; Frazier's tenor)
Is It Love Or Infatuation? (vocal: Bob Eberly) (too commercial: no worthwhile solos)
After You (vocal: Don Mattison) (nuttsy arrangement of recent hit: grand tenor sax; trombone; piano)
MEDLEY: *Moonglow / Can't We Be Friends?* (Dorsey's fair clarinet)
Parade Of The Milk Bottle Tops (Dorsey's best: McKinley's fine drumming; Dorsey's alto; trombone)

12:00 MIDNIGHT WOR
BENNY GOODMAN
Hotel Pennsylvania, NYC
Let's Dance (theme)
Minnie The Moocher's Wedding Day (grand arrangement: Benny; James; tricky brass)
Afraid To Dream (vocal: Martha Tilton) (swell recent song hit: recorded in July)
Moonlight On The Highway (good: Stacy; Krupa)
Once In A While (vocal: Martha Tilton) (James' nuttsy trumpet on 1st chorus of this hit tune; Benny)
Sugar Foot Stomp (WONDERFUL: James; Benny; clarinets)
Popcorn Man (vocal: Martha Tilton) (recently written by Will Hudson: fair)
More Than You Know (very likeable arrangement of a grand piece: Benny; Krupa)
The Dixieland Band (vocal: Martha Tilton) (colossal: Brown's trombone; Benny)
The Sheik Of Araby (James' colossal solo; fair saxes; Benny)
I Know That You Know (nuttsy: Benny's great work; Krupa)

12:30AM WABC
RED NORVO
Hotel St. Francis, San Francisco
GREAT! I still think Mildred Bailey is tops and how I love Norvo's soft-subtle swing.
Russian Lullaby (just released last week on Brunswick: Norvo's nice xylophone; saxes)
Loving You (vocal: Mildred Bailey) (grand: Mildred layin' 'em low; sweet trombone)
Yours And Mine (vocal: Stew Pletcher) (swell: Haymer's short solo; D'Amico; Red Norvo)
Night And Day (slow and sweet: muted trumpet; wonderful long solo by Norvo on xylophone; clarinet)
That Old Feeling (vocal: Mildred Bailey) (another swell commercial piece: Norvo)
The Lady is A Tramp (vocal: Stew Pletcher) (lousy song, but Haymer's nice tenor sax)
'Long About Midnight (vocal: Mildred Bailey) (great vocal)
I Never Knew (Pletcher's swell trumpet; Norvo's swell xylophone)

RECORDING SESSION

BENNY GOODMAN AND HIS ORCHESTRA
Recording session for Victor in New York City.
Benny Goodman (clarinet); Chris Griffin, Harry James, Ziggy Elman (trumpets); Red Ballard, Murray McEachern (trombones); George Koenig, Hymie Shertzer (alto sax); Art Rollini, Vido Musso (tenor sax); Jess Stacy (piano); Allan Reuss (guitar); Harry Goodman (bass); Gene Krupa (drums); Martha Tilton (vocal)
Let That Be A Lesson To You (vMT) / *Can't Teach My Old Heart New Tricks* (vMT) / *I've Hitched My Wagon To A Star* (vMT) / *Pop-Corn Man* (vMT)

MAXINE SULLIVAN
Recording session for Vocalion in New York City.
Maxine Sullivan (voc); Charlie Shavers (t); Buster Bailey (cl); Pete Brown (as); Claude Thornhill (p); John Kirby (b); O'Neil Spencer (d)
Easy To Love (vMS) / *The Folks Who Live On The Hill* (vMS) / *Darling Nellie Gray* (vMS) / *Nice Work If You Can Get It* (vMS)

FRIDAY 22 OCTOBER 1937

Hugh Pastoriza and myself decided to go down and see Benny Goodman and his great orchestra at the Madhattan Room of the Hotel Pennsylvania at 7th Avenue and 33rd Street. We invited Nancy Long and Carolyn Bade to go with us. Before leaving Bronxville we all had dinner at Hughie's house after which we caught the 8:09 train to Grand Central from where we took a taxi to the Hotel Penn because it was raining pretty hard. We got a table near the band at about 9:00, just after the Quartet had finished playing. We didn't get anything to eat but just paid the 75cents cover charge. Later on several other boys came: Morningstar, Pinger, Van Shilgan, Poe, Low, and Jack Lauder, but they sat at a different table. We all had an excellent time. I danced every dance with Carolyn and, during the all too often intermissions, we got autographs (Gordon Griffin, Martha Tilton, Vernon Brown, Ziggy Elman, Jess Stacy, Lionel Hampton, Gene Goodman, Gene Krupa, Art Rollini and Harry Goodman) and talked to them and listened to Teddy Wilson at the piano.

As far as I remember, the band played: *Afraid To Dream* (vocal: Martha Tilton); *Peckin'*; *Roll 'Em*; *Can't We Be Friends?* (Ballard's trombone); *Stardust*; *One O'Clock Jump* (something terrific); *My Honey's Lovin' Arms* (Rollini's tenor); *Remember* (Musso's tenor sax); *Bob White* (Martha Tilton singing – Benny Goodman whistling); *Loch Lomond* (vocal: Martha Tilton); *That Old Feeling* (vocal: Martha Tilton); *I Can't Give You Anything But Love* (vocal: Martha Tilton); *Caravan*; *Chlo-e*; *Stompin' At The Savoy* (Brown's nuttsy trombone; Rollini); *Me, Myself And I* (vocal: Martha Tilton); *Once In A While* (vocal: Martha Tilton); *Big John Special*, and many others.

Outstanding in the band were the great solos of Benny, Harry James and Vernon Brown and the great drumming of Gene Krupa which excited Carolyn very much. The sax solos by Rollini and Musso were also very good and the few solos that Elman and Griffin took were tops. In other words, the whole band is still tops having no recent changes in personnel except that Murray McEachern left 3 weeks ago to join Glen Gray's Casa Loma Band, now at the Hotel New Yorker. Vernon Brown, a slight, red-headed newcomer, has officially taken his place although, because of his newness to New York, the Union won't allow him to play more than 3 days a week with the band. Benny likes his hot solos very much and sure does have a right to. I'm not sure as to how smooth and sweet he can be but Ballard can do all of that with ease. I had a long talk with Ziggy Elman who told me that he got married two weeks ago and that Allan Reuss got married last month, making only 4 unmarried men in the band. Ziggy is having a lot of trouble with his lip and seemed pretty tired out. In fact, the whole band has been going at a terrific clip and all of them have had to take short rests. But the trumpeters have the hardest job because of their continual use of their lips and lungs. Krupa's work is muscular so he gets used to it. Shertzer is still the same good-natured fellow who leads the sax section splendidly. Ziggy promised to send me a picture of himself and, to my surprise, told me that McEachern took the solo in the Victor recording of *Can't We Be Friends?* He told us of how musicians get tired of the same band and how Art Shaw's band was getting nowhere. Tilton looked at this book with much interest and said that MCA had just gotten pictures of her. She seems very nice, is petite, and has a swell figure and a nice voice – the best vocalist with Benny since Helen Ward. The band recorded four commercial sides for Victor yesterday, including *Popcorn Man*. McEachern sat in with the band on these four sides. Another interesting thing was that Harry James played the drums in two numbers in the absence of Krupa. During the evening several dancers from Arthur Murray's gave an exhibition of 'The Big Apple' dance which is so popular now. They were good, but the dancers at the Savoy Ballroom in Harlem are much better.

We finally had to leave at 12:48 to catch the 1:00am train home to Bronxville from where Mr. Pastoriza drove Carolyn home to Hartsdale and Nancy home to Scarsdale. Hughie and I, after an excellent evening, got home at 2:45am.

SATURDAY 23 OCTOBER 1937

RADIO LOGS

7.00PM WABC
SATURDAY NIGHT SWING SESSION No67
CBS Studio No1, 485 Madison Ave, NYC
ELLA FITZGERALD and CHICK WEBB are guests this week.
Rose Room (CBS Band directed by Leith Stevens: clarinet; saxes)
If It's The Last Thing I Do (ELLA FITZGERALD singing swell with CBS Band)
Clap Hands! Here Comes Charlie (CHICK WEBB's great drums; Ross' tenor sax; trombone)
If You Were Someone Else (CBS Band: slightly commercial but good)
Oh, Lady Be Good (great: Toots Mondello on E-flat alto sax, magnificent tone)
Exactly Like You (KARAWANIS BROTHERS: Len on guitar; Jimmy on clarinet and trumpet; bass)
Rock It For Me (ELLA FITZGERALD and CBS Band going the nuts: new song written especially for Ella)
Caravan (colossal smooth arrangement: great clarinets & saxes; muted trumpet)

11:00PM WABC
BENNY GOODMAN
Hotel Pennsylvania, NYC
Let's Dance (theme)
In The Shade Of The Old Apple Tree
You're My Desire (vocal: Martha Tilton)
Am I Blue?
Where Or When (BG Trio)
Someday Sweetheart
Bob White (vocal: Martha Tilton)
Nagasaki (BG Quartet)
Yours And Mine (vocal: Martha Tilton)
Jam Session
Goodbye (closing theme)

12:30AM WABC
BOB CROSBY
Palomar Ballroom, Los Angeles
Heard this program at Carolyn Bade's house in Hartsdale after attending the Edgemont Dance in Scarsdale.
The Moon Got In My Eyes (vocal: Bob Crosby)
You Can't Have Everything (vocal: Kay Weber)
Squeeze Me (nuttsy, especially ending: Bob Zurke's piano)
The Loveliness Of You (vocal: Bob Crosby)
Little Rock Getaway (wonderful: Bob Zurke's piano; Yank Lawson's trumpet)
Roses In December (vocal: Kay Weber)
Bugle Call Rag (marvelous: Ray Bauduc's unsurpassable drums; Bob Haggart's nuttsy bass solo; Matlock's colossal low-register clarinet; Miller's tenor sax)

■ SUNDAY 24 OCTOBER 1937

RADIO LOGS

11:30AM WNEW
SUNDAY MORNING SWING CONCERT
International Casino, NYC
Why Talk About Love (ERSKINE HAWKINS playing a swell trumpet solo)
Nagasaki (Merle Pitts' WNEW Studio Band going good)
She's Tall, She's Tan, She's Terrific (ERSKINE HAWKINS' grand trumpet)
Satan Takes A Holiday (WNEW Band good: fair drum breaks; clarinets)
Marie (SAMMY WEISS singing a nuttsy hot vocal; Zippo's nice violin)
Swing Brother Swing (ELLA FITZGERALD singing the nuts: great)
In A Little Spanish Town (CHICK WEBB's Quintet: marvelous drumming)
A Study In Brown (WNEW Studio Band going darn good: trombone; tenor)
Swamp Fire (WNEW Studio Band concluding the program: pretty good)

■ MONDAY 25 OCTOBER 1937

RECORDING SESSION

FLETCHER HENDERSON AND HIS ORCHESTRA
Recording session for Vocalion in New York City.
Fletcher Henderson (p/ldr); Dick Vance, Russell Smith, Emmett Berry (t); John McConnell, Albert Wynn, Ed Cuffee (tb); Jerry Blake (cl/as/voc); Hilton Jefferson (cl/as); Elmer Williams, Ben Webster (ts); Lawrence Lucie (g); Israel Crosby (b); Pete Suggs (d/vib); Chuck Richards (voc)
If It's The Last Thing I Do (vCR) / *Sing You Sinners* / *You're In Love With Love* (vCR) / *Stealin' Apples*

WOODY HERMAN AND HIS ORCHESTRA
Recording session for Decca in New York City.
Woody Herman (cl/as/voc/ldr); Clarence Willard, Kermit Simmons (t); Joe Bishop (fh); Neal Reid (tb); Jack Ferrier, Ray Hopfner (as); Saxie Mansfield, Pete Johns (ts); Nick Hupfer (vln); Tommy Linehan (p); Oliver Mathewson (g); Walter Yoder (b); Frank Carlson (d)
I Double Dare You (vWH) / *Why Talk About Love?* (vWH) / *My Fine Feathered Friend* (vWH) / *You're A Sweetheart* (vWH)

■ TUESDAY 26 OCTOBER 1937

RECORDING SESSION

COOTIE WILLIAMS & HIS RUGCUTTERS
Recording session for Vocalion in New York City.
Cootie Williams (t); Juan Tizol (vtb); Otto Hardwick (as); Barney Bigard (cl/ts); Harry Carney (bar); Duke Ellington (p); Billy Taylor (b); Sonny Greer (d); Jerry Kruger (voc)
Jubilesta (2 takes) / *Watchin'* (vJK) / *Pigeons And Peppers* / *I Can't Give You Anything But Love*

RADIO LOGS

10:00PM WABC
BENNY GOODMAN
Camel Caravan, CBS Playhouse, NYC
Let's Dance (theme)
Changes (nuttsy: swell solos by Harry James, Musso, and Benny)
Once In A While (vocal: Martha Tilton) (swell: Harry James' trumpet on first chorus)
Camel Hop (grand: James and Musso with Krupa's great drums)
In A Mist (written by Bix Beiderbecke and played by Jess Stacy on the piano)
It Don't Mean A Thing If It Ain't Got That Swing (BG Quartet) (great)
Everything You Said Came True (vocal: Martha Tilton) (swell vocal)
Life Goes To A Party (just written by Harry James' and the band, and played for the first time: Musso's short, nuttsy solo; Stacy's piano; James' marvelous high-note trumpet; biting brass section; Krupa)
Goodbye (closing theme)

11:05PM WABC
TOMMY DORSEY
Hotel Commodore, NYC
Good.
La Golondrina (first time I've heard this number: Freeman's swell tenor sax)
Moanin' In The Mornin' (vocal: Edythe Wright) (very new piece: long and slow)
That Old Feeling (vocal: Edythe Wright)
The Morning After (vocal: Jack Leonard)
The Dipsy Doodle (vocal: Edythe Wright)
Who? (vocal: Jack Leonard & band) (swell)
Swing That Music
I'm Getting Sentimental Over You (theme)

11:30PM WJZ
JIMMY DORSEY
Congress Hotel, Chicago
Sandman (theme)
Just Lately (vocal: Bob Eberly)
The Moon Got In My Eyes (vocal: Bob Eberly)
Boston Tea Party (vocal: Don Mattison) (recorded on Decca: Dorsey's alto)
MEDLEY: *Body And Soul* / *How Am I To Know?* / *Rosetta* (nuttsy sweet medley)
Parade Of The Milk Bottle Tops (great, very relaxed: alto; trumpet; drums)
Sweet Leilani (vocal: Bob Eberly) (very sweet but good: 3 trombones)
By Heck (grand old piece: colossal trombone; Slack's ballsy piano; Dorsey's clarinet)
The Love Bug Will Bite You (vocal: Ray McKinley) (nuttsy: comical vocal)
I Cried For You

11:45PM WOR
ISHAM JONES
Hotel Lincoln, NYC
Lousy.
I Want A New Romance
In The Still Of The Night
Misty Moonlight (recently written by Isham Jones)
Why Talk About Love?

■ WEDNESDAY 27 OCTOBER 1937

RECORDING SESSION

CHICK WEBB ORCHESTRA
Recording session for Decca in New York City.
Ella Fitzgerald (voc); Mario Bauza, Taft Jordan, Bobby Stark (t); Sandy Williams, Nat Story (tb); Louis Jordan (as); Chauncey Haughton (cl/as); Ted McRae (ts); Wayman Carver (ts/fl); Tommy Fulford (p); Bobby Johnson (g); Beverly Peer (b); Chick Webb (d)
Just A Simple Melody (vEF) / *I Got A Guy* (vEF) / *Holiday In Harlem* (vEF) / *Strictly Jive*

RADIO LOGS

11:00PM WABC
BENNY GOODMAN
Hotel Pennsylvania, NYC
Let's Dance (theme)
When Buddha Smiles (nuttsy old piece: colossal sax section; tenor sax; Benny)
Tears In My Heart (vocal: Martha Tilton) (very good: swell arrangement and song)
Cherry (nuttsy: James' swell trumpet; rasping brass; Benny; saxes)
Bob White (vocal: Martha Tilton) (nice vocal; Benny whistling)
Swing Low, Sweet Chariot (swell: Musso's tenor sax; Krupa; trumpet)
Star Dust (marvelous Henderson arrangement: Harry James' trumpet)
The Lady Is A Tramp (vocal: Martha Tilton) (lousy piece, fair arrangement)
A Handful Of Keys (BG Quartet) (wonderful, especially Wilson's fine piano)
So Many Memories (vocal: Martha Tilton)
Swingtime In The Rockies (Musso's tenor)
Goodbye (closing theme)

11:30PM WMCA
WILLIE BRYANT
Apollo Theater, NYC
King Porter Stomp (WONDERFUL, very long colossal arrangement: ballsy long trombone solo; grand tenor sax and trumpet)

■ THURSDAY 28 OCTOBER 1937

RADIO LOGS

11:45PM WJZ
BOB CROSBY
Palomar Ballroom, Los Angeles
MARVELOUS! I heard this program in Jim Branham's car with Carolyn Bade. Because there's no school tomorrow we drove around all night having a good time.
She's Tall, She's Tan, She's Terrific (vocal: Nappy Lamare)
Squeeze Me
Bob White (nuttsy swing arrangement–the best I ever heard: Matlock's clarinet)
Remember Me (vocal: Bing Crosby) (Bob's famous brother BING singing the nuts: such swell informality)
South Rampart Street Parade (MAGNIFICENT!: Ray Bauduc's great drums)

12:00 MIDNIGHT WOR
BENNY GOODMAN
Hotel Pennsylvania, NYC
I heard the first half of this program in Jim Branham's car after driving around with the sweetest thing in the world (C.B.).
When You And I Were Young, Maggie
You And I Know (vocal: Martha Tilton) (very good: swell arrangement & song)
Can't We Be Friends? (colossal: Ballard's trombone)
Big John Special (MAGNIFICENT: Stacy; James)
Farewell, My Love (vocal: Martha Tilton) (swell ballad)
The Lady Is A Tramp (vocal: Martha Tilton & Benny Goodman) (fair)
Caravan (marvelous: Benny; Harry James' trumpet; Krupa's tom-toms)
That Old Feeling (vocal: Martha Tilton) (Stacy's intro)
Stompin' At The Savoy (nuttsy: Brown's ballsy trombone; Rollini)

■ FRIDAY 29 OCTOBER 1937

RECORDING SESSION

BENNY GOODMAN TRIO/QUARTET
Recording session for Victor in New York City.
Lionel Hampton (vib); Teddy Wilson (p); Benny Goodman (cl); Gene Krupa (d); Martha Tilton (voc)
Where Or When (BG Trio) / *Silhouetted In The Moonlight* (BG Trio, vMT) / *Vieni, Vieni* (BG Quartet)

■ SATURDAY 30 OCTOBER 1937

RADIO LOGS

7.00PM WABC
SATURDAY NIGHT SWING SESSION No68
Vine Street, Hollywood, Cal
Bob White (BOB CROSBY's entire orchestra playing the nuts: Smith's trombone)
I Can't Give You Anything But Love, Baby (The one and only LOUIS ARMSTRONG singing and playing grand trumpet with Crosby's band)
Squeeze Me (BOB CROSBY's Band going wonderfully: Bob Zurke's great piano; Eddie Miller's blue tenor sax; whole band swingin' something terrific!)
That Old Feeling (CONNIE BOSWELL singing sweetly: Lawson's trumpet)
The Penguin (RAYMOND SCOTT Quintet playing his latest piece: Harris' tenor)
War Dance For Wooden Indians (Scott's Quintet: Harris; Williams' drums)
Muskrat Ramble (LOUIS ARMSTRONG sitting in with Crosby's band: I never heard Armstrong play such great, inspired stuff)
South Rampart Street Parade (Crosby's Band playing some of the greatest Dixieland swing ever done: Matlock's colossal low blues clarinet. Too short!)

11:00PM WABC
BENNY GOODMAN
Hotel Pennsylvania, NYC
Makin' Whoopee
Farewell, My Love (vocal: Martha Tilton)
The Lady Is A Tramp (vocal: Martha Tilton & Benny Goodman)
Oh, Lady Be Good (BG Trio)
Love Me Or Leave Me
Once In A While (vocal: Martha Tilton)
Everybody Loves My Baby (BG Quartet)
You And I Know (vocal: Martha Tilton)
Life Goes To A Party

■ SUNDAY 31 OCTOBER 1937

George Fick and myself planned to go down to the Polo Grounds and see the New York Giants play the Chicago Bears in a professional football game. Much to our disgust we found that the seats were all sold out in the biggest crowd in 12 years. We finally went to the Savoy Ballroom after getting all mixed up on the damn subway, arriving there at

4:00pm when the Savoy Sultans began to play. We met these two white guys of God only knows what nationality. They thought that George and I were Italian brothers. I never laughed so much in my life. Much to our surprise we saw Jo Jones, Count Basie's fine drummer, and Frankie Newton, that grand trumpet player from the Onyx Club, with a nice white girl. The Savoy Sultans are a 9-piece combination who are not smooth but are very enthusiastic and give out plenty. The two trumpeters are fair and the two tenor sax soloists are better than fair. At 5:00pm Chick Webb's Band came in and began to play until 6:00. *Just A Simple Melody* (recorded with Ella Fitzgerald last week on Decca) and *Clap Hands! Here Comes Charlie* were the two outstanding numbers, being played twice each. After listening to the music until 7:30 we left to get the train home.

RADIO LOGS

11:30AM WNEW
SUNDAY MORNING SWING CONCERT
Criterion Theater, NYC
Yours And Mine (BILLIE HOLIDAY singing with COUNT BASIE at the piano: swell)
I Ain't Got Nobody (COUNT BASIE playing a grand piano: nutsy)
I'll See You In My Dreams (SAMMY SPERGEL playing good guitar)
Just A Simple Melody (THE ANDREWS SISTERS singing pretty good)
Melody In F (Merle Pitts' WNEW Studio Band playing swell: sax)
High, Wide And Handsome

11:30PM WJZ
JIMMY DORSEY
Congress Hotel, Chicago
Star Dust
I'm Getting Sentimental Over You
Flight Of The Bumble Bee
Once In A While (vocal: Bob Eberly)
Parade Of The Milk Bottle Tops
Time On My Hands
Dorsey Dervish
After You (vocal: Don Mattison)
An Old Flame Never Dies (vocal: Bob Eberly)
Waddlin' At The Waldorf

NOVEMBER 1937

Hotel Pennsylvania: **Benny Goodman**
Hotel Commodore: **Tommy Dorsey**
Hotel New Yorker: **Glen Gray**
Hotel Lincoln: **Isham Jones**

Apollo Theater: **Fletcher Henderson** (–4); **Count Basie** (5–11); **Andy Kirk** (12–18); **Four Ink Spots/Edgar Hayes** (19–25); **Erskine Hawkins** (26–)
Paramount Theater: **Tommy Dorsey** (3–16); **Bunny Berigan** (17–)
Loew's State Theater: **Ted Lewis** (4–10)

Cotton Club: **Cab Calloway**
Hickory House: **Joe Marsala**
Onyx Club: **John Kirby / Maxine Sullivan**
Famous Door: (opens at 66 W52nd on Nov 25) **Louis Prima**
Nick's: **Bobby Hackett**

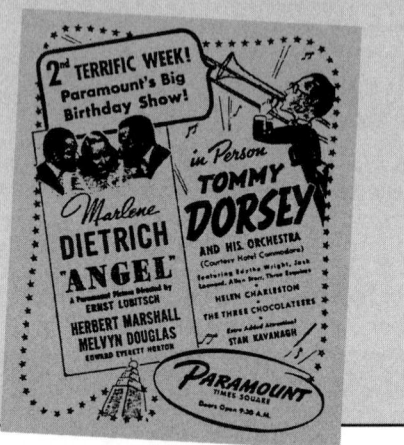

■ MONDAY 1 NOVEMBER 1937

RECORDING SESSION

BILLIE HOLIDAY & TEDDY WILSON ORCHESTRA
Recording session for Brunswick in NYC.
Buck Clayton (t); Prince Robinson (cl/ts); Vido Musso (cl/ts); Teddy Wilson (p); Allan Reuss (g); Walter Page (b); Cozy Cole (d); Billie Holiday (v)
Nice Work If You Can Get It / Things Are Looking Up / My Man / Can't Help Lovin' That Man

CHICK WEBB ORCHESTRA
Recording session for Decca in New York City.
Ella Fitzgerald (voc); Mario Bauza, Taft Jordan, Bobby Stark (t); Sandy Williams, Nat Story (tb); Louis Jordan (as); Chauncey Haughton (cl/as); Ted McRae (ts); Wayman Carver (ts/f); Tommy Fulford (p); Bobby Johnson (g); Beverly Peer (b); Chick Webb (d)
Rock It For Me (vEF) / *Squeeze Me* / *Harlem Congo*

RADIO LOGS

11:00PM WABC
GLEN GRAY
Hotel New Yorker, NYC
Trombonist Murray McEachern joined Glen Gray's Casa Loma band 3 weeks ago, replacing Fritz Hummel.
Goblin Band
Farewell My Love (vocal: Kenny Sargent)
Yankee Doodle Band (vocal: Pee Wee Hunt)
Whoa, Babe (vocal: Pee Wee Hunt)
Copenhagen
Smoke Rings (theme)

■ TUESDAY 2 NOVEMBER 1937

RECORDING SESSION

CHICK WEBB ORCHESTRA
Recording session for Decca in New York City.
Ella Fitzgerald (voc); Mario Bauza, Taft Jordan, Bobby Stark (t); Sandy Williams, Nat Story (tb); Louis Jordan (as); Chauncey Haughton (cl/as); Ted McRae (ts); Wayman Carver (ts/fl); Tommy Fulford (p); Bobby Johnson (g); Beverly Peer (b); Chick Webb (d)
I Want To Be Happy (vEF) / *Hallelujah!*

RADIO LOGS

10:00PM WABC
BENNY GOODMAN
Camel Caravan, CBS Playhouse, NYC
Let's Dance (theme)
Chicago (swell, fairly fast: Benny's 2 solos; James; Musso)
Time On My Hands (BG Trio) (sweet, but very good)
The Lady Is A Tramp (vocal: Martha Tilton) (lousy piece)
After You've Gone (guest DAVY NEWMAN playing an O.K. violin)
Unknown title (guest EMILIO CACERES playing a hot swing violin: swell parts but too fast)
Vieni, Vieni (BG Quartet) (nuttsy swinging, especially by Hampton; Krupa's fine breaks)
Farewell My Love (vocal: Martha Tilton) (swell vocal on recent hit piece)
Ridin' High (this week's 'killer-diller' requested by fan mail: rather fast with very sharp brass section; Benny's short solo; James' terrific solo with Krupa really beatin' it; Benny again; James again)
Goodbye (closing theme)

■ WEDNESDAY 3 NOVEMBER 1937

RECORDING SESSION

GLEN GRAY AND THE CASA LOMA ORCHESTRA
Recording session for Decca in New York City.
Glen Gray (as/dir); Sonny Dunham, Grady Watts, Frank Zullo (t); Pee Wee Hunt (tb/voc); Billy Rauch, Murray McEachern (tb); Clarence Hutchenrider (cl/as), Kenny Sargent (as/voc); Art Ralston (as/o/bsn); Danny d'Andrea (as); Pat Davis (cl/ts/fl); Joe Hall (p); Jack Blanchette (g); Stanley Dennis (b); Tony Briglia (d)
I've Got My Heart Set On You (vKS) / *Have You Met Miss Jones?* (vKS) / *In The Mission By The Sea* (vKS) / *Farewell, My Love* (vKS) / *I'd Rather Be Right* (vKS)

RADIO LOGS

6:35PM WABC
COUNT BASIE
Meadowbrook, N.J.
Basie's last night at the Meadowbrook. Recorded by John Hammond.
One O'Clock Jump (marvelous: Lester Young's great long tenor sax solo; Buck Clayton's nuttsy trumpet; marvelous rhythm section; nuttsy ending)
I Can't Get Started (vocal: Billie Holiday) (grand: Jones' nice drum breaks)
A Study In Brown (very nuttsy original arrangement: Lester Young's colossal tenor sax with Jo Jones' great, solid, clean drumming throughout; Basie's nuttsy tickling piano with Walter Page's great bass)
Rhythm In My Nursery Rhymes (vocal: Jimmy Rushing) (Basie's nuttsy piano intro; swell tricky saxes)
John's Idea (wonderful, whole band relaxed and swinging: grand tenor sax; Buck Clayton's soft trumpet with much feeling; Basie's simple but extraordinary swinging piano; more magnificent tenor sax and rhythm)
Good Morning Blues (vocal: Jimmy Rushing) (slow blues piece played with much feeling and relaxation; Clayton's blue ballsy trumpet; Basie's piano throughout)
Dinah (vocal: Jimmy Rushing) (great intro by rhythm section, especially Basie and Page's bass: Herschel Evans' nuttsy tenor sax; Young's tenor too; trumpet)

11:00PM WABC
BENNY GOODMAN
Hotel Pennsylvania, NYC
Alexander's Ragtime Band (swell snappy arrangement: Benny)
That Old Feeling (vocal: Martha Tilton) (swell sweet song)
Remember Me (BG Trio) (not very good: lousy tune with little swing)
Loch Lomond (vocal: Martha Tilton & Benny Goodman) (James' trumpet)
Darktown Strutters' Ball (nuttsy: very polished arrangement; James; trombones; clarinets)
If It's The Last Thing I Do (vocal: Martha Tilton) (good vocal)
Liza (BG Quartet) (tricky intro and ending: excellent work by all 4)
Blossoms On Broadway (vocal: Martha Tilton) (fair: a recent sweetish song)
Camel Hop (swell piece: James' grand trumpet & Krupa; Musso)
Bob White (vocal: Martha Tilton) (Benny whistling: this song is now a big hit)

11:30PM WMCA
FLETCHER HENDERSON
Apollo Theater, NYC
Beale Street Blues (swell arrangement but ragged: unsmooth trombone; good trumpet)
Avalon (good: nice trumpet by Dick Vance; good tenor sax; swell trombone)

■ THURSDAY 4 NOVEMBER 1937

RADIO LOGS

11:00PM WABC
CAB CALLOWAY
Cotton Club, NYC
Somebody Stole My Gal (vocal: Cab Calloway) (swell: Chu Berry's tenor sax; trumpet)
Miles Apart (vocal: Bennie Payne) (fair: too sweet with no solos)
How Am I To Know? (vocal: Cab Calloway) (very smooth: Berry; trumpet)
'Way Down Yonder In New Orleans (vocal: Cab Calloway) (nuttsy: Berry; trumpet)
Bugle Call Rag (good arrangement: screechy trumpet; Berry's short, nice sax solo)
Keep That Hi-De-Ho In Your Soul (vocal: Cab Calloway) (trombone team; trumpet; Berry)
In An Old English Village (lousy, first time on radio: trombone)
Nagasaki (vocal: Cab Calloway) (swell: Cab's wacky vocal; Berry's nuttsy tenor; good trombone)

11:30PM WJZ
BOB CROSBY
Palomar Ballroom, Los Angeles
Nuttsy, except the vocalists' and announcer's microphone was dead so I couldn't hear them.
Summertime (theme)
Sheik Of Araby (Matlock's clarinet; Smith; Miller's grand sax)
I Still Love To Kiss You Goodnight (vocal: Kay Weber) (Miller; Matlock)
Bob White (best arrangement yet: Lawson's brief trumpet; Miller & Smith the nuts)
Savoy Blues (nuttsy Dixieland piece: Matlock's intro; Miller; Lawson)
Unknown title (more good Dixieland: great solos by Lawson, Miller, Zurke, Bauduc)
Unknown title (featuring Bob Zurke's colossal piano backed by Bauduc's superb drums)
The Moon Got In My Eyes (vocal: Bob Crosby) (Lawson's trumpet: I couldn't hear the vocal)
Honeysuckle Rose (great: Matlock's ballsy, dirty clarinet; Smith's great trombone; Bauduc)

12:00 MIDNIGHT WOR
BENNY GOODMAN
Hotel Pennsylvania, NYC
Changes (excellent arrangement: James, Benny & Musso getting off!)
If It's The Last Thing I Do (vocal: Martha Tilton) (swell commercial song)
Someday Sweetheart (trombones on 1st chorus; Benny; James; ballsy saxes & brass)
So Many Memories (vocal: Martha Tilton) (very sweet and nice: good vocal)
Life Goes To A Party (nuttsy new piece: tricky wa-wa brass; James' trumpet; great ending)
Farewell My Love (vocal: Martha Tilton) (this song will be a big hit)
In The Shade Of The Old Apple Tree (kind of slow: saxes; Benny)
Blossoms On Broadway (vocal: Martha Tilton) (not very good: fair vocal)
Walk, Jennie, Walk (swell: James' grand trumpet; Benny; Gene Krupa)
I Can't Give You Anything But Love (vocal: Martha Tilton) (James; Stacy; Benny)

12:30AM WABC
RED NORVO
Hotel St. Francis, San Francisco
Goodbye Jonah (vocal: Stew Pletcher) (nuttsy vocal)
The Moon Got In My Eyes (vocal: Mildred Bailey) (marvelous slow, soft swing)
Paradise (that soft, delicate brass answered by the saxes that really sends me: Herbie Haymer's short but great tenor sax; Norvo's colossal xylophone; clarinet)
Harbor Lights (swing arrangement: Pletcher's nice trumpet; Red Norvo; Herbie Haymer)
So Many Memories (vocal: Mildred Bailey) (Mastren's trombone; Miller's swell piano)
Night And Day (swell: Red Norvo: saxes)
Bob White (vocal: Mildred Bailey) (featuring vocals and whistling)

■ FRIDAY 5 NOVEMBER 1937

RECORDING SESSION

BOB CROSBY AND HIS ORCHESTRA
Recording session for Decca in Los Angeles.
Bob Crosby (voc/ldr); Zeke Zarchy, Billy Butterfield, Yank Lawson (t); Ward Silloway, Warren Smith (tb); Matty Matlock (cl/as); Joe Kearns (as); Eddie Miller (cl/ts); Gil Rodin (ts); Bob Zurke (piano); Nappy Lamare (g/voc); Bob Haggart (b); Ray Bauduc (d); Kay Weber (voc)
Nice Work If You Can Get It (vBC) / *A Foggy Day* (vKW) / *I've Hitched My Wagon To A Star* (vBC) / *This Never Happened Before* (vKW) / *Little Rock Getaway* / *Squeeze Me*

JIMMIE LUNCEFORD AND HIS ORCHESTRA
Recording session for Decca in Los Angeles.
Jimmie Lunceford (ldr); Paul Webster (t); Eddie Tompkins, Sy Oliver (t/voc); Elmer Crumbley, Russell Bowles (tb); Trummy Young (tb/voc); Willie Smith (cl/as/bar/voc); Earl Carruthers (cl/as/bar); Ted Buckner (as); Dan Grissom (cl/as/voc); Joe Thomas (cl/ts/voc); Edwin Wilcox (p); Al Norris (g); Moses Allen (b); Jimmy Crawford (d)
Pigeon Walk / *Like A Ship At Sea* (vDG) / *Teasin' Tessie Brown* (vET & Band) / *Annie Laurie* / *Frisco Fog*

RADIO LOGS

10:45PM WJZ
JIMMY DORSEY
Congress Hotel, Chicago
I heard this program in Jim Branham's car with Carolyn, Hughie, Nancy Long, Nancy Noise and Jim.
Is It Love Or Infatuation? (vocal: Bob Eberly)
I Cried For You
Hollywood Pastimes

11:00PM WABC
GLEN GRAY
Hotel New Yorker, NYC
Heard this program in Jim Branham's car.
If It's The Last Thing I Do
Avalon
Have You Got Any Castles, Baby?
Tears In My Heart
Afraid To Dream
Limehouse Blues

■ SATURDAY 6 NOVEMBER 1937

RADIO LOGS

7.00PM WABC
SATURDAY NIGHT SWING SESSION No69
CBS Studio No1, 485 Madison Ave, NYC
Personnel of CBS Band under Leith Stevens: Nat Natoli, Chris Griffin, Lloyd Williams, Willis Kelly (trumpets); Joe Vargas, Roland Dupont (trombones); Toots Mondello, Art Manners, Henry Ross, George Tudor (saxes); Marty Dale (piano); Frankie Worrell (guitar); Lou Shoobe (bass); Billy Gussak (drums).
Rose Room (CBS Band directed by Leith Stevens: Manners' clarinet; Ross' tenor)
Exactly Like You (SAL FRANZELLA playing a swell clarinet)
Japanese Sandman (SAL FRANZELLA going the nuts on clarinet; swell bass)
The Lady Is A Tramp (CBS Band playing a lousy piece but grand solo by Dupont)
I Know Now (LARRY WYNN's WINNERS vocalizing the balls: they've got a great future)
I Got Rhythm (colossal vocalizing by LARRY WYNN's WINNERS: Wynn is white but the others are Negroes)
Oh! By Jingo! (wonderful arrangement: Dupont's great trombone; marvelous tenor sax)
The Dipsy Doodle (LOU 'RED' EVANS playing an ocarina—swell)
Jingle Bells / The Merry-Go-Round Broke Down (LOU 'RED' EVANS playing a double fife)
Shindig (wonderful new piece: nuttsy trumpet; grand drums; brass)

11:00PM WABC
BENNY GOODMAN
Hotel Pennsylvania, NYC
Let's Dance (theme)
You Showed Me The Way (vocal: Martha Tilton)
Popcorn Man (vocal: Martha Tilton)
That Naughty Waltz
Once In A While (vocal: Martha Tilton)
More Than You Know (BG Trio)
Blue Skies
Vieni Vieni (BG Quartet)
If It's The Last Thing I Do (vocal: Martha Tilton)
Life Goes To A Party
Goodbye (closing theme)

12.00 MIDNIGHT WMCA
JOE MARSALA
Hickory House, 144 W52nd Street, NYC
Personnel: Joe Marsala (clarinet); Marty Marsala (trumpet); Adele Girard (harp); Joe Bushkin (piano); Bobby Hackett (guitar); Art Shapiro (bass); Buddy Rich (drums).
Farewell Blues
Once In A While
Bob White
Someday Sweetheart
Basin Street Blues
Jim Jam Blues

12:30AM WABC
BOB CROSBY
Palomar Ballroom, Los Angeles
Colossal: Ken Frogley announced.
Between The Devil And The Deep Blue Sea (Lawson's great trumpet; Miller; Matlock)

Ebb Tide (vocal: Kay Weber) (commercial tune swung out on: Lawson and Miller the nuts)
Have You Got Any Castles, Baby? (vocal: Bob Crosby) (Miller; wa-wa brass; Matlock)
Gin Mill Blues (WONDERFUL: Bob Zurke's magnificent piano work; Eddie MIller's colossal blue tenor sax; Matlock's swell low clarinet; great ending– clarinets)
Remember Me (vocal: Bob Crosby) (nice vocal but I still don't like this song)
She's Tall, She's Tan, She's Terrific (vocal: Nappy Lamare) (ballsy: featuring Billy Butterfield's trumpet; Miller; Smith; Bauduc)
I Still Love To Kiss You Goodnight (vocal: Kay Weber) (Miller's 2 swell solos)
Pagan Love Song (marvelous, excellent relaxed swinging by whole band: Miller's nuttsy tenor sax; Bob Haggart's great bass solo; Bauduc's ballsy drums; Lawson's trumpet)

1:05AM WBBM
ROY ELDRIDGE
Three Deuces, Chicago
Pluckin' That Bass (Swell trumpet; good solid bassing throughout; nice piano)
Swing Is Here (Fast, high trumpet; fair alto sax; again that nuttsy high trumpet)
Heckler's Hop (Swell piece: nice alto sax; good piano; damn good trumpet; real solid drums)

■ **SUNDAY 7 NOVEMBER 1937**

RADIO LOGS

11:30am WNEW
SUNDAY MORNING SWING CONCERT
Criterion Theater, NYC
King Porter Stomp (Merle Pitts' WNEW Studio Band: nice clarinet)
I Hope Gabriel Likes My Music (ABE LYMAN Orch: Rose Bloom & Tiny Wolf singing)
Swing Begins (ADRIAN ROLLINI Trio: Rollini on vibraphone; Frank Victor on guitar; Haig Stephens on bass)
Satan Takes A Holiday (ADRIAN ROLLINI Trio playing great: Rollini's vibes; guitar)
Honeysuckle Rose (SUE MITCHELL singing the nuts with Merle Pitts' WNEW Studio Band)
Blues In B-flat (JOE MARSALA playing a wonderful blue clarinet)
Star Dust (Merle Pitts' WNEW Studio Band)
Marie (ADELE GIRARD's harp)

11:30PM WJZ
JIMMY DORSEY
Congress Hotel, Chicago
That Old Feeling
Caravan (Ray McKinley's good drumming)
MEDLEY: *Time On My Hands / Please / Dorsey Opus*
After You (vocal: Don Mattison)
Ebb Tide
Gone With The Gin (COLOSSAL, just written by the band: great dirty trombone; trumpet; sax; piano)
The Arkansas Traveler (swell: McKinley's nuttsy drumming; Dorsey's nice clarinet; sax)

11:30PM WABC
CAB CALLOWAY
Cotton Club, NYC
Getting Some Fun Out Of Life (vocal: Cab Calloway)
If It's The Last Thing I Do (vocal: Bennie Payne)
The Dipsy Doodle (nuttsy: whole band going the nuts; grand wacky trumpet; tenor sax)
Queen Isabella (great: Chu Berry's excellent sax; nuttsy trumpet; clarinet)
I've Got My Heart Set On You (vocal: Cab Calloway) (Berry's marvelous tenor sax)
At A Little Country Tavern (vocal: Cab Calloway) (very new song: good piano)
Peckin' (vocal: Cab Calloway) (swell: typical funny vocal; trombone; clarinet; Berry's tenor sax)
Savage Rhythm

■ TUESDAY 9 NOVEMBER 1937

RECORDING SESSION

BOB CROSBY AND HIS ORCHESTRA
Recording session for Decca in Los Angeles.
Bob Crosby (voc/ldr); Zeke Zarchy, Billy Butterfield, Yank Lawson (t); Ward Silloway, Warren Smith (tb); Matty Matlock (cl/as); Joe Kearns (as); Eddie Miller (cl/ts); Gil Rodin (ts); Bob Zurke (piano); Nappy Lamare (g/voc); Bob Haggart (b); Ray Bauduc (d); Kay Weber (voc)
Let's Give Love Another Chance (vBC) / *Vieni, Vieni* / *Silhouetted In The Moonlight* (vBC) / *I've Got A Strange New Rhythm In My Heart* (vBC) / *Why Should I Care?* (vBC)

RADIO LOGS

12:00 NOON WABC
CBS HOUSE BAND
'Swingin' The Blues', NYC
Call Of The Freaks (King Oliver used to play this tune: tenor sax; trombone)
Wistful And Blue (arranged by trumpeter Willis Kelly: trombone)
Wang Wang Blues (swell: clarinet)
Royal Garden Blues (nuttsy: Ross' peachy tenor sax; Manners' good clarinet)

Hugh Pastoriza, George Fick and myself got reserved tickets from Betty Grahl to see this week's Camel Caravan broadcast. We took the 8:09 train from Bronxville. Since we had plenty of time we went to the Commodore Music Shop first to hear some records, although we didn't have enough money to get anything. It sure was grand to walk up Broadway and see all the lights. There's no place in the world like it. We arrived at the CBS Theater at 53rd Street at 9:40pm. At 9:55 Benny Goodman was presented with a scribe from the Pilot Radio Co. for his outstanding radio work. Dan Seymour announced the show:

10:00PM WABC
BENNY GOODMAN
Camel Caravan, CBS Playhouse, NYC
Let's Dance (theme)
Blue Skies (colossal: Wilber Schwichtenburg's swell trombone; Rollini's grand tenor; Elman)
Nice Work If You Can Get It (vocal: Martha Tilton) (nuttsy arrangement; Elman's trumpet)
Once In A While (BG Trio) (good: Krupa especially on slow drum rolls & breaks)
China Boy (guest EMILIO CACERES on violin with swell guitar & baritone sax player)
Someday Sweetheart (grand: 4 saxes and trombone together; James' great trumpet; great ending)
I'm A Ding Dong Daddy (From Dumas) (BG Quartet) (I never heard it better!)
Blossoms On Broadway (vocal: Martha Tilton) (Tilton, in a green dress, singing swell)
Life Goes To A Party (GREAT: Musso's short tenor solo; terrific brass section; James & Krupa really inspired)
Goodbye (closing theme)

The Quartet in action on the show.

■ WEDNESDAY 10 NOVEMBER 1937

RADIO LOGS

11:00PM WABC
BENNY GOODMAN
Hotel Pennsylvania, NYC
I heard this program at Emmy Neiley's house in Bronxville with Carolyn Bade.
St. Louis Blues (magnificent 5-minute version: Griffin's great trumpet; Benny)
You Took The Words Right Out Of My Heart (vocal: Martha Tilton) (good: very new)
After You've Gone (BG Trio) (2 tempos: excellent work, especially Krupa)
Tears In My Heart (vocal: Martha Tilton) (swell arrangement of swell piece)
One O'Clock Jump (colossal: nice trombone; Stacy's excellent piano; trumpet)
So Many Memories (vocal: Martha Tilton) (little too commercial: nice vocal)
Vieni Vieni (BG Quartet) (just released last week: lousy piece but swell playing)
Bob White (vocal: Martha Tilton) (swell: brass; saxes; Benny)
Goodbye (closing theme)

12:30AM WABC
BOB CROSBY
Palomar Ballroom, Los Angeles
NUTTSY.
At The Jazz Band Ball (wonderful: Miller, Smith and Bauduc's great solos)
I Still Love To Kiss You Goodnight (vocal: Kay Weber) (good)
Nice Work If You Can Get It (vocal: Bob Crosby) (swell trumpet; Miller)
Dixieland Shuffle (nuttsy, slow Dixieland tempo: Lamare's nice guitar; Miller)
Have You Got Any Castles, Baby? (vocal: Bob Crosby) (Matlock's swell clarinet; Miller)
Tea For Two (great: featuring the one-and-only Bob Zurke at the piano)
So Many Memories (vocal: Kay Weber) (good: very little solo work)
South Rampart Street Parade (GREAT: Matlock's clarinet; Bauduc's drums)

■ THURSDAY 11 NOVEMBER 1937

Because today is Armistice Day there was no school. I spent the whole day just with Carolyn at her house in Hartsdale. I'll never forget this Armistice day because of the sweetest thing in the world!!!

RADIO LOGS

11:00PM WABC
CAB CALLOWAY
Cotton Club, NYC
Mama, I Want To Make Rhythm (vocal: Cab Calloway) (Cab's swell hot vocal)
Tears In My Heart (vocal: Cab Calloway)
Did You Know Noah? (vocal: Cab Calloway)
Marie (vocal: Cab Calloway)
Miles Apart (vocal: Bennie Payne)
The Hi-De-Ho Miracle Man (vocal: Cab Calloway)
She's Tall, She's Tan, She's Terrific (vocal: Cab Calloway)

11:00PM WEAF
LARRY CLINTON
RCA Studios, NYC
This is a commercial program sponsored by RCA and features Larry Clinton's very new, smooth swing orchestra.
A Study In Brown (theme) (written by Larry Clinton)
Satan Takes A Holiday (written by Larry Clinton)
True Confession (vocal: Beatrice Wain) (alto sax)
The Big Dipper (swell: nuttsy tenor sax; drums)
MEDLEY: *Roses Of Picardy / Bouquet Of Roses / Roses In December / One Rose*
I've Got My Heart Set On You
The Dipsy Doodle (vocal: Beatrice Wain)
Midnight In A Madhouse (written by Larry Clinton, his latest piece)

11:30PM WJZ
BOB CROSBY
Palomar Ballroom, Los Angeles
GRAND.
The Old Spinning Wheel (swell: Bauduc's bass drum intro; Lawson; Matlock)
This Never Happened Before (vocal: Kay Weber) (not very good, too commercial)
Bob White (best arrangement of this piece yet: Miller; Smith; grand ending)
Just Strolling (written by Joe Sullivan: Zurke's great piano work; brass & rhythm)
She's Tall, She's Tan, She's Terrific (vocal: Nappy Lamare) (Miller's nice tenor; Smith; Bauduc)
She's Funny That Way (slow tempo: Miller's grand, long blue tenor)
Remember Me (vocal: Bob Crosby) (very good swingy, rollin' arrangement: Miller; clarinets)
Panama (wonderful: Lawson's great trumpet; Miller's & Matlock's great solos)

12:00 MIDNIGHT WOR
BENNY GOODMAN
Hotel Pennsylvania, NYC
Big John Special (GREAT: James; Benny; Stacy; saxes & brass)
You Took The Words Right Out Of My Heart (vocal: Martha Tilton)
Laughing At Life (swell: nuttsy muted trumpet & sax; Stacy)
In The Still Of The Night (vocal: Martha Tilton)
If It's The Last Thing I Do (vocal: Martha Tilton)
Minnie The Moocher's Wedding Day (wonderful: Intro; Benny; James; great brass)
Farewell My Love (vocal: Martha Tilton) (good, but a steal from *Goodnight My Love*: Benny & Krupa)
Camel Hop (swell: nice soft trumpet; Benny; Krupa's great work; Musso)
Once In A While (vocal: Martha Tilton)
Vieni Vieni (stinking piece, fair arrangement but too fast: nice trumpet)

12:30AM WABC
RED NORVO
Hotel St. Francis, San Francisco
GREAT.
Rugcutter's Swing (slow swingy tempo: Pletcher's trumpet; Norvo's xylophone)
Everything You Said Came True (vocal: Mildred Bailey) (colossal sweet song; Haymer; Mastren)
Am I In Love? (swell: Miller's nuttsy piano; Purtill's solid drums; clarinet)
Whispers In The Dark (Herbie Haymer's nice tenor sax; Norvo's xylophone)
St. Louis Blues (vocal: Mildred Bailey) (Mildred singing colossally as only she can)
Yours And Mine (vocal: Stew Pletcher) (swell vocal; Haymer's short, nuttsy tenor sax)
Right Or Wrong (vocal: Mildred Bailey) (nuttsy: very new song released today on Brunswick)
Do You Ever Think Of Me? (great: Red Norvo really beating that old woodpile something terrific; smooth fast clarinet; Pletcher's trumpet)

■ FRIDAY 12 NOVEMBER 1937

RECORDING SESSION

BENNY GOODMAN AND HIS ORCHESTRA
Recording session for Victor in New York City.
Benny Goodman (cl); Chris Griffin, Harry James, Ziggy Elman (t); Red Ballard, Murray McEachern (tb); George Koenig, Hymie Shertzer (as); Art Rollini, Vido Musso (ts); Jess Stacy (p); Allan Reuss (g); Harry Goodman (b); Gene Krupa (d); Martha Tilton (voc)
You Took The Words Right Out Of My Heart (vMT) / *Mama, That Moon Is Here Again* (vMT) / *Loch Lomond* (vMT, BG) / *Camel Hop* / *True Confession* (vMT) / *Life Goes To A Party*

■ SATURDAY 13 NOVEMBER 1937

RECORDING SESSION

BOB CROSBY'S BOBCATS
Recording session for Decca in Los Angeles.
Yank Lawson (t); Warren Smith (tb); Matty Matlock (cl); Eddie Miller (cl*/ts); Bob Zurke (p); Nappy Lamare (g); Bob Haggart (b); Ray Bauduc (d)
Stumbling* / Who's Sorry Now? / Coquette / Fidgety Feet / You're Driving Me Crazy / Can't We Be Friends?

RADIO LOGS

7.00PM WABC
SATURDAY NIGHT SWING SESSION No70
CBS Studio No1, 485 Madison Ave, NYC
The guests are singer LEE WILEY and pianist MARLOWE MORRIS.
Swing Session Called To Order (CBS Band directed by Leith Stevens: great)
Sometimes I Feel Like A Motherless Child (LEE WILEY singing marvelously)
Stompin' At The Savoy (nuttsy: great clarinet and trumpet; Ross' tenor sax)
Sweet Sue (CBS Band: Hank Ross' great tenor sax, plenty solid, beautiful tone)
Caravan (MARLOWE MORRIS playing OK piano; poor piece for the piano)
Limehouse Blues (MARLOWE MORRIS playing swell piano, nice tickling)
You're My Desire (colossal slow, sweet swing: nice clarinet; clarinets; saxes)
Bob White (LEE WILEY singing colossally: 3 choruses of grand swing)

11:00PM WABC
BUNNY BERIGAN
Ohio
NUTTSY.
I Can't Get Started (theme)
So Many Memories (vocal: Gail Reese)
Can't Help Lovin' Dat Man (Bunny; Auld's tenor sax; Lee's trombone)
Miles Apart (vocal: Gail Reese)
Sweet Varsity Sue (nuttsy: Berigan; Lee's trombone; Georgie Auld's tenor)
I'd Love To Play A Love Scene (vocal: Gail Reese)
No One Else But You (vocal: Gail Reese) (nice trombones & saxes; Berigan)
The Prisoner's Song (wonderful: Dixon's clarinet; Auld; Wayland's bass; Wettling)

11:30PM WABC
BENNY GOODMAN
Hotel Pennsylvania, NYC
House Hop
I heard the first part of this program at Sally Noye's house in Scarsdale; the other part at Jim Poe's house in Bronxville.
Ridin' The Groove
You Took The Words Right Out Of My Heart (vocal: Martha Tilton)
When Buddha Smiles
You And I Know (vocal: Martha Tilton)

12:00 MIDNIGHT WMCA
JOE MARSALA
Hickory House, 144 W52nd Street, NYC
SWELL. I heard this program at Jim Poe's house in Bronxville.
Ferdinand Blues (theme) (nuttsy)
Smiling At Trouble
I Cried For You
Bob White (whole band singing swell)
Singin' The Blues (very appropriate tune tonight)
Goose Island Stomp
Star Dust

12:30AM WABC
BOB CROSBY
Palomar Ballroom, Los Angeles
Great.
Royal Garden Blues (colossal: wonderful relaxed solos by Matlock; Lawson; Miller)
Goodnight Kisses (vocal: Kay Weber)
Nice Work If You Can Get It (vocal: Bob Crosby) (Matlock; Lawson, etc)
Dixieland Shuffle (great: Smith's dirty trombone; Miller; Lamare; Lawson)
Remember Me (vocal: Bob Crosby) (swell swingin' after vocal: Miller)
Coquette (The Bobcats going magnificently: Miller; Smith; Matlock)
This Never Happened Before (vocal: Kay Weber)
Wolverine Blues (old piece written by Jelly Roll Morton: featuring Ray Bauduc's drums & Miller's tenor sax)

1:03AM WBBM
ROY ELDRIDGE
Three Deuces, Chicago
Wonderful.
Dismal Day (colossal slow blues: slow sendin' alto sax; nice piano; Eldridge)
Pluckin' The Blues (grand: nice solid fast bass; Eldridge's fine trumpet)
Swing Fever (Eldridge's GREAT fast, high trumpet; ballsy alto sax)
Heckler's Hop (great: Eldridge; piano; sax; real solid drums)

■ SUNDAY 14 NOVEMBER 1937

I got 3 old records today: Charleston Chasers' *Beale Street Blues* and *Basin Street Blues* (Columbia 2415-D); Duke Ellington's *Limehouse Blues* and *Echoes Of The Jungle* (Victor 22743); and Hoagy Carmichael's *Bessie Couldn't Help It* and Fess Williams' *Hot Mama* (Victor 22864).

RADIO LOGS

11:00AM WNEW
SUNDAY MORNING SWING CONCERT
Criterion Theater, NYC
The Snake Charmer (Merle Pitts' WNEW Studio Band playing good: clarinets)
The Dipsy Doodle (MILT HERTH on organ; WILLIE 'THE LION' SMITH on piano; O'Neil Spencer singing)
St. Louis Blues (SAMMY SPERGEL playing good electric guitar with band)
Getting Some Fun Out Of Life (Merle Pitts' WNEW Studio Band again: Weiss' drums)
I'm Confessin' (HARRY JAMES and VIDO MUSSO playing some great, relaxed, unrehearsed stuff; drums)
Rosetta (Merle Pitts' WNEW Studio Band: nice tenor sax; trumpet)
Annie Laurie (MAXINE SULLIVAN from the Onyx Club singing some marvelous stuff. She is a thin Negress who is said to be tops on vocals: very smooth)
Tiger Rag

■ TUESDAY 16 NOVEMBER 1937

RECORDING SESSION

BOB CROSBY AND HIS ORCHESTRA
Recording session for Decca in Los Angeles.
Bob Crosby (voc/ldr); Charlie Spivak, Billy Butterfield, Yank Lawson (t); Ward Silloway, Warren Smith (tb); Matty Matlock (cl/as); Joe Kearns (as); Eddie Miller (cl/ts); Gil Rodin (ts); Bob Zurke (piano); Nappy Lamare (g/voc); Bob Haggart (b); Ray Bauduc (d); Kay Weber (voc)
The Thrill Of A Lifetime (vKW) / *Be A Good Sport* (vBC) / *Every Day's A Holiday* (vBC) / *South Rampart Street Parade* / *Dogtown Blues* / *Sweet Someone* (vKW) / *Just Strolling* / *Panama* / *Big Apple Calls (When My Dreamboat Comes Home)* (vNL)

RED McKENZIE & HIS ORCHESTRA
Recording session for ARC in New York City.
Bobby Hackett (c); Vernon Brown (tb); Slats Long (cl); Babe Russin (ts); Fulton McGrath (p); Dave Barbour (g); Artie Shapiro (b); Stan King (d); Red McKenzie (comb/voc)
Farewell, My Love (vRM) / *You're Out Of This World* (vRM) / *Sail Along, Silvery Moon* (vRM) / *Georgianna* (vRM)

RADIO LOGS

12:00 NOON WABC
CBS HOUSE BAND
'Swingin' The Blues', NYC
Loveless Love (grand: Ross' tenor sax, etc)
Bluin' The Blues (colossal clarinet, etc)
Blue Again (vocal: Willis Kelly)
Black And Tan Fantasy (wonderful)
Junk Man Blues (written in 1922 by Red Nichols: swell)

10:00PM WABC
BENNY GOODMAN
Camel Caravan, CBS Playhouse, NYC
I heard this program at Dick Morningstar's house.
Let's Dance (theme)
Star Dust (swell: brass; Benny; James)
If It's The Last Thing I Do (vocal: Martha Tilton)
After You've Gone (BG Trio) (rather good, especially Benny)
You Took The Words Right Out Of My Heart (vocal: Martha Tilton)
Laughing At Life
Nagasaki (BG Quartet) (colossal stuff by all four)
Mama, That Moon Is Here Again (vocal: Martha Tilton)
Big John Special (stupendous: James; brass; Stacy)
Goodbye (closing theme)

■ WEDNESDAY 17 NOVEMBER 1937

RADIO LOGS

11:00PM WABC
BENNY GOODMAN
Hotel Pennsylvania, NYC
Smiles
You Can't Teach An Old Heart New Tricks (vocal: Martha Tilton)
Marie
Loch Lomond (vocal: Martha Tilton & Benny Goodman)
Once In A While (vocal: Martha Tilton)
Sweet Stranger
Vieni, Vieni
I've Hitched My Wagon To A Star (vocal: Martha Tilton)
Camel Hop
If It's The Last Thing I Do (vocal: Martha Tilton)

■ FRIDAY 19 NOVEMBER 1937

RECORDING SESSION

GLEN GRAY AND THE CASA LOMA ORCHESTRA
Recording session for Decca in New York City.
Glen Gray (as/dir); Sonny Dunham, Grady Watts, Frank Zullo (t); Pee Wee Hunt (tb/voc); Billy Rauch, Murray McEachern (tb); Clarence Hutchenrider (cl/as); Kenny Sargent (as/voc); Art Ralston (as/o/bsn); Danny d'Andrea (as); Pat Davis (cl/ts/fl); Joe Hall (p); Jack Blanchette (g); Stanley Dennis (b); Tony Briglia (d)
You Took The Words Right Out Of My Heart (vKS) / *The Waltz Lives On* (vKS) / *Thanks For The Memory* (vKS) / *Mama, That Moon Is Here Again* (vPWH)

■ SATURDAY 20 NOVEMBER 1937

RADIO LOGS

7.00PM WABC
SATURDAY NIGHT SWING SESSION No71
CBS Studio No1, 485 Madison Ave, NYC
EXCELLENT. The guests are pianist ART TATUM, guitarists CARL KRESS & DICK McDONOUGH, and the ANDREWS SISTERS.
Waddlin' At The Waldorf (CBS Band going great on swell piece)
I Got Rhythm (CARL KRESS & DICK McDONOUGH playing guitars)
Oh, Lady Be Good (CARL KRESS & DICK McDONOUGH again going marvelously)
Nice Work If You Can Get It (nuttsy: tenor; trombone; trumpet)
Gone With The Wind (ART TATUM, great blind colored pianist, playing a swell, intricate swing piano in the style that he originated. He's going to play at the Famous Door on 52nd Street when it reopens soon. Tatum is very underrated)
Sheik Of Araby (a jam session!!! Tatum on piano; Manners on clarinet; Ross' grand tenor sax; marvelous piano; trumpet)
Just A Simple Melody (ANDREWS SISTERS singing the nuts: trumpet)
It's The Natural Thing To Do (nuttsy swing arrangement: sax)
Honeysuckle Rose (Toots Mondello playing an absolutely great alto sax, such marvelous tone, and swinging)
Peckin' (grand arrangement: weak trumpet; nuttsy brass section)

■ SUNDAY 21 NOVEMBER 1937

RADIO LOGS

11:00AM WNEW
SUNDAY MORNING SWING CONCERT
Criterion Theater, NYC
Raggle-Taggle (Merle Pitts' WNEW Studio Band playing good: fair tenor sax)
China Boy (LLANA WEBSTER playing a nuttsy tenor sax: Weiss' nice drums)
Why Talk About Love? (ANDREWS SISTERS singing the nuts: swell)
Mary Lou (Merle Pitts' WNEW Studio Band going swell: very good solos by clarinet & trumpet)
Humoresque (CACERES TRIO: violin, clarinet, bass, guitar)
Abba Dabba (arranger & composer LARRY CLINTON leading WNEW Band)
The Lady Is A Tramp (SHIRLEY BROWN singing)
Farewell Blues (SAMMY SPERGEL playing that lousy electric guitar)

11:05PM WJZ
JIMMY DORSEY
Congress Hotel, Chicago
The Moon Got In My Eyes (Bob Eberly)
After You (vocal: Don Mattison) (swell arrangement of recent hit tune: nice trombone, piano, and alto sax solos)
Star Dust (first chorus a trombone solo by Bobby Byrne; second chorus a sweet trumpet solo)
I'm Getting Sentimental Over You (Byrne's nuttsy trombone)
Chicken Reel (a typical Dorsey swing arrangement: Ryan's solid bassing; Camarata's nice trumpet; Jimmy Dorsey's clarinet)
Is It Love Or Infatuation? (Bob Eberly) (good sweet ballad)
Flight Of The Bumble Bee (just released on Decca 2 weeks ago: fast, sweet trombone; Freddie Slack's swell piano solo; Ray McKinley's solid drum break before Dorsey's alto sax)
Night And Day (Bob Eberly) (Bobby Byrne's trombone outstanding)
Waddlin' At The Waldorf (colossal: great alto and tenor sax solos; McKinley's great drumming)
Sandman (theme)

11:30PM WABC
CAB CALLOWAY
Cotton Club, NYC
'Way Down Yonder In New Orleans (vocal: Cab Calloway) (Chu Berry's great tenor sax; clarinet)
Have You Ever Been In Heaven? (vocal: Bennie Payne)
At A Little Country Tavern (fair new piece: Payne's piano)
Somebody Stole My Gal (vocal: Cab Calloway)
Tiger Rag (fair arrangement: only solo by Chu Berry; Calloway's growls)
St. Louis Blues (vocal: Cab Calloway) (swell: very smooth sax section; nice piano)
Tears In My Heart (vocal: Cab Calloway) (good commercial song: fair flute)
I've Got My Heart Set On You (vocal: Cab Calloway) (Chu Berry's fair tenor sax)
Bugle Call Rag (very good: Chu Berry's swell tenor; trumpet; weak clarinet; brass)

■ MONDAY 22 NOVEMBER 1937

RECORDING SESSION

HUDSON-DeLANGE ORCHESTRA
Recording session for Brunswick in New York City.
Will Hudson (arr); Eddie DeLange (voc/ldr); Charles Mitchell, Howard Schaumberger, Joe Bauer (t); Edward Kolyer, Jack Andrews (tb); George Bohn, Gus Bivona (cl/as); Pete Brendel (as/bar); Ted Duane (cl/ts); Mark Hyams (p); Bus Etri (g); Doc Goldberg (b); Nat Pollard (d); Betty Allen (voc)
Rockin' The Town (vBA) / *Off Again, On Again* (vBA) / *Just An Error In The News* (vBA) / *My Heaven On Earth* (vBA)

RADIO LOGS

11:00PM WABC
GLEN GRAY
Hotel New Yorker, NYC
SWELL. Sonny Dunham rejoined the Casa Loma Band on November 3rd after having his own band for 2 months. He's one of the leading trumpet players today.
Sugar Foot Stomp (swell: Hutchenrider's clarinet; nuttsy trumpet; clarinets)
Have You Met Miss Jones? (vocal: Kenny Sargent) (very sweet new piece)
Mama, That Moon's Here Again (vocal: Pee Wee Hunt) (another very new song: tenor; clarinet)
Rosetta (Walter Smith's good trumpet; McEachern's nuttsy trombone; Joe Hall's good piano; clarinet; Davis' tenor)
Smoke Rings (grand theme: Hutchenrider's clarinet)
You And I Know (vocal: Kenny Sargent) (good arrangement of commercial tune)
Just A Simple Melody (vocal: Pee Wee Hunt) (swell recent piece: no solos)
Memories Of You (swell piece featuring Sonny Dunham's great trumpet)
Put On Your Old Grey Bonnet (vocal: Pee Wee Hunt) (swell old hit tune: nuttsy trombone; sax)

■ TUESDAY 23 NOVEMBER 1937

RECORDING SESSION

WOODY HERMAN AND HIS ORCHESTRA
Recording session for Decca in New York City.
Woody Herman (cl/as/voc/ldr); Clarence Willard, Kermit Simmons (t); Joe Bishop (fh); Neal Reid (tb); Jack Ferrier, Ray Hopfner (as); Saxie Mansfield, Pete Johns (ts); Nick Hupfer (vln); Tommy Linehan (p); Oliver Mathewson (g); Walter Yoder (b); Frank Carlson (d)
Let's Pitch A Little Woo (vWH) / *I Wanna Be In Winchell's Column* (vWH) / *Loch Lomond* (vWH) / *Broadway's Gone Hawaii* (vWH)

RADIO LOGS

12:00 NOON WABC
CBS HOUSE BAND
'Swingin' The Blues', NYC
Joe Turner Blues (very old, little-known piece: Hank Ross' great tenor sax)
In A Sentimental Mood (nice trumpet on 1st chorus; saxes; trombones; tenor sax)
Down And Out Blues (a rare old tune written in 1925: swell guitar solo)
Stormy Weather (vocal: Willis Kelly) (written in 1929: good trumpet; fair flute)
Jazz Me Blues (swell: Art Manners' ballsy clarinet)

10:00PM WABC
BENNY GOODMAN
Camel Caravan, CBS Playhouse, NYC
Let's Dance (theme)
All Of Me (colossal [Carolyn just told me she loved me]: great solos by Musso & James)
Loch Lomond (vocal: Martha Tilton) (nuttsy vocal)
Nice Work If You Can Get It (BG Trio) (good for a change)
Clarinet Marmalade (wonderful: Benny's marvelous clarinet work; GREAT trumpet; Krupa's colossal drumming)
I'm Like A Fish Out Of Water (vocal: Martha Tilton) (swell, very new: trumpet)
Runnin' Wild (BG Quartet) (colossal work, especially Benny & Hampton)
I've Hitched My Wagon To A Star (vocal: Martha Tilton) (very good commercial)
Vieni, Vieni (This week's 'killer-diller': I hate this song but the arrangement is very good; grand solo by Benny; James' raspy trumpet solo)
Goodbye (closing theme)

■ WEDNESDAY 24 NOVEMBER 1937

RADIO LOGS

11:00PM WABC
BENNY GOODMAN
Hotel Pennsylvania, NYC
I heard the first part of this program in Sally Noye's house and the second half in Nancy Long's house in Scarsdale.
In The Shade Of The Old Apple Tree
You Took The Words Right Out Of My Heart (vocal: Martha Tilton)
When It's Sleepy Time Down South
Goodnight My Love (vocal: Martha Tilton)
Someday Sweetheart
You Showed Me The Way (vocal: Martha Tilton)
Nobody's Sweetheart (BG Trio)
So Many Memories (vocal: Martha Tilton)
Big John Special

12:00 MIDNIGHT WABC
GLENN MILLER
Raymor Ballroom, Boston
On Moonlight Bay (Irving Fazola on clarinet)
The Moon Got In My Eyes (vocal: Kathleen Lane)
Humoresque (Chummy McGregor's piano; Bob Price's trumpet)
Time On My Hands (recently released on Brunswick)
Let's Give Love Another Chance

■ THURSDAY 25 NOVEMBER 1937 (THANKSGIVING)

Don Mortimer and Curtis Dewey from Memphis, both home from Governor Dummer Academy, and I took the 8:09pm train into New York City. We first went to see Benny Goodman's Orchestra at the Madhattan Room of the Hotel Pennsylvania, 33rd Street and Seventh Avenue, from 8:45 to 1:30. We each paid the cover charge of 75 cents, besides all the drinks that Curtis bought me (3 Cuba Libra's, etc). As usual it got very crowded with the young college crowd dominating and Goodman's Band causing great excitement among the dancers and 'sitters-out'. Since we went stag we didn't do any dancing but just sat and feasted our eyes on the band. We watched Krupa go mad; James forget his surroundings and really play some inspired stuff; Stacy's serious face as his mind made his fingers beat some colossal solid 'bank notes'; Goodman dividing his attention between smiling at friends in the crowd (including me) and his wonderful clarinet playing; James and Krupa clowning and really 'sending' each other; Reuss' solemn face broken by an occasional smile as he sees some pretty girl; little Hymie Shertzer leading the sax section with his alto. Later on Hugh Pastoriza, Fred Patrick, and Paul Mallory came down and joined us for a while. I only talked to James, Elman, Griffin and Rollini and didn't bother to get any more autographs. The personnel of the band is the same except that Vernon Brown left today to play with Milt Mezzrow at the Harlem Uproar House and has been replaced by Walter Mercurio who was with Tommy Dorsey for several months. He isn't very sure sure of himself and only takes fair solos. I doubt if he will stick with the band long. We all had a table right next to the band and had a marvelous time. We just sat and listened (and drank) all the time they played, until we had to leave. Everybody got the 1:00am train home except Curtis and myself. We decided to stay in all night and got the 6:15am train home. Curtis had a lot of money so we had a glorious time. After finally hearing the Goodman Quartet go to town we left the Hotel Penn at 1:30am with Henry Ferrou.

We took the subway up to 52nd Street where we first went to the Hickory House where Joe Marsala's Band was playing. Joe waved at me and smiled. We had several drinks at the bar watching the band really jam out! The two Marsala brothers, pianist Joe Bushkin, bassist Art Shapiro and drummer Buddy Rich (came from California last month and shows much promise) were outstanding. Harpist Adele Girard did the vocals.

We then went over to the Onyx Club where we stayed for an hour or so. The band was simply colossal and Negress Maxine Sullivan did her usual sweet-voiced, swingin' vocals which really did send me, even if I had already had 8 drinks so far tonight. I got the autographs of Maxine Sullivan, Buddy Rich and Buster Bailey. I can't remember clearly everything that happened but I remember meeting many college guys, particularly from Cornell and Dartmouth. I remember singing and truckin' a bit around the floor and kicking boxes around in back of the Onyx. Frankie Newton wasn't with the band. Nineteen-year-old Charlie Shavers, formerly with Lucky Millinder's Band, has taken his place. He is the nuts! As usual, Claude Thornhill was sitting at one of the tables. I remember Maxine Sullivan singing with all the lights out, except one on her. She sang: *Night And Day; It's Wonderful; Loch Lomond; Annie Laurie; I'm Coming Virginia*, etc.

> The **Famous Door**, musicians' hangout, has decided to make another try at it. Dying about a year after achieving an enviable reputation as a swing salon, it is opening Thanksgiving Evening (Thursday 25 November) at a new address, 66 West Fifty-second Street. Louis Prima's band, which has a good deal to do with the success of the original place, will officiate.
>
> **Nick's Tavern**, a not unknown place among aliens and residents of the Village, is pulling up stakes at 140 Seventh Avenue South and, either the last of this week or the first of next, moves across the avenue to 162 West Tenth Street. Bobby Hackett's band is going along. Mr. Hackett knows how to push the valve down on his trumpet but the band, particularly in the rhythm section, needs some more sessions together before it definitely confirms the belief of jam fans that it's going places. Incidentally, Mr. Nicholas Rongetti assures us that his new place will be structurally and atmospherically the same as the old.

Below: Louis Prima in action at the Famous Door.

We left the Onyx at about 3:30am and got in some guy's car (9 of us) and drove around to different dance halls and bars. Everything closes up at 4:30am so, after driving around some more, everybody went to their hotels except Dewey and I who had to wait around for the 6:15am train back to Bronxville. We went to a restaurant where we had some breakfast. It sure was funny to see Grand Central Station absolutely empty at 5:30am. We finally got the 6:15 train and slept from station to station. We got in Bronxville at 6:45. Dewey went to Mortimer's house and I went to Poe's house where I tried to get a little sleep. Poe woke me at 9:00am so I only got 2 hours' sleep. I saw Carolyn for a while that afternoon before I got terribly drunk on a quart of Scotch. What a weekend!!

RADIO LOGS

11:30PM WABC
BENNY GOODMAN
Hotel Pennsylvania, NYC
Makin' Whoopee
If It's The Last Thing I Do (vocal: Martha Tilton)
All Of Me
A Foggy Day (vocal: Martha Tilton)
Caravan
Bob White (vocal: Martha Tilton)
Vieni, Vieni (BG Trio)
You Showed Me The Way (vocal: Martha Tilton)
I Can't Give You Anything But Love, Baby (vocal: Martha Tilton)
One O'Clock Jump

11:30PM WJZ
BOB CROSBY
Palomar Ballroom, Los Angeles
Vieni Vieni (arranged by Bob Haggart)
Sweet Someone (vocal: Kay Weber)
Mama, I Want To Make Rhythm (vocal: Bob Crosby)
I've Got A Strange New Rhythm (vocal: Bob Crosby)
Gin Mill Blues
Be A Good Sport
This Never Happened Before (vocal: Kay Weber)
South Rampart Street Parade

■ FRIDAY 26 NOVEMBER 1937

Below: A picture taken by Hugh Pastoriza of part of Milt Mezzrow's new band consisting of 7 white men and 7 Negroes at the Harlem Uproar House at 51st Street and Broadway on the day after Thanksgiving. The band only lasted for a few weeks because of lack of business. It sure was colossal. It included Zutty Singleton (drums); Sidney DeParis, Max Kaminsky, Frankie Newton (trumpets); George Lugg, Vernon Brown (trombones); Bernard Addison (guitar); Elmer James (bass); Eugene Sedric (sax), John Nicolini (piano).

RADIO LOGS

12:00 MIDNIGHT WEAF
TEDDY HILL
Savoy Ballroom, NYC
Big John Special
Caravan
Parade Of The Milk Bottle Tops
My Blue Heaven (vocal: Bill Dillard)
Lonesome Nights (written by Benny Carter)
Three Little Words
Blue Skies
King Porter Stomp

12:30AM WJZ
LOUIS ARMSTRONG
Vogue Ballroom, Los Angeles
It's The Natural Thing To Do
Mahogany Hall Stomp
Darktown Strutters' Ball
On The Sunny Side Of The Street
Muskrat Ramble
At A Little Country Tavern
Cuban Pete
They All Laughed

■ SUNDAY 28 NOVEMBER 1937

RADIO LOGS

9:45PM WOR
ADRIAN ROLLINI QUARTET
Studios, NYC
Serenade For A Wealthy Widow (darn good: Adrian Rollini on vibraharp; Al Duffy on violin; Frankie Victor on guitar; Harry Clark on bass)
'Way Down Yonder In New Orleans (vocal: Helene Daniels)
Driftin' (written by Adrian Rollini and featuring his great vibraharp)
I Would Do Anything For You (vocal: Helene Daniels) (OK singing)
Vieni Vieni (played in 2 styles: Italian and modern swing—swell)

■ MONDAY 29 NOVEMBER 1937

RECORDING SESSION

ART TATUM
Recording session for Decca in New York City.
Art Tatum (p)
Gone With The Wind / Stormy Weather / Chloe / The Sheik Of Araby

GLENN MILLER AND HIS ORCHESTRA
Recording session for Brunswick in New York City.
Glenn Miller (tb/ldr); Pee Wee Erwin, Bob Price, Ardell Garrett (t); Jesse Ralph, Bud Smith (tb); Irving Fazola (cl/as); Hal McIntyre, Tony Viola (as); Jerry Jerome, Carl Biesecker (ts); Chummy MacGregor (p); Carmen Mastren (g); Rowland Bundock (b); Doc Cenardo (Carney) (d); Kathleen Lane (voc)
My Fine Feathered Friend (vKL) / *Humoresque* / *Doin' The Jive* (vKL& Band) / *Silhouetted In The Moonlight* (vKL)

RADIO LOGS

11:00PM WABC
GLEN GRAY
Hotel New Yorker, NYC
Muskrat Ramble (nuttsy: Sonny Dunham's wonderful trumpet; Davis' ballsy sax; trombone)
Once In A While (vocal: Kenny Sargent) (commercial but a swell hit tune now)
Queen Isabella (vocal: Pee Wee Hunt) (again Dunham's great trumpet)
Back Home Again In Indiana (grand: Murray McEachern's marvelous trombone solo!! Dunham; clarinet; Davis' tenor)
Time On My Hands (vocal: Kenny Sargent) (grand: 3 trombones; Dunham's swell high trumpet; clarinet)
Mama, That Moon's Here Again (vocal: Pee Wee Hunt) (Hutchenrider's clarinet; Davis' gutbucket sax)
I Can Dream, Can't I? (vocal: Kenny Sargent) (introduced by Gray last Wednesday)
Limehouse Blues (magnificent arrangement: great dirty, muted trombone; alto sax; Briglia's swell drumming; another great, soft, muted trombone; Pat Davis' colossal tenor sax; nuttsy ending!)

■ TUESDAY 30 NOVEMBER 1937

RADIO LOGS

12:00 NOON WABC
CBS HOUSE BAND
'Swingin' The Blues', NYC
Call Of The Freaks (swell blue trumpet; good clarinet; great trombone)
Blue Bayou (similar style to Red Nichols' *Wail Of The Winds*: trumpet; sax)
Yellow Dog Blues (one of W.C. Handy's first tunes: grand blue trumpet; clarinet)
Nothing But The Blues (marvelous: excellent clarinet; great tenor sax)

10:00PM WABC
BENNY GOODMAN
Camel Caravan, CBS Playhouse, NYC
I heard this program at my house with Fred Patrick.
Let's Dance (theme)
When It's Sleepy Time Down South (excellent arrangement: saxes & brass; Benny; Musso; Elman)
In The Still Of The Night (vocal: Martha Tilton) (good commercial: nuttsy muted brass)
China Boy (BG Trio) (swell, but lacking punch: Krupa's good drum break)
Rosalie (very new sweet piece, grand swinging by whole band: trumpet; Stacy; trombone)
Moonglow (BG Quartet) (a little commercial but nuttsy slow tempo: Hampton outstanding)
Sweet Stranger (vocal: Martha Tilton) (swell singing on another good commercial)
St. Louis Blues (EXCELLENT, GREAT: Benny; 5 clarinets; wonderful trumpet; Stacy; saxes)
Goodbye (closing theme)

11:00PM WABC
TOMMY DORSEY
Hotel Commodore, NYC
You And I Know (vocal: Edythe Wright)
Am I In Another World?
Just A Simple Melody
Just Lately (vocal: Edythe Wright)
Liza (very fast: Dorsey; Mince, etc)
Down With Love (vocal: Edythe Wright)
Rolling Plains (vocal: Jack Leonard)
Mendelssohn's Spring Song
You're A Sweetheart (vocal: Edythe Wright)
Who? (vocal: Jack Leonard) (successor to *Marie*)
I'm Getting Sentimental Over You (theme)

11:05PM WJZ
GLENN MILLER
Raymor Ballroom, Boston
Can I Forget You? (vocal: Kathleen Lane)
Doin' The Jive (vocal: Kathleen Lane & Band) (Fazola; Jerry Jerome)
Sleepy Time Gal (nuttsy arrangement: saxes; Fazola's clarinet)
Bob White (vocal: Kathleen Lane) (3 trombones: Glenn; Bud Smith; Jesse Ralph)

Peg O' My Heart (swell slow arrangement by Miller: Fazola's colossal clarinet)
Yours And Mine (vocal: Kathleen Lane) (Fazola again: sock drums)
Where Or When (vocal: Kathleen Lane) (nice slow)
Loveless Love (great swing piece featuring Jerry Jerome's nuttsy tenor sax; Fazola's clarinet)

Glenn Miller

Irving Fazola

Saxists Irving Fazola and Jerry Jerome

RAYMOR
253 Huntington Ave.
DANCING TONIGHT
and every evening
One of America's Greatest Bands
GLENN MILLER
Arranger, author and organizer
for Ray Noble and Jimmy Dorsey.
With His Sensational Band
Brunswick Records

NOVEMBER 1937

Kathleen Lane

Opposite page and above: Photographs of the Glenn Miller Band in action at the Raymor Ballroom in Boston. *All photographs taken by Don Mortimer*

11:30PM WJZ
JIMMY DORSEY
Congress Hotel, Chicago
Sweet Like You (vocal: Dorsey Trio) (swell alto sax by Jimmy Dorsey)
Caravan (Bobby Byrne's swell trombone; marvelous tenor sax)
Have You Got Any Castles, Baby? (vocal: Don Mattison)
Everything You Said Came True (vocal: June Richmond) (Dorsey's nice clarinet)
Parade Of The Milk Bottle Tops (excellent: sax; clarinets)
Sail Along, Silvery Moon (vocal: Bob Eberly)
Beebe (written by Jimmy Dorsey several years ago as a sax solo: Jimmy's marvelous alto sax)
A Foggy Day (vocal: Bob Eberly) (a recent Gershwin tune: good but too sweet)
Dusk In Upper Sandusky (originally called *Dorsey Stomp*: marvelous Dorsey; McKinley, etc)

12:00 MIDNIGHT WNEW
AL COOPER'S SAVOY SULTANS
Savoy Ballroom, NYC
Linger Awhile
On The Sunny Side Of The Street (vocal: Pat Jenkins)
You're Looking For Romance
If It Ain't Love
Coquette
Gates (written by the whole 9-piece band)
I Can't Give You Anything But Love (vocal: Pat Jenkins)

DECEMBER 1937

Hotel Pennsylvania: **Benny Goodman**
Hotel Commodore: **Tommy Dorsey**
Hotel New Yorker: **Glen Gray**
Hotel Lincoln: **Isham Jones**

Apollo Theater: **Erskine Hawkins** (–2); **Willie Bryant** (3–9); **Teddy Hill** (10–16); **Sunset Royals** (17–23); **Lucky Millinder** (24–30); **Tiny Bradshaw** (31–)
Paramount Theater: **Bunny Berigan** (–7); **George Hall** (8–14); **Russ Morgan** (15–28); **Fred Waring** (29–)
Loew's State Theater: **Leith Stevens CBS Swing Club / Maxine Sullivan** (9–15); **Noble Sissle** (16–22); **Rudy Vallee** (23–29); **Jimmie Lunceford** (30–);

Cotton Club: **Cab Calloway / Bill Robinson**
Hickory House: **Joe Marsala**
Onyx Club: **John Kirby / Maxine Sullivan**
Famous Door: **Louis Prima / Art Tatum**
Nick's: **Bobby Hackett**

■ WEDNESDAY 1 DECEMBER 1937

RECORDING SESSION

GLEN GRAY AND THE CASA LOMA ORCHESTRA
Recording session for Decca in New York City.
Glen Gray (as/dir); Sonny Dunham, Grady Watts, Frank Zullo (t); Pee Wee Hunt (tb/voc); Billy Rauch, Murray McEachern (tb); Clarence Hutchenrider (cl/as), Kenny Sargent (as/voc); Art Ralston (as/o/bsn); Danny d'Andrea (as); Pat Davis (cl/ts/fl); Joe Hall (p); Jack Blanchette (g); Stanley Dennis (b); Tony Briglia (d)
I Can Dream, Can't I? (vKS) / *Memories Of You* / *Let's Make It A Life-Time* (vKS) / *Song Of India*

HARRY JAMES AND HIS ORCHESTRA
Recording session for Brunswick in New York City.
Harry James (t/ldr); Buck Clayton (t); Eddie Durham (tb); Earl Warren (as); Herschel Evans (ts); Jack Washington (cl/bar); Jess Stacy (p); Walter Page (b); Jo Jones (d); Helen Humes (voc)
Jubilee (vHH) / *When We're Alone [Penthouse Serenade]* / *I Can Dream Can't I?* (vHH) / *Life Goes To A Party*

JIMMY NOONE AND HIS ORCHESTRA
Recording session for Decca in New York City.
Charlie Shavers (t); Jimmy Noone (cl); Pete Brown (as); Frank Smith (p); Teddy Bunn (g); Wellman Braud (b); O'Neil Spencer (d/voc); Teddy Simmons (voc)
Sweet Lorraine (vO'NS) / *I Know That You Know* / *Bump It* / *Four Or Five Times* (vO'NS) / *Hell In My Heart* (vTS) / *Call Me Darling, Call Me Sweetheart, Call Me Dear* (vO'NS) / *I'm Walkin' This Town* (vO'NS) / *Japansy* (vO'NS)

RADIO LOGS

11:00PM WABC
BENNY GOODMAN
Hotel Pennsylvania, NYC
Good, but too commercial. Mel Allen announced.
I've Got My Love To Keep Me Warm (swell: James' 2 solos; brass)
I've Hitched My Wagon To A Star (vocal: Martha Tilton) (fair: will be a hit)
Minnie The Moocher's Wedding Day (nuttsy: James; brass)
Loch Lomond (vocal: Martha Tilton & Benny Goodman) (good, to be released tomorrow on Victor: James' trumpet)
Dear Old Southland (grand: splendid solos by Elman, Rollini & Stacy)
True Confession (vocal: Martha Tilton) (very new sweet song, not very good: Stacy)
The Lady Is A Tramp (vocal: Martha Tilton) (stinky song: Mercurio's weak trombone)
Body And Soul (BG Trio) (swell song but little variety in arrangement)
Roll 'Em (wonderful: Stacy & Benny outstanding; James swell also; marvelous brass)

11:30PM WMCA
ERSKINE HAWKINS
Apollo Theater, NYC
Three Little Words (Avery Parrish playing a nuttsy, very fast, piano solo)
Peckin' (good: fair arrangement, but very good solos by piano, tenor & baritone saxes)

■ THURSDAY 2 DECEMBER 1937

RECORDING SESSION

BENNY GOODMAN AND HIS ORCHESTRA
Recording session for Victor in New York City.
Benny Goodman (cl); Chris Griffin, Harry James, Ziggy Elman (t); Red Ballard, Vernon Brown (tb); George Koenig, Hymie Shertzer (as); Art Rollini, Vido Musso (ts); Jess Stacy (p); Allan Reuss (g); Harry Goodman (b); Gene Krupa (d); Martha Tilton (voc)
Life Goes To A Party / *It's Wonderful* (vMT) / *Thanks For The Memory* (vMT)
BENNY GOODMAN QUARTET
Lionel Hampton (vib); Teddy Wilson (p); Benny Goodman (cl); Gene Krupa (d)
I'm A Ding Dong Daddy From Dumas

RADIO LOGS

11:10PM WABC
CAB CALLOWAY
Cotton Club, NYC
How Am I To Know? (vocal: Cab Calloway) (tricky trumpet; Chu Berry's nuttsy tenor sax)
Queen Isabella (swell: Doc Cheatham's nice trumpet; clarinet, Chu Berry)
Turning On My Heart (vocal: Cab Calloway) (lousy except for fair baritone sax)
Have You Met Miss Jones? (vocal: Cab Calloway) (lousy song but good Chu Berry)
Bugle Call Rag (Chu Berry's excellent solo; nice trumpet; swell clarinet)

12:00 MIDNIGHT WOR
BENNY GOODMAN
Hotel Pennsylvania, NYC
Always (grand old arrangement: Rollini's swell tenor; Benny; trombone)
Bob White (vocal: Martha Tilton) (very popular: vocal aided by trumpet)
Once In A While (vocal: Martha Tilton) (nuttsy hit song: James' swell sweet muted trumpet)
Oh Lady Be Good (BG Trio) (splendid: Wilson's great piano solo)
It's Wonderful (vocal: Martha Tilton) (played for the first time on radio: I heard Maxine Sullivan sing this at the Onyx Club last Thursday)

One O'Clock Jump (wonderful: Stacy's great piano; Musso's swell tenor; trombone; James)
Nice Work If You Can Get It (vocal: Martha Tilton)
Vieni, Vieni (BG Quartet) (Benny's great solo; Krupa's long, nuttsy break)
So Many Memories (vocal: Martha Tilton)

■ FRIDAY 3 DECEMBER 1937

RECORDING SESSION

BENNY GOODMAN AND HIS ORCHESTRA
Recording session for Victor in New York City.
Benny Goodman (cl); Chris Griffin, Harry James, Ziggy Elman (t); Red Ballard, Vernon Brown (tb); George Koenig, Hymie Shertzer (as); Art Rollini, Vido Musso (ts); Jess Stacy (p); Allan Reuss (g); Harry Goodman (b); Gene Krupa (d); Martha Tilton (voc)
If Dreams Come True / I'm Like A Fish Out Of Water (vMT) / *Sweet Stranger* (vMT)

RADIO LOGS

7:45PM WJZ
BUGHOUSE RHYTHM
San Francisco
NUTTSY: Announced by G. Archibald Presby with that great vocabulary of his spoken in such a sophisticated way. John Meakin directs the band. I heard this program at Maurine Van Meter's house.
Queen Isabella (written by Chu Berry: Harlow Burgess' great trumpet; Meakin's piano; sax)
Alligator Crawl (written by Fats Waller)
Announcer's Blues (written by Frankie Trumbauer & Harold Stokes: chimes; tenor sax; trombone)

11:00PM WABC
GLEN GRAY
Hotel New Yorker, NYC
SWELL: I heard this program at Ann Williams' house in Bronxville after the Arthur Murray Dancing Class.
Song Of India (swell: McEachern's trombone; Dunham's trumpet)
You Took The Words Right Out Of My Heart (vocal: Kenny Sargent)
Just A Simple Melody (vocal: Pee Wee Hunt)
Caravan
Let's Make It A Lifetime (vocal: Kenny Sargent)
Bob White (vocal: Pee Wee Hunt)
Paramour (great: Davis' nuttsy tenor)
Casa Loma Stomp (Gene Gifford's song and arrangement: trombone; trumpet)

11:30PM WJZ
LOUIS ARMSTRONG
Vogue Ballroom, Los Angeles
Satan Takes A Holiday
Darling Nellie Gray
Jungle Madness
That Old Feeling / An Old Flame Never Dies (vocal: Sonny Woods)
Swing That Music
Them There Eyes
When It's Sleepy Time Down South (theme)

■ SATURDAY 4 DECEMBER 1937

RADIO LOGS

7.00PM WABC
SATURDAY NIGHT SWING SESSION No73
CBS Studio No1, 485 Madison Ave, NYC
EXCELLENT. Program prepared by Phil Cohan and Ed Cashman; announced by Mel Allen and Paul Douglas.
It Don't Mean A Thing (nuttsy piece played in Duke Ellington's honor as he started his band 10 years ago today: wonderful arrangement; saxes; trumpet; brass)
Nagasaki (JOE SODJA playing a magnificent original swing guitar: 2 tempos)
Gypsy In My Soul (written by CLAY BOLAND of Penn College who played the piano and sung by JOE JENKINS a senior at Penn College– Phil Cohan's college)
Just A Simple Melody (TOMMY DORSEY'S whole band playing from the Hotel Commodore: Howard Smith's nuttsy piano; nice saxes and muted brass section. Dorsey is due to record this on Victor next week)
La Golondrina (TOMMY DORSEY'S band swinging another classic: Mince's clarinet; Pee Wee Erwin's great muted trumpet; Bud Freeman's colossal tenor sax with wa-wa brass and Tough's marvelous drums)
Body And Soul (ART TATUM playing great, intricate piano)
St. Louis Blues (A jam session led by ART TATUM: Tatum's colossal tickling on the piano; nuttsy clarinet; great tenor sax; good trumpet)
The Dipsy Doodle (Larry Clinton's recent hit swing tune played by Leith Stevens' CBS Band in an original arrangement: wonderful clarinet; tenor sax; Dupont's great trombone; swell trumpet)

11:30PM WABC
BENNY GOODMAN
Hotel Pennsylvania, NYC
Hugh Pastoriza and I ran the Open House at the Cafeteria in school so, after playing records, we got Goodman on the radio for dancing.
Changes
You Took The Words Right Out Of My Heart (vocal: Martha Tilton)
I Can't Give You Anything But Love, Baby (vocal: Martha Tilton)
(Stacy; James)
Tiger Rag (BG Trio) (Trio's best number: excellent solos by all three)
If It's The Last Thing I Do (vocal: Martha Tilton)
If Dreams Come True (swell: played for first time on the radio)
Smiles (BG Quartet) (colossal)
It's Wonderful (vocal: Martha Tilton)
Life Goes To A Party

■ SUNDAY 5 DECEMBER 1937

David Faulkner got some tickets to this morning's Sunday Swing Concert held at the New Criterion Theater at 44th and Broadway, broadcast over WNEW from 11:00 to 12:00 and announced by Martin Block. Faulkner took George Fick and myself and we went in on the 10:04 train. The theater was packed. The Benny Goodman Quartet almost broke up the show, it was so marvelous. In fact, it almost caused a riot. The applause was so terrific that Block had them play more numbers than they were supposed to: *Avalon* (colossal, especially Benny); *Nagasaki* (splendid); *Smiles* (marvelous, with nuttsy intro); *Vieni, Vieni* (great, Hampton & Krupa especially); *I'm A Ding Dong Daddy From Dumas* (magnificent).

After the broadcast, after walking around with Krupa for a while, we went to the Paramount Theater where we saw the movie 'Ebb Tide' and Frances Langford with Bunny Berigan's Orchestra on the stage. Berigan was colossal. He played *A Study In Brown; The Prisoner's Song; Caravan;* and *Frankie And Johnny*. The personnel of the band was: Bunny Berigan, Irving Goodman, Steve Lipkins (trumpets); Sonny Lee, Al George (trombones); Georgie Auld, Clyde Rounds (tenor sax); Joe Dixon (clarinet/alto sax); Mike Doty (alto sax); Joe Lippman (piano); Tom Morgan (guitar); Hank Wayland (bass); George Wettling (drums). I could only get Sonny Lee's autograph. He told me that the band was going to Boston next week; back to New York; and then to the Palomar in Los Angeles. After this we went to another theater where only movies were shown (much football). We got the 6:35 train home.

11:00AM WNEW
SUNDAY MORNING SWING CONCERT
Criterion Theater, NYC
Have You Got Any Castles, Baby? (Merle Pitts' WNEW Studio Band: trumpet; sax)
You Took The Words Right Out Of My Heart (SHIRLEY ROSS singing; Pitts' violin)
Chimes In The Spring (SAMMY SPERGEL's lousy electric guitar)
Between The Devil And The Deep Blue Sea (Merle Pitts' WNEW Studio Band going swell: Weiss; saxes)
Avalon (BENNY GOODMAN Quartet going the nuts: especially Wilson and Goodman)
Nagasaki (again the BENNY GOODMAN Quartet: MARVELOUS!!!)
Mama, I Want To Make Rhythm (DOLLY DAWN singing, George Hall directing band)
I Got Rhythm (Merle Pitts' WNEW Studio Band: Sam Weiss' nuttsy drumming; trumpet, etc)
Adios, Muchachos (Merle Pitts' WNEW Studio Band: Spergel's nice guitar; saxes; brass)
That Old Feeling (DOLLY DAWN singing, George Hall directing band)
Nagasaki (LLANA WEBSTER playing a long, colossal hot tenor sax)
Let That Be A Lesson To You (petite SHIRLEY ROSS singing)
Have You Met Miss Jones? (SHIRLEY ROSS again singing good: lousy song)
Pagliacci (overdone swing arrangement played by WNEW Studio band)
You Can't Stop Me From Dreaming (DOLLY DAWN singing pretty good)
Smiles (BENNY GOODMAN Quartet stupendous: tricky rhythm)
Vieni, Vieni (BENNY GOODMAN Quartet on a lousy piece: Krupa's swell break)
I'm A Ding Dong Daddy (From Dumas) (BENNY GOODMAN Quartet)

9:45PM WOR
ADRIAN ROLLINI QUARTET
WOR Studios, NYC
Chinatown, My Chinatown (colossal: Al Duffy's swell violin; Adrian Rollini on vibraharp; Frankie Victor on guitar)
Bob White (vocal: Helene Daniels) (Duffy and Rollini swell)
Messin' Around (written by Al Duffy and featuring his colossal violin: Rollini's vibraharp)
A Good Man Is Hard To Find (vocal: Helene Daniels) (fair vocal: Duffy & Rollini outstanding)
The Toy Trumpet (tricky work by instruments: Duffy's nuttsy violin)

Bunny Berigan and his Orchestra on the stage of the Paramount Theater.

MONDAY 6 DECEMBER 1937

RECORDING SESSION

TOMMY DORSEY AND HIS ORCHESTRA
Recording session for Victor in New York City.
Tommy Dorsey (tb); Pee Wee Erwin, Lee Castle, Andy Ferretti (t); Les Jenkins, Frank d'Annolfo (tb); Johnny Mince, Fred Stulce, Skeets Herfurt (cl/as); Bud Freeman (ts); Howard Smith (p); Carmen Mastren (g); Artie Shapiro (b); Dave Tough (d); Jack Leonard (voc)
I Can Dream, Can't I? (vJL) / *A Little White Lighthouse* (vJL) / *The One I Love* (vJL) / *Just A Simple Melody* / *I'm The One Who Loves You* (vJL) / *Little White Lies*

RADIO LOGS

11:00PM WABC
GLEN GRAY
Hotel New Yorker, NYC
Swing Low, Sweet Chariot
Sweet Someone (vocal: Kenny Sargent) (new sweet song: Rauch's trombone)
Mama, I Want To Make Rhythm (vocal: Pee Wee Hunt)
Rosetta (wonderful: Dunham; McEachern; Davis; Hutchenrider; Hall's good piano)
I Can Dream, Can't I? (vocal: Kenny Sargent) (nice intro: 3 trombones; bassoon)
Queen Isabella (vocal: Pee Wee Hunt) (swell, but no solos)
Sleepy Time Gal (3 trombones with baritone sax: Hutchenrider; Rauch's sweet trombone; Dunham's GREAT trumpet)
Twilight In Turkey (Tony Briglia's good drums; Hutchenrider; Dennis' bass)
Smoke Dreams (theme) (muted trombone and 3 clarinets)

TUESDAY 7 DECEMBER 1937

RADIO LOGS

12:00 NOON WABC
CBS HOUSE BAND
'Swingin' The Blues', NYC
Singin' The Blues (colossal: nuttsy saxes; trombone; trumpet in Bix's style)
New Orleans Twist (rather short and lacking solos: fine rhythm section)
Blue Turning Gray Over You (vocal: Willis Kelly) (nice trumpet)
Underneath The Harlem Moon (swell: corny trumpet; tom-toms)
Bluin' The Blues (wonderful: wa-wa brass; good clarinet; trumpet)

Dick Morningstar, Ed McNulty and myself took the 8:09 train to the city where we saw this week's Camel Caravan. We got reserved seats thanks to Betty Grahl. As usual, we got a great kick out of seeing Goodman again. Ella Fitzgerald was in the audience. The personnel was the same except that Vernon Brown is back on trombone, and Babe Russin has taken Vido Musso's place temporarily. We got the 10:45 train home.

10:00PM WABC
BENNY GOODMAN
Camel Caravan, CBS Playhouse, NYC
Let's Dance (theme)
Hallelujah (wonderful: unsurpassable trumpet section; Benny)
Bob White (vocal: Martha Tilton) (Tilton looking beautiful in a white dress)
Have You Met Miss Jones? (BG Trio) (not very good, too commercial)
I've Got My Love To Keep Me Warm (last year's hit tune: colossal saxes & brass; Harry James)
If Dreams Come True (introduced last Saturday, will be a tremendous hit: great muted brass with clarinets; Brown's trombone; Rollini)
Killer Diller (BG Quartet) (colossal: an original piece)
You're A Sweetheart (vocal: Martha Tilton)
Sugar Foot Stomp (grand, Henderson arrangement: James' great muted solo)
Goodbye (closing theme)

WEDNESDAY 8 DECEMBER 1937

RECORDING SESSION

GLEN GRAY AND THE CASA LOMA ORCHESTRA
Recording session for Decca in New York City.
Glen Gray (as/dir); Sonny Dunham, Grady Watts, Frank Zullo (t); Pee Wee Hunt (tb/voc); Billy Rauch, Murray McEachern (tb); Clarence Hutchenrider (cl/as), Kenny Sargent (as/voc); Art Ralston (as/o/bsn); Danny d'Andrea (as); Pat Davis (cl/ts/fl); Joe Hall (p); Jack Blanchette (g); Stanley Dennis (b); Tony Briglia (d)
I See Your Face Before Me (vKS) / *Bei Mir Bist Du Schoen* (vPWH) / *Time On My Hands* / *Sleepy Time Gal*

RADIO LOGS

11:00PM WABC
BENNY GOODMAN
Hotel Pennsylvania, NYC
What Does It Matter? (swell: no solos except for Benny)
Sweet Someone (vocal: Martha Tilton) (very new hit-to-be piece: no solos)
The Moon Is Low (BG Trio) (swell: Wilson's colossal piano; Krupa's solid drums)
Mama, That Moon's Here Again (vocal: Martha Tilton) (silly song: saxes; trumpet)
If Dreams Come True (nuttsy new piece: muted brass & clarinets; Brown; Rollini)
You Turned The Tables On Me (vocal: Martha Tilton) (splendid vocal: saxes; Benny)
Clarinet Marmalade (colossal fast arrangement: Benny's great clarinet with Krupa; trumpet)
It's Wonderful (vocal: Martha Tilton) (slow gliding saxes: swell to dance to)
Big John Special (great Henderson arrangement: James' great trumpet; Benny; Krupa)
Bob White (vocal: Martha Tilton) (swell: James' muted trumpet)

11:30PM WMCA
WILLIE BRYANT
Apollo Theater, NYC
Rhythm Jam (swelligant: nice tenor sax; Jones' good trumpet)
Sugar Foot Stomp (good: ragged saxes; Prince Robinson's nuttsy clarinet; Jones' fair trumpet)

FRIDAY 10 DECEMBER 1937

RECORDING SESSION

CAB CALLOWAY AND HIS ORCHESTRA
Recording session for Vocalion in New York City.
Cab Calloway (voc); Doc Cheatham, Shad Collins, Irving Randolph, Lammar Wright (t); DePriest Wheeler, Keg Johnson, Claude Jones (tb); Chauncey Haughton, Andrew Brown (cl/as); Chu Berry, Walter Thomas (ts); Benny Payne (p); Danny Barker (g); Milt Hinton (b); Leroy Maxey (d)
Every Day's A Holiday (vCC) / *Jubilee* (vCC) / *In An Old English Village* (vCC) / *(Just An) Error In The News* (vCC) / *Bugle Blues*

RADIO LOGS

12.00 MIDNIGHT WEAF
CHICK WEBB
Savoy Ballroom, NYC
Colossal. Personnel: Mario Bauza, Bobby Stark, Taft Jordan (trumpets); Sandy Williams, Nat Story (trombones); Garvin Bushell, Louis Jordan, Wayman Carver, Teddy McRae (saxes); Tommy Fulford (piano); Bobby Johnson (guitar); Beverly Peer (bass); Chick Webb (drums); Ella Fitzgerald (vocals)
I Found A New Baby (nuttsy: Wayman Carver's swell flute; high, hot trumpet; Sandy Williams' trombone; Fulford's piano; tenor sax)
After You (vocal: Ella Fitzgerald) (good song but not suited for Ella)

Bronzeville Stomp (great: Williams' great trombone; McRae's tenor; trumpet)
She's Tall, She's Tan, She's Terrific (vocal: Ella Fitzgerald)
Naughty Waltz (Bobby Stark's grand trumpet; Webb's grand drums throughout)
In A Little Spanish Town (Quintet: Garvin Bushell, clarinet; Wayman Carver, flute; Tommy Fulford, piano; Beverly Peer, bass; Chick Webb, drums)
You Showed Me The Way (vocal: Ella Fitzgerald) (colossal: Ella's marvelous slow vocal; Stark's trumpet)
Royal Garden Blues (great: marvelous trumpeting; Webb; Jordan's clarinet; Webb again)
Honeysuckle Rose (vocal: Ella Fitzgerald) (wonderful: Ella's great vocal; clarinet; tenor sax; clarinet again)

12:30AM WJZ
LOUIS ARMSTRONG
Vogue Ballroom, Los Angeles
Sugar Foot Stomp (Bingie Madison's nuttsy sax; Higginbotham's great trombone; clarinet; Louis' trumpet)
Public Enemy Number One (vocal: Louis Armstrong) (good: comical ending)
Fun For You (wonderful: Henry 'Red' Allen's colossal trumpet; tenor sax; Pops Foster's bass)
If We Never Meet Again (vocal: Louis Armstrong) (written by Louis)
Whoa, Babe (Henry 'Red' Allen's nuttsy trumpet again; great tenor sax)
Remember Me (vocal: Sonny Woods) (too sweet and slow)
Muskrat Ramble (slow, nuttsy tempo: colossal tenor sax by Greely Walton)
Algiers Stomp (colossal: Higginbotham; Red Allen; Madison's tenor)

■ SATURDAY 11 DECEMBER 1937

Hughie and I took the 9:27am train into the city. It is the first time we have been in the city in the day time in a long while. It sure was cold. We first went directly to Loew's State Theater where we saw the movie and stage show for 25 cents. The stage show was the nuts with many guys that we know from the CBS Swing Sessions taking part. As far as I could see, in the Leith Stevens Orchestra, I recognized Billy Gussak (drums); Lou Shoobe (bass); Walter Gross (piano); Frank D'Annolfo (trombone); Marty Marsala (trumpet); Nat Natoli (trumpet); Hank Ross (tenor sax); George Tudor (clarinet); and a couple of guys I never saw before. The numbers played were *Rose Room* (Stevens' Band, Ross' tenor, clarinet); *Nobody's Sweetheart* (Les Lieber the nuts on his fife); *Farewell Blues* (Stevens' Band, wonderful solos by Ross, trombone, Shoobe's bass); *Bob White* (Maxine Sullivan really singing the nuts; she's terrific); *Loch Lomond* (Maxine Sullivan again, Ross' tenor); *Nice Work If You Can Get It* (3rd number by Maxine Sullivan; great!!); *Margie / Chinatown, My Chinatown* (Tall Joe Sodja playing a swell, original, guitar); *Dipsy Doodle* (Stevens' Band, wonderful solos by clarinet, Ross' tenor, Marsala's trumpet).

After the show we walked up to the Music Corporation of America (MCA) where we got two pictures for nothing: one of Benny Goodman and one of Martha Tilton. We then wasted about 45 minutes taking the Fifth Avenue Open Bus up to 91st Street where I tried to find Dr. Richardson's offices so he could treat my ringworm. We never found him, however. We then took the elevated back to the RCA Building where we went to Rockwell-O'Keefe. We spent about an hour talking with Vincent Prior who works there. He is now personal manager of Willie Bryant's Band. He told us many interesting things: how Fats Waller is taking dope (I doubt it), how he saw Bunny Berigan walk into the Onyx Club drunk, and all about how Bob Crosby's Band is trying to leave Rockwell-O'Keefe for MCA, claiming R-O'K gave them a raw deal. He gave us a lot of pictures: about 10 of Jimmy Dorsey & Orchestra, 6 of Louis Armstrong & Orchestra, 2 of Mary Lou Williams, 2 of Willie Bryant, 1 of Bob Haggart, 2 of Bob Crosby, 2 of Kay Weber, 1 of Kathleen Lane, etc. He told us he would probably leave Bryant soon and go somewhere else. He sure is a swell guy. We said good-bye to him and went down to the Hotel New Yorker at 34th Street where Glen Gray's Casa Loma Orchestra had just finished playing for luncheon in the Terrace Room. Hughie asked Glen Gray, who was getting his coat to leave, where Murray McEachern was. He said that Murray, our old pal who we met when he played with Benny Goodman at the Pennsylvania Hotel across the street, was upstairs. We telephoned up to him and he came down to go home, after we had about a 10-minute talk. He told us that as the new arrangements came in he was getting more and more solos. He told us all about this camera he had, and about taking pictures. He reminded me of Vincent Prior: soft-spoken, intelligent, and dark. After Murray left, Hughie and I went upstairs in the Hotel New Yorker where I talked to M. S. Baker about getting into Hiram College of Hiram, Ohio. My brother and one of my sisters went there and enjoyed it and it looks like I'll end up there. We got the 5:25pm train home.

Fifty-second Street, between Fifth and Sixth Avenues, is finally coming to life after passing many months in the dog house. Specifically, the swing salons have been blossoming forth with favorite jam jupiters. A new **Famous Door** has opened with Louis Prima and boys; the Cafe Maria, site of the old Famous Door is now the **Swing Club**, with Wingy Mannone and fellow-conspirators presiding, and the **Onyx Club** has booked Stuff Smith and orchestra. All the retreats are of the traditional rectangular shape, noisy with music and the mutterings of jitterbugs and cloudy with smoke. The individual taste of the swing enthusiast is the prospective patron's best guide.

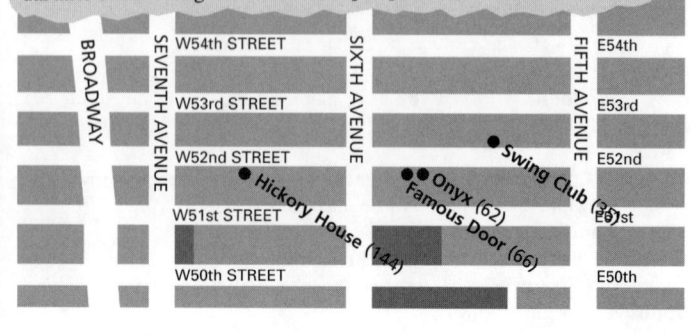

DECEMBER 1937

RADIO LOGS

7.00PM WABC
SATURDAY NIGHT SWING SESSION No74
CBS Studio No1, 485 Madison Ave, NYC
Down With Love (written by Harold Arlen: Hank Ross' swell tenor sax – Hank just got married last week)
Loch Lomond (MAXINE SULLIVAN giving a marvelous vocal; Ross' tenor sax)
N'Gona (CHAUNCEY MOREHOUSE playing some wonderful "N'Gona drums", 14 drums—something new: Shoobe's colossal bassing; Marsala's trumpet)
Ku-Li-A (means "come on and eat", very weird jungle piece with CHAUNCEY MOREHOUSE on drums, mostly tom-toms: whole band on swell vocal chorus; tenor sax)
Hittin' On All Six (JOHNNY CALI and TONY GATTUSO in guitar duet: little variety)
Swingin' Guitars (JOHNNY CALI and TONY GATTUSO again: swell)
The Lady is A Tramp (D'Annolfo's trombone; Ross' tenor; nice trumpet)
Nice Work If You Can Get It (MAXINE SULLIVAN: great, but too short)
Always (Leith Stevens' CBS Band: wonderful arrangement; Ross again, really groovin' it; clarinet; saxes & brass)

11:30PM WABC
BENNY GOODMAN
Hotel Pennsylvania, NYC
I heard this program at Emmy Neiley's house in Bronxville.
Dear Old Southland (colossal: wonderful tenor sax; Stacy's piano)
Sweet Someone (vocal: Martha Tilton) (swell sweet piece, good vocal)
If Dreams Come True (Benny certainly is playing this a lot; Brown's trombone)
Swingtime In The Rockies (great: Benny; Elman's grand trumpet)
Loch Lomond (vocal: Martha Tilton) (James' trumpet)
My Gal Sal (BG Quartet) (simply magnificent, especially Wilson & Benny)
Life Goes To A Party (great, what a brass section!! James; Krupa; Benny)
It's Wonderful (vocal: Martha Tilton) (fair: Benny's clarinet; time only permitted half of this piece)

1:00AM WBBM
ROY ELDRIDGE
Three Deuces, Chicago
Wonderful. Drummer Zutty Singleton left the band last month.
Minor Jive
That Thing (recorded on Vocalion: colossal, slow rhythm; Roy; alto sax; piano)
Gee, Jake, Whatta Snake (grand: Eldridge; alto sax; clarinet; Roy again)
Roaches And Incense (nuttsy: Eldridge's soft, muted trumpet; alto sax)
Shine (vocal: Roy Eldridge) (real hot vocal: Roy's wonderful, swingin' trumpet; drums)

■ SUNDAY 12 DECEMBER 1937

RADIO LOGS

11:00AM WNEW
SUNDAY MORNING SWING CONCERT
Criterion Theater, NYC
Marie (Merle Pitts' WNEW Studio Band)
If I Could Be With You One Hour Tonight (SHIRLEY BROWN singing)
Japanese Sandman (MURRAY GOLDEN playing a good, swing accordion)
Pagan Love Song (Merle Pitts' WNEW Make-Believe Ballroom Band)
Nice Work If You Can Get It (ANDREWS SISTERS: swell)
After You've Gone (swell: Merle Pitts' WNEW Make-Believe Ballroom Band; Sam Weiss' drums; nice tenor sax; clarinet)
I Ain't Got Nobody (SAMMY SPERGEL on electric guitar)
Weary Blues (Merle Pitts' WNEW Make-Believe Ballroom Band going swell)
Just A Simple Melody (ANDREWS SISTERS: they've got something!)

4:00PM WEAF
JIMMY DORSEY
Congress Hotel, Chicago
Excellent! This is a special benefit Swing Concert held for saxist Jimmy Cannon, formerly with Ray Noble. Tickets cost $1.50 for this show.
Sandman (theme) (swell slow theme used by Jimmy ever since he had a band)
Chicken Reel (colossal: Camarata's nuttsy trumpet; Dorsey's great alto)
Hollywood Pastimes (written by Jimmy Dorsey last spring in Hollywood: Jimmy's nice clarineting)
Parade Of The Milk Bottle Tops (written and arranged by Pat McCarthy—super-marvelous: wonderful in-the-groove tenor sax; nuttsy trumpet; Ray McKinley's nuttsy cymbals; Dorsey's great alto sax; nice sax run; swell, dirty trombone solo; clarinets; long, drawn-out ending; Freddie Slack's nice piano)
By Heck (very old piece recorded by Dorsey Brothers: marvelous trombone; Dorsey's swell clarinet; nuttsy trumpets; McKinley's marvelous drumming throughout)
Flight Of The Bumble Bee (very unusual swing arrangement, a little overdone: Bobby Byrne's fast, sweet trombone; hot trombone; Freddie Slack's swell piano solo; Dorsey's alto sax)
In A Sentimental Mood (Ellington's masterpiece featuring 19-yr-old Bobby Byrne's trombone; Jimmy Dorsey's great alto sax)
Put On Your Old Grey Bonnet (magnificent: COLOSSAL long, dirty trombone solo following Jimmy's clarinet; Freddie Slack's wonderful piano; McKinley's drums behinf muted brass and saxes; nuttsy trumpet by Toots Camarata; Jimmy's clarinet)
Dusk In Upper Sandusky (very fast, written by Larry Clinton: McKinley's cymbal intro; Jimmy's nice alto; brief trombone; Dorsey's fast, intricate alto; McKinley's long drum solo at end)

9:45PM WOR
ADRIAN ROLLINI QUARTET
WOR Studios, NYC
Nice Work If You Can Get It (vocal: Helene Daniels)
A Study In Brown (nuttsy: Rollini's vibraharp; Duffy's violin)
The Dipsy Doodle (vocal: Helene Daniels)
Caravan

■ MONDAY 13 DECEMBER 1937

RECORDING SESSION

ANDY KIRK AND HIS TWELVE CLOUDS OF JOY
Recording session for Decca in New York City.
Andy Kirk (bsx/ldr); Harry Lawson, Clarence Trice, Earl Thompson (t); Ted Donnelly, Henry Wells (tb); John Harrington (cl/as/bar); John Williams (as/bar); Earl Miller (as); Dick Wilson (ts); Mary Lou Williams (p); Ted Brinson (g); Booker Collins (b); Ben Thigpen (d); Pha Terrell (voc)
Lover, Come Back To Me (vPT) / *Poor Butterfly* (vPT) / *The Big Dipper* / *Bear Down*

GLENN MILLER AND HIS ORCHESTRA
Recording session for Brunswick in New York City.
Glenn Miller (tb/ldr); Pee Wee Erwin, Bob Price, Ardell Garrett (t); Jesse Ralph, Bud Smith (tb); Irving Fazola (cl/as); Hal McIntyre, Tony Viola (as); Jerry Jerome, Carl Biesecker (ts); Chummy MacGregor (p); Carmen Mastren (g); Rowland Bundock (b); Doc Cenardo (Carney) (d); Kathleen Lane (voc)
Every Day's A Holiday (vKL) / *Sweet Stranger* (vKL)

Today I went to Ferris' Music Store and bought Teddy Wilson's record of *Ain't Misbehavin'* and *Honeysuckle Rose* including Harry James, Red Norvo, etc. (Brunswick 7964)

RADIO LOGS

11:00PM WABC
GLEN GRAY
Hotel New Yorker, NYC
The Sheik Of Araby (good arrangement: Hutchenrider; nuttsy trumpet)
I Can Dream, Can't I? (vocal: Kenny Sargent) (typical Casa Loma sweet arrangement: trombones; Ralston's bassoon)
Mama, I Want To Make Rhythm (vocal: Pee Wee Hunt) (Rauch's brief hot trombone; clarinet; drums)
Diane (swell old piece: nice clarinet; Pat Davis' nuttsy tenor sax; clarinet again; good trumpet)

Satan Takes A Holiday (vocal: Pee Wee Hunt) (good original arrangement: colossal trombone)
In The Still Of The Night (vocal: Kenny Sargent) (Rauch's sweet, muted trombone; Ralston's bassoon)
How Am I To Know? (featuring 6 saxes: Gray; Davis; Hutchenrider; Ralston; Sargent; D'Andrea)
Pagan Love Song (great: wonderful soft, hot, muted trombone; Davis' tenor)

■ TUESDAY 14 DECEMBER 1937

RECORDING SESSION

GLEN GRAY AND THE CASA LOMA ORCHESTRA
Recording session for Decca in New York City.
Glen Gray (as/dir); Sonny Dunham, Grady Watts, Frank Zullo (t); Pee Wee Hunt (tb/voc); Billy Rauch, Murray McEachern (tb); Clarence Hutchenrider (cl/as), Kenny Sargent (as/voc); Art Ralston (as/o/bsn); Danny d'Andrea (as); Pat Davis (cl/ts/fl); Joe Hall (p); Jack Blanchette (g); Stanley Dennis (b); Tony Briglia (d)
Two Dreams Got Together (vKS) / *Drifting Apart* / *You Have Everything* (vPWH) / *I Cried For You* (vKS)

RADIO LOGS

12:00 NOON WABC
CBS HOUSE BAND
'Swingin' The Blues', NYC
Mood Indigo (one of Duke Ellington's finest compositions: nice clarinet)
Dallas Blues (swell, not a very original arrangement however: tenor sax)
St. Louis Blues (clarinet; trumpet)
Darkness On The Delta (good: colossal trombone with real guts; saxes)

10:00PM WABC
BENNY GOODMAN
Camel Caravan, CBS Playhouse, NYC
Let's Dance (theme)
Three Little Words (colossal: Brown's nuttsy, brief trombone; swell tenor sax; Benny & Krupa)
I Want To Be In Winchell's Column (vocal: Martha Tilton) (new: Benny)
Once In A While (BG Trio) (fair)
Josephine (great sax section; James' trumpet with Krupa; Benny's swell solo)
Dear Old Southland (marvelous: nuttsy trumpet intro followed by Benny's clarinet; weak trombone; grand tenor sax; Stacy's nice piano)
My Gal Sal (BG Quartet) (magnificent & wonderful, especially Benny & Lionel)
You Took The Words Right Out Of My Heart (vocal: Martha Tilton) (swell sweet piece: Brown's trombone; Benny)
I Found A New Baby (terrific: great brass; Benny outdoing himself in a great solo; Elman's magnificent hot trumpet with Krupa's nuttsy cymbals; Rollini's swell tenor sax; Elman & Krupa again)
Goodbye (closing theme)

■ WEDNESDAY 15 DECEMBER 1937

RADIO LOGS

11:00PM WABC
BENNY GOODMAN
Hotel Pennsylvania, NYC
Mel Allen announced.
Let's Dance (theme)
Walk, Jennie, Walk (swell: fast tempo; Benny; Brown's dirty trombone; Krupa)
I've Hitched My Wagon To A Star (vocal: Martha Tilton) (superb sax section; Benny)
China Boy (BG Trio) (great: Benny's fine clarinet; Krupa's cowbells)
Bob White (vocal: Martha Tilton) (swell arrangement but I'm sick of this tune: James' trumpet)
Rosalie (fine arrangement of fair current piece: nice trombone team; James)

Nice Work If You Can Get It (vocal: Martha Tilton) (nice relaxed vocal: Elman's trumpet)
If Dreams Come True (swell tempo featuring muted brass; Brown; Rollini)
Tea For Two (BG Quartet) (medium tempo with Benny outstanding)
Smiles (Ziggy Elman's colossal trumpet; Benny & Krupa; trombones)
Goodbye (closing theme)

11:30PM WEAF
JIMMY DORSEY
Congress Hotel, Chicago
Have You Got Any Castles, Baby? (vocal: Don Mattison) (clarinet)
In A Sentimental Mood (Bobby Byrne's trombone)
Hollywood Pastimes (Jimmy's clarinet)
Basin Street Blues (vocal: June Richmond) (nuttsy)
Love Me Or Leave Me (great: trombone)
Chicken Reel (great: Dorsey's alto; trombone)
Time On My Hands (nice)
Dorsey Opus (swell sweet piece)
Parade Of The Milk Bottle Tops (excellent, long arrangement)

12:00 MIDNIGHT WJZ
GLENN MILLER
Raymor Ballroom, Boston
Every Day's A Holiday (vocal: Kathleen Lane)
Time On My Hands (colossal sweet arrangement: great saxes; clarinet)
Sweet Stranger (vocal: Kathleen Lane)
Peg O' My Heart (another sweet Miller arrangement: nuttsy clarinet; saxes)
Doin' The Jive (vocal: Kathleen Lane & Band) (nuttsy original by Miller)
You Took The Words Right Out Of My Heart (vocal: Kathleen Lane)
Down South Camp Meetin' (wonderful Henderson arrangement: fine trumpet; clarinet; saxes; brass)
Let's Give Love Another Chance (vocal: Kathleen Lane) (swell piece: Fazola's clarinet)
Limehouse Blues (great: grand trumpet; nuttsy clarinet; Jerry Jerome's tenor sax)

12:00 MIDNIGHT WABC
TOMMY DORSEY
Hotel Commodore, NYC
Gypsy In My Soul (vocal: Edythe Wright)
Whispers In The Dark (vocal: Jack Leonard)
Candlelights (written by Bix Beiderbecke: nice saxes; Howard Smith's piano)
She's Tall, She's Tan, She's Terrific (vocal: Edythe Wright) (too fast)
That Old Feeling (vocal: Edythe Wright)
Who Knows? (vocal: Jack Leonard)
My Blue Heaven
Josephine (vocal: Jack Leonard)

12.30AM WJZ
CHICK WEBB
Savoy Ballroom, NYC
Wonderful.
After You've Gone (swell: Sandy Williams' nice trombone; Webb's drums)
Love Is The Thing So They Say (vocal: Ella Fitzgerald) (ballsy song)
My Blue Heaven (written by Walter Donaldson in 1928: Stark's nice trumpet; Williams' trombone; Bushell's high clarinet; colossal ending)
Love Is In My Heart (swell slow piece written by Webb: McRae's tenor; clarinet)
Don't Be That Way (nuttsy fast song: Webb's great drums; trumpet; sax; trombone)
Quaker City Jazz (in honor of Philadelphia's Jan Savitt: McRae's swell tenor)
Rock It For Me (vocal: Ella Fitzgerald) (great vocal)
Naughty Waltz

■ THURSDAY 16 DECEMBER 1937

RADIO LOGS

10:15PM WHN
JOE HAYMES
Roseland Ballroom, NYC
My Cabin Of Dreams (vocal: Barbara Burns) (great: marvelous tenor sax; trumpet; trombone; piano)

DECEMBER 1937

Dark Eyes (vocal: Barbara Burns) (wonderful: Dave Frankel's colossal trumpet; Charlie Bush's nuttsy solid drumming; Frankel's trumpet again; excellent tenor sax; Frankel's 3rd solo; ending)
Take My Word (swell slow fox-trot: swell muted trumpets with nice strong rhythm section, especially bass; fine sax section; nuttsy tenor sax)
Ubangi Man (written by Bunny Berigan: wonderful tenor sax; trombone; trumpet)

11:00PM WABC
CAB CALLOWAY
Cotton Club, NYC
Queen Isabella (Doc Cheatham's nice trumpet; Chu Berry's excellent tenor; clarinet)
Turning On My Heart (vocal: Cab Calloway) (fair new piece: Berry's tenor)
Chiquita (Rhumba with some fine string bassing throughout: trumpet, etc)
Jubilee (vocal: Cab Calloway) (again Berry taking an inspired solo; trumpet)
Harlem On The Prairie
Error In The News (vocal: Cab Calloway) (played for first time over radio)
Tiger Rag (fair arrangement: swell solos by Chu Berry; clarinet; trumpet)
I Still Love To Kiss You Goodnight (vocal: Cab Calloway) (lousy commercial tripe)
China Boy (great: Chu Berry; clarinet; trumpet)

11:15PM WEAF
LARRY CLINTON
RCA Studios, NYC
Every Day's A Holiday
I've Got My Heart Set On You
Remember (swell: fine clarinet; tenor sax; nice trumpets)
Scrapin' The Toast (vocal: Beatrice Wain) (swell new piece just recorded on Victor)
The Snake Charmer

11:30PM WEAF
JIMMY DORSEY
Congress Hotel, Chicago
Farewell My Love (vocal: Bob Eberly)
It's The Dreamer In Me (vocal: Bob Eberly) (music written by Jimmy Dorsey)
Nice Work If You Can Get It (vocal: Dorsey Trio) (nuttsy: Frazier's nuttsy tenor; dirty trombone; Ryan's solid bass; McKinley; clarinet)
Body And Soul (Bobby Byrne's trombone)
How Am I To Know? (Jimmy's clarinet)
Rosetta (grand: tricky trombone)
Put On Your Old Grey Bonnet (great: swell clarinet; marvelous trombone; Slack's terrific piano)
In The Still Of The Night (interrupted, and quite short)
Flight Of The Bumble Bee
One Rose Of Summer (fair)
Sandman (theme)

12:00 MIDNIGHT WOR
BENNY GOODMAN
Hotel Pennsylvania, NYC
Camel Hop (written by Mary Lou Williams: James; Rollini)
Farewell My Love (vocal: Martha Tilton) (good: Benny & Krupa)
Nice Work If You Can Get It (BG Trio)
Chlo-e (swell: fine trumpets; Benny & James)
Hallelujah (great arrangement: trumpets; Benny)
Bob White (vocal: Martha Tilton) (Benny whistling)
I'm A Ding Dong Daddy (From Dumas) (BG Quartet) (excellent: released today!)
I'm Like A Fish Out of Water (vocal: Martha Tilton)
One O'Clock Jump (magnificent: Stacy; tenor sax; Brown; Benny)

12.00 MIDNIGHT WNEW
CHICK WEBB
Savoy Ballroom, NYC
King Porter Stomp
Once In A While (vocal: Ella Fitzgerald)
Alabamy Home (wonderful)
Stop, Look, And Listen (dirty clarinet; trumpet)

So Rare (vocal: Ella Fitzgerald) (colossal, great)
I Got Rhythm (swell! Quintet: Garvin Bushell, clarinet; Wayman Carver, flute; Tommy Fulford, piano; Beverly Peer, bass; Chick Webb, drums)

■ **FRIDAY 17 DECEMBER 1937**

RECORDING SESSION

CHICK WEBB ORCHESTRA
Recording session for Decca in New York City.
Ella Fitzgerald (voc); Mario Bauza, Taft Jordan, Bobby Stark (t); Sandy Williams, Nat Story (tb); Louis Jordan (as); Garvin Bushell (cl/as); Ted McRae (ts), Wayman Carver (ts/fl); Tommy Fulford (p); Bobby Johnson (g); Beverly Peer (b); Chick Webb (d)
I Want To be Happy (vEF, 2 takes) / *The Dipsy Doodle* (vEF) / *If Dreams Come True* (vEF) / *Hallelujah!* (vEF) / *Midnite In A Madhouse*

Today I got Benny Goodman's record of *You Can't Teach My Old Heart New Tricks* and *Silhouetted In The Moonlight* with Martha Tilton singing both sides (Victor 25711).

■ **SATURDAY 18 DECEMBER 1937**

RADIO LOGS

7.00PM WABC
SATURDAY NIGHT SWING SESSION No75
CBS Studio No1, 485 Madison Ave, NYC
Panamania (Leith Stevens' CBS Band playing the nuts)
Bei Mir Bist Du Schoen (ANDREWS SISTERS girl trio singing swell: Bobby Hackett's trumpet)
Oh Lady Be Good (Toots Mondello playing a super-marvelous alto sax!)
When Your Heart's On Fire (very new swell piece from the Princeton Triangle Show)
Star Dust (BOBBY HACKETT playing GREAT trumpet in a subdued swing style in 2 tempos: marvelous Bixian tone)
Ku-Li-A (CHAUNCEY MOREHOUSE playing his tom-tom drums, swell if you don't get sick of the continual beat: tenor sax; vocal chorus)
Mazi-Pani (CHAUNCEY MOREHOUSE again on drums on another jungle piece!)
Nice Work If You Can Get It (ANDREWS SISTERS singing colossally)
Always (Leith Stevens' CBS Band: wonderful arrangement; Ross again, really groovin' it; clarinet; saxes & brass)

11:30PM WABC
BENNY GOODMAN
Hotel Pennsylvania, NYC
Big John Special (wonderful: 2 great trumpet solos; Stacy's piano)
You Took The Words Right Out Of My Heart (vocal: Martha Tilton) (trombone)
If Dreams Come True (swell: written by Edgar Sampson)
Bei Mir Bist Du Schoen (vocal: Martha Tilton) (new hit tune: Benny; Stacy)
Where Or When (BG Trio) (fair: Wilson's fine piano)
Darktown Strutters' Ball (colossal: Benny; Elman; Rollini)
I've Hitched My Wagon To A Star (vocal: Martha Tilton) (good)
Dinah (BG Quartet) (swell: different from record)
I Want To Be In Winchell's Column (vocal: Martha Tilton)
All Of Me (nuttsy tune and arrangement: great tenor sax)

12:00 MIDNIGHT WMCA
JOE MARSALA
Hickory House, 144 W52nd Street, NYC
SWELL.
Clarinet Marmalade (excellent clarinet by Joe; Marty's typical trumpet)
Nice Work If You Can Get It (vocal: Adele Girard)
Bob White (whole band singing swell original arrangement: Marty & Joe jammin' the nuts)

Star Dust (Joe's clarinet; Marty's muted trumpet; Joe Bushkin's piano)
Once In A While (vocal: Lou Hirst) (Bushkin's piano; Shapiro's bass)
Gold Mine In The Sky (fine jam arrangement: Bushkin; Joe; Marty)
Jim Jam Stomp (very fast piece: Marty's colossal trumpet; Bushkin's swell piano with Rich's drums; Artie Shapiro's colossal bass slapping; Ray Biondi's short violin break; Joe's great clarinet solo; Rich's nuttsy drums)

■ SUNDAY 19 DECEMBER 1937

Hughie, Robcliff Jones, Jim Poe and myself took the 3:23 train into 138th Street where we got off and walked over to 140th Street and Lenox Avenue where the famous Savoy Ballroom is located. We paid 35 cents apiece and went in at 4:00pm. Milt Mezzrow's mixed band was supposed to be there today but they have broken up through lack of engagements. Martin Block and Wingy Mannone were also to have showed up but while we were there (until 11:00pm) they never came. Hughie had to leave at 6:00 to go home, and Robcliff left at 8:45. Poe and I stayed until about 11:00 and had a colossal time doing some of our own particular dancing in Lindy-hop fashion. I got the autographs of the musicians in both bands, except the guitar player in Al Cooper's Savoy Sultans, Chick Webb himself, and Ella Fitzgerald who had a cold so couldn't sing. Webb was late so only drummed about half the time. Some other guys took his place during his brief absence. We were a little disappointed in Webb's Band. It seemed to lack that punch that it should have; there were too many commercials. Webb didn't do anything exceptional on the drums. McRae's tenor solos, Bobby Stark, and Taft Jordan were fine however. The Savoy Sultans were just the opposite. They aren't as polished and formal and well-known as Webb's Band, they are slightly ragged but how they swing! Especially on slow numbers. Ed McNeal plays a sensational, simple, grooving tenor sax. Rudy Williams, who is almost pure white, plays a screwy alto sax, but it sounds great. Sam Massenburg (a short fellow) and Pat Jenkins take turns out-doing each other on inspired trumpet solos. Taft Jordan often sat in with them and it sounded great. Grachan Moncur is a wonderful bassist who has wonderful technique and supports the rhythm section. Drummer Alex Mitchell, always smiling, beats hell as he plays a solid drum without any exceptional breaks. Al Cooper, who you would hardly know was the leader, plays an O.K. clarinet. Moncur is the only well-known member of the band. He has played in the recording bands of Bunny Berigan, Mildred Bailey, Bud Freeman and Teddy Wilson.

■ MONDAY 20 DECEMBER 1937

RECORDING SESSION

HUDSON-DeLANGE ORCHESTRA
Recording session for Brunswick in New York City.
Will Hudson (arr); Eddie DeLange (voc/ldr); Charles Mitchell, Howard Schaumberger, Joe Bauer (t); Edward Kolyer, Jack Andrews (tb); George Bohn, Gus Bivona (cl/as); Pete Brendel (as/bar); Ted Duane (cl/ts); Mark Hyams (p); Bus Etri (g); Doc Goldberg (b); Billy Exiner (d); Elyse Cooper (voc)
Definition Of Swing (vEC) / *You're Out Of This World* (vEC) / *Strictly Formal* (vEC)

RAYMOND SCOTT QUINTETTE
Recording session for Brunswick in NYC.
Raymond Scott (p/ldr); Dave Wade (t); Pete Pumiglio (cl); Dave Harris (ts); Ted Harkins (b); Johnny Williams (d)
War Dance For Wooden Indians / *The Penguin*

RADIO LOGS

12.00 MIDNIGHT WNEW
CHICK WEBB
Savoy Ballroom, NYC
My Blue Heaven (colossal: trumpet; clarinet)
Once In A While (vocal: Ella Fitzgerald)
What A Shuffle (nuttsy: Louis Jordan's alto sax; Sandy Williams' trombone)

DECEMBER 1937

I'll Come To The Point (vocal: Ella Fitzgerald) (swell new piece)
Midnight In A Madhouse
Tall, Dark, And Handsome
Rhythm In My Soul
I Want To Be Happy

12:30AM WJZ
EARL HINES
Grand Terrace, Chicago
Bear Down
Let's Make It A Lifetime
How Many Rhymes Can You Answer?
True Confession
My First Confession
Let's Give Love Another Chance
I've Hitched My Wagon To A Star
The Dipsy Doodle

■ TUESDAY 21 DECEMBER 1937

RECORDING SESSION

BENNY GOODMAN QUARTET
Recording session for Victor in New York City.
Lionel Hampton (vib); Teddy Wilson (p); Benny Goodman (cl); Gene Krupa (d); Martha Tilton (voc)
Bei Mir Bist Du Schoen, Part 1 (vMT)

ELLA FITZGERALD AND HER SAVOY EIGHT
Recording session for Decca in New York City.
Ella Fitzgerald (voc); Taft Jordan (t); Sandy Williams (tb); Louis Jordan (as); Teddy McRae (ts/bar); Tommy Fulford (p); Bobby Johnson (g); Beverly Peer (b); Chick Webb (d)
Bei Mir Bist Du Schoen / It's My Turn Now

RADIO LOGS

10:00PM WABC
BENNY GOODMAN
Camel Caravan, CBS Playhouse, NYC
I heard this program at Nancy Long's house in Scarsdale.
Let's Dance (theme)
Jingle Bells (nuttsy: Gordon Griffin's fine trumpet; tenor sax)
True Confession (vocal: Martha Tilton)
Someday Sweetheart (BG Trio) (very good)
One O'Clock Jump (excellent: Stacy; Russin; James)
Vibraphone Blues (BG Quartet) (Lionel Hampton singing his own tune)
Bei Mir Bist Du Schoen (vocal: Martha Tilton) (Elman's trumpet)

12.00 MIDNIGHT WNEW
CHICK WEBB
Savoy Ballroom, NYC
Clap Hands! Here Comes Charlie (Webb's great drumming; trumpet; clarinet)
True Confession (vocal: Ella Fitzgerald)
Sugar Foot Stomp (nuttsy: Bobby Stark's fine trumpet; Williams' trombone)
If Dreams Come True (grand new piece written by Edgar Sampson)
The Dipsy Doodle (vocal: Ella Fitzgerald)
Bronzeville Stomp (swell)
Bei Mir Bist Du Schoen (vocal: Ella Fitzgerald)
Royal Garden Blues

12:30AM WCCO
WOODY HERMAN
Hotel Nicollet, Minneapolis
Davenport Blues
Why Talk About Love? (vocal: Woody Herman)
Ain't Misbehavin'
Exactly Like You
Dupree Blues (vocal: Woody Herman)
Roses In December
Old Fashioned Love
Love Me Or Leave Me

■ WEDNESDAY 22 DECEMBER 1937

RECORDING SESSION

GLEN GRAY AND THE CASA LOMA ORCHESTRA
Recording session for Decca in New York City.
Glen Gray (as/dir); Sonny Dunham, Grady Watts, Frank Zullo (t); Pee Wee Hunt (tb/voc); Billy Rauch, Murray McEachern (tb); Clarence Hutchenrider (cl/as), Kenny Sargent (as/voc); Art Ralston (as/o/bsn); Danny d'Andrea (as); Pat Davis (cl/ts/fl); Joe Hall (p); Jack Blanchette (g); Stanley Dennis (b); Tony Briglia (d)
Sweet As A Song (vKS) / *I Could Use A Dream* (vKS) / *Girl Of My Dreams* (vKS)

RADIO LOGS

11:00PM WABC
BENNY GOODMAN
Hotel Pennsylvania, NYC
Milton 'Mezz' Mezzrow and Helen Ward are in the audience tonight.
Life Goes To A Party
Sweet Someone (vocal: Martha Tilton)
If Dreams Come True
Can't Help Lovin' Dat Man (BG Trio)
Alice Blue Gown
Josephine (marvelous arrangement)
It's Wonderful (vocal: Martha Tilton)
Avalon (BG Quartet)
Rockin' The Town (vocal: Martha Tilton)

12:30AM WCCO
WOODY HERMAN
Hotel Nicollet, Minneapolis
Weary Blues
Sweet Someone (vocal: Woody Herman)
Squeeze Me
Blue Hawaii
D-Flat Blues
Muskrat Ramble
Once In A While

■ THURSDAY 23 DECEMBER 1937

RECORDING SESSION

BUNNY BERIGAN AND HIS ORCHESTRA
Recording session for Victor in New York City.
Bunny Berigan, Irving Goodman, Steve Lipkins (t); Al George, Sonny Lee (tb); Mike Doty, Joe Dixon (cl/as); Clyde Rounds, George Auld (ts); Joe Lippman (p); Tom Morgan (g); Hank Wayland (b); George Wettling (d)
In A Little Spanish Town / Black Bottom / Trees / Russian Lullaby / Can't Help Lovin' Dat Man

Today, at Ferris' Music Store, I got Benny Goodman's record of *Life Goes To A Party* and *If Dreams Come True* (Victor 25726).

RADIO LOGS

6:10PM WEAF
TEDDY HILL
Savoy Ballroom, NYC
Queen Isabella (written by and featuring guest Chu Berry on tenor sax)

Darktown Strutters' Ball (swell arrangement: nice trumpet; trombone)
Swanee River (vocal: Bill Dillard) (very good: brass & sax ending)
Russian Lullaby (Russell Procope's clarinet; trombone)
My Cabin Of Dreams

10:00PM WHN
CLAUDE HOPKINS
Roseland Ballroom, NYC
Swinging Down The Lane (vocal: Beverly White)
Holdin' Your Man
Twelfth Street Rag
Loch Lomond (vocal: Beverly White)
Posin'
Cryin' My Heart Out For You
The Maid's Night Off
I Know That You Know

11:00PM WABC
BENNY GOODMAN
Hotel Pennsylvania, NYC
If Dreams Come True (Brown; Rollini)
A Foggy Day (vocal: Martha Tilton)
Three Little Words
Mama, That Moon's Here Again (vocal: Martha Tilton)
Nobody's Sweetheart (BG Trio)
Bob White (vocal: Martha Tilton)
The Man I Love (BG Quartet)
When Buddha Smiles
You Took The Words Right Out Of My Heart (vocal: Martha Tilton)

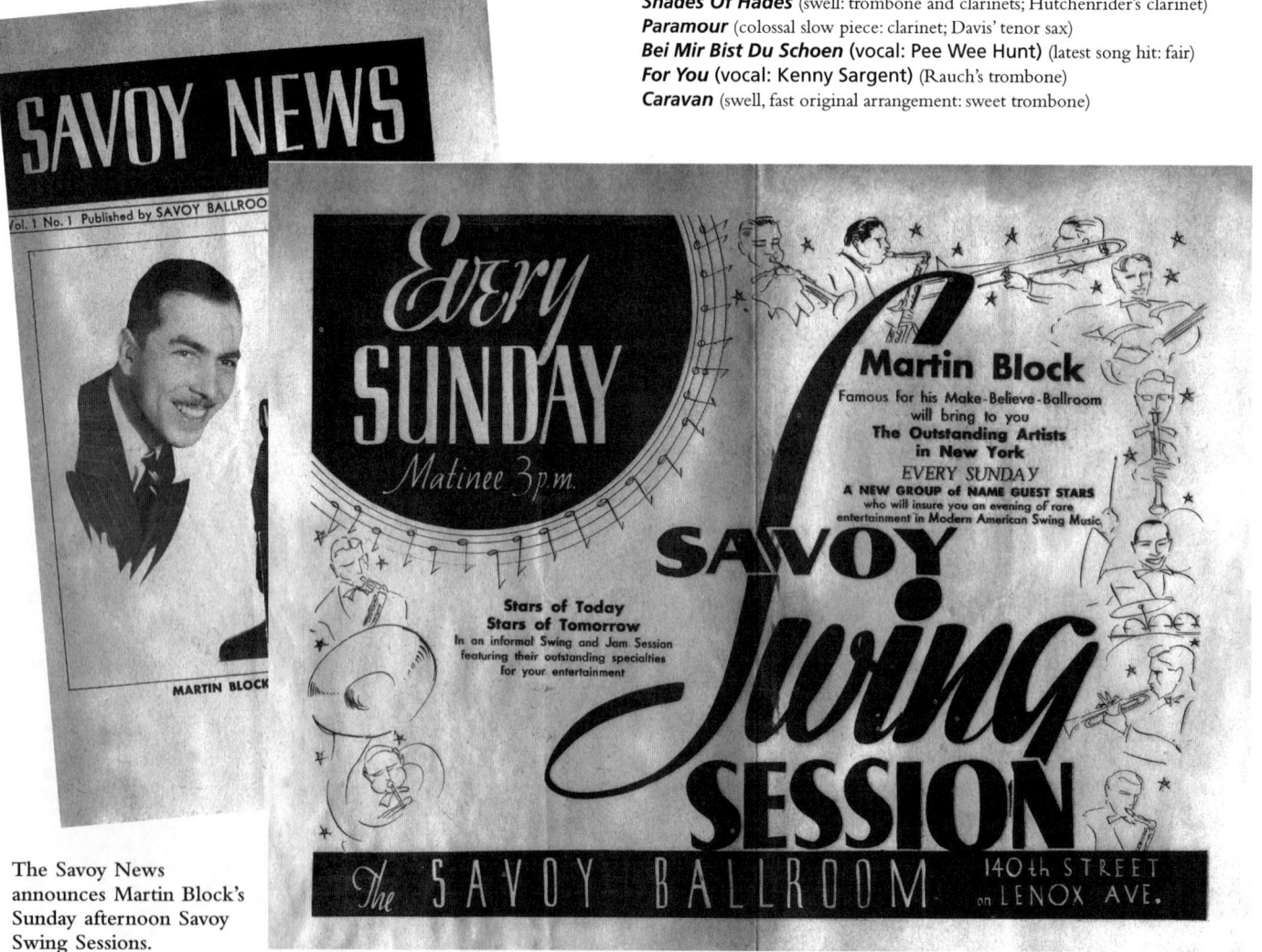

■ FRIDAY 24 DECEMBER 1937

Today, at the Commodore Music Shop in NYC, I bought Cootie Williams' *Swing, Baby, Swing* and *Sugar Hill Shim Sham* (Vocalion 3844); and Chu Berry's *Limehouse Blues* and *Back Home Again In Indiana* (Variety 587).

RADIO LOGS

9:30PM WJZ
TOMMY DORSEY
Kool-Raleigh Cigarette program, NYC
Star Dust (vocal: Edythe Wright)
Sweet Someone (vocal: Jack Leonard)
Candlelights
Once In A While (vocal: Three Esquires)
There's More Than One Santa Claus (vocal: Edythe Wright)
I Get A Kick Out Of You (vocal: Jack Leonard)
Lost
I Dream Of You (vocal: Edythe Wright)
If It's The Last Thing I Do

11:00PM WABC
GLEN GRAY
Hotel New Yorker, NYC
Dardanella (very old piece: Dunham's colossal trumpet; Hutchenrider's clarinet)
Once In A While (vocal: Kenny Sargent) (good: Ralston's bassoon)
Bob White (vocal: Pee Wee Hunt)
Shades Of Hades (swell: trombone and clarinets; Hutchenrider's clarinet)
Paramour (colossal slow piece: clarinet; Davis' tenor sax)
Bei Mir Bist Du Schoen (vocal: Pee Wee Hunt) (latest song hit: fair)
For You (vocal: Kenny Sargent) (Rauch's trombone)
Caravan (swell, fast original arrangement: sweet trombone)

The Savoy News announces Martin Block's Sunday afternoon Savoy Swing Sessions.

■ SATURDAY 25 DECEMBER 1937

RADIO LOGS

7.00PM WABC
SATURDAY NIGHT SWING SESSION No76
CBS Playhouse 3, NYC
The Dipsy Doodle (nuttsy: swell clarinet; colossal tenor sax; ballsy drums)
I Got Rhythm (TEDDY WILSON playing absolutely marvelous piano!!!)
Bei Mir Bist Du Schoen (JOHNNY HAUSER singing the nuts with a nuttsy sax chorus: Russ Case's trumpet)
Choppin' Wood (written by Hampton, featuring LIONEL HAMPTON playing some great vibraphone with Lou Shoobe on bass; Frankie Worrell on guitar; Teddy Wilson on piano; Billy Gussak on drums)
Always (Leith Stevens' CBS Band: magnificent tenor sax by Ross; swell clarinet; colossal saxes)
Honeysuckle Rose (JERRY KRUGER, female from the 18 Club on 52nd Street, singing the nuts)
Oh, Lady Be Good (LOU 'RED' EVANS playing a grand ocarina: real swing playing)
Moonglow (COLOSSAL!! HAMPTON & WILSON going marvelously; Gussak's drums)
China Boy (HAMPTON & WILSON and Gussak again layin' 'em low: simply grand)

11:30PM WABC
BENNY GOODMAN
Hotel Pennsylvania, NYC
Jingle Bells (Griffin's fine trumpet; Benny)
Loch Lomond (vocal: Martha Tilton) (Harry James' trumpet)
Sing You Sinners (great: Elman; Russin)
Once In A While (BG Trio) (fair)
Bei Mir Mist Du Schoen (vocal: Martha Tilton) (Ziggy Elman's trumpet)
If Dreams Come True (Benny; Brown; Rollini)
It's The Dreamer In Me (vocal: Martha Tilton)
Liza (BG Quartet) (excellent)
I Want To Be In Winchell's Column (vocal: Martha Tilton)

1:00AM WBBM
ROY ELDRIDGE
Famous Three Deuces, Chicago
Dismal Day
Blue Lou
Buzz Music
Heckler's Hop

■ MONDAY 27 DECEMBER 1937

Nancy Long, Barbara Doyle, Don Mortimer, Hugh Pastoriza, Roddy Snow, Dick Morningstar, Hal Johnson and myself went down on the 8:09 train to see Goodman's band. The photographs here were taken by Hughie and Don. As usual, we all had a great time and got the last train home. Some of the tunes played were: *So Many Memories* (vocal: Martha Tilton); *Bugle Call Rag*; *Blue Skies* (Rollini); *Once In A While*; *Sometimes I'm Happy* (James); *I've Got My Love To Keep Me Warm*; *Rockin' The Town* (vocal: Martha Tilton).

Teddy Wilson

Bob Inman reading *Down Beat*

The Benny Goodman Quartet with Harry James on drums

TUESDAY 28 DECEMBER 1937
RADIO LOGS
10:00PM WABC
BENNY GOODMAN
Camel Caravan, CBS Playhouse, NYC
I heard this program at Anne Wilson's house in Scarsdale.
Let's Dance (theme)
Sing You Sinners
Thanks For The Memory (vocal: Martha Tilton)
I Know That You Know (BG Quartet)
Bob White (vocal: Martha Tilton, Benny Goodman, Beatrice Lillie)
Sing, Sing, Sing

11:30PM WJZ
JIMMY DORSEY
Congress Hotel, Chicago
Nice Work If You Can Get It (vocal: Dorsey Trio)
I Want To Be In Winchell's Column
Bob White (vocal: June Richmond & Ray McKinley)
Blossoms On Broadway
Volga Boatmen (Bobby Byrne's hot trombone)
It's The Dreamer In Me (vocal: Bob Eberly) (Bobby Byrne's trombone)
Let That Be A Lesson To You
MEDLEY: *Moonglow / Can't We Be Friends?*
Put On Your Old Grey Bonnet

12:00 MIDNIGHT WNEW
AL COOPER'S SAVOY SULTANS
Savoy Ballroom, NYC
Gloomy Rhythm
Camels Are Swingin'
Am I In Another World?
Rhythm Doctor
Marie
On The Sunny Side Of The Street

■ WEDNESDAY 29 DECEMBER 1937

RECORDING SESSION

BENNY GOODMAN QUINTET
Recording session for Victor in New York City.
Lionel Hampton (vib); Ziggy Elman (t); Teddy Wilson (p); Benny Goodman (cl); Gene Krupa (d); Martha Tilton (voc)
Bei Mir Bist Du Schoen, Part 2 (vMT)

RADIO LOGS

11:00PM WABC
BENNY GOODMAN
Hotel Pennsylvania, NYC
If Dreams Come True
Thanks For The Memory (vocal: Martha Tilton)
More Than You Know (BG Trio) (swell)
Swing Low, Sweet Chariot (nuttsy: Russin; Elman)
You Took The Words Right Out Of My Heart (vocal: Martha Tilton)
Clarinet Marmalade
Stompin' At The Savoy (BG Quartet) (grand)
Makin' Whoopee
I've Hitched My Wagon To A Star (vocal: Martha Tilton)

■ THURSDAY 30 DECEMBER 1937

RECORDING SESSION

ART SHAW AND HIS NEW MUSIC
Recording session for Brunswick in New York City.
Art Shaw (cl/ldr); John Best, Malcolm Crain, Tom di Carlo (t); Harry Rogers, George Arus (tb); Les Robinson, Harry Freeman (as); Tony Pastor (ts/voc); Jules Rubin (ts); Les Burness (p); Al Avola (g); Ben Ginsberg (b); Cliff Leeman (d); Nita Bradley (voc)
Whistle While You Work (vTP) / *One Song* (vNB) / *Goodnight Angel* (vNB) / *There's A New Moon Over The Old Mill* (vNB) / *Non-Stop Flight* / *I'll Be With You In Apple Blossom Time*

RADIO LOGS

12:00 MIDNIGHT WOR
BENNY GOODMAN
Hotel Pennsylvania, NYC
Bei Mir Bist Du Schoen (vocal: Martha Tilton)
Star Dust (Henderson's marvelous arrangement)
Bob White (vocal: Martha Tilton) (swell arrangement but over-played: Benny's whistling)
Nice Work If You Can Get It (BG Trio) (good: tricky parts; Wilson)
Bugle Call Rag (excellent: magnificent solos by Benny; Rollini; Elman & Brown)
Loch Lomond (vocal: Martha Tilton)
If Dreams Come True (Benny plays it too much but it's still swell)
I Got Rhythm (BG Quartet) (wonderful: Benny's unsurpassable clarinet; Hampton)

■ FRIDAY 31 DECEMBER 1937

I heard all the bands on New Year's Eve at Bob Van Schilgan's house. Got home at 3:34am.

RADIO LOGS

7:45PM WJZ
BUGHOUSE RHYTHM
San Francisco
Rockin' The Town (recent hit tune played by Dr. John Meakin: good)
Subway (fast, recent modern piece depicting the subway: trumpet; tenor sax)
Auld Lang Syne (nuttsy swing style: Burgess' trumpet, etc)

11:55PM WOR
BENNY GOODMAN
Hotel Pennsylvania, NYC
I heard these 2 programs at Bobby Van Shilgan's house in Bronxville with Roddy Snow and Don Mortimer.
I'm A Ding Dong Daddy (From Dumas) (BG Quartet)

12:05PM WABC
BENNY GOODMAN
Hotel Pennsylvania, NYC
Life Goes To A Party
Loch Lomond (vocal: Martha Tilton)
If Dreams Come True
Roll 'Em

12:00 MIDNIGHT WNEW
JOHN KIRBY'S ONYX BAND
Onyx Club, 62 W52nd Street, NYC
The Dipsy Doodle (swell: exceptional informal vocals)
Someday Sweetheart (featuring Buster Bailey's clarinet)
Just Blues (grand: Kirby's solid bassing; Spencer's drumming, etc)
Nice Work If You Can Get It (vocal: Maxine Sullivan)
Onyx Spree (vocal: Leo Watson) (wonderful rhythm and jamming: nuttsy scat vocal)
Back Home Again In Indiana (colossal: Bailey's clarinet; Pete Brown's great alto sax; Watson's trombone)

12:30AM WABC
GLEN GRAY
Hotel New Yorker, NYC
Memories Of You (featuring Sonny Dunham on trumpet)
Bei Mir Bist Du Schoen (vocal: Pee Wee Hunt)
I Cried For You (vocal: Kenny Sargent)
Twilight In Turkey

JANUARY 1938

Hotel Pennsylvania: **Benny Goodman** (–15); **Bob Crosby** (17–)
Hotel Commodore: **Tommy Dorsey** (–26); **Red Norvo** (27–)
Hotel New Yorker: **Glen Gray**
Hotel Lincoln: **Isham Jones**

Apollo Theater: **Tiny Bradshaw** (–6); **Chick Webb** (7–13); **Noble Sissle / Maxine Sullivan** (14–20); **Duke Ellington** (21–27); **Claude Hopkins** (28–)
Paramount Theater: **Fred Waring** (–4); **Benny Goodman** (26–)
Loew's State Theater: **Jimmie Lunceford** (–5); **Count Basie** (20–26);

Cotton Club: **Cab Calloway / Bill Robinson**
Hickory House: **Joe Marsala**
Onyx Club: **John Kirby / Maxine Sullivan**
Famous Door: **Louis Prima / Art Tatum**
Nick's: **Bobby Hackett**

■ SATURDAY 1 JANUARY 1938

RADIO LOGS

7.00PM WABC
SATURDAY NIGHT SWING SESSION No77
CBS Playhouse 3, NYC
Rose Room (Leith Stevens' CBS Band: nuttsy)
Lazy Bones (PEE WEE HUNT singing)
The Cat Walk (colossal: written by Vincent Maffay, Willis Kelly & Billy Gussak; swell tenor sax by George Tudor)
Bei Mir Bist Du Schoen (HAZEL SCOTT singing the nuts and playing good piano: drums, etc)
Body And Soul (HAZEL SCOTT piano solo)
You're A Sweetheart (Leith Stevens' CBS Band swinging tenderly on a sweet piece)
Limehouse Blues (SONNY DUNHAM playing a colossal wa-wa trombone on his own arrangement)
Memories Of You (SONNY DUNHAM playing a colossal trumpet; swell trombone; saxes)
Mama, That Moon's Here Again (PEE WEE HUNT singing)
Tain't So (Leith Stevens' CBS Band on swell, smooth arrangement)

Mortimer, Pastoriza, Snow, Pinger, Jones, Sheldon Noseworthy, Long, and Sis Lake went down to see Goodman tonight but I didn't have enough money. They hollered my name over the following broadcast about ten times. It was funny as hell!!!

11:30PM WABC
BENNY GOODMAN
Hotel Pennsylvania, NYC
Camel Hop (colossal: James; Russin; Benny)
You're A Sweetheart (vocal: Martha Tilton) (grand)
Sing You Sinners (nuttsy: Elman; Benny)
I Must Have That Man (BG Trio) (swell)
Bei Mir Bist Du Schoen (vocal: Martha Tilton) (Elman)
Smiles (BG Quartet) (great stuff by all)
It's Wonderful (vocal: Martha Tilton) (nice sweet commercial made good by superb saxes & trumpets)
Swingtime In The Rockies (wonderful: good tenor; Benny; Elman with Krupa)
Rockin' The Town (vocal: Martha Tilton) (new piece, darn good: tricky brass & saxes)

12:00 MIDNIGHT WNEW
JOHN KIRBY'S ONYX BAND
Onyx Club, 62 W52nd Street, NYC
Linger Awhile (vocal: Leo Watson) (Pete Brown's nuttsy alto sax; Bailey; Frye's piano; Watson's colossal vocal)

Whoa, Babe (Bailey's great clarinet with Kirby's solid bass; wonderful soft, fast, muted trumpet; Brown's alto sax; Watson's fine original trombone; Spencer's long roll drum break; tricky ending)
Mood Indigo (muted trumpet on first chorus; Bailey's typical clarinet; muted trumpet again; Brown's nuttsy alto sax; Watson's trombone)
Darling Nellie Gray (vocal: Maxine Sullivan) (typical great vocal with fine backing from band: arranged by Claude Thornhill, recorded on Vocalion)
Twilight In Turkey (very fast—too fast: O'Neil Spencer's fair drums throughout; nice dirty trumpet; Bailey's clarinet)
Paul Revere (good, but cut short)

■ SUNDAY 2 JANUARY 1938

RADIO LOGS

11:00AM WNEW
SUNDAY MORNING SWING CONCERT
Criterion Theater, NYC
I Found A New Baby (Merle Pitts' WNEW Studio Band going good: tenor sax)
Nice Work If You Can Get It (DORIS DRAKE singing good)
Puddin' Head Jones (TINY BRADSHAW doing a swell, real hot vocal)
Oh, Lady Be Good (Merle Pitts' WNEW Make-Believe Ballroom Band)
That's What You Call Romance (SLIM Gaillard & SLAM Stewart: swell)
Mama, That Moon's Here Again (MILDRED CRAIG singing with WNEW Band)
Blue Room (Merle Pitts' WNEW Studio Band with George Tudor on tenor sax)
Big Boy Blue (TINY BRADSHAW singing)

11:00PM WEAF
JIMMY DORSEY
Congress Hotel, Chicago
I heard this program at Don Mortimer's house.
I Double Dare You
In A Sentimental Mood
Love Me Or Leave Me
Just Lately
Volga Boatmen (Bobby Byrne's hot trombone)
It's The Dreamer In Me (vocal: Bob Eberly)
You're A Sweetheart
Mama, I Wanna Make Rhythm (vocal: June Richmond) (swell hot vocal)
Listen To The Mocking Bird
Sandman (theme)

■ MONDAY 3 JANUARY 1938

RECORDING SESSION

COUNT BASIE AND HIS ORCHESTRA
Recording session for Decca in New York City.
Buck Clayton, Ed Lewis, Karl George (t); Dan Minor, Benny Morton, Eddie Durham (tb); Earle Warren (as/voc); Lester Young, Herschel Evans (ts); Jack Washington (bar); Count Basie (p); Freddie Green (g); Walter Page (b); Jo Jones (d); Jimmy Rushing (voc)
Georgianna (vJR) / *Blues In The Dark* (vJR)

RADIO LOGS

11:00PM WABC
GLEN GRAY
Hotel New Yorker, NYC
Good. John-Allen Wolf announced.
Swing Low, Sweet Chariot (pretty good: old spiritual swung)
I Can Dream Can't I? (vocal: Kenny Sargent) (introduced by the Casa Loma)
Mama, I Wanna Make Rhythm (vocal: Pee Wee Hunt)
Diane (swell: typical good solos by Pat Davis on tenor and clarinet)
Thanks For The Memory (vocal: Kenny Sargent)
You Have Everything (vocal: Pee Wee Hunt) (nuttsy trumpet by Dunham)
Girl Of My Dreams (vocal: Kenny Sargent) (very old sweet piece)
Pagan Love Song (swell fast arrangement: great muted trombone)

■ TUESDAY 4 JANUARY 1938

RADIO LOGS

10:00PM WABC
BENNY GOODMAN
Camel Caravan, CBS Playhouse, NYC
Let's Dance (theme)
I Can't Give You Anything But Love, Baby (no vocal: Elman; Stacy)
If Dreams Come True (great: Benny; Brown; Rollini)
Bei Mir Bist Du Schoen (vocal: Benny Goodman, Lionel Hampton, Martha Tilton) (6-minutes long: first 3 choruses by Quartet with vocals by Hampton & Benny; Elman's trumpet; Tilton's vocal with the band)
I've Hitched My Wagon To A Star (vocal: Martha Tilton)
Swing Low Sweet Chariot (swell: Russin; Elman; Brown)

11:00PM WABC
TOMMY DORSEY
Hotel Commodore, NYC
Can't Help Lovin' Dat Man (vocal: Edythe Wright)
I Can Dream Can't I? (vocal: Jack Leonard)
Song Of India
I'm Getting Sentimental Over You (swell in-between theme)
The Lady Is A Tramp
Bewildered (vocal: Jack Leonard) (played for the first time over the radio)
Just A Simple Melody (Howard Smith's piano)
I Live The Life I Love
Devil's Holiday

■ WEDNESDAY 5 JANUARY 1938

RECORDING SESSION

HARRY JAMES AND HIS ORCHESTRA
Recording session for Brunswick in New York City.
Harry James (t/ldr); Buck Clayton (t); Vernon Brown (tb); Earle Warren (as); Herschel Evans (ts); Jack Washington (cl/bar); Jess Stacy (p); Walter Page (b); Jo Jones (d); Helen Humes (voc)
Texas Chatter / Song Of The Wanderer (vHH) / *It's The Dreamer In Me* (vHH) / *One O'Clock Jump*

RADIO LOGS

11:00PM WABC
BENNY GOODMAN
Hotel Pennsylvania, NYC
Gene Krupa was sick tonight so Lionel Hampton played drums with the whole band. He's damn good.
Alexander's Ragtime Band (swell arrangement: Benny)
Thanks For The Memory (vocal: Martha Tilton)
Down South Camp Meeting (colossal: wonderful clarinets & trumpets)
Mama, That Moon's Here Again (vocal: Martha Tilton)
That Naughty Waltz (nuttsy: Benny; sweet trombone; Elman; Russin)
You're A Sweetheart (vocal: Martha Tilton) (good commercial)
China Boy (BG Trio) (nuttsy: Benny, Wilson, and Lionel Hampton on drums)
So Many Memories (vocal: Martha Tilton)
House Hop (great)
Between The Devil And The Deep Blue Sea (no vocal: Stacy; Russin)

11:35PM WMCA
TINY BRADSHAW
Apollo Theater, NYC
Bob White (vocal: Tiny Bradshaw) (very long hot arrangement with swell hot vocal)

■ THURSDAY 6 JANUARY 1938

RECORDING SESSION

BILLIE HOLIDAY & TEDDY WILSON ORCHESTRA
Recording session for Columbia in NYC.
Buck Clayton (t); Lester Young (ts); Benny Morton (tb); Teddy Wilson (p); Freddie Green (g); Walter Page (b); Jo Jones (d); Billie Holiday (v)
My First Impression Of You (vBH) / *When You're Smiling* (vBH) / *I Can't Believe That You're In Love With Me* (vBH) / *If Dreams Come True* (vBH)

TOMMY DORSEY AND HIS ORCHESTRA
Recording session for Victor in New York City.
Tommy Dorsey (tb); Pee Wee Erwin, Lee Castle, Andy Ferretti (t); Les Jenkins, Frank d'Annolfo (tb); Johnny Mince, Fred Stulce, Skeets Herfurt (cl/as); Bud Freeman (ts); Howard Smith (p); Carmen Mastren (g); Artie Shapiro (b); Maurice Purtill (d); Edythe Wright, Jack Leonard (voc)
You Couldn't Be Cuter (vEW) / *Just Let Me Look At You* (vJL) / *Smoke From A Chimney* (vJL) / *The Big Dipper* (vEW)

HARRY JAMES AND HIS ORCHESTRA
Recording session for Brunswick in New York City.
Harry James (t/ldr); Buck Clayton (t); Vernon Brown (tb); Earle Warren (as); Herschel Evans (ts); Jack Washington (cl/bar); Jess Stacy (p); Walter Page (b); Jo Jones (d); Helen Humes (voc)
Jubilee (vHH) / *I Can Dream Can't I?* (vHH)

JIMMIE LUNCEFORD AND HIS ORCHESTRA
Recording session for Decca in New York City.
Jimmie Lunceford (ldr); Paul Webster (t); Eddie Tompkins, Sy Oliver (t/voc); Elmer Crumbley, Russell Bowles (tb); Trummy Young (tb/voc); Willie Smith (cl/as/bar/voc); Earl Carruthers (cl/as/bar); Ted Buckner (as); Dan Grissom (cl/as/voc); Joe Thomas (cl/ts/voc); Edwin Wilcox (p); Al Norris (g); Moses Allen (b); Jimmy Crawford (d)
Margie (vTY) / *The Love Nest* (vDG) / *I'm Laughing Up My Sleeve* (vSO)

Today I bought Bob Crosby's Bobcats record of *Fidgety Feet* and *Stumbling* (Decca 1593), just released today.

RADIO LOGS

10:00PM WHN
CLAUDE HOPKINS
Roseland Ballroom, NYC
Scattin' At The Kit-Kat (good: nice fast clarinet; good brief tenor sax)
There's A Little White House (vocal: Beverly White)
Bob White (vocal: Beverly White) (rather ragged: tenor sax, etc)
Washington Squabble (featuring Claude Hopkins at the piano; clarinet)
Cryin' My Heart Out For You (vocal: Beverly White) (written by Hopkins)
Three Little Words (vocal: Beverly White) (rather long hot arrangement: Hopkins; clarinet)
Loch Lomond (vocal: Beverly White) (too ragged: more clarinet)

■ FRIDAY 7 JANUARY 1938

RECORDING SESSION

ADRIAN ROLLINI AND HIS ORCHESTRA
Recording session for Decca in New York City.
Johnny McGhee (t); Paul Ricci (cl); Adrian Rollini (bsx); Al Duffy (vln); Jack Russin (p); Frank Victor (g); Harry Clark (b); Buddy Rich (d); Pat Hoke (voc)
Bill / *Singin' The Blues* (vPH) / *The Sweetest Story Ever Told* (vPH)

RADIO LOGS

7:45PM WEAF
BUGHOUSE RHYTHM
San Francisco
Shades Of Haiti (rather old piece written by Larry Clinton: trumpet)
The Dipsy Doodle (Clinton's recent piece: bass; trumpets)
The Big Dipper (more recent piece by Clinton: Anthony Freeman on bass)

11:00PM WABC
GLEN GRAY
Hotel New Yorker, NYC
Always (recent Decca recording: Sonny Dunham's colossal trumpet; Davis' tenor)
I Could Use A Dream (vocal: Kenny Sargent) (very new song: Rauch's sweet trombone)
Just A Simple Melody (vocal: Pee Wee Hunt) (good: no solos)
Song Of India (nice arrangement: trumpet; bassoon)
You Took The Words Right Out Of My Heart (vocal: Kenny Sargent) (trumpet)
Mama, That Moon's Here Again (vocal: Pee Wee Hunt) (Davis' tenor; clarinet)
How Am I To Know? (swell: featuring 6 saxes; clarinet)
Maniac's Ball (swell old piece: Hunt's swell trombone; clarinet; trumpets)

12:00 MIDNIGHT WEAF
TEDDY HILL
Savoy Ballroom, NYC
Swell.
Ja-Da
Caravan
Back Home Again In Indiana
Three Little Words (featuring Sam Allen's fine piano)
Tune In On My Heart (new piece written by Joe Sanders)
Blue Rhythm Fantasy (a colossal swing tune partially written by Hill)
Sweet Stranger (vocal: Lilla Mae McLee)
Uptown Rhapsody (theme) (played in full)

12:00 MIDNIGHT WNEW
JOHN KIRBY
Onyx Club, 62 W52nd Street, NYC
MARVELOUS.
Tea For Two (vocal: Leo Watson) (nuttsy: wordless vocal; Pete Brown's alto; Shavers' trumpet)
Royal Garden Blues (Bailey's clarinet; Brown's alto; Charlie Shavers' trumpet leading the way)
Basin Street Blues (Buster Bailey's great medium tempo clarinet; trombone; alto sax; Frye's piano; trumpet)
A Brown Bird Singing (vocal: Maxine Sullivan) (very new piece sung by the great Maxine)
Caravan (vocal: Leo Watson) (nuttsy: Spencer's drum intro; Bailey's wonderful clarinet; Watson's colossal wordless vocal that really sent me!!! Brown's alto; trumpet)
Tea For Two (vocal: Leo Watson) (more relaxed swing dished out plenty with much gusto! Bailey's great clarinet; marvelous trumpet by Shavers; Watson's great vocal)

12:30AM WCCO
JIMMY DORSEY
Hotel Nicollet, Minneapolis
Dorsey Band's opening night at Hotel Nicollet.
I Want To Be In Winchell's Column (vocal: Bob Eberly)
In A Sentimental Mood
The Dipsy Doodle (vocal: June Richmond)
Sail Along, Silvr'y Moon (vocal: Bob Eberly)
Parade of The Milk Bottle Caps
More Power To You (vocal: Bob Eberly)
Farewell My Love (vocal: Bob Eberly)
Just Lately (vocal: Bob Eberly)
Chicken Reel

12:30AM WJZ
CHARLIE BARNET
Raymor Ballroom, Boston
SWELL.
Makin' Whoopee (colossal arrangement: Barnet's marvelous hot tenor sax)
True Confession (vocal: Charlie Barnet) (swell sweet piece and arrangement)
The Snake Charmer (fair piece with tiresome theme: drums; tenor sax)
Two Dreams Got Together
You Took The Words Right Out of My Heart
Bob White (vocal: Charlie Barnet) (terrific tenor sax by Charlie)
If Dreams Come True (vocal: Charlie Barnet) (swell new piece: tenor sax)
You're A Sweetheart (vocal: Charlie Barnet)
Sugar Foot Stomp (grand: swell hot trumpet solo; Barnet's great tenor sax)

■ SATURDAY 8 JANUARY 1938

Mrs Poe drove Jim Poe, Harvey Pinger and myself into New York City at 1:30 in her new auto. We were dropped off at 49th Street from where we went to Rockwell-O'Keefe in search of Vincent Prior. They told us that he wasn't working there any more and was in Columbus, Ohio. We then walked down to 42nd Street and Broadway where we paid 35 cents each to go in the Republic Theater where we saw a 2-hour burlesque stage show and several movies including a short about Cab Calloway. We left the theater at 6:15 and went up to 53rd Street on Broadway where the Columbia Broadcasting System's Playhouse 3 is located. The Saturday Night Swing Session was being held there tonight so we each tried to get tickets outside the entrance from people who had extra tickets. After about 10 minutes we all got tickets and went in. We got good seats downstairs in about the middle of the theater. We saw the band, under Leith Stevens' direction and Ed Cashman's directing, rehearse for 20 minutes before the broadcast. It sure was the nuts. I noticed Ed Cashman and Al Rinker up in the control room, announcers Paul Douglas and Melvin Allen on the stage with guests Maxine Sullivan and Chauncey Morehouse. The personnel of Leith Stevens' CBS Band was: Hank Ross, Toots Mondello, Art Manners, George Tudor (saxes); Joe Vargas, Wilbur Schwichtenburg, Roland Dupont (trombones); Willis Kelly, Russ Case, Nat Natoli, Cliff Natalie, Lloyd Williams (trumpets); Walter Gross (piano); Frankie Worrell (guitar); Lou Shoobe (bass); Billy Gussak (drums).

About 5 minutes before the broadcast, Fats Waller showed up so they had to change the broadcast around to make room for him. He also brought his two little sons along, one 9 yrs-old and the other 11 yrs-old. As usual, announcer Melvin Allen introduced the broadcast and then Paul Douglas announced the rest of the broadcast in his very informal way.

7.00PM WABC
SATURDAY NIGHT SWING SESSION No78
CBS Playhouse 3, NYC
Panamania (Schwichtenberg's nice trombone; Walter Gross' piano break; Russ Case's trumpet)
Nice Work If You Can Get It (MAXINE SULLIVAN singing as only she can in that sweet-swing voice of hers that sends chills up and down your back)
Bob White (MAXINE SULLIVAN again singing colossally; swell backing by band)
You're A Sweetheart (CBS Band on a fine sweet piece: Case's trumpet)
N'Gona (CHAUNCEY MOREHOUSE playing those 14 drums: good bassing)
After You've Gone (FATS WALLER sitting down and really beatin' the piano: funny vocals)
I Found A New Baby (KARAWANIS TRIO: 3 brothers playing bass, guitar and clarinet)

Casa Loma Stomp (KARAWANIS TRIO again: one of them doubles clarinet and trumpet)
ED CASHMAN talked about next week's Swing Session which is to be held in Hollywood.
Loch Lomond (MAXINE SULLIVAN singing great on Thornhill's arrangement: Ross' tenor sax)

After the broadcast we went outside to the stage door on 53rd Street where I got the autographs of Dupont, Tudor, Mondello, Case, Ross, Gussak, Natoli, Natalie and Worrell.

We then took the wrong subway trying to get to the Savoy Ballroom at 140th Street and Lenox Avenue. After walking about a mile we got there at 8:30 and paid 75 cents to get in. We all had a simply marvelous time listening to the bands, talking to the musicians, watching the Lindy-hoppers, and dancing ourselves. Teddy Hill's and Willie Bryant's Orchestras alternated every hour. Both of them were swell. Bryant's great personality leads his band which really plays some swell stuff most of the time. I don't like his girl vocalist, Billie Powell, particularly well. Prince Robinson, Charles Frazier, Manzie Johnson and Sonny White are the outstanding musicians with Reunald Jones' trumpet solos outstanding too. Teddy Hill's band was even better with some wonderful arrangements and such fine soloists as: Dickie Wells, whose trombone sounds more like a trumpet; Sam Allen on piano; John Gillespie on most of the hot trumpet choruses; and Robert Carroll's good tenor sax solos. Lilla Mae McLee is a pretty and very promising vocalist. I got all the autographs of both orchestras. I just missed getting Chu Berry's autograph who was there for a half hour. He used to play with Hill's band many years ago. Pinger and I had a very long visit with Teddy Hill. He told us his favorite musicians: Chu Berry (unsurpassable on tenor sax); Coleman Hawkins (great, but not as good as Berry); Johnny Hodges (easily the best alto saxist); Art Shaw (says Goodman is second to Shaw on clarinet as Shaw swings more); Roy Eldridge (real swinger, greater than Armstrong); Henry 'Red' Allen ("under key of G"); Gene Krupa (he doesn't think much of Webb, likes McKinley, Singleton, Bauduc). Hill is an old-timer, exceptionally polite and soft-spoken, who really knows swing and plays a nice alto sax while leading the band. Many Negro girls like to talk to the musicians and also to look at this scrapbook. I sure could go for one of them! Poe and I had a lot of fun Lindy-hopping. They had a colossal Lindy-hop contest at 12:00 and we left at 12:50.

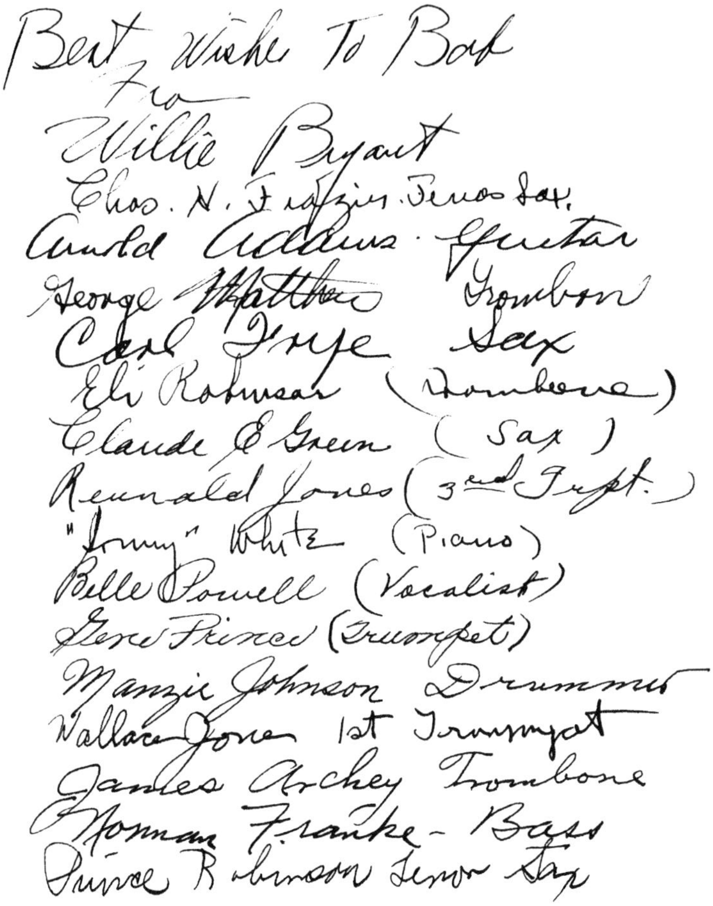

[Handwritten signatures:]
Best wishes to Bob
from
Willie Bryant
Chas. N. Frazier Tenor Sax
Arnold Adams - Guitar
George Matthews Trombone
Carl Frye Sax
Eli Robinson (Trombone)
Claude E Green (Sax)
Reunald Jones (3rd Trpt.)
"Sonny" White (Piano)
Belle Powell (Vocalist)
Gene Prince (Trumpet)
Manzie Johnson Drummer
Wallace Jones 1st Trumpet
James Archey Trombone
Norman Franke - Bass
Prince Robinson Tenor Sax

■ SUNDAY 9 JANUARY 1938

RADIO LOGS

11:00AM WNEW
SUNDAY MORNING SWING CONCERT
Criterion Theater, NYC
Melody In F (Merle Pitts' WNEW Studio Band: Weiss' drums; tenor sax)
Rockin' Chair Swing (TEDDY GRACE singing wonderfully: nuttsy)
Wabash Blues (SAMMY SPERGEL playing electric guitar: fair)
Posin' (EDYTHE WRIGHT singing with TOMMY DORSEY's Clambake Seven: good)
The Lady Is A Tramp (EDYTHE WRIGHT singing with TOMMY DORSEY's Clambake Seven: fair)
Like A Fish Out Of Water (MILDRED CRAIG singing)
Milenberg Joys (Merle Pitts' WNEW Studio Band playing swell: trumpet; tenor sax)
I Can't Give You Anything But Love (TEDDY GRACE singing great)
Start The Day With A Smile (MILDRED CRAIG singing with WNEW Band)

■ MONDAY 10 JANUARY 1938

RECORDING SESSION

MILDRED BAILEY & HER ORCHESTRA
Recording session for Vocalion in New York.
Jimmy Blake (t); Hank D'Amico (cl); Chu Berry (ts); Teddy Wilson (p); Allen Reuss (g); Pete Peterson (b); Dave Tough (d); Mildred Bailey (v)
I See Your Face Before Me (vMB) / *Thanks For The Memory* (vMB) / *From The Land of Sky Blue Water* (vMB) / *Lover, Come Back To Me* (vMB)

WILLIE 'THE LION' SMITH
Recording session for Decca in New York City.
Willie 'The Lion' Smith (p); O'Neil Spencer (d)
Passionette / *Morning Air*

■ TUESDAY 11 JANUARY 1938

RADIO LOGS

10:00PM WABC
BENNY GOODMAN
Camel Caravan, CBS Playhouse, NYC
Let's Dance (theme)
Blue Room (swell new arrangement: Benny; Stacy; Krupa)
It's Wonderful (vocal: Martha Tilton) (swell: Russin's tenor)
Solid Mama (nuttsy: Benny; Stacy; trumpets)
Body And Soul (BG Trio) (great: Wilson's colossal piano)
Let That Be A Lesson To You (vocal: Martha Tilton) (swell: trumpet)
Dizzy Spells (BG Quartet) (wonderful: written by the Quartet this afternoon)
Don't Be That Way (colossal recent tune by Edgar Sampson: wonderful brass & saxes; Benny; colossal tenor sax; Krupa; trombone)

11:00PM WABC
TOMMY DORSEY
Hotel Commodore, NYC
The Dipsy Doodle (vocal: Edythe Wright)
Log On The Fire (vocal: Jack Leonard)
When It's Sleepy Time Down South (swell: Freeman; Purtill's drums; Erwin; Mince)
Once In A While (vocal: Three Esquires)
Back In Your Own Backyard (good: Mince; Freeman; Erwin)
Rockin' The Town (vocal: Edythe Wright)
Bewildered (vocal: Jack Leonard) (Tommy Dorsey's trombone)
Just A Simple Melody (Howard Smith's piano; Dorsey)
A Little White Lighthouse (vocal: Jack Leonard) (Tommy Dorsey's trombone)
I've Gotta Swing (Mince; Smith's colossal piano; solid bass; Dorsey; Freeman)

■ WEDNESDAY 12 JANUARY 1938

RECORDING SESSION

BILLIE HOLIDAY & HER ORCHESTRA
Recording session for Columbia in NYC.
Buck Clayton (t); Lester Young (ts); Benny Morton (tb); Teddy Wilson (p); Freddie Green (g); Walter Page (b); Jo Jones (d); Billie Holiday (v)
Now They Call It Swing / *On The Sentimental Side* / *Back In Your Own Backyard* / *When A Woman Loves A Man*

WINGY MANONE AND HIS ORCHESTRA
Recording session for Bluebird in New York City.
Wingy Manone (t/voc); Joe Marsala (cl/as); Doc Rando (as); Bud Freeman (ts); Conrad Lanoue (p); Clayton Duerr (g); unknown (b); Danny Alvin (d)
Annie Laurie (vWM) / *Loch Lomond* (vWM) / *Down Stream* (vWM) / *Where's The Waiter?* (vWM) / *My Mariuccia Take A Steamboat* (vWM) / *In The Land Of Yamo Yamo* (vWM)

RADIO LOGS

11:00PM WABC
BENNY GOODMAN
Hotel Pennsylvania, NYC
Don't Be That Way (Russin; James; Brown)
Bob White (vocal: Martha Tilton)
Swingtime In The Rockies (Benny; Russin; Elman)
Oh, Lady Be Good (BG Trio) (magnificent, colossal)
Always (marvelous: Rollini; trumpets; Brown; saxes)
Thanks For The Memory (vocal: Martha Tilton) (Harry James' trumpet)
Make Believe (swell: Benny; Brown)
Runnin' Wild (BG Quartet) (marvelous Hampton)

11:30PM WMCA
CHICK WEBB
Apollo Theater, NYC
Midnight In A Madhouse (swell: McRae's brief tenor; Stark's fine trumpet; Sandy Williams' swell trombone)
True Confession (vocal: Ella Fitzgerald) (Ella singing magnificently; trombone; screwy trumpet)

12:00 MIDNIGHT WABC
TOMMY DORSEY
Hotel Commodore, NYC
The Big Dipper (vocal: Edythe Wright)
I Can Dream Can't I? (vocal: Jack Leonard)
Easy To Remember
Be With Us

■ THURSDAY 13 JANUARY 1938

RECORDING SESSION

DUKE ELLINGTON AND HIS ORCHESTRA
Recording session for Master Records in New York City.
Duke Ellington (p); Arthur Whetsel, Cootie Williams, Harold Baker (t); Rex Stewart (c); Joe Nanton, Lawrence Brown (t); Barney Bigard (cl); Johnny Hodges (cl/ss/as); Otto Hardwick (as/bsx); Harry Carney (cl/as/bar); Fred Guy (g); Hayes Alvis, Billy Taylor (b); Sonny Greer (d)
Steppin' Into Swing Society / Prologue to Black And Tan Fantasy / The New Black And Tan Fantasy

RADIO LOGS

10:00PM WHN
CLAUDE HOPKINS
Roseland Ballroom, NYC
China Boy (good: trumpet; nice clarinet)
Stop Stallin' (vocal: Beverly White) (written by Hopkins)
Monkey Business (swell: tenor sax; trumpet)
Rosalie (vocal: Beverly White) (lousy)
McGillicuddy's Stomp (first time on radio)
My Cabin Of Dreams (vocal: Beverly White)
Once In A While (vocal: Beverly White)
You Made Me Love You (vocal: Beverly White)

11:00PM WABC
CAB CALLOWAY
Cotton Club, NYC
I Know That You Know
Gypsy Smiles (vocal: Cab Calloway)
Jubilee (vocal: Cab Calloway)
Dear Old Southland
China Boy
I Like Music (With A Swing Like That) (vocal: Cab Calloway)
In The Still Of The Night
Sweet Stranger
Nagasaki (vocal: Cab Calloway)
Once In A While (vocal: Bennie Payne)

12:00 MIDNIGHT WOR
BENNY GOODMAN
Hotel Pennsylvania, NYC
If Dreams Come True (Benny; Brown; Rollini)
You Took The Words Right Out Of My Heart (vocal: Martha Tilton)
Blue Skies (colossal: Rollini; Elman)
Loch Lomond (vocal: Martha Tilton) (good: Harry James' trumpet)
Dizzy Spells (BG Quartet) (wonderful: Hampton)
It's Wonderful (vocal: Martha Tilton) (Russin's tenor)
Big John Special (magnificent: Stacy; 2 trumpet solos)
Once In A While (BG Trio) (fair)
Mama, That Moon is Here Again (vocal: Martha Tilton)

■ FRIDAY 14 JANUARY 1938

RADIO LOGS

12:15AM WABC
BOB CROSBY
Univ of Pittsburgh Junior Prom
Great.
I Still Love To Kiss You Goodnight (vocal: Kay Weber) (Miller's nice tenor)
She's Tall, She's Tan, She's Terrific (vocal: Nappy Lamare) (Matlock; Smith; Lawson)
Silhouetted In The Moonlight (vocal: Bob Crosby) (Miller featured on tenor chorus)

South Rampart Street Parade (WONDERFUL: written by Bauduc; arranged by Bob Haggart; Matlock's blue clarinet; great brass)
Summertime (theme)

12:30AM WJZ
ART SHAW
Raymor Ballroom, Boston
Nuttsy.
Non-Stop Flight (nuttsy: written by Shaw; magnificent solos by Pastor & Shaw)
Yours And Mine (vocal: Nita Bradley) (swell, slightly old, commercial)
Rosalie (vocal: Tony Pastor) (Pastor's fine tenor sax; Shaw's great clarinet)
Apple Blossom Time (marvelous: Tony Pastor's great tenor; nuttsy solos by trumpet & trombone)
One Song (vocal: Nita Bradley) (very new, swell piece in typical Shaw style with plenty of trumpets; Pastor)
The Lady Is A Tramp (vocal: Tony Pastor) (real hot vocal on a lousy song; Shaw's clarinet)
Ebb Tide (vocal: Nita Bradley) (more swell swinging on a sweet one: Shaw's clarinet)
Shoot The Likker To Me (marvelous, colossal: Pastor; Shaw; bassing; trumpets)

■ SATURDAY 15 JANUARY 1938

RADIO LOGS

7.00PM WABC
SATURDAY NIGHT SWING SESSION No79
Hollywood, California
Special one-hour swing broadcast from Hollywood with Paul Whiteman's Orchestra. Whiteman himself announced.

Paul Whiteman

In The Jug (JOE VENUTI playing a good violin: he used to be with Whiteman)
Jubilee (LOUIS ARMSTRONG singing a real hot vocal and playing great trumpet)
Stop, Look, And Listen (PAUL WHITEMAN Orchestra playing Freddie Van Eps' arrangement)
Mama Wants To Know Who Stole The Jam (CLEO BROWN singing and playing piano: swell)
Trombonist JERRY COLONNA giving his speech version of swing: funny?
Square Dance For An Egyptian Mummy (RAYMOND SCOTT Quintet playing Scott's latest piece: fair)
When It's Sleepy Time Down South (LORETTA LEE singing colossally on Armstrong's theme)
I Found A New Baby (nuttsy jam session!!! Louis Armstrong; 2 Teagardens; Buddy Christian on vibes; Charlie LaVere on piano; Perry Botkin on guitar; Johnny Williams on drums; Artie Miller on bass; Dave Harris on tenor sax. Outstanding were Louis Armstrong, Jack Teagarden and Johnny Williams)

11:30PM WABC
BENNY GOODMAN
Hotel Pennsylvania, NYC
Tonight is Benny Goodman's closing night at the Hotel Pennsylvania.
Remember (swell: Brown; Benny; tenor sax)
You Took The Words Right Out Of My Heart (vocal: Martha Tilton)
Happy Birthday (played for Gene Krupa's 29th birthday)
I Can't Give You Anything But Love, Baby (vocal: Martha Tilton)
Silhouetted In The Moonlight (BG Trio) (good)
Roll 'Em (great: Stacy; James; Benny's long solo)
I've Hitched My Wagon To A Star (vocal: Martha Tilton)
Nagasaki (BG Quartet) (colossal by all four)
Bei Mir Bist Du Schoen (good: no vocal; Elman's trumpet)

12:00 MIDNIGHT WNEW
JOHN KIRBY
Onyx Club, 62 W52nd Street, NYC
Just A Simple Melody (swell: Brown's alto; Frye's piano)
Paul Revere (vocal: Leo Watson) (rather short)
The Dipsy Doodle (vocal: Leo Watson) (colossal hot informal vocalizing by band with Watson's scat singing: Shavers' trumpet; Kirby's bass; trumpet again)
Bob White (vocal: Maxine Sullivan)
Two Dead Pans (vocal: Maxine Sullivan) (great: mostly vocal)
Dr Heckle And Mr Jive (vocal: Leo Watson) (Bailey's clarinet)
Linger Awhile (very long, colossal)

■ SUNDAY 16 JANUARY 1938

RADIO LOGS

11:00AM WNEW
SUNDAY MORNING SWING CONCERT
Criterion Theater, NYC
Limehouse Blues (Merle Pitts' WNEW Studio Band)
Caravan (DUKE ELLINGTON's Band: Tizol's trombone; Williams' trumpet; Bigard's clarinet; marvelous)
Back Room Romp (REX STEWART's 52nd Street Stompers: colossal)
That Old Feeling (IVIE ANDERSON singing swell with whole Ellington Band!)
Downtown Uproar (COOTIE WILLIAMS' Rugcutters: Cootie's great trumpet; Hodges' alto; Nanton's trombone; Carney's baritone sax; Ellington's piano; MARvelous!)
Clarinet Lament (written by and featuring BARNEY BIGARD on clarinet: magnificent)
Harmony In Harlem (JOHNNY HODGES' great soprano; 2 colossal trumpet solos)
A Sailboat In The Moonlight (JOHNNY HODGES playing terrific alto sax!!! He's easily the greatest alto saxist living!)
On The Sunny Side Of The Street (Hodges' magnificent alto sax; Williams' great muted trumpet; great vocal by IVIE ANDERSON — real hot and original; wonderful sweet trombone by Lawrence Brown; nobody can even come close to touching Ellington's style!)
Loch Lomond (Merle Pitts' WNEW Studio Band playing a fast original arrangement)
Frolic Sam

CARNEGIE HALL
SUNDAY EVENING, JAN. 16th
S. Hurok presents
BENNY GOODMAN
and his Swing Orchestra
SEATS NOW at CARNEGIE HALL

Around 7:00pm I took the train into Grand Central with Jim Poe and Bobby Van Schilgan who had tickets to the Benny Goodman Carnegie Hall Concert. I tried to get in on standing room but couldn't, so I went by myself up to the Savoy Ballroom to see Chick Webb and Count Basie in one of the most terrific battles of swing ever put on. It cost me 50 cents to get in. The place was absolutely jammed with people making it almost impossible to move. I like Basie better than Webb and he certainly did prove it although both were magnificent! I didn't have a chance to get any autographs. Many celebrities were there. The newspaper men gave the verdict to Basie but the ballot of the public there gave Webb a 2–1 victory. It was a memorable evening. I got the 1:10am train home, on which I met Poe, etc.

CARNEGIE HALL
Sunday Evening, January 16th, at 8:30

S. HUROK

presents

(by arrangement with Music Corporation of America)

BENNY GOODMAN
and his
SWING ORCHESTRA

I.

"Don't Be That Way" .... Edgar Sampson
"Sometimes I'm Happy" (from "Hit the Deck") .... Irving Caesar & Vincent Youmans
"One O'clock Jump" .... William (Count) Basie

II.

TWENTY YEARS OF JAZZ
"Sensation Rag" (as played c. 1917 by the Dixieland Jazz Band)
   E. B. Edwards
"I'm Comin Virginia" (as played c. 1926 by "Bix" Beiderbecke)
   Cooke-Heywood
"When My Baby Smiles at Me" (as played c. 1927 by Ted Lewis)
   Munro-Sterling-Lewis
"Shine" (as played c. 1929 by Louis Armstrong) Mack-Brown-Dabney
"Blue Reverie" .... Duke Ellington
"Life Goes to a Party" .... Harry James-Benny Goodman

III.

JAM SESSION
Collective improvision by a group of soloists to be announced. The length of the session is indeterminate, and may include one or more tunes.

A HISTORY MAKING.........BATTLE OF SWING
SUNDAY JAN. 16
The King OF THE DRUMS
The Royalist OF THE KEYBOARD
Chick WEBB vs **Count BASIE & HIS ORCHESTRA**
& AMERICAS OUTSTANDING...SWING BAND
The Aristocrat of Rhythm

Ella FITZGERALD FEATURED WITH CHICK

Chick Webb & HIS FAMOUS ORCHESTRA WILL PLAY NIGHTLY AT THE SAVOY
Special Matinee 3 P.M.
No Increase in Admission

Billie HOLLIDAY FEATURED WITH THE COUNT

LENOX AVE at 140' STREET.
SAVOY THE WORLDS FINEST BALLROOM

Benny and Cats Make Carnegie Debut Real Howling Success

Short-Hairs Shag, Long-Hairs Wag, Walls Sag, as Goodman's Gang Transforms Ancient Hall Into Modern Swing Emporium

By GEORGE T. SIMON

The first formal swing concert is history. It was made so Sunday, January 16, which, taking full possession of sedate, solid Carnegie Hall for the evening, proceed sand bristling and whistling swing cats and mystify several hundred long-haired sy to put in a rather smug appearance. Since several thousand enthusiastic cats can voicing their approval than a few hundred me

Benny Goodman 'Swings It Out' In Carnegie Hall

Capacity Crowd Swings in Seats as Band Wows 'Em in New Numbers and Old

Jam Session Included

Some There Hear Swing for First Time, and Like It

Concert by Benny Goodman and his Swing Orchestra, last night in Carnegie Hall.

PROGRAM
Don't Be That Way........Edgar Sampson
Sometimes I'm Happy, from "Hit the Deck."
    Irving Caesar and Vincent Youmans
One o'Clock Jump
    William (Count) Basie
Twenty Years of Jazz:
    Sensation Rag (1917)..E. B. Edwards
    I'm Comin' Virginia (1926)
        Cooke-Heywood
    When My Baby Smiles at Me (1927)
        Munro-Sterling-Lewis
Blue Revery.........Duke Wellington
Life Goes to a Party
    Harry James-Benny Goodman
Jam Session

SWING CONCERT FILLS CARNEGIE

Goodman Orchestra and Soloists Heard.

By IRVING KOLODIN.

Whether the local seismographs recorded it or not, an earthquake of violent intensity rocked a small corner of Manhattan last night as swing took Carnegie Hall in its stride. However, when the tremor had subsided, with midnight not far away, the only perceptible damage

GOODMAN IS HEARD IN 'SWING' CONCERT

Carnegie Hall Crowded for Orchestra's Rendition of 'New Kind of Music'

'JAM SESSION' A FEATURE

Soloists Join in Collective Improvisation — Virtuosity of Players Much Admired

By OLIN DOWNES

The writer of these lines, whose principal occupation it is to report performances of symphony and opera, is much interested in jazz and other forms of American popular music. He thinks, as Debussy put it, that there is only one music, which may exist in a dance, a folk song, a waltz or a symphony, and is often to be encountered in un-

---

■ **MONDAY 17 JANUARY 1938**

RECORDING SESSION

EDDIE CONDON & HIS WINDY CITY SEVEN
Recording session for Commodore in New York City.
Bobby Hackett (c); George Brunies (tb); Pee Wee Russell (cl); Bud Freeman (ts); Jess Stacy (p); Eddie Condon (g); Artie Shapiro (b); George Wettling (d)
Love Is Just Around The Corner / Beat To The Socks / Carnegie Drag / Carnegie Jump / Ja-Da

BUD FREEMAN TRIO
Recording session for Commodore in New York City.
Bud Freeman (ts); Jess Stacy (p); George Wettling (d)
You Took Advantage Of Me / Three's No Crowd / I Got Rhythm

---

* * * * * * * * * * * * * * * *

RAY BAUDUC — **BOB CROSBY AND HIS ORCHESTRA** — KAY WEBER

Tonight's their Gala Opening in the

MADhattan ROOM

Greet them tonight in the gay MADhattan Room! Dinner and supper dancing nightly except Sunday. Dinners from $2. Supper cover after 10 P.M. weeknights 75¢; Saturday and holiday eves, $1.

The place to go for a grand time!

HOTEL PENNSYLVANIA
James H. McCabe, Manager • Statler Operated
33RD STREET AND 7TH AVENUE

* * * * * * * * * * * * * * * *

RADIO LOGS

11:00PM **WABC**
GLEN GRAY
Hotel New Yorker, NYC
On January 29th Glen Gray's Band is going to play at President Roosevelt's Ball in Washington, D.C.
Imagination (nuttsy: trumpet, etc)
You Took The Words Right Out Of My Heart (vocal: Kenny Sargent)
Mama, That Moon's Here Again (vocal: Pee Wee Hunt)
Sugar Foot Stomp (great: clarinet; Hunt's trombone; trumpet)
I See Your Face Before Me (vocal: Kenny Sargent)
I May Be Wrong (vocal: Pee Wee Hunt) (colossal: Davis' tenor; trombone)
Memories Of You (wonderful: Dunham's marvelous trumpet; saxes)
Caravan (swell)
Smoke Rings (theme)

■ TUESDAY 18 JANUARY 1938

RECORDING SESSION

BARNEY BIGARD & HIS JAZZOPATORS
Recording session for Vocalion in New York City.
Rex Stewart (c); Juan Tizol (vtb); Barney Bigard (cl); Harry Carney (bar); Duke Ellington (p); Fred Guy (g); Billy Taylor (b); Sonny Greer (d)
Drummer's Delight / If I Thought You Cared

LIONEL HAMPTON AND HIS ORCHESTRA
Recording session for Victor in New York City.
Lionel Hampton (vib/voc); Cootie Williams (t); Johnny Hodges (as); Edgar Sampson (bar); Jess Stacy (p); Allan Reuss (g); Billy Taylor (b); Sonny Greer (d)
You're My Ideal (vLH) / *The Sun Will Shine Tonight* (vLH) / *Ring Dem Bells* (vLH) / *Don't Be That Way*

ADRIAN ROLLINI QUINTET
Recording session for Decca in New York City.
Bobby Hackett (c); Frank Victor (g); Harry Clark (b); Buddy Rich (d); Adrian Rollini (vib/xyl); Sonny Schuyler (voc)
Bei Mir Bist Du Schoen (vSS) / *Josephine* (vSS) / *You're A Sweetheart* (vSS) / *True Confession* (vSS) / *I've Hitched My Wagon To A Star* (vSS)

RADIO LOGS

10:00PM **WABC**
BENNY GOODMAN
Camel Caravan, CBS Playhouse, NYC
Let's Dance (theme)
Make Believe (swell smooth swing: James; Brown)
Don't Be That Way (colossal, magnificent; great: Benny; Russin's GREAT tenor sax; James; Brown)
Mozart's Quintet for String Quartet & Clarinet (Benny playing classical clarinet with the Coolidge String Quartet)
Honeysuckle Rose (BG Quartet) (great)
Mama, That Moon Is Here Again (vocal: Martha Tilton) (swell: fine vocal and Elman's trumpet)
Dear Old Southland (wonderful: trumpet intro; Russin's long solo; Stacy; James; Brown)

11:00PM **WABC**
TOMMY DORSEY
Hotel Commodore, NYC
You Took The Words Right Out Of My Heart (vocal: Jack Leonard)
Mendelssohn's Spring Song (Dorsey's muted smooth trombone; Freeman's great tenor)
Once In A While (vocal: Edythe Wright & Three Esquires) (Dorsey's soft, sweet muted trombone)
Loch Lomond (vocal: Edythe Wright) (a fine original arrangement: Mince's swell clarinet)
It's Wonderful (vocal: Jack Leonard) (good: nice, sweet commercial)
Song Of India (Tommy; Erwin's nice trumpet; Purtill's drums)
Bewildered (vocal: Jack Leonard) (going to be a hit, nice and sweet, like me)
Satan's Holiday (swell fast swing piece: Howard Smith's brief piano break)

12:00 MIDNIGHT **WABC**
BOB CROSBY
Hotel Pennsylvania, NYC
This is Crosby's first broadcast from the Hotel Pennsylvania. Benny Goodman's Band left it last Saturday night. John-Allen Wolf announced.
The Dipsy Doodle (swell: Matlock's blue clarinet; Miller's fine tenor; trombones; clarinets)
The Thrill of A Lifetime (vocal: Kay Weber) (Miller's good straight tenor; Matlock)
Nice Work If You Can Get It (vocal: Bob Crosby) (Dixielandish ending: Miller)
Yancey Special (wonderful arrangement of Meade Lux Lewis' tune: bass and piano open it up; weird parts; Haggart's solid bass throughout; Miller's brief solo; Zurke's nuttsy piano)
Sweet Someone (vocal: Kay Weber) (grand: Lawson's typical trumpet; Miller; Matlock)
She's Tall, She's Tan, She's Terrific (vocal: Nappy Lamare) (Miller; Matlock; Butterfield; Bauduc)
Why Should I Care? (vocal: Bob Crosby) (very new piece: Matlock; Miller)
Panama (another fine arrangement: Miller's grand tenor; swell ending)
Summertime (theme)

WEDNESDAY 19 JANUARY 1938

RECORDING SESSION

JOHNNY HODGES AND HIS ORCHESTRA
Recording session for Vocalion in New York City.
Cootie Williams (trumpet); Lawrence Brown (trombone); Johnny Hodges (soprano sax/alto sax); Otto Hardwick (alto sax); Harry Carney (baritone sax); Duke Ellington (piano); Fred Guy (guitar); Billy Taylor (bass); Sonny Greer (drums); Mary McHugh (vocal)
My Day (vMM, 2 takes) / *Silv'ry Moon And Golden Sands* (vMM)

COOTIE WILLIAMS & HIS RUGCUTTERS
Recording session for Vocalion in New York City.
Cootie Williams (t); Joe Nanton (tb); Johnny Hodges (as); Barney Bigard (cl/ts); Harry Carney (bar); Duke Ellington (p); Fred Guy (g); Billy Taylor (b); Sonny Greer (d)
Have A Heart (Lost In Meditation) / *Echoes Of Harlem*

GLEN GRAY AND THE CASA LOMA ORCHESTRA
Recording session for Decca in New York City.
Glen Gray (as/dir); Sonny Dunham, Grady Watts, Frank Zullo (t); Pee Wee Hunt (tb/voc); Billy Rauch, Murray McEachern (tb); Clarence Hutchenrider (cl/as), Kenny Sargent (as/voc); Art Ralston (as/o/bsn); Danny d'Andrea (as); Pat Davis (cl/ts/fl); Joe Hall (p); Jack Blanchette (g); Stanley Dennis (b); Tony Briglia (d)
My Heart is Taking Lessons (vPWH) / *Did An Angel Kiss You The Day You Were Born?* (vKS) / *Nutty Nursery Rhymes* (vPWH) / *This Is My Night To Dream* (vKS)

RADIO LOGS

11:00PM WABC
BOB CROSBY
Hotel Pennsylvania, NYC
SWELL. John-Allen Wolf announced.
Bob White (swell: Lawson's nuttsy trumpet; Miller's nice tenor; Smith's grand trombone)
True Confession (vocal: Kay Weber)
I've Hitched My Wagon To A Star (vocal: Bob Crosby) (fair song and arrangement)
Dogtown Blues (great slow Dixieland style: Lawson; Matlock's clarinet; great ending)
Rosalie (vocal: Bob Crosby) (lousy piece but fine arrangement: Lawson; Miller)
Stumblin' (8 Bobcats: colossal; weird intro; Miller's wonderful solo; Matlock; Zurke; Smith)
This Never Happened Before (vocal: Kay Weber) (nuttsy, brief clarinet)
Oh, Lady Be Good (wonderful relaxed swing: Miller's long, marvelous tenor sax solo; Lawson's nuttsy trumpet backed by Bauduc's ballsy drumming; colossal clarinet break by Matlock; Bauduc and Zurke going magnificently; swell ending)

11:30PM WMCA
NOBLE SISSLE
Apollo Theater, NYC
I Got Rhythm (swell: Sidney Bechet's nuttsy soprano sax; trumpet)

Maxine Sullivan   Noble Sissle

THURSDAY 20 JANUARY 1938

RADIO LOGS

11:00PM WABC
CAB CALLOWAY
Cotton Club, NYC
Dear Old Southland (nuttsy: Chu Berry's great tenor)
The One I Love (vocal: Cab Calloway) (trumpet; Berry's tenor)
Sometimes I'm Happy (nice arrangement: saxes)
Half-Moon On The Hudson (vocal: Cab Calloway)
Alexander's Ragtime Band (Berry; trumpet)
She's Tall, She's Tan, She's Terrific (vocal: Cab Calloway)
Once In A While (vocal: Bennie Payne)
Have You Met Miss Jones? (vocal: Cab Calloway)
Keep That Hi-De-Ho In Your Soul (vocal: Cab Calloway)
Three Swings And Out

12:00 MIDNIGHT WOR
BOB CROSBY
Hotel Pennsylvania, NYC
Arthur Whiteside announced.
The Last Round-up (lousy piece: grand solos by Miller; Smith; Matlock; Miller again)
Sweet Someone (vocal: Kay Weber)
I've Hitched My Wagon To A Star (vocal: Bob Crosby) (Miller's nice tenor sax)
Squeeze Me (colossal, real Dixieland rhythm: Miller's great tenor; Zurke; marvelous ending)
A Foggy Day (vocal: Kay Weber) (Miller's fine chorus)
Bei Mir Bist Du Schoen (vocal: Bob Crosby) (marvelous blue trumpet intro: Matlock; Zurke; Butterfield)
Wolverine Blues (wonderful old swing tune: trombones and clarinets; Matty Matlock's great blue clarinet in lower register; Bauduc's magnificent drumming!!!)
This Never Happened Before (vocal: Kay Weber) (nuttsy, brief clarinet)
Summertime (theme)

DIXIELAND DILEMMA

Following Benny into the Pennsy, a difficult task indeed, came Bob Crosby's crew the middle of this month. Caught in person opening night as well as over the air on its first broadcasts, the Dispensers were distributing their Dixieland in the customary digging style. Improvement was especially noticeable in the brass section, which had young Bill Butterfield shining more brilliantly than ever on some pretty, sending, hot passages, and Charlie Spivak's tone and phrasing on first trumpet supplying the band with the necessary feeling here-to-fore so sadly lacking in its rendition of ballads.

12.00 MIDNIGHT WNEW
CHICK WEBB
Savoy Ballroom, NYC
If You Should Ever Leave (vocal: Ella Fitzgerald) (Fulford; McRae)
Quaker City Jazz (nuttsy: trumpet; tenor sax)
The Dipsy Doodle (vocal: Ella Fitzgerald) (Sandy Williams' trombone)
Go Harlem (swell: Webb's drums; McRae's tenor, etc)
True Confession (vocal: Ella Fitzgerald) (great vocal)
I Found A New Baby

FRIDAY 21 JANUARY 1938

RECORDING SESSION

JOHNNY DODDS & HIS CHICAGO BOYS
Recording session for Decca in New York City.
Charlie Shavers (t); Johnny Dodds (cl); Lil Armstrong (p); Teddy Bunn (g); John Kirby (b); O'Neil Spencer (d/wb*/voc)
Wild Man Blues / *Melancholy* / *29th And Dearborn* / *Blues Galore* (vO'NS) / *Stack O'Lee Blues* (vO'NS) / *Shake Your Can* (vO'NS)

RED NORVO AND HIS ORCHESTRA
Recording session for Brunswick in New York City.
Red Norvo (xyl/ldr); Jimmy Blake, Zeke Zarchy, Barney Zudecoff (t); Al Mastren, Wes Hein (tb); Hank D'Amico (cl); Len Goldstein (as); Charles Lamphere (as/ts); Jerry Jerome (ts); Bill Miller (p); Alan Hanlon (g); Pete Peterson (b); George Wettling (d); Mildred Bailey (voc)
Always And Always (vMB) / *I Was Doin' Alright* (vMB) / *It's Wonderful* (vMB) / *Love Is Here To Stay* (vMB)

Hugh Pastoriza, Jim Poe, Dick Morningstar, Harvey Pinger and myself went down on the 7:31 train to Grand Central from where we took the subway to 33rd Street and 7th Avenue where we went into the Madhattan Room of the Hotel Pennsylvania. We all had a swell time. I got the whole band's autographs, plus arranger Deane Kincaide and vocalist Kay Weber. Kincaide is one of the finest arrangers today and also plays saxophone. He left Crosby's Band last year to join Woody Herman's Band but he said there's something about Crosby's Band that draws him back although Herman has a wonderful band. Kay Weber is the sweet vocalist who's been with Crosby's Band for a year and a half. She formerly sang with the Dorsey Brothers' Band when Bob Crosby also sang with it. She's fair looking and has a good sweet voice. We got a table right next to the Orchestra but didn't get anything to eat so we each paid 80 cents. At first the band played too many sweet songs, but later it really went to town. You know that Crosby replaced Goodman here last Monday. He isn't doing nearly the business that Goodman was doing. He's got a great band but I doubt if his Dixieland style will ever be as popular as Goodman's style. I can't remember all of the numbers played but here are a few: *Muskrat Ramble*; *Basin Street Blues* (vocal by Bob Crosby); *In A Minor Mood* (featuring pianist Bob Zurke); *Gin Mill Blues* (featuring Eddie Miller's clarinet); *Pagan Love Song*; *Steppin' Pretty*; *On The Alamo*; *She's Tall, She's Tan, She's Terrific* (vocal by Nappy Lamare); *I've Hitched My Wagon To A Star* (vocal by Bob Crosby); *Rosalie*; *I'm Getting Sentimental Over You*; *Stardust*; *Summertime* (featuring Charlie Spivak's trumpet); *Sweet Someone* (vocal by Kay Weber); *Between The Devil And The Deep Blue Sea*, etc. The whole band is rather young and clean cut, and presents a fine appearance. Every one of them is actually great and well-known. Saxist Gil Rodin is the most important man in this co-operative organization. He hires and fires the men, gets the spots, etc. The band just left Rockwell-O'Keefe, claiming they got a raw deal, and are now with the Music Corporation of America (MCA). Lawson takes most of the trumpet solos and is considered very great. Spivak also has a national reputation as being a most consistent trumpeter but doesn't take many solos. Bill Butterfield is a young chap who only joined the band last fall in Los Angeles. He plays a marvelous, blue trumpet. Most of

Ray Bauduc

Yank Lawson
Charlie Spivak

Bob Haggart

Ray Bauduc

JANUARY 1938

the great trombone solos are taken by Warren Smith, although Silloway took one tonight. Bauduc is my favorite drummer next to Krupa; Haggart is my favorite novelty bassist, although not as a solid bassist even though most people think he's the greatest bassist living. Zurke is a magnificent pianist with a terrific left hand. He replaced Joe Sullivan about a year ago and has done a great job, making many think that he's the greatest. He's been on crutches for several months with a bad leg. Eddie Miller is almost tops on tenor sax, is young and is a swell guy. Matty Matlock plays most of the clarineting and gets plenty of blue notes in.

Nappy Lamare

Joe Kearns   Matty Matlock   Eddie Miller

Charlie Spivak

Yank Lawson

Nappy Lamare

Eddie Miller

■ SATURDAY 22 JANUARY 1938

RADIO LOGS

7.00PM WABC
SATURDAY NIGHT SWING SESSION No80
CBS Studios, 485 Madison Avenue, NYC
Message From Mars (nuttsy weird new swing tune written by Sid Phillips from Jack Hylton's band in London: grand clarinet; straight sax; trombone)
Rockin' Chair (MILDRED BAILEY singing three lines to introduce herself)
'Long About Midnight (MILDRED BAILEY singing as only she can: wonderful!)
Azure (DUKE ELLINGTON playing his own composition at the piano: good)
If Dreams Come True (recently written by Edgar Sampson, nuttsy swing piece: nice smooth trombone; magnificent tenor sax; trombones)
Throw-Down Blues (CASPAR REARDON, back from Hollywood, playing a swell harp)
I Never Knew (RED NORVO playing a wonderful xylophone, colossal: tenor sax)
Snowball (MILDRED BAILEY singing a slow spiritual: she's got a great voice!)
The Dipsy Doodle (Great! Mondello's fine clarinet; colossal tenor sax; drums; trumpet)

■ SUNDAY 23 JANUARY 1938

RADIO LOGS

11:00AM WNEW
SUNDAY MORNING SWING CONCERT
Criterion Theater, NYC
Song Of India (Merle Pitts' WNEW Studio Band)
Whistle While You Work (MILDRED CRAIG singing)
September Morning In Harlem (Merle Pitts' WNEW Studio Band: played for first time over radio; tenor; trombone)
Brown Girl (LIL ARMSTRONG singing a slow piece: swell)
MEDLEY: *Night And Day / Dancing In The Dark* (Merle Pitts' WNEW Studio Band)
I Never Knew (RED NORVO's 7 Peppers— colossal: Haymer's grand tenor; clarinet; Jimmy Blake's nice trumpet; Red's wonderful xylophone beating!)
Honeysuckle Rose (MILDRED BAILEY singing colossally with Red's Peppers: clarinet)
Nagasaki (RED NORVO's 7 Peppers— marvelous jamming: nuttsy clarinet; Haymer's tenor; trumpet; Red)
With A Smile And A Song (Merle Pitts' WNEW Studio Band: Don Richards singing)
After You've Gone (Merle Pitts' WNEW Studio Band: good)
My True Confession (MILDRED CRAIG singing)
Sweet Bill From Sugar Hill (Merle Pitts' WNEW Studio Band)
Born To Swing (LIL ARMSTRONG singing good: she's got nice rhythm)
Ida (RED NORVO playing some magnificent, funny sounding, flat xylophone that really sent me! Played with a special mallet)
Rockin' Chair (MILDRED BAILEY singing wonderfully with Red)
I Got Rhythm (nuttsy parts: lousy electric guitar; Weiss' drums; tenor)

I went to see Duke Ellington today. I went by myself and got a ride to the subway from where I got off at 125th Street and walked over to the Apollo Theater where Duke Ellington's Famous Orchestra is playing a week's engagement. Ellington is a musical genius and easily one of the leading men in the music world. He writes hundreds of songs and arrangements, many of which have been national hits. His orchestra is also really marvelous. Most of its members have been with it for 10 years and are all leaders on their instruments. The whole band, thanks to Duke, has a certain style that no other band has ever accomplished. They can play plenty hot and when they play sweet with that magnificent sax section there's nothing like it in the world! The stage show was great except that Ellington didn't play enough. Here are the songs featuring Ellington's Band, besides several other tunes played as accompaniment to other stars:

Chatterbox (just released on Brunswick, marvelous: Stewart's nuttsy hot trumpet; Lawrence Brown; Johnny Hodges)
Echoes Of Harlem (featuring Cootie Williams playing a magnificent, muted, slow, hot trumpet!)
You Go To My Head (vocal: Ivie Anderson) (very new song, just introduced: red hot vocal)
I Want A Man Like That (vocal: Ivie Anderson) (a little swell comedy between Ivie and Sonny Greer; Ivie and Rex Stewart's trumpet carried on a funny conversation— Rex is great!)
Lionel Hampton came out on stage and said hello but couldn't play because of his contract.
Oh, Babe, Maybe Someday (vocal: Ivie Anderson) (Ivie singing a request from Bennie Payne, Calloway's pianist, who was in the audience: Cootie's trumpet)
On The Sunny Side Of The Street (vocal: Ivie Anderson) (magnificent! Hodges' wonderful long alto sax solo; Ivie's colossal vocal with Cootie trumpet backing her; Brown's great, smooth trombone solo)
I've Got To Be A Rug Cutter (vocal: Ivie Anderson) (swell exceptional piece: Stewart, Williams and Nanton playing first chorus; Ivie & trio of Stewart, Carney & Alvis singing; very hot ending, different from record)

The personnel of the band hasn't changed. It still has 2 bassists (Hayes Alvis & Billy Taylor), 4 trumpets (Jenkins, Whetsel, Williams & Stewart), etc. I got the 5:25 train home after a grand afternoon.

■ MONDAY 24 JANUARY 1938

RADIO LOGS

11:00AM WABC
GLEN GRAY
Hotel New Yorker, NYC
Great.
Minding My Business (colossal new piece: Davis' swell tenor; trombone; trumpet)
Did An Angel Kiss You? (vocal: Kenny Sargent)
Bei Mir Bist Du Schoen (vocal: Pee Wee Hunt) (swell arrangement: clarinet; Hall's piano)
Song Of India (another fine, original arrangement: trumpet; tenor sax)
Let's Make It A Lifetime (vocal: Kenny Sargent) (trombone; bassoon)
Sing A Nursery Rhyme (vocal: Pee Wee Hunt)
Who's Sorry Now? (grand old piece: 3 trombones; clarinet; trombone; saxes)
I Found A New Baby (wonderful! Dunham's great trumpet; Davis' ballsy tenor)

JANUARY 1938

■ TUESDAY 25 JANUARY 1938

RECORDING SESSION

ELLA FITZGERALD AND HER SAVOY EIGHT
Recording session for Decca in New York City.
Ella Fitzgerald (voc); Taft Jordan (t); Sandy Williams (tb); Louis Jordan (as); Teddy McRae (ts/bar); Tommy Fulford (p); Bobby Johnson (g); Beverly Peer (b); Chick Webb (d)
It's Wonderful / *I Was Doing All Right*

JIMMY DORSEY AND HIS ORCHESTRA
Recording session for Decca in New York City.
Jimmy Dorsey (cl/as); Shorty Sherock (t); Toots Camarata (t/voc); Bobby Byrne, Don Mattison (tb/voc); Bruce Squires (tb); Len Whitney (as); Dave Matthews (as/ts); Charles Frazier (ts); Freddie Slack (p); Roc Hillman (g/voc); Jack Ryan (b); Ray McKinley (d/voc); Bob Eberly (voc)
Doctor Rhythm (vDM,RH,BE) / *On The Sentimental Side* (vBE) / *How'dja Like To Love Me?* (vDM) / *I Fall In Love With You Every Day* (vBE) / *Love Is Here To Stay* / *Smoke From A Chimney* (vBE) / *It's The Dreamer In Me* (vBE) / *I Was Doing All Right* (vBE) / *My First Impression Of You* (vDM)

RADIO LOGS

10:00PM WABC
BENNY GOODMAN
Camel Caravan, CBS Playhouse, NYC
Let's Dance (theme)
Big John Special (magnificent Henderson arrangement: Stacy; James)
I See Your Face Before Me (vocal: Martha Tilton) (Brown's trombone)
Roll 'Em (Stacy; James; Benny)
Liza (BG Quartet) (Wilson's fine piano; Hampton's swell long solo)
You Took The Words Right Out Of My Heart (vocal: Martha Tilton)
Bugle Call Rag (wonderful, very fast: Benny; Rollini; Elman; Brown; Krupa)

■ WEDNESDAY 26 JANUARY 1938

RECORDING SESSION

BUNNY BERIGAN AND HIS ORCHESTRA
Recording session for Victor in New York City.
Bunny Berigan, Irving Goodman, Steve Lipkins (t); Al George, Sonny Lee (tb); Mike Doty, Joe Dixon (cl/as); Clyde Rounds, George Auld (ts); Fulton McGrath (p); Tom Morgan (g); Hank Wayland (b); Dave Tough (d); Gail Reese (voc)
Piano Tuner Man (vGR) / *Heigh-Ho* (vGR) / *A Serenade To The Stars* (vGR) / *Outside Of Paradise* (vGR)

CAB CALLOWAY AND HIS ORCHESTRA
Recording session for Vocalion in New York City.
Cab Calloway (voc); Doc Cheatham, Shad Collins, Irving Randolph, Lammar Wright (t); DePriest Wheeler, Keg Johnson, Claude Jones (tb); Chauncey Haughton, Andrew Brown (cl/as); Chu Berry, Walter Thomas (ts); Benny Payne (p); Danny Barker (g); Milt Hinton (b); Leroy Maxey (d)
One Big Union For Two (vCC) / *Doing The Reactionary* (vCC) / *Rustle Of Swing* / *Three Swings And Out* / *I Like Music (With A Swing Like That)* (vCC) / *Foolin' With You* (vCC)

RADIO LOGS

11:00PM WABC
BOB CROSBY
Hotel Pennsylvania, NYC
The Dipsy Doodle
This Never Happened Before (vocal: Kay Weber)
Rosalie (vocal: Bob Crosby)
Josephine
Beale Street Blues (vocal: Bob Crosby) (great! trumpet; trombone; clarinet; Zurke's colossal piano; nuttsy vocal)
Little Rock Getaway (written by Joe Sullivan, played by Bob Zurke)
Thrill Of A Lifetime (vocal: Kay Weber)
South Rampart Street Parade (wonderful!)

11:30PM WMCA
DUKE ELLINGTON
Apollo Theater, NYC
Chatterbox (magnificent! Rex Stewart's great cornet; Brown's hot trombone; Johnny Hodges; Rex Stewart again)
Once In A While (wonderful! no arrangement: real slow, colossal swing that sends you!! Hodges' terrific, sweet alto sax; Lawrence Brown's real sweet, smooth trombone)

For the thousands who were turned away from Carnegie Hall last night!

IN PERSON
BENNY GOODMAN AND HIS BAND

Starts Wednesday, Jan. 26th
At Regular Paramount Prices

PLUS Mae West in her newest screen sensation "Every Day's A Holiday"

PARAMOUNT TIMES SQUARE

Broadway Dances in Aisles For Goodman (and Mae West)

Whether it was Mae West and her new black wig or Benny Goodman and his own strange music hasn't quite been settled yet, but Times Sq. went crazy this morning in front of the Paramount Theater.

The place was supposed to open at 8 A. M., but a line started to form in front of the box office at 5 A. M., and less than ninety minutes later there were more than 2,000 persons stamping their feet in the early morning chill. By 7:30 A. M. the theater management put a riot call into the W. 47th St. station.

Sergeant Harry Moore and ten mounted policemen tried to keep things quiet along Broadway and around 43rd St., but it didn't work, and a few minutes later 'he doors had to be opened well ahead of schedule. By 7:45, 3,634 persons had filled every seat in the house and 1,800 more were crowded in the stairways and lobby

The picture, "Every Day's a Holiday," was put on twenty minutes early because the audience demanded it, and then at 10:04 A. M., the swing maestro appeared on the stage. From that moment on things went loudly nuts.

Couples started to shag in the aisles and the ushers couldn't do anything about it. When the aisles got too crowded, the couples marched on stage and continued their peculiar movements under the not-unhappy eye of Mr. Goodman

Swing satiated and happy, the mob left an hour later and the management was able to unlock its front doors and let another army in.

12.30AM WJZ
CHICK WEBB
Savoy Ballroom, NYC
Tea For Two (Fulford's piano; trumpet)
Heart Of Mine (vocal: Ella Fitzgerald)
Somebody Loves Me
Naughty Waltz
You Took The Words Right Out Of My Heart
Clap Hands! Here Comes Charlie
It's Wonderful (vocal: Ella Fitzgerald)
Copenhagen
King Porter Stomp

■ THURSDAY 27 JANUARY 1938

RECORDING SESSION

TOMMY DORSEY AND HIS ORCHESTRA
Recording session for Victor in New York City.
Tommy Dorsey (tb); Pee Wee Erwin, Lee Castle, Andy Ferretti (t); Les Jenkins, Frank d'Annolfo (tb); Johnny Mince, Fred Stulce, Skeets Herfurt (cl/as); Bud Freeman (ts); Howard Smith (p); Carmen Mastren (g); Artie Shapiro (b); Maurice Purtill (d); Edythe Wright, Jack Leonard (voc)
How Can You Forget? (vEW) / *More Than Ever* (vJL) / *There's A Boy In Harlem* (vEW)

HUDSON-DeLANGE ORCHESTRA
Recording session for Brunswick in New York City.
Will Hudson (arr); Eddie DeLange (voc/ldr); Charles Mitchell, Howard Schaumberger, Joe Bauer (t); Edward Kolyer, Jack Andrews (tb); George Bohn, Gus Bivona (cl/as); Pete Brendel (as/bar); Ted Duane (cl/ts); Mark Hyams (p); Bus Etri (g); Doc Goldberg (b); Billy Exiner (d); Mary McHugh (voc)
At Your Beck And Call (vMM) / *Doin' The Reactionary* (vMM)

At the conclusion of Tommy Dorsey's Engagement Wednesday, January 26th...

"THE MR. & MRS. of SWING"
RED NORVO AND MILDRED BAILEY AND THEIR ORCHESTRA
come to the
COMMODORE *Palm Room*

Starting at Supper
THURSDAY, JANUARY 27th
and at DINNER & SUPPER
nightly thereafter—except Sundays

Frank J. Crohan, Presid.

THE COMMODORE
RIGHT AT GRAND CENTRAL

NORVO'S OPENING

Red Norvo's opening at the Commodore Hotel, January 27th, proved to be just about the most sensational of the year. A capacity crowd, well-studded with celebrities including bandleaders Benny Goodman, Bob Crosby, Randy Mergentroid, Larry Clinton and others, cheered and whistled as Red and wife Mildred Bailey thrilled all with a grand display of real swing. Excitement became so tense that a member of the Norvo band fainted and had to be carried from the room.

■ SATURDAY 29 JANUARY 1938

I got six records today at the Commodore Music Shop: Sonny Greer's Memphis Men playing *Beggar's Blues* and *Saturday Night Function* (Vocalion 3012); Duke Ellington's *In The Shade Of The Old Apple Tree* and *Harlem Speaks* (Brunswick 6646); Duke Ellington's *Merry-Go-Round* and *Admiration* (Brunswick 7440); Cootie Williams' *Pigeons And Peppers* and *Jubilesta* (Vocalion 3922); Barney Bigard's *If You're Ever In My Arms Again* and *Get It Southern Style* (Variety 546); and Buster Bailey's *Dizzy Debutante* and *Afternoon In Africa* (Variety 668).

JANUARY 1938

RADIO LOGS

7.00PM WABC
SATURDAY NIGHT SWING SESSION No81
NYC
Farewell Blues (Leith Stevens' CBS Band playing magnificently! nuttsy trombone; Hank Ross' tenor)
Cowbell Serenade (featuring the composer, Walter Gross, on piano; Gussak's drums; tenor sax)
Funiculi, Funicula (The MERRY MACS vocalizing colossally: 3 girls & 1 boy)
Avalon (BENNY GOODMAN QUARTET, wonderful!! all four nuttsy)
Where Or When (slow swinging by BENNY GOODMAN TRIO: Teddy Wilson's piano outstanding)
I'm A Ding Dong Daddy (From Dumas) (BENNY GOODMAN QUARTET again playing simply magnificently!!! I never heard them better)
Alice Blue Gown (BOBBY HACKETT playing a colossal but brief trumpet solo)
Down With Love (Leith Stevens' CBS Band going swell on a grand arrangement: Ross' great tenor; nice brief clarinet)

11:00PM WABC
RED NORVO
Hotel Commodore, NYC
Red Norvo and Mildred Bailey opened 2 days ago at the Commodore, replacing Tommy Dorsey. I heard this program at Nancy Long's house.
Thanks For The Memory (vocal: Mildred Bailey)
Remember (colossal: great saxes; rhythm)
Tea Time (Norvo's wonderful xylophone!!!)
It's Wonderful (vocal: Mildred Bailey)
Moonglow (vocal: Terry Allen) (great sweet arrangement)
Bob White (vocal: Mildred Bailey) (good)
King Porter Stomp (magnificent, great)

12:00 MIDNIGHT WABC
BOB CROSBY
Hotel Pennsylvania, NYC
In A Minor Mood (magnificent piano by Bob Zurke)
Always And Always (vocal: Kay Weber)
Nice Work If You Can Get It (vocal: Bob Crosby)
Squeeze Me
Bei Mir Bist Du Schoen (vocal: Bob Crosby)
Bugle Call Rag

12:00 MIDNIGHT WNEW
JOHN KIRBY
Onyx Club, 62 W52nd Street, NYC
A Foggy Day
Exactly Like You (super-magnificent playing: Pete Brown's great alto sax; trumpet; clarinet)
Loch Lomond (vocal: Maxine Sullivan)
Moanin' In The Morning (vocal: O'Neil Spencer)

J. DORSEY FOR N. Y.

After an absence of almost three years, Jimmy Dorsey's band returns to New York on March 5th to commence an extended engagement in the New Yorker Hotel, announces a press-time report from Rockwell-O'Keefe.

Larry Clinton replaced Glen Gray there for the night of January 29, Casa Loma playing the President's Ball.

12:30AM WMCA
GLEN GRAY
Hotel Mayflower, Washington, D.C.
Grand. This is a special engagement for Gray's band at President Roosevelt's Birthday Party with proceeds going to fight Infantile Paralysis.
Melody In F-Minor (colossal: clarinet; McEachern's dirty trombone; Davis; Dunham)
I See Your Face Before Me (vocal: Kenny Sargent) (O.K. violin)
You Better Change Your Tune (vocal: Pee Wee Hunt) (trombone)
Sugar Foot Stomp (nuttsy: fair clarinet; great trombone; trumpet)
True Confession (vocal: Kenny Sargent) (swell commercial piece: Dunham's trumpet)
I May Be Wrong (vocal: Pee Wee Hunt) (Dunham's high trumpet)
Who's Sorry Now? (slow swing: 3 trombones; clarinet; saxes)
Limehouse Blues (Dunham's magnificent arrangement: Hunt's trombone; alto sax; trombone)

■ SUNDAY 30 JANUARY 1938

RADIO LOGS

11:00AM WNEW
SUNDAY MORNING SWING CONCERT
Criterion Theater, NYC
I Found A New Baby (Merle Pitts' WNEW Studio Band: nice tenor sax)
Down With Love (vocal by THE SMARTIES – 3 girls and a boy)
Happy Feet (HOT LIPS PAGE from Harlem singing and playing trumpet)
Ol' Man River (BILLIE POWELL, from Willie Bryant's band, singing lousy)
Who's Sorry Now? (BOB CROSBY'S 8 BOBCATS playing the nuts: Miller's tenor; Zurke's great piano; Matlock's nice clarinet; Smith's trombone)
Fidgety Feet (CROSBY'S Fidgety Feeted Boys going to town: Matlock; rhythm)
Nice Work If You Can Get It (MILDRED CRAIG singing O.K.)
Unknown Operatic Piece (Merle Pitts' WNEW Studio Band)
Bugle Call Rag (Featuring SAM SPERGEL's electric guitar which I don't like!)
Old Man Ben (HOT LIPS PAGE playing a nuttsy trumpet and singing a hot slow vocal)
You're Driving Me Crazy (BOB CROSBY'S BOBCATS really going to town: Miller's tenor; Matlock's clarinet; Lawson's trumpet; Haggart's long nuttsy bass solo; Bauduc's great drum breaks)
Beale Street Blues (BOB CROSBY'S BOBCATS with a swell vocal by Bob Crosby: Smith's nuttsy, dirty trombone; clarinets; Matlock's ballsy clarinet; what rhythm!; Zurke)
Dinah (THE SMARTIES singing good)
Bei Mir Bist Du Schoen (BILLIE POWELL vocalizing fair)
Stumblin' (BOB CROSBY'S BOBCATS playing great: Miller; Matlock; Smith; Lawson; Zurke, etc)

■ MONDAY 31 JANUARY 1938

RADIO LOGS

11:00PM WABC
GLEN GRAY
Hotel New Yorker, NYC
Swell. Pee Wee Hunt can't sing tonight because of a cold.
Down By The Old Mill Stream (swell old piece: Dunham's grand trumpet)
I Can Dream, Can't I? (vocal: Kenny Sargent) (very sweet: brief trombone)
You Have Everything
What Is This Thing Called Love? (nuttsy old piece: Davis' tenor; trombone)
You Took The Words Right Out Of My Heart (vocal: Kenny Sargent) (trumpet)
My Heart Is Taking Lessons (McEachern's fine hot trombone; clarinet; Davis' tenor)
Peg O' My Heart (very old piece: nuttsy muted brass intro; trumpets; trombones; Davis' tenor)
Caravan (rather fast arrangement: fair straight trombone; Davis' tenor sax; drums)

FEBRUARY 1938

Hotel Pennsylvania: **Bob Crosby**
Hotel Commodore: **Red Norvo**
Hotel New Yorker: **Glen Gray** (–26); **Jimmy Dorsey** (27–)
Hotel Lincoln: **Isham Jones**

Apollo Theater: **Claude Hopkins** (–3); **Savoy Sultans** (4–10); **Don Redman** (11–17); **Earl Hines** (18–24); **Count Basie** (25–)
Paramount Theater: **Benny Goodman** (–15); **Clyde McCoy** (16–)
Loew's State Theater: **Andy Sanella** (17–23)

Cotton Club: **Cab Calloway** / **Bill Robinson**
Hickory House: **Joe Marsala**
Onyx Club: **John Kirby** / **Maxine Sullivan**
Famous Door: **Louis Prima** / **Art Tatum**
Nick's: **Bobby Hackett**

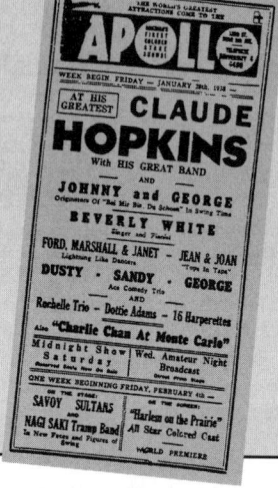

■ TUESDAY 1 FEBRUARY 1938

RADIO LOGS

10:00PM WABC
BENNY GOODMAN
Camel Caravan, CBS Playhouse, NYC
Let's Dance (theme)
When Buddha Smiles (great arrangement: Benny; saxes, etc)
Sunday In The Park (vocal: Martha Tilton) (very good new piece: brief trumpet)
Don't Be That Way (magnificent: Benny; Russin; James; Brown; Krupa)
Ooooo-oh Boom! (vocal: Martha Tilton & Benny Goodman) (very new novelty tune: swell vocal by Tilton and Goodman who introduced the following soloists: Russin; James; Krupa)
Dinah (BG Quartet) (wonderful fast swinging: Hampton & Benny outstanding)
Life Goes To A Party (great: uplifting trumpets; Russin; Benny; James)

11:00PM WABC
RED NORVO
Hotel Commodore, NYC
André Baruch announced.
You Can't Stop Me From Dreaming (swell: tenor; trumpet; George Wettling's drums)
Thanks For The Memory (vocal: Mildred Bailey) (Jerry Jerome's grand sweet-swing tenor sax)
I Double Dare You (vocal: Terry Allen) (Jerome's good tenor with Wettling's great drums)
Sweet Someone (vocal: Terry Allen) (nice clarinet; trombone)
Is That Religion? (vocal: Mildred Bailey) (swell words)
Tea Time (an original piece: clarinet)
I Was Doing All Right (vocal: Mildred Bailey) (clarinets)
Why Do I Love You? (swell: nuttsy brass; Jerome's tenor; drums; Norvo)
Smiles (grand: wonderful trumpet; Jerome's tenor)

■ WEDNESDAY 2 FEBRUARY 1938

RECORDING SESSION

DUKE ELLINGTON AND HIS ORCHESTRA
Recording session for Master Records in New York City.
Duke Ellington (p); Arthur Whetsel, Cootie Williams, Harold Baker (t); Rex Stewart (c); Joe Nanton, Lawrence Brown (t); Juan Tizol (vtb); Barney Bigard (cl); Johnny Hodges (cl/ss/as); Otto Hardwick (as/bsx); Harry Carney (cl/as/bar); Hayes Alvis, Billy Taylor (b); Sonny Greer (d)
Riding On A Blue Note / Lost In Meditation / The Gal From Joe's

GLEN GRAY AND THE CASA LOMA ORCHESTRA
Recording session for Decca in New York City.
Glen Gray (as/dir); Sonny Dunham, Grady Watts, Frank Zullo (t); Pee Wee Hunt (tb/voc); Billy Rauch, Murray McEachern (tb); Clarence Hutchenrider (cl/as), Kenny Sargent (as/voc); Art Ralston (as/o/bsn); Danny d'Andrea (as); Pat Davis (cl/ts/fl); Joe Hall (p); Jack Blanchette (g); Stanley Dennis (b); Tony Briglia (d)
What Is This Thing Called Love? / Melody In F Minor / Mindin' My Business

RADIO LOGS

8:30PM WEAF
TOMMY DORSEY
Kool-Raleigh Cigarette program, NYC
Annie Laurie (vocal: Three Esquires) (good new arrangement: Bud Freeman's tenor; Dorsey)
The Trombone Man (vocal: Edythe Wright) (novelty piece showing different stages of Dorsey's life)
Bewildered (vocal: Jack Leonard) (this tune will soon be a big hit)
Stop, Look, And Listen (nice: clarinets; Tommy; Johnny Mince; Freeman; Maurice Purtill's drums)
Tchaikovsky's Unfinished Symphony (sweet trombone solo by Dorsey)
MEDLEY: *Sweet Madness / Love, Your Magic Spell Is Everywhere / Love Is Just Around The Corner*
Who? (vocal: Jack Leonard) (swell arrangement: Pee Wee Erwin's trumpet; Dorsey's trombone; Freeman's tenor)

11:00PM WABC
BOB CROSBY
Hotel Pennsylvania, NYC
Grand. Kenneth Roberts announced.
Vieni, Vieni (great arrangement: Lawson; Bauduc; Miller; Matlock; Zurke)
Silhouetted In The Moonlight (vocal: Bob Crosby) (Eddie Miller's nuttsy tenor sax)
The Old Spinning Wheel (more great Dixieland jive: Ray Bauduc's drums; Yank Lawson's trumpet; Matty Matlock's clarinet)
Sweet Someone (vocal: Kay Weber) (nice sweet piece: Miller's swell tenor)
More Than Ever (vocal: Bob Crosby) (swell arrangement: grand ending)
In The Still Of The Night (vocal: Kay Weber) (good: nice trumpet)
Royal Garden Blues (colossal: Dixieland brass & Matlock; trumpet; Warren Smith's trombone; Bauduc)

11:00PM WNEW
JOHN KIRBY
Onyx Club, 62 W52nd Street, NYC
WONDERFUL! CBS announcer Paul Douglas witnessed this broadcast.
Linger Awhile (vocal: Leo Watson) (wonderful: good trumpet; Pete Brown's magnificent alto sax; clarinet)
Big John Special (vocal: Leo Watson & Band) (more colossal, ragged, give-out swing: wonderful vocal)
Whoa, Babe (colossal muted trumpet: Brown's great alto sax; O'Neil Spencer's drums; Watson's trombone)
Easy To Love (vocal: Maxine Sullivan) (a great vocal!!!)
That's Why I'm Blue (magnificent: Brown's alto sax; Charlie Shavers' trumpet; Buster Bailey's clarinet)
Rose Room (vocal: Leo Watson) (Kirby's great bassing; Watson's ballsy scat vocal)
The Dipsy Doodle (great)

■ THURSDAY 3 FEBRUARY 1938

RECORDING SESSION

BOB CROSBY AND HIS ORCHESTRA
Recording session for Decca in New York City.
Bob Crosby (voc/ldr); Charlie Spivak, Billy Butterfield, Yank Lawson (t); Ward Silloway, Warren Smith (tb); Matty Matlock (cl/as); Joe Kearns (as); Eddie Miller (cl/ts); Gil Rodin (ts); Bob Zurke (piano); Nappy Lamare (g/voc); Bob Haggart (b); Ray Bauduc (d); Kay Weber (voc)
It's Wonderful (vKW) / *In The Shade Of The Old Apple Tree* (vBC) / *Always And Always* (vKW) / *More Than Ever* (vBC) / *It's Easier Said Than Done* (vBC)

TOMMY DORSEY AND HIS ORCHESTRA
Recording session for Victor in New York City.
Tommy Dorsey (tb); Pee Wee Erwin, Lee Castle, Andy Ferretti (t); Les Jenkins, Frank d'Annolfo (tb); Johnny Mince, Fred Stulce, Skeets Herfurt (cl/as); Bud Freeman (ts); Howard Smith (p); Carmen Mastren (g); Artie Shapiro (b); Maurice Purtill (d); Jack Leonard (voc)
Annie Laurie (vQuartet) / *Oh, Promise Me* / *Shine On, Harvest Moon* / *Bewildered* (vJL) / *It's Wonderful* (vJL)

■ FRIDAY 4 FEBRUARY 1938

RECORDING SESSION

MAXINE SULLIVAN
Recording session for Vocalion in New York City.
Maxine Sullivan (voc); Charlie Shavers (t); Buster Bailey (cl); Pete Brown (as); Claude Thornhill (p); John Kirby (b); O'Neil Spencer (d)
It's Wonderful (vMS) / *Dark Eyes* (vMS) / *A Brown Bird Singing* (vMS) / *You Went To My Head* (vMS)

Bunny Berigan
ARTHUR T. MICHAUD, Personal Manager

February 4, 1938

Bob Inman,
133 Pondfield Road,
Bronxville, New York.

Dear Mr. Inman:

I'm really sorry I haven't been able to answer your note sooner, but broadcasts and hotel and stage appearances have a way of taking up more time than you'd think.

Thanks millions for your kind comments. They're mighty encouraging to me, and I appreciate them sincerely. I'm sending you my autographed photo.

Here's hoping you'll be in our unseen audience every time we take the air. And if we ever make a personal appearance in your vicinity, I hope you'll drop in to see and hear us swing out.

Until then, I am

Cordially yours,

Bunny Berigan

■ SATURDAY 5 FEBRUARY 1938

RECORDING SESSION

HUDSON-DeLANGE ORCHESTRA
Recording session for Brunswick in New York City.
Will Hudson (arr); Eddie DeLange (voc/ldr); Charles Mitchell, Howard Schaumberger, Joe Bauer (t); Edward Kolyer, Jack Andrews (tb); George Bohn, Gus Bivona (cl/as); Pete Brendel (as/bar); Ted Duane (cl/ts); Mark Hyams (p); Bus Etri (g); Doc Goldberg (b); Billy Exiner (d); Mary McHugh (voc)
Sunday In The Park (vMM)

Oliver Quayle and myself took the 9:27am train into N.Y.C. I had to go to the dentist first but, at 12 noon, we paid 40 cents each and went into the Paramount Theater at Times Square to see Benny Goodman and his band on the stage. He has been packing them in for almost two weeks now, breaking all records and causing a few riots with dancers in the aisles, etc. We got seats in the balcony where we met Lil Hettrick, Val Kuntz, and Betty Landon who left before we did. The movie was terrible. We had to see it twice so that we could see Goodman again. This is what they played:

Let's Dance (theme)
Dear Old Southland (colossal: Benny with his smile & clarinet; Red Ballard's trombone; Harry James; Vernon Brown)
Don't Be That Way
Loch Lomond (vocal: Martha Tilton) (Tilton singing swell in a long pink dress; she's plenty easy on the eyes)
Mama, That Moon Is Here Again (vocal: Martha Tilton) (good: no solos)
Bei Mir Bist Du Schoen (vocal: Martha Tilton) (Ziggy's show-off trumpet solo)
China Boy (BG Trio)
Body And Soul (BG Trio)
Limehouse Blues (BG Quartet)
Nagasaki (BG Quartet)
Sing, Sing, Sing (colossal long arrangement: James; Jess Stacy; Babe Russin; Benny; Gene Krupa)

STARTS TODAY Doors Open at 8:00 a.m.

"DRUM UP AND SEE US SOMETIME IF YOU WANTA GRAB A LITTLE LOAD OF SWING"

MAE WEST in "EVERY DAY'S A HOLIDAY"
A Paramount Picture with
EDMUND LOWE
CHARLES BUTTERWORTH
CHARLES WINNINGER
Walter Catlett · Lloyd Nolan
Herman Bing · Chester Conklin
and Louis Armstrong
Screen Play by Mae West
An Emanuel Cohen Production

in Person
BENNY GOODMAN
AND HIS ORCHESTRA
featuring
GENE KRUPA · TEDDY WILSON
LIONEL HAMPTON · MARTHA TILTON
and
CASS, MACK and TOPSY

PARAMOUNT

The band was dressed in light, greyish-blue formal suits while Benny wore a black tuxedo. They all looked kind of sick of playing the same numbers for two weeks although they always gave out excellently when they played. On the second show we saw they changed some numbers. The Trio played *Where Or When* and *After You've Gone*; the Quartet played *Avalon* and *Ding Dong Daddy*; and the band finished with *Bugle Call Rag*.

RADIO LOGS

7.00PM WABC
SATURDAY NIGHT SWING SESSION No82
CBS Theater, NYC
Hallelujah (Leith Stevens' CBS Band playing the nuts: great saxes and brass)
Margie (BOBBY SHORT, 11-yr-old boy, playing swell piano and singing a lousy vocal)
At The Jazz Band Ball (BOBBY HACKETT'S Jam band from Nick's Tavern playing some colossal jam stuff: Pee Wee Russell's dirty clarinet; Hackett's great trumpet; George Brunies' ballsy trombone; Eddie Condon's solid guitaring; Johnny Blowers' great drums)
You're A Sweetheart (Leith Stevens' CBS Band playing a magnificent arrangement: saxes & brass)
After You (FRANCES FAYE, from 52nd Street, singing a hell of a hot, wild vocal and beatin' some terrible piano!)
That's A-Plenty (BOBBY HACKETT'S Band again jammin' something terrific: Russell's terrific soft, dirty clarinet; Brunies' colossal trombone)
My Gal Sal (BUSTER BAILEY playing simply wonderful clarinet)
Dizzy Debutante (BUSTER BAILEY playing his own tune with aid of CBS Band: Russ Case's grand trumpet)
Blue Skies (Leith Stevens' CBS Band going sthe balls: nice trumpet; saxes; Hank Ross' tenor sax)

■ SUNDAY 6 FEBRUARY 1938

RADIO LOGS

11:00AM WNEW
SUNDAY MORNING SWING CONCERT
Criterion Theater, NYC
Oh, Lady Be Good (Merle Pitts' WNEW Band playing the nuts: clarinet)
Jazz Band Blues (BOBBY HACKETT'S Band playing some terrific jam: Pee Wee Russell; Hackett)
Jazz Me Blues (BOBBY HACKETT'S Band: Hackett's Bixian trumpet; Russell's clarinet; George Brunies' trombone)
Royal Garden Blues (Merle Pitts' WNEW Studio Band playing darn good: nice arrangement)
I've Gone Romantic Over You (KAY THOMPSON singing swell: Jack Jenney's trombone)
I Can't Give You Anything But Love (SLIM & SLAM [Slim Gaillard & Slam Stewart] playing some ballsy jive)
Bei Mir Bist Du Schoen (Merle Pitts' WNEW Studio Band playing a special arrangement: Pitts' violin)
If It's The Last Thing I Do (RED McKENZIE singing the nuts with Hackett's Band: Hackett's trumpet; Condon's guitar)
Love Is Just Around The Corner (BOBBY HACKETT'S Band playing marvelously: Russell; Brunies)
Sweet Sue (SAMMY SPERGEL playing a foul sounding electric harp)
You're A Sweetheart (Merle Pitts' WNEW Studio Band playing darn good: nice tune)
Unknown Title (SLIM & SLAM)
I Surrender Dear (JACK JENNEY, Kay Thompson's husband, playing nuttsy trombone)
The Criterion Blues (Merle Pitts' WNEW Studio Band: swell; trombone; tenor sax; saxes)
Blue Skies (KAY THOMPSON singing colossally: very original)
There'll Be Some Changes Made (RED McKENZIE singing with Hackett's Band: Russell's clarinet)

■ MONDAY 7 FEBRUARY 1938

RADIO LOGS

11:00PM WABC
GLEN GRAY
Hotel New Yorker, NYC
Minding My Business (nuttsy: Pat Davis' colossal tenor sax; trumpet; trombone)
You Took The Words Right Out Of My Heart (vocal: Kenny Sargent)
My Heart Is Taking Lessons (vocal: Pee Wee Hunt)
Oh, Lady Be Good (colossal, great!!! Sonny Dunham's trumpet; clarinet; trombone; tenor)
Did An Angel Kiss You? (vocal: Kenny Sargent) (trumpet)
Nutty Nursery Rhymes (vocal: Pee Wee Hunt)
Sleepy Time Gal (great!)
The World Is Waiting For The Sunrise (fast as light!!!)

■ TUESDAY 8 FEBRUARY 1938

RECORDING SESSION

ANDY KIRK AND HIS TWELVE CLOUDS OF JOY
Recording session for Decca in New York City.
Andy Kirk (bsx/ldr); Harry Lawson, Clarence Trice, Earl Thompson (t); Ted Donnelly (tb); Henry Wells (tb/voc); John Harrington (cl/as/bar); John Williams (as/bar); Earl Miller (as); Dick Wilson (ts); Mary Lou Williams (p); Ted Brinson (g); Booker Collins (b); Ben Thigpen (d); Pha Terrell (voc)
I Surrender Dear (vPT) / *Twinklin'* / *It Must Be True* (vPT) / *I'll Get By* (vHW) / *Little Joe From Chicago* (vBand)

RADIO LOGS

10:00PM WABC
BENNY GOODMAN
Camel Caravan, CBS Playhouse, NYC
Let's Dance (theme)
Memphis Blues (colossal new arrangement: Babe Russin; Benny)
Thanks For The Memory (vocal: Martha Tilton) (swell: trumpet)
The Lillie Stomp (BG Quartet) (written this afternoon in honor of Bea Lillie)
If Dreams Come True (nuttsy: clarinets & muted brass; Benny; Brown; Rollini)
Ooooo-oh Boom! (vocal: Martha Tilton & Benny Goodman) (first vocal by Tilton followed by Benny's vocal introducing solos by: Stacy; Griffin; Brown)
Bei Mir Bist Du Schoen (good, whole band playing: Benny & Krupa; Stacy's nice piano; Elman's trumpet)

■ WEDNESDAY 9 FEBRUARY 1938

RECORDING SESSION

GLEN GRAY AND THE CASA LOMA ORCHESTRA
Recording session for Decca in New York City.
Glen Gray (as/dir); Sonny Dunham, Grady Watts, Frank Zullo (t); Pee Wee Hunt (tb/voc); Billy Rauch, Murray McEachern (tb); Clarence Hutchenrider (cl/as); Kenny Sargent (as/voc); Art Ralston (as/o/bsn); Danny d'Andrea (as); Pat Davis (cl/ts/fl); Joe Hall (p); Jack Blanchette (g); Stanley Dennis (b); Tony Briglia (d)
You Better Change Your Tune (vPWH) / *The Old Apple Tree* (vPWH)

RADIO LOGS

11:30PM WMCA
SAVOY SULTANS
Apollo Theater, NYC
My Blue Heaven

FEBRUARY 1938

■ THURSDAY 10 FEBRUARY 1938

RECORDING SESSION

BOB CROSBY AND HIS ORCHESTRA
Recording session for Decca in New York City.
Bob Crosby (voc/ldr); Charlie Spivak, Billy Butterfield, Yank Lawson (t); Ward Silloway, Warren Smith (tb); Matty Matlock (cl/as); Joe Kearns (as); Eddie Miller (cl/ts); Gil Rodin (ts); Bob Zurke (piano); Nappy Lamare (g/voc); Bob Haggart (b); Ray Bauduc (d); Kay Weber (voc)
Please Be Kind (vKW) / *I Simply Adore You* (vBC) / *You're An Education* (vBC) / *Grand Terrace Rhythm* / *Wolverine Blues*

RED NORVO AND HIS ORCHESTRA
Recording session for Brunswick in New York City.
Red Norvo (xyl/ldr); Jimmy Blake, Zeke Zarchy, Barney Zudecoff (t); Wes Hein (tb); Hank D'Amico (cl); Len Goldstein (as); Charles Lamphere (as/ts); Jerry Jerome (ts); Bill Miller (p); Alan Hanlon (g); Pete Peterson (b); George Wettling (d); Mildred Bailey, Terry Allen (voc)
A Serenade To The Stars (vTA) / *More Than Ever* (vMB) / *The Week-end Of A Private Secretary* (vMB) / *Please Be Kind* (vMB)

NOBLE SISSLE'S SWINGSTERS
Recording session for Variety in New York City.
Noble Sissle (ldr); Clarence Brereton (t); Sidney Bechet (cl/ss); Gil White (ts); Harry Brooks (p); Jimmy Miller (g); Jimmy Jones (b); O'Neil Spencer (d/voc)
Viper Mad (vO'NS) / *Blackstick* / *When The Sun Sets Down South [Southern Sunset]* / *Sweet Patootie* (vO'NS)

■ SATURDAY 12 FEBRUARY 1938

I bought two records today at the Commodore Music Shop: Red Norvo's Septet playing *I Surrender Dear* and *Tom Boy* (Columbia 2977-D); and *Carnegie Drag* and *Carnegie Jump* by an All-Star Band (12-inch record costing $1.50) made by the Commodore Music Shop last week.

RADIO LOGS

7.00PM WABC
SATURDAY NIGHT SWING SESSION No83
CBS Theater, NYC
Nice Work If You Can Get It (Leith Stevens' CBS Band playing a nuttsy arrangement: tenor sax; trumpet)
Star Dust (CHARLIE TEAGARDEN playing wonderful trumpet: clarinet; drums)
Smiles (HENRY LOU 'RED' EVANS playing an ocarina: Shoobe's bassing)
The Dipsy Doodle (HENRY LOU 'RED' EVANS on ocarina with Shoobe)
Swingin' In The Corn Belt (Leith Stevens' CBS Band playing a swell, newly written, piece: Hank Ross' magnificent tenor sax)
Between The Devil And The Deep Blue Sea (VI MELE singing good and playing ballsy piano: clarinet)
I Can't Get Started (VI MELE playing nice, intricate piano)
The Cat Walk (written by Gussak, Vincent Maffay & Willis Kelly who is now in hospital: grand; ballsy tenor sax)
Ain't Misbehavin' (CHARLIE TEAGARDEN playing an inspired trumpet solo)
I Found A New Baby (Leith Stevens' CBS Band playing a colossal arrangement magnificently: trumpet)

■ MONDAY 14 FEBRUARY 1938

RADIO LOGS

11:00PM WABC
GLEN GRAY
Hotel New Yorker, NYC
Melody In F-Minor (swell original piece: clarinet; trombone; sax)
Two Dreams Got Together (vocal: Kenny Sargent) (sweet trombone; clarinet)
You Better Change Your Tune (vocal: Pee Wee Hunt) (Pat Davis' nuttsy tenor)
Song Of India (swell original arrangement: straight trumpet; sax)
This Is My Night To Dream (vocal: Kenny Sargent)
Just A Simple Melody (vocal: Pee Wee Hunt) (O.K. arrangement: clarinet)
Girl Of My Dreams (vocal: Kenny Sargent) (nice sweet vocal)
Dear Old Southland (colossal fast arrangement: dirty trombone; Stanley Dennis' bass solo; Davis' tenor)

12:00 MIDNIGHT WOR
RED NORVO
Hotel Commodore, NYC
Annie Laurie (vocal: Terry Allen) (nuttsy arrangement: brass & Red's xylophone; clarinet)
Thanks For The Memory (vocal: Mildred Bailey) (Jerome's swell tenor sax)
I Double Dare You (vocal: Terry Allen) (good)
Tea Time (clarinet; tenor sax; trombone; piano)
Please Be Kind (vocal: Mildred Bailey) (grand sweet piece: trombone)
Paradise (featuring Norvo's magnificent xylophone playing: tenor sax)
The One I Love (vocal: Terry Allen) (fair: nice vocal)
Honeysuckle Rose (vocal: Mildred Bailey) (Norvo & Bailey producing some gigantic stuff!!)
King Porter Stomp (wonderful: trumpet; great tenor sax; Norvo)

12:00 MIDNIGHT WJZ
CHICK WEBB
Levaggi's, Boston
Blue Room
I Simply Adore You (vocal: Ella Fitzgerald)
Unknown Title
D-Natural Blues
You're A Sweetheart (vocal: Ella Fitzgerald)
Unknown Title
If Dreams Come True (vocal: Ella Fitzgerald)
Harlem Congo (written by Chick Webb)

12:30AM WEAF
LOUIS ARMSTRONG
Grand Terrace, Chicago
Unknown Title
Two Dreams Got Together (vocal: Bobbie Caston)
Riffs
Sweet As A Song (vocal: Louis Armstrong)
Mr. Ghost Goes To Town (colossal: Red Allen's trumpet; great tenor sax; trombone)
This Is My Night To Dream (vocal: Sonny Woods)
If My Heart Could Only Talk
Mahogany Hall Stomp

■ TUESDAY 15 FEBRUARY 1938

RADIO LOGS

10:00PM WABC
BENNY GOODMAN
Camel Caravan, CBS Playhouse, NYC
Let's Dance (theme)
That Naughty Waltz (swell: solid saxes; Benny; Brown's trombone; James' muted trumpet)
Loch Lomond (vocal: Martha Tilton) (good to hear it again: James' trumpet)
Dixieland One-Step (guests LARRY SHIELDS-clarinet; EDDIE EDWARDS-trombone; BOBBY HACKETT-trumpet; TONY SBARBARO-drums; and Jess Stacy-piano: gigantic jamming!)
I'm Coming Virginia (Bobby Hackett playing colossal 'Bix-style' trumpet with guests)
When My Baby Smiles (more Dixieland with guests)
Mood Indigo (Goodman Band in short version of Ellington's piece)
Shine (Harry James playing great Armstrong-inspired trumpet)

Roll 'Em (Mary Lou Williams' great piece: Stacy; James)
Nagasaki (BG Quartet) (great work by all four)
Mama, That Moon Is Here Again (vocal: Martha Tilton) (swell: Benny; trumpet)

■ WEDNESDAY 16 FEBRUARY 1938

RECORDING SESSION

COUNT BASIE AND HIS ORCHESTRA
Recording session for Decca in New York City.
Buck Clayton, Ed Lewis, Harry Edison (t); Dan Minor, Benny Morton, Eddie Durham (tb); Earle Warren (as/voc); Lester Young, Herschel Evans (ts); Jack Washington (bar); Count Basie (p); Freddie Green (g); Walter Page (b); Jo Jones (d); Jimmy Rushing (voc)
Sent For You Yesterday And Here You Come Today (vJR) / *Every Tub* / *Now Will You Be Good?* (vJR) / *Swinging The Blues*

BOBBY HACKETT AND HIS ORCHESTRA
Recording session for Vocalion in NYC.
Bobby Hackett (c); Pee Wee Russell (cl/ts); Bernie Billings (ts); Dave Bowman (p); Eddie Condon (g); Clyde Newcomb (b); Johnny Blowers (d); Lola Bard (v)
You, You And Especially You (vLB) / *If Dreams Come True* (vLB) / *At The Jazz Band Ball* / *That Da Da Strain*

RADIO LOGS

11:00PM WABC
BOB CROSBY
Hotel Pennsylvania, NYC
Colossal.
At The Jazz Band Ball
That's Easier Said Than Done (vocal: Bob Crosby)
Goodnight Angel
I See Your Face Before Me (vocal: Kay Weber) (nice sweet piece: Eddie Miller's swell tenor)
Squeeze Me
I Double Dare You (vocal: Bob Crosby) (swell: fine trumpet; Miller's swell sax)
Please Be Kind (vocal: Kay Weber) (very new sweet piece introduced by Crosby)
The Dipsy Doodle

11:00PM WNEW
JOHN KIRBY
Onyx Club, 62 W52nd Street, NYC
MAGNIFICENT! Pianist Billy Kyle joined the band 2 or 3 weeks ago. He's marvelous and used to play with Lucky Millinder.
Big John Special (vocal: Leo Watson & Band) (colossal: Pete Brown's great alto sax; Charlie Shavers' ballsy trumpet; Kyle's piano; Watson)
Azure (Ellington's great piece played real slow and blue: clarinet; Kyle's great piano; Brown's alto)
It's Wonderful (vocal: Maxine Sullivan) (Maxine's magnificent singing, Kirby's fine bassing: what a voice!!!)
Dizzy Debutante (written by and featuring Buster Bailey: Kyle; Brown)
Allah's Holiday (vocal: Leo Watson) (an original, medium tempo, piece: vocal; Kyle, etc)

■ THURSDAY 17 FEBRUARY 1938

RADIO LOGS

11:00PM WABC
CAB CALLOWAY
Cotton Club, NYC
SWELL. Chu Berry on tenor sax steals the show on practically every number. He's terrific!!!
Marie
The Toy Trumpet
Body And Soul (vocal: Cab Calloway) (Berry's GREAT tenor)
The Greatest Mistake Of My Life (vocal: Cab Calloway)
Alexander's Ragtime Band (piano)
I Know That You Know
Paradise (vocal: Cab Calloway) (Berry's tenor; trumpet)
Sweet Stranger (vocal: Cab Calloway)
China Boy (good: clarinet)

12:00 MIDNIGHT WOR
BOB CROSBY
Hotel Pennsylvania, NYC
The Old Spinning Wheel
The One I Love (vocal: Kay Weber) (nice sweet piece: Miller's swell tenor)
Tea For Two (Bob Zurke; Eddie Miller)
Bei Mir Bist Du Schoen (vocal: Bob Crosby)
Yancey Special (Zurke's piano)
You're A Sweetheart (vocal: Kay Weber)
Unknown title
Panama

12:00 MIDNIGHT WNEW
TEDDY HILL
Savoy Ballroom, NYC
Merry-Go-Round
Sweet Lorraine
My Blue Heaven (vocal: Bill Dillard)
Three Little Words
Paradise (vocal: Bill Dillard)
Swingin' On C
Out The Window

12:30AM WEAF
WOODY HERMAN
Hotel Schrader, Milwaukee
Nuttsy. Opening night for Woody Herman at the Hotel Schrader in his home town.
Twin City Blues (colossal: Saxie Mansfield's blue tenor sax; Woody's clarinet)
My Night To Dream (vocal: Woody Herman) (rather commercial: Nick Hupfer's violin)
Mama, That Moon Is Here Again (vocal: Woody Herman) (swell brief piano passages; clarinet; Neil Reid's trombone)
One Rose Left In My Heart (vocal: Woody Herman)
Flugel Horn Blues (real low-down piece written & played by Joe Bishop on flugelhorn: trombone; tenor)
Exactly Like You (grand: Reid's ballsy trombone; Woody's clarinet; trumpet)
It's My Turn Now (vocal: Woody Herman) (some wonderful blues: trombone; clarinet)
Muskrat Ramble (Woody's fine clarinet; Bishop's flugelhorn; Saxie Mansfield's tenor)

■ FRIDAY 18 FEBRUARY 1938

RECORDING SESSION

BUSTER BAILEY & HIS RHYTHM BUSTERS
Recording session for Vocalion in NYC.
Charlie Shavers (t); Buster Bailey (cl); Pete Brown (as); Billy Kyle (p); James McLin (g); John Kirby (b); O'Neil Spencer (d)
Planter's Punch / *Sloe Jam Fizz*

RADIO LOGS

7:45PM WEAF
BUGHOUSE RHYTHM
San Francisco
Swanee River
Smuggler's Nightmare (colossal: saxes & brass; trumpet; rhythm)

FEBRUARY 1938

My Bronxville High School swing buddies, Hugh Pastoriza, Harvey Pinger, O. Quayle, Roach, Goldsmith, and myself took the NY Central Railroad commuter train to Grand Central station. We walked across to the Palm Room of the Hotel Commodore, right next to Grand Central, got there at 9:45pm, paid the 50 cents cover charge, and went in. We got a table right in front of the band and had a nuttsy time, enjoying Red Norvo's Band with vocalist Mildred Bailey. Robcliff Jones had brought Nancy Long by car from Hartsdale. Of course, many of us had the urge to dance to Norvo's subtle dance music. I danced a combination of swing, Lindy-hop and Peabody with Nancy.

This was the first time I have seen Norvo, as he hasn't been around NYC, except at a small club in Tuckahoe. I got the autographs of the whole band, while Hugh took flash pictures with his super new camera, which came out very well. I took an excellent picture of Hugh with drummer George Wettling. Wettling was very friendly and insisted that we mail him his picture pronto.

Eddie Sauter does most of the arrangements for the band although we saw Deane Kincaide down there. The band specializes in subdued swing and really sends you. The sax section is so smooth and Red's xylophone playing is so soft and imaginative. The rhythm section is O.K. being led by that fine drummer George Wettling.

To the Palm Room of the Commodore has come Red Norvo's orchestra and Mildred Bailey, swing songstress. Mr. Norvo and his boys have a proper regard for the ear-drums of their auditors and swing out in an altogether agreeable fashion. Particularly is Mr. Norvo's xylophoning productive of contagious rhythm. Miss Bailey is, needless to say, one of our more seasoned dispensers of lyrics, low-down and otherwise.

Mildred Bailey

Step to the NEWEST!
Step to the GAYEST!
Step to...

"THE MR. & MRS. of SWING"
RED NORVO & MILDRED BAILEY
AND THEIR ORCHESTRA
in the
COMMODORE
Palm Room
JOYOUS! REFRESHING!
...It's the Glorious New Dance Thrill!

NIGHTLY AT DINNER & SUPPER
(except Sundays)
Dinner $2. Never a Cover Charge at Dinner.
Special Supper $1.50. Cover after 10 P.M.
Weekdays 50c, Sat. & Holiday Eves. $1.

THE COMMODORE FRANK J. CROHAN Right at Grand Central
                President

Bill Miller takes some fine solos on the piano every once in a while. The brass section of only three trumpets and one trombone is very steady. Trumpet soloist Jimmy Blake from the Hudson-DeLange Band is only a kid and has much promise for the future. Of course, Zeke Zarchy has played with Crosby, Shaw, Goodman, etc. Trombonist Wes Hein (very friendly with a fine sense of humor) is very new and seems to be plenty good. The smoothness of the sax section (Jerry Jerome, Hank D'Amico, Len Goldstein and Charles Lamphere) really gave us a glowing feeling. Tenor saxist Jerry Jerome is marvelous. He came from Glenn Miller's Band and has been with Red for three weeks. He talked with us several times and is a real gentleman!

We had to leave the Palm Room at 12:55 and ran to catch the last train at 1:10.

Hugh Pastoriza and George Wettling

Jerry Jerome

Norvo saxes (l to r): Charles Lamphere, Len Goldstein, Hank D'Amico, Jerry Jerome

■ SATURDAY 19 FEBRUARY 1938

RADIO LOGS

7.00PM WABC
SATURDAY NIGHT SWING SESSION No84
CBS Theater, NYC
After You (Leith Stevens' CBS Band colossal: Hank Ross' fine tenor sax)
Meade Lux (ART SHAW playing clarinet on his own tribute to Meade Lux Lewis: great style)
Nothing (ART SHAW on clarinet with another rare original: colossal guitar & drums)
In The Shade Of The Old Apple Tree (PEE WEE HUNT singing O.K.: fair song)
The Toy Trumpet (Leith Stevens' CBS Band playing a new arrangement of Raymond Scott's tune: Russ Case's trumpet)
Memories (SONNY DUNHAM playing colossal trumpet: nice trombone; swell piece)
Streamline (ART SHAW playing fast piece magnificently: guitar; drums)
If Dreams Come True (Leith Stevens' CBS Band playing Edgar Sampson's recent piece: tenor sax)
I'd Do Anything For You (PEE WEE HUNT singing swell: Dunham's nuttsy trumpet)
Down With Love (Leith Stevens' CBS Band playing wonderfully: saxes; tenor sax)

12:00 MIDNIGHT WNEW
JOHN KIRBY
Onyx Club, 62 W52nd Street, NYC
Colossal. Heard this program at Robcliff Jones' house in Bronxville where I spent the night.
Stompin' At The Savoy (vocal: Leo Watson)
Tiger Rag (long and very fast: terrific!!)
Allah's Holiday (vocal: Leo Watson)
Easy To Love (vocal: Maxine Sullivan) (great!)
I Found A New Baby
Rose Room

■ MONDAY 21 FEBRUARY 1938

RADIO LOGS

12:00 MIDNIGHT WOR
RED NORVO
Hotel Commodore, NYC
Smiles (grand: Jimmy Blake's trumpet; Red's xylophone)
I Live The Life I Love (vocal: Mildred Bailey) (Jerome's swell tenor sax)
Moonglow (nuttsy, great Eddie Sauter arrangement: Red's xylophone)
Whatcha Gonna Do When There Ain't No Swing? (vocal: Mildred Bailey)
I Surrender Dear (colossal: Wes Hein's swell trombone; Hank D'Amico's clarinet; Jerome's tenor; Red)
I Double Dare You (vocal: Terry Allen) (Jerry Jerome's tenor)
From The Land Of The Sky Blue Water (vocal: Mildred Bailey)
Why Do I Love You? (Jerry Jerome's tenor)

12:30AM WEAF
LOUIS ARMSTRONG
Grand Terrace, Chicago
Mahogany Hall Stomp (great: Louis' great trumpet; tenor sax; trombone)
Thanks For The Memory (vocal: Bobbie Caston)
Keep In The Groove (colossal: Red Allen's trumpet; Higginbotham)
Sweet As A Song (vocal: Louis Armstrong) (featuring Louis' muted trumpet and vocal)
Honeysuckle Rose (swell: nice clarinet; wonderful tenor; trombone; Red Allen's trumpet; Pops Foster's bass solo)
This Is My Night To Dream (vocal: Sonny Woods)
I Double Dare You (vocal: Louis Armstrong)
Dinah (colossal: all Louis' marvelous trumpet)

■ TUESDAY 22 FEBRUARY 1938

RECORDING SESSION

BENNY GOODMAN AND HIS ORCHESTRA
Recording session for Victor in Detroit.
Benny Goodman (cl); Harry James, Ziggy Elman, Gordon Griffin (t); Red Ballard, Vernon Brown (tb); Hymie Shertzer, George Koenig (as); Arthur Rollini, Babe Russin (ts); Lionel Hampton (vib); Jess Stacy (p); Allan Reuss (g); Harry Goodman (b); Gene Krupa (d)
I Know That You Know

RADIO LOGS

10:00PM WABC
BENNY GOODMAN
Camel Caravan, Detroit, Michigan
Let's Dance (theme)
Blue Room (nuttsy: Benny; trombones; brass)
Sweet As A Song (vocal: Martha Tilton) (good: Benny's clarinet)
China Boy (BG Trio) (swell: Krupa)
My Melancholy Baby (swell: Benny; trombone)
Don't Be That Way (colossal: Russin; Brown; Benny; Krupa)
Smiles (BG Quartet) (great, especially Benny & Hampton)
I See Your Face Before Me (vocal: Martha Tilton) (good: Benny)
I Know That You Know (excellent, very fast: Hampton's vibes; Benny's great clarinet)

12:00 MIDNIGHT WOR
BOB CROSBY
Hotel Pennsylvania, NYC
Wolverine Blues
I See Your Face Before Me (vocal: Kay Weber)
Little Rock Getaway
It's Easier Said Than Done (vocal: Bob Crosby)
Gin Mill Blues (great: Bob Zurke's piano)
I Double Dare You (vocal: Bob Crosby)
Always And Always (vocal: Kay Weber)
South Rampart Street Parade

12:00 MIDNIGHT WABC
RED NORVO
Hotel Commodore, NYC
Unknown Title
I See Your Face Before Me (vocal: Mildred Bailey)
More Than Ever (vocal: Terry Allen)
Swing Fever
Please Be Kind (vocal: Mildred Bailey)
Tea Time
It's Wonderful (vocal: Mildred Bailey)
Bob White (vocal: Mildred Bailey)
Do You Ever Think Of Me?

12:00 MIDNIGHT WEAF
WOODY HERMAN
Hotel Schrader, Milwaukee
Unknown Title
True Confession (vocal: Woody Herman)
My Fine Feathered Friend
Beale Street Blues (vocal: Woody Herman)
Loch Lomond (vocal: Woody Herman)
In The Still Of The Night
Doctor Jazz (vocal: Woody Herman)

Woody Herman

■ WEDNESDAY 23 FEBRUARY 1938

RECORDING SESSION

RED NORVO AND HIS ORCHESTRA
Recording session for Brunswick in New York City.
Red Norvo (xyl/ldr); Jimmy Blake, Zeke Zarchy, Barney Zudecoff (t); Wes Hein (tb); Hank D'Amico (cl); Len Goldstein (as); Charles Lamphere (as/ts); Jerry Jerome (ts); Bill Miller (p); Alan Hanlon (g); Pete Peterson (b); George Wettling (d); Mildred Bailey, Terry Allen (voc)
Jeannine / Tea Time / How Can You Forget? (vTA) / *There's A Boy In Harlem* (vMB)

RADIO LOGS

11:00PM WNEW
JOHN KIRBY
Onyx Club, 62 W52nd Street, NYC
Linger Awhile (vocal: Leo Watson) (colossal: Leo Watson's ballsy scat vocal; magnificent solos by Kyle; Bailey; Shavers; Brown; Watson again)
Whoa, Babe (magnificent: Watson's hot trombone; O'Neil Spencer's long drum break; Buster Bailey; Billy Kyle)
Rose Room (wonderful: Kyle; Watson; Pete Brown)
My Yiddishe Momma (vocal: Maxine Sullivan) (first time on air)
The Dipsy Doodle (great trumpet; band vocal)
The Sheik Of Araby (Billy Kyle's great piano)

11:00PM WOR
BOB CROSBY
Hotel Pennsylvania, NYC
Honeysuckle Rose (colossal: Waller's piece in Dixieland manner; Eddie Miller; Matty Matlock; Ray Bauduc)
It's Wonderful (vocal: Kay Weber) (excellent arrangement of a sweetie: Eddie Miller's tenor)
Goodnight Angel (nuttsy Dixieland jam: Miller's tenor)
Beale Street Blues (vocal: Bob Crosby) (colossal: Bob Zurke's piano)
I Double Dare You (vocal: Bob Crosby) (hot arrangement: brass)
Squeeze Me (nuttsy arrangement and piece: brass; Zurke's piano)
Outside Of Paradise (vocal: Kay Weber)

11:30PM WMCA
EARL HINES
Apollo Theater, NYC
Marcheta (nuttsy: ballsy trumpet and Hines' grand piano)
Mama, I Want To Make Rhythm (a little ragged: nice trumpet)

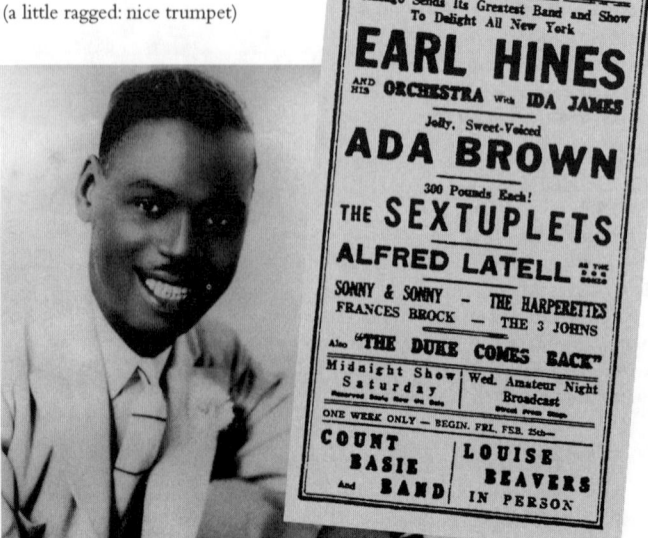

■ THURSDAY 24 FEBRUARY 1938

RECORDING SESSION

DUKE ELLINGTON AND HIS ORCHESTRA
Recording session for Master Records in New York City.
Duke Ellington (p); Wallace Jones, Cootie Williams, Harold Baker (t); Rex Stewart (c); Joe Nanton, Lawrence Brown (tb); Juan Tizol (vtb); Barney Bigard (cl); Johnny Hodges (cl/ss/as); Otto Hardwick (as/bsx); Harry Carney (cl/as/bar); Fred Guy (g); Hayes Alvis, Billy Taylor (b); Sonny Greer (d); Ivie Anderson (voc)
If You Were In My Place (vIA) / *Scrounch* (vIA)

GLEN GRAY AND THE CASA LOMA ORCHESTRA
Recording session for Decca in New York City.
Glen Gray (as/dir); Sonny Dunham, Grady Watts, Frank Zullo (t); Pee Wee Hunt (tb/voc); Billy Rauch, Murray McEachern (tb); Clarence Hutchenrider (cl/as), Kenny Sargent (as/voc); Art Ralston (as/o/bsn); Danny d'Andrea (as); Pat Davis (cl/ts/fl); Joe Hall (p); Jack Blanchette (g); Stanley Dennis (b); Tony Briglia (d)
Daddy's Boy (vKS) / *My Bonnie Lies Over The Ocean* (vPWH) / *You Go To My Head* (vKS) / *Dear Old Southland*

RADIO LOGS

11:00PM WABC
CAB CALLOWAY
Cotton Club, NYC
Alexander's Ragtime Band
I See Your Face Before Me
Sunday In The Park (vocal: Cab Calloway)
Minor Breakdown
Dear Old Southland
Trees (vocal: Bennie Payne)
The Hi-De-Ho Miracle Man (vocal: Cab Calloway)
I Simply Adore You
I Got Rhythm

11:30PM WABC
BUNNY BERIGAN
Arcadia Ballroom, Philadelphia
Heigh-Ho
Serenade In The Sky
A Study In Brown
In A Little Spanish Town
I Can't Get Started (theme)

■ FRIDAY 25 FEBRUARY 1938

RECORDING SESSION

ERSKINE HAWKINS AND HIS ORCHESTRA
Recording session for Vocalion in New York City.
Erskine Hawkins (t/ldr); Wilbur Bascomb, Marcellus Green, Sam Lowe (t); Edward Sims, Robert Range (tb); William Johnson (as); Jimmy Mitchelle (as/voc); Paul Bascomb (ts); Haywood Henry (cl/bar); Avery Parrish (p); William McLemore (g); Leemie Stanfield (b); James Morrison (d); Billy Daniels, Merle Turner (voc)
Carry Me Back To Old Virginny / Let Me Day Dream / Who's Sorry Now? / Lost In The Shuffle

■ SATURDAY 26 FEBRUARY 1938

After a dentist's appointment in the morning, George Fick and I went to the Apollo Theater, 125th Street, to see Count Basie. We got there at 2:45pm and saw Basie's Band plus movies and a

FEBRUARY 1938

Harlem's High Spot — and America's Leading Colored Theatre

APOLLO — At The 125th Street — America's Smartest Colored Shows! — THEATRE 125th Street Near 8th Av. — Telephone Un. 4-4490

ONE WEEK ONLY—BEGINNING FRIDAY, FEB. 25th

TWO OUTSTANDING HEADLINERS IN A GRAND SHOW—

LOUISE BEAVERS — The Noted Star IN PERSON

COUNT BASIE and HIS BAND

with JIMMY RUSHING

JELLI SMITH (As Father Neptune) — FRANCES WILLS (Acrobatic Marvel)

MASON - LA RUE and VIGAL — America's Funniest Trio

BILLY & BILLIE (Also New to Harlem—and Very Good) — HARPERETTES (16 of the Loveliest Dancing Girls In America)

Also the Sensation-Filled Racketeer Drama **'CITY GIRL'** RICARDO CORTEZ

MIDNIGHT SHOW SAT. Reserved Seats Now On Sale — WED.—AMATEUR NIGHT BROADCAST

stage show. Basie's Band is just about tops now. It is magnificent!! One of the solidest rhythm sections and an uplifting, steady brass section. To me Jo Jones is one of the greatest drummers alive; Walter Page is a big fellow who plays some great solid bass; Basie has a typical style of his own that makes him great, and Freddie Green on guitar is plenty O.K. Herschel Evans and Lester Young take turns in tenor sax solos that send you to 'booze'. Although seldom given a chance, Earle Warren, sweet vocalist, is the nuts on his alto sax. Trombonist and guitarist Eddie Durham is well-known for his fine arrangements. Buck Clayton is a fine trumpet player, especially on the mute with plenty of feeling, and leaving out the screeching. Yes sir! When that band gets hot it rocks you right out of your seat. Of course, you realize that Billie Holiday is, with Mildred Bailey and Ella Fitzgerald, the greatest woman blues singer today. She used to have red hair but today it was black. Jimmy Rushing is the big vocalist who is not only jovial but has a hot voice.

Farewell Blues (colossal)
Swingin' The Blues (great!!)
Underneath The Stars (vocal: Billie Holiday)
Nice Work If You Can Get It (vocal: Billie Holiday)
I Can't Get Started (vocal: Billie Holiday)
Easy Living (vocal: Billie Holiday)
One Never Knows, Does One? (vocal: Billie Holiday)
One O'Clock Jump (Evans; Young; Morton; Basie)
Rosalie (vocal: Jimmy Rushing) (Rushing singing colossally & truckin')
Boogie-Woogie (vocal: Jimmy Rushing) (funny blues vocal)
Rhythm In My Nursery Rhymes (vocal: Jimmy Rushing)

RADIO LOGS

7.00PM WABC
SATURDAY NIGHT SWING SESSION No85
CBS Theater, NYC
Liza (Leith Stevens' CBS Band stupendous: great tenor sax; Case's trumpet)
I'm Getting Sentimental Over You (EDDIE MILLER with some great tenor saxing: wonderful)
The Dipsy Doodle (CBS Band super-colossal: Hank Ross' magnificent tenor sax; ballsy clarinet; drums)
Body And Soul (BOB ZURKE playing Johnny Green's swell piece)
Little Rock Getaway (BOB ZURKE on Joe Sullivan's tune: magnificent style & technique)
Blue Skies (KAY THOMPSON singing colossally: excellent on difficult arrangement)
CARL CONS, of Down Beat, awarding All-American Musicians Poll trophies to the best orchestras: 1-Benny Goodman; 2-Tommy Dorsey; 3-Bob Crosby; 4-Duke Ellington. Cons congratulated the Swing Session as the outstanding promoter of swing.
Exactly Like You (jam session!!! Ellington & Zurke at pianos; Miller's tenor; Shoobe's bass; Case's trumpet; Mondello's clarinet; Worrell's guitar; Gussak's drums; Schwichtenberg's trombone)

11:00PM WOR
BOB CROSBY
Hotel Pennsylvania, NYC
The One I Love (vocal: Kay Weber) (swell: a new commercial played well)
D-Natural Blues (colossal, written by Fletcher Henderson: trumpet; Bob Zurke; Ray Bauduc)
More Than Ever (vocal: Bob Crosby) (Eddie Miller's nice tenor; nice trumpet; clarinet)
Can't We Be Friends? (featuring Miller's great tenor; Zurke's piano)
The Old Apple Tree (vocal: Nappy Lamare & Band)
Please Be Kind (vocal: Kay Weber) (nuttsy new piece: Miller's tenor sax)
Sweet Lorraine (GREAT: Miller's tenor; Nappy Lamare's guitar)

12:00 MIDNIGHT WMCA
JOE MARSALA
Hickory House, 144 W52nd Street, NYC
Bird Man Blues (theme) (colossal theme)
Down Stream (vocal: Lou Hirst)
I Want A Little Girl (vocal: Joe Marsala)
It's Wonderful
Always And Always
Jim Jam Stomp

■ SUNDAY 27 FEBRUARY 1938

RECORDING SESSION

TOMMY DORSEY AND HIS ORCHESTRA
Recording session for Victor in New York City.
Tommy Dorsey (tb); Pee Wee Erwin, Lee Castle, Andy Ferretti (t); Les Jenkins, Frank d'Annolfo (tb); Johnny Mince, Fred Stulce, Skeets Herfurt (cl/as); Bud Freeman (ts); Howard Smith (p); Carmen Mastren (g); Artie Shapiro (b); Maurice Purtill (d); Edythe Wright, Jack Leonard (voc)
Jezebel (vJL) / **Goodnight, Sweet Dreams** (vJL) / **'Deed I Do** (vEW) / **Moonlight On The Purple Sage** (vJL)

RADIO LOGS

11:00AM WNEW
SUNDAY MORNING SWING CONCERT
Criterion Theater, NYC
I Double Dare You (MILDRED CRAIG singing with Merle Pitts' WNEW Studio Band: tenor sax)
It Don't Mean A Thing (MIDGE WILLIAMS singing darn good)
Every Tub (COUNT BASIE Band swinging magnificently: 3 great tenor sax solos; Jo Jones' drums; trumpet)
One O'Clock Jump (COUNT BASIE Band – magnificent: Evans & Young on tenor sax; Buck Clayton's trumpet; trombone)
I Got Rhythm (SAMMY SPERGEL on electric guitar)
When The Heather Is In Bloom (MILDRED CRAIG singing with Merle Pitts' WNEW Studio Band)
Rosalie (COUNT BASIE Band – Jimmy Rushing singing the nuts)
Out The Window (COUNT BASIE Band: great tenor sax solos; trumpet)
Rockin' The Blues (Merle Pitts' WNEW Studio Band playing Pitts' new piece)
Mama, That Moon Is Here Again (MILDRED CRAIG singing)
Pagliacci (Merle Pitts' WNEW Studio Band playing a classic: Pitts' violin)
Love Is Like Whisky (MIDGE WILLIAMS singing)
Star Dust (Merle Pitts' WNEW Studio Band playing good: fair arrangement)
Sent For You Yesterday (COUNT BASIE Band – Jimmy Rushing singing: nuttsy, just recorded)
Swingin' The Blues (COUNT BASIE Band – magnificent: Young's tenor; Clayton's muted trumpet)
I Ain't Got Nobody (COUNT BASIE Band – Jimmy Rushing on swell vocal: Young's tenor sax; Jo Jones' drums)

5:00PM WHN
LUCKY MILLINDER
Roseland Ballroom, Brooklyn
Big John Special (great: Tab Smith's nuttsy alto sax)
Rosalie (vocal: Trevor Bacon)
Worried Over You
So's It (colossal: swell piano; Smith's alto; trumpet)
If It's The Last Thing I Do (vocal: Trevor Bacon)
For Dancers Only (grand: Smith's alto; swell brass & saxes)
Prelude To A Stomp (marvelous: more of Smith's alto; trumpets)
Come On With The Come On (another hot one: piano; trumpet; Smith's alto sax)

■ MONDAY 28 FEBRUARY 1938

RADIO LOGS

11:00PM WABC
JIMMY DORSEY
Hotel New Yorker, NYC
Dorsey Band's opened last night at Hotel New Yorker, replacing Glen Gray's Casa Loma Orchestra.
Dr. Rhythm (vocal: Dorsey Trio) (swell: McKinley's great drumming; Jimmy's alto)
Love Is Here To Stay (vocal: Bob Eberly) (swell new piece & arrangement: nice clarinet)
Bob White (vocal: June Richmond & Ray McKinley) (nuttsy novelty swing arrangement)
It's The Dreamer In Me (vocal: Bob Eberly) (nice sweet tune recently written by Jimmy: Dorsey's clarinet)
Parade of The Milk Bottle Caps (colossal Dorsey swing: McKinley's fine drums; Jimmy's screwy alto; trombone; clarinet)
You're A Sweetheart (vocal: Bob Eberly) (very original arrangement: Jimmy's straight clarinet; muted brass)
Mama, I Want To Make Rhythm (vocal: June Richmond) (nuttsy: Frazier's swell tenor; Slack's brief piano; drums)
Dusk In Upper Sandusky (Dorsey's own hot piece: Jimmy's colossal alto; McKinley's drums; cut short)

MARCH 1938

Hotel Pennsylvania: **Bob Crosby** (–3); **Benny Goodman** (4–)
Hotel Commodore: **Red Norvo**
Hotel New Yorker: **Jimmy Dorsey**
Hotel Lincoln: **Isham Jones**

Apollo Theater: **Count Basie** (–3); **Ethel Waters / Eddie Mallory** (4–10); **Willie Bryant** (11–17); **Buck & Bubbles** (18–24); **Floyd Ray / Nicholas Brothers** (25–31)
Paramount Theater: **Clyde McCoy** (–8); **Cab Calloway** (9–15); **Guy Lombardo** (23–29)
Loew's State Theater: **Milt Britton / Buck & Bubbles** (3–9); **Earl Hines** (10–16); **Louis Armstrong** (24–30);

Cotton Club: **Cab Calloway / Bill Robinson** (–8); **Duke Ellington** (10–)
Hickory House: **Joe Marsala**
Onyx Club: **John Kirby / Maxine Sullivan**
Famous Door: **Louis Prima / Art Tatum**
Nick's: **Bobby Hackett**

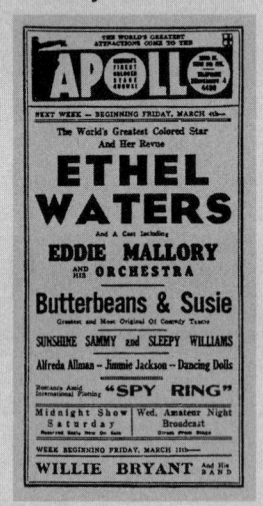

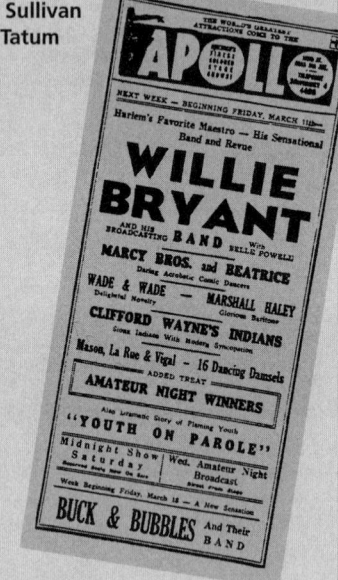

■ TUESDAY 1 MARCH 1938

RECORDING SESSION

MAXINE SULLIVAN
Recording session for Victor in New York City.
Maxine Sullivan (voc); Claude Thornhill (p/ldr); Bobby Hackett (c); Jimmy Lytell, Paul Ricci (cl/as); Bernie Kaufman (as); Babe Russin (ts); Eddie Powell (fl); John Kirby (b); Buddy Rich (d)
Moments Like This (vMS) / *Please Be Kind* (vMS) / *It Was A Lover And His Lass* (vMS) / *Dark Eyes* (vMS)

RADIO LOGS

9:15PM WHN
LUCKY MILLINDER
Roseland Ballroom, Brooklyn
Marie
Once In A While
Bei Mir Bist Du Schoen (vocal: Lucky Millinder)

10:00PM WABC
BENNY GOODMAN
Camel Caravan, Philadelphia
Let's Dance (theme)

Make Believe (swell: Benny; Harry James; Vernon Brown)
Always And Always (vocal: Martha Tilton) (good: Benny's clarinet)
Sweet As A Song (BG Trio) (nice new sweet piece)
Can't We Be Friends? (great: trombone; Benny; Gene Krupa; Babe Russin)
Sunday In The Park (vocal: Martha Tilton) (lousy piece, nice arrangement)
Lillie Stomp (BG Quartet) (fair original number)
One O'Clock Jump (magnificent!! intro; Russin; James; Benny)

11:30PM WOR
JIMMY DORSEY
Hotel New Yorker, NYC
The Big Dipper (swell: Frazier's nuttsy tenor; brass)
Sweet Someone (vocal: Bob Eberly)
The Dipsy Doodle (vocal: June Richmond)
In The Still Of The Night (vocal: Bob Eberly)
Chicken Reel (Toots Camarata's trumpet)
It's The Dreamer In Me (vocal: Bob Eberly)
Nice Work If You Can Get It
Darktown Strutters' Ball (vocal: June Richmond)
Arkansas Traveler

11:30PM WABC
BUNNY BERIGAN
Arcadia Ballroom, Philadelphia
Swanee River (good: George Auld's fine tenor; Dave Tough's drums)
Why Talk About Love (vocal: Gail Reese)
Heigh-Ho (vocal: Gail Reese)
Serenade To The Stars (vocal: Gail Reese)
Mama, I Want To Make Rhythm (vocal: Bunny Berigan)
You Took The Words Right Out Of My Heart (vocal: Gail Reese)
Louisiana (nuttsy: Bunny; Sonny Lee's trombone; Joe Dixon; Auld's tenor)
Black Bottom (colossal: Bunny; Auld's very long solo; Dixon)
I Can't Get Started (theme)

12:00 MIDNIGHT WABC
RED NORVO
Hotel Commodore, NYC
Bei Mir Bist Du Schoen
Thanks For The Memory (vocal: Mildred Bailey)
Tea Time
Sweet Someone (vocal: Terry Allen)
Lover Come Back To Me (vocal: Mildred Bailey)
I Never Knew (COLOSSAL)
Love Is Here To Stay (vocal: Mildred Bailey)
I Live The Life I Love (vocal: Mildred Bailey)

12:00 MIDNIGHT WOR
BOB CROSBY
Hotel Pennsylvania, NYC
South Rampart Street Parade
I Simply Adore You (vocal: Bob Crosby)
You're Driving Me Crazy
I See Your Face Before Me (vocal: Kay Weber)
Beale Street Blues (vocal: Bob Crosby)
The Old Apple Tree (vocal: Nappy Lamare & Band)
It's Wonderful (vocal: Kay Weber)
Little Rock Getaway

12:00 MIDNIGHT WJZ
CHICK WEBB
Levaggi's, Boston
Sugar Foot Stomp
Heart of Mine (vocal: Ella Fitzgerald)
Blue Skies
It's Wonderful (vocal: Ella Fitzgerald)
Don't Be That Way
I'm Thinking Of You Tonight
I Found A New Baby
Goodnight Angel
Copenhagen

■ WEDNESDAY 2 MARCH 1938
RADIO LOGS

8:30PM WEAF
TOMMY DORSEY
Kool-Raleigh Cigarette program, NYC
This broadcast featured all the tunes introduced by Tommy Dorsey. This coming week Tommy and the band are playing at Harvard, MIT.
The Dipsy Doodle (vocal: Edythe Wright)
I Can Dream Can't I? (vocal: Jack Leonard)
Satan Takes A Holiday
Once In A While (vocal: Edythe Wright & Three Esquires)
Down With Love (vocal: Edythe Wright)
If It's The Last Thing I Do (vocal: Jack Leonard)
I Live The Life I Love
You're A Sweetheart (vocal: Edythe Wright)
In The Still Of The Night (vocal: Jack Leonard)
Marie (vocal: Jack Leonard & Band)

11:00PM WABC
BOB CROSBY
Hotel Pennsylvania, NYC
I Double Dare You
Outside of Paradise (vocal: Kay Weber)
Goodnight Angel
It's Easier Said Than Done (vocal: Bob Crosby)
The Old Apple Tree (vocal: Nappy Lamare & Band)
I Simply Adore You (vocal: Bob Crosby)
Always And Always (vocal: Kay Weber)
South Rampart Street Parade

11:00PM WNEW
JOHN KIRBY
Onyx Club, 62 W52nd Street, NYC
Linger Awhile (vocal: Leo Watson)
Just A Simple Melody
Rose Room
Annie Laurie (vocal: Maxine Sullivan)
Royal Garden Blues
Paul Revere (vocal: Leo Watson)
Reckless Night Aboard An Ocean Liner
Whoa, Babe

11:30PM WOR
JIMMY DORSEY
Hotel New Yorker, NYC
Just A Simple Melody
One Rose Of Summer
How'dja Like To Love Me? (vocal: Don Mattison)
It's The Dreamer In Me (vocal: Bob Eberly)
Volga Boatmen
You Started Something (vocal: Bob Eberly)
Mama, That Moon's Here Again (vocal: June Richmond)
I Cried For You (vocal: Bob Eberly)
Waddlin' At The Waldorf

11:30PM WMCA
COUNT BASIE
Apollo Theater, NYC
Every Tub
Out The Window

12:00 MIDNIGHT WABC
RED NORVO
Hotel Commodore, NYC
Thou Swell
I Can't Face The Music (vocal: Mildred Bailey) (first time on air)
Rugcutter's Swing
The One I Love (vocal: Terry Allen)
The Weekend Of A Private Secretary (vocal: Mildred Bailey)

MEDLEY: *True Confession / You're A Sweetheart / One Song*
It's Wonderful (vocal: Mildred Bailey) (tenor sax; Red's xylophone)
From The Land Of The Sky Blue Water (vocal: Mildred Bailey) (Red's xylophone)
Get Happy

12:00 MIDNIGHT WEAF
LOUIS ARMSTRONG
Grand Terrace, Chicago
They All Laughed
Sunday In The Park (vocal: Bobbie Caston)
If My Heart Could Only Talk
Between The Devil And The Deep Blue Sea
This Is My Night To Dream (vocal: Sonny Woods)
True Confession
Tiger Rag

■ THURSDAY 3 MARCH 1938

RECORDING SESSION

DUKE ELLINGTON AND HIS ORCHESTRA
Recording session for Master Records in New York City.
Duke Ellington (p); Wallace Jones, Cootie Williams, Harold Baker (t); Rex Stewart (c); Joe Nanton, Lawrence Brown (tb); Juan Tizol (vtb); Barney Bigard (cl); Johnny Hodges (cl/ss/as); Otto Hardwick (as/bsx); Harry Carney (cl/as/bar); Fred Guy (g); Hayes Alvis, Billy Taylor (b); Sonny Greer (d); Ivie Anderson (voc)
I Let A Song Go Out Of My Heart / Braggin' In Brass / Carnival In Caroline (vIA)

Gene Krupa left Benny Goodman's Orchestra today at the end of a one-week engagement at Philadelphia's Earle Theater. Lionel Hampton will play drums with the band until a suitable replacement is found.

Billie Holiday leaves the Count Basie Band at the end of their Apollo Theater engagement.

RADIO LOGS

11:00PM WABC
CAB CALLOWAY
Cotton Club, NYC
Nagasaki (vocal: Cab Calloway)
The One I Love (vocal: Cab Calloway)
Three Blind Mice (vocal: Cab Calloway)
Three Swings And Out
Ooooo-oh Boom!
Azure
Sunday In The Park (vocal: Cab Calloway)
I Can Dream Can't I? (vocal: Cab Calloway)
China Boy

11:30PM WJZ
CHICK WEBB
Levaggi's, Boston
What A Shuffle
I Fall In Love With You Every Day (vocal: Ella Fitzgerald)
Blue Room
Midnight In A Madhouse
I'm Glad For Your Sake (vocal: Ella Fitzgerald)
Tea For Two
I Simply Adore You (vocal: Ella Fitzgerald)
Alabamy Home
Hallelujah

12:00 MIDNIGHT WOR
BOB CROSBY
Hotel Pennsylvania, NYC
South Rampart Street Parade
I See Your Face Before Me (vocal: Kay Weber)
Little Rock Getaway
You're An Education (vocal: Bob Crosby)
Yancey Special
In The Shade Of The New Apple Tree (vocal: Nappy Lamare & Band)
Please Be Kind (vocal: Kay Weber)
Sweet Lorraine

■ FRIDAY 4 MARCH 1938

Benny Goodman's Orchestra open a new engagement at the Madhattan Room of the Hotel Pennsylvania in New York City. Lionel Hampton plays drums with the band.

RADIO LOGS

11:00PM WABC
BENNY GOODMAN
Hotel Pennsylvania, NYC
Don't Be That Way
Thanks For The Memory (vocal: Martha Tilton)
Always
It's Wonderful (vocal: Martha Tilton)
When Buddha Smiles
Always And Always (vocal: Martha Tilton)
Dizzy Spells (BG Trio)
Mama, That Moon Is Here Again (vocal: Martha Tilton)

■ SATURDAY 5 MARCH 1938

RADIO LOGS

6.30PM WABC
SATURDAY NIGHT SWING SESSION No86
CBS Theater, NYC
After You (Leith Stevens' CBS Band)
Darling Nellie Gray (MAXINE SULLIVAN)
Whoa, Babe (JOHN KIRBY'S ONYX CLUB Band)

HE'S COMING MARCH 4th!
BENNY GOODMAN KING OF SWING and his Orchestra with GENE KRUPA • LIONEL HAMPTON TEDDY WILSON • MARTHA TILTON
MADHATTAN ROOM
Dinner and supper dancing except Sunday. Dinners from $2.
HOTEL PENNSYLVANIA
33RD STREET AND 7TH AVENUE

Billie Thru With Basie, In New Spot

NEW YORK CITY, Mar. 3— Fresh from a sensational engagement at the Apollo Theatre and her last with Count Basie and his orchestra Billie Holiday, one of the modern delineators of swing songs, will go into Clark Monroe's Uptown House in Harlem for an indefinite engagement.

Others in the Uptown House revue are: Clarence Weems, emcee; Joe Smothers, Mae Arthur, Bernice Robinson, Toy (Mad Genius) Wilson and Clark Monroe himself, whose ability as a dancer, is second to his ability as a host.

You're A Sweetheart (Leith Stevens' CBS Band, for Nat Natoli's birthday)
I Got Rhythm (Gene Krupa; Buster Bailey; Billy Kyle; John Kirby)
Hot Water Bottle (JOHN KIRBY'S ONYX CLUB Band)
Loch Lomond (MAXINE SULLIVAN)
Diga Diga Doo (Leith Stevens' CBS Band: Hank Ross' tenor)

8.00PM WJZ
TEDDY HILL
RCA Program, NYC
Merry-Go-Round (real swingin' out: trumpet; alto sax)
The Campbells Are Swingin' (low-down & ballsy)
It's Wonderful (vocal: Midge Williams)
Out The Window (Basie's tune: colossal!!)
Blue Skies (great: trumpet; alto)
I Cried For You (vocal: Midge Williams)
Jumpin' (magnificent: brass; tenor sax)
I Got Rhythm (Bob Carroll's tenor; piano)

11:30PM WABC
BENNY GOODMAN
Hotel Pennsylvania, NYC
Dear Old Southland
I See Your Face Before Me (vocal: Martha Tilton)
You Took The Words Right Out Of My Heart (vocal: Martha Tilton)
I Found A New Baby
I Can't Give You Anything But Love, Baby (vocal: Martha Tilton)
Can't We Be Friends?
Avalon (BG Trio)
I Know That You Know

■ MONDAY 7 MARCH 1938

RECORDING SESSION

EARL HINES AND HIS ORCHESTRA
Recording session for Vocalion in New York City.
Earl Hines (p/ldr); Freddy Webster, George Dixon (t); Ray Nance (t/voc); Louis Taylor, Kenneth Stuart, Joe McLewis (tb); Leroy Harris (cl/as); Budd Johnson, William Randall, Leon Washington (cl/ts); Claude Roberts (g); Quinn Wilson (b); Oliver Coleman (d); Ida Mae James (voc)
Solid Mama / Please Be Kind (vIMJ) */ Goodnight, Sweet Dreams, Goodnight / Tippin' At The Terrace / Dominick Swing*

RADIO LOGS

11:00PM WABC
JIMMY DORSEY
Hotel New Yorker, NYC
I Double Dare You (vocal: Don Mattison) (colossal)
I See Your Face Before Me (vocal: Bob Eberly)
Doctor Rhythm (vocal: Dorsey Trio)
It's The Dreamer In Me (vocal: Bob Eberly)
Parade Of The Milk Bottle Tops (wonderful tenor)
On The Sentimental Side (vocal: Bob Eberly) (Jimmy's alto sax)
Mama, That Moon's Here Again (vocal: June Richmond)
Just A Simple Melody (Freddie Slack's fine piano)
Dusk In Upper Dandusky (Ray McKinley's long drum solo)
Sandman (theme)

12:00 MIDNIGHT WJZ
CHICK WEBB
Levaggi's, Boston
Royal Garden Blues (swell: screwy trumpet; Webb's drums)
Sweet As A Song (vocal: Ella Fitzgerald) (nice muted trumpet)
King Porter Stomp (Ted McRae's tenor; Sandy Williams' trombone; Bobby Stark's trumpet)
Strictly Jive (nice arrangement: Bobby Stark's trumpet)
In The Shade Of The New Apple Tree (vocal: Ella Fitzgerald)
Stompin' At The Savoy (trombone; trumpet)
I'm Glad For Your Sake (vocal: Ella Fitzgerald)
That's A-Plenty (clarinet; Webb's drums; trumpet)

12:30AM WEAF
LOUIS ARMSTRONG
Grand Terrace, Chicago
A Heart Full Of Rhythm (vocal: Louis Armstrong)
Sunday In The Park (vocal: Bobbie Caston)
Prelude In C-Sharp Minor
I Double Dare You (vocal: Louis Armstrong) (Higginbotham's trombone)
Serenade To The Stars (vocal: Sonny Woods)
Climax Rag (Louis Bacon's nice trumpet; clarinet; Charlie Holmes' tenor)
Jubilee (vocal: Louis Armstrong) (Barbarin's drums; trumpet)
St. Louis Blues (Rupert Cole's clarinet; Red Allen's trumpet)
Muskrat Ramble (Luis Russell's piano; Bingie Madison's tenor sax)

■ TUESDAY 8 MARCH 1938

RADIO LOGS

10:00PM WABC
BENNY GOODMAN
Camel Caravan, CBS Playhouse, NYC
Let's Dance (theme)
Ti-Pi-Tin (swell: Benny; Babe Russin; Ziggy Elman)
It's Wonderful (vocal: Martha Tilton) (nice: Benny's clarinet)
Always And Always (BG Trio) (fair)
I Found A New Baby (great: Art Rollini; Elman)
Ooooo-oh Boom! (vocal: Martha Tilton & Benny Goodman)
Sweet Georgia Brown (BG Quartet) (colossal)
Please Be Kind (vocal: Martha Tilton) (swell: Russin)
King Porter Stomp (colossal: trumpets; Vernon Brown)

■ WEDNESDAY 9 MARCH 1938

RECORDING SESSION

BENNY GOODMAN AND HIS ORCHESTRA
Recording session for Victor in New York City.
Benny Goodman (cl); Harry James, Ziggy Elman, Gordon Griffin (t); Red Ballard, Vernon Brown (tb); Hymie Shertzer, Dave Matthews (as); Babe Russin, Lester Young (ts); Jess Stacy (p); Freddie Green (g); Walter Page (b); Lionel Hampton (d); Martha Tilton (voc)
Please Be Kind (vMT) */ Ti-Pi-Tin / oooOO-OH BOOM!* (vMT,BG) */ Always And Always* (vMT) */ Make Believe / The Blue Room*

BOB CROSBY AND HIS ORCHESTRA
Recording session for Decca in New York City.
Bob Crosby (voc/ldr); Charlie Spivak, Billy Butterfield, Yank Lawson (t); Ward Silloway, Warren Smith (tb); Irving Fazola (cl); Matty Matlock (cl/as); Joe Kearns (as); Eddie Miller (cl/ts); Gil Rodin (ts); Bob Zurke (piano); Nappy Lamare (g/voc); Bob Haggart (b); Ray Bauduc (d)
Jezebel (vBC) */ Do Ye Ken John Peel?* (vNL) */ How Can You Forget?* (vBC) */ There's A Boy In Harlem* (vNL)

THURSDAY 10 MARCH 1938

RECORDING SESSION

BOB CROSBY AND HIS ORCHESTRA
Recording session for Decca in New York City.
Bob Crosby (voc/ldr); Charlie Spivak, Billy Butterfield, Yank Lawson (t); Ward Silloway, Warren Smith (tb); Irving Fazola (cl); Matty Matlock (cl/as); Joe Kearns (as); Eddie Miller (cl/ts/voc); Gil Rodin (ts); Bob Zurke (piano); Nappy Lamare (g/voc); Bob Haggart (b); Ray Bauduc (d); Kay Weber (voc)
Yancey Special / Louise, Louise (vEM) */ At The Jazz Band Ball / Milk Cow Blues* (vNL) */ Tea For Two*

TOMMY DORSEY AND HIS ORCHESTRA
Recording session for Victor in New York City.
Tommy Dorsey (tb); Pee Wee Erwin, Lee Castle, Andy Ferretti (t); Les Jenkins, Earle Hagen (tb); Johnny Mince, Fred Stulce, Skeets Herfurt (cl/as); Bud Freeman (ts); Howard Smith (p); Carmen Mastren (g); Gene Traxler (b); Maurice Purtill (d); Edythe Wright, Jack Leonard (voc)
Yearning (vJL & band) */ I Never Knew / Oh, How I Hate To Get Up In The Morning / What'll I Do? / Comin' Thro' The Rye* (vEW)

TOMMY DORSEY AND HIS CLAMBAKE SEVEN
Recording session for Victor in New York City.
Tommy Dorsey (tb); Pee Wee Erwin (t); Johnny Mince (cl); Bud Freeman (ts); Howard Smith (p); Carmen Mastren (g); Gene Traxler (b); Maurice Purtill (d); Edythe Wright (voc)
When The Midnight Choo-Choo Leaves For Alabam' (vEW) */ Everybody's Doing It* (vEW)

RADIO LOGS

9:00PM WNEW
JOHN KIRBY
Onyx Club, 62 W52nd Street, NYC
Reckless Night Aboard An Ocean Liner (Pete Brown; Buster Bailey; Kyle)
Tea For Two (Leo Watson; Brown; Charlie Shavers)
The Blues (magnificent: Billy Kyle; Bailey)
Dark Eyes (vocal: Maxine Sullivan) (great!)
Royal Garden Blues (John Kirby's bass; Bailey)
Tiger Rag (featuring Buster Bailey's clarinet)
The Dipsy Doodle (vocal: Leo Watson) (great scat vocal)

11:00PM WABC
DUKE ELLINGTON
Cotton Club, NYC
This is opening night for Duke Ellington in the new Cotton Club Parade at the Cotton Club at Broadway & 48th Street, replacing Cab Calloway.
East St.Louis Toodle-Oo (theme)
Carnival In Caroline (vocal: Ivie Anderson) (written by Ellington for the new Cotton Club show: trumpet; clarinet)
If You Were In My Place (vocal: Ivie Anderson) (nice trombone; clarinet; Hodges' alto; trumpets)
The Skrontch (vocal: Ivie Anderson) (another new piece: Hodges' alto; Bigard's clarinet)
Braggin' In Brass (brand new: screwy trombones; Stewart's cornet; trombone; trumpets)
Azure (Ellington piece from last year: Bigard; Carney)
I'm Slappin' Seventh Avenue (Stewart's cornet; Ellington's piano)
I Let A Song Go Out Of My Heart (nuttsy tempo: Hodges; Carney's grand baritone; Bigard)
Chatterbox (Stewart's great cornet; Brown's trombone)

RADIO LOGS

11:30PM WABC
BUNNY BERIGAN
Arcadia Ballroom, Philadelphia
Back In Your Own Backyard
Serenade To The Stars (vocal: Gail Reese)
Heigh-Ho (vocal: Gail Reese)
Goodnight Angel

In A Little Spanish Town
Thanks For The Memory
Tain't So
The One I Love
The Prisoner's Song

11:30PM WABC
BENNY GOODMAN
Hotel Pennsylvania, NYC
Blue Room
Ooooo-oh Boom! (vocal: Martha Tilton & Benny Goodman) (Benny introduces Stacy; Griffin; Brown; Russin; James)
Ti-Pi-Tin
Please Be Kind (vocal: Martha Tilton)
Rosetta (BG Quartet) (Harry James on drums)
Big John Special (piano intro; Harry James' trumpet)
I See Your Face Before Me (vocal: Martha Tilton)
Swingtime In The Rockies

12:00 MIDNIGHT WEAF
ANDY KIRK
Grand Terrace, Chicago
Whistle While You Work (vocal: Pha Terrell)
Dear Old Southland (Mary Lou Williams' piano intro; clarinet)
Until The Real Thing Comes Along (vocal: Pha Terrell) (Dick Wilson's tenor sax)
Mellow Bit Of Rhythm (written by Mary Lou Williams: tenor sax)
You're An Education (good, refreshing swing: clarinet; drums)
I'm Glad For Your Sake (vocal: Pha Terrell)
I Never Slept A Wink Last Night (featuring Mary Lou Williams' piano)
How'd You Like To Love Me?

■ FRIDAY 11 MARCH 1938

RECORDING SESSION

FATS WALLER & HIS RHYTHM
Recording session for Victor in New York City.
Herman Autrey (t); Gene Sedric (cl/ts); Fats Waller (p/voc); Albert Casey (g); Cedric Wallace (b); Slick Jones (d)
Something Tells Me (vFW) / *I Love To Whistle* (vFW) / *You Went To My Head* (vFW) / *Florida Flo* (vFW) / *Lost And Found* (vFW) / *Don't Try To Cry Your Way Back To Me* (vFW) / *If You're A Viper* (vFW)

Hugh Pastoriza, Quayle, Pinger, Noseworthy and myself took Sis Lake, Barbara Stuart, Joan Rome, Dottie Kyser, Nancy Long and Lil Hetrick down to the Palm Room of the Hotel Commodore at Grand Central. We all took the 9:03 train in, arriving there at 9:49. Hughie and I, with Lake and Hetrick, got a swell table directly by the band. We had a magnificent time except that I brought the wrong girl. After a while it got very, very crowded, making it very hard to dance. It was about three weeks ago that I saw Red Norvo's band and was deeply impressed. This time he's still great. The band has that certain style of subdued swing that can play excellent sweet and hot music. The band plays perfectly together and the soloists can all send me. I think especially highly of tenor saxist Jerry Jerome, clarinetist Hank D'Amico, trombonist Wes Hein, drummer George Wettling, and Norvo himself. Blake, Peterson and Bill Miller are also grand. Some of the best numbers played were: *Honeysuckle Rose* (vocal by Mildred Bailey); *Tea Time; Azure; Lover Come Back To Me* (vocal by Mildred Bailey); *Do You Ever Think Of Me?; Why Do I Love You?; I Can't Face The Music* (vocal by Mildred Bailey); and *King Porter Stomp* (Jerome's great tenor sax solo & D'Amico's clarinet).

Jerry Jerome came over to our table a couple of times. Every Friday night he goes to the Onyx Club on 52nd Street and sits in with John Kirby's Band. We told him we'd see him there next Friday for the Onyx sure is a great place, with the greatest jam band I have ever heard.

■ SATURDAY 12 MARCH 1938

RADIO LOGS

7.00PM WABC
SATURDAY NIGHT SWING SESSION No87
CBS Theater, NYC
Blue Skies (Leith Stevens' CBS Band: Hank Ross' brief tenor; brass)
In A Happy Frame Of Mind (RAMONA singing and playing piano)
Ol' Man River (RAMONA singing and playing swell piano)
In The Shade Of The New Apple Tree (Ross' tenor sax; clarinet)
Beebe (JIMMY DORSEY's great alto sax on his own tune)
Dusk In Upper Sandusky (JIMMY DORSEY Band: Dorsey's alto & Ray McKinley's drums)

NAZIS ANNEX AUSTRIA AFTER HITLER ULTIMATUM

College Humor (RAY McKINLEY's screwy singing)
After You've Gone (jam session: Ramona; Dorsey's clarinet)
Toy Trumpet (good: fair trumpet; Shoobe's bassing)

11:30PM WABC
BENNY GOODMAN
Hotel Pennsylvania, NYC
If Dreams Come True
Always And Always (vocal: Martha Tilton)
Sweet Sue
I See Your Face Before Me (vocal: Martha Tilton)
Where Or When (BG Trio)
Naughty Waltz
Don't Be That Way
The World Is Waiting For The Sunrise (BG Quartet) (Harry James on drums)
Sugar Foot Stomp

■ MONDAY 14 MARCH 1938

RECORDING SESSION

MILDRED BAILEY & HER ORCHESTRA
Recording session for Vocalion in New York.
Jimmy Blake, Zeke Zarchy, Barney Zudecoff (t); Wes Hein (tb); Hank D'Amico (cl/as); Len Goldstein (as); Jerry Jerome, Charles Lamphere (ts); Bill Miller (p); Alan Hanlon (g); Pete Peterson (b); George Wettling (d); Red Norvo (xyl); Mildred Bailey (v)
Bewildered (vMB) / *I Can't Face The Music* (vMB) / *Don't Be That Way* (vMB) / *At Your Beck And Call* (vMB)

BOB CROSBY'S BOBCATS
Recording session for Decca in New York City.
Yank Lawson (t); Warren Smith (tb); Irving Fazola (cl); Eddie Miller (ts); Bob Zurke (p); Nappy Lamare (g/voc); Haig Stephens (b); Ray Bauduc (d)
March Of The Bobcats / *Palesteena* (vNL) / *Slow Mood* / *Big Foot Jump* / *The Big Crash From China* / *Five Point Blues*

■ TUESDAY 15 MARCH 1938

RECORDING SESSION

BUNNY BERIGAN AND HIS ORCHESTRA
Recording session for Victor in New York City.
Bunny Berigan, Irving Goodman, Steve Lipkins (t); Al George, Sonny Lee (tb); Mike Doty, Joe Dixon (cl/as); Clyde Rounds, George Auld (ts); C. Graham Forbes (p); Tom Morgan (g); Hank Wayland (b); Dave Tough (d); Gail Reese (voc)
Down Stream (vGR) / *Sophisticated Swing* (vGR) / *Lovelight In The Starlight* (vGR)

JIMMY DORSEY AND HIS ORCHESTRA
Recording session for Decca in New York City.
Jimmy Dorsey (cl/as); Shorty Sherock, Ralph Muzzillo (t); Bobby Byrne, Don Mattison (tb/voc); Sonny Lee (tb); Milt Yaner, Sam Rubinowich (as); Herbie Haymer, Charles Frazier (ts); Freddie Slack (p); Roc Hillman (g/voc); Jack Ryan (b); Ray McKinley (d/voc); Bob Eberly, June Richmond (voc)
Two Bouquets (vBE) / *I Can't Face The Music* (vJR) / *Joseph! Joseph!* (vJR) / *At A Perfume Counter* (vBE)

BILLIE HOLIDAY TO BE FEATURED IN ALL-WHITE BAND

Billie Holiday joins the Art Shaw Band at the Roseland-State Ballroom in Boston where they are booked for three months playing Tuesdays and Saturdays. The rare photograph above shows them together on the Roseland-State stage.

RADIO LOGS

10:00PM WABC
BENNY GOODMAN
Camel Caravan, CBS Playhouse, NYC
Let's Dance (theme)
Don't Be That Way (Benny; Hampton's drums; Vernon Brown)
Always And Always (vocal: Martha Tilton) (swell: Benny's clarinet)
Sweet Sue (Henderson arrangement: saxes; Benny; Babe Russin)
Lullaby In Rhythm (Edgar Sampson's latest piece: Russin; James; Brown)
The World Is Waiting For The Sunrise (BG Quartet)
Serenade To The Stars (vocal: Martha Tilton)
Ti-Pi-Tin (crappy song: Russin; James)

12:00 MIDNIGHT WNEW
COUNT BASIE
Savoy Ballroom, NYC
Out The Window
Melody In F
Marie
King Porter Stomp
Good Morning Blues (vocal: Jimmy Rushing)
I Found A New Baby
Basin Street Blues (vocal: Earle Warren)

■ WEDNESDAY 16 MARCH 1938

RECORDING SESSION

BUNNY BERIGAN AND HIS ORCHESTRA
Recording session for Victor in New York City.
Bunny Berigan, Irving Goodman, Steve Lipkins (t); Al George, Sonny Lee (tb); Mike Doty, Joe Dixon (cl/as); Clyde Rounds, George Auld (ts); C. Graham Forbes (p); Tom Morgan (g); Hank Wayland (b); Dave Tough (d); Gail Reese (voc)
Rinka Tinka Man (vGR) / *An Old Straw Hat* (vGR) / *I Dance Alone* (vGR)

JIMMY DORSEY AND HIS ORCHESTRA
Recording session for Decca in New York City.
Jimmy Dorsey (cl/as); Shorty Sherock, Ralph Muzillo (t); Bobby Byrne, Don Mattison (tb/voc); Sonny Lee (tb); Milt Yaner, Sam Rubinowich (as); Herbie Haymer, Charles Frazier (ts); Freddie Slack (p); Roc Hillman (g/voc); Jack Ryan (b); Ray McKinley (d/voc); Bob Eberly, June Richmond (voc)
It's The Dreamer In Me (vBE) / *Don't Be That Way* / *Love Walked In* (vBE) / *The Weekend Of A Private Secretary* (vJR)

JOE MARSALA'S CHICAGOANS
Recording session for Vocalion in New York City.
Marty Marsala (t); Joe Marsala (cl); Ray Biondi (vln); Joe Bushkin (p); Adele Girard (harp); Jack LeMaire (g/voc); Artie Shapiro (b); Buddy Rich (d)
Mighty Like The Blues / *Woo-Woo* (vJLM) / *Hot String Beans* / *Jim Jam Stomp*

■ THURSDAY 17 MARCH 1938

RECORDING SESSION

EARL HINES AND HIS ORCHESTRA
Recording session for Vocalion in New York City.
Earl Hines (p/ldr); Freddy Webster, George Dixon (t); Ray Nance (t/voc); Louis Taylor, Kenneth Stuart, Joe McLewis (tb); Leroy Harris (cl/as); Budd Johnson, William Randall, Leon Washington (cl/ts); Claude Roberts (g); Quinn Wilson (b); Oliver Coleman (d)
Jezebel (vLH) / *Jack Climbed A Beanstalk* (vRN)

RADIO LOGS

12:00 MIDNIGHT WOR
BENNY GOODMAN
Hotel Pennsylvania, NYC
I Found A New Baby
Please Be Kind (vocal: Martha Tilton)
Sometimes I'm Happy
I Love To Whistle (vocal: Martha Tilton)
Dinah (BG Quartet) (Harry James on drums)
Always And Always (vocal: Martha Tilton)
House Hop
Nice Work If You Can Get It (BG Trio)
Sweet Sue

■ FRIDAY 18 MARCH 1938

RECORDING SESSION

KANSAS CITY FIVE
Recording session for Commodore in New York City.
Buck Clayton (t); Eddie Durham (tb/elg); Freddy Green (g); Walter Page (b); Jo Jones (d)
Laughing At Life / *Good Mornin' Blues* / *I Know That You Know*

■ SATURDAY 19 MARCH 1938

Hugh Pastoriza and I went with Emmet Evans (in his car) to NYC for an all-night trip to do the town. We left Bronxville at 8:00 and drove all the way down to Greenwich Village at 7th Street. After walking around the picturesque streets we went, at 9:30, to Nick's Tavern where Bobby Hackett's great jam band plays. Hackett came to NYC from Boston last year, tried to start his own band without success, played guitar with Joe Marsala at the Hickory House, and finally formed his own band a few months ago. The band is still the same now except that the exceptionally fine drummer Johnny Blowers has left to join Bunny Berigan's Band, replacing Dave Tough who is to join Benny Goodman. We got a table right next to the band and had 4 drinks for the exceptionally cheap price of $1.50. We had a great time talking and kidding with the band. I got all their autographs and the new drummer, Vic Angle, is plenty O.K. Outstanding, however, are Hackett, Brunies, Russell and Condon. Russell came over to our table and was rather drunk. I asked him several questions even though he was foggy. He said that nobody could compare with Goodman's clarinet playing.

After enjoying ourselves thoroughly we left at 11:00 and drove up to the Hotel Pennsylvania to see Goodman's Band. I forgot to mention that we were there at 9:15 for a few minutes when Hughie and Emmet took some pictures and Harry James told me that he had no intentions of leaving Goodman. Lionel Hampton was drumming but Dave Tough is going to be the regular drummer from Monday. Harry James has been playing drums with the Quartet since Krupa left on March 3rd. This second time that we saw Goodman was from 11:00 to 11:30 when the band was exceptionally good, playing *King Porter Stomp* for 10 minutes. Dave Matthews is now on sax in place of George Koenig. At 11:30 we went over to the Hotel New Yorker to peek in on Jimmy Dorsey for 5 minutes. We didn't have enough money to go in. We then drove up to the Hotel Commodore where we saw Red Norvo from 12:00 to 2:00. I

Buster Bailey solos with the John Kirby Band at the Onyx

think we had the best time here. It was simply magnificent listening to Norvo's unsurpassable band with Mildred Bailey's great vocals. We sat at the same tables as members of the band. We had been down there twice before recently so we seem to be well-known. Jerry Jerome, Wes Hein, George Wettling, Jimmy Blake, Alan Hanlon and Norvo seem to like us tres bien. We were going to take Jerome up to the Onyx Club but because of a bad cold he couldn't go. I never will forget the band's renditions of *Peckin'*, *King Porter Stomp*, and *Non-Stop*. The band is going to be at the Commodore until May and may go into the Hotel Penn this summer.

At 2:00 we drove up to the Hickory House on 52nd Street where we saw Joe Marsala and his Band plus a saxophonist from Chicago and vocalist Sue Mitchell who were sitting in. The band played our request, *Christopher Columbus*, for 10 minutes with drummer Buddy Rich really playing colossally! At 2:30 we went over to the Onyx Club where it was as crowded as hell. We couldn't get very near the band. Maxine Sullivan sang a couple of songs and the band, under John Kirby's direction, played some great stuff. I noticed that Pete Brown was missing and some other fine alto sax player, resembling Benny Carter, was there in his place. After leaving the Onyx we looked in the Famous Door where Art Tatum and Louis Prima were playing. At 3:30 we drove all the way down to Nick's again where we had some more drinks and, to our surprise, met George Wettling again. We had seen him with Norvo at the Commodore 2-hours ago. He told us that he had to get up at 10:00am to make a record for Brunswick. He and another guy, a trumpet player, sat in with Hackett's Band. Wettling, Brunies, Condon and Russell were all wonderful, while Hackett played a little bit on the electric organ. At 4:00am when everything closed up we drove all the way from 7th Street to Bronxville in 30 minutes – a record time! Hughie and I left Emmet at 4:45 and tried to get into Robcliff Jones' house where we were to sleep. We had to climb a 30-foot rope to reach Robcliff's window so that he could let us in.

Art Tatum and Louis Prima at the Famous Door

■ SUNDAY 20 MARCH 1938

RADIO LOGS

11:30PM WABC
DUKE ELLINGTON
Cotton Club, NYC
Harlem Speaks (great: Williams; Brown; Carney; Hodges)
I See Your Face Before Me (vocal: Ivie Anderson) (fair: Hodges' alto)
I'm Slappin' Seventh Avenue (Stewart's cornet; Hodges)
Azure (very slow: Carney)
The Skrontch (vocal: Ivie Anderson) (nuttsy: Hodges' great alto; Stewart; Brown)
If You Were In My Place (vocal: Ivie Anderson) (Hodges' alto; Brown; Ellington)
Caravan

■ TUESDAY 22 MARCH 1938

RADIO LOGS

10:00PM WABC
BENNY GOODMAN
Camel Caravan, CBS Studio, NYC
Drummer Dave Tough joined the band at the Hotel Pennsylvania last night.
Let's Dance (theme)
Love Me Or Leave Me (colossal: Stacy; Tough's drums; trumpet)
Please Be Kind (vocal: Martha Tilton) (swell: Benny's clarinet)
If I Could Be With You (One Hour Tonight) (great: Russin; Stacy)
Stompin' At The Savoy (BG Quartet) (Dave Tough's drums)
One O'Clock Jump (GREAT: Russin; Brown; Benny; James; Stacy)

■ WEDNESDAY 23 MARCH 1938

RECORDING SESSION

CAB CALLOWAY AND HIS ORCHESTRA
Recording session for Vocalion in New York City.
Cab Calloway (voc); Doc Cheatham, Shad Collins, Irving Randolph, Lammar Wright (t); DePriest Wheeler, Keg Johnson, Claude Jones (tb); Chauncey Haughton, Andrew Brown (cl/as); Chu Berry, Walter Thomas (ts); Benny Payne (p/vib*); Danny Barker (g); Milt Hinton (b); Leroy Maxey (d)
Azure / Skrontch (vCC) / *We're Breaking Up A Lovely Affair* (vCC) / *Peck-A-Doodle-Do* (vCC) / *At The Clambake Carnival* / *Hoy-Hoy* (vCC)

TEDDY WILSON ORCHESTRA
Recording session for Columbia in NYC.
Bobby Hackett (c); Pee Wee Russell (cl); Tab Smith (as); Gene Sedric (ts); Teddy Wilson (p); Allen Reuss (g); Al Hall (b); Johnny Blowers (d); Nan Wynn (voc)
Moments Like This (vNW) / *I Can't Face The Music* (vNW) / *Don't Be That Way*

RADIO LOGS

7:45PM WJZ
GENE KRUPA
Oh, Lady Be Good
It's Easier Said Than Done (vocal: Helen Ward)
I Got Rhythm

■ THURSDAY 24 MARCH 1938

RADIO LOGS

12:00 MIDNIGHT WOR
BENNY GOODMAN
Hotel Pennsylvania, NYC
Don't Be That Way
Please Be Kind (vocal: Martha Tilton)
You Couldn't Be Cuter (vocal: Martha Tilton)
Dizzy Spells (BG Quartet)
I See Your Face Before Me (vocal: Martha Tilton)
When Buddha Smiles
I Got A Guy (vocal: Martha Tilton)
I Never Knew

■ FRIDAY 25 MARCH 1938

RECORDING SESSION

BENNY GOODMAN QUARTET
Recording session for Victor in New York City.
Lionel Hampton (vib/voc); Teddy Wilson (p); Benny Goodman (cl); Dave Tough (d)
The Blues In Your Flat / *The Blues In My Flat* (vLH) / *Sugar* / *Dizzy Spells*

■ SATURDAY 26 MARCH 1938

We went by car with Hugh Pastoriza to NYC where I went to radio station WEVD located on 44th Street & Broadway. Every Saturday WEVD has a jazz broadcast between 2 and 3:00pm. Gene King and Milt Gabler (owner of the Commodore Music Shop on 42nd Street) ask questions that are mailed to WEVD. I managed to answer all questions correctly so won 5 dollars worth of records. I had fun at the Commodore Music Store picking out the following free records: Mildred Bailey's *Lover Come Back To Me* and *Land Of The Sky Blue Water* on Vocalion; Bud Freeman Trio's (Stacy & Wettling) *Three's No Crowd* and *You Took Advantage Of Me* on Commodore 501 and *I Got Rhythm* on Commodore 502; Red Nichols Five Pennies' *On Revival Day* (Teagarden), both sides on Brunswick 6020; Red Norvo Septet's

Red Nichols

Old Fashioned Love and *Honeysuckle Rose* on Columbia 3059-D; Duke Ellington's *Braggin' In Brass* and *Carnival In Caroline* (Ivie Anderson) on Brunswick 8099; and Barney Bigard's *Moonlight Fiesta* and *Sponge Cake And Spinach* on Vocalion 3834.

RADIO LOGS

11:30PM WABC
BENNY GOODMAN
Hotel Pennsylvania, NYC
Honey Chile
Please Be Kind (vocal: Martha Tilton)
You Couldn't Be Cuter (vocal: Martha Tilton)
Sugar (BG Quartet)
Roll 'Em
Always And Always (vocal: Martha Tilton)
Ti-Pi-Tin
If Dreams Come True
Make Believe

■ MONDAY 28 MARCH 1938

RECORDING SESSION

JOHNNY HODGES AND HIS ORCHESTRA
Recording session for Vocalion in New York City.
Cootie Williams (t); Lawrence Brown (tb); Johnny Hodges (ss/as); Harry Carney (bar); Duke Ellington (p); Billy Taylor (b); Sonny Greer (d); Mary McHugh (voc)
Jeep's Blues / *If You Were In My Place* (vMM) / *I Let A Song Go Out Of My Heart* (vMM) / *Rendezvous With Rhythm*

■ TUESDAY 29 MARCH 1938

RADIO LOGS

9:30PM WABC
BENNY GOODMAN
Camel Caravan, CBS Playhouse, NYC
Let's Dance (theme)
I Never Knew (new arrangement: Vernon Brown's trombone)
You Couldn't Be Cuter (vocal: Martha Tilton)
Sweet Lorraine (BG Trio) (Lionel Hampton's drums)
Honey Chile (Edgar Sampson's latest: Brown; Babe Russin; Harry James)
Something Tells Me (vocal: Martha Tilton) (first time on air: Russin; Brown; James)
Sugar (BG Quartet) (swell)
On The Sentimental Side (vocal: Martha Tilton)
Wrappin' It Up (GREAT)

■ WEDNESDAY 30 MARCH 1938

RADIO LOGS

12:00 MIDNIGHT WOR
BENNY GOODMAN
Hotel Pennsylvania, NYC
Camel Hop (Bud Freeman; Harry James)
On The Sentimental Side (vocal: Martha Tilton)
Something Tells Me (vocal: Martha Tilton)
China Boy (BG Trio)
Always And Always (vocal: Martha Tilton)
Chlo-e
The Man I Love (BG Quartet)
Blue Skies
Honey Chile

APRIL 1938

Hotel Pennsylvania: **Benny Goodman**
Hotel Commodore: **Red Norvo**
Hotel New Yorker: **Jimmy Dorsey**
Hotel Lincoln: **Isham Jones**

Apollo Theater: **Cab Calloway** (1–7); **Teddy Hill** (8–14); **Jimmie Lunceford** (15–21); **Fats Waller** (22–28); **Stuff Smith** (29–)
Paramount Theater: **Tommy Dorsey** (13–19)
Loew's State Theater: **Rudy Vallee** (14–20); **Buddy Rogers** (28–)

Cotton Club: **Duke Ellington**
Hickory House: **Joe Marsala**
Onyx Club: **John Kirby** / **Maxine Sullivan** (–13); **Stuff Smith** (14–)
Famous Door: **Louis Prima** / **Art Tatum**
Nick's: **Bobby Hackett**

FRIDAY 1 APRIL 1938

Mortimer, Pinger, Morningstar and myself took the 8:09pm train down to see Benny Goodman at the Hotel Pennsylvania. We got a table fairly near the band and had a very funny and nuttsy evening. Among notables watching the band were drummer Ray McKinley, critic Johnny Hammond, and Bunny Berigan with part of his band from the Paradise Restaurant. With the exception of Dave Tough, whose drumming isn't nearly as good as Krupa's, the band sounds more relaxed and better than ever. Dave Matthews took a great solo on *Wrappin' It Up*. Bud Freeman sent me crazy! He's magnificent! All three trumpeters were great. Pinger and I took the subway home.

Bob Inman and Dick Morningstar practicing the Big Apple before truckin' on down to the Hotel Pennsylvania to be knocked out by Bud Freeman with the Benny Goodman Orchestra.

SUNDAY 3 APRIL 1938

Don Mortimer (home from attending Governor Dummer Academy) and I went to see Red Norvo at the Commodore Hotel which is next to Grand Central Station. We were there from 9:00pm until 12:49am when we had to leave to catch the 1:10am train to Bronxvillle. We had a colossal time talking and joking with band members, especially George Wettling and Jerry Jerome.

MONDAY 4 APRIL 1938

RECORDING SESSION

COOTIE WILLIAMS & HIS RUGCUTTERS
Recording session for Vocalion in New York City.
Cootie Williams (t); Joe Nanton (tb); Johnny Hodges (ss/as); Barney Bigard (cl/ts); Harry Carney (bar); Duke Ellington (p); Fred Guy (g); Billy Taylor (b); Sonny Greer (d); Jerry Kruger (voc)
A Lesson In C (vJK) / *Swingtime In Honolulu* (vJK) / *Carnival In Caroline* (vJK) / *Ol' Man River*

RADIO LOGS

? ?
BENNY GOODMAN QUARTET
Eddie Cantor program, NYC
I'm A Ding Dong Daddy (From Dumas) (BG Quartet) (magnificent)

TUESDAY 5 APRIL 1938

RADIO LOGS

09:30PM WABC
BENNY GOODMAN
Camel Caravan, CBS Playhouse, NYC
Let's Dance (theme)
Makin' Whoopee (swell: Gordon Griffin's trumpet)
I Fall In Love With You Every Day (vocal: Martha Tilton)
Tiger Rag (BG Trio) (excellent)
How'd You Like To Love Me? (vocal: Martha Tilton)
Roll 'Em (Jess Stacy; Harry James; Bud Freeman; Benny)

WEDNESDAY 6 APRIL 1938

RADIO LOGS

12:00 MIDNIGHT WOR
BENNY GOODMAN
Hotel Pennsylvania, NYC
Lullaby In Rhythm [Honey Chile]
It's The Dreamer In Me (vocal: Martha Tilton)
You Couldn't Be Cuter (vocal: Martha Tilton)
When Buddha Smiles
After You've Gone (BG Trio)
Please Be Kind (vocal: Martha Tilton)
Don't Be That Way
How'd You Like To Love Me? (vocal: Martha Tilton)
Clarinet Marmalade

FRIDAY 8 APRIL 1938

RECORDING SESSION

HUDSON-DeLANGE ORCHESTRA
Recording session for Brunswick in New York City.
Will Hudson (arr/ldr); Charles Mitchell, Rudy Novak, Joe Bauer (t); Edward Kolyer, Jack Andrews (tb); George Bohn, Gus Bivona (cl/as); Pete Brendel (as/bar); Charles Brosen (cl/ts); Mark Hyams (p); Bus Etri (g); Doc Goldberg (b); Billy Exiner (d); Jane Dover (voc)
Why Pretend? (vJD) / *China Clipper* / *The One I Love Belongs To Somebody Else* / *On The Alamo*

RADIO LOGS

9:30PM WABC
BENNY GOODMAN
Camel Caravan, CBS Playhouse, NYC
Let's Dance (theme)
Blue Room
You Couldn't Be Cuter (vocal: Martha Tilton)
After You've Gone (BG Trio)
Feeling High And Happy (vocal: Martha Tilton)
Lullaby In Rhythm
My Honey's Lovin' Arms
Always And Always (vocal: Martha Tilton)
Clarinet Marmalade

■ WEDNESDAY 13 APRIL 1938

RECORDING SESSION

BUD FREEMAN TRIO
Recording session for Commodore in New York City.
Bud Freeman (ts); Jess Stacy (p); George Wettling (d)
Keep Smilin' At Trouble / At Sundown / My Honey's Lovin' Arms / I Don't Believe It

■ THURSDAY 14 APRIL 1938

RECORDING SESSION

WOODY HERMAN AND HIS ORCHESTRA
Recording session for Decca in New York City.
Woody Herman (cl/as/voc/ldr); Clarence Willard, Malcolm Crain (t); Joe Bishop (fh); Neal Reid (tb); Jack Ferrier, Ray Hopfner (as); Saxie Mansfield, Pete Johns (ts); Nick Hupfer (vln); Tommy Linehan (p); Oliver Mathewson (g); Walter Yoder (b); Frank Carlson (d); Sonny Skylar (voc)
Calliope Blues (vWH) / *Twin City Blues* / *Carolina In The Morning* (vWH) / *I'm Saving Myself For You* (vWH) / *Laughing Boy Blues* (vWH,SS)

GENE KRUPA AND HIS ORCHESTRA
Recording session for Brunswick in New York City.
Gene Krupa (d/ldr); Tom DiCarlo, Tom Gonsoulin, Dave Schultze (t); Charles McCamish, Bruce Squires (tb); Murray Williams, George Siravo (as); Vido Musso, Carl Biesecker (ts); Milton Raskin (p); Ray Biondi (g); Horace Rollins (b); Helen Ward (voc)
Grandfather's Clock / *Prelude To A Stomp* / *One More Dream* (vHW)

■ MONDAY 11 APRIL 1938

RECORDING SESSION

DUKE ELLINGTON AND HIS ORCHESTRA
Recording session for Master Records in New York City.
Duke Ellington (p); Wallace Jones, Cootie Williams, Harold Baker (t); Rex Stewart (c); Joe Nanton, Lawrence Brown (t); Juan Tizol (vtb); Barney Bigard (cl); Johnny Hodges (cl/ss/as); Otto Hardwick (as/bsx); Harry Carney (cl/as/bar); Fred Guy (g); Billy Taylor (b); Sonny Greer (d); Ivie Anderson (voc)
Swingtime In Honolulu (vIA) / *I'm Slappin' Seventh Avenue (With The Sole Of My Shoe)* / *Dinah's In A Jam*

■ TUESDAY 12 APRIL 1938

RECORDING SESSION

JIMMIE LUNCEFORD AND HIS ORCHESTRA
Recording session for Decca in New York City.
Jimmie Lunceford (ldr); Paul Webster (t); Eddie Tompkins, Sy Oliver (t/voc); Elmer Crumbley, Russell Bowles (tb); Trummy Young (tb/voc); Willie Smith (cl/as/bar/voc); Earl Carruthers (cl/as/bar); Ted Buckner (as); Dan Grissom (cl/as/voc); Joe Thomas (cl/ts/voc); Edwin Wilcox (p); Al Norris (g); Moses Allen (b); Jimmy Crawford (d)
Down By The Old Mill Stream (vDG) / *My Melancholy Baby* (vDG) / *Sweet Sue, Just You* (vSO) / *By The River Sainte Marie* (vDG)

FATS WALLER & HIS ORCHESTRA
Recording session for Victor in New York City.
Herman Autrey, John Hamilton, Nathaniel Williams (t); George Robinson, John Haughton (tb); William Alsop, James Powell, Fred Skerritt (as); Gene Sedric, Lonnie Simmons (ts); Fats Waller (p/voc); Albert Casey (g); Cedric Wallace (b); Slick Jones (d)
In The Gloaming / *You Had An Evening To Spare* (vFW) / *Let's Break The Good News* (vFW) / *Skrontch* (vFW) / *I Simply Adore You* (vFW) / *The Sheik Of Araby* (vFW) / *Hold My Hand* (vFW) / *Inside* (vFW)

Roddy Snow, who just came to Bronxville on his Easter vacation, and I went down in his car to the Apollo Theater at 125th Street where we saw a movie and the stage show featuring Teddy Hill and his fine band. He was plenty O.K. Some of the numbers he played were *King Porter Stomp*, *China Boy* (with Sam Allen at the piano), and some with vocals by trumpeter Bill Dillard and a nice new girl singer. Solos were taken by Shad Collins, John Gillespie, Bill Dillard, Dicky Wells, Bob Carroll on tenor, Russell Procope on alto and clarinet, Sam Allen at the piano, and Bill Beason on the drums. Wells, Allen and Procope were best.

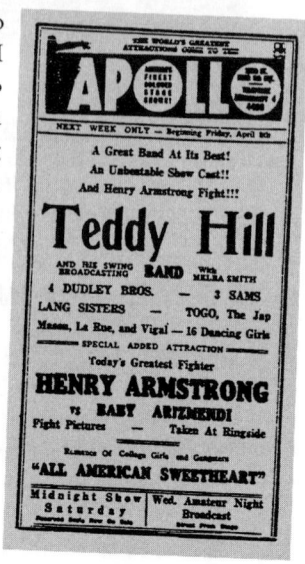

In the evening Roddy drove Morningstar, Pinger, and myself into NYC where we spent the whole night. We arrived at the Hotel New Yorker at 9:30 where we spent several hours listening to Jimmy Dorsey and his Band. Jimmy himself didn't get there until 10:30 because he was over at the Paramount Theater sitting in on a special jam session with his brother Tommy, Gene Krupa, and Bunny Berigan. Jimmy's band was a little too much on the sweet side while vocalist Bob Eberly led it in leader's absence. However, when the band gets going it has plenty of top-notch soloists and plenty of in-the-groove men. New men in the band are trombonist Russ Genner, formerly of the Saturday Night Swing sessions, who replaced Bruce Squires when the latter joined Krupa's new band. Ralph Muzzillo has replaced trumpeter Toots Camarata who is now with Norvo. Herbie Haymer has replaced saxist Dave Matthews who went with Benny Goodman. Soloists included Haymer and Frazier on tenors, Jimmy on clarinet and alto, Shorty Sherock on trumpet, Freddie Slack on piano, Ray McKinley on drums, and Bobby Byrne on trombone (Genner and Mattison took one solo apiece). Hot and comic vocals were done by June Richmond and Ray McKinley. We had a table right next to the band, making it easy to get autographs and to talk with the guys. I got most of the band's autographs in my book Rhythm On Record. We had interesting chats with Haymer who said that he got tired of Norvo's Band and left it. Mattison told us a little about the old Dorsey Brothers band. Late in the evening Kay Kyser and his vocalist came in and he and Jimmy had quite a conversation telling many jokes. Then there was the Ice Carnival. We left at 1:30 and drove down to Nick's Tavern on 10th Street. We were there from 2 to 3. Hackett's Band was sensational with Russell, Brunies, Condon and Bobby outstanding. I know of none who have more distinctive styles than these men, especially Russell. The Emilio Caceres Swing Trio were playing when Hackett rested. They are three Spanish men who play violin, guitar, baritone sax and clarinet. I got their autographs in Rhythm On Record along with those of Brunies and Condon. Red McKenzie happened to be there singing a few numbers. Guitarist Dick McDonough was there with a lady, but didn't play. To our disgust, we found that we had a flat tire outside of Nick's. We didn't have the right kind of jack so we had to have a garageman fix it. We finally got up to the Onyx Club at 3:30am where Stuff Smith just opened. He seemed only fair so we went to the Hickory House for ten minutes until it closed. Joe Bushkin was sitting in, with a couple of Negroes. It's a law in NYC that every nightclub has to close at 4:00am, so we had to come home. We didn't go directly home, however, but hunted for some place to get a bite to eat, without success. We finally reached Dick's house at five o'clock where we climbed in his window and got some breakfast. We finally went to sleep there at 6:00am with the sun up. Because I slept on the floor I woke up at 8:00. Two hours later I was in Scarsdale running the 440 dash.

■ FRIDAY 15 APRIL 1938

RECORDING SESSION

TOMMY DORSEY AND HIS ORCHESTRA
Recording session for Victor in New York City.
Tommy Dorsey (tb); Pee Wee Erwin, Lee Castle, Andy Ferretti (t); Les Jenkins, Earle Hagen (tb); Johnny Mince, Fred Stulce, Hymie Shertzer (cl/as); Skeets Herfurt (ts/voc); Deane Kincaide (ts); Howard Smith (p); Carmen Mastren (g); Gene Traxler (b); Maurice Purtill (d); Jack Leonard (voc)
Cowboy From Brooklyn (vSH) / *You Leave Me Breathless* (vJL) / *I'll Dream Tonight* (vJL)

GENE KRUPA AND HIS ORCHESTRA
Recording session for Brunswick in New York City.
Gene Krupa (d/ldr); Tom DiCarlo, Tom Gonsoulin, Dave Schultze (t); Charles McCamish, Bruce Squires (tb); Murray Williams, George Siravo (as); Vido Musso, Carl Biesecker (ts); Milton Raskin (p); Ray Biondi (g); Horace Rollins (b); Helen Ward (voc)
I Know That You Know / *Feelin' High And Happy* (vHW)

Roddy drove Nancy Long and myself into the Commodore Hotel where we saw Red Norvo play from 10:00pm until 2:00am. He was magnificent! Roddy and I took turns dancing with Nancy. We had a table near the band, and most everybody in the band recognized me and spoke to me. Jerry Jerome came over and talked a while with us. At two o'clock he went up to the Onyx Club to sit in. Wettling said he didn't have enough money to go anywhere so he was going to bed. There sure are a bunch of swell guys in that band. Since I last saw them there are two new members: Toots Camarata has replaced Zeke Zarchy and Jerome's teacher has taken Goldstein's place in the sax chair. After a long, very successful, engagement, the band is leaving the Commodore next week. At midnight the band broadcast over WABC. They played: *Hot Feet* (written by Red); *If You Were In My Place* (vocal by Mildred Bailey); *Drop Me Off At Harlem*; *Why Must I Be Neglected?* (vocal by Terry Allen); *'Long About Midnight* (vocal by Mildred Bailey); *Boy From Harlem* (vocal by Mildred Bailey); *Between The Devil And The Deep Blue Sea*; and *My Melancholy Baby*. We drove home in an hour, getting in at 3:00am.

■ SATURDAY 16 APRIL 1938

In the afternoon, Roddy, Pinger, Poe and I went into station WEVD at Broadway and 44th Street where Roddy and I watched Poe and Pinger answer questions on the Swing Quiz. This is the show that I was on a month ago when I won 2nd place and $5 worth of records. Poe got second place today but Pinger came in fourth. A Negro won it. Milt Gabler asks the questions. I think I'll go on it again in two weeks.

After buying three records at the Commodore Music Shop (Bob Crosby's *Grand Terrace Rhythm* and *John Peel*; Mildred Bailey's *'Long About Midnight* and *More Than You Know*; Barney

Bigard's *I Thought You Cared* and *Drummer's Delight*) Roddy, Pinger, Nancy Long, Barbara Doyle and myself went to the Hotel Pennsylvania where we saw Benny Goodman from 9:00pm until 1:15am. We drove in in the car. We had a ballsy time dancing and listening to the band. I still think Benny's band, with all it's new members, is as good if not better than before. Even Tough has improved. Noni Bernardi joined the band April 15. We saw Noni playing with Jimmy Dorsey's band last Thursday but he's now with Benny. Hymie Shertzer left the band several days ago to go with Tommy Dorsey. Milt Yaner replaced him until Noni came along. Had a long talk with Vernon Brown who told us that the band was going to Washington, D.C. tomorrow for a day, back to the Penn for 2 weeks and then on the road for a month or so. He said the band has made a lot of records this week (*Sweet Sue; Lullaby In Rhythm*, etc). A special Goodman album is to come out soon.

Barbara Doyle had to get the train but we missed it and had to take the subway home. After much trouble we finally got in Bronxville at 3:15am. In the last three nights I've gotten 13 hours sleep. What fun!!
Noni Bernardi

RADIO LOGS

11:30PM WABC
BENNY GOODMAN
Hotel Pennsylvania, NYC
How'd You Like To Love Me? (vocal: Martha Tilton)
Melancholy Baby (great: Gordon Griffin's trumpet)
Lullaby In Rhythm [Honey Chile]
I Let A Song Go Out of My Heart (vocal: Martha Tilton) (GREAT!)
Big John Special (Harry James; Bud Freeman)
Dizzy Spells (BG Quartet)
Serenade In The Night (vocal: Martha Tilton)
I Can't Give You Anything But Love, Baby (Freeman's tenor sax)

Harlem's High Spot — and America's Leading Colored Theatre

APOLLO THEATRE
125th Street Near 8th Av.
Telephone Un. 4-4490
At The 125th Street
AMERICA'S SMARTEST COLORED SHOWS!

One Week Only Begin. Friday, April 15th
JIMMIE LUNCEFORD and his Orchestra and Glee Club

One Week Only Begin. Friday, April 22nd
"FATS" WALLER and his BAND and REVUE
with MYRA JOHNSON AND CAST OF FORTY

COMING SOON!
NOBLE SISSLE and his Band AND REVUE

■ MONDAY 18 APRIL 1938

RECORDING SESSION

BEN POLLACK AND HIS ORCHESTRA
Recording session for Decca in Los Angeles.
Ben Pollack (ldr); Don Anderson, Bob Goodrich, Andy Secrest (t); Joe Yukl (tb); Opie Cates, Bud Carlton (as); Alan Harding, Mort Friedman (ts); Al Beller (vln); Bob Laine (p); Bob Hemphill (g); Slim Jim Taft (b); Graham Stevenson (d); Paula Gayle (voc)
You'll Be Reminded Of Me (vPG) / *After You've Gone* / *There's Rain In My Eyes* (vPG) / *Everybody's Doin' It* (vPG) / *This Is The Life*; *The International Rag* (vPG) / *Looking At The World Through Rose-Colored Glasses* (vPG)

■ TUESDAY 19 APRIL 1938

RECORDING SESSION

RED NORVO AND HIS ORCHESTRA
Recording session for Brunswick in New York City.
Red Norvo (xyl/ldr); Jimmy Blake, Zeke Zarchy, Barney Zudecoff (t); Wes Hein (tb); Hank D'Amico (cl); Len Goldstein (as); Charles Lamphere (as/ts); Jerry Jerome (ts); Bill Miller (p); Alan Hanlon (g); Pete Peterson (b); George Wettling (d); Mildred Bailey (voc)
Says My Heart (vMB) / *I Let A Song Go Out Of My Heart* (vMB)

RAYMOND SCOTT QUINTETTE
Recording session for Brunswick in NYC.
Raymond Scott (p/ldr); Dave Wade (t); Pete Pumiglio (cl); Dave Harris (ts); Fred Whiting (b); Johnny Williams (d)
The Happy Farmer

RADIO LOGS

9:30PM WABC
BENNY GOODMAN
Camel Caravan, CBS Playhouse, NYC
Let's Dance (theme)
Sweet Sue (great: saxes; James; Freeman)
I Let A Song Go Out Of My Heart (vocal: Martha Tilton)
Ti-Pi-Tin (swell: Freeman; James)
You Couldn't Be Cuter (vocal: Martha Tilton) (Bud Freeman's tenor)
Ciribiribin (Harry James' trumpet)
Don't Be That Way (BG Quartet)
Joseph, Joseph! (vocal: Martha Tilton) (Ziggy Elman's trumpet)

■ THURSDAY 21 APRIL 1938

RECORDING SESSION

MILDRED BAILEY & HER ORCHESTRA
Recording session for Vocalion in New York.
Jimmy Blake, Zeke Zarchy, Barney Zudecoff (t); Wes Hein (tb); Hank D'Amico (cl/as); Len Goldstein (as); Jerry Jerome, Charles Lamphere (ts); Bill Miller (p); Alan Hanlon (g); Pete Peterson (b); George Wettling (d); Red Norvo (xyl); Mildred Bailey (v)
Moonshine Over Kentucky (vMB) / *Rock It For Me* (vMB) / *After Dinner Speech* (vMB) / *If You Were In My Place* (vMB)

BUNNY BERIGAN AND HIS ORCHESTRA
Recording session for Victor in New York City.
Bunny Berigan, Irving Goodman, Steve Lipkins (t); Al George, Nat Lobovsky (tb); Mike Doty, Joe Dixon (cl/as); Clyde Rounds, George Auld (ts); Joe Lippman (p); Dick Wharton (g/voc); Hank Wayland (b); Johnny Blowers (d); Ruth Gaylor (voc)
Never Felt Better, Never Had Less (vRG) / *I've Got A Guy* (vRG) / *Moonshine Over Kentucky* (vRG) / *Round The Old Deserted Farm* (vRG) / *Azure*

RADIO LOGS

12:00 MIDNIGHT WOR
BENNY GOODMAN
Hotel Pennsylvania, NYC
That Naughty Waltz (swell: Vernon Brown; Harry James)
I Fall In Love With You Every Day (vocal: Martha Tilton)
Sometimes I'm Happy (GREAT: James; Bud Freeman)
One O'Clock Jump (Jess Stacy; Freeman; Brown; Stacy; James)
You Go To My Head (vocal: Martha Tilton) (swell)
Shine (BG Quartet) (colossal: Dave Tough; Lionel Hampton)
Swing In D-Flat Minor (good: Benny & Tough)
Always And Always (vocal: Martha Tilton) (fine commercial)

■ FRIDAY 22 APRIL 1938

RECORDING SESSION

JIMMY DORSEY AND HIS ORCHESTRA
Recording session for Decca in New York City.
Jimmy Dorsey (cl/as); Shorty Sherock, Ralph Muzzillo (t); Bobby Byrne, Don Mattison (tb/voc); Sonny Lee (tb); Milt Yaner, Sam Rubinowich (as); Herbie Haymer, Charles Frazier (ts); Freddie Slack (p); Roc Hillman (g/voc); Jack Ryan (b); Ray McKinley (d/voc); Bob Eberly (voc)
Popcorn Man (vRMK) / *I Love You In Technicolor* (vBE) / *At Your Beck And Call* (vBE) / *Cowboy From Brooklyn* (vRMK) / *Who Do You Think I Saw Last Night?* (vDM)

■ SATURDAY 23 APRIL 1938

RECORDING SESSION

RAYMOND SCOTT QUINTETTE
Recording session for Brunswick in NYC.
Raymond Scott (p/ldr); Dave Wade (t); Pete Pumiglio (cl); Dave Harris (ts); Fred Whiting (b); Johnny Williams (d)
Egyptian Barn Dance

RADIO LOGS

11:30PM WABC
BENNY GOODMAN
Hotel Pennsylvania, NYC
I Let A Song Go Out Of My Heart (vocal: Martha Tilton)
Always (colossal relaxed swing: Freeman; Benny)
Something Tells Me (vocal: Martha Tilton)
I'm A Ding Dong Daddy (From Dumas) (BG Quartet) (great: Hampton;Tough)
Please Be Kind (vocal: Martha Tilton) (excellent commercial)
Ti-Pi-Tin (nuttsy arrangement of lousy piece: Freeman)
Nice Work If You Can Get It (BG Trio)
You Couldn't Be Cuter (vocal: Martha Tilton) (wa-wa brass)

■ TUESDAY 26 APRIL 1938

RECORDING SESSION

BENNY GOODMAN TRIO
Recording session for Victor in New York City.
Lionel Hampton (d); Teddy Wilson (p); Benny Goodman (cl)
Nobody's Sweetheart

RADIO LOGS

9:30PM WABC
BENNY GOODMAN
Camel Caravan, CBS Playhouse, NYC
Let's Dance (theme)
Make Believe (swell: James; Brown)
On The Sentimental Side (vocal: Martha Tilton)
Don't Be That Way (great: Freeman; James)
Why'd Ya Make Me Fall In Love? (vocal: Martha Tilton) (first time on radio)
Nobody's Sweetheart (BG Trio) (Lionel Hampton on drums)
You Had An Evening To Spare (vocal: Martha Tilton)
House Hop (colossal: Elman; Freeman)
Goodbye (theme)

■ WEDNESDAY 27 APRIL 1938

RECORDING SESSION

TOMMY DORSEY AND HIS ORCHESTRA
Recording session for Victor in New York City.
Tommy Dorsey (tb); Pee Wee Erwin, Lee Castle, Andy Ferretti (t); Les Jenkins, Earle Hagen (tb); Johnny Mince, Fred Stulce, Hymie Shertzer (cl/as); Skeets Herfurt (ts/voc); Deane Kincaide (ts); Howard Smith (p); Carmen Mastren (g); Gene Traxler (b); Maurice Purtill (d); Edythe Wright, Jack Leonard (voc)
Marching Along With Time (vEW) / *I Hadn't Anyone Till You* (vJL) / *My Walking-Stick* (vEW)

HARRY JAMES AND HIS ORCHESTRA
Recording session for Brunswick in New York City.
Harry James (t/ldr); Ziggy Elman (t); Vernon Brown (tb); Dave Matthews (as); Art Rollini (ts); Harry Carney (bar); Jess Stacy (p); Thurman Teague (b); Dave Tough (d)
Out Of Nowhere / *Wrap Your Troubles In Dreams* / *Lullaby In Rhythm* / *Little White Lies*

George Fick and I took the train from Bronxville to 138th Street where we walked across to the Savoy Ballroom at Lenox and 140th Street. We saw continuous good music from the bands of the Savoy Sultans and Hot Lips Page. The Savoy Sultans small band really swung in a knock-out fashion and kept the Big Apple dancers groovin'.

■ FRIDAY 29 APRIL 1938

RECORDING SESSION

JIMMY DORSEY AND HIS ORCHESTRA
Recording session for Decca in New York City.
Jimmy Dorsey (cl/as); Shorty Sherock, Ralph Muzzillo (t); Bobby Byrne, Don Mattison (tb/voc); Sonny Lee (tb); Milt Yaner, Sam Rubinowich (as); Herbie Haymer, Charles Frazier (ts); Freddie Slack (p); Roc Hillman (g/voc); Jack Ryan (b); Ray McKinley (d/voc); June Richmond (voc)
John Silver / *Song Of The Volga Boatman* / *The Darktown Strutters' Ball* (vJR) / *Dusk In Upper Sandusky*

■ SATURDAY 30 APRIL 1938

RECORDING SESSION

EDDIE CONDON & HIS WINDY CITY SEVEN
Recording session for Commodore in New York City.
Bobby Hackett (c); Jack Teagarden (tb); Pee Wee Russell (cl); Bud Freeman (ts); Jess Stacy (p); Eddie Condon (g); Artie Shapiro (b); George Wettling (d)
Embraceable You / *Meet Me Tonight In Dreamland* / *Diane* / *Serenade To A Shylock*

RADIO LOGS

11:30PM WABC
BENNY GOODMAN
Hotel Pennsylvania, NYC
Benny Goodman's closing night at the Hotel Pennsylvania.
That Feeling Is Gone (vocal: Martha Tilton)
Sing, Sing, Sing (colossal: Benny; Freeman; James;Tough)
You Had An Evening To Spare (vocal: Martha Tilton) (nuttsy new piece)
Avalon (BG Quartet) (great: Hampton)
Don't Be That Way
Joseph, Joseph! (vocal: Martha Tilton)

MAY 1938

Hotel Lincoln: **Isham Jones**

Apollo Theater: **Stuff Smith** (–5); **Edgar Hayes** (6–12); **Count Basie** (13–19); **Don Redman / 4 Ink Spots** (20–26); **Chick Webb** (27–)
Paramount Theater: **Kay Kyser** (–3); **Bunny Berigan** (11–17); **Hal Kemp** (18–24)
Loew's State Theater: **Buddy Rogers** (–4); **Shep Fields** (12–18);

Cotton Club: **Duke Ellington**
Hickory House: **Joe Marsala**
Onyx Club: **Stuff Smith**
Famous Door: **Louis Prima / Art Tatum**

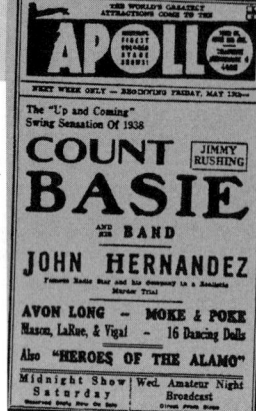

■ SUNDAY 1 MAY 1938

Benny Goodman and his orchestra play a benefit concert at Symphony Hall in Boston

■ MONDAY 2 MAY 1938

RECORDING SESSION

CHICK WEBB ORCHESTRA
Recording session for Decca in New York City.
Ella Fitzgerald (voc); Mario Bauza, Taft Jordan, Bobby Stark (t); Sandy Williams, Nat Story, George Matthews (tb); Louis Jordan (as); Garvin Bushell (cl/as); Ted McRae (ts); Wayman Carver (ts/fl); Tommy Fulford (p); Bobby Johnson (g); Beverly Peer (b); Chick Webb (d)
A-Tisket, A-Tasket (vEF) / *Heart Of Mine* (vEF) / *I'm Just A Jitterbug* (vEF) / *Azure*

RED NORVO AND HIS ORCHESTRA
Recording session for Brunswick in New York City.
Red Norvo (xyl/ldr); Jack Owens, Jack Palmer, Barney Zudecoff (t); Andy Russo, Al George (tb); Hank D'Amico (cl); Frank Simeone (as); Maurice Kogan, George Berg (ts); Bill Miller (p); Alan Hanlon (g); Pete Peterson (b); George Wettling (d); Mildred Bailey (voc)
Day Dreamin' (vMB) / *A Cigarette And A Silhouette* (vMB) / *Savin' Myself For You* (vMB) / *You Leave Me Breathless* (vMB)

■ TUESDAY 3 MAY 1938

RECORDING SESSION

ELLA FITZGERALD AND HER SAVOY EIGHT
Recording session for Decca in New York City.
Ella Fitzgerald (voc); Taft Jordan (t); Sandy Williams (tb); Louis Jordan (as); Teddy McRae (ts/bar); Tommy Fulford (p); Bobby Johnson (g); Beverly Peer (b); Chick Webb (d)
This Time It's Real / *What Do You Know About Love?* / *You Can't Be Mine* / *We Can't Go On This Way* / *Saving Myself For You* / *If You Only Knew* / *Spinnin' The Webb* / *Liza*

RADIO LOGS

9:30PM WABC
BENNY GOODMAN
Camel Caravan, Waltham, Mass
Let's Dance (theme)
I Can't Give You Anything But Love, Baby (trumpet; Stacy; Freeman)
Please Be Kind (vocal: Martha Tilton) (good commercial: Freeman)
Sampson's Stomp (Brown; Stacy Freeman; Elman)
The Dixieland Band (vocal: Martha Tilton)
Nagasaki (BG Quartet) (excellent work by all four)
I Let A Song Go Out Of My Heart (vocal: Martha Tilton)
Wrappin' It Up (magnificent: Matthews' alto; Freeman's tenor; Harry James)
Goodbye (theme)

■ WEDNESDAY 4 MAY 1938

RECORDING SESSION

GENE KRUPA AND HIS ORCHESTRA
Recording session for Brunswick in New York City.
Gene Krupa (d/ldr); Tom DiCarlo, Tom Gonsoulin, Dave Schultze (t); Charles McCamish, Bruce Squires, Chuck Evans (tb); Murray Williams, George Siravo (as); Vido Musso, Carl Biesecker (ts); Milton Raskin (p); Ray Biondi (g); Horace Rollins (b); Jerry Kruger (voc)
Since My Best Gal Turned Me Down / *Fare Thee Well, Annie Laurie* (vJK) / *Jam On Toast*

■ MONDAY 9 MAY 1938

RECORDING SESSION

MILDRED BAILEY & HER ORCHESTRA
Recording session for Vocalion in New York.
Jimmy Blake, Zeke Zarchy, Barney Zudecoff (t); Wes Hein (tb); Hank D'Amico (cl/as); Len Goldstein (as); Jerry Jerome, Charles Lamphere (ts); Bill Miller (p); Alan Hanlon (g); Pete Peterson (b); George Wettling (d); Red Norvo (xyl); Mildred Bailey (v)
Washboard Blues (vMB) / *My Melancholy Baby* (vMB) / *Round The Old Deserted Farm* (vMB) / *The Lonesome Road* (vMB)

■ TUESDAY 10 MAY 1938

RADIO LOGS

9:30PM WABC
BENNY GOODMAN
Camel Caravan, CBS Playhouse, NYC
Let's Dance (theme)
I Found A New Baby (great: Dave Matthews; Ziggy Elman)
That Feeling Is Gone (vocal: Martha Tilton) (swell: Bud Freeman)
At A Perfume Counter (good: Stacy; Freeman)
I Must Have That Man (piano duet: Jess Stacy & Teddy Wilson)
Joseph, Joseph! (vocal: Martha Tilton) (Freeman; Benny)
Lillie Stomp (BG Quartet) (swell)
I Married An Angel (vocal: Martha Tilton)
One O'Clock Jump (magnificent: Stacy; Freeman's tenor; Harry James; Vernon Brown)
Goodbye (theme)

■ WEDNESDAY 11 MAY 1938

RECORDING SESSION

BILLIE HOLIDAY & HER ORCHESTRA
Recording session for Columbia in NYC.
Bernard Anderson (t); Babe Russin (ts); Claude Thornhill (p); John Kirby (b); Cozy Cole (d); Billie Holiday (v)
You Go To My Head / *The Moon Looks Down And Laughs* / *If I Were You* / *Forget If You Can*

RADIO LOGS

12:00 MIDNIGHT WABC
BENNY GOODMAN
Convention Hall, Philadelphia
Don't Be That Way
On The Sentimental Side (vocal: Martha Tilton)
Sweet Sue
I Fall In Love With You Every Day (vocal: Martha Tilton)
Star Dust (swell: Benny)
Dizzy Spells (BG Quartet)
You Had An Evening To Spare (vocal: Martha Tilton)
Ti-Pi-Tin (Freeman; James)
Wrappin' It Up (Dave Matthews' alto sax; trumpet)

■ THURSDAY 12 MAY 1938

RECORDING SESSION

TOMMY DORSEY AND HIS ORCHESTRA
Recording session for Victor in New York City.
Tommy Dorsey (tb); Pee Wee Erwin, Lee Castle, Andy Ferretti (t); Les Jenkins, Earle Hagen (tb); Johnny Mince, Fred Stulce, Hymie Shertzer (cl/as); Skeets Herfurt (ts/voc); Deane Kincaide (ts); Howard Smith (p); Carmen Mastren (g); Gene Traxler (b); Maurice Purtill (d); Edythe Wright, Jack Leonard, Three Esquires (voc)
Now It Can Be Told (vJL) / *This Time It's Real* (vJL) / *Music, Maestro, Please* (vEW) / *All Through The Night* (vEW,3E)

■ MONDAY 16 MAY 1938

RECORDING SESSION

JIMMY DORSEY AND HIS ORCHESTRA
Recording session for Decca in New York City.
Jimmy Dorsey (cl/as); Shorty Sherock, Ralph Muzzillo (t); Bobby Byrne, Don Mattison (tb/voc); Sonny Lee (tb); Milt Yaner, Sam Rubinowich (as); Herbie Haymer, Charles Frazier (ts); Freddie Slack (p); Roc Hillman (g/voc); Jack Ryan (b); Ray McKinley (d/voc); Bob Eberly, Vi Mele (voc)
There's A Faraway Look In Your Eye (vBE) / *Any Old Time At All* (vVM) / *I Let A Song Go Out Of My Heart* (vVM) / *That Feeling Is Gone* (vDM) / *If You Were In My Place* (vVM) / *Arkansaw Traveler*

■ TUESDAY 17 MAY 1938

RADIO LOGS

9:30PM WABC
BENNY GOODMAN
Camel Caravan, CBS Playhouse, NYC
Let's Dance (theme)
I'll Always Be In Love With You (Freeman; Elman)
I Love To Whistle (vocal: Martha Tilton) (Freeman; Brown)
Moonglow (BG Quartet) (swell)
Star Dust (great: James; Benny)
Jazz Me Blues (colossal: Dixieland style with small group from band; Vernon Brown; Harry James; Dave Tough; Jess Stacy)
I Let A Song Go Out Of My Heart (vocal: Martha Tilton)
Who? (BG Trio) (great: Wilson; Tough; Benny)
Don't Be That Way (Harry James; Freeman's tenor; Vernon Brown)
Goodbye (theme)

BENNY GOODMAN and his SENSATIONAL ORCHESTRA
ONLY NEW YORK BALLROOM APPEARANCE
TONIGHT THE KING OF KINGS IS HERE!
FOR ONE NIGHT ONLY!
Admission LADIES 70¢ PLUS TAX GENTLEMEN 90¢ PLUS TAX
Scientifically Cooled
ROSELAND BROADWAY at 51st ST.

352 Swing Era Scrapbook
MAY 1938

RAYMOR
253 Huntington Ave.
DANCING TONIGHT
and every evening
One of America's Greatest Bands
GLENN MILLER
Arranger, author and organizer
for Ray Noble and Jimmy Dorsey.
With His Sensational Band
Brunswick Records

Photographs of the Glenn Miller Band taken during their April/May engagement at the Raymor Ballroom in Boston.
Top, l to r: Glenn Miller, trumpeter Johnny Austin, drummer Bob Spangler, and tenor saxist Tex Beneke.
Above: Drummer Bob Spangler and pianist Chummy MacGregor.
Left: Miller, Ray Eberle, Kathleen Lane, Hal McIntyre and Beneke.

MAY 1938 — Swing Era Scrapbook 353

■ MONDAY 23 MAY 1938

RECORDING SESSION

WINGY MANONE AND HIS ORCHESTRA
Recording session for Bluebird in New York City.
Wingy Manone (t/voc); Brad Gowans (v-tb); Al Kavich (cl/as); Wilder Chase (p); Bobby Bennett (g); Sid Jacobs (b); Danny Alvin (d)
Heart Of Mine (vWM) / *Let's Break The Good News* (vWM) / *Martha* (vWM) / *Mannone Blues* (vWM) / *The Flat Foot Floogie* (vWM) / *Little Joe From Chicago* (vWM)

GLENN MILLER AND HIS ORCHESTRA
Recording session for Brunswick in New York City.
Glenn Miller (tb/ldr); Johnny Austin, Bob Price, Gasparre Rebito (t); Brad Jenney, Al Mastren (tb); Willie Schwartz, Hal McIntyre (cl/as); Stanley Aronson (as/bar); Tex Beneke, Sol Kane (ts); Chummy MacGregor (p); Carmen Mastren (g); Rowland Bundock (b); Bob Spangler (d); Gail Reese, Ray Eberle (voc)
Don't Wake Up My Heart (vRE) / *Why'd Ya Make Me Fall In Love?* (vGR) / *Sold American* (vBand) / *Dipper Mouth Blues* (vBand)

■ TUESDAY 24 MAY 1938

RADIO LOGS

9:30PM WABC
BENNY GOODMAN
Camel Caravan, Boston
Let's Dance (theme)
Honeysuckle Rose (magnificent, never heard the band better or as relaxed: Vernon Brown; Harry James; Benny)
Cowboy From Brooklyn (vocal: Martha Tilton) (swell: Brown)
Oh, Lady Be Good (Benny with Teddy Wilson playing harpsichord)
Lullaby In Rhythm (nuttsy: Bud Freeman; Brown; Benny)
It's The Dreamer In Me (vocal: Martha Tilton) (swell)
Joseph, Joseph! (BG Quartet) (swell: Dave Tough's drums)
King Porter Stomp (COLOSSAL, great!!! very relaxed and in the groove: Benny; James; Brown; Freeman; Tough's cymbals)
Goodbye (theme)

■ THURSDAY 26 MAY 1938

RECORDING SESSION

BUNNY BERIGAN AND HIS ORCHESTRA
Recording session for Victor in New York City.
Bunny Berigan, Irving Goodman, Steve Lipkins (t); Ray Conniff, Nat Lobovsky (tb); Mike Doty, Joe Dixon (cl/as); Clyde Rounds, George Auld (ts); Joe Bushkin (p); Dick Wharton (g/voc); Hank Wayland (b); Johnny Blowers (d); Ruth Gaylor (voc)
Somewhere With Somebody Else (vDW) / *It's The Little Things That Count* (vRG) / *Wacky Dust* (vRG) / *The Wearin' Of The Green*

11:30PM WABC
BENNY GOODMAN
Footguard Hall, Hartford, Conn.
That Naughty Waltz (Vernon Brown's trombone)
Says My Heart (vocal: Martha Tilton) (Vernon Brown's trombone)
Don't Be That Way (Bud Freeman's tenor; Vernon Brown)
Cowboy From Brooklyn (vocal: Martha Tilton)
Sweet Sue (great: Bud Freeman, etc)
Please Be Kind (vocal: Martha Tilton)
Why'd You Make Me Love You? (vocal: Martha Tilton)
My Melancholy Baby (Gordon Griffin's trumpet; saxes)
I'm A Ding Dong Daddy (From Dumas) (BG Quartet)
Blue Skies

■ FRIDAY 27 MAY 1938

RECORDING SESSION

FLETCHER HENDERSON AND HIS ORCHESTRA
Recording session for Vocalion in Chicago.
Fletcher Henderson (p/ldr); Dick Vance, Russell Smith, Emmett Berry (t); John McConnell, Albert Wynn, Ed Cuffee (tb); Eddie Barefield (cl/as); Budd Johnson (as); Elmer Williams, Franz Jackson (ts); Lawrence Lucie (g); Israel Crosby (b); Pete Suggs (d/vib); Chuck Richards (voc)
Don't Let The Rhythm Go To Your Head (vCR) / *Saving Myself For You* (vCR) / *There's Rain In My Eyes* (vCR)

■ SATURDAY 28 MAY 1938

RECORDING SESSION

FLETCHER HENDERSON AND HIS ORCHESTRA
Recording session for Vocalion in Chicago.
Fletcher Henderson (p/ldr); Dick Vance, Russell Smith, Emmett Berry (t); John McConnell, Albert Wynn, Ed Cuffee (tb); Eddie Barefield (cl/as); Budd Johnson (as); Elmer Williams, Franz Jackson (ts); Lawrence Lucie (g); Israel Crosby (b); Pete Suggs (d/vib); Chuck Richards (voc)
What Do You Hear From The Mob In Scotland? (vCR) / *It's The Little Things That Count* (vCR) / *Moten Stomp*

■ SUNDAY 29 MAY 1938

The 'Carnival of Swing' (11am–4.45pm) at Randall's Island Stadium in New York City, organised by Martin Block, features more than 20 bands and attracts a crowd of 25,000.

■ TUESDAY 31 MAY 1938

RADIO LOGS

9:30PM WABC
BENNY GOODMAN
Camel Caravan, CBS Playhouse, NYC
Let's Dance (theme)
Alexander's Ragtime Band (good: Benny)
On The Sentimental Side (vocal: Martha Tilton) (good)
I'll Never Be The Same (BG Trio) (good)
I Never Knew (trumpet; swell brass; Benny)
The Blues (guests JOE TURNER singing & PETE JOHNSON playing piano)
Smiles (BG Quartet) (swell)
Says My Heart (vocal: Martha Tilton) (Bud Freeman's tenor)
Flat Foot Floogie (vocal: Band) (Matthews' alto; Benny)
Goodbye (theme)

JUNE 1938

Hotel New Yorker: **Henry Busse** (27–)

Apollo Theater: **Chick Webb** (–9); **Duke Ellington** (10–16); **Louis Armstrong** (15–28); **Tiny Bradshaw** (24–30)
Paramount Theater: **Sammy Kaye** (1–7); **Red Norvo / Mildred Bailey** (15–21); **Xavier Cugat / Frances Langford** (29–)

Paradise Restaurant: **Glenn Miller** (14–)
Cotton Club: **Duke Ellington** (–9)
Hickory House: **Joe Marsala** (–22); **Red Stanley & His Californians** (23–)
Onyx Club: **Stuff Smith**
Piccadilly Circus Bar: **Adrian Rollini Trio**

THURSDAY 2 JUNE 1938

RECORDING SESSION

GENE KRUPA AND HIS ORCHESTRA
Recording session for Brunswick in New York City.
Gene Krupa (d/ldr); Tom DiCarlo, Tom Gonsoulin, Dave Schultze (t); Charles McCamish, Bruce Squires, Chuck Evans (tb); Murray Williams, George Siravo (as); Vido Musso, Carl Biesacher (ts); Milton Raskin (p); Ray Biondi (g); Horace Rollins (b); Irene Day (voc)
If It Rains, Who Cares? (vID) / *Wire Brush Stomp* / *What Goes On Here In My Heart?* (vID) / *There's Honey On The Moon Tonight* (vID)

SATURDAY 4 JUNE 1938

I met Oliver Quayle at the Savoy Ballroom. We saw Edgar Hayes' fine band for the first time, and also the Savoy Sultans. We watched the two bands from 9:00 until 1:00am. The Lindy-hop contest at 12:30 was sensational. Hayes' Band has some excellent ensemble arrangements, with Hayes and Joe Garland writing most of the scores. Outstanding musicians are Hayes on piano, Joe Garland on tenor sax and Henry Goodwin on trumpet. Clarinetist Rudy Powell is way too corny. Coco Darling is the funniest bass player I've ever seen, although he isn't just showing off. He throws that bass around and gets a funny look on his face. One of the trombonists specializes on the growling rubber mute. It sounds swell but sometimes gets monotonous.

Personnel of Edgar Hayes Band:
Edgar Hayes (piano); Eddie Gibbs (guitar); Frank 'Coco' Darling (bass); Kenneth 'Kenny' Clarke (drums); Rudy Powell, Roger Boyd, William 'Slappy' Mitchner, Joe Garland (saxes); Bernard Flood, Leonard Davis, Henry Goodwin (trumpets); Clyde Bernhardt, R. H. Horton, David James (trombones).

MONDAY 6 JUNE 1938

RECORDING SESSION

COUNT BASIE AND HIS ORCHESTRA
Recording session for Decca in New York City.
Buck Clayton, Ed Lewis, Harry Edison (t); Dan Minor, Benny Morton, Eddie Durham (tb); Earle Warren (as); Lester Young, Herschel Evans (ts); Jack Washington (bar); Count Basie (p); Freddie Green (g); Walter Page (b); Jo Jones (d); Jimmy Rushing (voc)
Mama Don't Want No Peas An' Rice An' Coconut Oil (vJR) / *Blue And Sentimental* / *Doggin' Around*

TUESDAY 7 JUNE 1938

RECORDING SESSION

DUKE ELLINGTON AND HIS ORCHESTRA
Recording session for Master Records in New York City.
Duke Ellington (p); Wallace Jones, Cootie Williams (t); Rex Stewart (c); Joe Nanton, Lawrence Brown (tb); Juan Tizol (vtb); Barney Bigard (cl); Johnny Hodges (cl/ss/as); Otto Hardwick (as/bsx); Harry Carney (cl/as/bar); Fred Guy (g); Billy Taylor (b); Sonny Greer (d); Ivie Anderson (voc)
You Gave Me The Gate And I'm Swingin' (vIA) / *Rose Of The Rio Grande* (vIA) / *Pyramid* / *When My Sugar Walks Down The Street* (vIA)
Duke Ellington plays tom-toms on *Pyramid*.

RADIO LOGS

9:30PM WABC
BENNY GOODMAN
Camel Caravan, Cleveland, Ohio
Let's Dance (theme)
Shine On Harvest Moon (nuttsy: Freeman; trumpet)
Saving Myself For You (vocal: Martha Tilton) (grand new piece)
Flat Foot Floogie (vocal: Band) (ballsy parts: Benny; Matthews' alto; brass)
She's Funny That Way (piano duet: Jess Stacy & Teddy Wilson)
It's Been So Long (vocal: Martha Tilton) (revival of ballsy piece)
Diga Diga Doo (BG Quartet) (magnificent Hampton)
You Couldn't Be Cuter (vocal: Martha Tilton) (nice pop: Stacy)
I Know That You Know (colossal: Benny; one of Freeman's greatest solos; trumpet)
Goodbye (theme)

■ WEDNESDAY 8 JUNE 1938

RECORDING SESSION

BUNNY BERIGAN AND HIS ORCHESTRA
Recording session for Victor in New York City.
Bunny Berigan, Irving Goodman, Steve Lipkins (t); Ray Conniff, Nat Lobovsky (tb); Mike Doty, Joe Dixon (cl/as); Clyde Rounds, George Auld (ts); Joe Bushkin (p); Dick Wharton (g/voc); Hank Wayland (b); Johnny Blowers (d); Ruth Gaylor (voc)
The Pied Piper (vRG) / *Tonight Will Live* (vDW) / *(A Sky Of Blue And You) And So Forth* (vRG) / *(How To Make Love) In Ten Easy Lessons* (vRG)

WOODY HERMAN AND HIS ORCHESTRA
Recording session for Decca in New York City.
Woody Herman (cl/as/voc/ldr); Clarence Willard, Malcolm Crain (t); Joe Bishop (fh); Neal Reid (tb); Jack Ferrier, Ray Hopfner (as); Saxie Mansfield, Pete Johns (ts); Nick Hupfer (vln); Tommy Linehan (p); Oliver Mathewson (g); Walter Yoder (b); Frank Carlson (d); Sonny Skylar (voc)
The Flat Foot Floogie (vWH) / *Lullaby In Rhythm* (vWH) / *Don't Wake Up My Heart* (vWH) / *Laughing Boy Blues* (vWH,SS)

■ THURSDAY 9 JUNE 1938

RECORDING SESSION

CHICK WEBB ORCHESTRA
Recording session for Decca in New York City.
Ella Fitzgerald (voc); Mario Bauza, Taft Jordan, Bobby Stark (t); Sandy Williams, Nat Story, George Matthews (tb); Hilton Jefferson (as); Garvin Bushell (cl/as); Ted McRae (ts); Wayman Carver (ts/fl); Tommy Fulford (p); Bobby Johnson (g); Beverly Peer (b); Chick Webb (d)
Pack Up Your Sins (And Go To The Devil) (vEF) / *MacPherson Is Rehearsin'* (vEF) / *Everybody Step* (vEF) / *Ella* (vEF, TJ)

■ FRIDAY 10 JUNE 1938

RECORDING SESSION

WILL HUDSON AND HIS SEVEN SWINGSTERS
Recording session for Brunswick in New York City.
Will Hudson (arr/ldr); Joe Bauer (t); Gus Bivona (cl/as); Charles Brosen (cl/ts); Mark Hyams (p); Bus Etri (g); Doc Goldberg (b); Billy Exiner (d)
Lady Of The Night / *Hangover In Hong Kong* / *The Corrigan Hop*

■ SATURDAY 11 JUNE 1938

RECORDING SESSION

WILL HUDSON AND HIS ORCHESTRA
Recording session for Brunswick in New York City.
Will Hudson (arr/ldr); Charles Mitchell, Rudy Novak, Joe Bauer (t); Edward Kolyer, Jack Andrews (tb); George Bohn, Gus Bivona (cl/as); Pete Brendel (as/bar); Charles Brosen (cl/ts); Mark Hyams (p); Bus Etri (g); Doc Goldberg (b); Billy Exiner (d); Jane Dover (voc)
The Flat Foot Floogie (vBand) / *There's Something About An Old Love* (vJD) / *Break It Down* / *Break It Up*

■ SUNDAY 12 JUNE 1938

Don Mortimer and I went to see Duke Ellington today at the Apollo Theater in Harlem. The band didn't play quite enough to please us, but was great. Bassist Hayes Alvis has left and Arthur Whetsel has been replaced by Wallace Jones on trumpet. Ellington goes into hospital in three weeks for an operation.

The Benny Goodman & Count Basie Bands appeared at a concert at Madison Square Garden in New York. The concert was broadcast by station WHN.

RADIO LOGS

11:00pm WHN
COUNT BASIE & BENNY GOODMAN
Madison Square Garden, NYC
11:00PM **COUNT BASIE**
Farewell Blues (great! sax; drums)
Topsy (Basie's piano)
Rosalie (vocal: Jimmy Rushing)
I Found A New Baby
Blue And Sentimental
Everybody Loves My Baby
Jumpin' At The Woodside
Swingin' The Blues (colossal: tenor sax)
11:30PM **BENNY GOODMAN**
Joseph, Joseph! (vocal: Martha Tilton) (Ziggy Elman's trumpet)
Sampson Stomp (colossal: Brown; trumpet; Freeman; trumpet)
Something Tells Me (vocal: Martha Tilton) (Brown's trombone)
King Porter Stomp (great, very fast: James; Benny; James; Brown; Freeman; Tough)
Please Be Kind (vocal: Martha Tilton) (Freeman's tenor)
Don't Be That Way (Freeman's 2 ballsy solos; Brown; Tough)
Saving Myself For You (vocal: Martha Tilton) (nuttsy)
Wrappin' It Up (magnificent: Dave Matthews' alto sax; Harry James)
After You've Gone (BG Trio) (swell: Hampton's show-off drumming)
You Leave Me Breathless (vocal: Martha Tilton)
Limehouse Blues (BG Quartet) (swell)
12:15AM **COUNT BASIE**
St. Louis Blues
Every Tub
Rhythm In My Nursery Rhymes (vocal: Jimmy Rushing)
One O'Clock Jump
Boogie Woogie (vocal: Jimmy Rushing)
Doggin' Around

Above: Glenn Miller and his Orchestra at the Paradise Restaurant on Broadway where they opened on June 14th. Glenn and Tex Beneke are at the microphone. Bob Inman and Roddy Snow can be seen, far right, smoking pipes.

Blues In The Dark
Flat Foot Floogie
Harlem Shout

■ TUESDAY 14 JUNE 1938

RADIO LOGS

9:30PM WABC
BENNY GOODMAN
Camel Caravan, Boston
Let's Dance (theme)
Sweet Sue (great saxes; James; Freeman)
I've Got A Guy (vocal: Martha Tilton) (swell)
Don't Be That Way (Brown; Freeman)
You Leave Me Breathless (duet: Benny with Teddy Wilson playing harpsichord)
Make Believe
I Found A New Baby (BG Quartet)
I Hadn't Anyone Till You (BG Quartet, vocal: Martha Tilton)
Swingtime In The Rockies (very fast: Freeman; Elman's noisy trumpet)
Goodbye (theme)

■ WEDNESDAY 15 JUNE 1938

RADIO LOGS

11:30PM WABC
BENNY GOODMAN
Ritz Hotel Roof, Boston
You Leave Me Breathless (vocal: Martha Tilton)
Lullaby In Rhythm (Bud Freeman's tenor)
I Never Knew
Blue Room
My Gal Sal (BG Quartet)
Smiles
It's The Dreamer In Me (vocal: Martha Tilton) (Dave Tough's drumming)
Flat Foot Floogie (Bud Freeman)
Why'd You Make Me Love You? (vocal: Martha Tilton)
Can't We Be Friends?

■ MONDAY 20 JUNE 1938

RECORDING SESSION

DUKE ELLINGTON AND HIS ORCHESTRA
Recording session for Master Records in New York City.
Duke Ellington (p); Wallace Jones, Cootie Williams (t); Rex Stewart (c); Joe Nanton, Lawrence Brown (tb); Juan Tizol (vtb); Barney Bigard (cl); Johnny Hodges (cl/ss/as); Otto Hardwick (as/bsx); Harry Carney (cl/as/bar); Fred Guy (g); Billy Taylor (b); Sonny Greer (d); Ivie Anderson (voc)
Watermelon Man (vIA) / *A Gypsy Without A Song* / *The Stevedore's Serenade* / *La De Doody Do* (vIA)

■ WEDNESDAY 22 JUNE 1938

RECORDING SESSION

JOHNNY HODGES AND HIS ORCHESTRA
Recording session for Vocalion in New York City.
Cootie Williams (t); Lawrence Brown (tb); Johnny Hodges (ss/as); Harry Carney (bar); Duke Ellington (p); Billy Taylor (b); Sonny Greer (d); Mary McHugh (voc)
You Walked Out Of The Picture (vMM) / *Pyramid* / *Empty Ballroom Blues* / *Lost In Meditation* (vMM)

RADIO LOGS

11:30PM WABC
BENNY GOODMAN
Ritz Hotel Roof, Boston
Clap Hands, Here Comes Charlie (Bud Freeman's tenor)
Says My Heart (vocal: Martha Tilton)
You Leave Me Breathless (vocal: Martha Tilton)
Lullaby In Rhythm (Bud Freeman's tenor)
Saving Myself For You (vocal: Martha Tilton)
I Found A New Baby (BG Quartet)
I'll Always Be In Love With You
Don't Wake Up My Heart (vocal: Martha Tilton)
When You And I Were Young, Maggie (Dave Tough's drumming)
At A Perfume Counter

■ THURSDAY 23 JUNE 1938

RECORDING SESSION

BILLIE HOLIDAY & HER ORCHESTRA
Recording session for Columbia in NYC.
Charlie Shavers (t); Buster Bailey (cl); Ben Webster (ts); Claude Thornhill (p); Allan Reuss (g); John Kirby (b); Cozy Cole (d); Billie Holiday (v)
Havin' Myself A Time / *Says My Heart* / *I Wish I Had You* / *I'm Gonna Lock My Heart And Throw Away The Key*

ADRIAN ROLLINI QUINTET
Recording session for Decca in New York City.
Bobby Hackett (c); Frank Victor (g); Harry Clark (b); Buddy Rich (d); Adrian Rollini (vib/xyl); The Tune Twisters (voc)
Ten Easy Lessons (vTT) / *Small Fry* (vTT) / *I Wish I Had You* (vTT) / *On The Bumpy Road To Love* (vTT)

■ SATURDAY 25 JUNE 1938

12.00–1.30AM CBS Theater, NYC
SATURDAY NIGHT SWING SESSION 2nd Anniversary
LEITH STEVENS Conductor   PAUL DOUGLAS, MEL ALLEN Commentators
DUKE ELLINGTON ENSEMBLE Swing Group
SLIM AND SLAM Guitar and Bass   CONNEE BOSWELL Vocalist
BOBBY HACKETT'S JAZZ BAND with Gowans, Russell, Condon, Bowman, Caceres
LORETTA LEE Vocalist   CASPAR REARDON Swing Harpist
MODERNAIRES Vocal Swing Quartette
JACK AND CHARLIE TEAGARDEN Trombone and Trumpet Soloists
RAY SCOTT QUINTETTE Raymond Scott, Piano… Dave Wade, Trumpet… Dave Harris, Tenor Sax… Pete Pumiglio, Clarinet… Fred Whiting, Bass… Johnny Williams, Drums
JERRY COLONNA A Few Words on Swing
MILDRED BAILEY Vocalist   RED NORVO Xylophonist
BENNY CARTER Saxophone and Trumpet Soloist   LES LIEBER Hot Fife
MILLS BROTHERS Vocal Quartette   LOUIS ARMSTRONG Hot Trumpet
SATURDAY SWING CLUB BAND

■ TUESDAY 28 JUNE 1938

RADIO LOGS

10:00PM WABC
BENNY GOODMAN
Camel Caravan, Montreal, Canada
Benny Goodman's Swing School 1st Anniversary program.
Let's Dance (theme)
Changes
You Leave Me Breathless (vocal: Martha Tilton)
Lullaby In Rhythm (Bud Freeman)
Spring Is Here (vocal: Maxine Sullivan)
Canadian Capers (BG Quartet)
Fare-Thee-Well, Annie Laurie (vocal: Maxine Sullivan)
Clarinet Marmalade (Jimmy Mundy arrangement: Brown; James)
Goodbye (theme)

■ WEDNESDAY 29 JUNE 1938

RECORDING SESSION

MILDRED BAILEY & HER ORCHESTRA
Recording session for Vocalion in New York.
Jimmy Blake, Zeke Zarchy, Barney Zudecoff (t); Wes Hein (tb); Hank D'Amico (cl/as); Len Goldstein (as); Jerry Jerome, Charles Lamphere (ts); Bill Miller (p); Alan Hanlon (g); Pete Peterson (b); George Wettling (d); Red Norvo (xyl); Mildred Bailey (v)
So Help Me (vMB) / *Small Fry* (vMB) / *As Long As You Live You'll Be Dead If You Die* (vMB) / *Born To Swing* (vMB)

MAXINE SULLIVAN
Recording session for Victor in New York City.
Maxine Sullivan (voc); Claude Thornhill (p/ldr); Bobby Hackett (c); Jimmy Lytell, Paul Ricci (cl/as); Bernie Kaufman (as); Babe Russin (ts); Eddie Powell (fl); John Kirby (b); Buddy Rich (d)
Spring Is Here (vMS) / *Down The Old Ox Road* (vMS) / *St. Louis Blues* (vMS) / *L'Amour, Toujours L'Amour* (vMS)

■ THURSDAY 30 JUNE 1938

RECORDING SESSION

RED NORVO AND HIS ORCHESTRA
Recording session for Brunswick in New York City.
Red Norvo (xyl/ldr); Jack Owens, Jack Palmer, Barney Zudecoff (t); Andy Russo, Al George (tb); Hank D'Amico (cl); Frank Simeone (as); Maurice Kogan, George Berg (ts); Bill Miller (p); Alan Hanlon (g); Pete Peterson (b); George Wettling (d); Mildred Bailey (voc)
Put Your Heart In A Song (vMB) / *Wigwammin'* (vMB) / *The Sunny Side Of Things* (vMB) / *How Can I Thank You?* (vMB)

JULY 1938

Hotel New Yorker: **Henry Busse** (27–)

Apollo Theater: **Willie Bryant** (1–7); **Maxine Sullivan / Eddie Mallory** (8–14); **Edgar Hayes** (15–21); **Mills Brothers / Claude Hopkins** (29–)
Paramount Theater: **Xavier Cugat / Frances Langford** (–5); **Jimmy Dorsey** (13–19); **Gene Krupa** (27–)
Loew's State Theater: **Will Osborne / Nicholas Brothers** (14–20)

Onyx Club: **Stuff Smith**
Famous Door: **Count Basie** (11–)
Piccadilly Circus Bar: **Adrian Rollini Trio**

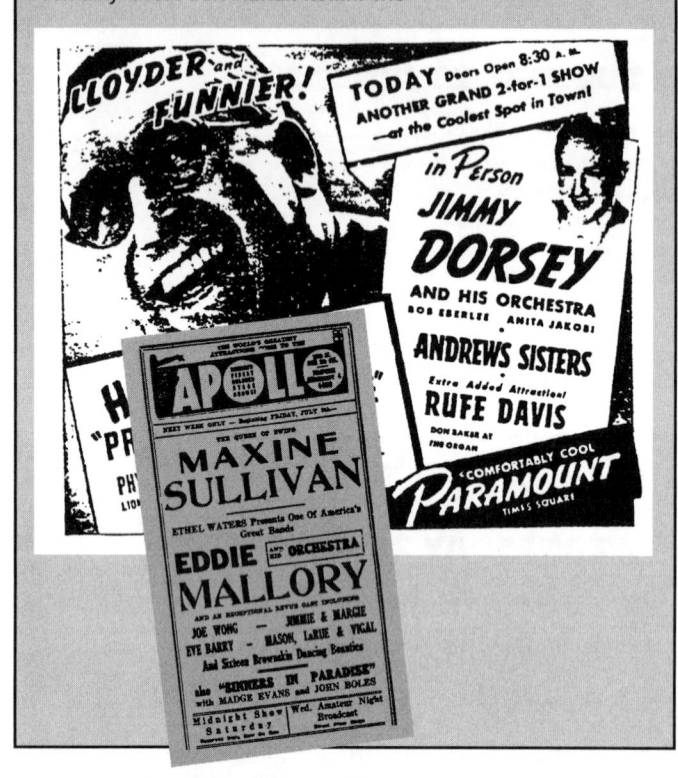

■ FRIDAY 1 JULY 1938
RECORDING SESSION

FATS WALLER & HIS RHYTHM
Recording session for Victor in New York City.
Herman Autrey (t); Gene Sedric (cl/ts); Fats Waller (p/voc); Albert Casey (g); Cedric Wallace (b); Slick Jones (d)
There's Honey On The Moon Tonight (vFW) / *If I Were You* (vFW) / *The Wide Open Places* (vFW) / *On The Bumpy Road To Love* (vFW) / *Fair And Square* (vFW) / *We, The People* (vFW)

■ SATURDAY 9 JULY 1938
RECORDING SESSION

TOMMY DORSEY AND HIS CLAMBAKE SEVEN
Recording session for Victor in Hollywood.
Tommy Dorsey (tb); Pee Wee Erwin (t); Johnny Mince (cl); Skeets Herfurt (ts); Howard Smith (p); Carmen Mastren (g); Gene Traxler (b); Graham Stevenson (d); Edythe Wright (voc)
My Own (vEW) / *A-Tisket, A-Tasket* (vEW)

■ MONDAY 11 JULY 1938
RECORDING SESSION

TOMMY DORSEY AND HIS ORCHESTRA
Recording session for Victor in Hollywood.
Tommy Dorsey (tb); Pee Wee Erwin, Lee Castle, Andy Ferretti (t); Les Jenkins, Earle Hagen (tb); Johnny Mince, Fred Stulce, Hymie Shertzer (cl/as); Skeets Herfurt (ts/voc); Deane Kincaide (ts); Howard Smith (p); Carmen Mastren (g); Gene Traxler (b); Maurice Purtill (d); Edythe Wright, Jack Leonard (voc)
Stop Beatin' Around The Mulberry Bush (vEW,SH) / *Lightly And Politely* / *I'll See You In My Dreams* (vJL) / *Panama* / *Washboard Blues*

TOMMY DORSEY AND HIS CLAMBAKE SEVEN
Recording session for Victor in Hollywood.
Tommy Dorsey (tb); Pee Wee Erwin (t); Johnny Mince (cl); Skeets Herfurt (ts); Howard Smith (p); Carmen Mastren (g); Gene Traxler (b); Maurice Purtill (d)
Chinatown, My Chinatown

■ TUESDAY 12 JULY 1938
RECORDING SESSION

BUD FREEMAN AND HIS GANG
Recording session for Commodore in New York City.
Bobby Hackett (c); Pee Wee Russell (cl); Dave Matthews (as); Bud Freeman (ts), Jess Stacy (p), Eddie Condon (g); Artie Shapiro (b); Dave Tough (d)
Tappin' The Commodore Till / *Memories Of You*
Marty Marsala (d) replaces Dave Tough:
Life Spears A Jitterbug / *What's The Use?*

■ FRIDAY 15 JULY 1938
RECORDING SESSION

TOMMY DORSEY AND HIS CLAMBAKE SEVEN
Recording session for Victor in Hollywood.
Tommy Dorsey (tb); Pee Wee Erwin (t); Johnny Mince (cl); Skeets Herfurt (ts); Howard Smith (p); Carmen Mastren (g); Gene Traxler (b); Maurice Purtill (d); Edythe Wright (voc)
The Sheik Of Araby / *You're As Pretty As A Picture* (vEW) / *As Long As You Live (You'll Be Dead If You Die)* (vEW)

WILL HUDSON AND HIS ORCHESTRA
Recording session for Brunswick in New York City.
Will Hudson (arr/ldr); Charles Mitchell, Rudy Novak, Joe Bauer (t); Edward Kolyer, Jack Andrews (tb); George Bohn, Gus Bivona (cl/as); Pete Brendel (as/bar); Charles Brosen (cl/ts); Mark Hyams (p); Bus Etri (g); Doc Goldberg (b); Billy Exiner (d); Jane Dover (voc)
The Night Is Filled With Music (vJD) / *Miracle At Midnight* (vJD) / *I Haven't Changed A Thing* (vJD) / *May I Have My Heart Back?* (vJD)

■ MONDAY 18 JULY 1938
RECORDING SESSION

GENE KRUPA AND HIS ORCHESTRA
Recording session for Brunswick in New York City.
Gene Krupa (d/ldr); Tom DiCarlo, Tom Gonsoulin, Dave Schultze (t); Charles McCamish, Bruce Squires, Chuck Evans (tb); Murray Williams, George Siravo (as); Vido Musso, Carl Biesecker (ts); Milton Raskin (p); Ray Biondi (g); Horace Rollins (b); Irene Day (voc)
Meet The Beat Of My Heart (vID) / *My Own* (vID) / *You're As Pretty As A Picture* (vID)

■ TUESDAY 19 JULY 1938

RECORDING SESSION

GENE KRUPA AND HIS ORCHESTRA
Recording session for Brunswick in New York City.
Gene Krupa (d/ldr); Tom DiCarlo, Tom Gonsoulin, Dave Schultze (t); Charles McCamish, Bruce Squires, Chuck Evans (tb); Murray Williams, George Siravo (as); Vido Musso, Carl Biesecker (ts); Milton Raskin (p); Ray Biondi (g); Horace Rollins (b); Leo Watson (voc)
Rhythm Jam / Nagasaki (vLW)

RADIO LOGS

9:30PM WABC
BENNY GOODMAN
Camel Caravan, Montreal, Canada
Benny Goodman has gone on a 3-week vacation to Europe so the band is led by Harry James. Jess Stacy and Dave Tough are also missing, replaced by Teddy Wilson & Lionel Hampton. Jo Jones drums on the Trio numbers.
Let's Dance (theme)
Down South Camp Meetin'
I Hadn't Anyone Till You (vocal: Martha Tilton)
Boo Hoo
Coquette (BG Trio) (Lionel Hampton, vibes; Teddy Wilson, piano; Jo Jones, drums)
Big John Special
You Leave Me Breathless (vocal: Martha Tilton)
Wrappin' It Up
Goodbye (theme)

■ THURSDAY 21 JULY 1938

RECORDING SESSION

LIONEL HAMPTON AND HIS ORCHESTRA
Recording session for Victor in New York City.
Lionel Hampton (vib/voc); Harry James (t); Benny Carter (cl/as); Dave Matthews (as); Herschel Evans, Babe Russin (ts); Billy Kyle (p); John Kirby (b); Jo Jones (d)
I'm In The Mood For Swing / Shoe Shiner's Drag / Any Time At All (vLH) */ Muskrat Ramble*

■ SUNDAY 24 JULY 1938

RECORDING SESSION

ART SHAW AND HIS ORCHESTRA
Recording session for Bluebird in New York City.
Art Shaw (cl/ldr); Chuck Peterson, John Best, Claude Bowen (t); George Arus, Ted Vesely, Harry Rogers (tb); Les Robinson, Hank Freeman (as); Tony Pastor (ts/voc); Ronnie Perry (ts); Les Burness (p); Al Avola (g); Sid Weiss (b); Cliff Leeman (d); Billie Holiday (voc)
Begin The Beguine / Indian Love Call (vTP&Band) */ Comin' On / Back Bay Shuffle / Any Old Time* (vBH) */ I Can't Believe That You're In Love With Me*

■ MONDAY 25 JULY 1938

RECORDING SESSION

TOMMY DORSEY AND HIS ORCHESTRA
Recording session for Victor in Hollywood.
Tommy Dorsey (tb); Pee Wee Erwin, Lee Castle, Andy Ferretti (t); Les Jenkins, Earle Hagen (tb); Johnny Mince, Fred Stulce, Hymie Shertzer (cl/as); Skeets Herfurt (ts/voc); Deane Kincaide (ts); Howard Smith (p); Carmen Mastren (g); Gene Traxler (b); Maurice Purtill (d); Three Esquires (voc)
Sweetheart Of Sigma Chi (v3E) */ Copenhagen / Symphony In Riffs*

■ TUESDAY 26 JULY 1938

RECORDING SESSION

RED NORVO AND HIS ORCHESTRA
Recording session for Brunswick in New York City.
Red Norvo (xyl/ldr); Jack Owens, Jack Palmer, Barney Zudecoff (t); Andy Russo, Al George (tb); Hank D'Amico (cl); Frank Simeone (as); Maurice Kogan, George Berg (ts); Bill Miller (p); Alan Hanlon (g); Pete Peterson (b); George Wettling (d); Mildred Bailey (voc)
Garden Of The Moon (vMB) */ Just You, Just Me*

RADIO LOGS

9:30PM WABC
BENNY GOODMAN
Camel Caravan, Montreal, Canada
Benny Goodman is still in Europe so the band is led by Harry James & Ben Bernie. Jess Stacy and Dave Tough are still missing, replaced by Teddy Wilson & Lionel Hampton. Jo Jones drums on the Trio numbers.
Let's Dance (theme)
Smiles
My Best Wishes (vocal: Martha Tilton)
Flat Foot Floogie (vocal: Ben Bernie)
Dinah (BG Quartet) (Ben Bernie, violin, vocals; Lionel Hampton, vibes; Teddy Wilson, piano; Jo Jones, drums)
Sweet Georgia Brown (BG Trio) (Lionel Hampton, vibes; Teddy Wilson, piano; Jo Jones, drums)
Lonesome Old Town (Ben Bernie's theme tune)
A-Tisket, A-Tasket (vocal: Martha Tilton & Ben Bernie)
Madhouse (Teddy Wilson plays Benny's clarinet solo on piano)
Goodbye (theme)

■ THURSDAY 28 JULY 1938

RECORDING SESSION

MILDRED BAILEY & HER ORCHESTRA
Recording session for Vocalion in New York.
Jack Owens, Jack Palmer, Barney Zudecoff (t); Andy Russo, Al George (tb); Hank D'Amico (cl); Frank Simeone (as); Maurice Kogan, George Berg (ts); Bill Miller (p); Alan Hanlon (g); Pete Peterson (b); George Wettling (d); Red Norvo (xyl); Mildred Bailey (v)
Now It Can Be Told (vMB) */ Jump, Jump's Here* (vMB) */ I Haven't Changed A Thing* (vMB) */ Love Is Where You Find It* (vMB) */ I Used To Be Color Blind* (vMB)

■ FRIDAY 29 JULY 1938

RECORDING SESSION

TEDDY WILSON ORCHESTRA
Recording session for Columbia in NYC.
Jonah Jones (t); Benny Carter (as); Ben Webster (ts); Teddy Wilson (p); John Kirby (b); Cozy Cole (d); Nan Wynn (voc)
Now It Can Be Told (vNW) */ Laugh And Call It Love* (vNW) */ On The Bumpy Road To Love* (vNW) */ A-Tisket, A-Tasket* (vNW)

AUGUST 1938

Hotel New Yorker: **Henry Busse**
Astor Roof: **Hal Kemp**

Apollo Theater: **Mills Brothers / Claude Hopkins** (–4); **Slim & Slam / Savoy Sultans** (5–11); **Sunset Royals** (12–18); **Hot Lips Page** (19–25); **Luis Russell** (26–)
Paramount Theater: **Chick Webb / Ella Fitzgerald** (10–16); **Phil Spitalny** (17–23)
Loew's State Theater: **Jimmie Lunceford** (18–24); **Don Redman** (25–31)
Strand Theater: **Ben Bernie** (24–30) First stage show at this theater

Onyx Club: **Stuff Smith**
Famous Door: **Count Basie**
Piccadilly Circus Bar: **Adrian Rollini Trio**

■ MONDAY 1 AUGUST 1938

RECORDING SESSION

JOHNNY HODGES AND HIS ORCHESTRA
Recording session for Vocalion in New York City.
Cootie Williams (t); Lawrence Brown (tb); Johnny Hodges (ss/as); Harry Carney (bar); Duke Ellington (p); Billy Taylor (b); Sonny Greer (d); Leon La Fell (voc)
A Blues Serenade (vLLF) / *Love In Swingtime* (vLLF) / *Swingin' In The Dell* / *Jitterbug's Lullaby*

■ TUESDAY 2 AUGUST 1938

RECORDING SESSION

COOTIE WILLIAMS & HIS RUGCUTTERS
Recording session for Vocalion in New York City.
Cootie Williams (t); Johnny Hodges (ss/as); Barney Bigard (cl/ts); Otto Hardwick (as/bsx); Harry Carney (bar); Duke Ellington (p); Billy Taylor (b); Sonny Greer (d); Scat Powell (voc)
Chasin' Chippies / *Blue Is The Evening* (vSP) / *Sharpie* (vSP) / *Swing Pan Alley*

■ THURSDAY 4 AUGUST 1938

RECORDING SESSION

DUKE ELLINGTON AND HIS ORCHESTRA
Recording session for Master Records in New York City.
Duke Ellington (p); Wallace Jones; Cootie Williams (t); Rex Stewart (c); Joe Nanton, Lawrence Brown (tb); Juan Tizol (vtb); Barney Bigard (cl); Johnny Hodges (cl/ss/as); Otto Hardwick (as/bsx); Harry Carney (cl/as/bar); Fred Guy (g); Billy Taylor (b); Sonny Greer (d); Scat Powell (voc)
A Blues Serenade / *Love In Swingtime* (vSP) / *Please Forgive Me*

BEN POLLACK AND HIS ORCHESTRA
Recording session for Decca in Los Angeles.
Ben Pollack (ldr); Don Anderson, George Thow, Clyde Hurley (t); Earle Hagen (tb); Opie Cates, Peyton Legare (as); George Hill, Mort Friedman (ts); Al Beller (vln); Bob Laine (p); Carroll Thompson (g); Jim Lynch (b); Graham Stevenson (d); Paula Gayle (voc)
Meet The Beat Of My Heart (vPG) / *Sing A Song Of Sixpence* (vPG) / *What Are You Doing Tonight?* (vPG) / *Naturally* (vPG) / *So Unexpectedly* (vPG) / *As Long As I Live* (vPG)

■ TUESDAY 9 AUGUST 1938

RECORDING SESSION

DUKE ELLINGTON AND HIS ORCHESTRA
Recording session for Master Records in New York City.
Duke Ellington (p); Wallace Jones, Cootie Williams (t); Rex Stewart (c); Joe Nanton, Lawrence Brown (tb); Juan Tizol (vtb); Barney Bigard (cl); Johnny Hodges (cl/ss/as); Otto Hardwick (as/bsx); Harry Carney (cl/as/bar); Fred Guy (g); Billy Taylor (b); Sonny Greer (d)
Lambeth Walk / *Prelude To A Kiss* / *Hip Chic* / *Buffet Flat*

RADIO LOGS

9:30pm WABC
BENNY GOODMAN
Camel Caravan, Manhattan Beach, NY
Benny Goodman, Jess Stacy and Dave Tough are back in the band.
Let's Dance (theme)
You Go To My Head (vocal: Martha Tilton)
Lullaby In Rhythm (Benny's clarinet; Bud Freeman's tenor)
Now It Can Be Told (BG Trio) (Ben Bernie, violin, vocals; Lionel Hampton, vibes; Teddy Wilson, piano; Jo Jones, drums)
Roll 'Em
A-Tisket, A-Tasket (vocal: Martha Tilton & Benny Goodman)
Honeysuckle Rose (BG Quartet) (Lionel Hampton, vibes; Teddy Wilson, piano; Jo Jones, drums)
Blue Interlude (vocal: Martha Tilton)
I Want To Be Happy
Goodbye (theme)

■ WEDNESDAY 10 AUGUST 1938

RECORDING SESSION

GENE KRUPA AND HIS ORCHESTRA
Recording session for Brunswick in New York City.
Gene Krupa (d/ldr); Tom DiCarlo, Tom Gonsoulin, Dave Schultze (t); Charles McCamish, Bruce Squires, Chuck Evans (tb); Murray Williams, George Siravo (as); Vido Musso, Carl Biesecker (ts); Milton Raskin (p); Ray Biondi (g); Horace Rollins (b); Irene Day, Leo Watson (voc)
Any Time At All (vID) / *Tutti Frutti* (vLW)

■ THURSDAY 11 AUGUST 1938

RADIO LOGS

11:30PM WABC
BENNY GOODMAN
Manhattan Beach, N.Y.
Makin' Whoopee
I've Got A Date With A Dream (vocal: Martha Tilton)
Stop Beating Around The Mulberry Bush
Blue Skies
You Go To My Head (vocal: Martha Tilton)
Make Believe
Swingtime In The Rockies (Bud Freeman)
Blue Interlude (vocal: Martha Tilton) (Jess Stacy's piano)
Three Little Words (Freeman; Vernon Brown)
What Goes On Here In My Heart? (vocal: Martha Tilton)

■ MONDAY 15 AUGUST 1938

RECORDING SESSION

GLEN GRAY AND THE CASA LOMA ORCHESTRA
Recording session for Decca in Los Angeles.
Glen Gray (as/dir); Sonny Dunham, Grady Watts, Frank Zullo (t); Pee Wee Hunt (tb/voc); Billy Rauch, Murray McEachern (tb); Clarence Hutchenrider (cl/as), Kenny Sargent (as/voc); Art Ralston (as/o/bsn); Danny d'Andrea (as); Pat Davis (cl/ts/fl); Joe Hall (p); Jack Blanchette (g); Stanley Dennis (b); Tony Briglia (d)
Yours, All Yours (vPWH) / *You Never Know* (vKS) / *At Long Last Love* (vKS) / *Hoboken Bucket*

■ TUESDAY 16 AUGUST 1938

RADIO LOGS

9:30PM WABC
BENNY GOODMAN
Camel Caravan, ??
Let's Dance (theme)
Down South Camp Meetin'
I Let A Song Go Out Of My Heart (vocal: Martha Tilton)
Don't Be That Way
'S Wonderful
My Walking Stick (vocal: Martha Tilton)
Runnin' Wild (BG Quartet)
A Pocket Full Of Dreams (vocal: Martha Tilton)
Three Little Words
Goodbye (theme)

■ WEDNESDAY 17 AUGUST 1938

RECORDING SESSION

CHICK WEBB ORCHESTRA
Recording session for Decca in New York City.
Ella Fitzgerald (voc); Mario Bauza, Taft Jordan, Bobby Stark (t); Sandy Williams, Nat Story, George Matthews (tb); Hilton Jefferson (as); Garvin Bushell (cl/as); Ted McRae (ts); Wayman Carver (ts/fl); Tommy Fulford (p); Bobby Johnson (g); Beverly Peer (b); Chick Webb (d)
Wacky Dust (vEF) / *Gotta Pebble In My Shoe* (vEF) / *I Can't Stop Loving You* (vEF) / *Ella* (vEF, TJ)

TOMMY DORSEY AND HIS ORCHESTRA
Recording session for Victor in Chicago.
Tommy Dorsey (tb); Charlie Spivak, Lee Castle, Yank Lawson (t); Les Jenkins, Buddy Morrow (tb); Johnny Mince, Fred Stulce, Hymie Shertzer (cl/as); Skeets Herfurt (ts/voc); Deane Kincaide (ts); Howard Smith (p); Carmen Mastren (g); Gene Traxler (b); Maurice Purtill (d); Edythe Wright (voc)
Ya Got Me (vEW) / *There's No Place Like Your Arms* (vEW)

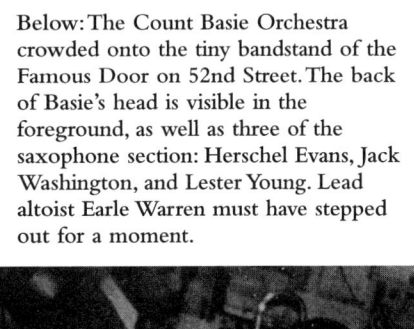

Below: The Count Basie Orchestra crowded onto the tiny bandstand of the Famous Door on 52nd Street. The back of Basie's head is visible in the foreground, as well as three of the saxophone section: Herschel Evans, Jack Washington, and Lester Young. Lead altoist Earle Warren must have stepped out for a moment.

■ THURSDAY 18 AUGUST 1938

RECORDING SESSION

CHICK WEBB ORCHESTRA
Recording session for Decca in New York City.
Ella Fitzgerald (voc); Mario Bauza, Taft Jordan, Bobby Stark (t); Sandy Williams, Nat Story, George Matthews (tb); Hilton Jefferson (as); Garvin Bushell (cl/as); Ted McRae (ts); Wayman Carver (ts/fl); Tommy Fulford (p); Bobby Johnson (g); Beverly Peer (b); Chick Webb (d)
I Let A Tear Fall In The River (vEF) / *Who Ya Hunchin'?*

ELLA FITZGERALD AND HER SAVOY EIGHT
Recording session for Decca in New York City.
Ella Fitzgerald (voc); Taft Jordan (t); Sandy Williams (tb); Hilton Jefferson (as); Teddy McRae (ts/bar); Tommy Fulford (p); Bobby Johnson (g); Beverly Peer (b); Chick Webb (d)
Strictly From Dixie / *Woe Is Me*

■ SATURDAY 20 AUGUST 1938

RADIO LOGS

5:30PM WABC
BENNY GOODMAN
Steel Pier, Atlantic City, N.J.
A special broadcast to Europe.
I Found A New Baby
I Hadn't Anyone Till You (vocal: Martha Tilton)
Make Believe
Don't Be That Way (Bud Freeman; Vernon Brown)
More Than You Know (BG Trio)
A-Tisket, A-Tasket (vocal: Martha Tilton & Benny Goodman)
Blue Interlude (vocal: Martha Tilton) (written by Benny Carter)
I'm A Ding Dong Daddy (From Dumas) (BG Quartet)
One O'Clock Jump (Jess Stacy; Freeman; Dave Tough; Brown)

BRONXVILLE HIGH SCHOOL—CLASS OF 1939

Bob Inman  — Carolyn Bade  — Hugh Pastoriza  — Dick Morningstar  — Nancy Long

Don Mortimer  — Barbara Fick  — Maurine Van Meter  — Harold Johnson  — David Faulkner

At Kelly's Stable, 52nd Street: Bob Inman (front left), Dick Morningstar, George Fick (centre), Don Mortimer (far right)

AFTERWORD by BOB INMAN

The scrapbooks were discontinued in the summer of 1938. My life found me with more important things to keep me busy. My father, Dr. Samuel Guy Inman, had been invited as guest professor at the University of Mexico. He decided to take me and my brother and sister, with my mother, to live in the great city from July 4, 1938 to August 26. So it was goodbye to hearing much jazz on the radio. I became ill with a high fever and lost 15 pounds which caused concern for me making the Bronxville High School varsity football team in September. I must say that I rapidly regained my weight and became co-captain of Bronxville's undefeated football team.

On the way home, just south of Monterrey, Mexico, a car cut our Chevy car off the road. As there were many wild jungle plants to slow down our impact, nobody was hurt. Mexico had a law that any car driven into Mexico had to be driven back to the United States, so we drove our mangled car, with two missing windows, all the way back to New York.

After graduating from Bronxville in 1939 I attended the very small Hiram Disciple college, near Cleveland, Ohio, from September 1939 until May 1941. Hiram was an excellent college, but I missed the swinging atmosphere of New York. The only jazz I can remember during this period was Max Kaminsky's Band and the Benny Goodman Orchestra at Cleveland's Trianon Ballroom.

Shortly after I transferred to Maryland University near Washington, D.C., war was declared against Japan in December 1941. I enlisted in the Army Air Corps which wanted us to finish college before becoming Aviation Cadets for pilot training. One wild time we had in 1942 was when we drove to see Benny Goodman's Band at the Mayflower Hotel in Washington. We had much fun trying to pick up vocalist Peggy Lee. She insisted on returning to the band bus instead of allowing us to drive her to her next band engagement.

The Air Corps called us to duty just before our scheduled graduation. My first base was Miami Beach where they tried to get rid of all weak 'cry-babies'. We spent many hours patroling the beach with machine guns, watching for German mini-submarines. Over the next 13 months I trained and flew several hundred hours, only to be 'washed out' after several accidents.

The Air Corps decided it did not need any more pilots, navigators, bombadiers or gunners, so they made me a crew member flying on Air Transport Command DC-3s. I was stationed at Orly Field in Paris and I was very fortunate to fly all over Europe. I remember waiting for Glenn Miller to land in December, 1944. We all concluded that Miller was 'crazy' to take-off from England in such terrible weather.

We heard some excellent jazz in Paris, including the Glenn Miller Band led by Ray McKinley. We saw Stephane Grappelli (Django Reinhardt was in London) at a ritzy Montmartre nightclub where naked women came down from the ceiling riding fake horses. The French franc was so worthless that we used them to light our cigarettes.

I was discharged from the Air Corps in January, 1946. Leaving my sweet French girl friend in Paris, I returned to the jazz clubs and theaters of New York.

Aaronson, Irving 37,39–40,53
Abba Dabba 285
Abadias 243,253
A Blues Serenade 360
A Brown Bird Singing 309,325
A Call To Arms 100,103
Achin' Hearted Blues 257
A Cigarette And A Silhouette 350
A Country Girl 29
Across The Field 76
Adam's Apple 164
Adams, Arnold 147,207,235–237,241,
  243–244,260
'A Day At The Races' [movie] 189
Addison, Bernard 105,188,288
Adios, Muchachos 294
Ad Lib 47
Admiration 189,196,322
A Fine Romance 38–39,42,49,51,56,
  60,64–66,72,88,107
A Foggy Day 280,288,291,302,317,
  323
Afraid To Dream 205,214,216,219–222,
  225,242,244,251–252,254,274–275,
  280
African Lullaby 250
After All 210
After Dark 24
After Dinner Speech 348
Afterglow 27,30–31,33,35,37,40,44,46,
  50,57,59,65
After Last Night With You 128
Afternoon In Africa 259,322
After Sundown 58,196
After The Ball Is Over 213
'After The Thin Man' [movie] 109
After You 192,213,267,269–270,272,
  274,278,281,285,295,326,331,336
After You've Gone 3,5,8–9,11,17,29,42,
  44–45,50,66,68,70,72–73,76,79,
  88–89,91,107,117,120,129–130,151,
  186,195,202,218,233,236,243,246,
  251,254,279,283,285,297–298,309,
  320,326,340,345–346,348,355
A Gold Mine In The Sky 265,267
A Good Man Is Hard To Find 43,49,
  273,294
A Gypsy Without A Song 356
A Handful Of Keys 26,90,172,191,204,
  216,220,248,254,277
Ah, But Is It Love? 104
A Heart Full Of Rhythm 337
A High Hat, A Piccolo, And A Cane 58,
  60,70,72,74,81,92
A Hopeless Love Affair 269
Ah, Sweet Mystery Of Life 161
Ah-Woo! Ah-Woo! To You 27
Ain'tcha 18
Ain't-cha Glad 104
Ain't Misbehavin' 15,21,26,32,38,58,
  65,95,97,100,116,126,187,195,200,
  220,224–225,233,254,297,301,327
Ain't Nobody's Business What I Do 31
Ain't She Sweet 35,37,47
Alabama Barbecue 62
Alabama Bound 185
Alabama Home 159,186
Alabamy Home 238,299,336

Alcott, Mary 46
A Lesson In C 345
Alexander, Darelle 42,62
Alexander, Meyer 210,213,219,223,
  231,235,241,246,253
Alexander's Ragtime Band 3–5,9,27,30,
  36,38,60–61,64,67,74,76,104–105,
  108,111,116,119,127–128,135,138,
  151–152,163,170,183,200,203,205,
  218,232–233,240,245,252,254,259,
  279,308,317,328,332,353
Alexander, Willard 10
Alexy, Bob 245,251
Algiers Stomp 34,81,296
Alkenza 64
Alibi Baby 153,174,203,207,244
Alice Blue Gown 255,301,323
A Little Bit Later On 13,17,23,31,35,
  87,115,233
A Little White Lighthouse 295,311
Allah's Holiday 328,331
All Alone 171
All By Myself 252,256
All Dark People Are Light On Their Feet
  144,169,178
*All Dressed Up Tonight And No Place To
  Go* 40,47
Allegheny Al 207,219,222,231,239
Allen, Betty 286
Allen, Bob 30,37,39,45,51,88
Allen, Charlie 117,231
Allen, Fred 114
Allen, Henry 'Red' 12,16,20,26,30,
  34,36,49,52,69–70,73,80–81,96,116,
  121,128,141,155–156,163,189,203,
  226,253,296,311,327,331,337
Allen, Melvin 132,135,145,149,164,
  169,183–185,187,202,204,216,238,
  250,260,267,292–293,298,309,357
Allen, Moses 52–53,69,74,111,188,
  190,205,280,308,346
Allen, Sam 12,17,76,138,151,159,161,
  169,173,309–310
Allen, Terry 323–324,327,331–332,
  335,346–347
All God's Chillun Got Rhythm 171,
  173–174,186,189,192,194,200–203,
  205,211,217,221,223–224,231,234,
  239,242,255–256,263–264,266,269
Alligator Crawl 129,261,293
All I Want 263
All My Life 9,13–15,17,19,22,30,35,
  41,43,48–49,57,59,61
All Of Me 124,205,286,288,299
All Over Nothing At All 178,223,232,
  244
All Right, All Right 43
All's Fair In Love And War 83,124
All The Jive Is Gone 7,244
All The World Is Oaksie-Doaksie 162
All Through The Night 351
All You Want To Do Is Dance 192,201,
  213
Alone 3,5
Alone Together 57
A Lonely Gondolier 39
Alone With You 165
A Lot Of Stuff 246,255

A Love Song Of Long Ago 163
Alston, Ovie 86,94
Alsop, William 346
Alvin, Danny 115,151,158,177–178,
  197,210,226–227,239,242,244,265,
  311,353
Alvis, Hayes 6,28,31,93,128,130,132,
  148,162,172,175,186–187,189,202,
  205,264,312,320,324,332,336,355
Always 3–4,26–27,30,32–33,35,37,
  43–45,52,54,82,88,96,100,114,121,
  124,140,145,154,160,183,194,209,
  214,222,261,272,292,297,299,303,
  309,312,336,344,349
Always And Always 318,323,325,331,
  333,335–337,340–341,346,349
Always With You 47
Amaral, Frank 18,23,167
Ambassador Hotel, LA 97
A Mellow Bit Of Rhythm 218,231,240,
  270,339
A Melody From The Sky 8,13
America Dances 40,52,58
A Message From The Man In The Moon
  174,198,202,207,211,221,225,
  231–232,235,239
Am I Asking Too Much? 34,36,38,45
Am I Blue? 157,169,175,184,187,211,
  225,253,262,276
Am I Dreaming? 207,220,236
Am I In Another World? 289,306
Am I In Love? 223,235,241,256,264,
  267,283
Am I Intruding? 92,110
Am I Wasting My Time? 166
Among My Souvenirs 270
An Apple A Day 82,87,90,93,96,103,
  107,111,116,118,124–125,151
Anderson, Bernard 351
Anderson, Don 348,360
Anderson, Edward 'Andy' 102
Anderson, Ivie 6,17–20,22,28,33,56,
  93,98,128,132,134,142,144–146,148,
  159,162,165–166,171–173,175,177,
  186,189,192,202,264,313,320,332,
  336,338,343–344,346,354,356
Anderson, Stuart 79,114,118,129,209,
  245,251
Andrews, Jack 179,201,237,286,300,
  322,325,345,355,358
Andrews, Lavern 73
Andrews Sisters 278,285,297,299
And So Do I 86
And They Said It Wouldn't Last 43
A New Sun In The Sky 57
Angle, Vic 341
Angry 90,96,100,118,166
Annie Laurie 211,224,255,280,284,
  287,311,324–325,327,335
Announcer's Blues 4,293
An Old Flame Never Dies 243,246,
  253,269,272,278,293
An Old Straw Hat 341
Another Perfect Night Is Ending 72,88
Answer 166
Antler's Club, Kansas City, Mo 234,
  236,243–244,246,251,255
Antonelli, Tony 171

Any Old Time 359
Any Old Time At All 351
Any Time At All 359–360
Anything But Love 95
Anything Goes 36,40,114,126
Anytime, Anyday, Anywhere 137,165,
  184,210,214,218,231,241
A Perfect Lover 84
A Pocket Full Of Dreams 361
Apollo Theater, NYC 2,5,7,12,16,23,
  25,27,32,53–54,66,76,78,83,86,91,
  99,106,111,114,117,124,126–127,
  129–130,144,159,166–167,184,189,
  197,201,214,222,236,247,250,254,
  260,264–266,268,277–279,292,295,
  307–308,312,317,320–321,324,326,
  332,334–336,344,346,350,354–355,
  358,360
A Porter's Love Song To A Chambermaid
  47,103,202,255,265,267
Apple Blossom Time 313
A Pretty Girl Is Like A Melody 25,34,
  43–44
April In Paris 142,171
Aragon Ballroom, Chicago 183
Arbello, Fernando 10,13,20,33,55,
  58–59,162,173,193
Arcadia Ballroom, Philadelphia 88,97,
  115,332,335,338
Archey, James 155–156,239
A Rendezvous With A Dream 33,55
A Rendezvous With You 37
Are You In Love With Me Again? 20
Are You My Love? 40
A Rhyme For Love 85
Aristocrat Of Harlem 70
Arkansas Blues 32
Arkansas Traveler 269,335,351
Arkansas Travelers 125
Arlen, Harold 58,297
Armstrong, Lil 318,320
Armstrong, Louis 2,5,7,16,21,23,53,
  89,112,120,122,135,139,144,
  155–156,162,168,184,195,203,228,
  252,273,277,289,293,296,311,313,
  327,331,334,336–337,354,357
Arnheim, Gus 92,95,97,99,123,
  165–166,171,174,184–185,196,
  201–203,207,211,218,220,222,234
Arnold, Harold 'Specs' 118,141,
  162–163,189,195
Aronson, Stanley 353
Arthur, Zinn 212,219–220,231–232,
  241,245
'Artists And Models' [movie] 228
Arus, George 171,174,211,214,223,
  259,273,306,359
A Sailboat In The Moonlight 166–167,
  175,188,196,198,215,218,223,231,
  234–235,239,241,243–244,313
A Serenade To The Stars 321,327
A Session Of Jam 146
Ask Me 59
A Simple Melody 271
(A Sky Of Blue And You) And So Forth
  355
As Long As I Live 186,360
As Long As You Live You'll Be Dead If

INDEX

You Die 357–358
As Long As You've Got Your Health 158, 171
A Solid Sender 32
Astaire, Fred 217,219,234,237, 242
A Star Fell Out Of Heaven 33,35,38, 42,44,46,50,52,54,56–61,64–65,67, 70,72,83
A Stolen Melody 236
A Stone's Throw From Heaven 267
A Strange Loneliness 269,273
A Study In Brown 90,114–115,121, 149,151,157,159,161,196,202–203, 215,218,221,223,236–237,239, 244–245,247–248,251–252,255,259, 263,267,270,272,276,279,283,294, 297,332
A Swingy Little Rhythm 56
At A Fair With Rex (Exposition Swing?) 22,33
At A Little Country Tavern 281,285, 289
At A Perfume Counter 340,351,357
A Thousand Dreams Of You 85,101,118
A-Tisket, A-Tasket 350,358–360,362
At Long Last Love 361
Atkins, Jack 233,246
At Sundown 79,122,346
At The Clambake Carnival 343
At The Codfish Ball 13,18,22
At The Jazz Band Ball 151,161, 163–164,167,170,183,207,238,269, 283,326,328,338
At The Rugcutters' Ball 17
At Your Beck And Call 322,340,349
Augustine, Johnny 36,40,46,52,55,73, 75,84,110
Auld, George 144,171–172,175,178, 186,189,194–196,198,202,204,208, 210–211,213,216,219,224–225,227, 231–232,234–236,239,244,248,252, 269,272,284,294,301,321,335, 340–341,348,353,355
Auld Lang Syne 306
Aunt Hagar's Blues 96,271
Austin, Johnny 352–353
Austin, William 267
Autrey, Herman 5,13,24–25,32,56,85, 94,123,134,148,186,253,269,339, 346,358
Avalon 98,110,178,183,200,207,220, 234,236,244,246,249,255,262,269, 271,279–280,294,301,323,326,337, 349
Avalon Town 16
Avola, Al 171,174,214,223,259,273, 306,359
A Waltz Dream 52
Away From Me 252
A Woman Can Change Her Mind 70
A Woman's Got A Right To Change Her Mind 90
Aw, Shucks! 76
Ayalla, Frank 89–90
Azure 162,165–166,171–173, 265, 320,328,336,338–339,343,348,350
Baby Girl 197,237
Baby, I Want You 260

Baby, Keep From My Heart 244
Baby, Won't You Marry Me? 254,256
Baby, Won't You Please Come Home? 251
Bach Goes To Town 255
Bach Invention 73
Bach Up To Me 25
Back Bay Shuffle 359
Back Home Again In Indiana 11,28–29, 45,50,88,100–101,137,143,186,210, 244,252,289,302,306,309
Back In Your Arms 131,219,242,247
Back In Your Own Backyard 119,137, 311,338
Back Room Romp 202,205,313
Bacon, Louis 155–156,337
Bacon, Trevor 264,334
Bade, Carolyn 112,185,223,249,253, 269–272,275–277,280,283,286,288, 362
Bailey, Buster 10,13,18,20,33,41,70, 119,127–128,137,144,151,159,161, 165,170,184,210,224,230,233, 256–257,259,272,274,287,306–307, 309,313,322,324–326,328,332, 337–338,342,357
Bailey, Mildred 11,47,72,77,98–99, 101–106,108–109,113,116–118, 126–127,130,135,137,155,169,179, 196,200,202–206,220–223,238,249, 253–256,263–265,267,274,280,283, 300,311,318,320,322–324,327,329, 331–333,335–336,339–340,342–343, 347–348,350–351,354,357,359
Baker, Abe 206
Baker, Harold 65,179,312,324,332, 336,346
Baker, Jerry 119
Baker, M. S. 296
Ballad In Blue 110
Ballard, Red 3,4,10,14,22–23,26,37, 44,67,75,88,96,105,107,128,135, 138–139,143,147,157,160,176,183, 189,204–205,239,253,274–276,283, 292–293,325,331,337
Balloonacy 70,150,263
Bamba 39
Bandana Days 152
Banks, Billy 8,19,153
Baptist Moan 266
Baranco, Wilbert 99
Barbarin, Paul 155,163,189,195,337
Barber, Charlie 216
Barbour, Dave 3,6,47,72,77,101,137, 284
Barcarolle 186,204,219,222,230,232, 242,245,267
Bard, Lola 328
Barefield, Eddie 111,117,235,353
Bargy, Roy 4–5,15,26,236,242,254
Barker, Danny 69,80,96,118,128,141, 162–163,189,253,255,295,321,343
Barnard, Vi 109
Barnes, Howard 131
Barnes Tavern, Nr Pelham, N.Y. 212, 215
Barnet, Charlie 18,22–23,29–31,33, 35–36,38–39,41,43–44,48,50,52,

54–55,57,64,78,104,115,167, 175–176,188–189,191,196,223,227, 230,232,238–239,309
Barrelhouse 70
Barrie, Clyde 43
Barry, Paul 151
Bartha, Alex 30,60,64,201,218,240, 254
Baruch, André 130,324
Bascomb, Paul 29,56,151,158,162, 165,232,332
Bascomb, Wilbur 29,56,158,162,232, 332
Basie, Count 76–78,80,83,89,97–98, 102,104,109–110,118,124,126,135, 137,155–157,184,191–195,197,202, 204–205,221,231,233–235,237, 239–241,243,245,248–249,253,255, 261–262,266,271,274,278–279,307, 314,324,328,332–337,340,350, 354–355,358,360,361
Basin Street Blues 3,15,17,22,30,36, 45,64,81,83,87,89–90,95–96,98, 100,103,108,112,115,129,144,172, 175,179,186,196,200,203,209–210, 212–213,221,225,236,240,244,254, 257,265,280,284,298,309,318,340
Bassman, George 122
Bauduc, Ray 4,8,9,13,25–26,42–43, 68,117,125–126,131,133,146,148, 151–152,157,159–161,163–164,166, 170,205,207–208,210,215,218,224, 230,269,274,276–277,279–284,311, 313,316–319,323–325,327,332–333, 337–338,340
Bauer, David 151
Bauer, Joe 10,13,25,72,80,82,101,108, 112,121,130,134,136,143,153,166, 171,178,186,207,210,213,230,286, 300,322,325,345,355, 358
Bauza, Mario 12,23,74,105,138, 277–279,295,299,350,355,361–362
Be A Good Sport 284,288
Beale Street Blues 79,83,124,138, 143–144,158,178,207,223,230, 235,257,262,272–273,279,284, 321, 323,331–332,335
Bean, Ralph 134
Bearcat Shuffle 8
Bear Down 297,301
Beason, Bill 12,17,138,159,173,346
Beat It Out 253
Beat To The Socks 315
Beautiful Lady In Blue 19
Beavers, Louise 114
Because I Love You 159,171
Because You're You 29,190
Bechet, Sidney 8,152–153,160,179, 317,327
Beebe 55,291,339
Beggar's Blues 322
Begin The Beguine 52,64,359
Beiderbecke, Bix 230,238,241,273, 276,295,298
Beigel, Les 185
Bei Mir Bist Du Schoen 295,299, 301–303,306–308,313,316–317,320, 323,325–326,328,334–335

Belaire, Ray 218
Belasco, Leon 73
Beller, Al 243,246,348,360
Belles Of Harlem 64,101
Bellizia, Frank 162
Ben Bernie Program, NYC [radio] 80
Beneke, Tex 352–353,356
Ben Marden's Riviera, N.J. 37,39–40, 53
Bennett, Bobby 6,8,18,27,44,66,165, 235,353
Bennett, Constance 195
Bennett, Jack 247,249
Bennett, June 186,221
Bennett, Mark 25,117,164
Benny, Jack 228
Berg, George 350,357,359
Berger, Manny 109,121
Bergman, Eddie 140,160
Berigan, Bunny 3,5–7,12–13,16,21, 25,28,32,36,39–40,42,45–46,49–50, 52,54–55,58,65–66,68,71,73, 75–76,81–82,84,87,90,93,95,99,101, 103,106,108–110,112–113,115–117, 119,121,125,129–130,135,143–144, 156–157,161,163–164,166–167,169, 171–172,175,177–178,183–187,189, 192,194–202,204,208,210–211,213, 216–217,219–221,224–227,231–236, 239,244,248–249,252,261,269–270, 272,274,278,284,292,294,296, 299–301,321,325,332,335,338, 340–341,345,347–348,350,353,355
Berlin, Irving 27–28,100,111,124, 127,140,216,218,256,272
Bernardi, Noni 9,13,25–26,42,117, 348
Bernhardt, Clyde 354
Bernie, Al 89
Bernie, Ben 80,359–360
Bernstein, Artie 65,170,188,243
Berry Brothers 63
Berry, Cappy 55
Berry, Chu 6,10,13,18,20,27,33,41, 52,58–60,69–70,79,119,127,137,165, 188,200,203,207,210,225,230, 233–234,241,246,255,262–263,266, 269,274,279,281,285,292–293,295, 299,301–302,310–311,317,321,328, 343
Berry, Emmett 119,127,137,200,236, 263,276,353
Berry, Howard 99
Berton, Vic 142
Bessie Couldn't Help It 284
Best, John 171,174,214,223,259,273, 306,359
Better Get Off Your High Horse 86,115
Better Luck Next Time 218
Between The Devil And The Deep Blue Sea 15,31,36–37,41,43,46,52,54,61, 69,79,81,89,93,95,117,121,124,128, 131,140,145,151,157,160,163,166, 174,182,209–211,215,220,232,240, 250–251,254,256,267,270,280,294, 308,318,327,336,347
Beverly Wilshire Hotel, LA 97
Bewildered 308,311,316,324–325,340

Be With Us 312
Biagini, Henry 135,165,171,175,178
Biamonte, Louis 35
Biesecker, Carl 137,186,211,213–214, 289,297,346–347,350,354,358–360
Biettel, Will 239
Big Apple Calls (When My Dreamboat Comes Home) 284
Bigard, Barney 6,28,31,33,92–93,128, 132,134,144–146,148,159,162–163, 165–166,171–177,186–189,192,238, 262,264,276,312–313,316–317,322, 324,332,336,338,344–346,348,354, 356,360
Big Boy Blue 105,108–109,117,121, 123–124,138,140,149,157,161–162, 165,175,218,233,235,243–244,251, 261,307
'Big Broadcast of 1937' [movie] 64
Big Chief De Sota 24,26,32,52,55–56, 58–59,65,67,84,88,98,100,102,162, 173,243
Big Foot Jump 340
Big John Special 4,18,22,28,31,34,43, 47,55–57,81,84,88,113,124,126,143, 145,158,163,165–166,172,174,177, 183,186,195,216,233,241,243,245, 248,251,256,262–263,267,275,277, 283,285–286,289,295,299,312,321, 324,328,334,339,348,359
Bill 308
Bill Bailey 46
Billie's Blues 28
Billings, Bernie 328
Binyon, Larry 139
Biondi, Ray 151,158,160,177,197, 226–227,242,300,341,346–347,350, 354,358–360
Bird Man Blues 333
Birmingham Breakdown 159
Bishop, Joe 76–77,83,86,95–96,118, 121,161–162,205,208,231,267–268, 276,286,328,346,355
Bishop, Wallace 117,231
Bismarck Hotel, Chicago 97
Bivona, Gus 130–131,179,201,219, 224–225,237,242,286,300,322,325, 345,355,358
Biwangi 39
Black And Blue 94,128
Black And Tan Fantasy 30,61,65,155, 273,285
Black Beauty 132
Black Bottom 167,169,175,194,196, 202,216,270,301,335
Black Bottom Stomp 145
Black Butterfly 93,144,159
Blackhawk Restaurant, Chicago 60, 69,97–99,101–106,109–110,113, 116–118,126–127,130,145,163,169, 265
Black Raspberry Jam 25
Blackstick 327
Blackstone Hotel, Chicago 97
Blair, Lee 155
Blake, Charlie 79,86,88,209,245,251
Blake, Jerry 9,127,137,200,203,263, 269,276

Blake, Jimmy 82,92,130–131,179, 201,215,219,224,237,240,242,311, 318,320,327,330–332,339–340,342, 348,351,357
Blanchette, Jack 5,25,112,115, 120–121,128,143,201,214,279,285, 292,295,298,301,317,324,326,332, 361
Blazing The Trail 24
Blend Of All Instrumentalists 69
Bloch & Sully 231
Block, Bert 77,80
Block, Martin 74,115,163,232,254, 270–271,294,300,302,346,353
Block, Ray 115
Block, Sid 10
Bloom, Kurt 167,196,223,232
Bloom, Mickey 129,132,183
Bloom, Rose 281
Blossoms On Broadway 279–280,282, 305
Blowers, Johnny 326,328,341,343, 348,353,355
Blow, Gabriel, Blow 57
Blue Again 285
Blue And Sentimental 354–355
Blue Ball 191,194
Blue Bayou 240,289
Blue Bonnet 227
Blue Brass 256
Blue Danube 130–131,134,138,148, 232,239,246
Blue Fantasy 215
Blue Flames 40,52,58,69,75,89–90, 113,123,127
Blue Grass 260
Blue Hawaii 157,159,163,165,170, 174,183,185,214,220,301
Blue Illusion 12,41
Blue Interlude 87,360,362
Blue Is The Evening 360
Blue Lou 10,41–42,58,88,96,100,102, 109,112–113,117,124,176,200,205, 207,234,251,256,303
Blue Memories 212
Blue Minor 43
Blue Moon 11,22,43
Blue Prelude 83,93,95–96,102, 108–109,114,118,121,124,127,140, 162,173,200,205,214,264,267
Blue Reverie 130
Blue Rhythm Fantasy 17,65,118,141, 150,157,173,223,231–232,234–235, 237,241,243,245,253,256,260, 264–265,268,309
Blue Room 38,118,156,204,236,239, 307,311,327,331,336–337,339,346, 356
Blue Skies 2,6,11,15,19,23,25,28,31, 38–39,41,43–44,52,64,67,69,72,83, 92,96,100,123,144,147,158–160, 171,174,183,197,200,204–205, 220–224,227,231,238,243,248, 251–252,256,280,282,289,304,312, 326,333,335,337,339,344,353,360
Blues 261
Blues Galore 318
Blues In B-Flat 255,281

Blues In C-Sharp Minor 18
Blues In Disguise 188
Blues In E-Flat 49,88,188,250
Blues In G Minor 37
Blues In The Dark 307,356
Blues, Why Don't You Let Me Alone? 257
Blue, Turning Grey, Over You 95,186, 262,295
Blue, William Thornton 4
Bluin' The Blues 61,285,295
Bob, Lola 39
Bobbin' Up And Down 44
Bob White 253,256–257,264,270, 274–277,279–280,283–284,288–289, 292–296,298–299,302,305–306, 308–309,312–313,317,323,331,334
Body And Soul 49,60,65,75,81,100, 103,114,117,128,134,140,146,189, 197,204–205,211,222,251,255,267, 273,276,292–293,299,307,311,325, 328,333
Bohn, George 'GiGi' 37,82,92, 130–131,179,201,215,219–220, 223–225,237,240,242,248,286,300, 322,325,345,355,358
Bojangles Of Harlem 46,53–54,59,62
Boland, Clay 293
Bolar, Abe 114,158
Boling, Arnold 13,24
Bonano, Sharkey 185,216
Bond, Amos 246–247
Bond, Ford 23
Bone, Red 112,121,130,134,153,166, 171,178,186,207,230
Bongo 220,232,241
Boogie Woogie 77,80,138,195,221,234, 236–237,245,255,333,355
Boo Hoo 115,117,124,133,138, 145–146,148,152,154–155,159–160, 164,166–167,171,175,194,201–202, 359
Boone, Harvey 17,65,179
Born To Love 188,217,221,225
Born To Swing 320,357
Bose, Sterling 44,64,67,75,137,172, 174–176,183–184,186,210–211, 213–214,216,218–219,222,231,234, 239–242,254–256
Boston Tea Party, The 29,42, 46–47,49, 55–61,67,70–71,76,79,83,86,88–89, 95–96,100,104,113,129,140,151,209, 245,251,276
Boswell, Connie/Connee 70,175,277, 357
Botkin, Perry 313
Bouncy Rhythm 113–114
Bouquet Of Roses 283
Bowe, Morton 207
Bowen, Claude 359
Bowers, Gil 4,8–9,13
Bowes, Major 201
Bowles, Russell 52–53,69,74,111,188, 190,205,280,308,346
Bowlly, Al 11,73
Bowman, Dave 328,357
Boyd, Roger 354
Boy From Harlem 347

Boy Meets Girl 56
Brackman, Al 192
Braddock, James J. 191
Bradley, Nita 306,313
Bradley, Ruth 184,186,194,196–198, 202,204,210–211,213,216,219,221
Bradley, Will 73
Bradshaw, Tiny 144,166,266,292, 307–308,354
Brady, Floyd 114,158
Brady, Willard 18,23,33,64
Braggin' In Brass 336,338,344
Branham, Jim 269,271,277,280
Braud, Wellman 8,101,189,292
Breakin' In A Pair Of Shoes 4,11,24
Breakin' It Up 33
Break It Down 273,355
Break It Up 355
Breakup 187
Breeze, George 97
Breidis, Vic 139
Brendel, Pete 37,82,92,130–131,179, 201,237,286,300,322,325,345,355, 358
Brereton, Clarence 8,152,327
Brierley, Jimmy 61–62,161,210–211, 223,251
Briglia, Tony 5,25,112,115,118, 120–121,128,143,201,212,214,279, 285,289,292,295,298,301,317,324, 326,332,361
Brinson, Ted 7–8,11,12,13,88,119, 157,218–219,297,326
Britton, Milt 334
Broadway's Gone Hawaii 286
Bronxville Field Club 141,195
Bronzeville Stomp 296,301
Brooklyn Roseland Ballroom 81,108, 111,117
Brooks, Billy 244
Brooks, Harry 8,327
Brosen, Charles 345,355,358
Brown, Al 250
Brown, Andrew 4,20,59,127,134,241, 246,295,321,343
Brown, Cleo 145,313
Brown, Ed 188,205,245
Brown, Eddie 162–163
Brown Girl 320
Brown, L. 109,121
Brown, Lawrence 6,18,28,31,90,93, 128,132,148,152,159,162,172,186, 262,312–313,317,320–321,324,332, 336,338,343–344,346,354,356–357, 360
Brown, Leonard 251,255
Brown, Les 97,106,135,232–235,237, 241,246,249
Brown Palace Hotel, Denver 97
Brown, Pete 210,224,230,257,259, 272,274,292,306–307,309,313, 323–325,328,332,338,342
Brown, Sam 251
Brown, Shirley 285,297
Brown, Vernon 273–275,277,284, 287–288,292–293,295,297–299, 302–303,306,308,312–313,316,321, 324–327,331,335,337,339–340,344,

INDEX

348–351,353, 355–356,360,362
Brunies, George 4,115,216,315,326, 341–342,347
Brunton, Jim 162
Bryant, Willie 12,15–16,32,83,87,91, 99,114,147,167,207,212,218,221, 223,225,231–232,234–237,239–241, 243–248,250–251,253,256,260,265, 277,292,295–296, 310,323,334,358
Buck & Bubbles 12,114,126,334
Buckner, Ted 280,308,346
Budge, Donald 228
Buffet Flat 360
Bughouse 109,250
Bughouse Rhythm [radio show] 38, 49,55,61,88,99,120,126,130,142, 146,151,158,214,233,237,293,306, 309,328
Bugle Blues 52,60,81,196,295
Bugle Call Blues 254,256
Bugle Call Rag 6,9,18,25,29,31,33,42, 65,69,75,80,87,91,93,96,98,100,103, 109,111,119,126–128,130–131,141, 148,150,158,161,183,185,197,204, 210,214–216,222,225,232,235, 239–240,242,245–246,255,257,265, 273,276,279,285,292,304,306,321, 323,326
Bullock, Chick 6,13,25,115
Bump It 292
Bunch, Bob 13,25,72,80,82
Bundle Of Blues 273
Bundock, Rowland 289,297,353
Bunn, Teddy 69,101,172,292,318
Burgess, Wallace Harlow 120,215,237, 293,306
Burke, Johnny 201
Burkhart, Johnny 97
Burness, Les 109,121,171,174,211, 214,223,259,273,306,359
Burning Down The House I Was Brought Up In 115
Burns, Bob 136
Burns, Barbara 'Honey' 41,43–45,47, 49,84,100,213–214,298–299
Burns, Howard G. 109
Burrill, Chester 8,152
Burroughs, Alvin 234
Bush, Charlie 116–117,213,299
Bushell, Garvin 20,59,127,134,241, 246,295–296,298–299,350, 355, 361–362
Bushkin, Joe 6,13,25,28,43,82,87, 112,116,121,133,140,142,147,151, 153,158,177,183,197,205,208,210, 225–227,234,236,239–240,242,244, 254,280,287,300,341,347,353,355
Busse, Henry 97,354,358,360
But Definitely 23,25,30,34,36–38,40, 42–43,49,54,78,83,102
Butterfield, Billy 280–282,284, 316–318,325,327,337–338
Butterfield, Erskine 152
Buzzin' 'Round With The Bee 152
Buzz Music 303
Byas, Don 253–254,256,262
Bye Bye Baby 32–33,35–37,39–40, 42–44,46–49,51–55,58,60,62,71,84,

87,99,103–104,111
Bye Bye Blues 52,80
Bye Bye Pretty Baby 241
By Heck 8,38,59,73,84,90,119,143, 146,164,225,276,297
Byrne, Bobby 10–11,27,29,33–34, 134,192,201,257–258,269,285,291, 297–299,305,307,321,340–341,347, 349,351
By The Fireside 73
By The River Sainte Marie 346
Cabin In The Sky 13
Caceres, Emilio 279,282,347
Caceres, Ernie 357
Caceres Trio 285
Caesar's Ghost 207
Cafe Maria, 52nd Street, NYC 296
Cahn, Sammy 142,207
Cali, Johnny 123,207,297
California, Here I Come 89,101,255
California Ramblers 125
Callin' Your Bluff 81,147,236,243
Calliope Blues 346
Call Me Darling, Call Me Sweetheart, Call Me Dear 292
Call Of The Freaks 282,289
Calloway, Blanche 2,23,65,83,96,222, 247,263,272
Calloway, Cab 4,12,20,27,32,50, 52–53,59,62–66,74,78,86,89,94,97, 99,101,103–105,109,111,114–115, 117,124,126–127,132,134,144,168, 192,201,222,225,230,233–234,241, 246,252,262–263,266,269,274, 278–279,281,283,285,292,295,299, 307,309,312,317,320–321,324,328, 332,334,336,338,343–344
Call Your Bluff 232
Camarata, Toots 10–11,27,29,33–34, 134,192,258,269,274,285,297,321, 335,347
Camel Caravan 26,29,34,36,41,47,53, 56,59,62,65,67,69,72,74–75,77,80, 82,86,88,90,93,96,100,104,108,111, 114,117,120,124,127,130,134,137, 143,147,152,158,165,170,174,178, 184,186,188,191,200,204,210,213, 219,222,231,235,241,246,253,257, 262,265,267–268,271,273,276,279, 282,285–286,289,295,298,301,305, 308,311,316,321,324,326–327,331, 334,337,340,343–346,348–351, 353–354,356–357,359–361
Camel Hop 130,133–134,137,140, 145,149,159,162–163,182,213,246, 273,276,279,283,285,299,307,344
Camels Are Swingin' 306
Campus Serenade 114,120,123,126, 130,162,165,197
Canadian Capers 204,231,233,267, 273,357
Candlelights 298,302
Can I Be Wrong? 16
Can I Forget You? 240,242,252–254, 262,273,289
Cannon, Jimmy 297
Canobie Lake Park, Salem, N.H. 206,233,243

Can't Help Lovin' Dat Man 144,146, 215,252,278,284,301,308
Cantor, Eddie 345
Can't Teach My Old Heart New Tricks 274
Can't We Be Friends? 73,140,143,145, 147,154,157,160,183,189,200, 204–205,214,233,239,274–275,277, 284,305,333,335,337,356
Can't You Hear Me Calling, Caroline? 255
Can't You Tell? 126
Captivators (CBS Band) 38,44,49,55, 57,75
Caravan 92,132,134,165,172,175, 177–178,183,185,188–189,196,204, 207,211,213–216,220–221,231–232, 234–236,239,241–242,244,246–247, 254–257,263,265,269–272,275,277, 281,284,288–289,291,293–294,297, 302,309,313,316,323,343
Carbonaro, Joe 79,209
Careless Love 156
Carelessly 130–131,143–144,150,154, 158,163–164,167,169,171,173–175, 177,179,182,185,189,195–196, 203–204,207,213,216,223,231,247
Carheart, Ruth 40,44,55
Carina Mucho 57
Carle, Frankie 67,86,88,90,100,108, 111–114,118,129,140,209,251
Carlon, Freddie 243
Carlson, Frank 76–77,83,86,114,118, 121,161–162,205,214,231,270,273, 276,286,346,355
Carlson, Simon 185
Carlstrom, Skippy 37,39
Carlton, Bud 243,246,348
Carmichael, Hoagy 27,43,45,50,86, 88,284
Carnegie Drag 315,327
Carnegie Hall, NYC 314–315
Carnegie Jump 315,327
Carneol, Jess 188,243
Carney (Cenardo), Doc 172,289,297
Carney, Harry 6,26,28,31,90,92–93, 128,130,132,143,148,162–163, 165–166,171–173,175,177,186–189, 202,205,262,264–265,312–313, 316–317,320,324,332,336,338, 343–346,349,354,356–357,360
Carnival In Caroline 336,338, 344–345
'Carnival of Swing' [concert] 353
Carolina In The Morning 346
Carrel, Harry 223,232
Carroll, Louise 86
Carroll, Patricia 217
Carroll, Robert 17,65,151,173,179, 310,337,346
Carroll Sisters 129
Carruthers, Earl 52–53,69,74,111, 188,190,205,280,308,346
Carry Me Back To Green Pastures 36,45
Carry Me Back To Old Virginny 332
Carry, Scoops 10,80,108
Carter, Benny 289,342,357,359,362
Carter, Frank 87,115
Carver, Wayman 12,23,74,105,113,

123,126,138,177,238,250,277–279, 295–296,299,350,355,361–362
Casa Loma Orchestra 2,5,9,25,112, 115,120,128,143,168,201,212,214, 275,278–279,286,292,295–296,298, 301,307,323–324,326,332,334,361
Casa Loma Stomp 38,79,121,203,214, 246,248,264,266,293,310
Casa Madrid, Louisville, KY 15
Casa Manana, Ft Worth, TX 42,54,62
Case, Russ 26,87,303,309,310,326, 331,333
Casey, Albert 8,13,24–25,32,56,85, 94,102,123,134,148,186,253–254, 269,339,346,358
Casey Jones 186
Cashman, Ed 39,75,156,238,250,260, 293,309–310
Casino Capers 79
Castle, Boots 220
Castle Farms, Cincinnati, Ohio 215–216,220–221,234
Castle [Castaldo], Lee 35,61,74,85,93, 119,230,254,271,295,308,322,325, 333,338,347,349,351,358–359,361
Castle, Selva 165–166,175,178
Caston, Bobbie 40,155,203,327,331, 336–337
Cates, Opie 59–60,92,348,360
Catlett, Sid 10,13,18,20,33,65,179
Cauldwell, Happy 20,188
'*Cause My Baby Says It's So* 144,163, 165,169,172,186,189,202–203,213, 215–216,227,239, 247,256
Cavernism 16,18,21,78,87,98–99,223
Changes 115,126,135,140,154,158, 205,225,276,280,293,357
Changing Of The Guard 223
Chansonette 39
Chant Of The Jungle 78
Chant Of The Weed 11
Chapel In The Moonlight 69,76,84,88, 91,95,98,102,108
Chapin, Mr. 107,113,138,153
Chapin, Patti 53
Chaplin, Saul 142,207
Characteristic Blues 153,160
Charleston Chasers 284
Charlie Barnet's History Of Jazz 45,48, 52,57
'Charlie Chan at the Olympics' [movie] 197
Charmaine 26,93,146,169,172
Chase, Frank 21,35
Chase, Ronnie 44,47
Chase, Wilder 353
Chasin' Chippies 360
Chatterbox 262,320–321,338
Chatterbox, Hotel William Penn, Pittsburgh 118,124
Cheatham, Doc 4,111,117,127,225, 241,246,269,292,295,299,321,343
Cheek To Cheek 203
Cherry 225,232,277
Chesterfield Dance Time 57
Chez Paree, Chicago 97
Chicago 30,279
Chicken A La Swing 188

INDEX

Chicken And Waffles 113,116,119,123, 125,145,157,169,172,188, 233,250
Chicken Reel 33,285,297–298,309,335
Chick Webb Stomp 177,243
Chimes At The Meeting 83
Chimes Blues 158
Chimes In The Spring 294
China Boy 14,16,29,44,59,67,74,80, 99,110,159,161–162,221,240,246, 251,255,282,285,289,298–299,303, 308,312,325,328,331,336,344,346
China Clipper 345
China Girl 19
China Stomp [Chinatown] 161,217
Chinatown, My Chinatown 37,39,56, 58,73,116,134–135,143,171,204, 208,294,296,358
Chinese Rhythm 97,274
Chiquita 299
Chlo-e 26,105,107,109,118,123,134, 138,145,160,178,182,221,234–235, 271,275,289,299,344
Choir Boy 140
Cholden, Abe 87,92
Chopin's Ghost 217
Chopin's Waltz in B Minor 73
Choppin' Wood 303
Chopsticks 94
Chorney, Ben 99
Chris And His Gang 188,200,234,244, 251,255–256,269
Christian, Buddy 313
Christmas Night In Harlem 46,87,93, 95,158
Christopher Columbus 8–10,13,15, 17–19,21–22,25–27,29–31,35–38, 41–43,45,49–50,52,54,58–60,62, 67–70,80,99,104,119,127,146,154, 165,177,185,200,203,207,210, 236–237,245–246,254,269,342
Chuberry Jam 255
Church Mouse On A Spree 55,60,254
Church Street Sobbin' Blues 158,272
Ciribiribin 271,348
Clap Hands, Here Comes Charlie 86, 101,111,119,131,138,146,172, 202–203,208,221,243,255,263,267, 275,278,301,321,357
Clap My Hands 8
Clarinet Lament (Barney's Concerto) 6,17,19,33,165,171,176,189,313
Clarinet Marmalade 48,87,89,112,142, 146,165,211,214,231,236,240,244, 247,269,286,295,299,306,345–346, 357
Clark, Buddy 42,49,52,54,58,175
Clark, Dick 3,4,10,14,22–23,26,37, 44,67
Clark, Harry 289,308,316,357
Clark, Pete 6,12,23,52,74,80–81,105, 138,155,177
Clarke, Kenneth 'Kenny' 354
Clarry Doodle 196
Classics In Jazz 188
Clay, Shirley 17,114,158,206
Clayton, Buck 109–110,118,138,170, 184,188,193,197,200,202,205,231, 233,237,240–241,245,248,253,256,

271,278–279,292,307–308,311,328, 333–334,341,354
Clementine 263
Climax Rag 337
Cling To Me 3
Clinton, Larry 205,211,219,267,283, 285,293,297,299,309,322–323
Close To Me 54,57,69,72
Close Your Pretty Eyes 61
Clouds 108,110,242,246,252,255
Clouds In My Heart 92,238
Cloudy 12,246
Cloutier, Norman 33–35,38,41, 43–44,47,51,55,57
Club Caliente, 66 W 52nd Street, NYC 93
Club 18, 18-20 W 52nd Street, NYC 303
Club Evergreen, N.J. 143
Coast To Coast 105
Cobbs, Alfred 162
Cocktails For Two 69,273
Cocktail Rhythm 124
Cocoanut Grove, Bridgeport, Conn 44–45
Cohan, Phil 39,75,238,250,260,293
Cohen, Ray 59–60,92
Cole, Caesar 116
Cole, Cozy 8–9,12–13,18,25–28,34, 44,52,65–66,69,77,80–81,94,104, 111,121,137,143,145,152,159,161, 165,170,235,251,278,351,357,359
Cole, Rupert 17,65,179,337
Cole, Teddy 108
Coleman, Emil 97
Coleman, Oliver 337,341
Coler, Lawrence 237
College Humor 340
College Widow 130
Collins, Booker 7–8,12–13,88,119, 157,218–219,297,326
Collins, Johnny 108
Collins, Park 176
Collins, Shad 12,17,20,59,127,134, 138,159–160,173,295,321,343,346
Colonna, Jerry 37,48–49,69,106,313, 357
Color Of Your Eyes 57
Colucci, Tony 123
Come Back, Sweet Papa 25,33,126
Come! Come! 264
Come On With The Come On 334
Comin' On 359
Coming Through the Rye 123,338
Comiskey Park, Chicago 191
Commodore Music Shop, NYC 116, 119,135,174,238,249,260,282,302, 322,327,343,347
Community Swing 106,186,211,214, 219,221,241
Condon, Eddie 12,13,25,27,30,32,82, 87,116,121,133,135,156,158,160, 177,226–227,315,326,328,341–342, 347,349,357–358
Coney Island, Cincinnati, OH 43–45, 47,221–223
Confessin' 79,80,221,235
Congo 127,221,232,236,240

Congress Hotel, Chicago 2–8,11,15, 17–20,22,69–70,78–79,83–84,87, 89–90,92,95,97,99,123,125–126, 128,131,133,140,143–146,148, 150–152,157,159–161,163–164,166, 170,274,276,278,280–281,285,291, 297–299,305,307
Connie's Inn, NYC 2,5,7,11–12,16, 23–24
Conniff, Ray 353,355
Conn Musical Instrument Store, NYC 156,168,192,249
Cons, Carl 333
Convention Hall, Philadelphia 351
Coolidge String Quartet 316
Cooper, Al 291,300,306
Cooper, Elyse 244,300
Cooper, Jane 89
Cooper, Jerry 37
Copenhagen 25,29,61,93,98,126,158, 172,177,206–208,244,278,321,335, 359
Copenhagen Swing 93
Copper Colored Gal 56,59,64–65,74, 76,88,90,93,96,105–106,111,118, 155,169
Copsey, Ralph 185
Coquette 56,126,151,173,188, 220, 232,234,241,252,260,284,291,359
Cordaro, Joe 4–5,15,26
Corky 8
Cornell University, Ithaca, N.Y. 179
Cornfed 95
Cottage By The Moon 43,50
Cotton Club, Culver City, Calif 60
Cotton Club Downtown 53,62–66, 74,78,86,89,94,97,99,101,104–105, 109,111,114,117,124,126–127,132, 134,142,144,146–147,156,159,162, 164–166,171–173,175,177,184,247, 262–263,266,269,274,278–279,281, 283,285,292,299,307,312,317,324, 328,332,334,336,338,343–344,350, 354
Cotton Club, Harlem 2,5
'Cotton Club Parade of 1936, The' 62,64,74,127
Count Me Out 255
Covey, Bill 185
Cowbell Serenade 323
Cowboy From Brooklyn 347,349,353
Cowboy Reel 109
Cradle Song 42
Craig, Mildred 307,311,320,323,334
Crain, Malcolm 171,174,214,223, 259,273,306,346,355
Crawford, Forrest 3,5–6,12–13,116
Crawford, Jimmy 52–53,69,74,111, 113,188,190,205,280,308,346
Crazy Blues 271
Crazy Rhythm 39–40,44,48,87,165, 177,187,195,216,239
Cream Of The Crop 92
Cream Puff 62,84,93,100,126,157
Creole Love Call 145
Crescendo In Blue 262,264
Criterion Theater, NYC 270,278, 281,284–285,294,297,307,311,313,

320,323,326,334
Crosby, Bing 89,109,175,179,186, 195,201,212,277
Crosby, Bob 9,12–14,16,21–23–27,30, 32–33,36,40,42–43,45,51,68,93, 95–96,100,115,117,125–126,128, 131–133,135,140,143–146,148, 150–152,156–157,159–161,163–164, 166,168,170,174,179,183,186,205, 207–208,210,212,215–216,218,220, 222,224–225,231,237,239–240,262, 267,269,274,276–277,279–284,288, 296,307–308,312,315–319,321–325, 327–328,330–338,340,347
Crosby, Everett 212
Crosby, George 212
Crosby, Israel 6,13,18,20,33,127,137, 200,207,263,269,276,353
Crosby, Ted 212
Cross Country Hop 37,220,23
Cross Patch 13,18,21–22,25–26,31,33, 35–38,40,44,46–47,50–51,54–55,70, 126,212
Crumbley, Elmer 52–53,69,74,111, 113,188,190,205,280,308, 346
Cruse, Vera 44–45
Cryin' Mood 134,138
Crying My Heart Out For You 12,24, 84,302,308
Cuban Pete 195–196,203,211,289
Cuban Swing 35
Cuddle Up A Little Closer 255
Cuffee, Ed 10,13,20,33,127,137,200, 263,276,353
Cugat, Xavier 168,354,358
Culley, Wendell 8,152
Cumberback, Clarissa 248
Cuomo, George 223,232
Curry, James 167
Cusumano, Bob 101,108,112
Daddy's Boy 332
D'Agostino, John 223,232
Dailey, Frank 59,90,104,165,171,184, 195,202,222,242,265,271
Dale, Carlotta 38,202,207,233,256, 270
Dale, Jimmy 260
Dale, Joe 223,232
Dale, Marty 37,262,280
Dallas Bender 48
Dallas Blues 13,22–24,185,204,223, 240,253,298
D'Amico, Hank 72,101,137,169, 202–204,206,255–256,263–265,274, 311,318,327,330–332,339–340,348, 350–351,357,359
Dance For Me My Darling 63
Dance Of Inspiration 35
Dancing Blue Devils 241
Dancing Derby 124
Dancing In The Dark 215,320
Dancing On The Ceiling 215
Dancing Till Dawn 37,41,43
Dancing Under The Stars 203,246,268
Dancing With Mince 151
Dancing With You 72,75,109,122
D'Andrea, Danny 128,143,201,212, 214,279,285,292,295,298,301,317,

INDEX

324,326,332,361
Daniels, Billy 29,56,91,158,232,332
Daniels, Helene 289,294,297
Daniels, Jerry 126
D'Annolfo, Frank 144,167,171, 295–297,308,322,325,333
Dano, Art 236
Darcy, Dan 215–216
Dardanella 32,45,70,75,89,123,227, 233,252,302
Dark Eyes 130,136,138,147,151,159, 164,200,207,213,223,225,233,236, 244,299,325,334,338
Darkness On The Delta 298
Darktown Blues 96
Darktown Lullaby 102
Darktown Strutters' Ball 5,15,19,34,36, 41,43,50,61,78,81,110–111,114,120, 138,149,157,166,216,219–220,225, 240–241,245,251,273,279,289,299, 302,335,349
Darling, Frank 'Coco' 354
Darling Nellie Gray 272,274,293,307, 336
Darling, Not Without You 52,61,65,79, 83,88,91,100,103,107
Davenport Blues 114,200,202,267,301
Davies, Ann Lee 59,90
Davis, Charles 158
Davis, Johnny 69
Davis, Leonard 354
Davis, Pat 5,25,70,79,83,87,112, 114–115,118,120–121,124,128,143, 201,212,214,279,285–286,289, 292–293,295,297–298,301–302,307, 309,316–317,320,323–324,326–327, 332,361
Davis, Ramona 62,125
Davis, Sammy 253
Dawn, Dolly 34,36–37,42,46–47,50, 54,115,192,294
Daybreak Express 148
Day Dreamin' 350
Day, Irene 354,358,360
Dead End Blues 148
Dean, Connie 236,243
Dean, Demas 8,152
Deane, Laura 23
Dear Diary 92
Dear Old Southland 4,11,29–30,80,87, 96,98,105,117,124,152,157–158, 165,176,188–189,197,209,231,251, 253,273,292,297–298,312,316–317, 325,327,332,337,339
Decca Stomp [Queen Isabella] 3,104, 118,205
Deck Of Cards 11
Dedicated To You 88,112,123–124,126, 138,148,159,169,176,186,195,251, 253
'Deed I Do 333
Deep Elm 92
Deep Forest 76,87,103,105,109,169, 270,273
Deep In The Heart Of The South 178, 249
Deep Sea Blues 19
Deep South 40,46,48

Definition Of Swing 300
De Jazz Wereld [magazine] 192
DeLange, Eddie 37,64,82,91–92,104, 108,110,130–131,149,151–152,168, 179,183–185,196,201,204,215,219, 223–225,237,240,242,247,286,300, 322,325
Delirium 61
DeLys, Gogo 32,40,42,52–53,58,73, 116,207
Demi-Tasse 163
Denniker, Paul 115
Dennis, Stanley 5,25,112,114–115, 118,120–121,124,128,143,201,214, 279,285,292,295,298,301,317,324, 326–327,332,361
Dent, Laforet 52–53,69,74,111
DeParis, Sidney 17,212,288
De Paris, Wilbur 118,162
DePew, Bill 3–4,10,14,22–23,26,37, 44,67,75,88,96,105,107,127,139,205
Derrick, Dorothy 119,127
Dese Dem Dose 105
Desperately In Love 254,256
Devil's Holiday 101,308
Devil's Kitchen 111
Devlin, Helen 220
Devoting My Time To You 23
Dewey, Curtis 286–288
D-Flat Blues 301
Diane 84,87,95,297,307,349
Diaz, Horace 18,23,33,64,76–77,86, 161
Di Carlo, Tom 171,174,211,214,223, 259,273,306,346,347,350,354, 358–360
Dick, Edith 60
Dickenson, Vic 114,158,206
Dickinson, Hal 50,52
Dictators (CBS Band) 36,39,41,44, 46–47,49,52–54,56,94
Did An Angel Kiss You The Day You Were Born? 317,320,326
Did Anyone Ever Tell You? 123
Did I Remember? 25,28,30–31,35–37, 40–42,44,46–49,52,54,56–61,65, 78–80,83,94
Did You Forget? 160
Did You Know Noah? 283
Did You Mean It? 64,70,72–73,75,80, 83–84,88–89,98,100,104,126
Diga Diga Doo 26,52,100,130,162, 174,337,354
Dillard, Bill 12,17,65,138,157, 159–161,169,173,272,289,302,328, 346
Diminuendo In Blue 262
Dinah 18,21,35,40,46–47,54,80,82, 87,96,100,102,111–112,115, 127–128,135,140,147,151,165,195, 202,205,221,236,243,261,267,273, 279,299,323–324,331,341,359
Dinah's In A Jam 346
Dinner Music For A Pack Of Hungry Cannibals 156,192,195
Dippermouth Blues 152,216,353
Dismal Day 284,303
Diven, Ernie 223,232

Dixieland Band 3–4,10–11,18,24,30, 38–39,43,55,78,88,209,246,248,251, 274,350
Dixieland One-Step 327
Dixieland Shuffle 13,33,43,49,51,68, 121,133,140,148,160,237,283–284
Dixie, Where Jazz Was Born 94
Dixon, Charles 244
Dixon, George 337,341
Dixon, Joe 10,13,25,72,80,82,101, 108,112,122,124,130,165–166,171, 174,185,189,192,194–196,198,200, 202,204,208,210–211,213,216, 224–225,227,230–232,234–236,239, 248,252,269,272,284,294,301,321, 335,340–341,348,353,355
Dixon, Lawrence 117,231
Dizzy Debutante 259,322,326,328
Dizzy Drumming 42
Dizzy Spells 311–312,336,343,348, 351
Djangology 187
D-Minor Blues 121
D-Natural Blues 327,333
Dr Heckle & Mr Jive 146,313
Doctor Jazz 161,169,173,196,205,214, 270,331
Doctor Rhythm 321,334,337
Dodds, Baby 157
Dodds, Johnny 157,318
Dodging A Divorcee 2,5,15,52,76,105, 115,211
Does Your Heart Beat For Me? 151,165
Doggin' Around 244,253–355
Dogtown Blues 125,152,157,212,284, 317
Doh, Ray, Me 46
Doin' The Jive 217,289,298
Doin' The Prom 36,42,53–54,56,58, 61–62
Doing The Reactionary 321–322
Doin' The Riviera 40
Doin' The Suzy-Q 87
Doing The Voom Voom 18,273
Doin' Things 16
Dolan, Skeets 215,219,225,230
Dominick Swing 337
Donaldson, Walter 298
Donnelly, Ted 7–8,11–13,88,119,157, 218–219,240,246,249,252,254,297, 326
Don't Be That Way 79,84,86,298, 311–312,316,324–325,331,335–336, 340–341,343,345,348–349,351,353, 355–356,361–362
Don't Blame Me 3
Don't Count Your Kisses 5,18,30
Don't Cry When He Is Gone 57
Don't Ever Change 178,186
Don't Kiss Me Again 184,196
Don't Let The Rhythm Go To Your Head 353
Don't Look Now 29,135
Don't Save Your Love 243
Don't Try To Cry Your Way Back To Me 339
Don't Wake Up My Heart 353,355,357
Don't You Care What Anyone Says? 163,

203
Don't You Know Or Don't You Care? 186,231,242,254,257,261,268
Don't You Miss Your Baby? 271
Door, Russell 40
Dornberger, Charles 166
Dorsey Dervish (Waddlin' At The Waldorf) 33,272,278
Dorsey, Donald 42
Dorsey, Jimmy 10–11,27,29,33–34, 54–55,60–61,109,119,134–135,156, 164,172,174–175,179,186,192,195, 201,230,243,247,249,255,257–258, 260,269,272–274,276,278,280–281, 285,291,296–299,305,307,309,321, 323–324,334–335,337,339–341, 344,347–349,351,358
Dorsey Stomp 291
Dorsey, Tommy 10,12–13,16,18–19, 21–23,25,34,36,41,47,66,72–73,75, 80,82,91,95,101–102,108–110, 112–116,121–122,124,126,129–132, 132,134–136,138,143–144,146–148, 151–153,155,158–159,162,164, 166–168,171,178,183,186,195–198, 201,204–205,207–208,210,213, 215–217,219–220,222–224,228–233, 235–237,239–240,242–247,249,253, 255–256,261,263,266–268,270–273, 276,278,287,289,292–293,295,298, 302,307–308,311–312,316,322–325, 333,335,338,344,347–349,351, 358–359,361
Dorsey Opus 281,298
Doty, Mike 130,134,136,153,166,171, 178,186,207,224,230–231,236,248, 254,269,294,301,321,340–341,348, 353,355
Double Breasted Lips 264
Double Or Nothing 231
Douglas, Beatrice 138,143,159
Douglas, Paul 25,39,68,89,95,106, 129,132,145,149,164,169,183,185, 187,202,216,238,250,260–261,267, 272,293,309,324,357
Dover, Jane 345,355,358
Dowell, Saxie 37
Dowling, Eddie 23
Down And Out Blues 286
Down Beat [magazine] 157,333
Down By The Old Mill Stream 75,84, 99,323,346
Downes, Cecil 44–45
Downey, Morton 57
Down Home Rag 65,76,78,92,135
Down South Camp Meetin' 4–5,29,31, 36–38,41,47,50,54,58,60,66,72,74, 80,86,92,107,119,127,130,136,138, 140,143,154,157–158,160,162,175, 179,183,207,210,214–215,230,239, 253,263,298,308,359,361
Down Stream 119,247,252,311,333, 340
Down The Old Ox Road 357
Downtown Uproar 130,144,173,313
Down With Love 271,289,297,323, 331,335
Do Ye Ken John Peel? 337,347

Doyle, Barbara 23,138–139,145–146, 304,348
Doyle, Cynthia (Sis) 66–67,77, 114, 118–119,121–122,129,138–139,163, 260
Doyle, Henry 114
Doyle, J. Howard 146,159,175
Doyle, John 18,23,33,64
Doyle, Mrs 114
Doyle, Tommy 139
Do You Ever Think Of Me? 203–204, 206,222,224,236,239,283,331,339
Do You Or Don't You Love Me? 20,34, 46,54,57
Drake, Doris 307
Dream Awhile 33,37,47,53,62,64,80, 99,102
Dreamboat 194
Dream Boy 26,190
Dream Lullaby 22,35
Drelinger, Art 9,109,117,121,157,161, 164,166
Driftin' 86,289
Driftin' Along 31,47–48
Drifting Apart 120,298
Drifting Changes 20
Drifting Tide 115
Drop Me Off At Harlem 83,166,204, 347
Druck, George 214
Drummer's Delight 316,348
Drummond, John 212
Drum Stomp [Crazy Rhythm] 235
Duane, Ted 37,82,92,130–131,179, 183,201,204,215,219,224–225,237, 286,300,322,325
Duchin, Eddie 97,126,144
Ducky Wucky 22
Duerr, Clayton 311
Duffy, Al 58,125,289,294,297,308
Dunham, Sonny 5,25,83,101,112, 114–115,118,120–121,128,156,192, 212,248,279,285–286,289,292–293, 295,298,301–302,306–307,309, 316–317,320,323–324,326,331–332, 361
Dupont, Roland 238,260–262,264, 280,293,309–310
Dupree Blues 161,171,263,301
Durham, Eddie 52–53,69,74,111,188, 190,205,231,237,239–240,271,292, 307,328,333,341,354
Dusk In A Chinese Cemetery 196
Dusk In The Desert 262
Dusk In Upper Sandusky 269,291,297, 334,337,339,349
Dust On The Moon 95
Earle Theater, Philadelphia 336
Easter Parade 39
East Of The Sun 214,220
East St. Louis 270
East St. Louis Toodle-Oo 98,132,134, 141,144–145,147,159,165,168,189, 338
Easy Like 66
Easy Living 184,196,207,216,218,237, 333
Easy To Love 33,72,79,81–83,87,

90,95–97,99–101,104–107,109–110, 112,123,125–127,217,274,324,331
Easy To Remember 4,144,162,173,268, 312
Ebb Tide 243,248,255,281,313
'Ebb Tide' [movie] 294
Eberle, Ray 352–353
Eberly, Bob 10,11,33–34,60,119,134, 192,258,269,272,274,276,278,280, 285,291,299,305,307,309,321, 334–335,337,340–341,347,349,351
Ebony Rhapsody 80,83,159,175
Eccentric 25,218
Echoes Of Harlem (Cootie's Concerto) 6,17–20,33,56,142,189,196,317,320
Echoes Of The Jungle 175,284
Eclipse 89
Edgar Steps Out 185
Edgewater Beach Hotel, Chicago 97
Edison, Harry 118,141,162,195,328, 354
Edwards, Eddie 39,75,327
Edwards, Joan 169
Edwards, Ralph 171,213
Eeny-Meeny-Miney-Mo 2,5,46
Egyptian Barn Dance 349
800 Club, 52nd Street, NYC 167
Elden, Bob 167
Eldridge, Roy 6,10,13,18,20,22,33, 41,52,60,80–81,108,145–146,154, 230,241,281,284,297,303,311
Elgin Revue 9–11,13–15,17–18, 20–21,23
Eli's Stomp 235,237,240,244,248
Ella 355,361
Ellington, Duke 5–6,17–20,22,27–28, 31,33,49,53,56,90,92–93,97–98,112, 126,128,130,132–134,142,144–148, 156,159,162–166,168–169,171–175, 177,184–189,192,197–198,201–205, 207, 216–217,247,254,262,264–265, 272–274,276,284,293,297–298,307, 312–313,316–317,320–322,324, 327–328,332–334,336,338,343–346, 350,354–357,360
Ellis, Bob 33,41,43
Elman, Ziggy 67,75,77,79–80,82–83, 86,88,90–93,96,100,105,107–112, 115,117,120,124–128,135,137,140, 147,153–154,156,158,163,176,180, 182–183,198,204–205,217,244,251, 253,257,262,274–275,282–283,286, 289,291–293,297–299,301,303, 306–308,312–313,316,321,325–326, 331,337,348–351,355–356
Emaline 39,104,198
Embraceable You 223,349
Emperor Jones 223
Empty Ballroom Blues 357
Empty Saddles 23,32,37–38,41,48–49, 53–55,61
Energetic Stomp 235,240
Engle, Vic 3,14
Ennis, Skinnay 30,37,39,45,51,88
Ens, Arthur 3,14
Erwin, Pee Wee 10,14,22–23,26,37, 44,67,122,129–132,134,136,138, 143–144,146–147,151,153,158–159,

162,164,166,171,178,183,186,201, 205,207–208,210,213,215,219–220, 222,232,235–237,239–240,244–246, 254–255,271,289,293,295,297,308, 311,316,322,324–325,333,338,347, 349,351,358–359
Erwin, Stuart 267
Estalie 218
Estelle 86,90,118
Estren, Joe 167,191
Etri, Bus 130–131,179,201,215,219, 224–225,237,242,286,300,322,325, 345,355,358
Evans, Chuck 350,354,358–360
Evans, Emmet 341–342
Evans, Herschel 109,118,138, 193–194,197,200,202,205,231,233, 235,237,239,244,248,253,271,279, 292,307–308,328,333–334,354,359, 361
Evans, Lou 'Red' 149,164,225,280, 303,327
Evenin' 77,104,253
Even Though It's The Colour Of Your Eyes 49
Everybody Calls It Swing 40,69,108
Everybody Knows My Baby 57
Everybody Loves My Baby 244,251, 273,276,355
Everybody Shuffle 247
Everybody Step 355
Everybody's Doin' It 338,348
Everybody's Swingin' It 20
Everybody Swing 65,106
Every Day 171
Every Day's A Holiday 284,295, 297–299
'Every Day's A Holiday' [movie] 321
Every Minute Of The Hour 12,19–20, 22
Every Now And Then 35
Every Once In A While 17,22
Everyone's Wrong But Me 178,206,223, 256
Everything I Have Is Yours 41
Everything Is Still Okay 20,29–30,33
Everything's In Rhythm With My Heart 11
Everything You Said Came True 265, 267,273,276,283,291
Every Tub 328,334–335,355
Exactly Like You 47,81,94,96,118,138, 146,152,154,165,179,202,215,221, 234,237,246,268,275,280,301,323, 328,333
Exiner, Billy 300,322,325,345,355, 358
Exposition Swing 31
Face To Face 143
Fair And Square 358
Fallon, Brad 163
Famous Door, 35 W52nd Street, NYC 5,7,12,16,344
Famous Door, 66 W52nd Street, NYC 278,285,287,292,296,307,324,334, 342,350,358,360–361
Fancy Meeting You 43,53,57–59,69

Fan It 121
Far Above Cayuga's Waters 179
Fare Thee Well, Annie Laurie 350,357
Fare Thee Well To Harlem 89
Farewell Blues 3,6,15,18,29,33,37–38, 40,50–51,55,130,144,172,196,205, 223,225,227,239,251,255,265,272, 280,285,296,323,333,355
Farewell My Love 271,277–280, 283–284,299,309
Farewell To Arms 270
Far In The Night 59
Farley, Ed 2–3,14,32,39–41,50,53,58, 60,64,66,74,143,215
Farr, Tommy 245
Farrell, Jimmy 188
Fascinating Rhythm 40
Fatso, Al 178
Faulkner, David 294,362
Faye, Frances 326
Fazola, Irving 59–60,65,92,185,211, 218,234,254–255,257,286,289–290, 297–298,337–338,340
Feather Your Nest 234–235,241
Fee Fi Fo Fum 223
Feelin' Gay 16
Feeling High And Happy 346–347
Feelin' Low 123
Feldman, Al 113,177,259
Felton, Happy 134
Fenton, Mildred 16,18,42,54,62,201
Ferdinand Blues 284
Ferrall, Jimmy 38,41,47,49,53,55
Ferretti, Andy 117,121,130,132,134, 136,153,166,171,178,186,201,207, 213,230,254,271,295,308,322,325, 333,338,347,349, 351,358–359
Ferrier, Jack 231,276,286,346,355
Ferris' Music Store 266,273,297,301
Ferrou, Henry 287
Fick, Barbara 362
Fick, George 269–270,277,282,294, 332,349,362
Fiddlesticks 42
Fidgety Feet 150,284,308,323
Fields, Shep 53,97,115,247,350
50 Million Sweethearts Can't Be Wrong 108
Fifty Second Street 88,118,142,162,201
52nd Street Fever 40,56
52nd Street Stomp 192
Fight On Pennsylvania 69
Filla, Thelma 42,48
Finale In E-flat 47
Financial Love 251
Finger Buster 22
Firecrackers 270
Fireman's Ball 220,223,240
First Rose of Spring 40
First Time I Saw You 211
Fishel, Bob 167,191,223,232
Fisher, Abby 27
Fisher, Eddie 125
Fishkind, Arnold 109,121,144,167, 171,189,194–195,198,216,239
Fitzgerald, Ella 9,12,23,74–75,77–81, 84,86–88,90,92–93,98,100,104–105, 108–109,111–113,115–116,119,

INDEX

123–126,128,133,135,137–138,146, 170,172,176–178,208,238,243,250, 254,259,275–279,293,295–296, 298–301,312,317,321,327,333, 335–337,346,350,355,360–362
Five Point Blues 340
Flaming Youth 273
Flanagan, Billy 33,64
Flany Doodle Swing 117
Flat Foot Floogie 353–356,359
Flato, Ludwig 223,232
Fleagle, Brick 90,205
Fleischmann Yeast [radio show] 195
Fleming, Frank 49,61,83–84
Fletcher, Milton 117,231
Flight Of A Haybag 4
Flight Of The Bumble Bee 73,179,188, 192,201,269,274,285,297,299
Flippen, Jay C. 200
Floatin' Down To Cotton Town 56,66
Floating On A Bubble 115
Flood, Bernard 354
Florida Flo 339
Flugelhorn Blues 267,328
Flying Fingers 151
Flying Off The Handle 114
Fool By My Side 109
Fooled 94
Fooled Again 101
Foolin' Myself 157,175,184,242,252
Foolin' With You 321
Footguard Hall, Hartford, Conn 353
Forbes, C. Graham 340–341
For Dancers Only 112,188,231–232, 244,246,256,260,334
Foresythe, Reginald 58,115
Forget If You Can 351
Formal Night In Harlem 87,109,115, 119,126,214
For Sentimental Reasons 70,72,74,77, 79,82–84,88,90–92,101–102, 124
For You 57,112,121,175,214,231,237, 266,302
Foster, Artie 9,13,101,108
Foster, George (ann) 204
Foster, George (d) 158
Foster, Pops 155,188–189,296,331
Foster, Ray 99–100,123,165–166,171, 174,185,196,202–203,207,211,218, 234
Found 145
Four And One-Half Street 163
Four Eaton Boys 40,44,55,115,123
Four In A Bar 246
Four Ink Spots 16,60,126,151,158, 161,174,185,212,218,278,350
Four or Five Times 18,34,50,54,292
Four Score And Seven Years Ago 90
Four Stars Quartet 149,223
Four Step Brothers 264
Fractious Fingering 25
Frank, Norman 244,260
Frankel, Dave 213,299
Frankie & Johnny 177,183,195,198, 213,221,232,272,294
Franklin, William 117,231
Franzella, Sal 230,270,280
Frazier, Charlie 83,134,192,225,236, 241,243–246,258,260,274,299,310, 321,334–335,340–341,347,349,351
Fredericks, Harry 237,260
Fredericks, Sonny 128
Frederico, Frank 59–60,92
Free For All 273
Freeman, Anthony 309
Freeman, Bud 6,8,13,25,34,41,72,80, 82,101,108,110,112,116,121–122, 124,129–132,134,136,143–144, 146–147,151–153,158–159,162,164, 166,178,183,186,201,204–205, 207–208,210,213,215,219,222, 230–232,236–237,239–240,242, 245–246,254–255,271,276,293,295, 300,308,311,315–316,322,324–325, 333,338,343–346,348–351,353–358, 360,362
Freeman, Henry/Harry/Hank 144, 174,214,223,259,273,306359
Freeman, Jay 48,142
Freeman, Jerry 97
Free Wheeling 259
French Casino, NYC 79,97
Friedman, Mort 243,246,348,360
Frisco Flo 59,62,94
Frisco Fog 280
Froeba, Frank 11,30–31,35,37,39, 48–50,55,57,60,64
Froggy Bottom 8,110,236,242–243,246
Frogley, Ken 280
Frolic Sam 92,172,187,233,238,261, 313
From The Land of The Sky Blue Water 311,331,336,343
From The Top Of Your Head 9
Frye, Don 172,230,259,272,307,309, 313
Fulbright, Richard 12,17,138,159,173
Fulford, Tommy 74,80–81,105,119, 126,138,177–178,238,250,259, 277–279,295–296,299,301,317,321, 350,355,361–362
Fuller, Walter 16,18,92,94,99,105,109, 117,231,244,246,248,251–252,256
Fulton Royal, Brooklyn 97
Fun For You 296
Funiculi Funicula 27,60,323
Fun In Swingtime [radio show] 157, 161,164,169,177,208,211,227,235, 244,252
Funk, Larry 97
Fuqua, Charles 126
Gabler, Milton 116,135,168–169,249, 260,343,347
Gadsby, Larry 215
Gage, Ed 167
Gaillard, Slim 307,326,357,360
Gale Artists, Inc 174
Gallodoro, Al 210,236,251
Galtman, Henry 167
Garber, Jan 97
Garbo Green 5
Garden Of The Moon 359
Garden Of Weeds 211
Garland, Joe 20,26,36,70,81,141,354
Garrett, Ardell 289,297
Garrett, Frances 244
Gates 291
Gattuso, Tony 74,85,93,119,207,297
Gayle, Paula 348,360
Gaylor, Ruth 37,64,123,130–131,189, 195,224,348,353,355
Gee, But It's Great To Meet A Friend 248
Gee! But You're Swell 88,92,105,115, 117,133,138,148,179,198,201
Gee, Jake, Whatta Snake 297
Geller, Harry 3–4,10,14
Genner, Russ 73,75,106,110,113,116, 119,125,129,132,140,156,169,172, 187,347
Gentleman Doesn't Believe 24
Gentry, Art 44,55,82,109,115,183
George, Al 224,236,248,269,294,301, 321,340–341,348,350,357,359
George, Karl 307
Georgia Jubilee 129,145
Georgianna 284,307
Georgia On My Mind 66,101
Gerhart, Ruth 38
Gerlach, Horace 195
Gershwin, George 50,149,170,185, 208,210,269,274,291
Get A Little Closer, Babe 78
Get Acquainted With Yourself 210
Get Happy 10,36,38,49,60,90,98,111, 250,336
Get It Southern Style 188,192,267,322
Get Rhythm In Your Feet 3
Get Thee Behind Me Satan 13
Getting Some Fun Out of Life 256,265, 271,273,281,284
Get What You Can While You Can 189
Get Yourself A New Broom 273
Gibbs, Eddie 354
Gibson, Al 240,248
Gibson, Andy 239,244,246,253,260
Gibson, Fredda 82,91,104,108,110
Gifford, Gene 114,121,203,208,293
Gill, Emerson 97
Gillespie, John 'Dizzy' 173,310,346
Gillespie, Jack 163
Gillrum, Clark 15
Gilson, Edson 99,130,142,215
Gin Mill Blues 117,126,131,135,145, 151,157,166,183,207,216,231,274, 281,288,318,331
Ginsberg, Ben 35,61,74,85,93,119, 171,174,214,223,259,273,306
Girard, Adele 89,140,144,146–147, 151,158,164,177–178,197,205,208, 210–211,225–227,231,234,236, 239–240,242,244,251,254,263, 280–281,287,299,341
Girl Of My Dreams 301,307,327
Git 7
Give Her A Pint (And She'll Tell It All) 12
Give Me That Old Fashioned Swing 52, 54
Gizar, Tito 64
Glad To Be Unhappy 43
Glen Island Casino 22,29–31,35–36, 38–39,41,43–44,48,50,52,54–55,57, 185,191,203,218,227
Glenn, Tyree 254,260,262
Glockenspiel 99
Gloomy Rhythm 306
Gluskin, Lud 32,40,44,55,58,92
Goblin Band 84,278
Goblin Market 203
Go For Yourself 248
Go Harlem 23,78,177,317
Goin' Haywire 237
Goin' Home 18,25,60,171,210,231, 240,243
Goin' Places 166
Goldberg, Doc 37,82,92,130–131, 179,201,237,286,300,322,325,345, 355,358
Goldberg, Ed 224–225,230
Golden, Murray 297
Goldfield, Harry 236
Gold Mine In The Sky 300
Goldsmith, Frank 329
Goldstein, Len 206,263–264,318,327, 330,332,340,347–348, 351,247
Gomar, Larry 210
Gone 104,109
Gone With The Dawn 234
Gone With The Gin 281
Gone With The Wind 185,188,196,202, 205,210–211,214,216–218,223–224, 227,232,234,237,239,241–242,244, 246,254–255,270,272,285,289
Gonsoulin, Tom 346–347,350,354, 358–360
Goodbye 3,11,15,33,35,43–44,46,61, 82,87,90,92,96–97,105,107,111,114, 118,123–127,130,133,137,140,160, 163,183,215,220,231–232,235,237, 241,246,248,253,257,262,265,268, 271,273,276–277,279–280,282–283, 285–286,289,295,298,349–351, 353–354,356–357,359–361
Goodbye Forever 131
Goodbye Jonah 254,263,273,280
Good-Bye To Love 171
Good Green Acres At Home 40
Good Gulf Program [radio], NYC 244
Goodman, Benny 2–11,13–15,17–18, 20–23,26–31,33–37,39,41,43–47,50, 53–54,56,58–62,64–67,69–70,72–83, 86–88,90–93,96–100,102,104–112, 114–118,120–121,123–128,130–135, 137–141,143–145,147,149,152, 155–160,162–167,170,172,174,176, 178–180,182,184,186–189,191,198, 200,204–205,210–214,216–217, 219–223,225–226,230–232,234–235, 237,239,241,243–244,246,248–254, 256–257,261–262,265–268,270–280, 282–289,292–299,301–308,311–316, 318,321–327,330–331,333–337, 339–341,343–351,353–357,359–363
Goodman, Freddy 198
Goodman, Gene 275
Goodman, Harry 3–4,10,14,22–23, 26,37,44,46,67,75,83,88,96,105,107, 117,128,135,139,176,180,204–205, 217,220,253,274–275,283,292–293, 331

Goodman, Irving 9,33,64,78,88,96, 107,154,167,189,192,194–195,198, 224,236,248,269,294,301,321, 340–341,348,353,355
Good Mornin' 166,183,188,196,201, 208,215,221,255
Good Morning Blues 231,240,248,266, 279,340–341
Goodnight 337
Goodnight Angel 306,328,332,335,338
Goodnight Kisses 284
Goodnight, My Love 75,79–80,83,90, 98–100,104–108,111–114,118, 122–123,125–128,130,133–135,140, 160,183,283,286
Goodnight, My Lucky Day 128
Goodnight, Sweet Dreams 333,337
Goodnight Sweetheart 73
Goodrich, Bob 348
Goodtime Charlie 100,118
Good Time Society [radio show] 151, 158,161,178,185,208,212,218,231, 235,240,245,253,256,265
Goodwin, Henry 354
Goody Goody 4–6,8,11,13,15,18–19, 21,24–25,28,48,72
Goose Island Stomp 284
Gordon, Kilborn 135
Go South, Young Man 246,262
Gotham Stompers 238
Gotta Dance My Way To Heaven 51
Gotta Go 212
Gotta Pebble In My Shoe 361
Gotwalls, Dave 167
Gowans, Brad 213,245,248,251,353, 357
Grab Your Partner And Swing 37,240
Grace, Teddy 113–114,118,129,140, 209,245,251,311
Grahl, Betty 127,282,295
Gramercy Square 3
Grandfather's Clock 346
Grand Terrace, Chicago 8,15–16, 18–22,31,35,37–38,41–43,47–48,52, 54,57–62,68–70,76,78,80,83,87,92, 94,97–99,102,105,109,118,186,188, 203,207,210–211,223,240,242–249, 252–255,257,262,270,301,327,331, 336–337,339
Grand Terrace Rhythm 20,327,347
Grand Terrace Swing [Big Chief De Sota] 10
Grappelli, Stephane 363
Gray, Glen 2,5,7–9,12,16–17,19,21, 23,25,27,38,69–70,78–79,83–84, 86–87,89–90,99,101,103,112, 114–115,118,120–121,124,126,128, 135,142–143,149,168,183,187,192, 201,203–204,208,212,214,266,269, 275,278–280,285–286,289,292–293, 295–298,301–302,306–307,309, 316–317,320,323–324,326–327,332, 334,361
Gray, Jerry 35,61,74,85,93,119,123
Gray, Maxine 30,37,39,45,51,88
Great Caesar's Ghost 137
Great Day 19,52
Great Lake Stomp 33

Green, Claude 'Fats' 236–237, 240–241,243–244,248,253,260
Green, Freddie 110,138,184,188,200, 205,231,256,271,307–308,311,328, 333,337,341,354
Green, J. 36
Green, Johnny 333
Green, Madeline 231
Green, Marcellus 29,56,158,232,332
Greenwald, Harry 109,121
Greer, Sonny 6,28,31,92–93,128,130, 132,134,148,159,162–163,165–166, 172–173,175,186,188–189,202,262, 264,276,312,316–317,320,322,324, 332,336,344–346,354,356–357,360
Griffin, Chris (Gordon) 22–23,26,37, 44,46,67,72,75,79,88,96,105,107, 125,128,135,138,140,146,154,163, 176,182–184,204–205,217,234,253, 274–275,280,283,286,292–293,301, 303,326,331,337,339,345,348,353
Grissom, Dan 26,29,52–53,69,74,111, 161,188,190,205,255,280,308,346
Gross, Walter 250,296,309,323
Grossinger Country Club, Ferndale, N.Y. 217
Guess Who? 26–27,36,46,146
Guion, King 255
Gussak, Billy 92,95,110,211,216,225, 260–262,280,296,303,307,309–310, 323,327,333
Guy, Fred 6,28,31,93,128,132,148, 162,172,175,186,188,262,312,316, 317,332,336,335,346,354,356,360
Gypsy Fiddler 101
Gypsy Fiddles Were Playing 69
Gypsy In My Soul 293,298
Gypsy Smiles 312
Gypsy Violins 59,90,104,165,195,202, 265
Hackett, Bobby 164,278,280,284,287, 292,299,307,315–316,323–324, 326–328,334,341–344,347,349, 357–358
Hagen, Earle 271,338,347,349,351, 358–360
Haggart, Bob 9,13,25–26,42–43, 68,117,125–126,128,131,146,151, 157,159,161,163,166,170,205,210, 212,218,274,276,280–282,284,287, 296,313,316,318–319,323,325,327, 337–338
Hail West Virginia 119
Half-Moon On The Hudson 317
Half Of Me 76,94,123,157
Hall, Al 343
Hall, Edmond 188,193,200,253
Hall, George 32,34,36–37,42,46–47, 50,53–54,66,86,97,99,114–115,126, 144,292,294
Hall, Joe 5,25,112,114–115,120–121, 124,128,143,201,214,279,285–286, 292,295,298,301,317,320,324,326, 332,361
Hall, Sleepy 21
Hallelujah! 35,47,63,95,100,104,106, 116,146,152,159,177,179,195–196, 202,205,212,221,232,236,279,295,

299,326,336
Hallelujah! Things Look Rosy Now 85
Hallett, Mal 15,24,55–59,66–67,76, 79,83,86,88,90,96–97,99–100,104, 108,111–114,118,129,140,196,201, 208–209,222,245,251,306
Halley, Eddie 34
Hallsey, Paul 270
Halstead, Henry 16,71
Hamilton, Dave [see Harris, Dave] 81, 90,95
Hamilton, Don 123
Hamilton, John 165–166,171,174, 185,196,202–203,211,218,346
Hammond, D. 240,254
Hammond, John 106,139,193,227, 279,345
Hampton, Lionel 44,46–47,80–83, 86,92,100,107,109,112,114–115, 117–118,123,127–128,131,135,139, 152–154,161,174,179,217,220, 222–223,225,235,241,243,251,253, 271,275,277,279,286,289,292,294, 298,301,303,306,308,312,316, 320–321,324,331,336–337,340–341, 343–344,349,354–355,359–360
Hand In Glove 99,104,115
Hands Across The Table 39,231
Handy, Elizabeth 13
Handy, W. C. 12,28,112,162,270,289
Hanging Around My Home 251
Hangover In Hong Kong 355
Hanlon, Alan 318,327,332,340,342, 348,350–351,357,359
Hanshaw, Annette 140
Happy As The Day Is Long 25,34,43, 65,69,80,119,146,246,253,267
Happy Birthday 113,313
Happy Birthday To Love 178,200,213, 222,236,246
Happy Days Are Here Again 115
Happy Feet 83,202,323
Harbor Lights 188,220,240,247,252, 280
Harding, Alan 348
Hardwick, Otto 6,28,31,93,128,132, 134,146,148,162,165–166,172–175, 186,189,262,264,276,312,317,324, 332,336,346,354,356,360
Hardy Brothers 16,18,27
Hardy, Jim 60
Hare, Paul 49
Harkins, Ted 300
Harlemania 39
Harlem Congo 177,238,278,327
Harlem Heat 46,54,87,90,104
Harlem Joys 225,231,234,239,242,263
Harlem On The Prairie 299
Harlem Shout 26,69,80,356
Harlem Speaks 19,134,175,322,343
Harlem Special 223,243
Harlem Uproar 132
Harlem Uproar House, NYC 111, 114,120,123–124,126,130,151,156, 162,165,287–288
Harmonica Ride 55,64
Harmonica Willie 272
Harmony In Harlem 262,313

Harper, Red 46
Harrington, John 7–8,11–13,55,88, 119,120,157,215,218–219,297,326
Harrington, Raymond 237
Harris, Al 139
Harris, Arville 4,158
Harris, Dave [see Hamilton, Dave] 103,110,113,116,119,122–123,125, 129,132,140,145,148–149,156,164, 169,172,177,185,187,192,195, 202–203,277,300,313,348–349,357
Harris, Joe 3–4,10,14–15,23
Harris, Leroy 337,341
Harris, Phil 97–98,227,252
Harris, Silly 23
Hart, Clyde 52,65,69,80,165,235
Hart, Phil 9,13
Hasse, Adrian 134
Hatton, Raymond 267
Haughton, Chauncey 8,114,152,206, 225,277–279,295,321,343
Haughton, John 346
Hauser, Johnny 121,217,265,267,303
Have A Heart (Lost In Meditation) 317
Have You Ever Been In Heaven? 246, 248,285
Have You Ever Been In Love? 253
Have You Got Any Castles, Baby? 213,220,225,231–232,235,237,240, 242–243,245,253,255,267,269–270, 274,280–281,283,291,294,298
Have You Met Miss Jones? 269,274,279, 286,292,294–295,317
Havin' A Ball 94,150,159
Having A Wonderful Time 195,202,213, 223,244
Havin' Myself A Time 357
Hawkins, Coleman 311
Hawkins, Erskine 2,27,29,56,86,91, 111,114,120,123–124,126,130,151, 156,158,162,165,184,189,197,232, 248,276,278,292,303,332
Hawthorne, Alice 158
Hayes, Billy 115
Hayes, Edgar 16,20,26,34,36,141,166, 185,201,214,261–262,278,350,354, 358
Hayes, Mutt 4–5,15
Haymer, Herbie 3,47,72,101,108,118, 137,169,179,202–206,255–256, 263–265,267,274,280,283,320, 340–341,347,349,351
Haymes, Joe 41,43–45,47,49,84,100, 110,116–117,160,213–214,298
Haynes, Ronald 118
Hay Straw 39
Hayton, Lennie 45,144,151,157
Hazlett, Chester 35
Head Over Heels In Love 80,91, 108–109,124,144
Heatherton, Ray 35,39,57,63
He Ain't Got Rhythm 96,100,105, 110–111,117,125,127–128,131,135, 138,140,172,234,251
Heart Of Mine 321,335,350,353
Heart Of Stone 232,237
Heat Wave 11,39,103,149,161,211
Heaven 98

INDEX

Heaven Help This Heart Of Mine 200, 202,210,218,221,227,244,248,254
Heavenly 240
Heckler's Hop 80,281,284,303
Hector, The Garbage Collector 126
He Does Me So Much Good 264
Heggins, Larry 129
Heidt, Horace 97,144,266
Heigh-Ho 321,332,335,338
Hein, Wes 318,327,330–332,339–340, 342,348,351,357
Helbock, Joe 272
Hell's Bells 188
Hell In My Heart 292
Hemphill, Bob 348
Hemphill, Shelton 'Scad' 20,36,70,81, 141,155,156
Henderson, Fletcher 8,10,13,19–22, 31,33,35,37–38,41–43,47–48,50,52, 54,57–62,68–70,114,119,126–127, 130,137,158,165–166,186,188,193, 195,200,203,207,210–211,214–216, 223,230,236,262–263,265–266, 269–270,273,276–279,295,298,306, 321,333,340,353
Henderson, Horace 10,13,20,33,137, 233–234,244,246,248,251–252, 255–256
Henderson Stomp 88
Henry, Eric 151
Henry, Haywood 29,56,158,232,332
Here Comes The King 61
Here Comes The Man With The Jive 39,44,145
Here Comes Your Pappy 30,43,128,143, 150,161,218,267
Here's Love In Your Eyes 37,43,46–47, 58,60,64,70,72–73,75,80,83,90,92, 99,107
Herfurt, Skeets 10–11,27,29,33–34, 213,230,254,271,295,308,322,325, 333,347,349,351,358–359,361
Herman, Woody 76–77,81,83,86,93, 95–97,100,102,108–109,112, 114–115,118,121,127,135,137,140, 143,147,161–162,168–169,171,173, 192,196,200,205,214,231,263–254, 267–268,270,273–274,276,286,301, 303,318,328,331,346,355
Herth, Milt 272–273,284
He's A Gypsy From Poughkeepsie 153
He's A Humdinger 90
He's Funny That Way 256
Hesitation Blues 17
Hettrick, Lil 325,339
He Walked Right In 167
Hey, Hey 74,93
Hibbert, Hugh 37,82,92
Hickory House, NYC 2,5,7,12, 15–19,21–23,25,27,30,32,38–40,50, 53,58,60,64,66,86–87,89,95,97–90, 114–115,118,126,138,140,142,144, 146–149,151,153,160,164,172,174, 177–178,184,196–197,201,205,208, 210–211,214,222–223,225–227, 230–231,234,236,239–240,242,244, 247, 251,254,263,266–267,278,280, 284,287,292,299,306–307,324, 333–334,341–342,344,347,350,354, 357
Hickory Lodge, Larchmont, N.Y 189,191,196
Hicks, Billy 167,192–194,239
Hicks, Bobby 271
Hidden Valley 31,34,44,49
Hi-De-Ho 50
Hi-De-Ho Romeo 246
Higginbotham, J. C. 12,16,20,26,36, 70,73,81,127,137,141,155–156,188, 296,331,337
High Dive 4
High Jive 256
High Society 216
High, Wide And Handsome 234,278
Hill, George 360
Hill, Teddy 5,12,17,27,65,76,99,103, 138,143–144,151,156–161,167,169, 173–174,230,272,289,292,301,303, 309–311,328,337,344,346
Hilliard, Harriet 186
Hillman, Roc 10–11,27,29,33–34, 134,192,195,257–258,321,340–341, 349,351
Himber, Richard 160
Hindenburg Disaster 166
Hines, Earl 5,15–16,18,23,25,76,78, 87,92,94,97–99,105,109,117,126, 129–130,192,196–197,231,270,273, 301,324,332,334,337,341
Hines Rhythm 231
Hinton, Milt 20,59,72,127,134,241, 246,255,295,321,343
Hip Chic 360
Hirst, Lou 72,300,333
Hitchcock, Bill 80
Hite, Les 107
Hittin' On All Six 297
Hnida, George 9,140
Hoboken Bucket 361
Hobo On Park Avenue 57,61,64,91, 104,108,110,149,184,196,204,215, 219,223
Hobo, You Can't Ride This Train 273
Hocus Pocus 42,62
Hodge-Podge 76,219
Hodges, Johnny 6,26,28,31,77,90,93, 128,130,132,134,143–144,146,148, 152,159,161–162,165–166,170–173, 175,186,189,205,262,264–265, 311–313,316–317,320–321,324,332, 336,338,343–346,354,356–357,360
Hodges, Joy 33
Hoffa, Portland 114
Hoffman, Harry 165
Hogan, George 39,84,106
Hohler, Bob 162,213
Hoke, Pat 308
Holden, Jerry 124
Holdin' Your Man 302
Hold Me Tight 84
Hold My Hand 346
Hold Your Hat 211
Holiday, Billie 26,28,53,57,65,72,81, 104,110,121,143–144,157,170,184, 188,191,193–194,197,202,204–205, 233–235,237–241,244–245,248,253, 256,274,278–279,308,311,333,336, 340,351,357,359
Holiday, Clarence 65
Holiday In Harlem 172,177,277
Hollenbeck, Ralph 37
Hollingshead, Elmer 212,261,270
Holly, Ed 38,44,47,51,55,57
'Hollywood Hotel' [movie] 235
Hollywood Pastime 29,186,280,297–298
Hollywood Restaurant, NYC 112, 115,121
Holmes, Charlie 155,189,337
Hometown Band 162
Honest And Truly 111,161,255
Honey 158
Honey Chile [Lullaby In Rhythm] 344
Honey, Keep Your Mind On Me 205
Honeymoonin' In Manhattan 195
Honeymoonin' On A Dime 257
Honey, Please Don't Turn Sour On Me 51
Honeysuckle Rose 6,11,15–16,20–22, 24,26,29–31,38–39,41,44,52,55, 58–59,61,64–65,69,72,79,83,86–87, 90,93,95,98,100,103–104,107–110, 115,117,119,121,124,126,129,131, 137,143–146,148,151,160,163, 165–167,169,172,175–176,178, 184–185,196,203–204,209,211, 213–216,218,220,223–224,230, 233–234,236–237,239,241,243, 249–251,253–256,264,268,270,272, 279,281,285,296–297,303,316,320, 327,331–332,339,344,353,360
Honey, Won't You Please Come Home 172
Hooray For Love 4
Hope, Frankie 104
Hope, Joe 22
Hopfner, Ray 276,286,346,355
Hopkins, Claude 2,7,32,53–54,62,76, 80,86,99,111,114,144,158,168,193, 206,222,236,252,266,302,307–308, 312,324,358,360
Hoppin' Off 234
Horne, Lena 8,19,65
Hors D'Oeuvres 185
Horten, Dick 38
Horton, R. H. 354
Host, Joe [see Joe Hostetter] 29–31, 35–36,39,44
Hostetter, Joe [see Joe Host] 18,23,33
Hot Club, 144 E42nd Street, NYC 168–169
Hot Club Stomp 188
Hot Coffee 78
Hotel Adolphus, Dallas 242, 254–257
Hotel Astor, NYC 2,5,7,12,16,23,27, 30,32,37,39,45,51,97,99,115,201, 222,360
Hotel Biltmore, NYC 97
Hotel Book-Cadillac, Detroit 97,267, 269
Hotel Bradford, Boston 100,104, 124, 142–145,148,151,158,161–162, 166–167
Hotel Capital, NYC 156
Hotel Commodore, NYC 23–24,27, 29,66–67,76,79,83,86,88,90,96–97, 99–100,104,108,111–114,118,122, 124,126,129–132,136,138,143–144, 146–148,151–152,158–159,162,164, 169,191,247,266–268,271–273,276, 278,289,292–293,298,307–308, 311–312,316,322–324,327,329,331, 334–336,339,341–342,344–345,347
Hotel Drake, Chicago 161
Hotel Edison, NYC 115
Hotel Francis Drake, SF 97
Hotel Gibson, Cincinnati, Ohio 169
Hotel Governor Clinton, NYC
Hotel Jefferson, St. Louis 97
Hotel LaSalle, Detroit 97
Hotel Lexington, NYC 2,5,7,12,16, 23–24,27,30,32–33,36,40,43,45,50, 52–53,58–59,61,65,97,99,114,122, 126,144,184
Hotel Lincoln, NYC 2,12,16,18–19, 21–23,25,27,31–32,35,37,41,47,49, 53,58,61,66,70,83,86,92,95,97,99, 101,109,114–115,126,131,144–146, 266,268,276,278,292,307,324,334, 344,350
Hotel Mayflower, Washington, D.C. 323,363
Hotel Netherland-Plaza, Cincinnati, OH 73,97–98,152,269,272–273
Hotel New Yorker, NYC 12,32,39, 52–54,66,86,97,99,126,144,151, 164–166,171,174,176,184–185,196, 201–203,207,211,218,220,222,233, 237,240,247,251,266,269,275,278, 280,286,289,292–293,295–297,302, 306–307,309,316,320,323–324, 326–327,334–335,337,341,344,347, 354,358,360
Hotel Nicollet, Minneapolis 301,303, 309
Hotel Pennsylvania, NYC 10,16,19, 23,27,66–67,70,72–80,82–83,86–88, 90–92,96–99,105–107,109–115, 117–118,121,123–127,129–131, 133–135,137–139,141,144–145,147, 149,152–153,157–159,163–164, 166–167,169,171–172,175,178,180, 183–187,194,196,198–199,201–202, 204, 208,210,213,216,219,222–223, 226,228,231–232,235–236,242, 245–247,253,256,266–267,270–280, 283–288,292–293,295–299,301–303, 306–308,312–313,315–318,321, 323–324,328,331–335,337,339–345, 348–349
Hotel Plaza, NYC 97
Hotel Plymouth, NYC 146,156
Hotel Ritz-Carlton, Boston 58, 60–61,64,193,207–208,210,212, 215–216,218,220,222,224–225,231, 233–235,237,239–240,243,245,248, 253,356–357
Hotel Roosevelt, NYC 97,115, 166
Hotel Roosevelt, New Orleans 93, 95–96,100,103,210–215,217–219, 221–222,224,231,234–234,237, 239–242

Hotel St. Francis, San Francisco 17,274,280,283
Hotel St. Nicholas, St.Paul-Minneapolis 68
Hotel Schrader, Milwaukee 328,331
Hotel Senator, Sacramento 97
Hotel Sherman, Chicago 97
Hotel Statler, Boston 163
Hotel Stevens, Chicago 97
Hotel Taft, NYC 32,34,36–37,42, 46–47,50,53–54,66,86,97,99, 114–115,126,144
Hotel Waldorf-Astoria, NYC 97
Hotel William Penn, Pittsburgh 97, 118,172,177
Hot Feet 347
'Hot Jazz' [book] 226
Hot Jazz [magazine] 192
Hot Mama 284
Hot String Beans 341
Hot Stuff 89,94,105,111,117
Hotter Than Hell 205
Hot Water Bottle 337
House Hop 18,22,26,28,37,70,77,80, 86,96,98,100,105,112,120,128,133, 137,140,186,188,194,243,246,272, 284,308,341,349
House Jack Built For Jill 44
How Am I To Know? 64,72,137,159, 172–173,175,185,203,205,240,242, 256,276,279,292,298–299,309
Howard, Darnell 117,231
Howard, Shirley 84
Howard Theater, Washington, D.C. 146
How Can I? 269
How Can I Thank You? 357
How Can You Forget? 237,322,332,337
How Carelessly 211
How Could You? 108,112,125,127,130, 135–136,143–145,147,152,154, 157–160,163,171,174–175,178–179, 183–185,195–196,210–211,216, 219–220,232,240,246,252–253,255
How Deep Is The Ocean? 53,211,213
How'dja Like To Love Me? 321,335, 339,345,348
How Do I Rate With You? 21
How Dry I Am 214
Howe, Dorothy 158–159,220,233, 237,240
How I Miss You 30
How Many Rhymes Can You Answer? 301
(How To Make Love) In Ten Easy Lessons 355,357
How Was I To Know? 91–92
How Ya, Baby? 269
How Ya Gonna Keep 'Em Down On The Farm 108
Hoy-Hoy 343
Hudson-DeLange Orchestra 37,64, 82,91–92,104,108,110,123,130–131, 149,151–152,168,179,183–185,196, 201,204,215,219–220,223–224,230, 237,240,242,247,249,264,270,286, 300,322, 325,330,345
Hudson, Will 37,61,64,66,73,76, 80–82,91–92,99,117,130–131,146, 179,183–185,196,201,215,219–220, 223–225,234,237,240,242,247, 273–274,286,300,322,325,345,355, 358
Huff Puff 98
Hughes, Rupert 74
Hula Heaven 159
Hulick, Bud 135
Humes, Helen 292,308
Hummel, Fritz 5,25,112,115,118,120, 128,143,201,214,278
Humoresque 67,171,175,178–179,204, 211,214,219–220,222,230–232, 239–240,254,268,270, 285–286,289
Humphrey, Willie 12,20
Hunt, Frances 100,104–105,107, 109–112,114–115,117–118,120–121, 123–128,130–131,133–135,137–138, 140–141,143–147,149,152,154, 157–160,162–163,243,246
Hunt, George 109,138,205
Hunt, Pee Wee 5,8,16,19,25,69–70, 78–80,83–84,87,89–90,101,103,112, 114–115,118,120–121,124,128,143, 168,183,187,201,203–204,208,212, 214,278–279,285–286,289,292–293, 295,297–298,301–302,306–307,309, 316–317,320,323–324,326–327, 331–332,361
Hupfer, Nick 76–77,86,102,109,114, 118,161–162,231,264,276,286,328, 346,355
Hurley, Clyde 360
Hurst, Lou 29
Husing, Ted 115
Hustlin' And Bustlin' For Baby 273
Hutchenrider, Clarence 5,9,25,69, 78–79,83,87,112,115,118,120–121, 124,128,143,201,214,279,285–286, 289,292,295,297–298,301–302,317, 324,326,332,361
Hutton, Ina Ray 135,197–198
Hyams, Mark 37,82,92,130–131,179, 201,215,237,286,300,322,325,345, 355,358
Hyde Park 19,173
Hyland, Bill 47,72,101,118,137,204
Hylton, Jack 20,167,238,320
Hymn To The Sun 186,205,213,232, 237,267
I Adore You 85,96,140
I Ain't Got Nobody 25,74,102,104, 186,244,253,265,278,297,334
I Can Dream, Can't I? 289,292,295, 297,307–308,312,323,335–336
I Can Pull A Rabbit Out Of My Hat 12,19,46,50,105
I Can See You All Over The Place 151
I Can't Believe That You're In Love With Me 117,130,174,234,270,308,359
I Can't Believe You Really Love Me 95
I Can't Break The Habit Of You 123, 131,146,151,166,172,178
I Can't Escape From You 29,36,39–41, 46–53,55,59–60,62,65–66,69,72,74, 76,107,115,120
I Can't Face The Music 335,339–340, 343
I Can't Get Started 12–13,19,23,30, 32,36,39,43,45–47,50,55,58,66,69, 71,73,75–76,81,84,87,90,95,99,101, 103,106,110,113,116–117,119,125, 156–157,178,196–198,200,202,208, 211,213,216,221,224,227,235,239, 279,284,327,332–333,335
I Can't Give You Anything But Love 17, 21,70,81,92,96,99–100,102,107–108, 114,118,124,127,143,162,173,201, 209,215–219,239,253,266,270,273, 275–277,280,288,291,293,308,311, 313,326,337,348,350
I Can't Lose That Longing For You 111, 113–115,121,124,131,133,137–138, 140,147–148,151–152,160,165,185, 209
I Can't Pretend 40,60,65–66,70,77,83, 89,118
I Can't Remember 28,39
I Can't Stop Loving You 361
I Could Be In Heaven 60
I Couldn't Be Mad At You 59
I Could Use A Dream 301,309
I Cried For You 26,101,112,118,124, 138,148,153,183,210,237,269,274, 276,280,284,298,306,335,337
I Dance Alone 341
Ida, Sweet As Apple Cider 19,69,99, 114–115,124,145,163,203,256,320
I'd Be A Fool Again 128
I'd Climb The Highest Mountain 118
I'd Do Anything Because I Love You 219
I'd Do Anything For You 331
I'd Like To See Some More Of Samoa 244,271
I'd Love To Play A Love Scene 269,284
I Don't Believe It 346
I Don't Know If I'm Coming Or Going 127,144,244
I Don't Know Your Name 5
I Don't Want To Make History 8,16,45
I Double Dare You 276,307,324, 327–328,331–332,334–335,337
I'd Rather Be Right 279
I'd Rather Call You Baby 253
I'd Rather Lead A Band 5,6
I Dream Of You 302
I Fall In Love With You Every Day 321, 336,345,349,351
If Dreams Come True 293,295,297–299, 301–303,306,308–309,312,320, 326–328,331,340,344
I Feel Like A Feather In The Breeze 5
If I Can Count On You 236
If I Could Be With You One Hour Tonight 35,46,49,56,60,67,87,143,179,185, 196,204,219,265,297,343
If I Could Have You 96
If I Could Only Count On You 232, 253,267
If I Had My Way 25,153
If I Had You 117,125,135,183,202, 210,216,222,237,240,242
If I Put My Heart In My Song 210,214, 219,222,224,231,234,239,241,256
If I Should 112
If It Ain't Love 291
If I Thought You Cared 316
If It Rains, Who Cares? 354
If It's The Last Thing I Do 254,256,259, 262,267–269,272,275–276,279–281, 283,285,288,293,302,326,334–335
If I Were You 351,358
If My Heart Could Only Talk 92, 100–101,104,109,115,147,327,336
I Found A New Baby 3–5,14,23,25–26, 30,33,35,44,49,55,58–59,75,82,84, 90,93,114–115,126,130,137,140,149, 151,160,162–163,172,177,184,189, 204,211,220,223,227,232,234,239, 242,295,298,307,309,313,317,320, 323,327,331,335,337,340–341,351, 355–357,362
If The Man In The Moon 255
If We Never Had Met 29
If We Never Meet Again 31–32,37–38, 43–44,47–50,52–54,56–61,64–65, 68–70,73,76,78–79,82–84,98,102, 105,108,296
If You Ask Me How Much I Love You 46–47,50
If You Leave Me 158,162
If You Love Each Other 196
If You Love Me 19,39
If You Only Knew 350
If You're A Viper 339
If You're Ever In My Arms Again 188, 192,223,322
If You Should Ever Leave 178,186,188, 200,203,207–208,210–211,214,218, 222–223,236–237,240,242–244, 246–247,256,270,317
If You Should Leave Me 114
If You Were In My Place 332,338, 343–344,347–348,351
If You Were Mine 246
If You Were Someone Else 254,271,273, 275
I Get A Kick Out Of You 37,39,203, 302
I Give My Heart To You 57–58
I Got A Guy 137,277,343
I Gotcha 17
I Got Plenty O' Nuttin' 19–20,60
I Got Rhythm 35–36,38,40–41,46–47, 59,61,64,71,74,76,80–81,89–90,95, 98,102,107–108,115,117–118,123, 128,135,137,140,143,156–157,163, 171,174,176,179,183,186–187,191, 207,209,212,214–216,219,247–248, 251,256,266–267,271,280,285,294, 299,303,306,315,317,320,332,334, 337,343
I Gotta Right To Sing The Blues 273
I Hadn't Anyone Till You 349,356,359, 362
I Hate To Leave You Now 273
I Hate Your Face 37
I Haven't Changed A Thing 358–359
I Hope Gabriel Likes My Music 5–6, 155,281
I Just Couldn't Take It Baby 251
I Just Made Up With That Old Girl Of Mine 27,32,52

INDEX

I Keep Remembering 271
I Kiss Your Hand, Madame 162,215
I Know Now 159,183,202,207,209, 215,218–220,224,227,232,234, 239–240,242–243,245–246,249,251, 259,262,267,280
I Know That You Know 9–10,35–36, 38,43,47,67,69,73,78–79,107,109, 115,118,127,134,160–161,169,179, 184,188,196,204,217,223,225,233, 240,244,266,270,274,292,302,305, 312,328,331,337,341,347,354
I Learned About Love From Her 101, 109
I Let A Song Go Out Of My Heart 336,338,344,348–351,361
I Let A Tear Fall In The River 362
I Like Music (With A Swing Like That) 312,321
I Live The Life I Love 308,331,335
I'll Always Be In Love With You 13,72, 76,83,105,178,235,351,357
I'll Be Glad When You're Dead, You Rascal You 22,24
I'll Be Loving You Always 73
I'll Bet You Tell That To All The Girls 12,19
I'll Be With You In Apple Blossom Time 306
I'll Chase The Blues Away 116,127
I'll Cling To The Moon 88
I'll Come To The Point 301
I'll Dream My Way To Heaven 121,146, 158
I'll Dream Tonight 347
I'll Follow You 18
I'll Forsake All Others 95,100,102,109, 114,121
I'll Get Along Somehow 157,232, 253
I'll Get By 44,59,170,326
I'll Keep Warm All Winter 120,123
I'll Never Be The Same 184,264,353
I'll Never Forget That I Love You 163
I'll Never Let You Go 36,39,42,46,51, 54,59
I'll Never Say I Love You 91
I'll Never Tell You I Love You Again 82, 151,196,214
I'll See You Again 225
I'll See You In My Dreams 101,109, 115,232,278,358
I'll Sing You A Thousand Love Songs 52, 80,84,93,103,109,145
I'll Stand By 11,31,54
I'll String Along With You 272
I'll Take The South 29,47
I Love To Sing-a 4,89,111,274
I Love To Whistle 339,341,351
I Love You 240
I Love You From Coast To Coast 100–101,114,240
I Love You In Technicolor 349
I Love You Just Enough 157
I Love You Truly 111,254,256
I'm A Ding Dong Daddy (From Dumas) 3,45,89,265,272,282,292,294,299, 306,323,326,345,349,353,362
I'm A Fool For Lovin' You 13,18–19

Imagination 252,316
I'm A Hi-De-Ho Romeo 262–263
I'm All Dressed Up 58
I'm A Lone Cowboy 39
I'm All Out Of Breath 151,185
I'm Always In The Mood For You 241, 253,262
I'm An Old Cowhand 23,26,30–31,36, 42,44,46,49–50,52,54–55,57–58, 60–61,63,67,69–70,87–89,95,98, 100,102,113,115,118,159
I Married An Angel 351
I'm At The Mercy of Love 56,62,89
I May Be Wrong 78,146,201,203,213, 219,222,236,242,254,260,316,323
I'm Betting On You 96
I'm Bubbling Over With Love 178,184, 202,204,256
I'm Building Up To An Awful Letdown 3–4,21,35
I'm Coming, Virginia 43,48,96,107, 159,224,232,237,253,270,287,327
I'm Confessin' 41,205,284
I'm Counting On You 260
I'm Crazy 'Bout My Baby 32,36,95, 103
I'm Dependable 246
I'm Doin' That Thing 106
I Met My Waterloo 273
I'm Face To Face With Love 127,137
I'm Feelin' Like A Million 173,201, 220,232,234,235,239,240,242,248, 268
I'm Getting Sentimental Over You 15, 18–19,21–22,24,34,36,58,60,63,67, 72–73,82,84,91,93,95,103,110,113, 115,118,122,124,130,136,146, 151–152,162,183,201,207,210,213, 231–232,236,242–244,246,251,265, 269,272,276,278,285,289,308,318, 333
I'm Glad For Your Sake 157,336–337, 339
I'm Gonna Clap My Hands 3,6,40,50
I'm Gonna Kiss Myself Goodbye 121, 166
I'm Gonna Lock My Heart And Throw Away The Key 357
I'm Gonna Put You In Your Place 186
I'm Gonna Sit Right Down And Write Myself A Letter 3,13,19,21,26,64, 254
I'm Grateful To You 25,52
I'm Happy, Darling, Dancing With You 171,173,185,196,202–203,210,219
I'm Hatin' This Waitin' Around For You 154,157,160,175,178–179,183,189, 196,203,220,240
I'm In A Crying Mood 177
I'm In A Dancing Mood 75,82,90,92, 100,109,119
I'm In My Glory 262
I'm In The Mood For Love 11
I'm In The Mood For Swing 359
I'm Just A Country Boy 270
I'm Just A Jitterbug 350
I'm Just Beginning To Care 30,52
I'm Just Wild About Harry 152

I'm Laughing Up My Sleeve 308
I'm Like A Fish Out Of Water 286, 293,299
I'm Nuts About Screwy Music 161,190
I'm One Step Ahead Of My Shadow 45, 59
I'm Painting The Town Red 120,130
I'm Pictulated Over You 16
Improvisation 149
Improvisation On A Piano 37
I'm Putting All My Eggs In One Basket 6
I'm Satisfied 18,98,148
I'm Saving Myself For You 346
I'm Shootin' High 3–4,6,59
I'm Sitting On Top Of The World 137, 143,178,214,222,239
I'm Slappin' Seventh Avenue (With The Sole Of My Shoe) 338,343,346
I'm Sorry I Made You Cry 94
I'm Surprised 57
I'm Talking Through My Heart 75,84, 142
I'm The Cuban Cary 92,97
I'm The One Who Loves You 295
I'm Thinking Of You Tonight 335
I'm Tootin' My Horn 37,46,48–49,53, 71,75
I Must Have That Man 110,205,233, 307,351
I'm Walkin' This Town 292
I'm Yours 39,273
I'm Yours For The Asking 243
In A Happy Frame Of Mind 339
In a Jam 31,144
In A Little English Inn 52
In A Little Gypsy Tea Room 55,58,88, 209
In A Little Hula Heaven 121,130,158, 166,175
In A Little Roadside Rendezvous 185
In A Little Spanish Town 71,82,93,250, 276,296,301,332,339
In A Little Wayside Inn 22
In A Minor Mood 148,212,225,237, 318,323
In A Mist 273,276
In An Old English Village 279,295
In A Sentimental Mood 18–20,22,24, 26,29–31,33,36–37,40–41,45,56–57, 61–62,75,79,92–93,96,132,166,169, 210,236,264,286,297–298,307,309
Indian Love Call 46,359
Indian Tom Toms 46
I Nearly Let Love Go Slipping Thru' My Fingers 25,33,36
I Need You Night And Day 47
I Need You So 30,32,45
I Never Knew 15,29,40,49,58,64,76, 93,99,102,109,146–147,169,175, 177–179,184–185,196,208,221,236, 243–244,247,251,270,274,320,335, 338,343–344,353,356
I Never Knew I Could Love Anybody 39
I Never Slept A Wink Last Night 84, 112,240,257,339
I Never Should Have Told You So 99, 105,116

Inge, Edward 17,65,179
Inka Dinka Doo 6,13,48,56,102
Ink Spots 100,108,113–114
In Little Town 233
Inman, Dr Samuel 245,363
Inman, John 189
Inman, Slim 95,245
In My Meditations 207
In My Seclusion 90
In My Solitude 220
In My Wildest Dreams 218
Inside 346
Inspiration 87,92,117,270
Instrumentalists 37–38,42,44,48–49, 69
International Casino, NYC 272,276
In The Chapel In The Moonlight 80
In The Gloaming 346
In The Groove 16,66,72,75,119
In The Jug 313
In The Land Of Yamo Yamo 311
In The Middle Of A Kiss 99,169
In The Mission By The Sea 271,279
In The Shade Of The New Apple Tree 336–337,339
In The Shade Of The Old Apple Tree 45–46,158,264,268,271,276,280, 286,322,325,331
In The Shadow Of Love 252
In The Still Of The Night 254,267,270, 273,276,283,289,298–299,312,324, 331,335
Introduction To A G String 62
In Your Own Little Way 167,175–176
Iona, Andy 184
I Ought To Have My Head Examined 238
I Owe You 253
I Remember 143,208
Iridium Room, NYC 97
Isaacs, Russ 207
I Saw A Kiss A-Sailing 265
I'se A-Muggin' 6,8,11,15,18,21,24,30, 37–39,43,45,49,69,76,95,98,108
I See Your Face Before Me 295,311,316, 321,323,328,331–332,335–337, 339–340,343
I Simply Adore You 327,332,335–336, 346
Is It Love Or Infatuation? 253,274,280, 285
Is It True Somebody Loves Me 223
Is It True What They Say About Dixie? 8,11,18,21,30,37,42,46,50,52–53,56, 58
Isle Of Capri 18,21,24,177,200,214, 217
Isn't Love The Strangest Thing? 6,17–18, 20,33
Ison, Earle 250
Is She Really The One For Me? 92
Is That Religion? 102,130,324
Is This Gonna Be My Lucky Summer? 185–186
I Still Love To Kiss You Goodnight 279, 281,283,299,312
I Still Want You 69
I Surrender Dear 3–4,6,11,28,44,

57–59, 76, 101–102, 142, 145, 151, 171, 174, 186, 194, 202, 206, 213, 235, 238, 253, 263, 326–327, 331
I Take To You 8, 30, 32, 40–41, 49, 54, 56, 61, 68
I Take Your Hand 147
It Ain't Necessarily So 50, 89, 105, 111
It Ain't Right 24, 27, 29, 35, 40–42, 44–45, 48–49, 52, 58, 62, 65, 98
It All Begins And Ends With You 30, 44, 47, 55, 57
It All Depends On You 38
It Can Happen 58
It Can Happen To You 43, 57, 67, 72
It Don't Mean A Thing If It Ain't Got That Swing 132, 145, 151, 160, 264, 272, 276, 293, 334
It Goes To Your Feet 171
It Had To Be You 109, 126–127, 187, 202
It Happened 18
It Happened In Chicago 62
It Happened Down In Dixieland 96, 105, 121, 161, 196, 264, 267, 273
It Happened To End 18
It Happens To The Best Of Friends 92
I Thought You Cared 348
It Looks Like Love 196
It Looks Like Rain In Cherry Blossom Lane 172, 175, 184, 186, 194, 201, 210–211, 216, 218–220, 223, 225, 231, 233–234, 236–237, 240, 242, 244, 246, 248, 254
It Must Be Religion 178
It Must Be True 185, 326
It Must Have Been A Dream 4, 5
I Told The Birds 145
It's A Long, Long Way To Tipperary 259
It's A Sin To Tell A Lie 24, 30–31, 35–36, 41, 48–49, 53–55, 58–59
It's Been So Long 3–6, 11, 15, 19, 35, 73, 354
It's De-Lovely 75, 79, 81, 83, 88–89, 92, 98, 104–105, 107, 109, 112
It's Easier Said Than Done 325, 331, 335, 343
It Seems I've Done Something Wrong Again 108
It's Got To Be Love 38, 44
It's Great To Be In Love Again 6, 9, 11
It's High Time 151
It's Like Reaching For The Moon 26, 37, 41, 55
It's Love Again 41
It's Love I'm After 64, 77, 79, 88, 90, 100, 113, 117, 185
It's My Turn Now 273, 301, 328
It's No Fun 13, 22–23, 25
It's Over Because We're Through 83, 147, 207, 212, 218, 260
It's Swell Of You 138, 142, 146, 148, 159, 166–167, 169, 173, 175, 179, 196, 204, 219, 238
It's The Dreamer In Me 299, 303, 305, 307–308, 321, 334, 335, 337, 341, 345, 353, 356
It's The Gypsy In Me 43, 48, 64
It's The Little Things That Count 353
It's The Natural Thing To Do 192,

200–201, 207, 211, 234, 254–255, 285, 289
It's The Talk Of The Town 54, 57, 239
It's Wearing Me Down 119, 127, 186, 244, 256, 269–270
It's Wonderful 7, 287, 292–293, 295, 297, 301, 307, 311–312, 316, 318, 321, 323, 325, 328, 331–333, 335–337
It's You I'm Talking About 10, 18–19, 42, 54
It's You In Love 49
It Was A Lover And His Lass 334
(It Was A) Sad Night in Harlem 28–29, 47, 55, 65, 173
I Used To Be Above Love 25, 50
I Used To Be Color Blind 359
I've A Strange New Rhythm In My Heart 259
I've Been A Fool Again 130–131, 151
I've Gone Romantic Over You 326
I've Got A Date With A Dream 360
I've Got A Dime 178
I've Got A Feelin' You're Foolin' 21
I've Got A Guy 348, 356
I've Got A Heavy Date 15, 18, 22, 49, 69
I've Got A New Lease On Love 148
I've Got A Note 40, 47
I've Got A Strange New Rhythm In My Heart 282, 288
I've Got Beginner's Luck 130, 140, 146, 148, 160–161
I've Got My Eye On You 194
I've Got My Fingers Crossed 21
I've Got My Heart Set On You 265, 279, 281, 283, 285, 299
I've Got My Love To Keep Me Warm 101, 104, 109, 112, 117, 123–125, 127–128, 130, 134–135, 137, 140, 142–143, 145–147, 151, 154, 157, 160, 162–163, 175, 182, 185, 197, 203, 223, 231, 292, 295, 304
I've Got Rain In My Eyes 134, 177
I've Got Something In My Eye 79
I've Gotta Right To Sing The Blues 52
I've Got The Blues 219, 222
I've Got The World On A String 13, 52, 87
I've Got To Be A Rug Cutter 128, 142, 148, 159, 165, 168, 171, 177, 189, 202, 264, 320
I've Got To Have You 253
I've Got To Swing 205, 237, 311
I've Got To Think It Over 257
I've Got Trouble With My Shadow 60
I've Got You Under My Skin 34, 78, 81, 86–87, 90, 95, 100, 103, 105–106, 108, 110, 115, 127, 159, 185, 211, 217, 263
I've Had The Blues So Long 96
I've Hitched My Wagon To A Star 274, 280, 285–286, 292, 298–299, 301, 306, 308, 313, 316–318
I've Lost Another Sweetheart 39, 44, 48, 52, 54–55, 189, 196
I've Waited A Lifetime 47, 49, 53, 55
I Wanna Be In Winchell's Column 286, 298–299, 303, 305, 309
I Want A Little Girl 140, 153, 172, 251, 333

I Want A Man Like That 320
I Want A New Romance 269, 272, 276
I Want The Whole World To Know I Love You 54, 58, 76
I Want To Be A Gypsy 219
I Want To Be Happy 105, 108, 111, 116, 124, 126, 140, 163, 165, 279, 299, 301, 360
I Want To Be With You 35–37
I Was Born To Swing 128
I Was Doin' Alright 318, 321, 324
I Was Saying To The Moon 100
I Wish I Could Shimmy Like My Sister Kate 130
I Wish I Had You 357
I Wish I Knew 124, 126, 135
I Wish I Were Aladdin 3
I Wish I Were In Love Again 163
I Wish I Were Twins 246
I Wish You Were My Love Affair 58, 60
I Wonder 35, 38, 61
I Wonder Who Made Rhythm 8
I Won't Take No For An Answer 236
I Would Do Anything For You 22–23, 30–31, 41, 62, 64, 74–76, 80, 83, 86, 102, 110–112, 121, 137, 186, 206, 266, 289
I Would Sing To The Moon 75, 79
Jack Climbed A Beanstalk 341
Jack Dempsey's 5, 7, 12
Jackson, Earl 234
Jackson, Franz 353
Jackson, Quentin 65, 179
Jacob, Jules 99
Jacobs, Pete 114, 206
Jacobs, Sid 353
Ja-Da 13, 21, 41, 54, 130, 148, 157–158, 163, 175, 196, 215, 230, 236, 243, 309, 315
Jaffe, Nat 99, 189, 211, 233
Jamaica Shout 62, 87, 177
Jamboree 82, 100, 126, 128, 130, 133, 143, 145, 147, 151, 159, 162, 164, 170, 224
Jamboree Jones 71, 79, 87, 89
James, David 354
James, Elmer 12, 20, 26, 34, 36, 141, 288
James, George 102
James, Harry 59–60, 92, 105, 107, 109–110, 112, 115, 117–118, 123–128, 130–131, 134–135, 137, 140, 145–147, 149, 152, 154, 156–160, 163, 165, 170, 174, 176, 178–180, 182–186, 191, 204–205, 211, 213, 216–221, 223, 231–232, 234, 239, 241, 243–244, 246, 248, 251, 253, 256–257, 262, 265, 267–268, 271, 273–277, 279–280, 282–286, 292–293, 295, 297–299, 301, 303–305, 307–308, 312–313, 316, 321, 324–325, 327–328, 331, 335, 337, 339–341, 343–345, 348–351, 353, 355–357, 359
James, Ida 87, 92, 94, 99, 105, 109, 117, 130, 196, 270, 337
Jammin' 134, 152, 159, 163–164, 176, 179, 196, 203, 208, 219, 221–223, 270
Jam On Toast 350
Jam Session 69–70, 72, 74–75, 82, 88, 98, 105, 109, 124–125, 137, 147, 151, 172, 174, 177, 183, 194, 219, 221, 244, 246,

252–253, 276
Janas, Judy 98
Jangled Nerves 13, 21–22, 42, 49, 54, 57–58, 64, 67, 69, 80, 83, 93, 98, 123, 188, 203, 207, 234, 244, 267
Japanese Sandman 38, 65, 100, 108, 114, 129, 203, 207, 222, 224, 239, 250, 280, 297
Japansy 292
Jarrett, Art 227, 252
Jason, Barbara 104
Jazz A La Carte 163
Jazz Band Blues 326
Jazzeroo 81, 95, 172
Jazz In Blue 18
Jazz Lips 146
Jazz Me Blues 21, 50, 79, 83, 93, 118, 144, 158, 177, 185, 196, 203, 223, 238, 242, 244, 265, 273, 286, 326, 351
Jazznocracy 29–30, 40, 112, 161
Jazz World [magazine] 168
Jealous 270
Jealous Blues 215
Jealous Of Me 269
Jeannine 332
Jean, Val 252
Jeep's Blues 344
Jefferson, Fred 212
Jefferson, Hilton 127, 137, 200, 236, 263, 276, 355, 361–362
Jelly Roll Blues 90
Jenkins, Freddy 189, 205, 262, 264, 320
Jenkins, Gordon 100, 114, 118, 143, 162, 248, 273
Jenkins, Joe 293
Jenkins, Les 101, 108, 112, 121, 130, 134, 138, 153, 166, 171, 178, 186, 198, 207, 213, 254, 271, 295, 308, 322, 325, 333, 338, 347, 349, 351, 358–359, 361
Jenkins, Pat 291, 300
Jenney, Brad 353
Jenney, Jack 326
Jenssen, Mel 5, 9, 25, 112, 115, 120, 212
Jerome, Jerry 137, 176, 186, 210–211, 213–216, 218–219, 231, 234, 237, 240, 254–256, 289–290, 297–298, 318, 324, 327, 330–332, 339–340, 342, 345, 347–348, 351, 357
Jes' Natch'ully Lazy 20, 50
Jessup, Red 82
Je Vous Adore 34
Jezebel 333, 337, 341
Jigglin' And Reelin' 34
Jim Jam 252
Jim Jam Blues 280
Jim Jam Stomp 300, 333, 341
Jim Town Blues 8, 33, 60, 62, 93, 119, 158, 211
Jingle Bells 50, 56, 80, 91, 95, 100, 106, 237, 280, 301, 303
Jingle Of The Jungle 62
Jitterbug Shuffle 109
Jitterbug's Lullaby 360
Jitterbug Special 233
Jitters 88, 103
Jive Stomp 165, 177
Jiving The Jeep 137
Jivin' The Keys 244

INDEX

Jivin' The Vibes 117
Joe Louis Truck 11
Joe Turner Blues 286
Johnny One Note 163
John's Idea 205,221,279
John Silver 349
Johns, Pete 276,286,346,355
Johnson, Arthur 120,201
Johnson, Bill 80
Johnson, Bobby 178,277–279,295, 299,301,321,350,355,361–362
Johnson, Budd 117,185,231,337,341, 353
Johnson, Charlie 243,246–247
Johnson, Countess 234,236,243–244, 246,251,255
Johnson, Ed 261
Johnson, Gene 114,158,206
Johnson, Harold 73,84,137,139–140, 182,195,304,362
Johnson, Howard 12,17,138,159,173
Johnson, Irene 31
Johnson, Ivy 260
Johnson, Jerry 273
Johnson, Keg 20,59,74,127,134,241, 246,255,262,266,269,295, 321,343
Johnson, Manzie 17,310
Johnson, 'Miss California' 60
Johnson, Otis 65,179,207
Johnson, Pete 353
Johnson, Walter 20,127,137
Johnson, William 29,56,158,232,332
Jones, Bobby 5,25,145,212
Jones, Claude 4,12,20,59,109,117, 127,134,233,241,246,295,321,343
Jones, Dick 10,13,25,72,80,82,101, 108,112,121–122,130,134,136,162, 230
Jones, Isham 2,5,83,99,101–102,109, 114–115,126,131,144–146,162, 266–268,276,278,292,307,324,334, 344,350
Jones, Jimmy 8,152–153,327
Jones, Jo 77,109–110,118,138,184, 188,193,197,200,202,205,221,231, 233,235,240–241,245,253,256,271, 278–279,292,307–308,311,328, 333–334,341,354,359–360
Jones, Joe 206
Jones, Jonah 6,8,18,26–27,44,57,64, 66,69–70,81,94,104,108,111, 115–116,124–125,140,145,165,235, 359
Jones, Orville 126,212
Jones, Reunald 17,65,179,295,310
Jones, Robcliff 84,123,139,182–183, 228,257,300,307,329,331,342
Jones, Slick 32,56,85,94,123,134,148, 186,253,269,339,346,358
Jones, Wallace 93,128,162,172,186, 251,260,332,336,346,354–356,360
Jones, Walter 114,158
Jones, Wardell 20,36,70,81
Jordan, Louis 74,90,100,104–105,111, 115,123,138,146,177–178,238, 277–279,295–296,299–301,321,350
Jordan, Taft 12,23,74,78–81,84,86,88, 90,104–105,119,126,128,138,146, 176–178,238,259,277–279,295, 299–301,321,350,355,361–362
Joseph! Joseph! 340,348–349,351,353, 355
Josephine 255,298,301,316,321
Joyce, Vicki 119
Juba Dance 273
Jubilee 292,295,299,308,312–313,337
Jubilesta 262,276,322
Judy 251
Julian, Louis 56
Jumpin' 337
Jumpin' At The Woodside 355
Jump, Jump's Here 359
Jump Steady 150
Jumpy 17–19,147
Jumpy Rhythm 31
June Night 58,117,158,198,266
Jungle Drums 123
Jungle Jitters 25
Jungle Madness 118,141,293
Junk Man 11,87,90,250
Junk Man Blues 265,285
Just A Little Girl 146
Just An Error In The News 286,295,299
Just A Quiet Evening 142,174
Just A Simple Melody 257,277–278, 285–286,289,293,295,297,308–309, 311,313,327,335,337
Just A Stone's Throw From Heaven 264
Just A-Wearyin' For You 34,47,263,266
Just Because You're You 270
Just Blues 306
Just Drifting Along 37,40,47,52–53,57, 60
Just Foolin' Myself 246
Just Lately 274,276,289,307,309
Just Let Me Look At You 308
Just Met Up With That Gal Of Mine 65
Just Naturally Swinging 123
Just One More Chance 171
Just Strolling 157,160–161,170,208, 283–284
Just To Remind You 131,145–147
Just You 206
Just You, Just Me 23,273,359
Kaetz, George 49
Kahn, Roger Wolfe 76,125
Kaiser, Dottie 160
Kaloah 63
Kaminsky, Max 10,13,25,41,72,80,82, 110,112,130,230,288,363
Kane, Sol 353
Kanter, Ben 243,246,255,262
Karawanis Brothers 264,275, 309–310
Karawanis, Jimmy 275
Karawanis, Len 275
Kassel, Art 97
Kaufman, Bernie 334,357
Kavelin, Al 97
Al Kavich 353
Kaye, Jenny 196,200
Kaye, Sammy 354
Kaye, Sharri 214
Kazebier, Nate 3,4,10,14,22–23,26, 67,139
Kearns, Joe 270,280,282,284,319,325, 327,337–338

Keeping Out of Mischief Now 82,120, 186,246
Keep In The Groove 331
Keep It In The Groove 244–245
Keep Me In Your Dreams 99,105
Keep On Smiling 102
Keep On The Right Side Of The Road 50
Keep Smilin' At Trouble 140,147,151, 160,178,254,346
Keep Swingin' 105
Keep That Hi-De-Ho In Your Soul 89, 97,103,279,317
Keep The Rhythm Going 16,24
Kelly, Paula 172,177,216–218,247, 255–256
Kelly, Willis 'Willie' 25,239,250, 260–262,265,273,280,282,285–286, 295,307,309,327
Kelly's Stable, 52nd Street, NYC 362
Kellsy, Walter 88
Kemp, Hal 5,27,30,32,37,39,45, 51, 88,129,132,350,360
Kennedy, George 33,64
Kenny, Nick 217
Kenton, Stan 185
Kentucky Hotel, Louisville, Ky 97
Kenyon, Eak 176,213–214,219,234, 237,242,257
Kern, Jerome 62,241
Kerr, Doris 40,48,92,99,101,110,137
Keyes, Joe 109
Kibling, Charles 218
Kick My Heart 29
Kiddin' On The Fiddle 58,125
Killer Diller 295
Kincaide, Deane 9,13,25–26,42,117, 231,240,264,318,329,347,349,351, 358–359,361
King, Alice 267
King, Art 234
King, Gene 343
King, Lawrence 38
King Of Swing 45,50,52,58,89
King, Paul 7–8,11–13,88,119,157, 218–219,252–254
King Porter Stomp 2,5,13,15,30,34,36, 38,52,58,60,65,68,73,76,78,80, 82–83,93,111,119,145,147,154,157, 169,173,183,188,191,210,223,234, 238,243,246,248,253,255,262,277, 281,289,299,321,323,327,337, 339–342,346,353,355
King, Saunders 126
King, Stan 3–5,12,15,284
King, Sylvia 218
King's Jesters 97
King, Tempo 112,115,121
Kinmore Hotel, Albany, N.Y. 175
Kinsey, Gene 171
Kirby, John 10,26,52,69–70,73,77, 80–81,104,121,143–144,152,159, 161,184,201,210,222–224,230,232, 247,257,259,266,272,274,278,292, 306–307,309,313,318,323–325,328, 331–332,334–339,342,344,351,357, 359
Kirk, Andy 7–8,11–13,84,88,110,112, 119,157,168,218–219,221,240, 242–249,252–255,257,262,278,297, 326,339
Kirk, Wilbert 8,152–153
Kirkpatrick, Don 12,17,23,65,179
Kissin' My Baby Goodnight 6,175
Kiss Me Again 164,166,171,198,234
Kit Kat Club, NYC 200
Klayman, Lou 25
Klein, Mannie 37,114,137,172, 186–188,243,250,255,261
Klinger, Frank 18,23
Knick-Knacks 233
Knock, Knock 30–31,33,37,41–42,46, 49,53–55,60,110
Knock Wood 210
Koenig, George 117,127–128,135, 176,180,204–205,217,253,274,283, 292–293,331,341
Kogan, Maurice 350,357,359
Kolyer, Edward 37,82,92,130–131, 179,201,215,219,224–225,237,240, 286,300,322, 325,345,355,358
KOOL Cigarette Program, NYC [radio show] 80,126, 130,195,201, 207,215,220,224,233,237,243,263, 270,302,324,335
Kostelanetz, André 35,39,57,63,73, 165,259
Kotsoftis, Ted 137,186
Koven, Jack 223,232
Kraft Music Hall, Hollywood [radio show] 109, 175,179,186,195,201
Kramer, Harry 212
Kress, Carl 11,15,21,26,32,103,114, 187–188,285
Kruger, Jerry 276,303,345,350
Krupa, Gene 3,4,6,9–10,14–15, 17–18,22–23,26,37,44,46–47,67,72, 74–77,79–80,82–83,86,88,90–91,96, 100,105–107,109,111,114–115,117, 123,127–128,131,133–135,137–140, 146,152–153,155,158,162–163,167, 170,174,176,178–179,183–184,186, 200,204–205,213,216–217,220–222, 230–232,235,238–239,243–244,253, 256–257,265,271,273–277,279,280, 282–283,286,289,292–295,297–299, 301,306–308,311,313,319,321, 324–326,331,335–337,343,345–347, 350,354,358–360
Ku-Li-A 297,299
Kuntz, Val 325
Kyle, Billy 70,73,81,96,118,124,128, 133,141,150,156,162,195,253,260, 263–264,268,328,332,337–338,359
Kyser, Dottie 339
Kyser, Kay 97,347,350
La Casino, Jamaica, Long Island, N.Y. 264
LaCentra, Peg 25,31,35,38,45,50,52, 58–59,61,65,74,79,85,89,119, 122–123,126,163,165,168,174, 178–179,182–184,188–189, 191–192,198,211,214,216,223,233
Lacey, Jack 25,188,243
La Cucaracha 246,256
La Cumparsita 90,270

Ladd, Bernie 84
La-De-De, La-De-Da 56
La De Doody Do 356
Lady From Broadway 19
Lady Of The Night 355
Lady's Bagatelle 96
Lafayette 273
La Fell, Leon 360
La Golondrina 83,276,293
Laine, Bob 243,246,255,262,348,360
Lake, Cynthia (Sis) 77,138,307,339
Lamare, Frank 115
Lamare, James 27,43,66
Lamare, Nappy 8,9,13,25–26,30, 32–33,36,40,42–43,51,68,96,117, 126,128,133,135,143–146,148, 150–152,157,159–161,166,170,183, 205,212,215,218,225,231,239,267, 269,274,277,280–284,312,316, 318–319,325,327,333, 335–338,340
Lambeth Walk 360
Lament For A Lost Love 163
Lament O Gitano 220
L'Amour, Toujours L'Amour 357
Lamphere, Charles 137,206,263–264, 318,327,330,332,340,348,351,357
Land Of Degradation 43
Land Of Jam 166
Landon, Betty 149–150,325
Landt Trio & White 115
Lane, Burton 61
Lane, Eleanor 34,47,51
Lane, Frances 115,118
Lane, Kathleen 175–176,210–211, 213–219,221–222,224,231,234,237, 239–242,254–257,286,289–291, 296–298,352
Lane, Rosemary 47
Lang, Bill 59
Lang, John 162
Langford, Frances 33–34,294,354,358
Langone, Frank 3,14
Lanoue, Conrad 3,13–14,17,27,43,66, 115,178,265,311
Larchmont Casino, N.Y. 26, 29–30
LaRocca, Nick 75
Larry Wynn's Winners 260–261,280
LaRue, Bob 97
Lassus Trombone 185
Last Night 198
Latch On 25
Lattimore, Harlan 11,17,65
Lauder, Jack 275
Laugh And Call It Love 359
Laughin' At Life 261,283,285,341
Laughing Boy Blues 346,355
Laugh Your Way Through Life 265
LaVere, Charlie 313
Lawnhurst, Vee 108
Lawrence, Jerry 92,186,203,271
Lawson, Happy 262
Lawson, Harry 7–8,11–13,88,119, 157, 218–219,297,326
Lawson, Yank 9,13,25–26,42–43,117, 125–126,128,131,144,146,148, 150–152,157,159–161,163–164,166, 170,183,205,208,210,212,215,218, 220,231,237,240,269,274,276–277, 279–284,312,316–319,323–325,327, 337–338,340,361
Lay, Ward 69,73
Lazy 242
Lazy Bones 103,307
Lazy Man's Shuffle 90
Lazy River 95
Lazy Weather 17
Leadbelly 12
Leary, Ford 109,115,118,121,144,164, 166–167,171–172,175,178,183,220, 233,237,240
Leaving Me 29
Lee, Clarence 94
Lee, Larry 97
Lee, Loretta 40,43,46,48,76,313,357
Lee, Peggy 363
Lee, Sonny 64,189,192,194–196,198, 200,202,204,208,210–211,216,219, 224–225,232,234,236,239,244,248, 269,272,284,294,301,321,335, 340–341,349,351
Leeman, Cliff 171,174,214,223,259, 273,306,359
Lees, Phil 176
Legare, Peyton 360
LeMaire, Jack 27,43,66,115,178,265, 341
Leonard, Jack 18–19,21–22,25,34,36, 41,47,72,75,80,82,91–92,101, 109–110,112,121–122,124,126, 129–131,134,136,138,143–144, 146–148,151–152,158–159,162,166, 178,183,186,195,201,204–205, 207–208,210,213,215,219–220, 222–224,230–233,235–237,239–240, 242–243,245–246,253–257,263, 267–268,270–273,276,289,295,298, 302,308,311–312,316,322,324–325, 333,335,338,347,349,351,358
Lessey, Bob 10,13,18,20,33,179
Lessons In Love 9
Lester, Norman 12
Let 'Er Go 201,224,235,240,263,269, 272–273
Let Me Be The One In Your Heart 31
Let Me Call You Sweetheart 66
Let Me Day Dream 332
Let Me Dream 271
Let's Break The Good News 346,353
Let's Call A Heart A Heart 34,61,65, 112,273
Let's Call The Whole Thing Off 134, 140,144–145,153–154,158,172,175, 178,183,185,195,203–204,217,219, 234,237,242,245,256
Let's Dance 27–28,33,35,46,61,64, 66–67,70,72–74,76,79,82,87,89–90, 92,97–98,107,109–111,128,137,147, 158,163,179,216,223,231,235,241, 246,253,257,262,265,267,271, 273–274,276–277,279–280,282, 285–286,289,295,298,301,305,308, 311,316,321,324–327,331,334,337, 340,343–346,348–351,353–354, 356–357,359–361
Let's Do It 121
Let's Face The Music And Dance 11,51, 55,60
Let's Get Together 48,86,88,92–93,98, 100,104,137,146,159,162,172, 176–177,238,243
Let's Give Love Another Chance 282, 286,298,301
Let's Go Ballyhoo 144
Let's Go Barrelhouse 39,125
Let's Have Another Cigarette 189, 234–235,237,239,243,245,248,251, 271
Let's Kiss And Make Up 171
Let's Make It A Life-Time 292–293, 301,320
Let's Pitch A Little Woo 286
Let's Put Our Heads Together 96
Let's Sing Again 24,30,33–37,39,43, 46,55,57,60
Let's Take A Trip To Jamaica 75
Let That Be A Lesson To You 274,294, 305,311
Let Yourself Go 5,6,10,15,24,36,39
Levaggi's, Boston 75,327,335–337
Lewis, Ed 138,205,231,239,271,307, 328,354
Lewis, Meade Lux 21,316,331
Lewis, Ted 61,144,201,230,278
Lewis, Teddy 20,22
Lido Casino, Larchmont, N.Y. 188, 190,213–214
Lieber, Les 160,168–169,187,211, 238–239,260,272,296,357
Liebestraum 121,124,129,131,136,146, 210,214,231,233,240
Life Goes To A Party 276–277,280, 282–283,292–293,297,301,306,324
Life Spears A Jitterbug 358
Life Without You 178
Lightly And Politely 358
Lights Out 4,5
Like A Fish Out Of Water 311
Like A Ship At Sea 280
Lillie, Beatrice 305,326
Lillie Stomp 335,351
Limehouse Blues 39,47,52,58,71,83, 92,98,100,105,110,126,131,134,137, 145,151,163,165,175,184,187,223, 233,244,251,253,268,280,284,289, 298,302,307,313,323,325,355
Lincoln Theater, Philadelphia 15–16, 18–19,21
Lindsey, Chick 110
Lindy Hop [dance] 164,261,300, 310–311,329
Lindy Hop 232,239
Lindy Hoppers 250
Linehan, Tommy 136,231,276,286, 346,355
Linger Awhile 58,111,232,270,291, 307,313,324,332,335
Linton, Charles 84,87–90,92–93,98, 100,104,111,113,137,146,172,177, 238,243
Lipkins, Steve 72,80,101,108,119,144, 167,171,189,194–195,198,224,230, 236,248,269,294,301,321,340–341, 348,353,355
Lippman, Joe 35,61,74,85,93,122,144, 167,171–172,189,194–195,198,200, 208,210–211,213,216,224,231–232, 236,248,269,294,301,348
Liss, Joe 47,72,101,137
Listen My Children, And You Shall Hear 205
Listen To The Mocking Bird 158,307
Little Girl Blue 161
Little Joe 137,169,238
Little Joe From Chicago 326,353
Little Old Lady 89,143,151,166,185, 192,209,213
Little Rock Getaway 159,210,218,276, 280,321,331,333, 335–336
Little White Lies 127,266,295,349
Live And Learn 94
Live And Love Tonight 273
Livery Stable Blues 75,185,265
Living From Day To Day 31,53,58–59, 234
Living In Seclusion 104
Livingston, Fud 10–11,27,29,33–34, 134,192
Liza 87,89,92,96,98,101–102, 114–115,124–125,127,133,137,140, 163,169,173,203–204,207–208,220, 222,225,235,240,255,272,279,289, 303,321,333,350
Lloyd, D. 130
Lloyd, Shirley 202–203
Lobovsky, Nat 348,353,355
Loch Lomond 224,257,268,272,275, 279,283,285–287,292,296–297, 302–303,306,308,310–313,316,323, 325,327,331,337
Loew's State Theater, NYC 2,5,7,12, 16,27,53,66,71–73,99,102,112,114, 126,144,184,197,201,222,238,247, 249,257,259,266,278,292,296,307, 324,334,344,350,358,360
Logan, Danny 179
Log On The Fire 311
Lombardo, Carmen 117
Lombardo, Guy 97,112,115,135,334
Lonesome Cabin 11
Lonesome Guitar 79
Lonesome Night 58,62,65,289
Lonesome Old Town 359
Lone Star 42
'Long About Midnight 77,86,86,202, 222,256,274,320,347
Long Ago And Far Away 23,41,45,61
Long, Kathleen 167
Long, Nancy 23,77,106,110,116,119, 126,129,139,145,182–183,201,209, 246,249,256–257,270,272,275,280, 286,301,304,307,323,329,339, 347–348,362
Long, Slats 25,47,121,144,284
Lookin' Around Corners For You 101, 116,124,130
Looking At The World Through Rose-Colored Glasses 348
Looking Down At The Stars 37
Look In Love 40
Looking For Love 185
Lopez, Vincent 2,5,7,12,16,23,53, 59–60,97,99,115

INDEX

Lost 6,8,12,15–16,18–19,21–22,24, 65,302
Lost Again 204,215,240
Lost And Found 339
Lost Ecstasy 144
Lost In Meditation 324,357
Lost In My Dreams 44,69,84
Lost In The Shuffle 332
Lost In Your Arms 84
Lost Love 186
Lost My Rhythm, Lost My Man 247
Lotta Sax Appeal 7
Louis 186
Louis, Joe 191,245
Louise 194,198,204,211,216,225,233
Louise, Louise 338
Louisiana 108,335
Louisiana Hayride 63
Lounging At The Waldorf 25
Love And Learn 85,99,105,113,119, 123,145
Love Came Out of The Night 16,21
Love In My Heart [Swing, Baby, Swing] 205
Love In Swingtime 360
Love Is A Merry-Go-Round 167, 171–172,184–185,189,196,198,202, 204,207,211,216–217,219–220,232, 236,245
Love Is A Powerful Thing 79
Love Is Good 206
Love Is Good For Anything That Ails You 119,123,128,144
Love Is Here To Stay 318,321,334–335
Love Is In My Heart 298
Love Is In The Air Tonight 248
Love Is Just Around The Corner 21,212, 269,315,324,326
Love Is Like A Cigarette 6,19
Love Is Like A Melody 49
Love Is Like Whisky 334
Love Is Never Out Of Season 166, 207–208,210,231
Love Is On The Air Tonight 233
Love Is The Reason 20,50
Love Is The Sweetest Thing 70,185
Love Is The Thing, So They Say 138, 239,241,251,298
Love Is Where You Find It 359
Loveless Love 32,45,73,103,214,217, 224,240,285,290
Lovelight In The Starlight 340
Love Locked Out 185
Lovely Liza Lee 21
Love Marches On 83,94–95,104–105, 107,110–111
Love Me 214,237
Love Me Or Leave Me 30,39,58,68,70, 72,78,84,91,99,114,141,161,163,178, 220,267,270,277,298,301,307,343
'Love On The Run' [movie] 109
Lover 38
Lover, Come Back To Me 297,311,335, 339,343
Love's Old Sweet Song 223
Love Song Of A Half-Wit 92,99
Love Song Of The Catskills 108
Love Walked In 341

Love Went Up In Smoke 24
Love, What Are You Doing To Me? 49
Love, What Are You Doing To My Heart? 87,90,98,165
Love Will Tell 47,53,62,115
Love, You Funny Thing 272
Love, You're Just A Laugh 12,23
Love, Your Magic Spell Is Everywhere 324
Lovin' Sam 208
Loving You 264–265,274
Low, David 110,117,138,195,275
Lowe, Francis 77
Lowe, Sam 29,56,158,232,332
Lowery, Fred 59
Lucas, Clyde 32,39,52–54,66,184
Lucas, Lyn 39,52,54
Lucie, Lawrence 12,20,26,34,36,52, 70,73,81,127,137,141,200,263,276, 353
Luckyology 150
Lucky Swings Out 31,33,45,73,141
Lugg, George 288
Lullaby In Rhythm [Honey Chile] 340, 345–346,348–349,353,355–357,360
Lullaby To A Lamp Post 189,196,232
Lulu's Back In Town 40
Lunceford, Jimmie 7,12,26,29–30, 52–53,61,69,74,99,111–112, 114–115,117,161,188–190,197,201, 205,239,255,280,292,307–308,344, 346,360
Lyman, Abe 86,97,99,115,164,281
Lynch, Jim 360
Lynebury, Barbara 114
Lyons, Francis 97
Lyons, Roger 83,115,162,166,171
Lytell, Jimmy 334,357
Mace, Tommy 17,27
McAdams, Garry 243,246,255,262
McCall, Louis 159
McCamish, Charles 346–347,350, 354,358–360
McCarthy, Charles F. 151
McCarthy, Joe 54
McCarthy, Pat 175,297
McConnell, John 200,263,276,353
McCook, Donald 3
McCoy, Clyde 324,334
McCracken, Bob 215–216
McCrae, Margaret 46,54,64,74–76, 78–79,81,96–98
McCrea, Bob 24
McDonough, Dick 11,21,28,31–32, 38,65,103,137,140,143,146,167, 186–188,285,347
McEachern, Murray 22–23,26,37,44, 58,61,67,72,75,78,83,86,88,90,96, 100,105,107,109–111,115,124, 126–128,131,133–135,147,152–153, 158–159,162–163,176,180,182–183, 204–205,216,220,223,231,235,239, 243–244,248,251,253,257,262, 274–275,278–279,283,285–286,289, 292–293,295–296,298,301,317, 323–324,326,332,361
McGarvey, Red 118,206,263–264
McGhee, Johnny 308
McGillicuddy's Stomp 312

McGinley, Dick 221
McGrath, Fulton 25,140,284,321
MacGregor, Chummy 176,214, 217–218,237,254,286,289,297, 352–353
McHugh, Mary 317,322,325,344,357
McIntyre, Hal 137,175–176,186,211, 213–214,216–219,231,234,237, 239–242,256,289,297,352–353
McKay, Carol 144,166–167,169, 171–172,175,183
McKay, Stewie 248
McKeever, Johnny 34,42,46–47,50, 54,115
McKenzie, Red 3,5,12,32,37,87,116, 125,284,326,347
McKinley, Barry 100,243
McKinley, Don 84
McKinley, Ray 10–11,27,29,33–34, 119,134,164,175,192,195,255, 257–258,269,274,276,281,285,291, 297,299,305,311,321,334,337, 339–341,345,347,349,351,363
McKinney, Ray 82
McLean, Connie 200
McLee, Lilla Mae 309–310
McLemore, William 29,56,158,232, 332
McLewis, Joe 337,341
McLin, Jimmy 121,151,210,257,259, 328
McMickle, Mike 209
McNeal, Ed 300
McNulty, Ed 295
MacPherson Is Rehearsin' 355
McRae, Ted 23,52,69,74,80–81,105, 119,126,138,172,176–178,208,238, 259,277–279,295–296,298–301,312, 317,321,337,350,355,361–362
Macey, Peter 264
Mack, Trudi 215–216
Mackay, Carol 59
Mackey Program (NBC) [radio] NYC 244
Mad Dogs And Englishmen 55
Madera, Oscar 8,152
Madhouse 4,8,27,49,58,60,69,110,112, 184,262,359
Madison, Bingie 155,189,195,203, 296,337
Madison Square Garden, NYC 355
Madriguera, Enric 247
Maelstrom 255
Maffay, Vincent 36,40,42,46,48,52,55, 66,84,87,89–90,99,102,110,113,119, 123,307,327
Maggie 82
Magic Key Program, NYC 82,103, 183
Magnolia 179,183,219,223
Magnolias In The Moonlight 57,69,118
Mahogany Hall Stomp 171,178,186, 195,202,217,219,289,327,331
'Maid of Salem' [movie] 128
Maisel, Jack 90,205
Make A Wish 251
Make Believe 36,48,312,316,335,337, 344,349,356,360,362

Make Believe Ballroom [radio show] 43,61,72,74,78,86,91,115,121,124, 145,148,163,254,271
Make Believe Ballroom 33,35,41,43–44, 48,57,59,74,76,78–79,83,86,88,92, 100,103,110,112,115,124
Makin' Whoopee 127,134,138,140,149, 179,232,257,277,288,306,309,345, 360
Mako, Gene 228
Mallory, Eddie 201,251,253–254,256, 260–262,266,334,358
Mallory, Paul 261,286
Malneck, Matty 28,161
Mama Don't Allow 21,23,109
Mama Don't Want No Peas An' Rice An' Coconut Oil 354
Mama, I Wanna Make Rhythm 246, 248,269,283,288,294–295,297,307, 332,334–335
Mama, I Want To Swing 263
Mama, That Moon Is Here Again 283, 285–286,289,295,302,307–309,312, 316,325,328,334–337
Mama Wants To Know Who Stole The Jam 313
Mandy 239,263
Man From Brandyville 38
Manhattan Beach Casino, Brooklyn 236
Manhattan Jam 134
Manhattan Matinée (CBS radio) 40, 46,62
Manhatters (NBC Band) 56,201
Maniac's Ball 70,309
Mann, Peggy 255,262
Manners, Art 36–37,40,42,46,48,52, 55,66,103,106,110,113,116,119,125, 129,132,140,156,164,169,172, 187–188,238,250,260,262,265,280, 282,285–286,309
Mannone Blues 353
Manone, Wingy 4,5,7–8,12–13, 15–19,21–25,27,43,66,115,177–178, 184,197,200,227,265,296,300,311, 353
Mansfield, Saxie 76–77,81,83,86,109, 112,114,118,121,161–162,205,214, 231,263,267–268,270,273,276,286, 328,346,355
Maple Leaf Rag 34,72,112,171
March Á La Swing 165
Marcheta 218,332
March, March On Down The Field 75
Marching Along With Time 349
March Of The Bobcats 340
Mares, Paul 167
Margie 110,161,196,206,248,296,308, 326
Marie 102,109,112,116,122,124,129, 143,152,161–162,183–184,186, 195–197,201,206,210,212–213,219, 223,227–228,231,234–237,239, 243–244,246,252,254,262–264, 266–267,272–273,276,281,283,285, 289,297,306,328,334–335,340
Marine Ballroom, NJ
Marjorie 98,118

INDEX

Mark Hopkins Hotel, SF 97
Marquetta 196
Marsala, Joe 4,6,8,13,17,27,30,32,43,
  66,87,112,115–116,121,126,138,
  140,142,144,146–149,151,153,156,
  158,164,172,174,177–178,184,
  196–197,201,205,208,210–211,214,
  222–223,225–227,230–231,234,236,
  239–240,242,244,247,251,254,263,
  265–267,278,280–281,284,287,292,
  299–300,306–307,311,324,333–334,
  341–342,344,350,354
Marsala, Marty 112,121,142,144,147,
  151,158,177,197,203,205,210,
  225–227,234,239–240,242,244,280,
  287,296–297,299–300,341,358
Marshall, Clydel 24
Martha 353
Martin, Hugh 106,216
Martin, Joe 101,109,115,131,145–146
Martin, Skippy 185
Marx, Albert 92
Marx, Frank 116
Mary Had A Little Lamb 18–22,24,26,
  28,30,36,38,41,43,53,58,62,110,157,
  218
Mary Lou 118,174,285
Mason, Russell G. 168
Massenburg, Sam 300
Massey, Harry 184
Masters, Art 171
Masters, Frankie 97
Mastren, Al 43,72,101,137,169,178,
  206,263–265,280,283,318,353
Mastren, Carmen 3–5,12,17,25,72,80,
  82,101,108,112,121–122,130,134,
  136,144,153,166,171,178,186,207,
  210,213,227,244,254–255,271,289,
  295,297,308,322,325,333,338,347,
  349,351,353,358–359,361
Mathewson, Oliver 231,276,286,
  346,355
Matlock, Matty 9,13,25–26,42–43,
  109,115,117,121,125,133,143–146,
  148,150–152,157,159–161,163–164,
  166,170,183,205,207,212,215–216,
  220,224–225,237,269,274,276–277,
  279–284,312–313,316–317,319,
  323–325,327,332,337–338
Matthews, Dave 59–60,92,258,321,
  337,341,345,347,349–351,353–355,
  358–359
Matthews, Eddie 151
Matthews, Emmett 102
Matthews, George 137,207,212,350,
  355,361–362
Mattison, Don 10–11,27,29,33–34,
  134,192,258,269,274,276,278,281,
  285,291,298,321,335,337,340–341,
  347,349,351
Maurice Casino, Asbury Park, N.J.
  196,203
Maxey, Leroy 4,20,59,127,134,241,
  246,255,295,321,343
Maybe 171–172
Maybe Someday 101
Mayfair Casino, Chicago 61
Mayfair Casino, Cleveland, Ohio 99

Mayflower 194
Mayhew, Bob 218
Mayhew, Jack 218
Mayhew, Nye 176,185,203,218
May I Have My Heart Back? 358
May I Have The Next Dance? 104
*May I Have The Next Romance With
  You?* 80,99,101,112,115–116,118,
  121,124,131,136,140,143,146,152,
  165,217
Mazi-Pani 299
Meade Lux 331
Meadowbrook Ballroom, N.J. 21,59,
  90,104,109–110,112–113,116–117,
  122,126,140,165,171,184,195,202,
  265,271,274,279
Meakin, Dr John (Jack) 38,49,55,61,
  88,120,126,142,146,158,214,233,
  237,293,306
Me And The Moon 21,33,35,38–39,
  41–46,48–50,53,55–56,60–61,84,100
Mean To Me 45,49,83,87–88,115,118,
  126,144,169–170,185,191,203,218,
  221
Meeker, Bobby 97
Meet Me In The Moonlight 163,185,
  243
Meet Me On The Down Beat 54,69
Meet Me Tonight In Dreamland 349
Meet The Beat Of My Heart 358,360
Melancholy 318
Melancholy Baby 348
Mele, Vi 172,174–176,178–179,
  183–185,267,327,351
Melody From The Sky 16,19
Melody In F 108,113,119,130,158,
  169,212,219,230,235,242,278,311,
  340
Melody In F-Minor 323–324,327
Melody In G 125
Melody Man 89,188
Memories 331
Memories Of You 51,55,236,286,292,
  306–307,316,358
Memphis Blues 78,93,112,124,137,
  151,162,171,177,271,326
Memphis Five 21
Me, Myself And I 178,188,194,197,
  205,213,219,223,225,231,233–243,
  248,252,256,265,267,273,275
Mendelssohn's Caprice 73
Mendelssohn's Spring Song 121,158,
  223,228,236,246,271,289,316
Mendelssohn's Swing Song 30,219
Mendelson, Julie 18,23
Mercer, Johnny 28,71,257
Mercurio, Walter 10,13,25,72,80,82,
  213,230,254,287,292
Mergentroid, Randy 322
Meroff, Benny 97–98,247,251,266
Merry-Go-Round 17–18,20,30,33,36,
  45–46,49,145,173,195,322,328,337
Merry Macs, The 323
Merry Madcaps 33–35,38,41,43–44,
  47,51,55,57
Merry Makers (CBS Band) 36,38,40,
  42,44,46–47,49,52,54,57,60,75,171,
  201

Merry Widow On A Spree 232
Message From Mars 320
Message To The Moon 185,203
Messin' Around 294
Messin' At The Meadowbrook 271
Methuselah Goes A-Riding 236
Metronome [magazine] 174,200,230
Metropolitan Theater, Boston 153,176
Me Without You 67
Mexicali Rose 61,134
Meyer, Joe 134,175,192,195,243,246
Meyers, Eddie 47,72
Mezzrow, Mezz 8,133,152,156,188,
  287–288,300–301
Michaels, Mike 35,61,74,116–117,213
Michels, Allen 30
Michels, Bob 129
Mickey Mouse's Birthday Party 90
Midnight 84,117
Midnight And You 50
Midnight At The Onyx 82,91,149,184,
  196,233–234,242
Midnight Blue 53,56–58,60,69–70,
  72–73,78–79,83,86,90,99–100,103
Midnight In A Madhouse 273,283,299,
  301,312,336
Midnight Lullaby 94
Mighty Like The Blues 341
Mikell, Gene 36,69–70,80–81,141
Milazzo, Jimmy 223,232
Milenburg Joys 16,42,70,88,233,245,
  251,311
Miles Apart 269,271,279,283–284
Milk Cow Blues 338
Milk Man's Matinee 78,89,115,168
Miller, Art 4,5,15,26,313
Miller, Bill 65,118,169,202,206,
  263–265,267,280,283,318,327,330,
  332,339–340,348,350–351,357,359
Miller, Buddy 7
Miller, Earl 119,157,218–219,297,326
Miller, Eddie 8–9,13,17,25–26,42–43,
  68,96,117,125–126,128,131,133,135,
  140,144–146,148,151–152,157,
  159–161,163–164,166,170,183,205,
  207–208,210,212,215,218,220,225,
  231,237,262,269,274,276–277,
  279–284,312,316–319,323–325,
  327–328,332–333,337–338,340
Miller, Glenn 59–60,73,92,99,106,
  135,137,172,174–176,178–179,
  183–186,192,210–215,217–219,
  221–222,224,231,234,237,239–242,
  254–257,286,289–291,297–298,330,
  352–354,356,363
Miller, Jimmy 8,152–153,327
Miller, Johnny 251
Miller, Marion 215,220–221
Millinder, Lucky 16,20,29–33,36,
  45–46,48–49,66,70–71,73,78,81,
  114,118,124,141,150,156,159, 162,
  184–185,192,195,201,230,260,
  263–264,266,268,287,292,328,334
Million Dollar Pier, Atlantic City, N.J.
  202–203,207,240,242
Mills Artists 168,192,197,249
Mills Blue Rhythm Band 250,262
Mills Brothers 2,86,105,357–358,360

Mills, Harry 88
Mills, Irving 133,168,192,224
Mills, Lincoln 114,158,206
Mince, Johnny 4–5,73,125,129–132,
  134,136,147,151–153,158–159,162,
  164,166,171,176,178,186,195,201,
  204–205,207–208,210,213,219,222,
  231–232,236–237,239–240,242,246,
  254–255,271,289,293,295,308,311,
  316,322,324–325,333,338,347,349,
  351,358–359,361
Minding My Business 320,324,326
Minnie The Moocher 50,52,62,64,74,
  117,234,262,274
Minnie The Moocher's Wedding Day 11,
  27,31,59,72,74,90,104,117,135,137,
  152,163,183,237,241,253,274,283,
  292
Minor, Dan 109,118,138,197,202,
  205,231,271,307,328,354
Minor Breakdown 332
Minor Jive 297
Minuet In Jazz 122,148,156
Miolla, Mike 84,106,110,116,119,125
Miracle At Midnight 358
Miro, Joseph 260–261
Miss Annabelle Lee 146
Mississippi 273
Missouri Misery 273
Mr Ghost Goes To Town 76,81,86,
  90–93,95,98,100–102,104,109–111,
  113–114,116–118,145–148,151–152,
  163,172,178,183,186,194,198,200,
  245,267,270,327
Mr. Sweeney's Learned To Swing 237
Mr T From Tennessee 89
Misty Moonlight 276
Mitchell, Alex 300
Mitchell, Charles 130–131,179,201,
  237,286,300,322,325,345,355,358
Mitchell, Sue 171–172,178,188,198,
  272–273,281,342
Mitchelle, Jimmy 29,56,114,120,123,
  126,130,151–152,158,162,165,197,
  232,332
Mitchner, William 'Slappy' 354
Mix Up 109
Moanin' In The Mornin' 271,276,323
Moanin' Low 143
Modernaires, The 357
Mole, Miff 45,158,178
Moments Like This 334,343
Moments Of Moments 23
Moncur, Grachan 300
Monday In Manhattan 40,62
Mondello, Toots 35,82,165,188,243,
  250,255,260–262,267,275,280,285,
  299,309–310,320,333
Monkey Business 312
Monopoly 39,42,45,51
Monopoly Swing 64,89,91,104,108
Monsoon 273
Montgomery, Jack 184,267
Mood Hollywood 45
Mood Indigo 4,30,46,73,146,203,217,
  298,307,327
Moon At Sea 241,263
Moonburn 5

INDEX

Mooney, Harold 126
Mooney, Joe 242,265
Moon Face 85
Moonglow 21,43,50,76,80,166,187, 243,274,289,303,305,323, 331,351
Moonlight And Cotton 114
Moonlight And Shadows 119,142, 146–147,151–152,159,163,165,179, 186
Moonlight Bay 137,213
Moonlight Fiesta 188,344
Moonlight Gardens, Cincinnati, Ohio 41,49,247
Moonlight On The Chesapeake 76
Moonlight On The Highway 245,251, 271,274
Moonlight On The Purple Sage 333
Moonlight Serenade 172,174–176, 210–217,241,256
Moonrise On The Lowlands 13,17
Moon Rose 5
Moonshine Over Kentucky 348
Moore, Bobby 138,193–194,197,205, 231
Moran, Leo 47
Morehouse, Chauncey 123,169,188, 243,297,299,309
More Power To You 253,309
More Than Ever 322,324–325,327,331, 333
More Than That 151
More Than You 53
More Than You Know 11,14,18,27,31, 35,47,66,77,79,98,115,133,147,158, 163,203,210,222,232–233,237,274, 280,306,347,362
Morgan, Al 4
Morgan, Dick 139
Morgan, Ray 203,217
Morgan, Russ 73,97,216,292
Morgan, Tom 109,121,144,167,171, 189,194–195,198,210,224,236,248, 269,294,301,321,340–341
Morley, Ed 138
Morning Air 311
Morningstar, Dick 77,81,84,87,89,99, 128,132,137,140,160,182,195,205, 208–209,275,285,295,304,318,345, 347,362
Morocco 40
Morres, Don 18,23,33,64
Morris, Marlowe 284
Morrison, James 29,56,158,232,332
Morrow, Buddy 85,93,119,361
Mortimer, Don 23,84,92,99,134–135, 137,140,147,176,187,190–191,194, 212,216–217,256,259–261,286,288, 291,304,306–307,345,355,362
Morton, Benny 17,65,179,231,271, 307–308,311,328,333,354
Morton, Jelly Roll 284
Morton, Lee 38
Mosley, Leo 155–156,212,215,221
Moten, Bennie 83,102,118,245,261, 273
Moten Stomp 353
Moten Swing 7,26,78,80,98,102,104, 118,157,191,202,233–234,245,248, 253,255
Moten Twist 240
Mother Goose 195
Mother Goose Marches On 231
Mound City Blue Blowers 32,125
Mountain Music 166,177,184,196, 202–203,210,221,248
Moynahan, Fred 163,213,218,245,251
Mozart, Micky 270
Mozart's Quintet for String Quartet & Clarinet 316
Mucci, Louis 206,263–264
Muddy Water 69
Muir, Billy 115
Mumma, Jim 270
Mundy, Jimmy 27–28,69,74,86,120, 127,142,146–147,175,243, 357
Murphy, Spud 237
Murray, Arthur 275,293
Murray's, Tuckahoe, N.Y. 100
Music Corporation of America (MCA) 192,249,275,296,318
Music Hall Rag 110
Music, Maestro, Please 351
Music Makes Me 40
Muskrat Ramble 13,24,30,33,51,128, 152,215,225,239–240,244,270,277, 289,296,318,328,337,359
Musso, Vido 44,46,67,69–70,72, 74–76,78–80,82–83,86–88,90–92,96, 100,105,107–109,111,115,117, 123–128,130–131,133–135,137–140, 143–147,152,154,156–159,162–163, 165,170,174,176,178–180,182–183, 191,204–205,213,216–217,219–220, 231–232,234–235,239,241,243–244, 246,248,251,253,256–257,262,265, 267–268,271,273–280,282–284,286, 289,292–293,295,346–347,350,354, 358–360
Mutiny In The Brass Section 29,174
Mutiny In The Parlor 6,8,19
Mutiny On The Bandstand 8
Muzzillo, Ralph 3,4,340–341,347, 349,351
My Baby Just Cares For Me 56
My Best Wishes 359
My Blue Heaven 31,35,50–51 54–55, 57,61,65,72,93,102,112,118,130,151, 155,159,161,173,175,205,208,211, 215–216,221,234,236–237,245–246, 251,268, 272,289,298,300,326,328
My Bonnie Lies Over The Ocean 332
My Buddy 126
My Cabin In The Ozarks 53
My Cabin Of Dreams 207,217,225, 231,234,236–237,240–241,244,248, 255–256,260–262,266–267,298,302, 312
My Day 317
My Dear 206
My Fine Feathered Friend 276,289,331
My First Confession 301
My First Impression Of You 308,321
My First Thrill 18,20,22,30,36,43,102, 194
My Future Just Passed 248
My Gal Mezzanine 127
My Gal Sal 2,72,179,210–211, 297–298,326,356
My Heart And I 5
My Heart is Taking Lessons 317,323,326
My Heart Is Under The Spell of The Blues 49
My Heart On Fire 92
My Heart's At Thy Sweet Voice 52
My Heart Stood Still 42
My Heart Wants To Dance 69
My Heaven On Earth 286
My Home Town Band 143
My Honey's Lovin' Arms 5,238,262, 272,275,346
My Kinda Love 158
My Kingdom For A Kiss 42–43,46–47, 50,55–56,68,96
My Last Affair [see also *This Is My Last Affair*] 108
My Little Buckaroo 142
My Little Fraternity Pin 233
My Little Friend 207
My Love Dreams Never Come True 112
My Man 278
My Marie 138
My Mariuccia Take A Steamboat 311
My Melancholy Baby 7,9,15,26,30, 34–35,39,41,43,45,76,80,83,90,94, 101,105,115,124,165,171,195, 201–202,217,233,265,331,346–347, 351,353
My Night To Dream 328
My Old Flame 19,107
My Own 358
My Romance 55
Myrow, Joe 232
My Secret Love Affair 255,271
My Silent Love 185,243
My Walking-Stick 349,361
My Wild Irish Rose 246,255
My Yiddishe Momma 332
Nagasaki 37,42,55,57,62,81,97–99, 102,105,108,110,112–113,116–118, 141,152,154,159,162,177,179,183, 188,197,202,210–211,216,222,233, 239,242,256,276,279,285,293–294, 312–313,320,325,328,336,350,359
Nana 59
Nance, Ray 337,341
Nanton, Joe 'Tricky Sam' 6,28,31,93, 128,130,132,134,145–146,148,159, 162,165,172,174–175,186,202,262, 264,312–313,317,320,324,332,336, 345–346,354,356,360
Napoleon, Phil 201,220,222–233, 237,240
Napoleon, Ted 23
Narcissus 208
Natalie, Cliff 99,144,167,171,309–310
Natoli, Nat 66,84,106,110,116,129, 132,156,167,169,187,250,260,280, 296,309–310,337
Naturally 360
Naughty Waltz 87,244,296,298,321, 340
Nautical Plaza, Revere Beach, Mass 206,213,215–216,218, 221,245,248, 251
Neiley, Emmy 139,283,297
Nelson, Dave 151
Nelson, Ozzie 2,5,7,12,33,53,97,99, 114,126,144,184,202–203, 222
Nero 94,123,129,149
Nestor, Gwynn 9
Never Felt Better, Never Had Less 348
Never Gonna Dance 46
Never In A Million Years 131,137, 143–146,149,159,161–163,165,167, 175,179,182–184,186,196,201–207, 213,222–223,251,256
Never More 58
Never Should Have Told You So 86,96, 109
Newcomb, Clyde 328
New Grand Terrace, Chicago 236
New Love 161
Newman, Davy 279
Newman, Douglas 203
Newman, Ruby 164,198
New Mayfair Casino, Cleveland, Ohio 105,265,267
New Orleans 273
New Orleans Twist 295
Newton, Frankie 8–9,12,17,133,138, 151,159,161,189,192,210,223–224, 230,232,257,259,272,278,287–288
N'Gona 297,309
Nice Work If You Can Get It 271,274, 278,280,282–286,293,296–299, 305–307,309,316,323,327,333,335, 341,349
Nicholas, Albert 52,155
Nicholas Brothers 334,358
Nichols, Lester 118,162
Nichols, Red 21,27,37,41,79,99,105, 142,146,285,289,343
Nicholson, Betty 223
Nicholson, Bobby 39
Nichol's Pinebrook Country Club, Conn 212,219,231–232, 241,245
Nickel In The Slot 18,21,25
Nickerson, Bert 30,201,218,240,254
Nick's Tavern, NYC 164,216,278, 287,292,307,324,326,334,341–342, 344,347
Nicolini, John 167,191,288
Night 104,108,112
Night And Day 36,38,59,67,127,130, 143,149,152,158–159,161,174–175, 178,183,185–186,208,211,213,217, 219,224,240,246,254,256,267,274, 280,285,287,320
Nightfall In Louisiana 262,269
Night In Manhattan 56
Nightmare 52,58–59,61,65,79,89, 122–123,157–159,259
Night Over Shanghai 174–175,179, 185,208,210–212,215,218,223,225, 234,236,244
Night Ride 142,179
Nitwit Serenade 18,35,57,234
Nixon Grand Th, Philadelphia 61,65, 72–73,96,103,108,119,129,146,150, 157,161
Noah's Ark 244
Noble, Ray 2,5,7,11,16,22,66,73,76,

86,97,99,106,130,132,137,297
Nobody 112
Nobody Lied 99
Nobody's Sweetheart 15,18,21,34,40,42, 48,54,77,94,99,103,112,114,120, 140,151,157,160,172,187,233,264, 286,296,302,349
Noise, Nancy 280
Nola 115,153,162,216
Noland, Bill 236,243–244,246,251
No More Tears 119,147
No, No, Brother, I Ain't The Man 215
No No Nora 114
Non-Stop 342
Non-Stop Flight 306,313
No One Else But You 284
Noone, Jimmy 292
'Noon Day Frolic' [radio show] 247, 249
No Other One 3
No Regrets 19,21,25,27–28,33,36–38, 41–42,49,52–53,58,60,65,67,70
Norman, Fred 76,111,114,158,206, 234,237,241,246
Normandie Ballroom, Boston 67, 168–169,171,173,263–264,267–268, 270,273
Norris, Al 52–53,69,74,111–113,117, 188,190,205,280,308,346
Norvo, Red 2–3,5,7,11–12,21,23–25, 27,29,47,72,89,97–99,101–106, 109–110,113,116–118,126–127,130, 137,164,169,179,191,196–197, 202–206,220–223,230,249–250, 253–256,263–265,267,274,280,283, 297,307,318,320,322–324,327, 329–332,334–336,339–344,347–348, 350–351,354,357,359
Norwegian Dance No. 7 233
Noseworthy, Sheldon 307,339
Not Enough 3
Not For All The Rice In China 39
Nothin' But The Blues 151,262,271, 289
Nothing 331
Nothing's Blue But The Sky 20,39,47, 51,55
Nothing Till Now 100
Notre Dame Victory March 81
Not Without You 57
Novak, Rudy 345,355,358
Now 99,116,123,140
Now It Can Be Told 351,359–360
Now Or Never 60
Now That Summer Is Gone 72,77,101
Now The Whole World Knows 146
Now They Call It Swing 311
Now Will You Be Good? 328
Now You're Talking My Language 131, 137,146
Noye, Sally 284,286
Number 2A 151
Number 32 220,223
Number 321 242
Nutty Nursery Rhymes 317,326
Oakie, Jack 162,200,267–268
Oakley, Helen 133,259
O'Bryan, Johnny 205

Ochi Chornya 39
O'Connell, James 37,82,92
Oderich, Jimmy 25,35,61,123
Ode To A Chimney Sweep 87
Off Again, On Again 286
Off To Philadelphia In The Morning 57
Of Thee I Swing, Baby 83
O'Hara, Edward 37,82,92,225
Oh Babe, Maybe Someday 6,19–20,22, 33,56,93,98,132,189,320
Oh, Babe! What Can The Matter Be? 118
Oh, Baby 17
Oh Baby, What I Wouldn't Do 116
Oh, Boy! 188
Oh! By Jingo! 280
Oh, Dear! What Can The Matter Be? 40,50,64,126
Oh, How I Hate To Get Up In The Morning 338
Oh, Lady Be Good 15,50,64,66,69, 76–77,80,87,93,95,107,109,117–118, 124,131,135,138,140,147,149,152, 154,163,165,183–184,202,211,213, 221,225,232,234–235,239,241–242, 245–246,248,251,253,272,275,277, 285,292,299,303,307,312,317,326, 343,353
Oh, My Goodness 30,37,42,44,46
Oh, Promise Me 325
Oh Say, Can You Swing? 86,93,96,104, 115,123,140,166
Oh, Sister! Ain't That Hot 140,142,208, 210,251,263
Oh, Susanna, Dust Off That Old Pianna 123
Oh, Yazoo 118
Oh, You 56
O'Keefe, Cork 102
Okey-Doke 153,160
Old Black Joe 105
Old Christmas Tree 95
Old Fashioned Love 106,108,146,157, 235,242,301,344
Old-Fashioned Swing 77,81,83,94–95, 102,109,115,186
Old Folks At Home 165
Old Joe's Hittin' The Jug 27,31,37,64, 94,108
Old King Cole 203,207–208,231,237
Old Louisiana 46
Old Man Ben 323
Old Man Harlem 257
Old Man Moon 264
Old Man Mose 4,24,38,52,100,162, 264
Old Plantation 134,165,173
Old Spinning Wheel 117
Oliver, King 282
Oliver, Sy 26,29,52–53,69,74, 111–112,161,188,190,205,280,308, 346
Ol' Man River 36,56,62,86,104,109, 125,130,145,155,212,323,339,345
Ol' Pappy 250
Olsen, George 97
O'Malley, Pat 223
On A Little Bamboo Bridge 108,124,

143–144,148,160
On A Summer Holiday 33,43,45
Once In A While 204–205,208,210, 213,219,222,232,235,239–240,242, 254,256,265,267,269,271,274–278, 280,282–283,285,289,292,298–304, 311–312,316–317,321,334–335
On Cocoanut Island 37,41,55
One Big Union For Two 321
O'Neil, Dolores 273
One In A Million 94,109,131,142,185
One More Dream 346
One Never Knows, Does One? 86,96, 104–105,107,111,113,138,333
One Night In Monte Carlo 22
One O'Clock Jump 202,205,221,241, 262,268,273,275,279,283,288,293, 299,301,308,333–335,343,349,351, 355,362
One Rose 46,255,283
One Rose Left In My Heart 328
One Rose Of Summer 299,335
One Song 306,313,336
One Step Ahead of My Shadow 52
One, Two, Button Your Shoe 33,61,65, 87,95,99,101,125,128,134
One, Two, Three Little Hours 128,166
On Moonlight Bay 172,174–176,179, 185,234,241–242,254,286
On Revival Day 343
On The Air 35,37,40–41,52,97,218
On The Alamo 6,10–11,19,42,54,62, 79,102,248,318,345
'On The Avenue' [show] 111
On The Beach At Bali-Bali 22,25–26, 29,35–38,47,53,58,67,88,90,100
On The Bumpy Road To Love 357–359
On The Isle Of Kitchy-Mi-Boko 195, 204,215,236,252
On The Sentimental Side 311,321,337, 344,349,351,353
On The Sunny Side of The Street 145, 161,179,217,225,263,289,291,306, 313,320
On The Trail Of The Lonesome Pine 202,271
On Wisconsin 71
On Your Toes 34,39
Onyx Club, 72 W52nd Street, NYC 2,5,7–8,12,16,23,27,30–32,35, 37–39,43–46,48–50,53,55,57,60,64, 66,69–70,76,86,94–95,97–99,101, 108,114–115,126
Onyx Club, 62 W52nd Street, NYC 144,147,164,172,184,201,222,226, 230,247,266,272,278,284,287–288, 292,296,306–307,309,313,323–324, 328,331–332,334–335,338–339,342, 344,347,350,354,358,360
Onyx Club Spree 165,306
Onyx Club Stomp 165
Ooh! Look-a There, Ain't She Pretty? 5,9,103
Ooooo-oh Boom! 324,326,336–337,339
Opus No 1 169

103,108,110,112,114,116–118,124, 140–141,143,161,167,188,195,231, 251,255,264,270
Oriental Yoga 210–211
Original Dixieland Jazz Band 61,75, 168
Original Dixieland One-Step 44,61, 233,264
Original Memphis Five 68
Osborne, Will 53,66,152,222,358
O Sole Mio 146
Ostrich Walk 143,183
Our Love Was Meant To Be 186,231, 235,253,266
Our Penthouse On Third Avenue 166, 186,202,204,207,211,215,223, 232–233,252
Out Of Nowhere 45,59,349
Out Of Space 39,79,83
Out Of The Blue 254
Out Of The World 55
Outside Of Paradise 321,332,335
Out The Window 271,328,334–335, 337,340
Out Where The Blues Begin 52–53,69
Over A Bowl Of Sushi-aki 58
Overheard In A Cocktail Lounge 232
Owens, Arline 105,146
Owens, Harry 97
Owens, Jack 146,350,357,359
Owens, Jesse 151,179,248
Oxley, Harold 112
Ozarks Are Calling Me Home 125
Packard, Jerry 44–45
Pack Up Your Sins (And Go To The Devil) 355
Pagan Fantasy 93
Pagan Love Song 25,33,43,84,89,96, 101,115,125,131,142,146,157,183, 210,231,234,262,281,297–298,307, 318
Page, Hot Lips 137,323,349,360
Page, Walter 77,109–110,118,138,184, 188,193,197,200,202,205,231,233, 240,245,253,256,271,278–279,292, 307–308,311,328,333,337,341,354
Pagliacci 294,334
Painting The Town Red 114
Pale Hands 46
Palesteena 340
Palisades Amusement Park, N.J. 29–33,35,45–46,48–50,52,56
Palmer Brothers 130
Palmer, Francis 243,246,255,262
Palmer, Gladys 81
Palmer House, Chicago 33,53
Palmer, Jack 350,357,359
Palmer, Skeeter 100
Palomar Ballroom, Los Angeles 27–28,30–31,33,35,37,43,46,97–98, 107,153,183,187,203–204,208,212, 216–217,220–221,223,225,232,234, 237,239,243–244,248,251,254–256, 265,267,274,276–277,279–280, 283–284,288,294
Panama 17,34,36,68,152,216,269, 283–284,316,328,358
Panamania 110,113,159,183,187,216,

INDEX

264,299,309
Panassie, Hugues 226
Papa Tree-Top Tall 43,45,47,64,73,79, 83,88,101,106,109
Paque, Glyn 163
Parade Of The Milk Bottle Tops 27,54, 135,175,269,274,276,278,289,291, 297–298,309,334,337
Parade To A G-string 216
Paradise 8,65,76,157,244,253,256,280, 327–328
Paradise Club, Atlantic City, N.J. 243, 246–247
Paradise Restaurant, NYC 48,97,142, 345,354,356
Paramount Theater, NYC 2,5,16,23, 27,32,53,66,86,89,99,126–129,134, 138,144,155,168,184,201,222,228, 247,266,278,292,294,307,321, 324–325,334,344,347,350,354,358, 360
Paramour 87,115,118,293,302
Parham, Charles 'Truck 80,108
Parks, Bert 40,46,91,105,107,127, 140,163,165–166,169,198, 251
Parks, Bob 18,23,33
Parlez-Moi D'Amour 39
Parrish, Avery 29,56,158,162,165, 197,232,292,332
Pasquall, Jerome 8,20,33,152
Passion 265
Passionette 17,124,185,311
Pastor, Tony 35,45,52,58–59,61,65, 74,79,85,89,93,119,122,158–159, 171,174,211,214,223,259,273,306, 313,359
Pastoriza, Hugh 23,66,68,70,73,76–77, 84,87,89,99,102,106,110,112,116, 119,123,125,127–129,136,138–139, 153–155,160,167–168,174,180, 182–183,187,192,195,205,208–209, 224,228,249–250,253,260–261, 270–272,275,280,282,286,288,293, 296, 300,304,307,318,329–330,339, 341–343,362
Pastoriza, Mr. 77,110,138,153,275
Pastoriza, Mrs 187,192
Paswonky 25
Patch Up Your Heart 214
Patrick, Freddy 249,253,261,270,286, 289
Paul Howard's Quality Serenaders 107
Paul Revere 307,313,335
Paul Taylor Chorus 179
Pavillion Royale, Long Island, NY 198,204–205,210–211,213,216,219, 221,225,231,233–235,239
Payne, Bennie 4,20,50,59,64–65,74, 78,101,105,109,111,117,127,134, 225,233–234,241,246,255,263,279, 281,283,285,295,312,317,320–321, 332,343
Peabody, The [dance] 329
Peace, Brother, Peace 210,235,244,248
Peanut Vendor 44
Pearl, Jack 201
Peck, Jack 184,267
Peck-A-Doodle-Do 343

Peckin' 92,124,127,154,167,170,175, 178–179,182–183,185,189,196,198, 200,202–204,207–208,211–212, 215–216,218,223,234,237,239,241, 244,248,253–254,256–257,260,270, 275,281,285, 292,342
Peer, Beverly 74,80–81,105,138,178, 238,250,277–279,295–296,299,301, 321,350,355,361–362
Peg O' My Heart 17,19,137,214,234, 290,298,323
Pennell, Ed 139
Pennell, Henry 139
Pennies From Heaven 33,79,81,83, 87–89,92,95–96,101–102,104,106, 108–109,112,122,134,152,194
'Pennies From Heaven'[movie] 89
Perfidia 233
Perkins, Jerry 55,76,79,83,86,88,90, 96,100,104,108,112–114,140,209, 245,251
Perlmutter, Sid 171,189,194–195,198, 231
Permit Me 16
Perry, Ronnie 359
Persoff, Sam 25,35,61,74,85,93,119, 123
Peter Piper 42–43,51,64,66–68,72,79, 110
Peterson, Chuck 359
Peterson, Pete 3,28,47,72,101,118, 137,202,206,263–264,311,318,327, 332,339–340,348,350–351,357,359
Peterson, Tweet 176,212–216,239,242
Petry, Fred 171,174,214,259
Philburn, Al 5,12
Phillips, Betty 240
Phillips, James 16
Phillips, Sid 320
Phillips, Sidney 38
Pianology 117
Piano Stomp [Shine] 235
Piano Tuner Man 321
Piccadilly Circus Bar, NYC 354,358, 360
Pickering, Ben 10,13,25,72,80,82
Pickin' The Blues 118
Pick Yourself Up 37,39,46,54,58–61,65, 83,90,94,99,110,129,185
Picture Me Without You 47,52,70,72, 76,140
Pigeons And Peppers 276,322
Pigeon Walk 280
Pilot Radio Co. 282
Pinger, Harvey 77,84,89,99,128–129, 132,137–138,141,182–183,226,275, 307,309–310,318,329,339,345, 347–348
Pinger, Mrs 128,137
Pioneer Palace, Cleveland, Ohio 243
Piron, A. J. 130
Pitt, Merle 272,276,278,281,284–285, 294,297,307,311,313,320,323,326, 334
Plantation Swing 206
Planter's Punch 328
Playland Casino, Rye, N.Y. 183–185, 196,204,215,219–220,223–225,

232–235,237,241,246,249
Please 281
Please Be Kind 327–328,331,333–334, 336–337,339,341,343–345,349–350, 353,355
Please Believe Me 4,8,21
Please Care For Me 96
Please Don't Turn Your Back On Me 62
Please Forgive Me 360
Please Keep Me In Your Dreams 94,104, 112,114
Please Leave Me Alone 55,60
Please Pardon Us, We're In Love 223
Pleasure Beach BR, Bridgeport, Conn 40,196,218,244,252
Pletcher, Stew 3,47,72,98–99,101, 103–106,110,113,116–118,137, 169,206,263–265,274,280,283
Plotkin, Ben 61,123
Pluckin' That Bass 281
Pluckin' The Blues 284
Poe, Jim 167–168,174,182,187,192, 249,269–270,275,284,288,300,309, 311,314,318,347
Poe, Mrs 309
Poinciana 89
Polka Dot Stomp 61,65
Pollack, Ben 59–60,92,107,139,211, 216,241,243,246,262,348,360
Pollard, Nat 130–131,179,201,237, 286
Polly Wolly Doodle 3
Ponce, Philip 112
Pons, Lily 35,165
Poor, Len 134,176
Poor Little Butterfly 89,297
Poor Little Rich Girl 175
Poor Robinson Crusoe 186,198,204, 216,232
Popcorn Man 196,201,223,264, 273–275,280,349
Poppa, Come Back Home 51
Porter, Cole 127,161,270
Porter, Dick 36,38,40,46,52,55
Porter, Yank 5,25
Posin' 186,200–201,203,205–207, 210–211,217,219–223,233–234,236, 240,242–248,251–252,254–257,262, 302,311
Powell, Billie 310,323
Powell, Eddie 188,243,334,357
Powell, James 346
Powell, Rudy 34,354
Powell, Scat 360
Powerhouse (Monkey Wrench Song) 110, 122–123,140,148,164,187,257
Powers, Ernie 24
Preble, Harry 92
Prelude To A Kiss 360
Prelude To A Stomp 118,147,239,244, 272,334,237,346
Presby, G. Archibald 38,49,120,146, 151,158,233,237,293
Price, Bob 254,286,289,297,353
Price, Joe 59
Prima, Louis 69,278,287,292,296, 307,324,334,342,350
Prince, Gene 237,244

Prince Of Wails 195,253
Prior, Vincent 113,135,156,168,174, 192,197,238,249,296,309
Pritchard, Billy 220,233
Privin, Bernie 236
Procope, Russell 12,17,138,159,173, 302,346
Prologue to Black And Tan Fantasy 312
Pryor, Roger 97
Public Enemy Number One 296
Puddin' Head Jones 307
Puddin' Head Serenade 11,13,221
Puerto Rican Dreams 189
Pumiglio, Pete 81,84,90,95,103,106, 110,113,116,119,122–123,125,129, 132,140,148–149,156,164,169,177, 187–188,192,203,300,348–349,357
Purple Shade 184
Purtill, Maurice 47,72,101–102,118, 137,179,203,206,255,263–265,283, 308,311,316,322,324–325,333,338, 347,349,351,358–359,361
Put On Your Old Grey Bonnet 57,121, 195,205,286,297,299,305
Put Your Heart In A Song 357
Pyramid 354,357
Quaker City Jazz 111,207,256,298, 317
Quayle, Oliver 325,329,339,354
Queen Isabella (Decca Stomp) 29,246, 263,281,289,292–293,295,299,301
Quenzer, Artie 243,246
Quintet of the Hot Club of France 187,217
Rachmaninov's Prelude 157
Raggin' The Scale 93,106,188
Raggle-Taggle 285
Rain 29,52,65
Rainbow On The River 64,95,105,111
Rainbow Room, NYC 2,5,7–9,12, 16–17,19,23,25,27,66,73,86,97,99, 101,103,114,118,121,124,126,142, 198
Rain In My Eyes 143,152
Rain In My Heart 188
Raisin' The Rent 251
Ralph, Jesse 137,174,176,186,211, 213–216,218–219,231,237,240,254, 256,289,297
Ralston, Art 5,9,25,112,115,120,128, 143,201,214,279,285,292,295, 297–298,301–302,317,324,326,332, 361
Ramona 246
Ramona [see Davis, Ramona] 42, 339–340
Randall's Island Stadium, NYC 353
Randall, William 337,341
Rando, Doc 311
Randolph, Anda 151
Randolph, Irving 20,59,72,127,134, 241,246,255,295,321,343
Range, Robert 29,56,158,165,232, 332
Rank, Bill 253
Rap Tap On Wood 33
Raskin, Milton 346–347,350,354, 358–360

Rauch, Billy 5,9,25,112,115,118, 120–121,128,143,201,214,279,285, 292,295,297–298,301–302,309,317, 324,326,332,361
Rausch, Cliff 37,82,92
Rausch, Harry 37,82,92
Ravazza, Carl 97
Ray, Floyd 334
Raye, Leah 227
Raye, Martha 139
Raye, Velma 69
Raymor Ballroom, Boston 64,71, 79–80,104,108,110,149,151–152, 157–159,172,174–176,178–179, 183–185,191,286,289–291,298,309, 313,352
Razaf, Andy 26–27,48,52,55,58–59, 115,120
Reardon, Casper 11,21,40,50,66,87, 89–90,98,110,119,132,187,192,225, 320,357
Rebito, Gasparre 353
Rebound 103,140,187
Reckless Night On Board An Ocean Liner 129,148–149,192,195,335,338
Red Cap 232
'Red Hot And Blue' [movie] 109–11
Red Hot Heat 245
Red Hot Penny 37
Redman, Don 5,7,11–12,17,65–66, 86,144,159,165,179,247,262,324, 350,360
Red Rhythm 16,20,30,33,45–46,49,73
Reed, Cappy 201
Reese, Gail 196,224–225,232, 234–236,239,248–249,269,272,284, 321,335,338,340–341,353
Reeves, Chick 76–77,86,161
Reeves, Talcott 17
Reichman, Joe 23,27
Reid Beach Casino, Asbury Park, N.J. 234
Reid, Neal 76–77,83,86,102,109,114, 118,121,161–162,196,205,214,231, 264,267,270,273,276,286,328,346, 355
Reinhardt, Django 363
Reisman, Leo 97
Remember 6,8,14,17,28,35,38,46,58, 62,86,98,103,107,112,126,137,140, 162,183,216,218,227,231,234,243, 255,255–256,267,275,299,313,323
Remember Me 220,233,254,264, 267–268,273–274,277,279,281, 283–284,296
Remember When 82,91,190
Rendezvous With A Dream 42,44, 47–48,50
Rendezvous With Rhythm 344
Reo, Tommy 248
Republic Theater, NYC 309
Reuss, Allan 3,4,6,10,14,22–23,26,37, 44,46,67,72,75,78,81,88,91,96, 104–105,107,117,128,135,143,152, 159,161,163,170,176,180,204–205, 220,251,253,267,274–275,278,283, 286,292–293,311,316,331,343,357
Reviso, Carl 17

Rexatious 90
Reynolds, Ellsworth 151
Reynolds, Helen 185
Reynolds, Jimmy 20
Rhapsody In Blue 62,208,210–211,254
Rhapsody Melody 266
Rhe Ta Ta Da Te De Tee De Dee De Da La 60
Rhyme For Love 98
Rhythmaires (CBS Band) 38,40,42, 44,46,49,53,55–56
Rhythm A La Carte 25
Rhythm Doctor 306
Rhythm Fantasy 169
Rhythm In My Nursery Rhymes 4,8, 22,24,30,80,83,205,239,252,279, 333,355
Rhythm In My Soul 88,124,301
Rhythm Is Our Business 29,61,112,188
Rhythm Jam 118,124,295,359
Rhythm Jamboree 108
Rhythm Of The Broadway Moon 8
Rhythm Of The Congo 31
Rhythm Of The River 78,89
Rhythm On The River 121,212
Rhythm Of The Tambourine 127,210, 223
'Rhythm On Record' [book] 106, 112–113,117,125,129,135–136,167, 226,249,347
Rhythm, Rhythm [I Got Rhythm] 161, 217
Rhythm Roundup 203
Rhythm Saved The World 10,13,16,18, 22
Rhythm Sundae 117
Ricci, Paul 12,13,308,334,357
Rich, Buddy 280,287,300,308,316, 334,341–342,357
Rich, Freddy 66,68–69,89
Richards, Chuck 16,20,29–33,36,45, 48–49,70,73,81,141,150,162,186, 188,195,200,203,207,210–211,223, 236,263,269–270,276,353
Richards, Don 320
Richards, Jimmy 48
Richardson, Dr. 296
Richmond, June 164,255,257,291, 298,305,307,309,334–335,337, 340–341,347,349
Riddel, Mary Elma 127
Ride, Red, Ride 16,23,30–31,33, 45–46,49,81,141,195,234
Ridin' A Riff 231,270
Ridin' High 88,104,109,111–112,117, 127,141,279
Riding On A Blue Note 324
Ridin' The Groove 284
Riffin' 20,22,25,41,54–55,57,92,118
Riffin' At The Ritz 61,64–67,81,87,89, 97,102,105,127,140,184,186,194, 207
Riffs 242,327
Rigamarole 30,37,45,60,94,126,237, 273
Right Or Wrong 264,283
Riley, John 162
Riley, Mike 2,3,14,32,39–41,50,53,

58,60,64,66,74,93,114,118,126,143, 196,215,220–221,236
Ring Dem Bells 98,215,316
Rinka Tinka Man 341
Rinker, Al 103,187–188,244,309
Rio, Rita 97
Rip Van Winkle 39,41,50,58,60,64
Riverboat Shuffle 30,32,207,233,270
River Man 27,31
Roach, Malcolm 329
Roaches And Incense 297
Roar, Lion, Roar 73
Robbins, June 92,95,99–100,123, 165–166,171,174,185,196,202–203, 207,211,218,234
Roberts, Caughey 109,138
Roberts, Claude 337,341
Roberts, Kenneth 131,152,220,231, 324
Robertson, Dick 115
Robeson, Orlando 54
Robins And Roses 10,18–19,21,23,25, 27–30,34,36–38,43,52,60,235
Rob(b)ins, Ruth 227,252
Robinson, Bill 53,63,66,86,99,114, 292,307,324,334
Robinson, Edgar 244
Robinson, Eli 237,240–241,244,248, 260
Robinson, George 346
Robinson, J. Russel 75
Robinson, Les 171,174,214,223,259, 273,306,359
Robinson, Prince 121,237,240,245, 248,251,260,278,295,310
Robison, Willard 39,265
Rock And Ride 98
Rockin' Chair 113,127,137,200,205, 234,238,253,320
Rockin' Chair Swing 176,188,196,198, 209–211,216,234,311
Rockin' In Rhythm 19,134,142
Rockin' The Blues 334
Rockin' The Town 286,301,304, 306–307,311
Rock It For Me 275,278,298,348
Rockwell-O'Keefe 102,113,135,156, 166–167,174,192,197,238,249,296, 309,318,323
Ro(d)gers, Harry 137,171,174,186, 214,223, 259,273,306,359
Rodin, Gil 9,13,25–26,42,117,139, 205,280,282,284,318,325,327, 337–338
Rodriguez, Nicholas 179
Rogers, Buddy 344,350
Rogers, Clyde 213–214
Rogers, Dorothy 152
Rogers, Ginger 217,219,234,237,242
Roll Along, Prairie Moon 5,14
Roll 'Em 121,123–124,130,135, 137–138,140–141,147,152,154,157, 162,179,183,205,222,234,241,245, 257–272,273,275,292,306,313,321, 328,344–345,360
Rolling Plains 289
Rollini, Adrian 9,11,21,31,68–69,84, 86,92,102–103,140,187,281,289,

294,297,308,316,354,357–358,360
Rollini, Art 3,4,10,14,22–23,26,37, 44,46,58,67,69,74–75,86,88,91,96, 105,107,109–110,115,117,124, 126–128,131,134–135,139–140,153, 158,163,176,183,204–205,216–217, 221,223,231,234,244,251,253, 256–257,262,274–275,277,282–283, 286,292–293,295,298–299,302–304, 306,308,312,321,326,331,337,349
Rollins, Horace 346–347,350,354, 358–360
Rollin' Sam 272
Roll Them Bones 65
Rome, Joan 339
Rongetti, Nicholas 287
Roosevelt, President F. D. R. 113
Rosalie 289,298,312–313,317–318, 321,333–334,355
Rosati, Gene 162–163,206
Rose In The Dark 48
Roseland Ballroom, Brooklyn 334
Roseland Ballroom, NYC 76,80,83, 91,93,95–98,100,102,104,110,112, 114,118,121,127,135,137,140,143, 147,153,162,165,168,171,175,178, 186,221,266,269, 298,302,308,312
Roseland Shuffle 109,197,205,235
Roseland-State Ballroom, Boston 340
Rose, Lila 15,24,196
Rose Marie 46
Rosenblum, Sam 35
Rose of The Rio Grande 16,25,62,354
Rose Room 8,16,35,41,70,81,83,93, 120,137,173,210–211,220,227, 231–232,244–245,252,264,270,273, 275,280,296,307,324,331–332,335
Roses In December 195,232,235,265, 267,269,271–272,274,276,283,301
Roses Of Picardy 53,126,283
Rosetta 3,6,13,16,36,45,76,84,95,98, 105,107,112,115–117,138,145,152, 172,178,215–218,234,239,242,256, 267,272,276,284,286,295,299,339
Ross, David 57,113,165
Ross, Hank 66,69,73,76,132,140,156, 169,187–188,203,211,225,238–239, 250,253,255,260–261,254,267,272, 275,280,282,284–286,296–297,299, 303,309–310,323,326–327,331,333, 337,339
Ross, Shirley 294
Rosselli, Jimmy 116,119,129,169,187, 250,260,264
Round The Old Deserted Farm 265, 348,351
Rounds, Clyde 10,25,72,80,82,101, 108,112,121,144,167,171,189, 194–195,198,224,230,236,248,269, 294,301,321,340–341,348,353,355
Royal Garden Blues 25,36,40,42,78, 81,90,94,96,115,121,161–162,169, 172,175,178,196,203,208,211,213, 219,230,232,238,250,265,267,282, 284,296,301,309,324,326,335, 337–338
Royal Hawaiian Hotel, Hawaii 97
Roxy Theater 12

INDEX

Rubin, Jules 223,273,306
Rubinowich, Sam 340–341,349,351
Rug Cutter's Swing 8,31,252,283,335
Runnin' A Temperature 57,74,161
Runnin' Ragged 54
Runnin' Wild 37,69,75,110–111,114, 138,140,144,154,158,165,175,205, 217,232,286,312,361
Rushing, Jimmy 76–78,80,83,96,98, 102,104,109–110,118,124,138,157, 194–195,197,202,205,231,233–234, 237,239–241,244–245,248–249,253, 261,271,279,307,328,333–334,340, 354–355
Russell, Edith 139
Russell, Johnny 83,87
Russell, Luis 5,7,32,40,86,108,155, 163,189,195,266,337,360
Russell, Pee Wee 69,315,326,328, 341–343,347,349,357–358
Russian Lullaby 216,221,232,256,263, 270,274,301–302
Russin, Babe 3,5,12,36–37,39–40,42, 46,48–49,52,54–55,66,69,71,76,82, 95,178,188,224,239,243,261,265, 284,295,301,303,306–308,311–312, 316,324–326,331,334–335,337, 339–340,343–344,351,357,359
Russin, Jack 9,308
Russo, Andy 350,357,359
Rustic Cabin, Palisades, N.J. 58
Rustle Of Swing 274,321
Rusty Hinge 123,138,145,166,172, 201,220
Ryan, Jack 134,175,192,258,269,285, 299,321,340–341,349,351
Ryerson, Frank 55–56,61,67,79,104, 113–114,129,140,209
Sacco, Tony 16,18
Sail Along, Silvery Moon 284,291,309
Sailin' 104
Sailing A Dreamboat 33,35,38,44,47, 51,55,57
Sailing Home 267
St. James Infirmary 127
St. Louis Blues 4–5,18–22,26,28,31, 37,40,42,44–45,47,50,52,59–60,69, 79,82,84,90–92,95,98–100,102–103, 106,116–117,119,124,126,129,142, 144,155,165,178,183–184,189, 196–197,203,207,209–211,213–214, 216, 218–219,222,225,231,233,239, 243,247,250–251,255,263,265, 269–270,283–285,289,293,298,337, 355,357
St. Louis Doodle 29
St. Louis Wiggle Rhythm 20,45,73
Salad, Sonny 260–261
Same Old Way 16
Sampson, Edgar 12,23,54,72,79,84, 86,104,108,111,123,126,177,234, 237,246,251,299,301,311,316,320, 331,340,344
Sampson's Stomp 350,355
Samuel, Morey 189,194–195,198
San Anton' 148,173
Sanders, Joe 60,145,163,265,309
Sanders, Ray 162,165

Sandman 3,5,60,115,119,182,269,274, 276,285,297,299,307,337
Sands, Bobby 114,158,206
Sanella, Andy 324
San Francisco 25,42,46–48,53,60–61,99
Saratoga 248
Sargent, Hugh 253
Sargent, Kenny 5,8,16–17,19,25, 69–70,78–79,83–84,87,89–90,101, 103,112,114–115,118,120–121,124, 128,143,183,201,203–204,208,212, 214,278–279,285–286,289,292–293, 295,297–298,301–302,306–307,309, 316–317,320,323–324,326–327,332, 361
Sarnelli, John 191
Satan's Holiday 42,316
Satan Takes A Holiday 153,158,169, 172,178,185,201,205–206,210,212, 215–216,218–219,221,223–225, 232–233,235–237,242,245,251, 256–257,263,271,276,281,283,293, 298,335
Saturday Night Function 322
Saturday Night Swing Session 25–26, 28,30,32,36,39,45,50,55,58,66,69,73, 75–76,81,84,87,89–90,92–93,95,99, 103,106,110,113,116,119,123,125, 129,132,135,140,145,149,156,160, 164, 167–169,172,177,183,185,187, 189,192,195,202,207,211,216,225, 233,238–239,250,255,260–261,264, 267,270,272,275,277,280,284–285, 293,297,299,303,307,309,313,320, 323,326–327,331,333,336,339,347, 357
Saunders, Joe 250
Sauter, Eddie 3,101,137,169,329,331
Savage Rhythm 246,281
Save Me, Sister 4,78,117,274
Savin' Myself For You 350,353–355, 357
Savitt, Jan 29,38–40,111,202,207,233, 256,259,270,298
Savoy Ballroom, Harlem, NYC 65,76, 78–79,84,87–89,92–93,97–98,100, 104,113,119,123,126,128,132,135, 137,143,146–147,153,156–157, 159–161,164,167,169–170,172, 176–177,179,185,191–194,197,202, 204–205,223,225,230,232,234–237, 239,241,243–244,246,248,250–251, 253–254,256,260–261,263–264,270, 272,275,277,289,291,293,295, 298–303,306,309–310,314,317,321, 328,340,346,349,354
Savoy Blues 26,36,96,279
Savoy Sultans 270,277–278,291,300, 303,306,324,326,349,354,360
Say It With Music 25,123,165,202, 207,234
Say Not 34,63
Says My Heart 348,353,357
Sbarbaro, Tony 75,327
Scafati, Sill 162
Scattin' At The Cotton Club 93
Scattin' At The Kit Kat 128,142,144, 164,166,169,171,173,177,179,185, 195–196,202,213,243,265,270,308

Schaffer, Bob 28
Schaffer, William 10,13
Schaumberger, Howard 130–131,179, 201,237,286,300,322,325
Schechter, Julie 25
Scherzinger, Vic 265
Schiller, Bill 165–166,171,175,178
Schleman, Hilton R. 106
Schnickelfritz Band, The 356
Schrafft's Restaurant, NYC 129
Schubert, Del 157,161,177,252
Schultze, Dave 346–347,350,354, 358–360
Schumacher, Ralph 242
Schumann, Bill 74,85,93,119
Schutt, Arthur 61,129
Schutz, Buddy 167,191
Schuyler, Sonny 316
Schwartz, Willie 353
Schwichtenburg, Wilbur [Will Bradley] 187,282,309,333
Scott, Cecil 12,17,20,34,80,121,138, 159
Scott, Hazel 49,57,103,264,307
Scott, Mabel 112
Scott, Raymond 44,48,73,95,103,110, 113,116,119,122–123,125,127,132, 140,145,148–149,156,158,164,169, 172,177,187–188,192,195,207,238, 277,300,313,331,348–349,357
Scrapin' The Toast 299
Scrounch 332
Sears, Jerry 31,151,158
Sebastian's Cotton Club, L.A. 93, 97–98,119,132
Secrest, Andy 348
Sedric, Gene 5,13,24–25,32,56,85,94, 123,134,148,186,253,269,288,339, 343,346,358
Seidel, Al 121
Selmer Music Store, NYC 156
Sensation 39,61,65,93,103,161,169, 202,256
Sent For You Yesterday And Here You Come Today 328,334
Sentimental And Melancholy 120–121, 145–146,149,157,160,165
Sepian Jazz 112
September In May 143
September In The Rain 149,151–152, 157,160,163,165–166,171,175–178, 182–184,186,188,195,203,205,208, 214–216,238,243,245
September Morning In Harlem 320
Serenade For A Wealthy Widow 27,29, 58,88,289
Serenade In The Night 100,117,125, 154,171,348
Serenade In The Sky 332
Serenade To A Shylock 349
Serenade To Nobody In Particular 10
Serenade To The Stars 335,337–338,340
Seymour, Dan 75,86,282
Shades Of Hades 17,25,79,90,212,302, 309
Shafter Octet 217
Shake Your Can 318
Shall We Dance? 165

'Shall We Dance' [movie] 217,219, 234,237,242
Shame On You 216,223
Shanghai Shuffle 42
Shapiro, Artie 8,13,17,27,43,66,115, 121,151,158,177–178,197,210–211, 225–227,234,242,265,280,284,287, 295,300,308,315,322,325,333,341, 349,358
Sharon, Sally 43
Sharpie 360
Shavers, Charlie 118,124,141,162,195, 263,268,274,287,292,309,313,318, 324–325,328,332,338,357
Shaw, Art 13,15,21,25,28,32,35,45,50, 52–53,58–59,61,65,74,77,79,85–86, 89,93,119,122,126,133,135,156–159, 163,167,171,174,185,211,214,220, 223,230,233,238,259,261,273,275, 306,311,313, 330–331,340,359
Shaw, Bert 19,31,35,37,41,47,49,58, 61,70,83–84,92,95,97,172,177, 215–218,247,256
Sheen, Jimmy 153–154
Sheik Of Araby 99,185,212,279,285
She Lived Down In Our Alley 140
Shepard, Howard 224
Sheppard, Bud 36–38,40,46,52, 54–55,71
Sherman, James 8,18,27,44,200
Sherock, Shorty 59–60,92,258,321, 340–341,347,349,351
Shertzer, Hymie 3,4,10,14,22–23,26, 37,44,67,75,88,96,105,107,109,117, 121,128–129,135,137,139,176, 204–205,217,253,274–275,283,286, 292–293,331,337,347–349,351, 358–359,361
She's Funny That Way 29,96,140,283, 354
She Shall Have Music 33,41–42,50,53, 55,59,100
She's Tall, She's Tan, She's Terrific 241, 253,262,269,274,276–277,281,283, 296,298,312,316–318
Shields, Larry 75,327
Shindig 264,280
Shine 21,33,48,63,81,88,109,130,134, 146,149,189,210–211,216,222,225, 231,234,254–256,297,327,349
Shine On, Harvest Moon 325,354
Shine On Your Shoes 40
Shine, William H. 156,168,192
Shoe Shine Boy 8,16,28,31–33,35, 39–40,43,46,52,55,60,77,81,83,110, 183,219,222,255,257
Shoe Shiner's Drag 359
Shoobe, Lou 36,40,46,52,55,66,76,81, 84,89–90,93,95,103,106,110,113,119, 122–123,125,132,140,156,164,169, 183,187–188,192,250,255,260,272, 280,296–297,303,309,327,333,340
Shoop, Jack 185
Shoot The Likker To Me, John Boy 237, 259,313
Short, Bobby 326
Should I? 43,45,84,103,114,124
Shout And Do It 78

Shout And Feel It 157
Shout And Scream 80
Shoutin' In That Amen Corner 103,223, 265
Showboat Shuffle 19–20,70,132,162,195
Showers, Earl C. 126
Siboney 200,210
Sidell, Al 140
Siegfield, Frank 74,85,93,119
Signorelli, Frank 3,5,12
Silent Love 166
Silhouetted In The Moonlight 277,282, 289,299,312–313,324
Sillman, Phil 9
Silloway, Ward 8–9,13,25–26,40,42, 117,133,205,280,282,284,319,325, 327,337–338
Silver Threads Among The Gold 99
Silv'ry Moon And Golden Sands 317
Simeon, Omer 13,117,231
Simeone, Frank 47,72,101,137,350, 357,359
Simmon, Earl 97
Simmons, Kermit 18,23,33,64,76–77, 86,161–162,231,264,276,286,292
Simmons, Lonnie 346
Simon, Gene 17,65,179
Simon, George 137,186
Simpkins, Arthur 'Georgia Boy' 33,52, 54,58–60,68–70,246,248,251, 255–256
Simply Grand 211,214,218,221,237
Simpson, Bill 115
Sims, Edward 29,56,158,165,232,234, 332
Since My Best Gal Turned Me Down 350
Sing An Old-Fashioned Song 3,5
Sing A Nursery Rhyme 320
Sing A Song Of Sixpence 360
Sing, Baby, Sing 40,42,44,46,48,52, 54–55,58,60,64,66,68,73,78,83,95, 106,112
Singin' In The Rain 76
Singin' The Blues 44,90,118,127,151, 178,183,196–197,208,225,242,262, 267,273,284,295,308
Singleton, Zutty 80,108,154,230,288, 297,311
Sing Me A Swing Song 17–18,21–23, 30–31,35–36,38,40,44,52,55,57–58, 79,100
Sing, Sing, Sing 10,28,31,33,42,46–47, 52,55,57,59–61,65,69,72,103,114, 128,135,140,146,154,183,200,204, 231,305,325,349
Sing You Sinners 276,303,305,307
Siravo, George 137,186,346–347,350, 354,358–360
Sissle, Noble 2,8,16,19,53,65–66, 152–153,160,179,230,292,307,317, 327
Sister Kate 264
Sittin' In The Sand 30
Sitting On The Moon 49,69,84,104
Sizzlin' Sam 47
Skeleton In The Closet 78–79,91,96, 101–102,109,119–120,122,155,166
Skerritt, Fred 346

Skies Are Blue 119
Skoller's Swingland Café, Chicago 244,246,248,251–252,255–256
Skolnick, Sam 10,13,25
Skylar, Sonny 346,355
Skyles, Jimmy 58,67
Slack, Freddy 59–60,92,134,192,201, 258,269,274,276,285,297,299,321, 334,337,340–341,347,349,351
Slap That Bass 134,140,165,183,196, 200,202,205,209,212,216,222
Sleep 34,72,245
Sleepy Time Gal 29,186,224,232,235, 256,289,295,326
Slew Foot 60
Slim & Slam 357,360
Slippery Horn 159
Slippin' Around 45
Sloe Jam Fizz 328
Slow Mood 340
Slummin' On Park Avenue 101,111, 116,118,123,127,131,133,136,138, 140,142,145–146,148–149,153,157, 161,164
Small Fry 357
Small Town Girl 18–19
Smarties, The 323
Smarty 186,201,205,233, 244–245,270
Smiles 213,216,222,239,243,251,253, 271,285,293–294,298,307,324,327, 331,353,356,359
Smiling At Trouble 284
Smith, Ben 114,158,206
Smith, Bessie 12,86,193
Smith, Bud 176,289,297
Smith, Buzz 18,23,33
Smith, Carl 'Teddie' 77,109,221
Smith, C.E. 102
Smith, Frank 292
Smith, Howard 137,153,166,171,178, 186,205,207,210,213,216,219–220, 222,231,237,239,243,246,254–255, 267,271,273,293,295,298,308,311, 316, 322,325,333,338,347,349,351, 358–359,361
Smith, Jabbo 114,158,206
Smith, James 5
Smith, J. D. 168–169
Smith, Joe 236
Smith, John 12,17,138,159,173
Smith, Leroy 7,12,16
Smith, Mamie 32
Smith, Raymond 6
Smith, Russell 127,137,200,263,276, 353
Smith, Stuff 5–8,11–12,16,18,21–23, 27,30–32,35,37–39,43–46,48–50,53, 55,57,60,64,66,69–70,76,86,94–95, 97–99,101,104,108–109,111–112, 114–116,124–126,144–145,147, 164–165,272,296,344,347,350,354, 358, 360
Smith, Tab 20,26,34,36,69–70,73, 80–81,96,118,128,141,150,162–163, 189,195,253,263–264, 268,334,343
Smith, Walter 143,201,203,212,214, 286
Smith, Warren 25–26,42,143–146,148,

151–152,157,159–161,163–164,166, 170,183,205,207–208,210,212,215, 218,237,240,253,269,274,277, 279–284,312,317,319,323–325,327, 337–338,340
Smith, Willie 26,30,52–53,69,74, 111–112,117,161,188,190,205,255, 280,308,346
Smith, Willie 'The Lion' 8,12,151, 185,210,230,257,284,311
Smoke Dreams 88,90,92,96,100–101, 103,105,109,112,116,121,123–124, 126–127,133,135,140,145,150, 157–159,174,255,295
Smoke From A Chimney 308,321
Smoke Gets In Your Eyes 44,213,246, 251,254
Smoke Rings 17,69,78–79,83–84,87, 89,103,114,118,124,143,203,212, 214,278,286,316
Smuggler's Nightmare 328
Snaps And Go 33
Snowball 109,320
Snow, Nan 247
Snow, Roddy 99,138,140,197,224, 226–228,249,304,306–307,346–348, 356
Snow, Valaida 23,27
Sobbin' Blues 93
Sodja, Joe 99,177,185,267,293, 296
So Do I 33,78,89,93,96,101,103–104, 106,108–109,121
Soft Horn 80
Soft Lights And Sweet Music 43
So Help Me 357
Solace 172,175
Sold American 353
Solid Mama 311,337
Solitude 15,51,55–56,60,84,132,158, 169,234,264
So Many Memories 257,268, 272–273, 277,280,283–284,286,293,304,308
Somebody Loves Me 15,75,76,82,88,105, 106,108,111,124–125,127,138,140, 145,157–158,183,196,251,271,321
Somebody Stole My Gal 279,285
Someday Sweetheart 3–4,13,15,23–24, 28,31,77,89,94,120,135,137, 157–160,174,177,194,215,220,233, 271,276,280,282,286,301,306
Someday We'll Meet Again 38,40
Some Of These Days 6,30–32,38, 49–50,59,70,72,74,78,101,117,124, 127,169
Someone To Care For Me 76,106,124
Something Has Happened To Me 88
Something Tells Me 339,344,349,355
Something To Sing About 265
Sometimes I Feel Like A Motherless Child 58,284
Sometimes I'm Happy 35,46,58,61–62, 68,73,75,86,89,96,111,114,118,127, 135,138,146,148,154,163,183,194, 206,209,234, 241,304,317,341,349
Somewhere With Somebody Else 353
Songcopators 99
Song Of India 112,122,129,136,138, 152,162,179,186,196,201,210,228,

235,244,247–248,252,273,292–293, 308–309,316,320,327
Song of The Islands 39,59,236,243
Song Of The Volga Boatman 263,349
Song Of The Wanderer 308
So Nice Of You 34,39,41,44,47–48,53, 57
Sonny Boy 161
Sontag, Sonny 186
Soon 42,272
Sophisticate 43
Sophisticated Lady 2,4,18,29–30, 39–40,61,64,132,134,147,152,237, 251,264
Sophisticated Swing 60,131,151, 204,215,234,240,248,270,273,340
So Rare 188,190,196,198,202,208, 211,215,219–220,223,225,231,235, 244–247,251–253,255,257,260,265, 267,299
So's It 334
So They Say 128,172
So This Is Heaven 8,11
So Unexpectedly 360
South American Joe 58
Southland Serenade 202
South Rampart Street Parade 43,133, 145–146,157,160,207,216,274,277, 283–284,288,313,321,331,335–336
South Sea Island Magic 35,45–47,52, 54,57–58,60,64,79,105
Southside Stomp 202,221,232,239,245
So You Won't Sing 251
Spain 221,237
Spangler, Bob 352–353
Spanier, Muggsy 243,246,255,262
Speakeasy 73
Speak Easy 203
Speakin' Of Dreams 195
Speak To Me Of Love 54
Spencer, O'Neil 20,26,36,70,73,81, 141,156,195,210,224,230,257,259, 272,274,284,292,306–307,309,311, 318,323–325,327–328,332
Spergel, Sammy 270,273,278, 284–285,294,297,311,323,326,334
Spinnin' The Webb 350
Spirits Of Rhythm 69,98,101,184, 201,222,247,266
Spitalny, Phil 32,222,228,360
Spivak, Charlie 59–60,73,92,137,186, 188,243,284,317–319,325,327, 337–338,361
Sponge Cake And Spinach 188,344
S'posin' 56,186,188
Spreadin' Knowledge Around 60
Spreadin' Rhythm Around 38
Spring Cleaning 134,151
Spring Fever Blues 74,78,86,88, 111–112,119,147,151,158,171,251
Spring Holiday 112
Spring In Vienna 22
Spring Is Here 357
Spring Song In Swing 130
Springtime In The Rockies 88,143
Square Dance For An Egyptian Mummy 313
Squeeze Me 162,169,262,267,276–278,

INDEX

280,301,317,323,328,332
Squires, Bruce 59–60,92,134,192,258, 321,346–347,350,354,358–360
Stabile, Dick 16,19,23,27,31–32, 35–37,41,47,49,53,58,61,66,70,80, 83,86,92,95,97,99,109,172,177, 215–218,247,255–256
Stacey, Jack 10–11,27,29,33–34
Stack O' Lee Blues 318
Stacy, Jess 3–4,6,9–10,14,22,26,37,44, 67,74–76,78,81–83,88,90–91,96,105, 107,110,112,115,117,123–124,128, 130,134–135,140,145–146,152, 160–163,176,178,183–184,204–205, 216,219,221,223,234–235,239,241, 244,248,251,253,256,262,267–268, 271,273–277,280,283,285–286,289, 292–293,297–299,301,308,311–313, 315–316,321,325–328,331,337,339, 343,345–346,349–351,354,358–360, 362
Stafford, George 8,243
Stage Fright 103
Stampede 137
Stanfield, Leemie 9,29,56,158,232, 332
Stanley, Red 354,357
Star Dust 2–3,5,11,13–14,16,20,27, 29–30,32,34–35,37,40,43,45,47–50, 55,58–59,61,65,69–70,72–73,76,80, 86–87,90,97,99,107,109,111,113, 123,126–130,136–137,140,142,147, 149,152,154,159,161,164,166–167, 172,175,179,183,186,188,194–195, 197–198,202,205,209–210,212–215, 217,219,224,236–237,239,241, 246–247,251,260,263–264,269–270, 272,275,277–278,281,284–285, 299–300,302,306,318,327,334,351
Stardust On The Moon 213,223, 231–232,235–236,243,251,255–256, 273
Stark, Bobby 12,23,74,105,138,238, 254,259,277–279,295–296,298–301, 312,337,350,355,361–362
Starr, Allen 130
Starr, Charles 253
Starrett, Paul 129,188,202
Stars Fell On Alabama 166
Stars In My Eyes 38–40,44,57
Start The Day With A Smile 311
Stay 13
Stay On The Right Side Of The Road 37,215
Steak And Potatoes 207,237,243
Stealin' Apples 10,203,276
Steele, Alphonse 96,128,144,253
Steel Pier, Atlantic City 29–30,51, 55–57,59–60,64,180,201–205, 215–218,222,239–240,242,251,254, 362
Stephens, Haig 86,103,140,187,281, 340
Steppin' Into Swing Society 312
Steppin' Pretty 8,143,157,170,318
Stern, Harold 97
Stevens, Leith 39,45,95,103,106,110, 123,129,132,140,145,149,156,160,

164,169,172,177,185,187,195,202, 211,216,225,250,255,260,267,270, 272,275,280,284,292–293,296–297, 299,303,307,309,323,326–327,331, 333,336–337,339,357
Stevenson, Graham 243,246,348,358, 360
Stevenson, Tommy 83
Stewart, Al 189
Stewart, Lucille 8
Stewart, Rex 6,17,20,22,28,31,33,90, 93,128,132,134,144–146,148,159, 162–163,165–166,171–175,186, 188–189,197,202,205,262,264, 312–313,316,320–321,324,332,336, 338,343,346,354,356,360
Stewart, Slam 307,326,357,360
Sticks And Stones 163
Still, Lois 59
Stokes, Harold 293
Stolen Melody 213
Stoll, Georgie 74,267
Stomp 117
Stompin' Around 69
Stompin' At The Onyx Club 145
Stompin' At The Renny 261
Stompin' At The Savoy 2–4,6,8,11,13, 15–16,21,24,26,29–33,35–38,40, 42–43,45–48,54,56,58,60,65,71–72, 76,78–79,82–84,86,88,92,99–100, 103–104,107,109,113,123–124, 126–128,130,135,137,140,143,154, 157,169,177,183,202,208,211,219, 223,237,240–242,250,253,275,277, 284,306,331,337,343
Stompin' Serenade 68
Stomp It Off 18
Stompology 152,217
Stompy Jones 18,92
Stone, Eddie 101,109,115,131,145–146
Stone, Gene 50,58,65
Stone, Jesse 126
Stoneburn, Sid 140
Stoopnagle 135
Stop Beatin' Around The Mulberry Bush 358,360
Stop, Look And Listen 4,16,21,29–30, 41,43,45,52,54,69,75,78,89,99, 103–104,123,125,138,153,169,185, 239,299,313,324
Stop Stallin' 312
Stop! You're Breaking My Heart 188, 205,207–208,210–211,214,218–219, 223,227,232,235,239–240,243–245, 254,257,262,267
Stordahl, Axel 'Odd' 143,210,230
Stormy Weather 114,125,179,227,286, 289
Story, Nat 23,74,105,138,277–279, 295,299,350,355,361–362
Strand Theater, NYC 360
Strange New Rhythm In My Heart 270
Strangers In The Dark 178,195–196, 203,216,218–219,232–233,241–242, 246,263–264,267
Streamline 89,93,331
Streamline Strut 38,76,83,104,118
Strictly Formal 300

Strictly From Dixie 362
Strictly Jive 254,277,337
Strike Up The Band 42
Strollin' Through The Park 215,218
Struttin' With Some Barbecue 143, 159–160
Stuart, Al 115,167
Stuart, Barbara 77,339
Stuart, Kenneth 337,341
Stuart, Nick 97–98
Stuff, Etc. 9
Stuff Stomp 70,98
Stuhlmaker, Mort 6,12–13,25,82,116, 226
Stulce, Fred 10,13,101,108,112,121, 130,134,136,153,166,171,178,186, 207,213,230,254,271,295,308,322, 325,333,338,347,349,351,358–359, 361
Stultz, Gene 35,61
Stumblin' 142,195,207,242,265,284, 308,317,323
Styles, Jimmy 15
Subway 306
Sugar 22,49,267,343–344
Sugar Blues 11,169
Sugar Foot Stomp 22,30,35–36,41,43, 47,50,58,64,80,86,96,105,118,123, 127,136–138,146,149,157,179,183, 210,220,232,235,239,243,246,248, 251,253,266,273–274,286,295–296, 301,309,316,323,335,340
Sugar Foot Strut 25,68,146,231
Sugar Hill Shim-Sham 205,302
Sugar Rose 5,21,26
Suggs, Pete 200,263,276,353
Sulkin, Harry 223,232
Sullivan, Joe 25–26,68,96,126,149, 151,157,160–161,170,208,210,283, 319,321,333
Sullivan, Maxine 188,211,224,230, 243,272,274,278,284,287,292, 296–297,306–307,309–310,313,317, 323–325,328,331–332,334–338,342, 344,357–358
Sultan Serenade 246,256
Sultan Serenaders 261
Summer Breeze 42,54
Summer Holiday 27,50
Summer Nights 100,109,111,115, 117–118,131,146,159,166,169,200
Summertime 24,28,30,32,36–37,40,43, 45,64,79,93,95–96,125,128,131,133, 140,144–145,159,164,170,183, 207–208,210,212,224,239,267,269, 274,279,313,316–318
Sumpin' 'Bout Rhythm 19,166
Sunday 111,114,236,266
Sunday In The Park 324–325, 332, 335–337
Sundays Are The Best For Somebody Else But Me 124
Sunny Disposish 86,243,273
Sunset Royal Serenaders 32,66,292, 360
Sunshine At Midnight 22,25,30,35,37, 40,42,56
Sun Showers 170

Suppose I Had Never Met You 53
Surrealism 232,261
Suzy-Q [dance] 261
Suzy Q 62
Swamp Fire 33,42,44,46,53,55,60,70, 167,179,235,256,276
Swanee River 156,158,161,166–167, 171,184,198,204,213,217,219,225, 235,263,266,302,328,335
Swanee Shuffle 273
Swartout, Gladys 49
Sweet Adeline 214
Sweet And Hot 38,44,55
Sweet And Lovely 185,254
Sweet And Low 35
Sweet And Swingy 237,246
Sweet As A Song 301,327,331,335,337
Sweet Bill From Sugar Hill 320
Sweet For The Eyes 94
Sweet Georgia Brown 56,244,246,253, 255,337,359
Sweet Heartache 148
Sweetheart, Let's Grow Old Together 83, 88
Sweetheart Of Sigma Chi 359
Sweethearts On Parade 260
Sweet Is The Word For You 121,130, 138,143,146,151–152,154,158–159, 162,171–172,174,205
Sweet Leilani 183–184,196,200,202, 217,219,221,237,242,251,254,269, 276
Sweet Like You 237,291
Sweet Lorraine 18,21,93,96,107,111, 115,125,144,151,159,171,208,218, 220,240,292,328,333,336,344
Sweet Madness 324
Sweet Mama 144
Sweet Misery Of Love 43
Sweet Mystery Of Love 32–33,35,37, 40–42,46–48,50,52,54–55,59,61
Sweet Night 237
Sweet Patootie 327
Sweet Someone 284,288,295,297, 301–302,316–318,324,335
Sweet Stranger 285,289,293,297–298, 309,312,328
Sweet Sue 8,18–19,21,35–36,38,44, 46,48,50,64,74,80,83,101,108,111, 130,140,145,157,164,170,179,211, 217,237–239,250,269,273,284,326, 340–341,346,348,351,353,356
Sweet Varsity Sue 248,284
Swift, Jack 60
Swing 35
Swing At The Onyx Club 69
Swing, Baby, Swing 302
Swing Begins 281
Swing, Benny, Swing 231
Swing, Brother, Swing 118,146,202, 235,250,253,276
Swing Club, 52nd Street, NYC 296
Swingerin' 18
Swing Feud 57
Swing Fever 15,56,79,108,284,331
Swing Fugue In E Flat 43,61
Swing Guitars 207,217
Swing High 29

INDEX

Swing High, Swing Low 112,119,123, 130–131,140,143,145–146,158,163, 167,183–185,251
'Swing High, Swing Low' [movie] 155
Swing In D-Flat Minor 349
Swing In The Spring 161
Swing Is Here 6,281
Swing Is The Thing 58
Swing Is The Word For It 135
Swing It 48
Swing It, Gate 112
Swing Low 9,20,41,47,56,62,84,171
Swing Low, Sweet Chariot 78,86–88, 92,100,108,126,135,146–147,159, 175,183,186,213–214,236,243,251, 277,295,306–308
Swing Me Crazy 49
Swing, Mister Charlie 6,39–40,60,94, 126
Swingin' Along 123
Swinging At The Daisy Chain 109–110, 118,157,205,233,237
Swingin' At The Hickory House 13, 22–24,177
Swingin' Down The Lane 111,114,266, 302
Swingin' For The King 41,44,104,113
Swingin' Guitars 297
Swingin' In E Flat 16,30,250
Swingin' In The Corn Belt 327
Swingin' In The Dell 360
Swinging In Harlem 56,130,162,197
Swingin' On C 328
Swinging On The Reservation 74,100, 104,113,123,146,148,174
Swingin' On The Swanee Shore 94,98–99
Swingin' The Blues [radio show] 253, 262,265,271,273,282,285–286,289, 295,298
Swingin' The Blues 203,328,333–334, 355
Swingin' Them Jingle Bells 85
Swingin' The Scales 93
Swingin' Uptown 21
Swingin' With The Fat Man 179
Swingland Café, Chicago 234
Swingola 40
Swing Pan Alley 360
Swing Session 169
Swing Session Called To Order 189,211, 239,261,284
Swing Song 246
Swing, Swing Mother-In-Law 54–55, 57,60,62,75–76,84,98,104,116,127, 145,165,187
Swing, Swing, Swing 104,117,127
Swing That Music 110,122,124, 129–130,138,146,155,159,201, 203,233,242,268,273,276,293
Swingtet, The 238–239
Swing Time 27
Swingtime In Honolulu 345–346
Swingtime In The Rockies 26,39,41,43, 49,52,56–57,59–60,66,70,75,79,83, 97,103,109,125,137,145,147,158, 160,165,183,189,204,206,209,223, 277,297,307,312,339,356,360

Swing With Luis 40
Swing Your Feet 100
'S Wonderful 15,89,95,115,361
Sylvia 50,65,74,103,233
Symphonettes, The 106
Symphony Hall, Boston 350
Symphony In Riffin' 59
Symphony In Riffs 55,76,83,157, 271, 359
Taft, Slim 10–11,27,29,33–34,348
'Tain't A Fit Night Out For Man Or Beast 8
'Tain't (No)Good 31,52–53,56,58,66, 78,82–87,89,102–105,111,161
'Tain't No Use 8,10,30,33–34,37–38, 42–43,45–47,52,54–55,57–58,61–62, 65,71,75,79,87,96,100,188,203,269
'Tain't So 227, 235,307,339
Take Another Guess 74–75,79–80,82, 87,92,97,99,105,113,118
Take It From The Top 172
Take Me Out To The Ball Game 39
Take Me To The Opera 35
Take My Heart 26,28–29,36–38, 40–46,51–53,56–57
Take My Word 58,299
Takin' It On The Lam 32
Talking To My Heart 73,79,92, 95,105
Talk With Sax 243
Tall, Dark, And Handsome 301
Tango Of Roses 210
Tappin' The Commodore Till 358
Tap Room Swing 9,11,69
Tatum, Art 156,285,289,292–293, 307,324,334,342,344,350
Taylor, Billy (b) 6,28,31,90,92–93, 128,132,148,162–163,172,186, 188–189,262,276,312,316–317,320, 324,332,336,344–346,354,356–357, 360
Taylor, Frank 162,245,248
Taylor, Louis 117,231,337,341
Taylor, Sammy 59–60,92
Tchaikovsky's Unfinished Symphony 324
Tea And Trumpets 205
Tea For Two 37–38,41,43,54,69,78,84, 87,95,102,109,114,140,147,154,160, 177,186,213,216–217,240,254,283, 298,309,321,328,336,338
Teagarden, Charlie 4–5,15,26,86–87, 89–90,99,114,161,211,251,313,327, 357
Teagarden, Jack 4–5,15,26,42,62, 86–87,89–90,95,98–99,114,139,161, 208,210–211,223,236,242,251,254, 257,313,343,349,357
Teague, Thurman 59–60,92,349
Tea On The Terrace 70,82–83,92–93, 95–96,98,100,102,106,108–110,117, 126,152,221,248,252
Tears In My Heart 255,263,265,277, 280,283,285
Teasin' Tessie Brown 256,280
Tea Time 323–324,327,331–332,335, 339
Templeton, Alec 255
Tennille, Frank 24,135
Terrell, Pha 7,12,88,110,112,119,157,

218–219,240,242–247,249,252–255, 257,262,297,326,339
Texas Chatter 308
Thanks A Million 4,5,24
Thanks For Everything 115,121, 130–131,136
Thanks For The Memory 285,292, 305–308,311–312,323–324,326–327, 331,335–336,339
Thanksgiving 83,98,197,205,239
That Da Da Strain 328
That Feeling Is Gone 349,351
That Foolish Feeling 80,82,152, 159–160, 163,165,171,239
That Man Is Here Again 86,108,125, 127
That Naughty Waltz 138,179,235,239, 280,308,327,349,353
That Never-To-Be-Forgotten Night 5
That Old Feeling 231,235,237,246, 254,256,265,267,269–272,274–277, 279,281,293–294,298, 313
That's A-Plenty 19,21,25,36,55,71,73, 75,82,92,101,123–124,140,144,152, 172,178,200,207,214,220,230–231, 236–237,245,251,326,337
That's Easier Said Than Done 328
That's How I Feel Today 188
That's Life I Guess 81,88,90,96,100, 111,123,162
That's My Home 273
That's Love 102
That Stolen Melody 186
That's What Love Did To Me 8
That's What Makes The World Go Round 37
That's What You Call Romance 307
That's What You Mean To Me 62,65, 95–96
That's Why I'm Blue 101,324
That's You, Sweetheart 3–5
That Thing 80,297
The Arkansas Traveler 281
The Beggar 50,78,101
The Big Apple [dance] 237,261,275, 349
The Big Apple 237,239–240,242,244, 246,248–249,252,254,263,266–267
'The Big Broadcast of 1937' 28
The Big Crash From China 340
The Big Dipper 267,283,297,308–309, 312,335
The Big Roar 52
The Bill Robinson 262
The Blues 223,338,353
The Blues In Your Flat 343
The Blues In My Flat 343
The Broken Record 4
The Bug Walk 109
The Buzzard 145
The Campbells Are Swingin' 337
The Cat Walk 307,327
The Chant 223
The Clock Strikes Three 218
The Continental 40
The Corrigan Hop 355
The Criterion Blues 326
The Curse Of An Aching Heart 32

The Day I Let You Get Away 4–5, 10–11,22,96
The Devil is Afraid Of Music 187
The Dipsy-Doodle 268,271–273,276, 280–281,283–284,293,296–297,299, 301,303,306,309,311,313,316–317, 320–321,324,327–328,332–333,335, 338
The Dream In My Heart 264
The Duke Steps Out 162
The Duke Swings Low 87
The Duke Swings Out 93
The Fireman's Ball 215
The First Thing I Knew Was You 64
The First Time I Saw You 167,171,184, 205,207,218,220,236–237,243,256, 269,274
The Folks Who Live On The Hill 243–246,252,255,257,274
The Gal From Joe's 324
The Gentleman Obviously Doesn't Believe 67
The Ghost Of Casey Jones 207
The Girl Friend 122,218
The Girl Of My Dreams 108
The Girl With The Light Blue Hair 164,177
The Glory Of Love 14,22,24,30–32, 35,38,48–49,52–53,56–57,59,78,80, 98,110,138,241,255
The Goblin Band 115,121
The Goona Goo 101,109–112, 116–118,121,126,128–130,138,144, 152,157,166,171,175,183,185,196, 203,209,211,213,232,236,241,243
The Goose Hangs High 77,83,98,108
The Greatest Mistake Of My Life 328
The Happy Farmer 348
The Harlem Bolero 262
The Harlem Twister 138
The Haywood Breakdown 166
The Hi-De-Ho Miracle Man 59,62, 64–65,74,97,103,115,117,283,332
The Hour Of Parting 220
The House Jack Built For Jill 64
The House Went Up In Smoke 30
Thief In The Night 233
The Image Of You 171,177–178,186, 196,202–204,207,211,213,216–218, 221,223,225,232,234–235,247,267
The Indian Jubilee 179
The International Rag 348
The Japanese Sandman 25
The Jig Waltz 165
The Jitters 140
The Jive Stomp 146
The Joint Is Jumpin' 269
The Key To My Heart 219
The Lady From Fifth Avenue 189,198, 201–202,210,215–216,220,231,234, 236,248,253
The Lady From Mayfair 124,127, 140
The Lady In Red 145
The Lady Is A Tramp 255,270,274,277, 279–280,285,292,297,308, 311,313
The Lady Who Couldn't Be Good 175
The Lady Who Couldn't Be Kissed 159,162,166,178,201–202,

INDEX

214–215,220,222,224,236–237, 241–242,244,255,264
The Lady Who Swings The Band 88, 114,118,209
The Land Of Jam 148,173
The Land Of Jazz 64
The Last Rose Of Summer 165
The Last Round-up 317
The Lillie Stomp 326
The Little Things 183
The Lonesome Road 88,104,351
The Love Bug Will Bite You 138, 143,148,151,161,165,179,196,203, 205,212,214,234,237,240,276
The Loveliness Of You 205,208,211, 215,218,234,239–240,242,248, 253,255–256,264,270,276
The Love Nest 308
The Lucky Swing 162
The Maid's Night Off 130,183,185, 215,240,242,266,302
The Man I Love 48,57,220,262, 302, 344
The Man On The Flying Trapeze 179
The Man With The Funny Horn 212,215
The Man With The Jive 46,58,66
The Mayor Of Alabam' 15,87,123, 146,177,217,265
The Meanest Thing You Ever Did Was Kiss Me 123
The Melody Man 29
The Melody Plane 68
The Merry-Go-Round Broke Down 188–189,196,211,215,222,225, 236–237,270,280
The Milkman's Matinee 64,153,162, 217
The Miller's Daughter, Marianne 189, 202,233,251
The Mooche 217
The Mood That I'm In 117,121,124, 144–146,148,150–152,157, 162
The Moon Got In My Eyes 192, 200–201,203,207,211,217,219, 224,234,240,242,245,253,257,265, 267,271,276,279–280,285–286
The Moon Is Grinning At Me 67,70,73, 87,90–92,101,104,114,124, 150
The Moon Is In The Sky 158,166,171, 175
The Moon Is Low 20,41,58,295
The More I Know You 24
The Moon Looks Down And Laughs 351
The Morning After 204–206,208,210, 213,219,221–223,231–232,236,245, 268,276
The Mother-In-Law's Necktie Party 211
Them There Eyes 245,293
The Music Goes Round And Around 39,50,60,64,93,215,221,236
The Naughty Waltz 172
Then Came The Indians 37
The New Birmingham Breakdown 128
The New Black And Tan Fantasy 312
The New East St. Louis Toodle-Oo 128,148

The Night Is Filled With Music 358
The Night Is Young 83,87–88,90, 98,101,109,123,126,140,223
The Night We Met 79
The Night Will Never End 110
Then I'll Be Happy 195
Then You Kissed Me 254
The Object Of My Affection 251
The Old Apple Tree 326,333,335
The Old Grey Bonnet 273
The Old Oaken Bucket 14
The Old Spinning Wheel 60,148,161, 164,174,183,202,208,222,267,283, 324,328
The Old Stamping Ground 210,230
The One I Love 295,317,327–328, 333,335–336,339
The One I Love Belongs To Somebody Else 345
The One Rose Left In My Heart 246
The Panic Is On 5,8
The Peanut Vendor 98,251
The Penguin 277,300
The Pied Piper 355
The Prisoner's Song 178,204,208,210, 213,221,224–225,233,272,284,294, 339
There Goes My Attraction 32,47,57, 75
There Goes The One I Love 55
There Is No Greater Love 6,16,18, 22,48,147
There Isn't Any Limit To My Love 39
There'll Be Some Changes Made 71, 105,157,161,183,212,220,326
There's A Boy In Harlem 322,332, 337
There's A Faraway Look In Your Eye 351
There's A Kitchen Up In Heaven 128
There's A Little White House 308
There's A Lull In My Life 137,143,145, 147–148,151,154,157–159,162–163, 165,167,171–172,174,177–178, 183–186,188–189,194–197, 200–201,203–205,208–210,212,215, 218,221,227,233–235,238,241
There's Always A Happy Ending 16, 25
There's A New Moon Over The Old Mill 306
There's A Small Hotel 26,31,33,35, 37–39,42,45,49,51,53,59,69–70, 76,115–116,220,264
There's Frost On The Moon 74,80,82, 91,95,98–99,104–105,107–109, 111–112,117
There's Heaven In My Heart 92
There's Honey On The Moon Tonight 354,358
There's More Than One Santa Claus 302
There's Music In The Air 79
There's No Place Like Your Arms 361
There's No Substitute For You 16,27
There's No Two Ways About It 189
There's Rain In My Eyes 348,353
There's Religion In Rhythm 39
There's Rhythm In Harlem 30
There's Somebody Else But Me 159
There's Something About An Old Love 355

There's Something In The Air 73–76, 78–79,86–87,93,98–101,105,111, 115–116,123–124,138,140
There's Something In The Wind 14
The Roar 97
The Rockin' Chair Swing 171
The Same Old Line 85
The Scene Changes 29–30,34,36, 40,46,51
These Foolish Things 21–22,26,28–29, 31,33–41,43,46,48–49,54, 57–59,65
The Shag 251,269
The Shag [dance] 261
The Sheik of Araby 143,173,188,216, 219,244,274,289,297,332,346,358
'The Singing Marine' [movie] 165
The Skeleton In The Closet 74,115
The Skipper 255
The Skrontch 338,343,346
The Snake Charmer 262,284,299,309
The South Side Stomp 78
The Stampede 69–70
The Stars Weep 41–42,46,54,61,67, 70,75
The State Of My Heart 36,56,58,67
The Stevedore's Serenade 356
The Stolen Melody 205
The Subway To Barnes 215
The Sunny Side Of Things 357
The Sun Will Shine Tonight 316
The Swampland Is Calling Me 151
The Sweetest Story Ever Told 308
The Swing Waltz 18
The Things I Want 207,213,215,219, 231–232,236
The Thrill Of A Lifetime 284,316,321
The Toothache 177,207
The Top Of The World 253
The Touch Of Your Hand 16
The Touch Of Your Lips 12,22,99
The Toy Trumpet 95,122,148,294,328, 331,340
The Trombone Man 324
The Trouble With Me Is You 131, 143
The Turkey is Going To Swing Tonight 42
The Uproar Shout 165
The Very Thought Of You 11,48
The Village Cut-up 49
The Viper's Swing 152
The Waltz Lives On 285
The Way You Look Tonight 36,40–41, 46–47,54,57,63–64,72,79,95,99, 101,196
The Wearin' Of The Green 353
The Wedding Of Jack And Jill 3
The Wedding Of Mr & Mrs Swing 59,78,84
The Weekend Of A Private Secretary 327,335,341
The Wheel Of The Wagon 251,254
The Wide Open Places 358
The World Is Waiting For The Sunrise 88,326,340
They All Laughed 130,134,144,146, 149–150,159,163,167,169–172,175, 183–185,194–196,198,202,208,212, 216–220,222,234,237,240,242,251, 254–255,273,289,336

They Can't Take That Away From Me 134,140,144,146,158–159,163, 166–167,171,173,177–179,183,186, 189,196–197,204,206–207,211,213, 215,218–219,234,236–237,239–240, 242,251,255,263,265,269
They Didn't Remember 37
The You And Me That Used To Be 159–161,163,166,175–177,179,183, 185,191,195–196,198,202–205,215, 219–220,225,234–237,245–246,248, 250,257
Thigpen, Ben 7–8,11–13,88,110,119, 157,218–219,242,246,297,326
Things Are Looking Up 278
This And That 207,212,225,243
This Is My Last Affair 74,80,84,98, 109,112,114–115,117,119,121,123, 126,131,134–135,137–138,140, 143,146,148,151–152,156,158–159, 169,172,175,183,185–186,201–202, 238,243,251
This Is My Night To Dream 317,327, 331,336
This Is The Life 348
This Never Happened Before 280, 283–284,288,317,321
This Time It's Real 350–351
This Year's Kisses 96,105,107,110–111, 114,117–118,123–124,127,131, 134–136,140,142,144–145,151,154, 157,161–162, 167,171,183
Thomas, Bill 12,23
Thomas, Joe (cl/ts) 52–53,69,74, 111–113,144,188,190,205,255,280, 308,346
Thomas, Joe (t/voc) 10,13,20,33,38, 147
Thomas, Walter 4,20,59,127,134,241, 246,295,321,343
Thompson, Carroll 360
Thompson, Earl 7–8,11–13,88,119, 157,218–219,297,326
Thompson, Kay 11,35,39,57,63, 187–188,195,244,326,333
Thomson, Glena Jane 35
Thomson, Scoop 64
Thornhill, Claude 73,187–188,224, 230,243,256,274,287,307,310,325, 334,351,357
Thou Swell 35,52,67,100,105,146,176, 335
Thow, George 10–11,27,29,33–34, 360
Three Blind Mice 237,336
Three Deuces, Chicago 80–81, 145–146,154,281,284,297,303
Three Esquires 18–19,21–22,34,36, 47,72,82,92,101,109–110,112–113, 121–122,124,126,129–131,138,143, 146–147,151–152,158–159,162,201, 204–205,208,210,213,215, 219,222, 230,239–240,242,267,271,302,311, 316,324,335,351,359
Three Little Words 35,48,50,53–54,57, 60,71–72,76,78,83,92,99–100,105, 109,115,138,140,175,188,195,197, 210,216,223,239,289,292,298,302,

308–309,328,360–361
Three Palmer Brothers 21
Three Peppers 147,151,153
Three Rhythm Boys 244
Three's No Crowd 315,343
Three Swings And Out 234,317,321,336
Three Symphonettes 216
Through The Courtesy Of Love 42,54–55,59,61,78,108,110,152
Throw-Down Blues 320
Thunder 29
Tia Juana 57
Tidal Wave 188
Tiger Fantasy 172
Tiger Rag 62,68,72,74–75,79–80,86,98,108,115,128,130,146,154–155,174,185,188,203,207,213,236,284–285,293,299,331,336,338,345
Till The Clock Strikes Three 189
Tilton, Martha 60,241,243–244,246,248,251,253,256–257,262,265,267–268,271–277,279–280,282–286,288–289,292–293,295–299,301–308,311–313,316,321,324–328,331,335–337,339–341,343–346,348–351,353–357,359–362
Tim & Irene 157,177
Time On My Hands 57,177,179,186,201,211,215,240,255,278–279,281,286,289,295,298
Time Out 231
Time Out For Love 163
Tin Roof Blues 40,69,146,157,161,169,210,222,251,263,269
Ti-Pi-Tin 337,339–340,344,348–349,351
Tippin' At The Terrace 337
Tizol, Juan 6,28,31,92–93,128,132,146,148,159,162–163,165,172,174–175,186–189,276,313,316,324,332,336,346,354,356,360
To A Sweet Pretty Thing 134,151–152,157,164,166,177,207
To Be Alone With You 42,53
Tobin, Joe 169
Today I'm A Man 221,236
Together We Live 100
Togue, Muriel 197
Tolbert, Skeets 212,215
To Mary With Love 70,72,78,84
Tom Boy 327
Tomorrow Is Another Day 175,196,211–212,216,220,231,235–236,239–240,251
Tompkins, Eddie 52–53,69,74,111–113,144,161,188,190,205,255–256,280,308,346
Tompkins, Tommy 'Red' 23
Tonight Will Live 355
Too Bad 31,55,59,65,102,123,171
Toodle-Oo 35,55,172,178,184,211
Too Good To Be True 15,18,27,31,39,42–43,50
Too Marvelous For Words 118,120,124,126,131,137,140,143–145,151–152,154,159–160,163,167,169,171–172,175,183–184,186,197,202,210–211,218,234,245

Too Much Imagination 76
Top Hat 41
Top Street Blues 239
Topsy 231,355
Tormented 13,16,19–23,30,35,40,42–43,91
Tough, Dave 6,10,13,25,34,41,72,80,82,101,108,110,112,116,121–122,124,129–131,134,136,143,146–148,151–153,158–159,162,164,166,171,178,186,200,204–205,207–208,210,213,215,219,222,228,230–231,238–240,254–255,271,293,295,311,321,335,340–341,343,345,348–349,351,353,355–360,362
Town Hall Tonight [radio] 114
Trans-Atlantic Auditorium, L.A. 196
Transcontinental 3,7
Trask, Billie 97
Travelin' Down The Trail 237
Trav'lin' All Alone 256
Traxler, Gene 10,13,25,80,82,101,112,121–122,130,134,136,153,166,171,178,186,207,213,254–255,271,338,347,349,351,358–359,361
Trees 8,54,72,108,157,166,169,176,183,194,210,234,239,263,273,301,332
Trianon Ballroom, Chicago 24,97,209
Trianon Ballroom, Cleveland, OH 97,106,110,112,363
Trice, Clarence 297,326
Trini, Anthony 186,221
Trombone Man 72,113,129
Tropical Moonlight 179
Trotter, Bobbie 264
Trouble Don't Like Music 74,112,215
Troubled Waters 18–19,264
Trouble In Mind 161
Troublesome Trumpet 8,93,96,99
Truckin' [dance] 261
Truckin' 5,11,18,28,65,142,210,248
Trudeau, Carmen 142,144–145,148,151,158,161,163,167,206,213,215–216,218,245,248,251
True Confession 283,292,301,309,312,316–317,320,323,331,336
Trueheart, John 9,12,23,74,80–81,105,138
Trumbauer, Frankie 4–5,15,25–26,42,86–87,89–90,99,102,114–115,118,127,208,211,237,273,293
Trumpet in Spades (Rex's Concerto) 28,132,144–145,189,264
Trust In Me 94,102,108,112,115–116,120–121,126,133,140,142,144,146,151,157,159,162–163,166,170–171,173,175,195,197,215,252
Tudor, George 260,280,296,307,309–310
Tumminia, Josephine 134
Tune In On My Heart 309
Tune Twisters, The 137,357
Tunnell, George 'Bon-Bon' 202,207,233,270
Turkey In The Straw 207,259

Turner, Buford 33
Turner, Charles 5,13,24–25,32,56,85,94,123,134,148,186,253,269
Turner, Joe 353
Turner, Merle 29,56,158,232,332
Turning On My Heart 292,299
Turn Off The Moon 134,162,165,171–174,179,185,196,203,210–212,221,223,233,237,254
Turn On That Red-Hot Seat 224
Tutti Frutti 360
12th Street Rag 95,104,115,129,221,231,234,237,241,246,256,302
Twenty-Four Hours A Day 54
29th And Dearborn 318
Twiddlin' My Thumbs 60
Twilight In Turkey 103,122–123,132,140,145,148,153,157,159,161–162,165,168,172,185,188,209,212,215,217,220,223,225,231,234,240,246,264,273,295,306–307
Twin City Blues 328,346
Twinkle, Twinkle, Little Star 97,123–124,127,130
Twinklin' 326
Two Bouquets 340
Two Cigarettes In The Dark 126,130
Two Dead Pans 313
Two Dreams Got Together 298,309,327
Two In Love 42,54
Two Sides To Every Story 47,58–62,70
Ubangi Club, NYC 83,87,94
Ubangi Man 194,211,216,225,244,270,299
Under A Blanket Of Blue 237
Under a Texas Moon 37
Underhill, Babs 159,189,269
Underneath The Harlem Moon 295
Underneath The Music Box 57
Underneath The Stars 333
Under The Spell Of The Blues 12
Under The Spell Of The Voodoo Drums 98,109
Under Your Spell 99
Unsophisticated Lady 26
Unsophisticated Sue 29
Until The Real Thing Comes Along 8,12,29,31–33,35–38,40–41,45,47–50,52–55,57–62,64–65,69,70–71,73–74,76,78,83,98,104,110,240,243,246,251,253,339
Until Today 31,33–34,36,39–40,42,45–47,51,55–58,61–62,64,68,70,93
Up On Your Toes 36
Uproar Shout 114,158
Upstairs 165
Uptown Downbeat (Blackout) 31,146
Uptown Rhapsody 12,65,143,161,309
Uptown Shuffle 54
Us On A Bus 13,19,22
Vagabond Song 65
Vallee, Rudy 292,344
Vampin' A Co-ed 49,99
Van, Betty 205,213,216,219–221,223,225,232,234,237,239
Vance, Dick 10,13,20,33,59,119,127,137,200,236,263,276,279,353
Van Eps, Bobby 10–11,27,29,33–34

Van Eps, Freddie 313
Van Eps, George 4–5,76
Van Meter, Maurine 174,267,269–272,293,362
Van Schilgan, Bobby 270,275,306,314
Van Steeden, Peter 114
Vargas, Joe 66,106,116,119,125,129,132,140,156,168,187,250,260,280,309
Vaughan, George 18,23,33,64
Vaughan, Wes 25
Venuti, Joe 16,18,21,42,54,62,145,167,215–216,313
Verrill, Virginia 40,44,54,56–57
Vesely, Ted 255,262,359
Vibraphone Blues 47,246,301
Vibraphonia 92
Vibrollini 86
Victor, Frank 84,86,92–93,103,140,187,281,289,294,308,316,357
Vieni, Vieni 277,279–280,282–283,285–286,288–289,293–294,324
Viggiano, Mike 27,43,66
Vilia 29,165
Village Cut-Ups 151
Vims Music Store, NYC 135,249
Viola, Tony 289,297
Viper Mad 327
Viper's Moan 147
Viper's Swing 123
Vogue Ballroom, Los Angeles 289,293,296
Volga Boatmen 305,307,335
Volpa, Harry 92–93
Von Zell, Harry 114
Voodoo 55
Vote For Mr. Rhythm 74,78,100
Voynow, Dick 120
Wabash Blues 40,50,148,252,311
Wacky Dust 353,361
Waddlin' At The Waldorf 156,172,186,189,225,255,278,285,335
Wade, Dave 35,66,76,95,103,106,110,122–123,125,129,132,140,148,156,164,169,172,177,187–188,192,348–349,357
Wade, Ed 4–5,15
Wah-Hoo! 11
'Waikiki Wedding' [movie] 170
Wail Of The Winds 79,99,105,142,146,289
Wain, Bea 259,283,299
Wait 93,118
Waitin' For Liza 11
Wake Up And Live 131,134,138,142,151,153,159,166–167,170,172,177–178,184,195–196,204,209–210,213,215–216,231,242,247
Wake Up And Sing 47,149
Walker, Bob 30,32–33,36,40,43,51
Walker, Mack 6,8,18,27,44,165,235
Walkin' And Swingin' 7,110,240,247,254
Walkin' Through Heaven 29,236
Walking Through The Park 104
Walk, Jennie, Walk 4–5,11,14,28,31,62,73,76,90,111,186,221,256,280,298
Wallace, Cedric 179,339,346,358

INDEX

Wallace, Louise 117,165,171,184,195, 202,242,249,265,271
Wallace Sisters 116
Waller, Fats 2,5,7,13,21,23–26,32,36, 38,56,66,85,94–95,99,102–103,106, 112,120,123,126,129,134,143,148, 157,162,167,186,192,249,253–254, 260–261,269,293,296,309,332,339, 344,346,358
Walton, Greely 296
Wang Wang Blues 45,66,103,183,200, 211,282
Wanted 125,130,144,148
War Dance For Wooden Indians 277, 300
Ward, Frankie 67,100,104,124, 142–145,148,151,158,161–163, 166–167,206,213,215–216,218,245, 248,251
Ward, Helen 2–11,13–15,17–18, 20–23,26–31,33,35–38,41,43,46,56, 58–62,64–70,72–74,79–83,86–88, 90–91,115,159,163,270,275,301, 343,346–347
Ware, James 153
Waring, Fred 41,45,87,216,292,307
Warmin' Up 18
Warner, Sam 150
Warnow, Mark 37,40,43,47–49, 53–57,61,64,81
Warren, Earle 205,231,235,245,248, 271,292,307–308,328,333,340,354, 361
Warwick, Carl 118,141,162,195
Washboard Blues 110,220,233,351,358
Washington, Al 21
Washington & Lee Swing 66,110
Washington, George 20,36,70,73,81, 102,127,137,141
Washington, Jack 109,138,205,231, 271,292,307–308,328,354,361
Washington, John 6
Washington, Leon 337,341
Washington, Ned 122
Washington Squabble 308
Was It My Heart? 174
Was It Rain? 115,119,124,126,128, 131,140,144–146,148,161–162,172, 185,194–195,205,208,251
Was That The Human Thing To Do? 169,175,184,196
Watchin' 276
Watermelon Man 356
Waters, Ethel 23,53,201,266,334
Watson, Ivory 126
Watson, Leo 172,223,230,259,272, 306–307,309,313,324,328,331–332, 335,338,359–360
Watson, Sandy 118,141
Watt, Don 76–77,86,161
Watts, Grady 5,25,112,115,118, 120–121,128,143,201,208,214,279, 285,292,295,298,301,317,324,326, 332,361
'Way Down Upon The Swanee River [see *Swanee River*]
'Way Down Yonder In New Orleans 19–21,40–41,45,47,50,65,73,79,87,

93,95,100,115–116,119–120,124, 126,146,148,151–152,162,171,183, 207,235,242,248,256,274,279,285, 289
Wayland, Hank 25,224,236,248,269, 272,284,294,301,321,340–341,348, 353,355
Wayman, James 167
Weary Blues 41,83,93,95,100,102,114, 169,196,232,239,264,273,297,301
Webb, Chick 12,23,54,66,74,78–81, 84,86–90,92–93,97–100,104–105, 111,113,115,119,123,126,128, 132–133,135,137–138,144,146,156, 167,170,172,174,176–178,189,193, 200,208,222,230,238,243,247,250, 254,259,275–279,293,295–296, 298–301,307,311–312,314,317,321, 327,335–337,350,354–355,360,362
Weber, Kay 10–11,51,68,95–96,100, 125,128,131,133,135,140,143–146, 151–152,157,159–161,163–164,166, 170,183,197,205,207–208,210,212, 215–216,218,220,222,224–225,231, 237,239–240,262,267,269,274,276, 279–284,288,296,312,316–318,321, 323–325,327–328,331–333, 335–336,338, 361
Webster, Ben 20,31,59,72,81,93,104, 111,117,127,134,263,276,357,359
Webster, Freddy 337,341
Webster, Llana 285,294
Webster, Paul 52–53,69,74,111–112, 188,190,205,280,308,346
We Can't Go On This Way 201,225, 350
Wednesday Night Hop 119,232,245, 254
We Don't Know From Nothin' 65
Weiss, Sam 17,25,35,43,61,227,250, 262,276,284–285,294,297,311,320
Weiss, Sid 3–5,12,17–18,23,33,64, 226–227,250,359
Welch, Jimmy 112,121
Welcome, Buddy 15,24,55–59,67,76, 79,83,86,88,90,96,100,104,108, 111–114,129,140,209,251
Welcome Stranger 10,16,19,23
We'll Rest At The End Of The Trail 17
We'll Ride The Tide Together 246
Wells, Dicky 12,17,138,159,173,310, 346
Wells, Henry 7–8,11–13,88,119,157, 218–219,240,242–245,247–249, 252–255,257,262,297,326
Wendell, Bill 166
Wendt, George 206,263–264
We're Breaking Up A Lovely Affair 343
We're In The Money 55,59,76,246,262
West, Mae 212,321
Westchester County Center 160,180, 182
Weston, Cliff 41,43–45,47,49,84,117
West Wind 5,8
We, The People 358
Wethington, Crawford 20,36,70,81, 141
Wetstein, Paul 204

Wettling, George 66,74,82,85,93,112, 119,122,133,135,143–144,156,167, 171–172,178,186,189,194–195,198, 200,202,211,213,216,219,224–226, 230,232,234–236,239,248,269,272, 284,294,301,315,318,324,327, 329–330,332,339–340,342–343, 345–351,357,359
Wharton, Dick 29,202,207,233,256, 348,353,355
What Are You Doing Tonight? 360
What A Shuffle! 172,208,300,336
What Can I Say After I Say I'm Sorry? 127
Whatcha Gonna Do When There Ain't No Swing? 25,45,69,113,202,241, 331
What Does It Matter? 6,30,295
What Do You Hear From The Mob In Scotland? 353
What Do You Know About Love? 350
What Goes On Here In My Heart? 354, 360
What Harlem Is To Me 151
What Is This Thing Called Love? 68, 148,323–324
What'll I Do? 212,338
What's Mine Is Yours 219
What's On Your Mind? 21
What's The Name Of That Song? 5–6, 15,18–19,24
What's The Reason (I'm Not Pleasin' You)? 11
What's The Use? 358
What's Your Story, What's Your Jive? 263
What The Heart Believes 37
What Will I Do In The Morning? 269
What Will I Tell My Heart? 88,117–118, 120,126–127,140,146,148,150–152, 155,157–158,161,165–166,175,203, 206,213,217,236,243,246
What You Mean To Me 90
Wheeler, DePriest 4,20,59,127,134, 241,246,295,321,343
When 203
When A Lady Meets A Gentleman Down South 37,44,50,53,55–56,60,67,69, 74,86,104,126,153,172
When A Woman Loves A Man 311
When Buddha Smiles 40,61,67,70,74, 79,82,91,134,138,140,158,183,202, 221,277,284,302,324,336,343,345
When Day Is Done 135,214
When Did You Leave Heaven? 33–34, 39,43,45,47,51–52,54–58,60–62, 64–68,70,72,74–76,78–79,83,87–88, 92,102,111,115,148, 255
When Dreams Come True 119
When I Dream About Hawaii 252
When I Get Low I Get High 12
When I Grow Too Old To Dream 31,92, 111,120,165,239,248,265
When I Look Into Your Eyes 210,215
When I'm So Close To You 43
When I'm With You 23,25,28,30–31, 34–43,46–47,49,52,54,60–62,64,67,

73,80,112,244
When Irish Eyes Are Smiling 234–235, 240,244,248,264,268
When Is A Kiss Not A Kiss? 72
When I Take My Sugar To Tea 165
When I Think Of You 183
When It's Sleepy Time Down South 155, 186,195,200,203,205,218,225,243, 256,273,286,289,293,311,313
When It's Twilight On The Trail 56
When Love Has Gone 5
When Love Is Young 123,143,146,151, 164,166,196
When My Baby Smiles 327
When My Dreamboat Comes Home 80, 87,117,144,146,151,155,157,165, 197,215,233,262
When My Sugar Walks Down The Street 354
When The Bride Comes Home 30
When The Heather Is In Bloom 334
When The Midnight Choo-Choo Leaves For Alabam' 338
When The Moon Hangs High 42
When The Poppies Bloom Again 131, 165
When The Sun Sets Down South [Southern Sunset] 327
When Two Love Each Other 169,171, 175,219,221
When We're Alone [Penthouse Serenade] 292
When We're In Love 233
When Will I Know? 118
When You And I Were Young, Maggie 82–83,88,98,107,115,133,135,142, 176,182,220–221,236,243,277,357
When You Gotta Swing, You Gotta Swing It 219
When You're Low 22
When You're Smiling 20,50,78,208,308
When Your Heart's On Fire 299
When Your Lover Has Gone 61
When You Wore A Tulip 232
Where Am I? 108
Where Are You? 80,82,108,131,137, 144–145,147–148,152,154,158,166, 172,175,178–179,183,185,191,197, 202,206–207,209,212–214,216, 219–220,231,240,245,255
Where Green Grass Grows Around 62
Where Is My Heart? 23
Where Is The Sun? 134,138,142–144, 148,161,165–167,172,177–178,196, 214–215,217,222,231,234,237,241, 252
Where Or When 174,177,185,198, 201–203,207–208,211–213,215–216, 218,220,222–223,225,231,233–234, 236–237,240,244–246,248,251–252, 254,256,263,267,276–277,290,299, 323,326,340
Where's The Waiter? 311
Where The Lazy River Goes By 79, 82,86,107
Where There's You, There's Me 20,38,47, 54
Whetsel, Arthur 6,28,31,93,128,132,

146,148,165–166,173,189,262,312, 320,324,355
Whispering 29,43,86,90,124,150,156, 207,215,222,224,236,239
Whispers In The Dark 188,205, 211, 214–216,222,224,227,232,235, 239–240,242,244–246,248,251–252, 254–255,262–263,267–269,271,283, 298
Whistle While You Work 306,320,339
White, Beverly 'Baby' 111,114,158, 206,236,266,302,308,312
White, Bob 3
White, Carl 64,218,240,254
White, Ernie 68,71,92,110,113,116
White, Gil 8,152,327
White, Harry 4,237,240
White Heat 19,35,37,65,109,184,221, 243
White, Morris 4,20,50,59,127,134, 241,246
White, Sonny 188,223,234,236–237, 240–241,243–244,246,248,250–251, 260,265,310
Whiteman, Paul 15,21,42,62,89,112, 118,125,161,208,210–211,217–218, 223,236,242,251,254, 257,313
Whiteside, Arthur 317
White Star Of Sigma Nu 100,116,183, 211,214,219,237
Whiting, Fred 162,348–349, 357
Whitmore, Charles 162
Whitney, Len 134,192,258,321
Whoa, Babe! 115,121,123,129,143, 152,158,161,165,178,183,188,209, 238,240,243,251,270,278,296,307, 324,332,335
Who? 46,72,75–77,107,118,223,243, 270–273,276,289,324,336,351
Who Do You Think I Saw Last Night? 349
Who Knows? 254,298
Who'll Be My Romance This Summer? 204
Who'll Be The One This Summer? 186
Who'll Buy My Violets? 108,124,131, 159,208,219,230,236,254,256,268
Who Loves You? 68
Who's Afraid Of Love? 94,109,113–114
Who's Sorry Now? 35,99,169,185,233, 270,284,320,323,332
Who's That Knockin' At My Door 116
Who's That Knocking At My Heart? 110,123
Who Wants Love? 256
Who Wants To Sing My Love Song? 65
Who Ya Hunchin'? 362
Why? 42
Why Can't We Do It Again? 219
Why Can't We Dream Again? 245
Why Do I Lie To Myself About You? 24, 40,52,55,57,60,62,86
Why Do I Love You? 324,331,339
Why'd Ya Make Me Fall In Love? 349, 353
Why'd You Make Me Love You? 353, 356
Why Must I Be Neglected? 347

Why Pretend? 345
Why Should I Care? 282,316
Why Shouldn't I? 35
Why Talk About Love? 236,272,276, 285,301,335
Why Was I Born? 110
Wigwammin' 357
Wilcox, Edwin 52–53,69,74,111,113, 188,190,205,280,308,346
Wild Cat 87
Wild Irish Rose 146
Wild Man Blues 318
Wiley, Lee 25,43,48,50,57–58,61,66, 284
Wild Party 40,102
Wilkins, Bruce 76–77,86,161,231
Willard, Clarence 76–77,83,86,161, 231,270,276,286,346,355
Will, Bob 176
Williams, Ann 293
Williams, Ben 162
Williams, Clarence 248
Williams, Claude 7–8,11–13,88,109, 119
Williams' College Glee Club 127
Williams, Cootie 6,17–18,20,28,31, 33,92–93,128,130,132,134,143–144, 146,148,152,159,162,165–166, 171–175,177,186–187,189,202,262, 265,276,302,312–313,316–317,320, 322,324,332,336,343–346,354, 356–357,360
Williams, Eddie 118,141,162
Williams, Elmer 10,12–13,20,33,127, 137,200,236,263,276,353
Williams, Fess 284
Williams, Griff 97
Williams, John (b) 118,141,162
Williams, John (saxes) 7–8,11–13,84, 88,119,157,218–219,297,326
Williams, Johnny (d) 37,42,54,58,66, 68–69,73,75,81,84,87,89–90,92,96, 103,106,110,113,116,119,122–123, 125,128–129,132,140,145,148–149, 156,163–164,169,172,177,183,185, 187–188,192,202–203,253,277,300, 313,348–349,357
Williams, Lloyd 95,119,132,156,169, 187,260,264,280,309
Williams, Mary Lou 7–8,11–13,84, 88,110,112,119,123,130,135, 137–138,157,179,218–219,240, 242–243,245,247,252–255,257, 296–297,299,326,328,339
Williams, Midge 151,158,334,337
Williams, Murray 64,76–77,86,161, 346–347,350,354,358–360
Williams, Nathaniel 346
Williams, Paul 143
Williams, Rudy 300
Williams, Sandy 12,23,74,80–81,88, 90,104–105,108,111,124,126,138, 176–178,238,259,277–279,295–296, 298–301,312,317,321,337,350,355, 361–362
Williams Sisters 151
William Tell 115,171
Will I Discover? 97

Will I Ever Know It? 10
Will I Remember? 110
Will Love Find A Way? 15
Will You Know Me When I'm Famous? 39
Wilmot, Jack 232–235,237,241,246
Wilshire Bowl, LA 97
Wilshire, Jack 99,105
Wilson, Anne 269–271,305
Wilson, Dick 7–8,11–13,88,110,112, 119,157,218–219,240,242–243,245, 247,249,252–255,297,326,339
Wilson, Edith 16
Wilson, George 102
Wilson, Jimmy 212
Wilson, Meredith 11
Wilson, Quinn 117,231,337,341
Wilson, Teddy 9,13–15,17–18,23,26, 44,46–47,68–69,72,75,77,79–81,83, 86,88–92,94,104,106–107,110,114, 121,128,135,138,140–141,143–144, 153,156,159–160,163,170,174,184, 188, 218,220,222,238,243,248,262, 266,268,271,275,277–278,292, 294–295,297,299–301,303–304,306, 308,311,321,323,343,349,351, 353–354,356,359–360
Winter, Al 237,245
Winter, Winona (Inman) 237
Wintertime Dreams 76,114
Wintz, Julie 87
Wire Brush Stomp 354
Wistful And Blue 137,174,178–179, 184,254,282
With All My Heart 2,8
With A Smile And A Song 320
With Love In My Heart 218,245
Without A Shadow of A Doubt 26,29, 36–38,42–43,46–47,49,52–55,57, 59–60,83
Without A Song 177
Without Your Love 165,184,188, 203–204,208,223,238,253
With Plenty Of Money And You 95,101, 104,106,109,115,118,126,130–131, 146,151,235
With Thee I Swing 72,74
Wobbly Walk 57
Woe Is Me 362
Wolf, John-Allen 88,166,307,316–317
Wolf, Tiny 281
Wolverine Blues 8,24,30,40,76,125, 128,144,147–148,151,158,196,205, 208,216,236,245,251,284,317,327, 331
Woman On My Weary Mind 32,42, 148,157,218
Wonderful Wintertime Dreams 96
Wood, Joe 270
Wooding, Sam 28
Woods, Ray 243,246
Woods, Sonny 40,108,155,203,293, 296,327,331,336–337
Woods, Stanley 60
Woo-Woo 341
Worrell, Frank 68–69,71,73,75,125, 129,132,156,169,187,250,260,280, 303,309–310,333

Worried Over You 157,243–244,246, 254,263,267,269,334
Would You? 16,20,22–23,25,36,39,47, 54,57
Would You Have A Cup Of Java With Me? 56
Would You Have A Cup Of Jello With Me? 44
Would You Like To Buy A Dream? 138, 143,256
Wrappin' It Up 265,344–345,350–351, 355,359
Wrap Your Troubles In Dreams 349
Wright, Edythe 10,13,18–19,21–22, 25,34,36,41,47,72,80,82,91–92,101, 108–110,112–113,121,124,126, 129–131,134,136,143–144,146–148, 151–153,158–159,162,164,166,183, 186,192,195,197,201,204–205, 207–208,210,213,215,219–220, 222–224,230–233,235–237, 239–240,242–244,253–256,263, 267–268,270–273,276,289,298,302, 308,311–312,316,322,324,333,335, 338,349,351,358,361
Wright, Lammar 4,20,59,127,134, 241,246,295,321,343
Wright, Mel 215
Wynn, Albert 200,263,276,353
Wynn, Larry 260,280
Wynn, Nan 183–185,196,201,204, 215,219–220,223–224,240,242,270, 343,359
Ya Got Me 361
Yancey Special 316,328,336,338
Yaner, Milt 137,237,340–341, 348–349,351
Yankee Doodle 202
Yankee Doodle Band 278
Yankee Doodle Never Went To Town 3,5, 30,112,188
Yeah, Man! 22,30–31,43,47–48,54,78, 80,104,110,118,124,157,197,205, 233,236,243,247–248,253,256
Yearning 338
Yearning for Love (Lawrence's Concerto) 28,93,162
Yellow Dog Blues 289
Yesterdays 106,232,241
Yes! We Have No Bananas 239
Yocum, Clark 24,55–59,67,79,209
Yoder, Walter 76–77,86,161–162,205, 231,273,276,286,346,355
Yorke, George 3,14
You 10,15,18–20,60,65
You And I Know 243,256,267, 273–274,277,284,286,289
You Are My Lucky Star 18
You Are The Reason For My Love 242
You Better Change Your Tune 323, 326–327
You Came To My Rescue 46–47,57,61, 124
You Can Call It Swing 16
You Can Depend On Me 33,81,83,86
You Can Tell She Comes From Dixie 78, 82,85,90,96,98,109,116
You Can't Be Mine 350

INDEX

You Can't Have Everything 205,212, 222,235,239,276
You Can't Live In Harlem 8
You Can't Pull The Wool Over My Eyes 14,16,28,31–33,40–45,48,50,52,57, 59,69,87
You Can't Run Away From Love Tonight 144,148,166,169,171–172,174,178, 183,185,194,198,201–202,204,211, 214,219,232,252
You Can't Stop Me From Dreaming 266,270,294,324
You Can't Teach An Old Heart New Tricks 285,299
You Couldn't Be Cuter 308,343–346, 348–349,354
You Do Me Good 274
You Don't Love Right 39,45,51
You Do The Darndest Things, Baby 64, 112,118,124,197
You Dropped Me Like A Red Hot Penny 39,42,44,48–49,54,56,61,111
You Forgot To Remember 3–4,30,33,64, 131
You Gave Me The Gate And I'm Swingin' 354
You Go To My Head 320,332, 349,351, 360
You Had An Evening To Spare 346,349, 351
You Have Everything 298,307,323
You Hit The Spot 2–7,11,31,38
You Leave Me Breathless 347,350, 355–357,359
You'll Be Reminded Of Me 348
You'll Have To Swing It 46,71,74,86, 109,123
You'll Never Go To Heaven 175,178, 189,202,218
You'll Wish You'd Never Been Born 273
You Look Lovely Tonight 147
You Made Me Love You 262,312
Youman, Vincent 177
You Never Know 361
You Never Looked So Beautiful 10,11, 13,24
Young, Andy 250
Young, Bob 97
Young, David 80
Young, Lester 77,104,109–110,118, 138,170,184,188,193–194,197,202, 205,218,231,233–234,239–241,245, 248,256,271,279,307–308,311,328, 333–334,337, 354,361
Young, Sterling 97
Young, Trummy 117,196,231,280, 308,346
You're A Heavenly Thing 44
You're An Education 327,336,339
You're As Pretty As A Picture 358
You're A Sweetheart 271,276,289,295, 307–309,316,326–328,334–337
You're Driving Me Crazy 143,165,174, 185,270,284,323,335
You're Everything Faithful 99
You're Everything Sweet 104,111
You're Giving Me A Song And A Dance 61,65,67–68,70,72,79–80,83,94

You're Gonna Wake Up And Think You're Dreaming 186
You're Gonna Wake Up Some Day 198,234
You're Here, You're There, You're Everywhere 112,123–124,128,138, 143,146,158,163,175,179,183, 210–211,214,221,224,231, 256
You're In Love With Love 276
You're Just A Little Different 127
You're Just The Kind 29
You're Laughing At Me 108,112,114, 117,123,125,131,133,138,140,146
You're Looking For Romance 167,196, 202,209,291
You're My Best Bet 87,92,98–99,105, 113
You're My Desire 130,183,185,196, 202,204,207,215,219–221,223, 232–233,237,240–241,245–248,260, 265,268,270,273,276,284
You're My Dish 253
You're My Everything 166,171
You're My Ideal 316
You're Not The Kind 24,26–27,30,33, 35,37–40,42–43,45,47–49,51–56, 59–61,64,67,72–73,82,91,118,164
You're Not The Kind Of A Girl For A Boy Like Me 41
You're O.K. 57
You're Out Of This World 271,284,300
You're Part Of Me 145
You're Precious To Me 176,178–179, 245
You're Still In My Dreams 69
You're The Cure For What Ails Me 4
You're The Only One To Blame 88
You're The Top 4
You're Too Good To Be True 83,89
You're Toots To Me 9
You're Wicky, You're Wacky, You're Wonderful 3
Your Minstrel Man 47
Yours, All Yours 361
Yours And Mine 170,173,201, 215–216,233,239–241,243–245,247, 252,254,256,262,265,269–270,274, 276,278,283,290,313
Yours To Command 267
Yours Truly Is Truly Yours 8
You'se A Viper 8,30,43,55
You Showed Me The Way 115,121, 123–127,130–131,134–135,137–138, 140–141,143–145,147–149,151,154, 158–161,163–166,169,171–172, 175–177,183,185,195–196,200,215, 239, 243–244,263,280,286,288,296
You Started Me Dreaming 10,13,18,21, 25,41
You Started Something 335
You Stepped Out Of A Dream 65
You Swing 101
You Took Advantage Of Me 39–40,42, 87,129,264,315,343
You Took My Heart 159
You Took The Words Right Out Of My Heart 283–286,293–294,298–299, 302,306,309,312–313,316,321,323, 326,335,337
You Turned The Tables On Me 35,37, 43,45–46,56–57,60–61,64,67,69–70, 72,76–77,80,82–83,87,89,91,100, 102,104,108,110,112,119,163,232, 295
You've Been Reading My Mail 134
You've Got Everything 90
You've Got Me Under Your Thumb 253
You've Got Something 86,88,100,113, 213,223,232–233,236,240,242,253, 256
You've Gotta Eat Your Greens 51
You've Gotta Eat Your Spinach, Baby 25,34,42,51
You've Got That Certain Something 99
You've Got To Swing It 79
You Went To My Head 325,339
You Walked Out Of The Picture 357
You Were Born To Love 202,207,218, 240
You, You And Especially You 328
Ysaguirre, Bob 17,65,179
Yukl, Joe 10–11,27,29,33–34,243, 246,348
Zarchy, Zeke 25–26,42,61,67,74–75, 79,85,93,119,122,164,205,237,280, 282,318,327,330,332,340,347–348, 351,357
Zaz-Zuh-Zaz 23,52,101,266
Zig Zag 103,120,124
Zimmer, Bill 146
Zimmers, Tony 25
Zippo 272,276
Zonky 157,252
Zoom Zoom Zoom 60
Zudecoff, Barney 318,327,332,340, 348,350–351,357,359
Zullo, Frank 112,115,118,120–121, 128,143,201,212,214,279,285,292, 295,298,301,317,324,326,332,361
Zurke, Bob 42,117,126,128,131,133, 143–146,148,151–152,157,159–161, 164,166,170,205,207–208,210,212, 215–216,218,220,237,239,262,274, 276–277,279–284,316–319,321, 323–325,327–328,331–333, 337–338, 340